An Encyclopaedia of Religions

An Encyclopaedia of Religions

By

MAURICE A. CANNEY

GYAN

Published by

Gyan Publishing House
5, Ansari Road
Daryaganj, New Delhi-110002
Phone: 011-47034999, 9811692060
E-mail: books@gyanbooks.com

Distribution Network
gyanbooks.com
India, USA, Canada, UK, Australia, France

ISBN : 978-81-212-2085-9 (PB)
First Published, 1921

2nd Impression 2021

Printed at: Gyan Press, Delhi.

An Encyclopaedia of Religions
Author: Maurice A. Canney

An Encyclopædia of Religions

By

MAURICE A. CANNEY

LONDON:
GEORGE ROUTLEDGE & SONS, LTD.
NEW YORK: E. P. DUTTON & CO.
1921

PREFACE

The science of Comparative Religion is still so young that information on many matters embraced by it has not found its way as yet into ordinary encyclopædias; and of special encyclopædias or dictionaries very few have been published. The great *Encyclopædia of Religion and Ethics*, edited by Dr. James Hastings, is a storehouse of learned discussion and information, but its size places it as a household work of reference beyond the reach of many readers. A felt gap is filled very usefully by the handy *Dictionary of Non-Classical Mythology*, compiled by Marian Edwardes and Lewis Spence; but, as its title indicates, much of the new material that belongs in a special sense to the domain of religion is excluded necessarily from such a work.

It may seem a bold undertaking to seek, as the present writer has done, to present in a volume of moderate size information about most of the ancient and modern religions, ethnic and historical. His excuse must be that certain cravings of his own impelled him many years ago to set out upon a journey along paths which at that time had not been trodden much, and to read more widely than is perhaps usual; that invitations since 1898 to contribute articles to four voluminous encyclopædias have formed an A B C habit which he finds it difficult to throw off; and that a work such as he has attempted here is as a matter of fact really needed. In any case, a work is provided which covers much of the ground claimed by Comparative Religion and is capable of subsequent expansion. If what is offered proves acceptable, new material may be added, particularly as the Science develops.

While it is true that much of the new material in this field has not been incorporated as yet in ordinary encyclopædias, it is true also that to matters of religion with which, by name at least, readers have become very familiar, a good deal of space has been given already in such works. In a field which is so vast, therefore, the present writer has preferred often to concentrate particularly on matters which are unfamiliar and on headings which are not to be found in ordinary encyclopædias. Many of the headings, here to be found, have never found a place as yet, he believes, in any other encyclopædia. These headings, with the matter included under them, it is hoped will not only interest the general reader, but also suggest to students, as they have suggested to the writer, subjects for special research.

The writer is well aware that there is much more to be said about many of the subjects treated, and in fact has himself dealt with some of them in much greater detail elsewhere. For example, with NAME, CHANGE OF, may be compared his article on "The Significance of Names" in the *Journal of the Manchester Egyptian and Oriental Society* (No. ix., 1921, pp. 21-37), and with ASHES and OATH his articles in Hastings' *Encyclopædia of Religion and Ethics* (vol. ii., 1909, pp. 112-114; vol. ix., 1917, pp. 436-438).

MAURICE A. CANNEY.

Knutsford.

CHIEF AUTHORITIES

[In the articles, books are referred to sometimes either by obvious abbreviations of the titles or by the names of the authors followed by the initial letters of the titles. *E.g.*, *The Dictionary of National Biography* is referred to as *D.N.B.*, S. Reinach's *Orpheus* as S. Reinach, *O.*]

W. E. ADDIS and T. ARNOLD, *A Catholic Dictionary*, 7th ed., 1905.

W. R. ALGER, *A Critical History of the Doctrine of a Future Life*, 10th ed., 1878.

T. W. ALLIES, *The Monastic Life*, 1896.

RICHARD ANDREE, *Ethnographische Parallelen und Vergleiche*, 1878; *Neue Folge*, 1889.

E. ANWYL, *Celtic Religion*, 1906.

T. W. ARNOLD, *The Preaching of Islam*, 1896.

H. H. BANCROFT, *The Native Races of the Pacific Coast*, 1875-76.

L. D. BARNETT, *Hinduism*, 1906.

L. D. BARNETT, *Antiquities of India*, 1913.

G. A. BARTON, *A Sketch of Semitic Origins, Social and Religious*, 1902.

G. A. BARTON, *The Religions of the World*, 1917.

W. BENHAM, *Dictionary of Religion*, 1887.

F. J. BLISS, *The Religions of Modern Syria and Palestine*, 1912.

J. H. BLUNT, *Dictionary of Sects, etc.*, 1903.

F. BOND, *Dedications and Patron Saints of English Churches*, 1914.

E. S. BOUCHIER, *Syria as a Roman Province*, 1916.

W. BOUSSET, *The Antichrist Legend*, 1896.

W. BOUSSET, *What is Religion?* 1907.

G. H. BOX, *Short Introduction to the Literature of the Old Testament*, 1909.

J. H. BREASTED, *Development of Religion and Thought in Ancient Egypt*, 1912.

C. A. BRIGGS, *The Higher Criticism of the Hexateuch*, 1897.

C. A. BRIGGS, *General Introduction to the Study of Holy Scripture*, 1906.

D. G. BRINTON, *The Myths of the New World*, 1868.

D. G. BRINTON, *Religions of Primitive Peoples*, 1897.

BROCKHAUS' *Konversations—Lexikon*.

E. G. BROWNE, *Literary History of Persia*, 1906.

E. A. W. BUDGE, *The Gods of the Egyptians*, 1904.

F. BUHL, *Kanon und Text des Alten Testamentes*, 1891, E.T. 1892.

F. W. BUSSELL, *Religious Thought and Heresy in the Middle Ages*, 1918.

A. BUTLER, *Dictionary of Philosophical Terms*.

CALWER, *Kirchenlexikon*, ed. P. Zeller, 1889, etc.

J. E. CARPENTER and G. HARFORD-BATTERSBY, *The Hexateuch*, 1900.

R. H. CHARLES, *Religious Development between the Old and the New Testaments*.

T. K. CHEYNE and J. S. BLACK, *Encyclopædia Biblica*, 1899-1903.

E. CLODD, *Myths and Dreams* (2), 1891.

E. CLODD, *Animism*, 1905.

G. A. COBBOLD, *Religion in Japan*, 1894.

C. M. COBERN, *The New Archeological Discoveries*, 1917.

T. C. CONYBEARE, *Myth, Magic, and Morals*, 1909.

S. A. COOK, *The Study of Religions*, 1914.

R. S. COPLESTON, *Buddhism Primitive and Present*.

C. CORNILL, *Introduction to the Canonical Books of the Old Testament*, 1907.

S. COULING, *The Encyclopædia Sinica*, 1917.

G. W. COX, *Mythology of the Aryan Nations*, 1870.

F. CUMONT, *The Mysteries of Mithra*, 1903.

F. CUMONT, *The Oriental Religions in Roman Paganism*, 1911.

W. A. CURTIS, *History of Creeds and Confessions of Faith*, 1911.

S. I. CURTISS, *Primitive Semitic Religion To-day*, 1902.

E. L. CUTTS, *Dictionary of the Church of England*.

T. W. RHYS DAVIDS, *Hibbert Lectures*, 1881.

W. L. DAVIDSON, *The Stoic Creed*, 1907.

C. J. DETER, *Abriss der Geschichte der Philosophie*, 1906.

The Dictionary of National Biography.

J. DOWSON, *A Classical Dictionary of Hindu Mythology and Religion*, 1879.

S. R. DRIVER, *Introduction to the Literature of the Old Testament*.

J. A. DUBOIS and H. K. BEAUCHAMP, *Hindu Manners, Customs, and Ceremonies*, 1897.

L. DUCHESNE, *Christian Worship*, 1904.

L. DUCHESNE, *Early History of the Christian Church*, 1909.

ÉMILE DURKHEIM, *The Elementary Forms of the Religious Life*.

J. EDKINS, *Religion in China*.

M. EDWARDES and L. SPENCE, *A Dictionary of Non-Classical Mythology*.

J. E. ERDMANN, *History of Philosophy*, 1890.

A. ERMAN, *A Handbook of Egyptian Religion*, 1907.

L. R. FARNELL, *The Cults of the Greek States*, 1896.

L. R. FARNELL, *Greece and Babylon*, 1911.

L. R. FARNELL, *The Higher Aspects of Greek Religion*, 1912.

J. N. FARQUHAR, *Modern Religious Movements in India*, 1919.

A. S. FARRAR, *Critical History of Free Thought*, 1862.

W. WARDE FOWLER, *The Religious Experience of the Roman People*, 1911.

J. G. FRAZER, *The Golden Bough*, 3rd ed., 1911 ff.

J. G. FRAZER, *Totemism and Exogamy*, 1910.

J. G. FRAZER, *Folk-lore in the Old Testament*, 1918.

J. GARDNER, *The Faiths of the World*, 1858-60.

L. M. J. GARNETT, *Mysticism and Magic in Turkey*, 1912.

A. S. GEDEN, *Introduction to the Hebrew Bible*, 1909.

A. S. GEDEN, *Studies in the Religions of the East*, 1913.

H. A. GILES, *Religions of Ancient China*, 1905.

T. R. GLOVER, *The Conflict of Religions in the Early Roman Empire*, 7th ed., 1918.

F. J. GOULD, *A Concise History of Religion*, 1907.

H. GRAETZ, *History of the Jews*, 1892.

G. B. GRAY, *A Critical Introduction to the Old Testament*.

Great Religions of the World, 1902.

C. R. GREGORY, *Canon and Text of the New Testament*, 1907.

J. J. M. de GROOT, *The Religious System of China*, 1892, etc.

J. J. M. de GROOT, *The Religion of the Chinese*, 1910.

H. GUTHE, *Kurzes Bibelwörterbuch*, 1903.

H. HACKMANN, *Buddhism as a Religion*, 1910.

A. C. HADDON, *Magic and Fetishism*, 1906.

K. R. HAGENBACH, *History of Christian Doctrines*, 1880.

H. R. HALL, *Ægean Archæology*, 1915.

PETER HALL, *Fragmenta Liturgica*, 1848.

P. S. P. HANDCOCK, *The Archæology of the Holy Land*, 1916.
A. HARNACK, *History of Dogma*, 1896, etc.
J. E. HARRISON, *Prolegomena to the Study of Greek Religion* (2), 1908.
J. E. HARRISON, *Themis, A Study of the Social Origins of Greek Religion*, 1912.
E. S. HARTLAND, *The Legend of Perseus*, 1894-96.
E. S. HARTLAND, *Primitive Paternity*, 1910.
E. S. HARTLAND, *Ritual and Belief*, 1914.
J. HASTINGS, *Encyclopædia of Religion and Ethics*, 1908 ff.
J. HASTINGS, *Dictionary of the Bible*, in one volume, 1909.
M. HAUG, *The Sacred Language, Writings, and Religion of the Parsis*, 2nd ed., 1878.
W. CAREW HAZLITT, *Dictionary of Faiths and Folklore*, 1905.
S. HEATH, *The Romance of Symbolism*, 1909
E. HERMANN, *The Meaning and Value of Mysticism*, 1916.
OSCAR HOLTZMANN, *The Life of Jesus*, 1904.
E. W. HOPKINS, *The Religions of India*, 1895.
J. A. HOULDER, *Short History of the Free Churches*, 1899.
MARK HOVELL, *The Chartist Movement*, 1918.
C. HUART, *A History of Arabic Literature*, 1903.
T. J. HUDSON, *The Law of Psychic Phenomena*, 1907.
F. VON HÜGEL, *The Mystical Element of Religion*, 1908.
F. VON HÜGEL, *Eternal Life*, 1912.
T. P. HUGHES, *Dictionary of Islam*, 1885.
J. HUNT, *Religious Thought in England*, 1870-73.
I. HUSIK, *History of Mediæval Jewish Philosophy*, 1918.

International Critical Commentary.

A. V. WILLIAMS JACKSON, *Persia, Past and Present*, 1906.
WILLIAM JAMES, *Varieties of Religious Experience*, 1906.
WILLIAM JAMES, *The Will to Believe*, 1908.
MORRIS JASTROW, Jr., *The Religion of Babylonia and Assyria*, 1898.
MORRIS JASTROW, Jr., *Religion Babyloniens und Assyriens*, 2 vols., 1905, 1912.
MORRIS JASTROW, Jr., *The Civilization of Babylonia and Assyria*, 1915.
A. JEREMIAS, *The Old Testament in the Light of the Ancient East*, 1911.
The Jewish Encyclopædia.
T. A. JOYCE, *Mexican Archæology*, 1914.
T. A. JOYCE, *Central American and West Indian Archæology*, 1916.
C. G. JUNG, *Psychology of the Unconscious*, E.T., 1915.

L. W. KING, *Babylonian Religion and Mythology*, 1899.
L. W. KING, *Legends of Babylon and Egypt in relation to Hebrew Tradition*, 1918.
C. F. KENT, *The Student's Old Testament*, 1910-14.
T. A. KLEIN, *The Religion of Islám*, 1906.
R. J. KNOWLING, *The Witness of the Epistles*, 1892.
K. KOHLER, *Jewish Theology*, 1918.

ANDREW LANG, *Custom and Myth*, 1893.
ANDREW LANG, *Myth, Ritual, and Religion*, 1899.
ANDREW LANG, *The Making of Religion*, 1900.
ANDREW LANG, *Social Origins*, 1903.
J. LEGGE, *The Religions of China*, 1880.
ARTHUR LLOYD, *The Creed of Half Japan*, 1911.
LUCIAN, *The Syrian Goddess*, translated by H. A. Strong, and edited by J. Garstang, 1913.

D. B. MACDONALD, *Development of Muslim Theology*, etc., 1903.
D. B. MACDONALD, *The Religious Attitude and Life in Islam*, 1909.
A. C. M'GIFFERT, *Protestant Thought before Kant*, 1911.
D. A. MACKENZIE, *Teutonic Myth and Legend*, 1912.
D. A. MACKENZIE, *Egyptian Myth and Legend*, 1913.
D. A. MACKENZIE, *Indian Myth and Legend*, 1913.
D. A. MACKENZIE, *Myths of Babylonia and Assyria*, 1915.
D. A. MACKENZIE, *Myths of Crete and Pre-Hellenic Europe*, 1917.
J. A. M'CLYMONT, *The New Testament and Its Writers*, 1901.
R. R. MARETT, *The Threshold of Religion*, 1909.
D. S. MARGOLIOUTH, *Mohammedanism*, 1911.
D. S. MARGOLIOUTH, *The Early Development of Mohammedanism*, 1914.
K. MARTI, *The Religion of the Old Testament*, 1907.
G. CURRIE MARTIN, *The Books of the New Testament*, 1909.
W. G. WOOD-MARTIN, *Traces of the Elder Faiths of Ireland*, 1902.
R. M. MEYER, *Altgermanische Religionsgeschichte*, 1910.
J. MOFFATT, *Introduction to the Literature of the New Testament*, 1911.
A. R. HOPE MONCRIEFF, *Classic Myth and Legend.*
G. F. MOORE, *The History of Religions*, 1913.
J. H. MOULTON, *The Treasure of the Magi*, 1917.
F. MAX MÜLLER, *The Sacred Books of the East.*

E. NAVILLE, *The Old Egyptian Faith*, 1909.
ARNO NEUMANN, *Jesus*, 1906.
R. A. NICHOLSON, *Literary History of the Arabs*, 1907.

W. O. E. OESTERLEY and G. H. BOX, *The Religion and Worship of the Synagogue*, 1911.
H. OLDENBERG, *Die Religion des Veda*, 1894.
H. OLDENBERG, *Ancient India*, 1898.
J. C. OMAN, *The Mystics, Ascetics, and Saints of India*, 1905.
J. C. OMAN, *The Brahmans, Theists and Muslims of India*, 1907.
J. C. OMAN, *Cults, Customs and Superstitions of India*, 1908.
MALACHIA ORMANIAN, *The Church of Armenia*, 1912.

E. H. PARKER, *Studies in Chinese Religion*, 1910.
G. T. W. PATRICK, *The Psychology of Relaxation*, 1916.
M. W. PATTERSON, *History of the Church of England*, 1909.
A. S. PEAKE, *Critical Introduction to the New Testament*, 1909.
W. M. FLINDERS PETRIE, *The Religion of Ancient Egypt*, 1905.
OTTO PFLEIDERER, *The Development of Theology in Germany since Kant*, 1890.
B. PÜNJER, *History of the Christian Philosophy of Religion*, 1887.

S. REINACH, *Orpheus*, 1910.
S. REINACH, *Cults, Myths and Religions*, 1912.
W. RIDGEWAY, *The Origin and Influence of the Thoroughbred Horse*, 1915.
Religious Systems of the World, 1908.
J. M. ROBERTSON, *Christianity and Mythology*, 1910.
J. M. ROBERTSON, *Pagan Christs*, 1911.
R. V. RUSSELL and R. B. HIRA LAL, *The Tribes and Castes of the Central Provinces of India*, 1916.
H. E. RYLE, *The Canon of the Old Testament*, 2nd ed., 1895.

W SANDAY, *Inspiration*, 1903.
P. D. CHANTEPIE DE LA SAUSSAYE, *The Religion of the Teutons*, 1902.
P. D. CHANTEPIE DE LA SAUSSAYE, *Lehrbuch der Religionsgeschichte*, 3rd ed., 1905.
SCHAFF-HERZOG, *Religious Encyclopædia*, 1883-4.
O. SEYFFERT, *Dictionary of Classical Antiquities*, 10th ed., 1908.
W. SIMPSON, *The Buddhist Praying-wheel*, 1896.
H. S. SKEATS and C. S. MIALL, *History of the Free Churches of England*, 1891.
SMITH and CHEETHAM, *Dictionary of Christian Antiquities.*
G. ELLIOT SMITH, *The Ancient Egyptians.*
G. ELLIOT SMITH, *Migrations of Peoples*, 1915.
G. ELLIOT SMITH, *The Influence of Ancient Egyptian Civilization in the East and in America*, 1916.
G. ELLIOT SMITH, *The Evolution of the Dragon*, 1919.
W. ROBERTSON SMITH, *The Old Testament in the Jewish Church*, 1892.
W. ROBERTSON SMITH, *The Religion of the Semites*, 1894.
W. ROBERTSON SMITH, *Kinship and Marriage in Early Arabia*, 1903.
LEWIS SPENCE, *The Mythologies of Ancient Mexico and Peru*, 1907.

W. B. SPENCER and F. J. GILLEN, *The Northern Tribes of Central Australia*, 1904.

C. SQUIRE, *The Mythology of Ancient Britain and Ireland*, 1906.
C. SQUIRE, *Celtic Myth and Legend.*
E. SQUIRE, *The Mythology of the British Islands*, 1910.
G. STEINDORFF, *Religion of the Ancient Egyptians*, 1905.

E. THURSTON and K. RANGACHARI, *Castes and Tribes of Southern India*, 1909.
E. B. TYLOR, *Primitive Culture*, 4th ed., 1903.

EVELYN UNDERHILL, *Mysticism*, 4th ed., 1912.
EVELYN UNDERHILL, *The Mystic Way*, 1913.

M. R. VINCENT, *A History of the Textual Criticism of the New Testament*, 1903.

H. WACE and W. C. PIERCY, *Dictionary of Christian Biography and Literature*, 1911.
L. A. WADDELL, *The Buddhism of Tibet*, 1895.
HUTTON WEBSTER, *Rest Days*, 1916.
MAX B. WEINSTEIN, *Welt- und Leben-Anschauungen*, 1910.
E. WESTERMARCK, *The Origin and Development of the Moral Ideas*, 1906-8.
E. M. WHERRY, *The Mohammadan World of To-day*, 1906.
O. C. WHITEHOUSE, *The Books of the Old Testament*, 1910.
A. WIEDEMANN, *Religion of the Ancient Egyptians*, 1897.
G. WILDEBOER, *The Origin of the Canon of the Old Testament*, 1895.
W. J. WILKINS, *Hindu Mythology*, 1901.
SIR MONIER MONIER-WILLIAMS, *Buddhism*, 1890.
SIR MONIER MONIER-WILLIAMS, *Brahmanism and Hinduism*, 4th ed., 1891.
H. B. WORKMAN, *Christian Thought to the Reformation*, 1911.
C. H. H. WRIGHT and C. NEIL, *A Protestant Dictionary*, 1904.

ENCYCLOPÆDIA OF RELIGIONS

A

Â. The name of a goddess in Babylonian-Assyrian religion. She is a consort, the "beloved one," of the sun-deity, Shamash (*q.v.*). The name seems to mean "lady" or "queen." See Morris Jastrow, *Rel.*

A. God A. is a designation used by anthropologists for a deity depicted in the MSS. of the Mayan Indians of Central America. His frequent appearance in the Dresden Codex and in the Codex Tro-cortesianus suggests that he was a god of great importance. He was clearly a god of death and hell, corresponding to the Aztec god Mictlan. His insignia include bells and a pair of cross-bones, and his symbolical bird is the owl.

AAH. An ancient Egyptian moon-god, who in course of time was merged with the lunar deity Thoth. His importance is proved by such names as Ah-mes ("born of Ah"; cp. Thoth-mes, "born of Thoth").

AB. The fifth month of the Jewish sacred year. The fifth month of the Babylonian calendar has the same name. It is sacred to the solar deity, Nin-gishzida. See Morris Jastrow, *Rel.*

AB, NINTH DAY OF. A Jewish fast-day (cp. Zechariah 8, 19), intended to commemorate the destruction of the two Temples (First, 586 B.C.; Second, A.D. 70). It falls about the beginning of August. The fast has been observed, with varying degrees of strictness, as a day of deep gloom. In early times no enjoyment whatever was permitted for twenty-four hours, from evening to evening. No work was allowed, only sad parts of the Law might be studied, and people went about without shoes or sandals. Bathing and anointing were of course forbidden. See the *Jewish Encycl.*, i., 1901; W. O. E. Oesterley and G. H. Box.

AB, FIFTEENTH DAY OF. A Jewish festival in the time of the Second Temple. It fell about the 15th of August. On this day the rich and poor maidens of Jerusalem, robed in white, are said to have repaired to the vineyards to dance with the young men and to give them an opportunity of choosing a bride. The Talmud gives various reasons for celebrating the day. One of them is that on this day wood was collected by priests and people for sacrificial use throughout the year. Josephus mentions (*B. J.* ii. 17, 6) a Feast of Xylophory ("Wood-bearing"), placing it on the 14th Ab. See the *Jewish Encycl.*, i., 1901.

ABACUS. A designation in architecture of the uppermost division of the capital of a column. It is variously formed or moulded in the different orders or styles of architecture. See J. H. Parker, *Gloss.*

ABADDON. Literally "(place of) destruction." A term used in the Wisdom-Literature of the Old Testament (Job 26, 6; Prov. 15, 11, etc.) as the equivalent of Sheol, the under-world of the Hebrews. The same word means "perdition" and "hell" in later Hebrew. The term occurs also in the New Testament (Rev. 9, 11), but in this case it is a proper name, a personification, Abaddon being a king or angel of the abyss, whose Greek name is Apollyon ("Destroyer"). See *Encycl. Bibl.*

ABBA. An Aramaic word meaning "father." It was used by Jesus and in his time as a title of God (so in Mark 14, 36).

ABBACOMITES. The Abbacomites or Abbates milites, count abbots, were laymen to whom abbacies were assigned for pecuniary profit. See *Cath. Dict.*

ABBATE. A Roman Catholic clergyman who has not taken full orders, but has received the tonsure.

ABBATES MILITES. Lay abbots of the 10th century, who appointed deans or priors to administer their abbeys and perform the spiritual duties. They were also called Abba-comités.

ABBÉ. The French name for an Abbot (*q.v.*). It is often used in France and Italy in a more general way as the title of an unbenificed priest.

ABBÉS COMMENDATAIRES. Abbots who were appointed by the king of France, and received one-third of the revenue of their convents. They were often laymen, noblemen's sons or literary men, and their office was a sinecure.

ABBESS. A designation of the superior of a community of nuns. The Abbess corresponds to the Abbot (*q.v.*), but the office is not so ancient. It was probably instituted in the time of Pope Gregory the Great (*c.* 591). Generally, only a professed nun could be elected, and the Council of Trent fixed the age at not less than forty years, at least eight years of which must have been spent in a convent. Like the Abbot, she has the ring, staff, and abbatial cross. Sometimes she commands the obedience of the monks of a related monastery (*e.g.* in the order of the Brigittines and of Fontevrault). She often possessed, under the ordinary, ecclesiastical patronage; but she could not choose confessors, dismiss a nun, etc. See *Cath. Dict.*

AB BETH DIN. Literally "father of the house of justice." This, according to tradition, was a title of the vice-president of the Jewish Sanhedrin, the President of which was called Nasi ("prince"). It seems more likely, however, that it was the title of the spiritual head of the people and so of the Sanhedrin, and that Nasi was the designation of the more secular head of the people (the High-priest). See the *Jewish Encycl.*, ix., 1905, under "Nasi"; W. O. E. Oesterley and G. H. Box.

ABBEY. A monastic community governed by an Abbot. See ABBOT.

ABBOT. The name means literally "father," and is

the designation of the head of a religious community of men. Another name for the same official is Prior, Rector, or Guardian. The office is as old as the third century. In the fourth century a number of monasteries, with abbots at their head, sprang up in Egypt. At first the abbots were laymen, but ordination soon became the rule, though it was not always strictly observed. They were required to be not less than twenty-five years old. The monks were allowed originally to elect their own abbot. The right, however, in the West was often exercised by temporal princes and lords. It is the duty of an abbot to govern the community, maintain discipline, and exercise the priestly office. A distinction has been drawn between these "abbates regulares" and other abbots, "abbates seculares," whose office is of the nature of an ordinary benefice. The Benedictine abbots have been allowed a large measure of freedom in the organisation of their convents. And abbots in general obtained special privileges, the heads of great monasteries being allowed to use the mitre, crosier, and ring ("abbates infulati"), and to perform some of the episcopal functions (*e.g.*, minor orders). Formerly abbots of such distinction might sit in the English Parliament. See *Cath. Dict.;* P. Zeller, *Calwer Kirchenlexikon*, 1889 etc.

ABBOT OF UNREASON. The Scottish name for one who took the principal part in Christmas revelries before the Reformation. The character is better known as the Lord of Misrule (*q.v.*). In Scotland he was suppressed by Act of Parliament in 1555. See W. C. Hazlitt.

ABBOTS IN COMMENDAM. Abbots commended to take charge of an abbey, until a regular abbot had been appointed.

ABBREVIATIONS. Words, titles, phrases, etc., in common use are often abridged. For example, "Reverend" as the title of a clergyman is usually written "Rev." The following are some of the most common abbreviations:

Abp.: Archbishop.
A.B.S.: American Bible Society.
A.D.: Anno Domini, in the year of Our Lord.
A.F.B.S.: American and Foreign Bible Society.
A.H.: Anno Hegiræ, in the year of the Hegira (622 A.D.).
D.O.M.: Deo optimo maximo, to God, best and greatest.
D.V.: Deo Volente, God willing.
F.C.: Free Church (of Scotland).
F.D.: Fidei Defensor, Defender of the Faith.
I.H.S.: The first three letters of the Greek word ΙΗΣΟΥΣ, Jesus.
: Jesus hominum Salvator.
A.M.: Anno Mundi, in the year of the world.
A.V.: Authorised Version of the Bible.
B.C.: Before Christ.
B.D.: Bachelor of Divinity.
Bp.: Bishop.
B.V.M.: Blessed Virgin Mary.
C.M.S.: Church Missionary Society.
D.D.: Doctor of Divinity.
D.G.: Dei Gratiâ, by the grace of God.
I.N.R.I.: Jesus Nazarenus, Rex Iudæorum, Jesus of Nazareth, king of the Jews.
I.O.G.T.: Independent Order of Good Templars.
J.U.D.: Juris Utriusque Doctor, Doctor of Civil and Canon Law.
LXX.: Septuagent Version of the Old Testament.
M.E.: Methodist Episcopal.
N.T.: New Testament.
O.S.B.: Order of St. Benedict.
P.E.: Protestant Episcopal.
P.P.: Parish priest.
R.I.P.: Requiescat in pace, May he rest in peace.
R.V.: Revised Version of the Bible.
S.J.: Society of Jesus (Jesuits).
S.P.C.K.: Society for Promoting Christian Knowledge.
S.P.G.: Society for the Propagation of the Gospel.
S.T.P.: Sacræ Theologiæ Professor, Professor of Theology.
U.P.: United Presbyterian.
V.D.M.: Verbi Dei Minister, Minister of the Word of God.
Xmas: Christmas.
Xtian: Christian.
Y.M.C.A.: Young Men's Christian Association.
Y.W.C.A.: Young Women's Christian Association.

ABBREVIATORS. A designation, first used about the beginning of the fourteenth century, of secretaries employed in the Papal Chancery. They were so called because they made short notes of decisions or replies made by the Pope, which they afterwards expanded. See *Cath. Dict.*

ABECEDARIAN HYMNS. Hymns in which each stanza or line begins with a letter of the alphabet. See ACROSTIC.

ABECEDARIANS. A German Anabaptist sect of the 16th century. They claimed to be directly inspired by God. Consequently they had nothing to learn from the Scriptures. Profane literature being equally useless to them, it was not necessary or desirable to learn to read. Divine truth, directly imparted, could best be learned from the most ignorant of men. The sect was founded by Nicholas Stork, a weaver, of Zwickau, and the Abecedarians are also known as "the Zwickau Prophets." See J. H. Blunt.

ABELITES. A religious sect in N. Africa in the 4th century. They are also called Abelians, Abeloites, and Abelonians. They objected to ordinary marriage, and contracted spiritual unions, taking their name from Abel, because they assumed that he had a wife, but never sought to procreate children. They adopted children in order to perpetuate the sect. These also had to abstain from sexual intercourse. The sect became extinct in the reign of Theodosius the Younger (408-450). See J. H. Blunt.

ABERDEEN, USE OF. Various places had liturgies of their own in the early days of the Church in Britain. These liturgies, which represented somewhat different modes of celebrating Mass, were called "Uses." Aberdeen was one of the places which had a use of its own.

ABERDEEN SERVICE. Forms of Divine Service composed by Henry Scougal (1650-1678), precentor in the Cathedral of Aberdeen, and professor of Divinity at King's College. They were prepared for the morning and evening service of the Cathedral Church of Aberdeen. They were in use until the Revolution, when the Presbyterians deemed written prayers unsuitable. See Peter Hall.

ABGARUS LETTERS, THE. Some correspondence purporting to have passed between Abgar Uchama (15—50 A.D.), King of Edessa, and Jesus. Jesus is besought by Abgar to visit Edessa. The letters are given by Eusebius (*Church History*, I, 13).

ABHIDHAMMA. The name of one of the three divisions ("the three baskets") in the final collection of Buddhist sacred books. The contents are partly metaphysical. See E. W. Hopkins.

ABHIDHAMMAPITAKA. The third division of the Buddhist Canon. See CANON, BUDDHIST.

ABHIDHARMA SECT. An early Buddhist sect in India of the School of the Hinayāna. The teaching was based upon the Commentary which Kātyāyaniputra wrote on the Abhidharma treatises. The sect was introduced into China about 394 A.D., and flourished until about 440 A.D. A. Lloyd finds no traces of it in Japan.

ABIB. The first month of the Jewish sacred year. Literally the month of "young ears of barley."

ABJURATION, OATH OF. An Act of 1701 required all clergy, members of the Universities, lawyers, and other persons who held public offices to abjure by oath the exiled House of Stewart. In the Roman Catholic Church a convert was formerly required to make a solemn abjuration of his former faith. In the Ritual of Strasburg (1742) he is asked: "Is it your firm purpose to renounce in heart and mind all the errors which it [the Catholic Church] condemns?" The modern convert in England is required to read and accept the Creed of Pope Pius IV. which denounces all doctrines which are considered erroneous. See *Cath. Dict.*

ABLUTION, ROMAN CATHOLIC. Ablution is the name applied to the water and wine used by a priest in the celebration of the Mass to wash his thumb and index-finger. "When he has consumed the Precious Blood, the priest purifies the chalice; he then, saying in a low voice a short prayer prescribed by the Church, holds his thumb and index-finger, which have touched the Blessed Sacrament and may have some particle of it adhering to them, over the chalice, while the server pours wine and water upon them. He then drinks the ablution and dries his lips and the chalice with the mundatory." (*Cath. Dict.*).

ABLUTIONS. Bathing the whole or parts of the body, as a religious practice, has been widely practised. It is well known that man in a primitive state regards rivers, springs, and wells as being often the abodes of deities. Water seemed to be a holy element. To bathe oneself in it meant to impart to oneself something of its divine life and power. This seems to have been the original idea in religious bathing. In course of time, however, the idea of purification came to prevail, and the washing away of external impurities became symbolical of the cleansing of the heart. Sin is, perhaps, regarded too as a real contagion, a disease, a kind of substance which may be washed away by bathing. The Incas of ancient Peru, after confessing their guilt, bathed in a river. It is a Vedic belief that sin may be removed by invoking the gods of water. The water-gods Varuna and Trita have power to wash it away. The later Brahmans regarded water as the "essence (sap) of immortality," and in modern India the waters of the Ganges have power, it is thought, to cleanse the blackest sinner. The Hindus shave their heads, and plunge into sacred streams. The Hebrews used consecrated water for the cleansing of impurities, and the modern Jews in Morocco preserve a reminiscence of the practice by throwing stones into the sea on New Year's Day. The Moors think that misfortune can be removed by ablutions. Ablutions are also practised to purify persons before they perform a sacred rite or come into contact with holy things (sacrifices, etc.). The Lapp wizard washes his body before sacrificing, as did also the ancient Egyptians, the Shinto priests of Japan, the ancient Greeks and Romans. Zoroastrianism regards impurity as a physical evil to be removed as quickly as possible. Brahmans and Hindus make daily bathing an important part of their religious exercises. In Lamaism the tips of the fingers are dipped in water before sacrifice. Jewish Rabbis wash the hands before praying. Mohammedans are commanded in the Koran to wash their faces and their hands up to the elbows, and to wipe their heads and their feet to the ankles, when they prepare for prayer (*Sur.* V., 8). Before reciting the liturgical form of prayer, therefore, they perform an elaborate ablution in which the acts are repeated three times. Where water is scarce, dust or sand serves as a substitute. In all such cases the idea is that any impurity might hurt the holiness of the deity and bring curses instead of blessings. Persons have been accustomed to bathe also after coming in contact with a corpse. The ablution removes the contagion of death. Sexual intercourse, again, has often (*e.g.* among the Babylonians, Hebrews, Arabs, Greeks) been regarded as defiling, and the defilement has been removed by bathing. Ablutions are necessary, again, after touching anything unclean (*e.g.* an unclean animal). Hindus and Brahmans live in constant fear of this defilement. The Hebrews dared not touch the dead carcase of a dog. If a living dog touches a Brahman, he plunges at once into water with his clothes on. It should be added that in ancient times ablutions have formed part of marriage ceremonials. Even deities, when they were united, bathed or were bathed. Thus the figure of Attis was bathed to represent her union with Cybele. Aphrodite bathed after her union with Adonis, and Hera after her marriage with Zeus. See E. Westermarck; J. G. Frazer, *G.B.; Adonis Attis Osiris*, 1906; W. R. Smith, *R.S.*, 1894; Monier-Williams, *Brahmanism;* J. A. Dubois and H. K. Beauchamp, *Hindu Manners, etc.*

ABODA ZARA. One of the treatises of the Mishnah (*q.v.*).

ABODE OF LOVE. See AGAPEMONITES.

ABOMINATION OF DESOLATION. A phrase occurring in the New Testament (Mt. 24, 15=Mk. 13, 14) in a passage in which Jesus is represented as speaking of his second coming. The "abomination of desolation" has been identified with the "man of sin" referred to in another apocalyptic passage, 2 Thess. 2, 1-12. The statue of an idol or false god seems to be meant, which causes desolation by being set up in opposition to the true God (so T. K. Cheyne). Another suggestion is that a statue of Caligula is intended (so Fr. Spitta). A third is that the "abomination" has reference to the Roman armies (so B. Weiss). See *Encycl. Bibl.*

ABORTION. Cases of miscarriage or abortion have sometimes received a religious significance. The Greenlanders thought an abortion became an evil spirit intent on avenging the crime. Artificial abortion is strongly condemned in the Christian religion (Tertullian, Augustine, etc.). It is also condemned by the sacred law of Zoroastrianism. See Edward Westermarck.

ABOTH. One of the treatises of the Mishnah (*q.v.*).

ABOTH DE-RABBI NATHAN. A Jewish treatise, being an exposition of the Mishnah treatise *Pirqê Ābōth* (*q.v.*). Of the two recensions which have been preserved, one is usually appended to the Babylonian Talmud (see TALMUD). Both have been published together by S. Schechter. The treatise is the work of a school (Tannaite), rather than of an individual author. An English version is included in M. L. Rodkinson's translation of the Babylonian Talmud, New York, 1900. See the *Jewish Encycl.*, i., 1901; W. O. E. Oesterley and G. H. Box.

ABRACADABRA. A mystic word or magical formula, used for the cure of fevers and agues. The letters were arranged in the form of a triangle, so that it was possible to read them in many different ways. The square piece of paper on which they were written was folded in the form of a cross. This was then worn as an amulet.

ABRAHAMITES. 1. A religious sect of the ninth century. They revived the teaching of the Paulianists, and denied the divinity of Christ. Their name was taken from Abraham or Ibrahim of Antioch. 2. A Bohemian religious sect, known also as Bohemian Deists. They appeared in 1782, and were so called because they claimed to represent the religion professed by Abraham before his circumcision. They were suppressed by force.

ABRAHAM-MEN. Beggars who wandered about the country seeking alms after the Dissolution of the Monasteries.

ABRAXAS STONES. Stones or gems having the word Abraxas or Abrasax engraved on them in Greek letters. Though of various shapes, the figure on them usually has a human trunk and arms, a cock's head, and two serpents' tails. They were used by the Gnostics, first by the Basilidians (*q.v.*), then by the Priscillians (*q.v.*), and afterwards generally. They were adopted by magicians and alchemists. They seem to have been used as talismans. Magicians in Egypt used them in the Hellenistic period. See Adolf Erman, *Handbook.*

ABRECH. A term occurring in the Old Testament (Genesis 41, 43). It is said that when Joseph was made grand-vizier of Egypt, the people "cried before him Abrech." The English version translates "bow the knee." This is unsuitable, because the form of the word is Causative ("make to kneel"). We should expect, moreover, an official title. This cannot be found in Egyptian. It has therefore been suggested that Abrech is a loan-word, being the equivalent of the Assyrian-Babylonian *abarakku*, a title of one of the five principal dignitaries of the empire. See *Encycl. Bibl.*

ABSOLUTION. To absolve is "to set free from" or "to acquit." Absolution is the act of pronouncing a person free from sin or penalty. According to the Christian idea of God, God Himself is strictly the only one who can do this. The Church, however, has taught that God deputed ministers, in the first instance the Apostles, to act for him. The crucial passage in the Bible is John xx., 23, "Whosesoever sins ye remit, they are remitted unto them, and whosesoever sins ye retain, they are retained." The origin and precise meaning of these words have been disputed. But in any case certain Church practices and doctrines have been connected with them. In the early days of the Christian Church anyone who had incurred its censure was required to do public penance involving exclusion from the Lord's Table. This having been duly performed, he was absolved publicly by Bishop and clergy, and re-admitted to Communion. In course of time and by slow degrees it came about that the sinner confessed privately to a priest and received from him alone the requisite absolution. At the Reformation the Church of England is commonly supposed to have renounced this practice. It cannot be denied, however, that there are passages in the Book of Common Prayer (the Holy Communion and Ordination Services) which do not altogether favour this view. In the Roman Catholic Church the practice has been maintained and elaborated. It has had, at least from 1215 (Innocent III.), a Tribunal of Penance, and has made the Sacrament of Penance consist of (1) Contrition or Attrition, (2) Confession, (3) Satisfaction, (4) Absolution. Confession is made in secret to the priest. The absolution afterwards pronounced by a duly authorised or delegated priest is a judicial act or sentence. There is a prescribed form of absolution in the Roman Ritual: "I absolve thee from thy sins, in the name of the Father, and of the Son, and of the Holy Ghost." See *Prot. Dict.; Cath. Dict.*

ABSTINENCE. See ASCETICISM.

ABSTINENTES. The name of a sect in Gaul and Spain at the end of the third century. Its members held that only by avoiding marriage could true holiness be attained. They found support in such New Testament passages as Matthew xix., 12, Hebrews xii., 14. The Christian life is that life of chastity which Jesus Himself led. The Abstinentes also objected to the use of meat. See J. H. Blunt.

ABUNDIA. The name of a goddess in German mythology who blesses marriage, brings good- or bad luck to spinners, etc. See P. D. Chantepie de La Saussaye, *Rel. of the Teutons*, 1902.

ABYSS, THE. In the Gnostic system of Valentinus "the Abyss" is the name of the unbegotten, invisible, ineffable Supreme Being, to whom the aeons owe their generation. The term is used in another sense in the New Testament (Revised Version). In Romans x., 7, it denotes Sheol, the Hebrew underworld (Authorised Version "the deep"). In Revelation ix., 1, 11, xi., 7, xvii., 8, xx., 1, 3 (Authorised Version "the bottomless pit") it is the abode of "the beast" and "the dragon," a place which seems to have been thought of as a lake of fire (cp Enoch x., 13).

ABYSSINIAN or ETHIOPIAN CHURCH. The early Church is said to have been founded, as a branch of the Christian Church, in A.D. 330 by Frumentius of Egypt or Phoenicia. In any case, a form of Christianity (Monophysite), in connection with Alexandria, was established in Abyssinia by the end of the sixth century. In the seventh century the country was practically isolated through the Mohammedan conquest of Egypt. Partly in consequence of this isolation, the Church has preserved a number of peculiar observances. The Jewish Sabbath is observed as well as the Christian Sunday. Circumcision is practised (though perhaps only for sanitary reasons), and certain foods are abstained from. The Books of Enoch and Jubilees (see APOCALYPTIC LITERATURE) are included in the sacred writings. The Virgin is worshipped, prayer is made to the saints, and great merit is attached to asceticism and monasticism. Some of these practices and observances seem to be due partly to Jewish influence, partly to an early connection with or migration from South Arabia. In 1540 the Abyssinians sought the help of the Portuguese against a threatened invasion by Mohammedans. Troops were sent, and the invaders were routed. The Pope then sought to convert the Abyssinians, and to effect this Jesuit missionaries laboured amongst the people. At length, after rebellion and bloodshed, proclamation of the Roman Catholic religion was made (1603). In 1632, however, perhaps in consequence of an attempt to abolish circumcision, the Jesuits were expelled, and the old Church was re-established. Since 1838 Roman Catholic missionaries have again worked in the country. Protestant missions have also been tried. Clerics are ordained by the *Aboun* (or *Abouna*), the head of the Church, an Egyptian monk nominated by the Alexandrian patriarch. His see, the centre of the Abyssinian Church, is at Axum. There are also such officials as a temporal head (*Etchigeh*), a head of the priesthood (*Nebrid*), and an ecclesiastical judge (*Lij Kancat*). The clergy are divided into priests, monks, and unordained clerks (*defteras*). The latter dance and sing in processions. There are a great many feast-days and fast-days. Paintings are hung in the Churches, and the cross is venerated. See *Prot. Dict.; Cath. Dict.*

ACACIANS. A school of Arians, followers of Acacius. See ARIANISM.

ACCA LARENTIA. A Roman goddess of the earth. She was worshipped as the protectress of the seed-corn, the guardian of the crops. It is said that she had twelve sons, and that she observed an annual sacrifice with them. The idea of the sacrifice having been to make the fields (*arva*) fertile, her sons were called Arval Brothers. The priesthood of that name is supposed to have been founded by Romulus who took the place of one of the brothers on his death. See O. Seyffert, *Dict.*

ACCAOPHORI. The name of a sect the members of which discarded the use of wine in the Holy Eucharist and substituted water. It is said that they were also called Hydroparastatae.

ACCEPTANTS. A name given to those theologians who accepted the papal Bull "Unigenitus" (1713) which condemned the views of the Jansenist leader Pasquier Quesnel (1634-1719). See JANSENISTS.

ACCEPTILATION. A word derived from Roman Law, and applied in theology to the doctrine of Duns Scotus, according to which the satisfaction rendered to God by Christ was not a full equivalent for the sins of mankind, but was graciously accepted by God as sufficient.

ACCOMMODATION. A term used in theology of a method of interpreting Scripture by which the words are accommodated or adapted to the needs of a discourse. Jesus himself, it is claimed, accommodated his teaching to his hearers by seeking to convey spiritual truths to them in a homely way.

ACELDAMA. A name compounded of two Aramaic words, and occurring in the New Testament as a designation of the field bought by Judas Iscariot, the disciple who betrayed Jesus, for some unknown purpose with the reward for his betrayal (Acts i., 19), or purchased by the priests as a place to bury strangers in. The Revised Version has Akeldama. The word is said to have been interpreted "the field of blood." But the best supported Greek reading is Acheldamach, which would give the unsuitable meaning "field of thy blood." On the other hand, assuming that Acheldamach is the correct form of the name, the second part of the word may be identified with another root. The name will then mean "field of sleep," *i.e.*, the sleep of death. See *Encycl. Bibl.*

ACEPHALI. A name applied to sects which had no recognised leader (the Monophysite Acephali), or who refused to follow their leader (the Nestorian Acephali); or to priests who refused allegiance to their diocesans and to suffragan bishops who would not obey their metropolitans. E. B. Tylor (*Primitive Culture*, i., 390) suggests that the term may well be used of those monsters who are reported by travellers to have existed without heads to their bodies.

ACHERON. In Homer several great rivers are represented as flowing through the world of the dead. One of these bears the name Acheron (river of woe). Later Legend imagines that the infernal regions are surrounded by these rivers. See O. Seyffert, *Dict.*

ACHIROPOETOS. Literally "made without hands." An expression used of pictures of Christ and the Virgin, which were supposed to have been executed miraculously, without human hands. There is one of these at Rome in the church of St. John of Lateran. St. Luke and angels are reputed to have been the artists.

ACŒMETAE. Literally "sleepless ones," an order of monks founded near Constantinople during the Patriarchate (A.D. 428-430) of Gennadius. They did not abstain from sleep altogether, but, in order that worship in their monastery should go on uninterruptedly, divided themselves into three "watches," each being of eight hours. A later name of the order was Studites, because during the episcopate of Gennadius a rich Roman consul, Studius by name, built a cloister for them in Constantinople. See J. H. Blunt.

ACOLYTE. Literally "one who follows," and so a ministrant or server. It is the highest of the four minor orders in the Church of Rome. The acolyte hands the priest wine and water at the Mass and carries the lights. He is now usually a layman.

ACOSMISM. A term used by Dr. Inge to denote the denial of reality to the visible world and the assertion that the only existence is "the intelligible world of ideas" in the mind of God. Examples of this attitude are the Neoplatonists, the mystic Eckhart, and the philosopher Spinoza.

ACROSTIC. A peculiar kind of verse-composition. The initial letters of the lines are made to form together a word or sentence. Religious psalms or hymns are sometimes composed in this way. There are examples in the Psalms of the Old Testament (*e.g.*, Ps. 119). In the 119th Psalm the stanzas run through the letters of the Hebrew alphabet. In Rabbinic literature this method of composition became very common. Sometimes the order of the alphabet was reversed, the hymn beginning with the last letter and ending with the first. See J. W. Etheridge, *Intr. to Heb. Lit.*, 1856.

ACT FOR UNIFORMITY. An act passed in 1549 for the purpose of introducing "uniformity of public worship." It required the new Liturgy of Edward VI. to be adopted throughout the kingdom. Refusal to comply with this command was punished by imprisonment or loss of benefice. There were other Acts of Uniformity in the reigns of Edward VI., Elizabeth, and Charles II.

ACT OF FAITH. See AUTO DA FE.

ACT OF SEPARATION. In 1843 a number of Scotch Presbyterian ministers and professors (470) signed a document by which they resigned their livings and in which they protested against attempts to interfere with the right of a congregation to choose its own minister.

ACT OF UNIFORMITY. An Act passed in the reign of Charles II. (1661). It required all clergymen of the Church of England to accept the Thirty-Nine Articles as the basis of uniformity in religion. Many clergymen were deprived of their livings for refusing to subscribe.

ACTA FRATRUM UNITATIS IN ANGLIA. An important folio work published (1749) by Count Nicolaus von Zinzendorf to explain the methods and principles of the Moravian Brethren (*q.v.*). John Wesley summarized the contents in a pamphlet (1750), "Contents of a Folio History," in which he fiercely attacked the Brethren as hypocrits and heretics. See J. E. Hutton, *History of the Moravian Church*, 1909.

ACTISTETES. A name derived from the Greek word *aktistos*, "uncreated." The sect of the Actistetes were so called because they claimed that Christ ought not to be called a created Being after his Incarnation, and therefore denied that he became truly man.

ACTS OF PAUL AND THECLA. See APOCRYPHAL BOOKS OF THE NEW TESTAMENT.

ACTS OF PILATE. *Acta Pilati* or *Anaphora Pilati*, a work which professes to give a record of the trial and death of Jesus, made for the Emperor Tiberius by Pontius Pilate, procurator of Judaea at the time of Jesus' death. The work is not genuine. See R. A. Lipsius, *Die Pilatus-Akten*, new ed., 1886. Cp. APOCRYPHAL BOOKS OF THE NEW TESTAMENT.

ACTS OF THE APOSTLES. One of the books of the New Testament which continues the Gospel story and gives in particular an account of the acts of the apostles Peter and Paul. Part of it reproduces the diary of a companion of Paul (the "we" sections). It is commonly considered to be the work of Luke, the reputed author of the third Gospel. Luke was a physician, and Adolf Harnack has recently sought to show that medical terms are common in both works. Harnack thinks Luke's material was in existence about 80 A.D. B. W. Bacon gives 85-90 as the approximate date. Other critics, however, deny the Lucan authorship and place the work as late as 120-130 A.D. P. W. Schmiedel places it between 105 and 130 A.D. See Adolf Harnack, *Luke the Physician*, 1907; W. C. Selleck, *New Appreciation of the Bible*, 1907; *Encycl. Bibl.*

ACTS OF THE SAINTS or MARTYRS. These are collections of stories about the Christian saints and martyrs. The most celebrated collection is that begun in the 17th century by the Jesuits and continued by the Bollandists (*q.v.*). Eusebius of Caesarea made two collections, one of which is still to be found at the end of Book viii. of his Church History. Simeon Metaphrastes compiled another about 900 A.D., probably making use of a collection (12 vols.) current in the Church of Constantinople. The West had its collection, "Legenda Aurea," made by Jacobus de Voragine (ob. 1298). Much of the material incorporated in the early collections is of doubtful value. Attempts have been made to sift it, however. In 1689 a Benedictine monk, Ruinart, published a folio volume, "Pure Acts of the Martyrs," and in 1748 Stephen Assemani published in two folio volumes, "Acts of the Holy Martyrs of the East and of the West." See *Cath. Dict.*

ACUANITES. Followers of Acuan, who was a leading Manichaean in Mesopotamia in the time of Epiphanius.

ADAD. A Babylonian deity. He was the god of storms and thunder. He is referred to in the Hammurabi (2150 B.C.) Code as one who might flood a man's field and destroy his harvest (§§45, 48). Another name for the same deity was Ramman (*q.v.*). See Morris Jastrow, *Rel.*

ADAD. The name, according to Macrobius, of the chief god of the Syrians, the name of his consort being Adargatis. He is the same as Hadad (cp. the Assyrian storm-god "Adad"), and is identified by Garstang with the chief god of the Hittites.

ADAMITES. A Gnostic sect which appeared in Africa in the second century. They were so called no doubt because they thought to live in a state of innocence, like Adam before the fall, though the name has also been connected with another Adam who is supposed to have founded the sect. They renounced marriage, and worshipped in nude condition, holding their meetings underground. Another sect holding some of their tenets appeared in Bohemia in 1421. They were a branch of the Beghards or Brethren of the Free Spirit (*q.v.*), and were called Picards (*q.v.*). Zisca slew a great many of them. See J. H. Blunt.

ADAM'S PEAK. A mountain summit in the South of Ceylon. Europeans have adopted the name from the Mohammedans. On the summit there is a hollow place which was supposed to resemble a footprint. Mohammedans said that it was made by Alī or Adam. Buddhists claim that it is the impress of the Buddha's foot. Hindus have claimed it for the god Siva, Portuguese Christians for St. Thomas. Many monasteries in Ceylon contain representations of this footprint made of wood. See further H. Hackmann.

ADAPA LEGEND. A legend in the Babylonian-Assyrian religion. It was found on the El-Amarna tablets (15th cent., B.C.). Adapa, a fisherman, son of Ea, is fishing in "the sea," when a storm arises. Though only a mortal, swept into the waters by the South Wind, he subdues the element, since it is under the control of his father, and breaks the wings of the storm-bird. Anu, God of Heaven, surprised at the disappearance of the south wind, asks the god Ilabrat, his messenger, the reason. He is informed, and thereupon requests Ea to send Adapa to him for trial. He does so, but advises his son to seek the protection of Tammuz and Gishzida, gods who guard the approach to the gate of heaven. Accordingly Adapa goes in mourning, explaining that he does so because "two gods have disappeared from the earth." This conciliates the two gods. They are prepared to plead his cause before Anu. The god's wrath is appeased. He is alarmed, however, that Adapa should have penetrated to heaven and seen its secrets. The only thing to do now is for the gods to make him one of themselves. He is therefore offered the food of life to eat and the waters of life to drink. But Ea had warned him not to eat or drink. He therefore refuses them and returns to earth. The lesson conveyed by the story seems to be that it is not good for man to live for ever. Ea, in his wisdom, prevents it. The legend is based upon "the nature-myth of the annual fight of the sun with the violent elements of nature." Gishzida and Tammuz are both solar deities, and Adapa seems to be identical with Marduk, a third solar deity. But the story has become more than a nature-myth. It is now a legend containing a moral or lesson. See Morris Jastrow, *Rel.*

ADAR. The twelfth month of the Jewish sacred year. The twelfth month of the Babylonian calendar has the same name. It was sacred to the seven evil spirits. The 15th day of the month was sacred to Shamash, Malkatu, and Bunene. An intercalated month is also called Adar, Second Adar. This is sacred to Ashur. See Morris Jastrow, *Rel.*

ADARGATIS. The name, according to Macrobius, of the chief goddess of the Syrians. It is equivalent to Atargatis (*q.v.*), who is identified by Garstang with the chief goddess of the Hittites.

'ADAWIYYA. An Arabian religious order. It was founded by Sheikh 'Adī ibn Musâfir al-Hakkârī, who took up his abode in the ruins of a Christian convent to the west of Mosul. After his death he became the patron saint of the Yazīdīs. See Clément Huart, *Arabic Lit.*, 1903.

ADDAI, TEACHING OF. An apocryphal book which was probably written about the middle of the third century, perhaps in or near Edessa. In this book it is said that in Edessa the early Christians heard the Old Testament read, and also "the New [Testament] of the Diatessaron." See C. R. Gregory, *Canon.*

ADECERDITAE. A name given to those who believed that Christ by descending into Hell was able to save many who were found there.

ADELOPHAGI. A name given to a sect, perhaps belonging to the end of the fourth century, the members of which would not eat in the presence of others. That is implied in their name which is derived from Greek words. But what precisely is meant is not clear. It may only mean that they would not eat with members of another sect. The Adelophagi seem to have denied the divinity of the Holy Spirit.

ADELPHIANS. One of the names given to the Euchites (*q.v.*). They were so called after one of their leaders, Adelphius of Mesopotamia. Treacherously enticed to disclose his views by Flavian, Bishop of Antioch, Adelphius was excommunicated and banished.

ADELPHOPOIIA. Literally "the making of (into) a brother." A religious rite which finds a place in old Greek prayer-books. It is similar to a rite which still survives in South Italy. In order to establish a blood-covenant between two persons, their blood is mingled. See F. C. Conybeare, *M.M.M.*, 1909, pp. 258f., and cp. BLOOD, COVENANT.

ADEPTS. A term used in Theosophy (*q.v.*). The adepts are those persons, members of a great Brotherhood, who possess the Secret Wisdom of Theosophy. They are living men whose evolution has reached a higher stage than that of ordinary humanity. See Annie Besant, "Theosophy," in *R.S.W.*

ADESSENARIANS. A name formed from the Latin word *adesse*, "to be present," and applied in the sixteenth century to Lutherans who held that in the Holy Eucharist Christ is really, and not merely figuratively, present, but who would not accept the Roman Catholic doctrine of transubstantiation.

ADIAPHORISTS. From the Greek term *adia'phora,* " things indifferent." The Leipzig interim of 1548 during the Protestant controversy in Germany used the term *adia'phora* of matters which Melanchthon and his party declared to be indifferent. Such matters were, *e.g.*, the use of pictures, candles, surplices, Latin hymns and vespers in the Roman Catholic Church, which the Lutherans, on the other hand, regarded as subversive of the faith.

ADIAPHORITES. An early religious sect, the members of which refused to recognise any distinction between the divine and human natures of Christ. See A. Harnack, *History of Dogma*, iv., 1898.

ADI BRAHMA SAMAJ. See BRAHMA SAMAJ.

ADI BUDDHA. The name in Lamaism for the one supreme Buddha from whom are ultimately derived the five celestial prototypes of the historical Buddhas. See H. Hackmann.

ADIGRANTH. The sacred book or bible of the Sikhs, compiled by Arjun in the sixteenth century. It was originally called the " Granth." The term Adigranth, First Book, was applied to it afterwards to distinguish it from a later collection of books. See E. W. Hopkins.

ADITI. An Indian goddess. Aditi (" Boundlessness ") is the mother of Varuna (*q.v.*) and the " mother of kings." All gods, men, and things are, in fact, identified with her. She has seven or eight children, of whom the chief, *the* Aditya (son of Aditi) is Varuna (*q.v.*).

ADITYAS. See ADITI and VARUNA.

ADMONITIONISTS. A name given to the Puritans who supported the " Admonition to the Parliament," a manifesto printed in 1572. The "Admonition" demanded extreme puritanical changes in the constitution of the Church. The principal authors were John Field (*d.* 1588) and Thomas Wilcox (*d.* 1608), and they were both imprisoned for libel in Newgate. The Admonitionists set up a secret conventicle at Wandsworth.

ADMONITION TO THE PARLIAMENT. A document drawn up by Puritans (1571) in the reign of Queen Elisabeth. It was Calvinistic, claiming that all rites and ceremonies in the Church of England should accord with the institutions of Apostolic times and with the teaching of Holy Scripture. All Roman Catholic practices, it contended further, should be abolished.

ADONAI. Literally " my Lord." A Hebrew name for the supreme deity. It is really a plural form (the so-called " plural of majesty "), the singular being *ādōn*, " lord." The Jews have a name for God which was considered too sacred to be pronounced. This consisted of the consonants JHVH. Where it occurs in the sacred texts, they pronounce in reading " Adonai " as a substitute for it. See JEHOVAH.

ADONIS. A deity of Semitic origin (Adonis=*ādōn* =lord), the personification of vegetation which dies yearly and revives as often. Legend represented that Adonis died while hunting from a wound inflicted by a boar, and that out of his blood Aphrodite (*q.v.*) made the anemone grow. Loved by both Aphrodite and Persephone, it was decided by Zeus that he should pass half the year with each goddess. In the Adonis-cult there was a yearly Festival of Adonis, observed by women. This spread from Phoenicia to Cyprus, Greece, Egypt and ultimately to Rome. First a figure supposed to represent Adonis' corpse received sad and solemn funeral rites: then its resurrection was celebrated with wild rejoicings. " Adonis-gardens " were a feature of the celebration. These were baskets or pots of earth sown with plants of various kinds that sprang up quickly and as quickly faded. The plants were afterwards thrown into the water. There is an allusion to them in the Old Testament (Isaiah xvii., 10, Revised Version margin, " plantings of Adonis "). It has been suggested that Adonis is another form of the Babylonian deity Tammuz (*q.v.*) who seems to have been honoured with a similar festival. See O. Seyffert, *Dict.;* J. G. Frazer, *Adonis Attis Osiris*, 1906.

ADONIS, RIVER. Lucian (§8) speaks of a marvellous portent in the region of the Byblians. " A river, flowing from Mount Libanus, discharges itself into the sea: this river bears the name of Adonis. Every year regularly it is tinged with blood, and loses its proper colour before it falls into the sea: it dyes the sea, to a large space, red: and this announces their time of mourning to the Byblians. Their story is that during these days Adonis is wounded, and that the river's nature is changed by the blood which flows into its waters; and that it takes its name from this blood " (transl. by H. A. Strong).

ADOPTION. The taking of a child into a family or clan to be treated as one of its born members often has a religious significance. In Athens and Rome sons were adopted, when necessary, not merely to perpetuate the race, but also to continue its religious rites. In China the eldest son of the principal wife occupies an important position, as the continuator of the ancestral line and the person upon whom devolves the charge of worshipping the ancestors. If the principal wife has no son, she adopts one. When adoption takes place, it is naturally celebrated by a more or less elaborate ceremony. Where importance is attached to the feeling of kinship, it has sometimes been the custom to make incisions and mingle the blood of adopters and adopted (cp. BLOOD). Mr. E. S. Hartland thinks that in the blood-covenant (see COVENANT), we have a survival of a rite of adoption into the clan. Such a practice is not merely a formality. The thought that the blood has been mingled acts as a powerful suggestion of kinship. Another practice is for the new mother, when a child is to be adopted, to pretend to give birth to him. Thus, when the goddess Hera adopted Hercules, she imitated a real birth. The same thing is done in Bulgaria, as well as among the Bosnian Turks and the Berawans of Sarawak. An example of a more elaborate and religious ceremony may be taken from India. Among the Brahmans, when a child is to be adopted, an auspicious day is first chosen. The portals of the house are decorated with garlands of leaves (*toranams*), and a pavilion (*pandal*) is erected. Then, when the ceremonies are to begin, sacrifice is made to Vigneshwara (the god of obstacles) and the nine planets. The new father and mother sit on a small daïs in the middle of the pavilion. The real mother is given a new garment, and a sum of money as " nursing wages." Carrying her son to the adoptive father, she is asked by him whether she hands over her child to be brought up. The answer is in the affirmative. Then a dish of water with powdered saffron in it is brought in. Next the priest (*purohita*) blesses it, mutters some prayers or formulas (*mantrams*), and performs some ceremonies. After this the real mother hands the dish to the new father, invokes fire as a witness, and says, " I give up this child to you; I have no more right over him." The new father takes the child on his knees and solemnly and ceremonially promises to bring it up as his own child. He and his wife next take a little saffron water in their right hands and drink it. Then they pour some into the hand of the child who has to drink it. They conclude the ceremony by saying: " We have admitted this child into our *gothram*, and we incorporate him into it." Other festivities follow. The ceremony among the Sudras and the Brahmans is almost identical; the only difference being that among the Sudras the new father and mother pour the saffron water on the feet of the child with one hand, while with the other they catch and drink it. See J. A. Dubois and H. K. Beauchamp, *Hindu Manners, etc.*, 1897; J. J. M. de Groot, *Rel. System of China*, 1894, etc.; E. S. Hartland, *Legend of Perseus*, 1894-96; J. G. Frazer, *G.B.*; E. Westermarck.

ADOPTIONISM. The doctrine according to which Jesus, as regards his human nature, was Son of God only by adoption. In the eighth century we hear of a special sect, the Adoptiani, which avowed this doctrine. The idea, however, was no new one. It was held by early Christian writers of Africa and Italy and was prevalent among Syriac and Armenian Christians. Elipandus, Archbishop of Toledo, and Felix, Bishop of Urgel, in Spain, held the doctrine at the beginning of the ninth century, and were condemned as heretics at the Council of Ratisbon. The doctrine was condemned again at Frankfort, Rome, and Aix la Chapelle.

ADORATION OF RELICS. The relics of departed saints and martyrs have been objects of worship in the Christian Church, and are still venerated by Roman Catholics. Such relics include their bodies, "fragments of their bodies, articles or portions of articles which they have used, such as clothes, vestments, rosaries, and the like"; in the case of Jesus, "the holy nails, lance, spear, or fragments of the True Cross"; and, in the case of Mary, "the girdle, veil, etc." (Addis and Arnold). The explanation given of this veneration is (1) that the saints were living members of Christ and their bodies the temples of the Holy Ghost; and (2) that God sometimes makes their relics instruments of healing and other miracles, and bestows "spiritual graces on those who with pure hearts keep and honour them." See *Cath. Dict.*

ADORATION OF THE CROSS. A ceremony observed in the Church of Rome on Good Friday. St. Thomas said that the cross was to be adored with supreme worship (*latria*), and Benedict XIV. quotes a verse of Lactantius which speaks of "adoring the cross." On Good Friday a crucifix being unveiled, priest and people kiss it and adore it on their knees. It is explained that the cross may be adored as representing something else. In this way "we may give to the cross relatively —*i.e.*, to the cross as carrying on our mind to Christ— the same honour which we give to Christ absolutely, *i.e.*, in himself. See *Cath. Dict.*; *Prot. Dict.*

ADRAMMELECH. According to a passage in the Old Testament, this was the name of a Babylonian deity. In II Kings xvii., 31, it is said that the Sepharvites whom the King of Assyria (Sargon) placed in the cities of Samaria "burnt their children in the fire to Adrammelech and Anammelech, the gods of Sepharvaim." It is difficult to identify the deity or to understand the allusion. Mr. L. W. King tells us (*Encycl. Bibl.*) that throughout the cuneiform inscriptions, "there is no allusion to human sacrifice, and in the sculptures and reliefs no representation of the rite has been discovered." The name used to be explained as equivalent to *Adarmalik*, "Adar the prince." This was supposed to be another name for the god Ninib (*q.v.*). But the supposition was a mere conjecture. On the other hand, if, as some scholars think, Sepharvaim is to be identified with Sippar, Adrammelech may have been a subsidiary name or title of Shamash the Sun-god, for the worship of this god was specially associated with Sippar. See *Encycl. Bibl.*

ADRANUS. A Sicilian god to whom dogs seem to have been sacred. Reference is made to his sacred dogs by Aelian (*Nat. An.*, xi., 20). Adranus was perhaps of Semitic origin. See W. R. Smith, *R.S.*

ADRASTEIA. A Greek goddess. Dr. L. R. Farnell (*Cults*, vol. ii., 1896) thinks that originally the name was a local title of Cybele. The cult of Adrasteia was established near Priapus, Cyzicus, and in the Troad, and it was in these localities in particular that Cybele was worshipped. In the later period she came to be regarded as a kind of twin-sister of Nemesis and was connected sometimes with Artemis. A plausible explanation of this development is offered by Farnell. "Cybele 'Αδράστεια meant the goddess of the city or locality in Phrygia that took its name from the Phrygian hero Adrastus. Then when the title was detached, it came to be interpreted as "the goddess from whom one cannot run away"; and this meaning may have been assisted by the confusion between the Phrygian Adrastus and the Argive hero, whose legend was a picture of inevitable fate. When afterwards this new sense of 'Αδράστεια came into vogue, she naturally became connected with Nemesis, and so accidentally with Artemis."

ADRIANISTS. The followers of a Dutch Anabaptist, Adrian Hamsted, who was for a time a minister in London. Edmund Grindal (*d.* 1583), Bishop of London and afterwards Archbishop of Canterbury, having deposed him early in the year 1561, he returned to Holland. The Adrianists would not accept the doctrine of the miraculous birth of Jesus.

ADRIATIC, MARRIAGE OF THE. An annual ceremony of early origin celebrated on Ascension Day at Venice. The Doge was rowed to the sea in his state barge, and threw a consecrated ring into the water. Pope Alexander III. originated the ceremony in 1174. From this custom Venice received the name "Bride of the Sea."

ADSALLUTA. The name of a goddess worshipped by the ancient Celts. Adsallūta was paired with a god Savus.

ADSMERIUS. Adsmerius or Atesmerius was one of the names given by the ancient Celts to a god who corresponded to the Roman Mercury.

ADULTERY. According to Hebrew law an adulterer must be put to death. In the ancient Egyptian religion it is an offence which excludes the guilty persons when they die from the kingdom of Osiris. The Babylonian Code of Khammurabi decrees that if the wife of a man be found committing adultery with another male, "they shall be bound and thrown into the water, unless the husband lets his wife live; and the king lets his servant live" (Chilperic Edwards, *The Oldest Laws in the World*, § 129). Brahmanic religion regards adultery as one of the worst sins, a sin against Varuna. A woman must beware of sacrificing with this guilt on her soul; but if confessed, "the guilt becomes less." Christianity condemns adultery equally in the case of husband or wife. Adultery is also condemned by primitive folk, though not by all. The god called Batara or Petara among the Sea Dyaks of Borneo punishes cases of adultery. So do Puluga, the supreme being of the Andaman Islanders; Leza, the supreme being of the Bantu people living between Lakes Tanganyika and Bangweolo, and of the Awemba. Elephant-hunters in East Africa think that if, during their absence, their wives are unfaithful, they themselves will be killed or wounded by the elephant. An Aleutian hunter of sea-otters believes that the same thing will prevent him from killing a single animal. Again it is thought by many of the indigenous tribes of Sarawak that "were the wives to commit adultery while their husbands are searching for camphor in the jungle, the camphor obtained by the men would evaporate" (J. G. Frazer). The Karens of Burma believe that the crops are blighted and the harvests spoiled by adultery or fornication. The same idea prevails among the Battas of Sumatra and the Dyaks of Borneo. See E. Westermarck; J. G. Frazer, *G.B.; E. W. Hopkins, The Religions of India*, 1895.

ADVENT. Literally "the coming," Latin *adventus*, the beginning of the ecclesiastical year, a season of preparation for the coming of Christ. It was first observed in the Western Church and thence was introduced into the Eastern Church as a period of penitence and fasting preliminary to the celebration of the Festival of Christmas or of the Nativity of Jesus. In the Greek Church it lasts forty days; and similarly in the Gallican Church of the sixth century it extended from the feast of St. Martin (Martinmas, November 11) to the Nativity, and was called "Quadragesima S. Martini." In the Church of England and of Rome the season has been restricted since the time of Gregory the Great to the four Sundays of Advent, the previous Sunday serving as a kind of introduction. During this season the Church "desires that her children should practise fasting, works of penance, meditation, and prayer, in order to prepare themselves for celebrating worthily the coming (*adventum*) of the Son of God in the flesh, to promote His spiritual advent within their own souls, and to school themselves to look forward with hope and joy to His second advent, when He shall come again to judge mankind" (Addis and Arnold). See A. Barry, *Teacher's Prayer Book; Cath. Dict.*

ADVENTISTS, SECOND. A religious body in America, the members of which believe that the second coming of Christ is to take place soon. The sect was founded by William Miller (1781-1849). The time of the second coming was definitely fixed, but has had to be altered from time to time. The Adventists observe various kinds of abstinence. There are various branches of the sect. One of them, the Seventh Day Adventists, fixes no definite date for the second coming. The members are so called because they regard the Sabbath as being still the seventh day.

ADVOCATUS DIABOLI. When a person is proposed for canonisation in the Roman Catholic Church someone is appointed as the "advocatus diaboli" to bring forward any objections to the proposal. On the other side, there is an "advocatus Dei," appointed to defend the person in question.

ADVOCATUS ECCLESIÆ. The "advocati ecclesiarum" were "advocate-protectors, princes or barons, or other powerful laymen, who, for a consideration, undertook to protect the property of a church or monastery, as well as the lives of the inmates" (Addis and Arnold). The Lateran Council (A.D. 1215) had to decree that they must be restrained from encroaching on the property entrusted to them. See *Cath. Dict.*

ADVOWSON. A term in Church of England Law, denoting the right of presentation to a vacant ecclesiastical benefice. The right belongs to the successor of the founder of the benefice who is commonly called the Patron. See *Prot. Dict.*

ADWAITA. The name of a sect among the Brahmans. Its adherents hold that the universe, with all its phenomena, has no real existence. The phenomena comprised in the universe are the result of illusion. "All animate and inanimate things are but parts of the Deity," the one eternal essence. See J. A. Dubois and H. K. Beauchamp.

ADYTUM. The most sacred part ("the holy of holies") of an ancient temple accessible only to priests. In Greek temples it was sometimes underground.

ÆGIR. A name occurring in Teutonic mythology. Ægir is the chief of sea-giants, and is commonly a personification of the calm open sea. He has a wife, Ran (*q.v.*), and nine daughters who represent together the sea's surf and rough waves. See P. D. Chantepie de la Saussaye, *Rel. of the Teutons*, 1902.

AEGIS. A name for the shield of Zeus. Homer imagines it to have been forged by Hephaestus. When Zeus shakes it, there is thunder and lightning. It is thus a storm and thunder-cloud figured as a shield. It is also borne by Athēnē, daughter of Zeus. See O. Seyffert, *Dict.*

ÆOLUS. A figure in Greek mythology. Homer imagines him to have been made keeper of the winds by Zeus. Later legend represents him as dwelling in one of the Æolian isles north of Sicily, Lipara or Strongyle, where he kept the winds imprisoned in a cave underneath a mountain. See O. Seyffert, *Dict.*

ÆON. Literally an "age" or "eternity." A term used by the Gnostics to denote an emanation from God. See Louis Duchesne, *Hist.*

ÆQUIPROBABILISM. One of the different forms or schools of Probabilism. It is the doctrine that the less certain opinion may be followed when it is as probable as the more certain. See A. Harnack, *Hist. of Dogma*, vii., 1899.

AERIANS. The followers of an Arian monk, Aerius. He was exiled from Sebaste in Armenia. He recognised no difference between a bishop and a presbyter, protested against prayers and offerings for the dead, and protested against the sacrifice of a paschal lamb in Christian worship. He also disapproved of fasting. The sect which he founded soon died out.

ÆSCULAPIUS. Asclepios (Latin *Æsculapius*) was worshipped by the Greeks as the god of Medicine. He is reputed to have been the son of Apollo (*q.v.*), the god of healing, by Coronis. One of the legends narrates that Coronis was secretly delivered of her child on a journey to the Peloponnēsus. She exposed him on a mountain, but he was suckled by a she-goat. According to another legend the boy was snatched by Apollo from the pyre on which his mother was about to be burnt, and was committed to the charge of a centaur, Chiron, who reared him and taught him how to cure all diseases. Homer and Pindar represent him as a hero endowed with the skill of a successful leech. He then appears as the god of healing worshipped throughout Greece in groves, on mountains, and by medicinal springs. He was able even to bring the dead to life. "Often the cure was effected by the dreams of the patients, who were required to sleep in the sacred building, in which there sometimes stood, as might be expected, a statue of Sleep or Dreaming" (O. Seyffert). The introduction of the worship of Æsculapius among the Romans is supposed to have been enjoined by the Sibylline Books. It took place about 290 B.C. It is said that the god used to reveal himself in the form of a snake. A coiled serpent and a staff are represented on his statues, and snakes were kept in his temples. J. M. Robertson points out that the title Saviour was given by the Greeks to Zeus, Helios, Artemis, Dionysos, Heracles, the Dioscuri, Cybelē, and Æsculapius. There is nothing surprising in this. Anyone may be called a saviour (cp., in the Old Testament, Judges iii., 9, II Kings xiii., 5). See O. Seyffert, *Dict.;* Reinach, *O.;* J. M. Robertson, *C.M.; P.C.;* J. G. Frazer, *G.B.*

AESHMA DAEVA. An evil demon in the ancient Persian religion. In *Yasna* lvii. of the Zend-avesta he is described as "the cruel demon Aêshemô." The word means "rapine" or "attack." In the Vendidad (*Fargard* xix), he is called "the impetuous rusher." The Asmodeus of the book of Tobit (iii., 8; see APOCRYPHA OF THE OLD TESTAMENT) has been identified with the Aeshma Daeva of Zoroastrianism. See Martin Haug.

ÆSIR. The name of some Teutonic deities. The Irish form of the name is ESIR. The Æsir have been identified by some with the Indian Asuras (*q.v.*). The gods figure in Danish mythology which tells of a conflict between the Æsir and the Vanir. See P. D. Chantepie de La Saussaye, *Rel. of the Teutons*, 1902.

ÆTERNALES. A sect mentioned by Danæus. The members believed that the present condition of the world will remain unchanged. It will not be altered even after the Second Coming of Jesus.

ÆTIANS. The followers of Aetius. Ordained deacon at Antioch A.D. 350, he was expelled on account of his Arian views. He returned in 358, but in 360 the Emperor Constantius summoned him to Constantinople and then banished him to Phrygia. He denied the doctrine of the Nicene Creed and agreed with the Homoiousians (*q.v.*) that the Son is like the Father. See ARIANISM.

AFFIRMATION. Persons (Quakers, etc.) who have conscientious scruples against taking an oath in a court of justice have been allowed since 1833 to make, instead, a solemn declaration. The permission has been extended gradually, a new Oaths Act having been passed as recently as 1888. In Scotland a person under age is required to make a "declaration."

AFFUSION. A term applied to the pouring of water on persons in Christian baptism (*q.v.*).

AFRINGĀN CEREMONY. A Parsee ceremony performed in honour of a deceased person or of an angel. In front of the fire, which burns in a vaselike vessel at the southern end of the ceremonial area, is placed a tray of wine and fruits, and on the left of the tray flowers are put. The chief officiating priest then pronounces a number of formulæ. After this the consecrated fruit and wine are partaken of by the priests and the other persons present, this being accompanied by solemn recitations. See Martin Haug.

AFRINGĀNS. A term used in the Zoroastrian religion of the "blessings which are to be recited over a meal consisting of wine, milk, bread, and fruits, to which an angel or the spirit of a deceased person is invited, and in whose honour the meal is prepared. After the consecration (which only a priest can perform) is over, the meal is eaten by those who are present" (Haug). There are special Afringāns for different occasions. See Martin Haug.

AFRIT. The name of a powerful demon in Mohammedan mythology.

AGAPÆ. This was a love- or charity-feast celebrated among the early Christians, in imitation, it is thought of common meals held among the Greeks (συσσίτια). It is mentioned in the New Testament. In the Epistle of Jude (vs. 12) it is said: "These are they who are hidden rocks (or spots) in your love-feasts when they feast with you, shepherds that without fear feed themselves." And it is referred to in I Corinthians xi. Rich and poor shared equally in the feast, the materials being supplied by those who could afford to contribute. "The Eucharist was always the chief act of worship. In the beginning it was celebrated at the end of a corporate meal. This is what we call the Agapé. In the second century the Agapé was already distinct from the Eucharist. It took place in the evening, while the Eucharist was celebrated at the morning meeting. A corporate meal, however frugal, was only suitable for restricted groups: as soon as the churches became crowded assemblies, it would be difficult to organize such banquets so as to secure order and decorum. The Agapé was still kept up, but less as an expression of a real corporate life than as a memory of the past, and also as a work of charity; but soon no one went to it except the poor and the clergy, and the latter took part in it rather as part of their duty than for their own benefit. Its recurrence did not coincide with that of the ordinary liturgical service. The Agapé became more and more rare, and finally fell into disuse" (Mgr. Duchesne). According to Duchesne, this must be distinguished from another kind of Agapæ of remote origin. This was a banquet in commemoration of deceased persons. It was still observed in the third and fourth centuries. See Louis Duchesne, *Hist.*; W. Soltau, *Das Fortleben des Heidentums in der altchristlichen Kirche*, 1906; *Cath. Dict.*; *Prot. Dict.*

AGAPEMONITES. The members of a conventual establishment called "Agapemone," "abode of love." The establishment was founded (1859) at Charlinch, near Bridgewater, Somerset, by Henry James Prince, a clergyman of the Church of England. It is now at Spaxton. The Agapemonites profess to devote themselves to spiritual contemplation, and to live in spiritual wedlock. See Hepworth Dixon, *Spiritual Wives*, 1868.

AGAPETAI and AGAPETOI. The words mean literally "beloved women" and "beloved men." They were men and women (spiritual wives) who lived together as "brothers and sisters" in the early Christian Church. The custom is eulogised in the "Shepherd of Hermas" dating from the end of the first or beginning of the second century. Tertullian however denounced it, and about the middle of the third century Cyprian, Bishop of Carthage, disallowed it. They are still referred to by Gregory of Nyssa in the fourth century. See F. C. Conybeare, *M.M.M.*, pp. 217 f.

AGAPETOS. There is reason to think that in the times when the Gospels of the New Testament were composed the Greek expression ὁ ἀγαπητός "the Beloved One" was a standing Messianic title. In this sense it seems to be used sometimes in the Gospels (*e.g.*, Mark i., 11; ix., 7). See J. Armitage Robinson, *Ephesians*, 1904; Allan Menzies, *The Earliest Gospel*, 1901.

AGDISTIS. A nature-goddess worshipped by a tribe of the Phrygians, equivalent to Atargatis.

AGGADA. See HAGGADAH.

AGHORIS. The Aghoris or Aghorpanthis are a class of Saiva mendicants in India, found now chiefly at Benāres and at Girnar near Mount Abu. They used to practise cannibalism, and still feed on human corpses and excrement. "The Aghoris now represent their filthy habits as merely giving practical expression to the abstract doctrine that the whole universe is full of Brahma, and consequently that one thing is as pure as another. By eating the most horrible food they utterly subdue their natural appetites, and hence acquire great power over themselves and over the forces of nature. It is believed that an Aghori can at will assume the shapes of a bird, an animal or a fish, and that he can bring back to life a corpse of which he has eaten a part" (R. V. Russell).

AGIONITES. One of the sects condemned by the Council of Gangra (between A.D. 360 and 380). The name may have been formed from the Greek word *hagios*, "pure."

AGIOSEMANDRUM. Literally "the holy caller" from two Greek words. In Turkey, where the use of bells is forbidden, this is a wooden instrument used instead of a bell in Christian churches.

AGLIBOL. A solar deity, worshipped by the Palmyrenes.

AGNI. An Indian deity. Agni, originally fire and then altar-fire, is one of the two greatest gods in the Rig Veda (*q.v.*), the other being Soma. Agni, in whom are the other gods, is regarded as a trinity (fire, lightning, sun; earth, atmosphere, heaven), and Hindu ritual prescribes the keeping up of "three fires." In the first hymn in the Rig Veda, Agni is described as "house-priest," "priest divine of sacrifice," "oblation priest," "lord of sacrifice and shining guardian of the rite." The Dabistān refers to "Agni-worshippers" as a sect existing in the seventeenth century. It is said that there are still in India "Agnihotri," fire priests who perform the Vedic sacrifices which entitle the worshippers to heavenly life. See E. W. Hopkins, and cp. E. B. Tylor, ii., 281, 386.

AGNIHOTRIS. A term used in Brahmanism of those Brahmans who duly perform all the sacrifices prescribed for those who hope to go to heaven.

AGNOITÆ. Literally "the Ignorant." A sect founded by Theophronius of Cappadocia in the fourth century. They were so called because they professed to have no knowledge regarding the omniscience of God. The followers of Themistius of Alexandria (c. 560) were also called Agnoitae because they professed no knowledge of the divinity of Christ.

AGNOSTICS. A term introduced by Prof. T. H. Huxley (1825-1895) as a convenient designation of those who refuse to claim any knowledge of supernatural beings and events or of a future life. Agnostics are not to be confused with Atheists (*q.v.*).

AGNUS DEI. The words mean "Lamb of God." It is a title of Christ in the First Epistle of John (29). It is also the name of a prayer, beginning with these words, in the Roman Catholic Service of the Mass. It is, further, the designation of medals of wax, silver, or gold, consecrated by the popes from time to time since the fourteenth century, and having stamped upon them the figure of a lamb bearing a cross. These medals were worn as amulets (*q.v.*).

AGONALIA. The word is derived from Agonius, a Roman god (Ovid, *Fasti*, i., 331). It is the name of a Roman festival in honour of the deities who guarded the State.

AGONICLITES. As the word suggests, this was the name of a sect which disapproved of kneeling in divine worship. The sect belonged to the seventh and eighth centuries, and was condemned in 726 by a Synod held at Jerusalem.

AGONISTICI. Literally "contenders," a name given to parties of Donatists (*q.v.*) who went about Africa trying to win converts. They seem to have been in existence in A.D. 317. They are also known by other names, such as Circuiti, Circumcellions (*q.v.*).

AGRAPHA. A name given to certain sayings which are supposed to have been uttered by Jesus, but have not been incorporated in the canonical Gospels. According to Papias, for instance, Jesus delivered a discourse on the Kingdom of God, in the course of which he said: "The days will come in which every vine shall produce ten thousand stems, and every stem shall give ten thousand branches, and every branch shall have ten thousand twigs, and on every twig shall be ten thousand grapes, and every grape when pressed shall yield twenty-five measures. And when a saint shall take a grape, another shall cry, 'Lo, I am a better grape, take me, and through me bless the Lord!' And in like manner a grain of wheat shall produce ten thousand ears, and each grain shall yield five 'double pounds' of pure white flour; and so on, with all the other fruits and seeds and vegetables in like manner. And all the creatures that eat of the things which are thus brought forth by the earth shall become gentle and peaceful one towards another, and be obedient unto man in every respect" (cp. the Apocalypse of Baruch, ch. xxviii.). Another supposed saying of Jesus about the Kingdom of God seems to have been current among the Encratites (*q.v.*) in the second century. One, Salome, asked the Lord how long death would continue to hold sway. The Lord answered, saying, "As long as ye women bear children; for I came to abolish the functions of woman." Salome said unto him, "Then have I done well in that I have not borne children." The Lord answered and said, "Eat of every plant save those which are bitter!" Salome then inquired when that which she asked should be revealed. The Lord said, "When ye tread down the garment of shame, when the two become one, the male with the female, neither male nor female." The same utterance, though in a rather different version, occurs in the Second Epistle of Clement (xii., 2-6). The Second Epistle of Clement (v. 2-4) gives another supposed saying of Jesus. "For the Lord said, 'Ye shall be like lambs in the midst of wolves.' But Peter answered and said, 'But what if the wolves should tear the sheep?' Jesus said to Peter, 'Let not the lambs, after they are dead, fear the wolves. And ye, in like manner, fear not ye those that kill you, and can do you no further hurt; fear rather him who after death has power over soul and body to cast them into the Gehenna of fire.'" Another short saying which is frequently quoted (Clem. Alex., *Strom.*, i., 28, 177, etc.) is: "Be ye skilful money-changers." Another saying given by Clement of Alexandria is: "Ask for great things, and at the same time small things shall also be given unto you; ask for heavenly things, and earthly things shall also be given unto you." See Oscar Holtzmann, *The Life of Jesus*, 1904.

AGRICULTURE. Primitive folk look with a feeling of awe and worship on the fertility of the earth. Originally Baal (*q.v.*) of the Canaanites and Astarte (*q.v.*) of the Phœnicians were gods of fertility and of the earth. Zoroastrianism recommends the diligent tilling of the soil. "What is the food that fills the Religion of Mazda?" asks Zoroaster. And the answer of Ahura Mazda is: "It is sowing corn again and again, O Spitama Zarathustra! He who sows corn, sows righteousness" (*Vendidâd*, iii., 23 *ff.*). Plato praises agriculture as providing, amongst other things, first-fruits for the gods and rich banquets for festivals. The deities, festivals, etc., connected with agriculture are dealt with under separate headings. See E. Westermarck.

AGUD. A term used among the islanders of the Torres Straits to denote a mystic potency in things. *Agud* seems to be a force, and not a personal being, and corresponds to the Melanesian *mana*.

AGYNIANS. A sect belonging to about A.D. 694. They held that marriage was not a divine institution, and therefore would hold no intercourse with women.

AHAU CHAMAHEZ. A tribal deity, god of medicine, in the religion of the Mayan Indians.

AHMADIYYAH. A Muhammadan sect founded in North India in recent years by Mirza Ghulam Ahmed of Qadian in the Punjab. According to E. M. Wherry, the sect really seems to be allied to that of the Babis in Persia (see BABISM). "The founder styles himself as the Mahdi-Messiah of the twentieth century. He claims to be a prophet and the Messiah of the last times." Many educated men have been influenced by the movement; "but perhaps this may be accounted for by its offering a refuge for men who can no longer continue with the orthodox schools." Orthodox Muhammadans regard the sect as heretical. See E. M. Wherry.

AHRIMAN. The personification of Evil in the dualistic religion of Zarathustra, Zoroastrianism. The Vendidad tells (*Fargard*, xix.) how Ahriman deputed one of the evil spirits who served him to destroy Zarathustra himself, and how Zarathustra defeated him by repeating a sacred formula. See Martin Haug.

AHSONNUTLI. The chief deity, creator of the heavens and earth, among the Navaho Indians of New

Mexico. Having the attributes of both sexes, he is called The Turquoise Hermaphrodite.

AHUNA-VAIRYA. The name of the oldest known creed or formula of the Zoroastrians. Martin Haug translates: "As a heavenly lord is to be chosen, so is an earthly master (spiritual guide), for the sake of righteousness, (to be) the giver of the good thoughts, of the actions of life, towards Mazda; and the dominion is for the lord (Ahura) whom he (Mazda) has given as a protector for the poor." Wilhelm Bousset gives as the translation (*What is Religion?* 1907, p. 159 *f.*): "The will of the Lord is the law of justice. The reward of heaven is for those who have worked in the world for Mazda. Ahura grants the kingdom to those who have helped the poor." In *Yasna* xix. of the Zend-avesta, Ahura-mazda is represented as saying: "These my parts of the Ahuna-vairya, when recited without mistake (and) without mispronunciation, are equal, O Spitama Zarathushtra! to a hundred of the other principal stanzas (Gâthas) recited without mistake (and) without mispronunciation. Even recited with mistakes (and) mispronunciation (they are) equal to ten other principals. And whoever, in this my world supplied with creatures, O Spitama Zarathushtra! shall recall (mentally) one part of the Ahuna-vairya, or in the course of recalling shall mutter it, or in the course of muttering shall chant it, or in the course of chanting prays to it, his soul will I, who am Ahuramazda, carry all three times over the bridge to paradise." See Martin Haug.

AHURA. A term used frequently in the Zoroastrian religion. It means "lord," and can be applied to men as well as to the Supreme Being. Commonly, however, it is used of the latter. Mazda is repeatedly addressed as "Ahura," or as Ahura-mazda (*q.v.*). A common expression is "the religion of Ahura." In *Yasna* xxxvii. of the Zend-avesta it is said: "Thus we worship Ahuramazda. . . . We worship him in calling him by the Ahura names which were chosen by Mazda himself, and which are the most beneficent." See Martin Haug.

AHURAMAZDA. The Supreme Being in the Zoroastrian religion. He is called by Zarathushtra "the Creator of the earthly and spiritual life, the Lord of the whole universe, in whose hands are all the creatures." He is said to be Light, and the source of light; wisdom and the intellect. The possessor of all such good things as the good mind, immortality, health, the best truth, devotion and piety, and abundance of all earthly blessings, he is ready to bestow these on the righteous man. At the same time he will punish the wicked. In Ahuramazda himself were united two principles or creative spirits, *speñtô mainyush*, "the beneficient spirit," and *angrô mainyush*, "the hurtful spirit." In course of time Spentô-mainyush was identified exclusively with Ahura-mazda, and Angrô-mainyush was regarded as an independent being, the organiser of the powers of evil. See Martin Haug.

AIRU. The second month of the Babylonian calendar. It was sacred to Ea. It seems to have been a particularly sacred month. The tenth day was sacred to Shamash, Malkatu, and Bunene. See Morris Jastrow, *Rel.*

AIRYAMAN. The chief god of healing in the Iranian pantheon. He is the equivalent of the Indian Aryaman, the good companion of Mitra and Varuna, that is to say, the third member of the great triad of the Adityas. A. Carnoy ("The Iranian Gods of Healing," *Journal of the American Oriental Society*, vol. 38) thinks that "the various indications which we possess about his character coincide in presenting him as a god of rain and of fertility who is essentially helpful to man. It is only reasonable to regard his functions of healer in Iran as a secondary but very natural development out of these elements." In the Pahlavi Vendidâd (xx.) it is said: "The longing for Airmân (Airyaman) destroys every disease and death, every sorcerer and witch, and every wicked courtezan." See Martin Haug.

AISLE. From Latin *ala*, "a wing," the wings of a Church or its lateral division. Churches in England have usually two aisles, one on each side of the nave or choir. Many churches, however, have only one. In continental churches there are commonly two, but in some cases three, aisles. "In many cases the aisles have had their origin in chantry chapels" (J. H. Parker, *Gloss.*).

AITKENITES. The followers of Robert Aitken (1800-1873), a clergyman of the Church of England, ordained in 1823. Leaving the Church of England, he became for a time a Wesleyan preacher. In 1840, however, he returned, and in 1849 he became Vicar of Pendeen in Cornwall. Aitken's experience of two types of Christianity led him to attempt to combine certain features of Methodism (*e.g.*, the ecstatic prayer-meetings) with the ritual and teaching of the High Church Party. See the *D.N.B.*, and J. H. Blunt.

AIZEN MYO-O. Japanese god of love.

AKA-KANET. A harvest-god worshipped by the Araucanian Indians of Chili.

AKALIS. A fanatical order of Sikh ascetics. The name Akāli means "immortal." After the death of Guru Govind, Bairāgi Banda introduced innovations which were resisted stoutly by some of the Sikhs. This section became the Akālis. "They constituted at once the most unruly and the bravest portion of the very unruly and brave Sikh army. Their headquarters were at Amritsar, where they constituted themselves the guardians of the faith and assumed the right to convoke synods. They levied offerings by force and were the terror of the Sikh chiefs. Their good qualities were, however, well appreciated by the Mahārāja, and when there were specially fierce foes to meet, such as the Pathāns beyond the Indus, the Akālis were always to the front" (Sir E. Maclagan, quoted by Russell and Hira Lāl). See R. V. Russell.

AKASAMUKHAS. Literally "Sky-facers." An order of Hindu ascetics, worshippers of Siva (*q.v.*). They are so called because with necks bent back they gaze at the sky. They spend their lives in this attitude. See Monier-Williams; E. W. Hopkins.

'AKIKA. Literally "the cutting off of the hair," an Arabian ceremony in the time of Mohammed performed on the birth of a child. The infant's head was shewed, and the scalp daubed with the blood of a sacrificed sheep. The ceremony was supposed to "avert evil from the child" and seemingly to place it under the protection of the community's god. Prof. Robertson Smith infers, however, from early references to an Arabian and Syrian practice that the oldest Semitic usage in Arabia and Syria was to sacrifice the hair of childhood, not in infancy, but on "admission to the religious and social status of manhood." See W. R. Smith, *R.S.*

AKITU FESTIVAL. The name in Babylonian-Assyrian religion of a festival in honour of Marduk (*q.v.*). Originally it was called Zagmuku (*q.v.*), New Year's Day, a festival belonging to another god. Akitu seems to have been a general name for festival, which in course of time was specially applied to Marduk's festival as the festival *par excellence*. See Morris Jastrow, *Rel.*

ALÆSIAGAE BEDE ET FIMMILENE. The names of two goddesses worshipped by some of the Ancient Teutons. In 1883 an altar erected by Frisian soldiers was found at Housesteads in the north of England. It bears two inscriptions, one of which runs: "To the god Mars Thingsus, and the two Alæsiagæ, Bede and Fimmilene." On the sides of the altar is depicted the "figure of a hovering female, with a sword (or staff) in the one hand and a wreath in the other" (Chantepie de la Saussaye, *R.T.*).

ALAGARSWAMI. A deity to whom special veneration is paid by the Kallans, a tribe or caste of the Madura district in Southern India. At the car festival he is represented as a long-eared Kallan carrying the boomerang and club, the favourite weapons of the caste. Although the Kallans sacrifice sheep to other deities, no blood sacrifice is offered to Alagarswāmi (the beautiful god). The essence of their religious belief is said to be devil-worship. See E. Thurston.

ALAGHOM NAOM. A goddess worshipped by the Tzental Indians of Mexico as the creator of mind and thought. She is called also Iztat Ix.

ALALA. The name of a deity in Babylonian-Assyrian religion. Consort of Belili, he is mentioned on a cuneiform tablet as one of the ancestors of the well-known deities. The name is found in incantations. He is perhaps to be connected with the bird Alallu, mentioned in the Gilgamesh epic (*q.v.*).

ALALLU. The name of a bird in the Babylonian Gilgamesh Epic (*q.v.*). Addressing Ishtar (*q.v.*), Gilgamesh says: "The bright-coloured alallu bird thou didst love; thou didst crush him and break his pinions; in the woods he stands and laments, 'O my pinions!'" There was originally perhaps some connection between Alallu and Alala (*q.v.*) who is referred to as one of the early ancestors of the gods. See Morris Jastrow, *Rel.*

ALAMOTH, UPON. A phrase occurring in the Old Testament (Psalm 46, title, etc.) as a musical expression or direction. It perhaps means "for sopranos," since the word *'Alāmōth* in Hebrew commonly means "maidens." See *Encycl. Bibl.*

ALASCANS. The Protestant party in the reign of Edward VI., which was led by the Polish refugee, John à Lasco. Lasco was much interested in the theology of Zwingli. Before coming to England he was Superintendent of the Reformed Churches at Emden in Friesland. Cranmer, who is said to have invited him to England, is thought to have been much influenced by his views. In London Lasco was made Superintendent of the Foreign Protestants. He worked in the interest of Puritanism, being opposed to the practice of kneeling at the Holy Communion, to the use of the surplice, etc. See M. W. Patterson, *Hist.*

ALB. An ecclesiastical vestment made of white linen. It was worn formerly in the Church of England, and is still worn in the Roman Catholic Church. It is a tunic with sleeves, and reached sometimes from head to foot. Other names for it were "camisia," "poderēs," and "linea." Its use was perhaps suggested by the under-garment or tunic worn by Greeks and Romans. A canon of the Fourth Council of Carthage (398) refers to its use by deacons; the Council of Narbonne (589) to its use by deacons, subdeacons, and lectores. Isidore says (595): "The poderes is a linen tunic worn by priests, fitting closely to the body and coming down to the feet; this is commonly called camisia" (quoted by Tyack). In later times the albs worn by English bishops were sometimes made of silk and coloured and embroidered. At the Reformation the use of the alb was regarded by the reformers as savouring of superstition. In 1571 Edmund Grindal (1519?-1583), then Archbishop of York, enjoined the churchwardens of his diocese to see that they were disused and destroyed. In the First Prayer Book of Edward VI. (1549) their use had been prescribed; but in the Second Prayer Book (1552) it was forbidden. In the Roman Catholic Church the priest still puts it on before saying Mass. See G. S. Tyack, *Historic Dress of the Clergy*, 1897; *Cath. Dict.*

ALBANENSES. A mediæval sect which derived its name from the diocese of Albi in Piedmont. It was a subdivision of the Cathari. The Albanenses had Manichaean leanings. They recognized two First Causes, a God of Light and a Prince of Darkness. Believing that God had not destined any creature to destruction, they held it sinful to take the life of animals. There were different parties in the sect, headed respectively by Balazinansa, Bishop of Verona, and John de Lugio, Bishop of Bergamo. See J. H. Blunt.

ALBATI. See WHITE BRETHREN.

ALBIGENSES. A general name given to sectaries who were found in great numbers in the district of Provence in Southern France at the beginning of the thirteenth century. One of the districts of Languedoc, Albigeois, of which Albi was the capital, seems to have given them their name. They were regarded as a Manichæan body and seem to have included adherents of the Cathari, the Waldenses, and the Paulicians, who had congregated in one district from various quarters. What their doctrines were, and to what extent they were heretical, it is difficult to say, since we have for the most part only the statements of their opponents to guide us. But in any case they were such as to bring them into collision with the Church of Rome; and from this and the further fact that they were nicknamed "the good people" we may infer that they were opposed to pontifical government and sought to live the simple life of the Apostles. They were condemned by Pope Calixtus II. in 1119 at Toulouse, and by Pope Innocent II. in 1139. In 1209 Simon de Montfort was commissioned by Pope Innocent III. to conduct a crusade against them. He was killed at the siege of Toulouse in 1218, but the crusade continued. The war itself changed its character, and peace was made in 1229 by which Louis IX. of France added to his possessions. But there was no peace for the Albigenses. They were handed over to the tender mercies of the Inquisition, and after suffering cruel torture and persecution were practically exterminated by A.D. 1244. See J. H. Blunt; *Prot. Dict.*

ALBINOS. From the Latin word for "white," a designation of persons having an irregularity in the skin. This irregularity (*leucosis*) affects the colour of the hair (white) and the eyes (the iris appearing red). The phenomenon appears also in animals. Since anything mysterious, startling, or uncanny sometimes engenders awe, Albinos have received religious veneration among certain races. Sometimes they have been made priests. On the other hand, they are sometimes looked upon with horror and disgust. The Hindus call them Kakrelaks, a name for loathsome insects. They will not allow them decent burial, but cast them into ditches. See Edward Westermarck; J. A. Dubois and H. K. Beauchamp, *Hindu Manners, etc.*

ALBIORIX. Albiorix, "king of the world," was one of the names given by the ancient Celts to the war-god, the deity who corresponded to the Roman Mars.

ALBRECHT BRETHREN. The followers of Jacob Albrecht, a German Lutheran, who founded a sect in Pennsylvania. See EVANGELICAL ASSOCIATION.

AL-BURĀK. Literally "the bright one." This is the name given to the animal on which Mohammed made his supposed journey to heaven. "After this, a white animal was brought for me to ride upon. Its size was between that of a mule and an ass, and it stretched as far as the eye could see. The name of the animal was Burāq. Then I mounted the animal, and ascended until we arrived at the lowest heaven, and Gabriel demanded that the door should be opened" (*Mishkātu 'l- Masābih*, quoted in T. P. Hughes, *Dict. of Islam*, 1885).

ALCANTARA, KNIGHTS OF. An order of knights established in Spain in 1177 in opposition to the Mohammedans.

ALCHEMY. Originally the art of transmuting base metals into gold and silver by a secret chemical process. Alchemy became associated with magic when alchemists thought to discover a solvent containing the original principle of all matter. This solvent was to prove a remedy for all diseases and a means of renewing youth and preserving life. A Chinese alchemist of the fourth century, Koh Hung, says that grease of jade mixed with the juice of herbs, will, if drunk, make one live a thousand years. "He who swallows gold will exist as long as gold." The efficacy ascribed by the Chinese to jade and gold is seen in the fact that they put them in the mouth of the dead to protect the body against putrefaction (see J. J. M. de Groot, *R.S.C.*). Some of the Hindus, again, have believed that they could attain "salvation during life" or present immortality by swallowing elixirs compounded of mercury and mica, the one being supposed to contain the essence of Siva, the other the essence of his wife Gaurī. The elixir, it was thought, repairs and rejuvenates the decaying particles of the body (see Monier-Williams). Alchemy was introduced into Egypt, and flourished there, in the Hellenistic period. The solvent of the alchemists was known in England as the "philosopher's stone," and those who possessed the secret were called "adepts." The adepts were taught the doctrines in mystical and symbolical language. In the Middle Ages the monks occupied themselves with alchemy.

ALCORAN. See KORAN.

ALDOBRANDINI, THE. The name of a Florentine family to which Pope Clement VIII. (1592) and other ecclesiastical dignitaries belonged.

ALEXANDRIAN CANON. The Bible of Greek-speaking Jews, the Septuagint (*q.v.*), includes, in addition to our canonical books of the Old Testament, the books commonly known to us as the Apocrypha. It has been customary therefore to speak of an Alexandrian Canon in distinction from the Palestinian Canon. This, as C. H. Cornill points out (*Intr.*), is hardly correct. "In strict correctness an Alexandrian 'Canon' should not be spoken of at all; for neither the number of the books admited nor their order is in agreement in the Greek Bible MSS. It is clear that the Greeks have allowed themselves to be guided simply by the principle of οἰκοδομή ('edification'): all writings of a religious character which they found edifying they read and held in high esteem. But such a proceeding would have been quite inconceivable if at the time of the birth of Christ there already existed in Palestine an official canon, and if the books had already at that time been separated into such as *defile the hands* [i.e., are canonical], and such as do not." See further CANON, OLD TESTAMENT.

ALEXANDRIAN CODEX. The Codex Alexandrinus (designated by the letter A) is a Greek manuscript translation of the Bible, belonging probably to the last half of the fifth century. It was so called from having been presented in 1098 to the patriarch of Alexandria. It was believed in Egypt to have been written by Saint Thecla; and a note in Arabic in the first of the four volumes says that she wrote it. But such traditions are not uncommon. Writing in 1907 Dr. Gregory says: "It is not a year since I visited a women's monastery in the East in which the abbess assured me that their beautiful manuscript had been written by an ancient saintly woman, whereas I found in it the name, and I think the date of the man who wrote it." In 1628 the Codex Alexandrinus was sent to King Charles I. as a present. It is now preserved in the British Museum. The first three volumes contain (with some gaps) the Septuagint Version of the Old Testament. The fourth volume contains the New Testament. But there are missing: Matthew i. to xxv. 6, John vi. 50-viii. 52, and II. Corinthians iv. 13-xii. 6. It also contains the genuine first Epistle of Clement of Rome and the homily known as Second Clement. See C. R. Gregory, *Canon;* M. R. Vincent, *Text. Crit. of the N.T.*

ALEXANDRIAN SCHOOL. When Alexandria became the centre of learning (second period 30 B.C. to A.D. 640), an effort was made to blend the wisdom or philosophy of the East and the West. Thus arose the Neo-Platonists (*q.v.*). The movement suggested a new style of treating theology, and gave rise to what is known as the Alexandrian or Alexandrine School. The chief representatives of this School were Clement of Alexandria and Origen. The Alexandrian School resolved to fight the Gnostic heresy with its own weapons, and developed a system of "Christian" Gnosis. See C. Bigg, *Christian Platonists of Alexandria*, 1886; *Neoplatonism*, 1895.

ALEXANDRIANS, EPISTLE TO THE. A work alluded to in the fragment of Muratori, the Italian historian and librarian. The Epistle was forged in Paul's name in support of the heresy of Marcion.

ALEXIANS. The name of a religious fraternity of laymen founded on the Lower Rhine in the fifteenth century. The name was suggested by that of St. Alexius, who devoted himself to a life of poverty in the time of Pope Innocent I. (402-417 A.D.). The Alexians devoted themselves to the work of tending the sick. They were known also as Nollards or Nollbrueder.

ALFHEIM. Alfheim would seem to have been one of the nine worlds in the cosmogony of the Ancient Teutons.

ALI, SECT OF. A Mohammedan sect. See SHI'AH.

'ALĪ-ILAHIS. A sect in Persia having many adherents. They regard 'Alī, the cousin of Mohammed and husband of his daughter, as "neither more nor less than an Incarnation or 'Manifestation' of God" (*Allah*). See E. G. Browne, *Lit. Hist. of Persia*, 1906.

AL-KITAB. Literally "the Book," another name for the Qur'ân (*q.v.*). "The book" of course means *the* book *par excellence*, the sacred book. Another name for the Qur'ân is Al-Furqân (see FURQAN).

ALKORAN. See KORAN.

ALLAH. The Arabic name for God (*the* God). It is cognate with the Hebrew *Eloah*.

ALLAH. Allah, the father of the Djinns, was a North Arabian deity. He appears sometimes as the consort of Allath (*q.v.*).

ALLATH. An Arabian goddess, identified with Athena. She was adopted by the Syrian Arabs. Her consort was Dusares (Dionysus). At Palmyra she was associated with the solar god Malakhbel. Herodotus calls her Alilat or Urania.

ALLATU. The name of a goddess in Babylonian-Assyrian religion. Originally a consort of Bel (*q.v.*) of Nippur, she was afterwards associated in turn with Ninazu and Nergal (*qq.v.*). She is the chief goddess of the subterranean cave in which the dead dwell, and seems sometimes, like Nergal, to have been depicted as a lion. As mistress of the underworld, she is regarded sometimes as the authoress of evil, though as a personification of the "earth" she seems also to have been considered a goddess of fertility. The El-Amarna tablets seek to explain Nergal's position in the world of the dead by the legend of a conflict between Nergal and Allatu. In the end she offers to marry him, and he spares her life. The legend seems to have been framed in imitation of the Marduk-Tiâmat story, Nergal corresponding to Marduk, and Allatu to Tiâmat. See Morris Jastrow, *Rel.*

ALLEGORY. A figurative manner of speaking in which the words are symbols, and are not to be understood in their literal meaning. The early Jewish rabbi Philo, a contemporary of Jesus, is noted for his allegorical interpretation of the Old Testament. Early Christian Fathers, such as Clement of Alexandria, Origen, Eusebius, Ambrose of Milan, followed his example. The ancient Stoics in like manner allegorised the poems of Homer, thereby explaining away many objectionable features in Greek mythology. The allegory in the "Arabian Nights" in which three rings represent the Mahommedan, Jewish, and Christian religions, has been repeated by Lessing in *Nathan the Wise.*

ALLELUIA. The Greek form of the Hebrew HALLELUJAH.

ALL-FOOLS' DAY. See APRIL FOOL'S DAY.

ALL-SAINTS' DAY. A Christian festival now held on the 1st of November. It took the place (A.D. 607) in the West of a pagan festival "To all the Gods." Among the Greeks the festival of all martyrs and saints seems to have been observed in the fourth century. It was Pope Gregory III. who fixed the day (about 731) as the 1st of November. Before this it had been the 13th of May. See *Cath. Dict.*

ALL SAINTS' SISTERHOOD, MARGARET STREET. A Church of England Sisterhood founded in 1851. The Sisters, whose headquarters are now All Saints' Convent, Colney Chapel, St. Albans, work as Hospital Nurses and District Visitors. They also work ecclesiastical embroidery and bake wafers for the Holy Eucharist. See Walter Walsh, "Sisterhoods, Ritualistic," in the *Prot. Dict.*

ALL SOULS DAY. Also called "Festa Animārum," "Animarum Commemoratio," "Omnium Fidelium Commemoratio." November the 2nd is observed as a day of commemoration of all the dead. Odilon, Abbot of Clugny, inaugurated the custom in A.D. 998.

ALMANACS. Registers of the days, weeks, months of the year, etc. The Hindu Almanac (*panchangam*) is compiled by learned priests (*purohitas*) Every priest must possess a copy, because it supplies information about auspicious and inauspicious days, propitious hours, lucky and unlucky constellations, etc. By studying it, he can give advice on the most varied matters. In China almanacs circulate freely. Here also they supply information as to favourable or unfavourable days. One of these popular almanacs gives details concerning "things to be avoided with regard to coffining." If the almanac does not suffice, a "day-professor" is consulted. See J. J. M. de Groot, *R.S.C.*

ALMEH. A name for certain singing girls in Egypt who attended festivals.

ALMOHADES. Originally the name of an Arabian religious sect founded in 1146 in the Atlas mountains by 'Abd al-Mu'min, a pupil of Abû 'Abdallah Muhammad Ibn Tûmart. The sect became militant and superseded that of the Almoravides (*q.v.*).

ALMONER. An ecclesiastical official attached to a royal court or a noble mansion with the duty of distributing alms. Before the French Revolution (1789) the Grand Almoner (*Grand Aumônier*) in France, who was usually a cardinal, was a very important dignitary. In England, there is a Lord High Almoner, an Anglican bishop or dean, who distributes the royal bounty. The Hereditary Grand Almoner is now hardly more than a name. In France the name Almoner is given to any kind of Chaplain.

ALMORAVIDES. Originally the name of an Arabian religious sect founded about the middle of the eleventh century by Abdallah-ben-Yasin. The sect became militant and gave its name to a dynasty which ruled in the eleventh and twelfth centuries in Africa and Spain. The prefix Al- is the Arabic definite article. Consequently, the name often appears as Moravids. See Chambers' *Encycl.*

ALMS. Relief given to the poor out of compassion. There seems to be a connection between sacrifice and the giving of alms. The deity enjoys only the spiritual part of the food offered; the poor receive often the substance. Sacrificial food is distributed among the poor. The goddess Artemis (*q.v.*), the god Mazda (*Yasna*, xxxiv., 5) benefited them in this way. The poor of ancient Arabia partook of meal-offerings made to the god Uqaiçir. Sometimes the almsgiving itself is a form of sacrifice. In the sacred books of India sacrifice and almsgiving are often mentioned. In the Egyptian "Book of the Dead" (*q.v.*), in the Zoroastrian prayer Ahuna-Vairya (*q.v.*), in the Koran, almsgiving occupies an equally important place as a part of religion. It is well known that the Jews associated almsgiving and sacrifice. "He that giveth alms sacrificeth praise" we are told (Ecclesiasticus, xxxv., 2). In the Mishnah it is said: "Through alms a man partakes of eternal life" (*Rosh hash-shanah* 3): and: "As sin-offering makes atonement for Israel, so alms for the Gentiles" (*Baba Bathra* 10*b*). In the Jewish synagogues and at the services of the early Christian Church alms were regularly collected. It has been said, too, that whereas in heathen guilds or clubs "charity was an accident, in Christian associations it was of the essence" (E. Hatch, *Organisation of the Early Christian Church*, 1881). Almsgiving is also closely connected with fasting. In Brahmanism sacrifice, fasting, and the giving of gifts are often spoken of together. In Mohammedanism almsgiving is enjoined after a fast, and in some cases (*e.g.*, of old people) it is a substitute for fasting. The Christian Fathers (*e.g.*, Augustine) say that what is saved by fasting should be given to the poor. See E. Westermarck; *Encycl. Bibl.*

ALOGI. A name used by Epiphanius and Augustine to describe those who did not accept St. John's doctrine of the Logos and who denied the authority of St. John's writings. The Montanist prophets based their claims on these writings. The Alogi, called into existence in Asia in the second century to combat Montanism, attacked the enemy by denouncing their sacred books. They rejected all the Johannine writings without distinction, ascribing the authorship to Cerinthus. See Louis Duchesne, *Hist.*

ALPHA AND OMEGA. The first and the last letter of the Greek alphabet. The expression is used in the New Testament to denote the eternity of Jesus. "I am the Alpha and the Omega, said the Lord God, which is and which was and which is to come, the Almighty" (Revelation, i., 8; cp. vs. 11 and xxi. 6, xxii. 13).

ALTAR. The Latin word is *altare* from altus "high." The Hebrew word *mizbēaḥ* means "a place of slaughter or sacrifice." It is represented closely by the Greek word *thusiastērion.* Sometimes, however, the word *bōmos* is given as the equivalent, which means literally "any raised place." This is the more primitive meaning of an altar. The altar was a place set apart for a holy purpose, that of sacrifice. As such it was natural to separate it from the ordinary soil on which men trod. This was done by raising it. Originally it was enough to pile up some of the earth, and earth altars were still in use among the Hebrews (Exodus xx., 24-26), Carthaginians, Romans, Greeks, and others. Afterwards a stone (cp. Judges vi., 11 ff.) or a heap of stones was used; and then a kind of table. When a stone has been consecrated to this use, it becomes holy, because the god is supposed to enter into it and make it his dwelling. The Old Testament contains many references to altars, those of later date relating to altars of rather elaborate construction (cp. I Kings ix., 25; II Chronicles iv., 1). The earlier Babylonian altar was of sun-dried brick. Stone was used later, and in Assyria altars of limestone and alabaster were common. At Nippur an altar twelve feet long and six wide was found. The height appears to have been from two to three feet. Like Hebrew and Phoenician altars, Assyrian altars had at the corners of the rim some kind of decoration resembling horns. The table rested on a solid piece of stone or on a tripod. When the Hebrews fled to the altar as a place of refuge, they caught hold of its horns (I Kings i. 50, ii. 28; cp. I Maccabees x. 43, Cicero, *De Natura Deorum* iii. 10). Besides the altars in temples and other sacred places, it has been the custom to have small household altars. Thus the Greeks and Romans had them in the courts of their houses. The Chinese may be said to have two kinds of domestic altar. In the house is an altar for sacrifice to the tutelar deities. While the coffin of a deceased relative is still in the house, the mourners offer the soul every evening burning candles and incense-sticks. Besides this, at a Chinese burial a table is placed in front of the soul-tablet and the coffin, and on it is set a sacrificial meal for the soul of the dead person. On it are placed also a censer or incense-sticks and candles. The "grave table" is "a square slab of granite, either placed on the ground, or upon a massive table-shaped pile of masonry; sometimes it is entirely of granite, and carved in front with characters or emblematic figures" (De Groot). At the left-hand side of the coffin is a small altar for sacrifices to the god of earth. This altar "consists of a rectangular slab of granite, seldom higher than one or two feet, fixed perpendicularly in the ground." The front of the slab bears such inscriptions as: "Ruler of the Earth," "God or Spirit of the Earth," "Active Animus of the Ground," "Spirit of the Felicitating Agencies." In the Christian Churches for some centuries the altars were usually of wood. In the fifth century altars of stone became common. This seems to have been suggested by the use of the tombs of martyrs in the Catacombs as substitutes for altars, the marble slab serving as a table. Stone altars were ordered in England in 705 by Egbert (*d.* 766), Archbishop of York. They had already been ordered in France in 509. On November 12, 1550, as a result of an Order in Council, it was commanded to "pluck down the altars." Matthew Parker (1504-1575), Archbishop of Canterbury, and Edmund Grindal (1519?-1583) were anxious to assure themselves that this order had been carried out. In 1857 it was decided that a stone altar may not be erected in churches. In the Church of Rome the altar "must consist of stone, or at least must contain an altar-stone large enough to hold the Host and the greater part of the chalice; and this altar, or the altar-stone, must have been consecrated by a bishop, or by an abbot who has received the requisite faculties from the Holy See" (Addis and Arnold). William Laud (1573-1645), Archbishop of Canterbury, gave offence to the Puritans by ordering the communion table or altar to be moved from the body of the church to the east end and to be placed altar-wise (see M. W. Patterson, *Hist.*; W. L. Mackintosh, *Life of William Laud*, 1907). See W. R. Smith, *R.S.*, 1894; Morris Jastrow, *Rel. of Babylonia and Assyria*, 1898; J. J. M. de Groot, *R.S.C.*, 1892, etc.; *Encycl. Bibl.; Prot. Dict.; Cath. Dict.*

AL-TASCHITH Or Al-Tashheth. A phrase occurring in the Old Testament (Psalm 75, 1 etc.) as a musical expression or direction. It seems to designate the tune ("Destroy not") to which a psalm is to be sung.

ALTRUISM. The word means literally "of or to others." It was first used by Auguste Comte (1798-1857) and his followers as a designation of unselfishness and interest in others as distinguished from selfishness and egoism.

ALUMBRADOS. A sect of Spanish mystics founded about 1520, and suppressed by the Inquisition. The Illuminati of a later date in Germany held similar principles.

ALVISS. A figure in Teutonic mythology. Alviss is a wise dwarf who presents himself before Thor (*q.v.*) and asks for his daughter in marriage. He is detained until the dawn of day which proves fatal to him. See Chantepie de La Saussaye, *Rel. of the Teutons*, 1902.

AMADHLOZI. A name given by the Zulus to their ancestral spirits who revisit them in the form of snakes. They may be distinguished from ordinary snakes by their frequenting huts, by their not eating mice, and by their not being afraid of people. "Common folk become harmless snakes with green and white bellies and very small heads; but kings become boa-constrictors or the large and deadly black Mamba" (Frazer). See J. G. Frazer, *G.B.*

AMAETHON. One of the deities worshipped by the ancient Celts. The name appears in late Welsh legend. Amaethon was the patron god of farmers.

AMALRICIANS. The followers of Amalric of Bena or Amaury of Bené, a Paris theologian at the end of the twelfth century, who taught Pantheism and held, amongst other things, that in Abraham was incarnate the Father, in the Blessed Virgin the Son, and in ourselves the Holy Ghost. His teaching was condemned by the University of Paris in A.D. 1204, by Pope Innocent III. in A.D. 1207, and by the Fourth Lateran Council in A.D. 1215. Amalric died in 1209. Several of his followers were burned as heretics.

AMARAPURA. The name of a sect (monks) in Singhalese Buddhism. The Amarapura Society arose at the beginning of the nineteenth century in opposition to the Siamese Society. The latter admitted only one special caste to the monkhood. The Amarapura Society gave entrance to three more. See H. Hackmann.

AMATERASU. One of the deities of the ancient religion of Japan known as Shintōism (*q.v.*). Amaterasu, the sun-goddess, is supposed to have been born from the left eye of Izanagi, the Creator. From her was descended Jimmu Tenno, the first human ruler of Japan, according to the Japanese, who ascended the throne on the seventh of April, 660 B.C. She is really a personification of the sun, which is symbolized by the mirror which figures as one of the chief emblems of Shintōism. Her shrine in Ise to which pilgrimages are made is called the Mecca of Japan. See G. A. Cobbold, *Religion in Japan*, 1894; D. Goh and Isabella Bishop, "Shintōism," in *R.S.W.*

AMATONGO. The term is used of the spirits of their ancestors by the Zulus. The "amatongo," particularly the heads of families, are worshipped. See ANCESTOR WORSHIP. The "amatongo" or ancestral spirits sometimes take possession of persons. Those who are thus possessed are stricken with a kind of disease (hysteria, convulsions). In some cases disease-possession becomes oracle-possession, and the possessed become professional diviners. See Tylor ii., 131 f.

AMBAGARHIA DEO. A Hindu deity, worshipped in Bhandāra by the Koshtis, the Marātha and Telugu caste of weavers of silk and fine cotton cloth in India. The original was one Kadu, headman of a village.

AMBARVALIA. A Roman festival during which

prayer was made to the deities of agriculture that the fields (*arva*) might be fertile and the harvest abundant. It was kept on the 29th of May. There was a solemn procession round the fields, in which the country people took part; and a hog, a ram, and a bull were sacrificed.

AMBISAGRUS. Ambisagrus, "the persistent," was one of the names given by the ancient Celts to a god who corresponded to the Roman Jupiter.

AMBO. Perhaps from the Greek *anabeinein* "to ascend," a platform in early Christian churches used as a pulpit. St. Chrysostom is said to have preached from an "Ambo." It stood in the nave of the church, and was used especially as a reading-desk. The Ambo is to be seen in churches in Rome. The earliest example is in the church of San Clemente, and belongs to about A.D. 1110. The Ambo was used for other purposes. "All church notices were read from it; here edicts and excommunications were given out; hither came heretics to make their recantation" (Addis and Arnold). See J. H. Parker, *Gloss.*, 1888; *Cath. Dict.*

AMBROSIA. A term derived from the Greek word *ambrŏtos*, "immortal." It is a name for the food of the gods in Greek Mythology. Human beings who were favourites of the gods were sometimes allowed to partake of it, and were supposed thereby to attain immortal youth and beauty. It was also a fragrant salve used by goddesses, and even by Jupiter. The drink of the gods was called nectar. In Hindu mythology the special beverage of the gods is called *amrita*.

AMBROSIAN CHANT. A hymn so called (Ambrosiānum), because it was supposed to have been composed by St. Ambrose. It is now commonly known as the "Te Deum laudamus." It was used in the fourth century by the Church in Milan.

AMBROSIAN LITURGY. Also called "Ambrosian Office," or "Ambrosian Missal." One of the most ancient liturgies, associated with the name of St. Ambrose, Bishop of Milan, because he adopted and adapted it.

AMBROSIANS. The followers of one Ambrose, a French Anabaptist. He claimed (*c.* A.D. 1559) to have received a divine revelation superior to that of Holy Scripture. His followers called themselves also Spirituals or "Pneumatiques."

AMELUNGEN SAGA. A Gothic heroic saga, a glorification of fidelity.

AMEN. A Hebrew word meaning literally "Yea," "Truly," or "Verily." Used first in ordinary speech, it was at an early date introduced into liturgies (see, *e.g.*, in the Old Testament, I. Chronicles xvi., 36=Ps. cvi., 48). The Jews in their synagogues pronounce it at the close of the parting benediction. The early Christians said it at the close of the prayer offered by the presbyter (I. Corinthians xiv., 16).

AMEN CORNER. This spot in London is so called on account of a procession of clergymen to St. Paul's Cathedral which used to take place annually on Corpus Christi Day. In the street called Pater-noster Row they chanted the "Pater-noster," and at the spot called Amen Corner said the "Amen." Ave Maria Lane commemorates the saying of the "Ave Maria," and Creed Lane the chanting of the "Credo."

AMENT. An Egyptian deity. She was a goddess of Thebes, though not one of the original deities. She is represented with the head of a sheep. See Alfred Wiedemann.

AMENTI. The region of the departed in the old Egyptian religion, the west-land, the underworld, in its Greek form written Amenthes. See Alfred Wiedemann.

AMERETÂD. Literally "immortality." One of the seven Ameshaspentas (*q.v.*), or celestial councillors, in the Zoroastrian religion. Ameretâd is usually mentioned together with Haurvatâd. Together they preside over vegetation, and preserve the good creation in its original uncorrupted state. See Martin Haug.

AMERICANISM. A name given by theologians to "an attenuated form of Catholicism which was propagated mainly in the United States by Father Isaac Hecker of the Paulist Order (d. 1888). Afterwards Archbishop Ireland, of St. Paul, Minnesota, became the accepted high priest of the movement. Americanism was introduced into Europe about 1890. "Its distinguishing doctrine was the characteristically American exaltation of good works over faith." Archbishop Ireland submitted to the Pope in 1899, after Leo XIII. had addressed a letter to Cardinal Gibbons of Baltimore. See S. Reinach, *O.*

AMESHASPENTAS. The designation of the seven archangels or celestial councillors in the Zoroastrian religion. In an old prayer found in the *Yasna haptaṇhaiti* we read: "We worship Ahuramazda, the righteous master of righteousness. We worship the Ameshaspentas, the possessors of good, the givers of good. We worship the whole creation of the righteous spirit, both the spiritual and earthly, all that supports (raises) the welfare of the good creation, and the spread of the good Mazdayasnian religion." Elsewhere they are described as "the immortal benefactors." They are now called Amshaspends. See Martin Haug.

AMIATA MANUSCRIPT. A manuscript of the Vulgate, named after Amiata, Codex Amiatinus. It was written by order of Ceolfrid (*d.* 716), abbot of Yarrow, shortly before A.D. 716, and is now preserved at Florence. The manuscript contains many Anglo-Saxon and Irish readings. See C. R. Gregory.

AMICE. An ecclesiastical vestment. The word (*amictus*) means "a wrap." It was also called "anaboladium" or "anabolagium" from the Greek *anaballein;* and "humerale" or "superhumerale," because it partly covered the shoulders. In an ancient missal at Narbonne it is referred to as *galea* or a helmet. In the Roman Catholic Church it is now "a piece of fine linen, oblong in shape, which the priest who is to say Mass rests for a moment on his head and then spreads on his shoulder," and is called the "helmet of salvation" (Addis and Arnold). The vestment is referred to frequently after the beginning of the ninth century. Originally it seems to have been a head-covering. This accounts for the Roman Catholic priest resting it on his head for a moment before he puts it on. Franciscan and Dominican friars, in fact, still wear it as a covering for the head. In course of time it was regarded as a decoration, and was often richly embroidered. Now, however, its only adornment is a cross. The origin of the clerical collar has been found in the Amice. It became "first a white collar with a necktie, and then the clerical collar as now usually worn, or the band or strip of linen stretched over a black stock" (Tyack). See G. S. Tyack, *Historic Dress of the Clergy*, 1897; *Cath. Dict.*

AMIDA. In Japanese Buddhism an abridged form of Amitâbha (*q.v.*), the name of one of the celestial Buddhas. See H. Hackmann.

AMITÂBHA. In Lamaism the chief figure among the five celestial prototypes of the historical Buddhas. The different heavens of the Buddhist system are here commonly represented as the "Paradise of Amitâbha." There is wonderful virtue and efficacy in the repetition of the name of Amitâbha. The priests repeat it thousands of times to save the soul of a dead person. See H. Hackman; J. J. M. de Groot, *R.S.C.*

AMITÂBHA SÛTRA. A sacred book among the Chinese Buddhists, the chief authority for the Chinese doctrine of the Western Paradise. See J. J. M. de Groot, *R.S.C.*

'AMM-ANAS. A South Arabian god for whom whole hecatombs of animals are said to have been slaughtered. See W. R. Smith, *R.S.*

AMMONIAN SECTIONS. The name usually given to the sections or divisions into which Eusebius divided the text of each of the four Gospels for the purpose of constructing a Harmony of the Gospels. Cp. CANONS OF EUSEBIUS, and see HARMONIES OF THE GOSPELS.

AMMONIANS. The followers of Ammonius Saccas, who founded a school of Neo-Platonism (*q.v.*) in the second century.

AMON. One of the principal Egyptian deities. Also called Amon Ra, he became prominent from the time of the eleventh dynasty as the deity of Thebes, where a magnificent temple was built for him. With him are associated the goddess Mut ("mother," a symbol of the sky) and the lunar deity Khons. As Amon represents the productive power of generation, he is sometimes rereferred to as the husband of his mother. He is frequently depicted as a man with a sceptre in his hands and two high feathers, royal emblems, on his head. Sometimes, however, since the ram was sacred to him, he is represented as a ram with great curving horns. Hymns to and decrees of Amon have come down to us. See Naville, *The Old Egyptian Faith*, 1909.

AMORAIM. A Rabbinic term. When the Jewish legal system was committed to writing a body of learned men were required to expound it. These were called Amoraim, the word being derived from the common Hebrew root *āmar*, "to speak." The Law had to be interpreted in the vernacular speech. In doing this, a duly qualified expounder might lay down new principles. These new principles, or additions to the Mishnah, were embodied in a collection of writings called the Tosefta. There was a Palestinian and a Babylonian School of Amoraim. See J. W. Etheridge, *Intr. to Heb. Lit.*, 1856.

AMOS, BOOK OF. One of the Minor Prophets of the Old Testament. Amos was a shepherd of Tekoa near Jerusalem, and preached about 800 B.C., extolling the practice of justice and condemning the superficial piety which thinks to please God by making frequent offerings. The book seems to have been edited and interpolated. See *Encycl. Bibl.*

AMOSITES. A small sect, an off-shoot of the Bohemian Brethren, followers of a farmer named Amos. In 1508 they sent word to the King and informed against the Brethren, saying that they were about to use the sword in defence of their cause. The King summoned a Diet, which issued on St. James's Day (July 25) the Edict of St. James which prohibited meetings of the Brethren and ordered their books to be burned. See J. E. Hulton, *History of the Moravian Church*, 1909.

AMPHICTYONIC LEAGUE. A union of twelve populations of Northern Greece, "which at stated times met at the same sanctuary to keep a festival in common, and to transact common business" (Seyffert). The league, which was supposed to have been founded by Amphictyon, met either at Delphi or near Pylae or Thermopylae, and protected the sanctuaries there. Each people sent two deputies ("pylagorae") and two "wardens of holy things" ("hieromnemones"). "When violations of the sanctuaries or of popular right took place, the assembly could inflict fines or even expulsion; and a state that would not submit to the punishment had a 'holy war' declared against it." The league is not heard of after the second century A.D. See O. Seyffert, *Dict.*

AMPHIDROMIA. A Greek Festival at which a child received its name. The child was first carried round the hearth by the nurse, after the friends of the parents had washed their hands.

AMPHITRITE. A goddess of the sea in Greek mythology.

AMRITA. The Indian equivalent of *ambrosia*, the gods' food of immortality. According to the Hindu epics, the gods required amrita to give them power to overcome the demons. A well-known legend relates that, by command of Vishnu, this amrita was obtained by churning the ocean. The juice called Soma was also the nectar of the gods. It was "the blood of trees" vitalized by the god Soma, for, as Professor Elliot Smith says (*Dr.*, 1919), in India the amrita was sometimes regarded as the sap exuded from the sacred trees of paradise. Amrita corresponds to the Persian Haoma, and to the mead of the gods in Teutonic mythology.

AMRITSAR. The sacred town of the Sikhs in India and the metropolis of their religion. It was so called, according to tradition, from the "Pool of Immortality" (*Amritsar*) which was said to have existed there from a remote period, some of the nectar of immortality (*Amrita*) having been spilt on the spot. The sacredness of the spot, however, is associated by the Sikhs with an event which is supposed to have happened in the time of Guru Ram-das (A.D. 1574-1581), the fourth Guru of their sect. It is said that an angry father married his beautiful and pious daughter to a cripple. She had to support herself and him by begging, and she carried her husband on her head in a basket. One day she left the basket for a little while near a pool. A lame crow came and went into the water, whereupon its lameness was cured. Observing this, the cripple followed its example, and he too was restored to health. Guru Ram-das therefore had a tank excavated, and laid here the foundations of the lake-temple, or Golden Temple, of the Sikhs. "To form an idea of the unique spectacle presented by this sacred locality," says Monier-Williams, "one must picture to one's self a large square sheet of water, bordered by a marble pavement, in the centre of a picturesque Indian town. Around the margin of this artificial lake are clustered many fine mansions, most of them once the property of Sikh chiefs who assembled here every year, and spent vast sums on the endowment of the central shrine. . . . In the centre of the water rises the beautiful temple with its gilded dome and cupolas, approached by a marble causeway. It is quite unlike any other place of worship to be seen throughout India, and in structure and appearance may be regarded as a kind of compromise between a Hindu temple and a Muhammadan mosque. . . ." See J. C. Oman, *Brahmans;* Monier-Williams, *B.H.*

AMSDORFIANS. The followers of Nicolas Amsdorf (1483-1565), Lutheran Bishop of Naumburg, and friend of Luther. He was the opponent of George Major of Wittenberg in a dispute about the saving efficacy of good works (A.D. 1552-54), which became known as the "Majoristic Controversy." The dispute was settled by the "Formula of Concord" (A.D. 1577).

AMSHASPENDS. See AMESHASPENTAS.

AMULETS. Objects supposed to possess magic power, and worn by people as a protection against evil. The wearing of amulets has been a common practice. The Babylonians seem to have used rings, seal cylinders, clay figurines, metallic statuettes, inscribed tablets, discs, etc. (Morris Jastrow, *Rel. Assyria*, 1898.) Egyptian mummies in the period of the New Kingdom were covered with amulets, which took the form of an eye, a heart, a sceptre, a crown, a beetle, etc. (Adolf Erman, *Handbook.*) Mohammedans not only wear such objects as a miniature copy of the Koran, chapters or verses of the Koran written on paper and folded, the Mohammedan creed on stone or silver, etc., but they also attach them to houses, animals, etc. (T. P. Hughes.) The Chinese place amulets over the grave or in the house of a dead person to remove evil influences in the calculation of an auspicious day for burial. These consist of small strips of yellow paper, on which are inscribed such words as, "The virgins of the dark spheres of the nine heavens are here present with imperial orders from Heaven to subdue unlucky influences." They also hang amulets on the walls of houses to purify them after a death, or on coffins to counteract bad influences. (J. J. M. de Groot, *R.S.C.*). Hindus value such objects as a jewel, a stone, a piece of paper or metal, a leaf inscribed with mystic words and formulae, as charms against evils of various kinds. Hindu women wear them as a protection against sterility. (Sir Monier Monier-Williams, *Brahmanism and Hinduism* (4), 1891.) For the same purpose, Kaffir women wear amulets made from the tail-hairs of a heifer and supplied by medicine-men, and Moorish women of Morocco carry a porcupine's foot. The women of Mecca wear a magic girdle, the women of Persia a mandrake. In other such cases, the object worn seems to be a talisman to bring good luck rather than an amulet to ward off evil. Thus, negresses in the interior of Western Africa have been known to carry small ivory figures of the two sexes, and amoug the Bechuana, Basuto, and Agni women dolls have been carried. (E. S. Hartland, *Perseus*, vol. I., 1894.) In England the practice of carrying amulets was common in the Middle Ages. These were often gems or coins having on them a figure of some religious hero or saint. (Brand's *Popular Antiquities*, ed. C. Hazlitt, 1905.) In Southern Germany the Alemanni as late as the end of the sixth century used herbs and amber as amulets. (P. D. Chantepie de La Saussaye, *Rel. of the Teutons*, 1902.) See also ABRAXAS STONES, CHARMS; J. M. Wheeler, *Footsteps of the Past*, 1895; A. C. Haddon, *Magic and Fetishism*, 1906.

AMYRALDISTS. The followers of Moses Amyraut, a French Protestant divine, Professor at Saumur (A.D. 1633-1664). Amyraut was a Calvinist, specially interested in the doctrines of Predestination and Grace. He held that the salvation of all men is desired by God, but can only be attained through faith in Christ, which is by God's grace possible for all men. Amyraut's teaching led to the formation of a school, especially amongst French and Swiss Protestants, of so-called "Hypothetical Universalists."

AN. The name borne by small monasteries or convents in Chinese Buddhism. See H. Hackmann.

ANA. Ana or Anu is mentioned as the name of an ancient Celtic goddess who was worshipped in Ireland. She was a goddess of abundance and prosperity, and is described as the mother of the gods. She would seem to have corresponded to Danu or Dôn (*q.v.*). See C. Squire, *Myth*.

ANABAPTISTS. The term is derived from a Greek word meaning "to baptise again," and was applied to a body of anti-sacerdotalists who came into prominence early in the sixteenth century. They were so called because, amongst other things, they disapproved of infant baptism, and required the members of their sect who had been baptised only as infants to be rebaptised. The movement began to develop under the influence of the "prophets of Zwickau," who became active in the year 1521. These were the followers of Thomas Münzer (1485-1525), Lutheran preacher at Zwickau in Saxony, who had absorbed the teaching of the mystic J. Tauler (1300-1361). Leaving Zwickau, Münzer went to Allstedt, and preached there for two years, calling for radical reforms in Church and State. He claimed that he had received a new revelation, and taught that in the kingdom of heaven now to be established on earth, all Christians must be equal and all goods be shared in common. Princes were summoned to join the new league started by Münzer. In 1524 he had to withdraw to Waldshut, on the borders of Switzerland, from which place as a centre the movement spread over the whole of Switzerland. The next year the "Peasant War" broke out, and found a supporter in Münzer. He moved in the same year to Mühlhausen, where he re-established his theocracy, gathering about him the discontented peasants and hillfolk. The result was a rebellion headed by "Münzer, with the sword of Gideon." The prophet was defeated at Frankenhausen on the 15th of May, 1525, and on the 30th of May was executed at Mühlhausen. Nine years later we find the theocracy re-established at Münster in Westphalia, under the guidance of a Protestant minister, Bernard Rothmann, and the burghers Knipperdolling and Krechting. These had joined John Matthieson and were reinforced by John Bockhold, a tailor from Leiden, who now became the leader of the militant Anabaptists. Gaining possession of Münster, they allowed Matthieson to proclaim himself a prophet. But his reign was short, for in a sortie against Count Waldeck, who was besieging the town of which he was bishop, he was killed. Bockhold succeeded him (1534), and was crowned king of the "New Jerusalem" or "New Zion" with the title John of Leyden. Churches were then destroyed, and lawlessness prevailed for a year. In 1535, however, the city was taken, and its king tortured and executed. The principles, however, lived on and were propagated in the Netherlands. Even before Münzer's death England seems to have been infected with the teaching, for in 1534 a royal proclamation was issued against persons holding similar views. In 1539 the opinions of the Anabaptists were condemned in a set of Injunctions. But the movement was everywhere changing its tone, and losing its revolutionary character, so that the followers of Menno Simonis (A.D. 1505-1561) in Germany, and of the mystic David Joris (1501-1556), of Delft, whose "Wunderbuch" ("Book of Miracles") was much studied, can hardly be called Anabaptists. Yet, harmless as the new body were compared with their forerunners, they were doomed to suffer cruel persecution. Further details will be found under BAPTISTS. See J. H. Blunt; *Prot. Dict.;* Brockhaus.

ANADYOMENE. A designation of Aphrodite as the goddess "rising out of" the sea.

ANAHITA. Another form of the name of the goddess Anaitis (*q.v.*), who was worshipped by the ancient Persians. She represents the celestial waters.

ANAITIS. The name of a goddess worshipped in Armenia. She was a goddess of fertility, and in her temple at Acilisena prostitution was practised even by daughters of the noblest families. This was an act of religion which did not prevent them from marrying afterwards. She seems to be a variant of Tanith and Athenê (*q.v.*). Her worship was afterwards displaced by that of the Virgin (Mary). Another form of her name is Anahita. See J. G. Frazer, *Adonis Attis Osiris*, 1906; J. M. Robertson, *P.C.*

ANAMMELECH. The name, according to a passage in the Old Testament, of a Babylonian deity worshipped by the Sepharvites whom the king of Assyria (Sargon) placed in the cities of Samaria. We are told (II. Kings xvii., 31) that "the Sepharvites burnt their children in the fire to Adrammelech and Anammelech, the gods of Sepharvaim." On the reference to human sacrifice see ADRAMMELECH. Anammelech seems to be for *Anumalik*, "Anu is the decider or prince." There is no evidence, however, that Anu (*q.v.*), the god of Heaven, was specially associated with Sippar. The Hebrew text is perhaps corrupt. Another suggestion is that Anammelech is a doublet, "a faulty variant of Adrammelech." See *Encycl. Bibl.*

ANANT. The infinite or eternal, one of the names of the Hindu god Vishnu.

ANANTA. The most powerful of the seven snakes worshipped by the Hindus. The earth is supposed to be supported on its head.

ANATHEMA. A word used in the Bible in the sense of "something devoted to destruction" (cp. BAN). It occurs, for example, in Romans ix. 3, Galatians i. 8, 9, I. Corinthian xvi. 22 (Revised Version). "Anathema sit" is equivalent to "let him be accursed." The expression was used in the early Christian Church, and has been retained in the Roman Catholic Church. The Council of Elvira (306) anathematized those who placed in the church libellous writings. "The Church has used the phrase 'anathema sit' from the earliest times with reference to those whom she excludes from her communion either because of moral offences or because they persist in heresy" (Addis and Arnold).

ANATHEMA MARANATHA. An expression occurring in a passage in the New Testament (I. Corinthians xvi., 22). The Authorised Version translates: "If any man love not the Lord Jesus Christ, let him be Anathema Maranatha." The Revised Version rightly places a stop after Anathema, and renders "let him be anathema . Maran atha." It explains Maran atha in the margin as meaning "Our Lord cometh." "Let him be anathema" means "let him be accursed" (see ANATHEMA). A better division of Maranatha, which is made up of two Aramaic words, is perhaps Marana/tha, "Our Lord, come!" This seems to have been an exclamation in use in the early Church.

ANCESTOR-WORSHIP. Though a person may be dead, his spirit, it has been widely held, is still active. And since the spirits of the dead may be harmful or helpful, it is important to make sure of their friendship, and if necessary to propitiate them by offerings, etc. Moreover, a proper treatment of ancestral spirits is a filial duty to one who still protects his family. In China, for instance, ancestor-worship plays a dominating rôle in religion. Ancestors are worshipped even in their lifetime. On their death, when they are regarded as protectors of their family or tutelary deities, there is naturally no abatement in this worship. The soul of an ancestor, which still lives in the grave or in ancestral tablets, has to be propitiated. The Hindu seeks happiness in a similar way; he is careful to make offerings to the fathers ("pitaras"). The Romans worshipped their ancestors as household patrons. The worship of ancestors was common among the ancient Teutons. The Swedes are said also to have worshipped men. King Ericus, for instance, was made one of the company of the gods. The worship of ancestors has been found also in North and South America, in Tanna, Tasmania, Tonga, New Zealand, the Malay Islands, Africa, Ceylon, Japan, etc. When a Zulu sneezes, he believes the sneezing is caused by the presence of the ancestral spirit. Sneezing is a good and healthy sign. He therefore praises the spirit, and asks various blessings. Some of the dark-skinned races, when white men have visited them, have thought that they were their own deceased kindred come back to them in a new form. The Divine Ancestor or First Man is naturally regarded as chief of the other ancestors, and so as a superior deity. He is then either closely connected with the Creator, as in the mythology of Kamchatka, or identified with him, as among the Zulus, though here his remoteness has lost him the respect of the worshippers. The Hindu Yama appears as First Man, solar God of Hades, and Judge of the Dead. See E. B. Tylor, *P.C.;* J. J. M. de Groot, *R.S.C.;* P. D. Chantepie de La Saussaye, *Rel. of the Teutons*, 1902; Monier-Williams, *Brahmanism*, 1891.

ANCESTRAL TABLETS. In China the Buddhists have adopted Chinese ancestor-worship. There is a special room in the monasteries containing tablets to the souls of cremated members of the communities. Offerings are made to the deceased persons on special days, and the sacred writings are read in front of the ancestral tablets. See H. Hackmann.

ANCHORITES. A class of HERMITS.

ANCIENT OF THE MOUNTAINS, THE. A supposed designation of the Chief of the ASSASSINS (*q.v.*), a Persian secret sect re-organised by Ḥasan-i-Ṣabbāḥ (*d.* A.D. 1123-24). He is also referred to as the "Old Man of the Mountain." The real meaning of the popular Persian expression is "the Mountain Chief." See E. G. Browne, *Literary Hist. of Persia*, 1906.

ANCIENT LITURGY OF THE CHURCH OF JERUSALEM. A Liturgy prepared by Thomas Rattray (1684-1743), nonjuring bishop of Dunkeld in Scotland. It is described as "The Ancient Liturgy of the Church of Jerusalem, being the Liturgy of St. James," restored to its original purity, with the Clementine Liturgy, and parts of the Liturgies of St. Mark, St. Chrysostom, and St. Basil, exhibited in parallel columns. It was published in 1744. See Peter Hall; and the *D.N.B.*

ANCIENT MERCHANTS' LECTURE. A theological lectureship founded in 1672. The lectures are delivered from October to May at the Memorial Hall, Farringdon-street, London. The object of the foundation is "to uphold the doctrines of the Reformation against the errors of Popery, Socinianism, and Infidelity" (*Congregational Year Book*). The lectures were founded by a wealthy London tradesman, and the lecturers were to be "the most eminent of the Dissenting ministers of the metropolis" (H. S. Skeats and C. S. Miall, *Hist.*).

ANCYRA, SEVEN MARTYRS OF. The Seven Martyrs of Ancyra were, according to the tradition, seven Christian virgins of great piety who suffered in Diocletian's persecution of 304 A.D. They were each about seventy years old. Commanded to act as priestesses of Diana and Minerva and to wash their statues, they refused. Thereupon they were taken naked to a lake and drowned in it, heavy stones being tied round their necks. Their "Acts" are supposed to have been written by an eye-witness named Nilus. See Wace and Piercy.

ANDRIAMANITRA. A name given by the Malagasy to a power which is supernatural, supernormal, or awe-inspiring.

ANELING. Another name for Extreme Unction (*q.v.*).

ANGELIACAE. The name of an order of nuns (also "Angelicals"), founded by Luigia di Torelli, Countess of Guastalla, at Milan, about A.D. 1530. They followed the rule of St. Augustine. See *Cath. Dict.*

ANGELIC BROTHERS. A community of Mystics or theosophic Pietists founded by J. G. Gichtel (1638-1710). He was banished from Regensburg, his native place, as an Anabaptist, and went to Amsterdam in 1668. The Gichtelians, as they were also called, neither married nor were given in marriage, and believed they had attained the state of angels. There are still adherents of the sect in Holland and Germany. Gichtel's letters, with a biography, were published in 1722 in seven volumes under the title "Theosophia Practica."

ANGELIC DOCTOR. Latin "Doctor Angelicus," a name given to Thomas Aquinas (1227-1274), whom Pope Pius V. in 1567 designated the "Fifth Doctor of the Church." He is said to have been so called from the part which he took in a controversy as to: "Utrum

Angelus possit moveri de extremo ad extremum non transeundo per medium."

ANGELICI. A sect referred to by Epiphanius (*Hær.* lx.) and Augustine (*Hær.* xxxix.). Why they were so called is matter of conjecture. The most likely reason is, as Augustine suggests, that they were worshippers of angels (cp. Colossians ii. 18 and the 35th Canon of the Council of Laodicæa). But it is possible also that they were so called either because they believed that the world was created by angels, or because they thought that they themselves had already attained the state of angels.

ANGELICI, THE. An order of monks founded by the Emperor Angelus Comnenus in 1191.

ANGELICS. A name taken by an Anabaptist sect in Silesia and Bohemia (*c.* A.D. 1596).

ANGELITAE. A name taken by the Jacobites or Monophysites (*q.v.*) of Alexandria, and suggested by the name of their first church, which was called the Angelium (A.D. 540).

ANGEL OF DESTRUCTION. Reference is made in the Old Testament to a destroying angel or angel of destruction (ii. Samuel xxiv., 16; ii. Kings xix., 35). The same idea is found elsewhere. Hadrian's castle was renamed the Castle of St. Angelo, because when Rome was smitten by a plague, the archangel Michael is said to have appeared on the castle holding a bloody sword. Slavonic folklore also knows of a Pest-maiden who visits countries and everywhere turns joy into sadness. More often these visitors, though they are believed to be at work, are invisible to man. See E. B. Tylor, *P.C.*

ANGELS. From a Greek word meaning "messenger." The Hebrew word *mal'ākh* has the same meaning. In English the word denotes messengers of God, superhuman beings. Angels are mentioned frequently in the Bible (Old and New Testament), but the idea of them developed gradually. In the earliest portions of the Old Testament, though mention is often made of superhuman beings with whom Jehovah took counsel, they are very rarely called "angels." The expression "angel of Jehovah" is common, but this means Jehovah himself in his human manifestation. In course of time, however, when it was no longer believed that Jehovah himself visited the earth in human form, the "angel of Jehovah" came to be regarded as an intermediary between God and men, a messenger sent by God to men (*cp.* Zechariah i. 11 *f.*). In the New Testament we hear of angels visiting men and women and bringing them divine messages (Matthew i. 20, ii. 13; Luke i. 19; Acts x. 3, 30). With this development came the idea of an inner circle of angels. Certain special messengers of Jehovah are distinguished from the general host of angels as chiefs, and are called "archangels" (cp. Daniel x. 13, xii. 1; Tobit xii. 15; Enoch xl.; and see I. Thessalonians iv. 16; Jude ix.). The number of these is sometimes given as seven. In Tobit xii. 15 one of these "chief princes" (Daniel x. 13) says: "I am Raphael, one of the seven holy angels, which present the prayers of the saints, and go in before the glory of the Holy One." In Revelation viii. 2 it is said: "And I saw the seven angels which stand before God; and there were given unto them seven trumpets." In Enoch (viii. 2) the seven angels "which stand before God" are said to be Michael, Gabriel, Raphael, Uriel, Chamuel, Jophiel, and Zadkiel. Seven, of course, is a sacred number, and the growth of an angelic hierarchy is a natural one. At the same time it is not unlikely that later Hebrew ideas of angelology and demonology were influenced by Persian ideas. Prof. Cheyne thinks that "manifestly this highest class of angels was suggested by the Zoroastrian Amesha Spentas or Amshaspands ('immortal holy ones'), who (like the counsellors of the king of Persia, Ezra 7, 14) are seven; and this seems to be confirmed by the reference to the archangels in the Book of Tobit, which also mentions the Zend name of the chief demon" (see AMESHA-SPENTAS; ASMODEUS). The tendency to distinguish between beneficent and maleficent angels might also be due to outside influence; but, as Prof. G. B. Gray says, "the Old Testament nowhere lays stress on the moral character of angels, or knows anything of their 'fall'; consequently, angels were divided, not into good and bad, but into those who worked wholly, and those who worked only partly, in obedience to God" (cp. Romans viii. 38; I. Corinthians xv. 24 *f.*). The idea of fallen angels first becomes prominent in the Apocryphal Book of Enoch (cp. xiv. 4-7, xv. 2). In the Gospels and in the Epistles of St. Paul, angels begin to lose their importance as intermediaries of revelation. While Jesus himself is with his disciples, he reveals to them the Father; and before leaving them he promises to send the Holy Spirit to guide and comfort them. St. Paul condemns the worship of angels; and it was one of the peculiarities of the Sadducees that they disbelieved entirely in the existence of angels. The existence of what are called "guardian angels" has been widely believed in, and the idea has been used by poets and painters. God, it is supposed, has appointed a special angel to take care of every believer. In support of this idea appeal has been made to Matthew xviii. 10 and Acts xii. 15. In Matthew xviii. 10 it is said: "See that ye despise not one of these little ones; for I say unto you that in heaven their angels do always behold the face of my Father which is in heaven." Another passage which is referred to sometimes is Luke xv. 10: "Even so, I say unto you, there is joy in the presence of the angels of God over one sinner that repenteth." According to the *Protestant Dictionary*, the invocation of angels "detracts from the unique glory of our ascended Lord, who is the alone Mediator between God and men; and sends the suppliant to seek other intercession than His." But there is, of course—without regarding the matter from the point of view of a High Churchman—something to be said on the other side. The Roman Catholic Church, we are told for instance, "shows to the angels that veneration or inferior honour which is their due, and, knowing from Christ's words that they are acquainted with things which pass on earth, she begs their prayers and their kind offices. It is true that St. Paul condemns the θρησκεία, or religion of angels, in writing to the Colossians (i. 16), but every scholar is aware that he is warning them against the Gnostic error which regarded angels as the creators of the world; and with equal reason, the same passage might be alleged as in condemnation of humility" (*Cath. Dict.*). See *Encycl. Bibl.; Prot. Dict.; Cath. Dict.*

ANGELS OF THE SEVEN CHURCHES. An expression occurring in the New Testament (Revelation i., 20). In Rev. i. 19 *f.* we read: "Write therefore the things which thou sawest, and the things which are, and the things which shall come to pass hereafter; the mystery of the seven stars which thou sawest in my right hand, and the seven golden candlesticks. The seven stars are the angels of the seven churches; and the seven candlesticks are seven churches." Angels here might mean "messengers" (cp. Matthew xi., 10; Luke vii., 24, etc.), delegates from the Asiatic Churches sent to Patmos. Or, it has been suggested, the reference might be to presbyteral colleges. It is more likely, however, that "angel" is used in its ordinary sense. Either angels were thought of as presiding over the Churches, or "angel of the Church" meant the prevailing spirit of the Church. See H. B. Swete, *Apocalypse of St. John* (2), 1907.

ANGELUS BELL. A bell which is rung morning,

noon, and night in Roman Catholic communities to summon the devout to the recitation of the Angelic Salutation, which is also called AVE MARIA (*q.v.*).

ANGLICAN. A designation of things and persons belonging to the Church of England. It is sometimes used particularly of the High Church Party.

ANGLICAN ORDERS. Roman Catholics have questioned the validity of Anglican Orders. "For us Catholics," say Addis and Arnold, "the question was decided by the Bull *Apostolicæ Curæ* (Sept. 13, 1896), which declared Anglican orders to be 'absolutely null and utterly void,' on the ground of defect of form in the rite, and defect of intention in the minister." The Hon. James Adderley says: "We are told that our Ordination Service is invalid (1) because there is no delivery of the Chalice to one who is to be ordained Priest, (2) because there are said to be no words to denote that the Priest is a Sacrificing Priest, (3) because there is no expressed 'intention' to make a Catholic Bishop or Priest." His reply to this is (1) that the delivery of the Chalice is a custom which was not in vogue until the eleventh century, and therefore can hardly be said to be essential, (2) that there can be no necessity to use the term 'Sacrificing Priest,' provided that we do really claim to ordain Priests, (3) that the intention of our Ordination Service is quite sufficiently expressed in the Preface, as follows: 'It is evident unto all men diligently reading Holy Scripture and ancient Authors, that from the Apostles' time there have been these Orders of Ministers in Christ's Church: Bishops, Priests, and Deacons. Which offices were ever more had in such reverent estimation, that no man might presume to execute any of them except he were first called, tried, examined, and known to have such qualities as are requisite for the same; and also by public prayer, with imposition of hands, were approved and admitted thereunto by lawful Authority. And therefore to the intent that these orders may be continued and reverently used and esteemed in the Church of England; no man shall be accounted or taken to be a lawful Bishop, Priest, or Deacon in the Church of England, or suffered to execute any of the said functions, except he be called, tried, examined, and admitted thereunto according to the Form hereafter following or hath had formerly Episcopal Consecration or Ordination.'" The Bull of Pope Leo XIII. was officially answered by the Archbishops of Canterbury and York. See *Cath. Dict.*; James Adderley, *The Catholicism of the Church of England*, 1908; M. W. Patterson, *Hist.*

ANGLO-CALVINISTS. A Romanist designation of the Church of England on the ground that its principles and formularies are Calvinistic.

ANGLO-CATHOLIC. A term which has become common in recent years as a designation of the Church of England. Those who belong to the High Church Party like to call themselves Anglo-Catholics. The claim is that the Church of England is as much a part of the original Catholic Church as the Church of Rome. The old Catholic Church existed in Britain before the mission of St. Augustine. This claim is well supported by history. For a popular presentation of the facts, see James Adderley, *The Catholicism of the Church of England*, 1908.

ANGLO-ISRAELITE THEORY. A theory, held by many people in Great Britain and America, that the English race is descended from one of the "lost tribes of Israel." It is said that the Israelites who were transported to Media became known as Sacae or Scythians. These Sacae afterwards overran Northern Europe and became known as the Saxons. The contention has no support in science or history. The attempt to show a relationship between the English and Hebrew language has resulted in endless misrepresentations and absurdities. The search for the "lost tribes" has, as a matter of fact, been carried on in nearly every part of the world. It has been fruitless as far as the original quest is concerned, but has brought to light much interesting knowledge.

ANGRO-MAINYUSH. In Zoroastrian religion, one of the two principles or creative spirits ("the hurtful spirit") which originally were thought of as united in Ahuramazda. The other spirit was called speñtô mainyush, "the beneficent spirit." In course of time Angrô-mainyush came to be regarded as a separate independent being opposed to Ahuramazda. As such he was the organiser of the forces of evil. He is described as "the deadly, the demon of demons," the "creator of evils." It was he who created the darkness of night. Having associated with him six councillors, he is himself called archdemon. See Martin Haug.

ANGUS. Angus, one of the sons of Dagda (*q.v.*), was a deity or divine hero revered by the ancient Celts in Ireland. He was a god of music and love, and seems to have resembled the British goddess of love, Dwynwen or Dwyn (*q.v.*). See Charles Squire, *Myth.*

ANGUTTARANIKAYA. One of the Buddhist sacred books in the second division of the Canon. See CANON, BUDDHIST.

ANIMA MUNDI. Literally "soul of the world." A name given by early philosophers to a vital, immaterial, non-intelligential force. To Plato the anima mundi was an intermediate agency between pure spirit and matter. The Stoics spoke of the Deity as the soul of the world. "Nothing that is itself destitute of life and reason can generate a being possessed of life and reason. But the world generates beings possessed of life and reason. Therefore, the world is itself possessed of life and reason" (Zeno in Cicero, *De Nat. Deor.* ii. 8). See William L. Davidson, *The Stoic Creed*, 1907.

ANIMAL MAGNETISM. The modern theory of animal magnetism is closely associated with the name of Anton Mesmer (MESMERISM), a Viennese physician, who came into prominence in 1780. Mesmer performed wonderful cures. His use of artificial magnets led him in time to believe in a magnetic fluid which, without the use of magnets, he could conduct to the bodies of his patients by movements of his own hands. "The Magnetic power was therefore evidently in man himself. It was an animal magnetism in opposition to the mineral one which belonged to the magnet and to the stars" (Münsterberg). See Hugo Münsterberg, *Psychotherapy*, 1909, and cp. HYPNOTISM, etc.

ANIMAL WORSHIP. Ancient or primitive peoples have regarded animals with awe and veneration, and attributed to them souls which survive like those of men and have power to bring good or evil. They have worshipped them in fear as possessing such qualities as strength and cunning in a high degree, or they have venerated them in gratitude as providing food. Thus, worship has been paid to whales (by the Kamchadahs), bears (*ibid.*), wolves (*ibid.*), fish (Tribes of Peru), monkeys (*ibid.*), sparrow-hawks (*ibid.*), tigers (*ibid.*), alligators (Philippine islanders). When the Ainos (of Yesso) slay a bear, they, as it were, apologise for doing so, doing obeisance and making fair speeches. Yet sometimes an animal when dead is treated with a kind of mockery (North American Indians, Ostyaks of Siberia). The Yakuts of Siberia worship the bear as their "beloved uncle." In many cases deities are supposed to be embodied in animals. The animals therefore are propitiated with food and fed on sacrifices. Serpents, for instance, have been special objects of veneration (*e.g.*, in Phoenicia, Babylonia, Egypt, Greece, Persia, India,

China, Tibet, Ceylon, etc.). In other cases animals have been worshipped as representatives of tribal ancestors, or as totems. Of course, where a transmigration of souls is believed in, the animal may be thought to be a reincarnation of an ancestor, and may be worshipped as such. The worship of such animals as the bull Apis, the bird Ibis, the hawk, the crocodile, etc., by the ancient Egyptians is familiar to everyone. The sacred cow is still worshipped by the Hindus. They worship also the monkey (*Hanuman*), the bull (*Basava*), the kite (the bird Garuda), snakes, fish, etc. (J. A. Dubois and H. K. Beauchamp; Monier-Williams). See E. B. Tylor, *P.C.*, vol. ii.; J. M. Wheeler, *Footsteps of the Past*, 1895; E. Clodd, *Animism*, 1905; F. J. Gould, *Concise Hist. of Religion*, 1907.

ANIMATISM. In reference to Hellenic worship, L. R. Farnell (*Greek Religion*, 1912) thinks that "where we find the object worshipped in and for itself as sentient and animate, a thunder-stone, moving water, a blazing hearth, we should describe the religious consciousness as animatism rather than animism, which implies the definite conception of souls or spirits." The use of the term animatism was suggested originally by R. R. Marett (1909) to describe, in distinction from Animism, a simple straightforward act of personification. It is an attitude which "is *not* Animism in the strict scientific sense that implies the attribution, not merely of personality and will, but of 'soul' or 'spirit.'" One of the examples given is that of the members of a Kaffir village who when a thunderstorm approaches, "rush to the nearest village and yell at the hurricane to divert it from its course."

ANIMISM. Originally the explanation of all natural phenomena by the theory of an immaterial soul (*anima*) as the principle of life. G. E. Stahl, the German physician (1660-1734), even maintained, like some of our modern mental healers, that the state of the body is dependent on the state of the mind, that, in fact, disease has its origin in the mind or soul. In modern usage the term animism is applied by E. B. Tylor and others to "the doctrine of souls and other spiritual beings in general." It therefore embraces the conception of the soul as an explanation of human and natural phenomena, or as a philosophy of religion. Primitive folk, we are told, have formed a conception of a world of spirits from their observation of dreams, shadows, reflections, echoes, and the phenomena associated with nervous disorders. Figures and scenes seen in dreams are believed really to exist. During sleep, something, the spirit, leaves the body to visit familiar or new friends and places, and if the sleeper be suddenly awakened, the spirit may not return. The spirit is conceived as a kind of shadowy breath or vapour. It is not found in man alone. Since plants, animals, and even inanimate objects also appear in dreams, a spirit is assigned to these as well. See H. Spencer, *Principles of Sociology;* E. B. Tylor, *P.C.;* E. Clodd, *Animism*, 1905.

ANIMISTS. The followers of the German physician G. E. Stahl. See ANIMISM.

ANNA KUĀRI. Anna Kuāri or Mahādhani is a Hindu deity, a fertility goddess, worshipped by the Oraons, an important Dravidian tribe in India, the members of which work as farm servants and labourers. Human sacrifices are offered to her.

ANNA PURNA. An Indian deity, the Corn-giving goddess of Madras. She corresponds to Durga or Devi.

ANNA-PRASANA CEREMONY. A Hindu ceremony which takes place as soon as a child is weaned. It is preliminary to the change of diet. An auspicious day having been chosen, a pavilion (*pandal*) is erected and decorated with wreaths (*toranams*) of mango leaves. The father, with a cup of *akshatas* (rice coloured with saffron), then invites his relations and friends to come to the feast, which they do, having first bathed. The mother, holding the child, sits by the side of her husband on a platform of earth in the centre of the pavilion. The priest approaches them and performs certain ceremonies (sacrifice to fire, etc.). After this the women sing verses wishing the child happiness, and perform the *aratti* ceremony (see ARATTI CEREMONY) over him. Next the father offers to his household gods, and has part of the banquet set aside for them. The married women, walking in procession and singing, bring a new dish of silver-plated copper, given by the maternal uncle, a cord of cotton thread, worn by Hindus round their loins to suspend the small piece of calico which covers their private parts. Having touched the child with these two articles, they pour a mixture (*paramanna*) into the dish. Then singing again they take the dish and place it before the household gods. It is then designated the "dish god." They carry it back, singing, to the child, and fasten the cord round its loins. Three of them then pour some of the mixture down its throat. The *aratti* (*q.v.*) concludes the ceremony. See J. A. Dubois and H. K. Beauchamp.

ANNAT. A term (also written ANN) used in Scots law. An Act passed by the Scottish Parliament in 1672 provided that on the death of a clergyman, the next half-year's stipend should be paid to his next-of-kin. This sum was called "Annat."

ANNATES. The income of a spiritual benefice for one year (annus), claimed by the Pope as First Fruits. At first the tax was levied only on bishoprics, but afterwards on abbeys, rectories, etc. They were withheld in 1534 in England, and appropriated by the crown to be devoted ostensibly to the Church of England. Queen Anne restored them to the Church, and the fund became known as Queen Anne's Bounty.

ANNIHILATION. The theory that the soul ceases to exist at death. Even those who believe in its survival sometimes think that there are exceptions. The Omahas think that a self-murderer is annihilated. The Thompson Indians (British Columbia) hold the same belief. It is said that some savages disbelieve entirely in the survival of the soul, but the cases cited are open to question. Some of the wild tribes of India (*e.g.*, the Bengalese Orāons and the Burmese Mishmis), for instance, are said to have no idea of a future life, though they believe that in the case of some persons a reincarnation takes place on earth (see E. W. Hopkins). To the primitive mind, the best way to annihilate an individual, or even an insect, is to eat him. This is one reason for cannibalism. To punish the wicked, the supreme deity of the Pawnees annihilates them. See E. Westermarck.

ANNIHILATIONISTS. A designation of those who believe that after death the wicked will be entirely annihilated.

ANNUNCIATION. A theological term for the tidings brought by the angel Gabriel to Mary when she was about to become "mother of the Lord" (see Lk. i.). The festival of the Annunciation is observed by the Church on the 25th of March. It is first referred to in the acts of the Tenth Council of Toledo (656) and of the Trullan Council (692). In England the festival is more commonly known as Lady Day (*q.v.*).

ANOINTING. The Egyptians, Greeks, Romans, and other ancient peoples were accustomed to anoint the body or parts of it with oil as part of their toilet. Among the Hebrews anointing with oil was combined with washing or bathing in water (Ruth iii., 3; Esther ii., 12; Ezekiel xvi., 9; Judith x., 3). Olive oil is frequently mentioned in this connection (Amos vi., 6; Micah vi., 15; Luke vii., 46). Even this ordinary anointing has become among some peoples a kind of religious duty. Brahmans anoint themselves with oil of sesamum or castor oil from head to foot, then rub themselves with herbs and finally bathe the body. On grand ceremonial occasions their guests are provided with some kind of ointment that they may anoint themselves in the same way. Another kind of anointing, practised by primitive folk, has a different significance. In this case, as in that of swallowing or inoculation, the idea is to get certain virtues imparted to one. The Australian Blacks used to cut out the caul-fat of a slain man and rub themselves with it in the belief that they would thus acquire his distinguishing qualities. The negroes of Southern Guinea hang up the head of a dead man that the drippings of his brain may fall on to a lump of chalk, which they afterwards use as a kind of ointment for the forehead. The Andaman Islanders rub the melted fat of a boar into the body of a young man when he is initiated into manhood. The Arabs of Eastern Africa anoint themselves with lion's fat, and the Central Australian tribes use the fat of the kangaroo, their totem. Such customs seem to throw light on the practice (*e.g.* among the Hebrews) of anointing kings, priests, and prophets with oil. By this action (now become symbolical) it was supposed that the good qualities of their predecessors were imparted to them. Another practice has been to anoint sacred pillars or stones with oil. This seems to have been a form of sacrifice, the oil being a substitute for the fat of an animal. The practice among the Arabs of smearing pillars with fat seems to prove this (see Robertson Smith). This kind of anointing was not confined to Hebrews (Genesis xxviii., 18) and Arabs. The image of Aphrodite was a white cone or pyramid. A cone was also in certain places the emblem of Artemis and Astarte. This cone was anointed with olive oil at a special festival. In the sanctuary of Apollo at Delphi, too, a sacred stone was anointed. Another idea is at work in anointing when it is practised in sympathetic magic. In Suffolk when a man cuts himself with a scythe, he "oils it to prevent the wound from festering." He does the same with a thorn which has run into his hand. In the Harz mountains people say that "if you cut yourself, you ought to smear the knife or the scissors with fat and put the instrument away in a dry place in the name of the Father, of the Son, and of the Holy Ghost. As the knife dries, the wound heals." Among the aborigines of Central Australia, when a boy has been circumcised, his mother rubs grease all over her body every day until the wound is healed. Cp., further, CHRISM and EXTREME UNCTION. See J. G. Frazer, *G.B.; Adonis Attis Osiris*, 1906; W. R. Smith, *R.S.;* J. A. Dubois and H. K. Beauchamp, *Hindu Manners, etc.; Encycl. Bibl.*

ANOMIANS. Another designation of the ANTINOMIANS (*q.v.*).

ANOMŒANS. A name given to the strict Arians. See ARIANISM.

ANRA-MAINYU. The personification of Darkness in the dualistic religion of Zarathustra.

ANSARS. An Arabian sect, more correctly called Nossairians (Nuseirîyeh, *q.v.*).

ANSHAR. The name of a deity in Babylonian-Assyrian religion. He is mentioned on a cuneiform tablet as one of the early ancestors of the gods. Anshar, perhaps another form of Ashur (*q.v.*), plays a part in the cosmology. He sends Anu, Ea, and Bel-Marduk (*qq.v.*) to destroy the monster Tiâmat. See Morris Jastrow, *Rel.*

ANTEDILUVIAN. Literally "before the deluge," the deluge referred to being that described in the Old Testament and commonly known as the Flood. The term is often used of anything antiquated or old-fashioned.

ANTHEMS. An abridged form of Antiphon, a piece sung in alternate parts. The words are verses from the Bible (Psalms, etc.), and are sung as solos or in chorus. In the reign of Elizabeth they were appointed to be sung at the morning and evening service of the Church of England. A similar part of the Roman Catholic Service is the Motet.

ANTHESTERIA. An Athenian festival, on which the souls of the departed were supposed to return from the nether world. Earthenware pots seem to have been filled with boiled food and placed in the streets for their entertainment. To prevent the ghosts from entering their houses, the people smeared the doors with pitch. They also fastened ropes round the temples "to keep out the wandering ghosts." See J. G. Frazer, *G.B.*

ANTHROPOLATRY. The worship of men. See ANCESTOR WORSHIP.

ANTHROPOMORPHISM. The style of thought and language that ascribes to the Deity human form and attributes.

ANTHROPOMORPHITES. Another name for the Syrian sect Audiani (*q.v.*).

ANTHROPOPHAGOI. Another name for CANNIBALS.

ANTI-ADIAPHORISTS. A name for the strict Lutherans as distinguished from the party of Melanchthon, the Adiaphorists (*q.v.*).

ANTIBURGHERS. A name taken by one of the divisions into which the Associate Synod or Secession Church of Scotland split up in 1747. The trouble arose over the burgess-oath which burgesses were required to take in certain corporate towns. One party maintained that it could not be taken by consistent Seceders. The other party, though they thought it inexpedient for Seceders to take the oath, would not refuse to do so. Those who refused to take the oath formed themselves into the "General Associate Synod" or "Anti-burgher Synod." Those who would not take it became the "Associate" or "Burgher Synod." Later on another split occurred owing to differences of opinion about the powers of the civil magistrate in matters of religion. It was felt by many that the views of the old Covenant required to be modified. In 1804 therefore a new Declaration of Principles or "Testimony" was put forth. Thomas McCrie (1772-1835), Archibald Bruce (1746-1816), James Aitken, and James Hog, however, professed to adhere "to the true constitution of the Reformed Church of Scotland," and in 1806 started the "Constitutional Associate Presbytery," the members of which were called also "Old Light Anti-burghers." Another division had in 1799 formed themselves into the "Original Burgher Presbytery" or "Old Light Burghers." In 1820 the "New Light" sections of the Burghers and Anti-burghers were re-united as the "United Secession." In 1827 the "Old Light Anti-burghers" united with the "Associate Synod of Protesters" (formed in 1820 in opposition to the "United Secession"), and the two bodies became the "Associate Synod of Original Seceders." Cp. BURGHERS. See J. H. Blunt.

ANTI-CALVINISTS. A designation of the Arminians (*q.v.*).

ANTICHRIST. The word is first found in the New Testament (I. John ii. 18, 22, iv. 3; II. John 7). In I. John ii. 18 we read: "Little children, it is the last hour, and as ye heard that antichrist cometh, even now have there arisen many antichrists, whereby we know that it is the last hour." In *vs.* 22 it is said: "Who is the liar but he that denieth that Jesus is the Christ? This is the antichrist, even he that denieth the Father and the Son." In I. John iv. 3 the words are: "And every spirit which confesseth not Jesus is not of God, and this is the spirit of the antichrist, whereof ye have heard that it cometh; and now it is in the world already." In II. John *vs.* 7 we read: "For many deceivers are gone forth into the world, even they that confess not that Jesus Christ cometh in the flesh. This is the deceiver and the antichrist." These are the only passages in which the term occurs. It means "one who opposes the Messiah (*Christos*)" and although the word only appears in the late Johannine passages, the idea itself is present elsewhere. In II. Thess. ii. 1-12 it is said that before the Second Coming of the Lord Jesus Christ there will be a falling away and "the man of sin (or lawlessness)" will be revealed, "the son of perdition, he that opposeth and exalteth himself against all that is called God or that is worshipped; so that he sitteth in the temple of God, setting himself forth as God." It is said also *vs.* 7 *f.*): "For the mystery of lawlessness doth already work; only there is one that restraineth now, until he be taken out of the way. And then shall be revealed the lawless one, whom the Lord Jesus shall slay with the breath of his mouth and bring to nought by the manifestation of his coming; even he, whose coming is according to the working of Satan with all power and signs and lying wonders, and with all deceit of unrighteousness for them that are perishing." Ideas belonging to the same world of thought are referred to in the Book of Revelation (xi.; xiii., 11 *ff.*). Outside the New Testament, moreover, there are many references (*e.g.* in Apocalyptic Literature and in the Early Fathers) to Antichrist which point to a body of tradition of which the New Testament statements are only fragments. The origin of these traditions is to be found partly in Jewish haggada, that method of exposition which consisted in "the working up of the historic and didactic parts of Scripture, an elaboration of them by the free use of the legendary element, suitable to the views and requirements of the age" (W. Fairweather, *The Background of the Gospels*, 1908). The starting-point for this may have been Daniel xi. 7 *f.* It should be noticed also that in Apocalyptic Literature (*e.g.*, *Sibyll.* iii. 63 *ff.*) Belial or Beliar, ruler of the evil spirits, "is already presented in an aspect closely resembling that of Anti-Christ" (W. Bousset). If we wish to trace these ideas farther back, much of the imagery may be reproduced from the conception of the dragon in the Babylonian creation-myth. The idea of Nero returning as a spirit from the underworld perhaps belonged originally to another tradition, but both traditions are combined in the Book of Revelation (xiii. and xvii.). The number of the Beast (666, Revelation xiii.) represented in Hebrew letters gives the name of Nero (see P. W. Schmiedel, *Johannine Writings*, 1908). Of course, the references to Antichrist have been regarded as prophecies, and some historical person has been looked for who seemed to fulfil the requirements. Other identifications (*i.e.*, besides Nero) have been: Mohammed, the Grand Turk, Napoleon I., Napoleon III., the Pope. See *Encycl. Bibl.;* W. Bousset, *The Antichrist Legend*, 1896.

ANTICONSTITUTIONISTS. A name given to those theologians who rejected the papal Bull "Unigenitus" (1713) which condemned the views of the Jansenist leader Pasquier Quesnel (1634-1719). See JANSENISTS.

ANTIDICOMARIANITES. Literally "opponents of Mary." A religious sect in Arabia, referred to by Epiphanius. They held that after the birth of Jesus, Mary and Joseph became the parents of other children.

ANTILEGOMENA. Literally "spoken against." A general designation of those books of the New Testament the authenticity of which was disputed in the fourth century. They were for a time regarded as uncanonical (see CANON). The Books in question are: Second Epistle of Peter, Ep. of James, Ep. of Jude, Ep. to the Hebrews, Second and Third Ep. of John, and the Book of Revelation. The term *homologoumena* was applied to the other books.

ANTINICAENS. Opponents of the Creed of Nicaea. See ARIANISM.

ANTINOMIANISM. Antinomian has been defined as "one who holds that the law is not a rule of life under the Gospel." The idea that to one who had become a true follower of Christ conscience was the only law might easily arise. Luke xvi. 16, "the law and the prophets were until John"; Romans vii. 6, "But now we have been discharged from the law, having died to that wherein we were holden, so that we serve in newness of the spirit, and not in oldness of the letter"; Galatians ii. 16, "knowing that a man is not justified by the works of the law, but only through faith in Jesus Christ, even we believed on Christ Jesus, that we might be justified by faith in Christ, and not by the works of the law"; and other passages would be appealed to in support of such a view. And the idea would soon be exaggerated and carried to extremes. This seems actually to have happened among certain sections of the Gnostics, and later among some of the religious sects in the Middle Ages. In such cases Antinomianism, from being a kind of superiority to law, degenerates into rejection and violation of the moral law. The term was first used, however, by Luther in reference to the views of John Agricola (1492-1566), called "Magister Islebius," from the name of his birth-place, Eisleben. In 1527 he maintained in opposition to Philipp Melanchthon (1497-1560) "that the law of God was not to be used to bring men to repentance, and that the preaching of the law was no work for a gospel minister" (J. H. Blunt). In 1538 he was bold enough to "declaim against the law, maintaining that it was neither fit to be proposed to the people as a rule of manners, nor to be used in the Church as a means of instruction; and that the gospel alone was to be inculcated and explained both in the churches and in the schools of learning." His followers were called Antinomians. His controversy with Luther, which ended in a recantation (1540), was called the "Antinomian Controversy." Since that time Antinomianism, in one form or another, has had its representatives in England. Amongst the troublesome parties with which Cromwell had to deal were "the violent fanatics and Antinomians who desired an immediate 'rule of the saints'" (M. W. Patterson, *Hist.*). In 1691 the republication of the works of Tobias Crisp (1600-1643) produced another "Antinomian Controversy" between Congregationalists and Presbyterians, the latter accusing the former of Antinomianism (see H. S. Skeats and C. S. Miall, *Hist.*). See J. H. Blunt; Brockhaus.

ANTIPAEDOBAPTIST. A designation, derived from the Greek, of one who objects to infant-baptism. See BAPTISTS.

ANTIPHONER. A name given to one of the four parts of the Mediæval Service-book of the Christian Church, the Missal (*q.v.*). It contained the antiphons sung by the choir and deacons at the celebration of High Mass. It was called also Grail or Gradual.

ANTIPHONY. A method of chanting in which two choirs sing in turn, responding as it were to each other. Some of the Old Testament Psalms are admirably adapted for this kind of singing. Ignatius is said to have introduced antiphony at Antioch in the second century. Ambrose is supposed to have used it at Milan in the fourth century, and thus to have introduced it into the Western or Latin Church.

ANTI-POPES. A designation of opposition popes, that is to say, of popes who have claimed the Papal Chair and set themselves in opposition to the canonically-elected occupant. There have been at least twenty-nine such popes. 1. Hippolytus (?), third century. 2. Novatian, A.D. 251. 3. Felix II., A.D. 355-365. 4. Ursicinus, A.D. 366-367. 5. Eutalius, A.D. 418-419. 6. Laurentius, A.D. 498-501. 7. Constantine II., A.D. 767. 8. Philip, eighth century. 9. Anastasius, A.D. 855. 10. Leo VIII., A.D. 956-963. 11. Boniface VII., A.D. 974. 12. John XVI., tenth century. 13. Gregory, A.D. 1012. 14. Sylvester III., A.D. 1044. 15. Benedict X., A.D. 1058. 16. Honorius II., A.D. 1061-1072. 17. Guibert, or Clement III., A.D. 1080-1100. 18. Theodoric, A.D. 1100. 19. Aleric, A.D. 1102. 20. Maginulf, A.D. 1105. 21. Burdin (Gregory VIII.), A.D. 1118. 22. Anacletus II., A.D. 1130-38. 23. Victor IV., A.D. 1159-64. 24. Pascal III., A.D. 1164-1168. 25. Calixtus III., A.D. 1168-77. 26. Innocent III., A.D. 1178-80. 27. Nicholas V., A.D. 1328-1330. 28. Robert of Geneva (Clement VII), September 20, A.D. 1378, to September 16, A.D. 1394. 29. Amadeus of Savoy (Felix V.), November, 1439, to April, 1449. See the *Catholic Encycl.*

ANTI-REMONSTRANTS. When Peter Walsh drew up the Petition of Remonstrance in 1666 which protested against the notion that if Catholicism were tolerated the safety of the State would be endangered, some of the Irish Catholics refused to sign it and were called Anti-Remonstrants.

ANTI-SCRIPTURALISTS. Richard Baxter (1615-1691), writing in 1650, refers to a sect of Puritans with this name. They were closely related to, or perhaps identical with, the Seekers (*q.v.*). With the latter they would seem to have attached more value to the present illumination of the Spirit than to the past revelation of the Scripture. See John Hunt.

ANTISTES. A title which has sometimes been applied to a Christian prelate or bishop.

ANTITACTICS. A term used by Clement of Alexandria in reference to "opponents" who held a dualistic philosophy and distinguished between God, the Father of all things who made all things good, and an Adversary, a rebel creature, who originated evil (Clem. Alex., *Strom.* iii., 4).

ANTITRINITARIANS. A designation of those who deny the doctrine of the Trinity. See TRINITY, UNITARIANS, and CHRISTADELPHIANS.

ANTITYPE. Literally, something which corresponds to, or is prefigured by, the type. But in theology the person who fulfils the idea of some prophetic type. Christ, *e.g.*, is the antitype of the paschal lamb.

ANTO. One of the gods of the Todas. Perhaps he is the same as Ön (Anto=Önteu). He seems to have been a giant. According to a legend, he rolled a large stone to the top of a hill with his hair.

ANTONINES. An order of monks founded towards the close of the eleventh century by Gaston, a gentleman of Dauphiné. Many people were suffering from a disease called St. Anthony's fire. Gaston's son became one of the afflicted. His father, praying before some relics of St. Anthony, vowed that if his son recovered he would found a hospital (1095). On the recovery of his son, he founded an order of monks, and established a hospital for the treatment of persons afflicted with St. Anthony's fire. The order flourished until the Revolution. "Benedict VIII. in 1297 ordained that the Antonines should live as canons-regular under the rule of St. Austin." See *Cath. Dict.*

ANTONY'S FIRE, ST. The name given to an epidemic which raged in France especially in 1089. It was so called because many of those who were attacked by it are supposed, on praying before the relics of St. Antony, to have been healed. St. Antony (A.D. 251-356) of Thebes had a great reputation as the father of monasticism and the ideal hermit.

ANTOSIANDRIANS. Opponents of the party of the German Protestant Andreas Osiander (1498-1552). See OSIANDRIANS.

ANTRIM, PRESBYTERY OF. An off-shoot of the Irish Presbyterians. They refused to subscribe to the Westminster Confession (*q.v.*), and formed themselves into an independent body in 1750.

ANTS. The Apalai Indians of South America drive away any demon of disease which may cling to their persons by allowing themselves to be stung by large ants. Certain Indians of Guiana, when a girl first shows signs of puberty, keep her for a month "in her hammock at the top of the hut," and expose her to the painful bites of large ants. This is said to be to strengthen her to bear the burden of motherhood. See J. G. Frazer, *G.B.*

ANTWERP POLYGLOT. An early printed edition of the New Testament in several languages. It was brought out at Antwerp under the auspices of Philip II., was edited by Benedict Arias Montanus, and was printed by Christopher Plantin. It is called also the Plantin polyglot after its printer. It contains the Greek text, the Syriac text both in Syriac and Hebrew letters, a Latin translation of the Syriac text and another of the Greek text, and the Latin Vulgate. The Greek text "agrees in the main with Robert Estienne's edition of the year 1550." See C. R. Gregory.

ANU. A Babylonian deity. He is described on an ancient Babylonian seal-cylinder as "Anu, the supreme, king of the Anunnaki" (spirits of the heavens). See Fr. Delitzsch, *Babel and Bible*, 1903, p. 74. The name seems to be found in inscriptions prior to the year 2300 B.C. Anu is the god of heaven. In the early religion, Anu Bel (*q.v.*), and Ea (*q.v.*) are the three great gods. Anu's consort is Anatum. According to one version of the great battle of the gods with the monster Tiâmat, Anu is sent to slay the monster. Anu also plays a part in the Adapa Legend (*q.v.*). He is brought into association with several other gods (*e.g.*, Ramman, Dagan), and in course of time is rather overshadowed by Ashur (*q.v.*). The sun's ecliptic is described as the "way of Anu," and the pole star of the ecliptic was specially identified with him. See Morris Jastrow, *Rel.*

ANUBIS. An Egyptian deity. Son of Osiris (*q.v.*), he is represented as having the head of a jackal or dog-ape. When the Greeks and Romans took over the worship they represented him as a dog. Like Hermes, with whom the Greeks identified him, he conducted the dead to the underworld (Amenthes), where with Horus (*q.v.*) he weighed their deeds in the balance before Osiris. In a tomb of the Old Empire has been found a slab of stone containing an invocation to Anubis. Anubis is entreated that the dead person may have a good tomb in the West, and may receive a plentiful supply of offerings on special feast-days. See E. Naville, *The Old Egyptian Faith*, 1909, p. 71.

ANUNIT. A Babylonian goddess. She is described (cylinder inscription of Nabonidus) as "the mistress of battle, bearer of the bow and quiver." Anunit is a feminine form corresponding to the masculine Anu (*q.v.*). She seems to be mentioned in inscriptions prior to the year 2300 B.C., but in course of time the name became another designation of Ishtar (*q.v.*). See Morris Jastrow, *Rel.*

ANUNNAKI. A term occurring in Babylonian-Assyrian religion. The derivation of the word is doubtful. It has been interpreted (Hommel) "gods of the watery habitation." In any case, the Anunnaki are a group of gods or spirits employed in the service of other gods. They are spirits of earth, while the spirits of heaven receive the name Igigi (*q.v.*). They figure in the Babylonian Creation and Deluge stories. See Morris Jastrow, *Rel.*

APADĀNA. A Buddhist sacred book, a book of stories of the saints, included in the collection appended to the second division of the Canon. See CANON, BUDDHIST.

APELLIANISTS. A Gnostic sect of the second century named after Apelles, who was for a time the disciple of Marcion (taught about A.D. 150). They were also called Apelleians or Apellites. Apelles seems to have held that matter was created by an inferior deity, hostile to God though created by Him; and that Jesus descended mysteriously from heaven and took a body composed of earth, air, fire, and water, which elements were dispersed again before his ascension to heaven. He criticised the prophets of the Old Testament and the Law of Moses, on the ground that they were often inspired, not by God the Creator, but by the inferior deity, the author of evil. He seems to have taught also that salvation depended upon being true to one's own faith, whatever it might be. See J. H. Blunt.

APHACA, POOL OF. A sacred pool among the Phoenicians. Once a year the heaven goddess is said to have come down into the waters "in the shape of a falling star." The worshippers of the goddess were accustomed to cast gifts into the sacred pool. If a gift was not accepted, the eddies cast it up. See W. R. Smith, *R.S.*

AP-HI. Ap-hi is worshipped by the Abchases of the Caucasus as the god of thunder and lightning. In time of drought an ox is sacrificed to him, and he is implored to send rain to revive the crops. He is one of the examples of a god of thunder being regarded as a god of fertility also. See J. G. Frazer, *The Magic Art*, 1911.

APHORISM. A short pithy saying expressing a general truth. The Hindus are fond of employing aphorisms (*slokas*), and many of these are of a moral or religious nature. The children learn them by heart in the schools. See J. A. Dubois and H. K. Beauchamp.

APHRODITE. The goddess of love in Greek religion. She appears under several aspects, some of them oriental. Other Greek names for her are: Aphro-gĕneia, the "foam-born"; Anadyŏmĕnē, "she who rises" from the sea; Kypris, the Cyprian; Aphrodite Urănia, "the heavenly"; Pandēmŏs, "all the people's." Thus she was goddess of the sea, especially the calm sea, and as such was worshipped by fishermen and sailors; she was goddess of the sky with its gales and storms. She was also goddess of the earth with its gardens and groves, its plants and flowers. As the goddess of love in a more and more refined sense, she became a goddess of marriage and married life, the goddess beloved by all. Early Greek legend represented that she was the daughter of Zeus and Dīonē. Aphrodite, however, was not always worshipped as the goddess of a purer love. At Paphos, the great and ancient seat of her worship, she seems to have shared, as a goddess of fertility, the licentious rites of other Asiatic deities, one of these being female prostitution. For her association with Adonis, see the article under that heading. In later Greek times the immoral form of her worship prevailed in Greece also. Aphrodite corresponds to the Roman Venus (*q.v.*). Her symbol or image was a white cone or pyramid. Minoan discoveries have thrown doubt on the theory that Aphrodite was originally a Semitic deity brought to Greece from Phoenicia or Cyprus. A Minoan Aphrodite is represented on monuments of the First Late Minoan period (*c.* 1600-1500 B.C.). H. R. Hall (*A.A.*) points out that "it is evident now that she was not only a Canaanitish-Syrian goddess, but was common to all the peoples of the Levant. She is Aphrodite-Paphia in Cyprus, Ashtaroth-Astarte in Canaan, Atargatis in Syria, Derketo in Philistia, Hathor in Egypt; what the Minoans called her we do not know, unless she is Britomartis. She must take her place by the side of Rhea-Diktynna in the Minoan pantheon." Professor G. Elliot Smith contends (*Dr.*) that this list of homologues can be extended to Mesopotamia, Iran, and India, to Europe and Further Asia, to America, and, in fact, to every part of the world that harbours goddesses. See O. Seyffert, *Dict.;* J. G. Frazer, *Adonis, Attis, Osiris.*

APHTHARTODOCETÆ. A general name for the Julianists of Armenia and the Gaianitæ of Egypt, the two divisions of the Monophysites (*q.v.*). They were so called because they attributed to Jesus' body *aphtharsia*, "incorruptibility." "The human nature they considered to have been so essentially united with the Divine nature of the Logos as to have become merged or absorbed in it, and therefore to have become possessed of the inherent and indestructible life of the Logos" (J. H. Blunt).

API. An Egyptian goddess. She is represented as having the body of a hippopotamus.

APIS. An Egyptian deity. At first a sacred bull in the temple of Ptah, he then became a god represented as a bull, and later still was regarded as an incarnation of Osiris (*q.v.*), and ranked next to Râ (*q.v.*). See Adolf Erman.

APITO. An earth-goddess worshipped in the West Indies (Antilles).

APOCALYPSE. The Greek name of the last book of the New Testament, more commonly known as the Revelation of St. John the Divine (*q.v.*).

APOCALYPSE OF BARUCH. See APOCALYPTIC LITERATURE.

APOCALYPSE OF PETER. See APOCRYPHAL BOOKS OF THE NEW TESTAMENT.

APOCALYPTIC LITERATURE. A general term for a collection of Jewish writings called "Apocalypses," *i.e.*, prophetic revelations of the future. An early example is found in the Old Testament in the book of Daniel (167-164 B.C.). The last book of the New Testament bears the Greek title "Apocalypse of S. John the Divine" (see REVELATION, BOOK OF), and some scholars think that a little Apocalypse has been incorporated in the Gospels (Matthew xxiv. 6-8, 15-22, 29-31, 34-35=Mark xiii. 7-9 *a*, 14-20, 24-27, 30; see Arno Neumann, *Jesus*, 1906, p. 148) and in 2 Thessalonians (2, 1-12). Other Apocalyptic writings are: the "Apocalypse of Baruch," preserved in Syriac, written by Pharisees (*c.* A.D. 50-90); the "Book of Enoch," preserved in Ethiopic, composite, the earliest portion having been written perhaps *c.* 200 B.C., the latest *c.* 64 B.C.; another "Book of Enoch" or "Book of the Secrets of Enoch," preserved in Slavonic, written about A.D. 1-50; the "Ascension of Isaiah," preserved in Ethiopic and partly in Latin, composite, written about A.D. 1-100; the "Book of Jubilees," preserved in Ethiopic and partly in Hebrew, Syriac, Greek, Latin, Slavonic, written about 40-10 B.C.; the "Assumption of Moses," preserved in Latin, written about 7-30 A.D.; the "Testament of the XII. Patriarchs," preserved in Greek, Armenian, and Slavonic, written about 130 B.C. - 10 A.D.; the "Psalms of Solomon," composite, written about 70-40 B.C.; the "Sibylline Oracles," written in Greek, composite, the earliest portions dating from the second century B.C., the latest from the third century A.D. See *Encycl. Bibl.;* W. Fairweather, *Background of the Gospels*, 1908. For New Testament Apocalypses, see APOCRYPHAL BOOKS OF THE N.T.

APOCALYPTIC NUMBER. In the New Testament Book of Revelation we read (xiii. 18): "He that hath understanding, let him count the number of the beast; for it is the number of a man; and his number is six hundred and sixty and six." This is what is meant by the Apocalyptic Number. It is supposed to indicate some name, since Greek and Hebrew letters were used to represent numbers. Prof. Schmiedel (*The Johannine Writings*, 1908) points out that in many copies of the Book of Revelation before the time of Irenaeus, that is to say, before A.D. 185, the number is given as 616. He therefore suggests that a name must be found the letters of which might in some way or other produce either of the numbers 666 or 616. He thinks that the name of the Emperor Nero meets the requirements, since it might be written N(e)ron K(e)s(a)r or N(e)ro K(e)s(a)r. The vowels *e* and *a* would not be expressed in Hebrew. The identifications are as follows:

N R O N K S R
50+200+6+50+100+60+200 = 666
N R O K S R
50+200+6 +100+60+200 = 616

Prof. Schmiedel points out that the number 666 alone has produced more than a hundred other solutions.

APOCARITES. A sect which appeared in the reign of the Roman Emperor Marcus Claudius Tacitus (A.D. 275-6). Its tenets were largely Gnostic and Manichæan. The Apocarites held also that the human soul is eternal and uncreated.

APOCATASTASIS. A Greek word meaning "restitution," and occurring in the New Testament. In Acts iii. 21 it is said that the heaven must receive Jesus "until the times of restoration of all things, whereof God spake by the mouth of his holy prophets which have been since the world began." Apocatastasis became a theological term denoting the doctrine, taught by Origen and others, that all men would be converted and admitted to everlasting happiness.

APOCATEQUIL. A deity in the mythology of the ancient Peruvians. He was connected with the night, and was called therefore by the Incan Peruvians "Prince of Evil." His name is said to mean "Chief of the followers of the moon."

APOCRISIARIUS. From the Greek *apokrinesthai* "to answer." A name given from the fourth to the ninth century to ecclesiastical or Papal emissaries to the Court of the Emperor. Their task was to bring important questions, civil and ecclesiastical, to the notice of the civil authority and to obtain answers to them. The same duty was performed at a later date by the Nuncio or Legate *a latere*. See *Cath. Dict.*

APOCRYPHA, INTERNATIONAL SOCIETY OF THE. A Society the object of which "is to make more widely known the theological, ecclesiastical, and literary value of the 'Books which the Church doth read for example of life and instruction of manners,' and to promote their more general study among the clergy and laity" (*Official Year-Book of the Church of England*). The Society publishes a Quarterly Journal.

APOCRYPHA OF THE OLD TESTAMENT. The word Apocrypha means literally "hidden," and, like the corresponding Hebrew word, denotes books which were withdrawn from public use as being unfit for public reading. Sometimes there is associated also with the word the idea that certain books are not suitable for the general public because they contain mysterious truths or esoteric doctrines. The early fathers applied the word "apocryphal" both to heretical works and to works which were not accepted as canonical or included in Sacred Scripture. Old Testament and New Testament Apocrypha, however, have been placed upon a very different level. While the New Testament Apocrypha (properly speaking) have been regarded as possessing very slight value, to some of the Old Testament Apocrypha has been ascribed a value almost, if not quite, as great as that of some of the canonical books. The Old Testament Apocrypha (proper) "the Church [of England] doth read for example of life and instruction of manners, but yet doth it not apply them to establish any doctrine" (Article vi.). The Roman Catholic edition of the Bible, the Douay Version, includes the Apocrypha (proper) with the exception of the "Prayer of Manasseh," "Third Esdras," and "Fourth Esdras," which were rejected by the Council of Trent as uncanonical. The books of the Apocrypha are as follows: 1. *The Third Book of Esdras*. This is the title in the Vulgate (*q.v.*). In the original Greek version, in the Septuagint (*q.v.*), and in the English Version, it is called "I. Esdras." The book is partly a compilation from the canonical Book of Ezra (*q.v.*). It perhaps belongs to the first century B.C. 2. *The Fourth Book of Esdras*. In the English Version it is called "II. Esdras." The Greek original has disappeared, and there are omissions in the Vulgate. The work is composite. It belongs perhaps to the first century after Christ. Sometimes it is called the "Apocalypse of Ezra." 3. *The Book of Tobit*. Preserved in Greek, Latin, Hebrew and Aramaic. It was written perhaps not later than the first century A.D. It is a romance of the Captivity, and is interesting on account of its angelology and demonology. 4. *The Book of Judith*. Preserved in Greek. It belong perhaps to the first century B.C. It is a romance, and perhaps to some extent an allegory. It describes how Judith, a noble Hebrew widow, delivers the city Bethulia from Holofernes, its besieger, by assassinating him. 5. *The Rest of the Book of Esther*. Additions to the Book of Esther (*q.v.*). In the Greek, Vulgate, and Douay Versions it is not a separate title. 6. *The Book of Wisdom*. Written in Greek under the assumed name of Solomon. It was perhaps written in the first century B.C. It is not all of equal merit, but there are many remarkable passages in the book. 7. *Jesus the son of Sirach*. Preserved in Greek, but a translation from Hebrew, much of a (perhaps original) Hebrew version having been recently discovered. It is better known as the *Book of Ecclesiasticus*. It probably belongs to the second century B.C. The book contains many remarkable passages, and is well worthy of study. 8. *Baruch the Prophet*. Preserved in Greek. It is composite. Part of it (the end) may have been written after 70 A.D. The Baruch meant is Jeremiah's amanuensis, the son of Neriah. Appended to it is a letter known as the *Epistle of Jeremy* (or Jeremiah), which belongs probably to the first century A.D. 9 *The Song of the Three Children*. Preserved in Greek. An addition to the Book of Daniel (*q.v.*), and not treated as a separate title in the Septuagint, Vulgate, and Douay Versions. 10. *The Story of Susanna*. In exactly the same category as No. 9. 11. *Of Bel and the Dragon*. In exactly the same category as Nos. 9 and 10. 12. *The Prayer of Manasses*. Preserved in Greek and Latin. It purports to have been written in prison by Manasseh, king of Judah. 13. *The First Book of Maccabees*. Preserved in Greek, but a translation from Hebrew. Written about 105 B.C. It is a historical work of great value, recording the history of the Jews in Palestine from 175 to 135 B.C. 14. *The Second Book of Maccabees*. Preserved in Greek. Of very much less value. The work is composite. The first part purports to give two letters written by the Jews of Jerusalem to the Jews of Egypt. The second part professes to be an abridgment of a lost work in five books by Jason of Cyrene. The above are the works which are commonly known as "the Apocrypha." Cp., further, PSEUDEPIGRAPHA. See *Encycl. Bibl.; Prot. Dict.; Cath. Dict.*

APOCRYPHAL BOOKS OF THE NEW TESTAMENT.

A large number of writings, purporting to have been written by apostles and designed to supplement the history contained in the New Testament. They group themselves for the most part under the headings *Gospels, Acts, Epistles, Apocalypses*. 1. GOSPELS. *a) Gospel according to the Hebrews*. It was originally in Aramaic. Only fragments have been preserved and not in the original language. These are found in the works of Jerome, Origen, Eusebius, and in Codex Tischendorf III. *b) Gospel of the Ebionites* or *Gospel of the Twelve*. Fragments are given by Epiphanius (*adv. Haer.* 30). *c) Gospel according to the Egyptians*. Quoted once by Clement of Alexandria. *d) Gospel according to Peter*. Referred to by Origen (*In Matth.* tom. 17, 10). A long fragment was discovered at Akhmim in 1885 (see the French Archaeological Mission's *Mémoires*, 1892). Another fragment is given by Serapion, Bishop of Antioch (A.D. 190-203). *e)* The *Logia*. Sayings of Jesus contained on a papyrus discovered by Grenfell and Hunt. *f) Protevangelium of James* or *Book of James*. This story of early events in the life of Jesus has been preserved in several languages, Syriac, Coptic, etc. The James is James the Just, and the book perhaps belongs to the first century. Mary's parents are said to have been Joachim and Anne. Published by K. v. Tischendorf, *Evangelia Apocrypha*. *g) Gospel of Nicodemus* or *Acts of Pilate*. Preserved in several languages, Coptic, Greek, Latin, etc. It treats of the Passion, Resurrection, and Descent to Hell of Jesus. It belongs perhaps to the early part of the second century. Published by K. v. Tischendorf (*op. cit.*). There is another work with the same title (see ACTS OF PILATE). 2. ACTS. The chief work is the *Acts of Paul and Thecla*. It has been preserved in Syriac, Greek, etc. It is a romance, the earliest of its kind, recounting the story of a virgin, Thecla of Iconium, converted by Paul. Published by R. A. Lipsius, *Acta Petri et Pauli*. There are also in existence fragmentary Acts of Paul, Peter, John, Thomas, Andrew and Philip. 3. EPISTLES. *a) Epistle of Paul to the Laodiceans*. A short document, preserved in Latin. *b) Epistle of Paul to the Alexandrines*. Mentioned in the Muratorian Canon (*q.v.*). *c) Third Epistle of Paul to the Corinthians*. Preserved in Armenian, Latin, and Coptic. 4. APOCALYPSES. *a) Apocalyse of Peter*. Preserved, in large part, in Greek. It contains part of a prophecy of Jesus about the last things and a description of the bliss of the blessed and the tortures of the damned. The work perhaps belongs to the early part of the second century. *b) Prophecy of Hystaspes*. It has not been preserved, but is quoted by Justin Martyr (*Apol.* I., 20, 44) and Lactantius (*Div. Inst.* vii. 15, 18), and is associated with the Sibylline Oracles. 5. PREACHING. *a) Teaching of the Apostles* or the *Didachè*. Preserved in Greek. It was first printed in 1883, having been recently discovered. It is partly a manual of ethics, partly a collection of rules and formulae. *b) Preaching of Peter*. Fragments are given by Heracleon and Clement of Alexandria. It contains warnings against Judaism, a lament of Peter, ethical maxims, and words of Jesus. See in Clark's "Ante-Nicene Library" the volume entitled *The Apocryphal Gospels, Acts, and Revelation*; A. Hilgenfeld, *Novum Testamentum extra canonem receptum* (2), 1876-84; and M. R. James in the *Encycl. Bibl.*

APOCRYPHANS. A general designation of religious sects which appealed for authority to apocryphal or private writings (*e.g.*, the Manichaeans and Gnostics).

APOLLINARIANS. The followers of Apollinaris (*d.* A.D. 390), Bishop of Laodicea. As against Arius, Apollinaris was anxious to maintain the Divinity of Christ. This led him to represent the human nature of Jesus in a way that was considered unorthodox. Making a distinction between *nous*, the rational soul, and *psyche*, the animal soul, Apollinaris argued that in Christ the divine Logos took the place of the human *nous*. In this way he thought the sinlessness of Christ was assured, since it is the human *nous* which is the seat of sin. He therefore virtually denied the perfect manhood of Christ. Apollinarianism was condemned by several synods from the year 362, particularly by the Council of Constantinople in A.D. 381. See J. H. Blunt.

APOLLO. A Greek deity, one of the most ideal figures in Greek mythology. According to legend, he was the son of Zeus by Leto (Latona), had as his twin-sister Artemis (Diana), and was born at the foot of Mount Cynthus in Delos. He seems to have been originally a god of light in general. Thus, having withdrawn in winter, he comes back in Spring to gladden the land with his brightness; he calms the wintry sea after the equinoctial gales; he protects the ripening crops, and receives in Autumn the first-fruits of the harvest; he is the patron of flocks and pastures, and slays rapacious beasts that come to do them harm. He is also a god of health and of prolific power, and gives help in war. As a god of streets and highways, his " rude symbol, a conical post with a pointed ending, stood by street-doors and in courtyards, to watch men's exit and entrance, to let in good and keep out evil, and was loaded by the inmates with gifts of honour, such as ribbons, wreaths of myrtle or bay, and the like" (O. Seyffert). Apollo is also a guardian and guide on the sea. As a god of health and averter of ills, he is one of the chief gods of healing. His son Asclepios (Æsculapius) is famous for his possession of the same power. Health and holiness, light and purity being closely allied, Apollo became a god of moral purity and civic righteousness. As such he is able to purify the penitent suppliant who is eager to make atonement for sin. Finally, he is a god of divination or prophecy and of music. With Zeus and Athene, Apollo forms a kind of divine triad. The worship of Apollo became naturalized among the Romans, and in B.C. 431 he was honoured with a temple as god of healing. In 212 B.C. the "Ludi Apollinares" were established. The symbols of Apollo include the bow and quiver, the lyre, the tripod, the bay, the dolphin, the snake. See O. Seyffert, *Dict.*; Chambers' *Encycl.*

APOLLYON. The Greek equivalent of the Hebrew name, Abaddon (*q.v.*).

APOLOGETICAL SOCIETY OF THE HAGUE, THE. Another name for The Haag Association for the Defence of the Christian Religion (*q.v.*).

APOLOGETICS. That branch of theology which is occupied specially with the defence of Christianity as a divinely-revealed system of religion. The term is still commonly used in Germany. In England the designation "Christian Evidences" seems to be preferred as a modern description. In the early days of the Church, Christian writers wrote "Apologies" in reply to charges brought against the "brethren," and in order to remove occasion of persecution. Thus one Quadratus addressed an Apology to the Emperor Hadrian (A.D. 117-138), which is referred to by Eusebius (*Church History*, iv. 3), Aristides and Justin addressed one to the Emperor Antoninus (A.D. 138-161). Justin, also famous for his dialogue (*c.* A.D. 135) with the learned Jew Trypho, wrote this Apology *c.* A.D. 152. In it he refutes the charges brought against the Christians and explains their meetings and religious practices. The essay is not free from inaccuracies. Later two Asiatic bishops, Melito, Bishop of Sardis, and Apollinaris, Bishop of Hierapolis, addressed Apologies to the Emperor Marcus Aurelius (A.D. 169-177). Of the former only fragments have been preserved by Eusebius (*Church History*, iv. 26). The latter has been lost, as has that also of Miltiades (Eus. *C.H.*, v. 17). Another Apology was that of Athenagoras, another Athenian philosopher. It was addressed to the Roman Emperors Marcus Aurelius and Commodus (A.D. 177-180). This has been preserved. All these apologies were followed by a number of Orations and Addresses to the Greeks. See Louis Duchesne, *Hist.*

APOLOGUE. A fable or parable with a moral. It is often a story in which animals or inanimate things figure. Aesop's fables are a classical example. There is also a good example in the Old Testament, in the apologue of Jotham (Judges ix. 7-15), which was perhaps drawn from a collection of popular apologues (see G. F. Moore, *Judges*, 1895). Mention may also be made of the fables of Bidpai or Pilpay, of which the oldest version that has been preserved is in Arabic, and dates from about A.D. 750 (*Kalilah wa Dimnah*).

APOLOGY OF ARISTIDES. An apology of, or defence of, Christianity addressed to the Roman Emperor Antoninus (A.D. 138-161). Aristides, an Athenian philosopher, eulogises the morals, practices and beliefs of the Christians as compared with those of barbarians, Greeks, and Jews. The work was published by Rendel Harris and Armitage Robinson in 1891 (*The Apology of Aristides*, Cambridge "Texts and Studies," vol. i.).

APOLOGY OF ATHENAGORAS. See APOLOGETICS.

APOPHIS-SERPENT. A monster often depicted on Egyptian mummy-cases.

APOSTATE. The word has been commonly used of one who abandons or renounces the Christian faith. In the early days of Christianity persecution led many to do this. The Emperor Julian was called the Apostate because he would not accept Christianity and wished to revive paganism. In England apostasy was formerly punished by civil penalties. An apostate can still be excommunicated. Addis and Arnold distinguish three kinds of apostasy. There is apostasy from the Christian faith when one "wholly abandons the faith of Christ, and joins himself to some other law, such as Judaism, Islam, Paganism, etc." There is apostasy from ecclesiastical obedience "when a Catholic wilfully and contumaciously sets at nought the authority of the Church." There is apostasy from a religious profession or from holy orders. The latter happens when one, "after having received major orders, renounces his clerical profession, and returns to the dress and customs of the world" (W. E. Addis and T. Arnold).

APOSTLE OF THE NORTH. A name given to John Macdonald (1779-1849), the missionary preacher.

APOSTLE SPOONS. Children at Baptism used to be presented with gilt spoons. These were called Apostle Spoons, because figures of the twelve Apostles were carved on the handles. Sometimes as many as twelve spoons were given. See Brand's Popular Antiquities, ed. C. Hazlitt, 1905.

APOSTLES. The Greek term *apostolos* means a "messenger" or a "delegate." In the Greek translation of the Old Testament it is given by Aquila (II. Kings xiv. 6) and by Symmachus (Isaiah xviii. 2) as the equivalent of the Hebrew word *shālīaḥ*, "one sent." After the destruction of Jerusalem the Hebrew term was used of those officials who collected from the dispersed the taxes due to the Jewish Patriarch (see Emil Schürer, *Gesch. des Jüd. Volkes*, ii. 532, 548). The Greek term is used especially of the twelve disciples chosen by Jesus as his constant disciples and deputed by him to preach the glad tidings of the Kingdom of God (Mark iii. 14, Luke vi. 13; Mark vi. 30, Luke ix. 10). The number twelve seems to have been suggested by the number of the tribes of Israel. The original apostles, as given in Matthew (x. 2), Mark (iii. 16), Luke (vi. 14), and Acts (i. 13) were: Simon, surnamed Peter; James of Zebedee, and John, the brother of James, surnamed Boanerges (*q.v.*); Andrew; Philip; Bartholomew; Matthew; Thomas; James of Alphæus; Thaddæus; Simon the Zealot; and Judas Iscariot. After the betrayal by Judas Iscariot, or Judas the man of Keriōth, Matthias was elected to fill his place. Afterwards Paul claimed equality with these apostles on the ground that he had received a direct revelation and commission from Christ. He describes himself (Galatians i. 1) as "Paul an Apostle, not of men, neither by man, but by Jesus Christ, and God the Father, who raised him from the dead." Of the Gospel he says, "neither did I receive it from man, nor was I taught it, but (it came to me) through revelation of Jesus Christ" (Galatians i. 12; cp. ii. 8, I. Corinthians i. 17, ix. 1, II. Corinthians iii. 2, etc.). Paul's claims were recognised, and the original inner circle seems to have been enlarged so as to include the "Apostle of the Gentiles" (Romans xi. 13). But the title seems in a restricted sense to have been conferred on a small outer circle including Barnabas (Acts xiv. 14), Silvanus (I. Thessalonians ii. 6), Andronicus and Junias (Romans xvi. 7). In a still more restricted sense reference is made to apostles in Luke xi. 49, Ephesians iii. 5, Revelation xviii. 20. The early work known as "The Teaching" shows in fact that in the sub-apostolic age there were a number of "apostles" who travelled about from one place to another as itinerant teachers or missionaries. The original apostles, however, had the unique advantage of being personally associated with Jesus, and, it is claimed, that they were witnesses of his resurrection (Acts i. 21 *f.*). They were in a sense his representatives (cp. Acts iii. 16, ix. 34). When new officers were chosen for the early Christian community we are told that these "they set before the apostles, and when they had prayed, they laid their hands on them" (Acts vi. 6). See *Encycl. Bibl.*; Grimm-Thayer, *Greek-English Lex. of the N.T.*, 1896; Prot. Dict.

APOSTLES' CREED. One of the principal creeds of the Christian Church. It does not belong to the apostolic age, but seems to have been called "The Apostles' Creed" because it was considered to embody apostolic teaching. It seems to have developed out of early baptismal formulas; and it is claimed that there are traces of a similar creed in the writings of Irenaeus (*c.* A.D. 115-202), Tertullian (born about A.D. 150), and Cyprian (born about A.D. 200). But Rufinus (*d.* A.D. 410) is the first to give a form of it which approximates to that which is now known as "The Apostles' Creed." His form of the Roman creed or "symbolum" reads: "I believe in God the Father Almighty; and in Jesus Christ, his only Son, our Lord, who was born of (*de*) the Holy Ghost of (*ex*) the Virgin Mary, was crucified under Pontius Pilate and was buried, rose again from the dead the third day, ascended into heaven, sitteth on the right hand of the Father, from thence he shall come to judge the quick and the dead; and in the Holy Ghost, the Holy Church, the Forgiveness of Sins, the Resurrection of the Flesh" (C. A. Heurtley, *De Fide et Symbols*, English edition, 1889). This is a shorter form than that in present use. The present Creed has in addition: "he descended into hell"; (I believe in) "the communion of saints"; "and the life everlasting." Marcellus, Bishop of Ancyra in Galatia (A.D. 336-341) gives in Greek a creed resembling that of Rufinus. The slightly longer form was no doubt in use in the Gallican and Italian Churches in the fifth or sixth century. Legend has it that the twelve articles of the Apostles' Creed were composed by the twelve Apostles, each of them contributing one article. The exact words of our Apostles' Creed are given (*c.* A.D. 730) by Pirminius, a Bishop in Gaul. See W. R. W.

Stephens, *Book of Common Prayer*, 1901; *Prot. Dict.; Cath. Dict.*

APOSTLES, TEACHING OF THE. See APOCRYPHAL BOOKS OF THE NEW TESTAMENT.

APOSTOLIC. A name applied to things relating to, derived from, or characteristic of the Christian Apostles (*q.v.*).

APOSTOLIC BRETHREN. 1. A Gnostic sect of the third century. 2. and 3. Another name for the APOSTOLICALS (*q.v.*).

APOSTOLIC CANONS and CONSTITUTIONS. The "Canones Apostolici" are eighty-five canons or precepts which purport to have apostolic authority and are supposed to have been communicated to the Church by Clement of Rome. They are first heard of in A.D. 494, when they were declared by Pope Gelasius and seventy bishops to be apocryphal. John Scholasticus, however, who afterwards became Bishop of Constantinople (A.D. 565), decided that they were of apostolic origin, and his decision was supported by the Trullan Council at Constantinople in A.D. 692 and by the second Nicene Synod in A.D. 787. They were therefore accepted in the Eastern Church. The verdict of the Western Church, on the other hand, has continued to be against them. In 1562 the Magdeburg Centuriators argued powerfully against the apostolic origin, and it would seem that in their present form they are not older than the fourth century. Some of them, it is now thought, belong to the sixth century. It has been suggested that the sources of sixty of the eighty-five canons may be found in the "Apostolic Constitutions" and the Canons of Nicaea (A.D. 325), Antioch (A.D. 341), and Ephesus (A.D. 431). The editor seems also to have had before him the "Teaching of the Twelve Apostles." It has also been pointed out that in many places the teaching is not apostolic, and things are mentioned which were of post-apostolic date and origin. The Canons are given in C. J. Hefele's *History of the Councils* (2nd German edition, 1873-1890), J. Mansi's *Collection of the Acts of the Councils* (1759-1781), and W. Beveridge's *Codex Canonum Ecclesiae Primitivae Vindicatus* (1678). The "Constitutiones Apostolicae" purport to have been dictated by the twelve Apostles in the first person to Clement of Rome. They are in eight books, and deal with the customs, homiletic teaching, liturgical forms, and official titles in the Eastern Church. William Whiston (1667-1752) translated them, and believed that he had discovered in them the true "primitive Christianity," which happened to be Arian. But the post-apostolic origin of the Constitutions is proved by absurd anachronisms, and in 1883 it was seen that a large part of one of the books was a reproduction of the "Teaching of the Twelve Apostles." C. J. Hefele assigns the work to the second half of the third century. The whole work is a compilation. It was perhaps put together by a Syrian between A.D. 364 and 378. The "Constitutions" will be found in J. P. Migne, *Patrologia Græca*, quarto, vol. i., 1857, and Pitra, *Juris Ecclesiastici Græcorum Historia et Monumenta*, vol. i., 1864. See F. von Funk, *Die Apostolischen Konstitutionen*, 1891; *Prot. Dict.*

APOSTOLIC FATHERS. Fathers of the Christian Church who lived in the period succeeding that of the Apostles. Their writings are commonly called patristic. The following are some of them: (1) *The Epistle of Barnabas*. Not written by Barnabas, Paul's fellow-traveller, however. It was probably composed between A.D. 70 and 137. The language is sometimes mystical. (2) *The Epistle of Clement to the Corinthians*. Written by Clement of Rome to the Church of Corinth. (3) *The Second Letter of Clement to the Corinthians*. The real author is unknown. It is part of an ancient homily belonging perhaps to the middle of the second century. (4) *The Epistles of Ignatius*, Bishop of Antioch. Seven letters of which there is a longer and shorter form. In their shorter and purer form they belong to the early part of the second century A.D. "The Catholic Church" is spoken of for the first time. (5) *The Epistle of Polycarp*, Bishop of Smyrna. A letter addressed to the Church of God at Philippi. It was probably written between A.D. 107 and 155. (6) *The Martyrdom of St. Polycarp*. Written soon after Polycarp's death (A.D. 155). (7) *Papias' Treatise on the Words of the Lord*. Only fragments have been preserved. Written A.D. 130. (8) *The Epistle to Diognetus*. The author is unknown, but it probably belongs to the second century A.D. It describes the manners of the early Christians. (9) *The Pastor or Shepherd of Hermas*. The work, which is allegorical, consists of Visions, Commandments, and Similitudes. It is referred to by Irenaeus and Clement of Alexandria. If the Hermas was the brother of Pope Pius (so Muratori), the work is to be dated between A.D. 140 and 156. See Lightfoot's editions of Clement (1869; new ed. 1890), Ignatius (1885), and Polycarp (1889); Funk's edition of the *Apostolic Fathers; Prot. Dict.; Cath. Dict.*; H. B. Swete, *Patristic Study*, 1902.

APOSTOLIC SUCCESSION. In a sense all ministers of the Christian Church who carry on the teaching of the Apostles share in the Apostolic Succession. They are doing the same work on the same authority. It may be claimed however, with reason, that the vitality of the Christian Church can best be explained on the supposition that a personal force or influence has since the days of Jesus, its founder, been transmitted from one person to another. The Apostles were the first agents; and there is therefore a deeper sense in the apostolic succession than is implied in a mere preaching of the Gospel. The power or influence of the Apostles may have been imparted to any person who came in contact with them, and may in this way have been disseminated widely. When therefore a person receives "a call" he may have come under this power or influence. In the Church of England the next step required is ordination, first as deacon, then as priest; but the Church of England "does not deny that men chosen in other ways are lawfully called to the ministry, and, in fact, from 1559 to 1662, presbyterian ministers often officiated and held dignities in the Church" (B. Whitehead, *Church Law*). The Church of England maintains that "episcopacy is necessary to the 'well-being,' but not to the 'being' of a Church, in other words, that it is the best form of ecclesiastical polity." If, however, it could be shown that the apostolic power or influence was directly and deliberately transferred to certain persons, and that through them it has been transferred uninterruptedly to others, apostolic succession will have a still deeper meaning than those already mentioned. This kind of apostolic succession is, as a matter of fact, claimed for the bishops of Rome, of the Greek Church, and of the Church of England. The Bishop of Rome claims to be the successor of the Apostle Peter. As regards the Church of England, the Catholic Church existed in Britain (Wales) before the Roman mission. The first Welsh bishop is supposed to have been Aristobulus, who is said to have died in A.D. 67. The claim is best supported in the case of the Greek Church (Antioch and Alexandria). The Church of Rome claims, in addition, a peculiar universal jurisdiction in virtue of its relationship to Peter, to whom Jesus is said to have addressed the words: "Thou art Peter, and upon this rock I will build my church . . . I will give unto thee the keys of the kingdom of heaven: and whatsoever thou shalt bind on earth shall be bound in heaven, and whatsoever thou shalt loose on earth, shall be loosed in heaven" (Matthew xvi. 18 *f.*). We are told that "it is

Peter only, who had any individual successor in his primacy and his universal jurisdiction" (Addis and Arnold). See *Prot. Dict.; Cath. Dict.*

APOSTOLICALS. 1. A twelfth century sect founded near Cologne and referred to by Evervinus (Jean Mabillon, *Veter. Analect. iii.* 152) and St. Bernard (*Serm. lxv., lxvi., in Cantica*). The members of the sect favoured celibacy, but were allowed to have spiritual sisters. They would not eat flesh, and regarded every meal as a Eucharist. They denied that there is an intermediate state after death, and disapproved of prayers for the dead, the invocation of saints, and infant baptism. 2. A mediæval sect, founded towards the close of the thirteenth century by Gerard Sagarelli of Parma. Sagarelli's followers, who belonged mostly to Lombardy and the Tyrol, were mendicants who went about bareheaded, unshorn, clothed in white, and accompanied often by "sisters," as they were not permitted to marry. They lived in expectation of the fulfilment of the prophecies of Joachim, Abbot of Flora, that is to say, in expectation of the rise of a new and purer Church. Coming into conflict with the civil power and the Church, the latter tried to suppress them by means of the Inquisition. Sagarelli suffered death by burning A.D. 1300. He was succeeded by Dolcino of Novara, who not only inveighed against the Pope, Bonifact viii., but put himself at the head of an army and fought against the papal troops. He was ultimately captured, and was executed in 1307 at Vercelli. See J. H. Blunt.

APOSTOLICI. Another name for the APOTACTICS (*q.v.*).

APOSTOLICON. In the Canon of Marcion (*c.* 144 A.D.) the New Testament consists of two parts: the Gospel and the "Apostle" or Apostolicon.

APOSTOLICUS. A title used at first generally of Christian bishops. Later it was used only of metropolitans or primates (so Pope Siricius, about A.D. 390). Later still (ninth century) it came to be used only of the Popes. See *Cath. Dict.*

APOSTOLOS. This name was given to a lectionary containing passages from the Acts of the Apostles in the early Christian Church. See LECTIONARIES.

APOSTOOLIANS. The followers of Samuel Apostool, a Baptist preacher at Amsterdam (A.D. 1664). The sect was an off-shoot of the Waterlanders, Dutch Baptists. The other division of the Waterlanders received the name Galenists from their leader, Galen Abraham de Haan.

APOTACTICS. A sect which seems to have advocated the renunciation of private property. Epiphanius and Augustine identify them with a sect having the name Apostolici. They took this name no doubt because they believed they were following the apostolic mode of life.

APOTHEOSIS. The deification of kings and heroes. This might take place during their life or on their death. The Roman Emperors sometimes claimed or were assigned divine honours in their life-time (*e.g.*, Julius, Augustus, Domitian, and Commodus). The Ancient Egyptians deified their kings in the same way. The deification and worship of ancestors has been widespread. See ANCESTOR-WORSHIP.

APOUATOU. The name of one of the deities in the early Egyptian religion. The meaning of the name is "he who opens the ways," and the ways referred to are the paths of unexplored regions. So, when the kings went to war, Apouatou was borne before them to show them the way. The deity was carried, in the form of a jackal or dog, on a kind of perch. At a later date he became merged in Osiris (*q.v.*). See Naville, *The Old Egyptian Faith*, 1909, p. 46.

APPARITIONS. Primitive folk believe that during sleep the soul leaves the body and makes journeys, sometimes of great distance. It may (so think, *e.g.*, the New Zealanders) on these journeys go to visit distant friends, even penetrating to the region of the dead. In like manner, the souls of the dead revisit the living. The reality of Apparitions has been contended for in modern times. It has been claimed, on the one hand, that the dead sometimes appear to the living, and on the other hand, that living people sometimes appear to others at a distance. The evidence for the theory of phantasms of the living seems to be increasing. We can hardly speak of "evidence" for phantasms of the dead. In any case, it is possible to explain most cases of apparition by Telepathy (*q.v.*). Cp. *Brand's Popular Antiquities*, ed. C. Hazlitt, 1905.

APPEALS, ACT OF. An Act of Parliament passed in the reign of Henry viii. (1533). It declared that the Church of England was empowered to deal with spiritual questions affecting it, and that appeals should be made to no higher authority than the Archbishop.

APPELLANTS. A name given to those theologians who rejected the papal Bull "Unigenitus" (1713) which condemned the views of the Jansenist leader Pasquier Quesnel (1634-1719). They were so called because they desired that the matter should be referred to a General Council. See JANSENISTS.

APPLES. In the Old Testament book, the Song of Songs, the apple (or the quince) is associated with love and marriage (ii. 3 and 4, viii. 5). A Hebrew Midrash states that in Egypt before the days of Moses the Hebrew women were delivered of children under the apple-trees. Among the Ottoman Jews it is the custom for a mother who is about to bear a child to put an apple on her head. Arab women eat fruit in order to make themselves fertile. Hartland notes that "among the Southern Slavs the bride is unveiled beneath an apple-tree and the veil is sometimes hung on the tree." Tuscan women, when they want children, get a priest to bless an apple. Then they pronounce over it an invocation to Saint Anne. In King-yang-fu in China the women resort to a goddess of fertility. Appearing in a dream, the goddess "gives fruit to the pilgrim, an apple or a peach if she is to have a boy, plums or pears if a girl." See E. S. Hartland, *P.P.*

APPLE-HOWLING. A name given to an old religious custom in England. It was observed at least in Devonshire and Cornwall. On Christmas Eve the parishioners walked in procession to the apple orchards, where, standing around a particular tree, they sprinkled it with cider, placed cakes of toast and sugar in its branches, and prayed for its fruitfulness. See W. Carew Hazlitt, and Sidney Heath.

APPROBATION. As a technical Roman Catholic term, this means "the formal judgment of a prelate, that a priest is fit to hear confessions." The approbation given "by the bishop, or one who has quasi-episcopal jurisdiction, is needed for the validity of absolution given by a secular priest, unless the said priest has a parochial benefice." See *Cath. Dict.*

APRIL FOOLS' DAY. A name for the 1st of April, which was observed in ancient Britain as a general festival. It was really the old Feast of the Vernal Equinox. It was called April Fools' Day on account of the playful revelry with which the festival was associated, as the beginning of the joys of Spring-time. The Spaniards and Swedes have observed the same custom. One of the customs at the Hindu Holi Festival is said to be "an exact reproduction of April Fools' Day." People are made "Holi fools" by being sent on useless errands, etc. See W. C. Hazlitt; E. W. Hopkins, *Religions of India*, 1895.

APSE. From a Greek word meaning "a wheel" or

"an arch." The apse was an architectural feature in the basilicas or halls of justice which were used by the Christians as places of worship in the early days of the Church. It was a "semi-circular or polygonal termination" to the aisles of a Basilica, in which the judges sat. The apse was retained in the Byzantine style of Church architecture, as may be seen in the Church of St. Sophia at Constantinople (sixth century). The semi-circular apse also became a feature in some of the churches in England built in the Norman style. Norwich Cathedral is a good example. "On the Continent the apse continued in use much later than in England, where the practice of making the east end of the churches square began early in the Norman period" (J. H. Parker). See J. H. Parker, *Gloss.; Cath. Dict.*

APSU. A name occurring in Babylonian-Assyrian religion. It is a personification of the "watery deep" and synonymous with Tiâmat. In course of time, it was represented that the gods were born of a union between Apsu and Tiâmat, a union, that is to say, between water, the first element, and chaos. See Morris Jastrow, *Rel.*

AQUÆI. A sect mentioned by St. Augustine, and probably to be identified with the Hydrotheitae.

AQUARIANS, THE. An early Church sect the members of which, instead of using wine in the Lord's Supper, used consecrated water.

AQUAVITA FATHERS. A name given to the Jesuats (*q.v.*).

ARABES, or ARABICI. An Arabian sect of the third century, the adherents of which believed that soul and body died together, only to be re-united and revived at the last day. They were converted by Origen at a council of Bishops held about A.D. 250.

'ARAFAH, THE MOUNT OF. See SERMON ON THE MOUNT, MUHAMMADAN.

ARAKHIN. One of the treatises of the Mishnah (*q.v.*).

ARAKH-SHAMNA. The name of the eighth month in the Babylonian calendar. It was sacred to Marduk (*q.v.*). The 15th day of the month was sacred to Shamash, Malkatu, and Bunene (*qq.v.*). See Morris Jastrow, *Rel.*

ARALÛ. A name for the nether-world in Babylonian-Assyrian religion. It is supposed to be a cave underneath the earth to which all the dead went. It seems also to be called "house of Aralû." In later usage it is also the name of the mountain within which the nether-world (Aralû itself) lay. See Morris Jastrow, *Rel.*

ARAMO. Aramo, "the gentle," was one of the names given by the ancient Celts to a god who corresponded to the Roman Jupiter.

ARATTI CEREMONY. A Hindu ceremony (also called ARTI) which only married women (not widows) and courtesans may perform. It is thus described by Dubois (ed. Beauchamp). "A lamp made of kneaded rice-flour is placed on a metal dish or plate. It is then filled with oil or liquefied butter and lighted. The women each take hold of the plate in turn and raise it to the level of the person's head for whom the ceremony is being performed, describing a specified number of circles with it. Instead of using a lighted lamp they sometimes content themselves with filling a vessel with water coloured with saffron, vermilion, and other ingredients. The object of this ceremony is to counteract the influence of the evil eye and any ill-effects which, according to Hindu belief, may arise from the jealous and spiteful looks of ill-intentioned persons." The ceremony is practised frequently, even daily, on behalf of distinguished persons, by courtesans or dancing-girls. The dancing-girls of the temples perform it twice daily over the images of the gods whom they serve. It is even performed over elephants, horses, etc. See J. A. Dubois and H. K. Beauchamp.

ARCHANGELS. See ANGELS.

ARCHBISHOP. An ecclesiastical title, first used in the fourth century A.D. Athanasius (*c.* 295-373) styled himself Archbishop. Originally bishops of the Christian Church in charge of a province and having suffragan bishops under them were called metropolitans. When in course of time the bishops of the greater cities themselves had suffragan bishops to assist them, these became metropolitans, and a new title "primate," "exarch," or "archbishop" was given to the old metropolitans. The only difference now between the terms "archbishop" and "metropolitan" is that a metropolitan always has suffragans. There seem to have been three archbishoprics in Roman times. These were London, York, and Caerleon. Menevia or St. David's afterwards took the place of Caerleon. In the sixth and seventh centuries Canterbury and York were the recognized archbishoprics. St. David's remained as before until it was amalgamated with Canterbury (*c.* A.D. 1147). In the eighth century Lichfield also was an archbishopric for a short time. This also was amalgamated with Canterbury. Ireland originally had four archbishoprics, Armagh, Dublin, Cashel, and Tuam, which have been retained by the Roman Catholics. The Protestants have now only two, Armagh and Dublin. There are now a number of colonial archbishops (Cape Town, Ottawa, Rupert's Land, Jamaica, Sydney, Melbourne, Brisbane). The Archbishop of Canterbury is "Primate of All England," and crowns the sovereigns of England. The Archbishop of York is called "Primate of England." The two Archbishops are independent; their authority is co-ordinate. Since 1850 the Roman Catholics have had an Archbishop of Westminster. The first holder of the office was Nicholas Wiseman. The superior dignity of an archbishop in the Roman Catholic Church is still marked by two insignia—"the *pallium* with which he is invested by the Holy See, and the *double cross* borne on his 'stemma' over his arms." He "has the right of carrying his cross throughout his province, except in the presence of the Pope or a Cardinal Legate" (Addis and Arnold). See *Prot. Dict.; Cath. Dict.*

ARCHDEACON. Originally an ordinary deacon (*q.v.*) chosen by a bishop to assist him. In course of time he acquired great power, and became almost equal to a bishop. It became necessary in the twelfth and thirteenth centuries to restrict his power and jurisdiction. In the Roman Catholic Church the office has now been entirely, and in the Greek Church almost entirely, abolished. In the Church of England the office is still an important one, but the dignity is inferior to that of a Dean (*q.v.*), and an archdeacon's powers and duties in no way compete with those of a bishop. He is the bishop's vicegerent in administrative matters, being in most cases appointed by the bishop himself. See *Prot. Dict.; Cath. Dict.*

ARCHES, COURT OF. An ecclesiastical court of the Church of England, so called because it used to be held by the Dean of Arches at the church in London called St. Mary le Bow ("Sancta Maria de Arcubus"). It is the Court of Appeal from all Diocesan Courts in the province of Canterbury. See, further, *Prot. Dict.*

ARCHIMANDRITE. A designation in the Greek Church of the dignitary who is placed at the head of a number of abbeys and convents.

ARCHONTICS. A second century sect named after an anchorite Archon, or after the angels or arch-spirits (Gk. *archontes*), who presided over seven of the worlds into which they divided the Universe. The sect originated in Palestine and spread to Armenia. The eighth world in their system of the Universe was a higher world ruled by the parent power. They are said to have denied the resurrection; and they did not recognise Baptism or the Holy Eucharist. They had their own apocryphal books. These, and not Holy Scripture, were their inspired and sacred works. They did not marry, regarding woman as a creation of the devil. See J. H. Blunt.

ARCHPRIEST. This was formerly the title of an officer in the Roman Catholic Church, and is said to date from the fourth century. He was at first attached to a cathedral as chief of the presbyters. Afterwards archpriests were appointed in the larger towns. In 1598, the missionary priests in England having no recognised head, Pope Clement VIII. appointed George Blackwell (1545?-1613) their superior as "Archpriest." Twelve priests were also nominated as his assistants. Blackwell was deprived of office in 1608 for taking an oath of civil allegiance which Pope Urban V. had condemned. He was succeeded by George Birket or Birkhead. On his death in 1614, William Harrison (1553-1621) was appointed. He was the last archpriest. After his death William Bishop (1554-1624) was made Bishop of Chalcedon and the first vicar-apostolic of England and Scotland. See *Cath. Dict.;* the *D.N.B.*

ARDIBAHISHT. The name of one of the archangels in the Zoroastrian religion. He was originally called *ashavahishta*, "the best righteousness." Ardibahisht represents "the blazing flame of fire, the light in luminaries, and brightness and splendour of any kind whatever, wherever it may exist" (Haug).

ARDI-EA. A figure in Babylonian mythology. In the Gilgamesh Epic (*q.v.*) Ardi-Ea is the ferryman who takes Gilgamesh across the waters of death to the fountain of life.

ARES. The Greek name for the god of war, Mars (*q.v.*).

AREVURDIS. An Armenian sect.

ARGENTEUS CODEX. A fragmentary manuscript of the Gothic translation of the Gospels. It is written in silver letters on purple parchment, dates from the sixth century, and is preserved in the University Library at Upsala. See C. R. Gregory.

ARGONAUTS. An ancient Greek legend, already well known in the time of Homer. A number of heroes sailed under Jason, son of Æson, in a fifty-oared vessel called the "Argo," to Colchis on the Black Sea to fetch the golden fleece of the ram on which Phrixus had fled. The fleece was held by Æetes, a magician. Æetes sets Jason a task, which seems impossible, and promises on its successful performance to hand over the fleece. Medea, Æetes' daughter, falls in love with Jason, and helps him by her witchcraft to overcome his difficulties. They then escape together. Seyffert points out that "as the story spread, all the Greek heroes that could have been living at the time were included among the number of the Argonauts" (*Dict.*).

ARHAT. In Buddhism "the Holy One," the ideal ancient monk, one who had gained entrance to Nirvâna by strictly obeying the teaching of the Buddha. In Lamaism sixteen of the chief apostles of the Buddha are called "Arhats." See H. Hackmann.

ARIANISM. The doctrines of Arius, a native of Libya, who was borne soon after the middle of the third century, and became a presbyter in Alexandria in A.D. 313. The Arian Controversy started from a criticism by Arius of a discourse on the Trinity delivered by Alexander his bishop. The Bishop having explained that the unity in the Trinity consisted in an indivisible unity of substance or essence, "a certain one of the presbyters under his jurisdiction, whose name was Arius, possessed of no inconsiderable logical acumen, imagining that the bishop entertained the same view of this subject as Sabellius the Libyan [see SABELLIANISM], controverted his statements with excessive pertinacity, advancing another error which was directly opposed indeed to that which he supposed himself called upon to refute. 'If,' he said, 'the Father begat the Son, he that was begotten had a beginning of existence: and from this it is evident that there was a time when the Son was not in being. It therefore necessarily follows that he had his existence (*hupostasis*) from nothing'" (Socrates, *Eccles. Hist.*). Alexander excommunicated Arius, and those who sympathised with him, who took a further step, denied the co-eternity and co-equality of the Son with the Father, and maintained that he differed from other beings in being created out of nothing as the first and highest of God's creatures. Arius was deposed at Alexandria in 321. In 323 a synod at Bithynia pronounced in his favour. But at the famous Council of Nicaea in Bithynia, convoked by the Emperor Constantine in 325, the doctrine of the Trinity was carefully defined in a way unfavourable to Arius, who was at the same time banished to Illyricum. The Nicene Creed declared that the Son was "begotten, not made, being of one essence (homoousion) with the Father," and anathematized those who say that "there was once when he was not," and "before he was begotten he was not," and "he was made of things that were not," or maintain that the Son of God is of a different essence (hupostasis or ousia) or created or subject to moral change or alteration." The great champion of orthodoxy was Athanasius (the "Father of orthodoxy"), who was born about A.D. 295, and became Bishop of Alexandria in 328. In the course of his struggles with the Arians, he suffered banishment five times, his opponents temporarily getting the upper hand. There was a re-action against the Nicene Formula after Constantine's death (337). Athanasius could be said at times to stand against the world ("Athanasius contra mundum"), and there was a period (A.D. 359 especially) of which it could be said that "the whole world groaned, and was astounded to find itself Arian" (Jerome). But a counter-reaction set in after the death of the Emperor Constantius (A.D. 361), and in A.D. 381 at the Council of Constantinople the Creed of Nicaea was re-affirmed. Arius, of course, was not the only leader, and Arianism had a number of able exponents. One of his earliest friends and sympathisers was Eusebius, Bishop of Nicomedia (*d.* 342), who became head of a party, the Eusebians. Another Eusebius (born about A.D. 270), Bishop of Caesarea and famous as a historian, also took part in the controversy. His followers also were called Eusebians as well as Semi-Arians. They maintained that the Son was "like in substance to the Father." Their teaching was therefore *Homoiousian* not *Homoousian.* Strict Arianism was represented by Aetius and his disciple Eunomius, whence they were called Aetians or Eunomians. They were also known as Anomœans or Heterousians, because they said that the substance of the Son was unlike (*anomoios*) that of the Father; or as Exucontians because they maintained that he was created from nothing (*ex ouk ontōn*). Another leader was Acacius, who contended simply that the Son is "like" the Father, and refused to use the phrase "like in substance or essence." His followers have been called Acacians or Homœans (from *homoios* "like"). The heterodox parties have also been called Antinicæans or Antinicenes as compared with the orthodox Athanasians or Nicenes. In the fifth century A.D. Arianism was expelled from the Roman Empire, but obtained a hold among the Vandals, Ostrogoths, Visigoths, Burgundians,

Suevi, and Lombards. It was through Arianism that these Teutonic tribes were introduced to Christianity. By the year 662, however, they had all passed over to the orthodox faith. See J. H. Newman, *The Arians of the Fourth Century*, new ed., 1891; H. M. Gwatkin, *The Arian Controversy*, 1889; J. H. Blunt, *Heresies, etc.*, 1903; *Cath. Dict.;* Chambers' *Encyclop.;* and Brockhaus.

ARIANROD. Arianrod appears as the name of a goddess revered by the ancient Celts in Britain and associated with the god Gwydion (*q.v.*). The name was popularly understood to mean Silver Wheel. Arianrod is said to have been the mother of Lleu (*q.v.*). See Squire, *Myth.*

ARICOUTE. A deity in the mythology of the Tupi tribe of Brazil. He is the god of darkness who is vanquished daily by his brother Timondonar, the god of light.

ARIEL. A name applied to Jerusalem in an Old Testament prophecy. Ariel (Arial) seems to mean "altar-hearth." When the city is besieged the slaughter in its streets will make it like an altar-hearth. The name has also been explained as meaning "lion of God" or "hearth of God." See *Encycl. Bibl.*

ARISTO, DIALOGUE OF. Eusebius refers (*Church Hist.*, iv. 6) to a Dialogue between Papiscus and Jason written by Aristo of Pella. The work, which was of an apologetic nature, has been lost. See A. Harnack, *Gesch. der altchristl. Lit. bis Eusebius* (1893 and 1897); Louis Duchesne, *Hist.*

ARK. For the ark of Noah, see DELUGE.

ARK OF THE COVENANT. A sacred chest among the Hebrews. It contained some sacred objects, but what these were originally is not stated. They were probably sacred stones, perhaps stones used in seeking oracles. It was not at first called the Ark of the Covenant. It was known at one time as the Ark of the Testimony (Exodus xxv. 22), and was supposed to have been so called because it contained the two stones on which were inscribed the ten commandments. It was an early belief that in some way or other the ark represented the presence of Jehovah. It was taken into battle that Jehovah Zebaoth, the god of war, might lead Israel's hosts to victory (I. Samuel iv. 3-8; cp. I. Sam. xvii. 45). According to later writers, those who had charge of it were themselves required to be priests or Levites (Joshua iv., 9, Priestly Code; I. Chronicles xv., 15). David transported it to Zion, his own city (2 Samuel vi. 7 *f.*), and Solomon set it in the most sacred part of his temple (I. Kings vi. 19). It came in course of time to be known as the Ark of the Covenant (Joshua iii. 6), because Jehovah was supposed to have made a covenant with his people. It was then thought to contain the documents relating to this covenant (I. Kings viii. 9). According to Exodus xxv. 10-22, xxxvii. 6-9 (Priestly Code), a magnificent golden cover was made for it. The Ark disappeared before the destruction of the temple. See H. Guthe, *Kurzes Bibelwörterbuch; Encycl. Bibl.*

ARMAGEDDON. In the New Testament (Revelation 16, 16; RV Har-Magedon) represented as the scene of the last great battle when the kings of the whole world shall be gathered together "for the war of the great day of God the Almighty." The writer seems to have had in mind "the mountain district (Hebrew *har*=mountain) of Megiddo." Assuming, however, that the writer was drawing upon a little apocalypse written in Hebrew, it has been suggested that he misinterpreted the second word of the expression. A very similar word would give the meaning "his fruitful mountain." This would mean "the mountain-land of Israel." H. Gunkel's idea that the name of a Babylonian goddess of the underworld (*Migadōn*) forms the second part of the expressions seems rather fanciful. See *Encycl. Bibl.*

ARMAITI. The name of a goddess or archangel in the Zoroastrian religion. She is the angel of the earth, personifies prayer, and is described as "the bountiful." Armaiti belongs to the number of the seven Amesha-spentas or archangels. The name originally means "devotion, obedience." She also appears as Spenta-Armaiti (Spendarmad), "the bountiful Armaiti." See Martin Haug.

ARMASITES. A seventh century sect founded by Harmasius, an Egyptian.

ARMENIAN CHURCH. The Armenian Church was firmly established as a branch of the Christian Church in A.D. 300 by Gregory the Illuminator (A.D. 257-325), who was supported by King Tiridates III. Gregory became its head or Catholicos (A.D. 302-318), the office for some centuries being made hereditary, and fixed the chief see at Etchmiazin near Mount Ararat. He conciliated the pagan priests by allowing the continuance of sacrifices for the dead, etc., but the formulae were christianized and the chief priests were made bishops. At first the Catholicos was ordained at Caesarea in Cappadocia. Monasticism was introduced in the fourth century by Basil (A.D. 330-379). In the fifth century Mesrop and Isaac the Great translated the Old Testament into Armenian and revised an already existing translation of the New Testament. They also translated Greek liturgies and homilies. This made the Armenians more independent. After the Persian conquest, the connection with Caesarea was broken (*c.* A.D. 370), and towards the end of the fifth century the Armenians declined to accept the decrees of the Council of Chalcedon (A.D. 451). The Church then became Monophysite (see MONOPHYSITES). Some of the members took up an extreme position, and in the seventh century existed as a sect called Paulicians. Since the time of the Crusades, some of the Armenians (*e.g.*, in Cilicia, Poland, and Russia), the Uniats, have recognised the Pope. In Turkey many of the clergy and laity amongst the "United Armenians" went over to Rome altogether in 1879. There has been change and development in Armenian worship. The Armenians used not to observe the Christmas Festival. They commemorated the Baptism of Jesus, the spiritual birth, and introduced a commemoration of the human birth later (*c.* A.D. 500). They observed the Jewish Sabbath as well as the Christian Sunday. Originally they practised Adult baptism, but they added Infant baptism later (eighth century). The Feast of the Annunciation was established in the ninth century. Protestant missionaries have had some success in Turkey. See F. C. Conybeare in *Prot. Dict.*, 1904, and in *R.S.W.*, 1908; *Cath. Dict.;* M Ormanian, *The Church of Armenia*, 1912.

ARMENO-CATHOLICS. A sect in Turkey and elsewhere, an off-shoot of the Armenian Church. In Turkey they form a nationality (*millet*) of their own with a special hierarchy. "In Russia the Armeno-Catholics have formed a community of their own, but it is subject to the control of the Roman Catholic bishop of Saratoff There are also to be reckoned a certain number in Galicia and in Hungary; these, however, have no relations with their co-religionists in the East" (Malachia Ormanian).

ARMENO-GREEKS. A body in the Ottoman empire which separated from the Armenian Church during the period of Byzantine rule. The sect was at one time very numerous, but its membership has now dwindled to a few thousands.

ARMENO-PROTESTANTS. A sect in Turkey, an off-shoot of the Armenian Church, due to the zeal of American missionaries. The Armeno-Protestants have endeavoured to form a special nationality (*millet*). "Their profession of faith is based on the principles of the Evangelical Church; a few of their number belong to the Episcopal and Baptist persuasions" (Malachia Ormanian).

ARMENO-RUSSIANS. A small sect in the Caucasus, an offshoot of the Armenian Church.

ARMINIAN BAPTISTS. See BAPTISTS.

ARMINIANS. The followers of Jakobus Arminius (1560-1608), who in 1603 was made professor at Leiden. Having engaged in a controversy on Predestination in which he championed the views of Calvin, he became himself in course of time a convert to Universalism, and was accused of Pelagianism. He met with determined opposition from his colleague at Leiden, Franz Gomarus (1563-1641), whose followers became known as Gomarists. After the death of Arminius (1609), the battle between his supporters and opponents continued. In 1610 the Arminians were so fiercely attacked that they drew up a remonstrance, which led to their being called Remonstrants. The remonstrance contained five articles. It claimed (1) that for Christ's sake all who believe in him and persevere in this belief to the end are saved by the grace of God; (2) that Christ died for all who by faith make his merit their own; (3) and (4) that a man can only have faith through Grace, but Grace is not irresistible; and (5) that those who believe can by the Spirit overcome sin, the world, the flesh, and the devil, but Scripture must decide whether those who have been born again can lapse. The Calvinistic party, or the Gomarists, became known as the Counter-remonstrants. Conferences were held at the Hague (1610) and at Delft (1613), but no reconciliation was effected. At the Synod of Dort (Nov. 13, 1618, to the end of April, 1619), to which representatives were sent from England, the Arminians, under Simon Episcopius, also called Bishop or Biscop (1583-1643), a Professor of Leiden, could not obtain a fair hearing. They therefore retired and were condemned and excommunicated in their absence. Hugo Grotius or de Groot (1583-1645), one of their leading men, was sentenced to life-long imprisonment, but escaped after two years. In 1630 some toleration was extended to them in Holland, and in 1634 an edict of toleration was passed. In the same year Episcopius opened a Seminary for Remonstrants in Amsterdam. Here he developed the ideas of Arminius and made them more universalistic. Henceforth Arminianism in Holland became more and more free in its interpretion of Scripture, the creeds, and ecclesiastical government. A certain kind of Arminianism has been represented in the Church of England from time to time. But compared with the later Dutch school, it has been of a moderate kind. In the reign of Charles I. those who were opposed to Calvinism were called Arminians, and in the time of Laud the Latitudinarians were described in the same way. See P. Zeller, *Calwer Kirchenlexikon*, 1889, etc.; J. H. Blunt; Chambers' *Encycl.*

ARNOLDISTS. The followers of Arnold of Brescia, a reformer and an opponent of the Papacy in the twelfth century. Arnold was a disciple of Abelard (A.D. 1079-1164). He preached in Brescia against the worldliness of the clergy and excited the people, whereupon he was cited before the Second Lateran Council (A.D. 1139), held under Pope Innocent II., which banished him from Italy. He removed to France, but the hostility of St. Bernard drove him to Zürich. In Zürich he stayed about five years. A rising against the papal government having broken out in Rome in A.D. 1143, Arnold repaired thither and preached against the secular rule of the Papacy and in favour of the revival of the ancient Roman republic. The insurrection continued for some years, and in the course of it Pope Lucius II. was killed (A.D. 1145). At the end of 1154 it was subdued by Pope Adrian IV. (Nicholas Breakspear), whereupon Arnold fled to Campania. Soon afterwards (A.D. 1155) the Emperor Frederick I. had him arrested and handed over to the Pope at Rome, where he was hanged and his body burned. He was afterwards held in great reverence by the Italians. The Arnoldists lived on into the thirteenth century. See Adolf Hausrath, *Arnold von Brescia*, 1891; *Die Arnoldisten*, 1895.

ARRHABONARII. A name formed from the Greek word *arrhabōn*, "a pledge," and given to a Polish sect or party, because its members held that in the Holy Eucharist the worshipper receives a pledge (not a present gift) of a gift to be enjoyed in heaven.

ARROWS, MAGIC. In the North American Indian myth of the Red Swan, the hunter Ojibwa makes use of three magic arrows. ' Among the Hindus the god of love (Kāma-deva) is represented as having five arrows, the arrow that puts to flight, the arrow that enchants, the arrow that fascinates, the love-kindling arrow, and the love-inflaming arrow. See Monier-Williams.

ARSUS. An Arabian deity, one of the heavenly twins, the evening star. Adopted by the Palmyrenes. Called also Monimus.

ARTAIOS. A god, perhaps of agriculture, worshipped by the continental Celts. Inscriptions to him have been found in France. The King Arthur of British legend was probably evolved out of an old hero-god worshipped by British Celts.

ARTEMIS. The Greek goddess corresponding to the Roman goddess Diana. She is said to have been daughter of Zeus and Lētō and twin-sister of Apollo, Delos having been the place of her birth, and she was worshipped in his shrines. Like Apollo, she carried bow and arrows. She was goddess of Light by night, of Nature, and of the Chase. As the latter, her favourite animal was the hind, and cakes made in the shape of this animal were offered at her festival (*Elaphēbŏlia*). As goddess of Light, she became goddess of the Moon, and in Attica at full moon round cakes were offered to her. Reverence was also paid her by girls and boys as the Guardian of youth. There were several Asiatic goddesses who bore the same name. Thus there was a Tauric Artemis, a Scythian deity, to whom human sacrifices were burnt and offered. There was a Perasian Artemis at Castabala in southern Cappadocia, whose priestesses walked over a charcoal fire, this being apparently a substitute for a human sacrifice by burning. A native goddess at Perga in Pamphylia, whose symbol was also a cone, was called Artemis by the Greeks; and the Sarpedonian Artemis of south-eastern Cilicia was probably another native goddess. See O. Seyffert, *Dict.*; J. G. Frazer, *Adonis Attis Osiris*, 1906.

ARTEMONITES. The followers of Artemon or Artemas who taught early in the third century and denied the Divinity of the Second and Third Persons in the Trinity. He held that Christ after his incarnation received a certain portion of the Divine Nature. We learn from a quotation in the Eccelsiastical History of Eusebius (v. 28) that the Artemonites tried to find support for their system in geometry and philosophy. "The sacred Scriptures have been boldly perverted by them; the rule of the ancient faith they have set aside, Christ they have renounced, not inquiring what the holy Scriptures declared, but zealously labouring what form of reasoning may be devised to establish their impiety. And should any one present a passage of divine truth, they examined first whether a connected or disjoined form of syllogism can be formed from it. But they abandon the holy Scriptures for the study of geometry; as being of the earth, they talk of the earth, and know not him that cometh from above. Euclid, therefore, is industriously measured by them. Aristotle and Theophrastus are also admired, and as to Galen, he is even perhaps worshipped by some."

ARTICLES OF THE CHURCH OF ENGLAND. Doctrinal statements put forth in the sixteenth century. There were a series of such Articles culminating in *The xxxix. Articles,* as finally revised and synodically sanctioned in 1571, which are now, reasonably interpreted, authoritative for the Church. The earlier series were: (1) *The x. Articles* of 1536. These rejected or ignored some of the seven Roman Catholic Sacraments, explaining only those of Baptism, Penance, and the Sacrament of the Altar. (2) *The xiii. Articles* of 1538. Influenced by the Confession of Augsburg, they bear the marks of an attempt to come to terms with the Lutherans. *The xiii. Articles* of 1538 found among Cranmer's papers were not put forth authoritatively. (3) *The vi. Articles* of 1539. These were reactionary, for they favoured Communion in one kind, clerical celibacy, vows of chastity, private masses, and auricular confession. (4) *The xlii. Articles* of 1553. To some extent influenced by the Confession of Augsburg, and largely the work of Cranmer and Ridley, these indicate a reassertion of the reforming spirit. (5) *The xi. Articles* of 1561. Put forth by Archbishop Parker on his own authority, these disallow private Masses and worship of images and relics, and re-admit Communion in both kinds. (6) *The xxxix. Articles* of 1563. These owed much to Archbishop Parker, and were based upon the xlii. Articles and the Würtemburg Confession of 1552. See *Prot. Dict.;* B. J. Kidd, *The Thirty-nine Articles,* 1908.

ARTICLES OF PRAGUE. The confession of faith of the Hussites. John Zisca issued it in the year 1420.

ARTIO. Artio was the name of a goddess worshipped by the ancient Celts. The name means "she-bear." On a bronze bas-relief discovered at Muri near Berne the goddess is represented as sitting with a huge bear in front of her. Originally, it would seem, the goddess herself was represented as a bear. Then she assumed a human form, but had a bear as her companion. Reinach points out that "the memory of the worship of the bear has persisted in the city of the bear (Berne) throughout the ages." See Anwyl; Reinach, *O.*

ARTOTYRITAE. A division of the later Montanists (*q.v.*) of Phrygia, who partook of bread (Gk. *artos*) and cheese (Gk. *turos*) at the celebration of the Lord's Supper. The cheese represented the fruit of the flock, as the bread did that of the ground.

ARUNDHATI MARRIAGE-VOW. A Hindu marriage custom. After the marriage-feast the couple go outside, accompanied by singing women, the guests, and the priest (*purohita*), and preceded by musicians. The priest calls their attention to a star, *Arundhati,* the chaste wife of Vasishta Rishi. The couple look at the star with due solemnity and vow to live together like Vasishta and Arundhati. See J. A. Dubois and H. K. Beauchamp.

ARUNGQUILTHA. Also written Arúnkulta, a term used among the Arunta of Central Australia to denote a mystic potentiality. The term seems to denote a force, and not a personal being. According to Strehlow, it is "a force which suddenly stops life and brings death to all who come in contact with it." According to Spencer and Gillen, "the name is applied indiscriminately to the evil influence or to the object in which it is, for the time being, or permanently, resident."

ARURU. The name of a goddess in Babylonian-Assyrian religion. In a Babylonian story of creation it is said that she, with Marduk, created mankind: "The Goddess Aruru created the seed of men together with him." She figures also in the Gilgamesh Epic (*q.v.*). Here she creates a human being out of a lump of clay, having already created Gilgamesh himself. See Morris Jastrow, *Rel.*

ARUSPICES, THE. Etruscan priests or diviners who predicted the future from an inspection of the entrails of sacrificial victims. They were introduced among the Romans.

ARVAL BROTHERS. An early Roman brotherhood (Fratres Arvales, "brothers of the fields") of twelve priests devoted to the worship of a goddess of cornfields, Dēa Dia, who seems to have been identical with Acca Lārentia. The brothers were life-members, and new brethren were co-opted. Under the Empire even the Emperors belonged to the Brotherhood. At their chief festival (1st, 2nd, and 3rd of May) a feature of the ceremonial in the temple of the goddess was a dance with the singing of the "Arval Hymn," which has been preserved and is one of the oldest Latin texts we possess. Part of the festival took place in a grove in which expiatory sacrifices were made for any damage done to the trees by lightning, etc. See O. Seyffert, *Dict.*

ARVAL HYMN. See ARVAL BROTHERS.

ARVEL BREAD. The name (also written Arvil and Arval) of loaves distributed among the poor at funerals in the North of England. See W. C. Hazlitt.

ARYA SAMAJ. A modern theistic church or society among the Hindus. It was founded by the reformer Dayānanda Sarasvatī, and to some extent in opposition to the Brāhma Samāj, since Sarasvatī still sought authority for his teaching in the hymns of the Veda. According to him, the only true non-human revelation is to be found in the four collections of Vedic hymns, and Agni, Indra, and Sūrya are merely different names for the One God. Sir Monier Williams received from him this definition: "Religion is a true and just view, and the abandonment of all prejudice and partiality—that is to say, it is an impartial inquiry into the truth by means of the senses and the two other instruments of knowledge, reason and revelation." In his will he appointed a Committee which was charged, amongst other things, to educate the poor in the principles of the Arya Samāj. Though Dayānanda professed a pure monotheism, he added to it the doctrine of metempsychosis. He denied that anyone, whether Christ or Krishna, could be an incarnation of the Deity, or that God, being absolutely just, could forgive sins. Thus he was equally free in his criticism of orthodox Brahmanism, Mohammedanism, and Christianity. See Monier-Williams, *B.H.;* J. C. Oman, *Cults;* R. V. Russell.

ASCENSION-DAY. One of the festivals of the Christian Church, also called Holy Thursday. It is kept on the fortieth day after Easter, and therefore was called Quadragesima, Tessarocostes or Tetracostes. The observance can be traced back to the fourth century, but is clearly of much earlier origin. Bishop Barry says that the comparative neglect of the festival in the Church of England, "which is now being partially corrected," is "entirely at variance with the intention of the Prayer Book" (*Teacher's Prayer Book*). In the Church of Rome, "in 1607 the Congregation of Rites ordered that the paschal candle should be lighted when Mass is sung and in vespers, on Easter Sunday, Easter Monday, Easter Tuesday, on Saturday in Low Week, and on Sundays till Ascension Day, when it is extinguished after the Gospel. The rite symbolises Christ's departure from the Apostles" (W. E. Addis and T. Arnold).

ASCENSION OF ISAIAH. See APOCALYPTIC LITERATURE.

ASCETICISM. The cultivation of the spiritual life by means of self-denial and severe religious exercises. Ascetics think to please God by imposing upon themselves suffering. A common form of such self-denial and self-torture is abstention from food (or fasting). "The ascetic element was not strongly marked in the Hebrew religion" (S. G. Smith, *Religion in the Making*, 1910); and asceticism is condemned in the Koran (*Sur.* lvii. 27). But, whether officially condemned or approved, the impulse to it has always been very strong (see William James, *Varieties of Religious Experience*, 1906). Christian ascetics have subjected themselves to all kinds of deprivation, living in caves, dens, or pits, going about like animals without clothes, eating rotten corn, etc. Hindus have exposed themselves naked to the violence of the weather, cut themselves with knives, eaten offal, etc. Monier-Williams tells of a Brahman who tortured himself by lying on a bed of arrows (as a substitute for a "bed of thorns") "He was seated in the usual way on the ground, but close to him on his right hand was his only bed—an iron framework resting on four short legs, and unprovided with mattress or coverlet, but studded instead with rows of iron spikes, somewhat blunted at the points, while at the pillow-end there was a spiky head-rest." Mohammedans have dragged about heavy chains or cannon balls, have lain on iron spikes, etc. Adherents of Zoroastrianism, the ancient Egyptians, and modern Jews have submitted to flagellation. Ancient Mexicans, as a preparation for festivals or as an expiation for sin, lacerated themselves and let the blood flow freely. Such beating is also connected with purification. As a preparation for the Jewish fast of atonement, for instance, some of the Jews purify themselves by ablutions, while others allow themselves to be scourged. Christians have in all ages suffered pain in order to atone for their sins; and the belief that atonement is possible in this way has prevailed among Mohammedans, adherents of Zoroastrianism, Hindus, and others. The Brahmans believe further that asceticism can produce superhuman power. Another idea which sometimes operates in asceticism is that the suffering will excite the compassion of the deity. A Fijian priest, after praying in vain for rain, is reported to have slept several nights on the top of a bare rock in the hope that the deity would take pity on him and send a shower. Another aim in asceticism is the mortification of the lusts of the flesh to such an extent that the proneness to sin may be reduced, and communion with God be rendered possible. Associated with this is the idea that matter and material things are evil by nature. This influenced the Essenes (*q.v.*) and the Therapeutae (*q.v.*) in their renunciation of the life of the world. A strict form of asceticism, apart from a simple monastic life, is foreign to the nature of Buddhism, though there are instances of it among Chinese Buddhists. Some of the latter not only brand themselves, but also burn off their fingers or give their whole body to the flames. Others incarcerate themselves. Another form of asceticism is celibacy. Cp. MYSTICISM. See E. Westermarck; Monier-Williams, *Brahmanism;* J. C. Oman, *M.A.S.I.;* H. Hackmann, *Buddhism.*

ASCHAFFENBURG, CONCORDAT OF. An agreement as to Papal rights made in 1448 between the Emperor Ferdinand III. of Germany and Pope Nicholas V.

ASCITÆ. A division of the Montanists at the end of the second century A.D. They took their name from the Greek word (*askos*) for a skin or bottle. Matthew ix. 17 ("Neither do men put new wine into old bottles: else the bottles break, and the wine runneth out, and the bottles perish: but they put new wine into new bottles, and both are preserved.") seems to have suggested to them the observance of festivals in which they danced on wine-skins. Cp. ASCODRUGITÆ.

ASCLEPIODOTIANS. The followers of Asclepiodotus, a disciple of Theodotus of Byzantium. He held that Jesus was no more than a man.

ASCODRUGITAE. A division of Montanists (*q.v.*) in Galatia at the end of the second century A.D. One of their practices was to put an inflated wine-skin (*askos*) on an altar and to dance round it. They held Montanus to be the Paraclete, who at times inspired them. The initiated were introduced to mysteries similar to those of the Gnostics (*q.v.*).

ASCODRUPITÆ, or ASCODRUTI. A division of the Marcosian Gnostics. They disapproved of externalities, outward signs, in religion, including the Sacraments, and attached all importance to purely spiritual knowledge.

ASCOPHITES. A sect which appeared about the year A.D. 173 and is referred to by Theodoret (*Hær. fab.* i. 10). They objected strongly to the Holy Eucharist, and seem to have refused to recognise the Old Testament.

ASGARDH. In the cosmogony of the Ancient Teutons, Asgardh was one of the nine worlds. It is said to have been on the Black Sea, and to have been the original home of the god Odhin (WODAN). See P. D. Chantepie de la Saussaye, *Rel. of the Ancient Teutons*, 1902.

ASGAYA GIGAGEI. A thunder-god in the mythology of the Cherokee Indians.

ASHEM-VOHU. An early sacred formula or creed in the Zoroastrian religion. In the *Hâdôkht Nask* of the Zend-avesta we read: "Zarathushtra asked Ahuramazda, O Ahuramazda! most munificent spirit, creator of the settlements supplied with creatures, righteous one! in whom alone is thy word, the enunciation of all good, of all that is of rightful origin? Ahuramazda answered him, In the Ashem-reciter, O Zarathushtra!" Haug translates the formula: "Righteousness is the best good, a blessing it is; a blessing be to that which is righteousness towards Asha-vahishta (perfect righteousness)." See Martin Haug.

ASHERAH. An object of worship referred to frequently in the Old Testament. A plural form, Ashērim, also occurs (II. Chronicles xxiv. 18). The Authorised Version wrongly translates "grove" or "groves." The use of Asherim is forbidden in Deuteronomy xvi. 21, and they are to be destroyed (Deut. vii. 5, xii. 3). "They were wooden poles set up like the stone pillars at sanctuaries. Their meaning is obscure, scarcely a phallic emblem, possibly a substitute for a tree as a residence of deity, or possibly originally boundary posts, regarded later as sacred. It has also been thought that there was a Canaanite goddess Asherah, equivalent to the great Semitic goddess Astarte, whose symbol or idol was the *Asherah* post (cp. xv. 16). But on this scholars are not agreed" (E. L. Curtis and A. A. Madsen, *The Books of Chronicles*, 1910). See *Encycl. Bibl.*

ASHES. The use of ashes in mourning customs is very familiar. The Hebrews and Greeks, for instance, strewed themselves with ashes or sat in them, as a sign of humiliation. Out of this practice developed the simpler one, that of a mere sprinkling. But the use of ashes as a sign of humiliation is not confined to mourning customs. Monier-Williams describes a Hindu ascetic who sat "perfectly motionless and impassive, with naked body smeared all over with white ashes, matted hair, and the forefinger of the upraised hand pointing to the heaven to which in imagination he seemed to be already transporting himself." In other ceremonies the ashes have a different significance: they are sacred. This can easily be understood in cases in which Fire is worshipped. For instance, the devout Brahman performs a religious ceremony before taking his mid-day meal, and consecrates his food by offering small portions to all the deities who have ministered to his wants, especially to Fire. In the course of this ceremony he takes up ashes from the fire and applies them to his forehead, neck, navel, shoulders, and head. It is natural also that the ashes of an ancestor or a hero should be regarded as sacred. Amongst Chinese Buddhists, for instance, the ashes of a monk who in his devotion to asceticism has immolated himself are treasured as those of a saint. Other uses of ashes are found amongst the Chinese. When a person dies suddenly in his sleep, they believe that he has been struck by a malicious agency. They exorcise this evil spirit by a ceremony in which a circle of ashes is made round the dead man. Again, they strew ashes in the bottom of the coffin of a deceased person. This is done by the sons, but they are unable to provide the ashes themselves because no fire is allowed in the dwelling of the dead person for some days after the decease. When therefore the corpse has been washed, they go round, dressed in sackcloth, to their neighbours to collect ashes. This is called the "begging for ashes." It is the custom to offer gifts for the dead. These often take the form of paper money, which is burned and placed in a paper wrapper in the coffin. See Monier-Williams, *Brahmanism;* J. J. M. de Groot, *R.S.C.*, 1892, etc.; and, for a number of other customs, Maurice Canney in Hastings' *E.R.E.*

ASHI. The name of a female angel in the Zoroastrian religion. The full form of the name is Ashish vanuhi (modernised into Ashishang), and means "the good truth." She is referred to as a daughter of Ahuramazda and a sister of the Ameshaspentas, as the inspirer of prophets and the giver of wealth. See Martin Haug.

ASHKENAZIM. A mediæval Jewish name for the Jews of German- and Slavonic-speaking countries, as distinguished from the Spanish and Portuguese Jews who were called Sefardim. See W. O. E. Oesterley and G. H. Box.

ASHTAROTH. See ASTARTE.

ASHTA-YOGA. A form of penance among the Hindus for obtaining forgiveness of sins. After a three days' fast the penitent goes to a temple of Siva, a cemetery, or a special kind of tree. Here he goes through a ceremony and paints a small circular mark (*tilaka*) on his forehead. Then he clears a clean space on the ground and stands on his head on it with his feet in the air. He performs six times, while in this position, a ceremony of inhaling and exhaling through the nostrils, thereby expelling from the body a nerve in which resides the Man of Sin. When the nerve has been expelled, he washes it and makes an offering to it. Then, by inhalation, he restores it to its original place. See J. A. Dubois and H. K. Beauchamp.

ASHTORETH. The name given in the Old Testament to a goddess of the Canaanites and Phoenicians (I. Kings xi. 5; II. Kings xxiii. 13). The correct form of the name is 'Ashtart, corresponding to the Greek Astarte (*q.v.*). The plural of the Hebrew, *'Ashtārōth*, is used in a general sense of heathen goddesses. In Deuteronomy vii. 13 occurs the peculiar expression "the 'Ashtoreths of thy flock," which, it has been suggested "appears to show that this deity, under one of her types, had the form of a sheep" (S. R. Driver, *Deuteronomy*, 1895). See *Encycl. Bibl.*

ASHUKU. One of the five celestial Buddhas in Japanese Buddhism. The Indian name is Akśobya. See H. Hackmann.

ASHUR. An Assyrian deity. The name means the "good one." Belit (*q.v.*) is sometimes represented as his consort. Ashur came to be placed at the head of the Assyrian pantheon. Great gods are associated with him, but he towers high above them all. He was first the patron god of the city of Ashur, to which he gave his name, and then extended his sway over the whole of Assyria. Wherever the kings fixed their official residence, the place became a centre for his worship. He had as his chief symbol a standard which could be carried into battle or moved about from place to place. It is possible that he was originally a solar deity. This is perhaps suggested by the standard which "consisted of a pole surrounded by a disc enclosed within two wings, while above the disc stood the figure of a warrior in the act of shooting an arrow" (Jastrow). Samsi-Ramman (*c.* 1850 B.C.) in an inscription describes himself as "the builder of the temple of Ashur." The Assyrian rulers, since they owed everything to this all-powerful god, the "king of gods" or "the guide of the gods," described themselves poetically as his offspring. Among other things, they owed to him their successes in war, and so in course of time he became purely a god of war. See Morris Jastrow, *Rel.*

ASH-WEDNESDAY. The name of the first day of Lent, the Christian penitential season which now lasts forty days. In early times it lasted thirty-six days, or six weeks, excluding Sundays. Addis and Arnold point out that this was nearly a tenth part of the year, so that "Christians were thought to render a penitential tithe of their lives to God." At the end of the fifth and in the sixth century the season extended from the first Sunday in Lent to Easter Day. Subsequently Ash Wednesday and the three following days were added. There is evidence that this must have happened before A.D. 714. The number of fast days then became forty, corresponding to the number of days Jesus is said to have fasted in the wilderness. The day was called "Ash Wednesday," "Caput jejunii," or "Dies Cinerum," because on the first day of Lent, penitents came to the church door clothed in sackcloth, to have penances imposed upon them. They then had to appear before the Bishop, and ashes were sprinkled on their heads. It became customary for the friends of the penitents to accompany them and to receive the ashes as well. Consequently in course of time the whole congregation came to share in this form of the penance. See *Cath. Dict.; Prot. Dict.*

ASMODEUS. An evil demon mentioned in the Book of Tobit (iii. 8), one of the apocryphal books of the Old Testament. The demon killed the seven husbands of Sara, daughter of Raguel, at Rages. Asmodeus may be the Aeshma Daeva (*q.v.*) of the ancient Persian religion.

ASPERGES. The first word of Psalm li., 7, in the Latin Version (in English "sprinkle [me]"). In the Roman Catholic Church it is used as a designation of the practice of sprinkling the altar, clergy, and people with holy water before the celebration of High Mass. See *Cath. Dict.*

ASPERSION. Literally "sprinkling." A designation of that mode of baptism (*q.v.*) in which an infant is sprinkled with water instead of being dipped in water or having water poured upon it.

ASSASSINS. In a passage in the New Testament (Acts xxi. 38) "Assassins" is given in the Revised Version as a rendering of the Greek word *sikarioi*. The Authorised Version translates "murderers." *Sikarioi* is formed from the Latin *sica*, a short sword which "cut-throats" (Grimm-Thayer, *Lexicon*, 1896) carried under their clothing (cp. Josephus, *Wars* ii 17, 6; *Antiquities* xx. 8, 10). The term seems to have been applied to some of the Jewish Zealots (*q.v.*).

ASSASSINS, THE. A sect which arose in Persia after the death of al-Mustanṣir (A.D. 1094), the supreme head of the Isma'ilis (*q.v.*), through the rivalry of his two sons, Musta'li and Nazir. Al-Mustanṣir is said to have been asked by Ḥasan-i-Ṣabbaḥ in whose name the Isma'ili propaganda should be conducted after his death, and to have received the reply, "In the name of my elder son, Nizar." He therefore carried on his propaganda in favour of this son, and his followers became known as "Assassins." The Crusaders called them Assassini, Assessini, Assissini, or Heissessini. It was once thought that the name was a corruption of Hasaniyyin, "followers of Ḥasan." Sylvestre de Sacy, however, has shown that the Greek chroniclers and Rabbi Benjamin of Tudela have preserved a form of the name (Χασισίοι; *Ḥashishin*) more nearly resembling the original. Benjamin of Tudela's designation, *Ḥashishin* represents, it is thought, the Arabic *Ḥashishiyyun*, a name which would have been given to the sect "because of the use which they made of the drug *Ḥashish*, otherwise known to us as 'Indian hemp.'" At this period the properties of the drug seem to have been known to only a few people in Persia. Its use by the Assassins seems to have been confined to one of the Degrees or Grades of Initiation into which the Order was divided. The head of the order was called the Chief-Propagandist or Grand Master (known in popular speech as "the Mountain Chief"). Immediately under him were the Grand Priors or Superior Propagandists. Then came the ordinary propagandists. The lower grades who received a lesser and varying kind of initiation, comprised Companions, Adherents, and Self-devoted Ones. The latter were the "ministers of vengeance of the Order" (the "Destroying Angels"), and were trained not only in the use of arms, but sometimes also in the use of foreign languages. To die on one of the Grand Master's errands of assassination was considered by them an honour and a sure way to future happiness. See E. G. Browne, *Literary Hist. of Persia*, 1906.

ASSEMBLY CATECHISM. A catechism or confession compiled by the Assembly of Divines in 1648

ASSEMBLY, GENERAL. The supreme ecclesiastical court of the Presbyterians in Scotland, Ireland, and the United States. In the Presbyterian State Church of Scotland, the General Assembly includes clerical and lay representatives from all the presbyteries, as well as representatives from the Universities and the royal burghs. At the annual meeting, which takes place at Edinburgh in May and is presided over by a Moderator, who is now always a clergyman, the King is represented by the Lord High Commissioner. The General Assemblies of the Free Church of Scotland and of the Presbyterian Church of Ireland are constituted in a similar way, but of course there is no royal commissioner.

ASSEMBLY OF DIVINES. See WESTMINSTER ASSEMBLY.

ASSERTION OF THE SEVEN SACRAMENTS. A reply to Luther written by King Henry VIII. Pope Leo X. on account of this book gave him the title of Defender of the Faith.

ASSOCIATE SYNOD. See BURGHERS.

ASSOCIATE PRESBYTERY. See ANTI-BURGHERS.

ASSUMPTION OF THE BLESSED VIRGIN. A Christian festival which is said to have been observed in the East and West before the sixth century. It is not observed in the Church of England, but in the Church of Rome is celebrated on the fifteenth of August. It is called in Greek *koimēsis* or *metastasis;* and in Latin *dormitio, pausatio, transitus,* or *assumptio.* The festival commemorates the taking up of Mary's body into heaven. There was a Gnostic or Collyridian tradition (see COLLYRIDIANS) that Michael brought back the soul of the Virgin Mary from Paradise to be reunited to her body, which was then carried by angels to heaven. See *Prot. Dict.; Cath. Dict.*

ASSUMPTION OF MOSES. See APOCALYPTIC LITERATURE.

ASSURANCE, THE. An oath which all persons who held positions of trust in Scotland were required to take on the accession of William III. Declaration had to be made that William was King *de jure* as well as *de facto*. The Episcopalian clergy who took the oath were allowed to retain possession of their benefices.

ASSURITANS. A sect, mentioned by St. Augustine, which arose in the time of Pope Liberius (*c.* A.D. 358). It was condemned by the Council of Bagai or Vaga in Numidia (A.D. 394).

ASTARTE. A goddess worshipped by the Canaanites and Phoenicians. The name appears in the Old Testament (I Kings xi. 5) as Ashtoreth, and a plural of this word (*Ashtārōth*) denotes heathen goddesses in general (Judges ii. 13, etc.). Other forms of the name are: 'Ashtart (Phoenicia), Ishtar (Babylonia and Assyria), 'Athtar (South Arabia), 'Astar (Abyssinia), 'Atar or 'Athar (Syria). Astarte was worshipped under different aspects in different places. It is clear that she played an important rôle as a goddess of fertility and generation. There was a great sanctuary of Astarte at Byblus, where her worship was associated with that of Adonis (*q.v.*), and another with a grove at Aphaca in Syria. Female prostitution was a prominent feature in her worship, as in that of Aphrodite (*q.v.*) to whom she corresponds. See *Encycl. Bibl.;* J. G. Frazer, *Adonis Attis Osiris*, 1906.

ASTATHIANS. A Greek designation corresponding to the Latin "Instabiles." The sect arose in Phrygia in the ninth century under the leadership of one Sergius, and was suppressed by the Emperor Michael Rhangabes (A.D. 811-813). The Astathians were perhaps a wandering body like the "Bohemians" and "Egyptians" of France in the Middle Ages.

ASTRÆA. Literally the "star-maiden." Daughter of Astraeus and Eos, or of Zeus and Themis. In the golden age she lived on earth as a goddess. She was the last of the gods to retire to the sky in the brazen age. She is represented in the Zodiac by the constellation Virgo.

ASTRAL BODY. An expression used in Spiritualism. It is claimed that "the power resides in the subjective mind of man to create phantasms perceptible to the objective senses of others." Some persons, it would seem, can not only create such phantasms, but also give them a certain amount of intelligence and power. An image can be thus created in sleep and even projected to a great distance, becoming visible and sometimes even tangible. The phenomenon is called by Orientalists the "projection of the astral body." See T. J. Hudson.

ASTRAL SPIRITS. Among the Greeks and Romans the heavenly bodies were supposed to have each a spirit or soul. In the Middle Ages deceased persons or fallen angels were sometimes thought of as astral spirits.

ASTROLOGY. The study of the stars. Astrology has played an important part in religion and magic as one of the occult sciences. It had a strong hold over the Babylonians. Babylonian astrologers carefully studied the stars and planets, and were enabled thereby —or so it was thought—to answer all kinds of questions about auspicious days, etc. Cuneiform texts show that there was an important official called the "court astrologer." The Hebrew writings have preserved few traces of the practice of the art, but this is no doubt due to the work of editors. On the other hand, it is forbidden by Mohammed, except as a help to travellers on the sea or through forests. Ancient and mediaeval astrologers undertook to calculate nativities, and to foretell a child's future from a study of the stars at the time of its birth. Mediaeval astrology also tells of star-souls and star-angels. The Hindus have family astrologers who draw up a horoscope or birth-record "of the exact time of the child's nativity, the constellation under which it was born, with a prophecy of the duration of its life, and the circumstances, good or evil, of its probable career" (Monier-Williams). In the villages the Brahman priest acts as astrologer, and the peasants consult him about every conceivable matter—about sowing and reaping, sneezing, the cries of animals, etc. The Chinese astrologers combine with the study of astrology the study of geomancy, in the belief that hills, mountains, etc., powerfully influence by their outlines the destiny of man. They have a Bureau of Astrology which selects auspicious days for important events, and to this are attached eighteen geomancers. See T. P. Hughes, 1885; Monier-Williams, *Brahmanism;* J. J. M. de Groot, *R.S.C.;* Morris Jastrow, *Rel. of Babylonia and Assyria*, 1898.

ASURA. A term in Indian religion. At first it meant the great and good spirit. The term is applied to Varuna (*q.v.*), but not to Varuna alone. Later it came to designate an evil spirit, or demon. See E. W. Hopkins.

ASVAMEDHA. The name of a horse-sacrifice among the Brahmans. It was the principal animal sacrifice, and there are special hymns for the occasion in the Rig-veda. "A horse was selected by a prince who aimed at supremacy and was let loose to roam at large for a year. Those who disputed his claim tried to capture the roving horse and to hold it against the original owner and all comers. If no one succeeded, the horse was brought back and sacrificed with long ceremonies, and the prince who held it was acknowledged as paramount sovereign." (Monier-Williams).

ASWATTA. A fig-tree regarded with great awe by the Hindus. Its large thin leaves, fanned by the wind, produce a refreshing coolness so that health-giving properties have been attributed to the tree. It is rendered sacred by the tradition that Vishnu (*q.v.*) was born under it. The tree even becomes an embodiment of Vishnu. It may not be cut down, its branches may not be lopped off, nor may its leaves be plucked (except in worship). The tree is sometimes ceremonially consecrated at great cost as the abode or embodiment of Vishnu. See J. A. Dubois and H. K. Beauchamp.

ASYLUM. A sanctuary or sacred spot, "within whose precincts those who take refuge may not be harmed without sacrilege" ("Encyclopaedia Biblica"). Among the Hebrews the asylum was at first the altar (I. Kings i. 50-53; I. Kings ii. 28-34). The Greeks fled to sanctuaries. We read in the Apocrypha of the Jewish high-priest Onias taking refuge in the famous sanctuary of Apollo and Artemis at Daphne near Antioch (ii. Maccabees iv. 33 *ff*). The Romans adopted the practice, and took refuge in sacred places (temples). Among the Central Australian Arunta a man, and even an animal, is safe in the immediate neighbourhood of an *ertnatulunga*, the sacred spot in a local totem centre. In Upolu (Samoan Islands) the asylum was found to be a sacred tree. At Maiva (South Eastern part of New Guinea), the temple (*dubu*) serves as an asylum. Among the Gallas it is a hut near the burial-place of the king; in Fetu on the Gold Coast it is the hut of the high-priest. In the Caucasus criminals, and even animals, take refuge in sacred groves. Among the Hebrews, when the old holy places were abolished, "six cities of refuge" (*'ārē miklat*) were appointed as asylums (Deuteronomy iv. 41-43; xix. 2 *f.*, 8-10). Amongst other peoples cities or villages have served the same purpose. In the island of Hawaii there were cities of refuge for non-combatants during a war. Among North American tribes the place of refuge is sometimes a whole village, sometimes a place of worship. Among the South-Central African Barotse it is a city of refuge or the tomb of a chief. Dr. Westermarck thinks that the right of sanctuary is explained, partly by the fear of shedding blood and disturbing the peace in a holy place, partly by the idea that a criminal, unless he is made friendly, might bring a curse on the deity. Christian churches became places of refuge, and long remained so; but something had to be done to check abuses. Consequently, "by the legislation of Justinian those guilty of certain specified crimes were to find no right of asylum in the churches" (Addis and Arnold). See E. Westermarck, vol. ii., 1908; *Encycl. Bibl.*

ATABEI. An earth-goddess worshipped in the West Indies (Antilles).

ATAGO. A Shinto god of Japan.

ATAGUCHU. The creative deity in the mythology of the Peruvians.

ATAHENTSIC. The name given to the moon by the Hurons. They regarded the moon as maker of the earth and man. Among the Northern Indians Atahentsic is the Death-goddess.

ATAHOCAN. The supreme deity of the Algonquin Indians. When in the seventeenth century they heard of the white man's Creator of heaven and earth, they identified him with Atahocan. It has been suggested that Iouskeha, the Sun, of the Hurons is identical with Atahocan.

ATARGATIS. A Syrian goddess. In one of the Apocrypha (*q.v.*) of the Old Testament (II. Maccabees 12, 26) we read that when Judas Maccabaeus defeated the Ammonites and Arabians, they took refuge in the Temple of Atargatis. Her worship is associated with that of sacred waters. At Ascalon there was a pool near her temple in which were sacred fish. One legend relates that she and her son plunged into the water and were changed into fish. Another represents that she "was born of an egg which the sacred fishes found in the Euphrates and pushed ashore" (Robertson Smith). Compare further 'ATHEH; and see W. Robertson Smith, *R.S.; Encycl. Bibl.*

ATAVISM. A scientific term denoting the reversion of an animal to its ancestral type. To the mind of primitive folk the phenomenon is explained by the doctrine of Transmigration of Souls (*q.v.*). See also METEMPSYCHOSIS.

ATEN. The name of a deity in the old Egyptian religion. Aten was the solar disc, and was regarded as a form in which Ra manifested himself. In the eighteenth dynasty Amenhotep IV. wished to raise the cult of the gods of Heliopolis above that of all the other gods. He assigned the first place to Aten, who became practically his sole god. He also changed his own name to Khuen-aten ("the splendour of the solar disc"). Naville thinks he was incensed against the college of the priests attached to the service of Amon at Thebes. Aten is always depicted as the disc of the sun with rays. See Naville, *The Old Egyptian Faith*, 1909.

ATHANASIAN CREED. One of the creeds or confessions of the Christian Church. It is also called "Quicunque vult" from its first words. It is printed in the Roman Catholic breviary and in the Book of Common Prayer of the Church of England. The latter speaks of it as "commonly called the creed of St. Athanasius." It is now widely recognised that it can be so called not as having been written by Athanasius, but at most merely as embodying his teaching. The style is Latin rather than Greek. The creed is not mentioned by Cyril of Alexandria, Pope Leo, the Council of Ephesus, or the Council of Chalcedon; and it is wanting in nearly all the MSS. of Athanasius' works. It has been suggested that it may have been composed by Bishop Vigilius of Thapsus (end of fifth century, A.D.), since for literary purposes he sometimes assumed the name of Athanasius. Other authors who have been suggested are: Victricius, Bishop of Rouen (c. A.D. 400); Hilary, Abbot of Lerins, afterwards Bishop of Arles (ob. A.D. 449); St. Vincent, a Gallican monk (earlier than A.D. 450); Venantius Fortunatus, Bishop of Poitiers (sixth century). A number of modern scholars have contended however that the creed was not the work of a single author and did not assume its present form until the ninth century. The creed has given rise to much controversy, many members of the Church of England objecting to its use on account of the damnatory clauses, or because it is not adapted to liturgical use. It is used in the French Protestant Church, but only as a hymn in the Church of Ireland. In the Protestant Episcopal Church of the United States it is not recognised in the Articles or Prayer Book. See *Prot. Dict.; Cath. Dict.*

ATHANASIANS. Followers of Athanasius the Great (c. 295-373). See ARIANISM.

ATHANASIUS CONTRA MUNDUM. See ARIANISM.

'ATHAR. A Syrian nature-goddess, equivalent to the Phoenician Astarte.

ATHARVA-VEDA. One of the four Vedas in Indian literature, the other three being the Rig-Veda, the Sáma-Veda, and the Yajur-Veda. Each Veda has three subdivisions, the Samhitá, Bráhmaṇa, and Sútra (*qq.v.*). The Atharva is the latest collection made from the first collection, the Rig-veda. The text and formulae of the Atharva-veda came to be used and are still used as charms and spells "to prevent or to cure diseases, to drive away demons, to frustrate sorcerers and enemies, to ensure victory in battle, to promote virility, to obtain a husband or wife, to arouse the passionate love of a man or a woman, to guarantee safety at an assignation, to allay jealousy, to stimulate the growth of the hair, and to secure a hundred other advantages both trivial and important" (Oman). See Monier-Williams; J. C. Oman, "Brahmans."

'ATHEH. A goddess worshipped at Tarsus as a partner of Baal (*q.v.*). The name occurs in combination with another in a Palmyrene inscription ('Athar-'atheh), the compound being apparently the equivalent of the Syrian Atargatis (*q.v.*). On coins 'Atheh is represented seated on a lion. At Hierapolis-Bambyce near the Euphrates the image of Atargatis was seated on a lion while it was worshipped. Hommel thinks that the East of Asia Minor was the oldest centre of 'Atheh's worship, and that it spread to Western Asia and North Syria. See *Encycl. Bibl.* under "Atargatis"; J. G. Frazer, *Adonis Attis Osiris*, 1906.

ATHEIST. One who does not believe in the existence of God. The Greeks called the early Christians "atheists" because they did not believe in the classic gods.

ATHENE. One of the three principal Greek deities. Also called Pallas Athene.

ATHINGANI. The name of a division of the Paulicians (*q.v.*) in Asia Minor. They were called "Attingians" or "Separates" in the days of the Empress Irene (A.D. 797-802) because they separated themselves from the dominant party, and refused to worship images, the cross, and relics. See J. H. Blunt.

'ATHTAR. A South Arabian god. The name corresponds to the Babylonian Ishtar (*q.v.*), and the Phoenician Astarte (*q.v.*), but in South Arabia the deity appears as masculine. 'Athtar is one of the gods of irrigation. Stags and gazelles seem to have been sacred to him. See W. R. Smith, *R.S.*

ATIUS TIRAWA. The chief deity, a creator-god, in the mythology of the Pawnees.

ATMA. A term used in Theosophy (*q.v.*). It is the name given to the Spirit in man. The vehicle of the Spirit is called Buddhi, the Spiritual Soul. Mrs. Besant explains that Atma and Buddhi "are the reflexions in man of the highest planes in the universe." See Annie Besant, "Theosophy," in *R.S.W.*

ATMAN. A common term in Brāhmanism. Ātman is spirit. It then becomes the Spirit, that mysterious Power which vivifies the body and is the Breath of Life, that divine afflatus which fills and inspires the sacred writers, that force which manifests itself in men, gods, and all material things, the primal and eternal essence, the Universal Soul. See Monier-Williams.

ĀTMĀRĀM. Soul of Rāma (King of Ayodhia, a great incarnation of Vishnu), one of the names of the Hindu god Rāma.

ATMIYA SABHA. Literally "Spiritual Society," a modern Hindu sect or church founded in 1816 by the reformer, Rāmmohun Roy (1772-1833). It met with great opposition from the orthodox priests which it did not survive, but it prepared the way for the foundation of a similar movement, the Brāhma Samāj (*q.v.*).

ATOMS. The atomic theory of the universe was originated by Democritus, the Greek philosopher, who was born at Abdera in Thrace about 460 B.C. Democritus was a disciple of Leucippus, whose teaching he developed. "According to this theory there are in the universe two fundamental principles, the Full and the Void. The Full is formed by the atoms, which are primitive bodies of like quality but different form, innumerable, indivisible, indestructible. Falling for ever through the infinite void, the large and heavier atoms overtake and strike upon the smaller ones, and the oblique and circular motions thence arising are the beginning of the formation of the world. The difference of things arises from the fact that atoms differ in number, size, form and arrangement. The soul consists of smooth round atoms resembling those of fire; these are the nimblest, and in their motion, penetrating the whole body, produce the phenomena of life. The impressions on the senses arise from the effect produced in our senses by the fine atoms which detach themselves from the surface of things. Change is in all cases nothing but the union or separation of atoms" (O. Seyffert, *Dict.*, *s.v.* "Democritus"). Epicurus (*b.* 342 B.C.) accepted the atomic theory, but in his teaching it assumed, in several respects, a different form. He gave it a more ethical and religious bearing. "It seemed to him to be most consonant with the theory of pleasure as the *summum bonum*, which was the ruling feature in Epicurus' philosophy, and it struck at the root of religious superstition by excluding the gods from arbitrary and capricious interference with the government of the world" (W. L. Davidson, *The Stoic Creed*, 1907). According to Epicurus, however, the soul is composed of no less than four elements—heat, air, vapour, and another unnamed; and while Democritus found no place for free will, Epicurus regarded it as a fact of experience, and attached great importance to it as a fundamental principle in ethics.

ATONEMENT. The act or practice of atoning or making expiation. See ATONEMENT, THE. The idea of atonement is dealt with further under ASCETICISM and SACRIFICE.

ATONEMENT, THE. "The Atonement" is the designation of one of the chief doctrines of the Christian religion. To atone means in English to give satisfaction, to set at one, to reconcile. The corresponding word in Hebrew is used in the sense of "to cover."

In Genesis xxxii. 20 Jacob says of Esau: "I will cover his face (Authorised Version 'appease him') with the present that goeth before me, and afterward I will see his face; peradventure he will accept me (Hebrew 'my face')." But there is reason for thinking that primarily the word meant "to wipe out." The word used in the New Testament (*katallagē*) and translated "atonement" in the Authorised Version (Rom. v. 11) means really "reconciliation" (so the Revised Version). In the ritual religion of the Old Testament guilt is removed by the offering of sacrifice. But an enlightened psalmist exclaims: "The sacrifices of God are a broken spirit; a broken and a contrite heart, O God, thou wilt not despise." Christian theories of the Atonement may be said to have arisen in answer to the question: "Why was Jesus destined to suffer a cruel death upon the cross?" The sudden termination of Jesus' career in a manner that seemed humiliating came as a shock and surprise to his disciples and followers. The Apostle Paul is the first to offer an explanation. In Romans iii. 25 we are told that God set forth (or purposed) Jesus "to be a *propitiation*, through faith in his blood, to shew his righteousness, because of the passing over of the sins done aforetime, in the forbearance of God." In Rom. iv. 25 it is said that Jesus "was *delivered up* for our trespasses, and was raised for our justification" (cp. viii. 3; II. Corinthians v. 21); in Rom. v. 10 and 11 that "if, while we were enemies, we were *reconciled* to God through the death of his Son, much more, being reconciled, shall we be saved by his life, and not only so, but we also rejoice in God through our Lord Jesus Christ, through whom we have now received the reconciliation" (cp. II. Corinthians v. 19). In Rom. v. 19 we read: "For as through the one man's disobedience the many were made sinners, even so through the *obedience* of the one shall the many be made righteous" (cp. x. 4; Galatians iv. 4). The conception of another writer is seen in St. John i. 29, "Behold, the Lamb of God, which *taketh away the sin* of the world," and x. 11, "I am the good shepherd, the good shepherd *layeth down his life* for the sheep" (cp. Rom. v. 6-8; I. Peter iii. 18). It is clear from such passages as these that the death of Christ was already explained in several ways. It was connected with the Old Testament idea of the fall of man and the atoning (appeasing) power of sacrifice, and with the prophetic and evangelic belief that God is propitiated by a life of penitence, obedience, and self-sacrifice. These ideas were afterwards developed in various ways. Athanasius (295-373), the "Father of Orthodoxy," explains that Jesus by paying the penalty incurred by all men satisfied God and delivered mankind from death. He offered up his sacrifice on behalf of all, "yielding his Temple to death in the stead of all, in order firstly to make men quit and free of their old trespass, and further to show himself more powerful even than death, displaying his own body incorruptible, as first-fruits of the resurrection of all" (*De Incarnatione*, xx., translated by Archibald Robertson). As to the cross, "if he came himself to bear the curse laid upon us, how else could he have 'become a curse,' save he received the death set for a curse? and that is the Cross. For this is exactly what is written: 'Cursed is he that hangeth on a tree'" (xxv.). Again, "as death must needs come to pass, he did not himself take, but received at others' hands, the occasion of perfecting his sacrifice. Since it was not fit, either, that the Lord should fall sick, who healed the diseases of others; nor again was it right for that body to lose its strength, in which he gives strength to the weaknesses of others also" (xxi.). Anselm (1033-1109), however, the founder of Scholastic Theology, is considered to have defined the doctrine more clearly and consistently (*Cur Deus Homo*). "In various ways Anselm seeks to illustrate and establish the truth of the *objective* necessity of the Atonement. The necessity is not found in the claims of Satan, nor in the character of man, but in the character of God and the claims of righteousness. But though there was a moral necessity for the death of Christ, His sufferings and death were perfectly voluntary. This is vindicated with great clearness against objections. And as it is shown that neither a sinless man nor an angel could have given the satisfaction which justice required, the necessity for a Redeemer who was both God and man is proved, and the connection is established between the two cardinal doctrines of the Deity of Christ and His atonement for sin. The voluntary death of such a person must have an incomparable value, and may well be accepted by God as a reason for righteously remitting the sins of even the vilest of men. It thus illustrates the love of the Father as well as of the Son. Mercy triumphs over guilt, while the claims of Justice are fully met" (E. S. Prout, Introduction to *Cur Deus Homo?*). The idea of a vicarious satisfaction is now generally accepted by orthodox Churchmen, and the atonement is regarded as complete and sufficient for all men. It may be said that on the whole the main stress is laid now on Jesus' self-sacrificing obedience unto death. Jesus effected the reconciliation not so much by his death as by his life. The "Mystical" theory also refuses to lay too much stress on his death. According to this Jesus made it possible for man and God to be at-one by his incarnation. Before this man could not enter into intimate relations with God. See *Prot. Dict.; Cath. Dict.;* Chambers' *Encycl.;* Brockhaus; A. Ritschl, *Die christliche Lehre von der Rechtfertigung und der Versöhnung*, 3 vols., 3rd ed. 1888-89, 4th ed. of vol. iii. 1895.

ATONEMENT, DAY OF. A Jewish festival, called in the Talmud "the great day," "the day," or "the great fast." The chapter in the Old Testament (Leviticus xvi.) which treats of its observance is composite, and there is no evidence that such a day was observed before the Exile. But in course of time it became the most important day in the ecclesiastical year. The Day of Atonement was instituted "that the Israelites might annually make a complete atonement for all sin, and that the sanctuary might be cleansed (Lev. xvi. 33). The leading idea of the entire Priestly Law found here its best expression" (I. Benzinger). Prof. Cheyne points out that the ritual of New Year's Day (*Rosh hash-Shanah*) had the same propitiatory character. It was believed "that the fate of man was decreed on New Year's Day (the festival of Creation), and that on the Day of Atonement the decree was 'sealed.' No wonder that the nine days which intervened between the first day of the seventh month (New Year's Day) and the tenth (the Day of Atonement) were regarded by the Jews as penitential days." On this day "the High Priest does not wear his gorgeous official dress, but the white robes of purity and consecration. The blood that is to expiate the people's sin must be brought directly into the presence of God, because the fullest expression must be given to the thought of atonement, because the innermost sanctuary must be cleansed from the stains with which it is defiled by the presence of a sinful people. He first offers a sin-offering for himself and the people. Enveloped in incense, he carries the blood before the holy mercy-seat, and besprinkles it therewith. Thus atonement is made for Israel, and its sin is taken away. Its holy things are consecrated; it stands there as a holy community in which God can dwell. His gracious presence in Israel is once more undisturbed. The second goat, which has been presented by the people for an expiatory purpose, but is not used as a sacrifice, can now be dedicated in order to carry the burden of the people's sins, laid upon it by confession, as being now forgiven and forgotten, away into the wilderness, beyond the consecrated circle of the camp, into a land where there is neither salvation nor mercy. The feeling of horror at the impurity of sin is so strongly expressed by this ceremony that the persons who have to do with the burning of the animal sacrificed, and with the driving away of the living one, are regarded as polluted, and have to be washed before they regain the holiness necessary for fellowship with Israel" (H. Schultz, *O.T. Theology*, vol. i., 1895). Cp. AZAZEL. See *Encycl. Bibl.*

ATTIS. A god worshipped in Phrygia and corresponding to the Syrian Adonis (*q.v.*). He is another personification of vegetation which dies yearly and yearly revives. He was born of a virgin, Nana, who conceived after eating an almond or placing it in her bosom. According to one account of his death he was killed by a boar. According to another he destroyed his manhood under a pine-tree, which became the embodiment of his spirit. From his blood grew violets. Attis is said to have been beloved by Cybele (*q.v.*), the Phrygian Mother of the Gods. The worship of Attis seems to have spread to Rome with that of Cybele (204 B.C.). Attis, in the form of a pine-log, decked with violets, was annually mourned at a Spring festival, part of the mourning consisting in self-mutilation. Afterwards he was sought for on the mountains, and was found on the third day. This resurrection was celebrated in a Festival of Joy (*Hilaria*), at which people, going about in disguise, made merry without restraint. There were also secret or mystic ceremonies connected with the worship of Attis. The god seems to have been originally a god of vegetation. See J. G. Frazer, *Adonis Attis Osiris*, 1906; O. Seyffert, *Dict.*

ATTRITION. In the Roman Catholic Church a distinction is drawn between Attrition and Contrition. The latter "is that sorrow for sin which has for its motive the love of God whom the sinner has offended." Attrition, on the other hand, is prompted by a lower motive, such, for instance, as "the fear of hell, the loss of heaven, the turpitude of sin" (Addis and Arnold).

AUDHUMLA. The name of a cow which figures in Teutonic cosmogony. It is regarded by some as symbolical of the clouds. See P. D. Chantepie de La Saussaye, *Rel. of the Teutons*, 1902.

AUDIANI. A sect founded by Audaeus of Mesopotamia in 338. He was a bishop of the Syrian Church, but was expelled for condemning the vices of the clergy.

AUFKLAERUNG, ZEITALTER DER. The period (eighteenth century) known in Germany as the "Period of Enlightenment." See ENLIGHTENMENT, PERIOD OF.

AUGEAN CODEX. The Codex Augiensis is a manuscript of part of the New Testament belonging to the end of the ninth century. It was so called from a monastery Augia Major or Dives on an island in Lake Constance. Dr. C. R. Gregory describes it as "a beautiful book." The manuscript, which is now preserved in Trinity College, Cambridge, England, contains the Epistles of Paul, with a few gaps. See C. R. Gregory.

AUGSBURG, CONFESSION OF. The most important confession of faith in the Lutheran Church, called in Latin "Confessio Augustana." In order to compose religious differences, Charles V. summoned a Diet of the States of the German Empire to meet at Augsburg in 1530. The Elector, John of Saxony, in view of this meeting, commissioned the Wittenberg theologians to draft articles of faith and present them to him at Torgau. In the execution of their task, these made use of articles which had been drawn up in Latin and German at Swabach and Marburg shortly before. The articles laid before the Elector at Torgau were in turn used by Philipp Melanchthon (A.D. 1497-1560), when, with the help of other theologians, he framed the Confession of Augsburg, which in Latin and German was presented to the Emperor on the 25th of June, 1530. It was intended to be a conciliatory statement of the beliefs of the Lutheran Protestants drawn up in such a way as to show as little divergence as possible from Catholic views. The Confession consists of two divisions. The first contains twenty-one articles of faith; the second consists of seven declarations or protests against abuses in the Roman Catholic Church. The twenty-one articles deal with the following matters: 1. God and the Trinity; 2. Original Sin; 3. The Son of God, the Incarnation, the Atonement, the Descent to Hell, the Ascension, the Second Coming; 4. Justification by Faith; 5. The Ministration of the Word and the Sacraments; 6. Obedience to God; 7. The One Church, its unity of doctrine and sacraments; 8. The Church, its Sacraments effective, even when administered by evil persons; 9. Baptism and the need of Infant Baptism; 10. The Lord's Supper, and the real presence of the Body and Blood of Christ; 11. Confession, its private use allowed; 12. Penance, contrition to be accompanied by good works; 13. The Use of the Sacraments, need of faith in their promises; 14. Church Government, duly appointed ministers; 15. Church Order, universal observance of Church Ceremonies; 16. Secular Government, legitimate authority of civil magistrates; 17. Christ's Second Coming to judgment; 18. Free-will and the Holy Spirit; 19. The cause of Sin, not in God; 20. Faith and Good Works, and the merit of Christ's sacrifice; 21. The Merits of the Saints as objects of imitation. The declarations against abuses deal with the following matters: 1. Withholding the Cup from the laity; 2. Compulsory Celibacy of the Clergy; 3. The Saying of Masses for money; 4. The Enumeration of sins in Auricular Confession; 5. Distinctions of Meat in Fasting; 6. Irrevocable Conventual Vows; 7. The Authority of Bishops, its growth and secular use. The Confession was too Protestant to please the Catholics, and too Catholic to please the Anabaptists and Swiss Reformers; but it was accepted by the Lutherans. Melanchthon afterwards thought himself at liberty to make certain changes, and in 1540, with the idea of reconciling Calvinists and Lutherans, he published a new edition in Latin (*Confessio Variata*). The Orthodox Lutherans would not accept these alterations, and the "Confessio invariata" became their standard. Both forms of the Confession, however, came to be recognised by the Reformed Churches of Germany. See the edition of the Confession by Th. Kolde (1896); also Brockhaus; J. H. Blunt; Chambers' *Encycl.*

AUGSBURG, DIET OF. See the preceding article.

AUGSBURG, INTERIM OF. Interim was a name given in Reformation times to edits given forth by the German Emperor pending the decision of religious disputes by a general council. The Augsburg Interim was made at a Diet of Augsberg in A.D. 1548. It provided that the Cup should not be withheld from the laity at the Lord's Supper, and allowed the clergy to marry.

AUGURY. The prediction of future events based on the close observation of the flight of birds, the state of the sky, etc., and the examination of the entrails of animals. Among the Romans there was a priesthood of Augurs or diviners, who were consulted about all kinds of matters, public affairs and private concerns. The predictions from the observation of birds received the special designation Auspices. The practice of augury has been noted among savages such as the Tupis of

Brazil, the Dayaks of Borneo, the Maoris, etc., as well as among representatives of ancient civilization.

AUGUSTINES. An order of nuns who claimed that their Order originated in a convent founded by St. Augustine at Hippo. The claim was no doubt suggested by a letter (no. 109) he wrote "in which he laid down a rule of life for the religious women under his direction, not binding them to strict enclosure, but requiring them to renounce all individual property" (Addis and T. Arnold). The Augustines devoted themselves to good works, especially among the sick.

AUGUSTINIANS. It has been claimed that the order of the Canons Regular of St. Augustine was founded by St. Augustine of Hippo (A.D. 354-430.) It is difficult, however, to prove that he composed any formal rule. All that can be said is that some of his writings (*e.g., De Moribus Clericorum*) may have suggested one. Addis and Arnold mention the argument that "if St. Augustine promulgated a rule and founded congregations which have had perpetual succession ever since, it seems impossible to explain how St. Benedict should have been universally regarded for centuries as the founder of Western monachism." The Augustinian Canons do not seem to be earlier than A.D. 816. In that year a rule was drawn up at Aix-la-Chapelle for observance among the canons of various Cathedrals. This rule did not forbid the holding of private property. In 1059 and 1063, however, at councils held in Rome, the rule was amended. Private property had to be renounced, and those who belonged to the Order had to live together. Those who conformed to this rule were called regular canons. It became known as the rule of St. Augustine. There were soon (12th century) many independent (that is to say, as regards Cathedrals) bodies of Canons Regular of St. Augustine or St. Austin in Europe. In England, where they were called Black Canons from their black cloaks, they had many houses. At the Reformation there were about 170. There were also Augustinian Hermits: otherwise known as Hermits of St. Augustine, Austin Friars, or Begging Hermits. The Order did not arise until A.D. 1265 when Pope Alexander IV. united several congregations. Pope Pius V. decided definitely that they were friars and not monks (1567). They gave up all property, and lived on alms. At the Dissolution they are said to have had thirty-two houses in England. There are now two houses in England, the one at Hoxton, London, the other at Hythe in Kent; and twelve houses in Ireland. Martin Luther was a member of the house of the Augustinian Hermits at Wittenberg. See *Cath. Dict.*; Chambers' *Encycl.*

AULD LICHTS. The United Presbyterian Church was formed in 1847 by the amalgamation of the Associate Presbytery or Secession Kirk and the Relief Church. But when this union took place, a few congregations stood aloof, and claimed to be the Old Seceders (that is to say, the original secession) or the Auld Lichts.

AUM. A sacred, mystic word in Brahmanism. It is pronounced with peculiar reverence, and its meaning is kept secret. The three letters may represent the three deities, Brahma, Vishnu, and Siva. See J. A. Dubois and H. K. Beauchamp.

AUREOLE. From the Latin *aureolus* "golden." In Christian Art the figure of a holy person is surrounded with gold. This is the Aureole as distinguished from the nimbus which covers only the head. "In theology it is defined as a certain accidental reward added to the essential bliss of heaven, because of the excellent victory which the person who receives it has attained during his warfare upon earth." See *Cath. Dict.*

AURICULAR CONFESSION. See CONFESSION.

AUSPICES. Properly, the special designation of predictions founded on the observation of birds in divination. See AUGURY.

AUSTIN FRIARS. See AUGUSTINIANS.

AUTGA. A Hindu deity, worshipped as the god of hunting by the Māls, a tribe of the Rājmahal hills in India.

AUTHORISED VERSION. Usually contracted and referred to as AV (margin of Authorised Version = AVmg). The English Version of the Bible published A.D. 1611. See BIBLE. The two versions of the Bible, Authorised and Revised, are often referred to together as E.V.

AUTOCEPHALI. Metropolitans, such as those of Cyprus or the Archbishops of Bulgaria, who were not subject to a patriarch.

AUTO DA FÉ. The Act of Faith was a name given to the public trial of those who were supposed to be heretics in the Roman Catholic Church. A special day was fixed from time to time by the Inquisition in Spain and Portugal for the examination of those who were accused of heresy. If the accused person was found guilty, he was handed over to the magistrate to be put to death, either by burning at the stake or by strangling. In Portugal the ceremony was held in a large theatre which could accommodate 3,000 spectators.

AUTOMATISM. A name given by F. W. H. Myers (1843-1901) to certain mental phenomena produced by an impulsive working of what is known as the subliminal self, the sub-consciousness, or the sub-conscious mind. Uprushes of sub-conscious knowledge into the ordinary consciousness, may and do produce, it is claimed, such phenomena as automatic speech or writing. Such Automatism often takes a religious turn. See William James, *Varieties of Religious Experience,* 1906.

AUTO-SUGGESTION. A hypnotized person is very susceptible to suggestion, so much so that the subject can be cured by suggestion of certain nervous diseases or of vices and bad habits. It is well known, moreover, that suggestion is, and has been, a great power in our daily life in the form both of heterosuggestion, suggestion coming from others, and auto-suggestion, suggestion made to ourselves. This has led to the discovery, it is claimed, that, without the use of hypnotism, a person can suggest to himself or herself the cure of diseases and bad habits. See T. J. Hudson; E. Worcester, S. McComb and I. H. Coriat, *Religion and Medicine*, 1908.

AVALIKITESVARA. The Indian name of the Chinese and Japanese Buddhist deity, Kwan Yin (Kwannon). In Lamaism the name appears as Avalokita. The deity is continually reincarnate in the Dalai Lama of Lhassa. See H. Hackmann.

AVATARS. A term used in Hindu mythology for incarnations of the Deity. Vishnu (*q.v.*), e.g., is supposed to have appeared in ten different incarnations. In the later writings called Purānas the number was increased to eleven (*Varāha Purāna*) and even to twenty or twenty-two (*Bhāgavat Purāna*). See E. W. Hopkins.

AVE MARIA. A prayer, also called the Angelical Salutation (Hail, Mary!) repeated daily by Roman Catholics before the canonical hours and after Compline. It consists of the words of the angel Gabriel ("Ave [Maria] gratia plena, Dominus tecum; benedicta tu in mulieribus"), those of Elisabeth to Mary ("et benedictus fructus ventris tui"), and a late addition ("Sancta Maria, Mater Dei, ora pro nobis peccatoribus nunc et in hora mortis nostrae"). The use of the whole prayer was enjoined by Pope Pius V. in 1568. The first two parts came into use towards the close of the twelfth century.

AVENGER OF BLOOD, THE. This is the English translation of a Hebrew expression occurring in the Old Testament. The Hebrew expression is *gō'ēl had-dām,* and the word *gō'ēl* means more properly "the reclaimer" or "the redeemer." When a person's blood had been unjustly shed, it was the duty of a member of his family or clan, especially of his nearest kinsman, to vindicate the rights of the dead person (II. Samuel xiv. 7, 11; Deuteronomy xix. 12; Numbers xxxv. 19, 21, 27). This vindicator was called the *gō'ēl had-dām*. See *Encycl. Bibl.*

AVERNUS, LAKE. A lake in Naples between the ancient Cumae and Puteoli. The hills which surrounded it were thickly wooded. This made the place dark and gloomy, and Homer and Virgil in their mythology have represented the place as the entrance to hell. Real places have often been so conceived. The Hebrews have their Gehinnom (Valley of Hinnom). The Baperi of South Africa think of a cavern, Marimatlé, in the same way. The North German peasants have connected the banks of the swampy Drömling, and the Irish the place Lough Derg, with the same idea.

AVERRHOISM. The teaching of an Arabian philosopher who became known as Averroes (1126-1198). His real name was Abû'l-Walîd Ibn Rushd. He was born at Cordova. He was suspected of heresy towards the end of his life, and was exiled. In his book "Decisive Discourse" he attempts to reconcile Moslem law and Science. See Clément Huart, *Hist. of Arabic Lit.*, 1903.

AVESTA, THE. The collection of the sacred books of the old Persians (see ZOROASTRIANISM). These sacred writings were collected and edited in the third century A.D. The text together with the commentaries which were added is known as the Zend-Avesta.

AVIGNON CAPTIVITY. A name given to the period (1305-1377) during which the Popes, from Clement V. to Gregory XI., resided at Avignon and were almost vassals of France. It is sometimes called the "Babylonish Captivity."

AWAKENING OF HERCULES. A Greek festival held about the month of January. In it were represented dramatically the burning of the god Hercules and his resurrection. See J. G. Frazer, *Adonis Attis Osiris*, 1906.

AWALOKITEÇWARA. In Chinese religion, one of the chiefs of the Western Paradise, the other being Amitâbha. The Chinese Buddhists say that Awalôkitêçwara conveys departed souls to Paradise in a ship ("the barge of mercy"). See J. J. M. de Groot, *R.S.C.*

AWONAWILONA. The creative deity in the mythology of the Zuñi of New Mexico.

AXE, DOUBLE-HEADED. The double-headed axe figures as a symbol or emblem of deities. It was borne for instance by the Asiatic deity Sandan of Tarsus, who corresponded to Hercules; by some of the Hittite deities of Boghaz-Keui; by Sandon of Lydia, another deity corresponding to Hercules. Sandon and Sandan are, no doubt, identical, and the deity in each case is Hittite. In Mycenaean and Minoan worship, again, the double axe appears frequently as a sacred emblem. In Crete it was associated with the sacred bull. See J. G. Frazer, *Adonis Attis Osiris*, 1906.

AXINOMANCY. A term composed of two Greek words and meaning "divination by an axe." The ancient Greeks practised this kind of divination, and believed that by means of it they could detect those who had been guilty of crime. The practice was to balance an axe upon a stake in such a way that it would turn or move.

AYNIA. Aynia or Aine was an ancient Irish deity. The goddess is associated principally with the North of Ireland. Popular legend suggests that at one time she was the moon-goddess. Near Dunany there is an immense stone, which is called "the chair of Aynia" or "the chair of the lunatics." It was believed that lunatics were drawn irresistibly to this chair. Sitting upon it three times, they became incurable. Even sane persons might lose their reason by sitting upon it. The influence of the goddess was felt particularly on the Friday, Saturday, and Sunday immediately following Lammas Day. Aynia seems to have been also a patroness of medicine and literature. According to W. G. Wood-Martin, herb and charm-mongers regarded her as equivalent to what they called the "vital spark." As patroness of literature, she rewarded the learned by leading them when they died into fairy realms. She came in fact to be regarded as the Queen of Fairies. One of her fairy haunts survives at Knocknanny, in the county Tyrone, in a rude stone monument which the peasants call "Aynia's Cove." Aynia seems to have been equivalent to the god who was worshipped as Minerva by the natives of Gaul. See W. G. Wood-Martin.

AYUNGANG. A deity (also known as Dharma Boja or Lānkan), the sun, worshipped by the Savaras (also known as Sawaras or Saoras), an important hill-tribe in Southern India. The deity is supposed to live in big trees.

AZAZEL. In the Hebrew ritual of the Day of Atonement the high-priest had to cast lots upon two goats. The one goat was to be a sin-offering for Jehovah, the other was to "be presented alive before the Lord, to make an atonement with him, and to let him go for a scapegoat into the wilderness" (Leviticus xvi. 8-10). The idea seems to have been that the goat which was sent into the wilderness bore away the sins of the people. The meaning of the word, however, has been disputed. Jewish interpreters thought Azazel was a place in the wilderness; others have taken it to be a designation of the goat itself, or even of the act of ritual ("complete dismissal"). But it seems clear that Azazel is a personal being contrasted with Jehovah. Azazel therefore was probably one of the demons to whom in post-exilic times sacrifices were made, or a kind of personal angel (so T. K. Cheyne), though "the first clear mention of a personal devil (Beliar= Satan, Sammæl, Mastema, Azazel) occurs in *The Testaments of the Twelve Patriarchs*, dating probably from the Maccabæan age" (W. Fairweather, *The Background of the Gospels*, 1908). Prof. Cheyne thinks that the author of the scape-goat ritual substituted this personal angel, "a fallen angel, evil no doubt, yet not altogether unfriendly to man," for the crowd of earth-demons to whom the people were accustomed to offer sacrifice. "This was obviously an offering to the devil," says Dr. Samuel G. Smith, "perhaps not seriously but rather as sending to him the sins of the people, a gift of his own come home" (*Religion in the Making*, 1910). See *Encycl. Bibl.*

AZIZUS. An Arabian deity, one of the heavenly twins, the morning star. Adopted by the Palmyrenes.

AZRAEL. In the Mohammedan religion this is the name of one of the four members of the highest group of angels, the others being Gabriel, Michael, and Israfil. Azrael is the "Angel of Death."

AZYMITES. From a Greek word meaning "without leaven." A name applied by Greek schismatics to the Christians of the Latin Church because they used unleavened bread in the Lord's Supper.

B

B. God B. is a designation used by anthropologists for a deity depicted in the MSS. of the Mayan Indians of Central America. He is represented as having a long truncated nose, and is described by Stempell as "the elephant-headed god B standing upon the head of a serpent" (Maya Codex Troano; see G. Elliot Smith, *Dr.*, p. 84). "Many authorities consider god B to represent Kukulkan, the Feathered Serpent, whose Aztec equivalent is Quetzalcoatl. Others identify him with Itzamna, the Serpent God of the East, or with Chac, the Rain God of the four quarters and the equivalent of Tlaloc of the Mexicans" (Herbert J. Spinden, *Maya Art*, p. 62). Prof. Elliot Smith identifies him with Chac, and contends that Chac (=Tlaloc) is simply an American form of the Indian rain-god Indra. "One and the same fundamental idea, such as the attributes of the serpent as a water-god, reached America in an infinite variety of guises, Egyptian, Babylonian, Indian, Indonesian, Chinese and Japanese, and from this amazing jumble of confusion the local priesthood of Central America built up a system of beliefs which is distinctively American, though most of the ingredients and the principles of synthetic composition were borrowed from the Old World."

BAAL. A Semitic word meaning "owner, proprietor, or possessor," it is used as the title of gods regarded as the owners or inhabitants of places or districts. Thus there was a Baal of Tyre, a Baal of Sidon, a Baal of the Lebanon, a Baal of Mt. Hermon, etc. In the Old Testament, the local deities are spoken of collectively as the Baalim or the Baals. As gods of fertility (Hosea ii. 5, 12), agricultural festivals were a feature of their worship (Hosea ii. 8, 13). One of the Baals who assumed a leading position in later times was called Baal-shamem, "the owner of the heavens." When the Israelites settled among the Canaanites they seem to have worshipped the Canaanite Baalim side by side with their own god Jehovah. Later on, however, they regarded Jehovah himself as the Baal of the land, though the rites of the old Baal cult survived even among the Israelites. The prophets of the eighth century denounced this idolatrous worship. See *Encycl. Bibl.*

BAAL BERITH. See BERITH MILAH.

BAAL-BERITH. A local Baal (*q.v.*) referred to in the Old Testament (Judges ix. 4), also called "El-berith" ("God of the covenant," Judges ix. 46). This was a Canaanite Baal who was worshipped at Shechem. In ordinary Hebrew *baal-berith* means "covenant ally," literally "possessor of covenant." Here, however, the god seems to be so called as "the Baal who presides over covenants, or rather over the special covenant by which the neighbouring Israelites were bound to the Canaanite inhabitants of the city" (W. R. Smith, *R.S.*). Or the covenant may have been between Shechem and neighbouring Canaanite towns. Another view is that the Baal was possessor of a covenant between himself and his worshippers. There was a temple of Baal-berith which is associated with several episodes in Hebrew history (Judges ix. 4, 27, 46). See *Encycl. Bibl.*

BAAL-HAMMON. A god who is often mentioned in Punic inscriptions. In the Old Testament (Ezekiel vi. 4, 6, and other passages) reference is made to *ḥammānīm* as places of idolatrous worship. This word has been connected with *ḥammā*, a late Hebrew word for "sun," and interpreted "sun images" or "sun pillars." *Baal-ḥammōn* might therefore mean "the deity which dwells in the sun-pillars." In "El-ḥammon," however, which occurs in another inscription, *ḥammon* seems to be the name of a place. See *Encycl. Bibl.*; W. R. Smith, *R.S.*

BAAL-MARCOD. The name of a god worshipped near Bairūt and referred to in inscriptions. The Semitic form of the name would mean "lord of dancing," or a god who required homage to be paid him in dances. See W. R. Smith, *R.S.*

BAAL-MARRIAGE. In marriages under the system of male kinship in Arabia, the wife—whether obtained by capture or by contract—"who follows her husband and bears children who are of his blood has lost the right freely to dispose of her person; her husband has authority over her and he alone has the right of divorce." Among the Arabians, Hebrews, and Aramaeans the husband in this kind of marriage was called *ba'al*, "lord" or "owner." Robertson Smith therefore describes it as Baal-marriage (cp. the term *be'ūlah* of a subject wife, Isaiah lxii. 4). In this way such a marriage is distinguished from a Beena-marriage (*q.v.*). Robertson Smith contends that before the separation of the tribes Beena-marriage or matriarchy was the universal practice among the Semites. But Prof. Wellhausen has proved that Baal-marriage or patriarchy can be traced back to primitive Semitic times. Dr. I. Benzinger thinks it "best to abandon all attempts to make out a genetic connection or evolutionary relation between the various kinds of marriage." One tribe "might count kin from the mother, being endogamous, or else marrying its young women to men of alien tribe only when the men consented to join the tribe of the wife and the children remained with the mother. Another tribe counted kin from the father and therefore sought for its wives, so far as these could not be found within the tribe, by capture of such welcome additions from other tribes" (*Encycl. Bibl.*). See W. Robertson Smith, *Kinship and Marriage in Early Arabia*, 1903.

BAAL-PEOR. The Baal of Peor, a Moabite god referred to in the Old Testament (Numbers xxv. 3; Deuteronomy iv. 3; Psalm 106, 29). The Israelites adopted the worship in Shittim. "And Israel yoked himself unto the Baal of Peor, and the anger of the Lord was kindled against Israel" (Numbers xxv. 3). It has been suggested (G. B. Gray) that the worship was possibly a local cult of Chemosh (*q.v.*). See *Encycl. Bibl.*

BAALSAMIN. A deity worshipped by the Phoenicians, Nabataeans, and Palmyrenes. The name means "the lord of heaven."

BAALZEBUB. The name of a local baal (see BAAL), a god of Ekron. Ahaziah, king of Israel, when he was ill sent messengers to consult the god's oracle (II. Kings i. 2, 3, 6, 16). The word has been commonly explained as "god of flies," that is to say, "a god who sends as well as removes a plague of flies"; but this is not very suitable. God of Zebub would be more suitable, but no such place is known. Prof. Cheyne would read Baal-zebul, "lord of the high house," a title such as any god with a fine temple might bear. He thinks that in contempt the late Hebrew narrator altered this to "god of flies." See *Encycl. Bibl.*

BAAL-ZEPHON. The name of a Phoenician god. The word *ẓāphōn* means "north" in Hebrew, whence Baal-zephon seems to mean "Baal of the North," or "the Baal whose throne is on the sacred mountain of the gods in the north" (Baethgen). The god is also referred to in Assyrian inscriptions (Baal-ṣapunu). Prof. Cheyne identifies Baal-zephon with Baal-Lebanon, "the Baal of Lebanon." See *Encycl. Bibl.*

BAANITES. Followers of Baanes, a disciple of Josephus Epaphroditus, who formed a sect of the Paulicians in Armenia (c. A.D. 810).

BABA. Literally "father," a title of honour in Persia and Turkey borne by distinguished ecclesiastics.

BABA BATHRA. One of the Jewish treatises or tractates which reproduce the oral tradition or unwritten law as developed by the second century A.D. and are included in the Mishnah (*q.v.*), a collection and compilation completed by Rabbi Judah the Holy, or the Patriarch, about 200 A.D. The sixty-three tractactes of the Mishnah are divided into six groups or orders (*sedarim*). Bābā Bathrā is the third tractate of the fourth group, which is called *Neziḳin* ("Damages").

BABA ḲAMMA. The name of one of the Jewish treatises or tractates which reproduce the oral tradition or unwritten law as developed by the second century A.D. and are incorporated in the Mishnah (*q.v.*), a collection and compilation completed by Rabbi Judah the Holy, or the Patriarch, about 200 A.D. The sixty-three tractates of the Mishnah are divided into six groups or orders (*sedarim*). Bāba Ḳammā is the first tractate of the fourth group, which is called *Neziḳin* ("Damages").

BABAKIYAH. The followers of Babek, upon whom is supposed to have fallen the mantle of the Persian Mazdak (founder of a Religious Communism). Babek claimed to be God incarnate. His followers are said to have practised the "extinction of the lamp" at their nightly festivals. According to Isfaraini, they assembled by night in the mountains and agreed upon all kinds of depravity with women and fluteplaying; they put out lamps and fires and each rises up to seize the female who sits nearest. But, as F. W. Bussell says, such charges are frequently levelled against all secret meetings of a suspected sect.

BĀBĀ MEṢI'Ā. The title of one of the Jewish tractates or treatises which represent the unwritten law or oral tradition as developed by the second century A.D. and are included in the Mishnah (*q.v.*), a collection and compilation completed by Rabbi Judah the Holy, or the Patriarch, about 200 A.D. The sixty-three tractates of the Mishnah are divided into six groups or orders (*sedarim*). Bābā Meṣī'ā is the second tractate of the fourth group, which is called *Neziḳin* ("Damages").

BABBAR. The name of a deity in the old Babylonian inscriptions. It means literally the "brilliantly shining one," and seems to have been another name for the sun, Shamash (*q.v.*). See Morris Jastrow, *Rel.*

BABEL, TOWER OF. A story in the Old Testament (Genesis xi.) the purpose of which was to account for a variety of languages amongst men and the dispersion of mankind. The story may have been suggested partly by the spectacle of a ruined temple-tower of Babylon. Bābel is, as a matter of fact, the Hebrew form of the native name Bāb-ili, "gate of God"; but the Hebrew narrator tries to connect it with a Hebrew word meaning "to confuse." The story, which is very anthropomorphic, is to this effect. The whole earth had originally one language. Mankind journeyed and found a place suitable to settle in, the plain of Shinar. They then proceeded to make bricks with clay and bitumen. They would build a city and also a tower reaching unto heaven. These would prevent them from being dispersed. But Jehovah, becoming alarmed, "came down to see the city and the tower." Having seen them he returns and takes counsel with the sons of God. If they do this, he says, "nothing will be withholden from them which they purpose to do." Then he adds, "Come, let us go down, and bring their speech into confusion." Thus, in the words of Dr. Samuel G. Smith, "to save the sanctity of the divine abode, the common language was confounded, the men were scattered abroad, the city building was abandoned, and a primitive explanation of the race question was left on record (*Religion in the Making*, 1910). See *Encycl. Bibl.*

BABISM. A religious movement in modern Persia. Bābism is an offshoot of Shiism (*q.v.*), the Persian state-religion. The Shiites recognised, after Mohammed, twelve Imams or vicars of God on earth. The last of these, Imam Mahdi, disappeared mysteriously A.D. 940. He communicated with the faithful, however, through privileged persons, each of whom was called Bāb or Gate. There were four of these in succession, and their period was called the "Lesser Occultation." The succeeding period was called the "Greater Occultation." The Shiite school known as Shaykhism maintained that between the Hidden Imam and his followers there must always be a "perfect man" to act as a channel of grace. Sayyid Kazim, one of these perfect men, died without naming a successor. Thereupon Mirza Ali Mohammad declared that he was the new Bāb or Gate, and Mulla Husayn soon became his devoted disciple (May 23, 1844). They were joined by followers of Sayyid Kazim and others, to whom the Bāb inveighed against the worldliness of the Mohammedan clergy and the injustice of the government. On a pilgrimage to Mecca he seems to have broken definitely with the faith of Mohammed, and in consequence his followers were soon made to suffer. He himself was next arrested, taken to Shiraz, and found guilty of heresy. In 1846 he made his escape to Ispahan, whence he was afterwards banished, first to Maku, and then to Chihrik, where he was closely confined, though he still contrived to send messages to his disciples. After this he gave out that he was the Imam Mahdi himself, and prophesied that there should come after him "He whom God shall manifest," one greater than himself. In his teaching he attached a peculiar sanctity to the number 19. He chose 18 disciples as "Letters of the Living," and called himself, as the nineteenth person, the "Point of Unity." His chief work, which became the Bible of Bābism, was called the "Bayan." His disciple Mulla Husayn was very active in spreading the faith, but was killed in 1849 while fighting with his co-religionists against the royal troops. There were several such Bābi risings in which the Bab's followers were mercilessly dealt with. The authorities now turned their attention once more to the Bab himself. After a mock trial at Tabriz he was condemned to death, and died a martyr at the age of twenty-seven. Other martyrdoms followed, especially in the year 1850. The movement tended to become more political. This, and an attempt on the life of the Shah, led to voluntary exile in Bagdad. In 1864 another movement had to be made first to Constantinople, and then to Adrianople. From 1850 until this time Subh-i-Ezel had been head of the Bābis. In 1866-67 an elder half-brother Beha gave out that he was " He whom God shall manifest." Subh-i-Ezel would not allow this. Thus a schism was caused, and the Behais, whose headquarters were moved in 1868 to Acre, became the more numerous and more powerful division. Amongst his other works, Beha produced one, the *Kitab-i-Akdas*, which became a new Bible and took the place of the *Bayan*. Beha, who came to be reverenced as God Almighty, died in 1892, and was succeeded by his eldest son, Abbas Efendi. The Bābis, who are said to number now one million, " have no places of worship of their own, but hold their meetings, generally after sundown, in the houses of various members of the community " (E. Denison Ross). The movement has spread to America. See E. Denison Ross in *G.R.W.;* E. G. Browne, *New History of the Bāb*, 1893

BABYLONIAN PSALMS. A number of Babylonian hymns and songs have been preserved, and are interesting as bearing some resemblance to the psalms of the Old Testament. The German scholar H. Zimmern has made a collection of the psalms of penance under the heading " Babylonian Penitential Psalms " (*Babylonische Busspsalmen*). He thinks that the impetus was given to this class of composition by national calamities rather than by personal grievances. The hymns often contain historical allusions, and sometimes include a prayer for the king. For specimens of these psalms, see Morris Jastrow, *Rel.;* W. Bousset.

BABY-TOWERS. In China it has been the practice to throw away the corpses of infants. In some parts of the Empire they have been left in urns or wooden boxes in the open country. In other parts structures called baby-towers have been built to receive them. These are round, polygonal, or square, and are constructed of stone blocks or of bricks. They have an aperture like a window into which the infants are dropped. Sometimes there are two apertures, one labelled " male infants," the other inscribed " female babies." On a slab of stone in front of such a tower may be found the inscription, " Pagoda or Tower for hoarding up bones " or " Place of Resort for Infants." See J. J. M. de Groot, *R.S.C.*

BACABS. A name given to four beings, upholders of the firmament, in the mythology of the Mayan Indians of Yucatan. Their names were Kan, Muluc, Ix, and Cauac. They represented the east, north, west, and south; and had as their symbolic colours yellow, white, black, and red.

BACCANARISTS. A religious order (also called " Paccanarists "), founded by one Baccanari or Paccanari of Trentino in 1798. Their proper title was Regular Clerks of the Faith of Jesus. Baccanari established his monastery in a country house near Spoleto with the idea of reviving the Jesuit Society of Jesus. The movement spread to France and Holland; but in 1804, when the Society of Jesus was re-established in Naples, it necessarily lost ground, and in 1814, on the restoration of the Jesuits, it ceased to exist. See *Cath. Dict.*

BACCHUS. One of the Greek names and the common Roman name for Dionysus, the god of wine.

BACULARII. An Anabaptist sect the members of which believed that Christians are forbidden in the Scriptures to carry any weapon but a staff.

BADI. A Malay term denoting something half-material, half-personal.

BADUHENNA, GROVE OF. A sacred grove where the Romans were defeated A.D. 28 (Tacitus, *Annals*, iv., 73).

BAELDAEG. The Anglo-Saxon form of Balder (*q.v.*), one of the gods of the Ancient Teutons.

BAETYLS. Since these objects are referred to as " bætyls, animated stones " (Sanchoniathon, Βαιτύλια, λίθους ἐμψύχους), the original meaning seems to be meteorites or supposed thunderbolts (see E. B. Tylor, *P.C.*). But the term is applied to small portable stones which were supposed to possess magic virtues.

BAGDAD, JEWS IN. The Bagdad Jew is described by E. J. Banks (*Bismya, or The Lost City of Adab*, 1912) as very superstitious. The following are examples of some of their superstitions. A wife may not look into a mirror, or sweep the floor of her house, or bring a saucepan into the house after sunset. " When her child dies, she forgets the old Hebrew Law, and takes a pig into the house to protect the other children from the evil eye; if the pig should die, a coat for the child is made from its skin." A large tomb in the desert to the East of Bagdad, which, though modern, is said to be the tomb of Joshua (Son of Nun), is a sacred place of pilgrimage for the Jewesses of the city. They gather also about a large English gun in a public square. Stroking it, they whisper their prayers, their troubles, and their hopes into its mouth. " They place lighted candles in tiny paper boats in the river, and, as the current bears them away, they read in the flickering flame whatever fate has in store for them."

BAGHARRA DEO. A Hindu deity, the tiger, worshipped as the protector of cattle against wild animals by the Kawars, a primitive tribe living in the hills of the Chhattisgarh Districts north of the Mahānadi in India.

BĀGHESHWAR. An Indian deity, the tiger god, worshipped by the Bharias.

BAGNOLENSES. A branch of the Cathari in the thirteenth century. They were also called Baiolenses, being named after Bagnolo or Baiolo, a town of Provence. They had much in common with the Albanenses (*q.v.*), and were perhaps forerunners of the Albigenses (*q.v.*). They held that matter was created by God alone, but that out of it an evil spirit made the four elements, earth, air, fire, and water, and so formed the world. See J. H. Blunt.

BAHAISM. A religion of Persian origin, a development of Babism (*q.v.*). At the end of the year 1852 many of the Babis were exiled to Bagdad by the Persian and Ottoman governments. One of the exiles was Bahā'u'llāh, an early disciple of the Bāb. His real name was Mīrzā Ḥusain 'Alī Nūrī, and he belonged to a powerful and noble family. He was born on the 12th of November, 1817. When he was nearly thirty he determined to consecrate all his energies to the cause of Bābism. He did not meet the Bāb, but he corresponded with him regularly. At Bagdad he became leader and organiser of the exiles. In the course of this work he became convinced that he was the Supreme Manifestation heralded by the Bāb, but he kept the conviction a secret from all but his most intimate friends. The party that gathered round Bahā'u'llāh grew to such an extent that in course of time it came to be considered dangerous. The leader was summoned to Constantinople. Before he left his movement underwent a new development. He declared himself to be the Supreme Manifestation of God prophesied by the Bâb. His followers were to be henceforth not Babis but Bahais. And he made the startling pronouncement that foreign peoples, infidels, were no longer to be considered unclean. " The times were distant since Moses, Jesus or Muhammad had brought them special laws. God would speak again, and this time, through His Supreme Manifestation, he would lead reconciled men toward progress, and regenerate them by love. Disdainful of the comforts of this world, they ought only to strive to develop their spirituality. Thus, the work begun by the Bāb would find in him its accomplishment and its end in the renovation and unification of all religions! " (H. Dreyfus). Bahā'u'llāh was four months in Constantinople. He was then sent to Adrianople (1864). Here he addressed letters to the rulers in Europe and America urging them to assist him in introducing universal fraternity and peace. In 1868 the Sultan banished him to 'Akkā, whither he was accompanied by his faithful disciples. They were at first imprisoned in the fortress and were treated rather harshly. After a time, however, they were released, and new-comers joined their colony, Buddhists, Parsees, Musulmans, and others. " One has not often, I think," writes H. Dreyfus, " had the opportunity of observing an economic and social phenomenon such as this little community composed as it was of individuals belonging to the most diverse and equally fanatical religions, having up to this time lived in the most different surroundings, accustomed to conceptions of existence often contradictory; and who had now come to carry into action the principles of detachment and of human fraternity, around the Prophet himself, which until then they had been powerless to realise in their native land. Their conduct was so perfect, their morality so high, their harmony so complete, that, although they have been there for forty years, no judge has had yet to intervene for them in any legal disputes." From 1869 to 1892 the leader dictated to some of his disciples a number of treatises. These included " The Most Holy Book " and " The Book of the Testament." When Bahā'u'llāh died at the end of May, 1892, his son 'Abdu'l-Bahā (b. May, 1844), who had been a tower of strength to his father, assumed the leadership. His opinions and advice have been sought on all hands by the Bahais. "Thus he is effectively the centre of this great movement, which having started from the Persian mountains, to-day re-unites people from all corners of the earth in one unique aim—that of the progress of humanity." Bahā'u'llāh exhorted the ministers of State to make some one language universal, and to institute tribunals of arbitration. He insists " that all nations should become one in faith and all men as brothers; that the bonds of affection and unity between the sons of men should be strengthened." The Bahais are required to live a spiritual life, but not a life of austerity and solitude. 'Abdu'l-Bahā says: " We were made to be happy and not sad; for joy, not for sorrow. Happiness is life; sadness is death; spiritual happiness is eternal life. It is a light that the night does not extinguish; it is an honour that shame does not follow, an existence which is not resolved into annihilation! For happiness the worlds and contingent beings have been created." See H. Dreyfus, *The Universal Religion: Bahaism*, 1909.

BAHMAN. Originally called Vohu-manô, "good mind," the name of a Zoroastrian god. Plutarch (" On Isis and Osiris," xlvi. and xlvii.) describes the deity as "the god of benevolence." Bahman " pervades the whole living good creation, and all the good thoughts, words, and deeds of men are wrought by him " (Haug).

BAHRĀM. According to R. V. Russell and R. B. Hīra Lāl, Bahrām of Nāchangaon near Pulgaon is the tutelary deity of the Wardha Dhangars. The Dhangars are the Marātha caste of shepherds and blanket-weavers in India.

BAIRAGIS. A general term for Hindu ascetics of any Vishnuite sect who are accustomed to go about naked, and pride themselves on having destroyed the power of sexual passion. This latter they are supposed to do either by practising great abstemiousness in eating and drinking, or by the use of drugs, or even by means of some such mechanical contrivance as a heavy weight fastened to the generative organs. Russell and Hira Lāl note that usually the term Bairagi is not applied to the Kabīrpanthi, the Swāmi-Nārāyan, the Satnāmi, the Sikh religious orders, or to the Chaitanya sect of Bengal. See J. A. Dubois and H. K. Beauchamp.

BAÏRAM. The Persian and Turkish name for one of the two great Mohammedan festivals. It follows the fast called Ramadan, and lasts three days or more. There is a second Bairam seventy days after the first. This last four days.

BAKHTASHIYEH. The Bakhtashiyeh or Baghdashiyeh are an order of Dervishes which was founded by Haji Bakhtash (d. 1357).

BĀLA GOPĀLA. A name for the child-god Krishna, a form of Krishna worshipped by modern Hindus. See E. W. Hopkins.

BALAAM'S ASS. Reinach remarks that one of the most curious episodes in the book of Numbers (see NUMBERS, BOOK OF) " is that of Balaam the prophet, whose ass seems to have been an echo of the worship of the ass, considered as an oracular animal." He compares the story (Numbers xxii.) with those animal-fables which were widely prevalent in ancient times (cp. the *Encycl. Bibl., s.v.* " Balaam," where Addis compares the Babylonian beast-stories, and the speaking horse in Homer's *Iliad,* xix. 404), and thinks that " the primitive stories which were combined and revised to form the Bible must have bristled with tales of animals." But he is obliged to admit that in the Bible as preserved to us animals only speak on rare occasions. There are only two instances—that of the serpent in the Book of Genesis and that of Balaam's ass in the Book of Numbers. Why are there not more? The truth may be that the Hebrew stories are not on a level with ordinary animal-fables, but were suggested by real psychical or spiritual experiences which seem to have been granted in unusually rich measure to the Hebrews. Balaam was requested by Balak, king of Moab, to go and curse the Israelites, that is to say, to bring them under the baneful influence of a powerful spell. Balaam at first refused to do this. He realized intuitively that this people was under the protection of the Divine Power. When at length he did consent to go, it was with great reluctance and hesitation. Now it has often been remarked that the mental state of a rider influences the animal which he rides. Balaam's uncertainty communicated itself to his ass, and the animal tried several times to turn back. The master beat the animal, and at length, we are told, the ass spoke and rebuked him. Of course animals do not speak. But it is nevertheless possible that Balaam heard a voice, and that he or his reporter believed that the voice proceeded from the animal. The words spoken have been altered in accordance with this idea. We now know that the hearing of a voice is a not uncommon psychical experience (cp. BURNING BUSH). And Balaam was just the kind of man to have had the kind of experience denoted by clairaudience (*q.v.*) and clairvoyance (*q.v.*). " Among the various nations of the world we find instances in which we are able to observe how certain persons, popularly regarded as a special type of men, distinct from their fellows, pass into ecstatic states, and in them make peculiar observations. Generally these experiences come to them during worship, or whilst they offer fervent prayer, or during some other powerful religious occupation of the mind. They get into a condition in which they are in a peculiar sense cut off from the world, but in which their souls are all the more active, and respond readily to influences which have no effect upon a man in his ordinary waking life. In this condition they see visions and hear voices and words, the significance of which is unknown to the ordinary man " (R. Kittel, *Scientific Study of the O.T.*, 1910). For the story of Balaam, see *Encycl. Bibl.;* G. B. Gray, *Numbers*, in the *I.C.C.*, 1903; A. R. S. Kennedy, *Leviticus and Numbers*, in the " Century Bible."

BÂLÂJI. Bâlâji is the name of one of the modern gods

of the Hindus, an incarnation of the Supreme Triad (Brahma-Vishnu-Siva). Sir Alfred C. Lyall states (*Asiatic Studies*) that he is one of the four most popular gods in the province of Berar in Central India. He thinks that not so very long ago he must have been a notable living man. Bâlâji is worshipped on Fridays as the younger brother of Rāma by the Dhangars, the Marātha caste of shepherds and blanket-weavers.

BALANCE OF OSIRIS, THE. A familiar representation in the religion of ancient Egypt. In the underworld, in the judgment-hall of Osiris (*q.v.*), the heart of a deceased person is weighed by Horus (*q.v.*) and Anubis (*q.v.*) to see whether it is lighter than truth. In a magical text of the Hellenistic period it is said: "he whose evil deeds are more in number than the good, is given to the Devourer of the underworld: his soul and his body are destroyed and he shall live no longer. He whose good deeds are more in number than the evil, he is received among the divine counsellors of the Lord of the underworld, while his soul goes with the glorious justified ones to heaven." See A. Erman.

BALDACCHINO. An Italian word for a canopy. It is supposed to be derived from Baaldak, the name by which Bagdad was known at the time of the Crusades. The Baldacchino is used in the Roman Catholic Church. The canopy placed over the high-altar hangs from the roof of the church or is supported on four pillars. Canopies may also be erected over a pulpit or above a bishop's throne, etc. Since the time of Constantine canopies resembling in shape the bowl of a cup have been suspended over the altar-table. Inside this canopy was hung a vessel containing the Holy Sacrament. This canopy was called *ciborium*. Its use in the Church of England has been declared illegal (Dec. 15, 1873). Baldacchino is also the name of a canopy held over the Roman Catholic priest as he carries the Host in procession on Holy Thursday, etc. See *Oath. Dict.*

BALDER. Also written Baldr, the name of a god in Teutonic religion (cp. Anglo-Saxon *bealdor* "prince"). He is a god of light. His original home was perhaps in Denmark, for he figures most frequently in Danish legends. In Denmark too are Baldersbrönd where he quenched the thirst of warriors by making water spring from the ground, and Baldrshöje where he is buried. Balder is said to have been wounded in a fierce struggle with Hotherus, son of a Swedish king, the two antagonists being rivals for the love of Nanna, the beautiful daughter of the Norwegian king Gevarus. Balder could only be wounded by Miming's sword, of which Hotherus had contrived to obtain possession. There are variations of the legend. According to another account, he was killed with mistletoe. All things had been put under oath not to harm him, except the mistletoe, which had been overlooked. In Norse mythology Balder has become more human: he is "the beaming hero, beloved of all" (C. de La Saussaye). Scenes from the legend of Balder seem to have been depicted on the two golden horns, dating from the fifth or beginning of the sixth century, found in Southern Jutland in 1639 and 1734. There is also reference to the legend in a magic formula (perhaps of the eighth century) found at Merseburg in 1841. See P. D. Chantepie de La Saussaye, *Rel. of the Teutons*, 1902.

BALKISHEN. The boy Krishna, one of the names of the Hindu god Krishna.

BALMARCODES. A shrine of the Punic or Phoenician god Baal Marcod, "the lord of dances," has been found not far from Berytus. In inscriptions of the Roman age this god is called Balmarcodes. His worship was introduced into Syria by the Phoenicians.

BĀLMĪK. A saint (also known as Bālnek) worshipped by the Mehtars, the caste of sweepers and scavengers in India. According to R. V. Russell and R. B. Hira Lāl, he is really the huntsman Vālmīki, the reputed author of the Rāmāyana, who in turn was originally a hunter called Ratnakār.

BALOR. A deity with an evil eye, one of the gods of the Irish Celts of the Fomorian cult.

BAMACHARI. A sub-division of the Hindu sect known as Saktas (*q.v.*). The Bamachari are left-handed Saktas, *i.e.*, worshippers of Sakti, the female force in Nature, personified as a goddess. They are so called as distinguished from the right-handed Saktas and the extreme Saktas. See J. C. Oman, *B.T.M.I.*

BAMBINO. An Italian word, meaning literally "babe." The term is used in art of the swaddled figure of the infant Jesus. The figure, carved in wood, in the church of the Ara Cœli at Rome (*Santissimo Bambino*) is supposed to possess the power of miraculously healing the sick.

BAMPTON LECTURES. A Church of England course of Lectures on Divinity delivered at Oxford, and named after their founder, the Rev. John Bampton. Bampton was a Prebendary of Salisbury Cathedral. He died in 1751, leaving a legacy of £120 per annum for the endowment of eight lectures. The lectures are delivered as sermons at Great St. Mary's, and are afterwards published. The object of the lectures is "to confirm and establish the Christian faith, and to confute all heretics and schismatics, upon the divine authority of the holy Scriptures, upon the authority of the writings of the primitive Fathers as to the faith and practice of the primitive Church, upon the divinity of our Lord and Saviour Jesus Christ, upon the divinity of the Holy Ghost, upon the articles of the Christian Faith as comprehended in the Apostles' and Nicene Creeds."

BAN. In the Old Testament we often read of things or persons being put under a ban, that is to say, being devoted to Jehovah by destruction. The term use (*ḥrm*, Greek ἀνάθεμα; Authorised Version "accursed thing"; Revised Version "devoted thing") is derived from a common Semitic root. It is the root from which harem (a place consecrated or set apart) comes. Amongst the things devoted to Jehovah were: idols (Deuteronomy vii. 25), Canaanite cities (Deut. xx. 16-18), enemies (I. Samuel xv.; cp. the Moabite Stone l. 16 *f.*), property (Micah iv. 13), and guilty persons (Joshua vii.). Sometimes the devoted thing seems to have been a kind of free-will offering or sacrifice to Jehovah. Leviticus xxvii. 28 says that "no devoted thing, that a man shall devote unto the Lord of all that he hath, whether of man or beast, or of the field of his possession, shall be sold or redeemed; every devoted thing is most holy unto the Lord. None devoted, which shall be devoted of men, shall be ransomed; he shall surely be put to death." Apparently the idea in such cases was to purchase by a vow the friendly aid of the deity. See *Encycl. Bibl.*

BANA. A term used in Singhalese Buddhism. Bana is a recitation which, even though the hearer does not understand the words, is supposed to act as a charm, averting illnesses and exorcising evil spirits. In connection with its use there is a custom called *pirit* (Pâli *parittа*). Laymen are accustomed to hire monks to read *bana* day and night without interruption. The ceremony usually lasts seven days, and is performed in the preaching-hall of a monastery or in some other suitable building. "The monks relieve one another in such a way that no smallest pause occurs to break the charm. A Buddhist relic lies on the platform where the monk is reciting, and a sacred cord encircles the whole building, beginning at the place of recitation and leading back to it again, so that by its means the working of the incantation may be substantially held together. Besides the two monks who read the *bana* simultaneously, there are usually others assembled in the building, who murmur with them and keep hold of the cord which encircles the sacred area. The festival ends with a procession and a mythological performance, which is often the cause of lavish expenditure. Thus the word of the Buddha's doctrine is perverted into a magic formula." See H. Hackmann.

BÂNAT SU'ÂD. An Arabic poem in praise of Mohammed. See BURDA.

BANBURY MAN. A name given to Puritans in the sixteenth and seventeenth centuries.

BAND OF HOPE. A name given (1855) to children's Societies the members of which have promised to abstain from intoxicants. The name is due to Jabez Tunnicliffe, of Leeds. One of the chief leaders in the movement was Stephen Shirley.

BANDA. A deified man, the principal deity of the Kharias, a primitive Kolarian tribe in India.

BANDANA. An annual festival, preliminary to marriage, among the Sunthāls, a wild tribe of India. The unmarried men and women "indulge together in an indescribable orgie, at the end of which each man selects the woman he prefers" (Hopkins).

BANDE NOIRE. When the French Revolution was supposed to have rendered useless many such buildings as castles, monasteries, churches, chapels, abbeys, societies were formed (*bande noire*) for the purpose of purchasing them, pulling them down, and selling the materials.

BANDS, CLERICAL. A kind of neckcloth or collar formerly worn by clergymen. They are mentioned as early as 1566 as part of the dress of the English clergy which was worn out of doors. They consist of two strips of linen which hang like a necktie. Barristers in England still wear something similar. Graduates at the Universities used to have them, and scholars at Christ's Hospital and Winchester School still have them. In the Church of England they have survived as part of the clerical Court dress. In France and Germany they are still worn. Their origin has been found in the broad collars generally worn in the Tudor period or in the ecclesiatical vestment known as the Amice (*q.v.*). See G. S. Tyack, *Historic Dress of the Clergy*, 1897.

BANGOR, USE OF. In the early days of the Church in Britain various places had liturgies of their own representing somewhat different modes of celebrating Mass. These were called "Uses," and Bangor was one of the places which had a use of its own.

BANGORIAN CONTROVERSY. A controversy in the Church of England (1717-1720) caused by a sermon preached by Dr. B. Hoadly (1676-1761), Bishop of Bangor, before King George I. on the text, "My kingdom is not of this world." In this sermon, which was published by Royal request, the Bishop laid stress on the fact that the Kingdom of God was spiritual and not temporal. Dr. Hoadly was censured by Convocation for denying the royal supremacy in ecclesiastical matters and for trying to subvert the discipline and government of the Church. The King, however, prorogued Convocation (1717). A great many pamphlets were written on one side or the other. See J. H. Blunt.

BANJĀRAS. An Indian caste of carriers and drivers of pack-bullocks, also known as Wanjāris, Labhānas, or Mukeris. Their favourite deities are Banjāri Devi, whose shrine in the forest is often a heap of stones; Mithu Bhūkia, who was originally a freebooter; and Siva Bhāia, the great brother to all women, who was wooed in vain by Māri Māta, the goddess of cholera. The Banjāras worship also their pack-cattle, practise witchcraft, and are said to offer human sacrifices. See R. V. Russell.

BANNERS. In the Roman Catholic Church banners are used in processions and services. Inside the church they are hung round or near the altar. "As the soldier in battle looks to the colours of his regiment, and while they float aloft, knows that the day may still be won, and is animated to do valiantly, so should Christians, as the Church by her sanction of banners reminds us, fix their gaze on that Cross of Christ which is the standard of their warfare, and be continually animated by the thought to fresh courage" (Addis and Arnold).

BANNS. A solemn proclamation of intended marriage made in Christian churches or in licensed public chapels. The proclamation is now ordered by Act of Parliament. In 1215 it had been made a general ecclesiastical law by the Fourth Lateran Council. See *Prot. Dict.*; *Cath. Dict*.

BANSHEE. The banshee is a female sprite or fairy in Irish folklore. Originally every family would seem to have possessed a banshee of its own, that is to say, "the spirit of one of its ancestors who always appeared to announce by its weird warning the approaching decease of any member of the family" (W. G. Wood-Martin); but she came to be identified with one of the ancient goddesses and to be associated particularly with aristocratic families. Often, too, she is the ghost of someone who has suffered violence at the hands of a progenitor of the family. W. G. Wood-Martin points out that the banshee resembles the guardian angel or saint of the Christian. She warned mortals of impending danger, and pointed out to them the right line of conduct to pursue. The moan of the wind in crevices of the rocks before a storm was supposed to be the wail of the banshee, and other strange noises (*e.g.*, in old houses) were explained in the same way. See W. G. Wood-Martin.

BAPHOMET. A name associated with the Templars. It has been explained as a cabalistic formation, an abbreviation, written backwards, of "templi omnium hominum pacis abbas," which means "abbot (or father) of the temple of peace of all men." An earlier explanation, however, is that the word is a corruption of Mahomet, and that the Templars venerated the prophet. Whatever Baphomet was, it seems to have been represented or symbolized by a small two-headed human figure.

BAPTISM, CHRISTIAN. A word formed from a Greek root meaning "to dip," and used as a special designation of one of the rites of the Christian Church. The practice seems to have been suggested by the Jews, who removed ceremonial uncleanness by bathing the body in water and required Gentiles to be baptised on becoming Jewish proselytes. But the rite, it is claimed, assumed a new significance. Whereas Jewish baptism was thought of only as a means of getting rid of ceremonial uncleanness, Christian baptism was regarded as "a baptism of repentance for the remission of sins." Jesus allowed himself to be baptised by John the Baptist. He did not himself baptise, however, and it has been questioned whether he himself instituted the rite. True, he is represented as having done so. In Matthew xxviii. 19, he is represented as saying to his disciples when he appeared to them after his crucifixion: "Go ye, therefore, and make disciples of all the nations, baptizing them into the name of the Father and of the Son and of the Holy Ghost." In Mark xvi. 16 we are told that he said: "He that believeth and is baptized shall be saved; but he that disbelieveth shall be damned." But there is evidence that the passage in Matthew's Gospel has been edited, and the passage in Mark's Gospel belongs to the last twelve verses which are widely recognised now to be a later addition. At any rate, the Christian community adopted the rite at an early date. When Peter appealed to the multitude on the day of Pentecost, saying, "Repent ye, and be baptized, each one of you, in the name of Jesus Christ for the remission of your sins, and ye shall receive the gift of the Holy Spirit" (Acts ii. 38), about three thousand persons are said to have been baptized. We need not suppose that people were required always to immerse themselves. The pouring of water on the head would no doubt often suffice. The Greek word for "to baptize" (Βαπτίζειν) could be used in a wide sense. It sometimes meant simply "to wash" (cp. Luke xi. 38; Mark vii. 4; Hebrews ix. 10). Persons were baptized at first "in the name of Jesus Christ" (Acts ii. 38, x. 48) or "in the name of the Lord Jesus" (Acts viii. 16, xix. 5). Afterwards, with the development of the doctrine of the Trinity, they were baptized "in the name of the Father and of the Son and of the Holy Ghost" (cp. Justin Martyr, *Apol.* i. 61). In Colossians ii. 11 *f.* St. Paul seems to compare baptism with circumcision. Since Jewish boys were circumcised on the eighth day after birth, this seems to suggest that infants were baptised in the early Christian community (cp. the references to "households" in Acts xvi. 15, 31-33, I. Corinthians i. 16). Towards the end of the second century we hear almost everywhere of "Catechumens." This was the name given to adult converts who were being prepared for baptism. The rite of initiation from the time of the apostles "included two principal parts: the bath, or baptism with water, and the laying on of hands. The first rite conveyed the special gift of remission of sin; it was the symbol of the purification of the soul, by conversion and grafting into Jesus; the second rite carried with it sanctification by the descent of the Holy Ghost upon the soul of the neophyte. As time went on, other ceremonies were introduced. Tertullian speaks not only of baptism and the laying on of hands, but also mentions unction, the consignation or imposition of the sign of the cross, and lastly, a mixture of milk and honey given the newly initiated to drink. And as he adds that all these ceremonies were practised by the Marcionites, they must date back at least to the first half of the second century" (Louis Duchesne). At baptism the catechumens "were required to renounce publicly, before the whole Christian assembly, Satan, his pomps, and his works, which meant, in fact, paganism, its worship and its lax morality. Then they declared their faith in Jesus Christ, and in token thereof they recited a profession of faith." This profession of faith was a form of the Apostles' Creed. The ancient ceremonial is largely retained in the Roman Catholic Church. "The priest meets the child at the door of the church; drives the devil from him; breathes thrice upon his face, to signify the new spiritual life which is to be breathed into his soul; puts salt into his mouth, as a sign that he is to be freed from the corruption of sin; signs him on the forehead and breast with the sign of the cross, and leads him into the temple of God. The recipient then, through his sponsors, professes his faith by reciting the Creed and the Our Father. Then the priest exorcises the child; anoints his ears and nostrils with spittle—after our Lord's example, who thus cured the deaf and dumb man—and asks him in three separate interrogations whether he renounces Satan, all his works, and all his pomps. He next anoints him with the oil of catechumens on the breast and between the shoulders. The ancient athletes were anointed before their contests in the arena, and in the same way the young Christian is prepared for the 'good fight' which lies before him. The priest pours water three times on his head, in the form of a cross, at the same time pronouncing the words 'I baptise thee,' etc. After baptism, chrism is put on the top of his head, to signify his union with Christ, the head of his Church; he receives a white garment, and a burning light in his hands, symbols of innocence and of the light of faith and charity" (Addis and Arnold). In the Church of England there are three forms of Service: one for the public baptism of infants, a second for the private baptism of children in houses, and a third for the baptism of those of riper years. In the public baptism of infants, the priest requests the sponsors to name the child, "and then naming it after them (if they shall certify him that the child may well endure it) he shall dip it in the water discreetly and warily, saying" the formula of baptism. "But if they certify that the child is weak, it shall suffice to pour water upon it." In practice, whether a child is weak or not, the latter method is now generally followed. After this "the priest shall make a cross upon the child's forehead" saying: "We receive this child into the congregation of Christ's flock, and do sign him with the sign of the cross," etc. In the baptism of those of riper years, the priest requests the godfather and godmother to name the person to be baptised, "and then shall dip him in the water, or pour water upon him." The controversies about baptism which have arisen from time to time are dealt with under separate headings. Cp. ABLUTIONS. See *Encycl. Bibl; Cath. Dict.; Prot. Dict.;* Louis Duchesne, *Hist.;* Chambers' *Encycl.*

BAPTISM OF BLOOD. A baptism of blood seems to have figured in the worship of Attis (*q.v.*). The worshipper stood in a pit while the blood of a bull which had been stabbed to death poured through a grating above his head. In this baptism he was born again to eternal life, and for a time he was dieted as a new-born child. The ancient Greeks purged a manslayer by smearing him with pig's blood, the idea perhaps being that the blood is accepted by the offended spirit "as a substitute for the blood of the guilty person" (J. G. Frazer, *Adonis Attis Osiris*, 1906). Sometimes a child receives a baptism of blood (*e.g.*, among the Gipsies of northern Hungary), the object being "to unite the child in the closest bond with the person whose blood is shed." See further E. S. Hartland, *Perseus*, 1894-1896.

BAPTISTERY. The name of a place or building specially set apart for the performance of Christian baptism. In ancient times it was a separate building attached to Cathedral churches. The baptistery was circular or polygonal with a bath in the middle, which in the West was called "piscina." There is a specimen at Ravenna in Italy belonging to about A.D. 430. The baptistery is now only a name for part of a church. "According to the Roman Rituale, it should be railed off, it should have a gate fastened by a lock, and be adorned, if possible, with a picture of Christ's baptism by St. John" (Addis and Arnold). See W. R. W. Stephens, *Common Prayer*, 1901.

BAPTISTS. A large body of Christians who object to infant baptism, and claim that, in the light of Scripture and of the original Greek term (*baptizein*), baptism is efficacious only when persons are baptized by immersion at an age at which they are able fully to understand the meaning of the rite. Baptism is a new birth ("Except a man be born again, he cannot see the kingdom of God") of which the recipient must be fully conscious, having been taught the truths of Christianity. Appeal is made to Romans vi. 4: "We were buried therefore with him through baptism into death, that like as Christ was raised from the dead through the glory of the Father, so we also might walk in newness of life"; and Colossians ii. 12: "having been buried with him in baptism, wherein ye were also raised with him through faith in the working of God, who raised him from the dead." The Baptists do not care to be identified with the Anabaptists of the sixteenth century, whose principles were certainly in some respects very different. Apparently they claim a kind of apostolic succession for their practices. Some of their principles, however, they find represented among such sects as the Cathari and Albigenses of the Middle Ages. In the twelfth century there were numbers of baptists among the Waldenses. Two leading opponents of infant baptism, Peter de Brueys and Arnold of Brescia, were condemned by the Lateran Council in 1139. Arnold of Brescia and Henry of Lausanne gathered around them many followers and organised a kind of Baptist Church at Toulouse in the south of France. Their followers were called Petrobrusians or Henricians. Coming down to later times, a connection is suggested with the Mennonites ("Dutch Baptists") of the sixteenth century, and more especially with the Brownists (*q.v.*) of the early part of the seventeenth century. A Baptist Church is said indeed to have existed in England in 1417. At any rate, we are told that "there were certainly Baptist 'churches' in England as early as 1589, and there could scarcely have been several organised communities without the corresponding opinions having been held by individuals and some churches established for years previous to this date" (H. S. Skeats and C. S. Miall). But Robert Browne and his successors seem to have been the founders of new denominations. Henry Jacob (1563-1624) is said to have changed the name "Brownists" into "Independents," and in 1616 to have established at Blackfriars, London, a community which claimed to be "The first Independent or Congregational Church in England." As far as this particular claim is concerned, "it is now clearly established that an Independent church, of which Richard Fitz was pastor, existed in 1568" (Skeats and Miall). But the importance of Henry Jacob's church remains. In course of time certain members of this congregation, having convinced themselves that baptism ought not to be administered to infants, separated, and in 1633 established a distinct church of which the minister was John Spilsbury. In 1639 there was another congregation which met in Crutched Friars. In the same year Roger Williams (1604?-1683) founded the first Baptist Church in North America at Providence. The spread of the movement in England after this was so rapid that in 1646 there are believed to have been forty-six congregations in and around London. In the reigns of Henry VIII. and of Elizabeth, the Baptists were numerous and important enough to attract the notice of the authorities and to suffer persecution. Since the reign of William III., in which they obtained a full measure of religious liberty, their progress has been unchecked. In 1908 there were 424,008 members of the Baptist Union (formed in 1813) in the British Isles; and in the United States the members numbered over 6,000,000. The Baptists have excellent Colleges, and send their missionaries to India, Ceylon, China, Palestine, the West Indies, Africa, Brittany, and Italy. Their church-government is congregational. The body has a number of sub-divisions. There are: General Baptists or Arminian Baptists (American Free-will Baptists) who believe that Christ died to save all men; and Particular Baptists who believe that he died to save only an elect number of persons. There are also Free-will Baptists, Old School Baptists, Six-Principle Baptists, Seventh-day Baptists, Se-Baptists, Scottish Baptists, Tunkers, Campbellites, and Hard-Shell Baptists. See John Hunt; J. H. Blunt; *Prot. Dict.;* Chambers' *Encycl.;* the *D.N.B.*

BARAITHA. A name given to additions to the Jewish Mishnah (*q.v.*). The term means literally "external," and its use corresponds to some extent to that of the term "apocrypha." The Baraithas are Tannaite traditions (see TANNAIM) which have not been incorporated in the Mishnah. See W. O. E. Oesterley and G. H. Box.

BARASHNOM OF NINE NIGHTS. A Parsee ceremony of purification, practised mostly by priests and lasting nine nights. The ceremony is described in the Vendidad (*Fargard* ix.). "The person who has to undergo the ceremony must drink the urine of a cow, sit on stones within the compass of certain magic circles, and while moving from one heap of stones to another he must rub his body with cow's urine, then with sand, and lastly wash it with water. This custom has descended from the most ancient times, when a purifying and healing influence was ascribed to the urine proceeding from so sacred an animal as the cow was to the ancient Aryans" (Haug). See Martin Haug.

BARBELIOTES. The Gnostic sect in Iberia referred to by Irenaeus, Augustine, and Epiphanius. It was named after Barbelos or Barbelo, a name which was perhaps framed out of two Hebrew words, *bar baalah*, "son of the Lady," or *bar baal*, "son of the Lord." The Barbeliotes claimed that Barbelo was the son of the Father by a mother named Jaldabaoth or Sabaoth. From him came Light who was anointed by the Father and became Christ. The sect received the name Borborians from the Greek word *borboros*, "filth" or "mud," probably on account of some of their secret practices. See J. H. Blunt.

BARCELONA, TREATY OF. A treaty made between Charles V. and Pope Clement VII. in 1529. The Emperor consented to receive his crown from the Pope's hands at Rome, and undertook as far as possible to prevent the reformed religion from spreading.

BARDESANISTS. The followers of Bardesanes (A.D. 154-222), a Syrian, who was born at Edessa in Mesopotamia. It has been thought that he was the tutor of Clement of Alexandria. He was the "last of the Gnostics," but developed a system of his own. He tried to explain the origin of evil by assuming two supreme principles, the one good, the other evil, which are co-equal. He asserted that the body of Christ was not real, but celestial, and he would not accept the doctrine of the resurrection of the body. He wrote many hymns which proved a successful means of spreading his teaching. See A. Hilgenfeld, *Bardesanes*, 1864.

BAREFOOTED FRIARS. There has been no distinct order of friars who have made it a practice to go barefoot; but a certain number of mendicant friars belonging to various orders (*e.g.*, Carmelites, Franciscans) have done so.

BARLAAMITES. The followers of Barlaam, a Calabrian abbot. He was an opponent of the Hesychasts, mystics among the monks of Mount Athos, who believed that by bringing the body into a state of perfect repose and fixing their gaze steadily on their own navels, they were able to cultivate the "inner light." Barlaam called them "omphalopsychi," and accused them of believing in two Gods, a God invisible, and a God visible. A Council held at Constantinople A.D. 1340 supported the Hesychasts and condemned Barlaam.

BAR-MITZVAH. Literally "Son of the Commandment," a Jewish designation given to a boy when he reaches his religious maturity, *i.e.*, when he is thirteen years of age. From this time he has to observe the whole Law. The occasion is marked by a special ceremony in the Synagogue at which the boy is called upon to read aloud or chant a portion of the Law, and by a festival in the home. See W. O. E. Oesterley and G. H. Box.

BARNABAS, EPISTLE OF. See APOSTOLIC FATHERS.

BARNABITES. The popular designation of the "Regular Clerks of the Congregation of St. Paul." They are called Barnabites because in the sixteenth century they preached in a church of St. Barnabas in Milan. The order was founded by St. Antonio Maria Zaccaria (in particular), Bartolommeo Ferrari, and Giacomo Antonio Morigena, and the foundation was sanctioned by Clement VII. in 1533. In 1579 St. Charles Borromeo, Archbishop of Milan, examined their constitutions, and finally approved and confirmed them. The Barnabites are a body of secular clergy who live in the world but devote their lives to the work of caring for the sick, instructing the young, preaching repentance, and sanctifying themselves. "Besides the three usual vows they take a fourth, never to seek any office or ecclesiastical dignity, and to accept no post outside of their order without the permission of the Pope. The habit is merely the black soutane worn by secular priests in Lombardy at the time of their foundation" (Addis and Arnold). They have now about twenty colleges in Italy, Austria, and France, their chief establishment being at Rome, where their General resides.

BARROWISTS. The followers of Henry Barrow (*d.* 1593). See BROWNISTS.

BARSANIANS. An offshoot of the Acephali (*q.v.*) in the second half of the fifth century A.D. They are said to have been followers of Barsanius, and have been identified with the Semidalites.

BARSANUPHITES. An offshoot of the Acephali (*q.v.*) at the end of the fifth century A.D. They took their name from one Barsanuphius.

BARSOM. In the Old Testament there is a reference (Ezekiel viii. 16, 17) to a practice of holding twigs towards the face in worship. The prophet reproves some of the Jews for doing this as well as for worshipping the sun. The Parsees have such a custom, aud the bundle of twigs which they use is called Barsom. In *Yasna* lvii. of the Zend-avesta the angel Sraosha (Srosh) is worshipped as "he who of Ahuramazda's creatures first worshipped Ahuramazda by means of arranging the sacred twigs (Barsom)" and as "he who first arranged the bundle of sacred twigs (Barsom), that with three, that with five, that with seven, and that with nine stalks, those which were as long as to go up to the knees, and those which went as far as the middle of the breast (he arranged them) to worship, to praise, to satisfy, and to extol the archangels." In one form of the ceremony with this bundle of sacred twigs, the twigs had to be arranged in a certain prescribed order while portions of a sacred book were being chanted. Thin metal wires are now generally used instead of twigs. See Martin Haug.

BARTHOLOMEW, MASSACRE OF ST. The name given to the well-known massacre of the Huguenots, because it took place on St. Bartholomew's Day, the 24th of August. Catharine de Medici, regent of France, planned that the Huguenots in Paris should be fallen upon and slaughtered on St. Bartholomew's Day, 1572. The signal was given by the ringing of a bell in the tower of the royal palace, and it is calculated that the number of persons who were killed exceeded 4,000. The provinces followed the example of Paris, continuing the slaughter for some weeks.

BARULI. A branch of the Albanenses in the twelfth century A.D. They maintained that Christ took a celestial kind of body and was not truly incarnate.

BASILIANS. A monastic order founded by St. Basil (*d.* 379), Bishop of Caesarea in Cappadocia. His mother Emelia and his sister Macrina had already founded monasteries in a desert region of Pontus when Basil, on his return from a visit to monasteries in Egypt, Palestine and Mesopotamia, established a monastic order of his own. Of his two rules, the Great and the Little, the Great comprised fifty-five articles, the Little three hundred and thirteen. These monastic rules now prevail in the Greek Church. St. Benedict himself seems to have taken hints from them. The Basilians have flourished in Southern Italy, Spain, Russia, Austrian Poland and Hungary. There is now a Basilian establishment at Plymouth, the College of St. Mary Immaculate. In Austrian Poland and Hungary these monks are called Ruthenians. See *Cath. Dict.*

BASILICA. A name applied to Christian churches about the beginning of the fourth century. In Rome before the time of Constantine the Christians seem to have used as places of worship the private basilicas of Roman palaces and sepulchral buildings (sometimes catacombs). In the age of Constantine they built basilicas of their own with distinctive features. In Syria many Christian basilicas have been unearthed in recent years, dating from the fourth century. The earliest of these are not characterised by distinctive features. "It is often only by the inscriptions that certain basilicas can be known as churches, since these are made in exact imitation of the public buildings of the Romans of the previous period" (Camden M. Cobern). "Between the fourth and fifth centuries there was some development in architecture, so that strange styles of capitals and a new and rich Christian symbolism appear. In the fifth century classic models of ornamentation are less and less used. The churches of this era, instead of the nine arches on either side of the nave as in the fourth century, now have seven and sometimes five arches, and the central nave becomes much wider and the apse arch much broader, while bands of chain and basket work ornament the mouldings. The churches are large and magnificent, often having splendid baptistries in connection with them, and vast inns for the accommodation of pilgrims; they often stand inside of strong forts, whose towers occasionally, as at Kasril-Benât, rise to six stories in height." The sixth century "saw the elaboration and perfection of all the architectural motifs that had been initiated and developed in the two centuries preceding." To this century belongs the church of St. Simeon Stylites at Kal'at Simân, described by H. C. Butler as the "most magnificent ruin of early Christian architecture in the world." One church, dated A.D 582, "very nearly anticipates by 500 years the Lombard and French Romanesque system, which has vaults constructed above the nave and side aisles." Cobern's account is based on Howard Crosby Butler's *Ancient Architecture in Syria*, 1910. See also the *Cath. Dict.*

BASILIDIANS. The followers of Basilides (*d.* about A.D. 139), one of the earliest of the great Alexandrian Gnostics (see GNOSTICS). He seems previously to have spent some time in Syria. Menander was one of his teachers. According to his own account, these also included St. Matthias and one Glaucias (otherwise unknown), who is supposed to have been associated closely with St. Peter. Basilides recognised one Supreme Being or First Cause, and called Him Abraxas. The letters of this name are supposed to give the number 365, like the name of the Persian sun-god Mithras. Abraxas has been explained as a Coptic word meaning "Hallowed by the Name." Basilides taught that from Abraxas sprang the Understanding or *Nous*, from the Understanding the Word or *Logos*, from the Word Providence, from Providence Power, from Power Wisdom, from Wisdom Righteousness, from Righteousness Peace. From these again sprang the higher angels, principalities, and powers; and from these the lower angels. The God of the Jews was only one of those angels of the lowest kind who created the world. Christ, the Son (*nous*) of the Supreme Being, was sent down to bring to man, who had become corrupt, heavenly knowledge. He joined himself to the man Jesus, and it was this man, not the

Christ, who was crucified. Regarding matter as evil, Basilides did not believe in the resurrection of the body. But he believed in a kind of metempsychosis or transmigration of souls. Saints and martyrs, he held, suffered because they had sinned in a previous stage of existence. Everyone had to atoue for his sins in this way, by living again in a different body. But in some people faith and godliness, are inborn. The Holy Spirit descended upon Jesus at his Baptism, and left him before his death. Basilides wrote some Commentaries. He did not recognise the Old Testament as authoritative, and rejected the Epistle to the Hebrews and the Epistles to Timothy and Titus. His followers seem to have developed and corrupted his teaching. See J. H. Blunt, and the literature under GNOSTICISM.

BASLE, CONFESSION OF. One of the most important of the Protestant confessions of faith drawn up in the sixteenth century (A.D. 1532-36). The Confession of Augsburg being considerd still too Catholic, the Confession of Basle was framed by Protestant ministers of Basle to repair these defects. It was reconstructed (A.D. 1536) by Bucer, Capito, and the theologians of Wurtemberg, renamed the Helvetic Confession, and accepted for all the Swiss churches at the Synod of Smalkalden. Another revision, made by Bullinger and published in Latin soon after 1560, was subscribed by all the Protestant Evangelical communities, having been first accepted by the magistrates of Mulhausen. Thus arose the name Mylhusian Confession. It was accepted by all the " ministers of the Church of Christ " in Switzerland " as a testimony to all the faithful that they remain in the unity of the true and ancient Church of Christ, teaching no new or erroneous doctrines, and having no connection with any sects or heresies; a fact of which all pious persons are invited to assure themselves by its perusal " (Preface). The Confession was accepted also by all the Reformed non-Lutheran communities in France and Flanders. See J. H. Blunt.

BASLE, COUNCIL OF. In accordance with decrees of the Council of Constance (A.D. 1414-1418) which recommended the convening of a general council every five years, Pope Martin V. summoned one to meet at Pavia in 1423. Difficulties having arisen with regard to this plan, the place was altered to Basle, and the date to July, 1431. Cardinal Julian Cesarini was nominated as papal legate and president. Many French and German bishops assembled at Basle; but in the meantime, Martin V. having died and his successor Pope Eugenius IV. having decided that there were objections to the suitability of Basle, the place of meeting was altered to Bologna. The bishops assembled at Basle under Cesarini opposed the transfer, and continued. The representatives from France and Germany had been joined by a few from Italy, Spain, and England. In 1432 the Pope sent a legate, Christopher, Bishop of Cervia, to confer with them, and in 1433 delegated other legates to be present, who were not well received. The next year a letter from the Pope seemed to have arranged matters, and the papal legates were admitted. In June 1435, however, the Council passed a decree for the reform of the Roman Chancery which the Pope would not sanction. A difference next arose among the members of the Council themselves on the question of removing the Council to Avignon or Ferrara, the majority deciding in favour of Avignon. The Pope, however, in October, 1437, formally transferred the Council to Ferrara. In May, 1439 those who remained at Basle under the Cardinal of Arles proceeded to depose Eugenius and to elect in his place Amadeus of Savoy, who became known as Felix V. In April, 1445, he abdicated, and the Council of Basle, now at Lausanne, recognised Nicholas V. See *Cath. Dict.*

BASMOTHEANS. A sect referred to in the Apostolic Constitutions (vi. 6), persons " who deny Providence, and say that the world is made by spontaneous motion, and take away the immortality of the soul." The name seems to be a variation or corruption of Masbotheans.

BASSINAM. A kind of ornament which plays a part in one of the ceremonies of a Hindu marriage. The ornament, decked with gold leaf or gold paper, and entwined with flowers, is placed on the foreheads of husband and wife as a protection against the evil eye of ill-disposed persons. See J. A. Dubois and H. K. Beauchamp.

BAST. The name of a goddess in the early religion of the ancient Egyptians. The Greek name is Bubastis. Bast delighted in music and dancing, and is commonly represented as holding in her hand the sistrum used by dancing-women, and on her arm a basket. As regards form, she is represented with the head of a cat. When later (*c.* 950 B.C.) Bubastis in the Delta became the capital of the Libyan ruler Sheshonk, Bast was made the official deity of his kingdom. A great festival was held in the town, a feature of which was the dancing and the playing of castanets. Erman reproduces a figure of Bast in the Berlin Museum in which she appears with a human head, but may be recognized by the basket on her right arm and by two cats which she holds one in each hand. See A. Erman.

BATH-KOL. Literally " daughter of a voice," a term occurring in Hebrew religion. It is a divine or heavenly voice, and, though the ordinary word for voice (*kōl*) is sometimes used alone in the same sense, it was called " daughter of a voice " for the sake of distinction. It was not thought of as an echo, but as a real voice which could be distinctly heard, though the author could not be seen. Sometimes it would roar like a lion, at other times murmur like a dove. A distinction is often made between the Bath-kol and the Holy Spirit. The Holy Spirit entered into a close relationship with the prophets and possessed them. The Bath-kol was something external. They could not possess it. The idea of the Bath-kol was no doubt suggested by certain psychological phenomena which are not uncommon even at the present day. Compare the experience of Saint Augustine (William James, *Varieties of Religious Experience*, 1906, p. 171). See the *Jewish Encycl., ii.*, 1902; and cp. W. O. E. Oesterley and G. H. Box.

BAU. The name of a goddess in the early religion of Babylonia (referred to before 2300 B.C.). A ruler of Lagash who added her name to his own and called himself Ur-Bau, built her a temple at Uru-azaga (" brilliant town "). She was the consort of Nin-girsu, the god of Girsu, another district of Lagash, and on New Year's Day, Zag-muk, called the Festival of Bau, bridegrooms were accustomed to offer presents to their chosen ones. There does not seem to be any connection between Bau and the Hebrew Bohu. Old inscriptions speak of her as the chief daughter of Anu (*q.v.*), the god of heaven. In incantation texts she is the great mother, the begetter and also the healer of mankind, in other words, the goddess of abundance and fertility. In processions the deities were carried in ships, and Bau's ship bore the name " the ship of the brilliant offspring." See Morris Jastrow, *Rel.*

BAV. An ancient Irish deity, the goddess of war. The name signifies rage, fury, or violence, and " ultimately came to be applied to a witch, fairy, or goddess, represented by the scarescald- or royston-crow " (W. G. Wood-Martin). Bav is represented in Irish tales of war and battle as a scald-crow screaming in anticipation of widespread carnage. In the South of Ireland it is said that the term is applied now to a scolding woman or virago.

BAXTERIANS. The followers of Richard Baxter (1615-1691). Baxter was the son of a well-to-do person, but his father being a gambler, the early years of his life were spent with his grandfather. He was mainly self-educated. In 1638, after trying a court-life, he was ordained and was appointed Head-master of a school at Dudley. He soon left this post to take up ministerial work. On the outbreak of the civil war in 1642 he sided with the Parliament, and retired to Coventry, where he became chaplain to the garrison. He afterwards acted as chaplain to Colonel Whalley's regiment, and was present at several sieges. Then, his health failing, he left the army, and quietly awaited his end. Meantime, he began to write his book "The Saints' Everlasting Rest" (published in 1650). He had formerly been preacher at Kidderminster (1641). His old parishioners now invited him to return, which he did. In 1660 he went to London and became one of the King's chaplains. Here he took an important part in preparing the "Reformed Liturgy." When the Act of Uniformity was passed, he left the Church of England (1662). In 1663 he went to live at Acton, and was occupied with literary work there until 1672, when the Act of Indulgence gave him an opportunity of returning to London. In 1685 he was brought before the brutal Judge Jeffreys and charged with libelling the Church in his "Paraphrase of the New Testament" (1685). He was condemned, fined, and imprisoned for nearly eighteen months. He died on the 8th of December, 1691. Baxter was remarkably catholic and tolerant for his period. He was viewed in one quarter as an Arminian, and in another as a Calvinist. See the *Reliquiae Baxterianae,* 1696; John Hunt; the *D.N.B.*

BAYAN, THE. The sacred book or Bible of Bābism (*q.v.*), the most important of the works written by Mirza Ali Mohammad.

BEADS. In the Roman Catholic Church, beads made of glass or other substances are used by worshippers to help them to remember a set number of prayers. A string of these beads is called a Rosary.

BEARD. We learn from the Old Testament that amongst the Hebrews the beard was shaved as a sign of mourning (Isaiah xv. 2; Jeremiah xli. 5, xlviii. 37). The Arabs touch the beard, or swear by it, as a token of good faith (Doughty, *Arabia Deserta* i. 250). The Hebrew priests were forbidden to shave off "the corner of their beard" (Leviticus xxi. 5), but Egyptian priests were accustomed to shave. On the other hand, the Egyptian god is represented as wearing a long beard. See *Encycl. Bibl.*

BECKMANITES. A religious sect founded by Mrs. Dora Beckman (*d.* 1883), of Alpena, Michigan. She claimed that in her person Christ was incarnate and had become "the bride of the Church."

BEDS, SACRED. It has been pointed out by Professor Elliot Smith (*Mi.*) that it is a familiar scene in ancient Egyptian pictures to find the mummy borne upon a bed, and that in a proto-dynastic cemetery, on a site excavated by Flinders Petrie at Tarkhan, corpses have been found lying upon beds. It may well be assumed that such beds, or some of them, came to be regarded as sacred. In the sanctuary of Men, the chief god of Antioch in Pisidia, Sir William Ramsay in his excavations found "three of the feet of the 'holy bed' used for the mystic marriage ceremony between the god and his goddess—in which service, according to immemorial tradition, Anatolian ladies, even those of highest rank, were expected to take part" (Cobern). In Ireland, as noted by W. G. Wood-Martin, there are a number of sacred spots known as Saints' Beds or Priests' Beds, to which devout persons, especially women, used to resort. St. Molaise's bed is near his house in the Island of Devenish. It is "a stone trough (coffin) sunk level with the surface of the ground, six feet in length and fifteen inches wide, in which people lie down and repeat some prayers, in hope of relief from any pains with which they may be affected." According to Lady Wilde, there is a stone receptacle called "The Bed of the Holy Ghost" in one of the wild desolate islands off the Western coast of Ireland. If one passed a night in it, it would heal all diseases, and to a woman would bring the blessing of children. In a depression or cavity of a slab of rock on Inishmore, now called Church Island, in Lough Gill, county Sligo, was a bed called "Our Lady's Bed." Women who desired children lay in it, turned thrice round, and repeated certain prayers. It is said that to "St. Patrick's Bed" on Croagh Patrick only barren women resorted. Here, after going round the bed seven times, they lay in it and turned round seven times.

BEDAWIYEH. An order of Dervishes, founded by Ahmed el-Bedawy (*d.* 1276). The Bedawiyeh, according to F. J. Bliss, follow ecstatic principles similar to those of the mother order, the Qadiriyeh (*q.v.*).

BEDIKATH CHAMETS. Literally "the search for leaven," a Jewish ceremony on the evening of the 13th Nisan, when, in preparation for the celebration of the Passover, the master of a house searches the house for leaven in order to remove or destroy it. See the *Jewish Encycl.;* W. O. E. Oesterley and G. H. Box.

BEELZEBUB. A name occurring in the New Testament (Matthew x. 25, xii. 24, 27, Mark iii. 22, Luke xi. 15, 18 f.). This is the reading of the Authorised and Revised Versions; but the margin of the Revised Version, following a better attested Greek reading (Βεελζεβουλ) has "Beelzebul." Beelzebul is the Aramaic form of Baalzebul, "lord of the mansion," which was altered in contempt to Baalzebub, "lord of flies" (Aramaic form, Beelzebub). The Jews of New Testament times seem to have interpreted "lord of the mansion" as "lord of the nether world." When Jesus healed one possessed with a devil, the Pharisees are said to have remarked: "This man doth not cast out devils, but by Beelzebub, the prince of the devils" (Matthew xii. 24). An older view (Lightfoot) was that Beelzebul was intended by the Pharisees to be understood "lord of dung," *zebul* being equivalent to the Hebrew word *zebel,* "dung." See *Encycl. Bibl.*

BEENA-MARRIAGE. A form of marriage which seems to have been common among the Semites in the period before the tribes separated. Robertson Smith brings forward evidence to show that "there was a well-established custom of marriage in Arabia in which the woman remained with her kin and chose and dismissed her partner at will, the children belonging to the mother's kin and growing up under their protection." J. F. McLennan has given the name *beena* marriages to marriages of this kind, because in Ceylon "unions in which the husband goes to settle in his wife's village" are so called. Robertson Smith accepts the term as applied to "regulated unions which really deserve the name of marriage." In the *beena* system of marriage it was the custom for the wife to receive her husband in her own tent; and a trace of this custom is found in Arabic, Syriac and Hebrew linguistic usage when the husband is said to "go in" (to the tent) to the bride (see Genesis xxxviii. 8; Deuteronomy xxii. 13; Judges xv. 1), whereas, as a matter of fact, the bride was brought in to the husband. There are other traces of *beena*-marriage or matriarchy in the Old Testament (*e.g.*, Genesis xxiv. 67; cp. the feminine tribal names: Keturah, Leah, Bilhah, Zilpah). In the case of Samson's marriage (Judges xiv.) the wife continued to belong to her own tribe. Cp. BAAL-

MARRIAGE. See W. Robertson Smith, *Kinship;* the *Encycl. Bibl.*, *s.v.* "Kinship."

BEES. The custom of "telling the bees" has been observed in this country. In Germany, on the death of the master or mistress of a house, it has been the practice to give the message to every bee-hive in the garden and to every beast in the stall. In addition to this, "every sack of corn must be touched and everything in the house shaken, that they may know the master is gone." See E. B. Tylor, *P.C.*

BEETLE. The Egyptian god Râ is sometimes represented as a glittering beetle, and the beetle was the special emblem of the god Khepera. The *scarabæus* or model of a beetle was one of the most popular talismans. According to the River Chaco Indians, the universe was created by a gigantic beetle.

BEFANA. An Italian word, a corruption of Epiphania, Epiphany. Befana is a figure in Italian folklore. She is a female spirit or fairy who is supposed to visit children on Twelfth Night and to put presents in the stockings which they have hung up before the fire. But she metes out punishment as well as reward. If a child has been naughty, she fills the stocking with ashes. Formerly it was the custom on Twelfth Night for a procession to pass through the streets carrying a figure called the Befana.

BEGGING HERMITS. See AUGUSTINIANS.

BEGHARDS. Associations of laymen modelled on those of the Béguines (*q.v.*). They are first heard of in the early part of the thirteenth century in Germany, the Netherlands, and the South of France. Later they became known in France as "bons garçons" or "boni pueri" and as "bons valets" or "boni valeti." They became vagrants and mendicants, and quickly degenerated. Having allied themselves with the Fraticelli and the Brethren and Sisters of the Free Spirit, and having given themselves up to Antinomianism, severe measures were taken against them. Called upon to suffer persecution after 1367, many of them preferred to join the third orders of the Mendicant fraternities. They were suppressed by Pope Innocent X. in 1650. See J. H. Blunt; *Cath. Dict.*

BEGOONI. Begooni or "the Runners" is another name for the Stranniki (*q.v.*), a Russian sect.

BÉGUINES. A Roman Catholic sisterhood. The founder is supposed to have been St. Begga (A.D. 700) or (more likely) Lambert le Bègues or le Bèghe who about the year 1184 established in Liège an institution for pious widows and single women. These women lived under a superior in an establishment consisting of a number of cottages, a chapel, a hospital, etc. The establishment was called a Béguinage or a Beginagium, and the sisters were known as Béghines or Béguines (also Beguinæ, Beguttæ). The only vow which they took was one of obedience and chastity while they remained in the Béguinage. They were free to leave when they liked. They devoted themselves to good works, including education. In the twelfth and thirteenth centuries they were active in France, Germany, and the Netherlands. In the fourteenth century many of them became associated with the Fraticelli and the Brethren and Sisters of the Free Spirit. They were suspected of immoral practices, and were condemned by the Council of Vienne (1311). Béguinages are still to be found in Belgium. The Béguinage of St. Elizabeth at Ghent forms in itself a little town within a town, like the Francke Institutes at Halle. There are also "Beguinenhaüser" in Germany, but these are almshouses and have ceased to be real Béguinages. See *Cath. Dict.;* J. H. Blunt; Chambers' *Encycl.*

BEHEMOTH. An animal referred to in the Old Testament (Job xl. 15-24). The term is the plural form of a Hebrew word which is common in the singular in the sense of "cattle." It seems to be an intensive plural meaning "colossal beast." The margin of the Revised Version gives "hippopotamus." This seems to be based on a supposed connection with an Egyptian word (*p-ehe-mōu*), but it is doubtful whether there was such a word. Prof. T. K. Cheyne regards Behemoth as a mythological monster, lord of the dry land, the other monster referred to in Job (xli.), Leviathan, being lord of the ocean. He thinks that the Hebrew notion of Behemoth was borrowed from the Egyptians, that of Leviathan from the Babylonians. The two monsters are referred to again in two apocryphal passages (Enoch lx. 7-9; 4 Esdras vi. 49-52). The passage in Enoch seems to lend strong support to the view that Leviathan is lord of the sea, and Behemoth lord of the dry land. See *Encycl. Bibl.*

BEHMENISTS. The followers of Jacob Behmen, Boehme, or Böhm (1575-1624), a German theosophist and mystic, born in Altseidenberg near Görlitz. Even as a boy, Boehme had strange religious experiences. Once he "was for seven days surrounded with a divine light, and stood in the highest contemplation, and in the kingdom of joys." In 1604 he became a master-shoemaker in Görlitz. In 1616 he published his "Aurora, or the Morning Redness," having written it some years earlier. This was the first of a number of books which brought him into conflict with the authorities. After a time he was summoned before the Elector of Saxony, and examined by six Doctors of Divinity. The court treated him favourably. On his return to Görlitz he died in 1624, after having gained many disciples. His works reveal a thorough knowledge of the Bible and a familiarity with the language of the mystico-philosophic alchemists of his time. His object was to explain the origin of things, the nature of God, and the existence of evil in the terms of a mystical philosophy. He has been studied with much sympathy and appreciation in Germany, Holland, and England. John Pordage (1607-1681), rector of Bradfield, Berkshire, wrote a commentary on his works. Jane Leade (1623-1704), an enthusiastic disciple, founded a sect, the Philadelphists, for the study of his philosophy. William Law (1686-1761), author of the "Serious Call," translated his writings. Sir Isaac Newton (1642-1727) took a great interest in them. See the biography of Boehme by Paul Deussen (1897); J. H. Blunt.

BEHRÂM. The name of one of the angels in the Zoroastrian religion. He was originally called *Verethraghna*, "killer of enemies." Behrâm is the giver of victory. He manifests himself under various forms to his worshippers (*e.g.*, as a wind, a cow, a horse, a camel, a boar, a boy of fifteen, a warrior). Zarathustra himself was one of his worshippers, and the angel rewarded him with strength of arm and general vigour of body. He was specially worshipped in a meal in which water was consecrated, the sacred twigs, Barsom (*q.v.*), were solemnly arranged, and an animal of reddish or yellowish colour was slain and cooked. No courtezan, criminal, or opponent of the Zoroastrian religion was allowed to take part in it. See Martin Haug.

BEIROBA. One of the modern gods of the Hindus, an incarnation of the Supreme Triad (Brahma-Vishnu-Siva). According to Sir Alfred C. Lyall, Kandoba, Vitoba, Beiroba and Bâlâji are the four most popular gods in the province of Berar in Central India (*Asiatic Studies*). He thinks that not so very long ago they must have been notable living men.

BEITULLAH. An Arabic expression meaning literally "the house of God." It is a name given to the temple of Mecca or the Great Mosque in which the Kaaba (*q.v.*) stands.

BEKHŌRŌTH. The name of one of the Jewish

treatises or tractates which reproduce the oral tradition or unwritten law as developed by the second century A.D. and are included in the Mishnah (*q.v.*), a collection and compilation completed by Rabbi Judah the Holy, or the Patriarch, about 200 A.D. The sixty-three tractates of the Mishnah are divided into six groups or orders (*sedarim*). Bekhōrōth is the fourth tractate of the fifth group, which is called *Ḳodāshim* (" Holy Things ").

BEL. The name of a Babylonian deity. He appears on the oldest monuments as En-lil, which means the " chief demon." He is " the lord of the lower world," the lower as compared with the upper or heavenly world. Becoming the great deity of Nippur, in course of time he " is released from the limitations due to his local origin and rises to the still higher dignity of a great power whose domain is the entire habitable universe " (M. Jastrow). He then became known as Bel, " the lord " *par excellence*, and was venerated in north and south alike. Nippur, however, remained his most important place of worship. It was called the " land of Bel." The great temple there called E-Kur or " mountain house " was continually repaired and added to by the kings of Nippur, each of whom wished to be known as " builder of the Temple of Bel at Nippur." Even the patron deity of the city of Babylon, Marduk, is sometimes honoured by having the name of Bel combined with his own. In the days of Khammurabi when Bel's powers were transferred to Marduk, the name was transferred as well. From about the twelfth century Marduk is referred to repeatedly as Bel. When Tiglathpileser I. wishes to announce that he rebuilt a temple to Bel he adds the word " old " to avoid confusion. The honour bestowed upon Marduk is referred to in a " Marduk hymn " in the Babylonian story of Creation: " Because he created the heavens and formed the earth, ' Lord of Lands ' father Bel called his name." Bel figures in the eleventh tablet of the Gilgamesh Epic as the rival of Ea (*q.v.*) and as wishing to destroy mankind. Bel is mentioned in the Bible in Isaiah xlvi. 1: " Bel has bowed down, Nebo has crouched " (Cheyne). See Morris Jastrow, *Rel. of Babylonia and Assyria*, 1898; H. Winckler, *History of Babyl. and Ass.*, 1907.

BEL AND THE DRAGON. An apocryphal addition to the Book of Daniel in which in the Greek, Latin and Douay Versions the fragment is actually included. See APOCRYPHA OF THE OLD TESTAMENT.

BELATUCADRUS. Belātucadrus, " the brilliant in war," was one of the names given by the ancient Celts to the god of war, the deity corresponding to the Roman Mars. Belātucadrus was held in high honour in ancient Britain. The name occurs in a number of inscriptions.

BELENUS. One of the gods worshipped by the ancient Celts. The name is rather like that of the Phoenician term Baal and of the Babylonian god Bel; but it is doubtful whether there was any connection between them. Reinach declares that " the Celtic divinity Belenus (Apollo) had nothing in common with a Baal." Ausonius states that Belenus was held in reverence by the Druids (*q.v.*) as a sun-god. In any case the name Belenus survived in Belinus, a mythical king of Britain, and in the Balin who figures in the *Morte D'Arthur*. See Anwyl; Squire, *Myth.*; Reinach, *O.*

BELFRIES. It has been held that the Irish round towers, which evidently once served a religious purpose, were watch-towers or belfries or both. Another suggestion is that they were pillars used for keeping alive the sacred fire of Bâl. In this connection Sidney Heath points out that " the early Irish colonists were worshippers of Bâl, and that the constant recurrence of the word Bâl in Irish place-names seems to indicate some connection with the early pagan settlements."

BELGIUM, CONFESSION OF. A Confession drawn up in A.D. 1561 by Belgian Protestants, who previously had called themselves " Associates of the Conference of Augsburg." Published in French in A.D. 1562, after having been framed in the Walloon language by Guy de Bres, it was approved by the Synod of Flanders (A.D. 1579), and confirmed by the Synod of Dort (A.D. 1619) and at the Hague (A.D. 1651). See J. H. Blunt.

BELI. Arianrod, who figures as a daughter of Dôn (*q.v.*) in the British mythology, is referred to also as the daughter of Beli. Beli, therefore, would seem to have been the father of the gods and the consort of Dôn, the mother of the gods. The Gaelic Bilé perhaps represents the same deity. Beli survived as the name of a legendary king of the Brythons. Bilé appears as the name of the ancestor of the first Celts who settled in Ireland. See Squire, *Myth.*

BELIAL. In the Old Testament " sons (or men) of Belial " is a familiar phrase for " good-for-nothing fellows," or, as the margin of the Revised Version translates it, " base fellows." The common explanation is that Belial (Heb. *Bcliyya'al*) is composed of two Hebrew words, *beli* " not " and *ya'al* " profit " and means literally " profitless." Another explanation is that it is a proper name, equivalent to Beliar. In that case, it would be a synonym for Satan. In 2 Corinthians vi. 14 *f.* it is said: " What fellowship have righteousness and iniquity? or what communion hath light with darkness? And what concord hath Christ with Beliar? " Prof. Cheyne connects the word Belial with Belili, the name of a Babylonian goddess of vegetation, " and hence of the underworld." He thinks that the Canaanites and Israelites probably regarded the name as a synonym for the abyss of Sheōl. It then came to be a symbol of insatiable destructiveness. See *Encycl. Bibl.*

BELIAR. A name for Satan in some of the apocryphal books (*Test of the Twelve Patriarchs;* the *Book of Jubilees;* the *Sibylline Oracles*).

BELIEVERS. A name given to those who believed in the claims of Joanna Southcott (1750-1814), the prophetess of Exeter. She was the daughter of a farmer, and for some years was in domestic service. She began to make converts in 1801. See the *D.N.B.*

BELILI. One of the deities in the old Babylonian pantheon. She seems to be referred to as the sister of Tammuz (*q.v.*), which suggests that she was one of the deities of vegetation. Her consort is Alala, and the two deities both belonged to the court of Allatu (*q.v.*).

BELISAMA. Belisama, one of the deities worshipped by the ancient Celts, corresponded to the Roman deity Minerva. The name means " the most warlike goddess." The British Celts regarded her as the tutelar deity of the River Ribble.

BELIT. One of the Babylonian deities, a goddess, mentioned in inscriptions prior to 2300 B.C. The name means " the lady " *par excellence*. Another form of it was Nin-Lil. Belit is the " mistress of the lower world." She received the title Nin-khar-sag, " lady of the high or great mountain," that is to say, the mountain on which the gods were thought to dwell. When in the days of Khammurabi Bel became Marduk, Belit did not at the same time become Marduk's consort. But Belit did apparently come to be applied in its general sense of " mistress " to the consort of the chief god. Thus Tiglathpileser I. speaks (*c.* 1140 B.C.) of Belit, " the lofty consort and beloved of Ashur "; and Nabopolassar, referring to the consort of Shamash at Sippar, speaks of " Belit of Sippar." As a general title, " mistress," the term is also applied to Ishtar (*q.v.*), Ashurbanipal apparently referring to her as "Belit mâti" or "the lady of the land." This would involve in course of time the transference of the qualities of Belit, the consort of Bel, to other consorts, just as the qualities of Bel were transferred to Marduk. From the names of the eight gates of Sargon's palace, it appears that Belit was a goddess of fertility. See Morris Jastrow, *Rel.*

BELL, BOOK, AND CANDLE. The expression has reference to a custom in the Roman Catholic Church. Since the eighth century, when a person has been condemned to suffer the greater excommunication, after the sentence has been read, a bell is rung, the book is closed, and a candle is put out.

BELLA PENNU. See BURA PENNU.

BELLONA. Two goddesses with this name were worshipped by the Romans. (1) One was the goddess of war, and seems to have been of Sabine origin. She is reputed to have been the sister or wife of Mars. The senate sometimes met in her temple in the Campus Martius. (2) The other goddess belonged originally to Comana in Cappadocia. Her worship was introduced among the Romans towards the beginning of the first century B.C. The priests and priestesses, who were Cappadocians and were called Bellonarii, at her festivals gashed their arms and loins with a two-edged axe and prophesied to the sound of drums and trumpets. Similar practices elsewhere suggest that this was regarded as a means of renewing a blood covenant. Robertson Smith points out (*R.S.*) that in the account of the worship given by Tibullus the blood is sprinkled on the idol; and that according to the Church Fathers "those who shared in the rite drank one another's blood" (on this practice cp. BLOOD). See O. Seyffert, *Dict.*

BELLONARII. See BELLONA.

BELLS. Bells have been used in religious worship from a remote period. They have been found among Buddhists and Brahmans and in the Shintoo temples of the Sun goddess in Japan. Bells are mentioned in the English translation of the Bible, but the words so translated do not seem to denote bells in our sense of the word. The Mohammedans object to the use of bells. In front of the porch before the door of a temple dedicated to Siva (*q.v.*), Monier-Williams noticed three long rows of bells. Whenever a worshipper entered the shrine, he rang one of the bells. In the shrine itself "there was a constant ringing of small portable bells and clapping of hands, as if to draw the attention of the deity worshipped to the prayers muttered by his worshippers." In the Hindu ceremony called Pañc'āyatana one of the sacred objects of worship is a small bell. At the adoration of the bell, the worshipper says: "O bell, make a sound for the approach of the gods, and for the departure of the demons. Homage to the goddess Ghaṇṭā (bell). I offer perfumes, grains of rice, and flowers, in token of rendering all due homage to the bell." Among the Lāmas of Tibet a bell forms part of the sorcerer's equipment (see L. A. Waddell). The bells already referred to were hand-bells. It is not known when exactly the large church-bells in Christian churches were introduced. It is possible that when in the early days of the Church basilicas or halls of justice were used as places of worship, the bells belonging to them were rung to call the people to divine worship. Paulinus, Bishop of Nola in Campania, however, is reputed to have introduced their use. In France they seem to have been used before the seventh century; and they were in use elsewhere in the ninth century (*e.g.*, in the Greek Church). In Germany and Switzerland they came into use in the eleventh century. In the tenth century the custom arose of giving them names. In the eleventh century we begin to hear of "the baptism of a bell." This is a popular expression for the ceremony of consecration, which is still observed in the Roman Catholic Church. "The bishop washes the bell with blessed water, signs it with the oil of the sick outside, and with chrism inside, and lastly places under it the thurible with burning incense. He prays repeatedly that the sound of the bell may avail to summon the faithful, to excite their devotion, to drive away storms, and to terrify evil spirits." It is explained that "this power of course is due to the blessings and prayers of the Church, not to any efficacy superstitiously attributed to the bell itself. Thus consecrated, bells become spiritual things, and cannot be rung without the consent of the ecclesiastical authorities" (Addis and Arnold). Small bells are also in use in the Roman Catholic Church. A bell is rung during Mass at the Sanctus and at the Elevation of the Host. See *Cath. Dict.;* Chambers' *Encycl.;* Monier-Williams, *Brāhmanism.*

BELTANE FIRES. The so-called Beltane Fires were lit in honour of the sun-god Bâl on the three great Druid festivals on May-day Eve, Midsummer Eve, and All Hallow-e'en. The custom is said to have survived until recently in Ireland, Scotland, and Cornwall. It was christianised by the Church, which made the fires symbolical of the shining light of John the Baptist (John the Baptist's Day = Midsummer Day). See Sidney Heath.

BEMIDBAR RABBAH. Bemidbar "in the wilderness" is the Hebrew name for the Old Testament Book of Numbers. Bemidbar Rabbah is the name of the Rabbinic commentary (*midrash*) on this book contained in the Midrash Rabbah. The work is composite, the second part being largely derived from another Midrash, Midrash Tanchuma. It seems to belong to the twelfth century. See the *Jewish Encycl.;* W. O. E. Oesterley and G. H. Box.

BENDIDEIA. An Athenian festival in honour of BENDIS (*q.v.*).

BENDIS. A Thracian goddess of the moon. The Greeks identified her with Artemis, Hecate, and Persephone. A public festival was held in her honour at Athens, which was called Bendideia.

BENEDICITE. One of the canticles in the Order for Morning Prayer in the Prayer-book of the Church of England. Shadrach, Meshach and Abed-nego, who figure in the Book of Daniel, are supposed to have sung it in "the burning fiery furnace." It is included in the Old Testament Apocrypha under the title "The Song of the Three Holy Children." In the Septuagint translation of the Bible it is inserted in the third chapter of Daniel (between verses 23 and 24). It was in use in the time of Chrysostom (A.D. 347-407) in the services of the Church.

BENEDICTINES. Orders of monks and nuns founded by St. Benedict (A.D. 480-543). Starting at Subiaco, near Rome, in A.D. 529, he removed his order to Monte Cassino, near Naples. While Benedict was still living, his disciple St. Maur founded a Benedictine monastery at Glanfeuil, near Angers, in France. In Spain others were founded about A.D. 633; and St. Placid, another disciple of St. Benedict, introduced them into Sicily. St. Augustine, when he came on his mission to England, having been abbot of a Benedictine monastery at Rome, brought the rule of St. Benedict with him. The English Benedictines became great missionaries. St. Willibrord (658-739), born in Northumberland, worked among the Frisians and the Dutch. St. Boniface or Winfried (A.D. 680-755), born at Crediton in Devonshire, laboured amongst the Germans and earned the title of "the Apostle of Germany." The rule of St. Benedict binds a monk to remain permanently in a monastery; to endeavour to live the perfect life; to observe chastity; to celebrate daily the divine office at the canonical hours; to live simply and labour devotedly. As copyists, students, and educationalists, the Benedictines have done a great work. Their clothing has long been black, whence they have been called "black monks." They were required to abstain from meat. Persons who were quite young could be admitted to the order. They were then educated in a monastery. This gave rise to monastic schools. The Venerable Bede or Bæda (*b.* about A.D. 673) is said to have entered the Benedictine abbey at Monkwearmouth when he was only seven years old. The order degenerated in course of time, but from time to time reformers arose such as Benedict of Aniane (A.D. 750-821), Peter the Venerable (*b.* A.D. 1094), Abbot of Cluny (1122), and St. Dunstan (A.D. 924-988). At a later date certain abuses led to the formation in France of the reformed congregation of St. Vanne (A.D. 1550) and of St. Maur (A.D. 1618). At the Revolution (A.D. 1792) the order was suppressed in France, but in the nineteenth century new foundations arose. In Germany, after being suppressed, the order has reappeared. At the Dissolution, the abbeys, priories, and nunneries were suppressed. The Benedictines, however, have reappeared in England also, and now have a number of houses. There is an English Benedictine monastery at Douai, and the Benedictines have done good work in Western Australia and New Zealand. There are also a number of abbeys in the United States. See Abbot Gasquet, *Henry VIII. and the English Monasteries*; *Cath. Dict.*

BENEDICTUS. The name of one of the canticles, the song of Zacharias (Luke i. 68-79), included in the Order for Morning Prayer in the Prayer-book of the Church of England. It is so called because the first word in the Latin version is "Benedictus." Formerly in the services known as the Canonical Hours (*q.v.*) it was sung at Lauds.

BENEFIT OF CLERGY. In Latin "privilegium clericale," originally the privilege allowed to clergy who were charged with felony (other than high treason or arson) of being tried only in ecclesiastical courts. Henry II. was anxious to abolish the privilege. So far from being abolished, however, in course of time it was extended, so that it was enjoyed not only by those who wore "habitum et tonsuram clericalem," but also by anyone who could read, except women and "bigami." It was afterwards extended to "bigami" (1547), then even to Peers who were unable to read, and early in the eighteenth century to others who were unable to read and to women. But a statute of 1487 had already provided that the privilege could not be claimed by a layman more than once, and to insure this he must be burned with a hot iron. When the privilege was extended to women they had to be burned and to spend less than a year in prison. The "privilegium clericale" was finally abolished in 1827. See *Prot. Dict.*; *Cath. Dict.*

BENI-ISRAEL. Literally "sons of Israel," the designation of a community of persons of Jewish origin settled in Bombay and other parts of western India. They keep the Sabbath strictly, observe the great feasts, and are careful to abstain from such flesh or fish as is regarded as unclean. They seem to have called themselves Beni-Israel because the Mussulmans could not bear to hear the name Jews (*Yehudim*).

BENSHEE. Another form of the word Banshee (*q.v.*).

BENTHEIM CONFESSION, THE. A German Confession of Faith in twelve articles drawn up by the authority of the ruling Count, who is said to have been a convinced Presbyterian. It is still authoritative. "No Confession in the long series is less controversial and partisan, more simple and charitable" (William A. Curtis).

BERĀKHŌTH. The title of one of the Jewish treatises or tractates which reproduce the oral tradition or unwritten law as developed by the second century A.D., and are included in the Mishnah (*q.v.*), a collection and compilation completed by Rabbi Judah the Holy, or the Patriarch, about 200 A.D. The sixty-three tractates of the Mishnah are divided into six groups or orders (*sedarim*). Berākhōth is the first tractate of the first group, which is called *Zerā'īm* ("Seeds").

BERCHTA. Another form of the name Perchta (*q.v.*).

BEREANS. A name taken by the disciples of John Barclay (1734-1798). The name is supposed to have been suggested by Acts xvii. 11, where the people of Berea are said to have "received the word with all readiness of mind, examining the scriptures daily." Barclay was originally assistant minister at Errol. Here he gave offence by his teaching, and was dismissed. He then became (1763) assistant minister at Fettercairn, Kincardineshire. Here again in 1772 he was inhibited from preaching. His next step was to found independent congregations at Sauchyburn and Edinburgh. At a later date he founded another in London. The views held by the Bereans were largely Calvinistic. They also attached supreme importance to the Bible as a revelation of God's being and character, and as the only revelation. See the *D.N.B.*

BERECYNTIA. A goddess referred to by Gregory of Tours. She was perhaps identical with Brigindu (*q.v.*).

BERITH MILAH. Literally "Covenant of Circumcision," the Jewish ceremony at which a boy is initiated into the covenant of Abraham. The godfather (*Sandek*), who took the child on his knees in the course of the ceremony, is sometimes spoken of as "Master of the Covenant" (*Baal Berith*). See W. O. E. Oesterley and G. H. Box.

BERKELEYISM. The philosophy of George Berkeley (1684-1753), Bishop of Cloyne, the Idealist. In 1709 Berkeley published an "Essay towards a New Theory of Vision." This was followed in 1710 by his "Treatise concerning the Principles of Human Knowledge," and in 1713 by his "Three Dialogues between Hylas and Philonous." The two latter are his chief works. The difference between a thing and an idea, according to Berkeley, "does not consist in the former being real and the latter notional, but in the former being complex and the latter simple; both are "notional beings." Instead of the world of Leibnitz, which consisted of quasi-spirits, we have one which consists solely of spirits and of their images or ideas. The principle which Leibnitz applies to some substances—that they have the power of thought and of will—is in this case applied to all alike. Instead of Leibnitz's Semi-idealism, we have here a consistent form of Idealism. Berkeley himself does not employ this name for his system. If he had wished to give it a distinctive title, he would probably have called it "spiritualism," possibly "notionalism," or "phenomenalism." Suffice it to say, that he takes up a position directly antagonistic to what he called, as we do, materialism, and that he is never tired of arguing against the mistaken notion involved in the "supposition of external objects," which really "subsist not by themselves, but exist in minds" (Erdmann). See J. E. Erdmann, vol. ii., 1892; and the *D.N.B.*

BERNARDINES. The followers of Bernard of Clairvaux; another name for the Cistercians (*q.v.*).

BERRETTA. A term formed from the Latin *birrus*, a mantle with a hood, and applied to a special kind of headgear worn by Roman Catholic priests and other ecclesiastics. Its use has been introduced into the Church of England by the ritualistic party. The Beretta is "a square cap with three or sometimes four prominences or projecting corners rising from its crown"

(Addis and Arnold). It often has a tassel on the top. The berretta of an ordinary cleric is black, of a bishop purple, of a cardinal red, of the Pope white. See *Cath. Dict.*

BES. An Egyptian deity who became popular in the period of the New Empire. He was regarded by the priests as an inferior kind of deity, as a demon in fact. Like a Greek satyr he was represented as half-animal half-human. He belonged to a class of grotesque beings who amused the great gods with music and dancing, and fought against adversaries of various kinds. His figure was used as a magical protection against evil creatures. In the Hellenistic Period Bes was esteemed highly as a protecting warrior, and he was represented as holding a shield in one hand and brandishing a sword with the other. See A. Erman.

BEṢĀ. The title of one of the Jewish treatises or tractates which reproduce the oral tradition or unwritten law as developed by the second century A.D. and are included in the Mishnah (*q.v.*), a collection and compilation completed by Rabbi Judah the Holy, or the Patriarch, about 200 A.D. The sixty-three tractates of the Mishnah are divided into six groups or orders (*sedarim*). Bēṣā is the seventh tractate of the second group, whch is called *Mō'ēd* ("Festival").

BETHESDA, POOL OF. In the New Testament reference is made (John v.) to a pool, Bethesda (or Bethsaida, or Bethzatha), the waters of which possessed healing virtues. "Now there is in Jerusalem by the sheep gate a pool, which is called in Hebrew Bethesda, having five porches. In these lay a multitude of them that were sick, blind, halt, withered, waiting for the moving of the water: for an angel of the Lord went down at certain seasons into the pool, and troubled the water; whosoever then first after the troubling of the water stepped in was made whole, with whatsoever disease he was holden." Bethesda seems to be for the Aramaic *Bēth-ḥesdā*, "house of mercy." But the best authorities read Bethsaida or Bethzatha. Bethsaida would be equivalent to the Aramaic *Bēth-tsaidā*, "place of fishing" or "fish-pool." Bethzatha is apparently for the Aramaic *Bēth-zaithā*, "place of the olive." It has been a common practice to bathe in sacred pools, and where the bather has had great faith in the healing properties of the waters, diseases of a nervous nature, (paralysis, etc.) have been cured. In modern times this has happened at Lourdes, for instance.

BETH HA-KENESETH. Literally "House of Assembly," the Hebrew name for a Synagogue (*q.v.*).

BETH HA-MIDRASH. Literally "House of Study," the Jewish name for a college in which higher instruction in the Jewish Law and Religion is given.

BETHLEHEMITES. 1. An order of monks who are said to have had a monastery at Cambridge in 1257. Matthew Paris (*d.* 1259) calls them "fratres Bethleemitae" and says that they wore a habit like that of the Friars Preachers, except that they had also on their breast a red and blue star. 2. A military order founded by Pope Pius II. in 1459 in opposition to the Turks. 3. An order founded about 1600 in Guatemala by the Spaniard Peter of Bétencourt. His foundation included a school, hospital, and convent. The Bethlehemites in 1687 were placed by Innocent XI. under the rule of St. Augustine. 4. The same name was applied to the Hussites (*q.v.*).

BEZPOPOFTSCHINS. A name for Russian dissenters who have abolished the office of pope or priest. They are sub-divided into a considerable number of sects.

BEZSLOVESTNI. Literally "the dumb," a name given to a Russian sect of the eighteenth century. On joining the sect, a member became speechless, consequently nothing, not even torture, has availed to gain information about the religious tenets of the Bezslovestni.

BHADRA-KĀLI. The deity of the Mukkuvans, the caste of sea fishermen on the Malabar coast of India. A goddess, she is represented by a log of wood kept in a hut which is called a temple. The Mukkuvans assemble four times a year, offer fruit to the log of wood, and sacrifice a cock.

BHAGA. A name, occurring in the Rig Veda, for the sun-god in Hindu religion. The word seems to have meant first "giver" and then "god." There is one hymn addressed to Bhaga which begins: "The early-conquering mighty Bhaga call we, the son of Boundlessness, the gift-bestower." See E. W. Hopkins.

BHAGAVAD GITĀ. One of the sacred wr tings, the Divine Song, of the Hindus. It is described as "the wonderful song, which causes the hair to stand on end." It is a revision (Krishnaite) of an earlier Vishnuite poem, and is treated with great reverence by the Vishnuites. "It is a medley of beliefs as to the relation of spirit and matter, and other secondary matters; it is uncertain in its tone in regard to the comparative efficacy of action and inaction, and in regard to the practical man's means of salvation; but it is at one with itself in its fundamental thesis, that all things are each a part of One Lord, that men and gods are but manifestations of the One Divine Spirit, which, or rather whom, the Vishnuite re-writer identifies with Krishna, as Vishnu's present form" (E. W. Hopkins). See E. W. Hopkins.

BHAGAVAT. A Buddhist title, meaning "the Blessed one. It is one of the titles of Gautama.

BHĀGAVATAS. An early Hindu sect the members of which worshipped Vishnu (*q.v.*) as Bhagavat. They held in reverence the holy-stone, and were guided by the Upanishads (*q.v.*) and the Divine Song or Bhagavad Gītā (*q.v.*). See E. W. Hopkins.

BHAGWĀN. The fortunate or illustrious, one of the names of the Hindu god Vishnu.

BHAINSĀSUR. A figure in Hindu mythology, the buffalo demon, invoked by the Jubbulpore Kols, a large tribe in India. Pigs are sacrificed to the deity for the protection of the crops. As R. V. Russell and R. B. Hira Lāl suggest, the pig itself was no doubt worshipped at one time by the Hindus. It seems possible "that the Hindus reverenced the wild boar in the past as one of the strongest and fiercest animals of the forest and also as a destroyer of the crops. And they still make sacrifices of the pig to guard their fields from his ravages. These sacrifices, however, are not offered to any deity who can represent a deified pig, but to Bhainsāsur, the deified buffalo. The explanation seems to be that in former times, when forests extended over most of the country, the cultivator had in the wild buffalo a direr foe than the wild pig." The breeding of pigs for sacrifices is made a special business by some of the Kumhārs, the caste of potters in India.

BHAIRON. A figure in Hindu mythology, the watchman of the temples of Mahādeo. He is represented riding on a black dog.

BHAKTAS. An early Hindu sect the members of which worshipped Vishnu (*q.v.*) as Vāsudeva. It is also the name of a modern order of mystics which was founded in 1876. These Bhaktas seek to attain "inebriation in God."

BHANDARIN. An Indian deity, worshipped as the goddess of agriculture by the Gadbas, a primitive tribe belonging to the Vizagapatam District of Madras.

BHARATA. One of the two sacred epics of early Hinduism, the other being the Rāmāyana (*q.v.*). The Bhārata (tale) is also called Mahā-Bhārata or Great

Bhārata. It was recognised as sacred by all sects. The work, which contains legends, myths, history, etc., is composite. Characters in the story were familiar to Pānini (probably of the fourth century B.C.), and the work was complete at the end of the sixth century A.D. The Bhārata reveals a great growth in an asceticism which is not of an exalted nature. See E. W. Hopkins.

BHARS. One of the wild tribes of Bengal. Another form of the name is Bhārats, which suggests a connection between the Bhārs and the great tribe known as Bhārata. The Bhārs hold in honour as sacred things, and perhaps as totems, the bamboo, the *bel*-tree, the tortoise, and the peacock. See E. W. Hopkins.

BHARWAN. An Indian deity, the protector of cattle, worshipped by the Gadbas, a primitive tribe belonging to the Vizagapatam District of Madras.

BHATS. An Indian caste, the caste of bards and genealogists.

BHAVANA RISHI. The caste deity of the Padma Sālēs, a Telugu-speaking caste of weavers in the Madras Presidency of India. "A festival in honour of this deity is celebrated annually, during which the god and goddess are represented by two decorated pots placed on a model of a tiger (vyagra vāhanam), to which, on the last day of the ceremonial, large quantities of rice and vegetables are offered, which are distributed among the loom-owners, pūjari, headman, fasting celebrants, etc." (E. Thurston).

BHEARTHA. An ancient Irish deity. In English the name of the goddess appears as Vera, Verah, Berab, Berri, Dirra, and Dhirra. She is conceived popularly as a being of great stature and forbidding mien. In the county Sligo there is a popular tradition that she was able to wade all the Irish rivers and lakes except Loch-da-ghedh, in which she was drowned. There still exists on the mountain near the lake a ruin called Cailleach-a-Vera's House. In the county Louth also there survives a sepulchral chamber called Cailleach Dirra's House. According to W. G. Wood-Martin, "in some parts of Ireland she is now looked upon as a banshee, and makes her appearance before the death of a member of some well-known families." See W. G. Wood-Martin.

BHIMSEN. An Indian deity, worshipped as the god of rainfall by the Baigas, who inhabit the eastern Satpūra hills in the Mandla, Bālāghāt and Bilaspur Districts.

BHUJARIYA. The name of a barley feast observed in the Central Provinces of India. Grains of barley are planted in a pot of manure on the seventh day of the month Sāwan. These grow very quickly into long stalks, and on the first day of Bhādon, the next month, the women and girls present the plants to their male friends to be placed in their turbans, throwing the manure into water. J. G. Frazer compares these plantings with the Gardens of Adonis (see ADONIS), which "are essentially charms to promote the growth of vegetation." See J. G. Frazer, *Adonis Attis Osiris*, 1906.

BHUMI DEVATA. A Hindu deity, worshipped once in three years as the earth goddess by the Jhodia, Pengu, and Kondhi divisions of the Porojas, a class of cultivators in India.

BHUTAS. The Bhūtas are demons worshipped by certain Hindu castes (*e.g.*, the Nalkes). The demon temple is called Bhūtasthānam. Usually it contains a number of images. "All castes in South Canara have great faith in Bhūtas, and, when any calamity or misfortune overtakes a family, the Bhūtas must be propiated. The worship of Bhūtas is a mixture of ancestor and devil propitiation. In the Bhūta cult, the most important personage is Brahmeru, to whom the other Bhūtas are subordinate. Owing to the influence of Brāhman Tantris, Brahmeru is regarded as another name for Brahma, and the various Bhūtas are regarded as ganas on attendants on Siva. Brāhmanical influence is clearly to be traced in the various Bhūta songs, and all Bhūtas are in some manner connected with Siva and Parvati" (E. Thurston and K. Rangachari). Among the many Bhūtas there are only two females, Ukkatiri and Kallurti.

BIANCHI. A fanatical sect found in Italy in 1399. Its members subsisted on bread and water, and always wore long white garments.

BIAS. In a very helpful work, Herbert Spencer has explained the influence of a number of different kinds of bias, educational, patriotic, social, political, theological. It is a common charge against theologians that they are biased. It is not sufficiently realized, on the other hand, by their opponents that men's views are distorted equally by an anti-theological bias. The theological bias cannot, of course, be denied. "Under its special forms, as well as under its general form, the theological bias brings errors into the estimates men make of societies and institutions. Sectarian antipathies, growing out of differences of doctrine, disable the members of each religious community from fairly judging other religious communities. It is always difficult, and often impossible, for the zealot to conceive that his own religious system and his own zeal on its behalf may have but a relative truth and a relative value; or to conceive that there may be relative truths and relative values in alien beliefs and the fanaticisms which maintain them. Though the adherent of each creed daily has thrust on his attention the fact that adherents of other creeds are no less confident than he is—though he can scarcely fail sometimes to reflect that these adherents of other creeds have, in nearly all cases, simply accepted the dogmas current in the places and families they were born in, and that he has done the like; yet the special theological bias which his education and surroundings have given him, makes it almost beyond imagination that these other creeds may, some of them, have justifications as good as, if not better than, his own, and that the rest, along with certain amounts of absolute worth, may have their special fitnesses to the people holding them." But the anti-theological bias also leads to serious errors, "both when it ignores the essential share hitherto taken by religious systems in giving force to certain principles of action, in part absolutely good and in part good relatively to the needs of the time, and again when it prompts the notion that these principles might now be so established on rational bases as to rule men effectually through their enlightened intellects. . . . It generates an unwillingness to see that a religious system is a normal and essential factor in every evolving society; that the specialities of it have certain fitnesses to the social conditions; and that while its form is temporary, its substance is permanent. In so far as the anti-theological bias causes an ignoring of these truths, or an inadequate appreciation of them, it causes misinterpretations." See Herbert Spencer, *The Study of Sociology*, 18th ed., 1897.

BIBLE. In Greek *Ta Biblia* is a plural expression meaning "The Books," just as we speak of "the Scriptures," meaning the Scriptures *par excellence*. In Low Latin the word *Biblia* came to be used as a singular, and this usage has been adopted in modern languages. The English Bible is a collection of books regarded as sacred and received as canonical. It includes books of the Old and New Covenants. See OLD TESTAMENT. The Roman Catholics accept also as canonical certain books which the English Churches regard as apocryphal. These are included in their Bible (see CANON OF THE OLD TESTAMENT). The ordinary English Bible, however, contains only the Old and New Testaments. The Apocryphal additions to the Old Testament (see APOCRYPHA OF THE OLD TESTAMENT) are only found in special editions of the whole Bible or in separate editions of the Apocrypha. In the English Versions, the Old Testament is translated from the Hebrew, the New Testament from the Greek. John Wycliffe (*d.* 1384) was the first to concern himself about a translation of the whole Bible into English. He himself seems to have translated the whole of the New Testament and part of the Old Testament. The whole work was completed and edited by John Purvey (1353?-1428?) before 1400. Nicholas de Hereford (*fl.* 1390), one of the leaders of the Lollards in Oxford, seems to have been responsible for the translation of a large part of the Old Testament. There are no verse-divisions in Wycliffe's Bible, but the matter is roughly divided into chapters. There are about 170 manuscripts of this Bible in existence. The first printed edition of the New Testament in English (1526) was the work of William Tyndale (*d.* 1536), who went direct to the original Greek. Afterwards he translated the Pentateuch (*c.* 1530), the following books of the old Testament as far as II. Chronicles, and the Book of Jonah (1531). Large use of this version was made when the Authorised Version was prepared, and Tyndale is considered to have set a standard of biblical translation. Tyndale's New Testament was printed and published at Worms. It was not yet possible to print a translation in England. The first English Bible which the Government allowed to be sold in England was the Bible of Miles Coverdale (1488-1568). His translation seems to have been first printed by Christopher Froschouer of Zürich in 1535. It was introduced into England in the same year by James Nicolson of Southwark. The work was not original, the translation being based upon the Bibles of Luther and Zwingli, with the help of Latin versions (especially the Vulgate) and of Tyndale's New Testament. In 1537 Coverdale revised and modified his version, which was then authorised by the King. In the same year Matthews' Bible was published. Thomas Matthews was a name assumed by John Rogers (1500?-1555), who was afterwards burnt at Smithfield in the Marian persecution. This was really a new edition of Tyndale's translation, which was completed by the addition of the Old Testament books after II. Chronicles from Coverdale's version. Next appeared Taverner's Bible (1539), which was no more than a revised edition of Matthews' Bible by Richard Taverner (1505?-1575), who wrote works in support of the Reformation. This was followed by the Great Bible or Cranmer's Bible (1539), another revision of Matthews' Bible. The printing of it in Paris was superintended by Miles Coverdale. It was, in fact, a revision of Matthews' Bible by Coverdale. From this Bible was taken the English version of the Psalms in the Prayer Book of the Church of England. Cromwell enjoined the use of the Great Bible in every parish church. Some years later some of the reformers who had fled to Geneva brought back the Geneva Bible (1557-1560), popularly called the "Breeches Bible," a version made by Protestant refugees. It was called the Breeches Bible because in Genesis iii. 7 in one edition it is said that Adam and Eve "sewed fig-tree leaves together, and made themselves breeches." This was for many years the most popular Bible in English homes. It was of a convenient size, and was supplied with notes. Another Bible of a later date (1568) was known as the Bishops' Bible. Matthew Parker (1504-1575), Archbishop of Canterbury, was occupied in the publication of this, a revision of the Great Bible, for some years (1563-68). Another version of the New Testament appeared in 1582. It was made at the College of Douay to meet the needs of English-speaking Roman Catholics, and was published at Rheims. The Old Testament was published at Douay, but not until 1609-10. This version is commonly known as the Douay Bible. The next version of the Bible was the famous one undertaken in the reign of James I. It became known as the Authorised Version, not because it was directly and officially authorised by King, Parliament, or Convocation, but because through its own merits it came to be regarded as authoritative. It was the work of six companies sitting at Westminster, Oxford, and Cambridge, and was based upon the Bishops' Bible with the help of the Genevan and Douay versions. The undertaking was discussed in 1604, seriously taken in hand in 1607, and completed in 1611. As Mr. Patterson truly says, it "has become a classic wherever the English tongue is spoken." He adds that "by the providence of God, it was written when the English language was in its simplest and most majestic form." But, beautiful and excellent as the Authorised Version is, yet another English version has been made necessary in recent years by the progress of scientific study. Since the time when the Authorised Version was made, much of its phraseology has become obsolete or even changed its meaning; scholars have a more thorough and accurate knowledge of the original and cognate languages of the Bible; new discoveries of ancient manuscripts, versions, and quotations have been made; and textual criticism has become a science. In June, 1870, therefore, an assembly of distinguished divines met in the Jerusalem Chamber in Westminster Abbey to start work upon a new version of the Bible. The New Testament was published in 1881, and the Revised Version of the whole Bible in 1885. In 1895 was published a Revised Version of the Apocrypha (Old Testament), "being the version set forth A.D. 1611 compared with the most ancient authorities and revised A.D. 1894." The work was done by three Committees, which were called the London, Westminster, and Cambridge Committees. See J. Paterson Smyth, *How we got our Bible*, 1889; M. W. Patterson, *Hist.;* the *D.N.B.*

BIBLE CHRISTIANS. See METHODISTS.

BIBLE COMMUNISTS. Another name for the PERFECTIONISTS (*q.v.*).

BIBLE SOCIETIES. Societies formed for the purpose of circulating copies of the Old and New Testaments. The First Bible Society seems to have been founded in Germany in 1712 by Baron Hildebrand von Canstein (1667-1719), the friend of the pietists P. J. Spener (1635-1705) and A. H. Francke (1663-1727). Called the "Cansteinsche Bibelanstalt," it was afterwards combined with the Francke Institutes at Halle. In 1780 a society called "The Bible Society" was formed in England with the object of supplying Bibles to soldiers and sailors. This afterwards became known as the "Naval and Military Bible Society." In 1792 a "French Bible Society" was formed for the purpose of circulating Bibles in French. In 1802 Thomas Charles (1755-1814) went to London to call the attention of religious people to the scarcity of Welsh Bibles in Wales. "Having been introduced to the committee of the Religious Tract Society, it was suggested by the Rev. Joseph Hughes, a Baptist minister, who was present, that there might be a similar dearth not only in Wales, but in other parts of the country, and that it would be desirable to form a society for the express purpose of circulating the Scriptures." On inquiry it was found that there was such a dearth, and "The British and Foreign Bible Society" was founded (1804). The Society "was founded on unsectarian principles, it being resolved that one-half of its committee should be elected from amongst Churchmen, and one-half from amongst Dissenters (H. S. Skeats and C. S. Miall). This is now the greatest society of the kind, and has branches in all parts of the British Empire. There is also a "National Bible Society of Scotland," which was formed in 1861. The Society next in importance to the British and Foreign Bible Society is the "American Bible Society," which was founded in 1816 at New York. There are similar societies in Germany and Russia. The income of the "British and Foreign Bible Society" is about a quarter of a million, and about five millions and a half of Bibles, Testaments, and portions of Holy Scripture are annually circulated in 409 languages and dialects" *London Diocese Book,* 1910). See Chambers' *Encycl;* Brockhaus; *Prot. Dict.*

BIBLIA PAUPERUM. Literally the "Bible of the Poor." The famous book with this title was a work giving pictures of the chief events recounted in the Old and New Testaments, to which were added short illustrative notes or texts in Latin or German. The book was treasured by the laity and used as a textbook by mendicant preachers in the Middle Ages. It was so called either because these mendicant preachers were known as Pauperes Christi, "Christ's Poor," or because it was intended for the "poor in spirit." The pictures were copied in sculptures, and on walls, glass, altar-pieces, etc. In Vienna are preserved an altar-piece of the twelfth century with a painting from the "Biblia Pauperum," and two copies of the book dated 1430. The book fell into disuse early in the sixteenth century. There was another book with the same title, "Biblia Pauperum," or "Poor Man's Bible," compiled by Bonaventura (A.D. 1221-1274). This book explains the contents of the Bible on mystical and allegorical lines.

BIBLICAL ARCHÆOLOGY, SOCIETY OF. A society founded in December, 1870. The special object of the Society was the collection of illustrations of archæology, history, arts, and chronology from the monuments of Ancient and Modern Assyria, Palestine, Egypt, and other Biblical Lands. Papers were read, and published in the "Proceedings" of the Society, which were issued monthly during the session.

BIBLIOMANCY. A term composed of two Greek words and meaning "divination by the Bible." The practice was to open the Bible haphazard, and to regard the first passage on which the eye fell as a special message or pronouncement. Or the first words of the Bible heard after entering a place of worship might be similarly regarded. Another form of bibliomancy is the ordeal of the Bible and the key. The way to detect a thief is to read to the apparatus Psalm 50. At the words "When thou sawest a thief, then thou consentedst with him," it will turn to the guilty person (see E. B. Tylor, *P.C.*).

BIBLIOTHECA. A term which has sometimes been used as a designation of the Bible. It came into use towards the end of the fourth century A.D.

BICORNI. Literally "idiots," a contemptuous designation of the Beghards (*q.v.*), used by mediaeval writers.

BIDDELIANS. Followers of John Biddle (1615-1662). In 1641 Biddle was made master of the free school of St. Mary-le-Crypt, Gloucester. In 1645 he was imprisoned on account of his religious opinions, but was soon released on bail. He was next summoned before a parliamentary commission at Westminster, and in 1647 was sent back to prison. In the same year, a work which he had published on the Holy Spirit, and in which he argued against the Godhead, was burnt as blasphemous by the hangman. Afterwards he was again released on bail, and then again imprisoned, this time in Newgate. In 1652 he was set free once more, in virtue of Cromwell's Act of Oblivion. By this time he had gained a number of followers. In 1654, however, he was imprisoned in Gatehouse, and in 1655 he became involved in a theological dispute and was banished to the Scilly Islands. He was allowed to return to London in 1658, and preached there until 1662. He was then arrested again, and, being unable to pay his fine, went to prison. Here he died. Biddle has sometimes been regarded as the founder of Unitarianism (*q.v.*) in England. See the *D.N.B.*

BIDDING PRAYER. A form of Christian prayer in which the people are "bidden" to prayer for certain persons. It is no longer in common use; but may be heard sometimes in Cathedrals, Inns of Court, and the Universities. Canon 55 of 1603 orders that "before all sermons, lectures, and homilies, the preachers and ministers shall move the people to join with them in prayer, in this form or to this effect as briefly as conveniently they may." The form then in use ran: "Ye shall pray for Christ's holy Catholic Church, that is, for the whole congregation of Christian people dispersed throughout the whole world, and especially for the Churches of England, Scotland, and Ireland: and herein I require you most especially to pray for the King's most excellent Majesty our Sovereign Lord *James*, King of England, Scotland, France, and Ireland, Defender of the Faith and Supreme Governor in these his realms, and all other his dominions and countries, over all persons, in all causes, as well Ecclesiastical as Temporal: ye shall also pray for our gracious Queen *Anne*, the noble Prince *Henry*, and the rest of the King and Queen's royal issue: ye shall also pray for the Ministers of God's holy Word and Sacraments, as well Archbishops and Bishops, as other Pastors and Curates: ye shall also pray for the King's most honourable Council, and for all the Nobility and Magistrates of this realm; that all and every of these, in their several callings, may serve truly and painfully to the glory of God, and the edifying and well governing of his people, remembering the account that they must make: also ye shall pray for the whole Commons of this realm, that they may live in the true faith and fear of God in humble obedience to the King and brotherly charity one to another. Finally, let us praise God for all those which are departed out of this life in the faith of Christ, and pray unto God that we may have grace to direct our lives after their good example; that, this life ended, we may be made partakers with them of the glorious resurrection in the life everlasting; always concluding with the Lord's Prayer." See *Prot. Dict.*

BIJAS. A term employed in Hinduism. Mantras (*q.v.*) are inspired Vedic texts which are supposed to possess great power as occult forces. Bijas are the radical letters or syllables of Mantras, the essential parts of them, or letters or syllables which represent the name of the deity to whom the Mantra is addressed, or letters or syllables which denote parts of the body over which the deity is supposed to preside. See Monier-Williams.

BIKKURIM. The name of one of the Jewish treatises or tractates which reproduce the oral tradition or unwritten law as developed by the second century A.D. and are included in the Mishnah (*q.v.*), a collection and compilation completed by Rabbi Judah the Holy, or the Patriarch, about 200 A.D. The sixty-three tractates of the Mishnah are divided into six groups or orders (*sedarim*). Bikkūrim is the eleventh tractate of the first group, which is called *Zerā'īm* ("Seeds").

BILOCATION. The expression denotes the power of being in two places at the same time. Certain persons are supposed to have possessed or to possess this power. In a biography of St. Alfonso di Liguori, translated by Cardinal Wiseman, the saint is said one day to have been in his own house and at the same time in church preaching a sermon. The writer of the biography of Apollonius of Tyana reports that his hero transported himself quickly and mysteriously from one place to another. Pythagoras is said to have had the same power. In modern times spiritualists have claimed that the same thing still happens. In 1905 Italian newspapers reported strange happenings in a family named Pansini. Two boys are said to have had a number of strange experiences. "The boys were at Ruvo one morning at 9 o'clock, and at 9.30, without knowing how or why, they found themselves at Molfetta, before the convent of the Capuchins." Again we are told that "one day the two boys were in the Piazza di Ruvo at 1.35 o'clock, and at 1.45, about ten minutes afterwards, were at Trani, before the door of the house of one of their uncles, Signor Girolamo Maggiore" (Joseph Lapponi, *Hypnotism and Spiritism*, 1907).

BIMBO-GAMI. A god of poverty in Japanese mythology.

BINDING AND LOOSING. Expressions occurring in the New Testament (Matthew xvi. 19, xviii. 18). In Matthew xvi. 18, Jesus is represented as saying to his disciple, Simon Peter: "And I also say unto thee, that thou art Peter (*Petros*), and upon this rock (*petra*) I will build my church; and the gates of Hades shall not prevail against it. I will give unto thee the keys of the kingdom of heaven: and whatsoever thou shalt bind on earth shall be bound in heaven: and whatsoever thou shalt loose on earth shall be loosed in heaven." On this passage the Church of Rome, of which Peter is supposed to have been the first bishop, bases its claim to supremacy. In Matthew xviii. 18, Jesus, addressing the disciples collectively, says: "Verily, I say unto you, what things soever ye shall bind on earth shall be bound in heaven: and what things soever ye shall loose on earth shall be loosed in heaven." The expressions were commonly used of decisions given by the Jewish rabbis. To bind was to forbid; to loose was to allow. See *Encycl. Bibl.*

BINZURU. Binzuru is one of the deities most widely revered in Japan in connection with the ancient national religion known as Shintōism (*q.v.*). The god of medicine, he "is usually a red lacquer figure of a man seated, and much defaced by the rubbings of centuries" (I. Bishop). Persons afflicted with disease make pilgrimages to celebrated images of the god. To cure the disease they rub that part of the god which corresponds to the afflicted part of their own persons. Then they rub themselves again. See "Shintōism" in *R.S.W.*

BIRADEVARU. Birādēvaru or Birappa is the patron saint of the Kurubas, a caste of hunters in Southern India. Horses and ponies being vehicles of the god, the Kurubas will not ride upon them. The Kurubas are ancestor worshippers, and treasure golden discs stamped with the figures of human beings. Their temples are dolmen-like structures. "In the open country near Kadūr in Mysore is a shrine of Birādēvaru, which consists of four stone pillars several feet in height, surmounted by flat slabs as a cap-stone, within which the deity is represented by round stones, and stones with snakes carved on them are deposited. Within the Kuruba quarter of the town, the shrine of Anthargattamma is a regular dolmen beneath a margosa (*Melia Azadirachta*) tree, in which the goddess is represented by rounded stones imbedded in a mound of earth. Just outside the same town, close to a pīpal tree (*Ficus religiosa*) are two smaller dolmen-like structures containing stones representing two Kuruba Dāsaris, one a centenarian, who are buried there" (E. Thurston and K. Rangachari).

BIRETTA. See BERRETTA.

BIRKATH ERUSIN. Literally the "Blessing of Betrothal," a feature in the Jewish marriage-service. God is blessed for having instituted marriage. "Blessed are Thou, O Lord, Who sanctifiest Thy people Israel by the rite of the canopy and the sacred covenant of wedlock." See W. O. E. Oesterley and G. H. Box.

BIRTH CEREMONIES. In Arabia soon after a child was born a sheep was sacrificed, and the infant's head was shaved and daubed with the sheep's blood. The sacrifice was meant "to avert evil from the child by shedding blood on his behalf," apparently to establish a kind of blood-brotherhood between the protector and the protected (see BLOOD). This ceremony was called 'AḲĪKA (*q.v.*). Another custom among some sections of primitive folk has been to spit on a child after its birth (*e.g.*, in Connemara) or at its naming (*e.g.*, among the Mandingos and among the Bambaras of Western Africa). The reason for this is that sometimes a person's saliva is supposed to possess the element of life. In order, apparently, to place a child under the deity's protection, the Arabs also hid it, as soon as it was born, under a cauldron, where it remained until dawn. Sometimes on the morning after birth a child's gums were rubbed with masticated dates and a name was given it. Robertson Smith thinks that "in general, the sacrifice, the naming, and the symbolical application of the most important article of food to the child's mouth all fell together, and marked his reception into partnership in the *sacra* and means of life of his father's group" (*Kinship*). See W. R. Smith, *Kinship;* E. S. Hartland, *Perseus*.

BISHNOIS. A Hindu sect, founded in the Punjab by a Panwār Rājpūt named Jhāmbāji (*b.* A.D. 1451). Jhāmbāji is supposed at an early age to have given evidence of a miraculous origin, and during a famine in 1485 he is said to have won a great reputation by providing food for all who had faith in him. He seems to have been a religious reformer, "who attempted to break loose from the debased Hindu polytheism and arrogant supremacy of the Brāhmans by choosing one god, Vishnu, out of the Hindu pantheon, and exalting him into the sole and supreme deity" (R. V. Russell). Some of his doctrines, as given by Russell and Hīra Lāl, are as follows: Bathe in the morning; Commit no adultery; Be content; Be abstemious and pure; Strain your drinking-water; Be careful of your speech; Examine your fuel in case any living creature be burnt with it; Show pity to living creatures; Do not steal; Do not speak evil of others; Do not tell lies; Never quarrel; Avoid opium, tobacco, *bhāng* and blue clothing; Do not cut green trees; Sacrifice with fire; Say prayers; meditate; Perform worship and attain heaven; Baptise your children if you would be called a true Bishnoi.

BISHOP. The word is given in the English Version of the Bible as a translation of the Greek word *episkopos* (Philippians i. 1; I. Timothy iii. 2; I. Peter ii. 25). In Acts i. 20 *episkopē* is translated "bishopric," but not, of course, in a technical sense. It has long been a matter of controversy whether "bishop" is used in the New Testament in the sense in which it was used later in the Christian Church. The word *episkopos* was taken over from the Greeks, among whom it denoted an "overseer" or a "superintendent" (cp. *episkopē*, visitation, oversight; and then office or charge generally). It seems to have been used particularly of the finance officers of Greek guilds. And it was just this kind of duty that the Christian *episkopos* was called upon to perform—the administration of the common fund of a kind of benevolent society. On the other hand, the word had already been adopted in the Greek translation of the Old Testament to represent the Hebrew *pāḳid*, which denotes an "overseer" in a more general sense (Judges ix. 28; Nehemiah xi. 9, 14, 22; II. Kings xi. 15). An earlier title for the officials of the early Christian Church was *presbyteros*, Presbyter or Elder (Acts xi. 30; xv.); and when *episkopos* first came into use the two terms seem to have been regarded as equivalent (Acts xx. 28; Philippians i. 1; I. Timothy v. 17; Titus i. 5, 7; I. Peter v. 1, 2). Moreover, these two terms seem to have other equivalents, such as *proïstámenoi*, "presidents" (I. Thessalonians v. 12; Romans xii. 8), *hēgoúmenoi*, "rulers" (Hebrews xiii. 7, 17), and *poiménes*, "shepherds" (Ephesians iv. 11). The question is: Did one of the Presbyters of a *collegium* come gradually in New Testament times to be elevated above the rest. It has been ably contended that this did happen, and that the government of the apostolic Church became monarchial. The power exercised by Diotrephes (III. John i. 9), it has been pointed out, seems to have exceeded that of ordinary presbyters. But Diotrephes is rebuked for desiring to exercise this power, so that it seems to have been a kind of usurpation; and in the time of Hermas and Irenaeus, bishops and elders or presbyters seem still to be placed upon the same level (Hermas, *Vision* ii. 4, iii. 9; *Similitudes* iii. 27; Irenaens, *Adv. Haeres.* iii. 3). Local conditions were not, however, the same everywhere. By the middle of the second century the monarchical episcopate was well established; and in Rome and elsewhere the development may have been more rapid than in other places (cp. Ignatius, *Epistle to the Romans*, ii., ix.; *Epistle to Polycarp* iv., vi.). In any case, it is difficult to prove that the monarchical episcopate is of apostolic origin. That it was, on the other hand, a natural and pre-ordained development is a legitimate contention. The Roman Catholic Church, however, insists on the apostolic origin of episcopacy. The Council of Trent says: "If anyone deny that there is in the Church a hierarchy instituted by divine ordinance, which consists of bishops, presbyters, and ministers, let him be anathema"; and "if anyone affirm that bishops are not superior to presbyters, or that they have not the power of confirming or ordaining, or that the power which they have is common to presbyters also, let him be anathema." It is claimed by Roman Catholics (though not by them alone) that "St. James the Less was beyond reasonable doubt bishop of Jerusalem"; that St. Paul having given Titus power to ordain presbyters, and Timothy directions as to receiving accusations against presbyters, these two were clearly "ecclesiastical officers superior to the clergy of the second order"; and that the Angels of the Churches mentioned in the Book of Revelation (i. 20) "answer to the idea of diocesan bishops and to nothing else." In the third century, according to Cyprian (*Ep.* lxviii.), bishops were chosen "by the vote of all the faithful and by the judgment of the bishops," and they were so elected in the West until the eleventh century. Bishops were then elected by the cathedral chapter. At first the election had to be confirmed by the metropolitan. The right of confirmation afterwards passed to the Pope, and in course of time in some cases the election itself. In Catholic Germany and Switzerland the right of election now belongs to the cathedral chapters; in France, Portugal, Spain, Naples and Sicily, Sardinia, Austria, and Bavaria to the Sovereign. In England the Pope chooses the Roman Catholic bishops. In the Church of England royal letters patent are sent to the Dean and Chapter of the Cathedral telling them to make a certain choice. In Protestant Germany the title Bishop has been dropped in favour of General-Superintendent. See D. Schenkel, *Bibel-Lexikon*; *Encycl. Bibl.*; Chambers' *Encycl.*; *Cath. Dict.*; *Prot. Dict.*

BISHOPS' BIBLE. An English version of the Bible, published in 1568. See BIBLE.

BISHOPS' BOOK, THE. A name given to "The Institution of a Christian Man," a manuel which was published in 1537. It was composed by a committee of bishops on the lines of and sometimes in the language of the Ten Articles, and its use was authorised for three years by Henry VIII. The book expounded the Apostles' Creed, the Sacraments, the Ten Commandments, the Lord's Prayer, the Ave Maria, Justification, and Purgatory. "It represented neither doctrinal advance nor doctrinal reaction" (M. W. Patterson, *Hist.*).

BISHRIYYA. An Arabian sect, regarded by the Sunnis (*q.v.*) as heretics. They hold that "the Will of God was one of His works, that since God is omniscient and knows what is profitable for man, it is impossible to suppose that He does not will it." See F. A. Klein.

BISMILLAH. An Arabic expression meaning "in the name of God (Allah)." The *bismillah* means the formula in which the name of God is mentioned.

BIZOCHI. A name used by Pope John XXII. for the Fraticelli in his Bull of A.D. 1317.

BLACK BARTHOLOMEW. A name given to St. Bartholomew's Day in 1662, because on that day all beneficed clergy had to comply with the provisions of the Act of Uniformity and accept the Book of Common Prayer.

BLACK BOOK. The report of the committee which King Henry VIII. nominated in 1535 to inquire into the condition and administration of the monasteries became known as the "Black Book."

BLACK CANONS. See AUGUSTINIANS.

BLACK FRIARS. See DOMINICANS.

BLACK-LETTER DAYS. These are the minor Holy Days noted in the Calendar of the Christian Church. They are so called in distinction from the major Holy Days, Red-letter Festivals, which were distinguished originally by red letters. See W. R. W. Stephens, *Common Prayer*, 1901.

BLACK MONKS. See BENEDICTINES.

BLACK POPES. A name given to the leaders of the Jesuit Society of Jesus in the time of Pope Pius IX. because of the influence which they exercised at Rome.

BLACK STONE, THE. A sacred stone in one of the corners of the Ka'ba, the square stone building at Mecca. See KA'BA and HAJJ, THE.

BLASPHEMY. In the Old Testament the word is equivalent to scorn or rejection of God. The Hebrews made such treatment of God a capital offence (Leviticus xxiv. 15). The people were forbidden lightly to use the name of God, and in course of time even to pronounce his true name was a profane act (Leviticus xxiv. 11). Jesus was accused of blasphemy when he claimed to be the Son of God (Mark xiv. 61-64; Matthew xxvi. 65), and Stephen was stoned because he was considered to have used "blasphemous words against Moses, and against God" (Acts vi. 13, vii. 56 *ff.*)

BLAVATSKY INSTITUTE, THE. The Blavatsky Institute was organized by a small group of disciples of H. P. Blavatsky. It is an activity within the Theosophical Society founded in 1875 by H. P. Blavatsky, H. S. Olcott, and W. Q. Judge. The promoters of the Institute believe in the teachings of Theosophy, and wish to give to those who desire it an opportunity to study them. The study of H. P. Blavatsky's works, and the application of her statements to the various problems, social, ethnical, philosophical and religious, which confront us in our complex civilization, constitute the main work. Intellectual and spiritual development receive equal attention. The fundamental laws of the Universe are learnt, and at the same time man is taught to obtain mastery over himself. It is stated that "it is not the object of this enterprise to furnish a retreat for misanthropes and hypochondriacs. Neither is it an infirmary for ghost-seers, visionaries, or dreamers, where they may revel to their hearts' content among the creations of their own fancy; nor is it to be a school for occultism, where magic arts are taught to the fool; but it is intended to be a place where those who earnestly aspire to spirituality may find the External conditions necessary to cultivate it, and to acquire the true 'magic staff' that will securely support them on their journey through Eternity." The Blavatsky Institute publishes a monthly journal called *The Path.*

BLESSED SACRAMENT, CONFRATERNITY OF THE. A Society founded in 1862 in the Church of England. With it was amalgamated in 1867 "The Society of the Blessed Sacrament." The Associates are priests and laymen. Grants of money are made to poor parishes for Altar linen and Eucharistic vestments. The Associates are asked to pray for the re-union of Christendom, the restoration of the Reserved Sacrament, "Sacramental Confession," and for the faithful Departed. Members of the Confraternity receive a medal. See Walter Walsh, "Ritualistic Secret Societies," in *Prot. Dict.*

BLESSINGS AND CURSINGS. In primitive times there was supposed to be a great power in a blessing or a curse. To have the blessing of a deity was to enjoy his friendly aid and protection; to have the curse was to encounter his disfavour and active hostility. A blessing or a curse was thus a kind of spell. Amongst the Hebrews it was an ancient practice to invoke a curse upon the enemy before commencing hostilities. Balak, King of Moab, summoned Balaam the prophet to come and curse the Israelites before he attempted to overthrow them (Numbers xxii.); and Goliath "cursed David by his gods" before advancing to battle against him (I. Samuel xvii. 43). Curses were added also to legal formulae to make them more impressive. Blessings might be used on the same occasions as cursings. Moses powerfully blessed his own people and effectively cursed their enemies (cp. Leviticus ix. 22, Numbers vi. 23-27). Fathers on their death-bed pronounced valued blessings on their children. There can be no doubt that, given a strong belief in the power of the god, the effect of a blessing or curse on the mind, and so on the life, of a person, might be very powerful. This, of course, is not the primitive, but the true psychological explanation. In the story in the New Testament known as the "Cursing of the Fig-tree (Matthew xxi. 19 *f.*; Mark xi. 13, 21 *f.*), the curse is so potent that it withers up the tree. Here we have not merely a mental effect, but one that is regarded as directly material. Jesus pronounced blessings in his discourses, as well as denunciations which might be called curses. See *Encycl. Bibl.*

BLOOD. Robertson Smith (*Religion of the Semites*, 1894, p. 233) notes that among the Semites the sacrificial use of blood "is connected with a series of very important ritual ideas, turning on the conception that the blood is a special seat of the life. But primarily, when the blood is offered at the altar, it is conceived to be drunk by the deity." He compares cases of the drinking of blood among other peoples. In Africa fresh blood is drunk by all the negroes of the White Nile. It is imbibed by Masai warriors, by the Gallas, and, as far as the men are concerned, by the Hottentots. Durkheim (p. 137) notes that in the tribes of Central Australia human blood is so holy a thing that it serves frequently to consecrate the most respected instruments of the cult. "For example, in certain cases, the nurtunja is regularly anointed from top to bottom with the blood of a man. It is upon ground all saturated with blood that the men of the Emu, among the Arunta, trace their sacred images. There is no religious ceremony where blood does not have some part to play. During the initiation, the adults open their veins and sprinkle the novice with their blood; and this blood is so sacred a thing that women may not be present while it is flowing; the sight of it is forbidden them, just as the sight of a churinga is. The blood lost by a young initiate during the very violent operations he must undergo has very particular virtues: it is used in various ceremonies. That which flows during the sub-incision is piously kept by the Arunta and buried in a place upon which they put a piece of wood warning passers-by of the sacredness of the spot; no woman should approach it. The religious nature of blood also explains the equal importance, religiously, of the red ochre, which is very frequently employed in ceremonies; they rub the churinga with it and use it in ritual decorations. This is due to the fact that, because of its colour, it is regarded as something kindred to blood. Many deposits of red ochre which are found in the Arunta territory are even supposed to be the coagulated blood which certain heroines of the mythical period shed on the soil." Elliot Smith has pointed out that blood was regarded as an elixir of life (*q.v.*), and that red ochre came to be used as a substitute for it. It was an Aztec belief that the sun was an animal, which was originally a man. The man had become transformed, and "had received the intense vitality necessary for the performance of his functions from the blood of the gods, voluntarily shed for that purpose" (Edwardes and Spence, p. 48). In the Central American system the sun is often represented as "a deity whose sole sustenance is human blood, and who must be well supplied with this gruesome pabulum or perish" (*ibid.*, p. 72). The Scandinavian god Heimdallr is nourished by the blood of sacrifices.

BLOOD, FIELD OF. See ACELDAMA.

BLOOD-BURIAL. An expression used in Chinese religion. It is a mark of filial devotion to allow a few days (sometimes seven) to elapse before a deceased parent is buried. When this is not done, the burial is called a "blood-burial," because the corpse is supposed still to have blood in it (J. Doolittle, *Social Life of the Chinese*, 1867, quoted by J. J. M. de Groot in *R.S.C.*).

BLOOD-LICKERS. See BLOOD.

BOANERGES. We read in the New Testament that Jesus gave this name to two of his disciples, James and John, the sons of Zebedee (Mark iii. 17). The name is interpreted by the Gospel writer "Sons of Thunder." The first half of the word might be a corrupt form of the Hebrew *b'nē* "sons of." The second part of the word is more difficult to explain. The most plausible suggestion is that the Hebrew or rather Aramaic word intended is *rĕgaz* "anger." *Rĕgaz* might be used of thunder, though "sons of anger" in the sense of "soon angered" seems more suitable. See *Encycl. Bibl.*

BOCHICA. A deity in the mythology of the Muyscas of Bogota. He is represented as a culture-hero, the teacher of building, agriculture, and laws; and as god of the dawn.

BODHISATTVAS. Literally "he whose essence is becoming enlightenment," a term used in Buddhism. A term applied to a Buddha at a certain stage in his development. Thus, when Gautama became incarnate and was born of Mâyâ, he was a Bodhisattva. Now "when a Bodhisattva undertakes the task of a Buddha, then his goal is Nirvâna: with that, naturally, all earthly relation comes to an end." But, "many of those lofty beings, who are in a position to tread the last way of life, are possessed by a strong craving to aid their fellow-beings around them, to lead them into the true way of knowledge, and this craving determines them to willingly forego the Buddhaship which they might attain, in order to live for countless years in the state of a Bodhisattva engaged in tasks of ministry to lower things. The Bodhisattva meanwhile exists in one of the many heavens, possesses divine powers, is filled with kindly intentions towards the suffering world below him, and is ready to help those who appeal to him." The Bodhisattva Avalokita is considered to be reincarnate regularly in the Dalai Lama of Lhassa. In Tibetan temples are to be seen on wall-paintings representations of Buddhas, Bodhisattvas, and saints. The Bodhisattva "is sumptuously adorned after the manner of an Indian Prince. The head is covered with a crown, the ornaments coming down over the ears; he wears bracelets, and has chains on his breast; precious stones, either real or imitation, are worn in profusion. The hair is not shaved off, but bound in a knot on the top of the head. Some Bodhisattvas show several heads or arms. Avalokita especially is often represented with eleven heads, with four or many more ("thousand") arms. The saints, on the other hand, generally wear the normal monk's habit and a monk's cap." See H. Hackmann.

BOEDROMIA. An Athenian festival held in honour of Apollo (*q.v.*) in his character of a god of battle (Boedromios). One of the months (September-October) was named after the god Boedromion. The festival took place on the sixth day of this month.

BOGOMILES. Literally "lovers of God" (from the Slavonic), a sect which appeared in Thrace and Bulgaria in the twelfth century. They are also called Bogarmitae, Massilians, and by orthodox members of the Greek Church Phundaites, "wearers of the girdle." The sect was founded by a monk named Basil, whose system of theology was dualistic like that of the Paulicians and Cathari. His followers had to live a life of poverty and asceticism. They did not accept all the books of the Bible, but only the Psalms, the Prophets, the Gospels, the Acts, the Epistles, and the Apocalypse; and they applied the allegorical key to the interpretation of Scripture. The world of matter and human beings was created, they held, by Satanael, who sprang from the Divine Being but rebelled against Him and opposed Him. The Logos, who also sprang from the Divine Being, took a phantom body and came down to earth to undo the work of the wicked Satanael. Alexius Comnenus (1048-1118) undertook to exterminate the heresy. In 1118 he invited Basil to a banquet, had him seized, and afterwards caused him to be burned at Constantinople. But the sect was not suppressed. In A.D. 1140 we find a Council of Constantinople anathematizing the followers of Basil, and in 1325 Bosnia was overrun with them. In this year Pope John xxii. wrote to the King of Bosnia inveighing against them. In the fifteenth century they appealed to the Turks to protect them against the King of Bosnia and the priests who were persecuting them. Soon after the invasion of Bosnia by Muhammad II. (1463), they seem to have gone over to Islam in large numbers. This, as Mr. T. W. Arnold says, in view of "the numerous points of likeness between their peculiar beliefs and the tenets of Islam," is quite intelligible. "They rejected the worship of the Virgin Mary, the institution of Baptism, and every form of priesthood. They abominated the cross as a religious symbol, and considered it idolatry to bow down before religious pictures and the images and relics of the saints. Their houses of prayer were very simple and unadorned, in contrast to the gaudily-decorated Roman Catholic churches, and they shared the Muhammadan dislike of bells, which they styled 'the devil's trumpets.' They believed that Christ was not himself crucified, but that some phantom was substituted in his place: in this respect agreeing partially with the teaching of the Qur'ān. Their condemnation of wine and the general austerity of their mode of life and the stern severity of their outward demeanour would serve as further links to bind them to Islam. . . They prayed five times a day and five times a night, repeating the Lord's Prayer with frequent kneelings, and would thus find it very little change to join in the services of the mosque." See J. H. Blunt; T. W. Arnold, *The Preaching of Islam*, 1896.

BOHEMIA, CONFESSION OF. A Bohemian confession approved by Luther, Melanchthon, and the Academy of Wurtemburg, and published in A.D. 1532.

BOHEMIAN BRETHREN. The Bohemian Brethren were descendants of the Hussites (*q.v.*). When the Taborites (*q.v.*), the extreme section of the Hussites, were finally conquered and dispersed, a remnant of them settled at Lititz on the borders of Moravia and Silesia. This remnant united with a remnant of the Calixtines (*q.v.*) in 1457 to form a religious body of Bohemian (and Moravian) Brethren, which took the name "Unitas Fratrum" or "The Unity of the Brethren." The unity they desired was that of a brotherhood of Christians (of every denomination) united on a broad basis of scriptural doctrine, practice, and worship. In 1467 The Brethren decided to organize a ministry of their own. Stephen, a Waldensian bishop, who claimed descent from the bishops of the early Church, consented to consecrate as their first bishop Michael Bradacius. Under George Podiebrad (*d.* 1471) the Brethren were persecuted. Under Luke of Prague (1497-1528) the Holy Scriptures became their only rule of faith and practice. In 1500 their churches in Bohemia and Moravia already numbered two hundred. In the time of John Augusta (1531-72) they issued "Confessions." In 1505 they published a Hymn Book, and in 1593 a Bohemian version of the Bible, the Kralitz Bible. The Bohemian Brethren, in fact, made great progress and became prosperous. But in course of time prosperity brought relaxation of discipline and excess of ambition. They had supported the Bohemian Protestants in their rising against Ferdinand II. These were routed at the Battle of the White Mountain in 1620, and the consequences were serious for the Bohemian Brethren. In 1621 their leading men were beheaded. Thousands of them afterwards fled, or were expelled, from Bohemia. A century later, when the remnant also left their native country, the refugees became known as Herruhuters or Moravians (see MORAVIANS). The members of the Unitas Fratrum were divided into three classes: the Beginners (*Incipientes*), the Proficient (*Proficientes*), and the Perfect (*Perfecti*). The ministers also, who were chosen from the Perfect, were of three kinds: Acolytes or Deacons, Pastors or Priests, and Bishops or Presidents. At the head of the Unitas Fratrum was a Council of Elders. See J. H. Blunt; *Prot. Dict.; Cath. Dict.;* Brockhaus.

BOHRAS. The Bohras or Bohoras (probably "traders") of India are a caste of traders, whose original home was Gujarāt. The sect is said to have grown up here through the activity of a missionary, Abdulla, who came from Yemen to Cambay in A.D. 1067. In 1539 the Bohras of India were joined by the Bohras of Arabia, and Surat became the headquarters of the sect. The Bohras are Muhammadans, and for the most part Shias of the Ismailia sect of Egypt. With a few exceptions (*e.g.*, the special importance attached to circumcision), the customs of the Bohras do not differ much from those of ordinary Muhammadans. See R. V. Russell.

BOLLANDISTS. The great Jesuit work "Acta Sanctorum" or Lives of the Saints was planned by Rosweid (*d.* 1629), a Flemish Jesuit. But John Bolland (1596-1665), who worked at Antwerp, was the first to make a real beginning with the undertaking. From 1635 George Henschen (1600-1681) collaborated with him, and by the year 1658 five folios had appeared. In 1660 Daniel Papebrock (1628-1714) also became a collaborator. After the death of Bolland there was a succession of Jesuit workers; but in 1794, by which time fifty-three volumes had been published, the undertaking was interrupted by the French Revolution. It was not possible to resume the work until 1837, when the Society of Jesus was commissioned to do so, and issued a prospectus "De Prosecutione Operis Bollandiani." In 1845 a new volume appeared. It has been followed by many more. The collaborators have been called Bollandists after John Bolland. See *Cath. Dict.*

BONA DEA. Literally "the good goddess," an Italian goddess of fertility. She was a patron goddess of women, and was worshipped in Rome only by women (and amongst them by the Vestal Virgins). Men were not allowed to enter her temple. She was evidently a goddess of healing, since healing plants, as well as tame serpents, were kept in her temple. Her symbol was a consecrated serpent. "She is represented in works of art with a sceptre in her left hand, a wreath of vine leaves on her head, and a jar of wine at her side." See O. Seyffert, *Dict.*

BONE-GATHERING CEREMONY. When a deceased person has been burnt, it has been the custom among some peoples to gather the bones and ashes together with great solemnity. Monier-Williams gives several descriptions of this ceremony as he saw it performed in India. One of them is as follows: "A Brāhman and five women were seated in a semi-circle round the ashes and bones of a young married girl of low caste, whose body had recently been burnt. Before them was an earthenware vase, and around it were flowers, fruits, and betel-leaves. The Brāhman had a metal vase shaped something like a tumbler in his hand containing consecrated or holy water. With a small round spoon or ladle he took out a small portion of the water and poured it into the hands of the woman, at the same time muttering texts and prayers. Then he poured water into the vase, and on the top of the water placed the fruit, flowers, and leaves. Next, he collected the half-calcined bones, and having put them carefully and reverentially into the vase, he made a hole in the ground a few yards off and buried it. I was told that the vase would be left there for ten days, when a Sraddha (offering to deceased ancestors) would be performed in the same place." Afterwards the ashes and bones are thrown into a sacred river, preferably the Ganges. See Monier-Williams.

BONI HOMINES. Another name of the Perfecti.

BONI PUERI. Another name of the BEGHARDS (*q.v.*).

BONI VALETI. Another name of the BEGHARDS (*q.v.*).

BON RELIGION. A primitive form of religion in Tibet, which preceded Lamaism. It "recognised nature spirits, which were worshipped by all sorts of powerful and terrible offerings; and it also paid reverence to the spirits of the dead. The religious functions were performed by priests, and there were the elements of a magic cult, the knowledge of which was a secret confined to the Bon priests. Sacrifices—especially human sacrifices—were obligatory." In course of time this religion, which did not disappear altogether, was completely mingled with Tantric Buddhism. See H. Hackmann.

BOOK OF "AM DUAT." Literally the book "of that which is in the underworld," a sacred book in the religion of ancient Egypt. It was inscribed on sarcophagi, or written on papyri which were placed in graves. There is a fuller form of the text reserved for royal use and an abridged form. The Dûat has twelve divisions, through each of which the Sun made an hour's journey at night. These divisions represent fields, cities, or dwellings through which runs a river. The Sun-god, journeying in his bark from West to East, meets every conceivable kind of spirit and demon, and encounters enemies whom he punishes, and faithful ones whom he rewards. The underworld received in different places a rather different colouring. The book which gives the Theban representation was the work of the priests of Amon, and the sun is identified with this god. We have in the Book of "Am Dûat," says Prof. Naville, "one of the best examples of the incoherences which reign in the religious ideas of the old Egyptians. It would indeed be difficult to disentangle from the midst of the fantastic scenes which pass before our eyes any unity of conception, beyond the fact that the subject is the course of the sun during the night, or rather of the king who has become that great god. If we would look for a key to the fantastic symbolism of the book, we should continually run against contradictions, and against conceptions which are in complete antagonism to one another." See A. Wiedemann; A. Erman, *Handbook;* E. Naville, *The Old Egyptian Faith*, 1909.

BOOK OF ARMAGH. A manuscript translation of the New Testament "in the emendated Irish text," written in A.D. 812, and now preserved in Trinity College, Dublin. See C. R. Gregory.

BOOK OF BEN SIRA, THE. Jesus the son of (Ben) Sira or Sirach is the reputed author of the Apocryphal book Ecclesiasticus. The work is also known as the Book of Ben Sira or The Wisdom of Jesus the son of Sirach.

BOOK OF CHAD. A manuscript translation of the Gospels, belonging to the seventh or eighth century. It contains the emendated Irish text of Matthew, Mark, and the beginning of Luke. The manuscript is preserved in Lichfield Cathedral. See C. R. Gregory.

BOOK OF CHANGES. The *Yih*, "Book of Changes," or *Yih-king*, "Classical Book of Changes," is one of the ancient books treasured by the Chinese. It gives the ancient political cosmogony. A very ancient work, it was remodelled and expanded by the founder (1122 B.C.) of the Imperial dynasty that ruled in the time of Confucius (551-479 B.C.). Confucius himself added appendices to the Yih. He said he would gladly give fifty years to the study of it. The book has been described as "the most ancient of the Chinese writings." And this would seem to be a true description, though Prof. Legge asserts that not a single character in the book is older than the twelfth century B.C. The Yih-king was one of five books that received the title of the "Five Classics." See James Legge, *Religions of China*, 1880; A. Terrien De Lacouperie, *The Oldest Book of the Chinese*, 1892; H. J. Allen, *Early Chinese Hist.*, 1906; E. H. Parker, *Studies*, 1910.

BOOK OF DEER. A manuscript translation, an emendated Irish text, of the Gospels, belonging to the eighth or ninth century. It is so called because formerly it was in the monastery of Deer or Deir in Aberdeenshire. It is now preserved in the Library of the University of Cambridge, England. See C. R. Gregory.

BOOK OF DIMMA. An Irish manuscript translation of the Gospels belonging to the ninth century. It is preserved in Trinity College, Dublin.

BOOK OF DURROW. An Irish manuscript translation of the Gospels belonging to the eighth century. It is preserved in Trinity College, Dublin.

BOOK OF HISTORY. The *Shu*, "Book of History" or "Book of Annals," or *Shu-king*, "Classical Book of History," is one of the five ancient books accepted by the Chinese as Classics. The Book of History deals with the patriarchal period and ends with the year 721 B.C. According to Prof. Legge (*The Religions of China*, 1880), this compilation is the oldest of Chinese books (see, however, BOOK OF CHANGES). See H. J. Allen, *Early Chinese Hist.*, 1906; E. H. Parker, *Studies*, 1910.

BOOK OF JASHER. The Book of Jasher (Revised Version, Jashar) is an ancient Hebrew song-book from which quotations are given in the Old Testament (Josh. x. 13; 2 Sam. i. 18). The Hebrew expression is *sēphĕr hayyāshār*, which is most naturally translated "the book of the righteous (or upright)." Yāshār can hardly be a proper name here. According to the Greek Version of the Old Testament (the Septuagint), the words of Solomon in I. Kings viii. 12 *f.* were to be found in the "Book of Songs." This in Hebrew would be *sēphĕr hashshīr*. Very likely in every case this was the original expression. Sēphĕr hashshīr (s-ph-r h-sh-y-r) was misread Sēphĕr hayyāshār (s-ph-r h-y-sh-r). The book was a collection of poems and perhaps also of narratives, which seems to have been made about 930 B.C., that is to say, soon after the time of Solomon. See *Encycl. Bibl.*

BOOK OF KELLS. An Irish manuscript translation of the Gospels, belonging to the seventh or eighth century. It is preserved in Trinity College, Dublin.

BOOK OF MOLING OR MULLING. An Irish manuscript translation of the Gospels belonging to the ninth century. It is preserved in Trinity College, Dublin.

BOOK OF ODES. The *Shī*, "Book of Odes," or *Shī-king*, "Classical Book of Odes," is one of the Chinese Classics. It contains "the popular songs of China, in which the people of the various states expressed their political and social emotions" (E. H. Parker). The odes were collected and edited by Confucius (551-479 B.C.). Prof. Giles quotes one as follows:

> Do not say, This place is not public;
> No one can see me here.
> The approaches of spiritual Beings
> Cannot be calculated beforehand:
> But on no account should they be ignored.

Prof. Legge quotes another ode, dating from the twelfth century B.C., and gives it in rhyme thus:

> With reverence I will go
> Where duty's path is plain.
> Heaven's will I clearly know;
> It's favour to retain
> Is hard;—let me not say
> 'Heaven is remote on high,
> Nor notices men's way.'
> There in the starlit sky
> It round about us moves,
> Inspecting all we do,
> And daily disapproves
> What is not just and true.

Prof. Giles thinks it is clear from the *Odes* "that the Chinese people continued to hold, more clearly and more firmly than ever, a deep-seated belief in the existence of an anthropomorphic and personal God, whose one care was the welfare of the human race." See James Legge, *Religions of China*, 1880; H. J. Allen, *Early Chinese Hist.*, 1906; H. A. Giles, *Religions of Ancient China*, 1905; E. H. Parker, *Studies*, 1910.

BOOK OF ORIGINS. The name given by H. Ewald to the Elohistic narrative which runs through the Hexateuch. It was so called because it seemed to form the framework or groundwork (German "Grundschrift"). See SUPPLEMENTARY HYPOTHESIS.

BOOK OF REWARDS AND PUNISHMENTS. The "Book of Rewards and Punishments" is said to be the most popular exposition in its modern form of the Chinese religion or system of ethics known as Taoism (*q.v.*). It does indeed claim to be the production of the reputed founder of Taoism, Lao-tsze himself (sixth century B.C.); but, according to Prof. Douglas, it can hardly have been published earlier than the fifteenth or sixteenth century A.D., that is to say, many centuries after Buddhism became known in China (A.D. 62). Some of the maxims of the book, as given by Douglas, are as follows: "Practise righteousness and filial piety, be affectionate towards your younger brothers and respectful towards your elder brothers. . . . Do no injury, either to insects, plants, or trees. . . . Rejoice at the success of others, and sympathise with their reverses, even as though you were in their place. . . . Bestow favours without expecting recompense. . . . Do not introduce vexatious reforms into the administration of the empire. . . . Don't shoot at birds, nor hunt animals. . . . Don't drive insects from their holes, nor frighten roosting birds. . . . Don't seek your own advantage at the expense of others. . . . Don't suck other men's brains. . . . Don't break asunder marriages. . . . Don't decry the excellences of others, nor conceal your own imperfections. . . . Don't put obstacles in the way of the promotion of men who are endowed with talents or worthy of praise. . . . Don't delight in picking and stealing. . . . Don't murmur against Heaven at your lot, nor accuse men. Don't scold the wind, nor abuse the rain. . . . Never say anything you don't mean. . . . Don't employ all your strength to accomplish your aims. . . . Live in harmony with your wife. Wives, respect your husbands. . . . Don't do anything which is not useful. . . . Don't leap over a well or a hearth. . . . Don't shout or get angry on the first day of the month, or in the morning. . . . Don't point rudely at the sun, moon, and stars. . . . Don't needlessly kill tortoises and serpents." Douglas's translation is based upon the French translation of Stanislas Julien. See Robert K. Douglas, *Confucianism and Taouism;* Frederic H. Balfour, "Taoism," in *R.S.W.*

BOOK OF RITES. The *Li*, "Book of Rites," or *Li-king*, "Classical Book of Rites," is one of the ancient books accepted by the Chinese as Classics. The Rites are those of the Imperial dynasty that was reigning in the time of Confucius (551-479 B.C.), and was founded in 1122 B.C. Prof. Parker states that the Book of Rites or Book of Abstract Principles has never been changed organically. And he quotes Confucius as saying: "The dynasty (1756-1122 B.C.) preceding that under which we live (1122-255 B.C.) continued the abstract principles of that before it (2205-1766 B.C.), and handed over the same principles to the dynasty now reigning." The Book of Rites was only in parts edited by Confucius and his disciples. A few quotations will give some idea of the nature of the work. "Every tree has its appointed time to perish, and every beast its appointed time to die, and he who cuts down a tree or kills an animal before their time is guilty of unfilial conduct (Douglas). . . . A woman is unable to stand alone, and therefore when young depends on her father and brothers, when married, on her husband, and after his death, on her sons (Douglas). . . . Sacrifice is not a thing coming to a man from without; it issues from within him, and has its birth in his heart. When the heart is deeply moved, expression is given to it by ceremonies; and hence, only men of ability and virtue can give complete exhibition to the idea of sacrifice" (Legge's translation of the "Book of Rites"). See R. K. Douglas, *Confucianism and Taouism;* H. A. Giles, *Religions of Ancient China*, 1905; H. J. Allen, *Early Chinese Hist.*, 1906; E. H. Parker, *Studies*, 1910.

BOOK OF SECRET BLESSINGS. The "Book of Secret Blessings" is an exposition in its modern form of the Chinese religion or system of ethics known as Taoism (*q.v.*). Next to the "Book of Rewards and Punishments" (*q.v.*), which it resembles, it is said to be the most popular religious work in China, being welcomed by Buddhists, Confucianists, and Taoists alike. "It has gone through many thousand editions, and has become a household word throughout the empire" (Douglas). Amongst its maxims, as summarized by Prof. Douglas, are these: "Publish abroad lessons for the improvement of mankind, and devote your wealth to the good of your fellow-men. In all your actions follow the principles of Heaven, and in all your words follow the purified heart of man. Have all the Sages of antiquity before your eyes, and examine carefully your conscience." See R. K. Douglas, *Confucianism and Taouism*.

BOOK OF THE ACTS OF SOLOMON. An old Hebrew record referred to in the Old Testament. In I. Kings xi. 41 we read: "Now the rest of the acts (or "words" or "matters") of Solomon, and all that he did, and his wisdom, are they not written in the book of the acts of Solomon?" It seems to have been a work based upon the annals of the reign of Solomon. It would appear to have included also narratives partly historical and partly biographical, which were intended to illustrate the wisdom and greatness of Solomon. The work was one of the sources used by the compiler of the Books of Kings. See Skinner, *Kings*, in "The Century Bible."

BOOK OF THE COVENANT. The name of several documents referred to in the Old Testament. (1) We read: "And Moses came and told the people all the words of Jehovah, and all the judgments: and all the people answered with one voice and said, All the words which Jehovah hath spoken will we do. And Moses wrote all the words of Jehovah, and rose up early in the morning, and builded an altar under the mount, and twelve pillars, according to the twelve tribes of Israel. . . . And he took the book of the covenant, and read in the audience of the people: and they said, All that Jehovah hath spoken will we do, and be obedient" (Exodus xxiv. 3, 4. 7). The document intended here is no doubt the section of the Hexateuch comprised in Exodus xx. 22-xxiii. 33, which is also known to scholars as the code of the covenant or the Greater Book of the Covenant (to distinguish it from No. 2 following). The code is part of the Ephraimitic narrative incorporated in the Hexateuch (see PENTATEUCH). "It contains several pentades of Words, a number of detached statutes, a few laws of a mixed type (probably redactional); but the main body of the code is made up of a series of pentades of judgments, which seem to be judicial decisions of cases arising in an agricultural community. These are not such as would arise among the nomads whom Moses led out of Egypt to Horeb" (C. A. Briggs). G. Wildeboer (*Canon of the O.T.*, 1895) points out that we have no certain knowledge about the promulgation of this book, and that since Deuteronomy, though often following its prescriptions closely, never mentions it, it must have had a private character. He adds that it could not have been a book for the people like Deuteronomy, but must have been a book for legal use. (2) In another passage we read: "And Jehovah said unto Moses, Write thou these words: for after the tenor of these words I have made a covenant with thee and with Israel" (Exodus xxxiv. 27). Here a "Book of the Covenant" is not actually mentioned, but is implied. It evidently consists of the preceding section, Exodus xxxiv. 11-28, the work of the Judaic writer. To distinguish it from book no. 1 (above), it has been designated by scholars the Little Book of the Covenant. It really represents another decalogue in addition to that of Exodus xx. 1-17 (see DECALOGUE). (3) Another book is referred to in II. King's xxii.-xxiii. and II. Chronicles xxxiv.-v. It is first spoken of as "the book of the law" (II. Kings xxii. 8, 11; II. Chronicles xxxiv. 15) or "the book of the law of Jehovah" (II. Chronicles xxxiv. 14) or simply "the words of the law" (II. Chronicles xxxiv. 19), and then as the "book of the covenant" (II. Kings xxiii. 2, 21; II. Chronicles xxxiv. 30) or "the law of Moses" (II. Kings xxiii. 25) or "the word of Jehovah by the hand of Moses" (II. Chronicles xxxv. 6). This "book of the covenant" is the book which was brought to light and introduced to the people in the eighteenth year of King Josiah (621 B.C.). It used to be thought that it was identical with the whole of our Pentateuch or of the Jewish "Torah." That view is no longer held by critical scholars. It has been demonstrated that "the Book of the Covenant," otherwise called "the Book of the Law," comprised "either a portion of our Deuteronomy or a collection of laws, Deuteronomic in tone, and, in range of contents, having a close resemblance to our Book of Deuteronomy" (H. E. Ryle). There are two lines of evidence. (1) It is clear from the description of the book that "in its most characteristic features, it approximated more closely to portions of Deuteronomy than to any other section of the Pentateuch." (2) When the historian speaks of "the law," he appears "to have in view the Deuteronomic section, and scarcely to be acquainted with any other." The arguments are summarized very lucidly by H. E. Ryle. The public recognition and acceptance of this deuteronomic work marks the beginning of the process of canonization. See H. E. Ryle, *Canon;* W. R. Smith, *O.T.J.C.* (2); C. A. Briggs, *Hex.*

BOOK OF THE DEAD. A book, that is to say, intended for the dead, the most important of the religious writings of the ancient Egyptians. Parts of it may belong to the remote period of the first Memphite dynasties. The Book contains prayers or addresses, hymns, and formulae for the use of a deceased person in the underworld. It was in use in the Middle Kingdom, but more so in the New Kingdom, and, later, portions were written on the walls of the tombs, the sides of the sarcophagi, the linen bandages, and on papyri folded within the body-cloths. Different portions or chapters were thought to be adapted to different tastes, emergencies, or means. With the magic help of the Book of the Dead, a soul on its journey through the underworld could overcome the evil spirits and win over the good ones. Prof. Naville gives this rubric from later papyri: "He who knows this book on earth, or on whose coffin it has been written, may come out from the day when he pleases, and again enter his dwelling, without anyone repulsing him. And there shall be given to him bread, beer, much flesh meat, upon the altar-table of Ra; he shall receive allotment of land in the garden of Aalu, and there shall be given to him grain, and he shall grow green (flourish) again, like what he was upon earth." A very interesting chapter or section has reference to the testing of the soul in the underworld. Arrived at the Hall of the Two Truths or Two Justices, the deceased person had to stand before the judgment-throne of Osiris, with whom sat the forty-two judges of the dead. The deceased had to justify himself, to make a confession, and to show that he had not been guilty of any of the forty-two sins. To test him, his heart was weighed in the scales by Horus (*q.v.*) and Anubis (*q.v.*). If he came through this ordeal satisfactorily, he received back his heart and in his old form became a new and eternal being. Other books based upon the Book of the Dead, supplementing it or reproducing the most important formulae, had a wide circulation. These included such works as: "The Book of the Breath," "The Second Book of the Breath," "The Book of Journeying in Eternity," "The Book of 'May my Name flourish'." It should be added that much of the matter in the Book of the Dead reveals a well-developed moral sense. See A. Wiedemann: A. Erman, *Handbook;* E. Naville, *The Old Egyptian Faith*, 1909.

BOOK OF THE KINGS OF ISRAEL. An old Hebrew record referred to in I. Chronicles ix. 1. It was one of the sources used by the compiler of the Books of Chronicles. The full title of the work seems to have been "The Book of the Kings of Israel and Judah." "This work, which is cited as an authority for reigns as early as that of Asa and as late as that of Jehoiakim, was clearly a comprehensive one, but not the canonical Books of Kings, because it is cited for matters not in those books—*i.e.*, genealogies (I. Ch. ix. 1), the wars of Jotham (II. Ch. xxvii. 7), and the prayer of Manasseh (II. Ch. xxxiii. 18) and the abominations of Jehoiakim (II. Ch. xxxvi. 8). Neither was it the sources mentioned in I. and II. Kings for the political history of Israel and Judah, since they were two distinct works." But it may have been dependent upon those sources, "or since the real historical material derived from this book apart from that in the canonical books is extremely meagre, it may have been dependent upon those books, a Midrash or commentary on them (Kuenen, *Einl.* p. 160). In their earliest form I. and II. Kings may have contained fuller information than in their present Massoretic form" (E. L. Curtis and A. A. Madsen). See E. L. Curtis and A. A. Madsen, *Book of Chronicles*, 1910.

BOOK OF THE LAW, THE. A document referred to in the Old Testament (II. Kings xxii. 8, 11) in connection with the reforms of King Josiah. In II. Kings xxiii. 2, 21, and II. Chronicles xxxiv. 30 it is called the Book of the Covenant (*q.v.*).

BOOK OF THE RESURRECTION. A N.T. apocryphal work. A Coptic version, found in Egypt, has been printed in recent years by the trustees of the British Museum. The work exhibits marked Egyptian (Gnostic) influence. "It describes the descent of Jesus into hell; the conquest of death; the defeat of the devil; the destruction of the gates, bolts, and bars of hell; the extinction of its fires; the overthrow of its blazing cauldrons; the liberation of Adam and Eve and all the children of men; the final condemnation of Judas Iscariot; the ascent from hell of the Lord Jesus; his resurrection; his enthronement at the right hand of the Father in his tabernacle of light in the seventh heaven; and the reconciliation of God with Adam and his sons" (Cobern).

BOOK OF THE WARS OF THE LORD. An ancient Hebrew book referred to in the Old Testament (Numbers xxi. 14 *f.*). The reference is as follows: "Wherefore it is said in the book of the Wars of the Lord, Vaheb in Suphah, and the valleys of Arnon, and the slope of the valleys that inclineth toward the dwelling of Ar, and leaneth upon the border of Moab." The book, it has been thought, was a collection of songs referring to Israel's wars against its neighbours, and it has been suggested that other passages in the O.T. (*e.g.*, Exodus xv. 1-19) were derived from it. Thus it may be supposed to have been a book like the Book of Jashar (*q.v.*). It was perhaps compiled about 900 B.C. Prof. Cheyne observes, however, with good reason, that the contents of the quotation hardly suggest a history or a collection of historical songs or ballads. The quotation suggests that the book "had reference to geography." There is perhaps some corruption in the text, though it is difficult to emend it satisfactorily. See *Encycl. Bibl.*

BOOK OF TORGAU. A confessional formula drawn up mainly by James Andreæ and Martin Chemnitz. It was designed as the basis on which the Lutherans might agree, and superseded the Swabian and Saxon Formula of Concord (*q.v.*) and the Maulbronn Formula. The Book of Torgau consisted of twelve articles. In 1577 A.D. Andreæ and Chemnitz, with the assistance of Selnecker, Musculus, Körner, and Chytræus, recast it at Bergen near Magdeburg as the Formula of Concord (*q.v.*). See William A. Curtis.

BOONBOLONG. A magic word among the natives of New South Wales. If it is uttered on the approach of the evil spirit which in the form of "a dwarf with monstrous head roams the woods at night and devours those whom he meets," the dwarf will pass by and do no harm. See D. G. Brinton, *Rel.*

BORBELITES. Another name of the BARBELIOTES (*q.v.*).

BORBORIANS. A name applied by way of reproach to the Barbeliotes (*q.v.*).

BORRELISTS. A division of the Dutch Baptists or Mennonites. The sect was founded by Adam Borrel in the second half of the seventeenth century. They correspond very largely to the English Quakers.

BORVO. Borvo, or Bormo, or Bormānus was one of the names of a god of the ancient Celts who corresponded to Apollo (*q.v.*). The name means "the boiling," and Borvo was the deity of thermal springs. The ancient Celts often associated a god with a goddess, but it is uncertain what relationship they had in mind. In any case, the god Borvo is paired with the goddess Damona (*q.v.*). See Anwyl, *Celtic Religion*, 1906: Reinach, *O.*

BOSTON DECLARATION, THE. The "Boston Declaration" is a Confession of Faith which was approved by the Synod of the New England Churches in 1680 A.D. It "is simply the Savoy Confession with the Cambridge Platform" (William A. Curtis). Cp. SAVOY DECLARATION and CAMBRIDGE PLATFORM.

BOTANOMANCY. Divination by means of plants. It was once a custom to write words and questions on leaves. When the leaves were blown about by the wind, some of them were supposed to come together in such a way as to answer questions.

BO-TREE. The name given in Buddhism to the tree under which Gautama received the revelation which changed his outlook on life. The Buddhist monks plant such a tree (*Ficus religiosa*) within the precincts of every monastery. Asoka sent one to Ceylon, which "still survives as a two-thousand-year-old rarity in the remarkable ruins of Anuradhapura." In Japan a substitute is found in an aniseed (*Illicium religiosum*) or in a Chinese juniper. See H. Hackmann.

BOUCHERA. A goddess worshipped by the Hijras (also called Khasuas), the community of eunuchs in India. The name appears also as Behechra.

BOURIGNONISTS. The followers of Madame Antoinette Bourignon de la Porte (1616-1680), a mystic and visionary. She was born at Lille. Madame Bourignon believed that she saw visions and was directly inspired by God to revive Christianity in its pure evangelic form. Admitted to a convent by the Archbishop of Cambray, she succeeded in making disciples of some of the nuns. She was afterwards head of a hospital, first in Lille, and then in East Friesland. She died at Franeker in Friesland. Her religion was a pietistic mysticism in which more importance was attached to emotion and inner feeling than to knowledge and practice. Madame Bourignon was an accomplished conversationalist and a prolific writer. Her principal followers have included

Bartholomew de Cordt, a Jansenist priest, and Peter Poiret, a Calvinistic minister, the editor of her works (25 volumes, 1676-84). The movement spread from Holland to Germany, France, Switzerland, and England. See J. H. Blunt.

BOURNEANS. The followers of one Bourne, a Birmingham preacher, who maintained that at the final punishment impenitent sinners would be totally annihilated.

BOWLS, MAGICAL. Morris Jastrow (*Civ.*) notes that at Nippur " hundreds of clay bowls, containing magical inscriptions in Aramaic and Syriac as a protection of the dead against evil demons, and dating from about the sixth century of our era, were found in graves of the uppermost layers in certain sections of the mound, as a proof that Nippur continued to be a sacred necropolis for Jews and Christians many centuries after it had ceased to be occupied, and at a time when all traces and even the recollection of its one-time grandeur had disappeared."

BOXERS. A secret society in China, one of the objects of which was to expel European missionaries from China. In 1900 the European Powers united to suppress them, and the expedition was successful.

BOY-BISHOP. In the Middle Ages it was a custom to elect one of the boys of the church or cathedral choir or of the grammar-school to act as boy-bishop from the 6th of December (St. Nicholas' Day) to the 28th of December (Holy Innocents' Day). The custom was perhaps intended as a commemoration of Jesus' act in setting a child in the midst of his disciples as a pattern of humility (Matthew xviii. 2-6). The boy-bishop was allowed to wear the episcopal dress, and to have a number of attendants who wore the priestly dress. With these he performed ceremonies (except Mass) in the church, and, going from house to house, blessed the people. The custom was discontinued in England by Henry VIII. (1542), but was revived by Queen Mary (1554). It was abolished, gradually, in the reign of Elizabeth. The Council of Basle condemned the practice (1431).

BOYLE LECTURES. A Church of England course of Lectures on Divinity founded by the Hon. Robert Boyle (1627-1691), one of the founders of the Royal Society. By his will he left £50 a year for eight sermons to be preached by " some preaching minister," the purpose of the lectures being to defend the Christian religion against notorious Infidels, Atheists, Deists, Pagans, Jews and Mohammedans. The lectureship may be held by the same preacher for three years. He must be " resident within the City of London or Circuit of Bills of Mortality," and deliver the lectures between Christmas and Midsummer of each year in some London Church. See the *London Diocese Book.*

BRACHITAE. A branch of the Manichaeans (*q.v.*), which seems to have belonged to the end of the third century A.D.

BRAGI. God of poetry in the religion of the ancient Teutons. Mention is made of Bragi's cup which every new king had to drain on ascending the throne of his father and by which he had to pledge himself. This Bragi must be distinguished from Bragi the Old or Bragi Boddason who seems to have been a historical person of the ninth century. See P. D. Chantepie de La Saussaye.

BRAHMA. The Indian deity from whom Brahmanism takes its name. Brahmā is the Creator, but not in the sense of being the original source of everything. He is the personal (masc.) manifestation of the one impersonal Essence or Being, Brahma (neuter). With him are associated, and often identified, Vishnu (*q.v.*) and Siva (*q.v.*). The two latter can, in fact, be worshipped as Brahmā, since the functions of the three gods are interchangeable. This is thought to account for the fact that there are not many temples to Brahmā himself. There is a temple to him near Idar or Edar, and another at Pushkara, and a legend associates him with the temple at Kalighat near Calcutta, one of the shrines of Siva's wife, Kali (Alexander Duff, *India and Indian Missions*, 1839, quoted by Oman). Brahmā is said to have performed a sacrifice at Pushkara which made the lake there sacred, so that to bathe in it is to be cleansed of all sin and to be made fit to enter Brahmā's heaven. Monier-Williams describes a visit to the temple at Pushkara. He found the actual shrine of Brahmā in the centre of a quadrangle. " In front of the entrance was the inevitable bell. I was allowed to look through the well-carved wooden gates at the image which was clearly visible in its sanctuary at the end of the vista of open columns. I observed that it had four black faces, each one of which was supposed to be directed towards one of the four quarters of the compass. In point of fact, however, three of the faces were made to look at the observer, each face having two great staring glass eyes. Covering the four-faced head was a broad red turban, and over that were hanging five umbrella-shaped ornaments. I noticed that the image was dressed in red clothes with flaps of coloured cloth hanging round the waist. On one side of the god's image was that of his wife worshipped here as Gāyatrī or Sāvitrī, and behind both was the image of Kāmadhenu—the sacred cow granting all desires. On the marble floor in front of the shrine was the carved representation of a tortoise—significant, no doubt, of Brahmā's connection with Vishnu (p. 108), out of whose navel he is fabled to have sprung, seated on a lotus." See Monier-Williams; E. W. Hopkins; J. C. Oman, *B.T.M.I.*

BRAHMACHARI. A name given to the young Brahman after he has obtained the right to wear the triple cord. He is invested with this cord at a special ceremony called the Upanayana. " It is well known that all Brahmins wear a thin cord, hung from the left shoulder and falling on to the right hip. It is composed of three strands of cotton, each strand formed by nine threads. The cotton with which it is made must be gathered from the plant by the hand of a pure Brahmin, and carded and spun by persons of the same caste, so as to avoid the possibility of its being defiled by passing through unclean hands. After a Brahmin is married his cord must have nine and not three strands" (Dubois and Beauchamp).

BRAHMAMAHA. A sectarian festival among the early Hindus in honour of Brahmā, a festival in which all the castes took part. It was a kind of harvest festival accompanied by athletic contests. See E. W. Hopkins.

BRAHMANAS. Each of the four Vedas in Indian Literature, the Rig-Veda, the Sáma-Veda, the Yajur-Veda, and the Atharva-Veda, has three sub-divisions, the Samhitá, Bráhmaṇa, and Sútra. The majority of the Bráhmaṇas were written before 480 B.C. They deal with prayer, ritual, dogma, sacrifice, and are much later than the Vedic hymns. " Their object is to connect the sacrificial songs and formulas with the sacrificial rite, by pointing out, on the one hand, their direct mutual relation; and, on the other, their symbolical connection with each other. In setting forth the former, they give the particular ritual in its details: in illustrating the latter, they are either directly explanatory and analytic, dividing each formula into its constituent parts, or else they establish that connection dogmatically by the aid of tradition or speculation. We thus find in them the oldest rituals we have, the oldest linguistic explanations, the oldest traditional narratives, and the oldest philosophical speculations. This peculiar character is common generally to all works of this class, yet they differ widely in details, according to their individual tendency, and according as they belong to this or that particular Veda" (A. Weber). Appended to the two Bráhmaṇas of the Rig-Veda is an Aran-yaka, a Forest-Book, and in the Forest-Book an Upanishad (*q.v.*). See A. Weber, *Hist. of Indian Lit.* (2) 1878; E. W. Hopkins.

BRAHMA SAMAJ. Literally "the Congregation of God," a modern theistic church founded at Calcutta in 1828 by the Hindu reformer, Rammohun Roy (1772-1833). After the death of Rammohun Roy, his successor, Debendranāth Tāgore (*b.* 1818), founded another church, "the Truth-teaching Society" (1839-1859), which was afterwards united with the Brāhma Samāj. In 1844 the latter was re-organised as the Ādi Brāhma Samāj, the First Congregation. The members of this took an oath, and were guided by a president and minister. A schism was nearly caused in the Church by a difference of opinion regarding the infallibility and authority of the Vedas. The movement, however, spread, and in 1850 Samājas were in existence in other provinces. In 1858 Keshub Chunder Sen joined the Brāhma Samāj, and soon began to advocate far-reaching reforms, such as the abolition of caste, child-marriages, and polyandry. Failing in his purpose here, in 1866 he founded a new church, the Brāhma Samāj of India as distinguished from the Ādi Samāj of Calcutta. In this church caste-restrictions and Brahmanism were abolished, but the religion was characterised by much emotionalism and ecstatic fervour. Sen, himself, though he denied that he made any claim to divine honours, came to receive divine honours. He certainly claimed to be divinely inspired, and assumed the power of a pope among his followers. His glory suffered an eclipse when in 1877 his young daughter (16) was engaged to a boy-prince (16). In 1880 he proclaimed Christianity to be the only true religion; but the Christianity he had in mind was hardly that of the Christian Churches, for he afterwards professed to find the true religion in an amalgamation of Christianity, Hinduism, and Mohammedanism. In 1878 Sen's opponents started another new church or society, and now there are said to be many such congregations in India. Cp. ARYA SAMAJ, and see E. W. Hopkins: Monier-Williams; J. C. Oman, *B.T.M.I.;* and R. V. Russell.

BRAHMANASPATI. Also called Brihaspati, one of the more recent of the Vedic gods, a personification of Prayer. In some texts he is identified with Agni or with Soma.

BRAHMANS. The priestly caste of India. The caste seems to have originated in the bards, ministers and family priests attached to the king's household in Vedic times. "Gradually then from the household priests and those who made it their business to commit to memory and recite the sacred hymns and verses handed down orally from generation to generation through this agency, an occupational caste emerged, which arrogated to itself the monopoly of these functions, and the doctrine developed that nobody could perform them who was not qualified by birth, that is, nobody could be a Brahman who was not the son of a Brahman" (Russell and Hīra Lāl). When the Sanskrit language ceased to be the language spoken by ordinary people, the Brāhmans alone held the key to the sacred books, and for a long time they enjoyed a monopoly of literacy and education. This made their intellectual, religious, and even administrative leadership secure. A change, however is taking place now through the action of the British Government, which has made education available to all. It is no longer possible for a Brāhman to learn all the Vedas and their commentaries. Hence the ordinary Brāhman devotes himself to one of the branches (or Shākhas) into which each Veda has been divided, and only to one Veda. This has given rise to a kind of sectarian division. In the Central Provinces most Brāhmans are either Rigvedis or Yajurvedis, who usually marry only followers of their own Veda. "Formerly the Brāhman considered himself as a part of Brahma, and hence a god. This belief has decayed, but the gods are still held to reside in the body: Siva in the crown of the head, Vishnu in the chest, Brahma in the navel, Indra in the genitals and Ganesh in the rectum. Most Brāhmans belong to a sect worshipping especially Siva or Vishnu, or Rāma and Krishna, the incarnations of the latter god, or Sakti, the female principle of energy of Siva. But as a rule Brāhmans, whether of the Sivite or Vishnuite sects, abstain from flesh meat and are averse to the killing of any living thing" (Russell and Hīra Lāl). See R. V. Russell, and cp. J. Dowson.

BRAIDISM. A name given to the hypnotic system used by the Scotch surgeon James Braid. Braid proved that the hypnotic state can be brought upon oneself by staring at a shining object, and is not dependent upon external energies such as mesmerism (*q.v.*) or animal magnetism (*q.v.*). He made his patients stare at a shining object, and produced hypnotism in this way. Braid was the first writer who employed the terms "hypnotism" and "nervous sleep" in this science. See J. Lapponi, *Hypnotism and Spiritism*, 1907; H. Münsterberg, *Psychotherapy*, 1909..

BRĀN. The Gaelic Bron or British Brān was one of the deities revered by the ancient Celts in Britain. He is said to have been the son of Llyr (*q.v.*). He is represented as the king of the Underworld, and the patron of bards and minstrels, and as being of immense size. See Squire, *Myth.*

BRANDING. The chiefs (āćāryas) of the two Hindu sects of Rāmānuja make a periodical visit of their dioceses, and in every large town hold a kind of confirmation. They confirm every child or young person who has been initiated by branding or stamping him as a true follower of Vishnu. "Boys may be branded at the age of seven or upwards; girls only after their marriage. A sacred fire is kindled, two golden instruments are heated, and the symbols of the wheel-shaped discus and conch-shell of Vishnu are impressed on the breast, arms, or other parts of the body." The same practice is observed by the Mādhva sect. "When I was at Tanjore," says Monier-Williams, "I found that one of the successors of Madhva had recently arrived on his branding visitation. He was engaged throughout the entire day in stamping his disciples and receiving fees from all according to their means." The worshippers of Siva are branded and stamped with the weapons and symbols of Siva (*e.g.*, the trident and the linga). See Monier-Williams.

BRASEN SEA. When Nebuchadrezzar, King of Babylon, sacked Jerusalem, his soldiers are said to have broken in pieces "the pillars of brass that were in the house of the Lord, and the bases and the brasen sea that were in the house of the Lord," and to have carried the brass to Babylon (2 Kings xxv. 13). The Brasen Sea was a laver.

BRASEN SERPENT. An object of veneration among the ancient Hebrews. According to the story in the Old Testament (Numbers xxi.), when the people were bitten by fiery serpents in the wilderness, the Lord said unto Moses (vs. 8): "Make thee a fiery serpent, and set it upon a standard; and it shall come to pass, that every one that is bitten, when he seeth it, shall live." Moses did so, making the serpent of brass: "and it came to pass, that if a serpent had bitten any man, when he looked unto the serpent of brass, he lived" (vs. 9). The idea of this story seems to be to account for the worship of serpents by the Hebrews. The worship has, as a matter of fact, been widespread, and "in some form or other the serpent had been worshipped ages before in Egypt" (Samuel G. Smith, *Religion in the Making*, 1910). It has been looked upon with fear and awe, because, amongst other things, to use the words of Genesis (iii. 1), the serpent is "more subtil than any beast of the field which the Lord God had made." When King Hezekiah proceeded to introduce extensive reforms, it is said that he "brake in pieces the brasen serpent that Moses had made, for unto those days the children of Israel did burn incense to it, and he called it a piece of brass" (2 Kings xviii. 4).

BREASTPLATE OF JUDGMENT. In the Old Testament the High Priest is said to have worn on the ephod a Breastplate (*khōshen*, Exodus xxviii. 4) or Breastplate of Judgment (*khōshen mishpāt*, Exodus xxviii. 15). This seems to have been a square kind of pocket fastened at each corner to the shoulder-straps of the ephod. The outer part was ornamented with precious stones.

BREECHES BIBLE. A popular name for the English version of the Bible (1557-1560) brought from Geneva. It was so called because in one edition it is said in Genesis iii. 7 that Adam and Eve "sewed fig-tree leaves together and made themselves breeches." See BIBLE.

BRETHREN OF CHELCIC. Peter of Chelcic was one of the spiritual descendants of John Hus (*c.* 1369-1415). He appeared in Bohemia some time after the final defeat and dispersion of the Taborites (*q.v.*), the extreme section of the Hussites, and by his pamphlets prepared the way for the foundation of the "Unitas Fratrum" (see BOHEMIAN BRETHREN). Peter of Chelcic described the Pope as Anti-Christ, attacked the morals of the priests in Bohemia, and contended that men could be saved solely by their own faith. Further, "he interpreted the Sermon on the Mount literally, denounced war as murder, opposed the union of Church and State, and objected to oaths and litigation. He declared that Christ's example and law were guide sufficient for any man." See C. H. H. Wright and C. Neil, *Prot. Dict.*, *s.v.* "Moravian Church."

BRETHREN OF JESUS. Reference is made in the New Testament to "brethren of Jesus." In Mark iii. 32 (Matthew xii. 47; Luke viii. 20) it is said that messengers came to Jesus and said: "Behold, thy mother and thy brethren without seek for thee." It is not absolutely necessary here to take brethren in its literal sense: "brethren" might mean kinsfolk. In Mark vi. 3, however, when Jesus began to teach in the Synagogue, we are told that the people exclaimed: "Is not this the carpenter, the son of Mary, and brother of James, and Joses, and Judas, and Simon? and are not his sisters here with us?" In this case real brothers and sisters seem to be meant. Again in Galatians i. 19 the writer says: "Then after three years I went up to Jerusalem to visit Cephas, and tarried with him fifteen days. But other of the apostles saw I none, save James the Lord's brother." In the interest of the perpetual virginity of Mary, the Mother of the Lord, it has been denied that the "brethren of Jesus" were literal brethren, and has been maintained that here the Greek *adelphoi* stands for *anepsioi*, children of two brothers or two sisters. But the expression used of Jesus in Luke ii. 7, *prōtotokon*, "first-born," clearly denotes that Mary had other children after the birth of Jesus.

BRETHREN OF MONTE SENARIO. Another name for the Servites (*q.v.*).

BRETHREN OF PURITY. A Muhammadan secret order of the tenth century. The Brethren composed an encyclopædia in fifty-one treatises which combined Aristotelian logic and physics with Neo-Platonic metaphysics and theology, and to which Jewish writers (such as Ibn Gabirol, Judah Halevi, Moses and Abraham Ibn Ezra) were much indebted. See Isaac Husik.

BRETHREN OF THE COMMON LIFE. A Dutch branch of the "Friends of God" (*q.v.*).

BRETHREN OF THE CROSS. A body which arose in Thuringia in 1414 under the leadership of Conrad Schmidt, who regarded himself as a reincarnation of Enoch. Schmidt "prophesied the downfall of Rome and the sacramental system, the imminent recognition by all mankind that salvation could only be attained by the whip. Joined by many of the vagrant Beghards, the united society suffered grievous persecution at the hands of Eylard Schöneveld and became nearly extinct" (F. W. Bussell). The Brethren lashed themselves in public twice a day, believing that the blood which they shed would mingle with the blood of the Saviour and wash away all sin.

BRETHREN OF THE FREE SPIRIT. The name of a sect which was originally called Ortlibenses (*q.v.*). The name and tenets seem to have been suggested by Romans viii., 2 and 14: "For the law of the Spirit of life in Christ Jesus hath made me free from the law of sin and death. . . . For as many as are led by the Spirit of God, they are the Sons of God." The Brethren claimed to be free from external ordinances and from the law of sin.

BRIDE OF THE NILE. A truncated cone of earth called the "bride" figures in a rite of irrigation performed at Cairo about the middle of August. The ceremony seems to be a charm to ensure a rich fertilisation of the land by water when the dam of earth across the canal of Cairo is cut. The "bride," set up in front of the dam at the river's side is washed down before the cutting of the dam. According to tradition, the bride was originally a young virgin who was thrown into the river as a sacrifice. Dr. Frazer thinks that the ceremony represents the marriage of the river as a male power to the cornland as his bride. See J. G. Frazer, *Adonis Attis Osiris*, 1906; E. W. Lane, *Modern Egyptians*.

BRIDGEWATER TREATISES. The Bridgewater Treatises "On the Power, Wisdom, and Goodness of God, as manifested in the Creation" were so called, because they were paid for from a fund left for the purpose by Francis Henry, Earl of Bridgewater, who died in 1829. Eight treatises were published, the authors being Thomas Chalmers, John Kidd, William Whewell, Charles Bell, Peter Mark Roget, William Buckland, William Kirby, and William Prout.

BRIEF. A Papal Brief or Breve is a letter written in modern characters on thin white parchment and issued from the Court of Rome. It is subscribed by the Secretary of Briefs, stamped in red wax with the Pope's signet-ring which bears a figure of St. Peter hauling in his fishing-net, and dated "a die Nativitatis." Before the date come the words "given at Rome at St. Peter's under the ring of the fisherman."

BRIGANTIA. It appears from several inscriptions found in the North of England that Brigantia was a goddess worshipped by the ancient Celts.

BRIGINDU. One of the goddesses worshipped by the ancient Celts. The name appears on an inscription found at Volnay near Beaune in Gaul. C. Squire connects her with the Brigit who was worshipped in Ireland as a kind of Minerva or Vesta. E. Anwyl thinks that she is perhaps to be identified with a goddess Berecyntia, who is referred to by Gregory of Tours. The goddess mentioned by Gregory would seem to have been a corn-spirit, for we are told that her image was borne on a wagon to the fields and vineyards to protect them. See Anwyl, *Celtic Rel.*, 1906; Squire, *Myth.*

BRIGIT. A goddess worshipped by the Irish Celts as the patroness of knowledge. She seems to have been also a goddess of fertility. When the Irish Celts were converted to Christianity, Brigit was transformed into Saint Brigit.

BRIGITTINES. An order founded in 1344 by St. Brigit (Brigitta) or Bridget (1302 or 1303—1373), a Roman Catholic saint, in Sweden. The community consisted of sixty nuns, thirteen priests, four deacons, and eight lay-brothers. It was thus a double establishment. The rule adopted was that of St. Austin. The order was called the Order of St. Salvator or the Order of the Saviour. It is also known as the Order of St. Brigit. It is claimed that the constitutions were divinely revealed to her. In Sweden the community was suppressed in 1595. There was a Brigittine house, Sion Convent, near Brentford, which was restored by Queen Mary, but suppressed in the reign of Elizabeth. In 1861 the convent of Sion House, Spettisbury, Dorsetshire, was founded by Brigittines from Portugal. In 1887 it was transferred to Chudleigh, Devonshire. A book which gives the confessions of St. Brigit, "Revelationes St. Brigittae" has been much read. See *Cath. Dict.*; Chambers' *Encycl.*

BRITINIANS. The name of a colony of Augustinian monks settled at Britini, Ancona.

BRITISH AND FOREIGN SCHOOL SOCIETY. Originally (1808) the Royal Lancasterian Society, founded in the interests of the Lancasterian System of Education (*q.v.*).

BRITOMARTIS. Literally "sweet maid," a Cretan goddess. She was identified sometimes with Artemis (q.v.). A goddess of Nature, of birth, and of health, she was supposed to protect sailors, fishermen, and hunters. As a goddess of the sea, she was called Dictynna, apparently from the Greek word *diktyŏn*, "a net." According to legend, to escape the attentions of Minos, her suitor, she leapt into the sea, fell into some nets, and was made a goddess by Artemis. Seyffert thinks that "she would seem originally to have been a goddess of the moon, her flight symbolizing the revolution of the moon round the earth, and her leap into the sea its disappearance." See O. Seyffert, *Dict.*

BRIZO. A goddess of Delos, worshipped particularly by women as one who protected mariners. Offerings were brought to her in small boats.

BROAD CHURCH. A Liberal party in the Church of England. There have always been Churchmen who have adopted a broad or liberal attitude in matters of doctrine (cp LATITUDINARIANS). Dr. Rashdall is certainly right when he claims: "It may safely be said that there has been no period in the history of the Church of England up to the days of the Oxford Movement at which there have not been thousands of the clergy who could only justify their position in its ranks by taking in a very loose and liberal sense some part or side of the authorised formulae" ("Clerical Liberalism" in the work *Anglican Liberalism*, 1908). But the particular attitude characterised as Broad Church may be said to have found one of its first representatives in John Colet (1467?-1519), Dean of St. Paul's (1504-1519), who was accused of heresy (1513-14) by Richard Fitzjames (d. 1522), Bishop of London. In the seventeenth century the movement made great headway. It may be said to have been represented by such men as Jeremy Taylor (1613-1667), Bishop of Down and Connor, the famous author, whose writings include the "Liberty of Prophesying" (1646); John Hales (1584-1656), Fellow of Eton (1613-49) and Canon of Windsor, who wrote a tract on "Schism and Schismaticks" (1642); William Chillingworth (1602-1644), who turned Roman Catholic for a time (1630), but afterwards repented (1634) and wrote a book "The Religion of Protestants a safe Way of Salvation" (1638); Thomas Tenison (1636-1715), Archbishop of Canterbury, who was noted for his "moderation towards dissenters"; Ralph Cudworth (1617-1688), Regius Professor of Hebrew at Cambridge (1645-88), who wrote "The True Intellectual System of the Universe" (1678); and the Cambridge Platonists: John Tillotson (1630-1694), Archbishop of Canterbury, who had to defend his orthodoxy in a course of lectures on the Socinian Controversy (1679-80); Edward Stillingfleet (1635-1699), Bishop of Worcester, who offered an olive-branch to the Presbyterians in his work "The Irenicum" (1659); John Hoadly (1678-1746), Archbishop of Armagh, one of whose friends was Thomas Chubb, the deist; and Gilbert Burnet (1643-1715), Bishop of Salisbury, who in 1699 published an "Exposition of the XXXIX Articles." Naturally the Broad Church attitude was well represented among the divines of the "rationalistic" eighteenth century. We may regard as members of the school such men as: Conyers Middleton (1683-1750), Fellow of Trinity College, Cambridge (1706), whose works on "Miracles" (1747 and 1748) caused a considerable stir; Arthur Ashley Sykes (1684?-1756), who published in 1742 "A Brief Discourse concerning the Credibility of Miracles and Revelation"; Francis Blackburne (1705-1787), Prebendary of York, who wrote an "Apology for the Authors of the Free and Candid Disquisitions"; John Hey (1734-1815), Norrisian Professor of Divinity (1780-95) at Cambridge, whose "Divinity Lectures" (1796) are remarkable for their candour and freedom; and Richard Watson (1737-1816), Bishop of Llandaff, who undertook to controvert Edward Gibbon (1776) and Thomas Paine (1796). The Broad Church attitude, however, has been identified more particularly with a school of theologians belonging to the nineteenth century who were influenced by a more scientific criticism of the Bible and by its representatives in Germany. In this school we may include: Sydney Smith (1771-1845), Prebendary of St. Paul's, the famous author of the "Plymley Letters" (1807); Richard Whately (1787-1863), Archbishop of Dublin, who chose as the subject of his Bampton Lectures (1822) "Party Feeling in Matters of Religion"; Thomas Arnold (1795-1842), the renowned Headmaster of Rugby School, author of "Principles of Church Reform" (1833); Julius Charles Hare (1795-1855), Archdeacon of Lewes, who translated German works and defended Niebuhr and Luther; Henry Bristow Wilson (1803-1888), Vicar of Great Staughton, Huntingdonshire (1850-1888), who was prosecuted for heterodoxy on account of views expressed in a contribution to "Essays and Reviews" (1860); Frederick Denison Maurice (1805-1872), Professor at King's College, London, who was charged with heterodoxy in 1851, and in 1853, after the publication of his "Theological Essays," was requested by the Council of King's College to resign; Mark Pattison (1813-1884), Rector of Lincoln College, Oxford (1861), who contributed an article to *Essays and Reviews;* John William Colenso (1814-1883), Bishop of Natal, who was deposed and excommunicated in 1863 by the Bishop of Cape Town on account of his critical works on the Pentateuch; Arthur Penrhyn Stanley (1815-1881), Dean of Westminster, who defended Bishop Hampden (1850), Bishop Colenso (1861), and the writers of "Essays and Reviews" (1861); Frederick William Robertson (1816-1853), Vicar of Trinity Chapel, Brighton, whose liberal sermons have been widely read in Germany as well as in England; Rowland Williams (1817-

1870), Professor of Hebrew at St. David's College, Lampeter (1850-62), who was prosecuted for heterodoxy on account of views expressed in a contribution to "Essays and Reviews" (1860); Benjamin Jowett (1817-1893), Master of Balliol College, Oxford (1870-93), who contributed an essay on the "Interpretation of Scripture" to "Essays and Reviews" (1860); Charles Kingsley (1819-1875), Canon of Westminster, the distinguished author; and Edwin Hatch (1835-1889), who chose as the subject of his Hibbert Lectures (1888) "Greek Influence on Christianity." See John Hunt; Leslie Stephen, *Hist. of English Thought in the Eighteenth Century;* A. I. Fitzroy, *Dogma and the Church of England*, 1891; *Anglican Liberalism* by Twelve Churchmen, 1908; the *D.N.B.*

BROSS FOUNDATION, THE. In 1879 William Bross, who was Lieutenant-Governor of Illinois from 1866 to 1870, transferred to the "Trustees of Lake Forest University" the sum of forty thousand dollars to found a memorial to his son Nathaniel Bross (*d.* 1856). When the income accumulated it was to be devoted to the purpose of stimulating the best books or treatises "on the connection, relation and mutual bearing of any practical science, the history of our race, or the facts in any department of knowledge, with and upon the Christian Religion." The donor wished "to call out the best efforts of the highest talent and the ripest scholarship of the world to illustrate from science, or from any department of knowledge, and to demonstrate the divine origin and the authority of the Christian Scriptures; and, further, to show how both science and revelation coincide and prove the existence, the providence, or any or all of the attributes of the only living and true God, 'infinite, eternal and unchangeable in His being, wisdom, power, holiness, justice, goodness, and truth.'" In 1900 the Trustees began to carry out the provisions of the trust. They decided to purchase and publish a series of books under the general title "The Bross Library." The first volume in this series was the "Evidences of Christianity" by William Bross's "very dear friend and teacher, Mark Hopkins, D.D." A prize, open to "the scientific men, the Christian philosophers and historians of all nations," was offered in 1902, and was awarded in 1905 to James Orr, D.D., Professor of Apologetics and Systematic Theology in the United Free Church College, Glasgow. His treatise, "The Problem of the Old Testament" (1906) was Volume III. of the "Bross Library." The Trustees have also invited eminent scholars to deliver courses of lectures before Lake Forest College. The first course, on "Obligatory Morality," was given in 1903 by Francis Landey Patton, D.D., LL.D., President of Princeton Theological Seminary. The second course, on "The Bible: Its Origin and Nature," was given in 1904 by Marcus Dods, D.D., Professor of Exegetical Theology in New College, Edinburgh. The third course, on "The Bible of Nature," was given in 1907 by Mr. J. Arthur Thomson, M.A., Regius Professor of Natural History in the University of Aberdeen.

BROTHERHOOD OF AS- SANUSI. An Arabian religious movement founded by Muhammad ibn Ali as-Sanusi in 1837. The Brotherhood is an order of Dervishes of a puritanical and reforming character. Its principles are strictly monotheistic. The original home of the order was at Jarabub in the eastern Sahara, but houses have been established throughout North Africa and Morocco. The head of the order, who resides in the African desert, claims that he is the Mahdi. See D. B. Macdonald, *Development.*

BROTHERHOOD OF ST. ANDREW, THE. A Church of England Brotherhood for laymen of all classes. "The rules binding on members are two: (1) The Rule of Prayer, to pray daily for the spread of Christ's Kingdom among men, especially young men, and for God's blessing upon the labours of the Brotherhood; (2) the Rule of Service, to make at least one earnest effort each week to lead some man nearer to Christ through His Church." There is a Junior Department attached to the Brotherhood. See the *Official Year-Book of the Church of England.*

BROTHERHOOD OF THE KOSMON DAWN. A religious brotherhood founded in 1918 by members of the so-called Faithist Churches as nearly as possible on the lines indicated in their sacred book, the Kosmon Bible Oahspe. The home of the Brotherhood, for the time being, is at "Rock," Crown Hill, South Devon. The objects are: (*a*) to found the Father's Kingdom on Earth through orphan babes, castaway infants, and foundlings under 3 years of age; (*b*) to provide a new way of living, and opportunities for a higher and holier development, whilst living upon and cultivating the land, thus providing for the spiritual as well as the corporeal man. All members work, sleep, and dine in the open as much as possible, and lead a simple life. In accordance with the teaching of the book Oahspe as to the desirability of purity and health, the children are encouraged to take sun, light and air baths. Vegetarianism is practised, as well as non-resistance to persecution and abuse. One of the conditions of life for the brethren is that "they shall abjure war, even, if necessary, by submitting to death rather than take part therein." See further *Kosmon Ray*, No. 1, 1919.

BROTHERHOODS, MODERN ANGLICAN. There are three well-known Brotherhoods. (1) "The Community of the Resurrection." This was founded at Pusey House, Oxford, in 1892. Since 1898 its centre has been the House of the Resurrection, Mirfield, to which was added in 1903 a College for training Candidates for the ministry. The Community itself consists of celibate Clergy who live under a Rule and share a common purse. "Each priest who joins the Community does so after a period of probation, and with the intention of remaining permanently in it, and is bound to it by simple vows." (2) "Society of St. John the Evangelist." This is a Society of Mission Priests of St. John the Evangelist who are commonly called the Cowley Fathers (Cowley St. John, Oxford). It was founded in 1865 by the Rev. R. M. Benson "for the cultivation of a life dedicated to God according to the principles of Poverty, Chastity, and Obedience, and is engaged in works both Missionary and Educational, at home and abroad, for the advancement of the Kingdom of Christ. Lay Brothers are united with the Clergy in Dedication to the Religious Life, who assist so far as they can in the works of the Society." (3) "Society of the Sacred Mission," Kelham, Newark-on-Trent. This is "an association of men bound together for the service of the Church." Its objects are: "1. By its rule and discipline to maintain the spirit of devotion and self-forgetfulness in the members: 2. To render such devotion effective by an organisation which allows of the concentration of many gifts upon a common plan." The House of the Sacred Mission is a recognised Theological College. See the *Official Year-Book of the Church of England.*

BROTHERS. In theosophy (*q.v.*) those who possess the Secret Wisdom form a great Brotherhood and are called Brothers. They are also called Adepts, Masters, Mahatmas (*q.v.*).

BROTHERS AND SISTERS OF PENANCE. The third Franciscan order, otherwise called Tertiaries (*q.v.*).

BROTHERS AND SISTERS OF ST. ALEXIUS. A more correct designation of the fraternity commonly known as Lullards (*q.v.*).

BROTHERS OF THE HOSPITAL OF ST. JOHN THE BAPTIST. Another name for the Knights of the Hospital of St. John of Jerusalem. See HOSPITALLERS.

BROTHERS OF VICTORY. A name by which the Minims (*q.v.*) were known in Spain.

BROWNIE. A kind of domestic fairy. Early references are found to it in Scotch writers. The brownie was supposed to visit houses and to help in the domestic work. It was "a very obliging spirit, who used to come into houses by night, and for a dish of cream to perform lustily any piece of work that might remain to be done: sometimes he would work, and sometimes eat till he bursted: if old clothes were laid for him, he took them in great distress, and never more returned" (Pinkerton quoted in Brand). Offerings of various kinds were made to the spirit. See *Brand's Popular Antiquities of Great Britain*, ed. W. C. Hazlitt, 1905. The Brownie corresponds to the German Kobold (Kabouter). "The *Kobold*, as a rule, likes to lend a helping hand in the field and stable; he feeds the cattle and threshes the grain, fetches water, and performs all manner of domestic duties. At the same time he is also capable of teasing, but, as a rule, only those who have deserved punishmen" (de La Saussaye). See P. D. Chantepie de La Saussaye, *Rel. of the Teutons*, 1902.

BROWNISTS. The forerunners in England of the Independents or Congregationalists, followers of Robert Browne (1550?-1633). After graduating at Corpus Christi College, Cambridge, Browne seems to have been ordained about 1573. After this he became Master of the Free School of St. Olave's, Southwark. At the same time he preached in the open air at Islington without a licence from the bishop. About the year 1578, preaching at Cambridge and in the neighbouring villages, he began to attack the parochial system, and to denounce ordination by bishops or by the presbytery. His brother obtained him a licence to preach from the Bishop of Ely, but he destroyed it. For this he was inhibited. He proceeded to Norwich about the year 1580, and formed an independent congregation, "the church," there, his assistant being Robert Harrison (*d.* 1585?). In 1581 the Bishop of Norwich was induced to take action against him, and he was imprisoned for "delivering unto the people corrupt and contentious doctrine." But through the influence of Cecil, Lord Burleigh, he was released. He then left England with his followers and settled at Middleburg in Holland. Here he wrote and issued books, which in England were not allowed to be circulated. One of these, published in 1582, was "A book which sheweth the life and manners of all true Christians, and how unlike they are to Turks and Papists and Heathen folk. Also, the points and parts of all Divinity, that is of the revealed will and word of God, are declared by their several definitions and divisions." In 1583 he quarrelled with Robert Harrison, and in 1584 he left Holland for Scotland. Having spent a few days in prison there, he returned to England. In England he was again imprisoned. His next field of action was Northampton where we find him preaching in 1586. In the same year he was excommunicated by the Bishop of Peterborough. After this he "submitted himself to the order and government of the Church." Thereupon he was made master of Stamford Grammar-school. From 1591 to 1631 he was Rector of Thorpe-Achurch in Northamptonshire. Before his death he was again imprisoned, this time for assaulting a constable. He died in Northampton gaol about the year 1633. Henry Barrow or Barrowe (*d.* 1593) succeeded Browne as leader of the Brownists. In consequence they became known also as "Barrowists." He was a Cambridge graduate and a barrister of Gray's Inn. In his advocacy of Brownist principles he was assisted by John Greenwood (*d.* 1593), a yonng clergyman. In 1586 they were both summoned to appear for examination before the Court of High Commission. From this examination it was clear that Barrow set himself in uncompromising opposition to the ecclesiastical government. He was, moreover, bitterly opposed to the use of fixed prayers and the taking of an oath. Greenwood's principles were found to agree closely with those of Barrow. They published an account of their examination and other works, and paid the penalty by going to prison. Subsequently (1593) they were hanged at Tyburn "for writing and publishing sundry seditious books and pamphlets, tending to the slander of the Queen and Government." In the same year another Brownist, John Penry (1559-1593), who wrote pamphlets under the pseudonym "Martin Mar-Prelate," was hanged in Southwark on the charge of exciting to rebellion. Henry Barrow was succeeded by Francis Johnson (1562-1618), who had been a Fellow of Christ's College, Cambridge, but was expelled in 1589 for preaching a "seditious" sermon. He went to Middleburg in Holland and was preacher to the English merchants there from 1589 to 1592. In 1592 he formed an independent church in London. In 1596, after being imprisoned several times, he went to Amsterdam, where he acted as Independent pastor and published works explaining Independent principles. Henry Jacob (1563-1624), precentor of Corpus Christi College, Oxford, joined the Brownists in Holland in 1593. In 1598, after a return to England, he was again in Holland, and in 1599 he entered into a controversy with Francis Johnson. He seems to have been convinced by a pamphlet which Johnson wrote the next year. Later on Jacob was associated with John Robinson (1576-1625), who emigrated to Amsterdam in 1608. In 1616, having returned to England, he established in Southwark "the first Independent or Congregational Church in England." Jacob regarded each côngregation as "an entire and independent body-politic, endued with power immediately under, and from, Christ, as every proper Church is and ought to be" (*Declaration and Plainer Opening of Certain Points*, 1611). In 1622 he emigrated to Virginia. Returning to London, he died there in 1624. He was succeeded in London by John Lathrop, Lothrop, or Lothropp (*d.* 1653), who emigrated to Boston in 1634. See John Hunt; D. Neal, *History of the Puritans*, 1732-1738; J. H. Blunt; the *D.N.B.*

BRUGGLENIANS. The followers of two brothers, Christian and Jerome Rohler, belonging to the Swiss canton of Brugglen. They gave out (A.D. 1746) that they were the two witnesses referred to in the Book of Revelation (Rev. XI. 3 *ff.*). Christian Rohler said he would ascend to heaven on a certain day and take his followers with him. The two brothers were executed in 1753.

BRUGPA SECT. A sect among the Tibetan Buddhists. Brugpa is another form of Dugpa. See DUGPA SECT.

BRUSIANS. The followers of Peter de Bruys, a religious sect of the twelfth century.

BRYANITES. A sect of the Methodists.

BUCHANITES. The followers of a Scotch lady, Mrs. Elspeth Buchan (1738-1791). She was the daughter of an innkeeper, John Simpson, near Banff. Originally an Episcopalian, about 1760 she married a potter, Robert

Buchan, and adopted his religion, that of the Burgher Secession. She separated from him in 1781. Shortly before this she began to prophesy the speedy coming of the millennium and promised that those who became her disciples would not die, but would witness the Second Coming of the Lord and with Him possess the earth for a thousand years. In 1783 Hugh White, minister of the Relief Church at Irvine, was persuaded that she was inspired. He became a follower, and his presbytery deposed him. Other followers joined them. They lived together, having renounced marriage and the ordinary duties of life, and awaited the Second Coming. In 1784, being expelled from Irvine, they moved into a farmhouse in Closeburn near Thornhill, Dumfriesshire. There were forty-six members of the community. They were supported mainly by the contributions of the wealthier disciples. In 1786 some of her followers left her and complained of trickery and extortion. Mrs. Buchan died in 1791, declaring on her death-bed that she was the Blessed Virgin and the woman referred to in the Book of Revelation (xii.). See Joseph Train, *The Buchanites from First to Last*, 1846; J. H. Blunt; the *D.N.B.*

BUDDHASĀSANA SAMĀGAMA. A modern reform party among the Buddhists. The movement originated in Burma in 1902, and was reorganized in 1903. The leader now is a European, Mr. Allan B. MacGregor, who was formerly a Roman Catholic. The aim of the society is to bring Buddhism " into close contact with Europe and its culture, for the needs of which this religion is held to be all-sufficing." There is a branch of the society in Ceylon. Here the members " have built a preaching-hall, in which on Sunday (!) evening there is usually a Singhalese sermon on Buddhist questions, at which the audience—mostly attired in European clothes—sit on benches as in a Christian church, the monk preaching from a kind of platform. They do not sing, but a creed is recited in unison at the close. In the background of the hall—somewhat in the position of a Christian altar—is a statue of the Buddha." See H. Hackmann.

BUDDHAVAMSA. A Buddhist sacred book included in the collection appended to the second division of the Canon. See CANON, BUDDHIST.

BUDDHI. A term used in Theosophy (*q.v.*). It is the name given to the Spiritual Soul in man, which is the vehicle of the Spirit or Atma (*q.v.*).

BUDDHISM. The religion founded by Gautama, afterwards called the Buddha, who seems to have been born about 567 B.C. Gautama's father was Suddhodana, a prince of the royal family of the Sākyas, a Rājput clan, which lived and ruled in the valley of the Ganges about 130 miles N. of Benares. The son was born under some tall trees in the Lambini Grove by the town of Kapilavastu, and lost his mother Māyā or Mahā-Māyā a week later. When he grew up he married his cousin, the daughter of the raja of Koli. At the age of twenty-nine, soon after the birth of a son, he was impelled to renounce the world in order to devote himself to the study of religion. Before doing so he visited his wife and child as they lay asleep and took a last look at them. This parting is called by Buddhists the "Great Renunciation." According to legend it was accompanied, like his birth, by miraculous signs. Mārā, the prince of evil, tried to turn him back, but without success. He went first to the kingdom of Magadha on the south of the Ganges, where he studied the philosophy of the Brahmans. Then, in company with five ascetics, he withdrew into the jungle and entered upon a course of austerities, which lasted six years. This period is called the "Great Struggle." At the end of it he abandoned the practice of austerities, and was abandoned by the five ascetics. Having bathed and eaten, he sat down under a banyan tree, and suffered again the onslaught of Mārā. Mārā was again defeated, and new light came to Gautama. From being a Bodhisattva, one who was destined to attain supreme wisdom, he became a Buddha or " enlightened one "; and the tree came to be known as the Bo-tree or " tree of enlightenment." The five ascetics had gone to Benares. Thither Gautama went, sought them out, converted them, and admitted them to the order of monks which he established. After thus " setting in motion the wheel of the law," the Master went about from place to place preaching. He also sent forth many disciples as missionaries. According to tradition, he was eighty years old when he died. Immediately after his death a Council is said to have been held at Rājagriha which established a fixed and authorised version of the sayings of the Master. The Vinaya and the Dharma were rehearsed, but no mention is made of the Abhidharma, the third division of the Buddhist Canon. About a hundred years later a second Council was held at Vaisālī to consider certain relaxations asked for by a section of the Buddhist monks. When these relaxations (or ten indulgences) were rejected by the Council, a schism took place. After about another century a third is said to have been held at Pātaliputra or Patna under the presidency of king Asoka (*d.* about 230 B.C.), which condemned all innovations and heresies. Asoka's work was of such importance that he has been called the " Buddhist Constantine." In some ways he did much more for Buddhism than Constantine is supposed to have done for Christianity. " Until his reign Buddhism was apparently confined to a comparatively restricted area in and about Magadha, and was perhaps little more than one of many sects of an all-embracing Hinduism. He gave it predominant influence and prestige. And by his zealous missionary endeavours, his direct inculcation of its principles, and by the example of his own life and practice, won respect and adherence to Buddhist teaching not only throughout the Indian peninsula from the north almost to the extreme south, but beyond its borders. As far as the available evidence enables us to form a judgement, it was Asoka who raised Buddhism from a narrow local sectarian faith to the position of a world-wide religion " (A. S. Geden, *Studies*). The thoughts and teachings of Asoka have been preserved in numerous edicts which he caused to be engraved on rocks and pillars throughout his empire. From these edicts it appears that he enjoined kindness and gentleness to animals as well as men, and toleration of other religions; that he appointed overseers or censors of public morals; and that he established hospitals for the care of men and animals. About three hundred years after the third Council, a fourth Buddhist Council met under the Indo-Scythian king Kanishka, who did for Northern what Asoka had done for Southern Buddhism. The purpose seems to have been to compose differences of opinion and to lay down rules for future guidance. Buddhism was introduced into Ceylon as the result of a mission sent there by Asoka. It has flourished in Ceylon with particular vigour. Indeed, the famous Buddhist monk and commentator Buddhaghosa, who lived there in the fifth century A.D., has been called the second founder of Buddhism. From Ceylon Buddhism spread to Burma, and then to the Malay peninsula, to Sumatra and Java, and to other islands of the Eastern Archipelago. In Kashmīr and Nepāl it appeared at an early date. It was carried to China in 62 A.D., and thence to Korea in 372 A.D., and to Japan in 552 A.D. It reached Tibet during the years 638-40 A.D., probably by way of Nepāl. Here it was developed about a century later by the Indian monk and saint Padma-Sambhava, the founder of Lāmaism. At about the close of the sixteenth century Tibetan Lamaism seems to have been introduced into Mongolia. From the sixth century Buddhism steadily declined in the land of its origin, and at the opening of the nineteenth century, although it was still supreme on the Himalayas, in Burma and in Ceylon, it had practically disappeared from India proper. It is said to have at the present time about 500,000,000 adherents in the world, and thus to be the religion of about one-third of the human race. The first and fundamental truth that the Buddha proclaimed was that existence itself is an evil, a source of pain and unhappiness. The desire for continuance of existence has, like other desires, to be suppressed. The second fundamental truth is an attempt to explain the origin of evil. Human life is linked to its beginnings by a chain of cause and effect. The first link of causation and the primary root of all evil is ignorance. With knowledge of the truth, false notions disappear. The formula known as the Buddhist confession of faith, though independent, gives expression to a thought similar to that of the Chain of Causation. To get rid of the evils of life, the causes of life itself must be suppressed or destroyed. The Buddha denied the existence of a soul in the sense of an individual and personal identity. There are five groups of elements (*skandhas*). These, when a person is born, unite together in various proportions (hence differences in character, disposition, etc.) to form the living sentient creature; and when he dies, they are dissolved again and perish. Apart from them no existence is possible. "The great aim of Buddhist teaching therefore is to show by what means the reconstitution of the skandhas may be prevented, and thus release obtained from existence with its weariness and sorrow" (Geden). When at death the skandhas are reconstituted and recombined a new individual arises in this or in some other world, and the link between the old and new existences is what is called *karma* or action. It is karma, and not the individual, that lives on. In the new existence (except for the Buddhas), the memory of the events of previous lives is lost, but penalty is paid for wrong-doing or reward is received for good deeds in a previous existence. This is what is meant by re-birth in Buddhism. The great aim of Buddhism is to break the chain of karma, and to extricate oneself from the mechanical round of re-births. To do this and to enter into the rest which is called Nirvana, one must become enlightened by treading in the Noble Eightfold Path. Nirvana is explained by E. Lehmann in Chantepie de la Saussaye's *Lehrbuch*. "The Nirvana is the condition in which the suffering life's endless reincarnations are abolished. It is declared to involve the extinction of Desire and of Cognition; and though we are not told that it also includes the extinction of Life, such an extinction would be in the logical consequence of Buddhism, since the evil from which man is to save himself, namely, suffering, consists precisely in existence." But "the Nirvana can only be defined negatively: not Desire, and not Consciousness, not Life, yet also not Death. Only this can be said positively concerning it,—that it is the condition in which the soul is freed from transmigration; only from the point of view of the endless births, with their life and death and death and life, is it possible to attach any conception whatsoever to the term Nirvana" (quoted by F. von Hügel). The two chief schools of thought and practice in Buddhism are called the Mahāyāna or the "Great Vehicle" and the Hīnayāna or the "Little Vehicle." They are also described, rather inexactly, as Northern Buddhism and Southern Buddhism. "The *Mahāyāna* system taught a kind of speculative theism, with which were united especially in Tibet elements of mysticism and fable, derived in large part from the ancient popular religions of the country. This system was moreover tolerant, gentler and more human than its rival, the Hīnayāna; and permitted greater freedom to the individual, both in action and belief, than did the simpler agnosticism and stern but unattractive morality which claimed to represent primitive Buddhism" (Geden). The Mahāyāna is often ascribed to Nāgārjuna, the thirteenth or fourteenth in succession of the Buddhist patriarchs. He is said also to have taught a "middle way" between the doctrines of the reality and of the deceptiveness of existence (the Middle Vehicle). This system is known in Tibet as the Mādhyamayāna. In Tibet the religion of the Buddha has been changed and modified by nature and devil worship; and the ritual, with its altars, processions, and incense resembles strikingly that of the Roman Catholic and Greek Churches. Buddhism in fact presents various types. "The Buddhism of Nepāl and Tibet differs from the Buddhism of Ceylon as much as the Christianity of Rome or of Moscow differs from that of Scotland or Wales. The Buddhism of Mongolia and China is far removed from either of these, and the Buddhism of Japan has peculiarities all its own" (T. W. Rhys Davids, *Hibbert Lectures*, 1881). An interesting problem is raised by the resemblance of some of the stories and parables which were in course of time attributed to Gautama and incorporated in the Buddhist scriptures, to passages in the New Testament Gospels. It has been maintained by some that Christianity borrowed from Buddhism, and by others that Buddhism borrowed from Christianity. "Albert J. Edmunds and Garbe earnestly advocate the indebtedness of Christianity to Buddhism. Such borrowing has not yet been fully proved, though shown to have been possible" (G. A. Barton, *Religions of the World*, 1917). See, in addition to works already mentioned: W. Bousset, H. Hackmann, Arthur Lloyd, F. W. Bussell.

BUDDHIST SACRED WRITINGS. See CANON, BUDDHIST.

BUDDHIST SOCIETY OF GREAT BRITAIN AND IRELAND. A Society founded in London in 1907. Its aim is to promote a better knowledge of Buddhism and to encourage the study of Pâli and Sanskrit literature.

BUDNAEANS. The followers of Simon Budnæus. They were drawn from the Antitrinitarians of Poland and Transylvania soon after 1565. In 1584 Simon Budnæus and his followers were excommunicated. They would not accept the doctrine of Jesus' miraculous birth.

BUFFALO, SACRED. The buffalo is worshipped by the Todas of South India as affording the main source of subsistence. They eat the male only once a year. A young bull calf is killed with special ceremonies by all the grown-up males of the village, and roasted by a sacred fire. "There is good reason for believing the Todas' assertion that they have never at any time eaten the flesh of the female buffalo" (Marshall, *Travels among the Todas*, 1873, quoted by W. R. Smith). At a funeral, when they kill a buffalo, the men, women, and children bewail its death. See W. R. Smith, *R.S.*

BUG BIBLE, THE. A popular designation of Matthew's Bible (1551). It was so called because in Psalm xci., 5, the passage, "Thou shalt not be afraid of the terror by night," is rendered "Thou shalt not be afraid of the bugges by night."

BULGARIANS. A name for the Catharists or Albigenses of mediæval times. They seem to have been so called because they came from, or were connected with, Bulgaria. Other forms of the name are: Bulgri, Bogri, Boulgares, Boulgres.

BULLA. An ornament worn by free-born Roman children. It was a round or heart-shaped box with an amulet inside it. In the case of patricians it might be golden, in that of poor families it was of leather. Boys discarded it when they were privileged to wear the toga virilis. Adults, however, occasionally wore it as a protection against the evil eye. See O. Seyffert, *Dict.*

BULL-ROARER. A convenient description of a sacred instrument, a kind of rattle (Australian *turndun*) used in religious mysteries in New Mexico, Australia, Africa, and even in ancient Greece. F. Cushing (*Adventures in Zuñi*) describes its sound as "a deep whirring noise." The Kurnai of Australia make boys listen to the din of the bull-roarer when they go through their mystic ceremony of initiation. The American Indians of Zuñi use it to summon men to the mysteries. In South Africa it has also, besides this use, magic power to raise a wind. It is noteworthy that among the Australian Kurnai women are strictly forbidden to look upon the *turndun*. As Spencer and Gillen have shown, the same prohibition extends to the *churinga*, a similar instrument with the same ritual significance, employed by the tribes of Central Australia. An identical instrument, it should be added, was used by palæolithic man in Europe. The identification with the Greek κωνος (cp. ῥόμβος) is due to Andrew Lang. He notes that an ancient scholiast on Clemens of Alexandria writes: "the κωνος is a little piece of wood, to which a string is fastened, and in the mysteries it was whirled round to make a roaring noise." The bull-roarer has survived as a toy; and in Scotland also as a thunder-spell.

BUNENE. One of the deities in Babylonian-Assyrian religion. In the great temple E-babbara at Sippar in the time of Nabubaliddin (c. 850 B.C.) Shamash, Malik, and Bunene form a triad. In a design added to the inscription of Nabubaliddin the two deities Malik and Bunene seem to be represented as attendants on the sun-god, "who drive the fiery chariot that symbolized the great orb." Bunene, though a male deity, becomes in time the consort of Malik. See Morris Jastrow, *Rel.*

BUPHONIA. This was in Athens another name for the Diipolia, a festival at which a bull was sacrificed. The term means "ox-murder." Robertson Smith points out (*R.S.*) that originally the term was a general one for the slaying of oxen for sacrificial feasts.

BŪRA PENNU. Among the Khonds of Orissa, Būra Pennu or Bella Pennu is the supreme creative deity, the Light-god or Sun-god. He is the good deity to whom is opposed as the deity of evil his consort Tari Pennu the Earth-goddess. Būra Pennu created the world a happy Paradise. Tari Pennu rebelled and introduced disease, poison, and every kind of disorder. The Khonds are divided into two sects. The Būra sect believe that Būra prevailed in the conflict; the Tari sect hold that the battle still continues. See E. B. Tylor, *P.C.*

BURDA. The Arabic word for "mantle." Mohammed presented his own *burda* to the poet Ka'b ibn Zuhair in recognition of some flattering verses which he had written. The poet showed his gratitude by writing another poem known as "Bânat Su'âd" from its opening words. In imitation of this panegyric, a later poet, Sharaf al-dîn Muḥammad al-Būṣîrî (A.D. 1211-1294) wrote another famous ode to the Prophet's mantle called "Qaṣîdat al-Burda," which has been translated into French, German, and English. See Clément Huart, *Hist. of Arabic Literature*, 1903.

BURDEN. Sometimes in the Old Testament this word stands at the head of prophecies (Isaiah xiii. 1, xv. 1, xix. 1, xxi. 1, etc.). In such cases the Hebrew word is *massā* from a root meaning "to lift up" (in this connection "the voice"), and the correct translation is "oracle" (so margin of the Revised Version, 2 Kings ix. 25).

BURGHERS. A name taken by one of the divisions into which the Associate Synod or Secession Church of Scotland split up in 1747. The division was due to difference of opinion regarding the religious clause of the burgess-oath which burgesses were required to take in certain corporate towns. This clause read: "I profess and allow with all my heart the true religion presently professed within this realm, and authorized by the the laws thereof; I shall abide at and defend the same to my life's end, renouncing the Roman religion called Papistry." The Burghers were not prepared to refuse to take this oath. The other division, however, the Anti-burghers, refused to do so. In course of time other divisions took place. In 1799 the Burghers separated into "Old Light Burghers" and "New Light Burghers." In 1820 the "New Light" sections of the Burghers and Anti-burghers joined forces as the "United Secession." In 1847 this joined itself to the "Relief Secession," a body which had seceded on the question of patronage and had formed itself in 1760 "into a Presbytery for the relief of Christians oppressed in their Christian privileges," and the two together became the "United Presbyterian Synod." The "Old Light Burghers" returned in 1839 to the Established Church. Cp. ANTI-BURGHERS. See J. H. Blunt.

BURHI MĀTA. An Indian deity, also called Thākurāni Māta, the goddess of smallpox and rinderpest, worshipped by the Gadbas, a primitive tribe belonging to the Vizagapatam District of Madras.

BURIAL CLUBS, EARLY CHRISTIAN. Burial guilds are referred to in a number of early Christian inscriptions discovered in recent years. By the will of Aristeas (Central Phrygia), for example, a sum of money is bequeathed to the "Society of Neighbours" to enable it every year to "cause the grave of my wife Aurelia to bloom with roses." Camden M. Cobern thinks "the burial club was almost certainly the first official society established under the auspices of Christianity. It was common among the pagans and the Jews, though not conducted probably on the same wide lines of charity and brotherhood as among the early Christians." Only by joining one of these clubs could even a hard-working labourer be sure of a decent burial in the first century.

BURIAL HILL DECLARATION, THE. The Burial Hill (Boston) Declaration of Faith was drawn up in 1865 A.D. by the National Council of Congregational Churches of the United States. It "impressively affirms the Synod's adherence to the faith and order of the Apostolic and Primitive Churches held by their fathers, and substantially as embodied in the Confessions and Platforms which the Synods of 1648 and 1680 set forth or re-affirmed" (William A. Curtis).

BURNETT LECTURES. A course of lectures so named after John Burnett (1729-84), an Aberdeen merchant. Originally the sum of money bequeathed by Burnett was to be applied to the foundation of two prizes to be awarded for the two best treatises on "The evidence that there is a Being all-powerful, wise, and good, by whom everything exists; and particularly to obviate difficulties regarding the wisdom and goodness of the Deity; and this independent of written revelation, and of the revelation of the Lord Jesus; and from the whole to point out the inferences most necessary and useful to mankind." Under a new scheme the prizes have since 1883 been converted into a lectureship on some subject illustrating natural theology. In 1887, for instance, Prof. W. Robertson Smith was invited to give three courses of lectures from October, 1888, to October, 1891, on "The primitive religions of the Semitic peoples, viewed in relation to other ancient religions, and to the spiritual religion of the Old Testament and of Christianity."

BURNING BUSH, THE. A phenomenon mentioned in the Old Testament (Exodus iii. 2-4). The vision is said to have been seen by Moses while he was tending the flock of Jethro, his father-in-law. "And the angel of the Lord appeared unto him in a flame of fire out of the midst of a bush: and he looked, and behold, the bush burned with fire, and the bush was not consumed. And Moses said, 'I will turn aside now, and see this great sight, why the bush is not burnt.'" Verse 5 continues: "And when the Lord saw that he turned aside to see, God called unto him out of the midst of the bush, and said 'Moses, Moses.' And he said, 'Here am I.'" The word used for bush here, *seneh*, seems to occur again in Deuteronomy xxxiii. 16, where Jehovah is referred to as "He that dwelt in the bush," *shōkeni seneh*. This would suggest that Jehovah, like the deities of other primitive folk, was sometimes thought of as making his abode in trees. But Renan was no doubt right in thinking that the original reading in Deuteronomy was *shōkeni sinai*, "he who dwells in Sinai." There is no reason to doubt that the Hebrews regarded fire as being sometimes a manifestation of the divine presence, or that they believed certain trees to be the abodes of deities. But this particular story need not be based upon such beliefs (cp., however, *Encycl. Bibl.*). Nor is it necessary to think, with Robertson Smith (*R.S.*), that "the original seat of a conception like the burning bush, which must have its physical basis in electrical phenomena, must probably be sought in the clear dry air of the desert or of lofty mountains." The story describes the kind of subjective vision which a prophet may well have seen. The seeing of a bright light and the hearing of a voice belong to psychic phenomena or experiences. See *Encycl. Bibl.*

BURNING OF THE GOD. In ancient times it was the practice in some countries (*e.g.* in Asia Minor) solemnly to burn a god either in effigy or in the form of a human representative. The idea of the rite seems to have been that in this way the incorruptible and immortal part of him was set free from the corruptible and perishable elements of human existence. The representative of the god was sometimes a king. Melcarth, the great god of Tyre, whom the Greeks identified with Hercules, seems to have been burnt in effigy in Gades (mod. Cadiz), an early Tyrian colony. It is said of Hercules himself that he burned himself to death and afterwards ascended to heaven. J. G. Frazer thinks this is a Greek imitation of the burning of Melcarth. The Cappadocian god Sandan, who also corresponds to the Greek Hercules, seems to have been burned in effigy at a periodical festival in Tarsus. The Assyrian king Sardanapalus, who is said to have founded the city of Tarsus, is also said to have burned himself on a great pyre. The story is not true of the Sardanapalus who is otherwise known as Ashurbanipal; but it is perhaps reminiscent of the practice of burning a king as a representative of the god. See J. G. Frazer, *Adonis Attis Osiris*, 1906.

BURNT OFFERING. See ALTAR, SACRIFICE.

BUSSUMARUS. Bussumarus, "the large-lipped," was one of the names given by the ancient Celts to a god who corresponded to the Roman Jupiter.

BUTO. The name of a goddess in the religion of the ancient Egyptians. She was the protecting goddess of Buto, the lower capital of Egypt, and took the form of a serpent. Her original name was Uto. In the religion of the late period Buto became the most important of the seven gods who spoke by oracles. See A. Erman.

C

C. God C. is a designation used by anthropologists for a deity depicted in the MSS. of the Mayan Indians of Central America. Since in one place he is represented as surrounded by a nimbus of rays, and in the Codex Tro-cortesianus is encircled by planetary signs, he would seem to have been a deity of astronomic significance; but his identification is very uncertain.

CABALA. A popularized form of the Hebrew term Kabbalah (*q.v.*).

CAINITES. A sect of the second century, the members of which placed Cain above Abel, and in fact, as F. W. Bussell says, converted the sinners of Scripture (Esau, Korah, the men of Sodom, Judas Iscariot) into saints. For them Abel represented the lower powers, while Cain was the messenger endowed with power from the higher regions.

CAITANYA SECT. A Hindu sect in Bengal, the followers of Caitanya. Caitanya was born in the year A.D. 1485. He came to be regarded as an incarnation of Krishṇa, which accounts for marvellous stories about his early years. Thus it is said that soon after his birth holy men visited his parents to pay homage to their new-born child and to offer him a present of rice, fruits, gold and silver. He is said also to have made himself master of Sanscrit grammar and literature with great rapidity. After spending some years in making religious pilgrimages he began to preach and to propagate his own view of Vaishṇavism or the worship of Vishnu in Bengal. "His success as a preacher was remarkable. Even his enemies were attracted by the persuasiveness of his manner and the magnetic power of his eloquence. The lower classes flocked to him by thousands." Leaving his two disciples, Advaita and Nityānanda to continue his work in Bengal, he himself settled at Kaṭak in Orissa not far from the temple of Jagan-nāth. "The first principle he inculcated was that all the faithful worshippers of Krishṇa (=Vishnu) were to be treated as equals. Caste was to be subordinated to faith in Krishṇa." And "the devotion of the human soul to Vishṇu was to be symbolized under the figure of human love." This devotion, similar to the tender affection of a girl for her lover, should be so intense that the worshipper loses "all individuality and self-consciousness in ecstatic union with his god." Such a state may be produced by constant repetition of the name of the deity, by singing, music, dancing or similar movements of the body. It is not known how or when Ćaitanya died. He disappeared in a mysterious way when he was forty-two years of age (c. A.D. 1527). After this he was deified and worshipped. The only question was "whether he was a full manifestation of the Supreme Being (Kṛishṇa) or only a descent of a portion (anśa) of his essence." It was decided that he was the very Krishṇa incarnate, and that "his two principal disciples, Advaita and Nityānanda, were manifestations of portions of the same deity." Another disciple, Haridās, was deified in Bengal as a separate divinity. See Monier-Williams.

ĆAITYAS. Originally the word Ćaitya meant the heap or mound under which the Buddhists placed the relics of their great saints. Then it came to denote a relic-structure within an assembly-hall, whereas a Stūpa meant a relic-structure outside in the open air. See STŪPAS.

CAJETANI. Another name for the Order of Theatines (*q.v.*).

CALEDONIAN ASYLUM, ROYAL. An institution founded by the "Highland Society of London" in 1814, and incorporated by Act of Parliament on June 14, 1815. See IRVINGITES.

CALF, GOLDEN. Reference is made in the Old Testament to worship of a golden calf by Israelites of the Northern kingdom. These images are said to have been set up in Dan and Bethel (I. Kings xii. 28 *ff.*; II. Kings, x. 29; Hosea x. 5), and in Samaria (Hosea viii. 5 *f.*). Reference is perhaps made also to their worship in Gilgal (Amos v. 4 *f.*; Hosea iv. 15, ix. 15, xii. 11). Apparently, however, they were not worshipped in the temple of Jerusalem or in the other sanctuaries of Judah. Aaron is said to have made a golden calf in the wilderness; but it is strange that nomads wandering in a wilderness should have thought of worshipping a golden calf. Some scholars have thought that the Israelites followed the example of the Egyptians in worshipping the bull. But Dr. Benzinger points out (*Encycl. Bibl.*) that the Israelites were not much influenced by the Egyptians, and as a matter of fact it was living animals that were worshipped by the Egyptians. The Israelites seem to have learned the worship from the Canaanites amongst whom the bull was the symbol of Baal. The prophetic writers condemn the worship as idolatry (Hosea viii. 5, x. 5; cp. the Deuteronomist in I. Kings xiv. 16, xv. 26, xvi. 26; II. Kings x. 29). See *Encyclop. Bibl.*

CALIXTINES. One of the sections into which the followers of John Hus (1369-1415; see HUSSITES) were divided. The name is derived from the Latin *calix* "cup" or "chalice"; and the Calixtines, "men of the Cup," were so called because they insisted on Communion in both kinds (*sub utraque specie;* bread and wine). They were called also Utraquists. This point, Communion in both kinds, was not one to which Hus himself attached importance. It was made important by one of his followers Jacobellus de Misa "the first to begin the practice of Communion in both kinds in Bohemia," and was adopted unanimously by the Hussites. While, however, the Calixtines were disposed to cherish and defend the practice peacefully, the other section of the Hussites, the Taborites proceeded under the guidance of John Ziska (1360-1424) to defend it by force of arms. In 1421 the Calixtines expressed their wishes in four articles ("Articles of Prague"). 1. "That the Word of God should be preached freely and without impediment throughout the kingdom of Bohemia." 2. "That the Sacrament of the Divine Eucharist should be freely administered in both kinds, that is, under the species of bread and of wine, to all Christians not disqualified by mortal sin, according to the command and institution of the Saviour." 3. "That any clergyman engaged in the pursuit of secular power, or of wealth and temporal goods, contrary to the precept of Christ, to the prejudice of his office, and to the injury of the State, should be forbidden such pursuits and made to live according to the Evangelical rule and Apostolic life which Christ lived with his Apostles." 4. "That all mortal sins, and particularly public ones, should be properly punished by those to whom the duty of suppressing them belongs, and by reason of the law of God." These articles were ratified and confirmed by the Council of Basle (1433) in the Compact of Prague. Eventually some of the Calixtines conformed to the Roman usage, while others joined the Taborites. See Blunt; *Prot. Dict.*; *Cath. Dict.*; *Brockhaus.*

CALVARIANS. A monastic association of priests founded on Mont Valérien near the Bois de Boulogne about 1635 by a priest named Hubert Charpentier. It was founded in honour of the Passion of Jesus Christ, and with the object of promoting Catholicism. Mont Valérien afterwards became known as *Colline de Calvaire.* In 1617 one Père Joseph founded a congregation of Calvarian nuns at Poitiers. In 1619 Virginia Braccelli established a congregation of Calvarian sisters at Genoa. See Schaff-Herzog; the *Cath. Dict.*

CALVARY. In the Gospel of Luke (xxiii. 33) it is said in the Authorised Version that Jesus was crucified at a "place which is called Calvary." The Revised Version has a "place which is called The Skull." The Greek word is *kranion*, which the Revised Version translates. The Authorised Version keeps the Latin word *Calvaria.* The parallel passages in the other Gospels preserve the Semitic word Golgotha.

CAMALDULES. An Order founded by Romualdus of Ravenna (950-1027). After establishing a number of monastic communities in different places, he established one at Campus Maldoli (Camaldoli) in the Apennines. This establishment, the Hermitage of Camaldoli, became the centre of his movement. In 1072 "there existed an order of Camaldules, not as a reformed branch of the order of the Benedictines, but as an independent association of anchorets. The prior was called 'major.' The members lived in separate huts, where they slept and ate. At certain hours they met in the prayer-house, and recited (not sang) the liturgy. They fasted often. Bread and water was their common diet: meat was not allowed. But the principal command was silence" (Schaff-Herzog). In course of time a monastery was built at Fontebuono in the neighbourhood of the Hermitage, and other monasteries arose in various places (in Venice, for instance) in place of hermitages. The severity of the original rule had been somewhat mitigated by Rudolph, the fourth major, in 1102, who introduced a common table and other changes. The Camaldules were abolished in Austria in 1782, and afterwards in France and Italy. In Naples, however, they were restored in 1822. See Schaff-Herzog; the *Cath. Dict.*

CAMAXTLI. A god of war among the Tlascaltecs or Tlascalans of Mexico.

CAMAZOTZ. A god of bats in the mythology of the Quiché of Guatemala.

CAMBRIDGE CAMDEN SOCIETY. A Society founded in 1839 "to promote the study of ecclesiastical architecture and antiquities, and the restoration of mutilated architectural remains." W. Walsh (*Prot. Dict.*, *s.v.* "Oxford Movement") quotes Francis Close (1797-1882), afterwards Dean of Carlisle, as saying in 1844 in a sermon that "as Romanism is taught *Analytically* at Oxford, it is taught *Artistically* at Cambridge—it is inculcated theoretically, in tracts, at one University, and it is *sculptured*, *painted*, *and graven* at the other. The Cambridge Camdenians build churches and furnish symbolic vessels, by which the Oxford Tractarians may carry out their principles."

CAMBRIDGE PLATFORM OF CHURCH DISCIPLINE. The Cambridge (New England) Platform of Church Discipline was drawn up by the Cambridge Synod in 1648 A.D. as a supplement to the Westminster Confession (*q.v.*) of 1646 A.D. The new Platform takes the place of the doctrine of Church government and discipline in chapters xxv., xxx., and xxxi. of the Westminster Confession. W. A. Curtis speaks of it as "a careful and minute application of Congregational principles to the details of the Puritan doctrine of the Church." See William A. Curtis.

CAMBRIDGE PLATONISTS, THE. A party of religious thinkers at Cambridge who were opposed to the party of William Laud at Oxford. Its chief representatives were Benjamin Whichcote (1609-1683), provost of King's College (1644-60), Ralph Cudworth (1617-1688), Regius Professor of Hebrew (1645-88), Henry More (1614-1687) of Christ's College, Nathanael Culverwel (*d.* 1651?), Fellow of Emmanuel College, and George Rust (*d.* 1670), Fellow of Christ's College (1649-59).

CAMEL, THE. Camels were used as food and offerings by the Arabs, but not by the Israelites. According to Nilus, among the Saracens, "the camel was not allowed to be killed and eaten except in a public rite, at which all the kinsmen assisted" (Robertson Smith). It was devoured by the Arabs in a sacramental meal while its blood and flesh were still warm. In the oldest known form of Arabian sacrifice, as described by Nilus, "the camel chosen as the victim is bound upon a rude altar of stones piled together, and when the leader of the band has thrice led the worshippers round the altar in a solemn procession accompanied with chants, he inflicts the first wound, while the last words of the hymn are still upon the lips of the congregation, and in all haste drinks of the blood that gushes forth. Forthwith the whole company fall on the victim with their swords, hacking off pieces of the quivering flesh and devouring them raw with such wild haste, that in the short interval between the rise of the day star which marked the hour for the service to begin, and the disappearance of its rays before the rising sun, the entire camel, body and bones, skin, blood and entrails, is wholly devoured" (*R.S.*). We read too of consecrated camels among the Arabs, which they released from service and allowed to roam at large. These might not be ridden, except in an emergency. But, though they seem sometimes to be spoken of as the property of the deity, they were not used for his service. At Rāmallāh in Palestine there are two springs, one of which is supposed to be inhabited by a camel.

CAMERONIANS. The name given to a body of Scotch Covenanters in the reign of Charles II. They were so named because one of their leaders was Richard Cameron. They claimed to be the true representatives of the principles of those who framed the original Covenant. Cameron was one of those responsible for the anti-monarchical Declaration which was read at Sanquhar in 1680. He was killed in the battle of Airdmoss in the same year. The Cameronians were organised in "societies," and were also called Society People. On the death of Cameron, James Renwick succeeded to the leadership. Renwick boldly disowned "the usurpation and tyranny" of James, Duke of York, and in 1688 was executed. In 1706 John Macmillan became leader of the Societies. In conjunction with Thomas Nairn, in 1743 he founded and organised a new body, "the Reformed Presbytery." Originally the Reformed Presbyterians were forbidden by a formal Act of Testimony to exercise the franchise or to take the oath of allegiance. In 1863, however, the Scotch synod decided that "while recommending the members of the Church to abstain from the use of the franchise and from taking the oath of allegiance, discipline to the effect of suspension and expulsion from the Church shall cease." A minority of the Reformed Presbyterians refused to accept this decision, and formed a new body with the same name. In 1876 the older and larger body of Reformed Presbyterians united with the Free Church of Scotland. See Schaff-Herzog; J. H. Blunt.

CAMERONITES. A School of theology founded by John Cameron (1579?-1625). Cameron was born and educated at Glasgow. In 1600 he went to France and taught Greek and Latin at Bordeaux. In 1602 he received an appointment at Sedan. After studying divinity at Paris, Geneva and Heidelberg for about three years, he went back to Bordeaux as protestant minister (1608-1617). In 1618 he removed to Saumur as professor of divinity. Here he put forward views which were similar to those afterwards adopted by Moses Amyraut (see AMYRALDISTS). "The substance of these opinions was that God wills the salvation of all men, and not of the elect only, that none are excluded from the possibility of salvation, and that those are saved who co-operate with God by using the power of judgment between good and evil which He infuses into their understanding for the choice of good" (Blunt) In 1620 Cameron returned to London, and in 1622 he became Principal of Glasgow University. He soon abandoned this position (1623) and went back to Saumur. The next year he removed to Montauban as professor of divinity. Here in 1625 he was stabbed by one of his opponents and died from the wound. His works were published in Latin and French in ten volumes (1616-42). See J. H. Blunt; the *D.N.B.*; and *Chambers' Encycl.*

CAMPBELLITES. The followers of Alexander Campbell (1786-1866). Born in Ireland, Campbell went to the United States in 1809. Here he became pastor of a Presbyterian church in Washington county, Pa. In 1827 he founded an independent sect which he called "The Disciples of Christ." The members of this sect are now known as the Campbellites. In 1840-41 he founded an institution called Bethany College and became its first president. The Disciples of Christ held that the Church of Christ was intended to be one and undivided; that its lost unity might be regained by a return to the Gospel in its original purity; that all the theological terms and doctrines of the schools must be abandoned and replaced by the original words, phrases, and ordinances of Holy Scripture; and that baptism should be by immersion. The officers of the local churches are elders and deacons. See *Harper's Encycl. of U.S. Hist.*, 1902.

CAMPBELLITES, AMERICAN. The followers of Thomas Campbell, who went from Ireland to America in 1807. They called themselves Reformed Baptists.

CAMULUS. Camulus, it would seem, was one of the deities worshipped by the ancient Celts. As a war-god, he would correspond to the Roman Mars; but he seems also in some respects to have resembled Jupiter as well. The name survived in Camulodūnum (Colchester), and perhaps in the Irish Cumhal who appears as father of Finn. See Anwyl; C. Squire, *Myth.*

CANDLEMAS. An ecclesiastical festival, so called on account of the candles which in the Roman Catholic Church are carried in procession. The festival is also called the "Purification of the Blessed Virgin Mary." It is observed on the 2nd of February in commemoration of the presentation of Christ in the Temple. In the Prayer Book of the Church of England it is described as "The Presentation of Christ in the Temple, commonly called the Purification of Saint Mary the Virgin." The purification thought of originally was that of the Levitical law (Lev. 12, 2), but two other events are now more prominent in the Roman Mass and office. "Candles are blessed and carried in procession to remind us how the holy old man Simeon met our Lord, took Him in his arms, and declared Him the light of the Gentiles and the glory of Israel. Next, in the collect, epistle, and the gospel there are marked references to the fact that our Lord was at the same time presented in the temple before God and redeemed with five holy shekels" (Lk. xii. 22; cp. Exod. xiii. 2, Num. viii. 16, xviii. 15—*Cath. Dict.*). The festival is said to have been kept at Antioch in 526 under the Emperor Justin, and was known in the West before 735. Baronius suggests that Pope Gelasius substituted it for the pagan Lupercalia which was kept in February (15) and was also a festival of purification and expiation. The lights were forbidden in the Church of England in 1548 by an order of the Privy Council. See *Prot. Dict.; Cath. Dict.*

CANDLES. The Chinese burn candles on their domestic altars. At sunset they place a burning candle in the "lantern of Heaven" which is suspended near the doorposts of the house. Candles are burned in front of the ancestral soul-tablets. Every evening, as long as the coffin of a deceased person is in the house, these candles are offered to the soul. In the funeral procession lighted candles are carried in lanterns hanging from curved poles. The lanterns bear inscriptions. "Their use in broad daylight shows decidedly that they are designed to pilot the soul, which lives in complete darkness, along the right path to the burial ground," and perhaps the inscriptions "are intended to prevent the soul from being led astray by other lanterns, which it may happen to see along the road" (de Groot). A peculiar kind of candle stands on the altar or in front of the altar in the temples of Tibetan Buddhists or Lāmas. This temple-lamp is "a short pedestalled bowl, into a socket in the centre of which is thrust a cotton wick, and it is fed by melted butter. As the great mass of butter solidifies and remains mostly in this state, the lamp is practically a candle. The size varies according to the means and the number of the temple votaries, as it is an act of piety to add butter to this lamp. One is necessary, but two or more are desirable, and on special occasions 108 or 1,000 small lamps are offered upon the altar. Sometimes a cluster of several lamps form a small candelabrum of the branching lotus-flower pattern" (Waddell). See L. A. Waddell; J. J. M. de Groot, *R.S.*

CANNON, WORSHIP OF. An example of the worship of a cannon is noted by E. S. Hartland (*P.P.*). "A cannon, old and useless and neglected, belonging to the Dutch Government, lay in a field at Batavia, on the island of Java. It was taken by the native women for a linga. Dressed in their best, and adorned with flowers, they used to worship this piece of senseless iron, presented it with offerings of rice and fruits, miniature sunshades, and coppers, and completed the performance by sitting astride upon it as a certain method of winning children" (I, 123). A similar superstition has been noted by E. J. Banks (*Bismya, or The Lost City of Adab*, 1912) among Jewish women in Bagdad. These gather about a large English gun in a public square, and stroking it, whisper into its mouth their prayers, their troubles, and their hopes.

CANON. The term Canon is commonly used (1) of a law or rule, (2) of a collection of sacred writings, especially of the Sacred Scriptures accepted by Christians, and (3) of a dignitary of the Church of England. The word is of course the same as the Greek *κανων*. It meant originally a reed or rod. It then came to mean a measuring rod, and was next "used for a plumbline or for a level, or a ruler, for anything that was a measure or a rule for other things" (C. R. Gregory). Then in the intellectual sphere it denoted a rule "that told a man what was right or what he had to do." The grammarians in Alexandria called the ancient Greek writers the canon, because they were regarded as patterns or models. They also called their rules for declensions, conjugations, and syntax "canons." In common usage canon denoted "a measure, a definition, an order, a command, a law." Joshua, as an ideal leader, is called by Philo (*c.* 20 B.C.-45 A.D.) a canon. The word is found in the New Testament. In Galatians vi. 16 it is said: "And as many as shall walk by this rule (*tō kanoni toutō*), peace be upon them and mercy." In II. Corinthians x. 13 (Authorised Version) it is said: "But we will not boast of things without our measure, but according to the measure of the rule (Revised Version "province"; Revised Version margin "limit"; Gk. *tou kanonos*) which God hath distributed to us, a measure to reach even unto you." In course of time the word came to be used in the Christian Church for a definite and certain decision, an ecclesiastical determination. At a synod at Antioch held in A.D. 266 one of Paul of Samosata's doctrines was said to be "foreign to the ecclesiastical canon." After this the ecclesiastical canon became a set phrase for the rule or custom of the Church. From A.D. 341 (Council at Antioch) the term "canons" was applied to the decisions of ecclesiastical councils. The term "canon" as applied to Holy Scripture was first used by the Greek Fathers of the fourth century. Cp. further CANON, OLD TESTAMENT. In the other sense of the term, a Canon is a residentiary member of a cathedral chapter. He is appointed by the Bishop or nominated by the Crown. There are also Honorary Canons who receive no emolument. They are appointed by the Bishop or Archbishop, and rank next after the residentiary Canons. Finally there are Minor Canons. These have to intone part of the Service. A good voice is therefore a necessary qualification for appointment. They are appointed by the Cathedral chapter. In some cases a professorship carries with it a canonry (*e.g.*, at Oxford, Cambridge, and Durham). "The clergy of every large church in ancient times were termed *canonici*, as being entered on the list (for this is one of the meanings of *κανων*) of ecclesiastics serving the church" (Addis and Arnold). See C. R. Gregory; *Cath. Dict.*

CANON, BUDDHIST. There are three collections of Buddhist sacred writings. We find (1) a Canon of the Southern Buddhists comprising books written in the Pāli language; (2) a Canon of the Northern Buddhists, comprising books written in Sanscrit; and (3) a Canon of the Chinese Buddhists, comprising books written in Chinese. As regards the fundamental features, the main divisions, and the most important books, the Canon is much the same everywhere; but there are great differences in details, and in the Canons of the Northern and Chinese Buddhists many later texts and commentaries have been introduced. In any case, there is not the same unity among the Northern Buddhists as there is among the Southern. "It is incorrect to speak, as is so often done, of Northern and Southern Buddhism as the only two great divisions into which Buddhism had been divided. There was a unity in Southern Buddhism; but there has been no such unity in Northern Buddhism. We may talk, indeed, of Northern Buddhisms; but it would be better to keep the Buddhism of each of the northern countries in which it has been adopted separate and distinct, both in our thoughts and our language" (T. W. Rhys Davids). Of the later books admitted into the Northern Canon (*e.g.* by the Buddhists of Nepaul), one is called "The Lotus of the true Law" and is a kind of mystery play (*Sacred Books of the East*, xxi.); the other is called "Lalita-Vistāra" and is an account of the birth and trials of the Buddha. The sacred collection of the Sikhs is called the "Adi-Granth" (*q.v.*). That of the Jains includes the "Gaina Sutras" (*Sacred Books of the East*, xxii.). The Southern Canon, however, must be taken as the original model. "Scholars generally agree that the canon of the so-called Southern Buddhism (prevailing in Ceylon, Burma, Siam), on the whole, presents the most original aspect of the sacred books" (H. Hackmann). In this Canon there are three principal divisions. It is therefore called the "Tipiṭaka" (Sanscrit, Tripiṭaka) or "The Three Baskets." (1) The first division is called the Vinayapiṭaka. It deals with the organization of the monastic life. There are three works in this division. (*a*) Suttavibhanga. This gives the precepts concerning monastic penances. (*b*) The Khandhakas. There are two books: the Mahâvagga and the Cullavagga. These give rules as to admission into the Order (Pâtimokkha), and as to dress, dwelling, etc. (*c*) Parivâra. This is a kind of appendix of later date giving details about the life of the community. (2) The second division is called the Suttapiṭaka. It deals with the Buddha's doctrine of salvation. There are four works in this division. (*a*) Dîghanikâya. Longer discourses of the master. (*b*) Majjhimanikâya. Discourses of medium length. (*c*) Anguttaranikâya. Discourses "arranged after numbers" (Hackmann). (*d*) Samyuttanikâya. Discourses arranged in groups. There is an appendix to this division called Khuddakanikâya, "a collection of different materials, sayings of the Buddha, songs, tales, legends, and the like." There are fifteen books, "some of which belong to the best-known and most impressive works of the Buddhist literature. They include the Dhammapada, a kind of hymn-book, which has been considered perhaps the most sacred and popular book of the Buddhist Bible (see *Sacred Books of the East*, x.); the Jâtaka which gives legends concerning five hundred and fifty previous existences of the Buddha; the Apadâna which gives stories of the saints; the Buddhavamsa which deals with twenty-four previous Buddhas; and the Cariyâpiṭaka which treats of thirty-four previous incarnations of the Buddha." (3) The third division is called the Abhidhammapiṭaka. It discusses "the psychological prolegomena of the Buddhist ethical system" (Hackmann). There are seven works in this division. (*a*) Dhammasamgani. This describes states or phenomena. (*b*) Vibhanga. This is a continuation. (*c*) Kathâvatthu. This refutes two hundred and fifty-two heresies. (*d*) Puggalapaññatti. This divides men into classes from the ethical standpoint. (*e*) Dhâtukathâ, (*f*) Yamaka, and (*g*) Patthâna are smaller treatises. The books included in the Southern Canon seem to have been committed to writing by about the beginning of the first century B.C. Earlier collections were recognised as authoritative in the time of Asoka (*c.* 250 B.C.). See H. Hackmann; Max Müller, *Sacred Books of the East;* T. W. Rhys Davids.

CANONICAL HOURS. Hours or times of prayer, which were prescribed by rule or canon. They were observed by the early Christians. In the days of persecution, there were Nocturns or Vigils, prayers at night. The early morning prayers were called Lauds. The following are the names of the canonical hours. 1. Matins, in Old English "Uhtsang," at break of day. 2. Prime, or "Primesang," at the first hour of the day, 6 a.m. 3. Tierce, or "Undersang," at 9 a.m. 4. Sext, or "Midday Sang," at 12. 5. Nones, or "Noon-Sang," at 3 p.m. 6. Vespers, or "Evensang," public evening service. 7. Compline, or "Night-sang," the closing service (Latin *complere*, to finish) of the day. See W. R. W. Stephens, *Common Prayer*, 1901; *Prot. Dict.*

CANON OF THE NEW TESTAMENT. The sacred writings of the earliest Christians were the canonical writings of the Old Testament. The authoritative words of their own Christian prophets at first circulated orally. The earliest written documents were letters written by the Apostle Paul to Churches which he had founded and which were in need of guidance. As in the case of the Old Testament the need for a sharply defined collection of sacred writings did not arise until other writings began to compete with those of the Church. This would not happen for some time. As Gregory says, at least in many districts, well on into the second century the word was still preached by wandering preachers, the Apostles. "Little by little it will have become known that the Gospels had been written. These Gospels will at first have been circulated in the immediate neighbourhood of the place in which each was written, and then have soon struck the great lines, if they were not already on one of them, and have reached Rome and Jerusalem and Alexandria. Wherever a Gospel was received, Christians will have compared its tenor with that which they had heard by word of mouth. But for a while the living voice of the evangelising preacher will have been preferred to the dead letter in the book. Many Churches will for a long while have had no Gospel or only one Gospel, and only after much waiting have gotten more. Church after Church, group after group of Christians had then a Gospel and an Epistle or two, a few Epistles. The tendency of the intercourse between the Churches was towards an increase in the collection of books; now one now another new one was added by friends to the old and treasured store of rolls." In course of time a fairly large number of books would be known to all the Churches alike, though some of them might not be held in equal esteem everywhere. Clement of Rome, writing in the post-Apostolic age, seems to be acquainted with nearly all of the books of our New Testament. We know that some of these books were already being made use of by unorthodox teachers (*e.g.*, Simon Magus, Cerinthus, Basilides). Basilides himself wrote twenty-four books on the Gospel. The Church Father Polycarp, according to Gregory, had in his hands all the Epistles of Paul, the First Epistle of Peter, the First Epistle of John, the Gospel of Matthew, and probably all the four Gospels. The Gnostic Valentinus (first half of second century) seems to have been acquainted with most of the books of the New Testament. The Gnostics had also books of their own, such as the Gospel of Truth, the Gospel of Perfection, the Gospel of Eve. Marcion, who left the Church and about the year 144 founded a Church of his own, set up his own canon of New Testament writings. He accepted only the Gospel of Luke, and ten Epistles of Paul (Galatians, Corinthians, Romans, Thessalonians, Ephesians [Laodiceans], Colossians, Philippians, Philemon). Melito, Bishop at Sardes (*fl.* 176 A.D.), seems to quote all the books of the New Testament, except the Epistle of James, the Epistle of Jude, the Second and the Third Epistle of John. Tatian, who severed his more direct connection with the Church about 172 or 173, in compiling his Diatessaron made use of the four Gospels. He seems also to have known most of the books of the New Testament. The Muratorian fragment belongs according to Gregory to about 170 A.D. It contains (as far as it has been preserved) a list of the books of the New Testament. "We have the four Gospels, Acts, the Epistles of Paul, the Epistles of John, Jude, the Revelation. So far as the fragment goes, it brings neither James nor the Epistles of Peter nor Hebrews. Of course, in the case of a copyist who was so extremely careless, there remains the possibility that in some place a line or several lines have been omitted. These Epistles are, however, Epistles that would be likely at first to be read more in the East than in the West." The Epistle to the Hebrews seems, however, to have been known at Rome as early as about 95 A.D. "There may have been some special reason for its omission in this fragment. Perhaps the author of the fragment thought, as Tertullian did, that Hebrews was written by Barnabas, and he may not have been inclined to put it into the list on that account" (Gregory). Irenaeus, in his great work on the Heresies, written between about the years 181 and 189, made use of the four Gospels, the Acts of the Apostles, the First Epistle of Peter, the First Epistle of John, the Book of Revelation, and all the Epistles of Paul except Philemon. He speaks of the Scriptures as having been handed down without corruption. Clement of Alexandria, according to Eusebius (*H.E.* vi. 14) made comments on all the Scriptures, including the books spoken against (*Antilegomena*), the Epistle of Jude and the rest of the Catholic Epistles. The Epistle to the Hebrews he regarded as the work of Paul. Tertullian does not seem to know anything of the Epistle of James, the Second Epistle of Peter, the Second and the Third Epistle of John. He knows of the Book of Revelation, and ascribes it to the Apostle John. He knows also of the Epistle to the Hebrews. This he ascribes to Barnabas. Origen accepts most of the books of the New Testament, including the Epistle of Jude, the Epistle to the Hebrews, and the Book of Revelation. His testimony as to the Epistle of James, the Second Epistle of Peter, the Second and the Third Epistle of John is somewhat uncertain. Dionysius of Alexandria (died about 265 A.D.) accepts the Epistle of James, the Second and the Third Epistle of John, and the Epistle to the Hebrews. The Book of Revelation he ascribes to an unknown John. The only books of the New Testament that he does not seem to accept are the Epistle of Jude and the Second Epistle of Peter. Cyprian of Carthage (died 258 A.D.) does not seem to have known of the Epistle of James, the Second Epistle of Peter, the Second and the Third Epistle of John, the Epistle of Jude, and the Epistle to the Hebrews. In the third century A.D., therefore, it cannot be said that our books of the New Testament were canonized, that is to say recognized as a whole as canonical. It is even possible that other works were considered of equal authority. Oscar Holtzmann (*Life of Jesus*) thinks that the Gospel of the Hebrews was assigned a rank equal to that of the Gospels of Luke and John. We next come to Eusebius, who wrote his Church History between about the years 305 and 325 A.D. He divides the writings of the three first centuries into three classes (*H.E.* iii. 25). These are: (1) the *acknowledged* books, the four Gospels, the Acts of the Apostles, the Epistles of Paul, the First Epistle of John, the Epistle of Peter, and perhaps ("if that appears perhaps just") the Revelation of John; (2) the *disputed* books, the Epistle of James, the Epistle of Jude, the Second Epistle of Peter, the Second Epistle of John, the Third Epistle of John, and the *spurious* books, the Acts of Paul, the Shepherd, the Apocalypse of Peter, the Epistle of Barnabas, the Teachings of the Apostles, and perhaps the Revelation of John and the Gospel according to the Hebrews; *heretical books*, the *Gospel* of Peter, Thomas, Mathias and others, the *Acts* of Andrew, John, and others. The Epistle to the Hebrews is included among the Epistles of Paul. Cyril of Jerusalem, in his Catechetical Lectures, written about 346 A.D., recommends a study of the four Gospels, the Acts of the Twelve Apostles, the Seven Catholic Epistles of James and Peter, John and Jude, and the fourteen Epistles of Paul. The Book of Revelation is not recommended. The next landmark in the history of the Canon is supposed to be the Council of Laodicea held in 363 A.D. The last canon gives a list of "canonized" books which includes all the books of our New Testament except the Book of Revelation. But the list seems to have been a later addition. The first complete list of New Testament books regarded as inspired scripture is given by Athanasius of Alexandria (367 A.D.). Later, we find Amphilochius, Bishop of Iconium in Lycaonia, rejecting the Book of Revelation and doubting the Second Epistle of Peter, the Second Epistle of John, the Third Epistle of John, and the Epistle of Jude. At the third Council of Carthage, held 397 A.D. a list of canonical books was drawn up corresponding to our list, and it was settled that "apart from the Canonical Scriptures nothing is to be read in Church under the name of Divine Scriptures." But the books were still far from being accepted universally. It is doubtful whether John Chrysostom (347-407 A.D.), Bishop of Constantinople, accepted all of them. Junilius (died after 550 A.D.) states that the Book of Revelation was questioned among Orientals. He himself does not seem to have accepted all the Catholic Epistles. Augustine, who became assistant Bishop of Hippo in 395 A.D., says that the Christian reader should place in the front rank those Canonical Scriptures which are received by all Catholic Churches, in preference to those which some do not receive. "Among those, moreover, which are not received by all, let him prefer those which more and more important Churches accept to those which fewer and less authoritative Churches hold. Should he, however, find some to be held by very many and others by very weighty Churches, although this cannot easily happen, yet I think that they are to be regarded as of equal authority" (after Gregory). On April 8, 1546, the Council of Trent recited a "catalogue of the sacred books," including those of the Apocrypha, and decreed that "if any one receive not, as sacred and canonical, these same books entire with all their parts, as they have been used to be read in the Catholic Church, and as they are contained in the old Latin Vulgate Edition," he should be anathema. The sixth article of the Thirty-Nine Articles of the Church of England says: "In the name of Holy Scripture, we do understand those Canonical books of the Old and New Testament, of whose authority was never any doubt in the Church." It then gives a list of the Old Testament books. There is no list of the New Testament books. In place of it we read: "All the books of the New Testament, as they are commonly received, we do receive and account them Canonical." It is then stated that the other books (the Old Testament Apocrypha) are read simply for example of life and instruction of manners, and a list is added. It has been suggested that a distinction is here drawn between the "Canonical" books and such "Canonical books as have never been doubted in the Church," and that the framers of the Article on a point on which scholars were greatly divided wished to leave the judgment free. See the separate articles on the books of the New Testament; articles on Canon and Bible in the Dictionaries and Encyclopaedias; C. R. Gregory; J. Moffatt, *Introd.*

CANON OF THE OLD TESTAMENT. The Jews divided their canonical writings into three groups: (1) The Torah or Law; (2) The Nebiim or Prophets; (3) The Kethubim or Writings (Hagiographa). The first group, the Torah, comprises the five books of the Pentateuch, called by the Jews "the five fifths of the law" (*chāmishshah chumshê ha-torāh*). The Hebrew name of each of the five books is derived from the initial word or words of the book. The second group, the Nebiim, is sub-divided into two main divisions: *(a)* The *Nebiim rishonîm* or Former Prophets comprising Joshua, Judges, I. and II. Samuel, and I. and II. Kings; *(b)* The *Nebiim akharônim* or Latter Prophets, comprising Isaiah, Jeremiah, Ezekiel, and the twelve Prophets. The Latter Prophets are further sub-divided sometimes into (i.) The Major Prophets (Isaiah, Jeremiah, Ezekiel) and (ii.) The Minor Prophets. The Minor Prophets were regarded as forming together a single book, and as such received the title "The Twelve" (Heb. *shenêm 'asar*; Aramaic *terêsar*; Greek *tō dōdekapropheton*). The third group, the Kethubim, is subdivided into three divisions: (i.) The Kethubim rishônim or Former Writings, Psalms, Proverbs, Job; (ii.) The Megilloth (*q.v.*) or the Five Rolls, Song of Songs, Ruth, Lamentations, Ecclesiastes, and Esther; (iii.) The Kethubim akharônim or Latter Writings, Daniel, Ezra, Nehemiah, I. and II. Chronicles. It seems strange that Joshua, Judges, I. and II. Samuel, and I. and II. Kings should be regarded as prophetical. But Samuel, of course, was a prophet; and Jewish tradition regarded him as the author of the Book of Judges as well as of the two Books of Samuel. Tradition also ascribed the Books of Kings to the prophet Jeremiah. As regards the Book of Joshua, Numbers xxvii. 18 speaks of Joshua as "a man in whom is the spirit," and Ecclesiasticus xlvi. 1 refers to him as "the successor of Moses in prophecies." As Prof. Sanday says (*I.*, 1903), "the idea was that the history of each successive generation was written by a contemporary prophet; and as the prophetic literature in the narrower sense does not begin until the reign of Jeroboam II. in Israel and Uzziah in Judah, the narratives of whose reigns fall in the second half of the Second Book of Kings, it was natural that the great bulk of the historical writings (Joshua—II. Kings) should be roughly described as the work of the older prophets" (p. 155). This was only a tradition; but as a matter of fact there was an element of truth in it, insofar as the books in their present form were put into shape by a prophetic school. The order of the Books of the Old Testament given above is that which is commonly followed in printed editions of the Hebrew Bible. In the Talmud (*Bâba bâthra 14b*), however, the order of the Latter Prophets is given as: Jeremiah, Ezekiel, Isaiah, the Twelve. The explanation of this remarkable order is fancifully explained as follows. "Since Isaiah lived before Jeremiah and Ezekiel, ought he not to have been put before them? [No.] Because Kings closes with destruction, Jeremiah is entirely occupied with it, Ezekiel begins with it, but ends with consolation, while Isaiah is all consolation: hence we connect destruction with destruction, and consolation with consolation." The same order is commonly followed in German and French manuscripts. The Massoretic scholars (7th-9th cent.), however, assigned Isaiah the first place, and this is the position of the book in Spanish manuscripts and in our printed Hebrew Bibles. The order of the Kethubim in the Talmud is: Ruth, Psalms, Job, Proverbs, Ecclesiastes, Song of Songs, Lamentations, Daniel, Esther, Ezra(—Nehemiah), Chronicles. Here Ruth is placed first as giving the ancestry of David, whose writings, the Psalms, come second. The other books are supposed to be in chronological order. The Massoretic scholars and usually the Spanish manuscripts arrange the books: Chronicles, Psalms, Job, Proverbs, Ruth, Song of Songs, Ecclesiastes, Lamentations, Esther, Daniel, Ezra. Thus they keep the five rolls or Megilloth together. German manuscripts generally follow the order found in our printed Hebrew Bibles. The three groups of canonical writings correspond to three stages in the growth of the Canon. The books were accepted only gradually. The terms "canon" and "canonical" are of course Christian. The Jews expressed the idea in a different way. Books which we call canonical are said by them to be books "that defile the hands" (*metamme'im ēth hay-yādayim*). The meaning of this expression seems undoubtedly to be that contact with the sacred writings involves a ceremonial washing of the hands. "The Pharisees," says Budde "(under protest from the Sadducees; cp. *Yad.* iv. 6) attributed to the sacred writings a sanctity of such a sort that whosoever touched them was not allowed to touch aught else, until he had undergone the same ritual ablution as if he had touched something unclean" (*Encycl. Bibl.*). According to a tradition preserved in Second Esdras Ezra was inspired to dictate ninety-four books, of which seventy were to be delivered only to the wise, while the other twenty-four were to be published. As far as Ezra himself is concerned, the legendary nature of the tradition is clear; but it seems to be no less evident, as Wildeboer says, "that toward the end of the first century of our era in Jewish circles a Canon of twenty-four books was recognized, and that gradually the part which Ezra had in the canonization of the Old Testament, viz., giving binding force to the Tora, was being extended to the entire Old Testament." The New Testament, it has been thought, may supply evidence that even in the New Testament period the Book of Chronicles was the last work in a Canon of twenty-four books. In Matthew xxiii. 35 we read: "that upon you may come all the righteous blood shed on the earth, from the blood of Abel the righteous unto the blood of Zachariah son of Barachiah, whom ye slew between the sanctuary and the altar" (cp. Luke xi. 51). The idea, it is supposed, was to refer to the first (Genesis iv.) and last book (II. Chronicles xxiv. 20-22) of the Old Testament. Since, however, it is uncertain which Zachariah is really referred to, it is not safe to attach much importance to the passage. The tradition as to Ezra and his companions was revived by David Kimchi (d. 1240) and Elias Levita (1472-1549), who stated that Ezra and his associates, the Men of the Great Synagogue, fixed the whole canon (Levita, *Massoreth ha-Massoreth*, p. 120, ed. Ginsburg). But the only Talmudic passage in which any support for this statement can be found is in *Baba bathra* 14*b*, and there is no satisfactory evidence of the existence of the Great Synagogue (*q.v.*). Moreover, as a matter of fact, some of the books of the third group (*e.g.*, Daniel) were clearly later than the time of Ezra. Daniel can hardly have been added to the Kethubim (Hagiographa) before the time of the Maccabees. And, assuming that the whole Canon was fixed at one time, it would in any case be very strange that Daniel should have been placed among the Kethubim instead of among the Prophets. It is useless to contend that he was not a prophet in the same sense as the others. He is recognized as a prophet in the New Testament (Matthew xxiv. 15; Mark xiii.). The Jewish tradition cannot be relied upon. Some of the books included among the Kethubim are found there, instead of among the Nebiim, because they were of late origin and were added to the Canon after the Prophetic group had been closed. The process of collection and canonisation was a gradual one. It is clear that an original collection, the Books of the Law, was gradually supplemented and enlarged. The division known as the Torah has a distinctive character: but, as Wildeboer says, "no one has succeeded in satisfactorily defining the specific difference between the Nebiim and Kethubim." It is noteworthy too that the Septuagint makes no distinction between the two groups (see ALEXANDRIAN CANON).

The process of growth and development can be seen from the very beginning. The Law itself grew. There was first the Ten Words inscribed on two tables of stone. Prof. Briggs (*Intr.*) thinks that, "if any document fulfils all the tests of canonicity, the Tables of the Law certainly do." There was next the Book of the Covenant (Exodus xxxiv., Judaic narrative; Exodus xx. 22-xxiii., Ephraimitic narrative), which Moses "read in the audience of the people" when God made a covenant with them (see BOOK OF THE COVENANT). After this came the promulgation of the Deuteronomic Code, which was found in the Temple in the reign of Josiah (621 B.C.). The event is recorded in II. Kings xxii.-xxiii.=II. Chronicles xxxiv.-xxxv. The book is described as "the book of the law" (II. Kings xxii. 8, 11) or "the book of the covenant" (II. Kings xxiii. 2, 21; II. Chronicles xxxiv. 30), or "the book of the law of Yahweh" (II. Chron. xxxiv. 14). Modern scholarship seems to have demonstrated that this book was nothing more than the Deuteronomic Code. The next stage brings us to the public recognition, through the influence of Ezra and Nehemiah, of the first division of the present Hebrew Canon, The Law. The account of this event is given in Nehemiah viii.-x. The Pentateuch, as promulgated by Ezra and Nehemiah in 444 B.C., was practically the Law as we have it. But only the Law was made authoritative by Ezra. Nehemiah viii.-x. speaks of nothing else. The Samaritans, moreover, adopted as their sacred book only the Pentateuch. This may be taken to prove that at late as 333 B.C. (according to Josephus' dating) or at any rate as late as about 410 B.C. (according to the calculation of many modern scholars) the Law stood alone (see SAMARITAN PENTATEUCH). It is true that in later times the Samaritans possessed a Book of Joshua. But it resembles the canonical book very little. As Wildeboer says, "it is really the beginning of a chronicle relating the history down to the time of the Roman emperors. Besides, the close connection of Joshua with the Pentateuch, taken together with the fact that Joshua is peculiarly the tribal hero of Ephraim, makes this exception quite explicable." In the case of the second group of writings, the Prophets, we have no historical accounts of a kind of public recognition or canonisation. But here again the process was gradual. The ultimate recognition of an authoritative group of prophetical writings was the result of a national crisis. The prophets were naturally speakers rather than writers, but at a comparatively early date they found it convenient to commit their words to writing. Thus a prophetic literature began to arise in the 8th century B.C. This was read even before the Exile, and during and after the Exile, was much studied. There is evidence of this in the books of Deuteronomy, Isaiah, Ezekiel, and Jeremiah. It is not difficult to account for the veneration with which this literature came to be regarded. The situation is well described by Robertson Smith (*O.T.J.C.*). "When the national existence with which the ancient religion of Israel was so closely intertwined was hopelessly shattered, when the voice of the prophets was stilled, and the public services of the sanctuary no longer called the devout together, the whole continuance of the spiritual faith rested upon the remembrance that the prophets of the Lord had foreseen the catastrophe, and had shown how to reconcile it with the undiminished trust in Jehovah, the God of Israel. The written word acquired a fresh significance for the religious life, and the books of the prophets, with those records of the ancient history which were either already framed in the mould of prophetic thought, or were cast in that mould by editors of the time of the Exile, became the main support of the faithful, who felt as they had never felt before, that the words of Jehovah were pure words, silver sevenfold tried, a sure treasure in every time of need." The prophetic writings gradually took firm hold of the hearts of the godly in Israel. Consequently, "these books had no need to be brought from Babylon with the approval of a royal rescript, or laid before the nation by the authority of a Tirshatha. The only form of public recognition which was wanting, and which followed in due course, was the practice of reading from the Prophets in the public worship of the synagogue. It required no more formal process than the natural use made of this ancient literature, to bring it little by little into the shape of a fixed collection." The collection was not at once formally fixed, because for Ezra's purpose, that of establishing a theocracy, the Priestly Law was of primary importance. When, and for what reasons, was it formally fixed? The strictly historical books known as "the former prophets" (Joshua, Judges, Samuel, Kings) immediately continue the narrative part of the Pentateuch, and are connected organically with it. It is reasonable therefore to suppose that these formed an early appendix, as it were, to the Law. "It is quite possible," says Wildeboer, "that the memory of the interval between the canonization of the historical books and of the prophetic writings proper is perpetuated by the order of the two groups of books and by the appellation based upon it, *Nebiim Rishonim* and *Aharonim.*" Wildeboer thinks that there is an element of truth in II. Maccabees ii. 13 which says that Nehemiah, "founding a library, gathered together the books about the kings and prophets and the books of David, and letters of kings about sacred gifts." Nehemiah collected a number of books; and this collection, which was held in high esteem, became the basis of the second and third parts of the Canon. At the same time he had no intention of ascribing canonical authority to this collection. A preeminent place in it was taken by the books of Joshua, Judges, Samuel, and Kings. These formed the foundation of the second division of the Canon, and in later times were rightly called Nebiim Rishonim. To this early collection was added in course of time the Nebiim Acharonim. It has already been mentioned that the Book of Daniel is not included in the second division of the Canon. The true explanation of this seems to be that it did not gain canonical recognition until after the division had been closed. It has been thought, moreover, that the Book of Daniel itself in ix. 2, where it speaks of "the books" (*ha-sephārim*) assumes as well known a collection of prophetic writings. There are excellent reasons for concluding that the Book of Daniel was composed between the years 168 and 165 B.C. (see DANIEL, BOOK OF). Another clue may perhaps be found in the fact that Isaiah xxiv.-xxvi., which probably belongs to about 332 B.C., is included in the collection. This would suggest that the prophetico-historical and the other prophetic writings were canonized some time after 332 B.C. and before 165 B.C. Wildeboer thinks that the date will probably have been about 200 B.C. Jesus ben Sira is thought to lend support to this view (xliv.-l.). When he mentions "the Twelve," it is supposed that he had in mind the technical name for the Twelve Minor Prophets. The Greek Ecclesiasticus may be placed between the years 130 and 120 B.C. The Hebrew original falls between the years 190 and 170 B.C. In the Prologue to Ecclesiasticus the grandson of Jesus ben Sira speaks of his grandfather as having "giving himself to the reading of the Law and the Prophets and other books of our fathers." Speaking of his own time, he says that "many and great things have been delivered unto us by the Law and the Prophets, and by others that have followed their steps." Such language has been taken to indicate that for some time the Law and the Prophets had been recognized as clearly defined groups. After the time of Ezra, it was apparently the scribes of Jerusalem who determined what books should be regarded as sacred. In the case of the third division of the Canon, the Kethubim, historical statements as to the canonization are again wanting. But clearly here, as in the other groups, the collection was formed gradually. The beginning seems to have been made with the Book of Psalms. In the New Testatment we actually find a reference (Luke xxiv. 44) to "the Law and the Prophets and the Psalms." The third group may be supposed to have existed for a time as an undefined collection. But, as Wildeboer says, it was not every book that could gain admission to this indefinite group. "There were admitted to it only books written in Hebrew or Aramaic, which treated of the ancient history (Ruth, Chronicles), or gave information about the establishment of the new order of things (Ezra-Nehemiah), or which were supposed to have been written by some famous person of ancient times (Proverbs, Ecclesiastes, Canticles, Lamentations, Daniel, perhaps Job also); while Esther obtained admission (after much controversy, as was the case with Ecclesiastes) because it was in complete harmony with the national sentiment of people and scribes alike." The Old Testament Canon seems to have been closed in the course of the second century, and not before. As Cornill says: "it was not Israel, not the Judaism of Ezra or of the Maccabees, that definitely fixed and established the Old Testament Canon, but only Talmudical Judaism at its early stages for the purposes of self-preservation." Hölscher thinks that there was pressing need for the Pharisees and Rabbis to assert the antiquity and authority of the classical writings. There had arisen a new literature which gave voice to the thoughts and hopes of the time, a literature such as had not previously existed, the Apocalyptic Literature (*q.v.*). It was eagerly accepted by the devout souls among the people, for it spoke of the realization of hopes in days not far distant, but within the reach of living men. And though it was really new, it professed to be old. It was received with such enthusiasm that, though it never really disputed the authority of the Torah and the other scriptures, it did as a matter of fact tend to overshadow the ancient literature. The books were put forward under the names and authority of the patriarchs. And, compared with the definite and detailed predictions of the Apocalyptic writers, what were the vague and general utterances of the prophets? What was the age of the Torah which Moses received compared to the revelations which Noah, Enoch, and even Adam received in the earliest days? The Apocalyptic literature in fact assumed an air of superiority. Thus the position of the really ancient literature seemed to be threatened. Something had to be done to defend it. The final fixing of the Canon was a blow aimed at the apocalyptic literature. The Rabbis had come to look upon the apocalyptic wisdom and the apocalyptic writings with anxiety and even to show pronounced hostility towards them. And the opposition was most bitter and pronounced just at that time when the principle of the Canon was established. See F. Buhl; H. E. Ryle; W. Sanday, *I.*; G. Wildeboer; W. H. Green, *Introd. to the O.T.*, 1899; G. Hölscher, *Kanonisch und Apokryph*, 1905; C. Cornill, *Intr.*

CANONS OF EUSEBIUS. Eusebius, in constructing his Harmony of the Gospels, divided the text of each Gospel into sections or small chapters. The indices or tables of these sections he called "canons" (Gk. *kanones*). See HARMONIES OF THE GOSPELS.

CANOPY. Above the altar in the temples of Tibetan Buddhists or Lāmas "is suspended a large silken parasol, the oriental symbol of royalty, which slightly revolves in one or other direction by the ascending currents of the warm air from the lamps. And over all is stretched a canopy, called the 'sky' on which are depicted the thunder dragons of the sky" (L. A. Waddell).

CANTICLES. One of the books of the Bible. It is included in the third division of the Canon (*q.v.*), that is to say among the Kethubim or Hagiographa. It is also one of the five books belonging to the sub-division Megilloth or "Rolls." Other names of the book are the "Song of Solomon" and the "Song of Songs" (i.e., the choicest of all songs). The theme of the Song of Songs is love. Older scholars (following Herder) regarded the book as a collection of independent love-songs. It is now held by many (following Ewald) to be a kind of drama. Whereas the older scholars recognised only two characters—King Solomon and a Shulammite (or Shunammite) maiden—later scholars have discovered three principal characters—King Solomon, a Shulammite (or Shunammite) maiden, and a young shepherd to whom she is betrothed—and a kind of chorus consisting of the "daughters of Jerusalem." King Solomon tries to win the affections of the maiden, but she remains true to her shepherd-lover, and true love triumphs (chap. viii. 5-7). Another explanation of the poem connects it with marriage customs which still prevail among the peasants of Syria. The customs have been described by J. G. Wetzstein. The substance of his descriptions is given in the *Encycl. Bibl.* (*s.v.* "Canticles"). "During the seven days after a wedding, high festivity, with scarcely interrupted singing and dancing, prevails. The bridegroom and the bride play the part of king and queen (hence the week is called the 'king's week'), and receive the homage of their neighbours; the crown, however, is at present in Syria (as in Greece) confined to the bride (contrast Song iii. 11). The bridegroom has his train of companions (to borrow the ancient term, Judg. xiv. 11), and the grander the wedding the more of these there are. The bride too has her friends (cp. 'daughters of Jerusalem,' Song i. 5, etc.), the maidens of the place, who take an important part in the reception of the bridegroom (cp. Ps. xlv. 14. Mt. xxv. 1-13)." This would suggest that in Canticles the "king" (King Solomon) represents the young husband, while the Shulammite (or Shunammite) maiden is his young wife. In any case, the poem is of a secular nature, however good the moral may be, and it is rather surprising that it should have gained admittance into the Canon. The explanation is that, owing to the mention of Solomon, it was believed to be of Solomonic authorship, and that it was interpreted as a spiritual allegory (so in the Fourth Book of Esdras). But the canonical authority of the book was certainly for a time a matter of controversy among Jewish scholars (see the passage from the Mishnah quoted under ECCLESIASTES). It is clear "that in the second century A.D. there was still vigorous dispute about some books of the Kethubim, viz., Proverbs, Ecclesiastes, Canticles, and Esther" (G. Wildeboer). As regards the date of Canticles, certain peculiarities in the language (Persian and Greek loan-words, etc.) seem to require a time not earlier than 300 B.C. See C. H. Cornill, *Intr.;* G. Currie Martin, *Proverbs, Ecclesiastes, and Song of Solomon* in the "Century Bible"; G. Wildeboer.

CAPUCHINS. An off-shoot of the Franciscans (*q.v.*), or rather of a branch of the Franciscans, the Observantines (*q.v.*). The Observatines adhered to the strict rule of Francis of Assisi. Matteo di Bassi of Urbino was one of them, being a member of the Observantine fraternity at Monte Falco. He came to the conclusion, however, that the hood (*capuche*) used by St. Francis was different from that adopted afterwards by the Franciscan monks. In 1526, therefore, he went to Pope Clement VII., and obtained permission "to put on a pyramidal capuche, to wear a long beard, to live as a hermit, and to preach wherever he liked, on the condition that he should report once every year at the provincial chapter of the Observants [Observantines]" (Schaff-Herzog). But the Observantines regarded him as an apostate. He was joined by others, and the new body was befriended by the Conventuals. In 1528 the Capuchins or Fratres Minores Capuzini were confirmed by Pope Clement VII. as a separate congregation, but were placed under the authority of the Conventuals. It was agreed that they should be allowed to live the hermit life, to wear beards, and to use the pyramidal capuche. "They should have only a vicar-general, and he should be confirmed by the general of the Conventuals; they should be subject to visitations from the chapter of the Conventuals; when walking in a procession, they should walk under the cross of the Conventuals, and not under a cross of their own, etc." (Schaff-Herzog). In 1619 they obtained more independence, when they were allowed to walk in procession under a cross of their own, and to have their own general. Before this the Order had spread from Italy to France, Germany, and Spain. In France and Germany the Order was abolished in the eighteenth century; but in Austria, Switzerland, and the British Isles it still flourishes. In 1534 an Order of Capuchin nuns was founded in Italy. See Schaff-Herzog; the *Cath. Encycl.*

CAPUTIATI. The followers of one Durand, a carpenter, a sect which appeared in Auvergne in 1182. They were so called from the caps or hoods which they wore. They proclaimed universal liberty and equality; and Durand professed to have received revelations from the Virgin Mary in the light of which he hoped to establish peace in the Church. They were suppressed by Bishop Hugo of Auxerre, who marched against them with troops. See Schaff-Herzog; J. H. Blunt.

CARBONARI. The word means literally "charcoal-burners" or "colliers." It was adopted as the name of a secret society, which was founded in the Abruzzi in 1808, the name being due to the fact that there were many charcoal-burners in that part of Italy. In organising the society, and arranging its ceremonial, the founders seem to have taken suggestions from freemasonry and Christianity. It had lodges, mystic rites of initiation, and four grades of members. In 1815 the Carbonari were a political force of considerable power and significance. Its members afterwards included the Italian poet Silvio Pellico (1788-1854), Lord Byron (1788-1824), and Guiseppe (Joseph) Mazzini (1805-1872). Mazzini, however, from the first seems to have shown dissatisfaction with the organisation of the Carbonari. He was amused at their ceremonies of affiliation, and "reflected with surprise and distrust that the oath which had been administered to him was a mere formula of obedience, containing nothing as to the *aim* to be reached . . . it was war to the Government, nothing more." The association which he himself founded later seems to have been intended to be an improvement upon that of the Carbonari. This new association was called "Young Italy." It was followed by another called "Young Europe." Cp. PACT OF FRATERNITY. See C. W. Heckethorn, *Secret Societies of All Ages*, 1874; and *Chambers' Encyc.*

CARDINAL. The term is explained as follows in C. H. Bowden's *Simple Dictionary for Catholics*. "A name first given (in the fourth century) to the priests having charge of the Roman parish churches or 'titles,' and now to the immediate counsellors and assistants of the Sovereign Pontiff, whose election rests with them. The college of Cardinals consists of six bishops, fifty priests, and fourteen deacons; but the number is seldom complete."

CARDINAL VIRTUES. According to Plato, the chief or cardinal virtues are four: Wisdom, Fortitude, Temperance and Justice. St. Ambrose suggested the addition of the three Christian virtues: Faith, Hope, and Love.

CAR FESTIVALS. These festivals are now characteristic of Hinduism. They are processions in connection with the more important temples. That in connection with the Temple of Jagan-nāth is famous. On these occasions "the idols are placed on huge massive cars supported on four large solid wheels, not made, like our wheels, with spokes and felloes. A big beam serves as the axle, and supports the car proper, which is sometimes fifty feet in height." The thick blocks forming the base have figures of men and women carved on them. "Several stages of carved planking are raised upon this basement, gradually diminishing in width until the whole fabric has the form of a pyramid." The car is decorated with garlands, etc., and the idol richly apparelled and bedecked with jewels is placed in the middle of it under a canopy. The car is drawn by thick cables, more than a thousand persons sometimes being harnessed to it. Seated on the car, around the idol, are dancing-girls who fan the idol, and many other persons who guide the car and spur on those who are dragging it. "The procession advances slowly. From time to time a halt is made, during which a most frightful uproar of shouts and cries and whistlings is kept up." The courtesans perform dances; and "as long as the procession continues, the drums, trumpets, and all sorts of musical instruments give forth their discordant sounds." And "finally, a great number of devotees crawl slowly before the car on hands and knees. Those who have nothing else to do shriek and shout so that even the thunder of the great Indra striking the giants would not be heard by them." See J. A. Dubois and H. K. Beauchamp.

CARIYĀPITAKA. A Buddhist sacred book included in the collection appended to the second division of the Canon. See CANON, BUDDHIST.

CARMELITES. An order of monks founded about 1156 A.D. at the Well of Elijah on Mount Carmel by a crusader named Berthold. There seem to have been hermits there already. The community established by Berthold received in 1209 a rule in sixteen articles from Albert, Patriarch of Jerusalem. By this the monks were required to live in separate cells, to renounce the possession of property, to abstain from meat, and to observe a strict fast for a certain period. They were recommended also to work with their hands and to observe silence. The rule was confirmed by Pope Honorius III. in 1224. In 1238 the Muhammadan danger made it necessary for them to leave Mount Carmel and establish themselves in Europe. The change required them also to abandon the life of hermits. In 1247, therefore, their rule was changed with the approval of Innocent IV., and they were confirmed under the title of Friars of Our Lady of Mount Carmel. They now became a mendicant order, and adopted a brown habit with white cloak and scapular. In England they became known as the White Friars. The scapular "consists of two stripes of gray cloth, worn on the breast and on the back, and connecting with each other on the shoulders" (Schaff-Herzog). It was believed that the pattern of this piece of dress was revealed to St. Simon Stock, general of the order (1245), by Our Lady herself. In 1431 the rule of the order was further relaxed by Pope Eugenius IV. This led to divisions. There arose Observantines or Discalced Carmelites who followed the stricter rule, and Conventuals or Calced Carmelites who followed the milder rule. Independent congregations were founded for the observance of the strict rule, such as the Congregation of Mantua, which owed its origin to Thomas Connecte. In 1452 an order of Carmelite Nuns was founded in France, but in course of time the strict rule was relaxed. St. Teresa, desiring a return to the strict rule, founded the Discalced Carmelite Nuns in Spain. With the help of St. Peter of Alcantara she founded there also reformed convents for men. In England there were at one time fifty-two Carmelite houses. See Schaff-Herzog; the *Cath. Dict.*

CARNIVAL. A word composed of two Latin terms and denoting either a farewell to flesh-meat or a solace of the flesh. It is an institution in Roman Catholic countries. A carnival is held on the three days preceding Lent. It "is a special season for feasting, dancing, masquerading, and mirth of all sorts," and is observed in Rome as well as in other places. "In itself this custom is innocent, although the Church from Septuagesima onwards assumes the garb of penance, and prepares her children, by the saddened tone of her office, for the Lenten season" (Addis and Arnold). See *Cath. Dict.*

CARPOCRATIANS. The followers of Carpocrates of Alexandria. Carpocrates (born in the first half of the second century) was a Platonist and a kind of Gnostic. His son Epiphanes, who was only seventeen years old when he died, was worshipped as a god at Cephalonia, where a temple and museum stood in his honour. Carpocrates "believed in one God, from whom emanated a whole hierarchy of angels. The visible world is their work. The souls of men first moved around the Father-God; then they fell into the power of matter, from which they have to be released to go back to their original state. Jesus, the son of Joseph, naturally born like other men, and subject as they are to metempsychosis was able, by a remembrance of what he had known in his first existence, and by power sent from above, to obtain dominion over the rulers of this world, and to re-ascend to the Father. It is in the power of all men by following his example, and by the method he used, to despise the creators of this world and to escape from them. They can achieve this equally well, or even better, than he did. This scheme of deliverance is consistent with all conditions of life, and with every kind of act" (Duchesne). Jerome charges the Carpocratians with mutilating the Gospels; Irenaeus accuses them of dealing in magic. The Carpocratians paid reverence not only to images of Jesus Christ, but also to those of Pythagoras, Plato, Aristotle, and other sages. They believed that Jesus imparted secret teaching to his disciples. The Carpocratian heresy was introduced into Rome by Marcellina (see MARCELLINIANS). See J. H. Blunt; Louis Duchesne, *Hist.*

CARTHUSIANS. An order of monks founded in the eleventh century by St. Bruno. Bruno went from Cologne, his birthplace, to Rheims, and there as "scholasticus" made a reputation as a teacher. Before long, however, he decided to retire from the life of the world. He left Rheims, went to Hugh, Bishop of Grenoble, and unburdened his soul to him, telling him that, with certain companions, he wished to live a life of severe austerity and self-discipline. Bishop Hugh pointed out to him a site in La Chartreuse (whence the name Carthusian) near Grenoble, a spot accessible only by a difficult and gloomy path, and here in 1086 with his followers he erected an oratory and small separate cells around it, as in the Lauras (*q.v.*) of Palestine. A few years later Bruno was summoned to Rome by his old pupil, now the Pope, Urban II., never to return to La Chartreuse. Later he founded convents at Squillace and La Torre in Calabria, and he retired to La Torre to end his days there († 1101). The Carthusians wore very rough and scanty dress, which included next to the skin coarse hair-shirts. They fasted almost without interruption. Sick or well, they would never touch flesh. But they ate fish when it was given to them as alms. On Sundays and Thursdays they ate eggs and cheese; on Tuesdays and Saturdays boiled pulse or herbs; on Mondays, Wednesdays, and Fridays they took only bread and water. They ate only bran bread. Except on special occasions, they had only one meal a day. They devoted themselves to some manual work, chiefly the transcribing of books, and to constant prayer and worship, alone and in common. For some time they seem to have had no written rule. The rules were first written down by Guigo, fifth prior of La Chartreuse (1228). In 1259 a collection of all the decisions of the chapter-general since 1141 was made by Bernard de la Tour. In 1581 a fourth compilation appeared (*Nova Collectio Statuorum Ordinis Cartusiensis*). In 1688 this was approved of by Pope Innocent XI. The name Chartreuse, which in England became Charterhouse, was given to all the monasteries of the order. In France at the beginning of the eighteenth century there were seventy-five monasteries. These were all swept away during the Revolution. There were nearly a hundred monasteries elsewhere. In England there were nine at the time of the dissolution. The Carthusian nunneries seem to have been founded in the thirteenth or fourteenth century. London still has its "Charterhouse," though it now serves a new purpose. The site, near Smithfield, with the surrounding land was purchased in 1349 by Sir Walter de Manny († 1372) as a burial-place for those who died from the "Black Death." In 1371 on the same land he founded a house of Carthusian monks. At the dissolution the prior was hanged for refusing to renounce the Pope's supremacy, and the monastery passed into the hands of the Speaker of the House of Commons, Sir Thomas Audley (1488-1544). In course of time it was purchased by Thomas Sutton (1532-1611), who founded a hospital and school, the hospital (home) for eighty men, by preference military men, the school for forty boys. The school was in course of time removed to Godalming. The Hospital remains, and now accommodates eighty Poor Brothers or pensioners. See Schaff-Herzog; W. Benham; the *Cath. Dict.*; *Chambers's Encycl.*

CASWALLAWN. A war-god worshipped by the British Celts. Probably the British warrior Cassivellaunus owes his name to him.

CAT, THE. In ancient Egypt the cat was regarded as a sacred animal, "especially in the nome of Bubastis, where cat-mummies may be counted by tens of thousands" (S. Reinach, *Cults*). The goddess Bast is figured with the head of a cat. It was a crime to kill cats; and it was forbidden in early times to export them from Egypt. Among the Greeks and Romans they were practically unknown. Not until the fourth century, when Christianity triumphed in Egypt, did the domestic cat begin to travel. The Greek monks when they left Egypt to preach in Europe took the cat with them. "Thus," says Reinach, "the cat, a local totem in Egypt, tamed and domesticated in that country only, spread over Europe when Egyptian paganism had vanished and all the barriers reared by the old cult had been levelled with the ground." In Scandinavian mythology the chariot of Freyja, a goddess of fertility, was drawn by cats. The Māngs, a low caste of the Marātha Districts in India, regard the cat as a sacred animal. Their most solemn oath is sworn on a cat.

CATACOMBS. Recent archæological discoveries have thrown new light on the Roman catacombs, underground passages and chambers, which were used by the early Christians for concealment from their persecutors, for burial, and for worship. "The catacombs represent the most notable monuments of primitive Christianity which have come down to us. They are entirely of Christian construction, and did not originate, as was formerly supposed, out of ancient stone quarries, but are hewn out of the tufa rock. The vastness of these labyrinths awakens astonishment when we consider the poverty of the early Christians" (Camden M. Cobern). The catacombe were dug along several of the principal streets leading out from Rome. "They are narrow passages with graves on the right and left, the number of which has been estimated at nearly two millions. They were evidently built on Jewish models, the Jews having made such underground cemeteries near Rome in pre-Christian time. Several of these Jewish catacombs remain, containing pictures which represent the olive branch, the dove, the palm, the seven-branched candlestick, and a number of inscriptions, prominent among which may be seen the Hebrew word שלום "Peace." Up to A.D. 70 the early Christians were legally regarded as Jews by the Roman Government, and could doubtless be buried in Jewish catacombs or in graves of their own without fear. Burial places, even of criminals, were sacredly respected by the Roman Empire, so that for several generations Christian cemeteries were not disturbed." The earliest of the catacombs, such as those of Domitilla, Priscilla, Commodilla, and the crypt of Lucina, date back to the first century; but the majority of those dug up (more than 50) during something over 300 years belong to the fourth century. Even after churches and cemeteries were built above ground, the catacombs continued in use. By the eighth century, however, they had been deserted, and from the tenth to the sixteenth they were almost entirely forgotten. In the catacombs have been found many beautiful inscriptions and paintings. Through the munificence of the Holy See, "there has been dug up a treasure of early Christian epitaphs and paintings, valuable beyond all expectations, which has given much unlooked-for information concerning the faith of the early Christians, their concepts of life, hopes of eternity, family relations, etc." (Anton de Waal, *Cath. Encyclopædia*). See A. P. Stanley, *Chr. Institutions*, 1882; and the *Cath. Dict.*

CATAFALQUE. The name given to a structure, usually empty, like a bier, placed in the centre or other suitable part of a Roman Catholic church while Masses are said for the dead. The term also includes the tapers, ornaments, etc., with which the structure is surrounded. Another name for the structure with all the decorations is castrum doloris or "castle of grief." The French name is chapelle ardente.

CATASTERISM. Translation into the stars. "The heroes of mythology, or even those of human society, continued to live in the sky in the form of brilliant stars. There Perseus again met Andromeda, and the Centaur Chiron, who is none other than Sagittarius, was on terms of good fellowship with the Dioscuri." To some extent the good or bad qualities of such heroes were then ascribed to the constellations. "For instance, the serpent, which shines near the northern pole, was the author of medical cures, because it was the animal sacred to Aesculapius" (Franz Cumont, *O.R.*).

CATECHISM. Catechism means properly teaching by word of mouth or oral instruction, but the term has come to denote a summary of Christian doctrine, usually in the form of question and answer. As a result of deliberations at the Council of Trent, Pope Pius IV. was commissioned to arrange for the drawing up of a Catechism for the Roman Catholic Church. This appeared towards the close of 1566 under the title "Catechismus Romanus, ex Decreto Concilii Tridentini, Pii V. Pont. Max. jussu editus." Since that time other Catechisms of various sizes have been prepared by Bishops. The Catechism incorporated in the Prayer Book of the Church of England (as far as the end of the explanation of the Lord's Prayer) was composed in 1549; but the latter part on the Sacraments was added, after the Hampton Court Conference, in 1604.

CATECHUMENS. A name formerly given to those who were being prepared for Christian baptism. The instruction often lasted for two or three years, and the catechumens were divided into classes. See *Cath. Dict.*

CATEGORICAL IMPERATIVE. An expression used by the German philosopher Immanuel Kant (1724-1804) to describe the fundamental law of the practical reason and the highest universal principle of morality. The principle is this: "So act that the maxim of your Will (or the subjective principle of your willing) can always stand at the same time as the principle of a universal law." As compared with the Categorical Imperative, the Hypothetical Imperative denotes mere rules of convenience for particular cases and definite circumstances. "To speak the truth is a Categorical Imperative. To take due exercise every day is a hypothetical imperative whose necessity depends on the hypothesis that I wish to keep well" (Butler). See C. J. Deter, 1906; Arthur Butler.

CATEQUIL. Catequil was one of the deities worshipped by the ancient Peruvians. He was the god of thunder, and as such was greatly feared. To propitiate him children were sacrificed. He was armed with a club and sling. See Lewis Spence.

CATHEDRAL. The church which contains the *cathedra* or seat of the bishop of a diocese and in which he performs the chief episcopal functions of the year. In the Roman basilicas the bishop's seat was a marble chair behind the altar. "This marble chair is often called the Cardinal's chair, because when the church was served by a Cardinal it was his seat" (J. H. Parker, *Gloss.*). The best example of the survival of the Bishop's chair in England is said to be that behind the altar in Norwich Cathedral. A few examples are to be seen on the Continent.

CATHOLIC APOSTOLIC CHURCH, HOLY. The title assumed in 1832 by the followers of Edward Irving (1792-1834). See IRVINGITES.

CATHOLIC EPISTLES. A name given from early times to certain of the New Testament Epistles, because they seemed to have been addressed to the whole (catholic) Church. The group originally was considered to include the First Epistle of John and the First Epistle of Peter. Afterwards it was extended (from the third century), and was made to comprise also the Epistles of James and Jude, the Second Epistle of Peter, and the Second and Third Epistles of John. These epistles were quite small books. They could easily be circulated. As Dr. C. R. Gregory says, James, the longest of the Epistles, would fill only about ten pages. To copy and distribute it widely will have been a simple matter.

CATHOLIC TRUTH SOCIETY, THE. The beginnings of a movement in the direction of the work of the Catholic Truth Society were suggested by the Anglican movement which began with the "Tracts for the Times." About a dozen persons, Roman Catholic priests and others, recognising the importance of cheap but attractive publications in support or in the service of the Faith, decided to contribute a pound each for this purpose. Three booklets were published, which not only excited interest but even realized a small profit. Dr. Coffin, Bishop of Southwark, when his attention was directed to the work, became an active sympathiser and patron. Early in 1884 a meeting was held at Messrs. Burns and Oates, the publishers, to consider the further development of the work, but no practical decision was arrived at. On November 5, 1884, a meeting was held at Herbert House, at which Bishop Vaughan presided. The Bishop had been approached by James Britten, had consented to become President of a new society, and had suggested that this new society should take up the name and work of "The Catholic Truth Society." The society was therefore formally re-established, with George Whitlaw as Treasurer, and Father Cologan and James Britten as Honorary Secretaries. The earlier Catholic Truth Society had been established in 1868 by Dr. Vaughan, Rector of St. Joseph's Missionary College, Mill Hill, Lady Herbert, and Father Bamfield. It had not been a great success. Its precursors had been a "Catholic Society for the Distribution of Prayer-Books, Catechisms, etc." (1832); and a "Catholic Tract Society" (1834), which had been amalgamated in 1838 with the "Catholic Institute," an organization for the printing and distribution of literature. In connection with the re-established "Catholic Truth Society," in 1888 an Annual Conference, somewhat similar to the Anglican Church Congress, was held. "Since then the Conferences have been an annual event in the Catholic life of England, and have afforded a platform for the delivery, by successive Archbishops, of important pronouncements affecting the action of English Catholics" (James Britten). In February 1887 the work of the "Catholic Truth Society" had grown to such an extent that special premises were taken. The Society now had important branches in Ireland, Scotland, Australia, New York, and other places. Off-shoots are the "Catholic Needlework Guild" and the "Catholic Guardians' Association." The aims of the Society have been condensed into four sentences. 1. To disseminate among Catholics small and cheap devotional works. 2. To assist the uneducated poor to a better knowledge of their religion. 3. To spread among Protestants information about Catholic Truth. 4. To promote the circulation of good, cheap, and popular Catholic works. The pamphlets written to spread among Protestants information regarding Catholic Truth "are unfortunately largely controversial, for in stating Catholic truth it is too often necessary to expose Protestant falsehood." In addition to pamphlets, the Catholic Truth Society publishes a number of larger works. Cardinal Newman, who had looked forward to seeing the establishment of a Catholic Society on the lines of the Anglican "Society for the Promotion of Christian Knowledge," is said to have found the realization of his dream in the Catholic Truth Society. Abbot Gasquet emphasises the great importance and absolute necessity of the work of the Catholic Truth Society. "There is hardly a paper, magazine, or book—that is perhaps too wide—so let me say there are few publications by non-Catholic writers which do not display an ignorance about Catholic matters which is simply amazing. Statements are made in such works which are wholly or partly false. Sometimes this is obviously intentional, but let us hope generally that it is done in ignorance." See Abbot Gasquet and James Britten, *The Catholic Truth Society.*

CAUSAL NEXUS, THE. The Causal Nexus (Pratītya Samutpāda) is a formula in Buddhism held in high esteem by all Buddhists. It is as follows:

> Ignorance produces the syntheses;
> The syntheses produce cognition;
> Cognition produces name and form;
> Name and form produce the sixfold sphere (sense surfaces and understanding);
> The sixfold sphere produces contact;
> Contact produces feeling;
> Feeling produces craving;
> Craving produces grasping;
> Grasping produces renewed existence;
> Renewed existence produces birth;
> Birth produces old age and death, grief, lamentation, distress, melancholy and despair.

The nexus forms a chain with twelve links. And "though the ideas underlying the connection of these twelve links are much disputed, it is clear that some sort of natural law is maintained, resulting in a new existence, and that in the series of causes craving and grasping are those which immediately produce this new existence" (H. Hackmann). See C. A. F. Rhys Davids, *A Buddhist Manual of Psychological Ethics*, 1909; H. Hackmann.

CAVES, SACRED. In Aegean religion there seems to have been nothing resembling a special religious building. Houses and palaces had small chambers or shrines. Apart from these, the worship of the gods on a large scale seems to have been pursued in the open air, or in graves, or in caves. To such places pilgrimages were made. See H. R. Hall, *A.A.*

CELESTINIAN HERMITS. A branch of the Franciscans (*q.v.*). The institution, which was named after Pope Celestine V. who authorised it, grew out of a desire to practise with greater strictness the rule of St. Francis.

CELESTINIANS. An order of monks founded about 1254 by the hermit Peter of Morone. In 1294 Peter of Morone became the "hermit Pope" Celestine V. His hermits then called themselves Celestinians or Celestines. They devoted themselves entirely to a contemplative life. They rose at 2 a.m. to say matins; "abstained perpetually from meat unless in case of illness, and fasted every day from the Exaltation of the Cross to Easter, and twice a week for the rest of the year" (*Cath. Dict.*). The Celestinians spread through France, Italy, and Germany, but the order has now almost disappeared.

CELLITE BROTHERS AND SISTERS. A more correct designation of the fraternity commonly known as Lullards (*q.v.*).

CENTEOTL. Centeotl was one of the deities worshipped by the ancient Mexicans. The name was that of a goddess, and means Maize-goddess. Centeotl was represented as bearing in her arms a child (the young maize), or as a frog with many udders. One of her descriptions is "the nourisher of men." Just as a young male was sacrificed to Tezcatlipoca (*q.v.*), a maiden, who personated Centeotl, was sacrificed to the goddess with other victims. "Before her death she took part in several symbolic representations which were expressions of the various processes in the growth of the harvest. The day before her sacrifice she sowed maize in the streets, and on the arrival of midnight she was decapitated and flayed" (Lewis Spence). A priest then donned her skin. J. M. Robertson compares the practice of the Babylonian priests who identified themselves with the Fish-god by wearing artificial fish-skins. See Lewis Spence; J. M. Robertson, "The Religions of Ancient America," in *R.S.W.; P.C.*, 1911.

CERDONIANS. A sect named after the Syrian Cerdo, who appeared in Rome in 138 A.D. A body of ascetics, they declined to marry, to drink wine, or to eat meat. They held that the birth and sufferings of Jesus were mere appearance.

CERINTHIANS. The followers of Cerinthus, who seems to have flourished about the end of the first century A.D., and to have been a contemporary of John of Asia. The principal authority for his teaching is Irenaeus. According to a story told Irenaeus by Polycarp, John of Asia actually met Cerinthus in Ephesus. On entering the baths at Ephesus one day he saw Cerinthus there, and left immediately saying: "Let us flee; the house may fall in, for it shelters Cerinthus, the enemy of the truth" (*Hær.* iii. 3). The doctrine of Cerinthus is stated by Irenaeus in the following passage (*Hær.* i. 26): "A certain Cerinthus in Asia taught that the world was not made by the Supreme God, but by a certain power entirely separate and distinct from that authority which is above the universe, and ignorant of that God who is over all things. He submitted that Jesus was not born of a virgin (for this seemed to him impossible), but was the son of Joseph and Mary, born as all other men, yet excelling all mankind in righteousness, prudence, and wisdom. And that after His baptism there had descended on Him, from that authority which is above all things, Christ in the form of a dove; and that then He had announced the unknown Father and had worked miracles; but that at the end Christ had flown back again from Jesus, and that Jesus suffered and rose again, but that Christ remained impassible, since He was a spiritual being" (as quoted by A. S. Peake). Hippolytus adds that Cerinthus taught that the world was made by an angel, and that the Law was given to the Jews by another angel, who was the God of the Jews. These angels were far below the Supreme Being. The teaching of Cerinthus has often been regarded as a mixture of Judaism and Gnosticism. J. M. Fuller more correctly speaks of it (*Dict. of Christ. Biogr.*) as a link connecting Judaism and Gnosticism. A. S. Peake agrees with Th. Zahn in regarding the Judaism of Cerinthus as only a learned myth. He points out that the representation of Cerinthus as a Judaizing Gnostic is due to Epiphanius and Philaster. "It is quite likely that what has given rise to it is the way in which Irenaeus connects Cerinthus with Carpocrates and the Ebionites." Irenaeus speaks of the Ebionites as holding views similar to those of Cerinthus and Carpocrates, and as using only the Gospel according to Matthew. "The point of contact between the Ebionites and Cerinthus lay in their denial of the supernatural origin of the humanity of Jesus; and this was extended by Epiphanius and Philaster to an acceptance of a mutilated Gospel of Matthew and a Judaizing legalism" (A. S. Peake). Epiphanius speaks of the Merinthians, and connects Merinthus with Cerinthus. Merinthus may be another form of the name Cerinthus, or it may be a nickname ("noose"). See Louis Duchesne, *Hist.;* Arthur S. Peake in Hastings' *E.R.E.;* Wace and Piercy.

CESSAIR. An ancient tribal deity in Ireland. She was worshipped there in pre-Celtic times. Later legend represents her as the first inhabitant of the island.

CHAC. A god of rain, thunder, and agriculture in the religion of the Mayan Indians. He was worshipped in Yucatan. With him were connected a number of subsidiary deities called the Chac. These were associated with the snake, the symbol of rain.

CHAGIGĀ. The title of one of the Jewish tractates or treatises which reproduce the oral tradition or unwritten law as developed by the second century A.D. and are included in the Mishnah (*q.v.*), a collection and compilation completed by Rabbi Judah the Holy, or the Patriarch, about 200 A.D. The sixty-three tractates of the Mishnah are divided into six groups or orders (*sedarim*). Chagīgā is the twelfth tractate of the second group, which is called *Mō'ēd* ("Festival").

CHALCHIHUITLICUE. One of the deities worshipped by the ancient Mexicans. She was the goddess of Water, wife of Tlaloc, the god of Rain. See TLALOC.

CHALDEAN RITE, CHRISTIANS OF. In ecclesiastical usage, according to the *Cath. Dict.*, the name Chaldeans denotes the Catholics who belong to the Church formed by conversions from Nestorianism. But it seems that the Christians of Persia, who claimed that Nestorius followed them, called themselves the *Chaldean Church* (F. W. Bussell, p. 152). The Chaldean Catholics are now distinguished from the Nestorians properly so-called by the name Meshihaya, which means "followers of the Messiah." The term Chaldean is not used in a linguistic sense. "The Catholics of the Syrian and Chaldean rites agree in the use of the Syriac tongue in the liturgy; the former, however, using the Western or Jacobite, the latter the Eastern or Nestorian, dialect" (*Cath. Dict.*).

CHALLA. The name of one of the Jewish treatises or tractates which reproduce the oral tradition or unwritten law as developed by the second century A.D. and are included in the Mishnah (*q.v.*), a collection and compilation completed by Rabbi Judah the Holy, or the Patriarch, about 200 A.D. The sixty-three tractates of the Mishnah are divided into six groups or orders (*sedarim*). Challā is the ninth tractate of the first group, which is called *Zerā'īm* ("Seeds").

CHAMON. A Syrian deity, dedications to whom have been found at Ham near Heliopolis, and in Dacia. Probably he is to be identified with Hermes (so E. S. Bouchier).

CHĀMUNDI. A figure in Hindu mythology, the queen of the demons. She plays an important part in the devil-charming or devil-driving of the Vannāns, a washermen caste in the Tamil and Malayalām countries of India.

CH'AN TSUNG. The name of one of the principal schools of thought in Chinese Buddhism. Ch'an means Buddhistic meditation, and tsung denotes School. The school was founded by Bodhidharma, the Patriarch of Indian Buddhism, who settled in China in A.D. 526. He urged the true disciples to cultivate the inner being, the heart, the nature, of Buddha, and not to concern themselves about externalities such as writings and ritual. The disciples must receive oral instruction, and must practise the "inward look" or deep abstraction. "The philosophy based upon this was the 'emptying of consciousness'—that is to say, the complete subjectivity of our human conceptions and impressions." Bodhidharma became known popularly as the Wallgazer. "Every outward manifestation was indeed superfluous as far as Bodhidharma's contemplative aim was concerned—whether worship, image, or recitation; and it may be that in those early times his school had really discarded these things, although, naturally, such is no longer the case." In course of time the school split up into five subdivisions, which all attached importance to objectivism and externals, and opposed the absolute subjectivism of the Ch'an school. See H. Hackmann.

CHAPTER, CATHEDRAL. An ecclesiastical body composed in the Church of England of the prebendaries, canons, and dean (who acts as president). In former times it governed the diocese whenever the see was vacant. Since the thirteenth century this is the case "only with regard to an archiepiscopal see" (*Prot. Dict.*). While the Dean and Chapter advise the bishop, they enjoy rights and privileges of their own, and often act independently. In the Roman Catholic Church "everywhere harmony and co-operation reign between the bishops and the cathedral chapters" (*Cath. Dict.*). In England every Catholic diocese has its chapter, consisting usually of ten canons and a provost.

CHAPTER, CONVENTUAL. An expression used in connection with the monastic life. Monks have long been accustomed to meet together every morning to hear a chapter (*capitulum*) of their rule read, and for other purposes. The term Capitulum or Chapter came in course of time to be applied both to the assembly and to the place of meeting. See the *Cath. Dict.*

CHAPTER-HOUSE. A Chapter-house may be either the room or hall in which the dean and chapter (canons) meet to transact business, or the meeting-place of the religious of a monastery. Before the thirteenth century Chapter-houses were usually rectangular. Now they are of various shapes (circle, parallelogram, octagon, etc.).

CHARCOT SCHOOL. A school of hypnotism founded by Professor Charcot of the Paris Salpêtrière. It is also called the Paris School, or School of the Salpêtrière. It "holds that hypnotism is the result of an abnormal or diseased condition of the nerves; that a great number of the phenomena can be produced independently of suggestion in any form; that the true hypnotic condition can be produced only in persons whose nerves are diseased; and that the whole subject is explicable on the basis of cerebral anatomy or physiology" (Hudson). A person must be in the condition which Charcot calls "neuromuscular hyperexcitability." See T. J. Hudson, *Psychic Phenomena*, 1907; Joseph Lapponi, *Hypnotism and Spiritism*, 1907.

CHARMS. The use of charms, like that of amulets (*q.v.*), has been common in all religions, and their nature has been very varied. It has been found that "in the hills of Northern India and as far as Madras, an approved charm for getting rid of a disease of demoniacal origin is to plant a stake where four roads meet, and to bury grains underneath, which crows disinter and eat" (Westermarck). In Morocco, it is said, the cross serves as a charm against the evil eye. Dr. Westermarck thinks that the chief reason for this is that the cross "is regarded as a conductor of the baneful energy emanating from the eye, dispersing it in all the quarters of the wind and thus preventing it from injuring the person or object looked at." Among the Tibetan Buddhists or Lamas great virtue is ascribed to the use of charms as a protection against evil spirits. One of the commonest charms is the repetition by monks of portions of the sacred writings. One of the best known of the sacred formulae is "Om! mani padme, hûm!" or "Om! the jewel in the lotos, hûm!" It is reputed to contain all happiness, knowledge, and capacity. "It is adorned with all sorts of mystic additions and interpretations; the six syllables represent the six divisions of the world, and each has its special appointed colour, etc." Many written charms, *mantras* or dhâranîs are also in use. The words need not be intelligible to the common people. "Such sayings are attached to walls or are carried on the person. In case of illness the person swallows such a charm, either by itself or mixed with some other ingredients. They have them reflected in a sacred mirror, which is commonly to be found in a temple; then the mirror is diligently washed, and the patient drinks the water which has been used for the purpose, and which is supposed to have absorbed the spirit of the formula" (Hackmann). Or the sacred words are written on rags, which are then hung up as flags. These prayer-flags are to be seen everywhere. A still more mechanical device is the prayer-cylinder. "The sacred formula (or a number of them) is printed on a long strip of paper rolled round the cylinder, which is enclosed in a box, and by means of a stick, which is the axle on which it revolves, it is fastened to a handle or in a case. Every turn of the cylinder sets the word in motion, and makes its wholesome influence operative." Sometimes wind or water is used to set the cylinder in motion. See H. Hackmann; E. Westermarck.

CHARTERHOUSE, THE. See CARTHUSIANS.

CHARTISM, CHRISTIAN. In connection with the Chartist political movement, a serious effort was made to form so-called Chartist churches. The best known church was at Birmingham, and was conducted by Arthur O'Neill and John Collins. The former definitely proclaimed himself a Christian Chartist. The principles of his movement are explained in the report of a sermon by him (*Parliamentary Papers*, 1843, p. cxxxiii., quoted by Mark Hovell). "The necessity of their new Church was evident, for the true Church of Christ ought not to be split up into opposing sects: all men ought to be united in one Universal Church. Christianity should prevail in everyday life, commerce should be conducted on Christian principles, and not on those of Mammon, and every other institution ought to be based on the doctrines of Christianity. Hence the Chartist Church felt it their duty to go out and move amongst the masses of the people to guide and direct them by the principles of Christianity. They felt it incumbent upon them to go out into the world, to be the light of the world and the salt of the earth. The true Christian Church could not remain aloof but must enter into the struggles of the people and guide them. The characteristic of members of a real Church was on the first day of the week to worship at their altar, on the next to go out and mingle with the masses, on the third to stand at the bar of judgment, and on the fourth perhaps to be in a dungeon. This was the case in the primitive Church and so it ought to be now." There was a similar church at Bath, conducted by Henry Vincent; and there were Christian Chartist churches in Scotland, especially at Paisley and Partick.

CHARTOPHYLAX. In the Eastern Church the Chartophylax, literally "keeper of records," originally corresponded to the Bibliothecarius of the Latins. In course of time, however, he assumed other duties. In Constantinople, and eventually, in other parts of the East he came to represent the bishop and to act like the archdeacon in the Western Church. The Uniate Greeks of the Austrian Empire still have their Chartophylax or Carthophylax, who directs the business of the episcopal chancery. See the *Cath. Dict.*

CHASCA. One of the gods worshipped by the ancient Peruvians. Chasca corresponded to Venus (*q.v.*).

CHAULA CEREMONY. A Hindu ceremony. Chaula means "tonsure," and this is made for the first time three years after the birth of a male child. The child is seated between his father and mother on a little earthen platform. Married women first anoint him with oil and bathe him in warm water. They then powder his forehead and other parts of his body, and put ornaments on him, "a long necklace of coral beads round his neck and two bracelets to match on his wrists."

The priest then draws near and, after performing some other priestly ceremonies, "traces on the floor in front of the child a square patch with red earth, which they cover with rice that has the husk on." On one side is now placed the idol Vigneshwara, and sacrifice and offerings are made to it. "The child is made to sit near the square patch, and the barber, after offering worship to his razor, proceeds to shave the child's head, leaving one lock at the top, which is never cut. While the barber is performing his part of the ceremony, the women sing, musical instruments are played, and all the Brahmins present remain standing in perfect silence. As soon as the barber has finished, they throw him the money due to him. This he picks up, and before retiring he also carries off the rice that has been scattered over the square patch." The child is then bathed again "to purify him from the defiling touch of the barber." After the women have again attended to his toilette, and the priest has performed some other ceremonies, the occasion is celebrated by a feast and the distribution of presents. See J. A. Dubois and H. K. Beauchamp.

CHAURASI DEVI. A goddess worshipped by the Kewats, a caste of fishermen and boatmen found chiefly in the Chhattīsgarh Districts of Drūg, Raipur, and Bilāspur in India. The goddess is painted on their boats, and is supposed to dwell in them and to keep them from sinking.

CHERUBIM. A class of angels often referred to in the Old Testament. In Genesis iii. 24 it is said that God "placed at the east of the garden of Eden the Cherubim, and the flame of a sword which turned every way, to keep the way of the tree of life." According to primitive Hebrew myth, therefore, they were powerful superhuman creatures who guarded the entrance to the earthly abode of the god or gods. Prof. Cheyne points out that "when the range of the supreme god's power became wider, when from an earth-god he became also a heaven-god, the cherub too passed into a new phase; he became the divine chariot" (*Encycl. Bibl.*). In I. Kings vi. 23 *ff.* there are said to have been huge figures of Cherubim in Solomon's temple, and according to Exodus xxv. 18 ff. there were small golden Cherubim on the lid of the ark in the Tabernacle. The derivation of the word is doubtful. It has been connected with the Greek word *gryps* "griffin." Lenormant thought he had found the word *kirubu* on a Babylonian amulet used as a synonym for *šidu* which denotes the winged bull of Assyrian palaces and temples. His theory has not been confirmed. But, whatever the etymology of the word, the Cherubim seem to resemble the winged genii which are often represented in Babylonian Art by the side of the tree of life. "These figures are usually human in form with human heads, but sometimes combine the human form with an eagle's head, and occasionally the human head with an animal body. They are shown in the act of fecundating the date-palm by transferring the pollen of the male tree to the flower of the female; and hence it has been conjectured that they are personifications of the winds, by whose agency the fertilisation of the palm is effected in nature (Tylor, *PSBA*, xii. 383 *ff.*)." The quotation is from Skinner. See D. Schenkel,*Bibel-Lexikon*, 1869; *Encycl. Bibl.;* J. Skinner, *Genesis*, 1910.

CHICOME COATL. A Mexican deity, a maize-goddess, sister of the great rain-god Tlaloc.

CHIETINI. Another name for the Order of Theatines (*q.v.*).

CHILDREN, SONG OF THE THREE. An apocryphal addition to the Book of Daniel. See APOCRYPHA OF THE OLD TESTAMENT and BENEDICITE.

CHILDREN'S CRUSADE, THE. See CRUSADES.

CHILIASM. The belief in and doctrines concerning a Millennium, or in a glorious and happy existence upon earth which was to last a thousand years. The Jews believed that this happy rule was to be introduced by the expected Messiah (*q.v.*). In its early form the doctrine was of a spiritual nature. Chiliasm, however, came in time to mean the expectation of a glorious Jewish or Jewish-Christian kingdom of a worldly character. This expectation was common in the days of Jesus, and was shared even by his most intimate disciples. Believers in the millennium are called Chiliasts or Millennarians.

CHIN. A moon-goddess in the mythology of the Muysca Indians of Bogota. She is associated with water, and is said on one occasion to have flooded the whole earth.

CHINAX. A tribal deity, god of war, in the religion of the Mayan Indians.

CHIROMANCY. Literally "divination by the hands," another name for palmistry, which has flourished in ancient Greece and Italy, and in modern India. "Chiromancy traces in the markings of the palm a line of fortune and a line of life, finds proof of melancholy in the intersections on the saturnine mount, presages sorrow and death from black spots in the finger-nails, and at last, having exhausted the powers of this childish symbolism, it completes its system by details of which the absurdity is no longer relieved by even an ideal sense" (E. B. Tylor).

CHITRAGUPTA. A god worshipped, as their divine ancestor, by the Kāyasths, the caste of writers and village accountants in India. On special occasions the Kāyasths worship also pen and ink.

CHITRAKATHIS. The Chitrakathis (also known as Hardās) are quite a small caste of religious mendicants and picture showmen found in the Marātha Districts of India. "The men sometimes paint their own pictures, and in Bombay they have a caste rule that every Chitrakathi must have in his house a complete set of sacred pictures; this usually includes forty representations of Rāma's life, thirty-five of that of the sons of Arjun, forty of the Pāndavas, forty of Sita and Rāwan, and forty of Harishchandra. The men also have sets of puppets representing the above and other deities, and enact scenes with them like a Punch and Judy show, sometimes aided by ventriloquism" (R. V. Russell). Their special god is Hari Vithal.

CHOLA PĀCHO. A Hindu deity, the lady of the sacred grove, worshipped by the Oraons, an important Dravidian tribe in India, the members of which work as farmservants and labourers. The goddess is supposed to give the rain which causes good crops.

CHRIST, THE. The Greek equivalent (*Christos*, "the one anointed") of the Hebrew *Messiah*, a designation of Jesus. There is a tendency in modern thought to distinguish between the Jesus of history and the Christ of religious experience. The idea is expressed in *Science and Health* (p. 334). "The invisible Christ was imperceptible to the so-called personal senses, whereas Jesus appeared as a bodily existence. This dual personality of the unseen and the seen, the spiritual and material, the eternal Christ and the corporeal Jesus manifest in flesh, continued until the Master's ascension, when the human, material concept, or Jesus, disappeared, while the spiritual self, or Christ, continues to exist in the eternal order of divine Science, taking away the sins of the world, as the Christ has always done, even before the human Jesus was incarnate to mortal eyes."

CHRISTENING. Initiation into the Christian religion, a popular designation of baptism (*q.v.*).

CHRISTIAN QUAKERS. Another name for the

Keithians (*q.v.*), the followers of George Keith (1639?-1716).

CHRISTIANITY. Christianity claims to be based upon the teaching of Jesus of Nazareth (*b.* shortly before the year 1 of our era), who seems to have come to regard himself as the Messiah (Christ) eagerly expected by the Jews, while interpreting the Messiahship in a new way. To Jesus the Kingdom of God meant a divine rule under the guidance of a spiritual Messiah, not in a national and political realm, but in the hearts and minds of men. The Kingdom was in the world, but not of the world. In the world in a real sense: not of the world in being raised above the world. Jesus was not the first to speak of God as a Father. But here again he brought a new interpretation. The sense in which he uses Father is not that of the stern (if just) master and ruler of the household, but that of the loving head and friend of the family. God as the Father is just but not stern, remorseful but not revengeful, reproachful but not vindictive. Full of kindness and love, on the first sign of penitence, he is ever ready to forgive. All are the children of God. Consequently all are brothers and sisters, who, being equally loved, should love one another equally. "Jesus had realized the life of God in the soul of man and the life of man in the love of God. That was the real secret of his life, the well-spring of his purity, his compassion, his unwearied courage, his unquenchable idealism: he knew the Father. But if he had that greatest of all possessions, the real key to the secret of life, it was his highest social duty to share it and help others to gain what he had. He had to teach men to live as children in the presence of their Father, and no longer as slaves cringing before a despot. He had to show them that the ordinary life of selfishness and hate and anxiety and chafing ambition and covetousness is no life at all, and that they must enter into a new world of love and solidarity and inward contentment" (W. Rauschenbush, *Christianity and the Social Crisis*, 1907). The kernel of Jesus' message or Gospel (*evangelium*) was not so much the preaching of the coming of the kingdom of God as this doctrine of the fatherhood of God. The model prayer which he gave to his disciples, and which even to-day is the real confession of faith that unites all Christendom (Arno Neumann, *Jesus*, 1906) begins with the words "Our Father." In his determination to carry out the will of the Father, he rejected the ordinances of the orthodox leaders of the people, and elected to pay the penalty of dath upon the cross. He was the Redeemer, though "not in the sense that his death was a propitiatory sacrifice, without which the God of love would not have been able to forgive us our sins." It was "his special work to redeem by guiding us from the letter to the spirit, from the feeling of a slave to the love of a child, from self-seeking to brotherly love, from the dominion of the visible to that of the invisible, and his death showed that he was ready and determined to offer, in order to procure these benefits, not his labour only, but also his life" (Neumann). He was the Saviour and Deliverer. "Jesus delivered religion from all national claims, from all national fetters, from ceremonial, from the letter of the law, and from the domination of erudition" (W. Bousset). The religion of Jesus was simple. In order to adapt it to the Graeco-Roman world, the Apostle Paul to some extent elaborated and transformed it. A community of disciples became a Church. The divine aspect of Christ was emphasized. Jesus became a Redeemer sent from heaven to deliver mankind from sin and death, and his death a vicarious sacrifice of atonement. The sacred acts of Christianity—such as Baptism and the Lord's Supper—began to receive a sacramental interpretation. Whether, and to what extent Jesus himself was a mystic is an open question. But in any case Paul and John (or the Johannine writers) found mysticism in the Gospel and developed the teaching along these lines. According to Evelyn Underhill (*M.W.*), Paul is in fact "the supreme example of the Christian mystic: of a "change of mind" resulting in an enormous dower of vitality: of a career of impassioned activity, of "divine fecundity" second only to that of Jesus Himself. In him, the new life breaks out, shows itself in its dual aspect; the deep consciousness of Spiritual Reality which is characteristic of the contemplative nature, supporting a practical genius for concrete things." When the Gospel of John was written (*c.* 100 A.D.), the Gnostic heresy, which was beginning to germinate in the time of Paul, had made considerable progress. The writer therefore opposes to it the true Christian *gnosis*. To the Johannine writers we owe the exposition of God as Spirit (John iv. 24), Light (I. John i. 5), Love (I. John iv. 8, 16). In the Apostolic Age Churches began to be organised on very much the same lines as Jewish Synagogues. There was of course a Christian community at Rome in the days of Paul, to which he addressed his Epistle to the Romans. It has been conjectured that this was founded by the Apostle Peter. At any rate, Peter, to whom (according to Matthew xvi. 18-19) the keys of the kingdom of heaven were committed, is regarded by Roman Catholics as its chief foundation, and the Pope as his successor is held to be "the vicar of Christ, the visible head of the Church, the doctor and teacher of all the faithful" (*Cath. Dict.*). In the second century the powerful appeal made by various types of Gnosticism led to the development in Christianity of its episcopal form of government and of a tendency to rely upon written creeds. The latter tendency was accentuated by the menace of a new heresy, that of Arius, who began to teach in Alexandria about 318 A.D. At the Council of Nicaea in 325 A.D. the so-called Nicene Creed was formulated. At the First Council of Constantinople in 381 A.D. it was reaffirmed and slightly supplemented. In the next century a great controversy arose between two schools of Christian thought—the school of Antioch and the school of Alexandria—which had developed during the third century about the two natures in Christ. In 451 A.D. the Council of Chalcedon sought to settle the matter, but neither of the extremes was satisfied. "The Monophysites, who believed in one nature, separated from the church. These form the Egyptian (or Coptic), the Abyssinian, and the Armenian churches to the present time. The radical Dyophysites, who believed in two natures, also separated and formed what is known as the Nestorian church. For some centuries they flourished, spreading eastward to Turkestan and China, but have now dwindled to a small remnant in Persia" (G. A. Barton, *Rel.*). The division of the early Church into the Eastern Church and the Western Church began when the Roman Empire was divided into an Eastern and a Western empire, and was completed in the Middle Ages. A marked difference between the two was that the Eastern Church was given to speculation and definition, while the Western Church concerned itself more with organization and administration. Monasticism took root and flourished in the East and West alike, but it assumed a rather different rôle. "In the East monasticism preserved its ascetic, quietistic character, but in the more vigorous West it developed into a civilising power of the highest importance" (Bousset). Bousset describes Christianity in the Eastern Church—the Greek Catholic Church—as sinking on the whole to a lower stage of religious life, through its attachment to fixed dogmas and self-sufficing acts and ceremonies. "Religion became entirely custom, usage as it had been when it was at the national stage of religious life; and from the time when the Byzantine Empire was subdued by advancing Islam the Oriental Church was split up into a number of insignificant, degenerate Churches closely united to the smaller Christian nations which were now arising in the East." In the West, on the other hand, the Roman Catholic Church did not lose its spiritual generating power. It developed the old traditional ecclesiastical features, drew to itself the spirit of Roman law and Roman world-empire, and assumed a political character. Its development owed much to the genius of St. Augustine and later of St. Francis of Assisi. The Middle Ages, after a period of darkness, produced a series of intellectual leaders who are known as the Schoolmen, such as Anselm (1038-1109 A.D.), Abelard, and Thomas Aquineas (1227-74). These expounded the doctrines of the Church (*e.g.*, the Atonement) in such ways as to commend them to the reason. Then other divines, seeking more direct knowledge of God and the Bible, interested themselves in a presentation of the Scriptures in the vernacular, and in mysticism. In the 14th century appeared the translation of the Bible by Wycliffe (1324-84) and the writings of Meister Heinrich Eckhart (*d.* 1329), John Ruysbroek (1293-1381), and John Tauler (1300-1361). On the one hand, it was felt that with the Holy Scriptures to guide him the meanest peasant might know the truth; and, on the other hand, that "the soul finds God in its own depths" (Ruysbroek). In the fifteenth century mysticism in a developed form passed into common life. "It was a mysticism which abandoned speculation for practice. Its keynote was the positive 'imitation' of Christ, and the reality of inward religion" (H. B. Workman). The outcome of this new movement on its intellectual side is seen in the *Imitation of Christ* of Thomas à Kempis (1380-1471), which Dr. Workman describes as "the most influential mystic writing the world has ever known." If the Protestant Reformation was not the result of the work of such men as Wycliffe, Huss (*d.* as a martyr in 1415), and Eckhart, they assisted humanists like Erasmus to prepare the way for it. The Reformation itself, as A. C. M'Giffert points out, was not exclusively nor even chiefly a religious movement. "It involved a break with the historical ecclesiastical institution and the organisation of new churches independent of Rome, but the break itself was as much political as religious both in its causes and in its results. Dissatisfaction with the existing order of things was widespread in Western Europe, and was coming to ever more active expression. It was not confined to one class of society, nor limited to one set of conditions. The period was marked by discontent and unrest, moral, religious, social, economical, and political. The conviction was growing that traditional customs and institutions needed adjustment to the new needs of a new age, and on every hand criticisms of the old were rife and programmes of reform were multiplying. For centuries the Church had been the most imposing institution in Europe, and the most influential factor in its life. Rightly or wrongly it was widely held responsible for current evils in every line, and every project for the betterment of society concerned itself in one or another way with the ecclesiastical establishment." The Reformation is closely associated with the name of Martin Luther (1483-1546), in whose teaching the most modern element was the idea of Christian liberty. He laid great stress on the doctrine of justification by faith. Another of the fathers of Protestantism was the great Swiss reformer, Huldreich Zwingli (1484-1531), though the differences between him and Luther were considerable. In his teaching the controlling place in Christian thought was given not to a personal religious experience, but to the absolute and unconditioned will of God. It was he rather than Luther that guided the reformed wing of Protestantism. The task of formulating and systematizing the teachings of Luther and Zwingli was undertaken chiefly by Philip Melanchthon (1497-1560) in the Lutheran camp, and by John Calvin (1509-64) in the Reformed. There was much in common between Melanchthon and Zwingli. "Both had the same conception of the authority of the Bible, of the relation of natural and revealed theology, of the oneness of law and gospel, and of the nature of faith" (M'Giffert). The theology of Calvin, however, who regarded man as a totally depraved being, and taught that his sins were borne vicariously by Christ, was the most widely accepted. The sixteenth century gave birth to many radical sects, which were not all the fruit of the Protestant Reformation. These included the Anabaptists and the Socinians. In England the break with Rome came in the reign of Henry VIII. In the reign of Edward VI. by the first Act of Uniformity (1549) the Book of Common Prayer was made the only lawful service book in the English Church. The second Act of Uniformity (1552) substituted a revised edition. In the reign of Elizabeth certain reformers who were called Puritans came into prominence. Many of the Puritans aimed simply at purifying and reforming the English Church from within. But some of them refused to belong to a national church, and formed independent churches of their own (*e.g.*, the Independents or Congregationalists). Thus arose the Separatists or Nonconformists. In the seventeenth and eighteenth centuries, through the influence especially of Philip Jacob Spener (representative of Pietism) in Germany, and of George Fox (d. 1690, representing the Friends) and John Wesley (representative of Evangelicalism) in England, mystical piety again asserted itself. Wesley, who came under the influence of the Moravians, and with whom was associated George Whitefield, sought to promote an evangelical revival in the Church, and ended by founding (1739) a new denomination (Methodism). In America a movement closely related to the evangelicalism of Wesley appeared in the New England theology of Jonathan Edwards and his school. At the same time the philosophical speculations of men like Descartes, Spinoza, Hobbes and Locke, and the scientific discoveries of men like Bruno, Copernicus, Galileo, Kepler, Gassendi, Bacon and Newton promoted rationalism in all spheres of thought. In England theology sought refuge to some extent in the Neo-Platonism of the Cambridge school, as represented by such men as Benjamin Whichcote, Henry More, Ralph Cudworth and John Smith (Cambridge Platonists), who laid "emphasis upon reason as a faculty by which we may enjoy a direct vision of spiritual realities hidden from the senses and inaccessible by the ordinary processes of discursive reason" (M'Giffert); but to a greater extent in the rational supernaturalism of theologians like John Tillotson and Samuel Clarke. The Deists (such as Tindal, Chubb, and Morgan) held that religion is primarily a means to virtue, and even opposed the divine claims of Christianity; but some of them at least regarded themselves as defenders of the true faith. In France Deism found wide acceptance, and in the writings of Voltaire and Rousseau was developed on more radical lines. In Germany rationalism in religion was promoted by the philosophy of Leibnitz and Kant. In America by the early Unitarians. In the nineteenth century a profound impression was made upon Christian thought by the philosophy of Kant and

Hegel, by the development of historical and literary criticism of the Old and New Testaments, by the spread of various types of Socialism (the Chartist Movement, etc.), and by the publication of Darwin's Origin of Species (1859). Christianity struggled to readjust itself, either by abandoning non-essentials (the Broad Church Movement in the Church of England; Modernism in the Church of Rome; various types of New Theology in the Free Churches), or by going back to traditions of Authority (proclamation of Papal Infallibility, 1870; the Oxford or Tractarian Movement in the Church of England). Turning to more recent times, the Roman Church seems to have taken its stand definitely for the mediaeval form of Christianity. In Protestantism modern Christian thought "is still endeavouring to adjust itself to the new intellectual universe called into being by modern science. The adjustment is not fully accomplished and there is consequently, much variety" (G. A. Barton). But the tendency seems to be to lay increasing stress upon a Christian life rather than upon Christian dogmas; and to regard religion as a system of living emotions rather than of dead intellectual errors. Mysticism, if of a rather new kind, is again making a strong and successful appeal (see Jane E. Harrison, *Rationalism and Religious Reaction*, 1919).

CHOREPISCOPUS. Chorepiscopus (Greek *chorepiskopos*) means literally "country-bishop." The word is first found in a canon belonging to a period late in the third century, and the office seems to have arisen in Asia Minor. The chorepiscopus was appointed by the bishop of a large diocese to take charge of and administer the more remote districts and was empowered to confer minor orders. Fifteen chorepiscopi are found among those who subscribed the Nicene canons. This has suggested that they were true bishops, "as far as order went, on a level with others, though they were sometimes consecrated by one bishop only" (Benham). The *Catholic Dictionary* thinks the better opinion is that, "notwithstanding the name, they were neither true bishops nor an order of clergy interposed between bishops and priests, but simply priests, invested with a jurisdiction smaller than the episcopal, but larger than the sacerdotal." The Council of Laodicea describes them as "circuit officers." In the Western Church frequent reference is made to them after the year 500 A.D. It appears that in course of time they were often not properly consecrated. After the middle of the eleventh century they disappeared. See Benham; Smith and Cheetham; the *Cath. Dict.*

CHOREUTAE. A name given to the Euchites (*q.v.*). They were so called because they danced. They trampled in this way on demons which they believed they could see. According to the teaching of the Euchites, everyone is born with a demon, which has to be expelled.

CH'ORTENS. A term used in Tibetan Buddhism or Lamaism. It means literally "receptacle for offerings." Intended originally as relic-holders, the Ch'ortens correspond to the Caityas and Stupās or "Topes" of Indian Buddhism. They "are now mostly erected as cenotaphs in memory of Buddha or of canonized saints." The Lāmaist Ch'ortens "generally adhere to the Indian type, but differ most conspicuously in that the dome in the commonest form is inverted. Both have more or less elaborate plinths, and on the sides of the capital are often figured a pair of eyes, like the sacred eyes met with in ancient Egyptian, Greek, and Roman vases, etc., and believed to be connected with sun-worship. Above the *toran* [square capital] is a bluntly conical or pyramidal spire, *Cūdāmani*, of thirteen steplike segments, typical of the thirteen Bodhisat heavens of the Buddhists. This is surmounted by a bell-shaped symbol (usually copper-gilt) called the *kalsa*, the handle of which forms a tapering pinnacle sometimes modelled after a small Caitya, but often moulded in the form of one or two or all of the following objects: a lotus-flower, a crescent moon, a globular sun, a triple canopy, which are finally surmounted by a tongue-shaped spike, representing the *jyoti* or sacred light of Buddha. And sometimes round the base of the *kalsa* is a gilt canopy or umbrella *(catra)*." See L. A. Waddell.

CHREMATHEISM. A term coined by E. W. Hopkins to denote a kind of worship which pervades the Rig Veda (*q.v.*). It is "the worship of more or less personified things, differing from pantheism in this, that whereas pantheism assumes a like divinity in all things, this kind of theism assumes that everything (or anything) has a separate divinity, usually that which is useful to the worshipper, as the plough, the furrow, etc." Chrematheism is not to be confused with Fetichism (*q.v.*). See E. W. Hopkins.

CHRISM. What is known as Chrism is still in use in the Greek and Roman Church. It was used also in, or soon after, the time of Tertullian, in the ancient Christian Church; and in the English Church until about 1552. Originally persons were anointed with simple olive oil. Chrism denotes in the Roman Church, as it did in the English Church, a compound of oil and balsam. In the Greek Church it denotes a compound of oil and forty different spices. The Maronites (*q.v.*), before their union with the Roman Church, mingled with the oil, saffron, cinnamon, essence of roses, white incense, and other spices. It appears that in England the parish priests obtained the chrism from the bishop, who consecrated it every year on Maundy Thursday. Chrism was used, as it is still in the Roman Church, in baptism, confirmation, ordination; the consecration of altar-stones, chalices, churches; the blessing of baptismal water; and also at royal coronations. It used to be the custom in England to anoint a king first with oil, and then with chrism. The chrism is now dispensed with. See Benham; the *Cath. Dict.*

CHRISTADELPHIANS. The small sect known as the Christadelphians arose during the American civil war. The founder was John Thomas, who was at one time one of the Disciples of Christ (*q.v.*). The Christadelphians ("Brethren of Christ") adopted this name because they claimed that being *in* Christ they were his brethren, and that they were the true representatives of the faith and practice of Apostolic times. Their congregations they called "ecclesias" to distinguish them from other churches which they regarded as "churches of the apostasy." Christadelphians do not accept the Trinity. "They believe in one supreme God, who dwells in unapproachable light; in Jesus Christ, in whom was manifest the eternal spirit of God, and who died for the offences of sinners, and rose for the justification of believing men and women; in one baptism only,—immersion, the 'burial with Christ in water into death to sin,' which is essential to salvation; in immortality only in Christ; in eternal punishment of the wicked, but not in eternal torment; in hell, not as a place of torment, but as the grave; in the resurrection of the just and unjust; in the utter annihilation of the wicked, and in the non-resurrection of those who have never heard the gospel, lack in intelligence (as infants), or are sunk in ignorance or brutality; in a second coming of Christ to establish his kingdom on earth, which is to be fitted for the everlasting abode of the saints; in the proximity of this second coming; in Satan as a scriptural personification of sin; in the millennial reign of Christ on earth over the nations, during which sin and death will continue in a milder degree, and after which Christ will surrender his position of supremacy, and God will reveal himself, and become Father and Governor of a complete family; in salvation only for those who can understand the faith as taught by the Christadelphians, and become obedient to it" (Schaff-Herzog). They profess in their Services to proclaim the Truth as set forth by Moses and the Prophets, Christ and the Apostles, in contradiction to "the writings and teachings of the Clergy of the Church of Rome and her Harlot Daughters the Church of England and Protestant Dissenters." See Schaff-Herzog; *Chambers's Encycl.;* J. H. Blunt.

CHRISTIAN BROTHERS. The Christian Brothers or more correctly the Brothers of the Christian Schools was an association which was founded in 1684 by the Abbé J. B. de la Salle (1651-1719) and elevated to the rank of a religious congregation by Pope Benedict XIII. in 1725. The object was to promote the Christian education of the people. The Brothers "bound themselves by vow to devote their lives to teaching in the schools, and wore the religious habit" *(Cath. Dict.)*. They were required to "be and remain laymen, equally with the professors and assistant teachers who were employed under them. And this has continued to be the practice of the congregation ever since." It has been claimed that J. B. de la Salle was the originator of primary schools, and that he founded a Sunday School at St. Sulpice (1699) before such institutions were thought of in England. See the *Cath. Dict.*

CHRISTIAN BROTHERS, IRISH. A religious congregation founded in Ireland in 1802 by Edmund Ignatius Rice (1762-1844), and modelled on the foundation of J. B. de la Salle (see preceding article). The efforts of Rice met with great success, and in 1820 the order of Christian Brothers, who devoted themselves to the work of educating poor children, was confirmed by Pope Pius VII. "The Brothers, after the establishment of the Irish system of national education in 1831, placed their schools for a time in connection with the Board, and accepted the grant; but finding that the rules of the Board as to the absolute division of secular from religious teaching were gradually leading them into concessions alien from the spirit of their founder and the Church, they withdrew from all connection with the Government, and have since carried on their schools independently" (*Cath. Dict.*). In 1896 the schools are said to have numbered three hundred. See the *Cath. Dict.;* the *D.N.B.*

CHRISTIAN COMMONWEALTH, THE. One of the publications which have been closely identified with a new development in religion and theology (cp. ESSAYS AND REVIEWS, LUX MUNDI, etc.) was the weekly journal which bore the name "The Christian Commonwealth." When Mr. R. J. Campbell was bitterly attacked as the apostle of the "New Theology" (*q.v.*), this journal boldly supported and defended him. Its allegiance never wavered, and the journal was recognised as the organ of that progressive movement in religion and social ethics which was associated with the name of Mr. R. J. Campbell. The adoption of the "New Theology" was commonly supposed to mark a great change in policy, but those who knew "The Christian Commonwealth" best claim that the development was a natural one, and that in all essential particulars the principles and policy of the paper had remained unchanged. The journal was founded in 1881 by Dr. W. T. Moore, Dr. John Kirton, and Mr. Henry Varley. Dr. Moore, an ardent follower of the Scottish American Alexander Campbell (see CAMPBELLITES), had come to England from Cincinnati, U.S.A., where he was minister of a large church, to carry on an evangelistic campaign in this country. In 1879 he founded with Mr. Timothy Coop in the North of England a paper called "The Evangelist." On moving to London, he produced with his coadjutors a new newspaper unlike any other religious journal published, and to this was given the name "The Christian Commonwealth." As explained in the first number, the editors aimed "to be liberal without being lawless: to be modern in our sympathies, thoughts and expressions, without being guilty of that popular spiritual vandalism which, whilst bearing the Christian name, attempts to destroy the whole Divine literature, and aims to remove the ancient monuments and landmarks. Our politics are not necessarily either Liberal or Conservative." They proclaimed that "Christianity comprehends true politics, which is another name for national righteousness, and we shall ardently co-operate with all those who labour for this result, by whatever name they may be called." One more statement is worth quoting. "We intend fearlessly to resist all attempted divorce between Commerce and Christianity, between wise legislation and national morality, between Law and its power and function to repress lawlessness. Wholesome laws are moral agencies, and sound legislation must stand on the side of truth and righteousness." In course of time Dr. Moore became sole editor. The "Christian Commonwealth" was the originator, it is said, of what was known as the Christian Unity Movement. It persistently attacked the evils of sectarianism and denominationalism. For four or five years it enjoyed the exclusive rights for the weekly serial publications of the sermons of Dr. Joseph Parker of the City Temple. Ultimately Dr. Parker's paper, "The Christian Chronicle" was absorbed by "The Christian Commonwealth." From 1901 the paper was edited by Mr. Albert Dawson.

CHRISTIAN DOCTRINE, FATHERS AND CONFRATERNITY OF THE. A Society of priests and laymen formed about 1560, under the leadership of one Marco Cusani of Milan, with the object of teaching children the Catechism on Sundays and countryfolk on Church holidays. Pope Pius V. in 1571 ordered a more general adoption of this kind of Society; and the Fathers and Confraternity of the Christian Doctrine received a fine church from Pope Clement VIII. in 1596. The Confraternity was raised by Pope Paul V. to the rank of an archconfraternity. See the *Cath. Dict.*

CHRISTIAN EVIDENCE SOCIETY. The Christian Evidence Society was instituted A.D. 1870. Its objects are: to declare and defend Christianity as a Divine Revelation; to controvert the errors of atheists, pantheists, secularists, and other opponents of Christianity: to counteract the energetic propagandism of Infidelity, especially among the uneducated: to meet the difficulties and strengthen the faith of the doubting and perplexed; and to instruct the young in the evidences of Christianity. It seeks to attain these objects by means of sermons and lectures, popular controversial addresses and discussions in halls and in the open air, classes and examinations, interviews and correspondence, and the distribution of tracts.

CHRISTIAN ISRAELITES. The followers of John Wroe (1782-1863). Wroe came under the influence of George Turner (d. 1821), of Leeds, who was a leader of the followers of Joanna Southcott (see SOUTHCOTTIANS): and when Turner died, he claimed to succeed him. Wroe went to Australia, New Zealand, and America, and gained many adherents. He professed to be a prophet, and announced that the Second Advent was close at hand. When it took place, Israel would be restored, as God had promised. "To this end it was necessary that there should be a great in-gathering of

Israel, that is of the lost tribes, which was to take place under the leadership of the Christian Israelites, divinely inspired for the work" (J. H. Blunt). See the *D.N.B.;* and J. H. Blunt.

CHRISTIAN QUAKERS. A name assumed by the followers of George Keith (1639?-1716). See KEITHIANS.

CHRISTIANS OF ST. JOHN. Another name for the Mandæans (*q.v.*).

CHRISTIAN SABBATH-KEEPERS' UNION. The objects of this Union are five. 1. To form a special bond of union between "immersed" Christians, irrespective of denomination, who observe the Seventh day of the week. 2. To spread the knowledge of the Sabbath of the Lord. 3. To help its members to obtain employment, also to look after their general welfare. 4. To cultivate a more intimate sociability and genuine sympathy between Sabbath-keepers. 5. To inculcate a spirit of mutual encouragement, support, and friendship among its members.

CHRISTIAN SCIENCE. The principles known as "Christian Science" were formulated and developed by Mary Baker G. Eddy. She was led to the discovery of her system in 1866, but her first pamphlet on Christian Science did not appear in print until 1876, though it had been copyrighted in 1870. She says she "had learned that this Science must be demonstrated by healing, before a work on the subject could be profitably studied." The text-book of Christian Science is called "Science and Health," and the first edition was published in 1875. The founder of Christian Science started the first school of Christian Science Mind-healing in Massachusetts about the year 1867 with only one student. In 1881 she opened the Massachusetts Metaphysical College in Boston, under the seal of the Commonwealth. She also acted as Pastor of the first established Church of Christ, Scientist; as President of the first Christian Scientist Association; and as sole editor and publisher of "The Christian Science Journal." During seven years over four thousand persons studied under her in her College. On October 1889 she closed her College in order to devote all her energies for a time to the revision of the book "Science and Health." The new edition was published in 1891, and the College was re-opened in 1899. A great number of people state that by reading Mary Baker G. Eddy's book they have not only been convinced of the truth of Christian Science, but have also been reformed and healed of various diseases. It is stated (in the form of testimonies) that these diseases have included cancer, fibroid tumor, epilepsy, cataract, heart disease, gastric catarrh, sciatic rheumatism, Bright's disease, deafness, consumption, insanity, etc. Such cures have been effected, it is claimed, not by ordinary mental science, but by Divine Science. "If God, the All-in-All, be the creator of the spiritual universe, including man, then everything entitled to a classification as truth, or science, must be comprised in a knowledge or understanding of God, for there can be nothing beyond illimitable divinity." The author of "Science and Health" uses the terms Divine Science, Spiritual Science, Christ Science, Christian Science, or Science alone, interchangeably. "These synonymous terms stand for everything relating to God, the infinite, supreme, eternal Mind. It may be said, however, that the term Christian Science reveals God, not as the author of sin, sickness, and death, but as Divine Principle, Supreme Being, Mind, exempt from all evil. It teaches that matter is the falsity, not the fact, of existence; that nerves, brain, stomach, lungs, and so forth, have—as matter—no intelligence, life, nor sensation." Disease and evil are the off-spring of mortal mind. "Science [Christian Science] not only reveals the origin of all disease as mental, but it also declares that all disease is cured by divine Mind. There can be no healing except by this Mind, however much we trust a drug or any other means towards which human faith or endeavour is directed. It is mortal mind, not matter, which brings to the sick whatever good they may seem to receive from drugs. But the sick are never really healed except by means of the divine power. Only the action of Truth, Life, and Love can give harmony." There is one basis for all sickness. "Human mind produces what is termed organic disease as certainly as it produces hysteria, and it must relinquish all its errors, sicknesses, and sins. I have demonstrated this beyond all cavil. The evidence of divine Mind's healing power and absolute control is to me as certain as the evidence of my own existence." There is really no pain in matter "Be firm in your understanding that the divine Mind governs, and that in Science [Christian Science] man reflects God's government. Have no fear that matter can ache, swell, and be inflamed as the result of a law of any kind, when it is self-evident that matter can have no pain nor inflammation. Your body would suffer no more from tension or wounds than the trunk of a tree which you gash or the electric wire which you stretch, were it not for mortal mind." As regards surgery, Mrs. Eddy writes as follows: "Until the advancing age admits the efficacy and supremacy of Mind, it is better for Christian Scientists to leave surgery and the adjustment of broken bones and dislocations to the fingers of a surgeon, while the mental healer confines himself chiefly to mental reconstruction and to the prevention of inflammation. Christian Science is always the most skilful surgeon, but surgery is the branch of its healing which will be last acknowledged. However, it is but just to say that the author has already in her possession well-authenticated records of the cure, by herself and her students through mental surgery alone, of broken bones, dislocated joints and spinal vertebrae." The Christian Science form of Service is simple but impressive. There is no sermon or address. Passages from the Bible with corresponding sections in "Science and Health" are read, and are allowed to speak for themselves. See Mary Baker G. Eddy, *Science and Health, With Key to the Scriptures*, 1907.

CHRISTIAN SCIENTISTS. The name given to those who accept the teaching of Mary Baker Eddy (see article above). Mrs. Eddy was the daughter of Mark and Mary Baker, and was born at Bow, New Hampshire, on July the 16th, 1821. In 1843 she married George Washington Glover, who had been associated with her brother, Samuel Baker, in Boston as a contractor and builder, and at this time had a good business in Charleston, South Carolina. He was a Mason, a member of Saint Andrew's Lodge, No. 10, and of Union Chapter, No. 3, of Royal Arch Masons. His married life was short, for within a year he became ill and died. Mrs. Glover returned to her parents. A son was born to her, whom she named after his father, but she was too ill to nurse him. On her recovery she was employed in writing political articles for the New Hampshire "Patriot," and in teaching occasionally at the New Hampshire Conference Seminary. After the death of her mother she became an invalid. She lived with her sister Abigail, and often for long periods was confined to her bed. In 1853 she contracted a second marriage with Daniel Patterson, a dentist. She had been separated from her child, and believed that in thus marrying again, she would be able to get him back. After a time they went to live at North Groton, New Hampshire. We are told that "she was bedridden most of the time they lived here." The next move was to a cottage in Rumney village. Here, in spite of a most careful observance of the laws of hygiene, and of homeopathic treatment from her husband, Mrs. Patterson's "spinal weakness was not overcome and the nervous seizures continued to occur with increasing violence." She "was wasting to a shadow under the most careful nursing, and her life was being consumed in ineffectual efforts to appease the ravishment of pain." At the same time she read the Bible daily, and, as her biographer says, "she more than ever pondered the cures of the early church." In 1862 she wrote to Phineas P. Quimby, of Portland, Maine, who had a reputation as a healer. She said she wished to come to him for study and healing. Her sister described Quimby as a charlatan, and tried to dissuade her from going. But Mrs. Patterson was determined to know whether he had discovered a truth which she had long been seeking. "I certainly do not want mesmerism or spiritualism, but I somehow believe that I must see what this man has or has not. I am impelled with an unquenchable thirst for God that will not let me rest. Abigail, there is a science beyond all sciences we have ever studied. It is Christ's Science. There is a fundamental doctrine, a God's truth that will restore me to health, and if me, then countless thousands. Has this man Quimby discovered the great truth or is he a blunderer, perhaps a charlatan as you say? I must know." In October, 1862, she arrived at the International Hotel, Portland, where Dr. Quimby had his offices. Dr. Quimby succeeded in giving her relief. Her biographer writes thus: "Gradually he wrought the spell of hypnotism, and under that suggestion she let go the burden of pain just as she would have done had morphine been administered. The relief was no doubt tremendous. Her gratitude certainly was unbounded. She was set free from the excruciating pain of years." But her interpretation of Quimby's success was different from his own. She imputed to him "a knowledge of God's law," an "understanding of the truth which Christ brought into the world and which had been lost for ages." She believed that he had a philosophy which could be reduced to philosophic arguments, and she tried to help him to put this into shape in writing. Mrs. Patterson was certainly for a long time under the influence of Quimby. On the strength of this fact extravagant claims have been made for him. They are: "that Quimby cured Mary Baker of her invalidism, that he gave her the germ ideas of her philosophy, that he presented her with manuscripts which she afterwards claimed as her own, that he focussed her mind, that he was the impetus of all her subsequent momentum." In the light, however, of her earlier history, and of the general character of the book which she afterwards published, as compared with the personal history of Quimby and with what is known of his efforts of composition, it seems pretty clear that in reality "she heard and saw only what was in her own mind and experience, and continued to identify publicly and privately her faith with Quimby's in the face of all the evidence to the contrary and his own occasional expostulation." In 1864 Mrs. Patterson went to live in Lynn, Massachusetts. On February the 3rd, 1866, she met with an accident, which was referred to in the Lynn "Reporter" as follows: "Mrs. Mary Patterson, of Swampscott, fell upon the ice near the corner of Market and Oxford streets on Thursday evening and was severely injured. She was taken up in an insensible condition and carried into the residence of S. M. Bubier, Esq., near by, where she was kindly cared for during the night. Dr. Cushing, who was called, found her injuries to be internal and of a severe nature, inducing spasms and internal suffering. She was removed to her home in Swampscott yesterday afternoon, though in a very critical condition." The next morning she was still semi-conscious, but was removed to her suburban residence. "On the third day, which was Sunday, she sent those who were in her room away, and taking her Bible, opened it. Her eyes fell upon the account of the healing of the palsied man by Jesus." Thereupon, we are told, she had a marvellous spiritual experience, which healed her. "Mrs. Patterson arose from her bed, dressed and walked into the parlor where a clergyman and a few friends had gathered, thinking it might be for the last words on earth with the sufferer who, they believed, was dying. They arose in consternation at her appearance, almost believing they beheld an apparition. She quietly reassured them and explained the manner of her recovery, calling upon them to witness it." Soon after this her husband deserted her. In 1873 she was divorced from him. In 1877 she married Asa Gilbert Eddy, an agent for a sewing-machine business, who had come to her for healing. He died in 1882. In 1883 Mrs. Eddy published the first number of the "Journal of Christian Science," now called the "Christian Science Journal." By the year 1888 thirty Christian Science academies were in existence. In 1889 Mrs. Eddy withdrew from the world, and retired to Concord. In 1894 was completed at Boston the original Mother Church of Christ, Scientist. In 1908 Mrs. Eddy removed to Chestnut Hill in the suburbs of Boston. She died in 1910. Cp. *CHRISTIAN SCIENCE*. See Sibyl Wilbur, *The Life of Mary Baker Eddy*, 1907.

CHRISTIAN SOCIALISM. See SOCIALISM, CHRISTIAN.

CHRISTIAN SOCIAL UNION, THE. A Society composed of Members of the Church of England and founded at Oxford as a result of the teaching of Charles Kingsley (1819-1875), Frederick Denison Maurice (1805-1872), and others. The Guild of S. Matthew (*q.v.*) had already been established in 1876 with rather similar aims. The objects with which the Christian Social Union was started, put in simple form, were three. 1. To claim for the Christian law the ultimate authority to rule social practice. 2. To study in common how to apply the moral truths and principles of Christianity to the social and economic difficulties of the present time. 3. To present Christ in practical life as the Living Master and King, the enemy of wrong and selfishness, the power of righteousness and love. The Union has now a number of Settlement Houses called "Maurice Hostels." The objects set before residents are: to share in the work of charitable agencies in the district, to take part in local government, to work clubs at the Settlement Houses, to aid in parochial work, and to study social problems in the district. See C. W. Stubbs, *Charles Kingsley and the Christian Social Movement*, 1899.

CHRISTLICH-SOCIALE PARTEI. A political party in Germany founded in Berlin in 1878 by the Court Preacher, Adolf Stoecker (1835-1909). It seeks to improve the condition of the working classes by working along the lines of a monarchical Christian Socialism. But the good seed of Christian Socialism is mingled with the poison of antisemitism.

CHRISTMAS DAY. The precise date on which the founder of the Christian religion was born is doubtful. The festival known as Christmas was a pagan festival adopted by the Christians and adapted to Christian use. As Arno Newmann says, it is not the day that matters, but the idea associated with it; and the birth of Jesus remains the most important event in the whole of history. "The celebration of the birthday of Jesus is not met with at all until after the beginning of the third century. Down to that time it was the day of His death that was observed, as being the birthday of the higher life. Even then the celebration is first found among heretical sects, and its adoption by the Church does not come until a later date, when its power had grown. The day was originally fixed as the 6th (at first also by accommodation the 10th) of January, now the feast of the Epiphany. Day of birth and day of baptism were regarded as identical, because in the baptism the 'Son of God' seemed to be born. We find this usage prevailing down to the end of the fourth century, particularly in the Eastern Church. Soon, however, religious policy, having the heathen in view, dictated the separation of the Birth from the Baptism. The 25th of December is first found as a real feast-day in Rome in 354 A.D. at the earliest. . . Under Bishop Liberius she [Rome] took the date as a substitute for the heathen solstice festival, calculating it from the spring equinox of the old calendar (25th of March), regarded as the date of the Annunciation. In place of the birthday of the invincible Sun-god (Helios=Sol=Mithra), she put that of Jesus Christ, the sun in men's hearts (cp. Malachi iii. 20). An official command was then sent to all places to observe the new festival. So, gradually, by the year 450 A.D. the 25th of December came to be observed throughout the Church except in Armenia" (Arno Neumann). See J. M. Wheeler, *Footsteps of the Past,* 1895; Oscar Holtzmann, *The Life of Jesus*, 1904; Arno Neumann, *Jesus*, 1906; J. G. Frazer, *G.B.*, Pt. iv., 2nd ed. 1907.

CHRISTO SACRUM. A society or association founded by Onder de Wijngaart Canzius, burgomaster of Delft in Holland (1797-1801 A.D.). The idea was to unite in one body all Christians, whatever their denomination, who believed in the divine nature of Christ and in the redeeming power of his Passion. For a time the association met with some success, but in 1838 it had to be dissolved. See Schaff-Herzog.

CHRIST SCIENCE. Another designation of Christian Science (*q.v.*).

CHRIST SCIENTIST. Another designation of Christian Scientist (*q.v.*). A place of worship is called "Church of Christ Scientist."

CHRONICLES, BOOKS OF. In Hebrew the Books of the Chronicles are called *Dibhrê hay-yāmim*, "affairs of the days" or events of the times. In the Septuagint the title is *Paraleipomena*, "things omitted" (in the older historical books). The English title was suggested by the name (*Chronicon*) which Jerome gave to the books. It would seem that originally the books of Chronicles, Ezra and Nehemiah were one work. They all have the same peculiarities of language and thought. The narrative which closes abruptly in Chronicles is resumed and continued in the Book of Ezra (see CANON OF THE OLD TESTAMENT). The Chronicler rewrites the history contained in the other books of the Old Testament from Genesis to II. Kings from a new standpoint, and takes hardly any account of the history of the Northern Kingdom. In I. Chronicles i.-ix. he gives the history from Adam to the end of the reign of Saul in the form of genealogies and statistics. In I. Chronicles x. to II. Chronicles xxxvi. the history runs parallel to that which is given in the books of Samuel and Kings from I. Sam. xxxi. to II. Kings xxv. 21. From the point at which David ascends the throne the history becomes more elaborate. The treatment of the Northern Kingdom suggests that it "had long ceased to possess any living interest." There are other indications, in addition to the Aramaic colouring of the books, that the Chronicles were separated from the fall of the Northern Kingdom by a long interval. In II. Chron. xxxvi. 23 Cyrus is given the title King of Persia. But the titles given to the Persian kings at the time were as a matter of fact "the King," the "Great King," the "King of Kings," the "King of the Lands." This suggests that the Chronicler wrote much later than the period of the Persian Empire. Again, in I. Chron. xxix. 7, in reference to the time of David, a sum of money is reckoned in darics, whereas this Persian coin was not introduced until the time of Darius I. (521-486 B.C.). Lastly, in I. Chron. iii. 19-24, six generations seem to be assigned to the descendants of Zerubbabel (*c.* 520 B.C.) in the Hebrew text and eleven in the Septuagint. This would give us either 400 or 300 B.C. A number of scholars favour the latter date for the compilation of Chronicles. The Chronicler seems to have made use of the earlier historical books. On his own admission he also used a number of works not included in the Canon of the Old Testament. Such works were: the "Words of Nathan, the prophet" (I. Chron. xxix. 29), the "Prophecy of Ahijah, the Shilonite" (II. Chron. ix. 29), the "Visions of Iddo, the seer" (II. Chron. ix. 29), the "Words of Iddo, the seer" (II. Chron. xii. 15), the "Midrash of the prophet Iddo" (II. Chron. xiii. 22), the "Words of Shemaiah, the prophet" (II. Chron. xii. 15), the "Words of Jehu, the son of Hanani" (II. Chron. xx. 34), the "Rest of the acts of Uzziah, first and last" (written by Isaiah the prophet, the son of Amoz; II. Chron. xxvi. 22), the "Vision of Isaiah, the prophet, the son of Amoz" (II. Chron. xxxii. 32), the "Words of Hozai" (II. Chron. xxxiii. 19), the "Words of Samuel, the seer" (I. Chron. xxix. 29), the "Words of Gad, the seer" (I. Chron. xxix. 29), the "Book of the Kings of Judah and Israel" (II. Chron. xvi. 11 etc.), the "Acts (or affairs) of the Kings of Israel" (II. Chron. xxxiii. 18), the "Midrash of the Book of Kings" (II. Chron. xxiv. 27). All this material has been treated in such a way as to enforce and illustrate a special point of view. "The Chronicler's survey is rather in the nature of a church history of Israel from the point of view of post-Exilic Jewish orthodoxy, than a mere narrative of events" (G. H. Box). He is particularly interested in the worship and music of the Temple. When material found in the books of Samuel and Kings is not calculated to further his purpose, he rejects it. Again, "there are many cases in which the chronicler modifies the material in Samuel and Kings in some degree, sometimes condensing a narrative greatly, sometimes expanding; at other times changing the significance of an event, or magnifying the size of an army, or disregarding historical fact" (W. R. Harper). The matter which is added to supplement that of the other canonical books is for the most part of the nature of moralising romance; but occasionally it seems to be based upon historical facts. For instance, in II. Kings there is only a brief account of the very prosperous reign of Uzziah. II. Chronicles xxvi. 6-15 supplements this by giving information about this prosperity, and Curtis and Madsen contend that this information is in substance historical. See *Encycl. Bibl.;* W. R. Harper, *The Priestly Element in the Old Testament*, 1905; C. Cornill, *Intr.;* G. H. Box; O. C. Whitehouse; E. L. Curtis and A. A. Madsen, *Chronicles* in the *I.C.C.*, 1910.

CHRONICLES OF THE KINGS OF MEDIA AND PERSIA. A document referred to in the Old Testament (Esther x. 2) as one of the sources of the Book of Esther. The reference is as follows: "And all the acts of his power and of his might, and the full account of the greatness of Mordecai, whereunto the king advanced him, are they not written in the book of the Chronicles of the kings of Media and Persia?"

CHRYSANTHEMUM, THE SIXTEEN-PETAL. The sixteen-petal Chrysanthemum of Japan is said to be a Buddhist emblem. But it has been found also on a tomb in Egypt by Dr. N. G. Munro, of Yokohama. "It is also given in the newly-discovered book of Jao as a 'seal,' with its appropriate though meaningless mantra: it comes to Japan *viâ* China and appears at Kyoto as the 'seal' of the god of Peace. In the twelfth century it appears as the *mon* or crest of the Emperor Toba, who was a religious-minded person, much devoted to the worship of the 'god of Peace.' It is to-day the Imperial Crest, sacred to the uses of the Imperial House. No subject may have it on anything that belongs to him; and yet, for the modest outlay of a halfpenny, he can procure at the (modern) Heian-Jingū, or Temple of the God of Peace, at Kyoto, amulets and charms, protective against evil, which bear the Imperial Chrysanthemum Crest" (A. Lloyd). See Arthur Lloyd.

CHULLA-GANDI. A reform party among the Buddhist monks of Burma. "The adherents of this party try to enforce a stricter observance of the monastic rules, as, for instance, that no luxurious gowns should be worn, even going so far as to prohibit the use of umbrellas and sandals, and to require that they should live on the food obtained by begging, that no one should accept money or gifts to himself personally, and that he should take no part in dances or popular festivals." See H. Hackmann.

CHULLIN. The title of one of the Jewish treatises or tractates which reproduce the oral tradition or unwritten law as developed by the second century A.D. and are included in the Mishnah (*q.v.*), a collection and compilation completed by Rabbi Judah the Holy, or the Patriarch, about 200 A.D. The sixty-three tractates of the Mishnah are divided into six groups or orders (*sedarim*). Chullin is the third tractate of the fifth group, which is called *Ḳodāshīm* ("Holy Things").

CHURCH. The Greek and Latin name for "church" is *ecclesia*, which meant originally "a legislative assembly of citizens" (cp. Acts xix. 32, 39, 41). The old English word "church" is derived from the Greek *kuriakos* (*oikos*), the "Lord's House." "It is used to designate alike a material fabric used for worship, a particular body of Christians, the whole body of baptized professing Christians, and the inner circle of true believers, whether now living or departed in the faith of Christ" (*Prot. Dict.*). The earliest well-preserved Christian churches in Syria date from the fourth century. See BASILICA.

CHURCH AND MEDICAL UNION. A Church of England Union or Society founded in 1908. The foundation seems to have been suggested by the work of healing carried on at Emmanuel Church, Boston, U.S.A. (see EMMANUEL CHURCH MOVEMENT). The object of the Union was to promote co-operation between the medical profession and the Church in the healing of the sick. A Committee, before the formal constitution of the Society, had undertaken "to collect as much evidence as possible in regard to the various healing movements both within and without the orthodox Christian Churches, and to endeavour to discover what was good in them and what was not." The principles of the Union as formally constituted were embodied in certain paragraphs in the Lambeth Report of 1908. They are these: (1) "The Committee believes that Christ still fulfils in Christian experience His power to give life, and to give it more abundantly; and that the faith, which realises His Presence, is capable of creating a heightened vitality of spirit, which strengthens and sustains the health of the body. The Committee believes that sickness and disease are in one aspect a breach in the harmony of the Divine purpose, not only analogous to, but sometimes at least caused by, want of moral harmony with the Divine Will; and that this restoration of harmony in mind and will often brings with it the restoration of the harmony of the body." (2) "The Committee believes that medical science is the handmaid of God and His Church, and should be fully recognised as the ordinary means appointed by Almighty God for the care and healing of the human body. The Committee believes that discoveries in the region of medicine and surgery come to man through Him who is the Light and the Life, the Divine Word." The work of the Union seems to have met with some success. See *Psychic Healing: An Account of the Work of the Church and Medical Union*, 1910.

CHURCH ARMY, THE. The Church Army was founded in 1882 by W. Carlile, Rector of S. Mary-at-Hill, and now Prebendary also of S. Paul's Cathedral. It is a Church of England Institution modelled in some respects on the Salvation Army (*q.v.*). As the designation Army implies, it enlists officers and soldiers, and does not disdain the use of brass bands. It has a Training Home in which working men and women are trained as "Church of England Evangelists" for mission work amongst their own people. The women act as Mission Nurses; the men as Reformatory Missioners, Mission Van Captains, Colporteurs, etc. Before they are commissioned they must now pass an examination. On doing so, the men are admitted by the Bishop of London as Lay Evangelists in the Church. In 1888 Mr. Carlile started Labour Homes in London and elsewhere to give a "fresh start in life to the outcast and destitute." In connection with the Church Army there are also such philanthropic agencies as cheap lodging-houses, an employment bureau, a cheap food depot, an old clothes department, and a dispensary. A few years ago the Army was presented with the Hempstead Hall Estate, near Haverhill, in Essex, comprising about 740 acres of mixed arable, pasture, and wood land, in order that it might be converted into a training test colony. There were included some farmhouses, and an old mansion which was converted into a labour home. "It is intended that the estate shall afford employment, at once healthy and instructive, for about fifty men at a time. These will be selected from the Army's London and provincial labour homes, and they will be kept at work hedging, ditching, digging, tending livestock, ploughing, and all the manifold occupations attendant upon a large mixed farm; and, provided they go through the period of training and testing satisfactorily, they will from time to time be drafted out to Canada, well equipped with a practical knowledge of the work which will probably form their lot in future years" ("The Daily Telegraph"). The men work in return for board. If they earn anything beyond this, it is placed to their credit and paid to them or used for them when they leave.

CHURCH ASSOCIATION, THE. The Church Association was instituted in 1865 "to uphold the doctrines, principles, and order of the United Church of England and Ireland, and to counteract the efforts now being made to pervert her teaching on essential points of the Christian faith, or assimilate her services to those of the Church of Rome, and further to encourage concerted action for the advancement and progress of Spiritual Religion." The Association seeks to resist what it believes to be innovations in the order of the Service as prescribed by the joint authority of the Church and State—whether in vestments, ornaments, gestures, or practices similar to those of the Church of Rome—and especially to prevent the adoration of the elements in the Lord's Supper, which, it contends, is contrary to the order of the Communion Service and the terms both of the Liturgy and Articles. "It seeks to resist all attempts to restore the use of the Confessional, and every exercise of that Priestly authority which was put down at the Reformation, and also to oppose the introduction of doctrines contrary to the teaching of the

Church, as set forth in her Liturgy and Articles." It seeks to attain these objects by means of public lectures and meetings, the use of the Press, Colporteurs, Lay Evangelists, Protestant Vans, Protestant Lay Missions; and through Appeals to Parliament to pass such measures as may be needed to restrain clergymen "from violating the order of their Church, and obtruding on their parishioners practices and doctrines repugnant to the Formularies and Articles of our Reformed Church."

CHURCHMEN'S UNION, THE. A Society in the Church of England. It was inaugurated at the Church House, Westminster, in 1898 for the advancement of liberal religious thought. The objects of the Union are stated to be five. (1) To maintain the right and duty of the Church to restate her belief from time to time as required by the progressive revelation of the Holy Spirit. (2) To uphold the historic comprehensiveness and corporate life of the Church of England, and her Christian spirit of tolerance in all things non-essential. (3) To give all support in their power to those who are honestly and loyally endeavouring to vindicate the truths of Christianity by the light of scholarship and research: and while paying due regard to continuity, to work for such changes in the formularies and practices in the Church of England as from time to time are made necessary by the needs and knowledge of the day. (4) To assert the rights and duties of the laity as constituent members of the Body of Christ. (5) To encourage friendly relations between the Church of England and all other Christian bodies. "Is the continuance of the Churchmen's Union necessary or useful? This question has been raised during the past year [1908-09]; but the Council feel that only one answer is possible. We gratefully acknowledge that real progress has been made in toleration for liberal religious views, and that open persecution of clergymen who hold them is now rare. But we cannot forget that the forces of reaction are strong, persevering and determined. They have captured to a large extent the machinery of the Church—Convocations, Diocesan Conferences, the so-called 'Representative' Church Council, and Training Colleges for clergy; and though the Episcopal Bench is now more liberal-minded than it was, this advance has not yet been followed by the majority of the clergy. There is, and there will be for many years to come, great need for such a body as ours to vindicate the value of liberal principles within our Church" (*Annual Report,* 1908-1909).

CHURCH OF THE DISCIPLES. A Church founded in 1826 by Alexander Campbell (1788-1866). His followers were also called Campbellites (*q.v.*).

CHURCH REFORM LEAGUE. The Church Reform League concerns itself solely with Church Reform. It is a non-party and non-political association, and does not deal with questions of doctrine. It advocates five principles of Reform. 1. That, saving the supremacy of the Crown according to law, and, in respect to legislation, subject to the veto of Parliament, the Church should have freedom for self-government, by means of reformed Houses of Convocation (which shall be thoroughly representative, with power for the Canterbury and York Convocations to sit together if desired), together with a representative body or bodies of the Laity. 2. That the Laity should have the principal share in the administration of Finance, and, within the fixed limits of Church order, a real control in the appointing of their Pastors, and in all matters of ecclesiastical organization and administration, a concurrent voice with the Clergy. That the Communicants of every Parish should have a recognized power to prevent the arbitrary alteration of lawful customs in ritual. 3. That all Ministers and Church Officers should be removable by disciplinary process, benefices being made tenable only during the adequate performance of the duties, and that a "Godly discipline" for the Laity should be established. 4. That all transfers by sale of next presentations and advowsons should be made illegal, but that where patronage is transferred to a Diocesan Trust reasonable compensation may be given. 5. That in each Diocese a Diocesan Trust be formed to receive and administer Diocesan and Parochial Endowments on lines similar to those on which the Ecclesiastical Commissioners administer their Trust. As an example of the spirit which animates the Church Reform League, its suggestions with regard to the election, number, and income of Bishops are significant and worth quoting. "Compared with freedom for legislation all else seems to us at present secondary. None the less, it is obvious that a better method for the nomination of our Bishops should be found than the choice of names by a Premier of any views or creed for approval by the King. It is notorious that within the lifetime of many of us such powers have been used for party purposes. Throughout the last century it was commonly so, and especially in the case of the Church in Wales. The appointments made by the Crown ruined the Church in Wales and paralysed the Church in England." Again, "surely it is time to do away with the income limit of £3,000 per annum that so seriously thwarts the founding of new sees. The work of the Church calls for a large episcopate; it in no way calls for a rich episcopate. On the contrary so large an increase of income is a drawback. The old sees have, indeed, heavy obligations attached to them that it may not be easy or wise to sever from them. No such obligations need attach to new sees. Hence to cripple our progress with such a condition, in itself a very doubtful blessing, is a spiritual folly. It only points a contrast that alienates the artisan, while it weakens a standard of living that is best and most effective when entirely simple and apostolic." See the Leaflets of the Church Reform League.

CHURINGA. Ritual instruments used by the tribes of Central Australia, especially the Arunta, the Loritja, the Kaitish, the Unmatjera, and the Ilpirra. "They are pieces of wood or bits of polished stone, of a great variety of forms, but generally oval or oblong. Each totemic group has a more or less important collection of these. Upon each of these is engraved a design representing the totem of this same group" (Émile Durkheim). Some of them have a hole at one end, through which a thread is passed. These serve as real bull-roarers. "By means of the thread by which they are suspended, they are whirled rapidly in the air in such a way as to produce a sort of humming identical with that made by the toys of this name still used by our children; this deafening noise has a ritual significance and accompanies all ceremonies of any importance." But not all churinga are bull-roarers. In any case, they are eminently sacred. They may not be touched or even seen at close quarters by women or by young men who have not been initiated into the religious life. They are kept in a special place, a kind of cave, called by the Arunta *ertnatulunga*, which they render so sacred that it is regarded as a sanctuary of the totemic group and as a place of asylum. Their properties are such that they can heal wounds, make the beard grow, and give men force, courage, and perseverance. They may be lent to another group, but when this happens, the original possessors weep and lament for two weeks. "They are taken care of, they are greased, rubbed, polished, and when they are moved from one locality to another, it is in the midst of ceremonies which bear witness to the fact that this displacement is regarded as an act of the highest importance." According to Spencer and Gillen, the churinga owe their power and sanctity to the fact that they serve as the residence of an ancestor's soul; according to Strehlow, to the fact that they are regarded as the image of the ancestor's body or as the body itself. Durkheim holds that their religious nature is due to the totemic stamp which they bear. It is the emblem that is sacred. See Émile Durkheim.

CIAGAT. A god worshipped by the Nicarao (of Nicaragua). He is probably identical with the Mexican Quetzalcoatl.

CICOLLUIS. Cicolluis was one of the names given by the ancient Celts to a god who corresponded to the Roman Mars. He was paired with the goddess Litavis (*q.v.*).

CIOACOATL. Cioacoatl or Chalchihuitlicue was the name of a goddess worshipped by the ancient Mexicans, the goddess of Water. She was the wife of Tlaloc (*q.v.*).

CIPALTONAL. The chief goddess of the Nicarao (of Nicaragua). She was equivalent to the Mexican Cipactonal. With the help of the god Tamagostad, she created the earth and mankind.

CIRCELLIONS. Another name for the CIRCUMCELLIONS (*q.v.*).

CIRCLE, THE. In the 13th century the circle was used in Christian art as a symbol of God. Three entwined circles, denoting the indissoluble union of the three persons, "were used as an abstract or geometric symbol of the Trinity" (Sidney Heath). The circle also symbolises eternity.

CIRCUITORES. Another name for the Circumcellions (*q.v.*).

CIRCUMAMBULATION. A mode of worship practised by the Hindus and other primitive folk. The worshipper must always keep his right side towards the object worshipped, following the course of the sun. Monier-Williams saw poor women who were probably not able to have a sacred Tulasi plant in their own homes. He noticed in one village, especially, "a woman who was in the act of walking 108 times round the sacred plant with her right shoulder always turned towards it. Her simple object, no doubt, was to propitiate the goddess with a view to securing long life for her husband and gaining a large family of sons for herself." Even sacred rivers are circumambulated. In the case of the Ganges, this takes six years (see Monier-Williams). Amongst the Lāmas of Tibet, it is the custom to proceed with the right hand to the wall in approaching the door of a temple. The Romans observed a similar practice in circumambulating temples. The Druids, on the other hand, kept the sacred structure to the left of them. Mr. Waddell points out that in the Scotch highlands "to make the *deazil*" is to "walk thrice in the direction of the sun's course around those" whom one wishes well. See L. A. Waddell.

CIRCUMCELLIONS. The Circumcellions were religious fanatics who took advantage of the strife between the Donatists (see DONATISM) and their opponents. They are commonly regarded as a section of the Donatists; but they were not desirable allies, and the Donatists themselves suffered by reason of their excesses. "It was a period of much social distress and disturbance in Africa. The Donatists, as ecclesiastical rebels, provided a rallying-point for all the discontented and seditious elements in the population. There was a breakdown of social order. Bands of dispossessed peasants and escaped slaves infested the country, committing abominable outrages and exposing themselves to death with fanatical enthusiasm. They sought to make common cause with the Donatists, and called themselves *milites Christi agonistici*, but are better known as *circumcelliones*, 'hut-haunters.' The Donatists were discredited by these excesses, and suffered in their suppression" (Hastings' *Encyclopaedia*). In A.D. 411, when Marcellinus, proconsul of Africa under the Emperor Honorius, pronounced sentence against the Donatists, he commanded that "if they have Circumcellions about them, and do not restrain and repress the excesses of these men, they shall be deprived of their places in the state." They were not totally suppressed until after A.D. 429, for they rendered assistance to Genseric, king of the Vandals, in his expeditions through Africa. See Schaff-Herzog, *Religious Encyclopaedia;* J. H. Blunt; Wace and Piercy; Hastings' *E.R.E.*, vol. iv., 1911.

CIRCUMCISION. Circumcision, the cutting away of the foreskin, was a rite common to a number of Semitic peoples in ancient times. It was practised by the ancient Arabs, and by the Edomites, Ammonites, and Moabites, as well as by the Hebrews. It was practised also by non-Semitic races. According to Herodotus and Philo, all Egyptians were circumcised; and according to other ancient writers the rite originated in Egypt and thence spread to the other peoples of Africa and to the Semites of Asia. In any case, as L. H. Gray says (Hastings' *E.R.E.*), the operation was practised almost everywhere except in Europe and non-Semitic Asia. "The Indo-Germanic peoples, the Mongols, and the Finno-Ugric races (except where they have been influenced by Muhammadanism) alone are entirely unacquainted with it. It can scarcely have been practised in pre-Aryan India (obviously we have no data regarding pre-Indo-Germanic Europe), for there is no allusion to it in Sanskrit literature, and no trace of it in modern India, even among peoples untouched by Hindu civilization." The real reasons for the operation are difficult to determine. Benzinger (*Encycl. Bibl.*) thinks that, in general, circumcision is to be regarded as a ritual tribal mark. It marked the initiation of the full-grown man into full membership of his clan. This involved something more. "Like all other initiation ceremonies of the kind in the Semitic religions, circumcism had attributed to it also the effect of accomplishing a sacramental communion, bringing about a union with the godhead." It should be noted, however, that among many peoples (including the ancient Arabs) the operation has been performed upon women as well as upon men. G. A. Barton is perhaps right in saying (Hastings) that in the beginning Semitic circumcision would seem to have been a sacrifice to the goddess of fertility. "Whether it was intended to ensure the blessing of the goddess, and so to secure more abundant offspring, or whether it was considered as the sacrifice of a part instead of the whole of the person, we may not clearly determine, though the writer regards the former alternative as the more probable." The idea of a sacrifice seems to be present in a custom found among the Borans. "The Borans, on the southern borders of Abyssinia, propitiate a sky-spirit called Wak by sacrificing their children and cattle to him. Among them when a man of any standing marries, he becomes a Raba, as it is called, and for a certain period after marriage, probably four to eight years, he must leave any children that are born to him to die in the bush. No Boran cares to contemplate the fearful calamities with which Wak would visit him if he failed to discharge this duty. After he ceases to be a Raba, a man is circumcised and becomes a Gudda. The sky-spirit has no claim on the children born after their father's circumcision, but they are sent away at a very early age to be reared by the Wata, a low caste of hunters. They remain with these people till they are grown up, and then return to their families" (J. G. Frazer). Frazer thinks that here the circumcision of the father seems to be regarded as "an atoning sacrifice which redeems the rest of his children from the spirit to whom they would otherwise belong." He thinks that the story told by the Israelites (Exodus iv. 24-26) to account for the origin of circumcision "seems also to suggest that the custom was supposed to save the life of the child by giving the deity a substitute for it." In the early days of Christianity the Judaeo-Christians wished to retain the rite of circumcision, but the Apostle Paul was instrumental in abolishing it. The Christian rite of baptism came to be substituted for it. The Jews circumcise children on the eighth day after birth (Gen. xvii. 12; Luke i. 59, ii. 21), and, as in Christian baptism, the name is given at the same time. But originally in both cases the rites may be supposed to have been celebrated at a later date, when the children attained puberty. See Schaff-Herzog; *Encycl. Bibl.; Chambers' Encycl.;* Hastings' *E.R.E.;* J. G. Frazer, *G.B.*, Pt. iii., 1912.

CIRCUMCISION, FEAST OF. In Judaism a father is required by the Mosaic Code to have his son circumcised on the eighth day after birth as a "sign" of the covenant with Abraham. The father in his benediction terms this act "admission into the covenant of Abraham"; but K. Kohler emphasises the fact that Circumcision is not a sacrament among the Jews, and does not determine membership in the Jewish community. Many rabbis have indeed held that Circumcision gave the Jew a place in "Abraham's bosom" which was denied to the uncircumcised. They thus made Circumcision equivalent to Christian baptism. But according to a number of passages in the Talmud, especially in the Tosefta, Circumcision was not believed to have power to save a sinner from Gehenna. We learn from Luke ii. 21 that Jesus was circumcised, and in the Church of England and of Rome the event is commemorated on the 1st of January. The first mention of the feast by its present name is in Canon 17 of a council held at Tours in 567 (*Cath. Dict.*). It was known also as the "Octave of our Lord."

CISTERCIANS. An order of monks founded at Citeaux (1098) (Cistercium; whence the name), near Dijon, in Burgundy, by St. Robert. Robert became first a Benedictine monk. But he wished to introduce a stricter observance of the Benedictine rule than that which he found to prevail. In 1075 he retired to the forest of Molesme, near Chatillon, and founded a small colony of hermits there. But again he became dissatisfied with the way in which the rule was observed. He retired to Haur, a forest in the neighbourhood, only to be recalled by the Bishop of the diocese. In 1098, however, with the permission of the papal legate, Archbishop Hughes of Lyons, he removed to Citeaux (Cistercium), near Dijon. Here he formed a community of hermits, who undertook to observe strictly the rules of St. Benedict (see BENEDICTINES). Then a monastery was built, of which Robert became Abbot. But again he was recalled, and was obliged to return to Molesme, where in 1108 he died. The successor of Robert at Citeaux, Alberic, succeeded in 1100 in having the monastery placed under the direct authority of the Pope. He also drew up the *Statuta Monachorum Cistertiensium*, which adopted the strict observance of the rule of St. Benedict. The habit of the order was changed from grey to white (in the choir, but black in the streets). In the time of Alberic's successor, the Englishman Stephen Harding († 1134), thirteen new monastries were founded. In 1113 Bernard, with a number of companions, was admitted into the Monastery of Citeaux. Two years later it became necessary to found four new monasteries, and Bernard was sent to found one of them at Clairvaux (whence his designation St. Bernard of Clairvaux). Bernard gave a great impetus to the movement. "Led by St. Bernard, and following the Pope, the order occupied one of the very first places in the Christian world. It crushed the heretics, Abelard, Arnold of Brescia, the Cathari, etc.; it preached the second crusade; it called into life the military orders of the Templars, of Calatrava, Alcantara, Montesa, Avis, and Christ. In 1143 the kingdom of Portugal declared itself a fief of the Abbey of Clairvaux; and in 1578 the abbey actually tried to make good its claims" (Schaff-Herzog). After St. Bernard the members of the order are sometimes called Bernardines. The Cistercians, under the strict observance of the rule of St. Benedict, abstained from meat, fish, eggs and grease, and usually from milk. They fasted from September 14th to Easter. But after the middle of the thirteenth century the discipline of the order began to be relaxed, and the order itself began to decline. In 1475, by a brief of Pope Sixtus IV., the monks of Citeaux were allowed the use of meat. In 1485, by order of the general chapter, it was allowed in all convents on three days in the week. There were protests against this which in course of time took the form of new congregations (see FEUILLANTS, TRAPPISTS). There were at one time eighteen hundred Cistercian abbeys. In England at the time of the dissolution, there were about one hundred houses for monks or nuns. See Schaff-Herzog; Benham; the *Cath. Dict.*; Brockhaus.

CITBOLONTUM. A tribal deity, god of medicine, in the religion of the Mayan Indians.

CITY TEMPLEISM. A name which was given to the New Theology (*q.v.*), or the teaching of Mr. R. J. Campbell, formerly minister of the City Temple, London.

CITY, THE. It has been pointed out by L. R. Farnell and others that in many cases the very origin of the *polis* or city was religious. "We have evidence that before the Homeric period the exclusive tribal-religious system had been transcended, and that certain tribes might share and maintain a common temple; for instance, the Delphic Amphiktyony had arisen before society had become predominatingly civic. The temple would be surrounded with sacrosanct ground, and this would serve as a rallying place for commerce and social union. Adjacent habitations could naturally arise, and the settlement could grow into a city, just as, in our early Middle Ages, a town might arise under the shadow of a monastery. The name 'Preston' points to such an origin: and names of cities such as 'Athenæ' the settlements of Athena, Alalkomenai the settlements of Athena Alalkomene, Potniai 'of the mistress,' Megara 'the nether shrine of Demeter,' indicate the same process of development. In these cases the temple is the nucleus of the expanding community. But also when, as perhaps happened more frequently, secular motives such as military security prompted the foundation, the bond that holds the city together is none the less religious" (L. R. Farnell). See L. R. Farnell, *Greek Religion*.

CIUAPIPILTIN. A name given to certain Mexican goddesses, goddesses of the cross-roads, who were thought to be the spirits of women who had died in childbirth. Since they were supposed to haunt cross-roads, temples were built and offerings made there to placate them. They were liable to afflict children with various diseases.

CLAIRAUDIENCE. It is well known that Socrates believed that a familiar spirit attended him and spoke to him sometimes, giving him advice. This advice generally took the form of a warning against some approaching danger. It is believed now that this and many other instances of the hearing of voices can be explained in the light of the modern study of psychic phenomena. Socrates, says Mr. Hudson, "was endowed with that rare faculty which, in one way or another, belongs to all men of true genius, and which enabled him to draw from the storehouse of subjective knowledge. In his case the threshold of consciousness was so easily displaced that his subjective mind was able at will to communicate with his objective mind in words audible to his senses. This phenomenon is known to spiritists as clairaudience." See T. J. Hudson.

CLAIRVOYANCE. The word has been defined to mean "the alleged power of seeing things not present to the senses." The power has been claimed as one of the phenomena of spiritism, and spiritists profess to be able to see things which are happening at a distance. T. J. Hudson says that "certainly the great bulk of phenomena which are popularly regarded as evincing clairvoyant power must now be referred to telepathy. It must be said, however, that many phenomena have been produced which cannot at present be accounted for on any other hypothesis than that of independent clairvoyance. Yet it is not impossible that, when the laws of telepathy are better understood, all so-called clairvoyant phenomena may be referred to that agency." Cp. TELEPATHY. See T. J. Hudson; Joseph Lapponi, *Hypnotism and Spiritism*, 1907.

CLAPHAM SECT. A name given by Sydney Smith (1771-1845) to a group of Evangelical philanthropists of the Church of England. They were so called because they lived in Clapham. One of them was the Vicar of Clapham, John Venn (1759-1813), a founder of the Church Missionary Society. Others were: Henry Thornton (1760-1815), first Treasurer of the Society for Missions, which became afterwards the Church Missionary Society; William Wilberforce (1759-1833), who carried the Bill for the abolition of slavery through the House of Commons; Granville Sharp (1735-1813), who formulated the principle "that as soon as any slave sets foot upon English territory he becomes free"; Zachary Macaulay (1768-1838), editor of the "Christian Observer," which was devoted to the cause of the abolition of the British slave-trade; James Stephen (1758-1832), who resigned his seat in the House of Commons because the Government refused to support the registration of slaves; and John Shore or Baron Teignmouth (1751-1834), the first President of the British and Foreign Bible Society. "The influence exerted by the co-operation of these men, and of the friends who came to visit them—men like Simeon and Dean Milner and Clarkson—was of vast importance in its day. The abolition of the slave trade, leading on to the abolition of slavery itself, was the work of this coteric. The Evangelical party found here their chief rendezvous. They started the *Christian Observer*, the only religious periodical of the day worth notice; they were the founders of the British and Foreign Bible Society, and of Exeter Hall as a place for religious meetings; and they wrought greatly on behalf of Church Missions to the heathen" (W. Benham, *Dictionary*). See Sir James Stephen, *Essays in Ecclesiastical Biography*, 1849; Benham; the *D.N.B.*

CLARISSES. The order of the Nuns of St. Clare. See POOR CLARES.

CLEMENT, EPISTLES OF. See APOSTOLIC FATHERS.

CLEWER SISTERHOOD, THE. A Church of England Sisterhood founded at Clewer near Windsor in 1849. The Sisters are engaged in educational work and in the conduct of Penitentiaries, Orphanages, and Convalescent Homes. Their *Manual* "advocates Auricular Confession, the Real Presence, the Eucharistic Sacrifice as a propitiation, and Prayers for the Dead" (Walsh). See Walter Walsh, "Sisterhoods, Ritualistic," in the *Prot. Dict.*

CLINICAL BAPTISM. In the early Christian Church persons who received baptism on the sick-bed were called *clinici* (from the Greek *klinē* "a bed"). They were of course baptised by the sprinkling or pouring of water over them, and in their case this form of baptism was considered valid. But *clinici* who recovered were not as a rule allowed to be ordained. This was decreed by the Council of Neo-Cæsarea (314 A.D.). The exceptions were to be made only when there was a great want of clergy, or when *clinici* had proved themselves to be particularly zealous Christians. See Schaff-Herzog; Benham; the *Cath. Dict.*

CLUNY, CONGREGATION OF. The Congregation of Cluny or Clugny represents a movement for the reform of the monastic life towards the end of the ninth century A.D. A new monastery was founded by Berno, Abbot of Gigny, in 912, at Clugny (*Cluniacum*) in Burgundy, and endowed by William Duke of Aquitaine. The reform took the form of a very strict observance of the rule of St. Benedict. It met with such favour and success that many other monasteries attached themselves to it. The rules of the Congregation (*Consuetudines Cluniacenses*) were finally collected by Peter the Venerable, the ninth abbot, whose authority was recognised by two thousand convents. The monastery of Cluny was the largest in Christendom. Its church, which was consecrated in 1131 by Pope Innocent II., "was one of the most magnificent built during the Middle Ages, ornamented with wall and glass pictures, and embroidered tapestries, and stocked with furniture of gold and bronze" (Schaff-Herzog). From the beginning of the twelfth century, however, the Congregation had begun to decline. In the thirteenth century discipline was greatly relaxed. At the Revolution the property of the Congregation of Cluny was confiscated by the Republican Government. The church was sold to the town of Cluny, and was then pulled down. In England, at the time of the dissolution there were thirty-two Cluniac houses. See Schaff-Herzog; Benham; the *Cath. Dict.*

COADJUTOR. In ecclesiastical usage, the term Coadjutor denotes "the assistant of an ecclesiastic who by sickness or age is prevented from fulfilling the duties of his office, and may be appointed temporarily or perpetually" (Schaff-Herzog). In ancient times it was not considered proper to appoint a successor to a bishop while the bishop was still alive. In the Church of England it was provided by Act of Parliament in 1869 that an Archbishop or Bishop, if incapacitated, might retire with a pension. A successor, a Coadjutor Bishop, is then elected and consecrated in the usual way. In the Church of Rome the Pope himself decides upon the right course of action. It was decreed by the Council of Trent that coadjutors "should be appointed at cathedral churches and monasteries only in cases of absolute necessity, and that they should never acquire the right of succession, except after a careful investigation of all circumstances by the Pope" (Schaff-Herzog). See Schaff-Herzog; Edward L. Cutts; the *Cath. Dict.*

COAT, THE HOLY. The relic known as the Holy Coat of Treves is preserved in the Cathedral of Treves. It has been claimed that it is the seamless coat worn by Jesus at the time of his Passion (John xix. 23). According to the "Gesta Trevirorum," the Empress Helena became possessed of it in the Holy Land and sent it (about 326 A.D.) to Treves. But there are several traditions. According to one of the legends it was brought to Treves by a maiden, and as she drew near to the city all the bells began to toll. In 1512 the coat was exposed for the veneration of the faithful. On the occasion of its exposure in 1844, in the presence of eleven bishops and more than a million laymen, several miraculous cures are said to have taken place. This led to a long controversy regarding the authenticity of the Coat, and to the secession of a number of members of the Church, who formed a new body called the "German Catholic Church" (Deutschkatholiken). The Coat was exposed as recently as 1891, when a number of cures were again reported. See William Benham; Schaff-Herzog; the *Cath. Dict.*; Brockhaus.

COATLICUE. One of the deities of the ancient Mexicans. She was the mother of the War-god Huitzilopochtli (*q.v.*), and became, when translated to heaven, the Goddess of Flowers.

COCCEIANS. A school of theologians in Holland which was led by J. Cocceius (1603-1669), a professor at Leiden. In 1669 Cocceius published a Hebrew Lexicon. But his peculiar system of theology, the Covenant or Federal Theology, was expounded in a work published in 1648, "Summa Doctrinae de Fœdere et Testamento Dei." He develops the idea of two covenants made by God with man, the first covenant, or covenant of works, made with Adam, and the second covenant, or covenant of grace, made with Christ. Cocceius "maintained that there is a strict unity between the Old and the New Testament, that a proper interpretation of the former makes it full of evangelical revelations, and that the fulness of the Divine Word is such that its language must bear many meanings, suited to many times and persons. It became a common saying that Cocceius saw Christ everywhere in the Old Testament, but that Grotius saw him nowhere" (J. H. Blunt). See J. H. Blunt; *Brockhaus*.

COCIDIUS. Cocidius was one of the names given by the ancient Celts to the war-god, a deity corresponding to the Roman Mars. Reverence was paid to Cocidius in ancient Britain.

COCK, THE. In China if there has been delay in burying a coffin, "it is not unusual to see on the way to the grave a live white cock with its feet tied standing upon the catafalque." From ancient times the Chinese have regarded the cock as an emblem of the sun. A Chinese book says: "The cock is the emblem of the accumulated Yang (*i.e.* the sun) and of the South. Etherial things which partake of the character of fire and of the Yang element, have the property of flaming up; hence, when the Yang rises above the horizon the cock crows, because things of the same nature influence each other." The cock seems therefore to be placed upon the catafalque because it contains Yang matter or vital energy. Another reason is that it is supposed to keep away spirits of darkness. It is commonly believed, moreover, that these cannot withstand daylight, and are put to flight every morning by the cock's crowing. To impart vitality to a soul-tablet marks are made on it with blood taken from the comb of a cock. When persons are lingering between life and death, or even when they are dead, the blood of a cock is supposed to have power to revive them. In funeral processions white cocks are preferred. In ancient times they were also preferred for exorcising purposes. See J. J. M. de Groot, *R.S.C.* Modern European Jews observe a ceremony in which a cock or hen (preferably a white one) plays a part. The bird serves as a kind of vicarious sacrifice on the day before the Day of Atonement. Usually a male person takes a cock, a female a hen. Psalm cvii. 17-20 and Job xxxiii. 23-24 are first recited, and then, the right hand resting on the animal's head, the bird is swung round the head three times. While this is being done, these words are said three times in Hebrew: "This be my substitute, my vicarious offering, my atonement. This cock [or hen] shall meet death, but I shall find a long and pleasant life of peace." The bird is afterwards killed and given to the poor; or it is eaten and its equivalent in money given to the poor. The ceremony bears the Yiddish name "Kaparath-Schlag." See Oesterley and Box. The cock appears as emblem of the Attis-priest in an inscription on an urn in the Lateran Museum at Rome. Lucian speaks (*Syrian Goddess*, § 48) of "a certain holy cock who dwells hard by the lake" (the sacred lake of Hierapolis). According to W. G. Wood-Martin, on some of the islands off the western coast of Ireland, it is the custom on St. Patrick's day to sacrifice a black cock in honour of the saint. The Gadbas, a primitive tribe belonging to the Vizagapatam District of Madras, offer a white cock to the sun and a red cock to the moon. When the Oraons, an important Dravidian tribe in India, the members of which work as farmservants and labourers, celebrate at the Sarhūl festival the marriage of the sun-god and earth-mother, the former is represented by a white cock and the latter by a black hen. After the marriage the cock and hen are sacrificed. The Vālans, a fishing caste in Southern India, hold a grand festival called Kumbhom Bharani (cock festival) in the middle of March, "when Nāyars and low caste men offer up cocks to Bhagavathi, beseeching immunity from diseases during the ensuing year" (E. Thurston and K. Rangachari). S. Couling notes that in Hongkong the form of oath for Chinese in Court was by cutting off a cock's head.

COCK FESTIVAL. The Nāyars, a Dravidian caste in Malabar, hold annually at Cranganore a festival in which the chief feature is the sacrifice of cocks. It is held in a temple dedicated to the goddess Kali, to which many pilgrims resort. The pilgrims take with them rice, salt, chillies, curry-stuffs, betel leaves and nuts, a little turmeric powder and pepper, and particularly a number of cocks. "The popular idea is that the greater the number of cocks sacrificed, the greater is the efficacy of the pilgrimage. Hence men vie with one another in the number of cocks that they carry on the journey. The sacrifice is begun, and then there takes place a regular scramble for the sanctified spot reserved for this butchering ceremony. One man holds a cock by the trunk, and another pulls out its neck by the head, and, in the twinkling of an eye, by the intervention of a sharpened knife, the head is severed from the trunk. The blood then gushes forth in forceful and continuous jets, and is poured on a piece of granite specially reserved. Then another is similarly slaughtered, and then as many as each of the pilgrims can bring. In no length of time, the whole of the temple yard is converted into one horrible expanse of blood, rendering it too slippery to be safely walked over. The piteous cries and death throes of the poor devoted creatures greatly intensify the horror of the scene. The stench emanating from the blood mixing with the nauseating smell of arrack renders the occasion all the more revolting" (T. K. Gopal Panikkar, *Malabar and its Folk*, 1900). The festival is known as the Bharani.

CODDIANI. One of the names given to the Gnostics. It is referred to by Epiphanius (*Hær.* xxvi. 3) who suggests that the name is connected with a Syriac word Codda meaning a dainty side-dish. The Gnostics might have been so called because they ate apart from others. See J. H. Blunt.

CODE OF HOLINESS, THE. The Code of Holiness or the Law of Holiness (commonly represented by the letter H) is the name given to a priestly document

Leviticus xvii.-xxvi.) incorporated in the Hexateuch. The book of the prophet Ezekiel is closely connected with it, and the booklet has even been ascribed to him. Another view is that it is "a codification of more ancient laws by Ezekiel prior to the composition of his own code." A third theory makes it later than Ezekiel, but earlier than the rest of the Priests' Code. C. A. Briggs is of opinion that "Ezekiel's resemblance to it in many respects implies a knowledge of its legislation whether he knew it in its present form of codification or not. It is probable that Ezekiel knew of it, but it is difficult to prove the existence of the code prior to Ezekiel." See C. A. Briggs, *Hex*.

CODE OF KHAMMURAPI. A Babylonian code of laws, the oldest code in the world, discovered at Susa in 1901 by M. J. de Morgan. Khammurapi flourished about 2100 B.C. Mr. W. St. Chad Boscawen points out that, although this is the oldest code of laws, "other tables of morality have existed, such as the Negative Confessions in the Egyptian Book of the Dead" (see BOOK OF THE DEAD). The following are examples of some of the laws (in the rendering of Chilperic Edwards): 109. If rebels meet in the house of a wine-seller and she does not seize them and take them to the palace, that wine-seller shall be slain. 110. If a priestess who has not remained in the sacred building shall open a wine-shop, or enter a wine-shop for drink, that woman shall be burned. 142. If a woman hate her husband, and say "Thou shalt not possess me," the reason for her dislike shall be inquired into. If she is careful, and has no fault, but her husband takes himself away and neglects her; then that woman is not to blame. She shall take her dowry and go back to her father's house. 143. If she has not been careful, but runs out, wastes her house and neglects her husband; then that woman shall be thrown into the water. 229. If a builder has built a house for a man, and his work is not strong, and if the house he has built falls in and kills the householder, that builder shall be slain. 250. If a mad bull has rushed upon a man, and gored him, and killed him; that case has no remedy. 251. If a man's ox is known to be addicted to goring, and he has not blunted his horns, nor fastened up his ox; then if his ox has gored a free man and killed him, he shall give half a mina of silver. See W. St. Chad Boscawen, *The First of Empires*, 1903; Chilperic Edwards, *The Oldest Laws in the World*, 1906.

CŒNOBIUM. Cœnobium was the name given to the place in which cœnobites lived together. Their superior was called *koinobiarchēs*. As distinguished from anchorites and hermits, cœnobites elected to live in common. Their name is derived from the Greek words *koinos bios* "common life." The monastic community of a cœnobium differs from that of a laura (*q.v.*) to the extent that the inmates of the latter have separate cells and live in solitude five days of the week.

COGITO ERGO SUM. This, according to René Descartes (1596-1650), the founder of speculative rationalism, is the basic principle of all philosophy. If we are to find in knowledge anything of abiding value we must start with the first grounds of Reason, and destroy all conventional assumptions (De omnibus nobis dubitandum, quae incerta). One thing it is impossible to deny—the fact that we exist. "For if I doubt or I deny, that means I must think, and the 'I' who thinks must exist" (Butler). "I think, consequently I exist." See C. J. Deter; Arthur Butler.

COGLERS. A sect founded by a man named Sirgood at Kirdford in Sussex. They were also called Coplers, and were believed to possess a "Book of Cople." They were teetotallers, and professed to be sinless.

COLLEGE. In Roman usage the word Collegium was a general term for an association. Political clubs were called Colleges. There were many associations or colleges, "which, although not united by any specifically religious objects, had a religious centre in the worship of some deity or other" (Seyffert). Religious societies were either established by the State, or formed by private individuals. In either case they had to be recognised and controlled by the Government. When Christian churches first arose in the Roman Empire they were regarded as colleges (*collegia*) and were considered to be illegal associations (*collegia illicita*). In modern times, apart from the ordinary uses of the term college, it is used often of that part of a Cathedral foundation in which the dean and Chapter reside. See O. Seyffert, *Dict.;* the *Cath. Dict.;* Smith and Cheetham.

COLLEGIANTS. The followers in Holland, and afterwards in Hanover, of John James, Hadrian, and Gisbert van der Kodde. The sect was founded in 1619. There was no official ministry. At their prayer meetings, held twice a week, any member of the congregation was allowed to pray or preach. They practised baptism by immersion. For a time a division was caused in the sect by John Bredenburg who had come under the influence of the teaching of Baruch Spinoza (1632-1677), but in course of time the breach was healed. See J. H. Blunt.

COLLYRIDIANS. A religious sect in Arabia, referred to by Epiphanius. The name is derived from the Greek word *kollurides*, "cakes," and the sect was so called because the women offered cakes or rolls to Mary and then ate them.

COLOURS, CHRISTIAN SYMBOLISM OF. The various colours are used to symbolise states and qualities. White denotes innocence, purity, virginity, faith, joy, life, and light. In ritual it is used on the festivals of the Circumcision, the Epiphany, Christmas, and Easter. Red denotes divine love, power, regal dignity, war, suffering, and especially the Passion of Jesus and the martyrdom of the saints. In ritual it is used on the festivals of Pentecost and of the Martyrs. Green denotes life, hope, plenty, mirth, youth, and prosperity. In ritual it is used on ordinary Sundays. Violet (or Purple) denotes sorrow, passion, suffering, humility, and truth. In ritual it is used during Lent, Holy Week, and Advent, as well as on Septuagesima, Quinquagesima, and Ash-Wednesday. Martyrs are depicted in purple garments. Black denotes death, despair, sorrow, humiliation, and mourning. In ritual it is used on Good Friday. Blue denotes sincerity, godliness, piety, and divine contemplation. Bright yellow denotes brightness, goodness, faith, and fruitfulness. Dull Yellow denotes faithlessness, deceit, and jealousy. See Sidney Heath.

COLUMBANUS, ST., RULE OF. Columbanus (about 543-615 A.D.) was born in Leinster, Ireland, and educated at Bangor. In 595 he founded a monastery on the Irish model in the Vosges, a school for the practice of asceticism and for sacred study. His work met with great success. Later, when he was banished from the country, he established himself in an abandoned church on the shore of the Lake of Constance. Finally he founded a monastery, Bobbio, on the Trebia, south of Pavia. This became a centre of learning. The community of Columbanus claimed a large measure of independence. In many points its leader refused to conform to the rites and rules of Rome. The life was one of great austerity. The monks had to observe, as far as possible, perpetual silence. Only one meal was taken, consisting of common vegetables, pulse, dough, and a small loaf twice-baked. Mortification had to be practiced in thoughts, words and movements. Columbanus is reputed to have composed two documents concerning his rule, the *Regula Columbani* and the *Regula Cœnobialis Fratrum de Hibernia.* "The former is a thoroughly biblical direction towards a Christian life in evangelical freedom: the latter orders that he who neglects to make the sign of the cross over the spoon before eating shall be punished by a sound whipping; that he who speaks to a layman shall be punished by singing a number of hymns, etc. But while the character of the *Regula Columbani* corresponds very closely with that of Columban's sermons, which are genuine, the *Liber Pœnitentialis Columbani*, which corresponds to the *Regula Cœnobialis*, is evidently spurious" (Schaff-Herzog). See Schaff-Herzog; the *Cath. Dict.*

COMARISTAE. A religious sect, the members of which held Pelagian views. They were so called after Theodore Comartius (d. *c. A.D.* 1595). Another name for them was New Pelagians (*q.v.*).

COMMANDMENTS, THE TEN. See DECALOGUE.

COMMERCE, PATRON SAINTS OF. There was a widespread dedication during the early Middle Ages of churches and fraternities to St. Nicholas of Myra in Lycia, and Professor G. Unwin (in the *Journal of the Manchester Egyptian and Oriental Society*, 1916, p. 13 ff.) has sought to establish a connection of these on the one hand with the spread of commercial usages and gild organisations from the Levant westwards, and on the other hand with the simultaneous spread of a particular method of city construction and city expansion which had been practised from the earliest historic times in Mesopotamia, and was especially exemplified in the foundation of Baghdad by the Caliph Mansur in 776 A.D. In the second century B.C. Delos was the principal intercontinental market for slaves. "The dedications to Isis, Hermes, and the Tyrian Hercules of the fraternities with clubhouses and chapels of the merchants who frequented it, point to their descent as institutions from a much earlier time, whilst, on the other hand, they were almost identical in their social and religious character with the merchant guilds of the early Middle Ages. One of the chief patron deities of commerce at Delos was naturally Poseidon; and later, in the second century A.D. a gild of merchants dedicated to Poseidon still existed at Tanais, at the mouth of the Don (Minns, *Scythians and Greeks*). Tanais, which had long been under the influence of a cosmopolitan Judaism, was a frontier post of that Levantine world, whose curious transitional blend of more primitive custom with Hellenism and with Christianity has been interpreted by Sir W. Ramsay and Professor Calder. Fraternities, at first Pagan, but afterwards Christian, played a large part in that world. The cult of Poseidon amongst seafaring merchants was displaced by the veneration of St. Nicholas of Myra in Lycia (Lawton, *Modern Greek Folklore*) to whom a church was dedicated by Justinian at Constantinople in 530 A.D. Until the rise of the Italian republics the Levantine region, of which St. Nicholas thus became the tutelary genius, remained the seat of active commerce in Europe and the intermediary through which the products and the technique of the more advanced industries of Mesopotamia and Central Asia, China and India slowly passed into the civilisation of the West. Greek and Syrian Christians were the first agents of this intercourse, as is shown by the earliest dedications of Florentine churches (Davidsohn, *Gesch. d. Florenz*) to St. Miniata, a Greek, in 250 A.D. and to St. Reparata, a Syrian, about 400 A.D.; but after the rise of Islam Arabs played a large part, and Offa's gold tribute to Rome in the eighth century was paid in Arab *dinars* (*Brit. Numis. Journal*, vol. v.)." From the ninth to the twelfth century the centre of this commerce and culture tended to gravitate towards Baghdad. The spread of St. Nicholas dedications began at the period of the Crusades. "In the last decade of the eleventh century Venice and Bari were contending for the possession of the saint's body and a large proportion of the churches erected at new ports or new markets throughout Northern Europe were dedicated to St. Nicholas." Unmistakable instances of the connection between St. Nicholas and new settlements of traders are found at Brussels, Ghent, Amsterdam, Middleburg, Leyden, Berlin, Hamburg, Leipzig, Frankfort-on-Maine, Prague, Stockholm, Paris, Rouen, Amiens, Chartres, London, Newcastle, Durham, Bristol, Liverpool, Yarmouth, Rochester. There are 385 dedications to St. Nicholas in England alone, many of them being in insignificant villages. The rapid spread of the cult of St. Nicholas at ports and markets seems to indicate "the activity of Levantine influences either through the migration of the traders themselves or through the adoption of their methods and traditions in the West."

COMMISSARY. In the Church of England a Commissary commonly denotes a clergyman or a layman who acts in England for colonial bishops in matters of business. The *Cath. Dict.* defines a Commissary as an ecclesiastic who is delegated by the bishop to exercise "a portion of the episcopal jurisdiction in a particular part of the diocese, especially with reference to licences, institutions, the examination of witnesses, etc."

COMMISSION CREED, THE. A Creed drawn up in America in 1883 A.D. by twenty-five commissioners. This creed, consisting of twelve Articles, is, in the opinion of W. A. Curtis, "one of the most successful modern Declarations," and has found wide acceptance. "It is catholic and evangelical in its doctrine; the historic difficulties in Calvinism are passed over; the language is simple, vigorous, and appropriate; even the doctrine of the Church in Art. X. is in such terms as would commend it to others than Congregationalists" (W. A. Curtis). See William A. Curtis.

COMMUNION, HOLY. A name given to the Christian institution (one of the Sacraments) which commemorates the Last Supper of Jesus with his disciples. It is also called the Lord's Supper; or the Eucharist, which means Thanksgiving, because according to the gospels of St. Matthew, St. Mark, and St. Luke, Jesus "gave thanks" before he broke and distributed the bread. The name Holy Communion emphasises the fact that "the Sacrament is a means of communion or fellowship with Christ Himself, and with all those, whether living or departed, who are members of His Body—the Church" (W. R. W. Stephens, *Book of Common Prayer*). It seems to have been suggested by the language of I. Corinthians x. 16.

COMMUNION OF SAINTS, THE. This expression, which is a translation of the Latin *communio sanctorum*, is the third clause of the third section of the Apostles' Creed in its present form, that is to say, of the common Creed of Western Christendom. It is not found in any Eastern Creed, nor is any allusion made to it in the *Commentary on the Apostles' Creed* by Ruffinus of Aquileia in Italy, which was written about 390. The first allusion to it seems to have occurred in a baptismal Creed of the South-Gallican Church, which is at least a century later. According to Heurtley, the clause can hardly be regarded as established before the close of the eighth century. It was therefore an insertion in the original creed. It is not even certain what the clause means. The Latin expression may, and has been, translated "communion of sacred things." The earliest comments take *sanctorum* to refer to persons rather than things. The Catechism of the Council of Trent takes it to refer to things rather than to persons, that is to say to participation in the Sacraments. Calvin explains: "Everyone of us must maintain brotherly concord with all the sheep of the flock, give due authority to the Church, and, in short, conduct ourselves as sheep of the flock." According to the Heidelberg Catechism, the clause means: "First, that believers, all and several, have communion in Christ and all His blessings, as His members; then, that each member is bound promptly and gladly to contribute the blessings he has received to the common good and to the salvation of all." It is contended by some of the Catholics of the Church of England that belief in the Communion of Saints involves prayers for the dead. According to the Roman Catechism the clause is an explanation of the foregoing words, "I believe in the holy Catholic Church." The *Cath. Dict.* explains: "The communion of saints consists in the union of the Church on earth, and connects the Church on earth with the Church suffering in Purgatory and triumphant in heaven." See the *Prot. Dict.*

COMMUNISM, RELIGIOUS. A movement of the nature of Religious Communism was promoted by Mazdak, son of Bambad, a Persian of Susiana. According to the Arab historian Tabari (838-923 A.D.), Mazdak counselled his followers to possess their estate and families in common, as an act of piety acceptable to God. God had placed the means of livelihood in the world that his servants might freely share them, but men had wronged each other and done injury to the poor. Mazdak forbade the slaughter of animals for food, and was himself an ascetic. He regarded his teaching as the revival of true Zoroastrianism. "Whatever the excesses of his followers, he appeared to have sincerely believed that the triumph of his communistic anarchy meant the defeat of the evil powers—the task which long ago Zoroaster had set before the nation" (F. W. Bussell).

COMMUNITY OF THE RESURRECTION, THE. An Anglican Brotherhood, which was founded in 1892, and consists of celibate clergy who live under rule and with a common purse, and devote themselves to pastoral, evangelistic, literary, and educational works. See BROTHERHOODS, MODERN ANGLICAN.

COMPANIONS OF MUHAMMAD. Muhammad is reported to have said: "God has chosen my Companions before all the worlds, with the exception of the prophets and the apostles." The Companions rank next after the prophets and apostles. Next come the Followers, men "who lived and had intercourse with the Companions even if but for a short time." Then come the Followers of the Followers; and after these the Khalifs (*q.v.*).

COMPITALIA. A popular Roman festival held in honour of the "lares compitales," that is to say, of the Lares, the good spirits of the departed, regarded as tutelary divinities of the cross-ways (*compita*). The festival was held four times a year. W. Warde Fowler thinks that the Lar was an object of worship on the land before it became such in the house. "The oldest Lar of whom we know anything was one of a characteristic Roman group of which the individuals lived in the *compita*, *i.e.* the spots where the land belonging to various households met, and where there were chapels with as many faces as there were properties, each face containing an altar to a Lar,—the presiding spirit of that allotment, or rather perhaps of the whole of the land of the familia, including that on which the house stood." The rejoicing, in which the whole familia, both bond and free, took part was free and jovial. "Each familia sacrificed on its own altar, which was placed fifteen feet in front of the compitum, so that the worshippers might be on their own land; but if, as we may suppose, the whole pagus celebrated this rite on the same day, there was in this festival, as in others . . . a social value, a means of widening the outlook of the familia and associating it with the needs of others in its religious duties." At the festival of the Compitalia, as at the Paganalia, small images of the human figure or round balls were hung on trees or doorways that they might swing in the wind. The common name for these figures was *oscilla*, but those of the Compitalia had a special name, *maniae*, of which the meaning has been lost. For the meaning of this custom see SWINGING, and cp. PAGANALIA. See O. Seyffert, *Dict.*; W. Warde Fowler.

COMPLINE. Compline was added by St. Benedict in the sixth century to the six Hours of Prayer which had previously been observed by devout Christians. See further CANONICAL HOURS.

COMPLUTENSIAN POLYGLOT, THE. An early printed edition of the Bible. It derived its name from Complutum, the Latin designation of Alcalá de Henares, a town in Spain. At the University of Alcalá Cardinal Francis Ximenes de Cisneros (1437-1517), Archbishop of Toledo, began in 1502 to prepare an edition of the Bible. It was to be a Polyglot, for his idea was to give in the Old Testament the Greek and Latin translations by the side of the Hebrew text, and in the New Testament the Latin translation by the side of the Greek text. The New Testament was finished first, and was printed, but not published, in 1514. The Old Testament was printed, but not published, in 1517. The volumes did not receive the approval of Pope Leo X. until March 22, 1520, and do not appear to have been in circulation before 1522. Dr. C. R. Gregory points out that in reference to the Old Testament the editors already reveal a tendency to overestimate the Latin Text of the Bible. "For, referring to the fact that they had placed the Latin text in the middle and the Hebrew and Greek at the sides, they said that the Latin text was like Jesus between the two thieves." See C. R. Gregory.

CON. Con or Cun, the "lord" or "father" of the mountains is a god of thunder worshipped by the Indians of the Andes. In time of drought he is appealed to to send rain. His sacred bird is the condor. Since a thunderstorm brings fertilising rain, a thunder-god comes to be regarded as a god of fertility. See J. G. Frazer, *The Magic Art*, 1911.

CONCH-SHELL, THE. Conch-shell trumpets were employed in temple services in Crete in Minoan times, and have long been in use as sacred instruments among the Hindus. Their use has been recorded also among the natives of Oceania and America. "The conch, which is necessary in every Hindu temple, is loudly sounded in the early morning, primarily to wake the deity, and secondarily to rouse the villagers. Again, when the temple service commences, and when the nivedya or offering is carried, the music of the conch is heard from the northern side of the temple" (E. Thurston and K. Rangachari). Some of the Mārāns, whose traditional occupation is sounding or playing on the sacred instruments, call themselves Vadakku-purattu, or belonging to the northern side.

CONCLAVE. The assembly of cardinals convened for the election of a new Pope, and the place where they assemble.

CONCORDAT. A concordat is defined in the *Cath. Dict.* as "a treaty between the Holy See and a secular State touching the conservation and promotion of the interests of religion in that State." The more famous concordats include that of Worms (1122), between Calixtus II. and the Emperor Henry V., which settled the question of investiture in such a way as "to leave intact in theory the universal pastorate of the successors of Peter"; that of Frankfort or Vienna (1446-8) between Popes Eugenius IV., Nicholas V. and the Emperor Frederic III., which agreed "to divide in a particular manner the patronage of ecclesiastical dignities in Germany"; that of 1515, between Leo X. and Francis I. by which the pragmatic sanction of Charles VII. was abolished, and the nomination to vacant bishoprics and abbeys was resigned to the crown of France; and that of 1801, between Pius VII. and the first Napoleon, by which the public practice of their religion was restored to the French nation.

CONFESSIO BOHEMICA. A confession of faith prepared for the Bohemian Brethren at Prague (1575) by a nnmber of learned divines. The Emperor, Maximilian II., attended a Diet at which it was presented to him. "It was a compromise between the teaching of Luther, and the teaching of the Brethren. In its doctrine of justification by faith it followed the teaching of Luther: in its doctrine of the Lord's Supper it inclined to the broader evangelical view of the Brethren." See J. E. Hutton, *Hist. of the Moravian Church*, 1909.

CONFESSIO HUNGARICA. The Confessio Hungarica (1570 A.D.), also called the Confession of Czenger, was in the main the work of Peter Melius. W. A. Curtis describes it as "the last and most important of a series of Synodic Declarations against the Unitarian movement in Hungary."

CONFESSIO HUNGARORUM. A Hungarian Confession of Faith. It was drawn up by Peter Melius, and was ratified by Synod. This Confessio Hungarorum (1560-62) "is the first general Calvinist Confession of the Church dealing with election and other topics, doctrinal and ecclesiastical" (W. A. Curtis). It is also called the Confession of Debreczen, or Confessio Agrivallensis, or Confessio Catholica.

CONFESSION. In the religion of the Mayan Indians "confession is made to the cacique, or local chief, if a member of the community is seriously ill and the patient believes that some sin of his commission may be the cause" (T. A. Joyce, *M.A.*).

CONFESSION (OF A MARTYR). Confessio or Confession, used as the equivalent of the Greek term *marturion*, has been applied from early times to the tomb of a martyr. "If an altar was erected over the grave, then the name 'confession' was given to the tomb, the altar, and the cubiculum or subterranean chamber, in which they stood" (*Cath. Dict.*). In the Vatican basilica there is a famous "confession" of St. Peter. See the *Cath. Dict.*

CONFESSION OF SEVEN CHURCHES IN LONDON. A Baptist Confession of Faith (1644 A.D.). Baptist divines were excluded from the Westminster Assembly (*q.v.*). They therefore published this Confession, in fifty-two articles, "for the vindication of the truth and information of the ignorant: likewise for the taking off of those aspersions which are frequently both in pulpit and print unjustly cast upon them." W. A. Curtis describes the articles as "Calvinistic throughout, apart from the Sacraments and Church polity."

CONFESSION OF THE AMERICAN FREE-WILL BAPTISTS. A Confession of Faith in twenty-one chapters. It was revised a third time in 1868. This Confession "is the most important and authoritative statement of Arminian Baptist views" (W. A. Curtis).

CONFESSION OF THE FRANKFORT COMMUNITY OF FOREIGNERS. A Confession of Faith (1554 A.D.) drawn up on behalf of exiles. In 1551 A.D. those who had taken refuge in London presented to Edward VI. a statement of their beliefs, "Compendium Doctrinae," composed by Martin Micron. The Frankfort Confession "is a revision of the earlier compendium under the influence of John à Lasco, their leader in England, and of Calvin" (W. Curtis).

CONFESSION OF WATERLAND, THE. A Mennonite Confession of Faith (1580 A.D.) drawn up in Dutch by De Ries and Gerardi. It is the most important of the Mennonite Confessions. "It consists of forty Articles, which deny the guilt of original or transmitted sin, affirm the conditional election of all, and universal atonement, condemn oaths, war, civil office, litigation, revenge, worldly amusements, infant baptism as unscriptural; approve of obedience to civil magistrates in all things not contrary to conscience and God's word; but on other points conform to the normal tenets of Protestantism" (W. A. Curtis).

CONFESSOR. In ecclesiastical usage the term Confessor has been used with different shades of meaning. In the early Christian Church it denoted at first one who confessed Christ by suffering death for him. It was thus synonymous with the earlier term Martyr (*q.v.*). In course of time, however, the word martyr was reserved for those who suffered death, while confessor was used of one who had displayed heroic sanctity and endured great suffering without dying. The term came also to be used of models of Christian piety who had not been exposed to great suffering. Thus in the calendar of the Anglican Church men like Augustine and Jerome are called Confessors. In the Roman Missal and Breviary the term is used of "all male saints who do not fall under some special class, such as Martyr, Apostle, Evangelist" (*Cath. Dict.*). The word was sometimes used of a singer or chorister, one who confessed to God with his voice in divine worship, and it is still so used in the Roman Catholic office on Good Friday. It was used again of one who confessed his sins, and so of a monk who devoted himself to a life of penitence. Finally, in the Roman Catholic Church it is used to denote the priest who hears confessions (*confessarius*). See Benham; the *Cath. Dict.*

CONFIRMATION. The Biblical Feast of Weeks or Festival of the First Fruits was transformed by Rabbinical Judaism into a historical feast when it was made the memorial day of the giving of the Ten Words on Mount Sinai. "The leaders of Reform Judaism surrounded the day with new charm by the introduction of the confirmation ceremony, thus rendering it a feast of consecration of the Jewish youth to the ancient covenant, of yearly renewal of loyalty by the rising generation to the ancestral faith" (K. Kohler). Kohler points out, however, that "Confirmation does not bestow the character of Jew upon the young, any more than the former rite of Bar Mizwah did upon the young Israelite who was called up to the reading from the Law in his thirteenth year as a form of initiation into Jewish life." The Jew becomes a member of the Jewish community by right of birth. In the Roman Catholic Church, Confirmation, conferred by the bishop, who lays his hands on the recipient, is held to be a sacrament: "a sacrament of the new law by which grace is conferred on baptised persons which strengthens them for the profession of the Christian faith" (*Cath. Dict.*). All baptised persons are qualified to receive this sacrament, and the twelfth year of age is considered the most suitable. The candidates are brought to the bishop by god-parents. At the time of Confirmation it is usual to take another Christian name, but this is not used afterwards in signing. In the primitive Church infants were confirmed immediately after baptism, and the practice still obtains in the Eastern Church. In the Protestant Churches, Confirmation is not held to be a sacrament.

In the Church of England, where, as in the Church of Rome, the bishop confirms, it is an ordinance "in which persons come to years of discretion, and previously baptized as infants, publicly take upon themselves the vows and promises made for them in their baptism by their godparents, and in which the gift of the Holy Spirit is specially sought for to strengthen in their resolutions those who submit themselves to the ordinance" (*Prot. Dict.*). It is administered also to persons baptized as adults. In the Greek Church the rite may be performed by a priest. In the Lutheran churches and in the Reformed Church of France, it is performed by pastors.

CONFUCIANISM. Confucianism, one of the three religions of China, owes its name to the great teacher Confucius (551-479 B.C.), but in a measure it existed before Confucius, just as Taoism (*q.v.*) did before Lao-tsze (6th century B.C.), its reputed founder. At the time of the birth of Confucius the power of the Emperor of China had almost disappeared. The appanage states of the vassal princes had become almost independent. Prof. Parker compares the condition of China to the state of France before the power of the vassal dukes and counts had been broken by Louis XI. "Not only were the vassal principalities, dukedoms, and counties insubordinate in relation to the king, but their own counts, barons, and squires were equally presumptuous towards themselves; and it was into this chaotic condition of society and policy, where each clever man was fighting for his own hand alone, that Confucius was ushered at his birth." According to later legend, his birth was accompanied by a number of marvels, but little is really known about his early years. He soon displayed an interest in ritualistic ceremonies; and at the age of fifteen he became devoted to study. At the age of nineteen he married. Soon afterwards he accepted a post as grain distributor. At the age of twenty-one he was promoted to be an estate-agent or a farm-overseer. When he was twenty-two he was already surrounded by a band of earnest students and disciples. He now earned his living by teaching philosophy. For years he taught others, and at the same time continued his own studies. He took lessons in music from a celebrated music-master. On a visit to the Imperial capital, whither he went particularly to obtain more exact information about the ancient rites and ceremonies, he met and consulted the Taoist philosopher Lao-tsze. According to one account Lao-tsze addressed him thus: "The bones of the people you speak of have all rotted away, and only their words remain. When a man of first rate qualities finds his opportunity, he makes his career; if he finds no opportunity, he betakes himself off like the grass carried away by the storm. I have always understood that a good trader keeps back his best wares: in the same way a man of first-rate qualities hides his potential virtues behind an expressionless face. Get rid of your superior airs and your multitudinous requirements, of your mannerisms, and your inordinate desires, none of which can be of any advantage to your body. This is all I have to say to you." Confucius is reported to have said to his disciples: "I know the capacity of a bird to fly, of a fish to swim, of a beast to get along; the last you can trap, the others take with a rod or an arrow; but when it comes to dragons, I am ignorant of how they ride the winds and clouds up to heaven. Lao-tsze, whom I have seen to-day, would seem to be of the dragon kind." In spite of Lao-tsze's reproof, Confucius' disciples soon numbered three thousand. When Confucius was thirty-six he was forced by the outbreak of a civil war to remove from Lu to the land of Ts'i. He returned after six years, and devoted himself for a time to the compilation and editing of the "Book of Odes" (*q.v.*) and the "Book of History" (*q.v.*). At the age of forty-seven, he was made Magistrate or Governor of one of the towns of Lu. This gave him an opportunity of putting his own principles of government into practice, and he met with such success that in course of time he was made Minister of Works. When the Duke, his master, had asked him whether his rule of government was adapted to the whole State he had replied: "Certainly, and not only to the State of Lu, but to the whole Empire." But enemies soon rose up to frustrate his work. "Honesty, morality and funeral etiquette advanced with such strides under the premiership of Confucius that neighbouring states began to grow uneasy. It was first thought advisable to conciliate the rising power by a cession of territory; but wilier counsels prevailed, and a successful effort was made to corrupt the new duke's heart with presents of beautiful singing-girls and fine horses. This moral collapse so distressed the philosopher that he left the country" (Parker). This happened in 496 B.C. Confucius went forth with his disciples to wander for thirteen years through the various feudal states, seeking, as Prof. Legge says, a ruler who would heed his instructions and had the goodness and the wisdom to follow them. A long and fruitless quest. The philosopher was sixty-eight years old when the Duke of Lu invited him to return. He accepted the invitation, but devoted the remaining five years of his life to the completion of his literary labours. His history of his own State (see SPRING AND AUTUMN ANNALS) begins with the year 722 B.C. and covers about two hundred and fifty years. His work as a historian marks a turning-point in the study of Chinese history. "All Chinese history previous to this date," says Prof. Parker, "is as vague and unsatisfactory as is our own European history previous to the founding of Rome in 753 B.C." When Confucius felt that he had not much longer to live he said: "No intelligent monarch arises; there is no ruler in the kingdom who will make me his master; my time has come to die." The philosopher only claimed to be a man with a divine mission. He was first described as "holy" by Mencius (372-289 B.C.) two hundred years later. Naturally it was reported in course of time that he possessed exceptional and extraordinary knowledge, but he said of himself: "I am never tired of learning myself, and never weary of teaching others." His mission was to teach men the way of perfection. "Self-control, modesty, forbearance, patience, kindness, orderliness, absence of effusiveness and passion, studiousness, industry, mildness, dutifulness, neighbourliness, fidelity, uprightness, moderation, politeness, ceremoniousness—these were the qualities which Confucius consistently practised and taught" (Parker). One of his rules was an anticipation of the Golden Rule. He said: "What you do not wish others to do to you, do not to them." Lao-tsze (see TAOISM) went even farther than this, for he said that good should be returned for evil. Confucius could not rise to this height. "What do you say," asked one of his disciples, "concerning the principle that injury should be recompensed with kindness?" The philosopher replied: "With what then will you recompense kindness? Recompense injury with justice, and recompense kindness with kindness." Prof. Parker suggests that as a practical man interested in good government Confucius could not approve of Lao-tsze's maxim. This indeed was the great difference between the two men. The one was a philosophical radical like Carlyle or Tolstoy; the other was a practical ruler and reformer. Confucius "probably did in common with the received traditions, more or less vaguely believe in a Supreme Maker, but he did not attempt to define or dogmatize as to what that Maker was, or how that Maker created. He preferred to discuss the practical character of things before his eyes, and was indifferent to the causes of those things. He says nothing about the future state, but holds that man continues, after what we call death, to live on" (Parker). Prof. Giles notes that in the one original work by Confucius, the "Spring and Autumn Annals" (*q.v.*) there is no allusion whatever to any interposition on the part of God in human affairs. It has been pointed out also that in the whole of the Confucian literature there is no purgatory or hell. Confucius shares the sacrifice that is made in China to the great men who have departed. Twice a year, in Spring and in Autumn, it is the duty of the reigning emperor to go to Peking and present offerings before the spirit tablets of Confucius. But according to Prof. Legge it is only the homage of gratitude that is given, and not the worship of adoration. See J. Edkins, *Religion in China*, 1878; James Legge, *The Religions of China*, 1880; R. K. Douglas, *Confucianism and Taouism*; H. A. Giles, *Religions of Ancient China*, 1905; James Legge, "Confucius the Sage and the Religion of China," in *R.S.W.*; E. H. Parker, *Studies in Chinese Religion*, 1910; cp. H. A. Giles, "Confucianism in the Nineteenth Century," in *Great Religions of the World*, 1902.

CONGREGATIONALISTS. For the origin of the Congregationalists or Independents, see BROWNISTS and cp. CHRISTIANITY.

CONSCIENCERS. Consciencers or Men of Conscience was the name by which the followers of the German wandering scholar Matthias Knutzen (*b.* 1646) were known. The greater number of his adherents were in Jena. Knutzen denied the divine inspiration of the Bible, and found a substitute for the sacred book in common science (the science common to all) or conscience. Conscience was his Bible, an authority superior to that of the secular government and the clergy. To do evil is to suffer grievous torture; to do good is to enjoy heaven. The supreme principle of the Consciencers was: "Live justly and honestly, and give everyone his due." They denied the existence of God, the devil, and a future life; the utility of governments and preachers, and the moral necessity of the institution of marriage.

CONSENSUS OF SENDOMIR. A Confession of Faith drawn up in Poland in 1570 A.D. by a joint-Synod of Lutherans, Calvinists, and Brethren. W. A. Curtis points out that "a notable feature is the complete mutual recognition of the Churches concerned, and the practical exhortation to avoid strife and promote fellowship by every possible means."

CONSENSUS OF ZÜRICH. A declaration made in 1549 A.D. and representing the agreement of Bullinger and Calvin on the question of the Lord's Supper. It consists of twenty-six articles. W. A. Curtis speaks of the Consensus as linking together the Churches of Zürich and Geneva and finding acceptance in other countries.

CONSISTORY. The Roman Emperors had their consistorium or privy council, and the word consistory has been adopted to denote a meeting of official persons to transact business, and also the place of meeting. In the Church of England every bishop has his Consistory Court, which is presided over by his Chancellor or Commissory. The *London Diocese Book* (1912) states that the Bishop of London's Consistory Court "has cognisance of all matters which arise locally within its limits, and administers generally all branches of Ecclesiastical Law." In the Roman Catholic Church the term Consistory is now used almost exclusively of "the ecclesiastical senate in which the Pope, presiding over the whole body of Cardinals, deliberates upon grave ecclesiastical affairs, and communicates to his venerable brethren, and through them to Christendom, the solicitudes and intentions of the vicar of Christ as to the condition of some Christian nation, or the definition of some Catholic doctrine" (the *Catholic Dictionary*). The ordinary meetings are secret, but from time to time public consistories are held, in which the decisions of the secret consistories are announced. In the Lutheran Churches the Consistory is composed of both lay and ecclesiastical officials. It often exercises the functions of a bishop. In the Reformed Churches it corresponds to the Session of the Presbyterian Church. See Schaff-Herzog; Benham; the *Cath. Dict.*

CONSTITUTIONISTS. A name given to those theologians who accepted the papal Bull "Unigenitus" (1713) which condemned the views of the Jansenist leader Pasquier Quesnel (1634-1719). See JANSENISTS.

CONSUBSTANTIAL. The Latin term *consubstantialis* is used as equivalent to the Greek term *homoousios*, which is used in the Nicene Creed to define the relationship of Jesus Christ the Son to God the Father. The word was purposely chosen in order to exclude the Arian doctrine. The Son is consubstantial, of the same substance, with the Father. Consubstantiality implies perfect equality and co-eternity. Compare SUBSTANCE.

CONSUBSTANTIATION. A technical term for the Lutheran doctrine relating to the bread and wine in the Lord's Supper or Eucharist. According to this doctrine the Bread and Wine are not converted into the Body and Blood of Christ (TRANSUBSTANTIATION): "the bread and wine remain bread and wine, though after the consecration, the real flesh and blood of Christ co-exist in and with the natural elements, just as a heated iron bar still remains an iron bar, though a new element, heat, has come to co-exist in and with it" (Schaff-Herzog). The followers of Luther, however, do not recognize a permanent consubstantiation, but confine the connection of the elements with the body and blood of Christ to the act of communion. See K. R. Hagenbach; Schaff-Herzog; W. Benham.

CONTEMPLATION, CHRISTIAN. A form of Silent or Mental Prayer. It differs from Meditation (*q.v.*), because there is a methodical use of the reason. See PRAYER.

CONTRITION. The Council of Trent defines contrition as "grief of mind and detestation of sin committed, with a purpose of sinning no more." The *Cath. Dict.* points out that, thus widely defined, Contrition includes Attrition (*q.v.*), but that the term has a narrower sense, being used to denote "that sorrow for sin which arises from consideration of God's goodness which sin has outraged, and which includes a resolution never to offend God (at least mortally) because God so deserves our love." See the *Prot. Dict.*; the *Cath. Dict.*

CONVENTUALS. A branch of the Franciscans (*q.v.*). In consequence of the action of Elias of Cortona, successor of Francis of Assisi as head of the Franciscans, in relaxing the strictness of the original rule of the Order, the Franciscans became divided into two great branches, the Conventuals, the milder party, and the Observantines, the severer party. The Conventuals decided to live in large convents. Efforts to reunite these bodies to the parent body only succeeded in the case of one of them, the Observantines (*q.v.*); the Conventuals have remained separate.

CONVERSION. In a religious sense, the term means a change of mind in matters of religion. This change is often supposed to come suddenly. This is the interesting question in religion: Is conversion ever really sudden? That a person should change from one religion to another after deep thought and long study is natural. That a person who has lived without religion for some years should suddenly change his mind seems to be supernatural. There are many interesting cases of conversion. Two of them are very familiar, those of Paul the Apostle and the Emperor Constantine the Great. Paul was a strict Pharisee and bitterly persecuted the early Christians. Suddenly, to all appearances, he changed his mind and became a Christian. The story is told in the Acts of the Apostles (ix. 1-18). "And Saul, yet breathing out threatenings and slaughter against the disciples of the Lord, went unto the high priest, and desired of him letters to Damascus to the synagogues, and that, if he found any of this way, whether they were men or women, he might bring them bound unto Jerusalem. And as he journeyed, he came near Damascus: and suddenly there shined round about him a light from heaven: And he fell to the earth, and heard a voice saying unto him, Saul, Saul, why persecutest thou me? And he said, Who art thou, Lord? And the Lord said, I am Jesus, whom thou persecutest: it is hard for thee to kick against the pricks. And he, trembling and astonished, said, Lord, what wilt thou have me to do? And the Lord said unto him, Arise, and go into the city, and it shall be told thee what thou must do. And the men which journeyed with him stood speechless, hearing a voice, but seeing no man. And Saul arose from the earth; and when his eyes were opened, he saw no man: but they led him by the hand, and brought him into Damascus" (vss. 1-7). In the first place it should be noticed that, although this conversion was no doubt quite unexpected, it was not sudden in the sense of being unprepared for. It was no doubt the last thing that Saul or Paul expected. But the fortitude and endurance of the Christians had made a great impression upon him. For a long time there had been going on in his subjective mind between two sets of ideas a conflict of which he was hardly conscious. On his way to Damascus, he fell into a kind of trance. The objective mind became dormant. The subjective mind, with its vast store of accumulated knowledge and experience, became abnormally active. The two sets of ideas struggled against one another for the mastery. The Christian overcame the Jewish, and, almost against his will, Paul became a Christian. This, we believe, is the true psychological explanation of all conversions of this kind. The hearing of a voice is what is known as clairaudience (*q.v.*). St. Paul's experience was a subjective one. Christianity had made already an overpowering impression without Paul's being aware of it. In any case he would have become a Christian in time. The event was hastened, and he was, as he himself described himself, "a child untimely born" (*ektrōma*, I. Corinthians xv. 8). The story of the conversion of the Emperor Constantine on the eve of his great battle with Maxentius is not so interesting, and is very likely a fiction, though it was suggested by the real occurrence of similar experiences. Constantine is supposed to have seen suspended in the air a cross together with the motto "Hoc signo vinces" ("By this sign thou shalt conquer"). If we accept the story as genuine, here again the conversion was already prepared for. Constantine had had opportunities of noting the virtues of the Christians. These had no doubt made a great impression upon him. The experience, too, was again subjective. The seeing of fiery crosses and other objects is a not uncommon experience when the subjective mind is abnormally active. Conversion, apparently sudden and certainly unexpected, is a very real thing. It is useless to scoff at the idea. The experience may come to anyone, even to the agnostic who has made up his mind that his views are settled once and for all. But it has next to be admitted that the experience is not confined to any one religion. Christians will claim of course that the Christian convert experiences a change different from that of all other converts. But it may be doubted whether there is any difference in the sense of relief and happiness felt by the convert to any religion at the time of conversion. Compare William James, *The Varieties of Religious Experience*.

CONVULSIONARIES. Convulsionnaires or Convulsionaries was a name given to the Jansenists (*q.v.*) after the year 1727. In that year a Jansenist François de Paris died, and at his tomb miracles are said to have taken place. Pilgrimages were made to the cemetery in which he was buried, and at the tomb people fell into fits of ecstasy and convulsion.

CORDELIERS. The name given in France to the Observantines (*q.v.*), one of the two great branches into which the Franciscans (*q.v.*) came to be divided.

CORINTHIANS, FIRST EPISTLE TO THE. Corinth, "the ancient Paris," as it has been called, was one of the cities in which the Apostle Paul lived and laboured. He resided there in the house of Aquila and Priscilla, and with them pursued the trade of tent-making. In spite of opposition, Paul's mission to the Corinthians was fruitful in so far as he succeeded in establishing a Christian Church amongst them. The dangers, however, to which a Church planted in such an "intellectual" atmosphere was exposed clearly caused the Apostle no little anxiety. None knew better than Paul that the claims of the intellect are very powerful until their weakness is demonstrated by the overpowering sense of divine intuition or inspiration. His own presence among the Corinthians was an inspiration. When he left them, as he was obliged to do after a time, the divine impulse had to be imparted by means of his written word and an ambassador (Timothy or Titus). Even the spoken word gives but a poor reflection of the light which has come by inspiration to a man like Paul. The written word probably reflects still less of it. And yet on this Paul had to depend largely for the strengthening of the faith of his Churches. He had to send letters, written in a hurry no doubt and when his mind was occupied with a number of different problems. After Paul's departure, the Church of Corinth seems to have suffered from divisions. It is a human weakness to form parties and to become attached to persons rather than to principles. In Christianity the essential thing is to have the mind of Christ or the Christ mind. "Wherefore," Paul has to declare to the Corinthians, "let no one glory in men. For all things are yours; whether Paul, or Apollos, or Cephas" (I. Corinthians iii. 21, 22). It would seem that it was at Ephesus, whither Paul had journeyed, that the Apostle received news of trouble at Corinth. It would also seem that three or four letters were sent to Corinth. In I. Corinthians v. 9 we read: "I wrote unto you in my epistle to have no company with fornicators." This seems to refer to a letter, now lost (though II. Corinthians vi. 14-vii. 1 may be a fragment of it; see next article), which was written before the letter now known as I. Corinthians. After this, Paul sent Timothy to Corinth. Then on receiving again an unsatisfactory report, he sent our I. Corinthians. "The genuineness of the Epistle has been almost universally admitted; it was regarded as axiomatic by the Tübingen school, and is accepted by all but the hypercritics who deny the authenticity of all the Pauline Epistles" (A. S. Peake). Internally the Epistle bears unmistakable marks of Paul's genius, character, and experience. The external evidence is also good. Clement of Rome, writing to the Church of Corinth about 95 A.D. says: "Take up the Epistle of the blessed Apostle Paul. What did he write to you at the beginning of the preaching of the gospel? In truth it was under the inspiration of the Spirit that he wrote to you concerning himself and Cephas and Apollos, because even then ye had formed parties." A verse of the Epistle is quoted by Polycarp with the words "as Paul teaches." The Epistle seems to have been used also by Ignatius. It is included in the list of Irenaeus and in the Muratorian Canon. Origen says that he had never heard of the genuineness of the Epistle being disputed. Clement of Alexandria refers to Paul's "Former Epistle to the Corinthians," and says that it contains the precept, "Brethren, be not children in mind." The Epistle treats in a very interesting way of a number of important questions, such as the Lord's Supper (xi. 17-34), Spiritual Gifts (xii.-xiv.), the Resurrection (xv.). See R. J. Knowling, *The Witness of the Epistles*, 1892; J. Massie, *I.* and *II. Corinthians*, in the "Century Bible"; J. A. M'Clymont, 1904; G. Currie Martin; Arthur S. Peake; J. Moffatt.

CORINTHIANS, SECOND EPISTLE TO THE. The Second Epistle to the Corinthians presents a number of difficult problems. At the same time the external evidence for its genuineness is not so good as for the first Epistle. Clement of Rome does not seem to have known of its existence. It seems, however, to have been used by Polycarp. It is included in the Canon of Marcion and in the Muratorian Canon. It is quoted by Irenaeus. This testimony is sufficient. Nor does the internal evidence argue against the genuineness of the Epistle. All that it militates against is the unity of the work. It has been said above (preceding article) that our First Corinthians seems to have been preceded by another letter. There is reason to believe that the same thing happened in the case of our Second Corinthians. In II. Corinthians ii. 4 we read: "For out of much affliction and anguish of heart I wrote unto you with many tears; not that ye should be made sorry, but that ye might know the love which I have more abundantly unto you." Paul, it appears, had written a very severe letter to the Corinthians. This can hardly have been our First Corinthians. "It is not comparable in the sharpness of its tone to the closing portion of II. Corinthians itself, which for concentrated and passionate invective has no parallel in the Pauline Epistles" (A. S. Peake). In the First Epistle Timothy was the messenger sent to Corinth. In the Second Epistle no mention is made of Timothy's visit, but Titus appears as Paul's messenger (II. Cor. vii. 5-15). In both Epistles there is reference to a person who has committed a grave offence, but the offender can hardly be the same. If the offender in the two Epistles be identical, as Peake says, in the Second Epistle "the grossness of the offence seems to be passed over altogether too lightly." It would seem therefore that Second Corinthians was preceded by another letter (other than our First Corinthians). It is not unlikely, moreover, that this letter was preceded by another visit of Paul, "a hasty visit to Corinth that he might set things right by a personal effort" (Massie). Compare II. Corinthians ii. 1, xiii. 1, 2, xii. 14. Now, it has been noticed that chapter ix. would be a more appropriate ending to Second Corinthians than chapter xiii.; that the tone of chaps. x.-xiii. differs from that of chaps. i.-ix.; and that at times chaps. x.-xiii. seem to reflect an earlier situation. All this (and more) has suggested that chapters x.-xiii. do not really belong to Second Corinthians. It has been conjectured further that in these four chapters are to be found the letter referred to in II. Cor. ii. 4 (the four-chapter letter) or at any rate part of it. Prof. Peake cannot help thinking that II. Cor. x.-xiii. formed part of the severe letter. "On the one side we have the description of a letter in the early chapters of II. Corinthians which it seems impossible to identify with our First Epistle; and then as corroborating this we have the surprising character of the last four chapters of II. Corinthians as part of the same letter which we find in the first nine chapters. It is difficult to believe that the two sections of the Epistle hold together. If II. Corinthians is a unity, we have the following state of things: Paul sends a very stern letter to Corinth, and is filled with regret for the writing of it, and apprehension as to its reception. In the joyful reaction caused by the good news of Titus, he writes a letter overflowing with affection at the beginning, and concluding with a sharpness of invective to be paralleled nowhere else in his Epistles." It has been said that, to judge by I. Cor. v. 9 our First Corinthians would seem to have been preceded by another letter. In Second Corinthians there is a short section (vi. 14-vii. 1) which does not fit well into its present context. It interrupts the progress of thought. If it is omitted, vi. 13 connects very well with vii. 2. The section seems to have been inserted here by mistake, and it has been conjectured that it really formed part of the letter referred to in I. Cor. v. 9. Bousset points out that Second Corinthians is deeply personal. "The nervous attractive personality of the Apostle speaks throughout it with the most extraordinary power." See R. J. Knowling, *The Witness of the Epistles*, 1892; J. Massie, *I. & II. Corinthians*, in the "Century Bible"; J. A. M'Clymont; G. Currie Martin; Arthur S. Peake; J. Moffatt.

CORPIANI. One of the names given to the Gnostics. The word is probably corrupt for Scorpiani.

CORPORATE REUNION, ORDER OF. An order founded in 1877 in the Church of England. Those who doubted the validity of the Orders of the clergy of the Church of England could, by joining the Order of Corporate Reunion, be re-ordained by "bishops" who had been consecrated by foreign Bishops whose Orders the Church of Rome recognised as valid. One of these "bishops" was F. G. Lee (*d.* 1902), Vicar of All Saints, Lambeth. After Lee's death the Order ceased to exist. See Walter Walsh, "Ritualistic Secret Societies," in the *Prot. Dict.*

CORPSE-CAKES. Corpse-cakes, according to E. S. Hartland ("Religion among the Indians of Guiana" in *The R.P.A. Annual* for 1918), figure in a funeral custom. "In the Highlands of Bavaria, when the corpse is placed upon the bier, the room is carefully washed out and cleaned. Formerly it was the custom for the housewife then to prepare the corpse-cakes. Having kneaded the dough, she placed it to rise on the dead body, as it lay there enswathed in a linen shroud. When the dough had risen the cakes were baked for the expected guests. To the cakes so prepared the belief attached that they contained the virtues and advantages of the departed, and that thus the living strength of the deceased passed over, through the medium of the corpse-cakes, into the kinsman who consumed them, and so was retained within the kindred."

CORPUS CHRISTI. Corpus Christi ("the body of Christ") is the name of a festival in the Roman Catholic Church, held on the Thursday after Trinity Sunday in honour of the transubstantiation. It was originally a local festival instituted in 1246 at Liège, by Robert, Bishop of Liège, at the special request of St. Juliana, a nun of Liège. Juliana had had a vision in which she seemed to be advised of the festival. In 1264 Pope Urban IV. published a bull which commanded that the festival should be celebrated throughout the Church;

but he died soon afterwards. He seems to have been influenced by another vision seen by a priest of Bolsena (the ancient Volsinium). Urban IV.'s decision was confirmed by Clement V., and the celebration of the festival was secured by succeeding Popes. It has long been the custom on Corpus Christi to carry the Blessed Sacrament about in a magnificent procession. In the Anglican Church the festival was removed from the Calendar at the Reformation, but in ritualistic churches its observance in some measure has been revived. See Benham; *Prot. Dict.; Cath. Dict.*

COUVADE, THE. The name given to a custom among primitive folk which requires a husband during the pregnancy of his wife or after the birth of the child to submit to various restrictions. Sometimes he has to abstain from all work, sometimes from certain kinds of work. One remarkable example is the case in which a husband is confined to his bed, like his wife. The custom as practised by the Yerūkalas, a vagrant gipsy tribe in India, for instance, is as follows. "Directly the woman feels the birth-pangs she informs her husband, who immediately takes some of her clothes, puts them on, places on his forehead the mark which the women usually place on theirs, retires into a dark room where there is only a very dim lamp, and lies down on the bed, covering himself up with a long cloth. When the child is born, it is washed and placed on the cot beside the father. Asafoetida, jaggery and other articles are then given, not to the mother, but to the father. During the days of ceremonial impurity the man is treated as other Hindus treat their women on such occasions. He is not allowed to leave his bed, but has everything needful brought to him" (John Cain, quoted by R. V. Russell and R. B. Hira Lāl). Hutton Webster (*R.D.*) suggests that "the practice of the *couvade* appears to be an outgrowth of the idea that under special circumstances the close ties uniting husband and wife engender a mystic sympathy between them, so that the acts of the one affect the welfare of the other."

COVENANTS. In Arabia when two groups undertook to aid each other to the death, or in other words when they undertook the duties of a common blood-feud, this compact or covenant was solemnized originally by a ceremony in which the blood of the two parties was commingled. At Mecca the form of oath among the group of clans afterwards known as "blood-lickers" was that "each party dipped their hands in a pan of blood and tasted the contents" (Robertson Smith, *Kinship*). In Herodotus (iii. 8) a custom is referred to in which blood is drawn and smeared on seven stones. Robertson Smith points out that "the later Arabs had substituted the blood of a victim for human blood, but they retained a feature which Herodotus had missed, they licked the blood as well as smeared it on the sacred stones." The idea of this ceremony was to unite the contracting parties in a bond of brotherhood. The smearing of blood on the sacred stones made the god also a party to the covenant. In old times men of the same stock, who had mutual obligations, seem to have borne a tattooed mark (*shart*). Professor Robertson Smith suggest that the mark of Cain was nothing else than "the *shart* or tribal mark which every man bore on his person, and without which the ancient form of blood-feud, as the affair of a whole stock, however scattered, and not of near relatives alone, could hardly have been worked." See W. R. Smith, *Kinship*.

COVENANT THEOLOGY. A name given to the theological teaching of J. Cocceius (1603-1669). See COCCEIANS.

COVERDALE'S BIBLE. The English translation of the Bible made by Miles Coverdale (1535). See BIBLE.

COWLEY FATHERS, BROTHERHOOD OF THE. An Anglican brotherhood inaugurated in 1865. The members devote their lives to missionary and educational works, upon the principles of poverty, chastity, and obedience. See BROTHERHOODS, MODERN ANGLICAN.

COYOTLINAUATL. A Mexican deity, the god of the guild of feather-workers.

COZAḤ. An Arabian deity. He was an archer-god, reference being made to his bolts as lightnings and his bow as the rainbow. He was worshipped by the Idumæans. In the sanctuary of Mozdalifa burned a fire sacred to Cozaḥ. This seems to have been the only sanctuary in Arabia which had "a place of burning." See W. Robertson Smith, *Kinship;* and *R.S.*

CRANMER'S BIBLE. Coverdale's Bible corrected and with a preface by Archbishop Cranmer (1540). See BIBLE.

CREATION. Since the outbreak of the great War, new material has been published in America which throws light on the earliest conceptions of creation. The bulk of this new material, according to L. W. King (*Legends of Babylon and Egypt in relation to Hebrew Tradition*, 1918), is furnished by some early texts, written towards the close of the third millennium B.C. "They incorporate traditions which extend in unbroken outline from their own period into the remote ages of the past, and claim to trace the history of man back to his creation. They represent the early national traditions of the Sumerian people, who preceded the Semites as the ruling race in Babylonia; and incidentally they necessitate a revision of current views with regard to the cradle of Babylonian civilization. The most remarkable of the new documents is one which relates in poetical narrative an account of the Creation, of Antediluvian history, and of the Deluge. It thus exhibits a close resemblance in structure to the corresponding Hebrew traditions, a resemblance that is not shared by the Semitic-Babylonian Versions at present known. But in matter the Sumerian tradition is more primitive than any of the Semitic versions. In spite of the fact that the text appears to have reached us in a magical setting, and to some extent in epitomized form, this early document enables us to tap the stream of tradition at a point far above any at which approach has hitherto been possible" (King, p. iii.). As regards the Old Testament narratives, it is now common knowledge that they present two versions of the story of creation—a primitive version (Gen. ii. 4b-25, Jehovistic) and a later version (Gen. i. 1-ii. 4a, Priestly). "In spite of the obvious differences, the two accounts have important features in common. Both show the influence of the ancient tradition by beginning with a scene of waste desolation; and the influence of inspired teaching by the omission of all polytheistic ideas. On the other hand the differences are also important: the Priestly account is cosmic; it deals with earth and heaven and all their hosts, with the dry land, and the firmament, and the waters above and below the firmament; the Primitive account is local, and is only concerned with a garden and its inhabitants, and the streams that water it. In the Priestly account anthropomorphic language is used as little as possible; but in ii. 4b-25 Yahweh is frankly spoken of as a man might be; He moulds a man out of dust, plants a garden, and takes a rib out of the man and builds it up into a woman. So far as the creation of the same beings is concerned the order is different; especially in ch. ii. the woman is formed last, as a kind of afterthought, to be the man's companion, and we are not told that God breathed into her the breath of life; whereas in ch. i. man and woman are formed by the same creative act in the likeness of God" (W. H. Bennett, *Genesis* in the "Century Bible"). In the Sumerian Version, according to L. W. King, the account of Creation is not given in full. Only such episodes are included as were directly related to the Deluge story. "No doubt the selection of men and animals was suggested by their subsequent rescue from the Flood" (p. 113). No attempt is made to explain how the universe itself had come into being. No less than four deities, including a goddess, are represented as taking part in the Creation, and when the deities (Anu, Enlil, Enki, and Ninkharsagga) undertake to create man, the existence of the earth is pre-supposed. Dr. King points out that the idea of a goddess taking part in creation is not a new feature in Babylonian mythology. "Thus the goddess Aruru, in co-operation with Marduk, might be credited with the creation of the human race, as she might also be pictured creating on her own initiative an individual hero such as Enkidu of the Gilgamesh Epic" (p. 111). And, although in the Sumerian text Ninkharsagga, the "Lady of the Mountains," appears for the first time in the character of creatress, "some of the titles we know she enjoyed, under her synonyms in the great God List of Babylonia, already reflected her cosmic activities" (*ibid.*). Turning to the ancient Egyptians, there is an interesting series of sculptures on the walls of the famous Queen Hatshepsut's temple at Deir el-Bahari in which she seeks to record her divine origin. "The scene in the series, which is of greatest interest in the present connection, is that representing Khnum at his work of creation. He is seated before a potter's wheel which he works with his foot, and on the revolving table he is fashioning two children with his hands, the baby princess and her 'double.' It was always Hatshepsut's desire to be represented as a man, and so both the children are boys. As yet they are lifeless, but the symbol of Life will be held to their nostrils by Heqet, the divine Potter's wife, whose frog-head typifies birth and fertility" (King, p. 106). Brinton points out (*R.P.P.*, p. 123) that this conception of the Creator as a moulder or manufacturer underlies many Creation myths. "Thus the Australians called him Baiame, 'the cutter-out,' as one cuts out a sandal from a skin, or a figure from bark. The Maya Indians used the term Patol, from the verb *pat*, to mould, as a potter his clay, Bitol, which has the same meaning, and Tzacol, the builder, as of a house. With the Dyaks of Borneo, the Creator is Tupa, the forger, as one forges a spear-blade; and so on." Frazer has shown (*Folk-lore in the O.T.*, vol. i.) that the legend of the creation of men out of clay is found among the Greeks, the Maoris, the Tahitians, the Melanesians, and others. Other conceptions are equally widespread. "The conception of the cosmic egg from which the universe is hatched, the heaven-born twins, the fecund mother of humanity who falls from heaven, are found not only in the older mythologies of India and China, Egypt and Babylon, but also in Scandinavian creation-story, Persian cosmogony, and the many world-legends of North and South America" (Edwardes and Spence, *Dict.*, p. 39). This is regarded as "a striking testimony to the world-wide similarity of the workings of the barbarian human mind." But it might also be said to be a remarkable demonstration of the diffusion of culture from a common centre.

CREATION-EPIC, BABYLONIAN. See MARDUK, EPIC OF.

CREDNE. The tutelar god of brasiers in the mythology of the Irish Celts.

CREED. The term Creed denotes in a specific sense a brief summary of the articles of Christian faith. The earliest designations of such a summary, however, were canon of faith or canon of truth (Greek), rule of faith, rule of truth, or symbol (Latin). In 1889 Dr. Rendel Harris discovered a Syriac translation of the long-lost Apology of Aristides, which represents a text dating back to the second century, the Apology itself having been written somewhere between A.D. 124 and 140. From this document Dr. Harris has restored a part of the creed of the Christian Church of that era. It reads: "We believe in one God Almighty, Maker of heaven and earth: And in Jesus Christ his Son . . . Born of the Virgin Mary . . . He was pierced by the Jews: He died and was buried: The third day he rose again; He ascended into Heaven . . . He is about to come to judge. . ." (see Camden M. Cobern). The three creeds in common use in the Christian Church are the Apostles' Creed, the Athanasian Creed, and the Nicene Creed (*qq.v.*). The Roman Catholic Church uses also the Creed of Pius IV., which was published in 1564 under the title Profession of the Tridentine Faith. "It consists of the Niceno-Constantinopolitan Creed with a summary of the Tridentine definitions. It now also contains a profession of belief in the definitions of the Vatican Council" (*Cath. Dict.*).

CREIRWY. A goddess of love in the mythology of the British Celts.

CRESCENT AND THE CROSS, THE. Another name for Mohammedanism and Christianity, the crescent being the symbol of the Saracens, and the cross the symbol of the Christians.

CRIOBOLIUM. A Roman sacrifice connected with the worship of the Asiatic goddess Cybele (*q.v.*). A ram was sacrificed, and, by a form of baptism with its blood, the person who made the offering was cleansed from pollution and born again ("in æternum renatus"). See O. Seyffert, *Dict.*, *s.v.* "Rhea"; J. M. Robertson, *C.M.*

CRISPIANS. The followers of Tobias Crisp (1600-1643), brother of Sir Nicholas Crisp, who raised a regiment for Charles I. (1643). Tobias Crisp was a clergyman of the Church of England, and in 1627 became Rector of Brinkworth in Wiltshire. His preaching became extremely Antinomian, and involved him in controversy with the Puritan Divines. After Crisp's death his discourses were published. But they did not attract much attention until they were republished by his son in 1690 in an edition which was recommended and authorised by twelve Independent ministers. In reply to Crisp's sermons, Dr. Daniel Williams (1643?-1716) published in 1692 a book with the title "Gospel Truth Stated and Vindicated." He was at the time Lecturer at Painters' Hall, London. In consequence of the controversy that arose on the publication of his book, he was dismissed from his lectureship. The Sermons of Tobias Crisp were republished in 1745. See J. H. Blunt; and the *D.N.B.*

CRISPINADES. The word Crispinades denotes acts of charity done at the expense of another. It is derived from Crispinus, the name of a saint and martyr. Crispinus fled from Rome to what is now Soissons, and with his brother Crispianus worked there as a shoemaker. Legend reports that he stole leather in order to make shoes for poor people. The two brothers were martyred in the year 287 A.D.

CRITICISM, HIGHER. Higher Criticism is the common, but rather unfortunate, designation of the modern critical study of the Bible. "Part of the phrase 'Higher Criticism' is a mere accident. Criticism, in its earliest stage, took the form of text-criticism. When, at a more advanced stage, it entered upon the inner study of Scripture, it called itself 'higher' in order to distinguish itself from the criticism of the text as a 'lower,' or preparatory form of study. The adjective is the result of a bare historical incident, having no merit in itself, deserving to be retained—if retained at all—solely on the ground of present convenience" (Henry S. Nash). As Prof. Nash says, the term "higher" offends people by suggesting a kind of superiority. Dr. C. A. Briggs (*Intr.*) explains in a very interesting way the questions which the Higher Criticism has to answer and the scientific principles by which it determines the questions. The questions are four. (1) As to the integrity of the writings; (2) As to the authenticity of the writings; (3) As to literary features; (4) As to the credibility of the writings. The principles are six. (1) The writing must be in accordance with its supposed historic position as to time and place and circumstances. (2) Differences of style imply differences of experience and age of the same author: or, when sufficiently great, differences of author and of period of composition. (3) Differences of opinion and conception imply differences of author when these are sufficiently great, and also differences of period of composition. (4) Citations show the dependence of the author upon the author or authors cited, where these are definite and the identity of the author cited can be clearly established. The other two principles relate to: (5) Positive testimony as to the writing in other writings of acknowledged authority; and (6) The silence of authorities as to the writing in question. As to Silence, there are a number of considerations. (a) Silence is a lack of evidence when it is clear that the matter in question did not come within the scope of the author's plans and purposes. (b) Silence is an evidence that the matter in question had certain characteristics which excluded it from the author's argument. (c) The matter lies fairly within the author's scope, and it was omitted for good and sufficient reasons which may be ascertained. (d) The silence of the author as to that which was within the scope of his argument was unconscious and therefore ignorance is implied. (e) When the silence extends over a variety of writings of different authors, of different classes of writings and different periods of composition, it implies either some strong and overpowering external restraint such as divine interposition, or ecclesiastical or civil power; or it implies a general and widespread public ignorance which presents a strong presumptive evidence regarding the reality and truthfulness of the matter in question. See further C. A. Briggs, 1906. See also for the history: C. A. Briggs, *Hex.;* Archibald Duff, *History of O.T. Crit.*, 1910; M. R. Vincent, *Text. Crit.*

CRITICISM, LOWER. The explanation of the expression "Lower Criticism" will be found under CRITICISM, TEXTUAL and CRITICISM, HIGHER.

CRITICISM, TEXTUAL. The critical examination of the text of documents. "One of the most necessary parts of the investigations of historians is to criticise the documents on which their researches are based, in order to be certain that the text which they are using really represents the original writing of the author. This criticism is usually known as *Textual criticism*, for the obvious reason that it deals with the *text* as opposed to the subject-matter. It is less commonly termed the *Lower* as opposed to the *Higher* criticism, which deals not with the text as written by the author or editor of the document in question, but with the sources and methods used by him in making the text. Thus Higher criticism approaches the subject at a point *higher* up the stream of its existence" (K. Lake). The critical study of manuscripts shows that corruptions have often crept into texts. The critic has to try to decide how these corruptions have arisen. In some cases a scribe or copyist has introduced changes on his own account through not understanding his copy. In other cases a text has been deliberately altered or corrupted because it seemed to contain something improper (unorthodox or profane). The Jewish scribes did not hesitate to make such alterations. In yet other cases corruptions are purely the result of accident. A word may be written twice over by mistake (dittography). When two clauses or lines end with the same or similar syllables, a copyist's eye may easily pass from the first to the second (homoioteleuton). Again, the same word may be written once when it ought to be written twice (haplography). Textual criticism classifies and compares manuscripts, noting their differences. It compares the text as quoted by various writers with the text of the original document. For instance, the quotations of the Old Testament found in the New Testament are carefully compared with the original Hebrew; the quotations of the New Testament in the writings of the Fathers of the Church are carefully compared with the original Greek. Textual criticism also compares the versions or translations of a document with the original (or the supposed original). In this way it often appears that the translator had before him a text different from the supposed original, and the true original text can be reconstructed. Valuable evidence may also be supplied by the examination of Lectionaries and Liturgies. In poetical compositions, textual criticism may attain important results by a careful study of the metre and its requirements (so, *e.g.*, in the Book of Isaiah). Something may also be gained in prose, as well as in poetical, compositions, by studying the ancient system of measuring books by the line, and the line by syllables (Stichometry). See F. Buhl; M. R. Vincent; K. Lake, *The Text of the N.T.*

CROCODILE. One of the sacred animals in ancient Egypt. Donald A. Mackenzie (*E.M.L.*) notes that "even the crocodile was associated with the worship of the corn god; in one of the myths this reptile recovers the body of Osiris from the Nile."

CROSIER. The crosier or pastoral staff which now serves as a bishop's emblem of office or symbol of authority may have developed out of an ordinary walking-staff. It may, however, have been suggested by the short hooked staff (*lituus*) which the Roman augurs bore. In any case, it did not become prominent as the symbol of a bishop until after the tenth century. It is like a shepherd's crook, being a long staff with a hook at the upper end. For a time it was borne also by abbots. A bishop held it, with the crook turned outwards, in his left hand; an abbot held it, with the crook turned inwards, in his right hand. The Anglican Prayer Book of 1549 directs that whenever the bishop celebrates the Holy Communion in the church or executes any other public ministration he shall have his pastoral staff in his hand, or else borne or held by his chaplain. The pastoral staff of an archbishop terminated in a floriated cross, instead of in a crook; that of a patriarch in a cross with two transverse bars; that of the Pope in a cross with three transverse bars. See Benham; Edward L. Cutts; the *Cath. Dict.*

CROSS. The cross in one form or another has been found to have been a wide-spread religious symbol in pre-Christian times. It was used, for instance, in ancient Egypt, Babylonia and Assyria, Crete, and Greece. In the palace of Knossos in Crete Sir Arthur Evans discovered an equilateral cross in marble, which he calls a "fetish cross." This, he thinks, occupied a central position in the Cretan shrine of the Mother Goddess. "A cross of orthodox Greek shape was not only a religious symbol of Minoan cult, but seems to be traceable in later off-shoots of the Minoan religion from Gaza to Eryx" (quoted by Donald A. Mackenzie, *Crete*). It it found on Babylonian cylinders, and as an amulet on

Assyrian necklaces. Mackenzie notes that the Maltese cross first appears on Elamite pottery of the Neolithic age. The "swastika," another form of cross, also known as the gammadion or crux gammata has been found at Knossos in Crete, at Troy, and at Cyprus; and appears on Greek pottery about the year 800. In the Christian era it reappears in the catacombs of Rome and elsewhere. It is found frequently, as Reinach says (*O.*) in the Buddhist art of India and China. Houssay and Elliot Smith think that the figure may have been derived from conventionalized representations of the octopus. The latter points out that a remarkable picture of a swastika-like emblem has been found in America. "The elephant-headed god sits in the centre and four pairs of arms radiate from him, each of them equipped with definite suckers" (*Dr.*, p. 175). Camden M. Cobern notes that among the early Christians a magic power came to be ascribed to the cross and other symbols for Christ. In a Christian tomb discovered in Palestine in 1913 "the most prominent features of the decoration were a garland of flowers surrounded by a cross and a cock." Here "the cross was probably merely an ornament, but the cock as 'herald of the dawn' almost certainly symbolized the hope of a future life." See Maurice A. Canney in the *Encycl. Bibl., s.v.;* O. Zoeckler, *The Cross of Christ*, 1877; M. Brock, *The Cross: Heathen and Christian*, 1880.

CROWN OF THE LAW. One of the names given to the sacred chest in which in Jewish synagogues the Torah (Law) is kept.

CRUSADES. The wars known as the Crusades were so called because the Christians who took part in them wore the cross as a badge. It was long a popular idea that the Crusaders' eagerness to gain possession of the Holy Land was due purely to an outbreak of religious zeal and unselfish chivalry in the twelfth century. But, as H. B. Workman points out (Hastings' *E.R.E.*), the conflict was simply a new form of an old struggle between East and West. "The conflict between Crescent and Cross was bound to be renewed under a new form, with a new champion of Christendom, and in a wider arena, no longer as a frontier war, but one of inter-continental character." There was of course at first a large amount of religious enthusiasm. But in course of time the enterprise degenerated, first into "a romantic tournament between the Christian knight and the Moslem warrior" (Schaff-Herzog), and then into what was little more than a commercial undertaking. To the eleventh and twelfth centuries the East was "what the New World was to the Elizabethan sailors" (H. B. Workman). "Motives of commerce, wealth, adventure, and religion were united." For convenience, the Crusades are usually divided into seven. The First Crusade (1096-1099) was decided upon at the Council of Clermont (Nov. 1095) under Pope Urban II. Before the main expedition was ready, a lawless multitude set forth under Peter the Hermit, Walter the Penniless, and Walter de Poissy, and met with disaster. The main Crusade was led by Godfrey of Bouillon, Hugh of Vermandois, Robert of Normandy, Robert of Flanders, Raymond of St. Gilles and Toulouse, and others. The Crusaders captured Antioch, and eventually Jerusalem (July, 1099). On the 22nd of July, 1099, Godfrey of Bouillon was elected king of Jerusalem or "Advocate of the Holy Sepulchre." His death occurred in July, 1100. The Second Crusade (1147) was due to the conquest of Edessa by the Muhammadans under 'Imād-al-Dīn Zengi, or Zanghis (Latinized, Sanguineus, 1127-1146). It was inspired by the preaching of St. Bernard of Clairveaux in France and Germany, and was led by the Emperor Conrad III. of Germany and King Louis VII. of France. The Germans under Otto of Freising met with disaster near Laodicea, and Louis was routed in Phrygia. The whole crusade was a failure, and the feeling against St. Bernard was very bitter. "He saved his fame as an inspired prophet by declaring the crusading armies unworthy of victory, and the defeat a divine punishment of their sins" (Schaff-Herzog). The Third Crusade was caused by the capture of Jerusalem by Kurd Saladin (Salāh-al-Dīn, *b.* 1137), Vizier of Egypt, in October 1187. The new crusade was preached by Pope Gregory VIII., and his call to arms was answered by Frederick Barbarossa, Emperor of Germany, Philip Augustus, King of France, and Richard I. (Cœur-de-Leon), King of England. The French king quarrelled with Richard and returned home. Richard I. severely defeated Saladin at Arsuf, but never succeeded in capturing Jerusalem. Ultimately he made terms with Saladin, by which the Christians were allowed free access to the Holy Sepulchre. Frederic Barbarossa was drowned during the crusade, but after the death of Saladin (March, 1193), the Germans gained a great victory. The Fourth Crusade was preached by Pope Innocent III. The Crusaders assembled at Venice; but Venice, indifferent to all motives except gain, demanded for their transfer to the Holy Land a greater sum than they were able to pay. They went therefore first to Dalmatia, and then to Constantinople, which they conquered in April, 1204. Venice had as a matter of fact by treaty with the Sultan of Egypt undertaken to divert the crusade. In 1212 Pope Innocent summoned a new crusade. "He was answered by the children." "In France arose a movement in 1212 which even the government was not able to suppress. Thousands of children, boys and girls, often of the tenderest age, took the cross, and rushed in feverish enthusiasm towards the Holy Land. Some swarms reached Italy; and there they melted away, by hunger and disease, in the waves, and in the slave-markets" (Schaff-Herzog). The Fifth Crusade was preached by Innocent III. in 1215, and the cross was taken by Andrew II. of Hungary (1217) and by the Emperor Frederick II. (1220). Frederick II. was excommunicated by Pope Gregory IX. for delaying to take the field, and in consequence could not prevail upon the Military Orders to fight under him. But he contrived to obtain the cession of Jerusalem, Bethlehem, and Nazareth, and in 1229 crowned himself King of Jerusalem. In 1244, however, the Templars and Hospitallers were defeated by the Charismians, allies of the Sultan of Egypt, and Jerusalem was sacked. The Sixth Crusade was led by Louis IX. of France (1248), who, however, never succeeded in reaching Jerusalem. He was defeated and captured on his way to Cairo. To secure his release, France had to pay a heavy ransom. In spite of this, he started on a new crusade, the Seventh Crusade, in 1270. As a preliminary he invaded and besieged Tunis. He died in August of the same year during the siege. Edward of England went to Tunis in October of the same year, and succeeded in saving Acre from the Muhammadans. The Crusades led to the institution of various orders of military monks. See Schaff-Herzog; Hastings' *E.R.E.*

CRYSTAL-GAZING. What is known as crystal-gazing consists in looking fixedly into a crystal, or into a mirror, or into water in a vessel or pond. Many persons who do this fall into a kind of daze or trance and see visions. There are reports of such visions in the Proceedings of the Society for Psychical Research. The phenomenon may be explained as due to the working of the subconscious mind. William James mentions the case of a lady who had the power of seeing these visions. "Miss X. has this susceptibility in a remarkable degree, and is, moreover, an unusually intelligent critic. She reports many visions which can only be described as apparently clairvoyant, and others which beautifully fill a vacant niche in our knowledge of subconscious mental operations. For example, looking into the crystal before breakfast one morning she reads in printed characters of the death of a lady of her acquaintance, the date and other circumstances all duly appearing in type. Startled by this, she looks at the 'Times' of the previous day for verification, and there among the deaths are the identical words which she has seen. On the same page of the 'Times' are other items which she remembers reading the day before; and the only explanation seems to be that her eyes then inattentively observed, so to speak, the death-item, which forthwith fell into a special corner of her memory, and came out as a visual hallucination when the peculiar modification of consciousness induced by the crystal-gazing set in." As Andrew Lang says, crystal-gazing in one form or another has been practised in most countries, and among primitive folk has served to increase the influence of priests and medicine-men. Where crystal-gazing is not understood, the visions seem to be supernatural. See T. J. Hudson; William James, *The Will to Believe*, 1908; Hastings' *E.R.E.*

CUCHULAINN. The Cuchulainn or Cuchullin who figures so prominently in the legends of ancient Ulster would seem to have been originally a solar hero or deity. "When in his full strength no one could look him in the face without blinking. The heat of his body melted snow and boiled water" (Squire). We are told that when he was a child he changed his name from Setanta to Cú Chulainn, "Hound of Culann." See Charles Squire, *Myth*.

CUERAVAHPERI. A Mexican deity, goddess of fertility and rain. At an agricultural festival held in her honour a victim was flayed, and the priest, arrayed in the skin, performed a ceremonial dance.

CULDEES. The Culdees appear as a religious order in the ancient British Church. They are mentioned chiefly in connection with Ireland and Scotland, and are not heard of after 1332 A.D. Their origin seems in fact to have been Irish. Culdees is a popular and later form of the original name. It was suggested by Culdeus, a term first used (A.D. 1526) by Hector Boece. The original Irish name seems to have been Céle dé "companion *or* servant of God" (compare Deicola). This assumed the Latinized forms Colidæi in Ireland, Calledæi and Keledei in Scotland, and Colidei in England. Culdees hardly seems to have been a general term for anchorites. "At first having the marks of anchorites, they gradually take on the appearance of secular canons . . . we find them filling a subordinate 'Levitical' position in cathedral establishments, chiefly engaged in the choral parts of the worship; they became especially associated also with charitable care of the sick and poor, and the distribution of alms. The latter seems to have been one of their earliest and most characteristic traits" (T. Jones Parry, *E.R.E.*). T. Jones Parry sees in the Culdees, not the drooping remnant of the disappearing Celtic Church, but "a recrudescence, a burst into flame of the old Celtic religion, stimulated perhaps by conflict with the rival Roman institution." The name, he thinks, was given by the people, and implies special devotion and piety, "a revival of religion at some given period, and not decay." See Schaff-Herzog; J. H. Blunt; Hastings, *E.R.E.*

CULLAVAGGA. A Buddhist sacred book, one of the Khandhakas, in the first division of the Canon. See CANON, BUDDHIST.

CULTUS. The term Cultus means veneration or worship, or in particular that form of public worship in which the special character of a religion is manifested most clearly. The Christian forms of cultus have been most elaborated in the Roman Catholic Church. In the more general sense of the term Roman Catholics distinguish three kinds of cultus—latria (Gk. *latreia*), dulia (Gk. *douleia*), and hyperdulia. Latria is the worship due to God alone. Dulia is the secondary veneration paid to saints and angels. Hyperdulia is that higher veneration which is paid "to the Blessed Virgin as the most exalted of mere creatures, though of course infinitely inferior to God and incomparably inferior to Christ in His human nature" (*Cath. Dict.*). See the *Cath. Dict.*; Brockhaus.

CUMBERLAND PRESBYTERIAN CHURCH. An American religious body which arose in Cumberland County, Kentucky, as the result of a "revival" under James McGready of the American Presbyterian Church. The revival began in 1797, and was so successful that more ministers than could be supplied were needed. To meet the need the Cumberland Presbytery ordained certain persons who had not had the usual education and training. This caused dissensions in the synod of Kentucky, and in 1806 the presbytery was dissolved. In 1810 the Cumberland Presbytery was re-organized by Finis Ewing, Samuel King, and Samuel McAdow as an independent presbytery. Its theology was mainly Calvinistic, but the doctrine of election and reprobation was rejected. "In the year 1813 the Cumberland Presbytery had become so large, that it divided itself into three presbyteries, and constituted the Cumberland Synod. This synod, at its sessions in 1816, adopted a confession of faith, catechism, and system of church order, in conformity with the principles avowed upon the organization of the first presbytery. The Confession of Faith is a slight modification and abridgment of the Confession of Faith of the Presbyterian Church. The Larger Catechism was omitted, and also some sections of the chapter on "God's Eternal Decrees." The form of government is Presbyterian" (Schaff-Herzog). In 1826 a College was established at Princeton, Kentucky. This was transferred in 1842 to Lebanon, Tenn., where a Cumberland University was founded. The University was divided into four branches, preparatory, academic, law, and theological. See Schaff-Herzog; J. H. Blunt.

CUNNINGHAM LECTURESHIP. A lectureship founded in 1862 by William Binny Webster, of Edinburgh, in memory of William Cunningham, D.D., Principal of the Free Church College, Edinburgh, and Professor of Divinity and Church History. The purpose was to advance the Theological Literature of Scotland. The Lecturer has to be a minister or Professor of the Free Church of Scotland, but occasionally a minister or Professor from other denominations may be appointed. He holds the lectureship for not less than two and not more than three years. He is at liberty to choose his own subject within the range of Apologetical, Doctrinal, Controversial, Exegetical, Pastoral, or Historical Theology, including what bears on Missions, Home and Foreign, subject to the consent of the Council. The lectures must be delivered publicly at Edinburgh, and must not be fewer than six in number. They must be printed and published within a year after delivery at the risk of the lecturer.

CURATE. In the Church of England the word Curate originally denoted a clergyman to whom was committed the cure of souls, that is to say the charge of a parish. The word is so used in the Prayer Book and its rubrics. In France the term is still so used, the incumbent of a parish being the Curé, while his assistant has the title Vicaire. In England a Curate now means one who is licensed to assist the incumbent of a parish. His correct description, however, is Assistant-curate. The incumbent is now called the Vicar (*q.v.*) or Rector (*q.v.*). The term Curate is not much used by Roman Catholics. But it is common in Ireland, where it denotes a priest who acts under the parish priest. See Benham; the *Cath. Dict.*

CURIA ROMANA. In its stricter sense the Curia denotes "the authorities which administer the Papal Primacy" (*Cath. Dict.*). In its wider sense, it denotes the body of authorities and functionaries who form the Papal Court, including the Congregations of Cardinals and the Cardinal Secretary of State. See the *Cath. Dict.*

CUTHBERT GOSPELS. A manuscript of the Gospels belonging to Lindisfarne and dating from the eighth century A.D. St. Cuthbert (*d.* 687), after being abbot of Lindisfarne, was made bishop (684). The manuscripts are now in the British Museum. "They are written in an Anglo-Saxon script, and contain between the lines a series of Northumbrian glosses" (C. R. Gregory).

CUYCHA. Cuycha was one of the deities worshipped by the ancient Peruvians, the rainbow, attendant on the sun and moon.

CYBELE. Cybele was originally a Phrygian deity, a goddess of fruitfulness. She was called also Agdistis after a sacred rock Agdus on Mount Dindymus, and Dindymene after the mountain itself, on which she was worshipped. Her priests were eunuchs. The Greeks identified her with Rhea, originally a Cretan goddess, and gave her Rhea's title, the "Mother of the Gods." As Rhea was accompanied by her Curetes, earth-born demons, so Cybele was attended by her Corybantes, priests who went into a frenzy on the festivals of the goddess. The Corybantes danced wildly to the music of flutes, horns, drums, and cymbals. Cybele had also mendicant priests "who roamed from place to place, as inspired servants and prophets of the Great Mother" (Seyffert). About 204 B.C. the worship of Cybele was brought to Rome, where she was called the "Great Mother." Her priest were called Galli (emasculated), and the chief of them or arch eunuch became known as the Archi-Gallus. A temple of the goddess was built on the Vatican Mount. Early in the second century A.D. sacrifices called the Taurobolium (*q.v.*) and the Criobolium (*q.v.*) were instituted in connection with the worship of Cybele. The offerer was cleansed from pollution and born again through a kind of baptism with the blood of bulls and rams. According to Augustine, Cybele was called the Virgo Coelestis. She is described also as a Saviour, and as healing little children by magical songs. According to another legend, her father exposed her as an infant on the mountain Cybelus, where she was suckled by panthers and other wild beasts. See O. Seyffert, *Dict.*; J. M. Robertson, *C.M.*; *P.C.*

CYNICS. The school of Greek philosophers known as Cynics was founded by Antisthenes of Athens (444-368 B.C.), who in later life became a disciple of Socrates. He founded his new School after the death of Socrates, and taught that as far as possible men should be independent of ordinary human needs. His clothing was an old cloak; his bed was the bare earth; his furniture consisted of a sack, a staff, and a bowl. The name Cynic is either derived from Cynosarges, the gymnasium in which Antisthenes taught, or was suggested by the mode of life of the Cynics, which, according to their opponents befitted a dog (*kuōn*) rather than a man. The Cynics claimed to be the true representatives of the teaching of Socrates, and they made a great impression on the Stoics (see STOICISM). They have been described as a kind of "mendicant order in philosophy." Their doctrines led them to flout and defy the conventionalities of life, to become self-sufficient and anti-social. They wished men to live in accordance with Nature. "They glorified the state of nature with inexhaustible eloquence and ingenuity, and they never wearied of anathematising the pernicious influence of civilisation" (Gomperz, *Greek Thinkers*, quoted by W. L. Davidson). The ideal man of Antisthenes was Diogenes of Sinope. Yet Cynicism at its best has a large element of the finest idealism. Anthisthenes teaches that pleasures of the world are not real pleasures, and that mere money is not real wealth. "You cannot buy uprightness with *material* coin; but you may be wealthy, though poor and lacking such coin, in *spiritual* riches. 'I hold to the belief,' he says, 'that wealth and poverty lie not in men's estate but in men's souls,' 'wealth of my sort will make you liberal of nature.' The soul is the great thing, and its health the first concern; and the discourse on this text that he gives is an advocacy of the wisdom, for the soul's sake, of sitting loose to the pleasures of the world, of moderating and suppressing one's desires, of finding the source of happiness and peace in the mind and inward being, not in external circumstances or the so-called good things of life, which are variable and uncertain and which perish in the using, leaving one unsatisfied" (W. L. Davidson). See William L. Davidson, *The Stoic Creed*, 1907; C. J. Deter; Max B. Weinstein, *Welt- und Leben-anschauungen*, 1910.

CYRENAICS. A school of Greek philosophers founded by Aristippus the Elder of Cyrene (365 B.C.). The philosophy seems to have been systematized by Aristippus the Younger, the grandson of Aristippus the Elder, since the latter left no writings. It has also been called Hedonism. "Its chief points were: (1) that all human sensations are either pleasurable or painful, and that pleasure and pain are the only criterions of good and evil; (2) that pleasure consists in a gentle, and pain in a violent motion of the soul; (3) that happiness is simply the result of a continuous series of pleasurable sensations; (4) that actions are in themselves morally indifferent, and that men are concerned only with their results" (*Chambers's Encycl.*). See *Chambers;* C. J. Deter.

D

D. God D is a designation used by anthropologists for a deity depicted in the MSS. of the Mayan Indians of Central America. In his hieroglyph, amongst other things a starry sky is represented by dots; and, like the Water-goddess I, he is depicted as wearing the serpent head-dress. This suggests that he was a moon-deity.

DABAIBA. The goddess Dabaiba was one of the deities worshipped by the ancient Americans. She was feared and propitiated, before the time of the Aztecs, as one who had power to control the thunder and lightning. To win her favour human victims were sacrificed. After being killed, they were burned "that the savoury odours of roasting flesh might be grateful in the nostrils of the goddess" (Bancroft). She was, it was said, the mother of the Creator. Her son, the Creator, mediated between the people and his mother. When rain was wanted, it was to him that the prayers were made. Bancroft mentions that "when the needs of the people were very urgent, the chiefs and priests remained in the temple, fasting and praying with uplifted hands; the people meanwhile observed a four-days' fast, lacerating their bodies and washing their faces, which were at other times covered with paint. So strict was this fast, that no meat or drink was to be touched until the fourth day, and then only a soup made from maize-flour." See H. H. Bancroft; J. M. Robertson, *P.C.*

DĀDŪ PANTHĪS. A modern Hindu sect. The founder, who flourished about A.D. 1600, was Dādū, a disciple of Rāmānanda; but the religious works of the sect are based on the precepts of the great reformer Kabīr (see KABĪR PANTHĪS). Monier-Williams describes them as being, like the Sikhs (see SIKHISM), Vaishṇava Theists. Some of their principles and precepts, as given by H. H. Wilson and E. W. Hopkins, are as follows: "He is my God who maketh all things perfect. O foolish one, God is not far from you. He is near you. God's power is always with you. . . . All things are sweet to them that love God. I am satisfied with this, that happiness is in proportion to devotion. . . . Sit ye with humility at the feet of God, and rid yourselves of the sickness of your bodies. From the wickedness of the body there is much to fear, because all sins enter into it. Therefore let your dwelling be with the fearless, and direct yourselves toward the light of God. For there neither sword nor poison have power to destroy, and sin cannot enter." See Monier-Williams; E. W. Hopkins; and R. V. Russell.

DĀGABAS. Dāgaba is the Pāli name for the casket in which the Buddhists placed the relics of their great saints. In course of time the word came to denote not only the casket but also the monument (Stūpa) in which the casket was placed (Pagoda). See STŪPAS and PAGODAS.

DAGAN. A Babylonian deity. Dagan appears as one of the gods before the time of Hammurapi. Afterwards we find the name used as the equivalent of Bel (*q.v.*). Anu and Dagan are sometimes mentioned instead of Anu and Bel. Eventually, however, Dagan disappeared altogether. It has been suggested that Dagan is the same as the Philistine god Dagon. He seems to have been regarded as the god of earth. See Morris Jastrow. *Rel.*

DAGDA. One of the gods worshipped by the ancient Celts in Ireland. It is thought that his name meant the "good god." He "played the seasons into being with his mystic harp" (Squire). He resembled the god Māth. One of his sons was Angus. See Squire, *Mythology*, 1906.

DAIKOKU. Daikoku figures in the religion of Japan known as Shintōism (*q.v.*) as the chief of the household gods. His image is to be found in every home. He is the leader and guide of all men, to whom offerings and incense are given continually. Those who have to earn their own living seek to propitiate him perpetually. "He is short and stout, wears a cap like the cap of Liberty, is seated on rice-bags, holds a mallet in his right hand, and with his left clutches the mouth of a sack which he carries over his shoulder" (I. Bishop). See "Shintôism" in *R.S.W.*

DAIRY-TEMPLES. The Todas, a tribe which inhabits the Nīlgiri plateau in India, have an elaborate dairy ritual. In connection with this they have what have been described as dairy-temples. "In addition to the dairies which in form resemble the dwelling-huts, the Todas keep up as dairy-temples certain curious conical edifices, of which there are said to be four on the Nīlgiri plateau, viz., at the Muttanād mand, near Kotagiri, near Sholūr, and at Mudimand. . . . The edifice at the Muttanād mand (or Nōdrs), at the top of the Sigūr ghāt, is known to members of the Ootacamund Hunt as the Toda cathedral. It has a circular stone base and a tall conical thatched roof crowned with a large flat stone, and is surrounded by a circular stone wall. To penetrate within the sacred edifice was forbidden, but we were informed that it contained milking vessels, dairy apparatus, and a swāmi in the guise of a copper bell (mani). The dairyman is known as the varzhal or wursol. In front of the cattle-pen of the neighbouring mand, I noticed a grass-covered mound, which, I was told, is sacred. The mound contains nothing buried within it, but the bodies of the dead are placed near it, and earth from the mound is placed on the corpse before it is removed to the burning-ground" (E. Thurston).

DALEITES. A religious sect, the followers of David Dale (1739-1806). David Dale was a weaver by profession. In conjunction with Richard Arkwright (1732-1792) about 1784 he erected cotton-mills at New Lanark, and became wealthy. He also became noted for his philanthropy. At first his religious views seem largely to have been in harmony with those of John Glas (1695-1773), who founded a sect of independent presbyterians at Dundee (see GLASSITES). But he came to differ from Glas to some extent, and therefore founded a congregation of his own in Glasgow and acted as its minister. The Daleites differed from the Glassites mainly in matters of discipline. "The Daleites did not keep aloof from other Christian bodies with the exclusiveness (so distinctive of petty sects) with which the Glassites regarded them, and they entertained somewhat different views respecting the office of elders, particularly holding that the apostolic description of an office-bearer, as being "the husband of one wife," forbade only the having more than one wife at the same time, while the Glassites generally held that an elder was disqualified for office by re-marriage after a first wife's death" (J. H. Blunt). Dale's daughter married Robert Owen (1771-1858). See J. H. Blunt; and the *D.N.B.*

DAMIANITES. The followers or school of Damianus or Damian, the Monophysite patriarch of Alexandria (570 A.D.). Damianus was accused of being a tetratheist, that is to say a worshipper of four Gods. Damianus maintained "that the Father is one, the Son another, and the Holy Ghost another, but that no one of them is God as such: they only possess the subsisting divine nature in common, and each is God, in so far as he inseparably participates in it" (Hagenbach). God Himself is the *autotheos*. See Hagenbach; J. H. Blunt.

DAMKINA. A Babylonian deity. The goddess Damkina appears sometimes as the consort of Ea (*q.v.*). The name means "lady of the earth." Ea and Damkina are appealed to by king Agumkakrimi and asked to grant him long life. Sargon calls her "Belit ilâni," the mistress of the gods. See Morris Jastrow, *Rel.*

DAMODAR. One of the names of the Hindu god Krishna.

DAMONA. One of the deities worshipped by the ancient Celts. Damona was the goddess of cattle. The name seems to be connected with a word either for "ox" (Irish) or "sheep" (Welsh): and Anwyl suggests that it is perhaps that of an ancient totem sheep or cow, just as the goddess Epona (*q.v.*) was originally perhaps a mare. A Celtic goddess is sometimes associated with a Celtic god. Whether they are to be regarded as mother and son, or as brother and sister, or as husband and wife is uncertain. The god who is paired with Damona is Borvo (*q.v.*). See Anwyl; Reinach, *O.*

DANCERS. The sect known as the Dancers made its first appearance, on the Lower Rhine, in 1374. The dancing was in honour of St. John, whose name the dancers introduced into their exclamations. They were "a crowd of men and women dancing hand in hand, either in pairs or in a circle, on the streets, in the churches, in private houses, wherever they might be, without shame, without rest, hour after hour, until they dropped from sheer exhaustion" (Schaff-Herzog). The movement spread throughout the Low Country and into France. "Children left their parents, and joined the wandering, crazy throng; wives forgot their houses, maidens their duties; all classes sent recruits." See Schaff-Herzog.

DANCING. Dances, or movements allied to dancing, have been practised widely in religious rites and ceremonies from very early times. Rhythmic movements of the body, to the accompaniment of musical instruments, however simple, seem to have been regarded as the most natural means of expressing both pious joy and devout sorrow. It seems also to have been felt that such movements served to put the worshippers in tune with the Infinite (to use a modern phrase). In a less refined form, as among dancing Dervishes, they have as a matter of fact been employed for the purpose of producing a frantic religious fervour, a divine ecstasy (see ECSTASY). According to a modern view of the matter, "the slow, measured, reverential movements characterising all religious rites of nearly every creed and race, have for their spiritual purpose the cultivation of repose and the economisation of the Infinite Force coming through man, so that it shall work the best results for him" (Prentice Mulford, *The Gift of Understanding*). In early Egypt and Babylonia religion seems to have provided the principal occasions for dancing. Thus dancing was first developed as an art in the processions of Apis, the black bull. The dancing of the Arabs is proverbial. Tristram (*Eastern Customs*) saw Mohammedans "leaping, bounding, swaying their arms and whirling round in time to the din of drums, trumpets and cymbals which followed them." As they danced, "the men chanted or rather yelled, verses of the Koran." The Circumcision Feast (*muzayyin*) was an occasion for manifesting joy by means of dancing. Dances have been a prominent feature in the worship of Krishṇa and Śiva in India. This kind of homage has been specially paid to Śiva in his character of lord of dancing. "Further, it is well known that in ancient times women were dedicated to the service of the temples, like the vestal virgins of Europe. They were held to be married to the god and had no other duty but to dance before his shrine. Hence they were called the god's slaves (*devadâsî*), and were generally patterns of piety and propriety" (Monier Williams, *Religious Thought and Life in India*). Among the Hebrews, dancing seems to have been practised in the earliest times. It was never entirely abolished. They danced in the vineyards on the Day of Atonement. On the Feast of Tabernacles the men performed a torch-dance. "They danced with torches, throwing them into the air and catching them again, often performing prodigies with a dexterity acquired by long practice" (Delitzsch, *Iris*). In the Old Testament itself we are told that on one occasion "David danced before the Lord with all his might" (II. Samuel vi. 14); and a psalmist exclaims, "Let them praise his name in the dance: let them sing praises unto him with the timbrel and harp" (Psalm CXLIX. 3). The Greeks devoted themselves to the art with peculiar zeal. "A whole world of dreams peopled the poetic Greece of long ago. In the hush of forests, before sacred altars, in sunshine, under starlight, bands of maidens crowned with oak-leaves, garlanded with flowers, passed dancing in honour of Pan, of Apollo, of Diana, of the Age of Innocence, and of chaste wedlock" (G. Vuillier, *A History of Dancing*). The Romans followed the example of the Greeks. But in ancient times dancing was practised solely in connection with religious rites and festivals. "Nemo fere saltat sobrius, nisi forte insanit" (Cicero, *Pro Mur.* vi. 13). In China, in ancient times, as in other countries, dances were performed during a funeral. It was commanded "that the Officers of the Shields at Great Funerals arrange the implements used at the execution of dances, and at the interment take them up, to store them away in the grave" (*Cheu li*, quoted by J. J. M. de Groot). The prevalence of dancing among primitive folk or savages is well known (so in Polynesia; see Gill, *From Darkness to Light in Polynesia*). See, in addition to the works already mentioned, R. Voss, *Der Tanz und seine Geschichte*, 1869; Lilly Grove, *Dancing*, 1895; *Encycl. Bibl.*

DAND DEVI. An Indian deity, the protector of men against the attacks of wild beasts, worshipped by the Gadbas, a primitive tribe belonging to the Vizagapatam District of Madras.

DANIEL, BOOK OF. Daniel is usually spoken of as a prophet, and it might have been expected that the Book of Daniel would be found in the second division of the Hebrew Canon of the Old Testament (*q.v.*); but as a matter of fact the book is included among the *Kethubim* (or Hagiographa). The book is really of a peculiar character, compared with the other books of the Old Testament. It is an example within the Canon of a class of literature which became very popular in later Judaism, Apocalyptic Literature (*q.v.*). The second part of the book records the visions of Daniel, which are supposed to have been seen in the time of Nebuchadnezzar (605-562 B.C.); the first part consists of ordinary narrative. Chapter i. tells how Daniel and his three friends were taken to Babylon in the reign of Jehoiakim, king of Judah, and were trained by command of Nebuchadnezzar in the language and learning of the Chaldeans. In chapter ii. we learn how by a kind of supernatural wisdom Daniel interpreted a dream which troubled Nebuchadnezzar and baffled his magicians. Chapter iii. describes how the three friends of Daniel, Hananiah, Mishael, and Azariah were cast into a burning fiery furnace for refusing to worship the golden image set up by Nebuchadnezzar, and how they were unharmed. In chapter iv. Daniel again appears as the successful interpreter of a dream which could not be interpreted by the Chaldeans. Chapter iv. describes an episode which has become proverbial. While Nebuchadnezzar was feasting, some mysterious handwriting appeared on the wall of the banqueting-hall, which Daniel alone was able to explain. In chapter vi. we learn how Daniel fell a victim to a plot devised by the nobles of King Darius, and how Daniel was cast into a den of lions, but was unharmed. Chapter vii. gives Daniel's account of his vision of the "four beasts," which are explained to mean four kingdoms. Chapter viii. gives the "horn" vision, in which, it is thought, the "little horn" represents Antiochus Epiphanes. Chapter ix. gives first a prayer of Daniel, and then the angel Gabriel's explanation of the seventy years of desolation predicted by Jeremiah, which is that they denote seventy "weeks of years." The book closes with a revelation concerning the future made to Daniel by an angel. Part of the Book of Daniel, as we have it, is in Aramaic (chapters ii. 4 *b*—vii. 28). This has suggested to some scholars that originally the whole book was in Aramaic. J. D. Prince, on the other hand, thinks that originally the whole book was written in Hebrew and translated into Aramaic. Then part of the Hebrew original was lost, and the gap was filled from the Aramaic translation. In any case, the style of the Book of Daniel is late, and there are other indications, internal and external, of lateness of date. The book must have been composed some centuries after the time of Nebuchadnezzar (605-562 B.C.). "It is practically certain that it was composed between the years 168 and 165 B.C., to encourage the faithful who were suffering in the persecution inaugurated by Antiochus Epiphanes" (G. H. Box). A. Kamphausen points out (*Encycl. Bibl.*) that the name Daniel is rare in the Old Testament. It is curious that in Ezra's time there was a priest named Daniel who had as his contemporaries a Mishael, an Azariah, and a Hananiah. This is "a coincidence of rare names which led Bleek to conjecture that our author had thrown back the contemporaries of Ezra by more than a century in order that he might represent them as living in the time of the 'exile' at a heathen court, and showing an example to his countrymen under the oppression of the heathen." See *Encycl. Bibl.;* S. R. Driver; C. Cornill; G. H. Box; O. C. Whitehouse; and the Commentaries by J. D. Prince (1899) and S. R. Driver (1900).

DANU. Danu or Donu was the name of an ancient Celtic deity. The name is the Gaelic equivalent of the British Dôn (*q.v.*).

DARBYITES. The followers of John Nelson Darby (1800-1882). In 1827 Darby became a Plymouth Brother. In 1847 he became the leader of a party within the community of the Plymouth Brethren. The Darbyites have also been called Separatists. See the *D.N.B.*

DĀRU'L HARB. A name given by the Muhammadans to any country which belongs to infidels, and has not been subdued, or to "a country in which peace has not yet been proclaimed between Muslims and unbelievers." The expression means "The Land of Warfare." It is distinguished from "The Land of Islâm" or Dâru'l Islâm (*q.v.*). See F. A. Klein.

DĀRU'L ISLĀM. A name given by the Muhammadans to one of the great divisions of the world. The expression means "The Land of Islâm." It denotes any country which has been subdued by Islâm, and in which the laws of Islâm prevails. The opposite expression is "The Land of Warfare," or Dâru'l Harb (*q.v.*). F. A. Klein explains that in certain circumstances the Land of Islâm becomes again a Land of Warfare. "(1) When the country is governed according to the laws of unbelievers instead of the laws of Islám; (2) when the country in question becomes joined to a Land of Warfare and no other Muslim country lies between them; (3) when no more protection remains for either Muslim or Zimmi, though they had, at first, enjoyed protection when the country was conquered by Muslims." On the other hand, "the Land of Warfare becomes a Land of Islám when the laws of Islám are promulgated in it and it is governed in accordance with the same, so that the Friday prayers and Muslim festivals are observed." See F. A. Klein.

DĀSARIS. A small caste of priests and mendicants in India. In the Central Provinces they are identified with the Sātanis, but elsewhere they are regarded as distinct. "The Dāsaris wander about, singing hymns to a monotonous accompaniment upon a leather instrument called *tappai* (perhaps a tabor). They are engaged by some Sūdra castes to sing their chants in front of the corpse at funerals. Others exhibit what is called the *Panda sewai*, that is, they become possessed by the deity and beat themselves over the body with a flaming torch" (R. V. Russell).

DASODA. A Hindu goddess, the foster-mother of Krishna.

DATTĀTREYA. A Hindu deity, one of the two gods (the other being Krishna) worshipped by the Mānbhaos, a caste in India, originally a religious sect or order.

DAVIDISTS. The followers of David of Dinant in the thirteenth century. David of Dinant, of whom little is known, has been regarded as a disciple of Amalrich (see AMALRICIANS). Erdmann, however, thinks it more likely that David "received his inspiration and his pantheism from Moorish commentators of Aristotle. David's doctrines were condemned, with those of Amalrich, at the Synod of Paris in 1209. He is said to have taught that "the *materia prima*, or the substratum of all corporeal things, the *nous* or the principle of all individual souls, and God or the source of the heavenly Essences, were one and the same, because they are indistinguishable in being" (Puenjer). See B. Puenjer: J. E. Erdmann; J. H. Blunt.

DAVIDISTS. One of the names of the followers of David Joris (or Joriszoon, *i.e.* Georgeson; c. 1501-1556). They were called also Jorists (*q.v.*).

DĀWAL MĀLIK. A Muhammadan saint worshipped by the Dhanoje Kunbis. The Kunbis are the great agricultural caste of the Marātha country in India. In Wardha and Berār their customs have been influenced by Islām.

DAZBOGU. Dazbogu was one of the gods worshipped by the ancient Slavs. He was a solar deity.

DEA DOMNANN. An ancient Irish goddess worshipped by the Celts or by the pre-Celtic population.

DEA GARMANGABIS. Dea Garmangabis, as appears from an inscription, was the name of a goddess worshipped by some of the Ancient Teutons.

DEA HARIASA. It would seem from an inscription that Dea Hariasa was the name of a goddess worshipped by some of the Ancient Teutons.

DEA HARIMELLA. Dea Harimella seems to have been a goddess worshipped by some of the Ancient Teutons. The name is found in an inscription.

DEA VAGDAVERCUSTIS. Dea Vagdavercustis was the name of a goddess worshipped by some of the Ancient Teutons. The name appears in an inscription.

DEA VERCANA. The name appears in an inscription. The goddess, Dea Vercana, was worshipped, it would seem, by some of the ancient Teutons.

DECALOGUE. Literally "(the) ten words," a Greek expression for the earliest collection of Hebrew laws. In Hebrew also they are called "the ten words." In English they are commonly known as the Ten Commandments. Two versions (Exodus xx. 1-17; Deuteronomy v. 6-21) or more (Exodus xxxiv. 14-26) are given in the Old Testament, which differ from one another in certain details. It seems clear that "the fact of these differences, if the argument from style were not sufficient to show it, points to the Decalogue having originally existed in a still shorter form. It argues also the freedom with which the compilers, the Elohist and the Deuteronomist, the one in the eighth or ninth, the other in the seventh century B.C., considered themselves at liberty to vary the form in which the fundamental Moral Code was transmitted. Both writers have introduced some touches of individual style and colouring into the explanatory clauses of the longer commandments, e.g. fourth and fifth. They have not thereby impaired the substantial accuracy of their record; but, by leaving impressed upon the Decalogue itself the literary stamp of the age to which they respectively belonged, they showed as conclusively as it was possible for them to show, that, in their days, the most sacred laws of Israel were not yet fenced about with any scrupulous regard for the letter apart from the spirit" (H. E. Ryle). W. E. Addis restores the decalogue of Exodus xx. as follows: 1. Thou shalt have no other gods beside me; 2. Thou shalt not make unto thee any (graven) image; 3. Thou shalt not take the name of Jehovah thy God for a vain end; 4. Remember the sabbath day to hallow it; 5. Honour thy father and thy mother; 6. Thou shalt do no murder; 7. Thou shalt not commit adultery; 8. Thou shalt not steal; 9. Thou shalt not bear false witness against thy neighbour; 10. Thou shalt not covet thy neighbour's house. This decalogue belongs to about the middle of the eighth century B.C. But it is claimed now that an older decalogue is found imbedded in Exodus xxxiv. 10-26. J. Wellhausen has reconstructed this decalogue as follows: 1. Thou shalt worship no other god; 2. Thou shalt made thee no molten gods; 3. The feast of unleavened bread shalt thou keep; 4. Every firstling is mine; 5. Thou shalt observe the feast of weeks; 6. And the feast of ingathering at the year's end; 7. Thou shalt not offer the blood of my sacrifice with leaven; 8. The fat of my feast shall not be left over till the morning; 9. The best of the firstfruits of thy land shalt thou bring to the house of Jehovah thy God; 10. Thou shalt not seethe a kid in its mother's milk. See H. E. Ryle; C. A. Briggs, *Hex.*, 1897; *Encycl. Bibl.*

DECLARATION OF THE CONGREGATIONAL UNION OF ENGLAND AND WALES. A Confession of Faith which appeared in 1833 A.D. and sets forth the "Faith, Church Order, and Discipline of the Congregational or Independent Dissenters." The Declaration has maintained its place as the official manifesto of the Union. "It is prefaced by seven preliminary notes which disclaim for it technical or critical precision, deny the utility of creeds as bonds of union, admit the existence of differences of opinion within the Union, but claim a greater harmony than among Churches requiring subscription" (W. A. Curtis). See William A. Curtis.

DECLARATION OF THORN. A Confession of Faith (1645 A.D.) recognised in Brandenburg and in Poland. "It was the Statement of Reformed Doctrine submitted to a Conference of Lutheran, Reformed, and Roman Catholic representatives, convened by the King of Poland, Vladislav IV., himself a Roman Catholic, in hope to allay his subjects' religious dissensions" (W. A. Curtis).

DEFIXIONES. Leaden tablets used by the ancient Greeks. The tablets were inscribed with the names of persons on whom an injury was invoked. They were "defixed" or bound with a nail. The custom spread to Italy; and similar tablets have been found in England (London, Gloucestershire, Yorkshire). See F. B. Jevons in the *Trans. of the Third Internat. Congress for the Hist. of Religions*, 1908, vol. ii., pp. 131-139.

DEISM. A term which has been used in various senses. "The term is now commonly applied to that view of the relation of God to the world which, in opposition to Atheism, affirms the existence of God, and in opposition to Pantheism, affirms the personal, independent, extra-mundane existence of God, but which at the same time, in opposition to Theism strictly so called, denies the continuous, ever-present action of God upon the world and His activity in it" (B. Pünjer). Pünjer observes that the roots of Deism, which was prepared for in politics by the doctrines of the Levellers and in philosophy by Francis Bacon, "lay in the sober, practical, common-sense character of the English people, and its beginnings took their rise in the characteristic movement of the English Reformation." J. B. Bury (*Hist. of Freedom of Thought*) speaks of the English deists as doing memorable work by their polemic against the authority of revealed religion. "The controversy between the deists and their orthodox opponents turned on the question whether the Deity of natural religion—the God whose existence, as was thought, could be proved by reason—can be identified with the author of the Christian revelation. To the deists this seemed impossible. The nature of the alleged revelation seemed inconsistent with the character of the God to whom reason pointed. The defenders of revelation, at least all the most competent, agreed with the deists in making reason supreme, and through this reliance on reason some of them fell into heresies. Clarke, for instance, one of the ablest, was very unsound on the dogma of the Trinity. It is also to be noticed that with both sections the interest of morality was the principal motive. The orthodox held that the revealed doctrine of future rewards and punishments is necessary for morality; the deists, that morality depends on reason alone, and that revelation contains a great deal that is repugnant to moral ideals."

DELUGE-STORY, BABYLONIAN. In the Babylonian Gilgamesh Epic (*q.v.*) Gilgamesh goes in search of Par-(*or* Ut-)napishtim to find out from him the secret of his immortality. Parnapishtim tells him that no man can escape death. Thereupon Gilgamesh asks how it is that he (Parnapishtim) has become immortal. In reply Parnapishtim tells him the story of a flood from which, as by a miracle, he was delivered. The city Shurippak had become corrupt. The gods determined to bring a deluge upon it. Their resolution was proclaimed by Anu (*q.v.*), Bel (*q.v.*), Ninib (*q.v.*), En-nugi, and Ea (*q.v.*). Parnapishtim is advised to build a ship and to load it with living things of every kind. Ea tells him to explain to the people that he is going to the "deep" to dwell with Ea, because Bel, the god of earth, has cast him out. As for them, a deluge is coming upon them. Parnapishtim builds a ship with six stories, and smears it without and within with bitumen. He then loads it with all that he has, with his family, silver, gold, cattle, etc. When the deluge is about to come, he enters and shuts the door. Then Ramman (*q.v.*) thunders, Dibbarra (*q.v.*), the god of war, lets loose his forces, Ninib works himself up into fury, the Anunnaki (*q.v.*) make their torches flash. The gods themselves tremble at the success of their activities. Ishtar (*q.v.*) groans like a woman in travail, and repents of the evil that has been wrought. The gods weep with her. Not until the seventh day does the storm begin to cease. Parnapishtim looks forth and weeps at the havoc that has been created, the disappearance of mankind. After a time the boat rests on Mount Nisir. Then Parnapishtim sends forth, first a dove, which returns, then a swallow, which returns, and finally a raven, which does not return. Parnapishtim now leaves the ship and offers a sacrifice to the gods. Bel is not allowed to share in it, because he caused the deluge. He, for his part, is angry that anyone should have escaped. He is told by Ninib that this is due to Ea. Ea reproves Bel, and admits that he saved Parnapishtim (or Adra-Khasis) by telling him in a dream the decision of the gods. At length Bel is reconciled. He goes on board the ship and blesses Parnapishtim and his wife. He declares that whereas before they were human, now they shall be gods. Parnapishtim's dwelling shall be "at the confluence of the streams." See Morris Jastrow, *Rel.;* S. Reinach, *O.*

DEMÁI. The name of one of the Jewish treatises or tractates which reproduce the oral tradition or unwritten law as developed by the second century A.D., and are included in the Mishnah (*q.v.*), a collection and compilation completed by Rabbi Judah the Holy, or the Patriarch, about 200 A.D. The sixty-three tractates of the Mishnah are divided into six groups or orders (*sedarim*). Dĕmái is the third tractate of the first group, which is called *Zerā'im* ("Seeds").

DEMIURGE. A term used in Gnosticism (*q.v.*). The Demiurge is the creator of the visible universe. For this purpose he is formed out of psychical substance by Hachamoth (*q.v.*). See VALENTINIANS.

DERCETO. A Syrian fish-goddess. According to Lucian, she was worshipped at Hierapolis. She is to be identified no doubt with Atargatis, in whom, according to Garstang (*The Syrian Goddess*, 1913), we have the embodiment of "that local aspect of the great Nature-goddess that typified the productive powers of waters (in generating fishes, etc.)." Derceto had other famous shrines at Carnion and Askelon. She resembles the Cretan Britomartis, and would seem to have been imported from Crete by the Philistines.

DERVISHES, WHIRLING. The Mowlawiyeh, one of the Dervish orders, have been called the whirling dervishes on account of a sacred dance which they practice. In Constantinople it is practised throughout the year, but in some places only during certain months. "The dancing is said to represent the revolving of the spheres as well as the circling movement of the soul caused by the vibration of its love to God. The participants wear voluminous bell-shaped skirts. After prayers led by the sheikh they file in stately procession before their master, reverentially saluting him with a low bow, each in turn. This function is repeated several times. Then follows the circling. When the dancer glides on to the floor his head is inclined and his arms are stretched out; the fingers of one hand are raised, those of the other are held drooping, symbolical of his being the medium of grace, received from heaven to be dispensed on earth. During the whirling the eyes are shut. As the pace increases the skirts spread out around the dancer like a wheel or disk. When exhausted he takes a rest, but, again resuming, glides into the circle for another round. On the floor there may be several dancing together or not more than one at a time. The dance may last, with brief pauses for prayer, for two hours, at the close of which the sheikh himself takes part" (F. J. Bliss). See T. P. Hughes; F. J. Bliss.

DERVONNAE. Dervonnae, the oak-spirits, was the name given to some goddesses who were worshipped as a group by the ancient Celts. Another group was called Proximae (*q.v.*).

DESWĀLI. A Hindu deity, god of the village, worshipped by the Mundas (also called Kols or Hos), a large tribe in Chota Nāgpur, India.

DETERMINISM. The doctrine of Determinism is opposed to that of the Freedom of the Will. "There is a dogmatic determinism, which, in order to glorify the majesty of God, excludes all other causality from human action but God himself (Luther, *De servo arbitrio*); and there is a philosophical determinism, which explains all human actions as results of surrounding circumstances (La Mettrie). There is a fatalistic determinism, which places God himself in the grip of an iron necessity (the ancient idea of Nemesis, Islam); and there is a pantheistic determinism, which makes even the faintest gleam of human freedom vanish into the darkness of a natural process (the Hindoos, Stoicism, Spinoza)"—Schaff-Herzog. It has been maintained that Determinism is not the only alternative. Other alternatives are Indeterminism (*q.v.*) and Self-determination (*q.v.*). See Schaff-Herzog; Arthur Butler; William James, *The Will to Believe*, 1908.

DEUTEROCANONICAL BOOKS. The Roman Catholic Church accepts (in accordance with the decrees of the Tridentine and Vatican Councils) certain books which are commonly regarded as apocryphal by other Christian Churches. Amongst these books are: Tobit, Judith, Wisdom of Solomon, Ecclesiasticus, Baruch, I. and II. Maccabees. The Old Testament Apocrypha (*q.v.*) are regarded, together with the other books of the Old Testament, as authoritative for dogmatic and ethical teaching. The Church of England, on the other hand, reads them "for example of life and instruction of manners, but yet doth it not apply them to establish any doctrine" (Article vi.). For convenience, however, since the sixteenth century Roman Catholics have used the expression "deuterocanonical of certain books (mentioned above) which are not included in the Jewish Canon (see CANON), and were admitted after the other apocryphal books into the Canon (as understood by Roman Catholics) of the Christian Church. The term "protocanonical" has been used of the books admitted earlier, but the use of the term is considered to be misleading and mistaken. See W. Sanday, *I.*

DEUTERO-ISAIAH. In the Book of Isaiah, chapters xl.-lv. differ so considerably in language and style from chapters i.-xxxix. and lvi.-lxvi. that they have been judged by critics to be of different date and authorship. The historic background is also different. Chapters xl.-lv. have therefore been designated Deutero-Isaiah to distinguish them from Isaiah (i.-xxxix.) and Trito-Isaiah (lvi.-lxvi.). See ISAIAH, BOOK OF.

DEUTERONOMY, BOOK OF. The Book of Deuteronomy, the fifth book in the first division of the Hebrew Canon of the Old Testament (*q.v.*), derives its name from the Septuagint, in which the words in chapter xvii. vs. 18, *mishneh hat-tōrah haz-zōth*, "the copy of this law," are translated *to deuteronomion touto*. Early Christian writers understood the term to mean either supplementary legislation or recapitulation of the law. G. F. Moore points out that to modern critics also it is the Second Legislation in the sense that it is an expansion and revision of older collections of laws such as the codes preserved in Exodus xxi.-xxiii., xxxiv. In the Hebrew Bible the book bears the title 'ēlleh haddebārim (the opening words) or debārim. The book discovered in the temple in the eighteenth year of king Josiah (622-621 B.C.) was not the whole Pentateuch, as used to be thought, but an early edition of the Book of Deuteronomy, which did not comprise the whole of the present book (see BOOK OF THE LAW). Deuteronomy, as we have it, "contains the last injunctions and admonitions of Moses, delivered to Israel in the land of Moab, as they were about to cross the Jordan to the conquest of Canaan; and with the exception of chaps. xxvii., xxxi., xxxiv., and a few verses elsewhere, is all in the form of address. It is not, however, one continuous discourse, but consists of at least three distinct speeches (i.-iv. 40; v.-xxvi.; xxviii.; xxix. f.), together with two poems recited by Moses in the hearing of the people (xxxii. f.). The narrative chapters record doings and sayings of Moses in the last days of his life, and are more or less closely connected with the speeches" (G. F. Moore). Only in a few sections do we detect the sources (JE and P) which have been so largely used in the other books of the Hexateuch. Deuteronomy has a thought, diction, and style of its own, which powerfully influenced a whole school of subsequent writers. This influence is manifest in the Books of Joshua, Judges, Kings, etc. The many resemblances between Deuteronomy and the Book of Jeremiah suggest either that the two books were produced at about the same time, or that Jeremiah was familiar with the ancient Deuteronomy, or even that he was the author of Deuteronomy. According to Moore, evidence of every kind "concurs to prove that the primitive Deuteronomy was a product of the seventh century." It seems to have been written at Jerusalem, both priests and prophets co-operating in its production. Moore thinks the book "will ever stand as one of the noblest monuments of the religion of Israel, and as one of the most noteworthy attempts in history to regulate the whole life of a people by its highest religious principles." To P (the Priestly Writer) have been assigned i. 3, xxxii. 48-52; xxxiv. 1*a*, 5*b*, 7-9; to JE earlier fragments, xxvii. 5-7*a*, xxxi. 14, 15, xxxi. 23, xxxiii., xxxiv. 1*a*, 1*b*-5*a*, 6, 10. To D (the First Deuteronomic Writer) have been assigned i. 1*f*., i. 4-iii. 13; iii. 18-iv. 28; iv. 32-40; v. 1-xxvi. 19; xxvii. 9*f*.; xxviii. 1-xxix. 8; xxx. 11-20; xxxi. 1-13; xxxi. 24-27; xxxii. 45-47; to D² (Second Deuteronomic Writer) iii. 14-17; iv. 29-31; iv. 41-49; xxvii. 1-4; xxvii. 7*b*-8; xxvii. 11-26; xxix. 9-28; xxx. 1-10; xxxi. 16-22; xxxi. 28-30; xxxiv. 11*f*. The Second Deuteronomic Writer would seem to have followed some time after the First. See Moore in *Encycl. Bibl.*; S. R. Driver, *Deut.*, in *I.C.C.*; J. E. Carpenter and G. Harford-Battersby, *The Hexateuch*, 1900; W. R. Harper, *The Priestly Element in the O.T.*, 1905; C. F. Kent, *Israel's Laws*, 1907; G. H. Box; O. C. Whitehouse.

DEVAK. A family god among the Rāmosis, a criminal tribe of the Bombay Presidency. The Devak is represented usually by a tree or a bunch of the leaves of several trees.

DEVI. A Hindu goddess, the earth-goddess, one of the names of the consort of Siva.

DEWĀKI. A Hindu goddess, supposed to have been the mother of Krishna.

DHĀMIS. A Hindu sect, founded by one Prannāth, who flourished towards the end of the seventeenth century. The founder's followers are known also as Prannāthi, and as Sāthi Bhai, brothers in religion, or Bhai, brothers. The name Dhāmi is derived from *dhām*, a monastery. The home of the sect was in the Panna State of Bundelkhand. The great object of the founder was to amalgamate the two religions of Islām and Hinduism. He supplied his followers with a book of faith called the Kulzam Sarup. In this were collected texts from the Korān and the Vedas. The book is supposed to be the only material object of worship. It is placed in all temples, and round it "a lighted lamp is waved in the morning and evening" (Russell and Hira Lāl). In practice, it is said, they worship the boy Krishna. The Dhāmis are strict vegetarians. Their priests are also celibates. The sect has adherents in Nepāl, where they are known as Pranāmi or Parnāmi. See R. V. Russell, vol. i., 1916.

DHAMMAPADA. A Buddhist sacred book, a kind of hymn-book, included in the collection appended to the second division of the Canon. See CANON, BUDDHIST.

DHAMMASAMGANI. A Buddhist sacred book in the third division of the Canon. See CANON, BUDDHIST.

DHARMES. A Hindu deity, the supreme god of the Oraons, an important Dravidian tribe in India, the members of which work as farm servants and labourers. The Oraons sacrifice to him a white cock. "They think that god is too good to punish them, and that they are not answerable to him in any way for their conduct; they believe that everybody will be treated in the same way in the other world. There is no hell for them or place of punishment, but everybody will go to *merkha* or heaven" (Father P. Dehon, quoted by R. V. Russell).

DHARNI. An Indian deity, worshipped as the goddess of good health by the Gadbas, a primitive tribe belonging to the Vizagapatam District of Madras.

DHARTI MĀTA. An Indian deity, Mother Earth. The Baigas regard her as the wife of Thākur Deo, and propitiate her for the sake of the crops.

DHĀTUKATHĀ. A Buddhist sacred book in the third division of the Canon. See CANON, BUDDHIST.

DIANKET. An ancient Irish deity. Dianket or Diancecht was the god of medicine. Legend relates that he was jealous of his own son and killed him. When on his son's grave there sprang up three hundred and sixty-five healing herbs, Dianket spitefully mixed them all up in utter confusion. He seems to have been equivalent to the god who was worshipped by the natives of Gaul as Apollo.

DIATESSARON OF TATIAN. Literally "Through Four," the Greek name of a Harmony of the Gospels made by Tatian (second century). The name indicates that four Gospels were used. The question has arisen: Were they our four canonical Gospels? The Gospel to the Hebrews, for instance, might have been used and not the Gospel of John. Dr. C. R. Gregory, however, points out that as a matter of fact Tatian begins with verses from the Gospel of John. The Harmony gave the gospel in a very convenient form, and was translated into Syriac and other languages. It was widely used. Theodoret (390-457 A.D.), as quoted by Gregory, refers to it thus: "This one [Tatian] also put together the Gospel called Diatessaron, not only cutting away the genealogies, but also the other things so far as they show that the Lord was born from the seed of David after the flesh. And not only the people of his society used this, but also those who follow the apostolical dogmas, not having known the evil tendency of the composition, but using it in simplicity as a short book. And I found more than two hundred such books held in honour in the

Churches among us, and gathering them all together I put them aside, and introduced instead of them the Gospels of the four evangelists." The Diatessaron was not in favour with the orthodox, because its author became a kind of Gnostic. But, as Dr. Gregory says, "from Theodoret's description it is perfectly clear that only our four Gospels were used in the Diatessaron. He would have pounced like a vulture on any sign of an apocryphal Gospel in it." The Diatessaron of Tatian, which was translated from a Syriac text into Arabic, "did a long service, and will certainly not have corrupted the Christianity of any reader, much as Theodoret was exercised about its use in the Churches near him." Ephraem the Syrian (*d.* 373) wrote a commentary on the work. James Aphraates, another Syrian writer, who lived about the middle of the fourth century, also commented on it. "As handed down in Arabic, it differs, both in text and in arrangement, from the text commented on by Ephraem; and both of these differ from the text commented on by Aphraates" (E. A. Abbott in *Encycl. Bibl., s.v.* "Gospels," § 107). The explanation seems to be that "at a very early period the Diatessaron was revised in the interests of orthodoxy." See C. R. Gregory.

DIBBARRA EPIC. Dibbarra or more correctly Girra is a Babylonian deity. He was a god of war and pestilence, a solar deity who in course of time came to be identified with Nergal (*q.v.*). In the Epic of Dibbarra he figures as the warrior, the god of war. He is attended by the god Ishum (*q.v.*), who describes his deeds. Dibbara sends a "governor" to attack Babylon. He is to kill young and old alike. Through the power of Dibbarra great slaughter is executed in the city. The blood of the inhabitants, the "servitors of Anu and Dagan," flows like water. On another occasion Dibbarra afflicts Uruk. The just and the unjust suffer alike. Then Ishum proposes a war against the gods, and of men against men, a kind of Armageddon (*q.v.*). Dibbarra consents. Country shall fight against country, house against house, man against man, brother against brother. Afterwards the Akkadian shall come and conquer all. By the Akkadian Hammurapi seems to be meant. After Dibbarra has wrought great havoc, Ishum seeks to appease his wrath. His entreaties are successful, and Dibbarra promises to bless those who acknowledge his power, praise, and honour him. The Babylonians seem to have hung in their houses tablets on which Dibbarra was glorified. See Morris Jastrow, *Rel.*, and cp. *Civ.*

DIDACHE. A shortened form (the first Greek word) of the title of "The Teaching of the Lord by the Twelve Apostles to the Gentiles," an early Christian work (probably written before 100 A.D.), discovered by Bishop Philotheus Bryennios in the library of the Jerusalem Monastery of The Most Holy Sepulchre in the Phanar of Constantinople.

DIGAMBARAS. The Digambaras or "sky-attire men" are one of the two main bodies into which the Jains (*q.v.*) have split up. They were so called because on principle they refused to wear any clothing. They argued that where there is no sin, there can be no shame.

DIGHANIKĀYA. One of the Buddhist sacred books in the second division of the Canon. See CANON, BUDDHIST.

DIKTYNNA. A Cretan goddess.

DIMOERITAE. Dimoeritae seems to have been another name for the followers of Apollinarius. Epiphanius called the Apollinarians Dimoeritae because, of the three parts that constitute perfect humanity (*sōma, psuchē, nous*), they held that Jesus assumed only two (*dimoiria*). Epiphanius says that "some (heretics) denied especially the perfect Incarnation of Christ, some asserted His Body consubstantial with His divinity, some emphatically denied that He had ever taken a soul; others not less emphatically refused to Him a mind" (*Haer* lxxvii.). J. M. Fuller thinks that probably the Dimoeritae existed as a sect only for a few years. See Wace and Piercy.

DINKAR. The sun, or he who makes the days, one of the names of the Hindu god Vishnu.

DIRONA. A goddess worshipped by the continental Celts, and regarded by the Romans as the consort of Mercury.

DISCIPLES OF CHRIST. The Disciples of Christ are a religious body which was founded in the United States by Thomas Campbell. Campbell was originally a minister of the Seceder Presbyterian Church in Ireland, who went to America in 1807. There his eagerness to reunite different bodies of Presbyterians brought him into conflict with the Presbytery. He left his own Church, and founded what he called the "Christian Association of Washington." His son, Alexander Campbell, after being educated at the University of Glasgow, became assistant to his father. In 1812 he and his father were baptized by immersion. "I have set out to follow the apostles of Christ, and their Master," said Alexander Campbell, "and I will be baptized only into the primitive Christian faith." In 1823 he began to publish a periodical, "The Christian Baptist," in which he pleaded for the restoration of the primitive gospel and practice. A complete union with the Baptist Churches seemed to be in sight, but in 1827 the Baptist Churches withdrew fellowship, and the Disciples became a separate body. "The special plea of the Disciples is the restoration of original apostolic Christianity, and the union of all Christians. They insist, that as, in the beginning there was one spiritual brotherhood—one body with one Lord, one faith, and one baptism—there should be but one to-day; that all party names, creeds, and organisations should be abandoned, and the Church have no creed but the Bible, no law but the Lord's, no name but the Master's; and that, as the basis of that primitive union was the common teaching of Christ and the Apostles, nothing is now essential to the conversion of the world but the union and co-operation of Christians with the apostles' teaching or testimony" (Schaff-Herzog). The Disciples have made great progress. They now have many representatives in England and Australia, and display missionary activity in China, India, Japan, Africa, the Philippines, Mexico, and the West Indies. "The creation of new educational foundations, the maintenance of an aggressive journalism, the organization of missionary and philanthropic agencies, and the encouragement of an effective evangelism in the churches have increased the numbers, intelligence, and consecration of the Disciples, until at the present time they are fifth among the great evangelical bodies of America" (Hastings' *Encyclopaedia*). See Schaff-Herzog; Blunt; Hastings' *E.R.E.*

DISCIPLES OF ST. JOHN. Another name for the Mandæans (*q.v.*).

DISCIPLINARIANS. A name given to those who in the reign of Queen Elisabeth wished to alter the constitution of the Church of England and to substitute for it the Presbyterian system of Calvin. They wished to abolish all ecclesiastical officers except presbyters. Their leader was Thomas Cartwright (1535-1603), who in 1565 attacked the use of the surplice. In 1569 Cartwright was appointed Lady Margaret Professor of Divinity at Cambridge, but the next year he was deprived of his professorship. The great work of Richard Hooker

(1554?-1600), "The Laws of Ecclesiasticall Politie," were directed against the Disciplinarians. See Blunt; the *D.N.B.*

DISHAI DEVI. An Indian deity, the goddess of the sheep-pen, worshipped by the Gadarias (also called Gădris), the occupational shepherd caste of northern India. When they enter the sheep-pen in the morning, they make obeisance to the sheep. This seems to indicate that Dishai Devi is really the deified sheep.

DIS PATER. Dis Pater, that is to say Dives Pater or Father Dives, was a name given by the Romans to a god who corresponded to the Greek god Pluto. His worship was commanded by the Sibylline Books. He was the ruler of the lower world, who stuns the dead with a mallet. Since he is represented as wearing a wolfskin, Reinach thinks that, like Orcus, he was originally a wolf. Caesar applies the name Dis Pater to a god worshipped by the Gauls as their ancestor. C. Squire suggests that this deity was Beli (*q.v.*), the father of the gods, consort of Dôn, the mother of the gods. The Gallic Dis Pater is represented in his images as wearing a wolf-skin and holding a long mallet. Another of his names Sucellus, means "the good striker." The deity was a nocturnal god. This, with the wolfskin, again implies that originally he was a wolf. See Edward Anwyl; Squire, *Myth.;* Reinach, *O.*

DIVINE SCIENCE. Another name for Christian Science (*q.v.*). One of Mary Baker Eddy's publications is entitled *Rudimental Divine Science* (1891; new edition, 1910).

DIWALI FESTIVAL. An Indian religious festival, known in Bengal as the Kali Poojah. In that province many victims, particularly sheep, goats, and buffaloes, are sacrificed. Elsewhere, on this occasion the Banias, a caste of bankers, moneylenders, and dealers in grain, etc., worship Ganpati or Ganesh, their principal deity, in conjunction with Lakshmi, the goddess of wealth. They open new account-books and worship them, and they pay reverence to a silver rupee or an English sovereign. See R. V. Russell and R. B. Hira Lāl.

DOCETISM. The term Docetism is derived from the Greek word *dokein* ("to seem, to appear"). The Docetæ were so called because they maintained that Jesus' body was not real or material, but only the appearance (*dokēsis*) of a body. They were opposed by Ignatius (*d.* 104 or 115?) or in the Ignatian Epistles, and even, it has been held, by the author of the Epistles of John (I. John i. 1-3, ii. 22, iv. 2 ff., II. John vii.). Docetism was of the nature of Gnosticism (*q.v.*). The Docetæ regarded matter as evil. "They rejected the idea of physical birth, as in the last degree degrading and unworthy of a divine saviour and teacher; the idea that he was begotten by a human father, of a woman, being, of course, still more repulsive to them" (F. C. Conybeare). See Blunt; *Prot. Dict.;* F. C. Conybeare.

DOCTRINAIRES. In 1562 Marcus de Sadis Cusani of Milan founded in Rome an association "Padri della Dottrina Christiana" with the object of instructing the people in the catechism. In France Caesar de Bus, a priest and Canon of Cavaillon, founded independently a similar association, the "Doctrinaires" or "Pères de la Doctrine Chrétienne." The members of this association were sent forth to catechise everyone they met in the streets. Caesar de Bus himself went from house to house catechising. The constitution of the association was confirmed in 1597 by Pope Clement VIII. See Schaff-Herzog.

DOCTRINE AND ERUDITION FOR ANY CHRISTIAN. The title of a book of Christian doctrine, published in 1537. It came to be known as the "King's Book" (*q.v.*).

DOCUMENTARY HYPOTHESIS, THE. This expression is used of one of the theories put forth by the Higher Critics (see CRITICISM, HIGHER) to explain the composition of the Hexateuch. It was noticed that in the book of Genesis certain sections might be distinguished from others by the use of the divine name Jehovah (correctly Yahweh) instead of Elohim, and, besides, that there were often duplicate accounts of the same events. In 1753 Jean Astruc claimed that a number of documents could be recognised in Genesis. He thought that at least nine had been used by the compiler of the book, two large and nine smaller documents. This is the Documentary Hypothesis, and as a whole it has held its ground. In 1798 C. D. Ilgen discovered that two documents (instead of one) were characterised by the use of the divine name Elohim, but the discovery did not receive due attention until it was revived by H. Hupfeld of Halle (1853). Ilgen believed Genesis to be composed of seventeen documents, all of them probably the work of three writers. J. G. Eichhorn, who published an Introduction to the Old Testament in 1780 (second edition 1787), gave more attention to the use of the divine names, systematized the new method, and called it the Higher Criticism. He also applied similar methods to Exodus, Leviticus, Numbers, and Deuteronomy, recognising in the three former the priests' code, and in the latter the law book of the people. The Documentary Hypothesis was followed for a time by the Fragmentary Hypothesis (*q.v.*). See C. A. Briggs, *Hex.*, 1897; Archibald Duff, *O.T. Crit.*

DODEKAPROPHETON. A Greek designation of the twelve Minor Prophets (*q.v.*). At an early date the Minor Prophets were regarded by the Jews (cp. Philo) as forming one book, and were spoken of collectively.

DOG, THE. The sacrifice of dogs is mentioned as a heathen practice in the Book of Isaiah (lxvi. 3). According to Al-Nadîm, they were sacred among the Harranians. The Harranians offered sacrificial gifts to the dog, "and in certain mysteries dogs were solemnly declared to be the brothers of the mystæ" (Robertson Smith, *R.S.*). Jacob of Sarug mentions "the Lord with the dogs" as one of the deities of Carrhæ. In the legend of the invention of the purple dye, the Tyrian Heracles or Melcarth is accompanied by a dog. Among the Muhammadans black dogs are supposed to have a demoniac character. In a hymn to the Egyptian god Amon-Ra it is said that "the gods gather as dogs round his feet." To the Greek goddess Hecate dogs were sacrificed. "In this case the victim was the sacred animal of the goddess to which it was offered; Hecate is represented in mythology as accompanied by demoniac dogs, and in her worship she loved to be addressed by the name of Dog. Here, therefore, the victim is not only a sacred animal, but an animal kindred to the deity to which it is sacrificed" (Robertson Smith). The cow and the dog are held in special reverence by the Naodas, a small caste in India. "The dog is sacred as being the animal on which Bhairava rides, and their most solemn oaths are sworn by a dog or a cow" (R. V. Russell and R. B. Hira Lāl). In Babylonia, it should be added, an important significance was ascribed to the movements and actions of dogs in divination. "A white dog entering a palace means siege of a city; a yellow dog, that the palace will escape disaster; a dog of mixed colours, that the enemy will plunder the palace. Dogs barking at the gates prognosticate a pestilence, mad dogs the destruction of the city, howling dogs the overthrow of the city" (Morris Jastrow, *Civ.*).

DOLCINISTS. The followers of Dolcino, a militant leader of the APOSTOLICALS (*q.v.*, 2).

DOLICHENUS. The god Jupiter Dolichenus takes

his name from Doliche near Aintab, which was north-west of Hierapolis. His worship seems to have been introduced to the Roman army by Syrian soldiers. Since he is associated with a bull and his consort with a lion, the god and goddess may be identified with the two chief deities of the Hittites.

DOLLS. In the course of excavations carried on at Tell Sandahannah in Palestine, the most striking find consisted of sixteen little human figures which date from the early Christian era. "These little 'revenge dolls' are bound in fetters of lead, iron, etc., through which the owners hoped to work magic on their enemies" (Camden M. Cobern). Robertson Smith notes that the Romans substituted puppets of rushes or wool for human offerings in the Argea and the worship of Mania (*R.S.*).

DOMINICA DE ROSA. Another name for Lætare Sunday (*q.v.*), the fourth Sunday in Lent.

DOMINICANS. An Order founded by Domingo de Guzman (1170-1221), or Dominic, of Calaruega, in Old Castile. In 1194 he was made a canon of the chapter of Osma. Here he helped Bishop Diego of Osma to introduce the rule of St. Austin. In 1204 he accompanied the Bishop to France, where they came into contact with the Albigenses. Bishop Diego was anxious to try to convert these heretics, and obtained permission from Pope Innocent III. to remain in Languedoc for a time. After his return and death, Dominic continued the work, aided by some earnest sympathisers, but without much success. At length Dominic decided that a new order was needed. He gathered a band of men round him in 1215, and then requested Pope Innocent III. to sanction the foundation of an order. The Pope did not approve of adding to the already existing orders. He declined at first to accede to Dominic's request. At length, however, he was prevailed upon to grant it "on the condition that the brotherhood should adopt the rules of some older, already recognised, order, and organize itself in the simple form of colleges of canons" (Schaff-Herzog). The rule adopted was that of St. Austin, with the addition of statutes of the Praemonstratensians. The members were to practise perpetual silence, to fast almost without intermission, to abstain altogether from meat, except in illness, to wear woollen garments, to accept poverty, etc. Their dress consisted of a black cassock and rochet. This was afterwards changed to "a white habit and scapular, with a long black cappa or mantle" (*Cath. Dict.*). In 1216 Pope Honorius III. fully confirmed Dominic's order, giving to it the title Fratres Prædicantes or Preaching Brothers. The order soon spread to Spain and France. Visiting Rome, Dominic was appointed Magister Sacri Palatii, Master of the Sacred Palace in the Pontifical Court, and this office has been held ever since by a Dominican. But he was not yet satisfied with the progress of his work. He felt that a more complete renunciation of worldly things was needed. Consequently, at a chapter-general held in 1220 "the order renounced the possession of property in any form or shape, and declared for complete poverty, and the daily begging of the means indispensable to the sustenance of life" (Schaff-Herzog). This renunciation had the desired effect. Greater progress was made, and at the chapter-general in 1221 as many as sixty monasteries were represented. After this the movement spread in every direction. In 1230 two chairs were held by Dominican monks in the University of Paris. The task of teaching, in particular, led to rivalry between the Dominicans and the Franciscans (*q.v.*), and the "Summa Theologiæ" of the Dominican Thomas of Aquinum became the cause of endless disputes. "The system of St. Thomas was so vast as to afford scope for the labour of many commentators and explicators, and a school hence arose, consisting chiefly of Dominicans, named Thomists. Franciscan theologians, among whom the chief was Duns Scotus, raised objections to portions of the teaching of St. Thomas: the problems of Realism and Nominalism were imported into the controversy; and the contentions of Scotists and Thomists, taken up often by men of inferior mental calibre, tended at last to make men weary of the scholastic philosophy altogether" (*Cath. Dict.*). In 1425 the prohibition as to the possession of property was revoked by Pope Martin V. This resulted in numerous bequests. Many churches and monasteries were built, and the Dominicans have enriched the world with some of the best examples of Gothic architecture. See Schaff-Herzog; the *Prot. Dict.*; the *Cath. Dict.*

DOMPELERS. A name by which the Tunkers (*q.v.*) are known in the Netherlands.

DON. In Welsh documents the gods of the Celts in Ancient Britain are sometimes referred to as the "Children of Dôn." The Goidels (Gaels) seem to have revered Danu or Donu (the Dôn of the Brythons or Britons) as the mother of the gods. They called the gods the "Tribe of the Goddess Danu." Dôn appears as the father of several of the heroes in British mythology. Gwydion and Govannon are sons of Dôn. Arianrod is a daughter of Dôn and of Beli (*q.v.*). The latter would seem to have been paired with Dôn as the father of the gods. See Squire, *Myth.*

DONAR. The name by which Thor (*q.v.*), the Teutonic god of thunder, was known to the High Germans.

DONATISM. Donatism was not a heresy, but a schism. During the persecution of the Christians under Diocletian, they were called upon to deliver up any copies of their sacred books they might have. Often they preferred to suffer martyrdom, and there grew up an unhealthy enthusiasm for the martyr's crown. Mensurius, Bishop of Carthage, tried to discountenance this. When called upon to deliver up his sacred books he hid them and substituted some heretical works. Mensurius died A.D. 311, and was succeeded by his archdeacon, Caecilian, who shared his views. Caecilian was consecrated by Felix, Bishop of Aptunga. The consecration provoked a storm which had long been brewing. The opponents of Mensurius and Caecilian warmly protested. They made three charges: (1) that Cæcilian was not worthy to hold the office; (2) that he had not been elected by the bishops of the whole province of Numidia; and (3) that he had not been properly consecrated, since Felix himself had been a *traditor*. Secundus, Bishop of Tigisis and Primate of Numidia, supporting the opponents of Cæcilian, consecrated Majorinus as a rival bishop. About A.D. 315 Majorinus was succeeded by Donatus Magnus, who was so called by his followers to distinguish him from another bishop of the same name. "Under him the sect became an organised community extending over all the provinces of North Africa, almost every town having its rival bishop and congregation" (*Prot. Dict.*). The aim of the Donatists was a good one. They felt that the Church ought to be pure, and consequently ought to exclude unworthy members. "Donatism represents an attempt—the final one for a thousand years—to resist the process of secularization by which the Church was gradually transformed from a community of holy persons into an institution of mixed character, offering to secure salvation for its members by means of grace over which it had sole control. . . . Insistence on a minimum of personal worthiness in the clergy at least was 'the last remnant of a much more earnest conception' of the Church. It was met by the defenders of Catholicism with a new emphasis on the objective character of the sacraments, and upon the holiness of the Church apart from the holiness or otherwise of its members and clergy. It was in the controversy with the Donatists, therefore, that the Catholic doctrine of the Church was completely developed" (*E.R.E.*). The case of the Donatists was examined and rejected a number of times by the orthodox Church. But they could not easily be suppressed, in spite of the fact that in course of time they split up into many sects (*e.g.*, Rogatists, Maximianists, Primianists). "As Donatus sought to divide Christ, so was Donatus divided by the divisions which arose daily amongst his own followers" (St. Augustine). In A.D. 411 the Emperor Honorius arranged for a conference of Catholic and Donatist bishops at Carthage. Marcellinus, pro-consul of Africa, presided, and 286 Catholic and 279 Donatist bishops were present. The president pronounced sentence against the Donatists. He warned all men to hinder their assembling in towns and villages, and to restore the churches to the Catholics. "Every bishop of the community of Donatus must, on his return to his home, return to the one true church, or at least not impede the faithful execution of the law." After this many of the Donatists returned to the Church. In A.D. 414 sterner measures were taken against those who remained. The Donatists continued to return to the Church in increasing numbers. They revived somewhat towards the end of the sixth century, but after the Saracen invasion in the seventh century they disappeared. Optatus, Bishop of Milevis in Numidia, wrote a treatise in seven books "On the Schism of the Donatists." See K. R. Hagenbach; J. H. Blunt; the *Prot. Dict.;* the *Cath. Dict.;* Wace and Piercy; Hastings' *E.R.E.*

DONGAR DEO. A Hindu village deity, god of the hills, worshipped by the Korkus, a Kolarian tribe in India.

DONNELLAN LECTURES. The Donnellan Lectureship takes its name from Mrs. Anne Donnellan who left a legacy in 1794 "for the encouragement of religion, learning, and good manners." It was founded by the Provost and Senior Fellows of Trinity College, Dublin. The lecturer delivers six lectures or sermons.

DORJE. The Dorje ("thunderbolt") is an instrument which forms part of the equipment of Buddhist monks in Tibet. It is thought that it represents the thunderbolt dropped by the Hindu god Indra (*q.v.*) from heaven, or that originally it was an instrument belonging to Gautama Buddha. In the latter case it is supposed that on Gautama's disappearance from earth, it floated through the air from India to Tibet. It is much used in the exorcism of evil spirits. Monier-Williams describes it as consisting of "a short bar, about four inches long, the two extremities of which swell out in globular form, or like small oval cages formed of hoops of metal." Hackmann describes it as being "a peculiar metal instrument, with a handle in the middle, at each end of which is fastened a bundle of four or eight birds' claws, tied together at the points." The instrument is waved to and fro. See Monier-Williams; H. Hackmann.

DOSITHEANS. One of the sub-sects of the class of Russian dissenters known as Popovtzi. The Dositheans, or followers of Dosithey, denounced both the Czar and the Church of Russia.

DOUKHOBÓRS. A Russian sect. The name means spirit-wrestler, and was used to describe those who were considered by the Orthodox Russian Church to be wrestling against the Holy Spirit (cp. the name Iconobórs, image-wrestlers, those who objected to the use of icóns or images). The sect began to come into prominence during the second half of the eighteenth century. It was the policy of Catharine II. to tolerate them, but they suffered some measure of oppression, being regarded as enemies of Church and State alike. At first they were tolerated by Paul also, but afterwards some of them were arrested and punished. Under Alexander I. (1801-25) they were allowed to congregate and to form a settlement at the "Milky Waters" near the sea of Azof. Here they organised themselves into an industrial, economic, and religious community. Their teaching was not enshrined in books, but was transmitted orally and in large part secretly. They acknowledged one God, believed in the pre-existence of souls, and denied the transmission of Adam's sin. They held Jesus to be the Son of God in the same sense in which other men are the sons of God, and believed that he is born and rises again spiritually in the heart of each believer. Men are enlightened by the inward word rather than by an external revelation. This inward light is smothered in most men by luxurious food and clothing. All men are equal, and, being the children of God, they do not require a Government. It is forbidden to go to war, to carry arms, and to take oaths. The true Church of God is world-wide and invisible, and has no common creed. The Scriptures are symbolical and mystical. The only true priest is the Christ within; no external priest is necessary; external sacraments have no efficacy. Marriage again needs no external ceremony. For the most part the Doukhobórs have been vegetarians, total abstainers, and non-smokers. During the years 1841-1844 the Doukhobórs were transported to the Caucasus. Here they formed three settlements, and, devoting themselves to agriculture and cattle-breeding, became prosperous. In course of time a dispute arose about their leadership, and two parties, the "Large Party" (followers of Peter Verígin) and the "Small Party" (followers of L. V. Kalmikóva's brother). Peter Verígin brought about a religious revival, which tended to enforce greater strictness. This conduced to aggravate trouble when the enforcement of conscription (introduced into the Caucasus in 1887) was in question. From being passive conscripts, the Doukhobórs became (after 1895) uncompromising objectors, with the result that they had to submit to persecution and punishment. They were imprisoned, flogged, even killed sometimes, and their settlements were broken up. So great was the suffering that Leo Tolstoy and others started a public agitation against the persecution. The result was that in 1898 the Doukhobórs, with certain exceptions, received permission to leave Russia. Funds were then raised and arrangements made for the migration of 7,363 members of the community to Canada. Here they established a Commune, called the "Christian Commune of Universal Brotherhood." This or the "Universal Community of Christian Brotherhood" is the name they prefer to be known by. See Aylmer Maude, *A Peculiar People: The Doukhóbors*, 1904; and cp. John F. Fraser, *Canada as it is;* W. Fairweather, *The Background of the Gospels*, 1908.

DOVE, THE. The dove had quite a peculiar sanctity among the Semites. Among the Syrians it was the holiest of birds, and anyone who touched it was taboo for a day. It was sacred among the Philistines; and among the Phoenicians, by whom it was associated with the goddess Astarte as her companion. Among the Hittites it was associated with the Goddess-mother. According to Al-Nadim, the Harranians would not sacrifice it. Its sanctity among the Arabs is clear from the fact that there are sacred doves at Mecca. The Hebrews did not use it for an ordinary sacrifice involving a sacrificial meal; but they offered it in sacrifices which were closely analogous to mystical rites. In Cyprus we hear of an earth goddess, who resembles Astarte and Aphrodite, and was known as "Our Lady of Doves." In Babylonia, Egypt, and Crete, again, we find turtle doves associated with the goddess of love. Among the Romans doves were sacrificed to Venus. In Russia the modern peasant never kills a dove, because it is the bird of the Holy Ghost (S. Reinach, *Cults*). In Christian art the dove is used as a symbol of baptism, and of the presence of the Holy Spirit. When doves are depicted drinking from a vase or chalice, they may symbolise the Eucharist also.

DREAM-THEORY. In the words of R. R. Marett, "this theory asserts that the prototype of soul and spirit is to be sought especially in the dream-image and trance-image."

DRUIDS. The Druids were a religious body which flourished in ancient times in Gaul and the British Isles. It is commonly supposed that they were so called because they were oak-worshippers, *drūs* being the word for "oak" in Greek. In this connection it is worth noting that for ordinary purposes they used the letters of the Greek alphabet. But the likeness of *drūs* to Druid may well be a mere coincidence. True, they venerated the oak, and preferred oak groves and oak leaves for their ceremonies and rites. But the worship of trees is a common feature in primitive religion. It is true also that they treated mistletoe with great reverence. "The mistletoe of the oak, which is a somewhat rare parasite, was gathered with great ceremony by the Druids, dressed in white robes; they detached it with a golden sickle, after sacrificing a white bull to the gods, and caught it in white cloths as it fell from the tree" (Reinach, *O.*). But here again reverence for the mistletoe might almost be described as natural. In any case, it was not peculiar to the Druids. In the Teutonic myth of Balder (*q.v.*) all objects were put under oath by Frigg (*q.v.*), not to harm Balder. But the mistletoe, which had escaped notice, was used as an arrow against Balder, and proved fatal to him. Probably the Druids were not so called on account of their reverence for the oak but because of their reputation for wisdom and knowledge. They were "the far-seeing" (dru-vid). This seems to have been the character in which they were known to Caesar. To him they were the learned, or professional, class as distinguished from the military class on the one hand and from the common people, on the other. To others they were even the philosophers as distinguished from those who were mere Seers (*Vates*). Posidonius and Strabo, for instance, discriminate between the three classes: Bards, Seers, and Druids. The Druids seem to have gained the reputation of philosophers through the resemblance of some of their teaching to the Pythagorean philosophy. According to Caesar, the Druids spread from Britain to Gaul about 500 B.C. Reinach thinks that we have evidence in the megalithic monuments that Druidism was fully developed earlier than this. He thinks that it flourished first in the neolithic period, particularly in Ireland. Then it spread to the continent. After the Roman conquest the Druids returned and rejoined their Irish confrères. The religious teaching of the Druids was not committed to writing. Their sacred principles and precepts were transmitted orally. This involved a great effort of memory, and accounts for the fact that the training of a novice lasted twenty years. The head of the clergy was called the Arch-Druid. He was elected for life. The clergy would seem to have ministered not merely as priests and healers, but also as arbitrators, judges, and teachers. Their teaching included astrology and history, as well as theology. The Druids were exempt from military service. According to Caesar, they used in some of their sacrifices great images of wickerwork. Sometimes criminals were placed inside these effigies and burnt. It is doubtful, however, whether human sacrifice was common. It would seem to have sufficed to take a few drops of blood from the victim and to burn only the wickerwork dummy. E. Anwyl thinks that "the use of wickerwork, and the suggestion that the rite was for purifying the land, indicates a combination of the ideas of tree-worship with those of early agricultural life." Suetonius says that the Emperor Claudius suppressed the Druids, but he would hardly seem to have done more than suppress some of their rites, if indeed he even did that. According to Diodorus Siculus, the Druids taught that after a certain number of years the souls of men came to life again and entered into other bodies. They would seem to have taught this kind of metempsychosis at first. Afterwards, however, they seem to have reduced the doctrine to "the migration of souls towards a region in the West" (Reinach). See Edward Anwyl; Reinach, *O.*; *Cultes, Mythes et Religion*, 1904-1908; *Chambers' Encycl.*; cp. J. M. Robertson, *C.M.*, and W. G. Wood-Martin.

DRUZES. A Mohammedan sect which owes its name to a Persian, Darázi. It arose in Syria early in the eleventh century, but its religious teachings had been systematized in Egypt by Khalif al Hákim bi-amr-illáh. The Khalif, supported by two Persians, Hamza and Darázi, had it publicly proclaimed at Cairo A.D. 1029 (A.H. 407) that he was an incarnation and manifestation of God. Darázi was nearly killed by the people for making this announcement. He fled to Mount Lebanon, whence the new faith was propagated. According to its teaching, God, who is a unity, has at different times manifested Himself in human form. Hákim bi-amr-illáh, the last of these incarnations, though he had disappeared A.D. 1033, would appear again and establish his kingdom. See F. A. Klein; and M. Th. Houtsma, *Encycl. of Islam*, 1913.

DUALITY OF MIND. According to T. J. Hudson, the doctrine of duality of mind has become a cardinal principle in the philosophy of many of the ablest exponents of what is called the New Psychology. He distinguishes the two minds in man by designating the one as Objective, and the other as Subjective. The difference between the two is stated as follows. "The objective mind takes cognizance of the objective world. Its media of observation are the five physical senses. It is the outgrowth of man's physical necessities. It is his guide in his struggle with his material environment. Its highest function is that of reasoning. The subjective mind takes cognizance of its environment by means independent of the physical senses. It perceives by intuition. It is the seat of the emotions, and the storehouse of memory. It performs its highest functions when the objective senses are in abeyance. In a word, it is that intelligence which makes itself manifest in a hypnotic subject when he is in a state of somnambulism." As regards the power of Suggestion over these two minds the following propositions are laid down. "1. That the objective mind, or, let us say, man in his normal condition, is not controllable, against reason, positive knowledge, or the evidence of his senses, by the suggestions of another. 2. That the subjective mind, or man in the hypnotic state, is unqualifiedly and constantly amenable to the power of suggestion." Two further propositions are as follows. "1. The objective mind is capable of reasoning by all methods,—inductive and deductive, analytic and synthetic. 2. The subjective mind is incapable of inductive reasoning." But, "given a general principle to start with," the subjective mind "will reason deductively from that down to all legitimate inferences, with a marvellous cogency and power." Another peculiarity of the subjective mind consists in its prodigious memory. "It would perhaps be hazardous to say that the memory of the subjective mind is perfect, but there is good ground for believing that such a proposition would be substantially true." It used to be thought that the subjective mind of a person could only be influenced by another objective mind (Suggestion). But it is now held that the objective mind of a person can influence its subjective mind (Auto-suggestion)—for instance by giving it certain directions just before the person falls asleep. See T. J. Hudson.

DUAT. The name of the underworld in Egyptian mythology. The region the sun traverses after it disappears in the West and before it rises in the East, a region bounded by two mountains. Maspero thought it lay on the same plane as the visible world but was beyond any regions known to the Egyptians. E. Naville thinks it was really thought of as a *lower* world, for, "if we may judge from different expressions which are applied to the Douat, and also from certain representations of it, we must think of it as lying below this world, and of the sun, when he sets, as descending lower than the visible world."

DUDHERA. A god worshipped as the protector of cattle by the Gowāris, the herdsman or grazier caste of the Marātha country in India. The Gowāris worship also the green pigeon, *haryal*.

DUGPA SECT. The Dugpa or Dukpa or Brugpa sect is a sect among the Tibetan Buddhists of the Red-cap school (see RED-CAP BUDDHISTS). Dharma-rāja, the spiritual ruler of Bhutān, claimed the title, "Chief of all the monks of the Dugpa sect." On his seal of office he gives himself a number of other titles, such as Defender of the Faith, Chief of all the Buddhas, Most learned in the holy Laws, An Avatār of God, Absolver of sins, etc. See Monier-Williams; H. Hackmann.

DULHA DEO. An Indian deity, the family god of the Agarias, a caste of iron-smelters and an offshoot of the Gond tribe. He is worshipped also by the cultivating caste, the Agharias, by the Audhelias, and by the Baigas. The Baigas revere him as the god who averts disease and accident. They offer him a reddish fowl or goat.

DUNKERS. An incorrect designation of the American Tunkers (*q.v.*).

DUNKIRK PRAYER-BOOK. A prayer-book published in 1791 for the use of English Protestants at Dunkirk in France. The title is: "The Book of Common Prayer compiled for the use of the English Church at Dunkirk, together with a Collection of Psalms." Attempts to establish a Church at Dunkirk entirely conformable to the Church of England had failed. In 1790 it was decided to open a Church and to call over a Minister from England. In view, however, of the existence of different sects and parties, it was determined to adopt a Form of Prayer of such a character that it might be calculated to offend no one and to satisfy all. Care was taken therefore to omit everything that might offend. The plan followed was that proposed by Dr. Samuel Clarke (1675-1729), Rector of St. James's, Westminster. Other alterations, not suggested by him, but well approved of by the Society for whose use the Prayers were printed, were made. The Liturgy was offered "with a degree of boldness to the examination of the public at large, but especially of the English inhabitants of Dunkirk, who are most concerned in the success of this establishment, which, if it be not conformable entirely to the Church of England, or to any other Church, at least claims affinity to all in everything essential to the proper mode of conducting public worship, and the cultivation of the morals of mankind." The whole management of the new religious establishment or Society was vested in a Committee of twelve members, chosen by the subscribers. See Peter Hall.

DURGĀ. Durgā is one of the deities worshipped by the Hindus. She is represented as the wife of Siva (*q.v.*) and the sister of Vishnu (*q.v.*). Hopkins points out that under various names (Pārvatī, Kālī, Umā, Bhavānī, Satī, etc.) she plays a great rôle in the 'revived' literature. He suggests that "Durgā was probably an independent local deity, subsequently regarded as Siva's female side." In a hymn she is described as the mother of the Vedas and Vedānta. She is known as the "hard" Durgā on account of the terror she inspires. One of the ways by which she used to be propitiated was by the sacrifice of human beings. Men were sacrificed to her yearly. Hopkins thinks that the Thugs (*q.v.*) originated among the worshippers of Durgā or Kālī. On principle they would not shed blood; but as a substitute for this, and as a protest against it, they throttled their victims. See Monier-Williams; E. W. Hopkins; J. C. Oman, *Cults*.

DUSARES. An Arabian deity, identified with Dionysus. He was the consort of Allath. Sometimes he was worshipped in the form of a large square stone.

DUSUQIYEH. An order of Dervishes, founded by Ib'rahim ed-Dusu'qi (*d.* 1278 A.D.), a celibate. The Dusuqiyeh, according to F. J. Bliss, follow ecstatic principles similar to those of the mother order, the Qadiriyeh (*q.v.*).

DUTCH CONFESSION, THE. A Confession or Creed drawn up in 1566. W. A. Curtis speaks of it as being a comparatively obscure work of uncertain origin, and as being of a milder Calvinism than the Belgic Confession of 1561 A.D. (see BELGIUM, CONFESSION OF). "Zwinglian indeed in character, reflecting in its eighteen articles the apologetic purpose of the Belgic Confession, but sharper in its anti-Romanist polemic" (William A. Curtis).

DUTCH REMONSTRANCE, THE. The Dutch "Remonstrance" of 1610 A.D. was a Creed or Confession of five articles, which modified the orthodox Calvinism from the standpoint of James Arminius (*d.* 1609). Drawn up by the preacher Uytenbogaert for presentation to the Estates of Holland and West Friesland, "it represented an even more serious and determined attempt than Amyraldism—its kindred though independent French counterpart—to break down the rigour of supralapsarian and infralapsarian Calvinism" (W. A. Curtis). Condemned by the Synod of Dort, "it exerted an extremely widespread influence, especially throughout the English-speaking world, pervading the Anglican Church and its great Methodist offshoot." See William A. Curtis.

DWYN. Dwyn or Dwynwen, a goddess of love revered by the ancient Celts in Britain, seems to have corresponded to the Roman Venus (*q.v.*). Her character resembled that of the Irish god Angus.

DYLAN. A figure in the mythology of the British Celts, associated with the waves of the sea, and probably a personification of them.

E

E. God E is a designation used by anthropologists for a deity depicted in the MSS. of the Mayan Indians of Central America. That he was a maize-god is shown by his head-ornament, the leafed ear of maize. He may therefore be equivalent to Centeotl, the Aztec maize-god. Schellhas (*Die Göttergestalten der Mayahandschriften*) identifies him with Yum Kaax, an obscure deity who was a lord of harvest.

EA. A Babylonian deity. The god Ea is mentioned before the time of Hammurapi. He became one of a great triad consisting of Anu (*q.v.*), Bel (*q.v.*), and Ea. Ea was a water-god, the giver of wisdom and fertility. As the giver of wisdom, he was also the protector of men against evil, whether this came from gods or demons. He was the god who removed pain, the god of physicians. He was the god of art and sculpture. When the god Marduk (*q.v.*) rose to power he was represented as being the son of Ea, and as having inherited all the virtues and honours of his father. Marduk appears in the Epic of Marduk as the creator of mankind (see MARDUK, EPIC OF), but it is likely that originally this rôle belonged to Ea. He is even said to have assigned to Anu, Bel, and Ea their domains. When he has finished the work of creation and the gods unite in praising him, Ea confers his own name upon him. In the story of the Deluge (see DELUGE-STORY, BABYLONIAN) Ea appears as the opponent of Bel (*q.v.*). Bel wishes to destroy all mankind. But Ea warns Utnapishtim, and advises him to build a boat. When Utnapishtim escapes, Bel is very angry; but Ea succeeds in pacifying him. In that part of the Gilgamesh Epic (*q.v.*) which recounts the adventures of Gilgamesh, Anu, Bel, and Ea are mentioned as the gods who have given him wisdom. The Persian Gulf was sacred to Ea, and in the Adapa Legend (*q.v.*) the fisherman Adapa is said to be the son of Ea, his protector. The god Nin-ib (*q.v.*) is called the first-born of Ea. Nabu (*q.v.*) also is said to be his son. The consort of Ea was Damkina (*q.v.*), but Belit (*q.v.*) also appears as his consort. See Morris Jastrow, *Rel.*

EABANI. One of the characters in the Babylonian Epic of Gilgamesh (see GILGAMESH EPIC). The goddess Aruru (*q.v.*) created him out of a lump of clay. He is a hairy creature who at first lives with animals. Afterwards he forsakes them and goes to Uruk. Here he becomes the companion of Gilgamesh and a hero like him.

EAGLE, TEMPLE OF THE. Reference is made to a "temple of the eagle" or "house of the eagle" in an inscription of Boghaz-Keui, and a double-headed eagle figures on Hittite sculptures. The eagle seems to have been one of the emblems of the chief god of the Hittites. That the eagle should be regarded with awe is natural. E. S. Hartland (*Ritual*) notes that "the Hidatsa of the North American prairies, after hunting eagles, build a sweat-lodge and purify themselves, singing a mystery-song or incantation."

EBELIANS. The followers of the German theologian J. W. Ebel (1784-1861). Ebel was Preacher at Koenigsberg (1816-1839). In 1839 he was deposed for erroneous teaching and immoral living.

EBIONITES. The Ebionites were an early Jewish-Christian sect. The name was derived from a Hebrew word (*'ebhyon*) meaning "poor." It was not chosen, it would seem, because there existed a leader of the sect named Ebion. The Ebionites were so called because they accepted the principle, "Blessed are the poor!" They seem to have arisen after the fall of Jerusalem (70 A.D.). J. M. Fuller (*Dict. of Christ. Biogr.*) rightly distinguishes between two types of Ebionism, an earlier type, Pharisaic Ebionism, and a later type, Essene or Gnostic Ebionism. Pharisaic Ebionism is described in the writings of Justin Martyr, Irenaeus, Hippolytus, Tertullian, and others; Essene or Gnostic Ebionism more especially in the writings of Epiphanius. The Pharisaic Ebionites were far more Jewish than Christian. They attached more importance to the Old Testament than to the New, and looked forward to a millennial kingdom of the Messiah, in which the earthly Jerusalem would be restored. Their ideal of perfection was legal righteousness. They held that Jesus was the Son of Joseph and Mary according to the ordinary course of human generation. But at his baptism, which was the turning-point in his life, he was anointed by election and then became Christ. He was the Christ of God in virtue of his perfect fulfilment of the Law. Naturally therefore all Ebionites must strictly observe the law, for "when Ebionites thus fulfil the law, they are able to become Christs" (Hippolytus, quoted by J. M. Fuller). This observance of the Law included circumcision, the sabbath, the sacrificial offerings, the distinction between clean and unclean food, etc. The Apostle Paul was regarded by the Ebionites as an apostate from the Law, and his Epistles were rejected by them. Their Gospel they called the "Gospel according to the Hebrews." This was a Chaldee version written in Hebrew characters, and is identified by Eusebius with the original Gospel of St. Matthew. The story of the miraculous birth of Jesus is excluded. It has been suggested that the Gospel according to the Hebrews, which was known in Egypt in the time of Trajan, was so called to distinguish it from the Gospel according to the Egyptians, which was in use among the Christians of Alexandria. The Ebionites in course of time even had their own Greek version of the Old Testament. This was made towards the end of the second century by Symmachus. Like the version of Aquila, it follows the Hebrew text exclusively and seems to have been intended for those "who declined the LXX adopted by the orthodox Christians, or the Greek versions of Aquila and Theodotion accepted by the Jews" (*Dict. of Christ. Biogr.*). After Symmachus we sometimes find the Ebionites called by Latin authors of the fourth and fifth centuries Symmachians. It is not always easy to distinguish between Pharisaic and Gnostic Ebionism, but in general the latter is characterised by features due to external influence. They accepted only the Pentateuch as authoritative, dividing the prophets of the Old Testament into two classes. The important class included Adam, Noah, Abraham, Isaac, Jacob, Aaron, Moses, and Jesus. As to Jesus or Christ, "some affirmed that He was created (not born) of the Father, a Spirit, and higher than the angels; that He had the power of coming to this earth when He would, and in various modes of manifestation; that He had been incarnate in Adam, and had appeared to the patriarchs in bodily shape; others identified Adam and Christ. In these last days He had come in the person of Jesus. Jesus was therefore to them a successor of Moses, and not of higher authority" (*Dict. of Christ. Biogr.*). The Gnostic Ebionites did not eat flesh or drink wine. Instead of wine in the Holy Communion, they used water. They practised frequent ablutions, were circumcised, and observed the Lord's Day of the Christians as well as the Sabbath of the Jews. On the other hand, they rejected the sacrifices of the altar. They did not abjure married life. In the time of Epiphanius (*d.* 403 A.D.) the Ebionites are represented as living in Rome, Cyprus, and particularly in the regions along the Dead Sea. They are sometimes called Peratici on account of their settlement at Peraea. See Schaff-Herzog; J. H. Blunt; Louis Duchesne, *Hist.;* Wace and Piercy.

ECCLESIASTES. The name of a book which is in some ways one of the most remarkable in the Old Testament. It is one of the five small works called Megilloth (*q.v.*) or "Rolls" by the Jews. The Hebrew name is Ḳoheleth. This is rendered *Ecclesiastes* by the Septuagint and *Concionator* by Jerome. Both of these words would give the meaning "The Preacher." The form of the Hebrew name is feminine. It might in an intensive sense ("the great orator," margin of Revised Version) be used of a person (cp. Sophereth in Nehemiah vii. 57). In chap. i., verse 1, the book is said to contain "the words of Ḳoheleth, the son of David, king of Jerusalem." In *vs.* 12 the author is represented as saying "I Ḳoheleth was king over Israel in Jerusalem." Ḳoheleth is thus identified with Solomon. A common use of the Hebrew root (to gather or assemble) has suggested that the title is descriptive, meaning "assembly," that is to say, a collection of wise sayings. The tone of the book is pessimistic. All is vanity and sorrow (i. 2, 18; ii. 1, 11, 23; xii. 8). "There is nothing better for a man than that he should eat and drink" (ii. 24). "Who knoweth the spirit of man—Doth it go upwards? or the spirit of beast—Doth it go downward to the earth?" (iii. 21). "But if a man live many years, and rejoice in them all; yet let him remember the days of darkness, for they shall be many. All that cometh is vanity" (xi. 8). Yet the pessimism is by no means a pessimism of abject despair. "A living dog is better than a dead lion" (ix. 4). A young man is exhorted to remember his Creator in the days of his youth (xii. 1); and all are urged to "fear God and keep his commandments, for this is the whole duty of man" (xii. 13). As Prof. O. C. Whitehouse says (*The Books of the Old Testament*, 1910), "the book reflects a period of national depression and hopelessness when the Jews were a subjugated people. It is evidently late, for the Hebrew abounds in Aramaisms and evidences of those later forms that are found in "New Hebrew" or the language of the Mishna. It cannot be much earlier than 200 B.C., and may, in fact, be even later." Ecclesiastes belongs to the third and latest division of the canonical writings, the Kethubim or Hagiographa. Its inclusion in the Canon at all was afterwards a matter of surprise and a subject of controversy. Echoes of this controversy are found in the Mishnah (200 A.D.). In the tractate *Yadaim* (iii. 5), quoted by G. Wildeboer (*Origin of the Canon of the Old Testament*, 1895), we read: "Rabbi Judah [*c.* 120 A.D.] said, Canticles defiles the hands [*i.e.*, is canonical; see CANON, OLD TESTAMENT], but Ecclesiastes is subject of controversy. Rabbi Jose [contemporary of the emperor Hadrian] said, Ecclesiastes does not defile the hands, and Canticles is subject of controversy. Rabbi Simeon said, The school of Shammai was laxer as to Ecclesiastes than the school of Hillel. Rabbi Simeon ben Azzai said, A tradition has been delivered to me from the lips of the seventy-two elders, on the day when R. Eleazar ben Azariah was raised to the presidency [of the Academy], that Canticles and Ecclesiastes defile the hands. Rabbi Akiba said: God forbid! No one in Israel ever contended that Canticles does not defile the hands! For the whole world together is not to be compared to the day on which Canticles was given to Israel; for all Kethubim are holy, but Canticles is most holy. If there was ever any controversy it was solely about Ecclesiastes. Rabbi Johanan ben Joshua, the son of R. Akiba's father-in-law, said: As [Simeon] ben Azzai reports, such was the controversy, and such was the decision." In *Shabbath* (fol. 30*b*) it is said: "The learned intended to withdraw the book Ḳoheleth; but gave up the intention on account of the beginning and end of the book." These doubts about the book were known to Jerome and other Christian scholars. The book owes its inclusion in the Canon largely no doubt to the fact that it professes to have been written by King Solomon. Two of the essential qualifications for admittance seem to have been (1) composition in Hebrew or Aramaic and (2) by a famous person of ancient times. See G. A. Barton, *Ecclesiastes;* G. Currie Martin, *Proverbs, Ecclesiastes, and Song of Solomon* ("Century Bible").

ECEBOLIANS. Ecebolius was a sophist of Constantinople whose religion was as changeable as that of the "Vicar of Bray." The ecclesiastical historian Socrates, referring to persons who consented to offer sacrifice under the Emperor Julian (reigned 361-363 A.D.), says: "Such was Ecebolius, a sophist of Constantinople, who, accommodating himself to the dispositions of the emperors, pretended in the reign of Constantius to be a very zealous Christian; while in Julian's time he appeared an equally ardent Pagan: nay, after Julian's death, he again made a profession of Christianity, prostrating himself before the church doors, and calling out, 'Trample on me, for I am as salt that has lost its savour'" (iii. 13). The term Ecebolian was applied to persons who changed their opinions in the sixteenth and seventeenth centuries. See J. H. Blunt.

ECHETÆ. Nicetas Choniates mentions a body of monks who bore this name. The Greek word from which it seems to be derived means to sound or (with Accus.) to make to sound. The monks followed the example of Moses and Miriam, and in divine service expressed their joy by dancing, etc. See J. H. Blunt.

ECLECTICISM. Eclecticism is the selection of ideas from various systems of philosophy to provide the material for a new philosophy. Roman philosophy was entirely eclectic. This is exemplified by the moral writings of Cicero, who had been influenced by the eclectics, Panætius and Posidonius. Neoplatonism (*q.v.*) was eclectic, since to a large extent it combined oriental ideas and doctrines with the doctrines of Pythagoras and Plato. The French philosopher Pierre Paul Royer-Collard (1763-1845) founded what has been described as an eclectic spiritualism. His pupil Victor Cousin (1792-1867) was another eclectic. See C. J. Deter; Arthur Butler.

ECSTASY. Really a Greek word, meaning, in its good sense "a trance." The root from which the word (*ekstasis*) is derived frequently signifies "to lose one's senses." As Emerson truly says ("Swedenborg; or the Mystic"), "all religious history contains traces of the trance of saints." He adds that "the trances of

Socrates, Plotinus, Porphyry, Behmen, Bunyan, Fox, Pascal, Guion, Swedenborg, will readily come to mind. But what as readily comes to mind, is the accompaniment of disease. This beatitude comes in terror, and with shocks to the mind of the receiver." Since Emerson's day, however, the branch of psychology to which phenomena such as ecstasy belong has become a serious study. Emerson seems to confuse different kinds of trances. A cataleptic trance is no doubt a kind of disease. A trance, in the sense of an ecstasy, while it is certainly not a normal state, is not abnormal to the extent of being a disease. If the claims of religion are to stand, ecstasy must be regarded as natural and intelligible. For religion not only recognises higher planes of existence and a life above the life of the world. It also asserts that there is, in human experience, contact between the higher and the lower world. A person in a state of ecstasy leaves for a time the life of the body and rises to a higher and a spiritual plane. The sense for spiritual things is quickened and intensified. The experience has been made in all ages. It has not been so common in modern times as it was in the days of the Hebrew prophets, because life has become more and more materialistic. The Hebrew prophets lived in closer touch with Nature and with God than any other prophets seem to have done. The human spirit entered into closer communion with the divine (cp. INSPIRATION). The question has been asked in Germany (O. Holtzmann): Was Jesus ecstatic? Our answer is that naturally he was. Like the great prophets, his predecessors, when he could escape from the crowd, "he walked with God" and was, as it were, lost to the things of the world. Philo (quoted by W. Sanday in *Inspiration,* 1903) well describes the state. With reference to Genesis xv. 12, where it is said that "about the setting of the sun a trance came" upon Abraham, it is explained that the sun represents the light of human reason which sets in order to give place to the Spirit of God. "So long then as our mind shines and stirs about us, pouring as it were noontide brightness into every corner of the soul, we are masters of ourselves and are not possessed; but when it draws to its setting, then it is natural that the trance of inspiration should fall upon us, seizing upon us with a sort of frenzy. For when the divine light begins to shine, the human sets; and when it sets below the horizon, the other appears above it and rises. This is what constantly happens to the prophet. The mind in us is expelled at the arrival of the Divine Spirit and returns again to its home at His removal. For it may not be that mortal dwell with immortal. So the setting of the reason and the darkness that gathers round it generates an ecstasy and heaven-caused madness." It has to be borne in mind that there is a natural (spontaneous) and an unnatural (artificial) form of ecstasy. But it was the ecstasy of natural experience that suggested the ecstasy of artificial stimulation. There can hardly be any comparison between the ecstasy of a Hebrew prophet and the ecstasy of a dancing Dervish. It is true that the two kinds appear in the Bible, but the Bible itself distinguishes between true prophets and false prophets, and between natural and artificial kinds of inspiration. Cp. William James, *The Varieties of Religious Experience.*

EDDA. A term denoting a species of Scandinavian or Norse literature. The Poetic Edda is a collection of songs. The word Edda means literally "grandmother." According to Reinach the collection was so called "as if the whole had been related by a grandmother." Chantepie de la Saussaye thinks that as applied to literature the sense "grandmother" is meaningless. According to another interpretation, Edda means "poetics." A third interpretation connects the word with the Icelandic school of Sæmund (died 1133). There is another Edda, the Snorra Edda, which is written in prose, but contains a number of verse quotations. The Edda is not a "bible." It consists of mythical and heroic songs. See P. D. Chantepie de la Saussaye, *Rel. of the Teutons,* 1902; Reinach, *O.*

EDGEITES. A sect which appeared at Rangoon. According to J. H. Blunt, they combined the principles and practice of the Baptists with those of the Plymouth Brethren.

'EDUYOTH. The title of one of the Jewish treatises or tractates which reproduce the oral tradition or unwritten law as developed by the second century A.D. and are included in the Mishnah (*q.v.*), a collection and compilation completed by Rabbi Judah the Holy, or the Patriarch, about 200 A.D. The sixty-three tractates of the Mishnah are divided into six groups or orders (*sedarim*). 'Edūyōth is the seventh tractate of the fourth group, which is called *Neziḳin* ("Damages").

EEVIL. Eevil or Aoibheil (or Aeibhinn) was an ancient Irish deity. A goddess, she appears as the guardian spirit of the warriors of the Dalcassian race.

EFFRONTES. A sect which arose in Transylvania about the year 1534. The Effrontes rejected the worship of the Third Person in the Trinity. "They professed to be Christians, but rejected the use of baptism, and substituted for it a strange custom of shaving the forehead until blood flowed, and then anointing the scarified surface with oil" (Blunt). Probably this practice was suggested by the reference to marks on the forehead in the Book of Revelation (Rev. xiii. 16, xx. 4). See J. H. Blunt.

EGOISTIC HEDONISM. See HEDONISM.

EGUNGUN. A god worshipped by the Yoruba tribes of the Slave Coast of Africa. He is supposed to have risen from the dead, and a powerful secret society was named after him. In the month of June he is honoured by an All Souls' festival, which lasts seven days.

EILITHYIA. A Syrian deity, mentioned by Lucian (§ 38).

EIR. One of the deities of the Ancient Teutons. The goddess Eir belongs to the retinue of Frija (*q.v.*), and is represented as the healer.

EKCHUAH. A tribal deity, god of travellers and traders, in the religion of the Mayan Indians. He corresponds to the Mexican god Yacatecutli.

ELAGABAL. A deity worshipped in Syria in Roman times. He was a sun-god, and had a magnificent temple at Emesa. The temple contained a sacred black stone. Later the sacred stone was transferred to the shrine at Rome (the Elagaballum).

ELEATICS, THE. A school of Greek philosophers founded in Elea by Xenophanes (*d.* about 470 B.C.). Other prominent representatives of the school were Parmenides (*b.* about 544 B.C.), Melissus, and Zeno (*b.* about 500 B.C.). According to Parmenides, Being alone can be cognized. There is no such thing as an empty space. Being is one, and excludes a multiplicity of individual things. A Becoming and a Multiplicity are only appearance. See J. E. Erdmann; C. J. Deter; Max B. Weinstein, *Welt- und Leben-Anschauungen,* 1910.

ELEPHANT, THE. When the birth of her son Gautama was foretold to Mahāmāyā in a dream, he appeared in the form of an elephant. Hence the animal was regarded as sacred by the Buddhists. The Hindu god Ganesa is represented with the head of an elephant, and in the MSS. of the Mayan Indians of Central America God B and God K are depicted as elephant-headed. It has been shown by Professor Elliot Smith not only that we find pre-Columbian representations of the elephant in America, but also that we can identify the species as Indian (*Nature*, Nov. 25, 1915). This suggests early contact between India and America. "The god who was most often depicted upon the ancient Maya and Aztec codices was the Indian rain-god Indra, who in America was provided with the head of the Indian elephant (*i.e.*, seems to have been confused with the Indian Ganesa) and given other attributes more suggestive of the Dravidian Nâga than his enemy, the Aryan deity. In other words the character of the American god known as *Chac* by the Maya people and as Tlaloc by the Aztecs, is an interesting illustration of the effects of such a mixture of cultures as Dr. Rivers has studied in Melanesia. Not only does the elephant-headed god in America represent a blend of the two great Indian rain-gods which in the Old World are mortal enemies, the one of the other (partly for the political reason that the Dravidians and Aryans were rival and hostile peoples), but all the traits of each deity, even those depicting the old Aryan conception of their deadly combat, are reproduced in America under circumstances which reveal an ignorance on the part of the artists of the significance of the paradoxical contradictions they are representing" (G. Elliot Smith, *Dr.*, 1919, p. 83). It should be added that Elliot Smith identifies God B with Chac and Tlaloc.

ELEPHANT, WHITE. One of the seven royal treasures which the ideal king, the king of kings, of the Buddhists (or rather of the pre-Buddhists), is supposed to possess. It is able to carry its master across the earth and to bring him back in time for the morning meal. Rhys Davids connects it with the mythical elephant Airāvata ("the Fertilizer"), "on which the sun-god Indra rides, the personification of the great, white, fertilizing rain-cloud, so rapid in its passage before the winds of the monsoon over the vault of heaven." See T. W. Rhys Davids.

ELEUSINIAN MYSTERIES. Greek initiation ceremonies, so called because according to legend they were first performed at Eleusis in Attica. L. R. Farnell (*Greek Rel.*) thinks that their expansion must have taken place before the composition of the Homeric hymn to Demeter, in whose honour they were celebrated, that is to say, not later than 600 B.C. In the mysteries the catechumens sought to enter into intimate personal relations with the Mother and the Maid. "An elaborate ritual of purification was prescribed whereby the candidate was spiritually prepared for this communion. And it has been supposed that the means of grace included a form of sacrament, the drinking of the sacred cup into which the personality of the goddess might be infused by transubstantiation; but the evidence does not allow us to interpret this part of the ritual with certainty. What is clear is that the fully initiated were privileged to see holy and mystic things, and that the revelation of these established between the individual and the great goddesses of life and death a close and personal tie, whereby his happiness after death was assured. By the time when these great mysteries of Eleusis became pan-Hellenic, this was probably their sole appeal to the peoples outside Attica—namely, their promise of posthumous salvation; and the craving for this grew ever stronger in the Hellenic world from the sixth century till the end of paganism." After the candidate had fasted and bathed in the sea with a young pig which was to be sacrificed, he entered the sacred place and drank of the sacred cup. "For a time his head and shoulders were covered by a cloth, so that he could not see what was happening about him" (Donald A. Mackenzie, *Crete*). Prof. G. Elliot Smith (*Dr.*) thinks the pig was bathed in the sea because it was "a surrogate of the cowry, which lived in the sea, and of the Great Mother, who was sprung from the cowry and hence born of the sea."

ELIXIR OF LIFE, THE. The search for an elixir of life, the Great Elixir, has not been confined to the alchemists of the Middle Ages. Much of what has gone by the name of religion, or philosophy, or science in all ages and in all countries represents a quest for something (some power or substance) that will confer upon mankind life, renewed life, and eternal life. From the ancient Egyptian ritual of rebirth to the modern cult of Christian Science, this has been the great quest. This is emphasized by Professor G. Elliot Smith in one of his remarkable essays ("The giver of Life" in the *Journal of the Manchester Egyptian and Oriental Society*, 1918, p. 53 ff.). Man's first and only concrete idea of death was associated with some physical injury which caused loss of blood ("the blood that is the life thereof"). From the fact that the effusion of the red fluid caused loss of consciousness and death, he inferred that blood was the substance of consciousness and life. This suggested that the defective vitality of persons might be remedied by offerings of blood. Blood "became an elixir to restore youth, to ward off danger to life (by adding to the vital substance), and to increase the supply of vitality to the dead, in whom life was not regarded as ended but simply reduced in volume." This belief in the efficacy of blood (or later of a substitute for blood, such as a fluid made of red ochre, or wine) as an elixir of life "not only exerted the most profound and far-reaching influence in early religious ceremonies and symbolism, but also was responsible for driving men to embark upon such diabolical practices as head-hunting and human sacrifice to obtain the blood which was credited with such potent magical value." Blood could revitalize. But since in the beginning man had to be born, it was further assumed that to enjoy new life, he must be re-born. "The portal of birth was regarded not merely as the channel by which a new life came into being, but also as the *giver* of life. The new being and its vital essence were considered to be actually created by what Semitic-speaking people still call 'the giver of life.' This 'giver of life' was simulated by the cowrie shell, which came to be regarded as an appropriate amulet to add vitality to living or dead, to ward off danger to life or to give renewed supply of life-substance to the dead. But the circumstances of its original symbolism made it also potent to increase the fecundity of women and to facilitate birth. When the moon also came to be regarded as a controlling influence over these physiological processes in women the moon was drawn into the circle of elixirs of life. This was the commencement of the belief in a sky-world and a heaven, and also the foundation-stone of astrology and astronomy." Then the pearl found in a shell and actually called by the Persians *margan* or "the giver of life" came to be regarded as a heaven-sent fragment of moon-substance and as the quintessence of life-giving substance. Magic shells were eagerly sought for, and incidentally provided the first coinage. The wearing of shell-girdles was responsible for the invention of clothing. Where the shell-amulets were not easily procurable, the practice grew up of making models of the cowries in stone or other materials. "In the deserts between the Nile and the Red Sea (the home of the cowrie cult), which must have been repeatedly traversed by the searchers after shells, the soft, plastic, yellow metal was found in considerable quantity, lying about unused and unappreciated." Models were made in gold, and in course of time gold itself acquired the reputation as a "giver of life" which at first belonged only to the *form* of the amulets made of it. Hence the value ascribed to gold, and its use as the basis of currency. See, further, G. Elliot Smith, *Dr.*

ELKESAITES. The Elkesaites or Elchasaites were an early sect to which a book called *Elkesai* was sacred. They seem to have been a branch of the Ebionites (*q.v.*), and flourished at the end of the second century A.D. The book *Elkesai*, which became known to Hippolytus, Origen, and Epiphanius, professed to contain angelic revelations. The revelation is said to have been made in the third year of Trajan (100 A.D.) to a member of the tribe of the Seres, a Parthian people who are supposed to have lived a life of perfect happiness, purity, and freedom from pain. The book of *Elkesai* "announced a new method of forgiveness of sin, asserted to have been revealed in the third year of Trajan, by which any person, no matter of what sins he might have been guilty (some of the very grossest are expressly mentioned), might obtain forgiveness by submitting to a new baptism with the use of a certain formula. . . . A similar baptism was prescribed as a remedy for the bite of a mad dog or a serpent or for disease" (*Dict. of Christ. Biogr.*). The Elkesaites observed the law of Moses, but rejected sacrifice and the eating of flesh. They held Christ to be simply the greatest of created beings and one of a number of manifestations of the Christ. They refused to acknowledge St. Paul. It is thought that the book of *Elkesai* was of Jewish origin. Its name seems to be Hebrew or Aramaic. If it is, it might perhaps mean "God is a shelter." It might, however, be Arabic. In that case it would mean simply "The shelter" (*'al-hashā*[*y*]). An Arabic author, En-hedim, of about 987 A.D., says that one El-Chasaiach founded a sect of Sabeans of the Desert. A special feature in their religion was the practice of frequent ablutions. See J. H. Blunt; Wace and Piercy.

ELLAMMĀ. A Hindu deity, goddess of the boundary, worshipped by the Paraiyans, a tribe or caste in India.

ELLERIAN SECT. A sect of religious enthusiasts in Germany, founded by Elias Eller (*b.* 1690). They were also called Zionites (*q.v.*).

ELNĀKHUM. One of the gods of the Todas.

ELOHIST. The name given by Higher Critics to one (or more) of the writers of the narratives of which the Hexateuch is composed. The writer was so called because his work was characterised by the use of the divine name Elohim instead of Jehovah (more correctly Jahveh or Yahweh). Critics now discriminate between a First Elohist and a Second Elohist. See PENTATEUCH.

ELY LECTURES, THE. The full title of the lectures founded by Zebulon Stiles Ely in the United States of America is "The Elias P. Ely Lectures on the Evidences of Christianity." The course of lectures was intended to comprise any topics serving to establish the proposition that Christianity is a religion from God, or that it is the perfect and final form of religion for man. Among the subjects may be: The Nature and Need of a Revelation; The Character and Influence of Christ and His Apostles; The Authenticity and Credibility of the Scriptures, Miracles, and Prophecy; The Diffusion and Benefits of Christianity, and The Philosophy of Religion in its Relations to the Christian System. The lectures are delivered in connection with the Union Theological Seminary.

EMBALMING. The ancient practice of embalming was specifically Egyptian. When Hebrew narrators say that it was applied in the case of Jacob and Joseph (Gen. 50, 2 f. 26), they are speaking of exceptions. It was not a Hebrew practice. The Egyptians believed in the continued existence of the human *Ka*, provided that the body of the deceased was carefully preserved. Hence the practice of embalming, to which reference is made by Herodotus (II. 86 ff.) and Diodorus Siculus (I. 91). Professor Elliot Smith explains that "from the outset the Egyptian embalmer was clearly inspired by two ideals: (*a*) to preserve the actual tissues of the body with a minimum disturbance of its superficial appearance; and (*b*) to preserve a likeness of the deceased as he was in life" (*Dr.*). To attain these ideals practical measures were taken, and various ritual ceremonies were performed (see MUMMIFICATION, INCENSE, LIBATIONS). The essential processes of mummification were salting, evisceration, drying, and smoking. The incision for eviscerating the body was made in the flank, right or left, or in the perineum. To prevent the general epidermis, as it was shed, from carrying the finger- and toe-nails with it, the ancient Egyptian embalmers made circular incisions around fingers and toes. Herodotus distinguishes three methods of embalming. In one method, the brain was withdrawn and the cavity filled with spices; then the bowels were removed and washed with palm wine, and the cavity was filled with myrrh, cassia, and other drugs; finally, after being kept for seventy days in natron (sub-carbonate of soda), the body was washed and swarthed in long strips of byssus smeared with gum. In another method "cedar oil was introduced into the body and removed after it had decomposed the viscera; the body was then laid in natron, which, according to Herodotus, wholly consumed the flesh, leaving nothing but the skin and bones" (*Encycl. Bibl.*). At an early stage in the evolution of mummification the wrapped body was converted into a portrait-statue of the deceased. Thus, in a mummy found at Mêdum by Flinders Petrie, "the superficial bandages were saturated with a paste of resin and soda, and the same material was applied to the surface of the wrappings, which while still in a plastic condition, was very skilfully moulded to form a life-like statue. The resinous carapace thus built up set to form a covering of stony hardness" (Elliot Smith, *M.*). Elliot Smith notes that "special care was devoted to the modelling of the head (sometimes of the face only) and the genitalia, no doubt to serve as the means of identifying the individual and indicating the sex respectively. The hair (or, perhaps it would be more correct to say, the wig) and the moustache were painted with a dark brown or black resinous mixture, and the pupils, eyelids and eyebrows were represented by painting with a mixture of malachite powder and resinous paste." It has been said that the practice of embalming was specifically Egyptian. It is in Egypt that we first hear of it, and it was there that it first developed. But it was not confined to Egypt. It has been found throughout the world. The Baganda embalm the bodies of their kings. Embalming was practised in the Canary Islands, in Persia by the Moslems, in Thibet, in Australia, in Tahiti, in Peru and other parts of America, and elsewhere. The methods employed often resemble so closely those used in ancient Egypt that one can hardly avoid the conclusion that Egypt was the centre from which, somehow or other, the custom spread all over the world.

EMDEN CATECHISM, THE. A Catechism (1554 A.D.) drawn up by John à Lasco. "It took the place of a larger Catechism for children based on Micron's Compendium, and also of a Lutheranizing substitute which an Emden pastor had prepared on his own authority. It became the recognized text-book and doctrinal norm of East Friesland, in whose dialect it is written" (William A. Curtis).

'EMETH. A *vox memorialis* sometimes used in Jewish literature to designate a group of books included in the Old Testament. The books are Job, Proverbs, and Psalms. 'Emeth is a common Hebrew word meaning "truth." The three consonants of which it is composed (אמת) correspond to the initial consonants of the three books, Psalms (ת), Proverbs (מ), Job (א).

EMMANUEL CHURCH MOVEMENT. Emmanuel Church is a church in Boston, U.S.A. The movement, also called the "Emmanuel Movement," is medico-religious in character. It began in an attempt to cure the poorest consumptives without removing them from their homes. "A Tuberculosis Class was formed under the direction of a distinguished medical authority. The treatment offered consisted of the most recent scientific method of combatting consumption, *plus* discipline, friendship, encouragement, and hope—in short, a combination of physical and moral elements." The success of this move led to an extension of the work. It was decided to render the same help to the morally and nervously diseased. The sympathetic approval and active co-operation of the leading neurologists in the country was first invited and obtained. One of the fundamental ideas of the movers is that all work of this kind should be under strict medical control. "We believe in the power of the mind over the body, and we believe also in medicine, in good habits, and in a wholesome, well-regulated life. In the treatment of functional nervous disorders we make free use of moral and psychical agencies, but we do not believe in overtaxing these valuable aids by expecting the mind to attain results which can be effected more easily through physical instrumentalities. Accordingly we have gladly availed ourselves of the services of the skilled medical and surgical specialists who have offered to co-operate with us, and we believe that our freedom in this respect and the combination of good psychical and physical methods have had much to do with our success." It will be clear at once that the Emmanuel Movement is not to be identified with Christian Science. It "bears no relation to Christian Science, either by way of protest or of imitation, but it would be what it is had the latter never existed." The Emmanuel workers believe in the existence of what is known as the Subconscious Mind and avail themselves largely of the power of Suggestion. They claim that by means of Suggestion it is possible not only to cure physical (nervous) disorders, but also to check or remove moral failings (*e.g.*, alcoholism). In England the Church and Medical Union (*q.v.*) worked on similar lines. The Psycho-Therapeutic Society (*q.v.*) did good work for some years (since 1901). Its field was rather wider, and it could perhaps claim to be more scientific. It was not specially identified with any particular religious denomination. See *Religion and Medicine* (1908), by E. Worcester, S. McComb, and I. H. Coriat.

EMMA-Ō. A god in Japanese Buddhism, lord of the underworld.

ENCRATITES. The name Encratites (Gk. "continent") describes probably not a single heretical sect, but heretics of a particular character belonging to a number of different sects. Such persons abstained from flesh, wine, and marriage (like the Essenes). Irenaeus applies the name to followers of Saturninus and Marcion. Such abstinence might of course be practised by orthodox Christians. But the Encratites who were heretics practised it because they believed that matter was essentially evil and was created by some hostile power opposed to the Supreme Being. "Epiphanius describes (*Haer.* 48) the Encratites as widely spread, enumerating seven different countries where they were then to be found. Evidently, therefore, there were in these countries heretics leading an ascetic life, though it would be unsafe to assert an absolute identity in their teaching" (*Dict. of Christ. Biogr.*). See J. H. Blunt; Wace and Piercy.

ENCYCLOPEDISTS. The name *Encyclopédistes* was given to the French scholars and thinkers of the eighteenth century who edited and contributed to the "Encyclopédie ou Dictionnaire raisonné des Sciences, des Arts et des Métiers," which was published in Paris in twenty-one volumes (1751-1764). The work was founded and edited by Denis Diderot (1713-1784) and Jean d'Alembert (1717-1783). Jean d'Alembert was co-editor only for a few years (till 1757), but he wrote the Introduction on the methods and correlation of the sciences. The other contributors included Marie François de Voltaire (1694-1778), Jean Jacques Rousseau (1712-1778), Baron Montesquieu (1689-1755), Etienne de Condillac (1715-1780), Claude Adrien Helvetius (1715-1771), and Baron Holbach (1721-1789). The writers were influenced by the philosophy (*Sensualism*) of John Locke (1632-1704) and David Hume (1711-1776): "nihil est in intellectu quod non prius fuerit in sensu." But this philosophy was transformed to suit the peculiar temper and circumstances of the age in France. "Instead of aiming at a transformation of the old theology into another pattern, as had been the object of the earlier English Deists, the French representatives of the movement advocated a general repudiation of theology and the substitution of an undogmatic religion in place of Roman Catholicism. To this end Voltaire applied the weapons of his caustic satire, and the Encyclopaedists added the weight of their accumulated knowledge. Indeed, Diderot (†1784) and his school represent a further stage in the downward transition from Deism towards Materialism" (Hastings' *E.R.E.*, *s.v.* "Deism"). It has been pointed out, however, that it is a mistake to suppose that Diderot's *Encyclopédie* is full of open and bold attacks on religion, Christianity, and the Roman Catholic Church. "Though the article on the Jesuits is written with great gusto for scandals, and though the article on the Pope vindicates the Gallican views of the episcopacy, the work as a whole is confessedly Roman Catholic, and the Reformation, with all that belongs to it, is treated in a supercilious manner as a vicious innovation; to which must be added that there is hardly any Christian dogma which is not accepted and defended,—such as those of the trinity, of inspiration, of the atonement, etc. But (and this is characteristic of the book) the reasons for the acceptance of the Christian dogmas are generally of such a quality that a flat rejection, for no reason whatever, could not have made the matter worse. Theism is preferred to atheism, because it is better for the development of human happiness to accept than to reject the idea of the existence of God. Christ is the first and foremost of all religious founders, because he revealed the best and highest morality, etc." (Schaff-Herzog). See Schaff-Herzog; J. H. Blunt; C. J. Deter; Max B. Weinstein, *Welt- und Leben-anschauungen*, 1910.

ENGLISH VIRGINS. See INSTITUTE OF THE BLESSED VIRGIN MARY.

ENIGORIO. The name (meaning Good Mind) of a figure in the mythology of the Iroquois Indians. Enigorio in his creative work is opposed and thwarted by his twin-brother Enigohatgea (Bad Mind).

ENLIGHTENMENT, PERIOD OF. The period of Enlightenment or Illuminism in Germany ("Zeitalter der Aufklaerung") was the period (eighteenth century) during which German thought was under the influence of John Locke (1632-1704) and the English deists, Marie François de Voltaire (1694-1778), Jean Jacques Rousseau (1712-1778) and the French Encyclopedists, and of the

German philosophers Gottfried Wilhelm Leibnitz (1646-1716) and Christian Wolff (1679-1754). See B. Puenjer.

ENMEDURANKI. A figure in Babylonian mythology, mythical king of Sippar and the seventh Antediluvian king in the list of Berossus. He was regarded as the founder of divination.

ENTHUSIASTÆ. Another name for the Euchites (*q.v.*).

ENTHUSIASTS. Writers of the Elizabethan period, such as John Jewel (1522-1571) and Thomas Rogers, in speaking of such heretics as the Familists (*q.v.*) and Anabaptists (*q.v.*), mention also a class of persons called Enthusiasts. This seems to have been a designation not of a distinct sect, but of such persons as the Familists and Anabaptists. During and after the Commonwealth period the term was applied to the Puritans. See Schaff-Herzog; J. H. Blunt.

ENTYCHITES. The sect referred to by Clement of Alexandria as the Entychites is perhaps the same as that referred to by Theodoret as the Eutychetæ (*q.v.*).

EONIANS. The followers of the Breton fanatic, Eon d'Etoile (*d.* 1148 A.D.). Eon claimed to be the Messiah, and when he died he was expected by the Eonians to appear again. Since his communism made him politically dangerous, the civil authorities imprisoned him. See J. H. Blunt.

EPHESIANS, EPISTLE TO THE. The Epistle to the Ephesians was the favourite epistle of Calvin, and was described by Coleridge as one of the divinest compositions of man. Dean Armitage Robinson describes it as the crown of St. Paul's writings. It is one of the four epistles now known as the Epistles of the Captivity, because in them Paul describes himself as a prisoner. Originally, it would seem, it was not addressed exclusively to the Church at Ephesus. This is suggested by a number of considerations. The words "in Ephesus" (i. 1) are wanting in our two best Manuscripts, and were not found in a number of ancient manuscripts known to Basil (360 A.D.). In spite of the fact that Paul had worked with success in Ephesus this Epistle contains no greetings to friends there (cp. Acts xx. 17-38). The author (to use the words of M'Clymont) "writes as if the Christian graces of his readers were only known to him by report, and as if his apostleship to the Gentiles were only known to them by hearsay (i. 15-19; iii. 1-4; iv. 17-22; cf. Col. i. 3-9)." The autograph of the Apostle is not added. The Epistle would seem to have been written not for a particular Church but for a number of Churches in Asia Minor. It was intended as a circular letter, an encyclical. "The capital of the Roman province of Asia was Ephesus. To Ephesus such a letter would naturally go first of all: and when in later times a title was sought for it, to correspond with the titles of other epistles, no name would offer itself so readily and so reasonably as the name of Ephesus. Accordingly the title 'to the Ephesians' was prefixed to it. And if, as seems not improbable, the opening sentence contained a space into which the name of each Church in turn might be read—'to the saints which are . . . and the faithful in Christ Jesus'—it was certain that in many copies the words 'in Ephesus' would come to be filled in" (Armitage Robinson). As a matter of fact, Tertullian says that the Epistle was also known by the title "to the Laodiceans." As regards the authenticity of the Epistle, the external evidence seems to be quite adequate. It seems to have been used by Ignatius and Polycarp. It is included in the Canon of Marcion and in the Muratorian Canon. It is ascribed to Paul by Irenaeus. It is more especially the internal evidence that has raised doubts in the minds of a number of scholars. It has been urged that it is un-Pauline in style and thought. But it is only un-Pauline in comparison with something that has arbitrarily been set up as a fixed standard of Paulinism. Scholars too often think of Paul as being an ordinary man like themselves. He was a genius. More than that, he was a man who had profound spiritual experiences, and, like the prophets, was from time to time possessed by a new spirit. A man of this kind never stands still. He never sees things in quite the same way yesterday, to-day, and to-morrow. His thought changes, his language changes under the impulse of divine intuitions. He may be lifted in a moment on to a different plane and use the language of that plane without having studied it in the ordinary way. This is not merely a supposition; it is a fact proved by experience. We must expect to find difficulties in the Epistles of Paul. And we need not expect to explain them all. The Epistle was probably written from Rome. It is catholic in nature. That does not militate against its Pauline origin. "We have no ground for the assumption that the conception of the Catholic Church must have been later than Paul, indeed it is quite in a line both with his thought and action. His attempt to keep the Churches together expressed in the collection for the saints at Jerusalem, his feeling that local idiosyncracies must be curbed by the general practice of the Church (I. Cor. xiv. 33, 36), his imperialist instincts which had controlled his missionary activity and which were nowhere so likely to find expression as in Rome, all urged him in this direction" (A. S. Peake). See J. Armitage Robinson, *St. Paul's Epistle to the Ephesians*, 1904; J. A. M'Clymont; G. Currie Martin; Arthur S. Peake; J. Moffatt.

EPHOD. A word occurring in the Old Testament with at least two different meanings. Sometimes it denotes a garment, probably a loin-cloth. The boy Samuel we are told was "girt with a linen ephod" (I. Samuel ii. 18). David, when he brought the ark up to Jerusalem and danced before Yahweh with all his might, wore only an ephod (II. Samuel vi. 14). At other times the word denotes something closely associated with the priests. Here it is not a vestment, but something which was borne or carried (I. Samuel xiv. 18; xxiii. 6, 9; xxx. 7), and it is used in divining or in consulting Yahweh. By some kind of manipulation it was made to answer questions. The ephod referred to in Judges viii. 27, xvii. f. and I. Samuel xxi. 9 seems to have been an image of Yahweh. If the ephod used in divining was in all cases an image, we may think of "a portable idol before which the lots were cast" (G. F. Moore). Something called an ephod figures also among the high-priest's ceremonial vestments. This seems to have been a kind of apron, to the shoulder-straps of which was attached an oracle-pouch ("breastplate of judgment"). "It is possible," says Prof. Moore, "that the primitive ephod—a corner of which was the earliest pocket—was used as a receptacle for the lots, from which they were drawn, or into which they were cast (see Proverbs xvi. 33); and that when it was no longer a common piece of raiment it was perpetuated in this sacred use, not worn, but carried by the priest; the ephod and oracle-pouch of the high-priest would then preserve this ancient association. The ephod of Gideon—perhaps also the ephod in the temple at Nob—was, however, an *agalma* of an entirely different character; what relation there may be between the ephod-garment and the ephod-idol, it is not easy to imagine." See *Encycl Bibl.*

EPHPHATHA. An Aramaic word found in the New Testament and represented in Greek letters. In the story of the healing of a deaf and dumb man in Mark vii. 32-37 we read: "And he took him aside from the multitude privately, and put his fingers into his ears, and he spat, and touched his tongue; and looking up to heaven, he sighed, and saith unto him, Ephphatha, that is, Be opened (Gk. *dianoichthēti*)." The word is a passive (Ethpe'el or Ethpa'al) of the verb *pĕthach* "to open."

EPICUREANISM. The philosophy of Epicurus of Samos (342-270 B.C.) owed much to the speculations of earlier Schools, for instance of the Cyrenaic School (see CYRENAICS) and of the Atomic philosophers (see ATOMS). In 306 B.C. he opened a school at Athens in a country-house and garden. Here he was held in the highest esteem by his pupils. And later every disciple was ardently devoted to the Master. "He even exalted him to the place of deity in his veneration. This comes out again and again in Lucretius, whose language in extolling Epicurus is that of the enthusiastic worshipper, disclosing whole-hearted and unbounded admiration" (Davidson). Epicurus wrote many works, but only extracts and summaries have been preserved. "We are fortunate, however, in possessing the philosophical masterpiece of a great Roman poet, who was, first and foremost, a follower of Epicurus—the famous didactic poem of Lucretius (95-52 B.C.), entitled *De Rerum Naturâ* ('On the Nature of Things'), in which the cosmology and general system of the Epicureans are worked out with considerable fulness and with great enthusiasm, and in which the strength of personal conviction aids the poetic imagination and adds force to the felicitous diction, so that the picture becomes at once vivid, fascinating, and impressive." According to the Epicureans the whole material universe was constructed, on fixed immutable laws, out of atoms in motion and the void. The laws are so fixed that no supersensible being can interfere with or alter them. The gods are located by Epicurus in the *intermundia* or spaces between the worlds (Gk. *diakosmoi*). Here, remote from the troubles and trials of earth, they have nothing to do with the affairs of mortal men. In their elaboration of the atomic doctrine, Democritus, Epicurus, and Lucretius, it is claimed (by Davidson and others), were the undoubted precursors of Tyndall, Huxley, Buechner, and Haeckel. The Epicurean doctrine of atoms and the void is used, however, to explain even Life and Mind. "In this view, Life is simply the result of particular collocations of particular atoms; and human consciousness, sensation, perception, reflection—the soul, with all its properties and functions—are the product of the elementary material particles, variously combining and reacting: life and consciousness alike are but 'modes of motion'" (Davidson). The soul itself is composed of very minute, smooth, round atoms. Pleasure and pain are explained on the same principle. "To the Epicurean, pleasure means simply the harmonious, and orderly movement of the atoms; while pain is the feeling that ensues when there are jarring and discord among them." Epicurus differed from Democritus (*b.* about 460 B.C.) in his application of the atomic theory, for he claimed that Free Will is the great fact on which ethics is based, and that it is a fact of our experience. C. J. Deter points out that Epicurus ennobled as much as possible the ancient conception of pleasure. Yet to him virtue was not an aim in itself, but was to be aimed at merely for its usefulness as a means to another end, a happy and pleasant life. To him personally his philosophy meant a virtuous and joyful life, spiritual and intellectual rather than sensual pleasure. But as in course of time it came to be interpreted by his disciples, it degenerated into a mere search for sensual pleasure. The stigma which attaches now to Epicureanism is of course due not to the original but to the degenerate form of the system. See William L. Davidson, *The Stoic Creed*, 1907; C. J. Deter; Max B. Weinstein, *Welt und Leben-anschauungen*, 1910.

EPISTLES OF DIONYSIUS OF CORINTH. Dionysius was Bishop of Corinth. He seems to have been bishop there in 165 A.D. and to have died before 198. His Epistles were addressed to the Christians of the Churches: to the Lacedæmonians, the Athenians, the Nicomedians, the Gortynians, the Amastrians, and the Cnossians (the people of Cnossos near Candia in Crete). Eusebius calls them "catholic letters to the Churches," perhaps with the idea of suggesting a comparison with the New Testament "Catholic Epistles" (*q.v.*). Eusebius (quoted by C. R. Gregory) tells us further: "And the same [Dionysius] speaks as follows of his letters as being treacherously treated: For when the brethren asked it of me that I should write letters, I wrote them. And these the apostles of the devil have mingled with tares, taking some things out and putting some things in. For whom the Woe is waiting. It is then not strange if some have laid their hands upon the work of treating the writings about the Lord treacherously, seeing that they have taken such counsel against letters that are not such as those are." Dr. C. R. Gregory thinks that the distinction here made between writings about the Lord and his own letters "that are not such" emphasises a difference between "the writings which belong in the service to the part God to Man and those which belong to the part Man to Man." He thinks that in the writings about the Lord probably Dionysius has in view the Gospels and possibly also the Epistles of the Apostles. See C. R. Gregory.

EPISTLES OF THE CAPTIVITY. Four of the Epistles ascribed to the Apostle Paul have been designated the "Epistles of the Captivity," because in all of them he describes himself as a prisoner. They are the Epistles to the Ephesians (cp. iii. 1, iv. 1, vi. 20), Colossians (cp. iv. 18), Philippians (cp. i. 7, 13), and the Epistle to Philemon (cp. vss. 10, 13). It is matter of dispute whether the place of imprisonment was Cæsarea or Rome.

EPONA. Epona was a goddess worshipped by the ancient Celts. She was the goddess of horses. The name means "equine spring," for which Reinach compares Hippocrene, the fountain of Parnassus brought forth by Apollo's steed Pegasus. E. Anwyl thinks that originally the goddess Epona had the form of a mare. Afterwards she was represented as a human being riding on a horse. As the protectress of horses, she was the only Gallic deity to find particular favour with the Romans. See Edward Anwyl; Reinach, *O.*

EPUNAMUN. The war-god in the mythology of the Araucanian Indians of Chili, probably of Peruvian origin.

ERASTIANS. A name given in England to those who hold that the Church should be subject to the State. The designation was suggested by the name Erastus, a name assumed by Thomas Liebler or Lieber (1524-1583), a German physician and theologian. As a theologian, Liebler defended the doctrines of the reformer Ulrich Zwingli (1484-1531), especially the doctrine that the external organization of religion is purely a civil matter, the spiritual part being entirely the concern of the individual conscience. In the reign of Charles I. many of the English Puritans were Erastians. Later, the Hanoverian bishops were "thorough-going Erastians" (Patterson). See J. H. Blunt; M. W. Patterson, *Hist.*; Brockhaus.

ERNATULUNGA. A name used by the Arunta of Central Australia for the sacred place in which their ritual instruments, the churinga, are kept.

'ERUBIN. The title of one of the Jewish treatises or tractates which reproduce the oral tradition or unwritten law as developed by the second century A.D. and are included in the Mishnah (*q.v.*), a collection and compilation completed by Rabbi Judah the Holy, or the Patriarch, about 200 A.D. The sixty-three tractates of the Mishnah are divided into six groups or orders (*sedarim*). 'Erūbin is the second tractate of the second group, which is called *Mō'ēd* ("Festival).

ESAUGETUH EMISSEE. The chief deity of the Creek Indians, a wind-god.

ESHARRA. In the Babylonian Epic of Marduk (see MARDUK, EPIC OF) Esharra is the name of the vault of earth which Marduk places over Apsu (*q.v.*), the Deep.

ESSAYS AND REVIEWS. A volume of theological essays written (with two exceptions) by clergymen of the Church of England and published in 1860. It is said in the Preface: "The Volume, it is hoped, will be received as an attempt to illustrate the advantage derivable to the cause of religious and moral truth from a free handling, in a becoming spirit, of subjects peculiarly liable to suffer by the repetition of conventional language, and from traditional methods of treatment." As a matter of fact the publication of the volume aroused a storm of protest and indignation among the orthodox, and charges were brought against it as being contrary to, or inconsistent with, the doctrines of the Church of England. The charges, however were not sustained. Some of them were withdrawn or rejected in the Court of Arches, others during the hearing before the Judicial Committee of the Privy Council. The first essay is on "The Education of the World," and was written by Frederick Temple. The writer was Headmaster of Rugby School. He afterwards became Archbishop of Canterbury. The second essay is on "Bunsen's Biblical Researches." It was written by Rowland Williams (1817-1870), who was at the time Vice-Principal and Professor of Hebrew in the Theological College of St. David's, Lampeter. The third essay is "On the Study of the Evidences of Christianity." The author was Baden Powell (1796-1860), Savilian Professor of Geometry in the University of Oxford. The fourth essay is on "Séances historiques de Genève. The National Church." It was written by Henry Bristow Wilson (1803-1888), Vicar of Great Staughton, Huntingdonshire. The fifth essay is "On the Mosaic Cosmogony." The writer, C. W. Goodwin (1817-1878), an Egyptologist, was a barrister. He afterwards became acting judge in the supreme court of China and Japan. The sixth article is on "Tendencies of Religious Thought in England, 1688-1750." It was written by Mark Pattison (1813-1884), who became Rector of Lincoln College, Oxford (1861). The seventh essay is "On the Interpretation of Scripture." The writer, Benjamin Jowett (1817-1893), was Regius Professor of Greek in the University of Oxford. He afterwards became Master of Balliol College.

ESSENES. The Essenes seem to have been a kind of monastic order among the Jews. As a well-defined body they do not seem to have arisen before the second century B.C. But there may have been small groups of them, resembling the bands of the prophets, at a much earlier date. It would be a quite natural development for disciples of men like Elijah to form themselves into societies like that of the Essenes. It would be equally natural for such societies, having cut themselves off to some extent from the common current of thought, to work out doctrines of their own. Essenism is not necessarily un-Jewish or due to foreign influence. As Mr. R. Travers Herford says (*Pharisaism*, 1912), they were ascetics and recluses, and stood apart from the main body of the Jewish people. They were ascetics "of more than Pharisaic strictness (for asceticism was not a characteristic feature of Pharisaism either in practice or theory), and they combined with the religion of Torah certain mystical doctrines of their own." W. Fairweather thinks that apparently the religious ideas of the Essenes were essentially Jewish with certain decided exceptions or modifications. "In respect of their belief in Providence, which was more absolute than that of the Pharisees; in respect of their veneration for Moses and the Law; and in respect of their sabbath observance, which was of the strictest possible type, they were Hebrews of the Hebrews. Apparently also, as a guarantee of ceremonial purity, their food was prepared and blessed by priests of Aaron's house, while the allegorical interpretation of Scripture had a place in their worship." The modifications, which he regards as alien elements, would arise from the fact of their standing apart from the main body of the Jewish people. The name Essenes might mean "the pious" or "the physicians." The former meaning is more likely. What we know about them is due to Philo, Josephus, the Jewish historian, and Pliny, the Roman historian. They preferred villages to towns, and lived chiefly in the neighbourhood of the Dead Sea. "Admission to the order was solemnised by the threefold gift of an apron, a white robe, and a mattock (symbols, presumably, of abstinence and purity), followed only upon a lengthened and double novitiate, and necessitated the taking of tremendous oaths of absolute obedience to the presidents, openness towards the members, and secrecy towards outsiders respecting the doctrines of the brotherhood" (Fairweather). Serious offenders were expelled from the order. The brethren lived a communistic life. "All their belongings were common property, administered by chosen stewards for behoof of the entire order. This applied to food, housing, and even clothing; while in every town provision was made for shewing hospitality to journeying brethren." They had many peculiar manners and customs. "While sending gifts to the Temple, they offered no animal sacrifices, deeming their own lustrations superior in point of purity. Theirs was a fellowship based not upon sacrifice, but apparently upon sacrament. Their midday common meal was at the same time a solemn diet of worship, a holy sacrament to which they came clad in white after having by a cold bath cleansed themselves on their return from the fields. A purifying bath had also to be taken in the event of contact with a foreigner, or even with an Essene of a lower grade. In bathing and in performing natural functions they behaved with extreme modesty." They probably abstained from flesh and wine. They abstained from all sexual intercourse, refused to use oaths, and rejected the use of oil for anointing. "Slavery and war they abhorred. Renouncing trade as tending to covetousness, they earned their livelihood by manual labour; the majority of them were engaged in agriculture. They were content with the same simple fare day by day; nor were their clothes and shoes replaced until utterly worn out." They were held in high repute as foretellers of the future. They held every object of sense to be ungodly, and sin to be a transgression of the law of nature. The soul of man really belongs to another world, the spiritual realm. "Having come out of the purest ether in order to be imprisoned in the body as the consequence of a fall into sin, souls, when freed at death from terrestrial bonds, soar again to the heights, happy to have escaped from their long servitude." It has been thought that the Essenes worshipped the sun. But it may be that their sun-worship was simply suggested by the reverence they paid to angels. A number of scholars and thinkers (including De Quincey, E. Planta Nesbit, and, more recently, Emil Berg) have urged that Jesus was educated among the Essenes, and that the religion of Jesus was a product of Essenism. But, as others have pointed out, there are radical differences between Essenism and the teaching of the gospels. The resemblances, as Fairweather says, extend only to minor details. See E. Planta Nesbit, *Christ, Christians, and Christianity*, 1899; the *Encycl. Bibl.*; W. Staerk, *Neutestamentliche Zeitgeschichte*, 1907; W. Fairweather, *The Background of the Gospels*, 1908.

ESTHER, BOOK OF. In the Hebrew Canon of the Old Testament the Book of Esther is one of the five books described as Megilloth (or "Rolls"). The book purports to be historical, but it is now widely regarded as a Jewish romance. It narrates that the Persian king Ahasuerus (Xerxes, 485-465 B.C.) repudiated his proud consort Vashti and made Esther, the adopted daughter of the Jew Mordecai, queen in her place. Haman, the Agagite, the enemy of Mordecai, hatches a plot to massacre the Jews. This plot is frustrated by Esther, with the result that Haman is hanged, and Mordecai promoted to take his adversary's place. The Jews were mercifully delivered, and in memory of this deliverance the Feast of Purim was observed on the 14th and 15th of the month Adar (Feb.-March). In II. Maccabees xv. 36 the Day of Nicanor, on which was celebrated Judas' defeat at Adasa of Nicanor the general of Antiochus Epiphanes, is referred to as being "the day before the Day of Mordecai." This Day of Mordecai seems to be identical with the Feast of Purim referred to in Esther ix. 22. The contents and language of the Book of Esther point to a late date for its composition. "In the Book of Esther the Persian empire is treated as a thing of the past, already invested with a halo of romance. The writer must therefore have lived some considerable time after Alexander the Great, not earlier than the third, probably in the second, century before Christ. The book presupposes moreover that the Jews had long been 'scattered abroad and dispersed' among the nations (iii. 8); this idea of a 'dispersion' (διασπορα) points to the time when large Jewish settlements were to be found within the domain of Greek civilisation. The same period is indicated by the passage about the conversion of vast multitudes to Judaism (ix. 27), for such a conception would have been impossible even in a romance, until Jewish proselytes had become numerous" (*Encycl. Bibl.*). A. Kuenen and C. Cornill assign the book to about 135 B.C. O. C. Whitehouse thinks "it probably arose after the Maccabaean war (165 B.C.), when the spirit of national exclusiveness in the Jewish people became intensified." The purpose of the book is to explain the origin of the Feast of Purim and to encourage the observance of it. See T. K. Cheyne and J. S. Black, *Encycl. Bibl.*; C. Cornill, *Intr.*; G. H. Box; O. C. Whitehouse.

ESUS. Esus, together with Teutates and Taranis, is mentioned by Lucan (*c.* A.D. 60) as one of the Gallic divinities. Esus, the eponym of the Essuvii, is said to have been a divine woodman; and the three gods, it appears, required human sacrifices. The triad, according to Reinach and Anwyl, does not represent a Celtic Trinity. It is composed simply of local deities who were "venerated by a few tribes to the north of the Loire" (Reinach). See Edward Anwyl; Reinach, *O.*

ETANA. A Babylonian deity. Etana may originally have been a historical person; but in any case he was deified and became a legendary figure. Shamash (*q.v.*), the sun-god, is his patron. When his wife finds it difficult to bring to birth a child, Etana beseeches Shamash to reveal to him "the plant of birth." He would seem to find it on a mountain with the help of an eagle. On another occasion Etana ascends with the eagle to the gates of the upper regions. As they ascend, the sea appears smaller and smaller, first like a pool, next like a belt, then like a gardener's ditch. They reach the gate of Anu (*q.v.*), Bel (*q.v.*), and Ea (*q.v.*). Thence the eagle wishes to carry Etana to Ishtar (*q.v.*), the mistress of the gods. Etana consents. They mount higher and higher. But their presumption is punished; they are cast headlong from the heights. In the Gilgamesh Epic (*q.v.*) Etana is one of the dwellers in the nether world. Etana's eagle, after the catastrophe, loses the favour of Shamash, and becomes hostile to the serpent of Shamash, trying to catch it. Shamash tells the serpent to ascend a mountain, tear open a wild ox and hide in its carcase. The eagle will descend with the other birds and can then be torn in pieces. The serpent does as he is told. The eagle is caught and destroyed. See Morris Jastrow, *Rel.*

ETHICAL HEDONISM. See HEDONISM.

ETHICAL SOCIETIES, THE UNION OF. If the Ethical Movement seems to be in conflict and rivalry with the Churches, it may nevertheless claim to be in a real sense a religious movement. The Gospel of the Ethical Movement, as expounded by W. M. Salter in his "Ethical Religion" should command the greatest respect. There are no doubt many persons to whom such a gospel comes as a great relief, consolation, and inspiration. Whether it is such a religion as can permanently satisfy the natural human craving for communion with a power beyond and above that of man may well be questioned. The general object of the Union of Ethical Societies is to advocate the supreme importance of the knowledge, love and practice of the Right. The principles of the Union are stated to be nine. (1) In all the relations of life—personal, social, and political—the moral factor should be the supreme consideration. (2) The love of goodness and the love of one's fellows are the true motives for right conduct; and self-reliance and co-operation are the true sources of help. (3) Knowledge of the Right has been evolving through the experience of the human race; therefore the moral obligations generally accepted by the most civilised communities should be taken as the starting-point in the advocacy of a progressive ideal of personal and social righteousness. (4) For each individual, after due consideration of the convictions of others, the final authority as to the right or wrong of any opinion or action should be his own conscientious and reasoned judgment. (5) The well-being of society requires such economic and other conditions as afford the largest scope for the moral development of all its members. (6) scientific method should be applied in studying the facts of the moral life. (7) The moral life involves neither acceptance nor rejection of belief in any deity, personal or impersonal, or in a life after death. (8) The acceptance of any one ultimate criterion of right should not be made a condition of ethical fellowship. (9) Ethical Fellowships are the most powerful means of encouraging the knowledge and love of right principles of conduct, and of giving the strength of character necessary to realise them in action. It is clear that the Ethical Societies have much in common with the Churches as far as good works are concerned, but the two conceptions of what constitutes true religion are widely divergent. "So far as the Churches are endeavouring to battle with the evils of Society and of the individual life, and to band the people together into religious communities for that purpose, the Ethical Societies welcome and endorse their efforts. But they have nothing in common with that view of Religion which lays the chief emphasis upon what a man believes and not upon what he does." Mr. H. Snell, a General Secretary of the Union of Ethical Societies, has drawn up a kind of Ethical Creed. Part of it may be quoted. "We believe first of all in making DUTY a religion. By duty we mean passionate loyalty to truth, justice, mercy, and right living. We do not believe that creeds, theologies, and priestly ceremonies are religion, and we are opposed to ceremonial beliefs being made a duty. We believe that what men call the 'good life' constitutes religion; that there is no religion except that, and we believe that man can lead the 'good life' without supernatural beliefs of any kind. We do not say that all supernatural theories are wrong, but we believe that the 'good life' is not dependent on belief in them. We believe that there is no salvation for mankind apart from character; and we believe that character is salvation. We have no collective beliefs concerning another life than this; but we believe that the life we have needs purifying and improving, and to this end we devote all our time and strength. As individuals we may or may not believe that a ready-made heaven is waiting for us when this life is over; but we unitedly believe that if the kingdom is to 'come on earth as it is in heaven' it must be by man's labour and self-sacrifice. We believe that perfection lies at the end and not at the beginning of human experience; that there was no Garden of Eden, no perfect man, and no Fall which brought sin into the world. We believe that although men fall daily, man is rising, and that he has risen from the beginning until now. We do not believe that Jesus encompassed all the possible good in his own personality, but that knowledge of the right evolves from age to age." There are more than twenty Societies federated in the Union.

ETHNOPHRONIANS. A name given in early times to those who mingled with Christianity pagan customs and superstitions. "Those who practised astrology, fortune-telling, divination, sortilege, or auguries, were all reprobated under this title" (J. H. Blunt).

EUCHARIST. A name given to the Christian institution which commemorates the Last Supper of Jesus. According to the gospels of St. Matthew, St. Mark, and St. Luke, Jesus "gave thanks" (*eucharistēsas*) before he broke the bread and gave it to his disciples. Hence the name Eucharist, which means Thanksgiving. Protestants prefer the title Lord's Supper or Holy Communion, and for the most part are not in agreement with Roman Catholics as to the meaning of the sacrament. Considered as a sacrament (as well as a sacrifice), the Eucharist, according to the *Cath. Dict.*, is the true body and blood of Christ under the appearance of bread and wine. "Like all the sacraments, it was instituted by Christ, and like them, it consists of an outward part—viz., bread and wine, or the appearance of bread and wine: and an inward or invisible part—viz., the body and blood of Christ with the grace which they impart to those who communicate worthily."

EUCHITES. A religious sect which became prominent in Syria towards the end of the fourth century A.D. Derived from a Greek word, the name means "the praying people." The original designation, formed from a Syriac word meaning "to pray," was Messalians or Massalians. The Euchites seem to have been confined to the East, where they existed for some centuries. Messalians are heard of as late as the twelfth century. The Euchites held that men are born with a demon which incites them to sin. This demon cannot be expelled by Baptism or the Eucharist. It can be expelled or subdued only by intense, concentrated prayer, continued until it produces a state from which all affections and volitions are banished. When this state is reached the soul is conscious of a union with God; the demon departs, and the Holy Spirit enters; the Holy Trinity can be seen with the bodily eyes. It was possible, the Euchites believed, to attain a passionless state of perfection in which a man became sinless. "The soul of him who was 'spiritual,' as they boasted themselves to be, was changed into the divine nature; he could see things invisible to ordinary men; and so some of them used to dance by way of trampling on the demons which they saw, a practice from which they were called Choreutae" (*Dict. of Christ. Biogr.*). The Euchites were monks, but, unlike other monks, they refused to support themselves by their labour, preferring to roam about begging. They were condemned by councils held at Side, Constantinople (426 A.D.), and Ephesus (431 A.D.). At Ephesus the Messalian book, *Asceticus*, from which passages were read, was anathematized. The Euchites suffered persecution both in Syria and Asia Minor. Amongst their leaders were Adelphius, Lampetius, and Marcian. See Schaff-Herzog; J. H. Blunt; Wace and Piercy.

EUDISTS. The Roman Catholic congregation known as Eudists derived its name from Jean Eudes (1601-1680). At an early age Eudes was admitted into the Oratory founded by Abbé de Bérulle in Paris. He became specially interested in missions, and left the Oratory with the intention of founding a congregation devoted to this work. In 1643 he founded his congregation of secular priests at Caen. The movement spread rapidly during his lifetime. The Eudists were attacked during the French Revolution, and many of them fled to England. The congregation was revived in 1826. It should be added that the Eudists are not required to make vows. See *Cath. Dict.*; Brockhaus.

EUDOXIANS. The followers of Eudoxius, who became Bishop of Antioch (357 A.D.). He was one of the leading Arians of the fourth century, and developed an extreme form of Arianism (*q.v.*). He was condemned by the Semi-Arian Councils of Seleucia (359 A.D.) and Lampsacus (365 A.D.). See J. H. Newman, *The Arians of the Fourth Century;* H. M. Gwatkin, *The Arian Controversy*, 1889; J. H. Blunt.

EUNOMIANS. A name given to the strict Arians (see ARIANISM) who belonged to the party of Bishop Eunomius. They were also known as Anomœans because they said that the Father and the Son were unlike, and as Exucontians because they said that the Son was made out of nothing.

EUNOMIO-EUTYCHIANS. The followers of Eutychius of Constantinople, a body of Eunomian heretics (see EUNOMIANS). Socrates, the ecclesiastical historian, seems to identify their tenets with those of the Eunomio-Theophronians (*q.v.*).

EUNOMIO-THEOPHRONIANS. The followers of Theophronius of Cappadocia (*flor.* about 370 A.D.), a body of Eunomian heretics (see EUNOMIANS). According to Sozomen, the ecclesiastical historian, Theophronius had given some attention to the works of Aristotle and composed an appendix to them with the title "Exercises of the Mind." Afterwards, on the strength of what he thought a deep knowledge of the terms of Scripture, "he attempted to prove that though God is acquainted with the present, the past, and the future, his knowledge on these subjects is not the same in degree, and is subject to some kind of mutation." The Eunomians repudiated and excommunicated Theophronius, whereupon he founded a new sect. Socrates, the ecclesiastical historian, states that the Eunomio-Theophronians baptized in the name of Christ alone, and not in that of the Trinity. See J. H. Blunt; Wace and Piercy.

EUPHEMITES. According to Augustine, Euphemites

was another name for Euchites (*q.v.*). According to Epiphanius, however, the Euphemites were pagans who in part had adopted the Christian form of worship: they had abandoned polytheism and devoted themselves to the worship of one God. See J. H. Blunt.

EUTYCHIANISM. The teaching of Eutyches, who was archimandrite of a monastery near Constantinople. In 448 A.D. he was definitely accused of heresy by Eusebius of Dorylaeum, at a synod convened in Constantinople. When Eutyches refused to present himself, deputies were sent to him to ascertain his views exactly. According to their report, he said that he was unable to find in the writings of the Fathers of the Church the doctrine that Jesus Christ subsisted of two Persons united in one Hypostasis; and that in any case he could not accept such a doctrine, as it is not found in Holy Scripture. He held that He who was born of the Virgin Mary was very God and very man, but that His body was not of like substance with ours. Summoned to come to the synod in person, Eutyches again refused. To those who were sent to question him again, he is said to have argued that the word *homoousios* ("of the same substance") does not occur in Holy Scripture, but was derived from the Fathers, as was also the affirmation of the two natures. Finally Eutyches presented himself, but his answers to the questions put to him were of the same kind, and were considered unorthodox. He was condemned to be "excluded from all priestly functions, from our communion, and from his primacy in his monastery." Eutyches and Dioscorus, patriarch of Alexandria, requested the Emperor to summon another synod. This was done, and in 449 the synod met at Ephesus, the chief opponent of Eutyches being Flavian, bishop of Constantinople. Eutyches was acquitted, but the synod became known as the Latrocinium or Robber Synod on account of its violence. "The Christian world was rent in pieces by its proceedings. Egypt, Thrace, and Palestine ranged themselves with Dioscorus and the emperor; Syria, Pontus, Asia, Rome, protested against the treatment of Flavian and the acquittal of Eutyches" (Wace and Piercy). In 451 a fourth great Council of the Church met at Chalcedon. At this the verdict of the Latrocinium was reversed, and Eutyches was condemned. It was decreed that Christ must be "acknowledged in two natures, inconfusedly, unchangeably, indivisibly, inseparably, the distinction of natures being by no means taken away by the union, but rather the property of each nature being preserved, and concurring in one person and one hypostasis, not parted or divided into two persons, but one and the same Son and Only-begotten, God the Word, the Lord Jesus Christ, as the prophets from the beginning have declared concerning Him, and the Lord Jesus Christ Himself has taught us, and the creed of the holy Fathers has delivered to us." Eutyches was crushed, but Eutychianism still exists. See William Benham; J. H. Blunt; the *Prot. Dict.*; Wace and Piercy.

EUTYCHETÆ. A sect of heretics mentioned by Theodoret. Theodoret seems to identify the Eutychetae with the Euchites (*q.v.*). Ittigius, on the other hand, identifies them with a sect mentioned by Clement of Alexandria, the Entychites, who, it would seem, owed their name to certain profligate practices. See J. H. Blunt.

EVANGELIARIUM. A lectionary containing passages from the Gospels was so called in the early Christian Church. See LECTIONARIES.

EVANGELICAL ALLIANCE, THE. The Evangelical Alliance was constituted in 1846 at a great Conference in Freemason's Hall, London, which was attended by eight hundred representatives of the Christian Churches. One of the resolutions passed was as follows: "This Conference, composed of professing Christians of many different denominations, all exercising the right of private judgment, and, through common infirmity, differing among themselves in the views they severally entertain on some points both of Christian doctrine and ecclesiastical polity, and gathered together from many and remote parts of the world for the purpose of promoting Christian union, rejoice in making their unanimous avowal of the glorious truth that the Church of the Living God, while it admits of growth, is one Church, never having lost, and being incapable of losing, its essential unity. Not, therefore, to create that unity, but to confess it, is the design of their assembling together. One in reality, they desire also, as far as they may be able to attain it, to be visibly one; and thus both to realize in themselves and to exhibit to others that a living and everlasting union binds all true believers together in the fellowship of the Church of Christ, 'which is His body, the fulness of Him that filleth all in all.'" The Alliance is based upon nine theological views which are usually understood to be evangelical. 1. The divine inspiration, authority, and sufficiency of the Holy Scriptures. 2. The right and duty of private judgment in the interpretation of the Holy Scriptures. 3. The unity of the Godhead, and the Trinity of Persons therein. 4. The utter depravity of human nature in consequence of the fall. 5. The Incarnation of the Son of God, His work of atonement for sinners, and His mediatorial intercession and reign. 6. The justification of the sinner by faith alone. 7. The work of the Holy Spirit in the conversion and sanctification of the sinner. 8. The immortality of the soul, the resurrection of the body, the judgment of the world by our Lord Jesus Christ, with the eternal blessedness of the righteous, and the eternal punishment of the wicked. 9. The divine institution of the Christian ministry, and the obligation and perpetuity of the ordinances of Baptism and the Lord's Supper. It is distinctly declared, however, that "this brief summary is not to be regarded, in any formal or ecclesiastical sense, as a creed or confession, nor the adoption of it as involving an assumption of the right authoritatively to define the limits of Christian brotherhood, but simply as an indication of the class of persons whom it is desirable to embrace within the Alliance." One of the practical resolutions agreed upon by the London Conference of 1846 and read at each Annual Meeting or Conference of the British Organization of the Evangelical Alliance lays special stress on this general Christian fraternity. "That, while they believe it highly desirable that Christians of different bodies, holding the Head, should own each other as brethren by some such means as the Evangelical Alliance affords, the members of the Alliance disclaim the thought that those only who openly join the society are sincere friends to the cause of Christian Union: that, on the contrary, they regard all those as its true friends who solemnly purpose in their hearts, and fulfil that purpose in their practice, to be more watchful in future against occasions of strife, more tender and charitable towards Christians from whom they differ, and more constant in prayer for the union of all the true disciples of Christ." Since its foundation the Evangelical Alliance has exerted itself on behalf of persecuted Christians not only in Europe but also in many countries beyond. In recent years it has endeavoured also to bring relief to Jews in Russia, and sufferers from famine in Armenia. It has tried to promote religious liberty in Malta, Russia, Spain, and other countries. See the Annual Reports of the Evangelical Alliance.

EVANGELICAL ASSOCIATION. The name assumed

by a religious sect founded in North America by Jacob Albrecht (*d.* 1808). In 1803 Albrecht was made presiding elder, or a kind of bishop, by the other preachers. The "Albrecht Brethren," as the members of the sect are also called, have much in common with the Methodists. Branches of the Evangelical Association were formed in Germany. See J. H. Blunt; Brockhaus.

EVANGELICAL UNION. The name assumed by the sect founded by James Morison (1816-1893). The members were also called Morisonians (*q.v.*).

EXCALCEATI. The Excalceati were an ancient sect who thought it necessary to follow the example of the prophet Isaiah and to walk barefoot. They were called also Gymnopodae. See J. H. Blunt.

EXCOMMUNICATION. A term used to denote exclusion from the ecclesiastical community. According to Ezra x. 8, those who had taken "strange" wives and refused to give them up were separated from the Jewish community. In Luke vi. 22 reference seems to be made to three different grades of Jewish excommunication. These apparently were (1) *niddûi*, a short term of thirty days; (2) *chêrem*, a much longer period; and (3) *shammattā*, complete exclusion. In St. Paul's epistles some kind of excommunication seems to be referred to in I. Cor. v. 3-5, II. Cor. ii. 6-11. In the Pastoral Epistles the rules of exclusion have become more precise (I. Tim. i. 20, v. 19 f.). In recent times several early Christian documents of excommunication have been discovered (Camden M. Cobern). The Roman Catholic Church distinguishes two kinds of excommunication, the major and the minor. "The minor kind is an ecclesiastical censure, by which a Christian is deprived of the right to participation in sacraments, and indirectly, as a consequence, of the right of receiving a benefice" (*Cath. Dict.*). The major excommunication "deprives of all ecclesiastical communion, and is equivalent in substance to *anathema*, from which it only differs in regard to the formalities by which the latter is surrounded." Article xxxiii. of the Church of England states that persons who are rightly cut off from the unity of the Church by open denunciation of it ought to be avoided by the faithful. "The rubric prefixed to the Communion Service provides that for notorious moral offences offenders may be denied the Lord's Supper, but the offence must obviously be proved by the judgment of some competent court" (*Prot. Dict.*).

EXERCISES, SPIRITUAL. Ignatius of Loyola wrote a work which he called "Spiritual Exercises," and which has served since as a guide for those who have desired to practice meditation and penance. The Jesuits have zealously practised spiritual exercises according to the method of Ignatius, and have won the title "men of the Exercises." The work was written in Spanish, but was translated into Latin (Engl. transl., *The Spiritual Exercises of St. Ignatius of Loyola*, 1849). "The person who makes the exercises is supposed to receive them from a director, and the exercises are arranged for a retreat of four weeks; they can, however, be adapted for a much shorter time. The exercitant begins with meditations on the end of man, and on the penalties of sin, that he may flee with horror from it; passes next to those on Christ's life and death, Christ being the model which we have to copy; and ends by contemplating the resurrection of Christ, happiness of heaven, etc., that he may learn to unite himself to God" (*Cath. Dict.*). See Schaff-Herzog; *Cath. Dict.*

EXODUS, BOOK OF. The Book of Exodus, the second book in the first division of the Hebrew Canon of the Old Testament (*q.v.*), bears in the Hebrew Bible the title *We-ēlleh Shemoth* (these being the opening words of the book) or simply *Shemoth*. The English title is derived, through the Old Latin and Vulgate, from the Septuagint. In the LXX the title is Exodus or Exodos Aiguptou ("Exodus from Egypt"; see Exodus xix. 1). The Book of Exodus carries on the history of Israel from the death of Joseph. But the circumstances have changed. "The twelve sons of Jacob with their children who went down into Egypt ('seventy souls') have so increased in numbers as to be a cause of alarm to the Egyptians; the narrative, which throughout Genesis preserves the form of a family chronicle, now at once becomes the history of a people (G. F. Moore). The contents of the Book of Exodus are as follows: Chapters i.-ii. describe the growth of the people in Egypt, the Egyptian oppression, and the early days of Moses. Chaps. iii. 1-vii. 13 tell of Moses' call to be the deliverer of his people. Chaps. vii. 14-xi. describe nine of the ten plagues sent by God to warn and frighten the Egyptians. Chaps. xii.-xiii. tell how the Feast of the Passover and the Feast of Unleavened Cakes were instituted, and how after the tenth plague, the destruction of the first-born of the Egyptians, the Israelites departed from Rameses. Chap. xiv. describes the passage of the Red Sea and the pursuit by the Egyptians. Chap. xv. gives Moses' Song of Triumph and Thanksgiving. Chap. xvi. tells how the Israelites journeyed to the wilderness of Sin, and were fed with Manna and Quails. Chap. xvii. recounts that they continued their journey to Rephidim, and found water at Massah (J) or Meribah (E). It describes also the battle with and victory over Amalek. Chap. xviii. tells of a visit made by Moses to Jethro and of its results. Chaps. xix.-xxiv. tell of the arrival of Israel at Sinai and of the preparation for the law-giving. Moses receives from God the Decalogue and the Book of the Covenant. Chaps. xxv.-xxxi. 18*a* tell how Moses received directions which amounted to "an entirely new law, very detailed instructions with regard to the institution of an official cultus" (Holzinger). Chaps. xxxi. 18*b*-xxxiv. tells of the making of the Golden Calf. Chaps. xxxv.-xl. describe how the instructions with regard to the institution of an official cultus were carried out. The Book of Exodus is of composite origin, and was compiled from a number of documents. The oldest of these were the Primitive Document (J; ninth cent. B.C.) and the early Elohistic Document (E; a little later). These were based partly upon oral tradition, partly upon written laws (*e.g.*, chaps. xx.-xxiii., xxxiv. 10-28). The combined narrative JE was compiled early in the seventh century B.C. Another stratum consists of additions made to J or E or JE by Deuteronomic editors (600 B.C.). The document known as P (Priestly Writer) is largely represented in the second half of the book. To this may be traced the chapters dealing with the institution of an official cultus (xxv.-xxxi. 18*a* and xxxv.-xl.). According to Driver, "it is probable that P was written, partly during the Babylonian exile, partly during the century that followed the return to Judah." Driver points out that, "as regards JE in general, it is to be remembered that the criteria distinguishing J and E from each other are less numerous and strongly marked than those distinguishing P from JE as a whole; so that, while there is hardly ever any doubt as to the limits of P, there are passages of JE in which, from the insufficiency or ambiguity of the criteria, the analysis is uncertain, and different critics may arrive at different conclusions." The Song of Moses or Song of Miriam, in the form in which it has been preserved (chap. xv. 1-18), is probably not of ancient date. It would seem to be an expansion of a very much shorter utterance—an utterance consisting only of vs. 1 (repeated in vs. 21). The expanded form may have been written in the sixth century B.C.; or even in Babylonia about 540-538, when, as Whitehouse says, "the expected restoration would naturally recall the memories ("former things") of the exodus (Isa. xliii. 1, 2, 16-17, xliv. 27, 28, xlvi. 9 ff., xlviii. 3, 21, l. 2, li. 9, 10)." The Book of Exodus contains several ancient codes of laws. There are the "Ten Commandments" (chap. xx., E), the "Book of the Covenant" (xx. 22-xxiii. 19, E), the Laws of the Two Tables (xxxiv. 10-28, J). See Moore in *Encycl. Bibl.;* J. E. Carpenter and G. Harford-Battersby; H. Holzinger, *Exodus*, 1900; W. H. Bennett, *Exodus* in the "Century Bible"; G. H. Box, *Intr.;* O. C. Whitehouse; S. R. Driver, *Exodus* in the "Cambridge Bible," 1911.

EXORCISM. The term "Exorcists" (*exorkistai*) occurs in the New Testament. It is used of persons who used a formula of conjuration in order to expel demons. Josephus (*Antiquities*, viii. 2, v.) says that God gave Solomon skill in expelling demons. "He composed such incantations also by which distempers are alleviated. And he left behind him the manner of using exorcisms, by which they drive away demons, so that they never return, and this method of cure is of great force unto this day; for I have seen a certain man of my own country, whose name was Eleazar, releasing people that were demoniacal in the presence of Vespasian and his sons and his captains and the whole multitude of his soldiers. The manner of the cure was this: He put a ring that had a root of one of those sorts mentioned by Solomon to the nostrils of the demoniac, after which he drew out the demon through his nostrils; and when the man fell down immediately, he abjured him to return into him no more, making still mention of Solomon, and reciting the incantations which he composed. And when Eleazar would persuade and demonstrate to the spectators that he had such a power, he set a little way off a cup or basin full of water, and commanded the demon as he went out of the man to overturn it, and thereby to let the spectators know that he had left the man; and when this was done, the skill and wisdom of Solomon was shown very manifestly" (Whiston's transl.). In the Wars of the Jews (vii. 6, 3) Josephus mentions a herb Baaras which was difficult to pluck. He adds: "Yet, after all this pains in getting, it is only valuable on account of one virtue it hath, that if it be only brought to sick persons, it quickly drives away those called demons, which are no other than the spirits of the wicked, that enter into men that are alive and kill them, unless they can obtain some help against them." In the New Testament we are told that Jesus cast out the spirits "with a word" or "by the spirit of God" or "by the finger of God." His disciples too were empowered by him to cast out demons both before and after his resurrection. In Mk. xvi. 17 Jesus, after his resurrection and before his ascension, is represented as saying that one of the signs that shall accompany those who believe will be the casting out of demons in his name. From Acts xix. 13 it seems that the sons or disciples of a prominent Jew at Ephesus used the name "as a spell in preference to the strings of names of gods and demigods and angels which were common in exorcisms both in Asia Minor and elsewhere" (*Ency. Bib.*). Justin Martyr says (*Apol.* ii. 5) that in cases in which every other kind of exorcism had failed, "the name of Jesus Christ who was crucified under Pontius Pilate" was potent to cast out demons. In his *Dialogue with Trypho* he admits that Jews were able to exorcise demons in the name of the God of Abraham or of Isaac or of Jacob, but he complains that they had adopted heathen practices, such as the use of perfumes and ligatures. There is frequent reference to the practice of exorcism in the early church. Catechumens were exorcised at baptism, and even afterwards. Baptismal exorcism has survived in the Roman Catholic Church. So also has the ancient practice (cp. Cyprian, *Ep.* 70) of exorcising inanimate things, such as holy oil and holy water. Cornelius, as quoted by Eusebius (*Eccles. Hist.*, vi. 43) refers to Exorcists as a special order of the clergy. A special form for the ordination of Exorcists is prescribed by what is known as the Fourth Council of Carthage. The bishop, in presenting a book of exorcisms, said: "Take this book and get it by heart, and have authority to lay hands upon catechumens and baptised persons possessed." Exorcists were forbidden by Innocent I. to exercise "their ministry on the possessed without express permission from the bishop, and this law is still in force" (*Cath. Dict.*). In the Roman Catholic Church the Exorcists are the third of what are known as the minor orders. In the Greek Church they are not recognised as an ecclesiastical order. Nor are they recognised by the Protestant Churches. By the seventy-second canon of the Church of England (1603) ministers are forbidden to attempt to drive out demons without a license from the bishop. In exorcism, as practised in ancient times by the Babylonians, use was made of ablutions, fumigations, and medicinal plants. See Benham; the *Cath. Dict.;* the *Encycl. Bibl.;* Chambers' *Encycl.;* Reinach, *O.*

EXOTIANS. Socrates, the ecclesiastical historian, describes how the Arians of Constantinople, "after having been in possession of the churches for forty years, in consequence of their opposition to the conciliatory measures of the emperor Thedosius, were driven out of the city, in Gratian's fifth consulate and the first of Theodosius Augustus, on the 26th of November" (v. 7). It seems from the chronicle of Alexandria and a decree of Justinian that the Arians who had to hold their services outside the city (*exo tēs poleōs*) were called Exotians. See J. H. Blunt.

EXTREME UNCTION. In the fifth chapter of the General Epistle of James (*q.v.*) it is said (vss. 14, 15): "Is any among you sick? let him call for the elders of the church; and let them pray over him, anointing him (or, having anointed him) with oil in the name of the Lord: and the prayer of faith shall save him that is sick, and the Lord shall raise him up; and if he have committed sins, it shall be forgiven him." James Adderley points out (*The Epistle of St. James*) that the Church of England has not made any special provision for the Unction, though it has done so for the Prayers. He thinks that a revival of the primitive and Catholic practice of anointing the sick should be prayed for. Since he wrote the practice has to some extent been revived. Originally, it would seem, the anointing with oil had a medicinal and therapeutic value. In Mark (vi. 13) it is said that the Apostles "cast out many demons, and anointed with oil many that were sick, and healed them"; and there are references to the practice in the Old Testament (*e.g.*, Ezekiel xvi. 9). A rule is given by Egbert, Archbishop of York (732-766), "That according to the enactment of the holy fathers, if any is sick he be diligently anointed with sanctified oil together with prayers." Extreme Unction is first spoken of as a sacrament by Hugo of St. Victor (*d.* 1141). Peter Lombard (*d.* 1164) distinguishes three kinds of consecrated oil—(1) that used for priests and kings and candidates for Confirmation; (2) that used for catechumens and newly baptized persons; (3) that used for the sick. Adderley suggests that probably at first Extreme Unction simply meant "the last of the unctions in a Christian's life." Then in course of time it came to mean the unction of a person dying or *in extremis*. But it did not become this in the Eastern Church. There, where the sacrament is called Prayer-oil, it is not confined to those who are dying. It is defined as "holy oil, a sacred rite and type of divine pity, supplied to those who turn from sin for redemption and sanctification, affording absolution of sins, and raising up from sicknesses, and filling with sanctification." In the Roman Catholic Church extreme unction is reserved for those who are in danger of death. It can only be given by a priest, and with a set form of words. In former times it preceded the Viaticum (*q.v.*); now it follows. The oil is applied in the form of a cross. See James Adderley, *The Epistle of St. James;* K. R. Hagenbach; *Prot. Dict.; Cath. Dict.*

EXUCONTIANS. A name given to the strict Arians (see ARIANISM) who belonged to the party of Aetius and Bishop Eunomius. They were so called because they taught that the Father and the Son were unlike (Gk. *anomoios*, whence the designation Anomœans), and that the Son was made out of nothing (Gk. *ex ouk ontōn*). They were also designated Eunomians.

EYES, CEREMONY OF PAINTING THE. A ceremony performed by the Kammālans (*q.v.*) of India, makers of god-images. The ceremony takes place when the eyes are added to the images. It is curious to find the Kammālans attaching the same importance to artificial eyes as the ancient Egyptians did. "After moulding into shape the wrappings of the mummy so as to restore as far as possible the form of the deceased, the embalmer then painted eyes upon the face. So also when the sculptor had learned to make finished models in stone or wood, and by the addition of paint had enhanced the life-like appearance, the statue was still a dead thing. What were needed above all to enliven it, literally and actually, in other words, to animate it, were the eyes; and the Egyptian artist set to work and with truly marvellous skill reproduced the appearance of living eyes. How ample was the justification for this belief will be appreciated by anyone who glances at the remarkable photographs recently published by Dr. Alan H. Gardiner. The wonderful eyes will be seen to make the statue sparkle and live. To the concrete mind of the Egyptian this triumph of art was regarded not as a mere technical success or aesthetic achievement. The artist was considered to have made the statue really live; in fact, literally and actually converted it into a 'living image.' The eyes themselves were regarded as one of the chief sources of the vitality which had been conferred upon the statue" (G. Elliot Smith, *Dr.*, 1919, p. 52).

EZEKIEL, BOOK OF. The Book of Ezekiel is one of the larger prophetic books in the Canon of the Old Testament. Ezekiel, the author, was one of those who with Jehoiachin was carried captive to Babylonia in 597 B.C. by Nebuchadrezzar. He was a priest as well as a prophet, and it has been suggested that "possibly he was singled out by Nebuchadrezzar as a chief man among the priests" (C. H. Toy). He represents a transition period, a period in which the prophets were giving place to the priests. Jeremiah also was a priest, and, as Prof. Harper says, the books of Haggai, Zechariah, and Malachi are far more priestly than prophetic. "Ezekiel, as a prophet, was alive to the dependence of the people on the immediate word of God, to the necessity, that is, of a constant living contact between the mind of God and the mind of man: but, as priest, he also saw that the people had reached a stage which demanded a more precise formulation of the law of worship. He lived on the verge of a great religious revolution—the abolition, namely, of idolatry, and the establishment of the sole worship of Yahwè in Israel. The religious leaders of Josiah's time, both priests and prophets, had with true insight insisted on the necessity of centralising the worship at Jerusalem in order to destroy the corrupt local cults. Ezekiel carries on the fight for ethical monotheism, not only by denouncing the worship of other gods than Yahwè as the source of the national misfortunes, but also, more effectively, by furthering that strict organisation of the cultus which alone could train the people to the purer worship of the one God of Israel" (C. H. Toy in the *Encycl. Bibl.*). The text of the Book of Ezekiel is in considerable disorder, but this is not due to composite authorship. The contents may be divided into three sections. (1) Chapters i.-xxiv. were delivered at the beginning of the siege of Jerusalem, and have in prospect its imminent destruction. This section contains the "Vision of the Chariot" (i. 1-iii. 15). Chapters xxv.-xxxii. contain oracles against foreign nations, against Ammon, Moab, Edom, Philistia, Tyre, Sidon, and Egypt. Chapters xxxiii.-xlviii. contain prophecies of Israel's restoration and triumph, with a vision of the restored theocracy. The last part of this section (xl.-xlviii.) and of the whole book is rather different in character from the rest of the work. It presents an ideal state; it puts forward "a conception which constitutes the germ of the doctrine of the *kingdom of God*" (Harper). There are many points of contact between Ezekiel and Jeremiah. Ezekiel would seem to have been familiar with discourses or writings of the earlier prophet; or it may be supposed that in some cases use was made of a common source. Compare Ezek. iii. 3 with Jer. xv. 16; Ezek. iii. 17 with Jer. vi. 17; Ezek. vii. 14, 27 with Jer. iv. 5-9; Ezek. xiii. with Jer. xiv. 13-16; Ezek. xiii. 10 with Jer. vi. 14; Ezek. xvi. 51 with Jer. iii. 11; Ezek. xviii. with Jer. xxxi. 29 f.; Ezek. xx. with Jer. xi. 3-8; Ezek. xxiv. 16-23 with Jer. xvi. 3-9; Ezek. xxix.-xxxi. with Jer. xlvi.; Ezek. xxxiv. with Jer. xxiii. 1-4; Ezek. xxxvi. 26 with Jer. xxiv. 7; Ezek. xxxvii. 24 with Jer. xxx. 9; Ezek. xxxviii. 15 with Jer. vi. 22. There are also points of contact between Ezekiel and the Code of Holiness (see LEVITICUS). The latest date given in the book of Ezekiel is 570 B.C. (xxix. 17). The text on which the Septuagint translation was based seems to have been shorter than the Hebrew text. See C. H. Toy in the *Encycl. Bibl.;* A. B. Davidson, *Ezekiel* in the "Cambridge Bible," 1892; C. Cornill, *Das Buch des Prophet Ezechiel*, 1886; A. Bertholet, *Das Buch Hesekiel*, 1897; R. Kraetzschmar, *Das Buch Ezechiel*, 1900; W. R. Harper, *The Priestly Element in the Old Testament*, 1905; C. Cornill, *Intr.;* G. H. Box; O. C. Whitehouse.

EZRA-NEHEMIAH, BOOK OF. The book of Ezra and Nehemiah originally formed one book in the Jewish Canon. In a passage of the Talmud (*q.v.*) the book of Nehemiah is evidently understood to be included in the book of Ezra (*Baba bathra* 14, 2; cp. Melito of Sardis in Eusebius, *HE*, iv. 26). The Jewish Rabbis Rashi and Aben Ezra regard Nehemiah i. 1 as directly continuing Ezra x. 44. The Massoretes by their liturgical divisions of Ezra-Nehemiah and by their appended Massoretic notes (at the end of Nehemiah) show that they regarded the two books as one. In the Septuagint they actually appear as one (Second Esdras). But, besides this, there is a close connection between Ezra-Nehemiah and the Books of Chronicles (*q.v.*), so close a connection that Ezra-Nehemiah would seem to have been compiled by the Chronicler as an immediate sequel to his books of Chronicles. As Prof. Harper says, "Ezra-Nehemiah takes up the history at the point where it stops in Chronicles and continues it until the building of the second temple is narrated, the two books, Chronicles and Ezra-Nehemiah, thus constituting a history of the temple and its worship from the time of the building of Solomon's temple until the restoration of worship in the days of Ezra and Nehemiah." Ezra-Nehemiah resembles

Chronicles in literary style and in vocabulary; and the opening words of the book of Ezra (i. 1-3*a*) are identical with the closing words of the Second Book of Chronicles (II. Chron. xxxvi. 22 ff.). The contents of the Book of Ezra may be divided into two sections: I., Chapters i.-xiii. 3; II., Chapter xiii. 4-31. In section I. Chapters i.-vi. describe the return of the Jews to Palestine and their experiences there from the first year of Cyrus as king of Babylon to the sixth year of Darius Hystaspis (538-515 B.C.). Chapters vii.-x. continue the history after an interval of about sixty years. They describe the arrival of Ezra in Jerusalem in the seventh year of Artaxerxes (458 B.C.) and his work as a reformer there. The contents of the Book of Nehemiah also divide themselves in the main into two sections. Chapters i.-vii. narrate (in the first person) events connected with the planning and carrying out of Nehemiah's visit to Jerusalem, and with his efforts at reform there. Chapters viii.-x. narrate (in the third person) events connected with the public reading of the "book of the Law of Moses" by Ezra, the celebration of the Feast of Tabernacles, etc.. Chapters xi.-xiii. 3 give statistics, and deal with the dedication of the walls of Jerusalem, etc. Section II. (chap. xiii. 4-31) gives an account (in the first person) of Nehemiah's second visit to Jerusalem and of his work as a reformer. It is clear that the compiler of the work Ezra-Nehemiah made use of a number of different sources. Part of the Book of Ezra is written in Aramaic (iv. 8-vi. 18 and vii. 12-26); and it has been mentioned already that the narrative in Ezra and Nehemiah is partly in the third and partly in the first person. The most important of the sources used were Memoirs of Ezra (*e.g.*, Ezra vii. 27-viii. 34, ix.) and Memoirs of Nehemiah (*e.g.*, Nehemiah i. 1-vii. 5*a*, xiii. 4-31). As regards the historical value of Ezra-Nehemiah, the Dutch scholar Kosters has tried to show that the first four chapters of Ezra are unhistorical, and that a return of exiles did not take place at all in the second year of Cyrus. R. Kittel, however (*The Scientific Study of the O.T.*, 1910), while admitting that Chronicles can only be accepted with great reservation as a record of history, thinks that the books of Ezra and Nehemiah, which are probably by the same compiler, are of a quite different type. "It is true that we must regard certain parts of these books with distrust, but in this case the books relate the history of a much later period than the Chronicles, and the narrator therefore is in a much better position, in that he speaks of events which were nearer to him in time than the events described in the Chronicles." C. F. Kent accepts the view that "many of the otherwise insuperable difficulties of Ezra-Nehemiah disappear, when it is recognized that, if at all historical, the work of Ezra must have followed, not preceded that of Nehemiah." As regards the date of Ezra-Nehemiah, internal evidence seems to point to the fact that the compilation was made between the years 300 and 250 B.C. See *Encycl. Bibl.*; H. E. Ryle, *Ezra and Nehemiah* in the "Cambridge Bible," 1893; C. Siegfried, *Esra, Nehemiah und Esther*, 1901; A. Bertholet, *Die Buecher Esra und Nehemia*, 1902; W. R. Harper, *The Priestly Element in the Old Test.*, 1905; C. F. Kent, *Israel's Historical and Biographical Narratives*, 1905; C. Cornill, *Intr.;* O. C. Whitehouse.

F

F. God F is a designation used by anthropologists for a deity depicted in the MSS. of the Mayan Indians of Central America. He is represented with black lines on his face and body. These, according to Schellhas, signify death wounds. In any case, the deity is a death-god and resembles God A (*q.v.*).

FAITHIST BROTHERS AND SISTERS. Members of a new religious community. The name is explained in the sacred book of the community—a work called *Oahspe*. "We cannot found the Father's Kingdom with any other members than such as say with all their hearts and mind and soul: Whatsoever Thou puttest upon me, O Jehovih, that will I do with all my wisdom and strength. To have faith in this way is to have Faith with practice: such a one is a Faithist in fact." See BROTHERHOOD OF THE KOSMON DAWN.

FAKIRS. The term Fakir means in Arabic a "poor man." The Fakirs in India are religious mendicants who, to excite pity, inflict tortures on themselves. They are feared, though not respected, by the people because their curses are believed to be very potent. It was formerly their practice to go about in a nude condition, but this practice is now forbidden. See Schaff-Herzog.

FALASHAS. The Falashas are a people in Abyssinia, whose religion incorporates a number of Jewish beliefs and practices. Their ancestors may have been Jews or proselytes to Judaism. But they observe also a number of pagan practices. Their sacred books include the canonical and apocryphal books of the Old Testament in Geez, a work *Ardit* which purports to be a book of secrets revealed to twelve saints, and a translation of Josephus called *Sana Aihud*. They practise circumcision and fasting, and keep some, but not all, of the Jewish Feasts (*e.g.*, Passover, Ingathering, Tabernacles). At the same time they believe in magic, and worship a goddess Sanbat. They offer sacrifices for the dead, pray for the dead, and use fire in a ceremony of purification for unchastity. See Schaff-Herzog.

FAMILIARS OF THE HOLY OFFICE. Spies who worked for the Inquisition (*q.v.*, ii.) or Holy Office in Spain.

FAMILISTS. The Familists or Familia Charitatis were a religious body founded by Henry Nicholas of Muenster. Nicholas went from Holland to England in the reign of Edward VI. and sought to make converts there. "The predominant trait of the sect was its mysticism, which gave rise to very peculiar doctrines of Moses as the prophet of hope, Christ as the prophet of faith, and Henry Nicholas as the prophet of love" (Schaff-Herzog). In the reign of Queen Elizabeth a proclamation was issued "against the Sectaries of the Family of Love." After this severe measures were taken against the Familists, and in the reign of James I. the sect died out. Nicholas was acquainted with David Joris. See Schaff-Herzog.

FARNOVIANS. The followers of Farnovius or Stanislaus Farnowski. Farnovius was one of the leaders of the anti-trinitarians in Poland in the sixteenth century. He was in fact an Arian or Unitarian. After his death, in 1615, the Farnovians amalgamated with the Socinians. See Schaff-Herzog; J. H. Blunt.

FATHER-MOTHER GOD. The name given to God by the founder of Christian Science (*q.v.*), Mary Baker Eddy. In "Rudimental Divine Science" (new edition, 1910) she says: "I mean the infinite and divine Principle of all being, the ever-present I AM, filling all space, including in itself all Mind, the one Father-Mother God. Life, Truth, and Love are this trinity in unity, and their universe is spiritual, peopled with perfect beings, harmonious and eternal, of which our material universe and men are the counterfeits." The Lord's Prayer, as expounded in the Christian Science Service, begins: "Our Father-Mother God, all-harmonious." See Mary Baker G. Eddy, *Science and Health*, 1907, p. 16 *f*.

FAUNUS. One of the oldest of the Italian deities. He was the god of forests, plains, fields, and shepherds. As such he came to be identified with the Greek god Pan (*q.v.*). He was worshipped also as a god of prophecy. "He revealed the future in dreams and strange voices, communicated to his votaries while sleeping in his precincts upon the fleeces of sacrificed lambs" (O. Seyffert). As a god of prophecy, he was called *Fatuus*. J. G. Frazer mentions (*G.B.*, Pt. II., 1911) that those who consulted the oracle of Faunus were required to be chaste, to eat no flesh, and to wear no rings. He explains that rings seem to have been regarded as magical fetters which prevented the egress or ingress of spirits. With Faunus was associated a goddess Fauna or Fatua. The festival Faunalia at which honour was done to the deity by peasants was celebrated on the 13th of February and the 5th of December. In legend Faunus is represented as the grandson of Saturn (*q.v.*), and as an ancient king of Latium who taught the people agriculture and cattle-breeding. To Faunus the god were assigned a number of Fauni or Fauns, just as to Pan (*q.v.*) were assigned a number of little Pans (*Paniskoi*), and to Silenus Silenuses. Like the Pans, Silenuses, and Satyrs (*q.v.*), the Fauns are represented as being to some extent in the form of goats. They were regarded as "merry, capricious beings, and in particular as mischievous goblins who caused night-mares" (O. Seyffert). J. G. Frazer points out that all such minor divinities in the form of goats partake more or less clearly of the character of woodland deities. "The Fauns are expressly designated as woodland deities; and their character as such is still further brought out by their association, or even identification, with Silvanus and the Silvanuses, who, as their name of itself indicates, are spirits of the woods." He points out further that there is a close connection between tree-spirits and corn-spirits. This is seen in the case of the Fauns. Though wood-spirits, they were supposed to foster the growth of the crops. In folk-custom the corn-spirit is frequently represented as a goat. Frazer agrees with Mannhardt that on the whole "the Pans, Satyrs, and Fauns perhaps belong to a widely diffused class of wood-spirits conceived in goat form." See *Chambers' Encycl.*; O. Seyffert, *Dict.*; J. G. Frazer, *G.B.*, Pt. V., vol. ii.

FEAST OF FOOLS. The Feast of Fools was a more or less christianized form of the pagan Saturnalia (*q.v.*). In the twelfth century it was celebrated as a Church festival throughout Italy, Spain, France, Germany, and England. See further BOY-BISHOP

FEATHERS' TAVERN ASSOCIATION. In the latter part of the eighteenth century a body of clergymen and laymen who demanded revision of the Liturgy of the Church of England, and particularly certain changes in the Athanasian Creed, used to meet in a place called Feathers' Tavern. From the name of the place they became known as the Feathers' Tavern Association.

FEBRONIANISM. Febronianism is a term used to describe certain views regarding the relations of Church and State which Roman Catholics describe as "an exaggeration of Gallicanism" (*Cath. Dict.*). The term is derived from the name Febronius, a name assumed for literary purposes by John Nicolas von Hontheim (1701-1790), who was suffragan bishop of Treves. Under this *nom de plume* there appeared in 1763 a work "De Statu Ecclesiae et de legitima Potestate Romani Pontificis," which attained great notoriety. The writer claimed that the power of the keys belonged to the whole body of the faithful, though the administration was committed to the bishops. The bishops received their power direct from God. The primacy of the Pope was only equivalent to the superiority of a Metropolitan to the other bishops of his province; and the authority of the Pope is not equal to that of the Episcopate as a body. The Pope's primacy was in the Church not over the Church, and from the Pope it was always possible to appeal to a General Council. In 1764 the book was condemned by Clement XIII. During the years 1770 to 1774 the author made considerable additions to his work. In 1778 he was persuaded by Pius VI. and the Archbishop of Treves to make a formal retraction of propositions in his book. In 1786 a schism was threatened by the Archbishops of Cologne, Treves, Mayence, and Salzburg, but in 1789 they returned to their allegiance. See *Prot. Dict.*; *Cath. Dict.*; Brockhaus.

FEDERAL THEOLOGY. A designation of the theological teaching of J. Cocceius (1603-1669). See COCCEIANS.

FE'E. A deity worshipped by the natives of Samoa, a war-god. The name really denotes the cuttle-fish. His sacred month in one district was May. "No traveller was then allowed to pass through the village by the public road; nor was any canoe allowed in the lagoon off that part of the settlement" (George Turner, *Samoa*, 1884). There were great festivities, in which featured games, club exercise, spear-throwing, and wrestling. In another district three months were sacred to the deity. "For the first month torches and all other lights were forbidden, as the god was about and did not wish to be seen. White turbans were also forbidden during the festivities, and confined to war" (*ibid.*).

FENRIS-WOLF. The Fenris-wolf or Fenrir-wolf is a figure in the mythology of the Ancient Teutons. He is represented as one of the offspring of Loki (*q.v.*). Like the Midhgardh-serpent (*q.v.*), he is represented as being a sea-monster, one of the giants. Legend tells of a struggle between Tyr (see TIU) and the Fenris-wolf, in which the God lost his right hand; and of a conflict between Vidharr (*q.v.*) and the wolf, in which the latter was slain. See P. D. Chantepie de la Saussaye, *Rel. of the Teutons*, 1902.

FERIÆ LATINAE. One of the principal of the movable festivals observed by the Romans. From being a celebration by the Latin race in honour of Jupiter Latiaris, it was converted by Tarquinius Superbus into a festival of the Latin League. "It's most notable ceremony consisted in the sacrifice of white bulls, a portion of whose flesh was distributed to each of the cities of the league represented at the sacrifice. If any city did not receive its portion, or if any other point in the ceremonial was omitted, the whole sacrifice had to be repeated" (O. Seyffert). J. G. Frazer points out that "at Rome swinging seems to have formed part of the great Latin festival (*Feriæ Latinae*), and its origin was traced to a search in the air for the body or even the soul of King Latinus, who had disappeared from earth after the battle with Mezentius, King of Caere." In this case, as in others, swinging was practised as a religious or rather a magical rite. At the Compitalia and Paganalia small images of the human figure or simply round balls were hung on trees or doorways to swing in the wind. Cp. COMPITALIA, PAGANALIA, and SWINGING. See O. Seyffert; W. Warde Fowler; J. G. Frazer, *G.B.*, Pt. iii., 1912.

FERMENTARIANS. A name formerly given by members of the Latin Church, who used unleavened bread in the Lord's Supper, to members of the Greek Church, who used leavened bread.

FETCHES. A term in Irish folklore. The fetch is an apparition, a kind of shadow of a living person. "If the apparition appears in the morning a happy longevity for the original may be confidently predicted; but if it appears in the evening the immediate dissolution of the living prototype may be as surely anticipated. When the Fetch appears agitated in its movements, a violent or painful death is indicated for the doomed prototype, who is known at the time to be labouring under some serious illness" (W. G. Wood-Martin).

FETICHISM. The term fetichism was introduced into the science of religions by De Brosses (*Du Culte des dieux fétiches*, 1760). "The Portugues navigators who first traded with Western Africa had noticed that the negroes of this region bestowed a kind of worship on material gods, such as stones or shells, which the Portuguese called *fetiches*, from a word in their own language [*feitiço*] derived from the Latin *factitius* (fabricated), used to denote small devotional objects" (Reinach, *O.*). Among anthropologists the term has come to be used in a great variety of applications. W. G. Aston in Hastings' *Encycl.* distinguishes five distinct classes of objects to which the term relates, "all of which fall under the general description of material objects worshipped, honoured, or esteemed for something more than their physical properties or commercial value." (1) Natural objects and phenomena, such as the sun, the sky, and the earth. (2) Material objects worshipped as representatives or symbols of a Nature-deity or deified man, such as the golden solar disk of the ancient Peruvians. (3) Material objects supposed to be the permanent or temporary abodes of a spirit, such as shells, bones, stones. (4) Non-religious magical appliances, charms, or amulets, which have a virtue quite independent of any gods or spirits, such as the claw of a lion worn to keep off danger. (5) Material things which are made the objects of a make-believe worship, such as the needle of the Japanese housewife.

FEUILLANTS. Feuillants was the name given to a reformed congregation of the Cistercians (*q.v.*), founded in 1577 by Jean de la Barrière.

FIDEISM. The French scholar Louis Bautain (1796-1867), Professor of Philosophy at Strasburg, wrote a thesis in which he maintained that human reason of itself has not the power to establish truth. According to Bautain, it is necessary to believe or have faith in truth as revealed by God and handed down from age to age. Bautain's thesis was condemned in 1834 by Gregory XVI. His doctrine was called Fideism. The same kind of teaching is called Traditionalism (*q.v.*). See Reinach, *O.*

FIFTH MONARCHY MEN. A religious sect which was particularly prominent in the time of Oliver Cromwell (1599-1658). Their views were Millenarian. Their name was due to the fact that they designated the Messianic reign, which they believed to be approaching, the fifth monarchy. The last of the four monarchies referred to in the Book of Daniel was the Roman. "It was represented by the fourth beast, which had ten horns, and among these horns came up a *little horn* previous to the final destruction of the empire, and just before the introduction of the millennial reign. Was not Oliver this 'little horn'?" The Fifth Monarchy Men included John Tillinghast (1604-1655), Rector of Trunch, Norfolk; Christopher Feake (*fl.* 1645-1660), Vicar of Christ Church, Newgate; and Vavasor Powell (1617-1670), the "metropolitan of the itinerants," who had previously been at the head of a band of travelling preachers. On one occasion, on a Sunday morning, when the Fifth Monarchy Men were assembled in Coleman Street to hear a sermon by John Canne (*d.* 1667?), Pastor of the English Independents in Amsterdam, Cromwell's officers surprised them. A "Narrative of the Sufferings of Fifth Monarchy Men" who were taken was published. At a later date a man named Thomas Venner (*d.* 1661) put himself at the head of a rising and proposed to take possession of London. His followers marched through the city, shouting, "Long live King Jesus!" Venner and others were captured, and executed for high treason. See John Hunt, *Rel. Thought in England*, 1870-73; J. H. Blunt.

FIKI, THE. A name by which the teacher of the Korân is known in the Libyan Desert.

FINGER, SACRIFICE OF. Amongst the natives of the Tonga Islands in the South Pacific Ocean it is a common practice to sacrifice a little finger when a superior relative is ill as a propitiatory offering to the gods for the sins of the sick man. It is said that there is scarcely a grown-up person who has not lost the little finger of both hands. See William Mariner's *Account of the Natives of the Tonga Islands* (ed. by John Martin, 2nd ed. 1818). The practice has been found among other peoples, and can be traced back as far as the Aurignacian Age (imprints of human hands with mutilated fingers). "The practice of finger-mutilation obtained among Bushmen, certain Australian tribes, and communities of Canadian Indians. Independent investigators have ascertained that it was usually associated with burial customs and the ravages of disease. Bush women sacrificed a joint of the little finger when a near relation died, and Canadian natives acted similarly during times of pestilence 'to cut off deaths.' Finger mutilation in Australia was, among other things, occasionally a mark of caste" (Donald A. Mackenzie, *Crete*). Mackenzie notes that references are made to finger mutilation in Gaelic stories. As he says, the practice had evidently a magical significance.

FIQH. An Arabic term used to designate the practical side of the religion of Islâm. It "consists of precepts and commandments to be obeyed, rules and customs to be observed, duties to be fulfilled." Klein explains that "it is generally called 'Fiqh' Science, Knowledge. Jurisprudence, and treats of the following subjects: Prayer, Almsgiving, Fasting, and the Pilgrimage to Mecca." See F. A. Klein.

FIRE, PASSING THROUGH. The ancient Irish would seem to have sacrificed human beings by burning them. A hint of this survived in the later custom of driving cattle through two fires to purify them. Toland in his *History of the Druids* (1814) says: "Two such fires as we have mentioned were kindl'd by one another on May Eve in every village of the nation (as well thro'out Gaule as in Britain, Ireland, and the adjoining lesser Ilands), between which fires the men and the beasts to be sacrific'd were to pass; from whence came the proverb, *between Bel's two fires*, meaning one in a great strait, not knowing how to extricate himself. One of the fires was on the carn, another on the ground. On the eve of the first day of November there were also such fires kindl'd, accompany'd (as they constantly were) with sacrifices and feasting" (quoted by W. G. Wood-Martin).

FIRE-SERMON. What is known as the "burning" fire-sermon is a sermon which was delivered on a hill by Gautama Buddha to a large gathering of monks. The part of the sermon which gave it its name is as follows: "Everything, O monks, is burning. The eye is burning; visible things are burning. The sensation produced by contact with visible things is burning—burning with the fire of lust, enmity and delusion, with birth, decay, death, grief, lamentation, pain, dejection, and despair. The ear is burning; sounds are burning; the nose is burning, odours are burning; the tongue is burning, tastes are burning; the body is burning, objects of sense are burning. The mind is burning; thoughts are burning. All are burning with the fire of passions and lusts." See Monier-Williams, *Buddhism*, 1890.

FISH, THE EMBLEMATIC. In early Christian art the fish appears as an emblem of Christ. The representation is found in the Catacombs of Rome. The letters of the Greek word for fish, IChThUS, interpreted as an anagram, served as a secret summary of Christian doctrine, being taken to represent "Jesus Christ, Son of God, Saviour." St. Augustine says: "ΙΧΘΥΣ is the mystical name of Christ, because he descends alive into the depths of this mortal life, as into the abyss of waters." In an early Christian inscription (not in the catacombs) Christians are spoken of as "the divine children of the Heavenly Fish" (Cobern). On the seal of Aberdeen Cathedral is depicted a Nativity-scene. The Blessed Virgin and St. Joseph are represented, but lying on the manger in place of the infant Saviour is seen a fish. The fish is used also (*e.g.*, in the catacombs) to symbolise Baptism and the Eucharist. The figure of three fishes entwined in the form of a triangle seems to symbolise baptism under the blessing of the Trinity. As a eucharistic symbol, we find in a picture dated to the second century the basket of loaves placed on a fish. See Sidney Heath and Francis Bond.

FISH AND ANCHOR. The fish as a sacred emblem in Christian art is associated sometimes with the Dove or the Anchor. Thus a fish and anchor appear on an inscription in the Catacombs dated A.D. 234. See the figures in Sidney Heath, p. 128, and Francis Bond, p. 259.

FISHPONDS, SACRED. In ancient times there were sacred fishponds at Edessa, Ascalon, and Hierapolis. At Hierapolis the Syrian goddess Atargatis is said to have come down into the fishpond once and then to have returned to heaven with one of the fish, the ancestor of the sign of the zodiac Pisces. The fishpond at Ascalon is said (by Diodorus) to have owed its sanctity to the fact that the goddess of the place had cast herself into the lake and assumed part of the form of a fish. Another explanation is that the goddess (Derketo or Atargatis) was drowned in the pool with her son Ichthys and devoured by fishes. Lucian (§45) says that the sacred fish at Hierapolis grew to a great size, were called by names, and would approach when called. He states also that an altar of stone stood in the midst of the lake. Xenophon (*Anab.* I., iv. 9) speaks of "tame fish looked upon as gods" in the Chalus, near Aleppo (Garstang in the *Syrian Goddess*).

FIVE FIFTHS OF THE LAW, THE. This was the name given by the Jews to the Pentateuch. See CANON OF THE OLD TESTAMENT.

FIVE FOUNDATIONS OF ISLĀM. The five foundations of Islām are five pillars of practical religion. They are: (1) witness to the creed; (2) the observance of prayer at the five stated periods; (3) the giving of alms; (4) fasting during the month Ramadan; (5) the pilgrimage to Mecca. See T. P. Hughes.

FIVE POINTS OF CALVINISM. In A.D. 1610 the Arminians (*q.v.*) or Remonstrants put forth Five Articles. In reply the Calvinists put forth Five Points of Calvinism: particular predestination, limited atonement, natural inability, irresistible grace, and the perseverance of saints. These points were defended by the Synod of Dort (1618, 1619). See Schaff-Herzog.

FLAGELLANTS. The name Flagellants was given to a body of religious persons who first attracted attention in the thirteenth century. To atone for the sins of the age, they went in processions with bare arms and shoulders, they lashed themselves and one another with scourges (*flagella*) until the blood flowed. The first body of Flagellants appeared at Perugia in 1260. Every member undertook to continue the penance for thirty-three days, the number of days corresponding to the number of years in the life of Jesus. The movement spread throughout Italy, and in course of time beyond the Alps. It broke out again, in a more extravagant form, after the plague known as the Black Death (1348). The Flagellants had now become heretics, and opponents of the Church. Pope Clement VI. anathematized them and prohibited their processions. But they were not entirely suppressed. They reappeared about the time of the Council of Constance (1414-1418), and were condemned by it. Afterwards they disappeared. See J. H. Blunt; *Prot. Dict.; Cath. Dict.*

FLAGSTONE OF THE FIRE. In the Church of Teach-na-Teinedh, or "the church of the fire," on the island of Inishmurray, off the Sligo coast of Ireland, there was formerly a flagstone called Leac-na-Teinedh, or "the flagstone of the fire." Until lately (according to W. G. Wood-Martin) it covered a miraculous hearth. "On this flag, or fire-stone, fire was always kept burning by the monks for the use of the islanders. In later times, when monks no longer inhabited the cashel, whenever a householder wanted kindling for the family fire, a sod of turf or a piece of wood deposited on this holy hearth ignited spontaneously."

FLOOD, THE. The Old Testament story of a great flood sent by God to destroy mankind (with a few exceptions) for their wickedness is well known. It is common knowledge too that a rather similar story has been preserved on Babylonian cuneiform tablets. Another story in the same series has recently come to light in documents published in America since the outbreak of the great War. "We have indeed recovered a very early, and in some of its features a very primitive, form of the Deluge narrative which till now has reached us only in Semitic and Greek renderings; and the stream of tradition has been tapped at a point far above any at which we have hitherto approached it" (L. W. King, *Legends of Babylon and Egypt*, 1918, p. 92). This is the Sumerian Version. It seems to have begun with a brief account of the Creation and the Antediluvian history. After the Flood, the chief duty of man is stated to be to build temples to the gods 'in a clean spot,' that is to say, 'in hallowed places.' The god (Anu or Enlil) founds five cities, and allots them to divine rulers. The name of the hero of the story is Ziusudu, and the description of him has 'great interest in furnishing us with a close parallel to the piety of Noah in the Hebrew Versions'" (p. 68). He is warned in a dream that a flood is to be sent "to destroy the seed of mankind." When the flood comes, it is accompanied by hurricanes of wind, but the hero is safe in a great boat which floats on the mighty waters. Then "the Sun-God came forth shedding light over heaven and earth." At the conclusion we read: "Ziusudu, the king, before Anu and Enlil bows himself down. Life like (that of) a god he gives to him. An eternal soul like (that of) a god he creates for him. In a . . . land, the land of Dilmun (?), they caused him to dwell" (King, p. 90). Frazer has shown (*Folk-lore in the O.T.*, vol. i.) that stories of a great flood are widespread, and that there are many points of similarity between them. D. G. Brinton (*R.P.P.*, p. 122) writes: "Look in what continent we please, we shall find the myth of a Creation or of a primeval construction, of a Deluge or a destruction, and of an expected Restoration." The Flood-stories have been explained, as Brinton says, as the remembrance of some local overflow. But this hardly accounts for the wide prevalence of such stories. A new explanation has therefore been proposed by G. Elliot Smith—that of transmission. "The Sumerian story of the Flood, which is at least as old as the beginning of the third millennium B.C., was transmitted not merely to Babylonia and Western Asia, but also to Greece and to the uttermost limits of Europe, where it is preserved in the folk-lore of Wales, Scotland and Ireland. And in the East it spread not merely to India, the Malay Archipelago, and China, but also to Oceania and both North and South America. Certain trivial and unessential incidents of the narrative crop up again and again throughout this wide domain, and proclaim the fact of the derivation of the common framework of all the versions, directly or indirectly, from one original source. Local circumstances supplied merely the corroborative detail and distinctive embellishments of each particular version. . . . The original story of the Flood was developed as the culmination of a series of legends of the destruction of mankind in which a flood played no part whatever. . . . In the earliest version, the 'Flood' consisted of the blood of a human victim whose throat was cut to provide the elixir of life to rejuvenate the king when his virile powers began to fail. In the next phase mankind as a whole replaced the original victim. In a third phase beer, to which red ochre was added to give it the proper colour as a substitute for blood, was employed in place of actual blood. Finally the blood-coloured mixture poured out upon the earth from seven thousand vessels was confused with the red waters of the annual inundation of the Nile. But as the destruction of mankind (which no longer formed a logical part of the story, once substitutes were found for human blood) had survived as the central incident of the narrative, the story-teller had to provide an explanation of it. Mankind was being punished for its sins, and instead of the slaughtered men providing the 'Flood' of blood, the blood-coloured waters of inundation were represented as inflicting the vengeance of the gods upon men" (*Journ. of the Manch. Eg. and Or. Soc.*, 1918, p. 17 ff.). This explanation is rather startling at first sight, but probably many facts could be adduced in support of it. For instance, "primitive people believe that unless the sun is regaled with the blood of mankind he ages rapidly. Hence the myth of the sending of Hathor-Sekhet to earth, and the holocaust of humanity. Such sacrifices on a large scale were frequent in ancient Mexico, and on one occasion some 70,000 people were immolated on the altars of the war-god Huitzilopochtli, the procession of victims stretching for over two miles" (Edwardes and Spence, *Dict.*, p. 146).

FLYING-HORSE. The "flying-horse" (or "wind-horse," Lungta) is one of the sacred figures or symbols of Tibetan Buddhists. It is supposed to be able to carry a man round the world in one day. If it is kept flying on a flag (see PRAYER-FLAGS), it will, it is thought, bring good fortune. It has been suggested that the flying-horse is identical with the mystic white horse of earlier Buddhism, which figures as one of the Seven Royal Treasures (see TREASURES, THE SEVEN ROYAL). See Sir Monier-Williams, *Buddhism*, 1890; cp. T. W. Rhys Davids.

FO. Fo or Fo-hi is a figure in the mythology of Chinese Buddhism, apparently a personification of idealized humanity. According to legend he was the first Chinese emperor.

FOMAGATA. One of the deities worshipped by the ancient Americans before the time of the Aztecs. He was the chief god of the Muyscas in northern South America. In Nicaragua he was worshipped as Fomagazdad. His wife bore the name Zipaltonal. Fomagazdad and Zipaltonal were regarded as the parents of the human race. They were propitiated by means of human sacrifices. See J. M. Robertson, *P.C.*

FOMORIANS. Deities worshipped by the pre-Celtic inhabitants of Ireland as gods of fertility, but regarded by the Celts as evil powers. They include Balor of the evil eye, Bres, Elatha, a god of knowledge, Indech, an earth-god, Net, a war-god, and Tethra, god of the underworld.

FORMULA OF CONCORD. The Formula of Concord was drawn up at Bergen, near Magdeburg, in 1577, as the basis on which Lutherans might agree. It was an improvement on the Book of Torgau (*q.v.*), which again was based upon the Swabian and Saxon Formula of Concord (*q.v.*) and the Maulbronn Formula. The Formula of Concord is in two divisions, the *Epitome* and the *Solida Repetitio et Declaratio*, and each division contains twelve articles. The "Prophetic and Apostolic writings both of the Old and of the New Testament" are declared to be the one and only "compendious rule and norm" by which all dogmas are to be judged. As subordinate standards of right doctrine, approval is given to the three "primitive Church Symbols," the "first, unaltered" Augsburg Confession, the Schmalkald Articles, and Luther's Smaller and Larger Catechisms. "In every article the conservative Lutheran position is maintained as against the Romanist and Melanchthonian, not to say against the Calvinist and Zwinglian and Anabaptist, and the victorious conclusions of the antecedent Lutheran controversies are firmly embodied, sometimes with moderated phraseology" (W. A. Curtis). See William A. Curtis.

FORSETE. Forsete or Forsite was the name of one of the gods of the Ancient Teutons. When Willebrord visited Helgoland, he found that the island was sacred to the god Forsete. Chantepie de la Saussaye thinks that among the Frisians he was regarded as a god of justice. The Scandinavians, in so far as they recognised him, made him the son of Balder (*q.v.*). See P. D. Chantepie de la Saussaye, *Rel. of the Teutons*, 1902.

FORTY MARTYRS, THE. No less than three different bands of Christians who suffered for their faith have been known as "The Forty Martyrs." Forty Christian soldiers are said to have been martyred at Sebaste in Armenia in 320 A.D. under Licinius. When ordered by the emperor to offer sacrifice they refused. Thereupon they were placed for a whole night in a pond of frozen water, and the next morning were thrown into fires. The Christians afterwards built churches in their honour. Another band of Christian martyrs is said to have suffered in Persia in 375 A.D. Thirdly, at Antioch in Syria forty virgins are said to have been martyred under Decius. See Wace and Piercy.

FOUNDATION-PILLARS FOR A LIFE OF JESUS. This expression has become familiar on account of the article on the Gospels contributed to the "Encyclopaedia Biblica" by P. W. Schmiedel of Zuerich. Schmiedel described nine passages in the Synoptic Gospels as "the foundation-pillars for a truly scientific life of Jesus." In order to prove the historicity of Jesus against those who seek to deny it, he selected nine passages which could not possibly have been invented, since they are incompatible with the worship in which Jesus came to be held. The passages are given, and explained briefly by Arno Neumann. Seven will be found on page 10 of his book (*Jesus*). The eighth and the ninth are discussed on page 86 f. and on page 76 note 2. It is not of course said that the Gospels contain only nine trustworthy passages. What is contended is that these nine passages cannot be accounted for on the supposition that Jesus did not exist as a historical person. They are guarantees for his historical existence and much more. See the *Encycl. Bibl.*, s.v. "Gospels," §§ 131, 139 f.; Arno Neumann, *Jesus*, 1906.

FOUNDATION-SACRIFICES. The practice of burying something at the foundation of a city is very ancient. In Palestine a human sacrifice was offered and buried in the structure of the building (cp. Josh. vi. 26). Usually the victim was a child, but at Gezer the skeletons of adults have been found. The children were often placed in jars, a form of burial that has been noted elsewhere (*e.g.*, in early Egypt, Babylonia, Assyria). See P. S. P. Handcock; and G. H. Payne, *The Child in Human Progress*, 1916.

FOUR-CHAPTER LETTER, THE. The "Four-chapter Letter" is a description given by certain New Testament scholars to four chapters in the Second Epistle to the Corinthians. It has been thought that these four chapters do not harmonise well with the earlier chapters of the Epistle, and that they are really an independent letter. See CORINTHIANS, SECOND EPISTLE TO THE.

FOURIERISM. The system of François Marie Charles Fourier (1772-1837). Fourier was the son of a draper, and it was some distasteful experiences in connection with business that excited his indignation against the conditions of trade and commerce. He was punished, when only five years old, for telling one of his father's customers the truth about some goods, and in 1799 as a clerk in Marseilles he had to superintend the casting into the sea of a great quantity of rice which had been held back at a time of scarcity in the hope of increasing the price and had become unfit for use. Fourier determined to try to discover a remedy for such a corrupt and immoral state of things. "He soon perceived that the only mode of ensuring truth, equity, and economy, either in productive or distributive industry, was to suppress the rivalry of interest between the producer and the consumer, by associating them together in a common union. The numerous advantages of other kinds capable of being realized by association if it were extended so as to embrace the domestic life of men as well as the operations of industry, convinced him that God must have ordained such an association as the natural destiny of man, and that the condition under which it could be formed would be discoverable by a careful study of the laws by which the nature of man was governed. The unity which he observed in all the works of God led him to the conviction that, the Creator being an infinite harmonious being, everything in nature must be an imitation of His attributes, and therefore that there exists in every order of creation similarity or universal analogy. The study of the universe around him led him further to the persuasion that all its harmonies are distributed in progressive series; and that every being in creation is subject to permanent attractions and repulsions in proportion to its respective functions and final destinies. Armed with these principles, he set himself to study first the natural impulses, attractions and repulsions of man, and then the mode in which these faculties could be combined progressively according to the general laws of series, satisfied that he should thus be led to the discovery of the principle of union of which he was in quest" (E. V. Neale). Fourier investigated the nature of man, and found in him three classes of inborn desires. The first class consists of the five senses. The second class comprises the four modes of affection: friendship, love, parental and filial, ambition or corporate affection. The third class embraces three intellectual desires: the desire of intrigue and rivalry; the desire of alternation; and the desire of combining different pleasures. How are these passions and desires to be satisfied duly? The five senses require physical health and vigour, as well as material wealth. The four moral affections require free scope for the development of groups of persons drawn together by similarity of tastes, etc. The three intellectual desires require free play for a spirit of rivalry and emulation. Fourier therefore combined men into social individuals called *phalanges*, who should dwell each in the *phalanstère* best suited to his taste, "cultivating each a sufficient quantity of land for the support of all the members of which it is composed, and carrying on, in combination with the agricultural operations forming the basis of its existence, such other industrial pursuits as the nature of the locality or climate suggested. The secret of securing the well-being of such a body, and of all the members composing it, consisted in such arrangements as would allow the groups into which its members would be drawn by their mutual attractions, to form themselves into a series methodically arranged, so that each group should be in direct rivalry with those immediately contiguous to it, and passing gradually into concord with those more removed from it, and as would at the same time link all the series thus formed to each other by a gradual transition" (Neale). See Edward Vansittart Neale, *The Characteristic Features of some of the Principal Systems of Socialism*, 1851; *Chambers' Encycl.*; cp. Guiseppe Mazzini, *Thoughts upon Democracy in Europe*, 1847.

FRAGMENTARY HYPOTHESIS, THE. This expression is used of one of the theories which has been put forth by the Higher Critics (see CRITICISM, HIGHER) to explain the composition of the Hexateuch. It followed the Documentary Hypothesis (*q.v.*). The Fragmentary Hypothesis was advocated, in particular, by Alexander Geddes (1737-1802) in England, and J. S. Vater in Germany. They believed that fragments of different date and authorship were added to one original Mosaic work. Geddes (as quoted by C. A. Briggs) thought it indubitable that: "(1) The Pentateuch in its present form was not written by Moses. (2) It was written in the land of Chanaan, and most probably at Jerusalem. (3) It could not be written before the reign of David, nor after that of Hezekiah." He believed, however, that "it was compiled from ancient documents, some of which were coeval with Moses, and some even anterior to Moses. Whether all these were written records or many of them only oral traditions, it would be rash to determine." The Book of Joshua he considered to belong closely to the Pentateuch, because it seems to have been "compiled by the same author, and because it is a necessary appendix to the history contained in the former books." W. E. Addis (*Documents of the Hexateuch*, i., p. xxvii.) thinks that in some respects the position of Geddes and Vater marked an advance upon that of Astruc and Eichhorn (see DOCUMENTARY HYPOTHESIS). "It extended the investigation from Genesis and the beginning of Exodus to the whole Pentateuch, and ceased to assume that the only documents in the Pentateuch were documents used by Moses. It argued, with justice, that the Pentateuch is composed of sections, some of which had no original connection with each other, and that even the documents which use the word Elohim or Yahweh [commonly pronounced Jehovah] may be, and are, of various origin." Its weakness consisted in failing to see "that the supposed 'fragments' might, on closer inspection, form themselves into two or three documents." See T. K. Cheyne, *Founders of O.T. Crit.*, 1893; C. A. Briggs, *Hex.*; A. Duff, *History of O.T. Crit.*, 1910.

FRANCISCANS. The Franciscans owe their name to Francis of Assisi (1172-1226), whose real name was Giovanni Francesco Bernardone. The son of a rich merchant, in his early manhood he became leader of a club to which the gay youths of Assisi belonged. He also fought in a battle between Assisi and Perugia. A severe illness marked a change in his life. It led him to take an interest in the poor and suffering, and to abandon his old pleasures. In 1206 he laid aside the clothes which he had been accustomed to wear, put on old garments, and devoted himself to a life of poverty. In 1209 when he heard a preacher read the passage in Matthew x. vss. 9 and 10 ("Get you no gold, nor silver, nor brass in your purses; no wallet for your journey, neither two coats, nor shoes, nor staff: for the labourer is worthy of his food. And into whatsoever city or village ye shall enter, search out who in it is worthy; and there abide till ye go forth"), the words appealed to him with all the force of a direct personal message, a message to go forth and preach. He now further simplified his dress, discarding shoes and the use of a staff, and before long he was joined by ten followers. His followers seem to have been exhorted to work for their daily bread, but in return to take only things necessary for life (not money). In 1210 he obtained from the Benedictines a plot of ground near Assisi called Portiuncula on which was an abandoned chapel of Our Lady of the Angels. Around this chapel the Franciscans established a convent consisting of rude huts. "From this humble site, which thus became the cradle of the order, thousands of monasteries were to be planted, missioners were to go forth to all parts of the world to preach, toil, and in many cases suffer martyrdom for the gospel of Jesus Christ, and a vast multitude of doctors and holy prelates were to issue, by whom the purity of the faith should be sustained, and its principles methodised and applied" (*Catholic Dictionary*). In 1210 Francis went to Rome to have his rule confirmed by the Pope, but he succeeded in obtaining from Innocent III. only verbal confirmation. The rule was not solemnly ratified until 1223, when, in a more compendious form, it was confirmed by Honorius III. The Order had already spread beyond Italy to Spain, Egypt, Africa, Greece, England, Hungary, and Germany. In 1219 as many as five thousand members were present at a general assembly. In 1220 Franciscans established themselves in England at Canterbury, and soon afterwards at Northampton. In course of time Franciscan convents arose in Oxford, London, Coventry, and in other places. Francis is said to have laid down twenty-seven precepts. "They prescribe the particular means by which the vow of poverty is to be carried out, regulate the dress to be worn, order that the friars shall go barefoot, specify the fasts to be observed, and enjoin a blind unlimited obedience to superiors for the love of God. The habit which he gave them was a grey gown of coarse cloth with a pointed hood or capuche attached to it, one undertunic and drawers, and a cord round the waist" (*Cath. Dict.*). After the death of Francis, his successor, the Minister-General Elias of Cortona relaxed the original strictness of the rule. This relaxation displeased many of the Franciscans and caused a division. Two branches of the Order grew up, Conventuals and Observantines. The Conventuals were the milder party and lived in convents; the Observantines were the severer party (in France they were called Cordeliers) and lived like hermits in poor dwellings. The Observantines in time became subdivided into Observants, Reformed, Discalced or Alcantarines, and Recollects. There arose also a distinct branch of Franciscans called Capuchins (*q.v.*). In 1897 Leo XIII. succeeded in re-uniting all the Franciscans except the Conventuals and Capuchins under the name of the Order of Friars Minor. The Franciscans have done a great work for humanity, and have produced many very eminent men. Naturally, their zeal and strictness have called forth opponents and rivals. Zoeckler describes the Dominicans (*q.v.*) as born rivals of the Franciscans. "The two orders fought for a time cordially together, side by side, as long as they had a common object; namely, to get access to the universities. But hardly were Bonaventura the Franciscan, and Thomas Aquinas the Dominican, installed as *doctores theologiae* at the University of Paris, before a strongly marked scientific difference between the two orders became apparent, and it continued to separate them during the whole period of the middle ages. The Franciscans were realists; the Dominicans, nominalists: the Franciscans leaned towards Semi-Pelagianism; the Dominicans were ardent disciples of Augustine: the Franciscans were Scotists; the Dominicans were Thomists: in the debate on the immaculate conception of Mary, the Franciscans said Yes, and the Dominicans No" (Schaff-Herzog). See Schaff-Herzog; the *Prot. Dict.*, 1904; the *Cath. Dict.*; Brockhaus.

FRANCKESCHE STIFTUNGEN. Philanthropic Institutions established at Halle (Schools, Home for Orphans, Dispensary, Printing-house, etc.) by the German pietist A. H. Francke (1663-1727). See PIETISM.

FRANKISTS. The followers of Jacob Frank (Jankiew Lejbowiez; 1712-1791). Frank at first put himself at the head of the Sabbatians (*q.v.*) in Podolia, South Russia. Then he had himself baptized and declared himself to be the re-born Christ. He was imprisoned for more than ten years. Frankists are to be found in Poland, Roumania, and Turkey. See Brockhaus.

FRATERNITY, PACT OF. A declaration of principles drawn up by Giuseppe (Joseph) Mazzini (1805-1872). See PACT OF FRATERNITY.

FREE CHURCH OF ENGLAND. A dissentient episcopal community. The Free Church of England originated in 1844 as a counteracting movement to the Oxford Tractarian movement. It regarded the episcopate as a distinction of "office not of order," and repudiated the historical succession of bishops. It held itself free "to preach in any parish, use a revised Prayer-book, associate the laity in the government of the Church, and hold communion with other Christians. It has annexed several churches of the Countess of Huntingdon's Connexion" (J. A. Houlder).

FREE CONGREGATIONS. Congregations founded in Germany in 1845 by Wislicenus of Halle and Julius Rupp (*b.* 1809) of Koenigsberg. They sought to develop a faith in harmony with reason. See FRIENDS OF LIGHT.

FREE RELIGIOUS ASSOCIATION. A very liberal Association founded at Boston in 1867. It "aims at the emancipation of religion from all sectarian limits, the reconciliation of faiths, and the application of the scientific method to the study of theology." See Schaff-Herzog.

FREE RELIGIOUS MOVEMENT, THE. The Free Religious Movement in London, the adherents of which meet in Steinway Hall, was founded by Dr. Walter Walsh. In 1912, after being deprived of his church through the verdict of the highest law court in Scotland, Dr. Walsh formed what he called a Free Religious Movement in Dundee. Subsequently he was appointed to succeed Mr. Voysey as Minister of the Theistic Church in London. But here again his utterances in course of time proved unwelcome to the members of the Church, and he was again ejected. Hence arose the Free Religious Movement in London. In the United States there is a Free Religious Association of America which has taken as its motto "World Religion and World Brotherhood"; in various parts of the Continent there has been a similar movement with the same name; and in Australia a Free Religious Fellowship has been formed. The Free Religious Movement towards World Religion and World Brotherhood, under the leadership of Dr. Walsh, has its source in that desire for unity which pervades the modern world. It is a reasoned effort to express and encourage that sweep towards universalism in religion and social ethics and politics which is the most powerful and hopeful impulse of our time. It seeks to relate man to his universe, and human beings to one another, by principals which are rational, scientific, ethical, and international. The movement is religious—not in the narrow ecclesiastical sense of the word—but in a broad, humanist and ethical sense. It is a constructive movement, springing from the spiritual oneness of humanity, and consciously directed towards the realisation of the greatest of human ideals—the ideal of social and international unity. To enable it to move with ease and rapidity, the Free Religious Movement does not encumber itself with creed or sacrament. Believing that for the accomplishment of the successive tasks of mankind ample wisdom and virtue dwell within the nature of man himself, it seeks to voice the truth of the ages as discovered by science, tested by reason, and approved by experience. It endeavours to support truth as disclosed to the growing intelligence of man by history and science. It asserts the undeniable right of everyone to think and speak his or her own thoughts; and therefore it assures to its leaders and speakers entire intellectual liberty; and to all its adherents and auditors perfect freedom of judgment. Believing that goodness and truth are inherent in human nature, it seeks for these in the immortal books of all ages and races; and regards with reverence all those who in every nation and time have laboured and suffered and lived and died for humanity. In the conviction that the goal of human unity can be reached only as men and women learn to think independently, fearlessly and rationally, the Free Religious Movement in all its activities keeps steadily before it the liberation of mind and conscience from servile submission to authority and tradition; and seeks association with all those who also are looking for a world which shall be enlightened by knowledge, guided by reason, and animated by love. See the Free Religious Addresses and Leaflets.

FRENCH PROPHETS. A body of fanatics which arose in France as a result of the persecution of Protestants and afterwards of Jansenists. Their fanaticism "found expression in convulsions and prophecies of the impending destruction of Church and State" (T. G. Crippen, Appendix to J. A. Houlder's *Free Churches*, 1899). Some of these enthusiasts came to England about the year 1706, and gained for a time a considerable following.

FREYJA. One of the chief of the Norse deities. She was one of the figures represented on the golden horns found in South Jutland in 1639 and 1734 and dating, it is thought, from the fifth or beginning of the sixth century. According to Snorri Sturluson (1178-1241), she was originally a human being. She is goddess of the dead and consort of Odhin (*q.v.*). They share the fallen heroes between them. She is a deity of sensuous love. In one myth she is said to be the wife of Odhr and to have borne him a daughter named Hnoss. Odhr is perhaps another form of Odhin. Freyja, the female deity, corresponds to the male deity Freyr (*q.v.*). She is identical with Gullveig-Heidhr, the Vanir-goddess (see VANIR). See P. D. Chantepie de la Saussaye, *Rel. of the Teutons*, 1902.

FREYR. One of the deities of the Ancient Teutons. Thor (*q.v.*) and Freyr became the chief gods of Sweden. Freyr was the god worshipped by the Ingvæones, and it is thought by some scholars that he is identical with their eponymous hero Ingv. He was the god of fertility. His symbol was the phallus, and there were processions in his honour in Spring. He was also the god of prosperity, peace, and love. Freyr, who was one of the Vanir (*q.v.*), was introduced into Norway, and it has been suggested that the war between the Vanir and the Æsir represents the conflict which then took place between the adherents of Freyr and the adherents of Odhin (see WODAN). See P. D. Chantepie de la Saussaye, *Rel. of the Teutons*, 1902.

FRIARS MINOR. The name chosen by Francis of Assisi for his followers. They are better known as Franciscans (*q.v.*).

FRIENDS, SOCIETY OF. The body of Christians known as the "Friends" and nick-named the Quakers (*q.v.*) was founded by George Fox (1624-1691 A.D.) as the result of a profound religious experience. As a young man, Fox was troubled for a time with religious despondency, and could find no comfort or help in the counsels of the priests and preachers of his age. He wandered about in great misery, with the Bible as his only companion. At length the clouds were dispersed, as they so often are in such cases, and his outlook was brightened in a wonderful way. He received a divine message to the effect that "There is one, even Christ Jesus, that can speak to thy condition." He now knew in what direction to seek for help. "I saw also that there was an ocean of darkness and death, but an infinite ocean of light and love which flowed over the ocean of darkness. In that I saw also the infinite love of God, and I had great openings." Such an experience as Fox had had seemed to prove to him that what men needed most was to seek spiritual enlightenment by kindling into flame the divine spark which exists in all of them. He had found that no priest nor religious rite is necessary to bring the soul into direct communion with God. He had re-discovered, he thought, the original secret of Christianity, and was prepared to devote himself heart and soul to the task of reviving primitive Christianity. In 1647 he started on a missionary campaign, which only ended when his life did. He wandered about England as a preacher, urging the people to "look to Christ within" and to "follow the inward light." He met with great success. After he had laboured alone for four years, he was joined by other preachers. In the seventh year of his work there were more than sixty. In the eighth year there were preachers in Asia and Africa, as well as in various parts of Europe. About twenty years after the formation of the body known as the Friends, William Penn (1644-1718) joined them. The Friends flourished in spite of persecution. Many of them were fined and imprisoned, particularly between the years 1650 and 1689. In 1682 a settlement was made in America, and in a few years there were thousands of Friends in the American Colonies. The body in America in 1827 split into two divisions, one of which became known as the Hicksites (*q.v.*). The principles of the Friends have been summarized as follows: (1) God's Spiritual Light that lighteth every man; (2) the indwelling of the Spirit with the disciple; (3) the Headship of Christ in His Church; (4) the priesthood of all believers; (5) the freedom of the Gospel Ministry; (6) the spiritual equality of the Sexes; (7) Spiritual Baptism, and Spiritual Communion; (8) the unlawfulness of war to the Christian; (9) the unlawfulness of oaths; and (10) the duty of brotherly love, and of simplicity of life. The members of the Society of Friends worship in silence, unless some member of the congregation is moved by the Spirit to preach or offer prayer or give praise. "But this silence is itself intended to be occupied with religious acts. Highest of these is the direct communion of the soul with its Maker and its Lord, in rapt devotion, in thanksgiving and prayer. But there are services, in these hours of silence, adapted to every degree of religious experience and every serious mood of mind. One of the most profitable of these is self-examination. . . . Another exercise is religious meditation. At worst, every attender can force himself to think on profitable themes by repeating to himself texts of Scripture, or the verses of some suggestive hymn. 'Sometimes a light surprises' the humble worshipper; his thoughts are led on and upward by a higher Power; new meanings of texts flash upon his mind, a new illumination is given to the path of duty, and in answer to the prayer breathed forth by his inmost soul, he feels conscious of a closer union with God, and strengthened for his future warfare with the world, the flesh, and the devil. And, if some brother or sister is led to offer vocal service, it often happens that the word of exhortation or reproof or comfort, or the earnest petition to the throne of grace, harmonizes with the private exercise of mind which the hearer has passed through, confirming his faith, and invigorating his resolution" (Schaff-Herzog). The Friends have been great philanthropists. See Schaff-Herzog; J. H. Blunt; *Prot. Dict.*; *R.S.W.*

FRIENDS OF GOD. A name (Gottesfreunde) assumed by German mystics in the fourteenth century. They included such men as: Henry Eckhart, "Master Eckhart" (*c.* 1260-1329); Rulman Merswin (1307-1382), author of "The Book of the Nine Rocks"; Nicolas of Basle (1330-1383); John Tauler (*c.* 1300-1361); and Henry Suso or Seuse (von Berg; 1295-1366), author of the "Book of Eternal Wisdom." See MYSTICISM, CHRISTIAN.

FRIENDS OF LIGHT. A religious sect of German origin. It originated in 1841, when Leberecht Uhlich (1799-1872), with fifteen other clergymen, formed a "Union of Protestant Friends." The members of this Union were also called the "Friends of Light." They held that Christianity ought to be brought into harmony with the faith of reason. In 1844 a great meeting was held at Goethen. A lecture was delivered by Wislicenus of Halle, and the Friends of Light declared that they could not allow their faith to be determined by Holy Scripture. In 1845 Wislicenus and Julius Rupp (1809-1884), of Koenigsberg, were dismissed from their churches by the Prussian Government. In 1846 they formed Free Congregations in Koenigsberg and Halle. Other congregations soon arose in other towns. See Brockhaus; J. H. Blunt.

FRIGG. Another form of the name Frija (*q.v.*).

FRIJA. One of the chief deities of the Teutons. Frija is a goddess who in the legends of the Lombards appears as Frea, and in those of the Frisians as Fria. She is mentioned in one of the Merseburg Charms (*q.v.*). In the Balder Myth, where she appears as Frigg, she aids Balder (*q.v.*) by making nearly all objects harmless. Frija is the consort of Odhin or Wodan (*q.v.*). She gives advice to Wodan, or sometimes even frustrates his plans. And, like him, she knows the fate of men. Swine and cats were sacrificed to her. Her worshippers also threw sacrificial cakes into wells and then drank of the water. See P. D. Chantepie de la Saussaye, *Rel. of the Teutons*, 1902.

FRINGES. One of the commands in the Old Testament is (Deuteronomy xxii. 12): "Thou shalt make thee fringes upon the four corners of thy vesture wherewith thou coverest thyself." The Hebrew word (*tsitsith*) seems to mean "twisted cords." These fringes were originally tassels attached by a blue cord (cp. Numbers xv. 38) to the four corners of the outer garment, a kind of shawl. The modern name for this garment is Talith (*q.v.*).

FRITHSTOOL. The Frithstool or Freedstool, literally "the seat of peace" was a seat or chair placed near the altar in certain churches. Such seats still survive in churches at Hexham and Beverley Minster. The frithstool was the most sacred place of refuge for those who claimed "sanctuary" (see SANCTUARY). Frequently the seats were of stone. See J. H. Parker, *Gloss.*

FRODHI-PEACE. Frodhi-peace is the Norse name for an idea which has prevailed in many parts of the world—the idea of a golden age in the past. Frodhi in the saga appears as one of the first of the Danish kings. He resided at Leire on Seeland. He is called the Prince of Peace, because during his reign, for a time at least, peace reigned supreme. No man harmed his neighbour. This continued until the king, developing a taste for gold, obtained from the king of Sweden two giantesses, Fenja and Menja, to grind gold, peace, and happiness. Instead of gold, the giantesses ground for him calamity and vengeance. They were at length carried off in ships of the enemy, but they made the ships sink by grinding salt on them. This accounts for the saltness of the sea. See P. D. Chantepie de la Saussaye, *Rel. of the Teutons*, 1902.

FRONTLETS. In the Old Testament it is said (Deuteronomy vi. 8) with reference to the words of God: "And thou shalt bind them for a sign upon thine hand, and they shall be for frontlets between thine eyes." In course of time the passage came to be interpreted literally, and it became the custom to wear frontlets, that is to say, small boxes containing prayers written on parchment. The Hebrew term is Totâfoth (*q.v.*).

FUDO. A deity worshipped by the Japanese Buddhists. It is thought that he corresponds to the Indian deity Siva (*q.v.*). "His appearance is fierce and angry, the face often coloured black; in his right hand he holds a sword, and in his left a rope; tongues of flame form the background." Fudo is a god of fire, and apparently also of wisdom. See H. Hackmann.

FUJUFUZE SECT. A sub-sect of Japanese Nichirenism (see NICHIREN SECT). They were extremists. Their principle was known as *Fuju fuze*. A. Lloyd explains that this means "not giving and not receiving," and may be translated *intransigeant*. The Emperor Iemitsu (died 1651) proscribed both the Fujūfuze Nichirenists and the Christians. See Arthur Lloyd.

FULLA. The name of one of the deities of the Ancient Teutons. In one of the Merseburg Charms (*q.v.*) the name seems to occur as Volla (*q.v.*).

FUNG-SHUI. A Chinese term meaning wind-water, in other words, the climate as regulated and determined by the winds that bring rain or drought. It is important that a Chinese grave should be so placed that the body and soul may be under the good influence of *fung-shui*. To secure this the Chinese consult *fung-shui* professors, a class of specialists who know how to find the most lucky spots for graves, as well as the best sites for temples and houses. "These *fung-shui* professors mostly take as the basis of their determinations of suitable spots for the dwellings of the living and the dead, the forms and configurations of the hills, the windings of the rivers and brooks, as well as the shapes of houses, temples, and rocks; in short, everything on earth, according to them, may modify those influences of wind and rain" (de Groot). Until a suitable spot for the grave can be found, the body must remain unburied. See J. J. M. de Groot, *Rel. of the Chinese*, 1910; Hastings' *E.R.E.*, vol. v., 1912.

FURIOUS HOST. Another name for the Wild Hunt (*q.v.*).

FURQAN. Al-Furqân is another name for the Qur'ân (*q.v.*). The root of the verb means "to separate or distinguish." Furqân therefore means that which distinguishes between truth and error, or that which is divided into sections. The Hebrew *pereq* also means a section (cp. the collection of sayings called *Pirqê Ābôth*).

FYLFOT, THE. The Christian symbol known as the *fylfot* (cp. the Fylfot Cross in heraldry) is identical with the Swastika, a sacred emblem of the Buddhists. It figures in the Catacombs and in mediæval churches. Cp. CROSS.

G

G. God G is a designation used by anthropologists for a deity depicted in the MSS. of the Mayan Indians. The employment of the sun-sign in his hieroglyph indicates that he is a sun-god. He is sometimes provided with the symbol of death, apparently because he needed human blood to sustain him.

GADADHAR. Wielder of the club or gada, one of the names of the Hindu god Vishnu.

GAGA. A Babylonian deity. Gaga was one of the minor gods. In the Epic of Marduk (see MARDUK, EPIC OF) Gaga appears as a messenger sent by Anshar to Tiâmat to announce the coming of Marduk. The message is received by Lakhmu (*q.v.*) and Lakhamu, and causes consternation among the Igigi (*q.v.*). See Morris Jastrow, *Rel.*

GALATIANS, EPISTLE TO THE. As far as genuineness is concerned, the Epistle of Paul to the Galatians is one of the least disputed of the Pauline Epistles. It has been said that "it bears on every line of it the sign manual of the Apostle" (Currie Martin). There are indeed statements in it which cannot easily be reconciled with other statements in other Epistles and in the Book of Acts, but there is a broad basis of agreement. The Epistle seems to be quoted by Justin the Gnostic, Polycarp, Theodotus, Justin Martyr, Athenagoras, and other early writers. It is included in the Versions and Canons of the second century A.D. In spite of all this, it is not without its difficulties. One of these is presented by the term "Galatians." In the Acts of the Apostles "Galatia" seems to denote only a broad strip of the Roman province of Galatia in Asia Minor, running from the South-west to the North-east, a territory inhabited by a mixed population of Phrygians, Greeks, Romans, Jews, and Celts (Acts xvi. 6; xviii. 23). But in the time of the Apostle Paul the term seems to have denoted also the whole Roman province, which included Antioch, Derbe, Lystra, and Iconium. It used to be thought that the Galations of Paul's Epistle were the inhabitants of the Galatia of the Acts of the Apostles (North Galatian theory). It is now held by many scholars that the Galatians of the Epistle were inhabitants of the southern towns (South Galatian theory). W. M. Ramsay maintains "that the Churches to which the Epistle was addressed were no other than those of Antioch, Iconium, Lystra, and Derbe, which were planted by Paul in his first missionary journey, and of which we have an account in Acts xiii., xiv." (McClymont). Some of the passages in the Epistle, it is thought, can be best explained as referring to customs and laws peculiar to the province of South Galatia in Roman times. "The main points that can be elucidated by reference to the current customs in the province of South Galatia are those of adoption, the making of wills or covenants, and the special character of the tutor or *paidagogos* (cf. Gal. iii. 24) found in the Galatian letter" (Currie Martin). In Galatians iv. 13 Paul says: "but ye know that because of an infirmity of the flesh I preached the gospel unto you the first time." This has been supposed to militate against the South Galatian theory since there is no reference to the illness of Paul in Acts. On the other hand, as Prof. Peake says, it is hardly likely that North Galatia could have been a place to which Paul could have gone in consequence of illness. "For either he was taken ill when passing through it to another district, or he went there to regain his health. Against the former it must be said that the road through North Galatia led nowhere where he was likely to go, against the latter that the climate was singularly unfitted for an invalid." McClymont thinks that the Epistle was written in the period of transition from II. Corinthians to Romans, towards the close of the year 57 A.D. Ramsay assigns it to about the year 53 A.D., the time when the Apostle was about to commence his Third Missionary Journey. He thinks that it was written at Antioch in Syria. The main object of the Epistle was to counteract a Judaising tendency in the Galatian Church. An interesting feature in the Epistle is the emphasis laid on the independent character of Paul's apostleship. He says, for instance (i. 11 f.): "For I make known to you, brethren, as touching the gospel which was preached by me, that it is not after man. For neither did I receive it from man, nor was I taught it, but through revelation of Jesus Christ." See J. A. McClymont; G. Currie Martin; Arthur S. Peake, *Intr.*; J. Moffatt, *Intr.*

GALILEE, THE. In Christian architecture this term is applied to a porch or chapel at the entrance of a Church. There are many examples in Cathedrals and old Priory Churches. The term is applied also sometimes "to the nave, or at least to the western portion of it, and in some churches there are indications of the west end of the nave having been parted off from the rest, either by a step in the floor, a division in the architecture, or some other line of demarcation" (J. H. Parker, *Gloss.*). St. Stephen's Chapel at Westminster had formerly at the west end a galilee which formed a kind of vestibule or ante-chapel. Durham Cathedral has at the west end of the nave a galilee dedicated to St. Cuthbert. It was built for the use of the women. Sidney Heath explains that the term "is thought to have been applied to porches situated on the north side of a conventual church or cathedral for the reason that when the Crusaders and pilgrims entered the Holy Land from the north, Galilee was the frontier province."

GALLI. According to Lucian, the Galli were sacred servants in the temple of Hierapolis. They were castrated and wore female attire.

GALLICAN PSALTER. The Gallican Psalter was the second (387) of the three revisions of the Book of Psalms made by Jerome. Under Pope Pius V. it was substituted in general ecclesiastical use in the Roman Church for the Roman Psalter (*q.v.*), the version made by Jerome in 383. The Gallican Psalter was so called because it was introduced primarily into Gaul by Gregory of Tours. It was introduced afterwards into Germany, England, and Spain. Cp. VULGATE.

GAMES. Robertson Smith has emphasized the joyful character of the ancient religions known to us. When men met their god they feasted and were glad together. Ordinary acts of worship are all brightness and hilarity. This is true also of the religions of primitive peoples And indeed it may be said of any religion that gloom and sadness are signs of degeneracy and decay. Games and the principal forms of art seem to have been born of religion, and for a long time they retained a religious character. Worship was not merely an act of religion but also a form of recreation (in the best sense of the word). "The state of effervescence in which the assembled worshippers find themselves must be translated outwardly by exuberant movements which are not easily subjected to too carefully defined ends. In part, they escape aimlessly, they spread themselves for the mere pleasure of so doing, and they take delight in all sort of games. Besides, in so far as the beings to whom the cult is addressed are imaginary, they are not able to contain and regulate this exuberance; the pressure of tangible and resisting realities is required to confine activities to exact and economical forms. Therefore one exposes oneself to grave misunderstandings, if, in explaining rites, he believes that each gesture has a precise object and a definite reason for its existence. There are some which serve nothing; they merely answer the need felt by worshippers for action, motion, gesticulation. They are to be seen jumping, whirling, dancing, crying and singing, though it may not always be possible to give a meaning to all this agitation" (Émile Durkheim). Durkheim thinks that religion would not be itself if it did not give some place to play, to art, and to all that serves to recreate the spirit which has been fatigued by the too great slavishness of daily work.

GANAPATI. Ganapati or Ganpati. Another name for Ganesa (*q.v.*), or Ganesh, one of the gods of the Hindus.

GANDHARVA. A Hindu god, guardian of the sacred Soma plant.

GANDHMALIS. A caste of village priests connected with the temples of Siva or Mahādeo in Sambalpur and the Uriya States in India. Another name assumed by some members of the caste is Thānāpatis ("Masters of the sacred place"; *Gandh* in Gandhmāli means "incense"). R. V. Russell and R. B. Hīra Lāl think that the Thānāpatis are priests of the temples in towns and large villages whose calling has gained for them considerable social estimation, whereas the Gandhmālis are village priests who occupy a more menial position. The Gandhmālis are generally Saivas. "They consider that their ultimate ancestor is the Nāg or cobra and especially observe the festival of Nāg-Panchmi, abstaining from any cooked food on that day" (Russell).

GANESA. Gaṇeśa, also called Gaṇa-pati, is one of the gods of the Hindus. He is one of the sons of Śiva (*q.v.*). His worshippers once formed one of the great Hindu sects. The name Ganesa means "lord of hosts," and the god was so called because he was supposed to be in command of the hosts of messengers and servants which surrounded Siva, that is to say, of the evil demons and the good angels. But he is not a fighting commander, a god of war; he is simply a tutelary village deity, a god of luck and misfortune. He seems in particular to be in charge of those spirits who contrive obstacles and difficulties. He is invoked to remove these. Thus, at the literary festival on the 2nd of February, Ganesa is invoked, not as a god of learning corresponding to Sarasvatī (*q.v.*), the goddess of learning, but as the god who might put obstacles in the way of literary accomplishment. At the present day Ganesa is worshipped in conjunction with all the other gods, and his images and shrines are found throughout India. "What the Gaṇeśa or Gaṇa-pati of the present day really represents is a complex personification of sagacity, shrewdness, patience, and self-reliance—of all those qualities, in short, which overcome hindrances and difficulties, whether in performing religious acts, writing books, building houses, making journeys, or undertaking anything. He is before all things the typical embodiment of success in life; with its usual accompaniments of good-living, plenteousness, prosperity, and peace. This is the true secret of his popularity" (Monier-Williams). But though he is mainly a god who removes obstacles, he may become a god who brings them. Hence his names Vighneśa and Vighna-rāja, "lord of obstacles." In sculpture Ganesa is figured with the head of an elephant and riding on a rat. Both elephant and rat are emblems of wealth. The elephant is a great consumer of grain, and the rat is associated with overflowing granaries. See Monier-Williams; E. W. Hopkins; J. A. Dubois and H. K. Beauchamp; R. V. Russell.

GANESH PRASĀD. Gift of Ganesh, one of the names of the Hindu god Ganpati or Ganesh.

GANGĀDHAR. The holder of the Ganges, one of the names of the Hindu god Siva.

GANGAMMĀL. A Hindu deity, worshipped as the goddess of cholera by the Paraiyans, a tribe or caste in India.

GARUDA. A figure in Hindu mythology, the king of birds, half-man and half-eagle, on which the god Vishnu rode.

GÂTHAS. The Gâthas, or sacrificial hymns, are the most ancient part of the Zendavesta (*q.v.*), the oldest collection of writings sacred to the old Persians. They constitute an original or old Avesta, as compared with a later and new Avesta. They are included in that division of the Zendavesta known as the Yasna.

GAYATRI PRAYER. A Hindu prayer or formula, regarded as the most powerful of the Mantras (*q.v.*). A good Brāhman should use this Vedic prayer daily, morning and evening. The ten Sanskrit words, supposed to be full of mystery and deep allusions, are translated by Monier-Williams: "Let us meditate on that excellent glory of the Divine Vivifying Sun: may he enlighten our understandings." Monier-Williams compares its sacredness with that of the Lord's Prayer among Christians. It was so sacred that it was deified and Gayatri became a goddess. See Monier-Williams; E. W. Hopkins; J. A. Dubois and H. K. Beauchamp; J. C. Oman, *Cults*.

GDID AL ISLAM. A Jewish sect of about 2,000 persons in Khorassan.

GEFJON. One of the deities of the Ancient Teutons. The goddess Gefjon shared with Odhin (WODAN) the knowledge of the fate of men. She was also the patron deity of those who died as maids. Gefjon is perhaps to be identified with the goddess Freyja (*q.v.*). See P. D. Chantepie de la Saussaye, *Rel. of the Teutons*, 1902.

GELUGPA SECT. An order of monks in Lamaism. It was founded by Tsong Kapa, who came from North-West China. Great reverence is paid to the founder, who is supposed to have been directly inspired by Atiśa, the great teacher of the eleventh century. Tsong Kapa "strove to reinstate the original stern rules of life by means of discipline, such as that their clothing should be made from rags sewn together, their food be obtained by begging, a strict retirement be observed during the Was season, earnestness in meditation, and so on. On the other hand, he established an ornate and strictly regulated ritual." The monks are celibates, but otherwise do not adhere strictly to the rules of the founder of the order. Their headgear and outer garments are yellow. See H. Hackmann.

GEM, THE WONDROUS. One of the seven royal treasures which the king of kings, the ideal king, of the Buddhists, or rather of the pre-Buddhists, is supposed to possess. It is described as being of the purest species and perfect in every way. It is said that "when the great king of glory, to test that wondrous gem, set all his fourfold army in array, and raised aloft the gem upon his standard-top, he was able to march out in the gloom and darkness of the night, and all the dwellers round about began their daily work, thinking, 'The daylight hath come.'" Rhys Davids points out that in the Vedic hymns Indra slays the demon of darkness with the lightning, which is called his jewel. He thinks that in the wondrous gem "we have a reminiscence of the poetry and mysticism of that Animism which is so hard to kill." See T. W. Rhys Davids.

GEMARA. The designation of a part of the Jewish Talmud (*q.v.*). In course of time the two constituents of the Talmud came to be distinguished as Mishnah (this being the text) and Gemara (the commentary). Gemara has commonly been taken to mean "completion," but there is reason to think that, in this connection, the word really means "learning." There are two recensions of the Jewish Talmud, a Palestinian and a Babylonian. The Palestinian Talmud is sometimes called "Gemara of the people of the West." In both the Palestinian Talmud (completed in the fourth century) and the Babylonian Talmud (completed by the end of the fifth century) the Gemara is incomplete, but it is much more extensive in the latter. The Gemara represents the teaching of the Amoraim (*q.v.*). See W. O. E. Oesterley and G. H. Box; C. A. Briggs, *Intro.*

GENESIS, BOOK OF. The name of the first book of the first division of the Hebrew Canon of the Old Testament (*q.v.*) is in the Hebrew Bible "Berēshith." This is the opening word of the book, "In-the-beginning." In the Septuagint the title is "Genesis kosmou" or "Beginning of the World." The common abbreviation of this, "Genesis" (cp. Philo, *De Abrahamo*, § 1), has suggested the title which the book bears in the English Bible. The book has two main divisions. The first, chapters i.-xi. 26, gives the Primaeval History of Mankind, including stories of the Creation, of a great Flood, of the dispersion of peoples, etc. The second, chapters xi. 27-l., gives the History of the Ancestors and Patriarchs of the Israelites, including stories of Joseph's adventures in Egypt. The work is composite, having been compiled from the Priestly History and Law-book (P) and the Prophetic (or Popular) History (JE). The compiler himself has made alterations and additions. G. F. Moore points out that the Genesis of P was much shorter than the account of the same period in JE. Within JE it is often possible to separate the two independent documents J and E. As S. R. Driver says, "the method of the compiler, who combined J and E together, was sometimes, it would seem, to extract an entire narrative from one or other of these sources (as xx. 1-17 from E; xxiv. from J); sometimes, while taking a narrative as a whole from one source, to incorporate with it notices derived from the other; and sometimes to construct his narrative of materials derived from each source in nearly equal proportion." The use of different documents is proved not only by striking linguistic differences, but also by the presence of duplicate narratives. There is a double account of the creation, for instance (ch. i. 1-ii. 4 *a* and ch. ii. 4 *b*-25). Compare also ch. vi. 9-13 with vi. 5-8, vii. 1-5 with vi. 18-22, viii. 20-22 with ix. 8-17, xv. with xvii., xx. with xxvi. 1-11, xxi. 22-32 with xxvi. 12-31, xxviii. 10-22 with xxxv. 9-15, xxxii. 22-32 with xxxv. 9-13, xxxvi. 15-19 with xxxvi. 40-43. The composite character of the Book of Genesis has long been recognized. A more recent discovery has been that there are remarkable parallels to some of its stories in the literature of Babylonia, Egypt, and Persia. The Babylonians had similar traditions about Creation and a Deluge (see DELUGE-STORY, BABYLONIAN). The Egyptian Tale of Two Brothers resembles the story of Joseph in Genesis (see *Encycl. Bibl., s.v.* "Joseph"). There are now a number of scholars who hold that the traditions and institutions of Israel were powerfully influenced by the culture of Babylonia. But even when this is admitted, it is claimed that the Israelite version of the Flood (for instance) "is no mere copy of the Assyrian-Babylonian, for the biblical narrative is stamped by the genuine characteristics of the Israelite spirit" (K. Marti, *Religion of the O.T.*). A comparison of the traditions of other peoples raises the whole question of the character of the Book of Genesis as a historical source. It cannot be regarded as history in the modern sense of the term, that is to say, as "an authentic record of actual events based on documents contemporary, or nearly contemporary, with the facts narrated" (Skinner). But if it be regarded as a collection of legends, there are, nevertheless, as Prof. Skinner says, three ways in which such legends may yield sound historical results. "In the first place, a legend may embody a more or less exact recollection of the fact in which it originated. In the second place, a legend, though unhistorical in form, may furnish material from which history can be extracted. Thirdly, the collateral evidence of archaeology may bring to light a correspondence which gives a historical significance to the legend." See *Encycl. Bibl.;* Carpenter and Harford-Battersby, *Hex.;* W. H. Bennett, *Genesis* in the "Century Bible"; S. R. Driver, *The Book of Genesis*, 7th ed., 1909; A. R. Gordon, *The Early Traditions of Genesis*, 1907; John Skinner, *Commentary on Genesis*, 1910; G. H. Box, *Intr.;* O. C. Whitehouse.

GENEVA CATECHISM, THE. The "Geneva Catechism" was prepared by Calvin in 1536 A.D. It included a brief "Confession of Faith" in twenty-one articles. In 1541 A.D. the Catechism was recast in French, and in 1545 in Latin. It was translated afterwards into many languages, and came into regular use in Scotland. "It is clear without being superficial, simple without being childish, lacking in the picturesque, but well arranged, comprehensive, and dignified. If it was excelled, it was only by its offspring, the Heidelberg Catechism and the Westminster Shorter Catechism" (W. A. Curtis).

GENISTAE. A Jewish sect referred to by Justin Martyr. J. H. Blunt suggests that Genistae is only another name for the Nazaræans (*q.v.*) spoken of by Epiphanius. He thinks the name should rather be Genitae. The sect would seem to have claimed that they represented the true stock of Abraham. See J. H. Blunt.

GENIZAH. The Jews are careful to prevent copies of the Scriptures which have been used in public worship from falling into profane hands, even when they have become old, dirty, and unfit for service. From early times, therefore, they have been accustomed to stow away (to hide) worn-out manuscripts in a kind of lumber-room in the Synagogue. This place is called *Genizah*, "place of hiding." The Genizah had a further use. Books were placed there which, though highly esteemed, were not considered suitable for use in the Synagogue services. They were said to be hidden, and were called "hidden books" (*sephārim genūzīm*). The question was raised by some of the Rabbinic scholars, whether some of our canonical books (*e.g.*, Proverbs, Ezekiel) ought not to be hidden. Cp. CANON, OLD TESTAMENT. See G. Wildeboer; W. O. E. Oesterley and G. H. Box; A. S. Geden, *Intr. to the Hebrew Bible*, 1909.

GEONIM. Geonim, "Princes," was the title given to the leaders of the Jewish Academies of Sura and Pumbeditha in Babylonia from 589 to 1040 A.D. The Geonim were "the official heads of dispersed Judaism in things judicial as well as spiritual" (Oesterley and Box).

GERDHR. One of the deities of the Ancient Teutons. Gerdhr is a beautiful young giantess, who plays a part with the god Freyr (*q.v.*). The god beheld her one day and sent his servant to persuade her to give herself up to him. After nine nights she yielded. Chantepie de la Saussaye thinks "the chief meaning of this myth is doubtless the awakening of the earth in spring, although not all details, of course, are transferable." Gerdhr is represented as a daughter of the giant Gymir. See P. D. Chantepie de la Saussaye, *Rel. of the Teutons*, 1902.

GERMAN CATHOLICS. A religious body in Germany whose aim at first was to reform the Roman Catholic Church. In 1844 they seceded under the leadership of Johannes Czerski and Johannes Ronge. Soon after 1845 a difference arose between the two leaders as to a confession of faith, which resulted in a separation. In 1848, owing to a rising, the German Catholics in Austria were completely suppressed. In 1850 in Germany they allied themselves with the Free Churches, but for political reasons the alliance did not endure. In 1859 an attempt at union took shape in a League of Free-Religious Churches, and in 1863 in a Religious Reform Union.

GESTA ROMANORUM. The *Gesta Romanorum* or "Deeds of the Romans" is a Latin collection of anecdotes which seems to date back to about the beginning of the fourteenth century. The stories inculcate a moral and were intended for the use of Christian preachers. Most of them begin with the words, "There was an Emperor of Rome," but the events related are pure fiction. The collection is of great interest as throwing light on the morals of the times and as containing the germs of many famous tales, such as the story of the caskets introduced into Shakespeare's "Merchant of Venice." An English translation of the collection is included in Bohn's "Antiquarian Library." See William Benham; Schaff-Herzog.

GHANSIĀM. The dark-coloured or black one, one of the names of the Hindu god Krishna.

GHĀSI SĀDHAK. An Indian deity, a god worshipped as the protector of horses against disease by the Ghasias (also known as Sais), a caste of Orissa and Central India. The occupation of the members of the caste is to cut grass, tend horses, and act as musicians at village festivals. At the Dasahra festival they worship also the sickle and the horse.

GHATOIA DEO. An Indian deity, a god of ferries and river-crossings. He is worshipped among the Dhīmars (also known as Kahārs, or Bhois, or Pālewārs, or Barauas, or Machhandars), the caste of fishermen and palanquin-bearers, that is to say, by those of them who are employed on ferry-boats. He is also the principal deity of the Dhobis (also known as Wārthis, or Barethas, or Chaklas, or Rajaks, or Parits), the professional caste of washermen, being the god of the landing-place (*ghāt*) on the river.

GIBBITES. The followers of John Gib of Borrowstounness in Scotland. They were also called Sweet Singers (*q.v.*).

GIBIL. A Babylonian deity. Gibil was a fire-god. But Nusku (*q.v.*) appears also as a fire-god, and the two seem to have been amalgamated. Both gods are sons of Anu (*q.v.*). Gibil or Nusku is the chief counsellor of the gods and the god of civilization. He is the founder of cities. It is he who (as fire) brings sacrifices into the presence of the gods. He came to be identified with Nergal (*q.v.*). See Morris Jastrow, *Rel.*

GILGAMESH EPIC. The great national epic of the Babylonians, which preserves a number of ancient traditions. Gilgamesh is the name of the hero. He was probably an ancient king who was afterwards deified. He became a solar deity, subordinate to Shamash (*q.v.*). The epic begins by representing the "walled Uruk," city of Ishtar (*q.v.*) as in a state of siege. Next we find Gilgamesh in possession of the city either as its saviour or its conqueror. Gilgamesh is a hero of great strength and power. He displeases the inhabitants of Uruk by taking captive their virgins and their wives. They beseech Aruru (*q.v.*), his creator, to raise up a rival to him. The goddess Aruru thereupon creates a divine hero Eabani. Eabani is a hairy creature, and in other respects resembles an animal. Gilgamesh sends a hunter to catch him, but Eabani frightens him. Gilgamesh then sends with him Ukhat, one of the harlots of Ishtar. Ukhat entices and gains control of Eabani. He returns with her to be her companion or the companion of Gilgamesh. The tablets containing the immediate continuation of the story are defective. We next find Eabani undertaking to fight in company with Gilgamesh against a terrible enemy Khumbaba. The enemy is overcome. Ishtar the goddess then seeks the love of the heroic Gilgamesh. But the hero repulses her, because she has slain those that once she loved. Ishtar appeals to Anu (*q.v.*), her father, the god of heaven, who creates a divine bull Alû to destroy Gilgamesh. The bull is attacked by Gilgamesh and Eabani together and killed. Eabani adds insult to injury by throwing the divine bull in Ishtar's face. Ishtar, with her prostitute attendants, the Kizrêti, the Ukhâti, and the Kharimâti, makes lamentation for the bull. Gilgamesh offers the horns of the bull to Lugal-Marada, king of Marad, his own native place. Gilgamesh now loses his companion. Eabani becomes ill and dies. Then he is himself stricken with disease. He decides to go in search of a "distant one," one who is immortal, his ancestor Parnapishtim or Utnapishtim. On the way he has to confront lions and scorpion-men. Finally he must cross a great sea. On this side of the sea he finds the sea-goddess Sabitum.

He beseeches her to allow him to cross. She tells him that the only person who can take him safely across is the ferryman Ardi-Ea. Ardi-Ea is persuaded to take him. At length Gilgamesh reaches Parnapishtim, tells him of his adventures and heroic deeds, and seeks his help. Parnapishtim tells him that it is impossible to escape death. Gilgamesh is naturally curious to know how in that case Parnapishtim has attained immortality. In reply Parnapishtim tells him the story of his escape from a deluge. This is a Deluge-story resembling that of the Bible. Parnapishtim was delivered from the flood and made a god. After the recital of the deluge-story, Gilgamesh is made to fall into a deep sleep. The wife of Parnapishtim then prepares magic food made of charm-root. Gilgamesh eats it and is partly healed of his disease. Ardi-Ea is told to take him to the place of purification and wash his sores. When this has been done, Gilgamesh is cured. Parnapishtim then tells him of a plant that restores youth. Ardi-Ea helps Gilgamesh to find it. But as he holds it, it is snatched out of his hand by a demon. Gilgamesh has to return to Uruk without it. On his return he wanders from temple to temple seeking to find out what has become of Eabani. At length Nergal causes the spirit of Eabani to appear to him. Gilgamesh inquires the nature of the land in which he is now dwelling. Eabani says he cannot tell him, apparently because it will not bear telling. He curses Ukhat as the cause of his death. See Morris Jastrow, *Rel.;* Reinach, *O.*

GIPSIES. In mediaeval times Egypt was supposed to be the home of the gipsies. This accounts for the name, which is probably an abbreviation of "Egyptian." It is held now that the gipsies spread from India. They have been identified with the Doms, a great caste of menials and scavengers in Hindustān and Bengal. Leland has pointed out that Romany is almost letter for letter the same as Domni, the plural of Dom in the Bhojpuri dialect of the Bihāri language. He thinks that Romany-Rye, "a gipsy gentleman," may be well compared with the Bhojpuri Domni Rai, "a king of the Doms." The Bhojpuri-speaking Doms are said to have many points of resemblance with the gipsies of Europe. The gipsy grammar is said to be connected closely with that of Bhojpuri. See R. V. Russell, *s.v.* Kanjar.

GIRDHARI. He who held up the mountain, one of the names of the Hindu god Krishna

GIR-RA. A Babylonian deity. The name was read originally Dibbarra. Gir-ra was a god of pestilence and war. See DIBBARRA EPIC.

GITA GOVINDA. In the Vishnu Purāna (see PURĀNAS) Govinda (*q.v.*), "cow-boy," is a title given to the man-god (Krishna). The Gita Govinda is a mystical poem, composed in the twelfth century A.D., which glorifies the cow-boy god. See E. W. Hopkins.

GIṬṬIN. The name of one of the Jewish treatises or tractates which reproduce the oral tradition or unwritten law as developed by the second century A.D., and are included in the Mishnah (*q.v.*), a collection and compilation completed by Rabbi Judah the Holy, or the Patriarch, about 200 A.D. The sixty-three tractates of the Mishnah are divided into six groups or orders (*sedarim*). Giṭṭin is the sixth tractate of the third group, which is called *Nāshim* ("Women").

GLASSITES. A religious sect founded by John Glas (1695-1773). Glas was for some years (1719-1728) minister of Tealing in Forfarshire. Glas developed doctrines on the kingdom of Christ and the relations between Church and State which brought him into conflict with the Solemn League and Covenant and the Westminster Confession. In 1728 he published his views in a book "The Testimony of the King of Martyrs concerning His Kingdom." He contended that national establishments of religion find no support in the New Testament; that congregations have the right to appoint their own teachers and to share in the government of the Church; and further that civil magistrates have no right to interfere in religious matters. On the publication of his book the Synod of Angus and Mearns suspended him "for holding tenets inconsistent with the established government of this Church, and declining to come under engagements to forbear venting them." The General Assembly of the Church of Scotland, on being appealed to, deposed him from the ministry (1730). Glas then became pastor of an independent congregation; and in course of time other Glassite congregations were formed in Scotland, England, and America. The teaching of the sect was developed by Glas's son-in-law, Robert Sandeman (1718-1771) to such an extent that the sect became better known as Sandemanians (*q.v.*). See J. H. Blunt; the *D.N.B.;* and *Chambers' Encycl.*

GLOSSOLALY. A term meaning "speaking with tongues." See TONGUES, GIFT OF.

GNA. One of the deities of the Ancient Teutons. The goddess Gna belongs to the retinue of Frija (*q.v.*), and is represented as his messenger.

GNOSTICS. The Gnostics claimed to possess a deeper insight and knowledge (*gnōsis*) than that which was supplied by the faith (*pistis*) of ordinary Christians. The basis of Gnosticism which flourished in the second century A.D. "was an eclectic philosophy of religion chiefly Hellenic in character, though in union with many Oriental elements, cosmical speculations, and mystic theosophy similar to what we find in Hinduism" (H. B. Workman). It was concerned with two main problems: the nature of the Absolute, and the origin of evil; and "was essentially an esoteric Christianity, which differed widely in its tenets according to its local habitation—Alexaudria, Syria, Asia Minor, or Rome—and the degree of admixture of East and West." In Syria one of the earliest Gnostics was Saturninus of Antioch, who flourished in the reign of Trajan. But quite a multitude of sects sprang up on this soil, which had been prepared by Simon Magus. These included the Ophites, Naassenes, and Peratae, which mingled Christianity with snake-worship. Spreading to Alexandria, celebrated forms of Gnosticism came to be associated with the names of Basilides, Valentinus, and Carpocrates. The best known of these is that of Valentinus (*fl.* 140 A.D.). It is throughout a nuptial Gnosticism in which there are perpetual syzygies, marriages, and generations. In Roman Gnosticism the leader was Marcion. Duchesne (*Hist.*) thinks that amid the diversity of the various Gnostic systems certain common and fundamental conceptions are easily discernible. "1. God, the Creator and Lawgiver of the Old Testament, is not the True God. Above him, at an infinite distance, is the Father-God, the supreme First Cause of all being. 2. The God of the Old Testament knew not the True God, and in this ignorance the world shared, until the appearance of Jesus Christ, who did indeed proceed from the True God. 3. Between the True God and creation is interposed a most complicated series of beings, divine in their origin; at some point or other in this series, occurs a catastrophe, whch destroys the harmony of the whole. The visible world—often including its creator—originates in this primal disorder. 4. In humanity there are some elements capable of redemption, having come in one way or another from the celestial world above the Demiurge. Jesus Christ came into the world to deliver them from it. 5. As the incarnation could not really amount to a true union between divinity and matter, the accursed, the Gospel story is explained as a moral and transitory union between a divine æon and the concrete personality of Jesus, or again, by a simple semblance of humanity. 6. Neither the passion nor the resurrection of Christ is therefore real; the future of the predestinate does not permit of the resurrection of the body. 7. The divine element which has strayed into humanity, that is, the predestinated soul, has no solidarity with the flesh which oppresses it. Either the flesh must be annihilated by asceticism (rigorism), or at least the responsibility of the soul for the weaknesses of the flesh must be denied (libertinism)." Gnosticism possessed great vitality. Even when defeated in the Church, it persisted by taking refuge underground. "For a thousand years we find it living a subterranean existence, ever and anon coming to the surface in some new heresy, the roots of which lie deep in the older Gnosticism, or rather in the religions older even than Gnosticism to which Gnosticism was so largely indebted. In the third century it appears in the formidable movement known as Manichaeism, so called from Mani (*b.* 215), the founder of the sect" (H. B. Workman). See F. W. Bussell.

GOD. According to M. Récéjac, the most perfect notion of God which has ever been conceived is "the Being forever communicating Its own essence" (quoted by E. Hermann, *Mysticism,* 1916). Matthew Arnold's definition of the God of the Bible and of Christianity is "The Eternal, not ourselves, that makes for righteousness." Another definition is the "Friend behind phenomena" (Bevan).

GODSTONES. A name given sometimes by the peasants of the North of Ireland to the white stones or lumps of quartz crystal which the ancient Irish buried with the dead. White quartz stones have been found also in primitive internments in the Hebrides and in the neighbourhood of Dundee. W. G. Wood-Martin thinks that "the custom of burying white water-worn stones or pieces of fractured quartz or crystals may have been practised contemporaneously in Scotland and Ireland." The custom survived into Christian times. The grave of St. Brecan, in Aran, when it was opened, was found to contain a number of rounded stones.

GOFANNON. One of the deities worshipped by the ancient Celts, the patron god of metal workers. Gofannon figures in late Welsh legend. He is the son of Danu or Dôn (*q.v.*). In Irish mythology, where the name appears as Goibniu, he is celebrated also as a divine hero who brewed an ale of immortality. He is represented also as a wonderful architect. See Anwyl; Squire, *Myth.*

GOLD. Among the Hindus, gold, silver, and copper are all held sacred, but a special sacredness is ascribed to gold. "When a man is at the point of death, a little gold, Ganges water, and a leaf of the tulsi or basil plant are placed in his mouth, so that these sacred articles may accompany him to the other world. So valuable as a means of securing a pure death is the presence of gold in the mouth that some castes have small pieces inserted into a couple of their upper teeth, in order that wherever and whenever they may die, the gold may be present to purify them" (R. V. Russell and R. B. Hira Lāl). According to G. Elliot Smith (*Dr.,* 1918) gold first acquired its value from being used for making models of shells (especially cowries). In course of time people who lived at a distance from the sea experienced difficulty in obtaining the shells which they wore as amulets on girdles and necklaces. Hence they took to manufacturing, at first in clay and stone, imitations of the shells. "But at an early period in their history the inhabitants of the deserts between the Nile and the Red Sea (Hathor's special province) discovered that they could make more durable and attractive models of cowries and other shells by using the plastic yellow metal which was lying about in these deserts unused and unappreciated. This practice first gave to the metal gold an arbitrary value which it did not possess before. For the peculiar life-giving attributes of the shells modelled in the yellow metal came to be transferred to the gold itself." Thus gold itself acquired the reputation of being a giver of life. Elliot Smith points out that the earliest Egyptian hieroglyphic sign for gold was a picture of a necklace of golden amulets which probably represented cowries; and he suggests that this emblem became the determinative of the Great Mother Hathor, not only because she was originally the personification of the life-giving shells, but also because she was the guardian deity both of the Eastern wadys where the gold was found and of the Red Sea coasts where the cowries were obtained. Hence she became the Golden Hathor, the prototype of the Golden Aphrodite.

GOLDEN ROSE. From the thirteenth century the Popes have been in the habit of sending a golden rose occasionally, as a mark of distinction, to Catholic sovereigns or other persons of eminence, as well as to churches, sanctuaries, or Catholic cities. "Originally, it was a single flower of wrought gold, coloured red; afterwards the golden petals were decked with rubies and other gems; finally, the form adopted was that of a thorny branch, with several flowers and leaves, and one principal flower at the top, all of pure gold" (*Cath. Dict.*). The rose is anointed, fumigated, and blessed by the Pope on Lætare Sunday (*q.v.*), or as it is also called on this account "Dominica de rosa." It was awarded to Joanna of Naples in 1366; to Henry VIII. by three Popes; to Queen Mary in 1555; to the Republic of Lucca in 1564; to Maria Theresa in 1668; to the Cathedral of Capua in 1726; as well as to other persons and institutions. See Schaff-Herzog; the *Cath. Dict.; Chambers' Encycl.*

GOLOKA. Go-loka is one of the paradises or heavens of the Hindus. It is the heaven of Krishṇa (*q.v.*), that of Śiva (*q.v.*) being Kailāsa, and that of Vishnu (*q.v.*) being Vaikuṇṭha. It is the paradise reserved for the faithful followers of Krishna. See Monier-Williams.

GONDHALIS. A caste of wandering beggars and musicians in the Marātha Districts of the Central Provinces of India and in Berar. R. V. Russell and R. B. Hira Lāl give the following as a specimen of a Gondhali religious song:

"Where I come from and who am I,
This mystery none has solved;
Father, mother, sister and brother, these are all illusions.
I call them mine and am lost in my selfish concerns.
Worldliness is the beginning of hell, man has wrapped himself in it without reason.
Remember your *guru*, go to him and touch his feet.
Put on the shield of mercy and compassion and take the sword of knowledge.
God is in every human body."

There are passages here which remind us of the New Testament.

GONDS, RELIGION OF THE. The Gonds, whose numbers were given in 1911 as three million, have been described as being perhaps the most important of the non-Aryan or forest tribes in India. The name Gond would seem to be practically equivalent to the name Khond. It has been pointed out that while the Gonds call themselves Koi (or Koitūr), the Khonds call themselves Ku. There seems to be sufficient evidence "to establish a probability that the Gonds and Khonds were originally one tribe in the south of India, and that they obtained separate names and languages since they left their original home for the north. The fact that both of them speak languages of the Dravidian family, whose home is in southern India, makes it probable that the two tribes originally belonged there, and migrated north into the Central Provinces and Orissa" (R. V. Russell and R. B. Hīra Lāl). The Gonds worship as their great God Bura Deo (originally, it is thought, the *sāj* tree). They worship also their ancestors, deified human beings, certain animals, implements and weapons. Some of their village gods are common to them and the Hindus. Their village gods include: Bhīmsen, the god of strength; Ghor Deo, the horse god; Holera, the god of cattle; Ghansiām Deo, a deified prince; and Doctor Deo, a deified physician. They have, besides, a number of special tribal gods. These include: Pharsi Pen, the battle-axe god; Matiya, the god of mischief; Ghangra, the bell god; Chāwar, the cow's tail; Pālo (a piece of cloth); and Sale, apparently the god of cattle-pens. Sometimes they think of their gods collectively as Bura Deo. They have also household gods, which include: Jhulān Devi, the cradle goddess; Nāg Deo, the cobra god; Nārāyan Deo, the sun. The Gonds used to offer human sacrifices to the goddess Kāli and to the goddess Danteshwari (of Bastar); and the sacrifices to Kāli at Chānda and Lānji persisted into the nineteenth century. "The victim was taken to the temple after sunset and shut up within its dismal walls. In the morning, when the door was opened, he was found dead, much to the glory of the great goddess, who had shown her power by coming during the night and sucking his blood" (Russell and Hīra Lāl). The goddess is perhaps a deification of the tiger. The Gonds also, or some of them (*e.g.*, a tribe in the hills of Amarkantak and to the south-east in the Gondwāna country), have been charged with cannibalism; but they only eat persons belonging to their own family or tribe. The cannibalism, if practised, may be ritualistic. The Holi festival is held in common with the Hindus. Stones are set up, usually by the roadside, in memory of dead persons. Sometimes a small stone seat is made in front for the deceased to sit on. This seems to be because ghosts and devils are supposed to be unable to sit on the bare ground. The Gonds seem to have believed originally that the spirits of the dead continued to hover about their old homes and villages; but in course of time they developed or borrowed a doctrine of reincarnation, according to which souls are born again in children of the same family. See R. V. Russell.

GONTIYALAMMA. One of the deities worshipped by the Mālas of Southern India. She is the special caste deity of the Mālas of the Godāvari district.

GOOSE, THE. The goose was associated with the ancient Egyptian god Amen or Amon, and was the symbol of the god Seb or Keb. Among the Greeks, the goose was associated with the worship of Asklepios, the god of healing. "The Romans declared that they kept geese on the Capitol to honour the vigilance of these birds, which had frustrated a nocturnal attack attempted by the Gauls; this was a later explanation of a custom founded on the sacred character of the goose" (S. Reinach, *O.*). The Britons of the time of Caesar kept geese which they were forbidden to eat.

GOPAL. A Hindu deity, another name for Krishna.

GORTHÆANS. Eusebius in his Ecclesiastical History (iv. 22), in referring to seven sects among the Jewish people, says: "Of these, also was Simeon, whence sprang the sect of Simonians; also Cleobius, from whom came the Cleobians; also, Dositheus, the founder of the Dositheans. From these also sprang the Gorthæans, from Gorthæus, and the Masbothœans, from Masbotheus." They are mentioned also by Epiphanius (Hær. xii.), in conjunction with the Essenes, the Sebuæ, and the Dositheans, as one of the sects of the Samaritans. See J. H. Blunt.

GOSAINS. Gosain (also Gusain, Sanniāsi, Dasnāmi) is a designation of the orders of religious mendicants of the Sivite sect in India. Sanniāsi is explained as meaning one who abandons the desires of the world and the body. Dasnāmi means the ten names (*i.e.*, of the ten orders). The ten orders of the Gosains are described as: Giri, peak of a hill; Puri, a town; Parbat, a mountain; Sāgar, the ocean; Ban or Van, the forest; Tīrtha, a shrine of pilgrimage; Bhārthi, the goddess of speech; Sāraswati, the goddess of learning; Aranya, forest; and Ashrām, a hermitage. Certain ascetics in these orders are called Dandis and Abdhūts. The Dandis take their name from a bamboo staff (*dand*), which they carry. Like the Sanniāsis, they claim to have become part of the deity (Siva). Another class of Gosains are called Rāwanvansis after Rāwan, the demon king of Ceylon, in whose character they go about. The Gosain mendicant provides himself with a begging-bowl, with a pair of tongs used for kindling a fire, and, if possible, with the skin of a tiger or panther to sit and lie down on. In former times he was accustomed to go about naked. The rule of the orders is celibacy, property passing to a man's *chela* or disciple; but it is now the practice of most Gosains to marry. See J. C. Oman, *M.A.S.;* and especially R. V. Russell.

GOTTESFREUNDE. A name assumed by German mystics in the fourteenth century. The word means Friends of God (*q.v.*).

GOVINDA. Govinda is one of the names given to the Supreme Being by Nānak (1469-1538 A.D.), the founder of Sikhism (*q.v.*). But he preferred the name Hari.

GRAECUS VENETUS. This is the name given to a Greek translation in manuscript of a large part of the Old Testament. The manuscript, also called Codex Venetus, was discovered in the library of St. Mark's Church, Venice. It belongs probably to the fourteenth or fifteenth century. The author seems to have been a Jew who translated direct from the Hebrew text, but compared earlier Greek versions. The books included are: the Pentateuch, Proverbs, Ruth, Canticles, Ecclesiastes, Lamentations, and Daniel. The work was published in 1784, and again by O. Gebhardt in 1875. In some respects the translation "recalls that of Aquila, in its literality and the attempt to render Hebrew terms by Greek words of similar origin and derivation. It is, however, entirely independent of the earlier version" (A. S. Geden). See H. B. Swete, *Intr. to the O. T. in Greek*, 1900; A. S. Geden, *Intr. to the Hebrew Bible*, 1909.

GRAIL, HOLY. The derivation of the word "grail" is doubtful. The most probable identification is with the Latin *gradalis* = cratalis (from *crater*), "cup." The story of the Holy Grail, as is clear from the Arthurian legend, centres round some precious object which was lost and could be found only by the truly pure seeker (such as Sir Galahad). In the Christian version of the Middle Ages the grail is thought of usually as the cup used by Jesus at the Last Supper or the vessel used by Joseph of Arimathæa to catch the blood which flowed from Jesus' wounded body. The Christian legend, however, is an adaptation or transformation of a legend which originally had nothing to do with Christianity. Its proximate origin, as far as it can be traced, is Celtic. The legend seems to have passed from Wales to France, where it was transformed (by Chrétien de Troyes (1180-90) in *Le Conte del Graal;* and by Robert de Borron (1180-99) in *Le petit St. Graal*). It was then reintroduced into Wales (*Mabinogi of Peredur, Son of Evrawc,*

13th cent.). The ultimate origin of the legend may have been Oriental. Miss M. A. Murray (*Journal of the Manchester Egyptian and Oriental Society*, 1917, p. 15 f.) thinks that that portion of the Grail romance which relates to Joseph of Arimathæa is Egyptian in origin. At the beginning of the legend the route taken by Joseph indicates that the whole action takes place in Egypt. The names of the principal characters in the story show an Egyptian origin. Further proofs of the Egyptian origin are to be found in the passages which relate to the Grail itself and to Josephes. The reference to a "wooden ark" points to a Christian ceremony, though a ceremony not in use in the Western Church. In the Coptic celebration of the Eucharist a wooden ark plays a large part. Again, in the consecration of Josephes Coptic ritual may be recognised; and the vestments with which Josephes was clothed appear to be those in use in the Coptic and Byzantine Churches. Another interesting proof of the connection with Egypt is found in the name of the castle in which the Grail was finally housed—Corbenie. The Arabic Qurbān is the usual name in the Coptic Church for the Eucharist. Castle Corbenie may therefore be explained "The House of the Eucharist." In any case, the legend in its wanderings gathered up a number of curious features. With the cup or chalice is associated sometimes a lance and a sword. S. Reinach (*O.*) points out that the chief episode in the Finnish collection of popular poems, the *Kalewala* (belonging in its present form to the age of Charlemagne) is the theft of a sacred object. See A. Nutt, *Studies on the Legend of the Holy Grail*, 1888, and No. 14 of *Popular Studies*.

GRĀMSIRI. An Indian deity, worshipped by the Chasas (also known as Tasas or Alias), the chief cultivating caste of Orissa. The god is represented by a stone outside the village. The Chasas worship also their agricultural implements (hoes, hatchets, etc.).

GRAND PRIORY OF THE ORDER OF THE HOSPITAL OF S. JOHN OF JERUSALEM IN ENGLAND. See HOSPITALLERS.

GRANNUS. The name Granni or Grannus, "the brilliant," appears as that of a god of the ancient Celts who corresponded to Apollo (*q.v.*). Grannus was a god of healing, who presided over thermal springs. The popularity of such a god is easily explained, and it is not surprising to find that the worship of Grannus was adopted by the Roman soldiers. A religion is often supposed to demonstrate its divine character by its success in healing bodily ailments. The god Grannus is paired with the goddess Sirona, but what relationship was intended is uncertain. See Anwyl; Reinach, *O.*

GRANTH, THE. The Granth, that is to say, "the Book," is the name of the sacred book or Bible compiled for the Sikhs (see SIKHISM) by their fifth Guru, chief, or teacher Arjun. It was called afterwards Ādigranth, or First Book, to distinguish it from a larger Bible which was compiled by the tenth Guru or teacher Govind. One of the books which Govind added to the original Granth was composed by himself. This was called the Book of the Tenth Guru. See Monier-Williams; E. W. Hopkins; *R.S.W.*

GRAPHOLOGICAL SPIRITISM. That kind of spiritism in which writing is employed as the medium of communication. See SPIRITISM.

GREAT SYNAGOGUE. Reference is made in the Jewish Mishnah, Gemaras and Midrash to a body of persons designated "the Men of the Great Synagogue." The Talmud represents that they consisted of one hundred and twenty (or eighty-five) persons learned in the Scriptures, that the body was founded or presided over by Ezra, and that after the exile they stood at the head of the state. One of the works they were supposed by the mediaeval Jews to have accomplished was the fixing of the whole Canon of the Old Testament. As to this the statements on which the idea was based are found in the tractate of the Mishnah called Ābōth (i. 1, 2) and in a Baraitha (*q.v.*) of the Talmud (*Bābā Bathrā*, fol. 15*a*). In Ābōth we read that: "Moses received the Torah from Sinai and delivered it to Joshua, and Joshua to the elders, and the elders to the prophets, and the prophets to the men of the Great Synagogue. They said three things: Be deliberate in judgment, and raise up many disciples, and make a fence to the Torah. Simon the Just was of the remnants of the Great Synagogue." In the Baraitha we are told that: "The men of the Great Synagogue wrote Ezekiel and the Twelve, Daniel and the Roll of Esther, whose sign is קנדג." These statements in themselves, however, do not imply more than that the men of the Great Synagogue were one of the means of transmitting the Torah and that they edited certain of the books of the Old Testament. But in any case the story of the work of the men of the Great Synagogue bears traces of being unhistorical (*e.g.*, Simon the Just belonged to the time of Alexander the Great), and the very existence of the Great Synagogue has been shown to be very doubtful. The statements about it are conflicting. It appears at one time as a permanent institution, at another time as lasting a hundred years. According to mediaeval Jewish scholars, it exercised a very great influence in religious matters. As G. Wildeboer says: "Jewish scholars after the fall of Jerusalem had an entirely false idea of the older times. Israel was not ruled by the Scribes before the year 70 A.D. What are we to imagine under the name Great Synagogue? A senate? Certainly not; it is supposed to have been a religious body." A. Kuenen argues powerfully for the view that the story is a legend based upon the narrative in Nehemiah viii.-x. "If now it be assumed that the historical basis of the legend is the assembly in Nehemiah viii.-x., then we cannot attribute to it the rôle ascribed to it by tradition. For this assembly did not legislate, but adopted a legislation." So A. Kuenen says that "the Talmudic Great Synagogue is an unhistorical conception, a transformation of the assembly which under Ezra and Nehemiah adopted the complete Mosaic law book." Subsequently the Sōpherim antedated the domination of their predecessors, and ascribed a prolonged existence to the assembly. In place of the men of the Great Synagogue we have to put "the older scribes." "The latter really accomplished what is ascribed to the former. They constituted no governing assembly, but were some of them priests, others not: some members of the Sanhedrin, others outside of that body" (Wildeboer). See G. Wildeboer, *Canon;* C. A. Briggs, *Intr.*

GREEK VERSIONS, OLD TESTAMENT. The translation of the Old Testament known as the Septuagint failed in course of time to satisfy the leaders of Jewish thought. It was considered too free, and wanting in dignity and precision. In consequence of this feeling new translations came into existence during the second century or at the beginning of the third century A.D. The chief of these were associated with the names of Aquila, Theodotion, and Symmachus. (1) The Version of Aquila seems to have been the earliest of the three. "It also represents most fully the reaction of Jewish sentiment against the freedom with which the Seventy had treated the Hebrew text" (A. S. Geden). The name of the author is in Greek Ἀκύλας. It seems to be identical with Onkelos, the traditional name of the author of a Targum on the Pentateuch (see TARGUM).

Epiphanius says that Aquila's translation was produced in the twelfth year (A.D. 128-29) of the reign of the Emperor Hadrian (A.D. 117-38). Jewish tradition states that he was a disciple (c. A.D. 100) of Rabbi Akiba. The fragments of the translation which have been preserved show that it was slavishly literal and full of Hebraisms. The version "seems to have been welcomed by the Jews, who found in it what they required, a Greek Bible free from Christian associations, and conformed to the Hebrew Canon and style; and it has been supposed to have been more or less formally authorised in Palestine, and to have remained in use there by Greek-speaking Jews until the time of the Muhammadan Conquest in the seventh century" (A. S. Geden). (2) The version of Theodotīōn was not much, if at all, later than that of Aquila. Theodotion is said by Epiphanius to have been a native of Pontus and an adherent of Marcion (flourished about A.D. 150), and is mentioned by Justin Martyr (c. A.D. 160). His translation was clearly not based upon the Hebrew text, but upon the accepted Greek text, of which it was evidently intended to be a revision. "His Hebrew scholarship appears to have been hardly equal to that of Aquila, for he sometimes transliterates Hebrew words where the latter translates, apparently for no other reason than that he was in doubt or ignorance as to the meaning" (A. S. Geden). Theodotion's translation of Daniel entirely supplanted that of the Septuagint. Only fragments of the rest of his version have survived. (3) Symmachus seems to have been the latest of the three translators. Irenaeus does not mention him. This may be regarded as an indication of his date. Moreover, as H. B. Swete says, "so far as we can judge from the fragments of his version which survive in Hexaplaric MSS, he wrote with Aquila's version before him, and in his efforts to recast it made free use of both the LXX and Theodotion." Epiphanius speaks of him as a Samaritan, and says that he lived under Severus (A.D. 193-211). It has been thought that Severus here is a mistake for "Verus," that is to say Lucius Verus (A.D. 161-180). Cp. further HEXAPLA. See F. Buhl, *Canon;* H. B. Swete, *Intr. to the O. T. in Greek*, 1900; A. S. Geden, *Intr. to the Hebrew Bible*, 1909.

GREY FRIARS. A name by which the followers of Francis of Assisi, the Franciscans (*q.v.*) were known in England. They were so called because the colour of their gowns and hoods was grey.

GRIHASTHAS. The word means literally "householders," and corresponds to "laity." It designates one of the two chief classes into which the disciples of the Hindu religious reformer, Svāmi Nārāyana (b. about 1780), are divided. The other chief class consists of the "holy men" or clergy, Sādhus (*q.v.*).

GUECUBU. An evil power (also called Aka-kanet) in the mythology of the Araucanian Indians of Chili, a power to whom or to which all misfortunes were ascribed.

GUILD OF ALL SOULS, THE. A society founded in 1873 in the Church of England, "for the purpose of propagating a belief in the existence of Purgatory, and of encouraging the practice of Prayers for the Dead, and the offering of Masses to release their souls from Purgatorial pains" (Walsh). See Walter Walsh, "Ritualistic Secret Societies" in *Prot. Dict.*

GUILD OF HEALTH. A Society founded in 1905 and reconstituted in 1918. It has been designed to promote a deeper interest in the relation between the spiritual life and bodily health. The promoters believe that by strengthening our grasp upon Eternal Realities, we find re-enforcement for the life in us, which quickens all the functions of body as well as those of mind. This truth has supplied the vital element of certain societies, in which it is combined with doctrines and practices which tend to draw the mind from the essential faith of Christianity. From these the members of the Guild of Health would dissociate the vital truth to which they bear witness. That truth is constructive, and it is by a constructive teaching alone that it is possible to put an end to the steady movement of good people from the Church into these societies, and to revive within the Church a right proportionate emphasis upon this neglected part of Christian doctrine. In other words, it is desired by the Guild to emphasize the great Christian truth which has been put forward in the movements known as Christian Science, Higher Thought, Faith Healing, etc., without accepting all the characteristic opinions which seem to its promoters to diverge seriously from the Christian Gospel. The objects of the Guild are: (1) The study of the influence of spiritual upon physical well-being; (2) the exercise of healing by spiritual means, in complete loyalty to scientific principles and methods; (3) united prayer for the inspiration of the Holy Spirit in all efforts to heal the sick; (4) the cultivation, through spiritual means, of both individual and corporate health. The Chairman of the Committee is the Rev. Harold Anson (12, Fellows Road, London, N.W. 3).

GUILD OF S. MATTHEW. A Society founded in 1876 by a small number of Anglican clergy who were inspired by the teaching of Charles Kingsley (1819-1875). Their objects were three. 1. To get rid, by every possible means, of the existing prejudices, especially on the part of "secularists," against the Church, her sacraments and doctrines; and to endeavour to "justify God to the people." 2. To promote the study of social and political questions in the light of the Incarnation. 3. To promote frequent and reverent worship in the Holy Communion, and a better observance of the teaching of the Church of England, as set forth in the Book of Common Prayer. The character of the work of the Guild is well explained in one of its Reports. "Believing, as we do, that the great fact of the Incarnation is the foundation of Christian teaching and practice, we cannot see how or why the Christian Church should not consider every question bearing upon the welfare, secular and spiritual of man. We feel the absolute need of preaching in season and out of season 'the Gospel of the Kingdom,' the fact that the Church is a real living society on this earth, working for the greatest good of the greatest number, and embodying in her sacraments and in her creeds the strongest assertions of true 'liberty, equality, and fraternity' ever given to the world, doing this, too, on far higher grounds than can possibly be taken by any 'secular' creed or society. Does the secularist talk of fraternity? We tell him there is no merely theoretical basis of true fraternity so grand or sure as the fact of the Fatherhood of God. Of equality? Nowhere is it embodied so grandly as in Holy Baptism and in the Holy Communion; nowhere have its principles been carried out to their logical conclusions so thoroughly as in the Communistic Church of Jerusalem. Of liberty? The priests and bishops of the English Church have constantly led the people to victory over kings and pope alike. Of the rights of labour? Bible history, as apart from Bible biography, begins with a 'strike' (Ex. v. 45), and some of the bitterest denunciations of the prophets both of the Old and of the New Testaments are launched against those 'who keep back by fraud the hire of the labourers who have reaped their fields.' Of patriotism? The English Church welded the incoherent Saxon kingdoms into one nation. The representative government of later times was modelled after the earlier councils of the Church. Of the wider bond of the brotherhood of nations? St. Paul preached it for the first time in Europe, in the teeth of the exclusive Greeks at Athens. The Hebrew prophets—nay, more, our Lord Himself—reiterated it in equally exclusive Judæa. The Catholic Church is the only true international." Cp. CHRISTIAN SOCIAL UNION, and SOCIALISM, CHRISTIAN. See C. W. Stubbs, *Charles Kingsley and the Christian Social Movement*, 1899.

GUKUMATZ. A tribal deity, god of creation, in the religion of the Mayan Indians. He is called also Kukulkan (*q.v.*).

GULA. A Babylonian deity. Gula was a goddess of healing. She was the "great physician," a "life-giver." But she could bring on diseases as well as heal them. Sometimes she is associated with Nin-akha-kuddu, the goddess of spells and purification. She was the consort of Ninib (*q.v.*). There was a festival (Si-gar) in her honour in Iyyar, the second month. See Morris Jastrow, *Rel.*

GURAIYA DEO. A Hindu deity, the principal deity in Hoshangābād of the Pārdhis, a low caste of wandering fowlers and hunters in India. His image, a human figure, embossed in silver, is kept in a leather bag. He is also one of the special deities of the Ahirs, a caste of cowherds, milkmen and cattle-breeders. As such, he dwells in the village cattle-stalls, and is worshipped once a year.

GURAOS. A caste of village priests of the temples of Mahādeo or Siva in the Marātha Districts of India. They claim to have been originally Brāhmans, who were degraded from their status on account of some ritual negligence. It seems more likely that "the caste is not of Brāhmanical origin but belongs to a lower class of the population" (R. V. Russell). The Guraos are allowed to repeat the Rudra Gayatri or sacred verse of Siva, but they are permitted to study only the Sāma Veda. According to the *Bombay Gazetteer* (quoted by Russell and Hira Lāl), "the Jain Guraos are probably Jain temple servants who have come under the influence partly of Lingāyatism and partly of Brāhmanism."

GURMUKHIS. A special sect, in the Nāgpur country in India, of the Koshtis (or Koshtas), the Marātha and Telugu caste of weavers of silk and fine cotton cloth. They are followers of a saint named Koliba Bāba, who "is said to have fed five hundred persons with food which was sufficient for ten and to have raised a Brāhman from the dead in Umrer" (R. V. Russell).

GURU. Religious teachers or spiritual guides among the Hindus. Usually they are Brahmans.

GUSTAV-ADOLF-VEREIN. The Gustavus Adolphus Association was founded at Leipzig in 1832 by Superintendent Grossmann in honour of Gustavus II. Adolphus (1594-1632), King of Sweden. The aim of the Association was to relieve Protestant communities, wherever they were oppressed, especially in Catholic countries. A. S. Farrar points out that the Association "was one of the first means of promoting Christian union." See A. S. Farrar, *Crit. Hist. of Free Thought* ("Bampton Lectures"), 1862; Brockhaus.

GWYDION. Gwydion was one of the gods or divine heroes revered by the ancient Celts in Britain. He is said to have been one of the sons of Dôn (*q.v.*). He resembles the Teutonic Odhin or Wodan (*q.v.*) in so many respects that the two gods have been thought to be identical. Professor Rhŷs has suggested the equation Gwydion = Wodan = Indra (Hibbert Lectures on *Celtic Heathendom*, 1886). Gwydion is represented as a Culture-hero. He was not only skilled in war-craft, but also wonderfully inspired as a poet. He was associated with a goddess Arianrod, who figures as the mother of Lleu (*q.v.*). See Squire, *Myth.*

GYMNOPODAE. Another name for the Excalceati (*q.v.*).

GWYNN. A god of the underworld in the mythology of the British Celts. An owl figures as his companion.

H

H. God H is a designation used by anthropologists for a deity depicted in the MSS. of the Mayan Indians of Central America. On his forehead appears the scale or skin-spot of a serpent; but the meaning of the sign is uncertain.

HAAG ASSOCIATION FOR THE DEFENCE OF THE CHRISTIAN RELIGION, THE. An association founded in Holland in 1785 as a result of the publication, in 1782, of Joseph Priestley's "History of the Corruptions of Christianity." Its object was to oppose the anti-Christian tendencies of the age. It sought to defend the more orthodox and conservative positions against the attacks of the rationalists, and of extreme critics like D. F. Strauss. After 1860, however, it became active rather in the ethico-religious field; "and, in spite of the truth and beauty they contain, its publications on slavery, war, capital punishment, woman's emancipation, and other questions of a similar import, lie far out in the periphery of Christian apologetics" (Schaff-Herzog). The Association is known also as "The Apologetical Society of the Hague." See Schaff-Herzog.

HABAKKUK, BOOK OF. Various dates have been assigned to the prophecy of Habakkuk. Betteridge (1903) favours the year 701 B.C. Peiser thinks the prophecy was composed about the year 609 B.C. by a Jewish prince who was familiar with Assyro-Babylonian literature. Whitehouse favours, for the major portion of the oracles, a date a little before 600 B.C. Happel thinks the prophecy was composed about 170 B.C. Kent is perhaps right in thinking that there is good reason for dating the original sections of the Book of Habakkuk in 605-4 B.C. He thinks "it is evident that the situation is precisely similar to that described by Jeremiah: and Habakkuk's teachings are closely parallel to those of Jeremiah in the same period. The rule of Jehoiakim, under Egyptian supremacy, represented injustice and violence to the true followers of the prophets. Habakkuk, as well as Jeremiah, recognized that the fate of the faithful seemed, for the moment at least, to implicate the very justice of Jehovah himself. At the same time, after the great victory at Carchemish, the advancing Chaldeans were recognized as Jehovah's agents, commissioned to overthrow the existing *régime* of violence and oppression." The third chapter of the book is called "Prayer of Habakkuk the Prophet." It is a post-exilic psalm; but, as Cornill notes, it is not one of the latest products of post-exilic literature, since it is imitated in Psalm lxxvii. 17-20. He further points out that "the circle of thought in which the poem moves is that of eschatology tinged with apocalyptic: its mode of expression is the artificial archaising style of such passages as Deut. xxxii., II. Sam. xxiii. 1-7, Pss. lxviii. and xc., in common with which it has a corresponding superscription." See C. Cornill, *Intr.;* G. H. Box; O. C. Whitehouse; C. F. Kent, *The Sermons, Epistles and Apocalypses of Israel's Prophets,* 1910.

HACHAMOTH. A term used in Gnosticism (*q.v.*). Hachamoth is the illegitimate offspring of Sophia, Wisdom, one of the thirty æons of the Pleroma, and is expelled from the Pleroma. She forms out of psychical substance the Demiurge or creator of the visible universe. See VALENTINIANS.

HACHIMAN. One of the native deities of Japan, the god of war. When the Ryōbu-Shinto (*q.v.*) was introduced in Japan, Hachiman came to be regarded as a Buddha. "One of the natural consequences of the system known as Ryōbu ("two parts") was that, by treating the native gods of Japan as merely incarnations of one or other of the Buddhas, and as therefore entitled to the worship of the Buddhists, the Japanese were enabled to introduce into their Buddhism many non-Buddhist elements" (Arthur Lloyd).

HADATHIYYA. An Arabian sect, regarded by the Sunnis as heretics. See HA'ITIYYA.

HADITH. An Arabic word meaning "tradition." The term is used to denote the body of traditions regarding Muhammad, and is equivalent to the Sunna (*q.v.*).

HÆVA. Hæva or Awai is the name of a goddess worshipped by some of the Ancient Teutons. The name appears on an altar discovered in the Netherlands. The altar was erected by a man and his wife, who would seem to have worshipped Hæva as a goddess of fertility.

HAGGADAH. In the Jewish (Talmudic) interpretation of the text of Scripture a clear distinction is made between two methods of exposition, one of which is called Haggadah, and the other Halakah. Haggadah means literally "telling" or "narration"; Halakah means "rule" or "binding law." The one method was legalistic and casuistic, the other illustrative and homiletical. The term Haggadah "acquired an extended significance covering the whole field of the non-halakic part of the old Rabbinical literature, all that is spiritual and homiletical as well as all that is merely illustrative, such as stories and legends of biblical and post-biblical heroes and saints, and folklore generally." Halakah embraces "all that belongs to the strictly legal or ritual element in Scripture, or can be deduced therefrom, including discussions of such points" (Oesterley and Box). It also covers usages, customs, ordinances and decrees which have little or no Scriptural authority. Haggadah became a special kind of oratory in the synagogue. "The Haggadah, which is intended to bring heaven down to the congregation, and also to lift man up to heaven, appears in this office both as the glorification of God and as the comfort of Israel. Hence religious truths, moral maxims, discussions concerning divine retribution, the inculcation of the laws which attest Israel's nationality, descriptions of its past and future greatness, scenes and legends from Jewish history, comparisons between the divine and Jewish institutions, praises of the Holy Land, encouraging stories, and comforting reflections of all kinds form the most important subjects of these discourses" (L. Zunz, quoted by Oesterley and Box). In course of time thirteen rules of Halakah and thirty-two rules of Haggadah were elaborated. Wogue (quoted by C. A. Briggs) sums these up. "These forty-five rules may all be reduced to two fundamental considerations. (1) Nothing is fortuitous, arbitrary, or indifferent in the Word of God. Pleonasm, ellipsis, grammatical anomaly, transposition of words or facts, everything is calculated, everything has its end and would teach us something. The casual, the approximate, the insignificant and inconsequential flower of rhetoric, all that belongs to the setting in human language, are strange to the severe precision of Biblical language. (2) As the image of its author, who is one by Himself and manifold in His manifestations, the Bible often conceals in a single word a crowd of thoughts; many a phrase, which appears to express a simple and single idea, is susceptible of diverse senses and numberless interpretations independent of the fundamental difference between literal exegesis and free exegesis, in short, as the Talmud says, after the Bible itself, the divine word is like fire which divides itself into a thousand sparks, or a rock which breaks into numberless fragments under the hammer that attacks it. These two points of view, I repeat, are the soul of the Midrash in general; the latter above all serves as the common basis of the *Halakah* and *Haggadah,* and it explains, better than any other theory, the long domination of the midrash exegesis in the synagogue." See C. A. Briggs, *Intr.;* W. O. E. Oesterley and G. H. Box.

HAGGAI, BOOK OF. The prophet Haggai is referred to in the Book of Ezra (v. 1, vi. 14). With a certain Zechariah he came forward in the second year of Darius Hystaspis (520 B.C.) to arouse the zeal of the people and to urge them to undertake without delay the rebuilding of the ruined temple. The Book of Haggai contains four prophecies, each of which is dated from the year of the reign of the Persian monarch. The first, ch. i. vss. 1-11, was delivered on the 1st day of the sixth month in the second year of Darius. To this is added, vss. 12-15, a section which states that, as a result of the prophet's words, a beginning was made with the work on the 24th day of the same month. The second prophecy, ch. ii. vss. 1-9, was delivered on the 21st day of the seventh month; the third, ch. ii. vss. 10-19, and the fourth, ch. ii. vss. 20-23, on the 24th day of the ninth month. The prophet rebuked the people for dwelling in ceiled houses, while the House of Jehovah lay in ruins. He declared that a severe famine from which the people and land were suffering was a punishment for this indifference. The concluding prophecy is Messianic. The descendant of David, Zerubbabel, shall set up the messianic kingdom, and shall be as a signet on the Lord's hand. It is possible that Haggai had seen the Temple of Solomon (cp. ii. 3). In that case he must have been over seventy years old at the time of his prophetic activity. In 538 B.C. Cyrus had given permission to the conquered peoples whom he found in Babylon to return to their own countries and rebuild cities and temples. Not many of the Jews took advantage of this concession. C. F. Kent takes the view that "the conditions of the Judean community reflected in the sermons of Haggai and Zechariah and the memories of Nehemiah indicate conclusively that there had been no general return of the exiles from Babylon. Rather the hope of a general return was still in the future. The audience to which the prophets Haggai and Zechariah spoke was the little community which had grown up about the ruins of the temple." See C. Cornill, *Intr.;* G. H. Box; O. C. Whitehouse; C. F. Kent, *The Sermons, Epistles and Apocalypses of Israel's Prophets,* 1910.

HAGIOGRAPHA. The third group into which the books of the Old Testament are divided. The Hebrew name is Kethubim, "Writings." The Jews have subdivided the Kethubim into three smaller groups. (1) Poetical books, also called "The Former Writings" (Kethubim rishônim): Psalms, Proverbs, Job. (2) The five Megilloth (*q.v.*) or Rolls: Song of Songs, Ruth, Lamentations, Ecclesiastes, Esther. (3) A miscellaneous group, sometimes called "The Latter Writings" (Kethubim akharônim): Daniel, Ezra, Nehemiah, I. and II. Chronicles. This is the order in printed editions of the Hebrew Bible. In the Talmud (*q.v.*) the order is: Ruth, Psalms, Job, Proverbs, Ecclesiastes, Canticles, Lamentations, Daniel, Esther, Ezra (Ezra-Nehemiah), Chronicles. Jerome gives the order: Job, David (=Psalms), Solomon (=Proverbs), Ecclesiastes, Canticles, Daniel, Chronicles, Ezra-Nehemiah, Esther. The three groups into which the books of the Old Testament are divided ((1) Law, (2) Prophets, (3) Hagiographa) mark the stages in the growth of the Canon. The third group is of a rather miscellaneous character. This is accounted for by supposing that some of the books were written, or received recognition, too late to be included in the second group. But if the Hagiographa formed as it were an undefined collection, the rules of canonicity were strictly adhered to, and it was not every book that could gain admission. "There were admitted to it only books written in Hebrew or Aramaic, which treated of the ancient history (Ruth, Chronicles), or gave information about the establishment of the new order of things (Ezra-Nehemiah), or which were supposed to have been written by some famous person of ancient times (Proverbs, Ecclesiastes, Canticles, Lamentations, Daniel, perhaps Job also); while Esther obtained admission (after much controversy, as was the case with Ecclesiastes), because it was in complete harmony with the national sentiment of people and scribes alike" (G. Wildeboer). See G. Wildeboer, *Canon;* H. E. Ryle, *Canon.*

HAIR, THE. In the Old Testament one of the legal enactments is said to have been: "Ye shall not round off the corners of your hair, nor shalt thou disfigure the corners of thy beard" (Lev. xix. 27). The Israelites were commanded not to cut off or shave the hair about the temples. This had come to be regarded as a heathen custom. We learn from Herodotus (iii. 8) that certain Arab tribes were accustomed to remove these locks at a certain age in honour of their god Orotal, and Jeremiah seems to allude to the custom (ix. 25) when he speaks of *ketsûtsê pē'ah,* "those who have the corners of their head polled." But the prohibition in Leviticus is probably directed against the practice of offering the hair as a sacrifice. It is likely that in ancient times the Hebrews sacrificed the hair of the head and the beard to some deity (cp. Baruch vi. 30 ff.). Some such custom prevailed widely in the East and in Greece. "When Egyptian boys or girls had recovered from sickness, their parents used to shave the children's heads, weigh the hair against gold or silver, and give the precious metal to the keepers of the sacred beasts, who bought food with it for the animals according to their tastes" (J. G. Frazer). In the worship of the Phoenician goddess Astarte, the sacrifice of women's hair was accepted as a substitute for the sacrifice of their chastity (cp. Lev. xix. 29). In some parts of Greece maidens before marriage sacrificed their hair to Artemis. Boys went to Delphi to offer their hair (the seat of strength) to Apollo. Elsewhere men dedicated locks of their hair to Zeus. Similar customs have been noted among primitive folk in modern times. Thus the Australians deposit hair (as the seat of human strength) with the dead. The use of hair as a charm may be explained on the principle of imitative magic. In ancient Mexico the goddess of maize was called "the long-haired mother." During her festival "the women wore their long hair unbound, shaking and tossing it in the dances which were the chief feature in the ceremonial, in order that the tassel of the maize might grow in like profusion, that the grain might be correspondingly large and flat, and that the people might have abundance" (E. J. Payne, quoted by J. G. Frazer). The natives in Western Australia blow hair plucked from their thighs and arm-pits in the direction from which they desire rain. In the case of the Hebrew Nazirite, the hair was allowed to grow long until the period of his vow had expired, when, we may suppose, the hair was offered as a sacrifice (Numbers vi. 5). "As soon as a man takes the vow to poll his locks at the sanctuary, the hair is a consecrated thing, and, as such, inviolable till the moment for discharging the vow arrives; and so the flowing locks of the Hebrew Nazirite or of a Greek votary like Achilles are the visible marks of his consecration" (W. R. Smith). Among the Hindus the hair was regarded as the special seat of bodily strength. Indeed, evidence has been collected which "appears to indicate that the belief of a man's strength and vigour being contained in his hair is by no means confined to the legend of Samson, but is spread all over the world" (R. V. Russell). See S. R. Driver and H. A. White, *The Book of Leviticus,* in "Sacred Books of the Old Testament," 1898; B. Baentsch, *Exodus-Leviticus-Numeri,* 1903; *Encycl. Bibl.;* W. Robertson Smith, *R.S.;* J. G. Frazer, *G.B.,* Part I., vol. i., p. 28 ff.

HĀ'ITIYYA. An Arabian sect, regarded by the Sunnis as heretics. The Hā'itiyya, together with the Hadathiyya, accepted the view of the Christians that at the last day Christ would come to judge all creatures. They ascribed to him a divine character. But "they asserted the existence of two gods, the one eternal, the most High God, and the other not eternal, that is Christ." See F. A. Klein.

HAJJ, THE. The name of a pilgrimage made by the Muhammedans to the holy house at Mecca, the Ka'ba (*q.v.*). It is the fifth of the foundations of Islam. Every Muslim, male or female, is commanded to make the pilgrimage at least once in his life (*Qur'ān,* xxii. 28; ii. 153, 192; iii. 90; v. 2). The black stone, "built up in one of the corners of this temple forms an object of special veneration to the pilgrim." To make the pilgrimage the Muslim must be a free man of full age, of sound reason, and in good health. He must also have the necessary means to provide for himself and for his family at home. "A woman must be accompanied by her husband or some near relation." Before setting out the pilgrim is required to repent of his sins, pay his debts, give alms, etc., say a prayer and read certain verses of the Qur'ān. He must take with him a pious and charitable man as his companion. The journey must be made for the most part by night, and the pilgrim must not dismount till the day has become hot. On the road to Mecca there are a number of stages called starting-places. The pilgrims are assigned different starting-places according to the places from which they have come. On reaching his starting-place, the pilgrim has to observe five customs. "(1) He bathes and cleans his whole body, proposing to himself to do it for the sake of the pilgrimage, he pares his nails, combs his beard: and (2) he divests himself of his clothes and assumes the pilgrim's sacred robe, consisting of two seamless wrappers, one being wrapped round the waist and the other thrown loosely over the shoulder, the head being uncovered." As long as he wears the pilgrim's garb, he must not pare his nails, nor shave his body, nor indulge in any kind of sexual intercourse. Before he enters Mecca, he has to bathe nine times. Having entered the holy mosque, he approaches the Ka'ba and says: "Praise be to God, peace on his servants." "After this he approaches the Black Stone and touches it with his right hand and kisses it saying: 'My pledge I have delivered, my vow I have fulfilled, bear thou witness that I have done it.'" If it is not possible to touch the stone with his hand, he is allowed to touch it with a stick. He then performs the ceremony of going round the Ka'ba, the *Tawaf* or circumambulation (cp. CIRCUMAMBULATION). He goes round the Ka'ba seven times. "The first three processions he performs at a quick step; the last four times at the usual walking pace. It is desirable that every time he passes before the Black Stone, he should touch it either with his hand or with a stick and kiss it." The next ceremony is "the walking between Safá and Marwa," two hills beyond the temple gate. After this, preparation must be made for the Feast of the Sacrifice. On the 9th of Zu'l-Hijja the pilgrim proceeds to mount 'Arafát. Here near the mosque he spends part of the day and the night. Thence he proceeds to Muzdalifa, where he spends another night. Before continuing his journey, he has to provide himself with a number of little stones or pebbles. His next destination is a place called Miná, where there are three heaps or pillars of pebbles. On reaching one of these heaps called Jumratu'l-'Aqaba he throws the seven stones of the 'Aqaba, thus performing the ceremony of "the throwing of stones." At Miná the pilgrim then observes the Feast of the Sacrifice. After this he is allowed to shave his head, and to return to Mecca, where he again goes round the Ka'ba seven times. Before returning home he goes to Miná and repeats the ceremony of stone-throwing, and before leaving Mecca finally he performs a farewell circumambulation (seven times). See F. A. Klein.

HALAKAH. One of the Rabbinic methods of interpreting the text of Scripture, the other being HAGGADAH.

HALJA. One of the deities of the Ancient Teutons. The name Halja is the same as Hel (*q.v.*).

HALLOWEEN. The Eve of All-Saints' Day (*q.v.*).

HALO. The bright ring which surrounds the heads of saints. It first appears about the head of Jesus in the third century. "In the early fourth century it seems generally reserved for Christ and the angels, but by the end of this century the Virgin and the Apostles are similarly decorated, and by the fifth century it begins to be used for any of the 'saints'" (Cobern).

HAMZAVIS. A Dervish order, founded about the beginning of the sixteenth century by Sheikh Hamza. The founder was put to death for heterodoxy, and his adherents seem to have been from the first in bad repute with the orthodox. "To judge, however, from their Litany, they appear to be a singularly pious sect, and they enjoy the reputation of being most conscientious in all their dealings, living only for their doctrines, regardless of the things of this world" (L. M. J. Garnett).

HAND, THE. It is noted by Donald A. Mackenzie (*Crete*) that "the Aurignacian custom of leaving imprints of bands on rocks is prevalent in modern times in Australia and elsewhere." In India such imprints are still made on houses to charm them. Edgar Thurston (*Omens and Superstitions of Southern India*, 1912) writes: "At Kadure, in the Mysore Province, I once saw impressions of the hand on the walls of Brahman houses. Impressions in red paint of a hand with outspread fingers may be seen on the walls of mosques and Mohammedan buildings." In the Old Testament reference is often made to the hand of God, and in Christian art a hand appears as a symbol of God the Father. In the earliest Christian representation, that found in a tomb of the Catacombs dated A.D. 359, the Divine Hand issues from a cloud. The hand is seen again in the Bayeux tapestry (Church of S. Peter), in the Romsey crucifix, and in Lenton Church, Notts., on the Norman font. G. C. Niven notes (*Dedications and Patron Saints*) that in modern Jerusalem a large hand is painted rudely over the main doorway of many houses. This hand, called the "hand of power," is the Hand of God. See Sidney Heath and Francis Bond.

HANUMĀN. A deity in Hinduism. Hanumān is the divine ape. He is worshipped, in particular, by the disciples of Rāmānand. Hanumān helped Rāma (*q.v.*) to recover his wife Sītā from the demon Rāvana. He has therefore been worshipped as a model of faithful and devoted service. It is believed that if his favour can be gained, he will bestow great muscular strength. Monier-Williams thinks that the original Hanumān who helped Rāma was a man, the chief of some wild ape-like aboriginal tribes. See Monier-Williams; E. W. Hopkins.

HAOKAH. A thunder-god in the mythology of the Sioux Indians. His countenance had two halves, expressing on the one side laughter (when he was depressed) and on the other tears (when he was cheerful).

HAOMA. The equivalent in the Later Avesta of the Indian Soma. In the pre-Zoroastrian nature-worship Sauma (=Haoma) appears as an intoxicating drink which has the power to confer immortality. It was repudiated by Zarathustra, but Haoma, "the Averter of Death," reappeared later as a deity to whom the Parsi prays for wisdom. See J. H. Moulton.

HARDAUL. A deified person (perhaps, as R. V. Russell and R. B. Hira Lāl suggest, the deified Rājpūt horseman) worshipped by the Kurmis, the representative cultivating caste of Hindustān. He is represented by an image of a man on horseback carrying a spear in his hand, and clay horses are offered to him.

HARE, THE. The Hebrews were forbidden to eat the hare. The reason given is that it chews the cud and does not part the hoof. Apart from the fact that the hare does not chew the cud, we may infer that it was not eaten because a certain sanctity attached to it. The Britons of the time of Caesar kept hares which they were forbidden to eat, and the Germans of the eighth century abstained from the flesh of hares. The Algonquian Indians of North America worship a god whom they call Manibozho, "The Great Hare."

HARI. Hari is the name given by preference to the Supreme Being by Nānak (1469-1538 A.D.), the founder of Sikhism (*q.v.*). He used also such names as Brahmā and Govinda.

HARIHARA. Hari-hara is a late dual name used in Hinduism to denote the two gods Vishnu (*q.v.*) and Siva (*q.v.*) regarded as one.

HARI VITHAL. An Indian deity, the special god of the Hardās or Chitrakathis (*q.v.*), a caste of religious mendicants and picture showmen found in the Marātha Districts of India.

HARMLESS PEOPLE. A name given to the Junkers (*q.v.*), a religious body in America.

HARMONIAL PHILOSOPHY, THE. The teaching of an American, Andrew Jackson Davis (*b.* 1826). The philosophy of life and the theory of disease taught by Davis resembles the teaching of Quimby (see QUIMBYISM). In 1850 he published an account of his philosophy in a book entitled "The Great Harmonia." Georgine Milmine quotes a number of his statements.

"There is but one Principle, one united attribute of Goodness and Truth . . . Truth is positive Principle; error is a negative principle, and as Truth is positive and eternal, it must subdue error, which is only temporal and artificial . . . Power, Wisdom, Goodness, Justice, Mercy, Truth, are the gradual developments of an eternal and internal Principle, constituting the Divine, original Essence . . . *disease* is *discord* . . . this disease originates in a want of equilibrium in the circulation of the spiritual Principle throughout the organism . . . those physical developments which are called *diseases*, are simply evidences of constitutional or spiritual disturbances; and consequently, that there is but one 'disease,' having innumerable symptoms." See Georgine Milmine, *The Life of Mary Baker G. Eddy and the History of Christian Science*, 1909.

HARMONIES OF THE GOSPELS. Theophilus, who was Bishop of Antioch about the years 181 to 190 A.D., is said by Jerome to have made a harmony of the Gospels by "fitting together into one whole the things said by the four evangelists." This work has been lost, but a work of the same kind has been preserved in the Harmony of Tatian (second century), which is otherwise known as the Diatessaron (*q.v.*). The plan of such Harmonies as these was to combine the narratives of the four Gospels into a single consecutive story. Another kind of Harmony, of which a great number have been produced from early times down to the present time, is more of the nature of a synopsis. The narratives of the four (or three) Gospels are arranged in parallel columns so that their agreements and differences may be seen at a glance. Of this kind apparently was the Harmony of Ammonius, which has been lost. Ammonius lived at Alexandria in the time of Origen (185-254 A.D.). He is said by Eusebius to have constructed his Harmony by making the text of Matthew's Gospel the basis and setting by the side of it the parallel passages in the other Gospels. Eusebius himself compiled a Harmony on a system of his own. He first divided the four Gospels into sections or little chapters. "Then he prepared lists, canons, of the various possible or actual combinations of these chapters, and thus of the Gospels with each other. There were ten of them. The first list contained the numbers of the sections in which all four Gospels agreed with each other. The second list or canon gave the numbers of the sections in which Matthew, Mark, and Luke coincided with each other. The third canon offered the sections in which Matthew, Luke, and John agreed. The fourth canon has the sections in which Matthew, Mark, and John go together. The fifth canon is occupied by the sections in which only Matthew and Luke agree. The sixth canon is devoted to the sections in which Matthew and Mark are alike. The seventh canon shows in which sections Matthew and John are of one mind. The eighth canon numbers the sections in which Luke and Mark unite. The ninth canon tells us in which sections Luke and John alone are found. And finally, the tenth canon recounts the sections in which each Gospel stands totally alone." Eusebius "put on the margin in red ink under every number of a section the number of the canon in which it belonged" (C. R. Gregory). In 1537 Andreas Osiander (1498-1552) published a *Harmonia Evangelica*, and in 1553 appeared Calvin's *Harmonia ex tribus Evangelistis Composita*. Some of the best known modern Harmonies are: K. von Tischendorf's *Synopsis Evangelica*; A. Wright's *Synopsis of the Gospels in Greek*; Stevens and Burton, *A Harmony of the Gospels*, 1896; S. D. Waddy, *A Harmony of the Four Gospels in the Revised Version*, 1895.

HARMONITES. A religious community founded by George Rapp (1757-1847). Rapp was born at Iptingen in Württemberg. He founded his society in 1805. It aimed at establishing a life of "harmony" in Church and State. The Harmonites had all things in common and objected to marriage. In 1814 they founded the city of New Harmony in Indiana, and in 1824 the city of Economy in Pennsylvania. They are also known as the Harmony Society, or the Harmonists, or the Rappists. See J. H. Blunt; Brockhaus.

HARMONY SOCIETY. A community founded in Pennsylvania in 1805 by George Rapp (1757-1847). See above.

HATHOR. One of the deities worshipped by the ancient Egyptians. Hathor, which means "House of Horus," was originally one of the names of the goddess of the sky (cp. NUT). Then as the chief of the goddesses, the complete embodiment of feminine godhead, she became the divine model of womanhood, as well as the goddess of joy and love. Another designation of the goddess is "the Eye of the Sun (Râ)." She is represented in such a way as to suggest a connection with the cow. Sometimes she appears as an ordinary woman, but with "a headdress which recalls the ancient celestial cow, consisting of two horns between which appears the sun" (Erman). At other times she appears with the head of a cow, or with a head half-human half-cowlike. In the Hellenistic period she had developed into a goddess of the dead, unless Wiedemann is right in thinking that the Hathor, Lady of the Underworld, was of independent origin. See Alfred Wiedemann; Adolf Erman, *Handbook*; Naville, *The Old Egyptian Faith*, 1909.

HATTEMISTS. The followers of Pontianus van Hattem, who was a disciple of Spinoza (see SPINOZISM). Van Hattem was pastor of Philipsland in Zealand, but was deposed for heresy in 1683. Advocating a kind of mystical pantheism, he denied the doctrine of original sin, and urged that there is in reality nothing in man that can offend God. Men are punished by their sins; they are not punished by God for their sins. Such doctrine seemed to lead to Antinomianism. See Schaff-Herzog; J. H. Blunt.

HAUPTBRIEFE, THE. The term *Hauptbriefe*, the "chief or great Epistles," is used by German New Testament scholars of a group of letters ascribed to Paul the Apostle. The letters are: Galatians, I. and II. Corinthians, and Romans. These four Epistles have been accepted as Pauline even by scholars who have taken up a very radical position with regard to many other writings in the New Testament. They have been rejected in particular by a Dutch school of Theologians, of whom W. C. van Manen may now be regarded as representative. Prof. van Manen's position, however, has won few adherents. For W. C. van Manen's views, see the *Encycl. Bibl.* See also R. J. Knowling, *Witness*; J. Moffatt, *Introd.*

HEBREWS, EPISTLE TO THE. The New Testament writing known as the Epistle to the Hebrews raises a number of problems. Two of these are suggested at once by the title. Is the book really an Epistle? And who are the Hebrews? Currie Martin thinks that the book has no features of an epistle, except in its close. This theory has been put forward by Wrede. He thinks that it is a treatise to which the concluding verses were added by an editor. The idea of the editor will have been to convert the treatise into a Pauline Epistle. Against this A. S. Peake argues that "if the editor had wished in the closing verses to pass the Epistle off as Paul's, he would surely have spoken with much greater definiteness and identified the writer with Paul far more clearly." It is not correct, Peake thinks, to say that the work is a mere abstract treatise. The constant references to the conditions and perils of the community are of such a kind that its history and present situation can to a large extent be reconstructed. Next, as regards the persons to whom the letter is addressed. "Hebrews" suggests at once Jews. Currie Martin, however, thinks that the word need not denote a purely Jewish community here, and points out that elsewhere Gentiles are addressed as the seed of Abraham (Galatians iii. 7, 29). To this it may be objected that merely to refer to Gentiles as the seed of Abraham is very different from addressing a writing to "Hebrews" in the sense of Gentiles. But Currie Martin, of course, adds other reasons for thinking that the writing was addressed to Gentiles as well as to Jews. Yet his reasons, and those of scholars who take the same view, are hardly convincing. Prof. Peake argues more strongly for the view that the writing was addressed to Jewish Christians. They were Jewish Christians who were in danger of falling back into Judaism. This is proved definitely, Peake thinks, by the use made in the Epistle of the Old Testament. "It is quite beside the mark to say that the Old Testament was regarded as authoritative by Gentile as well as by Jewish Christians. It is more to the point to observe that the grounds of acceptance were very different. The Jew whether Christian or not accepted the Old Testament as the sacred book of his nation, his belief might be confirmed by Christianity, but it was essentially independent of it. With the Gentile Christian the case was altogether different. The Old Testament meant nothing to him apart from his Christianity. It was as an integral portion of his new religion that he recognised its authority. Of what use then was it to supply a Gentile in danger of apostasy from Christianity with arguments drawn from a book in which he believed simply because he was a Christian? The author's argument has force only if his readers accepted the Old Testament independently of their acceptance of the Gospel, and this suits Jewish Christians but not Gentiles. It may be added that, even setting aside the inconclusive details, there are many phrases in the Epistle which point much more naturally to Jewish Christian than to Gentile readers, but where the main argument is so conclusive it is less necessary to lay stress on minor points." Another problem is the question of authorship. According to Clement of Alexandria, the Epistle was written in Hebrew by Paul, and translated into Greek by Luke. According to Origen, the thoughts are Paul's, but they were written down from memory by another person, who added annotations of his own. This person may have been either Clement of Rome or Luke. In the Western Church, however, for a long time the Epistle failed to win acceptance. "Augustine and Jerome were alike hesitant about it, but yielded to Eastern opinion and accepted the Pauline authorship, and this secured its acceptance in the Western Church." It does not seem to have been used by Hermas, Justin Martyr, or Irenaeus. It is not included in the Canon of Marcion or in the Muratorian Canon. The external evidence therefore supports the view, suggested by the style and contents, that Paul was not the author of the Epistle. Who then was the author? Tertullian ascribes the work to Barnabas. Luther suggested Apollos, and the suggestion has been favoured by a number of modern scholars. Others have thought of Silas. Harnack has now come forward with the theory that the author was Priscilla. See J. A. M'Clymont; G. Currie Martin; Arthur S. Peake, *Intr.;* J. Moffatt, *Intr.*

HEDONISM. Hedonism in its ancient form is represented by the philosophy of Aristippus (see CYRENAICS). But the name has been given to certain forms of a modern philosophy that originated with Jeremy Bentham (1748-1832) and J. S. Mill (1806-1873). *Psychological Hedonism* starts with the principle that all desire is desire for pleasure. *Ethical Hedonism* urges that pleasure ought to be pursued as being the highest good. It denies that all desire is for pleasure. *Egoistic Hedonism* teaches that the pleasure to be aimed at is the pleasure of the individual. *Universalistic Hedonism* holds that the pleasure to be achieved must be the pleasure not only of self but also equally of others. Bentham's Hedonism has been called *Consistent Hedonism,* because he held that the only difference between pleasures is one of quantity. See Arthur Butler; C. J. Deter.

HEIDELBERG CATECHISM, THE. The "Heidelberg Catechism" (1563 A.D.) was prepared by Zacharias Bär or Ursinus and Caspar Olewig or Olevianus, of Heidelberg, with the full approval of the Elector Palatine, Frederick III. They were, in fact, commissioned by him "to prepare a manual which should serve alike for teaching the young and for settling the constant differences in doctrine between Lutherans, of both schools, and Calvinists, of which Heidelberg had become the continual scene" (W. A. Curtis). They executed their task with great success. "The Catechism, though it had detractors, soon established itself in every Reformed land and language." See William A. Curtis.

HEIMDALLR. The name of a god in Norse literature. "He is the guardian of the gods, and sits at the edge of heaven to guard the bridge against the mountain giants. He requires less sleep than a bird, and both by day and night can see a distance of one hundred miles. He is, moreover, the possessor of the *Gjallarhorn* (loud-resounding horn), whose sound is heard throughout the universe, and which lies hidden under the world-tree until the final catastrophe" (Chantepie de la Saussaye). He plays a prominent part in the Necklace-myth, struggling with Loki (*q.v.*) for the possession of the necklace. See P. D. Chantepie de la Saussaye, *Rel. of the Teutons,* 1902.

HEKT. An Egyptian deity. Hekt was a goddess, and is represented with the head of a frog. In Abydos she was regarded as one of the two deities created by Ra (*q.v.*) out of himself, the other deity being the god Shu (*q.v.*). Wiedemann points out that lamps which date from Coptic times have the image of a frog with the inscription, "I am the resurrection." This suggests that Hekt "played some part in the doctrine of the resurrection." It was believed that frogs were generated spontaneously from mud. See A. Wiedemann; Adolf Erman, *Handbook.*

HEL. One of the deities of the Ancient Teutons. The goddess Hel is said to be one of the offspring of Loki (*q.v.*). Hel appears to Balder (*q.v.*) in a dream, when he is wounded, and tells him he will soon be at rest in her arms. But she represents a place more than a person, one of the abodes of the dead. It came to be regarded as a place of gloom, darkness, and misery; but not, it would seem, as a place of punishment. We hear of warriors going there. See P. D. Chantepie de la Saussaye, *Rel. of the Teutons,* 1902.

HELIAND. The "Heliand" (that is to say, Heiland or Saviour) is an Old Saxon poem written in alliterative verse and dating from the ninth century. It gives the story of Jesus, based, it is thought, on Tatian's Harmony of the Gospels (see DIATESSARON). The story is adapted to suit the Saxon surroundings. The disciples have become brave warriors with Jesus as their hero chief. "He is not the Man of Sorrows, nor yet the heavenly Son of God of the Catholic church, but now the brave Teutonic chief, who valiantly leads his men to victory, and then again the wealthy, generous Teutonic popular king, who gloriously traverses his land to teach, judge, heal, and to battle, and who in the end in defeat itself outwits the enemy and gains the victory—a Christ different certainly from that of the Gospels, but one that was living and real to the Saxons" (de la Saussaye). See P. D. Chantepie de la Saussaye, *Rel. of the Teutons*, 1902; Brockhaus.

HELIOLITHIC CULTURE. An expression which has come into use among certain ethnologists in recent years. It is explained by Professor Elliot Smith in his *Migrations of Peoples.*" "Between 4000 B.C. and 900 B.C. a highly-complex culture compounded of a remarkable series of peculiar elements, which were associated the one with the other in Egypt largely by chance, became intimately interwoven to form the curious texture of a cult which Brockwell has labelled 'heliolithic,' in reference to the fact that it includes sun-worship, the custom of building megalithic monuments, and certain extraordinary beliefs concerning stones. An even more peculiar and distinctive feature, genetically related to the development of megalithic practices and the belief that human beings could dwell in stones, is the custom of mummification."

HELVETIC CONFESSIONS. The "First Helvetic Confession" or the "Second Confession of Basel," as it was also called, was the result of a conference of representatives of the Reformed cities of Switzerland held at Basel in 1536 A.D. The Confession was prepared by Bullinger, Myconius, Grynaeus, Leo Judae, and Megander. "Their work, after discussion, was unanimously accepted and subscribed by the delegates, and became the first general Swiss Confession, the first 'Reformed' Confession of national authority" (W. A. Curtis). The "Second Helvetic Confession" was the work of Henry Bullinger. It was composed originally in 1562. In 1565 it was, in a somewhat revised form, approved universally in Switzerland, except at Basel. In 1566 it was presented to the Diet at Augsburg by the Elector Palatine, Frederick III., and in the same year was accepted by the Reformed Church in Scotland. It was accepted in Hungary in 1567, and in France and Poland in 1571. W. A. Curtis thinks that in theological ability and in doctrinal interest few Confessions can bear comparison with it. "It's doctrinal standpoint is characteristic of the author and the time—a combination of the positions of Zwingli and Calvin, with an unbending attitude towards Rome, whose Tridentine Confession was being formulated at the self-same time; with a courteous tone towards Lutheranism; with a firm adherence to the ancient Catholic Creeds, which are printed in the preface as authoritative; and with an underlying conviction that the doctrinal re-union of Christendom was possible upon a Scriptural basis alone, Confessional revision and readjustment being a Christian duty as better knowledge of the Word of God was attained." See William A. Curtis.

HELVIDIANS. The followers or adherents of Helvidius, a layman who died at Rome in the latter part of the fourth century A.D. Helvidius denied the perpetual virginity of the Virgin Mary and deprecated the tendency to rank celibacy above matrimony. His work on the subject has perished, and is known only from quotations in the tract "Contra Helvidium" written by Jerome against the author. Gennadius states that Helvidius was "a disciple of Auxentius," the Arian, and "an imitator of Symmachus," the pagan; but it is difficult to find any support for these statements. See Schaff-Herzog; J. H. Blunt; Wace and Piercy.

HEMERO-BAPTISTS. A Jewish sect, so called ("every-day baptists") because they practised ceremonial ablutions every day. Like the Sadducees, they did not believe in a Resurrection (Epiphanius, *Hæres.* xvii.). They are referred to by Hegesippus (Eusebius, *Hist. Eccles.* iv. 22) and Justin Martyr (*Dial. cum Tryph.*). See J. H. Blunt.

HENOTICON, THE. The Henoticon or "Instrument of Union" was an edict put forth by the Emperor Zeno in 482 A.D. with the idea of establishing unity between the Monophysites (*q.v.*) and the Church. It was consequently of the nature of a compromise. It was probably composed by Acacius, Patriarch of Constantinople. It condemned Nestorius, approved the anathemas of Cyril, and recommended acceptance of the creeds of Nicaea and Constantinople, but ignored, or seemed to ignore, the Council of Chalcedon. It professed to be addressed to the bishops and people in Alexandria, Egypt, Libya, and Pentapolis. It did not attain its object. "Like every endeavour, however well meant, to cover radical differences by a vague comprehensiveness, it not only failed to secure union but aggravated the divisions it was intended to cure, and created a schism which divided the East and West for nearly 40 years, lasting down to the reign of Justinian and the popedom of Hormisdas" (*Dict. of Christ. Biogr.*). See J. H. Blunt; the *Cath. Dict.*, *s.v.* "Monophysites"; Wace and Piercy.

HENRY BRADSHAW SOCIETY. A Society founded in November, 1890. It was named the Henry Bradshaw Society in honour of the scholar and antiquary, Henry Bradshaw (1831-1886), who was Librarian of the University of Cambridge. It was founded for the purpose of printing liturgical manuscripts and rare editions of service books, and illustrative documents, on an historical and scientific basis, especially such as bear upon the history of the Book of Common Prayer, or of the Church of England. One volume at least appears every year, and every volume bears a device commemorative of Mr. Bradshaw. The works edited by the Society are not published.

HEPATOSCOPY. The examination of the liver of animals in divination. "The sacrificial animal was believed to be united to the deity to whom it was dedicated. The soul of the animal was attuned to the deity, so that it was possible by the examination of the animal soul to understand the mind of the deity who controlled future events. The sanctity attached to blood not unnaturally suggested that the seat of the soul was in the liver, one-sixth of the blood in the human body, for example, being contained in it. To read the soul of the animal, and thus divine the purpose of the god, was effected by studying the conformation and the markings on the liver of the sheep, which was the animal invariably used. These are never precisely the same in any two animals, and most elaborate directions were given for reading the signs" (A. S. Peake, *The Bible*, 1913).

HEPTAPLA, THE. A name sometimes given in early times to Origen's Hexapla. See HEXAPLA.

HERA. According to Lucian, the name of a Syrian goddess, the patron-deity of Hierapolis, "the sacred city." Her temple was visited by many pilgrims—Arabians, Babylonians, Cilicians, Phoenicians, and others. She seems to be equivalent to the chief goddess of the Hittites.

HERACLES. Heracles (Latin Hercules) is one of the oldest and most famous of the heroes in Greek mythology. "Indeed, the traditions of similar heroes in other Greek tribes, and in other nations, especially in the East, were transferred to Heracles; so that the scene of his achievements, which is, in the Homeric poems, confined on the whole to Greece, became almost extensive with the known world; and the story of Heracles was the richest and most comprehensive of all the heroic fables" (O. Seyffert). He is represented as the son of Zeus by

Alcmēnē, the wife of Amphitryon. The strongest man on earth, he figures in works of art as the ideal of manly strength. See A. R. Hope Moncrieff.

HERMENEUTICS. The term is of Greek origin and denotes the science of interpretation. It has been used especially of the interpretation or exegesis of the Bible. Thus S. Davidson (1806-1899) published in 1843 a work called *Sacred Hermeneutics*. The term is old-fashioned, and is no longer in common use.

HERMESIANISM. The principles or philosophy of the Roman Catholic theologian George Hermes (1775-1831). Hermes is described by Erdmann as a Semi-Kantian. In 1805 he published a work "Investigations relating to the Inner Truth of Christianity," and in 1819 "Philosophical Introduction to Christian-Catholic Theology" (2nd ed. 1831). The latter work was censured by Gregory xvi. in 1835. Hermes held that philosophical inquiry ought to begin by questioning everything that hitherto had been regarded as self-evident. As regards Christianity three preliminary questions have to be asked. 1. "Is it possible for us to decide regarding the truth in what ways it is attainable and whether any of these ways is applicable to the proof of Christianity?" 2. "Is there a God, and what is his nature?" 3. "Must a supernatural revelation of God to men be admitted as possible, and under what universal conditions must it be deemed actual?" As regards a God, "in opposition to Kant and Fichte, it is asserted that the certainty of the existence of God is not a moral certainty, but that it is a physical necessity for the theoretical reason to hold as real a certain, eternal, absolute, unchangeable, personal, creative first cause of the transitory world. It is otherwise as regards the attributes of God, where theoretical and practical reason, belief and assumption, unite in making us certain of the incomprehensible power, knowledge, and goodness, as well as of the holiness, freedom, and love of God, in virtue of which God wills our happiness, which, just because He wills it eternally, is therefore eternally willed and hence will endure eternally. In spite of this faith, rendered irrevocably certain through the theoretical and practical reason, it must not be misunderstood, that much that transcends the power of reason to conceive, as *e.g.*, the infinitude of the divine attributes, can become certain to us only by the way of experience; especially, that the real nature of God remains to us, even after actual revelation, uncognizable" (Erdmann). As regards the third question, "whereas the existence of God is securely established by the theoretical reason, the above-mentioned attributes of God by the theoretical and practical reason, revelation in general, and a definite revelation in particular, is guaranteed only by the obligatory reason, so that, therefore, it remains a moral necessity." See J. E. Erdmann; *Cath. Dict.*

HERMETICAL BOOKS. Certain religious books attributed to the Egyptian god Thoth or Hermes Trismegistos. According to Seleucus in Iamblichus they numbered 20,000; according to Manetho 36,525. Clement of Alexandria seems to have known of forty-two. C. R. Gregory (*Canon*) thinks that perhaps "these large numbers apply to the lines contained in the books; in that case the great difference between the numbers would be intelligible."

HERRNHUTER. The Herrnhuter were the successors of the Bohemian Brethren. After the battle of the White Mountain (1620), in which the Bohemian Protestants were routed, the Unitas Fratrum was dispersed, and many of its members left Bohemia. In 1721 the greater part of the remnant of them also abandoned Bohemia, and settled in Lusatia on the estate of Nikolaus Ludwig von Zinzendorf (1700-1760). This settlement was named Herrnhut, "The Lord's Watch," and the settlers became known as Herrnhuter. See further MORAVIANS.

HERTFORDSHIRE HERMIT, THE. A name given to James Lucas (1813-1874), who lived near Hitchin, slept on cinders, and did not wash.

HEXAPLA, THE. Besides the Septuagint (*q.v.*) and the versions of Aquila, Theodotion, and Symmachus (see GREEK VERSIONS, OLD TESTAMENT), other Greek versions of the Old Testament were known to Origen (*c.* 185-86 A.D.—251-54 A.D.). Two of these, designated *Quinta* and *Sexta* he made use of in his Octapla. Eusebius and Jerome mention a third version, designated *Septima*. Origen sought to provide a critical edition of the Septuagint in the first half of the third century A.D. He first collected all existing Greek versions of the Old Testament. "He then proceeded to transcribe the versions in parallel columns, and to indicate in the column devoted to the Septuagint the relation in which the old Alexandrian version stood to the current Hebrew text." The work was called Hexapla because there were six columns. They were as follows: (1) the Hebrew text in Hebrew; (2) the Hebrew transliterated in Greek characters; (3) the Greek of Aquila; (4) the Greek of Symmachus; (5) the Septuagint; (6) the Greek of Theodotion. Origen also compiled a Tetrapla, that is to say, an edition in which the first two columns were omitted. The Hexapla, when the book of Psalms is in question, is sometimes referred to as the Octapla, apparently "because in the Psalter of the Hexapla there were two additional columns which received the *Quinta* and *Sexta*" (H. B. Swete). Similarly it was sometimes called Heptapla in reference to portions where a seventh column appeared. Origen "sought to determine the true primitive form of the Greek [which had become corrupt], and by an elaborate system of obelisks and other artificial marks inserted in the text to guard it from the possibility of further corruption. Unfortunately this system, owing to its detailed and highly-elaborate character, lent itself most easily to the cause of error. Copyists transposed Origen's asterisks, obelisks, etc., omitted them altogether, or inserted at wrong points, thus defeating the object which their author had in view, and introducing new variations and confusion" (A. S. Geden). The fragments of the Hexapla which have been preserved are collected in F. Field's *Origenis Hexaplorum quae Supersunt Fragmenta*, 2 vols. 1876. See H. B. Swete, *Intr. to the O.T. in Greek*, 1900; A. S. Geden, *Intr. to the Hebrew Bible*, 1909.

HIBBERT LECTURES. The Hibbert Trust was founded by Robert Hibbert (1770-1849), who had been a merchant and slave-owner in Jamaica. The trustees used the funds until 1878 to promote the higher education of candidates for the Unitarian Ministry. In 1878 they decided to establish a lectureship designed to promote thorough research into religious problems from an independent standpoint, that is to say, apart from any bias towards any particular church, system, or creed. The lecturers have been scholars of the highest distinction in England, Germany, and France.

HICKSITES. The followers of Elias Hicks (1748-1830), who was a distinguished preacher of the Society of Friends (see article) in the United States of America. His followers are also called Hicksite Friends. Hicks caused a schism in the Society by developing rationalistic views. He repudiated the dogmas of the Trinity and the Atonement, denied the miraculous conception and the deity of Jesus, and questioned the divine authority of Holy Scripture. See J. H. Blunt; *Chambers' Encycl.*

HIERACITES. The Hieracites were not exactly a sect but a school. The leader of this school, which arose at the beginning of the fourth century, was Hierax of Leontium in Egypt. He is said by Epiphanius and Augustine to have denied the resurrection of the body and the existence of a visible Paradise; and to have said that Melchizedech was the Third Person of the Trinity, and that infants cannot inherit the kingdom of God. Further, he held, it is said, that the body must be mortified in every way. Marriage must be rejected, and meat and wine abstained from. See J. H. Blunt.

HIGHER THOUGHT, THE. The "Higher Thought," also known as the "New Thought," may be described as a modern idealistic and mystical philosophy of a practical character. Some of its principles are, indeed, by no means new. As Horatio W. Dresser says (*Health and the Inner Life*, 1907), "for untold ages the 'New Thought' has been old in India." But the application of the principles is new. Mr. Dresser says further of the designation "New Thought": "This is the latest of mind-cure terms and at present the most popular. It came into vogue in 1895, and was used as the title of a little magazine published for a time in Melrose, Massachusetts. The term was apparently a convenient designation, inasmuch as for its devotees it was literally a 'new thought' about life. But critics soon assailed it on the ground that the doctrine was not new, and in England the term 'Higher Thought' was substituted." The Higher Thought lays great emphasis on the power of the mind. This power, many will think, is greatly exaggerated; but it will be admitted that much of the Higher Thought is of the highest ethical and religious value. Its value is recognized even by persons like the agnostic author of *The Churches and Modern Thought* (see p. 400 in the Popular Edition, 1908). One of the best exponents of the philosophy is Ralph Waldo Trine. "The great central fact of the universe," he says, "is that Spirit of Infinite Life and Power that is behind all, that animates all, that manifests itself in and through all; that self-existent principle of life from which all has come, and not only from which all has come, but from which all is continually coming" (*In Tune with the Infinite*, 1906). Further, "the great central fact in human life, in your life and in mine, is the coming into a conscious, vital realization of our oneness with this Infinite Life, and the opening of ourselves fully to this divine inflow." And "in the degree that we open ourselves to this divine inflow are we changed from mere men into God-men." As the Infinite Spirit is behind all and has created everything, "we, through the operation of our interior, spiritual, thought forces, have in like sense creative power." As in the New Theology, great stress is laid on the idea that God is immanent as well as transcendent. This being granted, "in the degree that we open ourselves to the inflowing tide of this immanent and transcendent life, do we make ourselves channels through which the Infinite Intelligence and Power can work." The bearing of such doctrines as these upon the question of mental healing is obvious. Another able exponent of this kind of philosophy is Orison Swett Marden. The teaching of his book *Peace, Power and Plenty*, and of much of the Higher Thought, is summarized in the Preface. "The author attempts to show that the body is but the mind externalised, the habitual mental state out-pictured; that the bodily condition follows the thought, and that we are sick or well, happy or miserable, young or old, lovable or unlovable, according to the degree in which we control our mental processes. He shows how man can renew his body by renewing his thought, or change his body, his character, by changing his thought. The book teaches that man need not be the victim of his environment, but can be the master of it; that there is no fate outside of him which determines his life, his aims; that each person can shape his own environment, create his own condition; that the cure for poverty, ill-health, and unhappiness lies in bringing one's self through scientific thinking into conscious union with the great Source of Infinite life, the Source of opulence, of health, and harmony. This conscious union with the Creator, this getting in tune with the Infinite, is the secret of all peace, power, and prosperity. It emphasizes man's oneness with Infinite Life, and the truth that when he comes into the full realization of his inseparable connection with the creative energy of the universe, he shall never know lack or want again. This volume shows how man can stand porter at the door of his mind, admitting only his friend thoughts, only those suggestions that will produce joy, prosperity; and excluding all his enemy thoughts which would bring discord, suffering, or failure." Some of the essays of Prentice Mulford are very striking. See Ralph Waldo Trine, *In Tune with the Infinite*, 1906; *What all the World's a-seeking*, 1907; O. S. Marden, *Peace, Power, and Plenty*, 1909; Prentice Mulford, *The Gift of the Spirit*, 1908; *The Gift of Understanding*; James Allen, *From Poverty to Power* (6), 1909; *The Mastery of Destiny*, 1909.

HIJRAS. The members of the community of eunuchs in India (also known as Khasuas). They are either persons who were born deformed or who have been made eunuchs by amputation. When admitted into the community, they become Muhammadans. The mutilation is effected usually in the performance of a religious vow. The Hijras worship the goddess Bouchera or Behechra, a sister of Devi. "As a further fulfilment of their vow, the Hijras pull out the hair of their beards and moustaches, bore their ears and noses for female ornaments, and affect female speech and manners" (R. V. Russell).

HINAYĀNA. When the widened form of Buddhism known as Mahāyāna, or the Great Vehicle, was developed, the older form received the name Hīnayāna or the Little Vehicle. See VEHICLES, THE THREE.

HINDUISM. The earliest form of Indian religious observance derived from the ancient literature is known as Brāhmanism. The term Hinduism is applied to later and modern developments. "Brahmanism, founded on these sacred books and claiming to fulfil their precepts, is the religion of *Brahmā*, the Creator, or of the *Brāhmans*, the priestly and privileged class, charged with the preservation of doctrine and the maintenance of the rites" (A. S. Geden, *Studies*). The revealed literature of the Veda was succeeded by a sub-Vedic literature, which is hardly inferior in authority. This is related to six recognised philosophical systems, which trace their origin more or less directly to the Upanishads. The systems are known as the Vedanta, founded by Vyasa; the Mimamsa, founded by Jaimini; the Sankhya, founded by Kapila; the Yoga, founded by Patanjali; the Nyāya, founded by Gotama; and the Vaiseshika, founded by Kanāda. The names of the founders or authors, it should be added, are only traditional. Other literary sources of the religious usages and beliefs are the two great epic poems, the *Mahābhārata* and the *Rāmāyana*. To these the later Puranas owe much of their information and inspiration. The *Bhagavadgītā* (later Bhāgavata Purāna) was the religious text-book of the Bhāgavatas, the worshippers of *Bhagavad*, the Lord or Blessed One—a body which represented, not a sectarian form of religion, but a more mystical kind of devotion. The origins of the movement may be hardly less ancient than the orthodox ritual and creed of the Brāhmans. In any case, Brāhmanism was confronted in course of time by many more popular forms of belief and worship. Hinduism "is the general title for all the forms under which the religious consciousness of the people of India has found expression; and the link or internal connection between the diverse creeds which pass under this name is of the very slightest—a recognition of common divinities and temples, and of the rights and prerogatives of their priests, the Brāhmans. There is no common article of faith or obligation of morality, and the adherence to forms or religious duties is often superficial, and in recent times especially is greatly relaxed. The real and most powerful bond of union is social. A Hindu is born, not made. Caste has been, and is at the present time, the compelling influence which welds into the semblance of a unity the multitude of diverse and often conflicting professions which claim to be parts of the Hindu faith" (Geden). Of the many sects which have arisen, the two great groups are known as the Vishnuite and the Sivaite. In the year 1800—which marks the beginning of quite new developments—Hinduism, which, according to J. N. Farquhar, was the religion of at least three-fourths of the population of the peninsula, consisted, in the main, of these two great groups of sects and of a mass of wandering celibate ascetics, who were held to be outside society. "The Vishnuite sects were very numerous, both in the North and in the South, and they were perhaps, on the whole, more homogeneous than the worshippers of Siva. The leading Vishnuite sects declare Vishnu to be the one God, and yet they recognize the existence of all the other divinities of the Hindu pantheon. They also hold that Vishnu has been incarnate among men a great many times, the latest and chief incarnations being Rāma and Krishna. Worshippers of Siva declare that Siva is the one God, but recognize also all the other gods. A special group of Sivaite sects has to be noticed, namely, those who pay honour to the wife of Siva as Kālī or Durgā. Both Vishnuites and Sivaites worship idols, but among Sivaites the phallic symbol is more usual than images of the god. Both sects worship their gurus, that is, their teachers, as gods. Both are fully orthodox in the sense that they retain and enforce with great strictness the ancient Hindu rules of conduct which are summed up under the word *dharma*. Both sects claim to be Vedāntists, but each has its own interpretation of the philosophy" (J. N. Farquhar). Perhaps the most celebrated of Vishnuite teachers was Rāmānuja, who lived about 1100 A.D., and opposed the doctrine which denied the real existence of the phenomenal world and identified all souls with the one Brahma. According to Rāmānuja, Brahma is "an all-penetrating, all powerful, all-knowing, all-merciful Being. He is not an undifferentiated Unity, for the manifold world of reality exists in Him; souls and the material elements form His body but not His nature; they are subordinate to Him as our body is to our spirit, and exist in Him with a relative independence. All that lives is in process of transmigration (*samsāra*), from which the soul can free itself—through the knowledge of Brahma, not through good works; the soul is then raised into the world of Brahma, to an eternal, blessed life, and participates in Brahma's divine qualities, except in His power to emit and to rule the world and to receive it back into Himself" (F. von Hügel, *E.L.*). See, in addition to the works already mentioned, E. W. Hopkins; W. Bousset; G. A. Barton, *Rel.*, 1917; F. W. Bussell. Various castes, sects, reform-movements, etc., are treated under separate headings.

HIRIADEVA. An object of worship among the Kurumbas of Southern India, represented by a rough stone set up either in a cave or in a circle of stones.

HISTOPEDES. The Eunomians (*q.v.*) are said to have been so called because they baptised persons with their feet upright (*histos*) in the air (Epiphanius, *Haer* lxxvi.; Theodoret, *Hæret. fab.* iv. 30).

HISTORY OF GAD THE SEER. A record referred to in I. Chronicles (xxix. 29). See HISTORY OF SAMUEL THE SEER.

HISTORY OF NATHAN THE PROPHET. A record referred to in I. Chronicles (xxix. 29). See HISTORY OF SAMUEL THE SEER.

HISTORY OF SAMUEL THE SEER. A record referred to in I. Chronicles (xxix. 29). We read as follows: "Now the acts of David the king, first and last, behold they are written in the history (or 'acts' or 'words') of Samuel the seer, and in the history of Nathan the prophet, and in the history of Gad the seer; with all his reign and his might, and the times that went over him, and over Israel, and over all the kingdoms of the countries." These do not appear to have been independent works. "There can be little doubt that these are nothing more than references to the narratives in which Samuel, Nathan, and Gad are mentioned in our books of Samuel. The order is the same as that in which they appear in the earlier historical books. If the Chronicler knew anything about these men with which we are not familiar from the books of Samuel, he kept that information to himself. Where he does mention Nathan (c. 17) and Gad (c. 21), he simply uses material found in II. Samuel (cc. 7, 24). He probably quoted the acts of these three men, instead of simply referring to the one book which contained all of them, since such an enumeration of works would emphasise the importance of David's reign" (E. L. Curtis and A. A. Madsen). See E. L. Curtis and A. A. Madsen, *Commentary on the Books of Chronicles*, 1910.

HITTITE RELIGION. The Hittites came into contact with Babylonia and Egypt towards the end of the third millennium B.C. In the fourteenth century they appear as a firmly-established power with an extensive dominion and with a capital at Boghaz-Keui. The name of their chief deity, the "Lord of Heaven," a storm-god, is not known, but representations of him have been preserved in sculptures. With him is associated a goddess, the Great Mother. A sculpture in the sanctuary near Boghaz-Keui represents the ceremonial marriage of the two deities with its rites and festivities. The goddess is represented as having a young companion, a youth, who seems to have been worshipped as the patron of agriculture. On some of the sculptures the god is represented as a Bull, while one of the special emblems of the Great Mother is the Lion. On one sculpture the goddess is worshipped in a ceremonial feast or communion. Again, in many small clay and bronze images found in Northern Syria, "the goddess is represented as naked, with her hands proffering her breasts" (J. Garstang, *The Syrian Goddess*). The Hittite power began to wane in the 12th century, and came to an end before 700 B.C. But the goddess survived, and her cult was pursued, with modifications, especially at Pessinus in Phrygia, and at Comana in the Taurus, where the Romans identified her with Bellona. See J. Garstang, *Land of the Hittites*, and his Introd. to H. A. Strong's translation of *The Syrian Goddess*, 1913.

HLIN. One of the deities of the Ancient Teutons. The goddess Hlin, who belonged to the retinue of Frija (*q.v.*) and Freyja (*q.v.*), appears as a goddess who protects people against peril.

HLUDANA. One of the deities of the Ancient Teutons. The goddess Hludana is mentioned on inscriptions as having been worshipped by fishermen. See P. D. Chantepie de la Saussaye, *Rel. of the Teutons*, 1902.

HŒNIR. A deity in the religion of the Ancient Teutons. The god Hœnir is sometimes one of a triad, the other two gods being Odhin (*q.v.*) and Lodhurr or Loki (*q.v.*). He is accompanied by the wise Mimir because he is himself dull. His precise nature is unknown. E. H. Meyer regards him as equivalent to the Enoch (Henoch) of the Bible. See P. D. Chantepie de la Saussaye, *Rel. of the Teutons*, 1902.

HOFFMANNITES. A religious community founded by Christian Hoffmann in 1848. Another name for them is Jerusalem Friends (*q.v.*).

HOKKE SECT. Another name for the Japanese Buddhist sect Nichiren (*q.v.*).

HOLDA. Holda is a figure in Teutonic mythology. She belongs more especially to Northern Germany. In modern folklore she is represented sometimes as leading the host of the dead when it rushes through the air (see WILD HUNT). Sometimes she is represented as a goddess of fertility. See P. D. Chantepie de la Saussaye. *Rel. of the Teutons.*

HOLLER. One of the deities of the Ancient Teutons. The god Holler was worshipped by the Frisians as the "Lord of the lower world."

HOLY CROSS, SOCIETY OF. A Society founded in 1855 by Anglican clergymen with the idea of cultivating a deeper spiritual life. The leading spirit was Alexander Heriot Mackonochie (1825-1887). In 1862 Mackonochie was appointed the first vicar of St. Alban's Church, Holborn. He became an advanced ritualist, and in 1867 was prosecuted under the "Church Discipline Act" in the provincial Court of Arches. On his acquittal here, appeal was made to the judicial committee of the privy council, and the former judgment was reversed. This decision Mackonochie did not consider binding. His opponents, however, continued to attack him. In 1882 he resigned the living of St. Alban's, Holborn. The church has become famous for its ritualistic practices. See the *D.N.B.*

HOLY DROP. Mr. F. L. Farīdi (quoted by R. V. Russell and R. B. Hira Lāl) speaks of the *samarchhanta* or Holy Drop as being a remarkable feature at the Khojāh's death. The Khojāhs are a small Muhammadan sect of traders belonging to Gujarāt in India, who retain some Hindu practices. They meet for prayer at a lodge called the Jama'at Khāna. "The Jama'at officer asks the dying Khojāh whether he wishes for the Holy Drop, and if the latter agrees he must bequeath Rs. 5 to Rs. 500 to the Jama'at. The officer dilutes a cake of Karbala clay in water and moistens the lips of the dying man with it, sprinkling the remainder over his face, neck and chest. The touch of the Holy Drop is believed to save the departing soul from the temptation of the Arch-Fiend, and to remove the death-agony as completely as among the Sunnis does the recital at a death-bed of the chapter of the Korān known as the Sūrah-i-Yā-sīn."

HOLY MAID OF KENT, THE. In the reign of Henry VIII, this name was given to Elizabeth Barton (1506?-1534). Originally a domestic servant, she became subject to trances and visions and gave forth messages which were supposed to be inspired. Her clients included the King, Edward Bocking (d. 1534), William Warham (1450?-1532), Archbishop of Canterbury, John Fisher (1459-1535), Bishop of Rochester, and Sir Thomas More (1478-1535). When King Henry divorced Catherine of Aragon, Elizabeth Barton denounced him, and prophesied that he would die soon after his marriage. Afterwards she declared that in the sight of God he was no longer king. Eventually an Act of attainder was passed against her; and in April 1534 she was executed at Tyburn with her chief accomplices. See M. W. Patterson, *Hist.*; the *D.N.B.*

HOLY OFFICE. Another name for the Inquisition (*q.v.*).

HOMA. The word Homa is explained in Garrett's "Classical Dictionary of India" as "a sort of burnt-offering which can be made by Brahmans only. It is only made on special occasions, such as the celebration of a festival, the investiture of a young Brahman with the sacred thread, marriages and funerals. The method of making it is as follows: During the utterance of Mantras, five species of consecrated wood, together with the Dharba grass, rice and butter, are kindled and burnt, and the fire is then kept burning as long as the festival or ceremony lasts. Great efficacy is ascribed to this rite." See J. C. Oman, *Cults.*

HOME-ATECIAGUAT. A deity worshipped by the Nicarao (of Nicaragua). He is probably the Mexican Omeciuatl.

HOME-ATELITE. A deity worshipped by the Nicarao (of Nicaragua). He is probably the Mexican Ometecutli.

HONGWANJI SECT. A Japanese Buddhist sect. Hongwanji sect is another name for the Shin sect (*q.v.*).

HŌRĀYŌTH. The title of one of the Jewish treatises or tractates which reproduce the oral tradition or unwritten law as developed by the second century A.D., and are included in the Mishnah (*q.v.*), a collection and compilation completed by Rabbi Judah the Holy, or the Patriarch, about 200 A.D. The sixty-three tractates of the Mishnah are divided into six groups or orders (sedarim). Hōrāyōth is the tenth tractate of the fourth group, which is called Nezīkīn ("Damages").

HOREBITES. After the death of John Hus (1369-1415) some of his followers became known as Calixtines (*q.v.*), others as Taborites (*q.v.*). The Taborites were the militant party. The Horebites were a sub-division of these. They were so called because they gave the name Horeb to a mountain in Bohemia on which they encamped.

HORNS OF CONSECRATION. In Minoan religious scenes is found a ritual object shaped like the horns of an altar. H. R. Hall (*A.A.*) thinks that it was not really a horned altar, but "something which was used in religious exercises." It is associated with the sacred double-axe or the sacred pillar.

HORSE, TREASURE OF THE. One of the seven royal treasures which the king of kings, the ideal king, of the Buddhists, or rather of the pre-Buddhists, is supposed to possess. It is described as "all white, with a black head and a dark mane, wonderful in power, flying through the sky, the charger-king whose name was Thunder-Cloud." Rhys Davids thinks the idea was borrowed from ancient mythology. He compares the idea of the horses of the sun, made familiar to us by the Greeks. See T. W. Rhys Davids.

HORSES, SACRIFICE OF. The sacrifice of the horse has been noted among a number of peoples. The ancient Persians are said to have sacrificed a horse every month to Cyrus. The Vedic Aryans and, according to Pliny, the Romans sacrificed horses. The Massagetæ, who were found to the East of Scythia, sacrificed a horse to the Sun, their only deity. According to Ridgeway, the horse-sacrifice was a characteristic of the religion of the Teutonic and Scandinavian peoples. The Illyrians, Greeks, and Persians preferred white horses. Dr. Jung points out that "legends ascribe properties to the horse, which psychologically belong to the unconscious of man; horses are clairvoyant and clairaudient; they show the way when the lost wanderer is helpless; they have mantic powers. In the Iliad the horse prophesies evil. They hear the words which the corpse speaks when it is taken to the grave—words which men cannot hear." In folklore horses are symbolical of wind, fire, or light, etc. See William Ridgeway, *T.H.*, 1905; C. G. Jung, *Psych.*, 1915.

HORUS. An Egyptian deity. (1) Horus was one of

the names of the sun-god. As such he bears a number of different cognomens, according to the districts in which he was worshipped. Thus we have "Horus the Elder" (Greek Aroëris) of Letopolis; "Horus of the Two Eyes" of Shedennû; "Horus Lord of Not Seeing" of Letopolis; "Horus on the Two Horizons" (Greek Harmakhis) of Heliopolis; "the Golden Horus"; "Horus the Bull" (Saturn); "the Red Horus" (Mars); "Horus the Opener of that which is Secret" (Jupiter). Horus the Sun-god is represented as a falcon or as a man with a falcon's head. Since the Egyptian word for falcon, *heru*, is also Arabic, Naville finds in it support for the view that the original home of the conquering Egyptian was in Arabia. In several chronologies Horus is represented as the last of the prehistoric divine kings. The legendary epoch is represented as the age of the "companions or followers of Horus." Naville explains that "on the threshold of history, we find Horus and his companions, a clan, a tribe who had the falcon as their sacred animal or their god; every king is himself a Horus, and in the oldest inscriptions that we possess, the king is not designated by his prenomen, or personal name, he is *a Horus* with this or that qualification or description added." (2) Horus, the son of Isis, first referred to as "Horus the child," and represented with human form, is one of the chief characters in the Osiris myth. He was blended with Horus the Sun-god at an early date, and is also represented as hawk-headed. In the Osiris myth Horus fights with Set (*q.v.*), and is declared victorious. The gods assembled in the hall of Keb (*q.v.*) greet him with the words: "Welcome, Horus, son of Osiris, courageous, just, son of Isis and heir of Osiris!" See Alfred Wiedemann; Adolf Erman, *Handbook;* Naville, *The Old Egyptian Faith*, 1909.

HORUS, THE EYE OF. In the Osiris myth, when Horus fights with Set (*q.v.*) he loses an eye. Thoth (*q.v.*) thereupon spits on the eye and heals it. Horus takes it and offers it to his father Osiris, who eats it. The eye of Horus thus became the prototype and model of all gifts, and frequent reference is made to it. Thus when the officiating priest drew the bolt of the door of the temple he said: "The finger of Set is withdrawn from the eye of Horus, that is excellent. The finger of Set is withdrawn from the eye of Horus, that is excellent. I loosen the leather behind the god." See Alfred Wiedemann; Adolf Erman, *Handbook;* Naville, *The Old Egyptian Faith*, 1909.

HOSEA, BOOK OF. Hosea, the son of Beeri, is assigned in the Old Testament the first place among the Minor Prophets (*q.v.*). He was a prophet of the Northern Kingdom. The book of Hosea falls into two parts. The first part (chaps. i.-iii.) recounts the unhappiness of his domestic life. He had married a wife who proved herself to be unfaithful. And he came afterwards to realize "that his own tragic domestic experiences had opened his eyes to the appreciation of those supreme truths regarding Jehovah's character and will which constituted his message and made him a prophet" (C. F. Kent). The second part of the book (chaps. iv.-xiv.) contains a series of addresses or sermons. The superscription to the book would seem to have been added by a later editor. References in the book itself seem to many scholars to suggest that Hosea's work must have begun before 740 and ended before 735 B.C. The background of chaps. i.-iii., it is thought, reflects the closing years of the reign of Jeroboam II. Afflictions and punishment seem to be thought of as still in the future. The background of chaps. iv.-xiv., it is thought, "agrees precisely with what we read in II. Kings xv. of the internal dissensions which rent the northern kingdom after the fall of the house of Jehu, when Menahem called in the Assyrians to help him against those who challenged his pretensions to the throne" (*Encycl. Bibl.*). See Hosea vii. 3-7, 16; x. 15; v. 13; vii. 11; viii. 9; xii. 2. There seems to be no allusion, on the other hand, to the events of the Syro-Ephraimite war (735 B.C.) or to the first invasion of Tiglath-pileser iv. (734 B.C.). O. C. Whitehouse, however, thinks that a careful examination of Hosea's book gives a different result. The "utter social disorganisation" of the Northern Kingdom," as depicted, points, he thinks, to "a period subsequent to rather than before the invasion of 734-2." Such passages as vi. 1, 2, 8-9, vii. 9, viii. 4, ix. 15, xii. 12 "are best explained when Tiglath Pileser's campaign is placed in retrospect." The pathetic appeals in x. 12-14, xi. 5-8 are best understood if they are assigned to the date 726-5 B.C. And xii. 1 refers, he thinks, to the double-dealing of King Hoshea (II. Kings xvii. 4). According to Prof. Whitehouse, "725, rather than 735, is the closing date of Hosea's oracles." C. Cornill describes the book as "individual and subjective in character to a degree that is hardly paralleled in the case of any other prophetic writing." Variations of metre have been noted, but these may well be explained as due to the quickly-changing moods of the prophet. See *Encycl. Bibl.;* C. Cornill, *Intr.;* G. H. Box; O. C. Whitehouse; C. F. Kent, *The Sermons, Epistles, and Apocalypses of Israel's Prophets*, 1910.

HOSPITALLERS. Hospitallers is the designation of a number of charitable brotherhoods in the Roman Catholic Church, "associations of laymen, monks, canons, and knights, which devoted themselves to nursing the sick and the poor in the hospitals, while at the same time observing certain monastic practices, generally according to the rule of Augustine" (Schaff-Herzog). In 1190 Count Guido of Montpellier founded there the Hospital Brethren of the Holy Spirit. The order was confirmed by Pope Innocent III. in 1198, and the "Hospitale S. Spiritus in Saxia" at Rome became its mother-house. In 1212 the Hospitallers of Burgos were founded. In 1280 arose the Brethren of Charity of Blessed Mary, and established its mother-house in the hospital "Les Billets" in Paris. Hospital Sisters were instituted also, who devoted themselves to the work of educating and protecting girls, as well as to the care of the sick. The Knights of St. John of Jerusalem and the Teutonic Knights (*q.v.*) started as Hospitallers. The former grew out of the Brothers of the Hospital of St. John the Baptist. About the middle of the eleventh century a convent and hospital dedicated to St. John the Baptist had been built at Jerusalem by merchants of Amalfi, with the object of caring for pilgrims to the Holy Sepulchre. Later, after the conquest of Jerusalem by the Crusaders, the hospital was separated from the convent, and received the gift of a manor from Duke Godfrey of Bouillon. Raymond du Puy, who succeeded Abbot Gerard in 1118, became Master of the Order of the Brothers of the Hospital of St. John the Baptist. He drew up a rule for the order, which was confirmed by Pope Calixtus II. in 1120. The Brothers had to take the three vows of poverty, chastity, and obedience. Knights now began to join the order, and it became more and more military. From the task of protecting pilgrims on their way to the Holy City, they proceeded to that of defending the Holy Sepulchre, and then to that of making war upon infidels. In course of time, too, there grew up a rivalry between them and the Knights Templars which led to a pitched battle between them (1259). In 1187 the Hospitallers removed to Markab in Phoenicia, in 1193 to Acre, in 1291 to Cyprus. In 1310 they took forcible possession of the Island of Rhodes. Driven from here by Sultan Solyman the Magnificent in 1523, they removed to Candia (Crete). In 1530 the Emperor Charles V.

granted them possession of the Island of Malta. Here they remained until 1798, when, through treachery, the Island was surrendered to the French. In 1800 the island was captured by the English. Afterwards the headquarters of the order were first at Catana and then at Ferra. Since 1799 most of the branches of the order have been suppressed. There is a revived order or Society in the Church of England, called "The Grand Priory of the Order of the Hospital of S. John of Jerusalem in England," with its headquarters at St. John's Gate, Clerkenwell, London. What is now the Anglican Church of St. John the Baptist, Clerkenwell, was before the dissolution of the monasteries the Priory of the Knights of St. John of Jerusalem (consecrated in 1185). The revived order has a new character. "Its efforts are purely philanthropic: it distributes charity to convalescents who have just left hospital, maintains cottage hospitals and convalescent homes in the country, and an ophthalmic hospital at Jerusalem. It has founded the street ambulance system, and was chiefly concerned in the origination of the Red Cross Society" (Chambers). See Schaff-Herzog; *Cath. Dict.; Chambers's Encycl.;* Brockhaus.

HOU CHI. A figure in the ancient religion of China. The House of Chou is said to have originated with him. On certain occasions he was worshipped as the Associate of God, and his aid was often sought in hours of distress or danger. In the *Odes*, as quoted by H. A. Giles, he is represented as having been miraculously born and protected. His mother conceived after treading in a footprint of God. In due time, "her firstborn came forth like a lamb. There was no bursting, no rending, no injury, no hurt, in order to emphasise his divinity. . . . He was exposed in a narrow lane, but sheep and oxen protected and suckled him; he was exposed in a wide forest, but woodcutters found him; he was exposed on cold ice, but birds covered him with their wings." Hou Chi was wonderfully successful in teaching the people husbandry. See Herbert A. Giles, *Religions of Ancient China*, 1905.

HOUSE-CLEANING, FESTIVAL OF. One of the two annual festivals of the Urālis is the Thai nombu, held in the month Thai (December—January). On this occasion the whole house is cleaned. The Urālis referred to dwell in the jungles of Dimbhum in the Coimbatore district of Southern India.

HOW-TOO. Chinese god of earth, whose worship was associated with that of mountains, rivers, and hills. He was a special object of worship to the emperor.

HTUBHTUM. A tribal deity, god of gems, in the religion of the Mayan Indians.

HUEHUETEOTL. One of the gods worshipped by the ancient Mexicans, the Fire-god. Hnehneteotl was another name for Xiuhtecutli.

HUGUENOT SOCIETY OF LONDON, THE. A Society founded in 1885 for the purpose of collecting and publishing information relative to the History and Genealogy of the Huguenots, especially of those who took refuge in the United Kingdom. The Society's chief publications are: (1) the History and Registers of all the French and Walloon Churches formerly existing in the United Kingdom; and (2) Proceedings, containing reports of meetings, papers read at meetings, and miscellaneous information.

HUITZILOPOCHTLI. Huitzilopochtli, which means "the Humming-bird on the left," was the name given to the god of war by the ancient Mexicans. It would seem to have been a popular name which came into use instead of the original name, Mextli. J. M. Robertson compares the story of the birth of Huitzilopochtli to that of the birth of Mars. One day, when a widow Coatlicue or Coatlantona entered the Temple of the Sun, a ball of bright-coloured feathers fell at her feet. Picking it up, she put it in her bosom. By touching it in this way, she became impregnated and in course of time gave birth to Huitzilopochtli. Her son was born with a spear in one hand, a shield in the other, and a plume of humming-bird's feathers on his head. The feathers appeared also on his left leg. Huitzilopochtli became a great hero in the eyes of the Aztecs. When his mother died she was translated to heaven, and became the Goddess of Flowers. Juno, too, the mother of Mars, when she became pregnant was a virgin. She was impregnated by touching a flower. Robertson (*R.S.W.*) thinks that originally Huitzilopochtli was, like Mars, a sylvan deity. He was the god of the Spring and Summer Sun. Then, since war was usually begun in spring, the God of Spring became the God of War. Lewis Spence holds that the humming-bird was the original totem of the Aztecs. Its pugnacity and courage would commend it to a warlike tribe. Their standard was, in fact, a miniature of Huitzilopochtli, and was called Huitziton or Paynalton, the "little humming-bird" or "little quick one." The totem became the national war-god of the Aztecs. The adoption of a solar cultus, according to Spence, came later. At Huitzilopochtli's festival in December "an image of him was modelled in dough, kneaded with the blood of sacrificed children, and this was pierced by the presiding priest with an arrow, in token that the sun had been slain, and was dead for a season." See Lewis Spence, *Myth.;* J. M. Robertson, "The Religions of Ancient Mexico," in *R.S.W.;* Reinach, *O.;* J. M. Robertson, *P.C.*

HULARIA. The special deity of the Golars (also known as Gollams, Gollas, Golas, Golkars), the shepherd caste of the Telugu country in India. Hularia is worshipped as the protector of cattle against disease and wild beasts.

HULSEAN LECTURES. The Hulsean Lectures were founded from a fund bequeathed by John Hulse (1708-1790) to Cambridge University. Among other foundations was to be that of Christian Advocate and Christian Preacher, or Hulsean Lecturer. The Lecturer was to deliver and publish twenty sermons yearly on the evidences of Christianity or on the difficulties of the Bible. In course of time the number of lectures or sermons was reduced, and in 1860 the Christian Advocateship was made a Hulsean Professorship.

HUMAN SACRIFICE. Lucian (§ 58) states that the Syrians sacrificed their children. Describing a special kind of sacrifice, he says: "They adorn live victims with ribbons and throw them headlong down from the temple's entrance, and these naturally die after their fall. Some actually throw their own children down, not as they do the cattle, but they sew them into a sack and toss them down, visiting them with curses and declaring that they are not their children, but are cows" (transl. by H. A. Strong). See further G. H. Payne, *The Child in Human Progress*, 1916..

HUMANISM. Humanism is the name given by F. C. S. Schiller, of Oxford, to a form of Pragmatism (*q.v.*) which he has himself developed. The name of the philosophy seems to be due "to the fact that it makes 'man the measure' (*homo mensura*), or bases itself in human nature and human experience" (Davidson). The appeal is to experience and consequences. "Truth, in order to be true, must have practical results, it must work—yea more, in the wider humanism, it *consists* in consequences, more especially if these are *good*. Our beliefs are determined by practical interest. We believe what serves our purpose, or what points to an end which we desire, or what satisfies our needs: we disbelieve what serves no purpose, or what has proved to be misleading or inadequate to meet our wants. So, too, of morality: human needs and their satisfaction determine between right and wrong, and give us the ethical notions." W. L. Davidson points out that pragmatism or humanism on its negative side is a protest against *a priorism* and Absolutism, neither of which submits to experience. "Indeed, it owes its existence to reaction against that extreme intellectualism which so long ruled, where man was contemplated simply as a rational being, his emotive and his volitional nature being ignored. It is, consequently, essentially inductive in its method, and breathes the scientific spirit throughout. It will not permit truth to be relegated to a transcendent sphere to which experience has no access, nor will it allow experience to be dictated to by mere unverified and unverifiable *a priori* conceptions." The defects of Humanism, according to W. L. Davidson, are (1) that it over-emphasizes action or the will, and (2) that, though strong psychologically, it is weak metaphysically. See William L. Davidson, *The Stoic Creed*, 1907.

HUMANITY, RELIGION OF. A designation of the system of religion formulated by Auguste Comte (1797-1858). See POSITIVISM.

HUNABKU. A tribal deity, god of creation, in the religion of the Mayan Indians. He is perhaps identical with Hunahpu.

HUNAHAU. A tribal deity, lord of the underworld, in the religion of the Mayan Indians. He is represented sometimes as a skeleton with skulls and cross-bones; and corresponds to the Mexican god Mictlantecutli.

HUNAHPU. A tribal deity, god of creation, in the religion of the Mayan Indians.

HUNPIKTOK. A tribal deity, god of war, in the religion of the Mayan Indians.

HUNTINGDON'S CONNEXION, THE COUNTESS OF. The followers of Selina, Countess of Huntingdon (1707-1791). The countess was the wife of Theophilus Hastings, ninth earl of Huntingdon. Her husband's sister, Lady Margaret Hastings, married Benjamin Ingham (1712-1772), who at Oxford was one of the members of the "methodist" society of Charles Wesley (1707-1788). John Wesley (1703-1791) was leader of his brother's society. Through her brother-in-law the Countess of Huntingdon made the acquaintance of the Wesleys. In 1738 John Wesley, and Peter Boehler, who had been ordained by Zinzendorf, founded a religious "society" in Fetter Lane, London, of which the Countess became a member. In 1739 Wesley opened a methodist chapel in London, and in 1740 he withdrew from the Fetter-lane Society. In the same year (1740) he abandoned Calvinism. George Whitefield (1714-1770) then became leader of the Calvinistic methodists, and an opponent or a rival of John Wesley. The Countess of Huntingdon supported Whitefield, and in 1748 made him one of her domestic chaplains. He was an attractive preacher, and even Lord Bolingbroke, Lord Chesterfield, and Horace Walpole were glad to listen to him. In 1761 the Countess opened a chapel at Brighton, and in 1765 another at Bath. In 1768 she opened a College, Trevecca College, at Talgarth, near Brecon, that her "chaplains" might be suitably trained. Other chapels were opened at Tunbridge Wells (1769), Worcester (1773), and Spa Fields, London (1779). At length the bishops refused to ordain her candidates for Orders. Domestic chaplains were not supposed to officiate in public chapels. The result was a secession from the Church of England in 1783, and an independent "ordination" (the first) in the chapel at Spa Fields. In 1789 a chapel was opened at Swansea. In 1790 the Countess made a will, and drew up a "plan of association" for perpetuating the Connexion. In the following year she died. In 1792 a college was opened at Cheshunt in Hertfordshire, and in 1797 another chapel at Canterbury. The Cheshunt College was removed to Cambridge in 1906. In 1910 it was decided to sell the site of the Spa Fields Church, and remove the Church to Golders Green, Hampstead. See J. H. Blunt; the *D.N.B.;* and the Annual Reports of "The Countess of Huntingdon's Connexion."

HUNTINGTONIANS. The followers of William Huntington (1745-1813), who was a coalheaver originally. He became a preacher, and preached in Surrey and Sussex. Removing to London, he ministered first to a congregation in Margaret Street, Cavendish Square, and then built "Providence Chapel" in Titchfield Street, London, where he preached for some years (1783-1810). In 1811 he opened the "New Providence Chapel" in Gray's Inn Lane, London. Huntington appended S.S. to his name, which is supposed to have stood for the words "Sinner Saved." "This popular preacher of his day seems to have acquired considerable influence by preaching in an exaggerated form the two doctrines of Faith and Indefectible Grace, which were made so prominent by the Methodists and the Calvinistic clergy, and by spicing his sermons with coarse humour" (J. H. Blunt). Rowland Hill (1744-1833) was one of those with whom he entered into controversy. Before he became rich, Huntington reproved the bishops for "rolling their fat carcases about in chariots." Afterwards he excused himself for riding in a chariot by referring to Acts xxi. 15, "And after those days we took up our carriages, and went up to Jerusalem." Huntington's works include *God the Guardian of the Poor*, and *The Naked Bow*. See J. H. Blunt; and the *D.N.B.*

HUNTOH. A tribal god in the religion of the Mayan Indians.

HURAKAN. A figure in the mythology of the Quiché Indians of Central America, a wind-god. Hurakan, who seems to correspond to the Mexican Tezcatlipoca, is in fact one of the central heroes of the Quiché sacred book, the Popol Vuh.

HUSSITES. The name Hussites, as that of a religious sect or school, was suggested by that of John Hus or Huss (1369-1415), the Bohemian. The name was given to his followers by his opponents. But his followers were, in reality, divided into two sections known as the Calixtines (*q.v.*) and the Taborites (*q.v.*). In 1401 John Hus became Dean of the Faculty of Arts in the University of Prague. In 1402 he was appointed also preacher in the Chapel of Bethlehem at Prague. With a natural gift of eloquence, he was inspired with enthusiasm by the writings of John Wycliffe (*d.* 1384). His denunciation of ecclesiastical abuses and his popularity as a preacher, however, soon brought him enemies. He was accused of being a rebel, a heretic, and a Wycliffite. At length the Emperor Sigismund persuaded him to submit his case to the Council of Constance (1414-15), promising him protection. The promised protection was not given, and Hus was thrown into prison. He was formally accused of denying Transubstantiation (*q.v.*), of teaching the heresies of Wycliffe, of inciting the people to enter upon a religious warfare and of causing strife between the civil and spiritual powers. He was condemned of heresy, degraded from the priesthood, and burnt. The literary remains of Hus consist of sermons, tractates, letters, and hymns. The Letters, as edited by E. de Bonnechose, were translated into English in 1846. John Hus's "De Ecclesia" (1413) bears unmistakable marks of the influence of the writings of John Wycliffe. See J. H. Blunt; *Prot. Dict.;* Brockhaus.

HUTCHINSONIANS. A school of theologians which came into evidence at the beginning of the eighteenth century. The founder was John Hutchinson (1674-1737), who was for some time steward of the household of the Duke of Somerset. The Duke procured him a sinecure office as purveyor of the royal stables of George I., which provided him until his death with a salary of about £200 a year. This enabled him to devote much of his time to the writing of books. He was a skilful mechanic, and invented an improved timepiece for determining longitude. He had some acquaintance with natural science, and acquired a knowledge of Hebrew. Hutchinson's main purpose seems to have been to prove that the Bible is supreme not only in the field of religion, but also in the sphere of science and theology. A number of eminent men became known as Hutchinsonians, though some of them were not inclined to acknowledge their indebtedness to the founder of the school. Hutchinson attached great importance to the study of the original Hebrew of the Bible. "He had embraced, in a very dogmatic spirit, some extraordinary doctrine about the perfection of the Scriptures, that is, the original Scriptures in the Hebrew language. He found deep meanings in recondite etymologies, and supposed that the Hebrew Bible contained all knowledge, human and divine. Hutchinson was also a zealous student of nature, and found the fact of Noah's Deluge proved by chinks in the earth, and sea-shells on the tops of mountains. The rise of Paganism he traced to the neglect of the Hebrew language. The heathen worshipped the air instead of the Deity. The same, or similar idolatry, is very prevalent now, through our language being Pagan, and partly through the influence of Greek and Roman learning. The Bible was written to cure the madness of the naturalists and the star-gazers. Modern philosophers, as, for instance, Sir Isaac Newton and Dr. Samuel Clarke, are 'idiots in respect of languages, and in respect of things ignorant.' Newton's doctrine of a vacuum in nature with the laws of gravitation are continual subjects of condemnation; and especially a theory to which Newton seems to have given some countenance, that in nature God sometimes works without the mediation of a second cause. Hutchinson found in the Hebrew Elohim the name of the Trinity, who agreed together that if man fell, one of them would become incarnate. This Trinity has its emblem in the elements which constitute nature—light, fire, and air. The persons in the Godhead are made so distinctly three intelligent agents that Unitarians, or such as believe in the absolute personal unity of the Deity, are said not to worship the God of the Christian revelation" (John Hunt). The Hutchinsonian theology was thought to be a convenient weapon to use against liberal churchmen who were supposed to be under the influence of such writers at Matthew Tindal (1653?-1733), author of the rationalistic work "Christianity as Old as the Creation" (1730), and John Toland (1670-1722), author of "Christianity not Mysterious" (1696). It was adopted for this purpose by Julius Bate (1711-1771), Rector of Sutton; by George Horne (1730-1792), afterwards Bishop of Norwich, who published "A Fair, Candid, and Impartial Statement of the Case between Sir Isaac Newton and Mr. Hutchinson"; and by William Jones (1726-1800), commonly known as "Jones of Nayland," who wrote a tract "An Essay on the First Principles of Natural Philosophy" with the object of refuting Sir Isaac Newton (1642-1727) and Samuel Clarke (1675-1729). The works of Hutchinson himself include *Moses' Principia*, 1724, and *Glory Mechanical, or the Agent of Nature, and Manner of their Agency Explained*. See John Hunt; J. H. Blunt; and the *D.N.B.*

HUTITES. The followers of John Hut, Huta, or Hutter, of Moravia, in the sixteenth century. They seem to have shared all things in common. See J. H. Blunt.

HYDROMANCY. The term Hydromancy means divination by means of water. We seem to have an example of this in the Old Testatment, where it is said, "Is not this (cup) that in which my lord drinketh, and whereby he divineth?" The ancient Babylonians poured oil into a vessel of water, and from the movements of the oil, in accordance with fixed rules of interpretation, deduced omens. A modern parallel has been found in the Travels of Norden (*c.* 1750), in which a Nubian sheikh is reported as saying: "I have consulted my cup, and I find that you are Franks in disguise, who have come to spy out the land." W. H. Bennett compares the modern custom in which the tea-leaves or coffee-grounds in a cup are made to give information about persons' fortunes. See W. H. Bennett, *Genesis* in the "Century Bible"; J. Skinner, *Genesis* in the *I.C.C.*

HYPOTHETICAL UNIVERSALISTS. A name given to persons who adopted the teaching of Moses Amyraut. See AMYRALDISTS.

HYPSISTARIANS. A fourth century sect referred to by Gregory of Nyssa and Gregory of Nazianzum. The term means "followers, or worshippers of the Most High." The Hypsistarians appeared in Cappadocia. They recognized only the Most High as God. They observed the Jewish Sabbath, but disapproved of circumcision and sacrifices. As symbols of the Deity, they used fire and lights. See J. H. Blunt.

HYSTERIA. A festival (Gk. ὑστηρια) at Argos at which swine (ὗς) were sacrificed to Aphrodite. It was held on New Year's Day, and was characterized by scenes of wild frenzy. In consequence of this emotional excitement, the term came to be applied to the excitement itself, and eventually was adopted in medicine to describe emotional derangements of a similar kind. "Thus both the terms 'hysteria' and 'lunacy' are intimately associated with the earlier phases in the moon-goddess's history; and their survival in modern medicine is a striking tribute to the strong hold of effete superstitiou in this branch of the diagnosis and treatment of disease" (G. Elliot Smith, *Dr.*, 1919).

I

I. Goddess I is a designation used by anthropologists for a deity depicted in the MSS. of the Mayan Indians of Central America. In the Dresden MS. she wears on her head a knotted serpent, and holds in her hands a vessel from which water streams. She is represented also as a death-deity with cross-bones, apparently because her activities as a water-goddess sometimes brought floods.

IBLIS. A name of the devil in Muslim theology. Another name is Shaitân. He was created of fire and was originally called 'Azâzil. The Qur'ân represents that he was a kind of angel who was expelled from Paradise and stoned.

IDHUNN. One of the deities of the Ancient Teutons. She is a goddess, and is represented as the wife of Bragi (*q.v.*). "Idhunn has the golden apples of youth in her keeping. She falls into the clutches of the giant Thjazi, but the Æsir compel Loki to bring her back again" (Chantepie de la Saussaye). See *Rel. of the Teutons*, 1902.

IDISI. The Idisi are divine figures in Old Teutonic mythology. They are mentioned in the Merseburg Charms (*q.v.*) as female beings who, like the Walkyries (*q.v.*), were active during battles.

IERMAOGUACAR. An earth-goddess worshipped in the West Indies (Antilles).

IGIGI. An order of superhuman beings in Babylonian religion. The name means "the strong ones." The Igigi seem to correspond to the Anunnaki (*q.v.*); but the former are spirits of heaven, the latter of earth. They are sent forth on missions by the higher gods such as Anu (*q.v.*), their father, Bel (*q.v.*), Ninib (*q.v.*), Marduk (*q.v.*). They are found throughout the whole period of the history of Babylonia and Assyria. In the Epic of Marduk (see MARDUK, EPIC OF) the army of Tiâmat (*q.v.*) is described as "all the Igigi"; and when Marduk has conquered and set all the world in order, he is adored and praised by the Igigi. See Morris Jastrow, *Rel.*

IGNATIANS. Another name for the Jesuits (*q.v.*). They were so called because their founder was Ignatius of Loyola (1491-1556).

IGNORANTINES. The abbot Baptiste de la Salle founded the Ignorantines or Fratres Ignorantiae or Frères ignorantins, or Frères des écoles chrétiennes in France at the beginning of the eighteenth century. The body was strongly supported by the Jesuits. "Its purpose was to give free instruction to people, not only in religion, but also in the elements of secular education, and thereby prevent any idea inimical to the Roman Church entering or taking possession of the young mind." See Schaff-Herzog.

IJMÂ'. Ijmâ' is an Arabic word meaning "agreement." The term is used to designate "the unanimous agreement of the Muslim nation, or rather of the representatives of the same, the learned doctors of Islám, called the Mujtahidín, on certain legal or theological questions, and corresponds with the Christian term 'the unanimous consent of the Apostolic Fathers.'" The Ijmâ' is the third foundation of Islâm. The agreement is of three kinds: (1) of word; (2) of action or practice; (3) of silence or tacit assent. See F. A. Klein.

IKTO. A deity in the mythology of the Sioux Indians, worshipped as the inventor of language.

ILAMATECUTLI. A Mexican deity. She seems to have been a maize-goddess. "She, Teteoinnan and Xilonen were associated in a peculiar form of sacrifice in which the victim was decapitated, and which perhaps represented the reaping of the maize-ear" (T. A. Joyce).

ILLUMINATI. The designation of the French Familists in Picardy, who in 1634 combined with the followers of Peter Guérin. "They claimed a special revelation as to the proper means whereby to attain Christian perfection. This perfection resulted in 'deificatio,' the θεωσις so often recurring in the Greek Fathers. The outcome was antinomian, for 'no act was sinful in the case of the deified'" (F. W. Bussell). The Illuminati were exterminated by the ministers of Louis XIII.

IMÂM, THE. An Arabic word meaning a "leader" in religion, from a root *'amma* "to have precedence" or "to lead." The word designates one who has been appointed to be the vice-regent of Muhammad and the leader of the Muslim nation. The office was established after the death of the Prophet. To be qualified for the Imâmate, a person must be a (1) Muslim, (2) a sane man of full age, (3) a free man, (4) not impious, (5) a just man, and (6) a Quraish. "It is the duty of every Muslim to obey the Imâm inwardly and outwardly, so long as his commands and prohibitions are in harmony with the doctrines of Islám. Should he give orders contrary to the same, *i.e.*, positively wrong, or objectionable, he is not to be obeyed. When he commands what is allowable, if his orders are such as tend to promote the interests of the Muslim nation, they are to be obeyed; if not, there is no obligation on the Muslim to obey them." The rightful successor of Muhammad was Abu Bakr. But the Shi'ahs contend that Muhammad nominated 'Ali. See F. A. Klein.

IMHOTEP. An Egyptian deity. Originally Imhotep was a learned man, an architect to the early king Zoser, and an author. He was afterwards made into a god, the patron of scribes, and regarded as a son of Ptah (*q.v.*) of Memphis. As patron of scribes he was also patron of learning. "Before the scribe dipped his pen in the water-jar he poured out a few drops as a libation to Imhotep, the physicians venerated him as patron of their science, and the people finally accepted him wholly as a god of medicine, Asklepios as the Graeco-Egyptians called him" (Erman). See A. Wiedemann: Adolf Ermann, *Handbook*.

IMMACULATE CONCEPTION. Since December the 8th, 1854, the doctrine of the immaculate conception of the Mother of Jesus (Immaculate Conception of the Blessed Virgin) has been one of the accepted dogmas of the Roman Catholic Church. It was decreed by Pope Pius IX. But, it is pointed out in the "Catholic Dictionary," that a distinction has been drawn, and has to be drawn, between active and passive conception. Active conception is the generative act of the parents. Passive conception is the reception into the body of a rational soul infused by God. "It is the passive, not the active, conception which Catholics have in view when they speak of the Immaculate Conception. For there was nothing miraculous in Mary's generation. She was begotten like other children. The body, while still inanimate, could not be sanctified or preserved from original sin, for it is the soul, not the body, which is capable of receiving either the gifts of grace or the stain of sin." The doctrine of the Immaculate Conception was first advocated and defended publicly by Duns Scotus (1265 or 1274-1308), the "Doctor Subtilis." It became afterwards a matter of fierce controversy between the Franciscans, who were Scotists, and the Dominicans, who were Thomists (followers of Thomas Aquinas, 1225 or 1227-1274). See *Cath. Dict.; Prot. Dict.*

IMMATERIALISM. The term Immaterialism is sometimes used of the doctrine of the immortality of the soul. It is also employed to describe the philosophy of George Berkeley (1685-1753). His system is so called as being the opposite of Materialism. It is known also as Idealism. Berkeley denied the existence of matter as an absolute substance. See BERKELEYISM.

IMPECCABLES. A name assumed by the sect otherwise known as Brethren of the Free Spirit (*q.v.*). The name was due to the belief that they were free from sin.

IMPLEMENTS, WORSHIP OF. On special occasions it is a common practice among the occupational castes in India to worship their implements or tools. The Murhas, for instance, a Dravidian caste of navvies and labourers found in Jubbulpore and the adjoining districts, invoke their implements as follows: "Oh! my lord the basket, my lord the pickaxe shaped like a snake, and my lady the hod, come and eat up those who do not pay me for my work!" The Prabhus, the Marātha caste of clerks and accountants, on the fifth day after the birth of a child, worship their pens, paper, and ink. See R. V. Russell.

INARI. A Japanese rice-goddess, with whose worship is associated the cult of the fox.

INCENSE. The *Encycl. Bibl.* defines incense as "the perfume arising from aromatic substances during combustion, and the substances themselves which are burned to produce the perfume." The use of incense in ritual and religious ceremonies has been widespread. It is referred to frequently in the Old Testament, where incense appears either as the concomitant of certain oblations or as an offering by itself; and in later Jewish literature we read often of the perfuming of garments by fragrant smoke, and the use of fumigatories after meals. In Psalm cxli., 2, Rev. viii. 3, v. 8, the sweet smoke which rises heavenwards seems to have become a symbol or vehicle of prayer, but this is a comparatively late conception. An earlier conception is represented by such passages as Gen. viii. 21 where Jehovah is said to have smelled with pleasure the odour of a burnt offering (cp. Lev. xxvi. 31). Another conception, by no means primitive, is that incense or fumigation with the smoke of incense is a powerful cleansing medium. Incense was much used in the religion of the Babylonians and Assyrians. In Sabaean inscriptions, again, mention is made of various substances used for incense. In ancient Egypt, as Cheyne says (*E.Bi.*), the offering of incense by a king is a frequent subject on the monuments, and great quantities of incense were consumed in the temples. It was an important feature in Roman religion. W. Warde Fowler states that when the Magna Mater of Pessinus was brought to Rome, "all Rome poured out to meet her, and burned incense at their doors as she passed by." He notes also that among the things which the Christian Church inherited from the Roman religion as symbolic elements in worship was the use of holy water and of incense. In Greek religion, according to MacCulloch (Hastings' *Encycl.*), "incense as such was not used before the eighth century B.C., and is first mentioned in Euripides"; but later it came to be used in large quantities. In the Roman Catholic Church incense is used "before the introit, at the gospel, offertory and elevation in High Mass, at the Magnificat in vespers, at funerals, etc." (*Cath. Dict.*); but it is said to be certain from Tertullian and many other early writers down to St. Augustine that the religious use of incense was unknown in the primitive Church. In the Church of England it does not seem to have been used in divine service in the period after the Reformation, but its use was revived by the ritualistic party in the 19th century. In recent years the study of the lower religions has revealed the fact that the use of incense is more world wide than it was formerly supposed to be. It was much used, for instance, in the religion of ancient Mexico. To return now to the problem of the origin of the use of incense. Robertson Smith (*R.S.*) suggested that the religious value of incense was originally independent of animal sacrifice, since, as a matter of fact, frankincense was the gum of a very holy species of tree, which was collected with religious precautions. "Whether, therefore, the sacred odour was used in unguents or burned like an altar sacrifice, it appears to have owed its virtue, like the gum of the *samora* tree, to the idea that it was the blood of an animate and divine plant." More recently much new light has been thrown on the subject, at any rate as far as ancient Egypt is concerned, by Dr. A. M. Blackman and Professor G. Elliot Smith. According to the former, the burning of incense before a corpse or statue in Egypt was part of the procedure considered necessary to give it a new life: it was intended primarily to convey to it the warmth, the sweat, and the odour of life. Then, according to Elliot Smith, from being an animating force, incense came to be regarded as a divine substance. Incidentally, "as the grains of incense consisted of the exudation of trees, or, as the ancient texts express it, 'their sweat,' the divine power of animation in course of time became transferred to the trees." This, in fact, is probably the origin of the sacredness of trees; "it was acquired from the incense and the aromatic woods which were credited with the power of animating the dead." The custom of burning incense, originally a ritual act for animating the funerary statue, developed ultimately into an act of homage to the deity. See A. M. Blackman, "The Significance of Incense, etc.," in the *Zeitschrift für Ägyptische Sprache und Altertumskunde*, Bd. 50, 1912; G. Elliot Smith, *Dr.*, 1919.

INCUBI. Male demons, satyrs, and fauns, who were supposed to visit women and have sexual intercourse with them.

INDEPENDENT METHODISTS. A separatist Methodist body which arose in 1810. They differ from other Methodists chiefly in their rejection of a paid ministry.

INDEPENDENTS. See BROWNISTS.

INDETERMINISM. Indeterminism is the opposite of Determinism (*q.v.*). It is explained by William James in the following way. Indeterminism says that the parts of the universe already laid down "have a certain amount of loose play on one another, so that the laying down of one of them does not necessarily determine what the others shall be. It admits that possibilities may be in excess of actualities, and that things not yet revealed to our knowledge may really in themselves be ambiguous. Of two alternative futures which we conceive, both may now be really possible; and the one become impossible only at the very moment when the other excludes it by becoming real itself. Indeterminism thus denies the world to be one unbending unit of fact. It says there is a certain ultimate pluralism in it; and, so saying, it corroborates our ordinary unsophisticated view of things. To that view, actualities seem to float in a wider sea of possibilities from out of which they are chosen; and *somewhere*, indeterminism says, such possibilities exist, and form a part of truth." See William James, *The Will to Believe*, 1908.

INDEX OF PROHIBITED BOOKS. The Index Librorum Prohibitorum is a list of prohibited books made by the Roman Catholic Church. The Council of Trent at first appointed a Commission to compile an Index of Prohibited Books, but afterwards it referred the whole matter to Pope Pius IV. In 1564 Pius IV. issued an index known as the Index Tridentinus. Subsequently a Sacred Congregation was constituted with power to deal with the matter. Its more complete organization was due to Sixtus V. "The Congregation of the Index of Prohibited Books consists of a competent number of Cardinals, and has a secretary taken from the Order of Preachers, and a great number of theological and other professors who are called Consultors, the chief of whom is the Master of the Apostolic Palace, the primary and official Consultor of this Congregation" (Ferraris, quoted in the *Catholic Dictionary.*). Rules as to the principles and methods by which the Congregation was to be guided were laid down very fully in 1753 by Benedict XIV. It is the duty of the Congregation of the Index to prepare also an Index Librorum Expurgandorum, a list of books which may be read when they have been expurgated. See Schaff-Herzog; the *Prot. Dict.;* the *Cath. Dict.*

INDRA. One of the deities in the religion of Hinduism. The precise nature of Indra is difficult to determine. He has been regarded as a Storm or Rain God, or as a Fire God. More probably, however, he represents Lightning. Hopkins points out that he is variously depicted by the poets. He "is armed with stones, clubs, arrows, or the thunderbolt (made for him by the artificer, Tvashtar), of brass or of gold, with many edges and points. Upon a golden chariot he rides to battle, driving two or many red or yellow steeds; he is like the sun in brilliancy, and like the dawn in beauty; he is multiform, and cannot really be described; his divine name is secret; in appearance he is vigorous, huge; he is wise and true and kind: all treasures are his, and he is a wealth-holder, vast as four seas; neither his greatness nor his generosity can be comprehended; mightiest of gods is he, filling the universe; the heavens rest upon his head; earth cannot hold him; earth and heaven tremble at his breath; he is king of all; the mountains are to him as valleys; he goes forth a bull, raging, and rushes through the air, whirling up the dust; he breaks open the rain-containing clouds, and lets the rain pour down." Indra came to be regarded for a time as the most powerful god of all, the All-god. See Monier-Williams; E. W. Hopkins.

INDULGENCES. An Indulgence is a remission of the temporal punishment due to sin after contrition has been shown (*contritio cordis*), confession has been made (*confessio oris*), and absolution has been given. The practice is peculiar to the Roman Catholic Church. In ancient times atonement (*satisfactio*) for great sins could only be made by many years of severe penance. In course of time, however, a lesser work, but a specific good work, in virtue of the "treasure of merits" accumulated by the saints, was substituted for a greater work. Such a work might take the form of alms to the poor, to churches, and to monasteries, or of pilgrimages, etc. Indulgences may be plenary (*indulgentia plenaria*) or partial (*indulgentia minus plena*); temporal or perpetual; particular, that is to say, for a special diocese, or general, that is to say, for the whole Church. One of the most famous of the plenary indulgences granted by the Roman Catholic Church is that of her jubilee. Other well-known examples are the indulgence granted to the dying by priests, and the indulgence given with the Pope's blessing. "The most celebrated local indulgences are gained by visiting the seven chief churches and privileged altars at Rome; by pilgrimages to the holy places in Palestine; or visiting the stations mentioned in the Missal" (*Catholic Dictionary*). Indulgences are granted also to persons who wear rosaries, scapulars, medals, etc. "With respect to the natural consequences of sin, such as disease, infamy, etc., the Roman Church does not pretend to possess any power; but with respect to those punishments which God inflicts on sinners, either in this world or in purgatory, she claims to have absolute jurisdiction conferred upon her by Christ, with the power of the keys. . . . If, now, the Church should remit those punishments from mere mercy, and without any *satisfactio*, she would violate the divine justice, which demands that every sin shall be balanced by a good work. But how, then, does the *indulgentia* of the Church enter into the transaction? Partly through the doctrine of good works as *opera operata*, that is, as values which can be transferred from one to another; and partly through the doctrine of *communio sanctorum*, or the co-ownership of the Church in the inexhaustible fund of good works which Christ and the saints have left, and of which they have no need themselves" (Schaff-Herzog). See Schaff-Herzog; William Benham; the *Prot. Dict.;* the *Cath. Dict.*

INFALLIBILITY OF THE POPE. The decree of the infallibility of the Pope was proclaimed in 1870 at the last meeting of the Vatican Council (*q.v.*). It was afterwards confirmed by the Pope. In the papal bull "Pastor Æternus" it is defined as follows: "Therefore faithfully adhering to the tradition received from the beginning of the Christian faith, for the glory of God our Saviour, the exaltation of the Catholic Religion, and the salvation of Christian people, the Sacred Council approving, we teach and define that it is a dogma divinely revealed, that the Roman Pontiff, when he speaks *ex cathedra*, that is, when in discharge of the office of pastor and doctor of all Christians, by virtue of his extreme Apostolic authority, he defines a doctrine regarding faith or morals to be held by the universal Church, by the Divine assistance promised to him in blessed Peter, is possessed of that infallibility which the Divine Redeemer willed that his Church should be endowed with for defining doctrine regarding faith or morals; and that therefore such definitions of the Roman Pontiff are irreformable of themselves, and not from the consent of the Church. But if anyone, which may God avert, presume to contradict this our definition, let him be anathema" (*Pastor Æternus*, quoted in Benham). The *Catholic Dictionary* is no doubt correct in claiming that the doctrine is simply the logical consequence of principles already accepted. Its exposition of the doctrine is interesting. "The Pope in himself is subject to error like other men; his infallibility comes from the spirit of God, which on certain occasions protects him from error in faith and morals. He has no infallibility in merely historical or scientific questions. Even in matters of faith and morals he has no inspiration, and must use the same means of theological inquiry open to other men. He may err as a private doctor; nor is any immunity from error granted to books which he may write and publish. Even when he speaks with Apostolic authority he may err. The Vatican Council only requires us to believe that God protects him from error in definitions on faith or morals when he imposes a belief on the Universal Church." The doctrine was not accepted unanimously, and led to the formation of the body known as Old Catholics (*q.v.*). See Schaff-Herzog; William Benham; the *Prot. Dict.*, 1904; the *Cath. Dict.*

INFRALAPSARIANISM. Infralapsarianism denotes certain doctrines taught by the Calvinists. For his own glory God created the world. It was his purpose to allow man to fall, and from among the fallen to choose many for salvation. These he would send His Son to redeem; the rest he would leave to suffer the punishment due to their sins.

INGERSOLL LECTURESHIP. In pursuance of the last will and testament of George Goldthwait Ingersoll, his daughter, Miss Caroline Haskell Ingersoll (*d.* Jan. 26, 1893), bequeathed to Harvard University in Cambridge, Massachussets, a sum of money to be regarded as a fund for the establishment of a Lectureship on a plan somewhat similar to that of the Dudleian lecture. One lecture was to be delivered each year, on any convenient day between the last day of May and the first day of December, on the subject "The Immortality of Man." The lecture was not to form part of the usual college course, nor to be delivered by any Professor or Tutor as part of his usual routine of instruction, though any such Professor or Tutor may be appointed to such service. The choice of the lecturer was not to be limited to any one religious denomination, nor to any one profession, but might be that of either clergyman or layman, the appointment to take place at least six months before the delivery of the lecture. The lecture was to be called "The Ingersoll Lecture on the Immortality of Man." The lecturers have already included the late Professor William James of Harvard University, Professor Josiah Royce of Harvard University, and Prof. William Osler of Oxford University.

INGHAMITES. The followers of Benjamin Ingham (1712-1772). As a student at Queen's College, Oxford, Ingham became a Methodist. The "four young gentlemen of Oxford" who were "the first Methodists," and one of whom was John Wesley (1703-1791), formed themselves into a society in November, 1729, and were afterwards joined by others, including Benjamin Ingham. In 1735 he went with John and Charles Wesley (1707-1788) on a missionary journey to Georgia. On his return he went with John Wesley to Hernnhut. After this Ingham proceeded to Yorkshire, and with the help of Moravian friends, founded societies there. He had come under Moravian influence in his travels. In course of time there were as many as eighty societies. In 1741 Ingham married Lady Margaret Hastings, sister of Lord Huntingdon This brought him into close connection with the Countess of Huntingdon (1707-1791), who was the founder of "Lady Huntingdon's Connexion." He also became closely acquainted with Count von Zinzendorf (1700-1760), founder of the Herrnhuter or the Moravian Brethren. He expressed a willingness to unite his forces to those of Wesley, but Wesley would not hear of the union unless he returned to "the old Methodist doctrine." Subsequently Ingham became interested in the teaching of Glas and Sandeman (see GLASSITES). He sent two of his preachers to study their principles, with the result that they came back and converted the majority of Ingham's followers. In 1851 the number of Inghamite chapels had dwindled to nine. See J. H. Blunt; and the *D.N.B.*

INNERE MISSION, DIE. The Inner or Home Mission movement in Germany was founded by J. H. Wickern (1808-1881) of Hamburg. It now has Associations or Branches throughout Germany. The aim of the movement is to revive true Christian feeling, and to help those who are in need, whether spiritual or bodily. Thus it has established Schools, Refuges, etc. See A. S. Farrar, *Crit. Hist. of Free Thought* ("Bampton Lectures"), 1862; Brockhaus.

INQUISITION, THE. The Inquisition (Inquisitio hæreticae pravitatis), also called the "Holy Office" (Sanctum Officium), is the name of a spiritual tribunal in the Roman Catholic Church whose duty it has been to detect, repress, and punish heretics. In the ancient Church this was one of the duties of the bishops. Under the Roman Emperors Theodosius and Justinian there were special officials, "inquisitors," to prosecute before the civil tribunals persons who opposed the national creed. In the eleventh, twelfth, and thirteenth centuries the sects known as the Cathari, the Waldenses (q.v.), and the Albigenses (*q.v.*) were thought to be a danger both to Church and State. Legates were empowered therefore by several Councils to check the abuse, and in 1215 the bishops were urged by the Fourth Lateran Council to take special measures. These consisted in part in binding parishioners by oath to inform against heretics. The measures taken by Innocent III. were approved and improved by the Council of Toulouse (1228). Gregory IX. in 1232 and 1233 "appointed the Dominicans a standing commission of inquisitors in Austria, Germany, Aragon, Lombardy, and Southern France" (Schaff-Herzog). In 1248 Innocent IV. instituted a special tribunal, the Inquisition, to deal with the matter; and in his bull *Ad exstirpanda* of 1252 he enacted that to extract a confession from a suspected person, use must be made of torture, if necessary. Persons found guilty were punished by confiscation of property, "loss of civil and ecclesiastical privileges, rigorous confinement, and death, either by a simple execution, or by incarceration and the flames" (Schaff-Herzog). The Inquisition was introduced into Italy, Spain, Germany, France, Portugal and the Netherlands. It could not establish itself in England, Sweden, Norway, or Denmark. It was abolished first in France. See, further, the following article.

INQUISITION, SPANISH. The Inquisition was used against the Jews and Moors in Aragon in the thirteenth century. Nicolaus Eymericus († 1393), the author of the "Inquisitor's Manual" (Directorium Inquisitorum), was Inquisitor-General for forty-four years. But the strict rules of procedure laid down by him were not fully introduced until 1481. In 1483 Torquemada was appointed Inquisitor-General for fifteen years. He organized the movement in Spain, and availed himself of the help of spies who were called "Familiars of the Holy Office." In 1492 an edict of banishment was proclaimed against all the Jews in Spain who refused to embrace Christianity. Thousands of Jews left the country, but many remained behind. Those who remained occupied the attention of the Inquisition for centuries. Torquemada was succeeded by Diego Deza (1499-1506), and Diego Deza by Ximenes (1507-1517). Under the latter, according to Llorente, 2,536 persons suspected of heresy were put to death. The Inquisition was very active in the sixteenth century. After 1770, however, its powers began to be curtailed, and in 1808 they were abolished for a time. They were not finally abolished until 1834. It was computed by Llorente, who from 1790-1792 was secretary to the tribunal of Madrid, that during its 330 years of existence the Spanish Inquisition condemned 30,000 persons to death. Hefele, the writer of the article "Inquisition" in Wetzer and Welte, defends the Inquisition and questions the statements of Llorente. He does so also in his "Life of Cardinal Ximenes" (Engl. Transl. 1860). "First, there is the general fact of the greater relative severity of penal justice in all countries alike, till within quite recent times. The Carolina, or penal code, in force under Charles V., condemned coiners to the flames, and burglars to the gallows. Burying alive and other barbarous punishments were sanctioned by it, none of which were allowed by the Inquisition. In England, in the sixteenth century, persons refusing to plead could be, and were, pressed to death. The last witch burned in Europe was sentenced in the Canton Glarus by a Protestant tribunal as late as 1785. Secondly, Llorente omits to draw attention to the fact that the Spanish kings obliged the Inquisition to try and sentence persons charged with many other crimes besides heresy—*e.g.*, with polygamy, seduction, unnatural crime, smuggling, witchcraft, sorcery, imposture, personation, etc. A large proportion of criminals of this kind would, down to the present century, have been sentenced to death on conviction in any secular tribunal in Europe. Thirdly, Llorente does not pretend to base the above statement as to the number executed by the Inquisition on written documents, but on calculations of his own making, in some of which he can be proved to be inexpert and inexact" (*Catholic Dictionary*). See H. C. Lea, *Hist. of the Inquisition of the Middle Ages*, 1888; Schaff-Herzog; *Chambers' Encycl.;* the *Prot. Dict.;* the *Cath. Dict.;* Brockhaus.

INSPIRATION. To be inspired in the religious sense of the word is to be stirred and influenced by an outside power, a power which is higher than anything human. To Christians inspiration denotes the direct influence of the divine upon the human mind. To the Jews of old it meant often an audible communication made by God to man; or at least it was represented in this way. The messages which God gave to certain persons in this way were at first proclaimed orally to the people in general by prophets and preachers; they were subsequently committed to writing. Afterwards it often happened, where the literary art was sufficiently developed, that a person wrote down at once the message which he believed he was inspired to deliver. In any case, such messages were gathered into books, which came to be regarded as sacred. Nearly every religion has its sacred books. It is claimed for the sacred books of Christianity that they are inspired above all others. It used to be claimed that they were verbally inspired, that is to say, that every word or phrase was, as it were, dictated by God. That claim has, it may be said, been abandoned by the majority of people. Is there such a thing at all as inspiration by an outside power? Do certain books belong to a class by themselves? There are many persons now who assert that the Bible is no more inspired than the Korân, or the Vedas, or the Zend-Avesta, or even than the Essays of Emerson. Now there is no reason to deny that in a measure all these non-Jewish and non-Christian writings are inspired. But there are grounds for thinking that Jewish writings were inspired in a peculiar and unique sense. It is not uncommon to find individuals revealing a gift or genius which is truly marvellous. Shakespeare, even if the groundwork of some of his works is not entirely original, stands in a class by himself. And, although it is not so common, we find also whole nations (or certain nations as a whole) displaying some remarkable gift or genius. The Germans, for instance, have a marvellous genius for music. One need only live amongst them to realize how widespread this gift is. The Jews of old had a peculiar and marvellous genius (or taste, to use a milder term) for religion This stands out clearly in their history. They had this marvellous gift, and the early Christians inherited it. No people has sought God so earnestly or listened so intently for his voice. Just as Germany has produced a Mozart, a Mendelssohn, and a Beethoven, Palestine has given birth to prophets of extraordinary power. And just as in Germany a musical genius of a quite exceptional character might arise, so it might be expected that among the Jews, in other words in the sphere of religion, a Prophet would appear who would reveal God to man in a quite peculiar way. Inspiration, we have said, is claimed for certain books. It may be said, however, that books never can be inspired to the same extent that men are. In moments of inspiration a man comes into communion with a power outside of himself, above himself, with God. He is spoken to by God. God breathes his spirit into him. In what language does God communicate with man? In no human language, it may be said. Spirit communes with spirit. The man has acquired a spiritual power, and is able to impart it, or some of it, to other people (cp. what is said under APOSTOLIC SUCCESSION). The spiritual power of Christianity, and in fact of every religion, is handed on far more by persons than by writings. God does not deliver his message in human language. The prophet, therefore, who wishes to express it in words, spoken or written, has to translate it in terms of human speech. To do this adequately is impossible. It is often said, with a sneer, of someone who claims to have received a divine message that he cannot tell us what it is, and that when he attempts to do so he only succeeds in saying something commonplace. The truth is it is extremely difficult to give human expression to a divine impression. Inspiration is a very real experience. In earlier times, when prophets lived in closer contact with nature and in more intimate communion with God, the experience known as inspiration seems to have been more frequent and to some extent better understood. The references to it in the Christian Bible are well known. There are other references which are not so familiar. Though, as Prof. Sanday says, Philo (*c.* 20 B.C.-45 A.D.) "lays stress rather on the inspired person than on the inspired book," he speaks of "sacred scriptures" (*hierai graphai*), "sacred books" (*hierai bibloi*), "the sacred word" (*ho hieros logos*), of "oracles" (*chrēsmoi*), etc. Philo clearly regarded every word of the Scripture text as sacred. If it did not give a suitable meaning when translated literally, it had to be explained allegorically. According to Philo, Jeremiah spoke "in the person of God Himself" (*ek prosōpou tou Theou*). He claims that there is "nothing superfluous" in the Law. It is clear, moreover, that "he regarded the Greek translation as itself a product of divine inspiration as much as the original. He is the first to add to the story of Aristeas—which made the Seventy translators produce a harmonious text by comparing their versions together—the further touch that this harmony was obtained, not by comparison of results, but by supernatural aid: the translators, according to him, were inspired prophets who 'did not produce one one rendering and another another, but all the same words and expressions as though some invisible prompter were at the ear of each of them'" (Sanday). Philo regards all good men as inspired (*e.g.*, Plato, the "most sacred"; Heraclitus, the "great and renowned"; Parmenides, Empedocles, Zeno, Cleanthes), and he had had personal experience of inspiration himself. Yet he "never quotes as authoritative any but the Canonical Books," and "it is clear that he attributes to them an authority which is really unique in its kind." To turn to another writer, Josephus (A.D. 37-38 to about A.D. 110), who represents the views of the Pharisees in Palestine during the second half of the first century A.D. Josephus speaks of "sacred books" (*hierai Bibloi*), "sacred writings" (*hiera grammata*), "books of sacred scriptures" (*hierōn graphōn Bibloi*), etc. Josephus "speaks of 'the Deity (*το Θειον*) being present with' a writer; of 'holding converse with God': of 'being possessed or inspired by God'; of 'being filled with Deity': of 'being in a state of Divine inspiration'; of 'the Spirit of God taking hold of' the prophet; of 'the Divine gift passing over' from one person to another. Josephus is almost as explicit as Philo in regard to the manner of inspiration. He describes Balaam as prophesying 'not as master of himself but moved to say what he did by the Divine Spirit'" (Sanday). He speaks of the Jewish Scriptures as the "decrees of God" (*Theou dogmata*). Every Jew from the day of his birth recognises them to be such by instinct, and is prepared "cheerfully to lay down his life in their behalf." In these writings "not a soul has ventured either to add, or to remove, or to alter a syllable" (Josephus, *Contra Apionem*, i. 8). And they do not disagree and conflict with one another. Such writers as Philo and Josephus would seem to have regarded all the books of the Jewish Canon as equally inspired. Some of the Jewish scholars, however, holding the theory of the Synagogue that the whole Canon was fixed at one time, and on this assumption finding it difficult to explain the position of some of the books (*e.g.*, Daniel) among the Hagiographa (*q.v.*), argued that there was a difference in inspiration. This was the line taken by Moses Maimonides (A.D. 1135-1204), David Kimchi (died A.D. 1240), and Abarbanel (born A.D. 1437). They supposed that the second group of books, the Prophets, were inspired by the "spirit of prophecy," the third group of books, the Hagiographa, by "the holy spirit." The Torah was revealed, peh 'el peh, the Nebiim (Prophets) by the *ruach ha-nebuah*, and the Kethubim (Hagiographa) by the *ruach ha-kodesh*. The theory, however, as G. Wildeboer points out (*Canon of the O.T.*, 1895) was peculiar to these later Jewish scholars. It finds no support in the New Testament or even in the Talmud. We have already suggested that in a so-called inspired book there must be a human element, inasmuch as it is difficult for a writer to give expression in human language to a divine impression. When the Swiss or Helvetic *Consensus Formula* (A.D. 1675) taught the literal inspiration of Holy Scripture, it took up an impossible position. A standard work on the subject is W. Sanday's *Inspiration*, 1903 ("Bampton Lectures," 1893).

INSTITUTION OF A CHRISTIAN MAN, THE. The title of a book of Christian doctrine, published in 1537. It was drawn up by a committee of bishops of the Church of England, and came to be known as the "Bishops' Book" (*q.v.*).

INSTITUTE OF THE BLESSED VIRGIN MARY. A religious order founded by an English lady, Mary Ward (1585-1645). Educated as a Roman Catholic, Mary Ward left England in 1606 and went to St. Omer. Here she entered the convent of the Colettines as a lay sister. In 1607, however, she left it with the idea of founding a similar convent for English ladies. With the intention of building a house under the rule of St. Clare (see POOR CLARES), she obtained from the Archduke Albert of Brussels a piece of ground at Gravelines. Meantime, she lived with the English ladies who had joined her in a hired house at St. Omer. After living for a time under the strict rule of St. Clare, she suddenly became persuaded that she had received a call to a somewhat different kind of work. In 1609 she left the Poor Clares. In course of time she became convinced that her vocation was to found a teaching order, "recruited from the ranks of her Catholic countrywomen, not cloistered, nor under obedience to any other order, but living under the rule of the Society of Jesus, and bound by terminable, not perpetual, vows" (*Cath. Dict.*). In 1611 therefore she founded in England the first community of the "English Virgins." A few years later she established a similar community at St. Omer. Other establishments soon grew up in Italy, and at Liège and Munich. But the foundress was not exempt from persecution. On several occasions she had to flee from one country to another, and for a time her houses were closed by order of Pope Urban VIII. Afterwards, however, her Institute again met with hearty approval, and since the death of Mary Ward it has flourished greatly. It is said to do excellent work in educating girls of every class in Bavaria. Hungary, Roumania, Italy, and other parts of the Continent. See the *Cath. Dict.*; the *D.N.B.*

INTINCTION. Intinction is the name given to the mode of administering the Eucharist to the laity in the Greek Church. The consecrated bread is broken into pieces, dipped in the consecrated wine, and given to the communicant in a spoon. It is claimed that the custom dates back to the time of Chrysostom (*b.* A.D. 347). It was sometimes followed in the Western Church, but the custom was condemned by Pope Julius I. (337-352) as unscriptural. See William Benham; Schaff-Herzog.

INTROIT. In the Roman Catholic Church, Introit is the name of the anthem sung at the beginning of the Mass or Communion Service. It is sung after the Confiteor, and when the priest has ascended the altar. It consists of an antiphon, Gloria Patri, and usually of part of a Psalm. Sometimes, however, use is made of other passages of Scripture, and even of passages from uninspired (*e.g.*, apocryphal) writers. The introduction of introits is ascribed by the "Liber Pontificalis" to Pope Celestine (423 A.D.), by Le Brun and Benedict XIV. to Gregory the Great (595 A.D.). The use of them is enjoined in the first Prayer Book of Edward VI., and psalms are prefixed to the Collects for the purpose. In the revision of 1552, however, these were removed. The *Protestant Dictionary* (1904) is distressed by the fact that "both the term and practice have been adopted by Ritualists of the Church of England." See William Benham; Smith and Cheetham; the *Cath. Dict.*

INTUITIONISTS. It has been truly said that there have been intuitionists in nearly all ages. The fact is proved by the history of what is called heresy. In modern times, however, the name has been assumed by persons who have been influenced by the progress of Science and historical criticism. Such men as Ralph Waldo Emerson and Theodore Parker in America, and Thomas Carlyle in England, are representatives of intuitionism. J. H. Blunt says that intuitionism, as represented by Emerson and Theodore Parker, indicates "the repudiation of all religion dependent on an external revelation, and looks to the intuitions of the soul as the only guide of humanity." He thinks that this means the substitution of the idolatry of self for the worship of God. This is an absurd view of the matter. The intuitions of the soul have led men to hold fast to the worship of god, and to the belief in His existence, when all other arguments have failed to satisfy them. Job was an intuitionist. To despise or undervalue intuitionism is to reject or undermine one of the firmest foundations of religion. See William Benham.

INVISIBLES. Some of the Reformers were so called because they "denied the perpetual visibility of the Church, and in answer to the inquiry of Romanists as to the whereabouts of the Church before the time of Luther, asserted that it was invisible" (William Benham).

INWARD LIGHT, THE. See FRIENDS, SOCIETY OF.

IOSKEHA. In the mythology of the Hurons two of the principal gods are Ioskeha and Tawiscara (the "White and Dark Ones"). In a conflict between them Tawiscara was overcome. Ioskeha then founded the human race, slew the great frog which had swallowed up the waters of the earth, and learned from the great tortoise, the upholder of the earth, the secret of making fire.

IRA. A Babylonian deity, god of pestilence. He figures in the Babylonian story of the Deluge.

IRMINSUL. The Irminsul was an old Saxon shrine. It is mentioned in connection with the destruction of Eresburg by Charles the Great in 774 A.D. Rudolph of Fulda says: "The Saxons worship in the open air a tree-trunk of considerable size; this they call in their language Irminsul, which in Latin would be universalis columna, that is to say, the column which sustains everything." But the Irminsul would seem to have embraced more than a tree-trunk, for reference is made to it also as a temple, a grove, or an image. It is likely that the first part of the term is a word meaning "large" or "mighty" (universalis). It is not, it would seem, the name of a god. Irmin, however, does also seem to have been an eponymous tribal hero; and he seems sometimes to be identified with the god Tiu (*q.v.*). For the worship of a tree compare YGGDRASIL.

IRRATIONALISM. W. Windelband has given the name Irrationalism to the philosophical system of Schopenhauer (1788-1860), and to the later theological and philosophical speculations of F. W. J. von Schelling (1775-1854). Josiah Royce thinks this kind of philosophy, which is based on the teaching of Kant, may be summarized as follows: "The world as we see it exists only in our ideas. We all have a common outer show-world because we all possess a common deeper nature, wherein we are one. You are essentially the same ultimate being that I am. Otherwise we should not have in common this outer projected world of seeming sea waves, star clusters, and city streets. For, as ideas, those things have no outer basis. As common to us all, they must have a deep inner basis. Yet this their basis can't be anything ultimately and universally rational. For in so far as we actually have reason in common, we think necessary, clearly coherent, exactly interrelated groups of ideas, such, for instance, as the multiplication table. But about the star clusters and the sea waves there is no such ultimate rational unity and coherency. . . . The world of the true idealism is n't so much the world of the rational and divine self, as it is the world of the deep unreason that lies at the very basis of all of our natures, of all our common selfhood. Why should there be any world at all for us? Is n't it just because we are all actually minded to see one? And is n't this being minded to see a world as ultimately and brutally unreasonable a fact as you could name? Let us find for this fact, then, a name not so exalted as Fichte's high-sounding speech would love. Let us call this ultimate nature of ours, which forces us all alike to see a world of phenomena in the show forms of space and time, simply our own deep common Will. Let us drop the divine name for it. Will, merely as such, is n't precisely a rational thing; it's capricious. It wills because it does will; and if it wills in us all to be of such nature as to see just these stars and houses, then see them we must, and there is the end of it." See Josiah Royce, *The Spirit of Modern Philosophy*, 1896.

IRVINGITES. The followers of Edward Irving (1792-1834). After studying at the University of Edinburgh, Irving went to Haddington as a schoolmaster (1810-12). In 1812 he was selected as the first master of a school at Kirkcaldy. Here three years later he obtained the Presbyterian license to preach. In 1819 he preached in S. George's, Edinburgh, before Andrew Thomson (1779-1849), its minister, and Thomas Chalmers (1780-1847), then minister of Tron parish, Glasgow. Towards the end of the same year he became assistant to Dr. Chalmers. In 1822 he went to his native place Annan in Dumfriesshire to be ordained. He had already in 1821 accepted a call to the Caledonian Chapel, Hatton Garden, London, which at the time was far from flourishing. "The Caledonian Church had been placed under the pastoral care of two worthy ministers, who were successively called to parochial charges in the Church of Scotland; and by their removal, and for want of a stated ministry, it was reduced to great and almost hopeless straits" (Edward Irving). One of the stipulations for appointment was that the minister should be able to preach in the Gaelic tongue; but through the influence of the Duke of York, who was President of the Royal Caledonian Asylum, this stipulation was set aside. The "Royal Caledonian Asylum" was instituted in 1815 by the Highland Society of London for "Supporting and educating the children of soldiers, sailors and marines, natives of Scotland, who have died or have been disabled in the service of their country; and also the children of Indigent Scottish Parents, residing in London not receiving Parochial Relief." The Institution was not opened for the reception of children until December, 1819. In that year premises had been acquired in Cross Street, Hatton Garden, London. The Caledonian Chapel was evidently connected with this institution. In July 1822 Irving began his work in London. By degrees he filled the chapel, and there came a time when it was invaded by streams of noble and fashionable hearers. The invasion is said to have been due in the first instance to a reference by George Canning (1770-1827) in the House of Commons. Canning said he had heard a Scotch minister in one of the most poorly endowed churches preach the most eloquent sermon he had ever listened to. The scene outside and inside the chapel is described by William Hazlitt (1778-1830). "You can scarcely move along for the coronet-coaches that besiege the entrance to the Caledonian Chapel in Hatton Garden; and when, after a prodigious squeeze, you get in so as to have standing-room, you see in the same undistinguished crowd Brougham and Mackintosh, Mr. Peel and Lord Liverpool, Lord Landsdowne and Mr. Coleridge. Mr. Canning and Mr. Hone are pew fellows, Mr. Waithman frowns stern applause, and Mr. Alderman Wood does the honours of the Meeting! The lamb lies down with the lion, and the millennium seems to be anticipated in the Caledonian chapel, under the new Scotch preacher" (*The Round Table*). Hazlett also gives a description of Irving himself. "Mr. Irving's intellect itself is of a superior order; he has undoubtedly both talents and acquirements beyond the ordinary run of every-day preachers. These alone, however, we hold, would not account for a twentieth part of the effect he has produced: they would have lifted him perhaps out of the mire and slough of sordid obscurity, but would never have launched him into the ocean-stream of popularity, in which he 'lies floating many a rood';—but to these he adds uncommon height, a graceful figure and action, a clear and powerful voice, a striking, if not a fine face, a bold and fiery spirit, and a most portentous obliquity of vision, which throw him to an immeasurable distance beyond all competition, and effectually relieve whatever there might be of common-place or bombast in his style of composition" (*The Spirit of the Age*). In 1825 Irving published a book, "Babylon and Infidelity Foredoomed," which he dedicated to James Hatley Frere (1779-1866), a person with curious views about prophecy. In 1826 a number of students of prophecy, amongst whom was Edward Irving, began to meet together at Albury Park, Surrey, in the house of Henry Drummond (1786-1860) to deliberate about prophetical questions. In May 1827 was opened a new church in Regent Square which had been specially built for Irving. Thus Irving became minister of the National Scotch Church, London. In 1828 he went to Scotland on a preaching tour. On this occasion he visited Rosneath, where he made a great impression upon many persons, including an invalid, Mary Campbell. In the same year Alexander John Scott (1805-1866) became Irving's assistant. Scott, who afterwards became the first Principal of Owens College, Manchester (1851-57), was one of those who believed "that the supernatural powers once bestowed upon the Church were not merely the phenomena of one miraculous age, but an inheritance of which she ought to have possession as surely and richly now as in the days of the Apostles" (Oliphant). The same idea had already occurred to Irving, and he seems to have been impressed more and more by Scott's convictions. In 1830 James Macdonald, a disciple of Scott, cured his invalid sister by telling her in the words of Psalm xx. to "Arise, and stand upright." He then wrote to Mary Campbell, who apparently was on her death-bed, and conveyed to her the same command. She has herself described the effect of the message. "I received dear brother James M'Donald's letter, giving an account of his sister's being raised up, and commanding me to rise and walk. I had scarcely read the first page when I became quite overpowered, and laid it aside for a few minutes; but I had no rest in my mind until I took it up again, and began to read. As I read, every word came home with power; and when I came to the command to arise, it came home with a power which no one can describe; it was felt to be indeed the voice of Christ; it was such a voice as could not be resisted. A mighty power was instantaneously exerted upon me. I felt as if I had been lifted from off the earth, and all my diseases taken from me at the voice of Christ. I was verily made in a moment to stand upon my feet, leap and walk, sing and rejoice" (Norton, *Memoirs of J. and G. Macdonald*). In the same year, apparently before her cure, Mary Campbell received the gift of tongues. Irving himself, writing later (1832) in "Fraser's Magazine" says that "the Holy Ghost came with mighty power upon the sick woman as she lay in her weakness, and constrained her to speak at great length and with superhuman strength in an unknown tongue, to the astonishment of all who heard and to her own great edification—for 'he that speaketh in an unknown tongue edifieth himself.'" Towards the end of 1830 Irving and some Evangelical clergymen began to conduct prayer meetings in order "to seek of God the revival of the gifts of the Holy Ghost in the Church." The Presbytery of London had already begun to doubt his orthodoxy. Early in November 1831 Irving preached two sermons on the extraordinary gifts of the Spirit, and several members of the congregation began to reveal the miraculous gift of tongues. In 1832 the Scotch Presbytery in London decided "that the said Rev. Edward Irving has rendered himself unfit to remain the minister of the National Scotch Church aforesaid, and ought to be removed therefrom, in pursuance of the conditions of the trust-deed of the said church." Irving's congregation sought an asylum in a large room in Gray's Inn Road. But here only the principal services were held. Irving preached for a time in various places out of doors. Later, he removed to a house in Newman Street. This contained a large picture gallery which was to serve as his new church. The ministerial organisation now underwent a change. Robert Baxter of Doncaster declared prophetically "that the Church no longer retained the privilege of ordaining, and that all spiritual offices were henceforth to be filled by the gifted, or by those specially called, through the gifted, by the Spirit of God" (Oliphant). Irving himself on April the 5th, 1833, was re-ordained as "angel over the Church in Newman Street." Irving died on December the 8th, 1834. Writing in 1836, Robert Baxter (*Irvingism*) describes the chapel and its arrangements. "The room adopted for their meetings was fitted up in the usual style of pews and galleries, as in a church; instead of a pulpit, however, there was constructed at the upper end of the church a raised platform, capable of containing perhaps fifty persons. In the ascent to this platform are steps, on the front of the platform are seven seats; the middle seat is that of the angel; the three on each side of the angel are elders. Below them on the steps, and in a parallel line, are seven other seats belonging to the prophets, the middle seat being allotted to Mr. Taplin as the chief of the prophets. Still lower in a parallel line are seven other seats appropriated to the deacons, the middle seat being occupied by the chief deacon. This threefold cord of a sevenfold ministry was adopted under direction of the utterance. The angel ordered the service, and the preaching and expounding was generally by the elders in order, the prophets speaking as utterance came upon them." In 1832 the followers of Irving had taken the title of the "Holy Catholic Apostolic Church." In July 1835 there were twelve apostles, who ordained angels and elders. The ritual of the Church developed considerably after this. In 1854 a fine chapel was opened in Gordon Square, London. It possesses a good liturgy. The ministry now comprises angels, elders, prophets, evangelists, and pastors, and is supported by tithes. See Robert Baxter, *Irvingism, its Rise, Progress, and Present State*, 1836; Mrs. Oliphant, *The Life of Edward Irving*, 1862; J. H. Blunt; the *D.N.B.*

ISAIAH, BOOK OF. The book of the prophet Isaiah is one of the most remarkable products of Hebrew prophetic genius found in the Old Testament. The prophet himself describes in the sixth chapter of the book named after him the powerful religious experience that made him a prophet. The event took place about the year 740 B.C., the year in which "the startling news came of the death of the great King Uzziah who for nearly half a century had brought to Judah strength and increasing prestige" (C. F. Kent). The prophet went up to the temple at Jerusalem to worship, and there in a wonderful vision felt the presence of Jehovah and realized that he had received a divine call. No doubt he was ready for the call; but when it came it did so with all the force of a new inspiration and revelation. "When Isaiah went forth from the temple, the world was richer because a new prophet had entered upon his life-work" (C. F. Kent). So great was the prophet's fame that other authors wrote afterwards in his name. Chapters xl.-lxvi., for instance, of the present book of Isaiah were clearly not by the prophet whose call is described in chap. vi. This portion of the book is now commonly described as II. Isaiah or Deutero-Isaiah. Kent thinks that the original prophecies of Isaiah fall naturally into eight or nine divisions. "The general introduction, chapter 1, is followed by a group of social sermons, 2-5, to which also belongs 9^{8}-10^{4}. These represent the first period of Isaiah's activity, from 740-735 B.C. The second stage of Isaiah's work, which was in connection with the crisis of 734 B.C., is recorded in 7 and 8. These chapters are introduced by an account of the prophet's call, in 6, and are supplemented by the messianic prophecies in 9^{1-7}, 11, 12. The next group contains a collection of foreign prophecies, 13-23, of various dates. Some of these are from Isaiah, but the majority are, apparently, from otherwise unknown later prophets. Chapters 24-27 are a very late apocalypse, describing Jehovah's final judgment of the world. The original sermons in 28-31 were delivered in connection with the crisis of 701 B.C.

Chapters 34, 35 contain another post-exilic apocalypse. The historical chapters, xxxvi., xxxvii., tell of Isaiah's work in the fourth and last great period of his activity, while 38 and 39 record certain events preceding the invasion of Sennacherib in 701 B.C." A number of critics distinguish a Trito-Isaiah as well as a Deutero-Isaiah. To Trito-Isaiah are assigned chapters lvi.-lxvi., and they are supposed to have been written about 450 B.C. The outlook and environment seem to be quite different from those of Deutero-Isaiah. The surroundings are not Babylonian, but Palestinian. See T. K. Cheyne, *Intr. to Book of Isaiah*, 1895; G. A. Smith, *The Book of Isaiah*, 1899; B. Duhm, *Das Buch Jesaia*, 2nd ed., 1902; K. Marti, *Das Buch Jesaia*, 1900; J. Skinner, *Isaiah*, in the "Cambridge Bible"; O. C. Whitehouse, *Isaiah*, in the "Century Bible"; G. H. Box, *The Book of Isaiah*, 1908; C. Cornill, *Intr.;* G. H. Box, *Intr.;* O. C. Whitehouse; C. F. Kent, *The Sermons, Epistles, and Apocalypses of Israel's Prophets*, 1910.

ISHTAR. A Babylonian deity. The goddess Ishtar, "the brilliant goddess," is described as the kind mother. But she came to be regarded as the goddess of war. It is possible that in this two-fold character she represents two aspects of Venus (*q.v.*), morning and evening star. She appears also as Anunit (*q.v.*) and Nanâ (*q.v.*). In the Assyrian pantheon one of her titles is "the queen of Kidmuru." She has become more than ever a goddess of war, and as such is placed by the side of Ashur (*q.v.*), but not as his consort. She is described as "mighty over the Anunnaki." She is the lady, Belit, of battle. In the Gilgamesh Epic (*q.v.*) Ishtar seeks the love of the hero Gilgamesh. Gilgamesh not only rejects her (here a goddess of love), but even upraids her for cruelty. Her love turns to hate. Anu (*q.v.*), the god of heaven, creates for her a divine bull, which is to destroy Gilgamesh. But, with the help of his friend Eabani, he kills it. Eabani even throws the carcase into Ishtar's face. Ishtar is represented elsewhere as having in her train the Kizrêti, Ukhâti, and Kharimâti. These represent three classes of harlots, who were devoted to her worship, as the goddess of fertility. In the story of the deluge (see DELUGE-STORY, BABYLONIAN), where even the gods are represented as trembling at the fury of the storm, Ishtar groans like a woman in travail. At Nippur clay figurines of Ishtar have been found which in one way or another represent her as the goddess of fertility. But Ishtar absorbed the qualities of all the other goddesses. See Morris Jastrow, *Rel.*

ISHUM. A Babylonian deity. Ishum is one of the gods mentioned before the time of Hammurapi. He was a solar deity. He appears as the messenger of Nusku (*q.v.*) and as the attendant of Dibbarra. It is he who recounts the deeds of Dibbarra (see DIBBARRA EPIC). He is himself a warrior and wages war as an agent of Dibbarra. See Morris Jastrow, *Rel.*

ISIS. An Egyptian deity. The goddess Isis was sister and wife of Osiris (*q.v.*), sister of Set (*q.v.*) and Nephthys (*q.v.*), and mother of Horus (*q.v.*). In the Osiris myth (*q.v.*) Isis is the devoted wife who watched over her husband and tried to protect him against the plots of his enemy Set. "She was his safeguard and warded off enemies, for she was subtle, with an excellent tongue, her word did not fail, and she was admirable in command." When at length Set succeeded and caused the dead body of Osiris to disappear, Isis sought it without wearying. When she found it, Anubis (*q.v.*), commissioned by the god Ra (*q.v.*), put the members together, and Isis breathed into the body new life for a second, but not earthly, existence. After a time Isis gave birth to a son Horus (*q.v.*). When Horus grew up he fought against Set and prevailed. In the Greek period Isis assumed a compound form among the people and became Isis-Hathor-Aphrodite. In Alexandria she became patroness of mariners. This character was, no doubt, as J. G. Frazer suggests, assigned to her by the sea-faring Greeks. Frazer also thinks that the epithet of *Stella Maris* as applied to the Virgin Mary as the guardian of tempest-tossed sailors was suggested by the similar worship of Isis. The original significance of the goddess Isis is difficult to determine. Frazer gives reasons for thinking that Osiris was the corn-god and Isis the corn-goddess. She is spoken of in inscriptions as "creatress of the green crop" and "mistress of bread." The Greeks identified her with Demeter, the Romans with Ceres. In later times the conception of Isis was refined and spiritualized. She became the model of a tender mother and true wife. She resembles the Madonna. "Indeed her stately ritual, with its shaven and tonsured priests, its matins and vespers, its tinkling music, its baptism and aspersions of holy water, its solemn processions, its jewelled images of the Mother of God, presented many points of similarity to the pomps and ceremonies of Catholicism" (Frazer). The figure of Isis and the infant Horus has sometimes been mistaken for that of the Madonna and child. The animal sacred to Isis was the cow. Hence she is represented as wearing horns, or even as having the head of a cow. See A. Wiedemann; J. G. Frazer, *Adonis, Attis, Osiris*, 1906; Adolf Erman, *Handbook;* Naville, *The Old Egyptian Faith*, 1909; Reinach, *O.*

ISLAM. The Arabic word *'Islâm* means "the act of resignation or submission." Muhammad himself gave this name to his religion. "The true religion with God is Islam," he says (*Qur'ân* iii. 17). Again, "whoso desireth any other religion than Islam, that religion shall never be accepted from him, and in the next world he shall be among the lost" (*ibid.* iii. 79). Muhammad is also represented as saying, "This day have I perfected your religion for you, and it is My pleasure that Islâm be your religion" (*ibid.* v. 5). The sources for the religion, called "the traditional proofs," are the *Qur'ân* (KORAN), the *Sunna* (*q.v.*), the *Ijmâ'* (*q.v.*), and the *Qiâs*. These are the foundations for the doctrines of the religion. See F. A. Klein.

ISMA'ILIYEH. A branch of the Muhammadan Shi'ah sect. Whereas the Shi'ahs find the true Imâm in Mûsâ al-Qâsim, the second son of Ja'afar as-Sâdiq, the Isma'iliyeh trace the succession from his eldest son, Ismâ'îl. The sect was founded in Persia in the middle of the eighth century. In the ninth century new life was infused into it by the zeal and the missionary activity of 'Abdu-llâh ibn Maymun. Missionaries went out in all directions. "They captivated the ignorant multitude by the performance of marvels that were taken for miracles and by mysterious utterances that excited their curiosity. To the devout they appeared as models of virtue and religious zeal: to the mystics they revealed the hidden meaning of popular teachings and initiated them into various grades of occultism according to their capacity. Taking advantage of the eager looking-forward to a deliverer that was common to so many faiths of the time, they declared to the Musalmans the approaching advent of the Imâm Mahdî, to the Jews that of the Messiah, and to the Christians that of the Comforter, but taught that the aspirations of each could alone be realised in the coming of 'Ali as the great deliverer" (T. W. Arnold). In these and other ways the Isma'iliyeh were able to unite together a very large number of persons of different faiths. According to F. J. Bliss, there is a large body of Isma'iliyeh in Syria at the present time, though the majority of the members are secret adherents. They send yearly tribute to a Sultan

Mohammed Shah in Bombay, who claims to be descended from the Old Man of the Mountain. Lord of the Assassins. They believe him to be an incarnation of the Deity. They believe also that God dwells in a virgin who lives on the edge of the Syrian desert. "This girl is called the ro'dhah, which may be translated a greensward or pleasaunce. As long as she remains a virgin she is regarded as sacred, and the Isma'ilians wear bits of her clothing or hair from her person in their turbans. But should she marry—and she may do so honourably—search is made for a successor, who must be a girl born on a certain day in the year, and who should conform to certain characteristics regarding her height and the colour of her hair and eyes" (F. J. Bliss). A government official, who surprised the Isma'iliyeh at a service of adoration of the ro'dhah, found her seated in a white robe on a high chair and wearing on her head a wreath of fresh flowers. The worshippers knelt before her and chanted sacred songs. F. J. Bliss thinks that the cult of the ro'dhah is an ancient form of nature-worship which was retained when the local inhabitants accepted the strange ideas of the Isma'iliyeh. "In the resultant synthesis both sets of ideas may have undergone alteration. In its present form this nature-worship appears to be symbolic rather than sensual. There is evidence that woman is venerated as the symbol of the earth-mother." The cults of the Isma'iliyeh, the Druses, and the Nuseiriyeh are secret. In all of them initiation plays an important part. See T. P. Hughes; T. W. Arnold; F. J. Bliss.

ITALAPAS. One of the principal deities in the mythology of the Chinook Indians. He assisted Ikanam in the creation of men, and then instructed them.

ITH. In Irish mythology Ith figures as one of the deities in the world of the dead.

ITZAMATUL. A tribal deity, a god of healing, in the religion of the Mayan Indians. He was known also as Kabul.

ITZAMNA. A deity worshipped by the Maya Indians in Yucatan. He was reputed to be the inventor of letters, and resembles the Mexican god Tonacatecutli.

IXCHEBELYAX. A tribal deity, goddess of embroidery and art, in the religion of the Mayan Indians. She resembles the Mexican deity Xochiquetzal.

IXCHEL. A tribal deity, goddess of child-birth, in the religion of the Mayan Indians.

IXTAB. A deity in the religion of the Mayan Indians. She was the goddess who received the souls of those who hanged themselves.

IXTLILTON. A Mexican deity, medical god of children. A sacrifice was offered to him when a child first began to speak. Children who were afflicted with any malady were given to drink "black water" or *tlilatl*, which was kept in little jars in the temple of the god.

IZANAGI. In Shintōism (*q.v.*), the ancient religion of Japan, Izanagi figures as the Creator. He is the Father of all the heroes and demi-gods of Japanese mythology and history, who are the chief objects of worship in Shintōism. One of the principal symbols of this religion is a mirror. A Japanese legend (quoted by G. A. Cobbold) preserves a beautiful tradition concerning this mirror. "When the time was come that Izanagi and his consort should return together to the celestial regions, he called his children together, bidding them dry their tears, and listen attentively to his last wishes. He then committed to them a disc of polished silver, bidding them each morning place themselves on their knees before it, and there see reflected on their countenances the impress of any evil passions deliberately indulged; and again each night carefully to examine themselves, that their last thoughts might be after the happiness of that higher world whither their parents had preceded them." Izanagi gave birth to Ama-terasu, the sun-goddess, from whom again was descended Jimmu Tenno, who is supposed to have been the first human sovereign of Japan. See G. A. Cobbold, *Rel.*

IZAZALVOH. A tribal deity, goddess of weaving, in the religion of the Mayan Indians.

IZDUBAR. This, according to the original decipherment, was the name of the hero of the great national epic of the Babylonians. The name is now read as Gilgamesh. See GILGAMESH EPIC.

J

JABARIYYA. The name of an Arabian sect, which differs from the Sunnis on the question of predestination. The name is derived from a root meaning "to compel." The Jabariyya think that God's unalterable decree compels men to act as they do. "Man, according to their view, is forced to act as he does like a feather in the air which the wind moves about at will, and he has neither power, nor will, nor choice any more than an inanimate agent, and therefore no acquisition." See F. A. Klein.

JACOBINS. A name by which the Dominicans (*q.v.*) became known in France. They were so called from the house of St. Jacob, in which a monastery was founded.

JAGANNĀTH. Lord of the world, one of the names of the Hindu god Vishnu.

JAINISM. The Jains are the followers of the religious reformer Jina. Jina, however, like Buddha, is not a name but a title. The real founder of Jainism would seem to have been Mahāvīra Jñātriputra. Both Jainism and Buddhism may be said to represent revolts against Brahmanism. Of the two systems, Jainism appears to have had the start of Buddhism; and in any case it may be regarded as a religion intermediate between Brahmanism and Buddhism. Another name for the Jains is Nirgranthas. The Nigranthas claimed Nātaputta as their founder. It would seem, therefore, either that Nātaputta was one who prepared the way for Mahāvīra, or that he was identical with Mahāvīra. In course of time the Jains split up into two main bodies, the Śvetāmbaras, "white-attire men," and the Digambaras, "sky-attire men," that is to say, naked devotees. The Digambaras insist that ascetics must be naked. The Jains differ from the Buddhists in this, among other things, that they attach the greatest importance to asceticism. The term Jina means "conqueror," and Mahāvīra held that the passions must be conquered by mortification of the flesh. The Digambaras argued that where there is no sin there can be no shame. Their nakedness implied the conquest of sin. The Śvetāmbaras arose in protest against this type of Jainism. They object even to nude images of the twenty-four Jinas or chiefs venerated by the Jains. They differ further from the Digambaras in admitting women into their order of ascetics, and in having sacred books of their own. The Jains in general practically worship their chiefs or Jinas as gods. They also worship the female energy. They do not believe in an All-Spirit, but they believe in individual souls or spirits existing in stones, plants, drops of water, particles of fire, etc. They cherish three moral gems or jewels, Right-knowledge, Right-intuition, and Right-conduct. Their five principles of Right-conduct are: "(1) Non-injury, (2) kindness and speaking what is true (in so far as the truth is pleasant to the hearer), (3) honourable conduct, typified by 'not stealing,' (4) chastity in word, thought, and deed, (5) renunciation of earthly interests" (Hopkins). The first principle is followed to an extravagant extent, since, among other precautions against killing living creatures they "often wear muslin before their mouths to catch minute insects" (Monier-Williams). It is a rule with the Jains that their hair, instead of being cut off, must be plucked out. Hence they have been called "hair-pluckers." The Jains believe in re-incarnation on earth. In this way salvation is attained by degrees. After twelve years of strict asceticism the Jain may commit suicide. The Jains do not erect Stūpas or Dāgobas to hold relics. See Monier-Williams, *Buddhism*, 1890; E. W. Hopkins; J. A. Dubois and H. K. Beauchamp.

JALIA. One of the deities worshipped by the Savaras (also known as Sawaras or Saoras), an important hill-tribe in Southern India. The deity, who is very malevolent, appears to be regarded in some places as male and in others as female.

JAMES, THE EPISTLE OF. The Epistle of James is one of a small group of New Testament writings which since the end of the second century have been known as "Catholic Epistles," because they are addressed to Christians in general. Eusebius (c. 325 A.D.) described it as a disputed book, that is to say, as a book not universally accepted by the Church. In the fourth century, however, it was definitely recognised as canonical (Council of Laodicea, 364 A.D.; Council of Carthage, 397 A.D.). The epistle is very Hebraic in tone and language, and it has been widely held that the James whose name it bears was "James, the Lord's brother" (Galatians i. 19), who became president of the Church at Jerusalem. The opening words, "James, a servant of God and of the Lord Jesus Christ, to the twelve tribes which are of the Dispersion, greeting," have been supposed to favour this view. But these words may well be editorial. The fact is that the Epistle of James is a puzzling writing. It may either be very early or rather late. It was evidently written by a Jew for Jews. There is little, if anything, in it that is distinctively Christian, and it is not referred to by Christian writers before the time of Origen. One is inclined to think, with Spitta, that it is a pre-Christian Jewish writing which was afterwards adapted to Christian use. Von Soden also holds that, at any rate parts of the epistle are of Jewish origin. New theories have been propounded by G. Currie Martin and J. H. Moulton. Currie Martin's theory was first explained in *The Expositor*. "The idea, briefly expressed, is that James, the brother of the Lord, may have made a collection of sayings otherwise not preserved, and have made these the basis of short homilies or reflections, which are collected together in this present work. It may not have been designed at all as a letter in the first instance, but after the death of James some of his disciples may have realised the value of such a record, and brought them all together in his name, and sent them out with his authority" (*Books of the N.T.*, 1909). The theory of J. H. Moulton is explained and commended by Prof. A. S. Peake. J. H. Moulton thinks that the epistle, which contains a number of sayings of Jesus not recorded elsewhere, was addressed not to Christians but to Jews. "This has the very great advantage that it explains why a Christian writing should be so destitute of avowedly Christian elements. The writer would not damage his appeal by specific references to Christ, above all to the scandal of His cross. But he included many sayings of Jesus in the hope that their own intrinsic beauty and worth would commend them to the readers and prepare them for a truer estimate of the crucified Nazarene whom they hated and despised. This involves that, as other scholars have suggested, the references to Christ were not a part of the original composition." See the Commentaries by J. B. Mayor and R. J. Knowling; the *Encycl. Bibl.*; J. A. M'Clymont; G. Currie Martin; Arthur S. Peake, *Intr.*; J. Moffatt, *Intr.*

JANĀRDAN. Protector of the people, one of the names of the Hindu god Vishnu.

JANGAMS. The Jangams or Jangamas are a Sivite order of wandering religious mendicants in India. Worshipping as their one and only deity Siva or Mahādeo, they act as priests or *gurus* to the Sivite sect of Lingāyats. Their great festival is the Shivrātri (Siva's night). The Jangams "reject the poems in honour of Vishnu, Rāma, and Krishna, such as the Bhāgavad Gita and Rāmāyana; they also deny the authority of Brāhmans, the efficacy of pilgrimage and self-mortification, and the restrictions of caste; while they revere principally the Vedas and the teaching of the great Sivite reformer Shankar Achārya" (R. V. Russell). They wear and worship the *lingam*, the phallic sign of Siva, and are vegetarians.

JĀNKI. A Hindu goddess, apparently another name for Sita, the wife of Rāma.

JANSENISTS. The Jansenists were a school rather than a sect. They were so named after Cornelius Jansen or Jansenius (1585-1638). The theological question to which they attached special importance was that of Grace. In 1588 L. Molina (1535-1600), a Spanish Jesuit, published a work "On the Agreement of Free-Will with Grace and Predestination." His views have been summarized as follows: "(1) A reason or ground of God's predestination is to be found in man's right use of his free will. (2) That the *grace* which God bestows to enable men to persevere in religion may become the *gift* of perseverance, it is necessary that they be foreseen as consenting and co-operating with the Divine assistance offered them, which is a thing within their power. (3) There is a mediate prescience, which is neither the free nor the natural knowledge of God, and by which he knows future contingent events before he forms his decree. (4) Predestination may be considered as either general (relating to whole classes of persons) or particular (relating to individual persons). In general predestination there is no reason or ground of it beyond the mere good pleasure of God, or none on the part of the persons predestinated; but in particular predestination (or that of individuals) there is a cause or ground of it in the foreseen good use of free-will" (Blunt, p. 330). The Dominicans (Thomists) regarded these views as Semi-Pelagian. The Jesuits denied that they were such, and maintained that they might be held. This led to hot disputes. In 1597 Pope Clement VIII. instituted Congregations de Auxiliis (concerning the helps, *i.e.*, of grace) to investigate the views of Molina. These held a number of sessions, which were continued under Pope Paul V. In 1607 the College of Cardinals met and deliberated, with the final result that "the theologians of each party were allowed to hold and teach their respective opinions, provided they did not stigmatise their opponents with theological censures" (Addis and Arnold). Cornelius Jansen became in 1617 Professor at Louvain, and in 1635 Bishop of Yprès. He was greatly interested in the study of St. Augustine, and prepared a great work "Augustinus." Before he could publish it, he died (1638). When it was published (1640), the Jesuits succeeded in getting it suppressed; and on its reappearance it was condemned by the Inquisition (1641) and by Pope Urban VIII (1642). It found a vigorous defender in Antoine Arnauld (1612-1694), Doctor of the Sorbonne. In 1649, however, Nicolas Cornet, a Jesuit father, submitted to the Sorbonne five propositions which he professed to have drawn from the "Augustinus." The Parliament, however, took the matter out of the hands of the Sorbonne, and referred it to an assembly of the clergy. In 1653 Pope Innocent X. condemned the propositions in a Bull "Cum occasione." The five propositions were as follows: I. "Some precepts of God are impossible to just men, wishing and striving (to obey them), according to the strength which they then have; also they lack grace which would make them possible." II. "Resistance is never made in the state of fallen nature to interior grace." III. "For merit and demerit in the state of fallen nature, there is not required in man freedom from necessity, but freedom from compulsion is sufficient." IV. "The Semi-Pelagians admitted the necessity of prevenient interior grace for single actions, even for the beginning of faith; but they were heretical in holding that grace to be of such a kind that the human will could resist or yield to it." V. "It is Semi-Pelagian to say that Christ did shed His blood for all men together." Jansen's friend, Jean du Verger de Hauranne, who in 1620 became the Abbé de St. Cyran, had founded a Jansenist Society called the Port Royal Society. Its original members included Antoine Arnauld, Le Maître, De Sericourt, and De Saci. Others who became members of the Society were: Nicole, Fontaine, and Blaise Pascal (1623-1662). In 1638 the Port Royal Society removed from Paris to the monastery of Port Royal des Champs near Versailles. In 1643, when St. Cyran died, Antoine Arnauld became leader of the Port Royalists, who had removed in the meantime to a farm called Les Granges in order to make room for a body of nuns from Port Royal de Paris (Marie Angélique Arnauld's Sisters). When Jansen's five propositions were condemned by the Pope, Arnauld was expected to approve of their condemnation. But Arnauld was not prepared to admit that the propositions could be found in the book of Cornelius Jansen. Moreover, he drew a distinction between things *de facto* and *de jure*. Whatever the tendency of Jansen's views *de jure* might be, the terms of the propositions *de facto* were not his. "The dictinction was pressed home, and while infallibility was allowed to the Court of Rome in synod assembled 'de jure' in matters of doctrine its complete fallibility was shewn from several historical instances, in which it was seen that the Holy See had often erred in matters of fact" (J. H. Blunt). The Jansenists could agree to the condemnation of the propositions regarded from the *de jure* point of view. Arnauld's reasoning was condemned by Pope Innocent X. (1654). It was condemned also by the Sorbonne, and Arnauld was driven from the ranks of its Doctors (1656). The next important step in the controversy was the publication by Blaise Pascal of his "Provincial Letters" (1656). These attacked not only the doctrines, but also the morals of the Jesuits. Pascal was a satirist, and satirists always exaggerate. But the letters contained a great deal of truth, and at the time were of great service to the Jansenists. "No one who has read the 'Provincial Letters' is likely to lose the impression which they make; it may be said without exaggeration that they touch every chord of the human heart, and the sudden transitions from logic and wit to sublime and pathetic eloquence produce an effect which can neither be resisted or effaced" (*Cath. Dict.*). In 1665 Pope Alexander VII. demanded submission to the condemnation *de facto*. The Bishops of Alet, Angers, Beauvais, and Pamiers would only silently submit on the question *de facto*. In 1669 the new Pope, Clement IX., restored them to the papal favour, which they had lost. This was called "the peace of Clement." Antoine Arnauld was succeeded by Pasquier Quesnel (1634-1719), of the Oratory of Cardinal Bérulle. In 1671 he published a work, "Moral Reflexions on the Gospels" (enlarged later). He was afterwards banished to Orleans, and finally sought refuge in Brussels. In 1708 Quesnel's book was condemned by the Pope. In 1710 the Port Royalists of France were suppressed or exterminated. In 1713 the papal bull "Unigenitus" condemned one hundred and one propositions drawn from Quesnel's book. But the bull raised a constitutional question. Those who accepted it formed a party called the Constitutionists or Acceptants. Those who rejected it constituted another party called the Anticonstitutionists, Appellants (because they wished to appeal to a general Council), or Recusants. The Bull "Pastoralis Officii" of Clement XI. excommunicated all who wished to refer the matter to a general Council. In 1727 a Jansenist deacon, François de Paris, died, and miracles are supposed to have taken place at his tomb in the cemetery of St. Médard. People made pilgrimages to the tomb and fell into ecstasies and convulsions. On this account the Jansenists were called Convulsionnaires or Convulsionaries, and from this time Jansenism in France began to decay. The Jansenist Church of Holland has maintained itself down to the present time. It is an independent Roman Catholic Church, and claims to be Old Roman or Old Catholic. When the Old Catholics (*q.v.*) were in need of an episcopal successor of the apostles to consecrate Prof. J. H. Reinkens (1821-1896) as their bishop, they applied to the Jansenist Church of Holland. See J. H. Blunt; *Prot. Dict.*; *Cath. Dict.*; Brockhaus.

JAR-BURIAL. In early Egypt, Babylonia, Assyria, and Palestine it was the custom sometimes to bury children in jars. In Palestine the children were sometimes foundation-sacrifices; but at other times they were ordinary human sacrifices. At Taanach twenty jar-buried infants were found near a rock altar. Their proximity to the altar suggests that the infants in this case were sacrificed in the ordinary way. See P. S. P. Handcock.

JASONDHIS. A small caste in India, a branch of the Bhāts. They sang the *jas* or hymns in praise of the chiefs at the Gond and Marātha festivals. Some of them, known also as Karohla, now go about as religious mendicants, singing the praises of Devi. "They carry an image of the goddess suspended by a chain round the neck and ask for gifts of *tilli* (sesamum) or other vegetable oil, which they pour over their heads and over the image. Their clothes and bodies are consequently always saturated with this oil. They also have a little cup of vermilion, which they smear on the goddess and on their own bodies after receiving an offering" (R. V. Russell and R. B. Hira Lāl).

JĀTAKA. A Buddhist sacred book, a book of legends, included in the collection appended to the second division of the Canon. See CANON, BUDDHIST.

JAWARAS. The Jawaras, sown by the Hindus, correspond to the gardens of Adonis. The sowings takes place before the sowing of the spring crop of wheat and other grains, at the beginning of the harvest of the crop, and sometimes also a third time during the rains. The wheat sown before the sowing of the spring crop is supposed to give a forecast of the success of the latter.

JEBAWI'YEH. Another name for the Sa'adi'yeh (*q.v.*), an order of Dervishes.

JEHOVAH. The Hebrew divine name Y-h-v-h has long been pronounced by Christians "Jehovah." Modern scholars, however, think that the word should be pronounced Jahveh or Yahveh (or Yahweh). See TETRAGRAMMATON, and YAHWEH.

JEHOVIST. More correctly Jahvist or Yahwist (see JEHOVAH). The name has been given to one (or more) of the writers of the narratives of which the Hexateuch is composed. The writer was so called because his work was characterised by the use of the divine name Jehovah (more correctly Jahveh or Yahweh) instead of Elohim. Critics now discriminate between a First Jehovist, a second Jehovist, and a Third Jehovist.

JEREMIAH, BOOK OF. The book of the prophet Jeremiah itself gives an account of the origin of the work. This is contained in chapter xxxvi. In the fourth year of Jehoiakim, son of Josiah, king of Judah (604 B.C.), Jeremiah, after he had prophesied orally for twenty-three years, was commissioned by Jehovah to write out all the oracles which had been revealed to him. The prophet therefore sought the help of Baruch, who wrote down the book at his dictation. The next year Baruch read the roll in the Temple in the hearing of a great assembly of people on the occasion of a fast. The roll was afterwards read before the princes. The king then commanded that it should be brought to him and read aloud. When three or four double columns had been read, the king threw the roll into the fire. Thereupon Jehovah commissioned the prophet to take another roll and write in it all the words that were in the first roll. This was done. The words of the original roll were written out again, "and there were also added to them many other similar words." As Cornill says, "it follows from this that we possess no authentic reports from the first half-period of Jeremiah's active ministry, but only a *résumé* given by himself, in which he had striven to recapitulate its fundamental thoughts and ideas in as brief and impressive a way as possible." And the original document cannot have been very voluminous, for it was read through twice in a single day. The earliest sections in the Book of Jeremiah would seem to be: chapters i., ii.-vi., vii.-x., xi.-xii. 6, xxv., xviii. These may be prior to the fourth year of Jehoiachim. But even here there are passages which cannot be due to the prophet himself. "Ch. iii. 6-18 breaks the connexion between iii. 5 and 19; ix. 22-x. 16, which itself consists of three discourses, dissevers the immediately continuous verses ix. 21 and x. 17 from each other; xii. 4 stands in an altogether unsuitable and impossible place" (Cornill). The original roll was utilised in the composition of the existing Book of Jeremiah, but it has not been preserved in its original form. In many ways the Book of Jeremiah has undergone considerable reduction. An example of this may be found in chapter iv. verses 5-31. The foe referred to in this prophecy, the "foe from the North," was probably the Scythians. We learn from Herodotus (i. 105-8) that about 625 B.C. the Scythians overran Western Asia, and advanced through Palestine as far as Ashkelon, with the intention of invading Egypt. By the time the prophecy was committed to writing, however, about 604 B.C., the Chaldaeans had become dangerous, and were beginning to march from the North. It has been suggested that the prophecy was adapted or modified in parts to meet the new situation. The whole prophecy extends to chapter vi. vs. 30; and Driver points out, as an instance of adaptation, that the "lion" and "destroyer of nations" in chapter vi. 7 are terms that apply better to an individual leader like Nebuchadnezzar than to a horde. The book of Jeremiah is remarkable, regarded as a prophetical work, for the amount of biographical material that it contains. This material is due to an editor, no doubt to Baruch. It is to be found in chapters xix.-xx. 6, xxvi.-xxix., xxxiv., and xxxvi.-xlv. Chapters xlvi.-li. contain a number of oracles uttered against foreign countries. It has been contended that none of these oracles contains words actually spoken by Jeremiah. This is an extreme position. Some of them no doubt are not Jeremian. But as regards others, as Cornill says, "on *a priori* grounds we should expect to find discourses against the heathen in the Book of Jeremiah, for no other prophet had the feeling from the outset that his commission included his having been sent to the nations outside Israel as well, to the same degree as Jeremiah (i. 5, 10; xxxvi. 2; xviii. 9 ff.; cp. also xxvii. 2 ff.); and if the announcement in xxv. 15-24 is certainly authentic, this inclines us to take a favourable view of its actual execution." The Septuagint exhibits a shorter form of text than the Hebrew of the Book of Jeremiah. Whitehouse thinks the Septuagint version is based on a shorter and earlier edition of the collected prophecies of Jeremiah. Cornill thinks "a connexion of the words of Jeremiah with the Baruch-narratives must have been effected some considerable time before the LXX." See S. R. Driver, *The Book of the Prophet Jeremiah*, 1906; C. Cornill, *Intr.*; G. H. Box; O. C. Whitehouse; A. S. Peake, *Jeremiah*, in the "Century Bible," 1910; C. F. Kent, *The Sermons, Epistles and Apocalypses of Israel's Prophets*, 1910.

JERUSALEM FRIENDS. A religious community founded in 1848 at Kirschenhardthof, near Marbach, in Württemberg by Christian Hoffmann. Their idea was to establish the Kingdom of God, and this kingdom was to be in Palestine. Consequently, in the year 1868 they began to send out colonists to the Holy Land. Other names for them are the Temple Society, the Temple Union, the German Temple, and the Hoffmannites. See C. Hoffmann, *Mein Weg nach Jerusalem*, 1881-1884; Brockhaus.

JESUATS. A congregation founded by St. John Colombini, a high official of Sienna. Colombini, becoming convinced that he ought to devote his life to the service of God, converted his house into a hospital and lived a life of austerity. Urban V. confirmed the order in 1367. Alexander VI. required the Jesuats to add to their title the words "of St. Jerome." Paul V. allowed them to receive holy orders. In course of time they were called "Aquavita Fathers," because many of them practiced distillation and pharmacy and made alcoholic liquor. See *Cath. Dict.*

JESUITS. The Roman Catholic order known as the Jesuits or the Society of Jesu (Societas Jesu) was founded by Ignatius of Loyola (1491-1556), after whom the Jesuits are called sometimes Ignatians. Ignatius was driven from the Spanish universities of Alcala and Salamanca because he was thought to have an undesirable influence on the students, and went to the University of Paris, where he gained the sympathy of Francis Xavier, James Laynez, Alphonsus Salmeron, Nicholas Bobadilla, Simon Rodriguez, and Peter Faber. These companions, after practising the "Spiritual Exercises" of Ignatius, in 1534 took with him a solemn vow. According to Alban Butler (as quoted in the *Cath. Dict.*), the tenor of it was "to renounce the world, to go to preach the gospel in Palestine, or, if they could not go thither within a year after they had finished their studies, to offer themselves to his Holiness to be employed in the service of God in what manner he should judge best." Before long there were added to the society Claude de Jay of Savoy, Codure of Dauphiné, and Pasquier Brouet of Picardy. All the members described themselves as of the Company of Jesus. Ignatius decided to place his order under "a general whom all, by their vow, should be bound to obey, who should be perpetual, and his authority absolute, subject entirely to the Pope, but not liable to be restrained by chapters" (Albion Butler, *l.c.*). On Sept. 27, 1540, Pope Paul III. confirmed the order by the bull "Regimini militantis ecclesiæ," and in April 1541 Ignatius became its first general. The membership of the Society was, and is, divided into four grades: (1) Novices, (2) Scholastics, (3) Coadjutors, and (4) Professed. "Novices are admitted only after a minute and searching examination of their character and social circumstances. The novitiate lasts for two years, which are spent in houses established for the special purpose. Time is there regulated from hour to hour. Reading, meditation, prayer, and devotional exercises, alternate with nursing in the hospitals, travels as beggars, menial services, and ascetic practices. A course of training is gone through which enables the novice to completely break his individual will, and prepares him to be a fit instrument for the will of the society. The term of probation ended, the novice takes the three monastic vows of poverty, chastity, and obedience, and enters one of the colleges of the society as a scholastic. There he studies grammar, rhetoric, and literature for two years, and philosophy, physics, and mathematics for three; teaches these subjects through all the classes of the college for five or six years; studies theology for five or six years, and finally completes his education by going through another novitiate of spiritual exercises. . . . After the second novitiate, the scholastic is ordained a priest, and becomes an active member of the society, either as coadjutor or professed, adding to the three common monastic vows, in the former case, that of zealous devotion to the education of the young, in the latter, that of undertaking any task which the Pope might see fit to confide to him" (Schaff-Herzog). According to the *Catholic Dictionary*, the professed of the four vows (professi quatuor votorum) now form only a small class. In any case, the Jesuit course of training is a very long and thorough one, and it is not surprising that it has produced great scholars and men of considerable administrative power. Their fault has been an over-zealous, and, in the view of their opponents, unscrupulous devotion to their cause. They are supposed to act, and to have acted, very largely on the principle that the end justifies the means. They have been charged with mixing themselves up in all sorts of political plots and intrigues. Nor can it be denied that the charge is a lawful one But unfortunately there have been times when plots and intrigues have been the order of the day. To succeed in one's efforts and to promote one's cause, good or bad, meant to meet one intrigue with another, one plot with another plot. When a plot has failed, the promoters of it have represented themselves to be the most innocent of men, and their opponents, whose plot has succeeded, the most execrable of monsters. This is not said by way of excusing the Jesuits, but as a protest against the many exaggerated statements made by their opponents. See Schaff-Herzog; the *Prot. Dict.*, 1904; the *Cath. Dict.*; Brockhaus.

JEWEL-LOTUS FORMULA. The "Jewel-lotus" formula is a formula or prayer used by the Tibetan Buddhists. It consists of six syllables, and is supposed to have been composed by the tutelary deity of Tibet, the Bodhisattva known as Avalokiteśvara or Padmapāṇi. The prayer runs: "Om! the Jewel in the Lotus! Hūm!" The first and last words are not real Sanskrit words, but ejaculations having some mystic meaning. There are only two real Sanskrit words in the formula. The prayer seems to have an occult meaning. Monier-Williams says that no other prayer in any part of the world is repeated so often. "Every Tibetan believes it to be a panacea for all evil, a compendium of all knowledge, a treasury of all wisdom, a summary of all religion." The word Om seems to have been borrowed from the Hindus. Naturally good use was made of the Jewel-Lotus formula in prayer-wheels or prayer-cylinders (see PRAYER-CYLINDER). See Monier-Williams, *Buddhism*, 1890; H. Hackmann.

JEZREELITES. The followers of James Jershom Jezreel, a name assumed by James White (1840-1885). The sect was also called "The New and Latter House of Israel" (*q.v.*).

JHAGRA KHAND. A Hindu deity, the two-edged sword, worshipped by the Kawars, a primitive tribe living in the hills of the Chhattisgarh Districts north of the Mahānadi in India.

JHULĀN DEVI. A deity worshipped by the Gonds in India as a cradle goddess.

JIHÂD. An Arabic word which means "a contending" or a striving. Muhammed commanded his followers to fight against unbelievers, and to win them over to Islâm or to exterminate them. The Jihâd thus became a sacred duty. It is defined by a learned Muslim doctor as "the calling on unbelievers to receive the true religion and fighting those who do not receive it." At first Muhammad simply delivered his message, and sought to win adherents by means of discussion and argument. But after his flight to Madina "he gave out that God had allowed him and his followers to defend themselves against the infidels, and, at length, pretended that he had Divine leave even to attack them and destroy idolatry and set up the true Faith by the sword" (Klein). The duty of fighting is emphasised in parts of the Kur'ân. "And when the sacred months are passed, kill those who join other gods with God wherever ye shall find them; and seize them, besiege them, and lay wait for them with every kind of ambush: but if they shall convert, and observe prayer, and pay the obligatory alms, then let them go their way, for God is Gracious, Merciful" (Sura, ix. 5). "Let those then fight on the path of God, who barter this present life for that which is to come; for whoever fighteth on God's path, whether he be slain or conquer, we will in the end give him a great reward" (iv. 76). "Say to the infidels: If they desist (from their unbelief), what is now past shall be forgiven them; but if they return (to it), they have already before them the doom of the ancients! Fight then against them till strife be at an end, and the religion be all of it God's. If they desist, verily God beholdeth what they do: But if they turn their back, know ye that God is your protector: Excellent protector! excellent helper!" (viii. 39-41). The infidels are first to be called upon to embrace Islâm. If they do so, no war is necessary. If they refuse to submit or to pay tribute; or if, having submitted, they refuse to continue to pay tribute; or if, whether Muslims or not, they rebel against the

Imâm (*q.v.*), the Jihâd must take its course. Cp. ZIMMIS, and see F. A. Klein.

JINN. In Muslim theology the Jinn (from *janna*, "to conceal" or "to hide") are an order of beings who are something between men and angels (Genii or demons). Some of them are good, others evil. "And there are among us good, and others among us of another kind; we are of various sorts" (Qur'ân lxxii. 11). They were created of fire. "We created man of dried clay, and the Jinn had been before created of subtle fire" (xv. 26, 27). They listen to the reading of the Qur'ân. "Say: It hath been revealed to me that a company of Jinn listened and said—'Verily we have heard a marvellous discourse (Qur'ân), etc.'" (lxxii. 1). They also hear what passes in heaven. "O company of Jinn and men, if ye can overpass the bounds of the Heavens and the Earth, then overpass them. But by our leave only shall ye overpass them" (lv. 33). They are also called "the stoned ones" because the good angels throw stones at them. "Moreover we have decked the lowest heaven with lights, and have placed them there to be hurled at the Satans, for whom we have prepared the torment of the flaming fire" (lxvii. 5). F. A. Klein points out that five orders of Jinn are distinguished. (1) Jânn, (2) Jinn, (3) Shaitân, (4) 'Ifrit, (5) Mârid. "The terms Jinn and Jánn are often used to designate the whole species, good and bad. The weakest among them are the Jánn, the strongest the Márid. Their chief abode is said to be the mountains of Qáf, which are supposed to encircle the world." Muhammad's conception of the Jinn seems to have been derived, through the Jews, from the Persians. See F. A. Klein.

JI SECT. A small Japanese Buddhist sect which is said to have been founded by Kūya, a priest of the fifteenth century. Kūya was called Odorinembutsu, "dancing nembutsu," because he went about the country dancing and repeating the Nembutsu. His idea was to convert the people to a religious life. He was a prince of the imperial house. The founder of the Ji Sect, however, according to A. Lloyd, is identified more generally with Ippen-Oshō (1239-1289 A.D.). Ippen was another itinerant preacher, "and to this day the head of the Ji sect, which has its chief temple at Fujisawa on the Tokaido, is supposed to spend all his time in itineracy." See Arthur Lloyd.

JIZO. A figure in the mythology of Japanese Buddhism, a patron-god of women, children, and travellers. He carries a pilgrim staff, and as the protector of travellers, his image is often found at cross-roads.

JIZZA. A kind of tribute, also called a capitation-tax or a captivity-tax, imposed by the Muhammadans on people who have become subject but have not embraced the Muslim faith. See ZIMMIS.

JOACHIMITES. The followers of Joachim (*c.* 1130-1200) of Floris in Calabria. Joachim was Abbot of the Cistercian monastery of Floris. He wrote books on the prophecies of the Old and New Testament, and on the doctrine of the Trinity. He held, as regards the Trinity, that "the three divine Persons were one God only in the same sense as many human persons are all men or Christians one with each other and with Christ" (*Cath. Dict.*). This teaching was condemned by the Fourth Lateran Council (1215). As regards the New Testament, influenced, as he claimed, by special spiritual revelations. Joachim wished to persuade the clergy to seek inward spiritualization by renouncing the world, in the manner of the apostles, and practising a rigid monasticism. This counsel appealed forcibly to some of the Franciscans. The teaching in the work "The Eternal Gospel," which was compiled and edited by one of his disciples (probably a Franciscan), helped considerably to prepare the way for the millenarianism of the thirteenth century. P. Puenjer gives the outlines of "The Eternal Gospel" as follows: "The history of the Christian Church runs through three great periods: the Age of the Father, extending from the creation of the world to John the Baptist; the Age of the Son, from the incarnation of Christ to the year 1260; and the Age of the Holy Spirit, which was regarded as beginning with that year. This last period is prepared by a boundless increase of abominations in the Church and life, as well as by the appearance of the Antichrist, who is more or less distinctly indicated as Frederick II. The characteristic of this new Age is to be derived from the contemplative life in which, with the right understanding of Scripture, the whole of previous history will come to appear in its true light." See J. H. Blunt; B. Puenjer.

JOANNAS. Another name for the Southcottians (*q.v.*), the followers of Joanna Southcott (1750-1814).

JOB, BOOK OF. The most remarkable of the Hebrew writings belonging to the class called Wisdom-Literature (*q.v.*). It deals with the problem of suffering, seeking to find an answer to the question, Why do the righteous suffer? Job, from the land of Uz, is a "perfect and upright" man. When the story opens he is also prosperous and happy, having been blessed with wealth and children. Satan, however, suggests to God that Job's piety would not be proof against misfortune. Let Job be put to the trial, and its worthlessness would soon appear. God allows Satan to test this perfect and upright man, and he is overtaken by one misfortune after another in quick succession. Job loses not only his possessions, but also his sons and his daughters. God will not allow his life to be taken; but he is smitten with a sore disease, either Elephantiasis, or the Oriental Boil, or Ecthyma. So deplorable is his condition that his wife advises him to "renounce God and die." But in spite of all his sufferings, Job did not sin with his lips. He now retires to a place outside the town and sits in ashes. Hither came three friends, Eliphaz, Bildad, and Zophar, to console with him. Out of respect for Job's grief they sat with him in silence seven days and nights. Then they sought to convince him that his sufferings were due to sin. Job cannot, and will not, admit this. This debate between Job and his three friends occupies a large part of the book. At the end of chapter xxxi., after Job has made a direct appeal to God, it is said: "The words of Job are ended." Afterwards, however, a new speaker, Elihu, is introduced (xxxii.-xxxvii.). Elihu dwells upon the love and providential wisdom of God manifested by the regulated course of the world. As to the suffering of the righteous, he points out that it is God's instrument of education. "If man misinterprets this educative character of suffering, he thereby commits a grave sin, and is justly punished by God: if, however, he recognises its true character and takes it to heart, the suffering becomes to him a source of infinite blessing, the highest practical proof of the divine love towards him" (Cornill). The Book of Job consists of five parts. (1) The Prologue, chapters i.-ii., written in prose. (2) The Debate between Job and his friends, chapters iii.-xxxi., written in poetry. (3) The Speeches of Elihu, chapters xxxii.-xxxvii., written in poetry (except xxxii. 1-6). (4) The Speech and Answer of Jehovah, chapters xxxviii. 1-xlii. 6, written in poetry. (5) The Epilogue, chapter xlii. 7-17, written in prose. It has been thought that the Speeches of Elihu (xxxii.-xxxvii.) have no claim to be regarded as an original part of the book. There is no reference to Elihu in the prologue or the epilogue. Chapter xxxviii., vs. 1, appears to be the direct continuation of xxxi. 40. When

Job's friends have been silenced, and Job addresses himself to God Himself, we should expect the reply of Jehovah to follow immediately. "Instead of this being so, six chapters here intervene, with a new speaker who up to this point has not received the smallest mention or notice, and who never gets the smallest notice later in the book, and whose self-introduction (xxxii. 6-xxxiii. 7) cannot be regarded as particularly happy" (Cornill). But, as Cornill says, the genuineness of the Speeches of Elihu is quite possible. Up to this point the problem raised in the book has found no solution. The poet, gifted as he clearly was, must have had some solution to offer. This is found in the Speeches of Elihu. "In the entire range of Holy Writ there are few passages which in profundity of thought and loftiness of feeling can compare with the Elihu-speeches: in content they form the summit and crown of the Book of Job, and furnish the only solution of the problem which the poet, from his Old Testament standpoint, is able to give, for the true and final solution was shut out from him" (Cornill). The date of the Book of Job is difficult to determine. According to an old Jewish tradition Moses was the author. The thought and language would seem to indicate a quite late date, a date, that is to say, not earlier than 400 B.C. See A. B. Davidson, *The Book of Job*, 1893; A. S. Peake, *Job*, 1904; C. Cornill, *Intr.;* G. H. Box; O. C. Whitehouse.

JOCAKUVAGUE MAOROCON. A sky-god worshipped in the West Indies (Antilles).

JODO SECT. A Japanese Buddhist sect founded A.D. 1175. The teaching is concerned specially with the western Paradise, which is ruled by Amida, Kwannon, and Daiseishi; and great veneration is paid to these holy ones. It is Amida in particular who grants admission into Paradise. See H. Hackmann.

JODO-SHIN SECT. The original name of a Japanese Buddhist sect, which afterwards received the name Shin Sect (*q.v.*).

JOEL, BOOK OF. The book of Joel deals with "the great and terrible day of the Lord." The immediate occasion for the prophecy was a plague of drought and locusts. "Recent writers have vividly described the appalling nature of this calamity. In great swarms which obscure the sky these ravenous insects sweep over large areas, destroying all vegetation, and leaving the land as barren as a desert" (C. F. Kent). There are no indications of the date of the book in the opening verse. It has therefore to be inferred from internal evidence. The period with which the prophet is familiar is one in which "comparative peace prevailed in Palestine, although the memories of past invasions and wrongs are still fresh in the mind of the prophet" (C. F. Kent). The prophet does not allude to a king or to princes; the elders and the priests are the prominent officials (i. 14; i. 9, 13, ii. 17). Jehovah's heritage has already been scattered among the nations (iii. 2-3). The Greeks are represented simply as slave-traders (iii. 6). The services of the Temple are properly maintained. The interruption of the regular sacrifices is regarded as a great misfortune (i. 9, 13, ii. 14). In fact, the writer seems to assume the existence and the Services of the Second Temple. "With this agree the features that the whole people can, and is called upon to, assemble in the Temple (i. 14; ii. 16), that the trumpet blown upon Mount Zion is heard throughout the whole land (ii. 1), because it consists only of Jerusalem and its immediate environs" (Cornill). It used to be thought that on the whole the criteria suit a date in the early part of the reign of Joash, king of Judah (837-801 B.C.). But the force of the evidence against an early date and in favour of a very late one has accumulated in recent research. Merx (quoted by Cornill) seems to be correct in saying that the diction of Joel "is the flowing diction of the scholar who is deeply read in the ancient literature, not the spontaneous beauty which marks the creations of genius." And Cornill thinks that Holzinger has demonstrated convincingly that Joel's language exhibits the character of the latest period of Hebrew literature. The mention of Jerusalem's "walls" (ii. 9) implies a period subsequent to Nehemiah; and it is thought that there are clear indications of the influence of the great priestly reformation of about 400 B.C. Prof. Whitehouse finds in iii. 19 ("Egypt shall become a desolation, because of the violence done to the men of Judah, because they shed innocent blood in their land") a reference to the destruction of the Jewish temple in Elephantine about 409 B.C., "of which we are informed in the Aramaic papyri recently discovered in that spot." Prof. Cornill would assign the book to about 400 B.C. "In the Book of Joel we possess a compendium of late Jewish eschatology written about the year 400—if anything rather later than earlier—as developed from later prophecy, with its tendency to flow over into apocalypse: in its whole tone and spirit Joel belongs altogether to apocalyptic, although in outward form it has preserved more of the character of older prophecy than Zechariah and Daniel." See S. R. Driver, *Joel and Amos*, 1897; in "Cambridge Bible"; C. Cornill, *Intr.;* O. C. Whitehouse; C. F. Kent, *The Sermons, Epistles and Apocalypses of Israel's Prophets*, 1910.

JOHANNITES. Another name for the Waterlanders (*q.v.*).

JOHN, THE GOSPEL OF. The Gospel of John presents a different view of Jesus from the view presented on the whole in common by the three other (Synoptic) Gospels, and it is now almost a commonplace of criticism to say that it represents a distinct and different style of literature. Arno Neumann writes as follows (*Jesus*): "It cannot be placed earlier than the second century, and arising as it did as a protest against Judaising parties and as a defence of ideas of religion conceived in an unhistorical way, all the details in the story, as regards localities, time, and personal characteristics, have been adapted to the requirements of that Christian philosophy in which the Gospel is steeped, or have been misplaced through its influence. To the author of this Gospel Jesus is the 'Word of God,' that is to say, the second person of the Godhead, who existed before Abraham, and in fact took part in the creation of the world (i. 1-3; viii. 5, 8; xvii. 5). Holding this view, he is naturally obliged to represent the appearance of Jesus as the thinly-veiled manifestation of a Divine being. Thus the Jesus of John is neither baptized nor tempted, does not waver in Gethsemane, has foreknowledge of everything, prays only for the sake of the bystanders (xi. 41 f.); when hanging on the cross says 'I thirst,' only in order to fulfil an Old Testament prophecy (xix. 28); calls upon his betrayer to hasten his wicked deed (xiii. 26 f.): and by a brief word 'I am He' makes 500 Roman soldiers recoil and bend the knee (xviii. 5 f.). The author's conception of the religion of Jesus, pervaded throughout by the spirit we have indicated, is certainly sublime enough, but it is far removed from the simple, sober, naïve facts of history as we find them in the Gospels according to Mark, Matthew, and Luke." This estimate of the Fourth Gospel, however, is perhaps based upon a misunderstanding of its language and purpose. At the beginning of the third century it became known as "the spiritual gospel." That was and is an accurate description. It is a spiritual gospel, and has to be interpreted spiritually. God is Spirit. Jesus, fully understanding the nature of God, Spirit, realized his own eternity, and the closeness of his union with God. It is quite conceivable that there was among the Evangelists one John who penetrated deeper than did the others into the spiritual essence of the gospel of Jesus. It is quite natural that, this being so, he should wish to write a new and rather different account of the work and teaching of Jesus. "He is said to have done so on the entreaty, and with the subsequent approval, of the Apostle Andrew and other leading members of the Church, in order to supplement the teaching of the three Gospels already published, and to counteract the errors which were beguiling some from the simplicity of the faith" (M'Clymont). Neumann admits that at times there are statements in the Fourth Gospel which point us to an original element overlooked by the other Evangelists. Examples are given by O. Holtzmann. It is only in the Fourth Gospel (ii. 19) that the saying upon which the accusation in Mk. xiv. 58 and the mockery in Mk. xv. 30 were based is represented as having been actually uttered by Jesus himself and in the right connection. From John x. 1-6 it is possible to disentangle a parable of Jesus traditionally handed down to the Evangelist (but no longer to be found in the Synoptic tradition), the genuineness of which can hardly be doubted. The Johannine Gospel is the only Source, apart from the apocryphal Gospel of Peter, that correctly gives the day of Jesus' death in so far as it places it on the day before the beginning of the Passover festival, while according to Mk. (Mt., Lk.) Jesus was crucified on the first day of the actual festival. The same accuracy characterises the date of the anointing in Bethany (John xii. 1). Irenaeus accepted the Fourth Gospel as the work of the Apostle John. This would suggest that it was accepted also by his teacher, Polycarp, who had been a disciple of John. In a letter to Florinus, Irenaeus writes (177 A.D.) as follows: "I can describe the very place in which the blessed Polycarp used to sit when he discoursed, and his goings out and his comings in, and his manner of life and his personal appearance, and the discourses which he held before the people, and how he would describe his intercourse with John and with the rest who had seen the Lord, and how he would relate their words. And whatsoever things he had heard from them about the Lord and about His miracles, Polycarp, as having received them from eye-witnesses of the life of the Word, would relate altogether in accordance with the Scriptures" (after M'Clymont). It has of course been disputed whether the John of the Fourth Gospel was the Apostle John, the son of Zebedee. But the character of the Gospel, with its knowledge of the inmost thought of Jesus, is best explained by accepting the authorship of this intimate friend of Jesus, who "held most tenaciously to the belief that he had found the Way, the Truth, and the Life" (W. Sanday). See J. A. M'Clymont; Oscar Holtzmann, *The Life of Jesus*, 1904; Arno Neumann, *Jesus*, 1906; P. W. Schmiedel, *The Johannine Writings*, 1908; C. F. Nolloth, *The Person of Our Lord and Recent Thought*, 1908; W. Sanday, *The Life of Christ in Recent Research*, 1907; G. Currie Martin; Arthur S. Peake, *Intr.;* F. C. Conybeare, *Hist. of N.T. Crit.*, 1910.

JOHN, THE FIRST EPISTLE OF. John, the son of Zebedee, would seem to have earned the title "the disciple whom Jesus loved" (John xix. 26) in the lifetime of his Master. This would indicate that he was in closest sympathy with Jesus. And the importance of loving Jesus with a perfect love, and of being loved by him in return, would naturally impress itself upon him with great force. We are told in the Gospel of John that the disciple whom Jesus loved was present at the crucifixion. We are told, moreover, that after the crucifixion one of the soldiers pierced Jesus' side with a spear, whereupon there came out blood and water. Now the First Epistle of John dwells much upon the idea of divine love. In chapter iv. vs. 16 we read: "And we know and have believed the love which God hath in us. God is love; and he that abideth in love abideth in God, and God abideth in him." And the same epistle says of Jesus: "This is he that came by water and blood, even Jesus Christ; not with the water only, but with the water and with the blood." These facts make it psychologically probable that John, the son of Zebedee, was really the author of the First Epistle of John. Psychological considerations suggest that he was also the John who wrote the Fourth Gospel (see JOHN, THE GOSPEL OF). The Epistle is probably quoted by Polycarp, and, according to Eusebius, it was made use of by Papias. It is quoted as the work of John by Irenaeus, Tertullian, Clement of Alexandria, and Origen. It appears as his work in the Muratorian Canon. It cannot be established that the false teaching attacked in the epistle is of the nature of a somewhat developed form of Gnosticism. If any particular heresies are attacked they are nothing more than doctrines of a Docetic tendency. It has to be borne in mind that before heresies arise as schools of thought, the ideas which they represent have suggested themselves to many individual minds. Moreover, a writer who is thoughtful and far-sighted, long forsees the lines along which arguments or thoughts opposed to his own may develop. He anticipates them without supposing that he is attacking a particular heresy. The Epistle, like the Gospel, has penetrated to the real kernel of the teaching of Jesus. As Currie Martin says, it "is full of the most beautiful thoughts exquisitely expressed, and as a practical treatise upon the love of God as finding its truest expression in the love of our fellow-men, ranks alongside Paul's great teaching on the same subject in I. Cor. xiii." See P. W. Schmiedel, *The Johannine Writings*, 1908; G. Currie Martin; Arthur S. Peake, *Intr.*

JOHN, THE SECOND EPISTLE OF. In the Second Epistle of John there is again reference to false teachers (vs. 7), but it is not necessary to think that particular schools of thought are referred to. The terms, however, are rather more severe than those of the First Epistle. Emphasis is again laid on love, "and in its few sentences we have the further expressions 'truth' and 'the world' used in the sense in which they are employed both in the First Epistle and in the Fourth Gospel" (Currie Martin). The Epistle is quoted as the work of John by Irenaeus and Clement of Alexandria; and seems to be recognised as his by the Muratorian Canon. The Epistle begins: "The elder unto the elect lady and her children, whom I love in truth." It is a problem whether "the elect lady and her children" designates an individual or a church. Schmiedel thinks a church or community is meant. He points out that elsewhere the community is thought of as the Bride of Christ (Ephesians v. 31 f.; Revelation xix. 7) who had been exalted to heaven, just as in the Old Testament the people of Israel is the Bride of God. "Since Christ is called 'the Lord,' the community might be called 'the lady.' It deserves to be called 'elect' because it consists of all the chosen. Its children are, of course, the members of the community." According to Schmiedel, the epistle was meant for the whole church. But vs. 13 seems to require an individual church. "The statement that the elect lady is greeted by her elect sister is incompatible with a Catholic destination of the Epistle; it could only mean that one Church greets another. In that case the elect sister may possibly be identified with the Church in Ephesus, where the author presumably was writing. It is accordingly probable that the elect lady should be identified with one of the Churches of Asia, perhaps with Pergamum, as Findlay has suggested" (A.

S Peake). See P. W. Schmiedel, *The Johannine Writings*, 1908; G. Currie Martin; Arthur S. Peake, *Intr.*

JOHN, THE THIRD EPISTLE OF. The Third Epistle of John is addressed to an individual, one Gaius. Reference is made also to two other individuals. One of these, Diotrephes, "loveth to have the pre-eminence and receiveth us not . . . prating against us with wicked words; and not content therewith, neither doth he himself receive the brethren, and them that would he forbiddeth, and casteth them out of the Church." Of the other, Demetrius, it is said that he "hath the witness of all, and of the truth itself." The writer again warns his reader, not against an heretical school, but against certain self-willed, self-assertive Christians who are inclined to interpret the truth in a way of their own. There always are such persons. Even in the lifetime of Jesus there will doubtless have been people who were faithful adherents of his, but who did not agree on every point with other adherents. John, through his intimacy with Jesus, gained a deeper understanding of the Master's teaching than was possible for many other followers. As he grew older, the persistent misunderstanding which he found in others perhaps made him a little intolerant and impatient. In the Third Epistle emphasis is again laid on "the truth." John naturally felt that there can be no deviation from the truth. He did not sufficiently realize perhaps that to many people the truth must come gradually, unless it come by a sudden inspiration. In any case, the Third Epistle is not different in style and outlook from the Second. "The affinities with the Second Epistle are so close that we may assume that it was written by the same author and in all probability at the same time. In that case it is possible that the letters were sent to the same destination. It is a plausible suggestion that the letter referred to in *v.* 9 is the Second Epistle, and that the writer sends this letter to Gaius to guard against the suppression of his letter to the Church by Diotrephes" (A. S. Peake). Eusebius includes the Epistle among the disputed books. See J. A. M'Clymont; P. W. Schmiedel, *The Johannine Writings*, 1908; G. Currie Martin; Arthur S. Peake, *Introd.*

JOHNSONIAN BAPTISTS. A sect founded by John Johnson (1706-1791). Johnson was in charge of the Byrom Street Baptist Chapel, Liverpool, from about 1741 to 1747-8, when he had to leave on account of his doctrinal views. His followers opened a chapel in Stanley Street, Liverpool, in 1750, and placed him in charge of it. Johnsonian Baptists arose in other places. They existed for some time at Wisbech in Cambridgeshire See the *D.N.B.*

JŌJITSU SECT. An early sect of Chinese Buddhists. Kumarajīva brought it to Singanfu in 401 A.D. In course of time it was absorbed by the Tendai (*q.v.*). "It appeared in Japan only to disappear again" (A. Lloyd). The members of the Jōjitsu sect were opponents of the doctrines of the Sarvāstivādins (*q.v.*).

JONAH. The prophet Jonah is said to have started on his sea-voyage from Joppa. At Joppa a sea-monster was worshipped. It has been suggested therefore that this worship "may have provided a theme for the writer of the allegory of Jonah" (E. S. Bouchier).

JONAH, BOOK OF. The book of the prophet Jonah is in the form of a historical narrative, and the history purports to be that of a prophet Jonah ben Amittai, of Gath-hepher in Galilee, who lived in the time of Jeroboam II. It is not possible, however, to regard the work as a product of this early period. The language is sometimes that of the latest style of Hebrew; at other times it is modelled on that of late books (compare Jonah iii. 9 with Joel ii. 14; Jon. iv. 2 with Jo. ii. 13, Exod. xxxiv. 6, Psalms lxxxvi. 15, ciii. 8). It has been pointed out also that the introduction of marvellous features is in the style of the books of Chronicles and Daniel. The book is in fact a parable, the fundamental idea of which, as Cornill says, clearly points to a very late period. "It is a protest against the pernicious arrogance of the Judaism that followed Ezra, which is jealous because God is so gracious, and which is in danger of losing its faith because Jahve does not extirpate and annihilate the heathen, as later prophecy had hoped and promised that He should." The book teaches that God is not merely a God of the Jews, but also of the Gentiles. The story of Jonah is referred to in the New Testament (Luke xi. 29 ff.; Matthew xii. 39 ff.). On this account many persons would like to regard it as historical. But the story is not necessarily referred to as anything more than a story, which was familiar to everyone. It should be noted that in the original Hebrew Jonah is swallowed not by a "whale" but by a "great fish." The second chapter of the book is composite, and is clearly a later insertion. If the book is interpreted as an allegory, C. H. H. Wright explains that "Jonah represents Israel fleeing from the duty imposed on the nation in its prophetic character as a witness for God. The sleep of Jonah, the storm on the sea, Jonah's bold confession of faith when aroused from slumber, admit of easy explanation. The world-power is actually represented in the prophets as a sea-monster (see Isa. xxvii.; Jer. li. 34). That sea-monster is represented as, in the person of Nebuchadnezzar, swallowing up Israel (li. 34). Bel, the god of Babylon, is forced to disgorge his prey (li. 44). Israel's duration in exile is represented by Hosea as lasting for three days" (Hosea vi. 1). See C. H. H. Wright, *Intr. to the O.T.*; C. Cornill, *Intr.*; G. H. Box; O. C. Whitehouse; C. F. Kent, *The Sermons, Epistles and Apocalypses of Israel's Prophets*, 1910.

JONATHAN, TARGUM OF. The Aramaic translation (interpretation) of the Prophetical Books of the Old Testament. The Targum on the Prophets is more paraphrastic than the Targum (of Onkelos) on the Pentateuch. See TARGUM.

JORISTS. The followers of David Joris (or Joriszoon, *i.e.*, Georgeson; *c.* 1501-1556). Originally an Anabaptist; after receiving, as he asserted, visions and revelations, he founded a sect of his own. The Jorists or Davidists regarded their leader as the true Christ.

JOSHIS. The Joshis (also known as Jyotishis, Bhadris, Parsis) are the caste of village priests and astrologers in India. For the most part they are Brāhmans. "The Joshi officiates at weddings in the village, selects auspicious names for children according to the *nakshatra* or constellation of the moon under which they were born, and points out the auspicious time or *mahūrat* for all such ceremonies and for the commencement of agricultural operations. He is also sometimes in charge of the village temples" (R. V. Russell).

JOSHUA, BOOK OF. The Hebrew Canon of the Old Testament (*q.v.*) groups the Book of Joshua, not with the books of the Pentateuch, but with the Prophets. The book of Joshua is the first of the "Former Prophets." In the Greek Bible it bears the title Ἰησους or Ἰησους υἱος Ναυη, in the Syriac "The Book of Joshua, the son of Nun, the disciple of Moses." Modern scholars connect the book with the Pentateuch, and speak of the six books as the Hexateuch. The book continues the account of the great movement which began with the exodus from Egypt. The Sources of "Joshua" represent a continuation of the sources used in the Pentateuch. The book deals with the conquest and division of Canaan under the leadership of Moses' successor, Joshua. The contents may be divided as follows: (1) Chapters i.-xii. the advance of Israel and the conquest of Canaan; (2) Chapters xiii.-xxi. the allotment of the land among the tribes; (3) Chapters xxii.-xxiv. accounts of the final measures taken by Joshua, of his farewell address, and of his death and burial. The conclusion of the book therefore resembles that of the book of Deuteronomy. Joshua of course is only the hero of the book and not the author. The greater part of the book was committed to writing long after the events happened which it purports to describe. We have evidence of this in the frequent recurrence of the formula " unto this day " (cp. iv. 9, v. 9, vi. 25, vii. 26, viii. 29, ix. 27, etc.). The book in fact was not the work of a single author, but is composed of a number of different works. There are conflicting statements and duplicate accounts (cp. xi. 21 f. with xv. 13 ff.; xiv. 6 ff. with xv. 13 ff.). On the whole the book of Joshua represents the conquest of Canaan as having been effected by a united Israel under the leadership of Joshua; but a different conception of the conquest has also found its way into the book. In chapters xiii.-xix. " there are considerable fragments of an account of the conquest which, like Judg. i., represented it, not as the work of Joshua at the head of all Israel, but as slowly and incompletely achieved by the several tribes; and in i.-xii. it is possible to distinguish an older and simpler account of the invasion from a later version of the same story in which a tendency to magnify the events and exaggerate the miraculous character of the history is conspicuous" (G. F. Moore in *Encycl. Bibl.*). It has been possible, in fact, to detect and distinguish the same documents P (Priestly writer), J (Jehovist), E (Elohist), and D (Deuteronomist), which are found interwoven in the books of the Pentateuch, and the basis of the book is a deuteronomic history of Joshua. The book is much more deuteronomic than the first four books of the Pentateuch. See *Encycl. Bibl.;* W. H. Bennett, *Joshua*, in "Sacred Books of the Old Testament"; C. Steuernagel, *Das Buch Josua*, 1899; Carpenter and Harford-Battersby; G. H. Box; O. C. Whitehouse.

JOTUNHEIM. Jotunheim was one of the nine worlds in the cosmogony of the Ancient Teutons.

JUDAISM. The religion of the Jews, as developed from the religion of the ancient Hebrews. Before the settlement of the Hebrew tribes in Palestine their religion seems to have resembled that of other nomadic Semites. Each tribe probably had its own deity. Some of the tribes, however, before the settlement seem to have adopted the god Yahweh, for the statement (E) that the name Yahweh was not known before the time of Moses (Exod. iii. 1-14) is hardly true of all the tribes. " There are indications that Yahweh may have been a divine name in North Arabia for a thousand years before Moses, and that emigrants from this region to Babylonia and Palestine had carried the name to those countries" (G. A. Barton, *R.W.*). In the time of Moses Yahweh's presence with his people came to be represented by a box or ark, containing presumably a sacred stone; and his commands were orally transmitted in ten sentences. The ten commands (Exod. xxxiv.) seem to have been: 1. Thou shalt worship no other god. 2. Thou shalt make thee no molten gods. 3. The feast of the Passover thou shalt keep. 4. The firstling of an ass thou shalt redeem with a lamb: all the first-born of thy sons thou shalt redeem. 5. None shall appear before me empty. 6. Six days thou shalt work, but on the seventh thou shalt rest. 7. Thou shalt observe the feast of ingathering (of dates). 8. Thou shalt not offer the blood of my sacrifice with leavened bread, neither shall the sacrifice of the Passover remain until the morning. 9. The firstlings of thy flocks thou shalt bring unto Yahweh, thy God. 10. Thou shalt not seethe a kid in its mother's milk. With the conquest of Palestine and the union of the tribes, life became gradually more settled. The shrines of the old inhabitants were taken over, and agricultural feasts became a prominent feature in the worship of Yahweh. The sanctuary, with one or two exceptions (the temple of Shiloh, I. Sam. i.-v.; and Solomon's temple), was a high place open to the sky. In the time of Elijah and Elisha we note the beginnings of a new development. More stress begins to be laid on ethics, and in a new form of the ten commandments (E) ritualistic requirements almost disappear (see DECALOGUE). In the period of the eighth-century prophets (755-690 B.C.) the development is carried further by Amos, Hosea, Isaiah, and Micah. These prophets introduced a practical monotheism, and Isaiah began to preach the Messianic Hope (see MESSIAH). Then Hezekiah sought to centre the worship of Yahweh in the temple of Jerusalem (II. Kings xviii. 1-6, 22). In the reign of King Manasseh (686-641), however, a religious reaction led to the restoration of the old shrines and the revival of heathen Semitic customs. To check this degeneracy the prophetical school composed about 650 B.C. the Deuteronomic law (*i.e.*, the kernel of the book of Deuteronomy [*q.v.*]). This was found in the temple in the reign of Josiah, and prompted the king to introduce a great religious reform. Worship was again centred at Jerusalem; the old shrines were removed, and the survivals of heathen Semitic religion (sacred pillars, *asherahs*, etc.) were abolished. We may see here the fruit of Hosea's teaching. " Hosea's condemnation of the worship at the local sanctuaries and his supreme doctrine of love and kindness toward man and all of God's creatures, reappear in many of the enactments found in the prophetic law-book of Deuteronomy. His teachings regarding the love of God, the character and effects of sin, the necessity of repentance, God's readiness to forgive, and the duty of love and kindness from man to man, are the essence of that gospel which Jesus proclaimed to all the world" (C. F. Kent, *The Kings and Prophets of Israel and Judah*, 1909). A further landmark is reached when we come to the prophet Jeremiah, who reiterates and enriches the teachings of Hosea. As Barton notes, he contributed four great and potent ideas to the religion of Israel: theoretical monotheism; the conception of Yahweh as God of the nations as well as of the Jews; the doctrine of the inwardness of religion; and the idea of individual responsibility. With Hosea, Jeremiah also conceived of Israel's relationship to Yahweh as that of a covenant of marriage, and represented God as a God of love. The capture of Jerusalem by Nebuchadrezzar in 586 B.C. and the destruction of the temple was enough to revolutionize the ideas of the Jews. It led Ezekiel, the prophet-priest, who had been one of those deported by Nebuchadrezzar to Babylonia in 597, to dream of the rehabilitation in Palestine of a Hebrew state, in which prophetic ideals would be blended with the ritual law. " Above all, he was an idealist, who believed firmly in the ultimate future of his race" (C. F. Kent). He, again, emphasized the great principle of individual responsibility. Second Isaiah (*fl.* in Babylonia from about 550 B.C.) encouraged the Jews to take advantage of the decree of Cyrus by returning to Palestine, and further conceived of Israel as the " suffering Servant of Yahweh" who had been chosen to bear the chastisement due not only to its own sins but to the sins of the nations. It was perhaps during his time that the Code of Holiness took shape. This was followed later by the document known as P—an elaboration of the priestly law and a re-editing of the earlier history in the light of it. Later still, in the time of Ezra and Nehemiah (*fl.* 444 B.C.), with the adoption of this priestly law in Palestine as the fundamental law of Jewish religion, Judaism in the specific sense of the name was born—a compromise between the idealism of the prophets and the ritualism of the priests. Most of the Jews who were settled in Babylonia preferred to remain there, but they too accepted the priestly law. The papyri from Elephantine in Egypt show that the Jewish colony, though it had a temple there, did not accept the new law at once. With the rebuilding of the temple at Jerusalem, a hymn-book was introduced, and the Samaritans, who built a rival temple on Mt. Gerizim, became a separate sect. In the Greek period, after the conquest of Palestine by Alexander (332 B.C.), the Jews became more widely dispersed, many of them settling in Alexandria, where they came under the direct influence of Greek thought. The prophets ceased (*c.* 250 B.C.), and were succeeded (after 200 B.C.) by the apocalyptists, many of whom wrote in Greek. Hellenic philosophy was one thing. When imperial force was used to impose upon the people Hellenic religion (168 B.C.), the Jews rebelled and found salvation in the Maccabees. Between this time and the birth of Philo (*c.* 20 B.C.), several Jewish parties or sects—the Pharisees, the Sadducees, and the Essenes—arose; the oral traditions of the law were started, and schools of oral tradition became active (the School of Hillel, the School of Shammai). Philo Judaeus (b. about 20 B.C.) was contemporary with Jesus. His doctrine of the Logos exercised a great influence on later Christian thought. "Though Philo was a good and loyal Jew, he stood, so to speak, apart from the real centre of Jewish intellectual and spiritual development. He was on the one hand too closely dependent on Greek thought, and on the other had only a limited knowledge of Jewish thought and tradition. The Bible he knew only in the Greek translation, not in the original Hebrew; and of the Halaka, which was still in the making in Palestine, he knew still less" (Isaac Husik). The Synagogue, as we know from the New Testament, was already firmly established in the time of Jesus. It seems to have originated much earlier, perhaps in Babylonia. When Jerusalem was destroyed in 70 A.D. Jabneh (Gk. Jamnia) had already become an important centre of Jewish learning. Here the oral law was now further developed, and the traditions were formulated in what came to be known as the Mishnah (200 A.D.). This, with the Gemara, which contains traditions later than the Mishnah, constitutes what is known as the Talmud, of which there are two recensions, one Palestinian (4th cent.), the other Babylonian (6th cent.). After the Bible, the Talmud is the chief religious book of Judaism. From the sixth to the eleventh century the rabbinical school in Babylonia (the Geonim) enjoyed a great reputation for interpretation. In the Middle Ages Judaism was interpreted on orthodox or unorthodox lines by many famous philosophers and exegetes. The exegetes included Rashi (1040-1105), Ibn Ezra (1093-1138), and Kimchi (1160-1235). The philosophers included Ibn Gabirol (1021-1058), Judah Halevi (*b.* in the last quarter of the 11th cent.), Ibn Daud (*b.* about 1110), Moses Maimonides (1135-1204), and Levi ben Gerson (1288-1344). The theological system of Maimonides largely shaped the intellectual life of the Jews for centuries. Maimonides propounded thirteen articles of faith. These, "in setting forth a Jewish *Credo*, formed a vigorous opposition to the Christian and Mohammedan creeds; they therefore met almost universal acceptance among the Jewish people, and were given a place in the common prayer-book, in spite of their deficiencies, as shown by Crescas and his school" (K. Kohler). His first five articles were: 1, the existence; 2, the unity; 3, the incorporeality; 4, the eternity—of God; 5, that He alone should be the object of worship. His tenth article is divine Providence. Moses Mendelssohn (1729-1786), who belongs to a much later period, is revered not only as a philosopher, but as the emancipator of the modern Jew from the thraldom of the Ghetto. What is known as Reform Judaism started in Germany about 1845. It has recast the ancient belief in the election and mission of Israel. On the one hand, the founders "have reinterpreted the Messianic hope in the prophetic spirit, as the realization of the highest ideals of a united humanity. On the other, they have rejected the entire theory that Israel was exiled from his ancient land because of his sins, and that he is eventually to return there and to restore the sacrificial cult in the Temple at Jerusalem. Therefore, the whole view concerning Israel's future had to undergo a transformation. The historic mission of Israel as priest of humanity and champion of truth assumed a higher meaning, and his peculiar position in history and in the Law necessarily received a different interpretation from that of Talmudic Judaism or that of the Church" (Kohler). The movement known as Zionism (*q.v.*), through the activities of Theodor Herzl, began to make great progress after 1895. On the whole, it is, or has become, nationalistic and cultural rather than religious. "The nationalists expect the Jewish nation to awaken from a sleep of eighteen hundred years to new greatness in its ancient home, not as a religious, but as a political body, and in renouncing all allegiance to the priestly mission of Israel and its ancestral faith they are as remote from genuine Orthodoxy as from Reform Judaism." Dr. Kohler emphasizes the necessity of distinguishing two opposite fundamental tendencies in Judaism, the one expressing the spirit of legalistic nationalism, the other that of ethical or prophetic universalism. "These two work by turn, directing the general trend in the one or the other direction according to circumstances. At one time the centre and focus of Israel's religion is the Mosaic Law, with its sacrificial cult in charge of the priesthood of Jerusalem's Temple; at another time it is the Synagogue, with its congregational devotion and public instruction, its inspiring song of the Psalmist, and its prophetic consolation and hope confined to no narrow territory, but opened wide for a listening world. Here it is the reign of the *Halakah* holding fast to the form of tradition, and there the free and fanciful *Haggadah*, with its appeal to the sentiments and views of the people. Here it is the spirit of *ritualism*, bent on separating the Jews from the influence of foreign elements, and there again the spirit of *rationalism*, eager to take part in general culture and in the progress of the outside world" (p. 13). See G. A. Barton, *R.W.*, 1917; *Rel. of Isr.*, 1918.

JUDE, THE EPISTLE OF. The Epistle of Jude, one of the group of New Testament Epistles known as Catholic or General Epistles, consists of only twenty-five verses. The writer calls himself "Judas, a servant of Jesus Christ, and brother of James" (vs. 1). He is commonly taken to be the Jude or Judas mentioned in Matthew xiii. 55 as one of the brethren of the Lord. Hegesippus, as quoted by Eusebius, has preserved a tradition that two grandsons of this Jude were summoned before the Emperor Domitian to give an account of their faith. The emperor found their religion to be harmless, and sent them away in peace. Tradition further tells that they died at an advanced age in the reign of Trajan. If the epistle was composed by the grandfather of these men, its date would be between 60 and 70 A.D. But the name Judas was a common one. The Jude of the Epistle may have been an otherwise unknown person, as Currie Martin suggests, the description "brother of James" being an editorial insertion. In any case, the epistle can hardly be assigned to a very early date. Eusebius speaks of it as one of the disputed writings, and Origen also evidently knew that its authorship was disputed. It is mentioned, however, in the Muratorian Canon, and is quoted by Clement of Alexandria and Tertullian. One of the curious features of the book is its use of apocryphal writings. Thus, in vs. 14 the Book of Enoch seems to be quoted, and in vs. 9 the Assumption of Moses. It is thought that this use of Apocrypha accounts for the tardy recognition of the book. But there is another very curious feature. There is a close resemblance between the Epistle of Jude and the Second Epistle of Peter—so close a resemblance that one must have copied the other. "In the judgment of most scholars Jude is the original from which 2 Peter borrowed. It is in the first place curious that, if 2 Peter were the earlier, Jude should have contented himself with extracting simply the section against the false teachers. But, apart from this general improbability, when we come to place the two documents side by side and test them, it is generally easy to explain why the author of 2 Peter has altered Jude, but it is not easy to see why, if Jude had 2 Peter before him, he should have altered his original to the form that we find in his Epistle. Obscurities in 2 Peter can in some cases be cleared up by reference to Jude" (A. S. Peake). The reference to false teaching has been taken to suggest some form of antinomian Gnosticism such as became prevalent in the second century. But the false teaching was not necessarily Gnosticism. Currie Martin thinks the epistle may have originated in Egypt, "because the churches there appear to have been more generally fond of apocalypse, and also liable to the errors in teaching and practice to which this epistle refers." See the *Encycl. Bibl.;* J. A. M'Clymont; G. Currie Martin; Arthur S. Peake, *Intr.;* J. Moffatt, *Intr.*

JUDGES, BOOK OF. The Book of Judges in the Hebrew Canon of the Old Testament (see CANON, i.) is grouped with the books described as the "Former Prophets." It purports to deal historically with a period embracing more than three centuries. The Judges were heroes who arose from time to time to lead the Israelite tribes against their enemies, and whose success resulted in their becoming judicial rulers and in a sense the forerunners of the Israelite monarchs. The Hebrew word for these and other judges is *Shōfetīm.* It has been pointed out by G. F. Moore, C. H. H. Wright, and others that the same word (*Suffetes*) was used in Carthage, a Phoenician colony, of rulers there (Livy, *Hist.* xxx. 7), who were sometimes called also by the Romans reges, consules, and dictators. The Book of Judges divides itself into four sections. The first (chap. i. 1-ii. 5), which is introductory, describes the conquest of Canaan after the death of Joshua (see JOSHUA, BOOK). It is really an old account of the conquest; it differs from that of the Book of Joshua and represents that the conquest was made, not simultaneously by all the tribes acting together under the leadership of Joshua, but gradually by individual tribes acting independently. The second section (chap. ii. 6-iii. 6) has been described as a Prelude to the history, "a moralising summary" (Whitehouse) of the story that is to follow. The third section (chap. iii. 7-xvi. 31), which is "the real kernel of the history," recounts the adventures of twelve judges. The chief of these were Othniel, Ehud, Deborah (with Barak), Gideon, Jephthah, and Samson. The minor judges were Shamgar, Tola and Jair, Ibzan, Elon, and Abdon. In chapter 9 a story is introduced which describes how one Abimelech became "king" of the Canaanite town, Shechem. The story has been regarded by some scholars as "a kind of prelude to the history of the kingdom of Saul" (Moore). But as Prof. Moore says, Abimelech was simply king of a town of the Canaanites, among whom the city-kingdom was a common form of government. "That he was also recognized as king by purely Israelite towns or clans is not intimated, and is not a necessary inference from the fact that he has the Israelites at his back in his effort to suppress the revolt of the Canaanite cities (955)." The fourth section of the book (chaps. xvii.-xxi.) is of the nature of an appendix or a supplement. It tells the adventures (xvii.-xviii) of a man named Micah who had an image and priest, a Levite, of his own. These were carried off by the Danites. It tells further (xix.-xxi.) of a war between the Israelites and the Benjamites, in which the latter were nearly exterminated. The Book of Judges is composite. In the sixth century B.C. a Deuteronomistic author (D) would seem to have composed a "History of Israel under the Judges." From this are derived chapters ii. 6-xvi. 31. This writer (D) obtained his information about the Judges from a work known as the "Prophetical Writings" or JE. This in turn was composed in the seventh century B.C. by an author or compiler (R_{JE}) who made use of two early narratives, a "Judaic History" (J, ninth century B.C.) and an "Ephraimite History" (E, somewhat later). The author of the present Book of Judges after the Exile supplemented D's work by adding from JE Judg. i. 1-ii. 5 and chapters xvii.-xviii., xix.-xxi. As regards the chronology of the Judges, Whitehouse points out that "there is nothing to forbid the assumption that some (*e.g.*, Samson and Jephthah, Barak, and Ehud) ruled contemporaneously." Unless we assume this, the period between the Exodus and Solomon would exceed the length (480 years) given in the First Book of Kings (vi. 1). See G. F. Moore, *Judges* (1895) in the *I.C.C.*, and *The Book of Judges* (1898) in the "Sacred Books of the Old Testament" (Engl.); C. H. H. Wright, *Intr.;* G. H. Box; O. C. Whitehouse.

JUMPING, AS A RELIGIOUS CEREMONY. J. G. Frazer mentions a number of instances in which some religious or magical virtue is ascribed to jumping over a thing or person (cp. THRESHOLD). In Russia on the Eve of St. John (Mid-summer Eve) young men and maidens, carrying a straw figure of the mythic hero Kupalo, jump over a bonfire in couples. Among the Baganda of Central Africa, "when the beans were ripe, a woman would call her eldest son to eat some of the first which she cooked; if she neglected to do so, it was believed that she would incur the displeasure of the gods and fall ill. After the meal her husband jumped over her, and the beans might thereafter be eaten by all." According to J. Roscoe (*The Baganda*), the act of stepping or leaping over a woman is accepted as a ritual substitute for cohabitation with her. And among several Bantu tribes cohabitation is enjoined as a religious and magical rite on certain solemn occasions, such as the circumcision of a child. The Baganda fisherman treats ceremonially the first fish taken. Some he takes to the god Mukasa. The remainder he partakes of with his wife after she has cooked them. Afterwards he jumps over her. Again, "in Uganda, when a man returns from a journey, his wife takes some of the bark cloths from the bed of one of his children and lays them on her husband's bed; and as he enters the house, he jumps over one of his wives who has children by him, or over one of his children. If he neglects to do this, one of his children or one of his wives will die." In Uganda, before an army set out, the general and all the chiefs, to ensure success, had either to cohabit with their wives or to jump over them. See J. G. Frazer, *G.B.*, Pt. II., 1911; Part III., 1912; Part V., vol. ii., 1912.

JUMPING DANCE OF ECHTERNACH. A festival held annually on White Tuesday at Echternach in Luxemburg. It would seem that in the eighth century the malady known as the Dance of St. Vitus (Chorea Sancti Viti) was prevalent here. The Jumping Dance is a festival of thanksgiving for its cessation. It has been described as follows: "The procession starts from the bridge, accompanied by several bands of music; the pilgrims of both sexes form in rows, and spring first four steps forward and three back, then eight steps forward and three back, and so on, continually increasing the steps forward, but making no change in those backward, until they reach the church, when they fall on their faces and begin to pray" (*Notes and Queries*, quoted by J. H. Blunt). See J. H. Blunt; Brockhaus.

JUNKERS. A religious body in America. E. Planta Nesbit finds in their habits and modes of thought many striking points of resemblance to the Essenes (*q.v.*). The Junkers call themselves "Brethren." The designation "Harmless People" is one by which they are often known. "They live in little villages and groups of farms. They permit marriage, like one sect of the Essenes did, but still hold celibacy in the highest honour" (Nesbit). See E. Planta Nesbit, *Christ, Christians, and Christianity*, 1899.

JURUPARI PIPES. Sacred instruments used in religious mysteries by the natives of Brazil. They serve the same purpose as the bull-roarer (*q.v.*); and just as women among the Australian Kurnai are forbidden to look upon the *turndun*, the Brazilian women are prohibited from seeing the jurupari pipes on pain of death.

JUSTIFICATION BY FAITH. According to Roman Catholic doctrine, as stated in C. H. Bowden's *Simple Dictionary for Catholics* (1906), Justification is "not only the remission of sin, but the sanctifying and renewing of the interior man by the voluntary reception of grace and gifts, whence a man, from being unjust and an enemy, becomes just and a friend of God, that he may be heir according to the hope of life everlasting (Tit. iii. 7)." According to Article xi. of the Church of England, "We are accounted righteous before God, only for the merit of our Lord and Saviour Jesus Christ by Faith, and not for our own works or deservings: Wherefore, that we are justified by Faith only is a most wholesome Doctrine, and very full of comfort."

K

K. God K is a designation used by anthropologists for a deity depicted in the MSS. of the Mayan Indians of Central America. Like God B, he is given an ornamental nose. He may in fact be simply a variant of B. In that case, he is probably to be identified with the rain-god Chac (= Tlaloc). There is good reason to suppose that B's proboscis really represents an elephant's trunk, and not merely a funnel through which gales were emitted (see G. Elliot Smith, "Pre-Columbian Representations of the Elephant in America," in *Nature*, Nov. 25, 1915).

KA, THE. Ka is a term used in the religion of the ancient Egyptians. Every living person was "lord of a ka." He received it at his birth. When the Sun god created the two primeval gods he stretched out his arms behind them, whereupon they received the ka and became animate. Erman points out that "this stretching out the arms must be specially connected with the investing with a ka, for from the earliest times two outstretched arms signified a ka." The ka is not the same as the soul, for the Egyptians speak of a soul as well, which at death flies away like a bird. The ka, though never seen, is supposed to have the same form as its possessor, or, as Erman says, to be "exactly the counterpart of the man." Salomon Reinach speaks of it as a man's double, a kind of tutelary genius or guardian angel. After death, it was supposed, the ka continued to take an interest in its old body, and sometimes to re-animate it. Food was placed in the grave to sustain it. Even the gods were supposed to have kas. As an instance of the close identification of the ka with the living body, Naville points out that the expression "to thy ka" came to be used instead of "to thyself." See Alfred Wiedemann; Adolf Erman, *Handbook;* Edouard Naville, *The Old Egyptian Faith*, 1909; Reinach, *O.*

KA'BA. The name of the temple to which devout Muhammedans make pilgrimages. It is "a square primitive stone building at Mecca, which Muslims believe to have been built by Abraham, and to which the pagan Arabs had from ancient times performed pilgrimages as to their national sanctuary, on which occasion they performed the very same rites and ceremonies now observed by the Muslim Pilgrims." The "black stone," which "is built up in one of the corners of this temple, forms an object of special veneration to the pilgrim." See F. A. Klein; and compare HAJJ, THE.

KABBALAH. A Hebrew word meaning literally "tradition." It is used especially in connection with the mystical teaching of a movement in the thirteenth century. These Kabbalists attached importance to every letter in the Bible on the ground that it conveyed some secret meaning to the initiated. The teaching is found in an extravagant form in a large work called the *Zohar*, which in its present form belongs to the thirteenth century. Kabbalistic interpretation follows three principles. "(1) *Notariqon*—to reconstruct a word by using the initials of many, or a sentence by using all the letters of a single word for initial letters of other words: (2) *Ghematria*—the use of the numerical values of the letters of a word for purposes of comparison with other words which yield the same or similar combinations of numbers; (3) *Temura*—the permutation of letters by the three Cabalistic alphabets, 'Atbaeh, 'Albam, and 'Athbash" (C. A. Briggs). See C. A. Briggs, *Intr.*

KABIR PANTHIS. A modern Hindu sect founded by Kabīr. Kabir seems to have lived partly at Benares and partly at Magar, near Gorakhpur, between the years 1488 and 1512, and to have been originally a Muhammadan. In course of time, however, he became a disciple of Rāmānanda. The followers of Rāmānanda, the Rāmānandis, worship Vishnu (*q.v.*) under the form of Rāma, the hero-god. Kabir, in his further development, became a reformer, and strove "to free the Vaishṇava creed from the useless and senseless incrustations with which it had become overlaid" (Monier-Williams). He assailed all worship of idols, and represented Vishṇavism as strictly monotheistic. The externalities of religion are of no importance; all that matters is the state of the "inner man." Monier-Williams describes him as "the first to attempt a partial bridging of the gulf between Hindūism and Islām." Kabir is claimed by the Sikhs as one of their prophets. See Monier-Williams; E. W. Hopkins; *R.S.W.;* and R. V. Russell.

KABOI. A deity worshipped by the Karaya Indians of Brazil. He is said to have led his people from the lower to the upper regions of the earth.

KABRAKAN. A tribal deity in the religion of the Mayan Indians. He is described as the destroyer of mountains.

KADAMPA SECT. A sect founded in the eleventh century among the Buddhists of Tibet. The movement was in the direction of reform. See YELLOW-CAP BUDDHISTS.

KADAVUL. A divine being conceived by the Paraiyans, a tribe or caste in India, as the supreme, omnipresent, personal spiritual Being, the source of all. "Kadaval possesses no temples, and is not worshipped, but he is the highest conception of Paraiya thought" (E. Thurston).

KAD BHAGAVADI. A Hindu deity, god of the jungles, the special god of the Paniyans, a tribe in India.

KĀDIRS. The Kādirs (also known as Kādans) are a tribe inhabiting the Ānaimalai or elephant hills and the great mountain range which extends thence southward into Travancore, in Southern India. Their religion, which has been described as an "ejaculatory religion, finding vent in uttering the names of the gods and demons," consists in the worship of stone images or invisible gods. Thurston and Rangachari mention five gods. Paikuttātha is "a projecting rock overhanging a slab of rock, on which are two stones set up on end." Athuvisariamma is "a stone enclosure, ten or fifteen feet square, almost level with the ground." There is a representation of the god within the enclosure. Vanathavāthi is worshipped anywhere as an invisible god. Iyappaswāmi is a stone set up beneath a teak tree, and worshipped as a protector against various forms of sickness and disease. In the act of worshipping, a mark is made on the stone with ashes. Māsanyatha is "a female recumbent figure in stone on a masonry wall in an open plain near the village of Ānaimalai, before which trial by ordeal is carried out." See E. Thurston.

KADRIYAH, THE. A Muhammadan religious order which established itself in Timbuctoo early in the sixteenth century. They were afterwards encouraged by the Wahhábis (*q.v.*) to propagate their faith more zealously. "Their missionary work bears an entirely peaceful character: it is founded merely upon personal example and good teaching, upon the natural influence of the teacher over the pupil, and upon the spreading of higher civilization" (Oskar Mann). See T. W. Arnold; Oskar Mann, "Mohammedanism" in *Great Religions of the World*, 1902.

KAILĀSA. Kailasa is one of the paradises or heavens of the Hindus. It is the heaven of Siva (*q.v.*), that of Vishnu (*q.v.*) being Vaikuṇṭha, and that of Kṛishṇa (*q.v.*) being Go-loka. Kailāsa is in the Himālaya, and the temple there is said by Monier-Williams to be one of the wonders of India and even of the world. Kailasa, a city constructed on a triangular plan, is sometimes called Parvata, "mountain." "It is a charming place. Siva rules over it, and it is here that he resides with his wife Parvati" (Dubois and Beauchamp). Kailasa is the paradise reserved for the faithful followers of Siva. See Monier-Williams; J. A. Dubois and H. K. Beauchamp.

KALANDARĪYEH. An order of Dervishes, an offshoot of the Bakhtashiyeh (*q.v.*). They practise celibacy, and have an establishment in Aleppo.

KĀLAPĀT. A Hindu deity, the tutelary god of the Taonlas, a small non-Aryan caste of the Uriya States in India, the members of which are generally farm-servants and labourers. The Taonlas worship also the cobra, and on the festival of Nawākhai a cattle-goad as the symbol of their calling.

KĀLI. Kālī is one of the deities worshipped by the Hindus. The name is one of those given to the wife of the god Siva (*q.v.*), and under this name she appears in her most terrible form. "It is this goddess who thirsts for blood, and especially for human blood: and if the blood of animals is not offered to her, she takes that of men. In one of the Tantras kings are directed to appease her by blood, and even by human sacrifice" (Monier-Williams).

KALOU. A name given by the Fijians to a power that is supernatural, supernormal, or awe-inspiring.

KAMA. A term used in Theosophy (*q.v.*). It denotes the emotional and passional nature in man.

KĀMA. A Hindu deity corresponding to Cupid. S. G. Roberts notes (*Calcutta Review*, 1902) that he is more like Eros than the tiny little god of Roman mythology. "He has beautiful attributes. His bow is of the sugar-cane: his arrows are tipped with flowers; and his bow-string is a chain of bees—a pretty touch that recalls the swallow song of the Homeric bowstring." The Hindu Cupid, however, is a married man.

KAMBATA. Kambata or Kamata is an annual feast, lasting about a fortnight, held in honour of the god Kamataraya by the Kota, an aboriginal tribe of the Nilgiri Hills of India. The only work permitted on the second day of the festival is the digging of clay and the making of pots.

KĀMDHENU. The sacred cow in Hindu mythology, the giver of all wealth.

KAMI-NO-MICHI. Kami-no-michi, the "Way of the Genii, or Spirits," is the Japanese equivalent of the Chinese Shinto. The expression is often rendered "Way of the Gods." According to D. Goh, however, there are no gods (in the ordinary sense) in Shinto; and Kami is a word used by Japanese subjects in speaking of their sovereign and by servants in addressing their master. See SHINTŌISM.

KAMMĀLANS. A Tamil caste. A more original form of the name is Kannālan, which means one who rules the eye or one who gives the eye. The Kammālans make images of gods for the temple. When the eyes are added, a special ceremony takes place, the ceremony of painting the eyes of images. Before this ceremony the block or lump is treated by the craftsman with no special honour. The Kammālans claim descent from Visvakarma, the architect of the gods. There is an artisan caste of Kammālans in Malabar, but they are regarded as a lower caste, and are not allowed to enter temples or Brāhman houses. See E. Thurston.

KĀNAPHĀTS. Literally "Ear-splitters." An order of Hindu ascetics, worshippers of Siva (*q.v.*). They are so called because they put heavy rings in their ears. See E. W. Hopkins.

KANDRĀPAT. A Hindu deity, a goddess, perhaps a deified tiger, worshipped by the Dehri Sudhs, a sub-caste of the Sudhs, a cultivating caste in the Uriya country in India. She is supposed to dwell always on the summits of hills.

KANEL. Kanel or Xkanel was a tribal god of fertility in the religion of the Mayan Indians.

KANHAIYA. One of the names of the Hindu god Krishna.

KANIKA DEVI. A Hindu goddess. The original was a maiden who is held to have been an incarnation of Pārvati. She is worshipped by the Komtis (or Komatis), a Madras caste of traders.

KANIYANS. A caste of astrologers in Southern India. In Malabar the name is spelt and pronounced Kanisan. According to Thurston and Rangachari, it is a Malayālam corruption of the Sanskrit word for astrologer, *Ganika*. Centuries ago the Kaniyans already enjoyed a great reputation as diviners. They practise sorcery and exorcism as well as astrology. They worship the sun, the moon, Ganēsa and Subramanya, Vishnu, Siva, and Baghavati. Logan (quoted by Thurston and Rangachari) explains that two things are essential to the astrologer, a bag of cowry shells and an almanac. "When anyone comes to consult him, he quietly sits down, facing the sun, on a plank seat or mat, murmuring some mantrams or sacred verses, opens his bag of cowries, and pours them on the floor. With his right hand he moves them slowly round and round, solemnly reciting meanwhile a stanza or two in praise of his guru or teacher, and of his deity, invoking their help. He then stops, and explains what he has been doing, at the same time taking a handful of cowries from the heap, and placing them on one side. In front is a diagram drawn with chalk on the floor, and consisting of twelve compartments (rāsis), one for each month in the year. Before commencing operations with the diagrams, he selects three or five of the cowries highest up in the heap, and places them in a line on the right-hand side. These represent Ganapati (the belly god, the remover of difficulties), the sun, the planet Jupiter, Sarasvati (the goddess of speech), and his own guru or preceptor. To all of these the astrologer gives due obeisance, touching his ears and the ground three times with both hands. The cowries are next arranged in the compartments of the diagram, and are moved about from compartment to compartment by the astrologer, who quotes meanwhile the authority on which he makes the moves. Finally he explains the result, and ends with again worshipping the deified cowries, who were witnessing the operation as spectators." See E. Thurston.

KARGYUPA SECT. A sect in Lamaism, founded by a lama named Marpa. The adherents pay special reverence to a disciple of Marpa, Milaraspa. Great importance is attached to the exorcism of demons, in which art Milaraspa won great renown. A peculiarity of the Kargyupa sect at first was that the members meditated in caves or deserts. See H. Hackmann.

KARMA. A term used in Theosophy (*q.v.*). The word means "action," and is applied to the immutable law of cause and effect. In virtue of this law, persons are re-incarnated. "Every debt incurred must be duly paid in this or in some other life, and as the wheel of life turns round it brings with it the fruit of every seed that we have sown" (Annie Besant, "Theosophy," in *R.S.W.*).

KARRAMIYYA. An Arabian sect, regarded by the Sunnis as heretics. They derived their name from Muhammad ibn Karrâm, and were also called the Mujassima or Corporealists. They "not only admitted a resemblance between God and created beings, but declared God to be corporeal." They split up into twelve different sects, each holding somewhat modified ideas about the corporeality of God." See F. A. Klein.

KĀRTTIKEYA. Another name for Skanda (*q.v.*), one of the gods of the Hindus.

KARUA. An Indian deity, the cobra, worshipped by the Bharias.

KARUVANDARĀYA BOMMADEVA. The caste god, according to F. R. Hemingway, of the Uppiliyans. "He has no temple, but all the Uppiliyans in a village join in offering him an annual sacrifice in Tai (January-February), before the earth is scraped for the first time in the season for making saltpetre" (quoted by E. Thurston and K. Rangachari). The Uppiliyans, Upparas, or Uppaligas of Southern India are employed in the manufacture of salt.

KĀSHINĀTH. The lord of Benāres, one of the names of the Hindu god Siva.

KATAPHANG. A ceremony observed every year by the Nicobars, a people inhabiting the archipelago between the Andaman Islands in the Bay of Bengal and the northern coast of Sumatra. On this occasion the *elpanam*, certain structures used as a guest-house for strangers and as a town-hall for public gatherings, are cleaned out with singing and dancing, and the rubbish is cast into the sea. Then the doors of the houses in the *elpanam* are closed, and the people go back to their dwellings. For a month they must observe silence, and are not allowed to show a fire or light, or to smoke a cheroot. "The natives believe that during this time the evil spirits from the jungle visit the *elpanam*. When the month is up, a great feast is given to the spirits and they are sent back to the jungle" (Hutton Webster, *R.D.*).

KATAPHRYGIAN CHURCH, THE. The Kataphrygian Church means the Church according to the Phrygians. The followers of Montanus were so called because they were so numerous in Phrygia. See MONTANISM.

KATHĀVATTHU. A Buddhist sacred book, a book on heresies, in the third division of the Canon. See CANON, BUDDHIST.

KĀYASTHS. The caste of writers and village accountants in India. According to R. V. Russell and R. B. Hira Lāl, the most probable hypothesis as to their origin is that they were an off-shoot of Brāhmans of irregular descent. "The reason for this is that the Kāyasths must have learnt reading and writing from some outside source, and the Brāhmans were the only class who could teach it them."

KEB. An Egyptian deity. Keb was god of the earth, the husband of Nut (*q.v.*), the female personification of the sky. Keb and Nut were the offspring of Shu (*q.v.*) and Tefnet (*q.v.*), and in their turn gave birth to Osiris (*q.v.*) and Set (*q.v.*), Isis (*q.v.*) and Nephthys (*q.v.*). By the Greeks Keb is identified with Kronos. The animal sacred to him was the goose. See Alfred Wiedemann; Adolf Erman, *Handbook;* Edouard Naville, *The Old Egyptian Faith*, 1909.

KEDĀRNĀTH. The lord of cedars, one of the names of the Hindu god Siva.

KEENS. An Irish term denoting lamentations for the dead in loud and mournful notes and verses. In a *keen* "the pedigree, land, property, generosity, and good actions of the deceased person and his ancestors are diligently and harmoniously recounted in order to excite pity and compassion in the hearers, and to make them sensible of their great loss in the death of the person they lament" (O'Brien, *Dictionary*). The *keener*, or person who makes lamentation, usually is an old woman. Three hours must elapse after death before wails of grief are raised. Otherwise, the noise might hinder the soul from leaving the body. See W. G. Wood-Martin.

KEITHIANS. The followers of George Keith (1639?-1716), who was for a time a missionary of the Society for the Propagation of the Gospel. He gave literary assistance to Robert Barclay (1648-1690), the Quaker apologist, and went to Holland and Germany as a missionary with George Fox (1624-1691) and William Penn (1644-1718). In 1689 he emigrated to America. On his return to England, he collected a congregation in Turners' Hall, Philpot Lane. Here he preached and officiated for some years (1695-1700). In 1700 he became a clergyman of the Church of England, and afterwards was made Rector of Edburton in Sussex. He and his followers called themselves Christian Quakers. George Keith's works include "The Deism of William Penn and his Brethren" (1699), "The Standard of the Quakers Examined" (1702), and "A Journal of Travels" (1706). See J. H. Blunt; and the *D.N.B.*

KELIM. The name of one of the Jewish treatises or tractates which reproduce the oral tradition or unwritten law as developed by the second century A.D. and are included in the Mishnah (*q.v.*), a collection and compilation completed by Rabbi Judah the Holy, or the Patriarch, about 200 A.D. The sixty-three tractates of the Mishnah are divided into six groups or orders (*sedarim*). Kēlim is the first tractate of the sixth group, which is called Ṭohorōth (" Purifications ").

KENŌMA. A term used in Gnosticism (*q.v.*). The Kenoma is the inferior world which is opposed to the Pleroma (*q.v.*). See VALENTINIANS.

KENOSIS. A term used in Christian theology. The word is Greek, and means "emptying." The verb occurs in the Epistle to the Philippians (ii. 7). The whole passage (*vss.* 5-11) is as follows: "Let this mind be in you, which was also in Christ Jesus, who, being in the form of God, thought it not a thing to be snatched to be equal with God, but emptied himself (*heauton ekenōsen*), and took upon him the form of a servant, and was made in the likeness of men. And being found in fashion as a man, he humbled himself, and became obedient unto death, even the death of the cross. Wherefore God also hath highly exalted him, and given him a name which is above every name, that at the name of Jesus every knee should bow, of things in heaven, and things in earth, and things under the earth, and that every tongue should confess that Jesus Christ is Lord, to the glory of God the father." Hilary of Pictavium (A.D. 350) explained this passage to mean that although the Divine Logos had entered into Christ he did not at once make full use of it, but willed to remain in a state of humiliation (just as he could will not to sin) until his exaltation. A later explanation was that Christ, although he knew that his nature was divine, would not make use of the divine majesty (as a thing to be snatched at). A modern idea of the Kenosis is that Christ identified himself with humanity (apart from the fact that he willed not to sin) so entirely that he shared its infirmities even as regards human knowledge. His knowledge does appear to have been limited. To take only one subject, it must be frankly admitted, as Prof. W. Sanday says (*I.*), "that even when deductions have been made, as some deductions must be made, on critical grounds, there still remains evidence enough that our Lord while upon earth *did* use the common language of His contemporaries in regard to the Old Testament; that He did speak—if not of Daniel as the author of the book which bears his name, yet of Moses as the author of the Pentateuch, and of David as the author of one of the later Psalms; and that He did apply to His own day some part at least of the story of Jonah and the story of Noah as literal narrative." Conseqently, "many of the most reverent and most careful of our theologians" have been forced to conclude "that limitations of knowledge might be and were assumed along with other limitations by Him Who was in all things made like unto His brethren, though without sin." See J. B. Heard, *New Wine in Old Bottles*, 1862; C. Gore, *Bampton Lectures*, 1891; W. S. Swayne, *Our Lord's Knowledge as Man*, 1891; Bodington, *Jesus the Christ*, 1892.

KERIDWEN. A goddess of the under-water Elysium in the mythology of the British Celts. A draught from her mystic cauldron called Amen had power to inspire those who drank it. Originally she would seem to have been a goddess of fertility.

KERĪTHŌTH. The title of one of the Jewish treatises or tractates which reproduce the oral tradition or unwritten law as developed by the second century A.D. and are included in the Mishnah (*q.v.*), a collection and compilation completed by Rabbi Judah the Holy, or the Patriarch, about 200 A.D. The sixty-three tractates of the Mishnah are divided into six groups or orders (*sedarim*). Kerīthōth is the seventh tractate of the fifth group, which is called *Ḳodāshīm* (" Holy Things ").

KESHO. Having long, fine hair, one of the names of the Hindu god Krishna.

KETHUBIM. The Hebrew name of the third of the groups into which the books of the Old Testament are divided. The word means "Writings." See further HAGIOGRAPHA.

KETHŪBŌTH. The name of one of the Jewish treatises or tractates which reproduce the oral tradition or unwritten law as developed by the second century A.D. and are included in the Mishnah (*q.v.*), a collection and compilation completed by Rabbi Judah the Holy, or the Patriarch, about 200 A.D. The sixty-three tractates of the Mishnah are divided into six groups or orders (*sedarim*). Kethūbōth is the second tractate of the third group, which is called *Nāshīm* (" Women ").

KHAMBESHWARI. A Hindu deity, the tutelary goddess of the Sudhs, a cultivating caste in the Uriya country in India. She is represented by a wooden peg.

KHALIFS. The Arabic word *khalif* means "a successor" or "substitute." The term is used of the successors of Muhammad. The first four Khalifs were Abu Bakr, 'Umar, 'Uthmân and 'Ali. These, according to the Sunnis, were the "rightly directed Khalifs." They were also Companions of Muhammad (see COMPANIONS OF MUHAMMAD). See F. A. Klein.

KHANDHAKAS. Two Buddhist sacred books in the first division of the Canon. See CANON, BUDDHIST.

KHANDOBA. An Indian deity, the principal god of the Marāthas, the military caste of southern India. Khandoba (= *khand-aba*, sword-father) is a warrior incarnation of Mahādeo, and is regarded as the tutelary deity of the Marātha country. The Kaikāris or Kaikādis (also called Bargandis), for instance, a wandering tribe of basket-makers, worship him as a god of war. The Dhangars, the Marātha caste of shepherds and blanket weavers, on the other hand, who worship him on Sundays and identify him with the sun, revere him as a family god. Khande Rao or Khandoba is also the favourite god of the Hindu and Muhammadan Bhils.

KHARAK DEO. One of the special deities of the Ahirs, a caste of cowherds, milkmen, and cattle-breeders in India. He seems to be the spirit or god of the place of assembly of the cattle (the *khirkha*).

KHARIMATI. Attendants upon the Babylonian goddess Ishtar (*q.v.*). See GILGAMESH EPIC, and UKHAT.

KHAWARIJ. A Muslim sect which differs from the Sunnis on the question of the Imâmate (see IMAM). They revolted from 'Ali, who according to the Sunnis was one of the four "rightly directed Khalifs." because he submitted the decision of his right to the

Khalifate to arbitration when it was challenged. "They blamed 'Ali for referring a matter concerning the religion of God to the judgment of man." The Khawârij also declined to recognise 'Uthmân. See F. A. Klein.

KHEPRE. An Egyptian deity. The word means "he who is becoming," and Khepre is referred to as the sun god. He is represented in the form of a beetle. The sun god was created "while as yet there was no heaven, when neither serpent nor reptile was formed. He came into being in the form of Khepre, and there was nothing that was with him in that place where he was." The sun god is referred to also as Re (Râ), Horus, Harakhti, Atum, etc. See A. Wiedemann; Adolf Erman, *Handbook*.

KHERMATA. A Hindu deity, worshipped as the mother of the village by the Kurmis, the representative cultivating caste of Hindustān.

KHLISTI. The Khlisti or "Self-slashers" are a subsect of the Russian dissenters known as Bezpopovtzi (*q.v.*). The body seems to have been formed about 1645 by Daniel Philipitch, a deserter from the army, who claimed to be divine. The Khlisti received the name "self-slashers" or "flagellants" because one of their practices is to lash themselves. They are ascetics and regard married life as sinful. One of their beliefs is that Christ and the Virgin from time to time appear among them. "Their meetings are marked by solemn dances, becoming wild like the dervishes' ritual waltzes, ending in convulsions, catalepsy, or prophesying with tongues" (F. W. Bussell). These dances are held in secret. See Schaff-Herzog; J. H. Blunt.

KHNUM. An Egyptian deity. The god Khnum was regarded as sculptor or modeller and creator. He is represented as a ram or with a ram's head. At Elephantine Khnum was worshipped as the cataract god. He is described as "he who created all that is, who formed that which is existent, the father of fathers, the mother of mothers." See A. Wiedemann; Adolf Erman, *Handbook*.

KHONDS. The Khonds or Kandhs are a Dravidian tribe found in the Uriya-speaking tract of the Sambalpur District and the adjoining Feudatory States of Patna and Kālāhandi in India. The Khonds used to offer human sacrifices to the Earth-Goddess, Tāri Pennu or Bera Pennu, which were believed to insure good crops. "The mode of performing these tribal sacrifices was as follows. Ten or twelve days before the sacrifice, the victim was devoted by cutting off his hair, which, until then, had been kept unshorn. Crowds of men and women assembled to witness the sacrifice; none might be excluded, since the sacrifice was declared to be for all mankind. It was preceded by several days of wild revelry and gross debauchery. On the day before the sacrifice the victim, dressed in a new garment, was led forth from the village in solemn procession, with music and dancing, to the Meriāh grove, a clump of high forest trees standing a little way from the village and untouched by the axe. Here they tied him to a post, which was sometimes placed between two plants of the *sankissār* shrub. He was then anointed with oil, ghee and turmeric, and adorned with flowers; and 'a species of reverence, which it is not easy to distinguish from adoration,' was paid to him throughout the day. A great struggle now arose to obtain the smallest relic from his person; a particle of the turmeric paste with which he was smeared, or a drop of his spittle, was esteemed of sovereign virtue, especially by the women. The crowd danced round the post to music, and addressing the Earth said, 'O God, we offer this sacrifice to you; give us good crops, seasons, and health.' On the last morning the orgies, which had been scarcely interrupted during the night, were continued till noon, when they ceased, and the assembly proceeded to consummate the sacrifice. The victim was again anointed with oil, and each person touched the anointed part, and wiped the oil on his own head. In some places they took the victim in procession round the village, from door to door, where some plucked hair from his head, and others begged for a drop of his spittle, with which they anointed their heads. As the victim might not be bound nor make any show of resistance, the bones of his arms and, if necessary, his legs were broken; but often this precaution was rendered unnecessary by stupefying him with opium. The mode of putting him to death varied in different places. One of the commonest modes seems to have been strangulation, or squeezing to death" (J. G. Frazer, *G.B.*). See E. Thurston; and R. V. Russell.

KHONSU. An Egyptian deity, another name for Thoth (*q.v.*), the moon god. Khonsu was worshipped at Thebes "in purely human form as a child" (Erman).

KHUDDKANIKAYA. A Buddhist sacred work, a collection of songs, tales, legends, etc., added as an appendix to the second division of the Canon. See CANON, BUDDHIST.

KHUMBABA. A figure in the Babylonian Epic of Gilgamesh (see GILGAMESH, EPIC OF). Khumbaba is a terrible foe fought against and overcome by Gilgamesh and his companion Eabani (*q.v.*).

KHURIA RĀNI. A Hindu deity, the principal deity in Sargūja of the Korwas, a Kolarian tribe of the Chota Nāgpur plateau in India. Khuria Rāni is the tutelary goddess of the Khuria plateau. Animal sacrifices are offered to her.

KIANG-SHI. A Chinese term. A *kiang-shi* is a horrible spectre which comes forth from a coffin and catches and kills those who pass by. It chooses the night for its raids, because daylight paralyzes its powers. It has a body, and is therefore stronger and more malicious than other disembodied ghosts. To kill its prey, it commonly sucks its blood. "Its body is covered all over with long, white hair, and its nails are exceedingly long, which reminds us of a belief, also prevalent among Europeans, that the hair and nails continue to grow after death. The best way to render a *kiang-shi* harmless is to destroy everything, coffin and all, by fire, or to take the corpse out of the coffin, and fry it in a big iron pan. It may also be reduced to the dead state by belabouring it with a broom" (J. J. M. de Groot). The Chinese believe that if a corpse remains too long unburied, it may change into a *kiang-shi*, and kill the inmates of the house. See J. J. M. de Groot, *Rel. of the Chinese*, 1910.

KIDDŪSHIN. The title of one of the Jewish treatises or tractates which reproduce the oral tradition or unwritten law as developed by the second century A.D. and are included in the Mishnah (*q.v.*), a collection and compilation completed by Rabbi Judah the Holy, or the Patriarch, about 200 A.D. The sixty-three tractates of the Mishnah are divided into six groups or orders (*sedarim*). Kiddūshīn is the seventh tractate of the third group, which is called Nāshīm ("Women").

KIL'AYIM. The name of one of the Jewish treatises or tractates which reproduce the oral tradition or unwritten law as developed by the second century A.D. and are included in the Mishnah (*q.v.*), a collection and compilation completed by Rabbi Judah the Holy, or the Patriarch, about 200 A.D. The sixty-three tractates of the Mishnah are divided into six groups or orders (*sedarim*). Kil'āyim is the fourth tractate of the first group, which is called *Zerā'īm* ("Seeds").

KILHAMITES. The followers of Alexander Kilham (1762-1798), the founder of the Methodist New Connexion (*q.v.*).

KINA-VERSE. A form of Hebrew metre used in lamentations. See LAMENTATIONS, BOOK OF.

KING'S BOOK. A book of Christian doctrine published in 1543. It was a revised and reactionary version of the book published in 1537, and known as the "Bishop' Book" (*q.v.*). The real title of the King's Book" was the "Necessary Doctrine and Erudition for any Christian Man." See M. W. Patterson, *Hist.*

KINGS, BOOKS OF. The books called First and Second Kings in the Hebrew Bible are described in the Septuagint as the Third and Fourth Books of Kingdoms (the First and Second being the books called in Hebrew First and Second Samuel). The contents of the books naturally divide themselves into three sections. These deal (1) with the reign of Solomon (I. Kings i.-xi.); (2) with the history of the divided kingdom to the Fall of Samaria (I. Kings xii.-II. Kings xvii.); (3) with the history of Judah from the Fall of Samaria (II. Kings xviii.-xxv.). The history of Solomon is treated very fully. The second section (2) is chiefly concerned with the history of the prophets Elijah and Elisha. The third section (3) deals for the most part with the religious reformation of Josiah and with events in which the prophet Isaiah was concerned. For information on all these and other matters the author indicates that he used a number of Sources. These included the "Book of the Acts of Solomon" (I. Kings xi. 41), apparently "a series of narratives descriptive of the glory of Solomon" (Whitehouse); the "Book of the Chronicles of the Kings of Israel"; and the "Book of the Chronicles of the Kings of Judah." The two latter works seem to have been of the nature of official annals kept by a minister called the Recorder (*Mazkir*). It is clear that "they were mainly if not exclusively of a *political* character, containing much valuable information regarding the doings of the several kings" (Skinner). These three Sources are referred to for information which the compiler has not included in his history, but there can be little doubt that they were used to some extent for information which he has included. A number of primary Sources, however, can be detected. These include a Court-memoir of the reign of David (I. Kings i., ii.), Temple-archives (I. Kings vi., vii.). Elijah-stories, Elisha-stories, and Isaiah-stories. In the three latter different cycles of stories have been distinguished. There are Early Ephraimite Elijah Stories, Gilgal Elisha and Elijah Stories, and Samaria Elisha Stories. There are two or three cycles of Isaiah Stories. The Septuagint has preserved in I. Kings viii. (after vs. 53) an utterance by Solomon (II. Kings viii. 11, 12 in a corrupt Hebrew text) which would seem to have been derived from a "Book of Songs" or from the "Book of Jashar" (*q.v.*). The utterance, as restored with the help of the Septuagint, may be rendered thus:

> The sun in the heavens did Yahweh give,
> But in darkness deep did he will to hide.
> "Now build me a dwelling in which to live,"
> He said, "for ever to be and abide."

The contents and structure of the Books of Kings were greatly influenced by the Book of Deuteronomy (*q.v.*; cp. CANON OF THE OLD TESTAMENT). Events in the reigns of the successive monarchs of Israel and Judah, and the characters of the monarchs, as Whitehouse says, "are estimated from the religious and legal standpoint of the Book of Deuteronomy, which enforced the legitimacy of the single sanctuary at Jerusalem only, and forbad the worship of the high places with their stone pillars and *Ashērim* (mistranslated 'groves')." And the books as we have them show signs of having been edited by more than one Deuteronomic redactor. The first was the redactor who edited all the historical books from Genesis (ii. 4b) to II. Kings (xxiv. 7). This redaction belongs perhaps to about 600 B.C. The second redactor was a later one who, amongst other things, continued the history from II. Kings xxiv. 7. This redaction may belong to about 560-555 B.C. The hand of a third redactor of a different character has been detected. This was a writer belonging to the later Priestly School (P; *e.g.*, I. Kings viii. 1-11). See I. Benzinger, *Die Buecher der Koenige*, 1899; C. F. Burney, *The Books of Kings*, 1903; J. Skinner, *Kings* in the "Century Bible"; C. F. Kent, *Israel's Historical and Biographical Narratives*, 1905; G. H. Box, *Intr.;* O. C. Whitehouse.

KING'S EVIL. King's Evil was the name formerly given to the disease now known as scrofula. It was believed in England and France for many centuries that this evil could be cured by the touch of the king. The act of touching was regarded as a religious act, for in England until 1719 the Prayer Book contained a special service to accompany it. King Charles II. is said to have "touched" thousands of persons. Samuel Johnson (1709-1784) is said to have been the last child to receive a king's touch.

KINGU. A demon in Babylonian mythology. In the Epic of Marduk (see MARDUK, EPIC OF) Kingu appears as the chief of the monsters who accompany Tiâmat (*q.v.*). Tiâmat makes him ruler of the gods, and gives him the tablets of fate. In the great battle between Tiâmat and Marduk, the latter captures Kingu and snatches from him the tablets of fate.

KINICH AHAU. A tribal deity, a sun-god, in the religion of the Mayan Indians.

ḲINNIM. The Jewish Mishnah, a collection and compilation completed by Rabbi Judah the Holy, or the Patriarch, about 200 A.D. (see MISHNAH), comprises a number of treatises or tractates which reproduce the oral tradition or unwritten law as developed by the second century A.D. There are sixty-three tractates, divided into six groups or orders (*sedarim*). Ḳinnim is the eleventh tractate of the fifth group, which is called Ḳodāshīm ("Holy Things").

KIRCHENTAG. Kirchentag or Church Diet was the name given in Germany to a periodical convention of laymen and ministers of the Lutheran, the Reformed, the United Evangelical, and the Moravian Churches. The object of the conventions, of which the first took place in 1848, was to promote the interests of religion on the basis of evangelical principles held in common. The first convention was attended by more than five hundred delegates. It was agreed "(1) that the evangelical church communities of Germany should form a unity; (2) that the unity should not have the form of a union, abolishing the differences of confession, but only the form of a confederacy; (3) that the confederacy, based on the common evangelical principle of the confessions, should leave to each Church to arrange its relations to the State, its constitution, its ritual, and doctrinal system, as it pleased; while (4) the confederacy as such should represent the unity, bear witness against the non-evangelical churches, administer advice and support, defend the rights and liberties which belong to every evangelical church, etc." (Schaff-Herzog). The confederacy was not established, and the Kirchentag has not been convened since the year 1871. It is agreed, however, that its discussions have had a considerable influence upon the religious life of Germany. See Schaff-Herzog; William Benham.

KISHAR. A Babylonian deity. In the Epic of Marduk (see MARDUK, EPIC OF) Anshar and Kishar are represented as the second pair of deities created. The first pair were Lakhmu (*q.v.*) and Lakhamu. Apsu (*q.v.*)

and Tiâmat were already in existence. The pairs represent the male and female principles. In this case Anshar is the male and Kishar the female. The first pair of deities, Lakhmu and Lakhamu are of the nature of monsters. The second pair, Anshar and Kishar, are of a character intermediate between that of monsters and that of gods proper. Anshar played a great rôle as Ashur (*q.v.*) afterwards. Kishar disappears.

KISHI BOJIN. A Japanese goddess. She is represented carrying a child and a pomegranate.

KITUNG. One of the deities worshipped by the Savaras (also known as Sawaras or Saoras), an important hill-tribe in Southern India. Associated with the deity are sacred groves.

KIZRETI. Attendants upon the Babylonian goddess Ishtar (*q.v.*). See GILGAMESH EPIC, and UKHAT.

KNIGHTS OF MALTA. In 1530 the Knights of the Hospital of St. John of Jerusalem came into possession of the Island of Malta. They held it for more than two centuries, and became known as the Knights of Malta. See HOSPITALLERS.

KNIGHTS OF RHODES. The Knights of the Hospital of St. John of Jerusalem came to be known as the Knights of Rhodes, because for over two centuries they were in possession of the Island of Rhodes. See HOSPITALLERS.

KNIGHTS OF THE HOSPITAL OF ST. JOHN OF JERUSALEM. An order of Hospitallers (*q.v.*).

KNIPPERDOLLINGS. B. Knipperdollinck was born at Münster and became leader of the Anabaptists there. In 1534 he was Bürgermeister. He supported "John of Leiden" (Bockold), and was executed with him in 1536. His followers were called Knipperdollings.

KNOT, SACRED. A Russian example of the sacred knot is quoted by R. R. Marett in the formula: "I attach five knots to each hostile infidel shooter. . . . Do ye, O knots, bar the shooter from every road and way. . . . In my knots lies hid the mighty strength of snakes —from the twelve-headed snake." Knots are represented as playing some part in Minoan religious worship.

KOBOLD. A spirit in German folklore resembling a brownie (*q.v.*).

KOHELETH. Literally the "Preacher," the Hebrew name of the Book of Ecclesiastes (*q.v.*).

KOJI-KI. A god in Japanese Buddhism, regarded as a patron of seafarers.

KORAN. The Koran is the sacred book of the Muhammadans. The word, which means the "reading" or the "lectionary," is more correctly written Kur'ân or Qur'ân. The work contains the revelations which are supposed to have come to Muhammad through the angel Gabriel. These are given in one hundred and fourteen Suras (*q.v.*) or chapters. "The style in which the Qur'ân is written is a kind of rhyming prose, *i.e.*, language having a final rhyme, without being measured, a style much in use in the time of Muhammad, and liked by the Arabs, and in which their soothsayers and poets used to speak" (Klein). The Qur'ân is supposed to contain all knowledge. Muhammad says that "he who reads a letter or syllable of the Qur'ân receives for it the recompense of a good action, and this action is worth ten other good actions." Again, "the Qur'ân contains a thousand times and twenty thousand letters: he who reads it with the desire of receiving a reward from God, and with patience, will receive (in Paradise) a 'Houri' as wife." Muhammad professes to have received divine and miraculous revelations. Muslim doctors say that these came to him by direct inspiration of the Angel Gabriel, "the Angel of Inspiration," or in visions in which the Angel Gabriel appeared to him, or by communication from God Himself when the prophet was awake or asleep. The revelations were not arranged in one book in the Prophet's lifetime. An amanuensis wrote them down as he uttered them "on any material that happened to be at hand, such as palm-leaves, bones, stones, leather, etc." After his death they were repeated for a time from memory by the "Readers" of the Qur'ân. The necessity of fixing and writing down the Koran was suggested by the multiplication of various readings. The Khalif Abu Bakr (632-634 A.D.) ordered Zaid bin Thabit to collect the various portions of the Qur'ân into one book. No copies of this first edition, however, have been preserved. It did not in any case put a stop to the multiplication of various readings. Khalif 'Uthman (644-655 A.D.) therefore had a new recension made. Persons having a thorough knowledge of the Qur'ân were called by Muhammad Qur'ân-readers. The Suras are divided into Suras revealed before the flight of Muhammad to Madina, "Mecca Suras," and Suras revealed after the flight, "Madina Suras." The Suras are arranged as to length and not according to chronology. "The long Suras were placed first and the short ones last. Within the Suras, some portions have been arranged in chronological order, others on the ground of similarity of matter; but in a variety of instances passages are joined together without any regard to either chronology or similarity of subject. Thus we find verses revealed at Mecca in the midst of Madina Suras, and passages revealed at Madina mixed up in the earlier Mecca Suras, and occasionally most heterogeneous materials put together without any regard to logical connexion at all" (Klein). The Qur'ân is not free from contradictions, and God Himself is represented as saying (ii. 100): "Whatever verse we abrogate, or cause thee to forget, we will bring a better one than it, or one like it." It is not certain that Muhammad could read or write. Devoted followers have maintained that he could not, and that therefore his revelations must certainly have been received from God. But in any case he had other means of obtaining religious information, and, as Klein says, it is "evident that by far the greater portion" of the Qur'ân "consists of materials collected from Jews, Christians, Sabeans, and pagan Arabs." J. M. Rodwell gives the following transliteration of the first Sura as an example of the rhyming prose in which the Qur'ân is written:

> Bismillahi ' rahmani ' rrahheem.
> El-hamdoo lillahi rabi ' lalameen.
> Arrahhmani raheem.
> Maliki yowmi-d-deen.
> Eyaka nahoodoo, waéyaka nestaeen.
> Ihdina 'ssirat almostakeem.
> Sirat alezeena anhamta aleihim, gheiri-'l
> mughdoobi aleihim, wala dsaleen. Ameen.

There are many commentaries on the Qur'ân. One of the best known is that of Al Baidâwi (685 A.H.). The Qur'ân has been translated into English by George Sale, J. M. Rodwell, and E. H. Palmer. See J. M. Rodwell, *The Koran*, 1861; G. L. Hurst, *Sacred Literature*, 1905; F. A. Klein, *The Religion of Islam*, 1906; T. Noeldeke, *Geschichte des Qorāns*, part I., second edition, 1909.

KORATEU. Korateu or Kurzkarv, son of Teikirzi, is one of the gods of the Todas. He seems to have been a river god.

KORAVAS. A nomad tribe in India. In different localities they are known by different names. According to Thurston and Rangachari, the members of the tribe are known as Korava from the extreme south to the north of the North Arcot district; north of this district they are called Koracha or Korcha, and in the Ceded Districts they become Yerukala or Yerakala. They live by basket-making and fortune-telling. According to the Census Report of 1901, the Koravas worship Subrahmanya, the son of Siva; the Yerukalas Vishnu in the form of Venkatēswara and his wife Lakshmi. Other gods include Kolāpuriamma, the goddess of Kolhapūr, the chief town of the native state of that name in the Bombay Presidency; and Perumālswāmi, the god of Tirupati, the great place of pilgrimage in the North Arcot district. In the southern districts the domestic god of the Koravas is said to be Sathavu. The Koravas are notorious thieves, and are said to worship as the presiding deity of the criminal profession Moothēvi, the goddess of sleep, who is supposed to keep them awake and alert while she sends their victims to sleep. The Korava women, when telling fortunes, use a winnowing fan and grains of rice. Good or evil is prophesied according to the number of grains found on the fan. "They carry a basket, winnow, stick, and a wicker tray in which cowry shells are imbedded in a mixture of cow-dung and turmeric. The basket represents Kolāpuriamma, and the cowries Pōlēramma. When telling fortunes, the Korava woman places on the basket the winnow, rice, betel leaves and areca nuts, and the wicker tray. Holding her client's hand over the winnow, and moving it about, she commences to chant, and name all sorts of deities. From time to time she touches the hand of the person whose fortune is being told with the stick. The Korava women are very clever in extracting information concerning the affairs of a client before they proceed to tell her fortune" (Thurston and Rangachari). The practice of the couvade, or the custom according to which the father takes to his bed when a baby is born, is found amongst the Koravas. A Tamil proverb says that if a Korati [Korava] is brought to bed, her husband takes the prescribed stimulant. See E. Thurston.

KOTAS. The Kotas are found on the Nilgiri hills and plateau in India. According to Shortt (*Tribes of the Neilgherries*, 1868), "some rude image of wood or stone, a rock or tree in a secluded locality, frequently forms the Kota's object of worship, to which sacrificial offerings are made; but the recognised place of worship in each village consists of a large square of ground, walled round with loose stones, three feet high, and containing in its centre two pent-shaped sheds of thatch, open before and behind, and on the posts (of stone) that support them some rude circles and other figures are drawn. No image of any sort is visible here" (quoted by E. Thurston and K. Rangachari). According to Thurston and Rangachari, the sheds are dedicated to Siva and his consort Parvati under the names of Kāmatarāya and Kālikai. Other deities are Mangkāli, Vettakaraswāmi, Adiral, Udiral, Māgāli, and Māriamma. Māgāli, to whom outbreaks of cholera are supposed to be due, "is represented by an upright stone in a rude temple at a little distance from Kotagiri, where an annual ceremony takes place, at which some man becomes possessed, and announces to the people that Māgāli has come." See E. Thurston.

KRALITZ BIBLE. The name given to the Bohemian version of the Bible which was published in 1593. It was the work of the Bohemian Brethren (*q.v.*).

KRISHNA. Krishṇa, one of the heroes of the Epic poem Mahā-bhārata (see BHARATA), was regarded as one of the incarnations of the Hindu god Vishnu (*q.v.*). In the Bhāgavata-purana he is said to have been a son of Vasudeva. His father entrusted him to the care of the wife of a herdsman named Nanda. Krishna began, even as a child, to perform miracles. On one occasion he protected the wives of the herdsmen against the anger of Indra (*q.v.*) by raising on his finger the mountain-range Govardhana. He had eight favourites among the wives or daughters of the cowherds. In the Vishnu Purāna, which represents the most extravagant form of Krishnaite Vishnuism, Krishna is described as a black child, the son of Nanda, and is called Govinda, the cowboy. "Here he puts a stop to Indra-worship, overpowers Siva, rescues Aniruddha, marries sixteen thousand princesses, burns Benares, and finally is killed himself, he the one born of a hair of Vishnu, he that is Vishnu himself, who in 'goodness' creates, in 'darkness' destroys, under the forms of Brahmā and Siva" (M.-W.). Krishna was deified, and his worship became more popular than that of any other of the later deities. See Monier-Williams; E. W. Hopkins; J. A. Dubois and H. K. Beauchamp.

KUAN-TI. The Chinese god of war. Originally a man, who met his death in A.D. 220, he was afterwards deified. S. Couling notes that he is to the military what Confucius is to the literary classes, and that somehow he has come to be regarded also as a god of literature.

KUDUMI. A name by which the medicine-man is known among castes and tribes of Southern India. "His office implies a more or less intimate acquaintance with the curative herbs and roots in the forests, and their proper application to the different ailments resulting from venomous bites or stings. . . . He prays over sprains and cricks, and binds the affected parts with the sacred cord made of the hair taken from the patient's head" (*Madras Mail*, 1907, quoted by E. Thurston and K. Rangachari). He is supposed to possess a magic influence over wild animals and snakes.

KUKULKAN. A tribal god worshipped by the Mayan Indians of Yucatan. In one account he appears as the god of fevers. He is equivalent to the Mexican god Quetzalcoatl. The Quiché called him Gukumatz, and the Tzental described him as "the feathered snake that goes in the waters." T. A. Joyce (*M.A.*) thinks that the description typifies "the ripple, born both of wind and water, the aspect of which suggests feathers, and the motion a serpent." He became a god of creation.

KUL-DEVI. An Indian deity, the goddess of the family, worshipped by the Dhangars, the Marātha caste of shepherds and blanket-weavers. Also the household deity of the Gajars, a large caste in India. The word *kul* means family.

KULINKARS. Kulinkars or Teikhars is one of the gods of the Todas.

KUTCHI. A term used among the Australian Dieri to denote a mystic potency in things. *Kutchi* seems to be a force, and not a personal being, and corresponds to the Melanesian *mana*.

KWANNON. Kwannon or Kwanyin is a Chinese and Japanese title given to a deity who corresponds to the Sanskrit Avalokitesvara (*q.v.*). G. A. Cobbold thinks she represents an apotheosis of Mercy, a kind of allegorical Mater Misericordiae who ministers untiringly to all sorrow and distress. "In Japan the shrines and statues of Kwannon are to be met with everywhere: many of her images being of enormous size, richly gilt and beautifully wrought. Sometimes the statues are kept concealed from view, either on account of alleged miraculous properties, or for some other reason of special sanctity" (G. A. Cobbold, *Religion in Japan*, 1894).

KWEI. A Chinese term. The *kwei* are evil spirits, a subdivision of Yin (*q.v.*), the darkness-soul of the universe. A man's *kwei*, also called *poh*, is supposed to represent his passions and vices. Everything that is evil comes from the kwei, regarded as devils, spectres, or demons. The kwei swarm everywhere. No one can escape from them. They are in frequented places, as well as in lonely spots. "Public roads are haunted by them everywhere, especially during the night, when the power of the *Yin* part of the universe, to which spectres belong, is strongest. Numerous, in fact, are the tales of wretches who, having been accosted by such natural foes of man, were found dead by the roadside, without the slightest wound or injury being visible: their souls had simply been snatched out of them. Many victims of such encounters could find their way home, but merely to die miserably shortly after. Others, hit by devilish arrows, were visited with boils or tumors, which carried them off, or they died without even any such visible marks of the shots" (J. J. M. de Groot). See J. J. M. de Groot, *Rel. of the Chinese*, 1910.

KWOTEN. One of the gods of the Todas.

KWOTO. Kwoto or Meilitars appears as one of the gods of the Todas.

L

L. God L is a designation used by anthropologists for one of the deities depicted in the MSS. of the Mayan Indians of Central America. He occurs only in the Dresden MS. One half of his face is painted black, which suggests to Schellhas the description "The Old Black God." But it should be noted that God M is even blacker. Possibly God L is to be identified with the God Votan of Central America, who in turn corresponds to the Aztec earth-god Tepeyollotl.

LABADISTS. The followers of the French pietist and mystic Jean de Labadie (1610-1674). Labadie was at first a Jesuit priest. Afterwards he went over to the Reformed Church (1650); and finally he became a separatist. In 1666 he settled with his followers in Holland. The Labadists, who did not survive long after the death of their leader, practised great austerity, desiring to follow the example of the apostolic community. Moreover, they sought diligently the "inward light." B. Puenjer points out that P. J. Spener (1635-1705), the father of German Pietism (*q.v.*), was strongly influenced by the profound mysticism of Labadie. See J. S. Blunt.

LABARTU. An evil goddess or demon in Babylonian mythology. In a series of incantation texts she is represented as a horrible monster who threatens the life of the mother at childbirth. On a bronze plaque, belonging probably to the later Babylonian period, she is represented holding a serpent in each hand, and with swine sucking at her breasts. "She kneels on an ass, and is apparently being driven off in a boat by the demon to her left, who brandishes a weapon or whip in his uplifted hand" (Morris Jastrow, *Civ.*). In one text she is described as "Mistress of the dark-haired men." To cure a sick man possessed by her or her power and to draw the evil out, a clay image of her was placed over his head.

LABARUM. The Labarum was the military standard used by the Emperor Constantine in his campaigns. It was an adaptation of the ordinary standard of the Roman cavalry, the "vexillum." The ordinary standard was "a square piece of cloth stretched on top by a cross-bar, and suspended from a gilt spear surmounted by an eagle of victory" (Schaff-Herzog; see O. Seyffert's *Dict.*, *s.v.* "Signum"). In consequence of the vision of a cross seen by Constantine before his victory over Maxentius (312 A.D.), it was given a Christian character and adopted as the standard of the whole army. On the banner itself were placed Christian emblems. Above it, in place of the Eagle of Victory, was put the monogram of Christ. This consisted of the first two Greek letters in the name of Christ intersected to form a kind of cross (☧). The monogram was enclosed within a crown of gold. In course of time the name Labarum came to be applied to the monogram alone. See Smith and Cheetham; Schaff-Herzog; the *Prot. Dict.*; the *Cath. Dict.*

LABBAIS. A caste of betel vine growers in Southern India. They are described as "a Musalman caste of partly Tamil origin" (*Madras Census Report*, 1901). H. A. Stuart (*Manual of the North Arcot District*) says that the Labbais of the North Arcot district are "very particular Muhammadans, and many belong to the Wāhabi section. Adhering to the rule of the Korān, most of them refuse to lend money at interest, but get over the difficulty by taking a share in the profits derived by others in their loans. . . . They seem to have a prejudice against repairing houses, and prefer letting them go to ruin, and building new ones." See E. Thurston and K. Rangachari.

LACTICINIA. Lacticinia, literally "foods made of milk," is an ecclesiastical term denoting "all those kinds of food which are derived from the mammalia in a more or less indirect way" (Schaff-Herzog). Such foods are milk, butter, cheese, and sometimes eggs. All lacticinia were forbidden during fasting by the Council of Laodicea (351 A.D.) and the Trullan Council of 692 A.D. In the Eastern Church for the most part the rule is still observed. In the Roman Church the use of lacticinia was forbidden on the fasting days of Lent. In other cases, in consideration of climate, etc., papal dispensations have been, or may be, granted. "In England, as in other countries, the extent to which lacticinia may be used in Lent is determined by the indult published in each year" (*Cath. Dict.*). See Schaff-Herzog; the *Cath. Dict.*

LADY DAY. In England the festival of the Annunciation (*q.v.*), which commemorates the bringing of the news by the angel Gabriel of the coming birth of Jesus to Mary, is commonly called Lady Day. The day of the festival is the 25th of March.

LÆTARE SUNDAY. The fourth Sunday in Lent is called in the Roman Catholic Church Lætare Sunday from the first word (*Laetare*, Rejoice) in the antiphon of the introit of the mass. It is also known as Mid-Lent Sunday or Refreshment Sunday (*Dies refectionis*), or "Dominica de rosa." The last name is due to the fact that on this day the Pope blesses the golden rose, an ornament sent to Catholic sovereigns or other persons of distinction, as well as to churches, sanctuaries, and cities. See Schaff-Herzog; the *Cath. Dict.*

LAKHMU. A Babylonian deity. In the Epic of Marduk (see MARDUK, EPIC OF) Lakhmu and Lakhamu are represented as the first deities created. Lakhamu is simply the feminine form of Lakhmu. Apsu (*q.v.*) and Tiâmat (*q.v.*) were already in existence. Apart from this Epic, Lakhmu and Lakhamu do not play active parts among the gods. Lakhmu came to be popularly regarded simply as a mythical monster.

LAKSHMI. A deity in Hinduism. Lakshmī, the wife of Vishnu (*q.v.*), is the goddess of beauty and fortune. She is not mentioned as a goddess in the Rig Veda, but became popular as an object of worship afterwards. A feast to Lakshmī is held on the 2nd of February. This is a literary festival. Such things as pens, inkstands, and books are cleaned and worshipped. The explanation of this is that in Bengal the Vishnuites have made Sarasvatī, the goddess of learning, the wife of Vishnu, and have identified her with Lakshmī. Lakshmī is worshipped by the Ramaites (*q.v.*) in conjunction with Vishnu. See Monier-Williams; E. W. Hopkins.

LĀLBEG. A saint worshipped by the Mehtars, the caste of sweepers and scavengers in India. He is supposed to have been originally one Ghāzi Miyān, a saint worshipped in the Punjab. At the Dasahra festival a cock is offered to him. The Mehtars are known also as Lālbegis.

LAMENTATIONS, BOOK OF. The book of Lamentations is one of the books of the Old Testament included among the Five Rolls or Megilloth. In the Jewish Canon the book bears the title "How!" because a lament usually begins with this word. There are five lamentations in the book, and all of them are concerned with the destruction of Jerusalem. All the chapters, except chapter v., are alphabetical, that is to say, each verse (in chap. iii. every third verse) begins with a letter of the alphabet. In the Septuagint Version the following words are prefixed to the book: "And it came to pass, after Israel was led into captivity, and Jerusalem laid waste, that Jeremiah sat weeping, and lamented with this lamentation over Jerusalem, and said . . ." The first four chapters are composed in what has become known as the "Kina-verse." The elucidation of the Kina-verse owes much to K. Budde. "He had observed that wherever the Hebrew text yields a song of lamentation a well-defined and characteristically constructed form, clearly distinguishable from its context, shows itself, and that this consists of two members of unequal length so arranged that the second is the shorter. The second shorter member is everywhere sharply marked off, and therefore as a rule follows on the first longer clause ἀσυνδέτως: normally a first clause was composed of three, a second of two, words" (Cornill). Both Jewish and Christian tradition regards Jeremiah as the author of the book, and there is no reason to doubt his authorship. The lamentations are for the destruction of Jerusalem in 586 B.C., and the descriptions in part seem to be those of an eye-witness. The English and German Bibles follow the Septuagint and Vulgate Versions in connecting Lamentations closely with the Book of Jeremiah. But if Jeremiah was the original author, it must at least be admitted that the work was afterwards edited and added to. There are passages which can hardly have been written by Jeremiah (*e.g.*, v. 7; ii. 9; iv. 17; with v. 7 compare Jeremiah xxi. 29-30). See C. Cornill, *Intr.;* G. H. Box; O. C. Whitehouse.

LAMIÆ. Female demons or spirits who were supposed to visit men and have sexual intercourse with them. The belief is found among the ancient Assyrians and the modern Arabs, as well as among other peoples.

LAMMAS DAY. The word Lammas is either the Anglo-Saxon *Hlaf Maesse,* Loaf-mass, or is a corruption of Lamb Mass. The day is the first of August, and if Lammas is loaf-mass, it was so called because it was an old Saxon custom to make offerings of new grain on that day. In the Sarum Manual the day is, in fact, called "Benedictio Novorum Fructuum." If Lammas is Lamb Mass, the name may be due to the fact that lambs also were offered. Dr. C. J. Casher notes that the tenants of the chapter of York Minster used formerly on the 1st of August to pay a tribute of a live lamb (*Prot. Dict.*). It is curious that in Italy it has been a practice at Easter to eat a baked image of a lamb. In the Roman Church Lammas has been explained as equivalent to Lamb Mass, and as due to the fact that St. Peter (to whom Jesus addressed the words "Feed my lambs") was the patron of lambs. It is remarkable that on the same day, the 1st of August, a festival known as the Feast of Peter's Chains has been celebrated at Rome since the beginning of the seventh century. The Roman Breviary relates that the Empress Eudocia, wife of Theodosius the Younger, on a visit to Jerusalem obtained the chains with which Peter had been bound (Acts xii.) and brought them to Constantinople. One of them she placed in the church of St. Peter there, the other she sent to her daughter Eudoxia, wife of Valentinian III., at Rome. According to another tradition, St. Peter was bound with chains at Rome during the Neronian persecution. In the Acts of Pope Alexander a St. Balbina is said to have found the chains of St. Peter, presumably these. Elsewhere it is said that Pope Alexander instituted a feast on the 1st of August and built the church *ad Vincula*. In the Greek Church the corresponding feast is kept on the 16th of January, and in the Armenian Church on the 22nd of January.

LAMPETER BRETHREN. A Society of Welsh students formed at Lampeter College by Henry James Prince, who was himself a student there (having entered in 1836). The members met together for prayer, "revival," and study of the Bible.

LAMPETIANS. One of the names given to the Euchites (*q.v.*). They were so called after one of their leaders, Lampetius, a priest who had been ordained in 458 A.D. by Alypius, Bishop of Caesarea in Cappadocia.

LAMPS, FEAST OF. 1. According to the Jewish historian Josephus (*Antiquities*, xii. 7, 7), the Jewish Feast of Dedication, which commemorates the re-dedication of the Temple by Judas Maccabæus (164 B.C.) after the conflict with Antiochus Epiphanes, was popularly known as the Feast of Lights or Lamps. It was so called, and in the Talmud the Feast of Illumination, because illumination was a prominent feature in the festival. 2. The Hindus observe a Feast of Lamps in autumn in honour of Lakshmī, wife of Vishṇu (*q.v.*), or of Pārvatī (Bhavānī), wife of Śiva (*q.v.*). This festival, of which again beautiful illuminations are a feature, is called Dīvālī or Dīpālī or Dīpāvalī. Monier-Williams gives a description of it, as held at Benares. "All the boats of the river are lighted up, and the city, under the serene sky of an Indian autumn, is a blaze of calm effulgence." 3. A Feast of Lamps is observed by all Buddhists. With the early Buddhists it was simply a day of rejoicing on the termination of the rainy season (Vassa). Among the Tibetan Buddists a Feast of Lamps held on the twenty-fifth day of the tenth month (Nov.-Dec.) is the occasion of celebrating the ascension to heaven of the reformer Tsong Khapa (see YELLOW-CAP BUDDHISTS). All buildings, including temples, tombs, and monasteries, are magnificently illuminated. See Monier-Williams, *Buddh-*

ism, 1890; *Brāhmanism*, 1891; W. O. E. Oesterley and G. H. Box; J. C. Oman, *Cults*.

LANCE, THE HOLY. Tradition relates that the Empress Helena discovered the head of the lance which pierced Jesus' side during the Passion. This lance was preserved for a time in the Church of the Holy Sepulchre. Afterwards it is supposed to have found its way to Antioch, where in 1098 it was discovered by one Peter Bartholomew or Peter Abraham in the Church of St. Peter. The lance was borne in front of the crusaders, who had become disheartened, and encouraged them to attack the Muhammadans. In course of time it travelled to Constantinople; but in 1492 it was presented by Bajazet II. to Innocent VIII., and the iron with which it was inlaid is now preserved in the basilica of the Vatican. According to another tradition, Rudolph of Burgundy presented to Henry I. of Germany a holy lance made out of the nails with which Jesus was fastened to the cross. In honour of this lance Innocent VI. in 1354 established a festival. The knife used in the Greek Church to pierce the bread of the Eucharist is also called a "holy lance." See Schaff-Herzog; Benham; the *Cath. Dict*.

LANCASTERIAN SYSTEM OF EDUCATION. Regarded purely from an educational standpoint, the system of Joseph Lancaster (1778-1838) was similar to that of Andrew Bell (1753-1832). It occurred to them both to try a system of mutual instruction by the scholars of their schools. This reduced the cost of teaching, and removed, or seemed to remove, the difficulty caused by a lack of adult teachers. Andrew Bell, whose system was called the Madras System of Education, had experienced this difficulty in Madras, where he was Superintendent of the Madras Male Orphan Asylum. The system of instruction in the Bell Schools and Lancaster Schools was the same. There was an important difference, however, as regards the nature of the religious teaching. Both kinds of schools were religious institutions; but in the Lancaster schools the religion taught was "undenominational," all denominational catechisms being excluded, whereas in the Bell schools use was made of the catechism and liturgy of the Church of England. In 1808 a "Royal Lancasterian Society" was founded. This afterwards became the "British and Foreign School Society." Lancasterian Schools began to multiply, and the name Lancaster was associated with undenominationalism. In 1811 the "National Society for the Education of the Poor in the principles of the Established Church" was founded, and Bell was made Superintendent. It should be added that Andrew Bell has the first claim to be regarded as the original inventor of the new system of education, the "Monitorial System." See *Chambers' Encycl.*; the *D.N.B.*; M. W. Paterson, *Hist.*

LAND OF ISLĀM, THE. See DĀRU'L ISLĀM.

LAND OF WARFARE, THE. See DĀRU'L HARB.

LAODICEANS, EPISTLE TO THE. In the Muratorian fragment, which contains references to books of the New Testament, it is said: "There is also an Epistle to the Laodiceans, another of the Alexandrians forged in Paul's name for the heresy of Marcion, and many others which cannot be received in the Catholic Church, for it is not fitting to mingle gall with honey." Tertullian says that "To the Laodiceans" was a title by which the Epistle to the Ephesians was known. Colossians iv. 16, which speaks of the "Epistle from Laodicea," seems to imply an epistle to Laodicea. A plausible theory is that the epistle now known as the Epistle to the Ephesians was really a circular letter. In that case it was known to some people as the Epistle to the Laodiceans. In Ephesians i. 1 the words "in Ephesus" are omitted in the two best manuscripts. An Epistle to the Laodiceans actually exists in Latin, but it is clearly a forgery. The oldest copy belongs to about the year 546 A.D. See C. R. Gregory; J. Moffatt, *Intr.*

LARGER CATECHISM, THE. The Larger Catechism of the Westminster Divines was one of the results of the consultations of the Westminster Assembly (*q.v.*). It was produced with the Westminster Confession (*q.v.*) in 1647 A.D. The conclusions were those of the Confession, but use was made also of Herbert Palmer's "Catechism" and James Ussher's "Body of Divinity." In 1648 the Scottish Assembly approved it as a "Directory for catechizing such as have made some proficiency in the knowledge of the grounds of Religion." There are one hundred and ninety-six questions and answers. See William A. Curtis.

LARVÆ. The Larvæ of whom the Romans stood in such dread were ghosts or terrible spectres, "the souls of dead people who could find no rest, either owing to their own guilt, or from having met with some indignity" (Seyffert). They resembled the Lemures, spectres of the night. On three days in May special rites, *Lemuria*, were performed with a view to expelling ghosts from the house. See O. Seyffert, *Dict.*

LATERAN COUNCILS. The Lateran Councils were General Councils of the Roman Catholic Church held in the Church of St. John Lateran, the chief Church of Rome. This Church was built near the Lateran palace which belonged to the family of the Plautii Laterani. There were five important Lateran Councils. (1) The First Lateran Council (Ninth General Council) was held in 1123 A.D. under Pope Calixtus II. (1119-1124). It dealt principally with the question of Investiture. (2) The Second Lateran Council (Tenth General Council) was held in 1139 A.D. under Pope Innocent II. (1130-1143). It excommunicated Roger of Sicily, who supported the claims of the Antipope Anacletus II. (see ANTI-POPES). (3) The Third Lateran Council (Eleventh General Council) was held in 1179 A.D. under Pope Alexander III. (1159-1181). It dealt with the question of the Election of Popes and with discipline. (4) The Fourth Lateran Council (Twelfth General Synod) was held in 1215 A.D. under Pope Innocent III. (1198-1216). The Council passed seventy decrees concerning discipline and doctrine. It declared that in the Mass the bread and wine are transubstantiated into the Body and Blood of Christ (see TRANSUBSTANTIATION). (5) The Fifth Lateran Council (Eighteenth General Council) began in 1512 A.D. under Pope Julius II. (1503-1513), and ended in 1517 under Pope Leo X. (1513-Dec. 1521). It condemned the Pragmatic Sanction (France, 1438; Germany, 1439) and approved the French Concordat. See K. R. Hagenbach; *Prot. Dict.*; *Cath. Dict.*

LATITUDE-MEN. Under the rule of Oliver Cromwell, clergymen of the Church of England, from 1653 to 1660, who readily adapted themselves to the undenominationalism which he established, were, according to the account of a writer in 1662 (S. P. Cambridge), called Latitude-men. Not long afterwards the forerunners of the Broad Churchmen (*q.v.*) received the name Latitudinarians (*q.v.*).

LATITUDINARIANS. A term which came into use about the year 1670 to describe those who took a "broad view" of Christian doctrine and of the relationship between Christian Churches. The Latitudinarians were forerunners of the later school of divines known as Broad Churchmen (*q.v.*). They attached importance to the moral, rather than to the doctrinal character of Christianity. "In words, in modes of speech, and generally in their mode of thinking," says John Hunt, "they are all in some respects at variance with the words, and frequently with the tone of the Articles and formularies of the Church of England. It is not that they teach what might be called new truth, but that they look at the old truth in new ways. They were men of progress, who did not think it a sin to differ either from the Fathers or the Reformers. Other parties did this, and denied that they did it. The Latitudinarians, on the other hand, recognized such differences in different ages, as the necessary conditions of mental and spiritual development." But in spite of the general agreement of Latitudinarians, two schools may be distinguished, one of which was more philosophical than the other. The Latitudinarians have included: Gilbert Burnet (1643-1715), Bishop of Salisbury; William Chillingworth (1602-1644), Prebendary of Salisbury; Ralph Cudworth (1617-1688), Regius Professor of Hebrew at Cambridge; Benjamin Hoadly (1676-1761), Bishop of Winchester; Henry More (1614-1687); John Smith (1618-1652); Jeremy Taylor (1613-1667), Bishop of Down and Connor; John Tillotson (1630-1694); Benjamin Whichcote (1609-1683); Provost of King's College, Cambridge; Daniel Whitby (1638-1726); Precentor of Salisbury Cathedral; and John Wilkins (1614-1672), Bishop of Chester. M. W. Patterson explains Latitudinarianism as being due to two tendencies. "A century of religious strife and religious confusion had produced in many men a sense of sheer weariness; they were willing to drop the shibboleths of contending factions and ground themselves on what they considered to be "fundamental Christianity." This sense of weariness was reinforced by the appeal to reason; strife about "non-fundamental" matters was not only wearisome, but also seemed to many men irrational. The appeal to reason and the advocacy of toleration for Protestant Dissenters were the chief features of Latitudinarianism." The explanation rather seems to suggest that the movement was produced by the peculiar circumstances of a particular age. The fact seems to be that Latitudinarianism, in the best sense of the word, goes back to the distant past, being a gradual, but natural and inevitable growth from the seeds of the Gospel. See John Hunt, *Rel. Thought in England*, 1870-73; A. I. Fitzroy, *Dogma and the Church of England*, 1891; M. W. Patterson, *Hist.*; the *D.N.B.*

LATROCINIUM. Latrocinium or "Robber Council" was a name given by Pope Leo to a council which met at Ephesus in 449 A.D. and acquitted Eutyches, who had been condemned as a heretic at the Synod of Constantinople held in 448. The council was so called on account of the violence of its proceedings. See further EUTYCHIANISM.

LATTER-DAY SAINTS. Another name for the Mormons (*q.v.*). The correct description of the Mormon organization is "The Church of Jesus Christ of Latter-day Saints." Mormons is only a popular designation.

LAUDS. One of the seven Canonical Hours (*q.v.*) contained in the mediaeval Service-book known as the Breviary or Hour Book. The office of Lauds was said or sung at break of day.

LAURA. The Greek word *laura* means properly an alley or a lane, but in ecclesiastical usage it came to denote a community of hermits who lived in separate cells. The hermits lived in solitude for five days of the week, making baskets or doing some other manual work, and subsisting on bread and water. On the first and last days of the week they took their meals together, and worshipped together in the common chapel. In the fourth and fifth centuries A.D. there were Lauras in Egypt, Syria, and Palestine. Pachomius of Tabenna in Upper Egypt († about 349 A.D.) organized his monks in a Laura, but he allowed three monks to occupy one cell. He is said to have supported himself by weaving shaggy tunics, and to have abstained much from food and sleep. Euthymius of Palestine († 473 A.D.) established a Laura six miles from Jerusalem, and another later on the road from Jerusalem to Jericho. Euthymius is said to have healed sick persons by his prayers. Sabas of Palestine († 531 A.D.) founded a Laura on the river Kidron. The Laura forms a transition between the hermit life of St. Antony, "the founder of asceticism," and the monastic life of St. Basil and St. Benedict. Several great monasteries are now called Laura (*e.g.*, the monastery on Mt. Athos). See Smith and Cheetham; the *Cath. Dict;* Wace and Piercy.

LAW, THE. The designation of the first of the three groups into which the books of the Old Testament are divided. The Hebrew name is Torah. It embraces Genesis (called in Hebrew *Berēshīth*), Exodus (*Shemōth*), Leviticus (*Vayyikrā*), Numbers (*Bemidbar*), and Deuteronomy (*Debhārīm*). The first of the three groups to attain canonical authority, "it so far overshadowed the other divisions that even in the New Testament the one name 'Law' is used to cover the rest. Even our Lord, as reported to us, so far accepts the current formulas as to apply the term 'Law' both to Prophetical Books and Psalms" (W. Sanday). The Jews regarded it as the one primary revelation, all else being secondary. "Even as far back as the Book of Ecclesiasticus, the Law as given by Moses was identified with Wisdom itself. This idea was developed by the Rabbis, who regarded the Law as existing before the Creation, and saw in it the plan on which God had made the worlds. No second revelation like it was possible. It had exhausted all the revelation which God could give to man." It is called "the jewel of jewels." In the tractate *Sanhedrin* (x. 1) it is said: "Whoever asserts that the Torah is not from heaven (from God), hath no part in the world to come." And again (fol. 99a): "Whoever saith, that Moses wrote so much as a single verse out of his own knowledge, he (is a liar and) a contemner of the word of God." The Law was officially adopted and canonized by Ezra (444 B.C.). The book that was brought to light in the reign of Josiah (621 B.C.) was not the whole Law but the Book of Deuteronomy (see BOOK OF THE COVENANT). Another name for The Law is The Pentateuch. Cp. PENTATEUCH and CRITICISM, HIGHER. See W. Sanday, *I.*; G. Wildeboer; H. E. Ryle.

LAZARISTS. The Lazarists are more correctly known as the "Congregation of the Priests of the Mission." The congregation was founded by St. Vincent of Paul in 1624. In 1632 it was confirmed by a bull of Urban VIII., and the same year was established in the College of St. Lazare at Paris. It had three objects: (1) the improvement of its own members by means of daily prayer, meditation, etc.; (2) the instruction of people living in the country towns and villages by means of missions; (3) the training of those who wished to become priests. "As a rule, eight months in the year were devoted to missions, which were conducted nearly on the same plan on which Redemptorist and Passionists missions are conducted at the present day" (*Cath. Dict.*). During the French Revolution the College of St. Lazare was plundered by the mob. At a later date the Lazarists were granted a house in the Rue de Sèvres. They are now actively engaged in mission work in many parts of the world. See *Prot. Dict.; Cath. Dict.*

LAZARISTS. Lazarists was the name of a religious and military order in the time of the Crusades. The members devoted themselves in the Holy Land to the care of lepers.

LEAGUE OF LIBERAL CHRISTIAN THOUGHT AND SOCIAL SERVICE. A league founded in connection with the New Theology (*q.v.*). A more convenient designation is "The Liberal-Christian League." The

President was Mr. R. J. Campbell. The objects, briefly described, were spiritual fellowship, theological freedom, and social regeneration. The League, as originally constituted in June 1908 was called "The League of Progressive Thought and Social Service," or, more popularly, "The Progressive League." By February 1909 the subscribing membership had increased to between three and four thousand. Mr. Campbell said of the League (*The New Theology*, popular edition): "Not only does it aim at providing spiritual fellowship for those whose religious sympathies are with the New Theology, but it seeks to articulate the social movement of the age from the side of liberal Christianity." Some time before the actual foundation of the League the "Christian Commonwealth" had begun to register the names of persons who were prepared to unite in such a movement. The objects, as defined more completely, were fivefold. (1) To provide a common meeting-ground and fellowship for those who are in sympathy with liberal Christianity and all progressive religious thought. (2) To study impartially the various manifestations of religious experience, and to make known the assured results of the historic and scientific study of religion. (3) To promote the systematic study of social questions from the spiritual and moral as well as from the economic point of view in the light of the best available knowledge and experience; to create a sense of individual, civic, and national responsibility for removing unjust social conditions; to encourage men and women to be trained and organized for social work. (4) To work for a social and economic reconstruction of society which shall secure the fullest opportunities and the most favourable environment for individual development, and shall have as its goal co-operation for life instead of competition for existence. (5) To promote the development of international goodwill by concentrating attention upon and seeking to strengthen the forces that make for peace and union among the nations. The League had three departments. (1) League Studies Department. The purpose of this is obvious. (2) Social Service Department. The members of this department were to do practical work of a useful social character. (3) League Service Department. In this department, the service took the form of arranging meetings, bazaars, concerts, etc., in aid of the funds. A corps of special preachers, Pioneer Preachers, was organised, "whose work is to carry the League gospel into fresh fields." See the popular edition of R. J. Campbell's *New Theology*.

LEAGUE OF PROGRESSIVE THOUGHT AND SOCIAL SERVICE. The original name of the "New Theology" organization which was afterwards called the "League of Liberal Christian Thought and Social Service" (*q.v.*).

LEAGUE OF THE CROSS. The Catholic Total Abstinence League of the Cross is a Roman Catholic Temperance Society which was founded in 1873 "for the purpose of uniting Catholics in a holy warfare against intemperance, and of thereby raising the religious, social, and domestic state" of the Catholic people (*Cath. Dict.*). The members, who must be Roman Catholics, pledge themselves to observe total abstinence and to live as good, practical Catholics. See the *Cath. Dict.*

LEAGUE PIONEERS. A corps of special preachers whose work was to carry into fresh fields the gospel of the "League of Liberal Christian Thought and Social Service" (*q.v.*).

LECANOMANCY. A species of divination. In the practice of Lecanomancy use was made of a bason and of wedges of gold or silver which were marked with certain characters. "The wedges were suspended over the water, and the demon formally invoked, when he gave the response in a low hissing sound passing through the fluid" (James Gardner, *Faiths of the World*).

LECTIONARIES. A general name for service-books containing passages from the New Testament adapted for public reading in the early Christian Church. Such books also had special names. Thus, a lectionary consisting of passages from the Gospels was called an Evangeliarium. A lectionary consisting of passages from the Acts of the Apostles was called an Apostolos. The passages were adapted in this sense that an alteration was often made at the beginning and the end to make the opening and the close of the reading intelligible, and that sometimes an interesting detail (a whole verse perhaps) was added from another Gospel. Lectionaries often afford help in the work of textual criticism (see CRITICISM, TEXTUAL). It must be admitted, however, that "not only is their testimony almost valueless on small points of wording, but it also carries no weight when narratives are in question which have parallels" (K. Lake). Lectionary systems are believed to be of great antiquity. But of those which have been preserved there is none in Greek earlier than the eighth century or in Syriac earlier than the sixth century A.D. See K. Lake, *Text of the N.T.*, 1904; M. R. Vincent, *Textual Crit. of the N.T.*

LECTISTERNIA. The Roman festivals known as *Lectisternia* were borrowed from the Greeks. They were banquets offered to the gods, whose images were placed for the purpose on couches (*lecti*). At first such banquets were provided for three pairs of non-Roman deities, for Apollo and Latona, Heracles and Artemis, Hermes and Poseidon, each pair being assigned a separate *lectus*. Later, they were offered to the six pairs of Roman deities, Jupiter, Juno, Neptune, Minerva, Mars, Venus, Apollo, Diana, Vulcan, Vesta, Mercury, and Ceres. "Rude copies of the wooden statues of these gods, which stood in the Forum, have come down to us on a Gallo-Roman altar at Navilly (Côte-d'Or)"—Reinach. Robertson Smith thinks that the closest parallel to the *lectisternia* is found in the Hebrew table of Shewbread (*q.v.*). See W. Robertson Smith, *R.S.*; O. Seyffert, *Dict.*; Reinach, *O.*

LEGEND, THE GOLDEN. The term legend means literally "something to be read," and originally corresponded largely to the term story. In mediaeval times *Legenda* or *Legendarii* (*libri*) denoted collections of extracts from the lives of saints and martyrs to be read as lessons in divine service. The practice of reading such lessons had grown up in days when the stories of the saints, as given for instance in such works as the "Acta Martyrum," the "Acta Sanctorum," and Eusebius's book on the martyrs of Palestine, were more historical. It appears that in the time of Augustine the custom of reading the passions of the martyrs on their anniversaries was general in the Christian churches of North Africa. In course of time, however, this kind of literature degenerated. An example of this degeneracy is provided by the "Golden Legend" (*Legenda Aurea*) of Jacobus de Voragine, who was so called from his birthplace Varaggia near Genoa. Jacobus was Archbishop of Genoa in the thirteenth century. His work, divided into 177 chapters, was the earliest collection in the West of the Lives of Saints. It became popular, was translated into a number of languages, and passed through more than seventy editions before 1500; but, though curious, interesting, and in some ways instructive, it is of slight historical value. It is quite uncritical. It is thought that the book provided the model for the "Legenda Angliae" of John Capgrave (1393-1464), a work printed by Caxton. The *Cath. Dict.* suggests that the work of Capgrave prepared the ground for the great compilation of the Bollandists (*q.v.*). See Benham; Schaff-Herzog; the *Cath. Dict.*

LEIPZIG COLLOQUY. A German Confession of Faith (1631 A.D.). It was the result of a conference convened by the Electors of Brandenburg and Saxony with the idea of uniting the Reformed and Lutheran forces against the forces of Roman Catholicism. The Colloquy obtained a certain measure of authority in Brandenburg, but " the times were not ripe for a real understanding " (W. A. Curtis).

LEONISTS. The name Leonists was given to the followers of Peter Waldus, the Waldenses (*q.v.*), because the community was founded (1177) at Lyons. They have also been called Paupĕres de Lugdūno, " Poor of Lyons," and Sabatati.

LEUCETIUS. Leucetius, the god of lightning, was one of the deities worshipped by the ancient Celts. He was identified with the Roman god Mars.

LEVELLERS. The followers of John Lilburne (1614?-1657) in the time of Oliver Cromwell. The Levellers formed an ultra-republican party. In 1638 Lilburne was imprisoned by the Star Chamber for publishing unlicensed books. Afterwards he fought for the Parliament (1642-1645). In 1649 he persuaded a part of the army to mutiny in support of his extreme republican views. He soon had to surrender to Cromwell. He was several times exiled or imprisoned. The Levellers ascribed supreme importance to practical piety. The conscience and the inner voice of the heart were regarded as more authoritative than the dogmas of the Church, however Scriptural these might be. " The supreme principle of the Levellers was that the will of the people is the highest law of a country, and that all authorities obtain their rights only through the consent of the people. On the basis of this principle they wished a purely democratic constitution in the State; and they were the first to demand an absolute separation of Church and State on the ground that all union between them leads to intolerable constraint of conscience and to endless civil misery. Every religious confession, and even atheism itself, should find toleration; and every ecclesiastical community should regulate its own affairs in entire independence " (B. Puenjer). See B. Puenjer; the *D.N.B.*

LEVITICUS, BOOK OF. The Book of Leviticus is the third book in the first division of the Canon of the Old Testament (*q.v.*). In the Hebrew Bible it bears the title *Way-yikra* " and he called." This is the first of the opening words of the book: " And Jehovah called unto Moses and spake unto him." The title in the Septuagint is *Leu(e)itikon* and in the Vulgate *Leviticus.* In each case the word Book is to be supplied. The English title is borrowed from the Vulgate. The " Levitical book " is so called not because it deals specially with the Levites, who in fact are mentioned only once (xxv. 32 ff.), but because it contains " the law of the priests." In the Mishnah (*q.v.*) it is called either Torath cōhănīm, " Law of Priests," or Sēpher cōhănīm, " Book of Priests," or Sēpher kŏrbănoth, " Book of Offerings." The subject-matter and linguistic characteristics of the Book of Leviticus show that it belongs entirely to the priestly stratum of the Hexateuch, which is commonly designated P. But though the book as a whole is clearly distinguished from the other main strata of the Hexateuch, J (the Jehovistic or Judahite), E (the Elohistic or Ephramite), and D (the Deuteronomic), it is not itself a literary unity. As Prof. G. A. Barton says (*Jewish Encycl.*), Leviticus as it stands is not " a consistent code of laws formulated at one time, but is the result of a considerable process of compilation." There are sections in P which differ linguistically from other sections; there are duplicate laws which imply diversity of date and origin. This has led to the separation within the main stratum P, or the Priests' Code, of other strata which have been designated Pɢ, Pʜ, Pᴛ, and Ps. These symbols may be explained in the order given. The letter G in Pɢ is an abbreviation of the German word Grundschrift, "groundwork." Pɢ denotes the matter which formed the groundwork or basis of the Pentateuch, a legal and historical nucleus, to which was added from time to time matter of a different and varied character. The theme of this nucleus or kernel is, as Prof. Kennedy says, " the history of the establishment of the theocracy and of the introduction of those laws, institutions, and rites by which the divine sovereignty received visible expression." To Pɢ belong in Leviticus the directions concerning the consecration of the priesthood (Lev. ix.-x.), the Day of Atonement (Lev. xvi.), the sacred calendar (xxiii. 4-8, 23-25, 33-38), the lamps and shewbread (xxiv. 1-9). According to Kennedy Pɢ was composed about 500 B.C.; according to Kent, somewhere between 450 and 400 B.C. The letter H in Pʜ is an abbreviation of the word " Holiness." Pʜ, or H alone, is a section of the Book of Leviticus (xvii.-xxvi.) which is distinguished by linguistic and other characteristics of its own. The underlying thought of this Code of Holiness may be found in Lev. xxii. 31-33: " Ye shall observe my commands and do them: I am Jehovah. And ye shall not profane my holy name; but I will be treated as holy among the Israelites. I am Jehovah who maketh you holy, who brought you out of the land of Egypt, to be your God: I am Jehovah " (cp. xix. 2; xx. 7, 8, 26, xxi. 6-8, 15, 23; xxii. 9, 16). Holiness, both moral and ceremonial, is insisted upon. The Code of Holiness, like the Book of the Covenant (Exodus xx. 24-xxiii. 19) and the Deuteronomic Code (Deut. xx.-xxvi.), opens with a law regulating altar sacrifices and ceremonies (Lev. xvii.), and closes with an exhortation (Lev. xxvi.). Even Pʜ, short as it is, is a compilation from various sources, and has been interpolated to some extent by P. In ch. xvii., for instance, vss. 1, 2, 15, 16, and references to " the tent of meeting " and " the camp " in vss. 3, 4, 5, and 6 are interpolations. So are verses 1, *2a*, *8b*, 21 and 22 in ch. xix. An interesting and important question with regard to the Code of Holiness is: What is the precise relationship of the Code to the Book of Ezekiel? There are many parallels and resemblances between Ezekiel and H. They are given fully in Carpenter and Harford-Battersby (i. 147 f.). Ezekiel was a priest as well as a prophet, in fact he was born a priest. In 597 B.C. he was taken captive to Babylonia. Here he devoted himself at first to the work of a preacher. Towards the close of his career, however, he occupied himself with the preparation of the Code contained in Ezek. xl.-xlviii. (572 B.C.). Now, while this code reproduces many of the ceremonial laws, etc., of the pre-exilic temple, it contains also regulations which are quite new (*e.g.*, xliv. 7, 8, xliv. 13). It was not actually adopted as a whole, but it prepared the way for the priestly codes that were ultimately accepted. It is further noteworthy that in all Ezekiel's laws and exhortations the greatest stress is laid on the holiness of Yahweh and on the necessity that his people also should be holy. And, as we have seen, the same stress and emphasis are found in the Code of Holiness. Kent concisely presents the resemblances between H and Ezekiel as follows: " The impressive refrain, *I am Jehovah*, is repeated forty-six times, and is one of many common characteristics that distinguish these laws. The same expression is also found seventy-eight times in Ezekiel, and not once in the writings of his earlier contemporaries, Isaiah and Jeremiah. There are many other striking points of contact both in vocabulary and idiom. The unusual formula beginning, *Every man of the house of*

Israel (Lev. xvii. 3, 8, 10, 13, 15), is found nowhere else in the Old Testament except in Ezekiel, where it is very common (*e.g.*, Ezek. xiv. 4, 7, 8, xliv. 10, 12). The social crimes especially prohibited in the Holiness Code (*e.g.*, xviii. 8, xx. 10-12, 17, xix. 13, 15, 36, xx. 9, xxi. 1-5) are denounced by Ezekiel in terms almost identical (*e.g.*, xxii. 10, 11, xviii. 7, 8, 12, 16, xxxiii. 15, 25, xlv. 10, xxii. 7, xliv. 25, 20). A like emphasis is also laid on the sanctity of the temple (cf. Lev. xix. 30, xx. 3, xxi. 12, 23, xxvi. 2 and Ezek. v. 11, viii. 6, xxiii. 38, 39). Both seek to guard the priesthood from all possible defilement. Thus in language, thought and purpose, Ezekiel and the laws of the Holiness Code are bound together by closest ties." The question then that arises is: Did H influence Ezekiel, or did Ezekiel influence H? According to G. A. Barton, this remains an open question. Various critics, however, have decided for the probability of the one view or the other. Wellhausen, Kuenen, Baentsch, and Addis think H is later than Ezekiel. Barton, Kennedy, Kent, and others think H is earlier. According to Kent, "a detailed comparison of the two systems leads to the conclusion that both come from the same priestly circles and approximately the same date, but that Ezekiel was acquainted with the major portion of the laws in the Holiness Code." He thinks the original draft of H was made between the first and final captivity (597-586 B.C.). Kennedy too regards it as "a pre-exilic document, dating probably from near the close of the monarchy." Barton again thinks it probable that it was compiled in Palestine. In the symbol P_T the T is an abbreviation of the Hebrew word *tōrōth*. P_T denotes a stratum composed of old sacrificial *tōrōth*, or priestly "decisions." In Ps the S is an abbreviation of the word "Secondary." Ps denotes secondary strata of the Priests' Code. Returning to P as a whole, Barton thinks that in its main features it was in the hands of Ezra and Nehemiah. The Book of Leviticus, however, "is not the work of the P who wrote the account of the sacred institutions, but of an editor who dislocated that work at many points, and who combined with it the Holiness Code and other elements." There is another interesting question: Was the Levitical ritual influenced by Babylonian institutions? The remarkable Babylonian Code of Khammurapi (*q.v.*), which was discovered in 1901 and 1902, goes back to about the year 2250 B.C., and it is itself no doubt a compilation from much earlier laws and customs. At two periods in their history the Israelites came into direct contact with Babylonian culture, so that if one nation was powerfully influenced by the other, it would not be surprising. P. Haupt claims that the Levitical ritual was so influenced. He even finds in it a number of Babylonian loan-words. Barton and Kent, however, decide, no doubt rightly, that any deep Babylonian influence is to be doubted. The external analogies are certainly striking, but, in the words of Kent, "the majority of the Old Testament laws are informed by a spirit and purpose which have no ancient parallel." See J. E. Carpenter and G. Harford-Battersby, 1900; C. F. Kent, *Israel's Laws and Legal Precedents*, 1907; E. Kautzsch, *Die Heilige Schrift des Alten Testaments*, 3rd ed. 1908-10; S. R. Driver and H. A. White, *Leviticus* in "Sacred Books of the Old Testament": Hebrew, 1894; English, 1898; A. Dillmann, *Exodus und Leviticus*, 1897; B. Baentsch, *Exodus-Leviticus*, 1900; A. Bertholet, *Leviticus*, 1901; D. Hoffmann, *Das Buch Leviticus*, 1905-6; A. R. S. Kennedy, *Leviticus and Numbers* in the "Century Bible."

LIBANOMANCY. A species of divination. Libanomancy was practised with frankincense (*libanos*). Frankincense was thrown into the fire, and observation was made of the manner in which it burned and of the odour which it gave forth. "If it burned quickly and sent forth an agreeable smell, the omen was favourable, but if the reverse happened, it was unfavourable" (James Gardner, *Faiths of the World*).

LIBATIONS. The practice of offering libations of blood, water, wine, and even of milk and beer, has been widespread. Libations of blood or of wine are referred to frequently in the Old Testament (cp. Ecclesiasticus l. 15, where wine is clearly a surrogate for blood). They usually appear as a mere accessory to a fire offering, but there is good reason to suppose that the libation of blood is a common Semitic practice and is really older than fire-sacrifices. The libation of wine may be regarded as a surrogate for the primitive blood-offering. There is no certain reference to libations of water in the Old Testament, but in the practice of later Judaism water was poured out at the Feast of Tabernacles. "One of the most striking ceremonies of the Feast of Tabernacles was the libation of water which was made every morning during the seven days of the feast at the same time as the libation of wine accompanying the morning holocaust. The water was carried up from Siloam through the water-gate, and poured into a basin on the top of the altar at the S.W. corner, the wine being poured into another. The bringing of the water into the precincts was accompanied by trumpet-blasts and loud jubilation" (*Encycl. Bibl.*, *s.v.* "Sacrifice"). In North Semitic ritual, however, the libation usually consisted of wine, which, even when it went with a fire-offering, was poured out on the ground. "The Greeks and Romans poured the sacrificial wine over the flesh, but the Hebrews treated it like the blood, pouring it out at the base of the altar" (Robertson Smith). That milk was a very ancient Semitic libation is indicated by its use in ritual both by the Arabs and by the Phoenicians. Among the Babylonians and Assyrians libations were offered to the gods and to the dead. A large votive tablet of Ur-Enlil (*c.* 3000 B.C.), unearthed at Nippur, for instance, shows the ruler in the act of offering a libation to Enlil. In a story of the descent of the goddess Ishtar to Aralû, worshippers whose dead had gone like Ishtar to "the land of no return" are instructed to turn in prayer to Tammuz and to pour out libations of pure water and oil to him (Morris Jastrow, *Civ.*). In ancient Egypt libations of blood or of a liquid substitute for blood and of water are a common feature in ritual and religion (see further below). Among primitive folk, too, the pouring out of blood has great religious significance. Take the tribes of Central Australia for example. The men of the Emu (totem) trace their sacred images on ground saturated with blood. In some of the clans the young men open their veins and let streams of blood flow on to a sacred rock, evidently with the idea of revivifying the virtues of the rock and of reinforcing its efficacy (Émile Durkheim). What then is the origin of the act of pouring out libations? As far as ancient Egypt is concerned, new light has been thrown on this question by Dr. A. M. Blackman and Professor G. Elliot Smith. From a study of certain passages in the Egyptian texts inscribed in the subterranean chambers of the Sakkara Pyramids of the Fifth and Sixth Dynasty, Dr. Blackman thinks the idea in the mind of the Egyptians is quite clear. "The corpse of the deceased is dry and shrivelled. To revivify it the vital fluids that have exuded from it [in the process of mummification] must be restored, for not till then will life return and the heart beat again. This, so the texts show us, was believed to be accomplished by offering libations to the accompaniment of incantations." In some passages the libations are said to be the actual fluids that have issued from the corpse. In others a different notion is introduced. "It is not the deceased's own exudations that are to revive his shrunken frame but those of a divine body, the [god's fluid] that came from the corpse of Osiris himself, the juices that dissolved from his decaying flesh, which are communicated to the dead sacramentwise under the form of these libations." Professor Elliot Smith thinks that the Proto-Egyptians clearly believed in the validity of a general biological theory of the life-giving properties of water. "Groping after some explanation of the natural phenomenon that the earth became fertile when water was applied to it, and that seed burst into life under the same influence, the early biologist formulated the natural and not wholly illogical idea that water was the repository of life-giving powers. Water was equally necessary for the production of life and for the maintenance of life." These general biological theories were current at the time of the Sakkara Pyramid texts, and had possibly received specific application to man long before the idea of libations developed. The original object of the offering of libations was to animate the statue of the deceased and so to enable him to continue the existence which had merely been interrupted by the incident of death. "In course of time, however, as definite gods gradually materialized and came to be represented by statues, they also had to be vitalized by offerings of water from time to time. Thus the pouring out of libations came to be an act of worship of the deity; and in this form it has persisted until our own time in many civilized countries." Later, water became also an essential feature in any act of ritual rebirth. Cp. MUMMIFICATION, and see W. Robertson Smith, *R.S.*; A. M. Blackman, "The Significance of Incense and Libations in Funerary and Temple Ritual" in the *Zeitschrift für Ägyptische Sprache und Altertumskunde*, Bd. 50, 1912; G. Elliott Smith, *Dr.*

LIBERAL-CHRISTIAN LEAGUE, THE. A convenient designation of the League which had as its full description the designation "League of Liberal Christian Thought and Social Service" (*q.v.*). Cp. NEW THEOLOGY.

LIFE AND LIBERTY MOVEMENT, THE. A modern reform movement in the Church of England, which started in a series of conversations between friends. The chairman of the Council, which takes general control of the movement, is the Rev. W. Temple. The movement aims at reforming the present conditions of the government of the Church, and demands more liberty for a fuller expression of Life. More liberty means self-government. If the Church has not given effective witness to the Mind of Christ in regard to such matters as International Relations, Industrial Order, Wealth and Poverty, etc.; if there are abuses in the system of its administration which disqualify it for effectively proclaiming the way of justice and love to others; this is due largely to its being without any means of self-expression so that it is hampered by restrictions which, in present conditions, it is powerless to alter. The Movement, therefore, accepts in general outline the scheme of reform set forth in the *Report of the Archbishops' Committee on Church and State*. But it would go further. It would make membership of all councils and the right to vote for them open to women on the same terms as to men; and it insists that the Church Council should have power to legislate on all matters relating to ecclesiastical endowments, property, patronage, and tribunals. Further, it demands a more vigorous prosecution of attempts at mutual understanding with other religious bodies with a view to re-union.

LIGHT OF GLORY. An expression used in connection with the Beatific Vision (VISION, BEATIFIC).

LIGHTNING BEFORE DEATH. The expression "lightning (or lightening) before death" used to be employed to describe a phenomenon which has often been observed in sick persons just before death. In the "Festivous Notes" on *Don Quixote* by Edmund Gayton (1608-1666) the lines occur:

> "Not that I lightning or fell thunder feare,
> Unless that lightning before death appear."

In Ray's "Proverbs" it is said: "This is generally observed of sick persons, that a little before they die their pains leave them, and their understanding and memory return to them; as a candle just before it goes out gives a great blaze." See Robert Nares, *Glossary*, 1822.

LIGORIANS. Another name for the Redemptorists. They were so called because the congregation was founded by St. Alphonsus Maria de Liguori.

LI-KING. One of the Chinese Classics. *Li* is the "Book of Rites" (*q.v.*). The word *King* simply means "Classic."

LIMBO, or LIMBUS. The Latin word Limbus means "fringe" or "border." In Roman Catholic theology the term has been used since the Middle Ages to denote one, or rather two, of the places of departed spirits. Good men, after their souls have been purified in purgatory (*q.v.*), go to heaven. Bad men go to hell. What was the state of the saints of the Old Testament, the good men who died before the gospel was proclaimed by Christ? They were gathered into "Abraham's bosom" or, in other words, into the *Limbus Patrum*, there to remain "in an intermediate state between blessedness and punishment until the descent of Christ into Hades" (Schaff-Herzog). What, again, is the state of infants who have died without baptism? They are gathered into a special place, the *Limbus Infantium*. It has been held by some theologians (by Augustine, for instance) that here they are not only excluded from the joys of heaven, but even suffer some measure of pain. According to the majority of theologians, however, they are simply excluded from heaven. They are not condemned to suffer any "pain of sense." Having never sinned, they enjoy natural happiness. The happiness attained in heaven differs from this in being supernatural. See Benham; Schaff-Herzog; the *Prot. Dict.*; the *Cath. Dict.*

LIMENTINUS. A Roman god or spirit mentioned by Augustine as the protecting spirit of the entrance to a house. See THRESHOLD, THE.

LINGA. The Linga, that is to say, the phallus, or male sexual symbol, plays a great rôle in the worship of the Hindu god Śiva (*q.v.*). The god is commonly represented by an image of it. Members of the modern sect called Lingāyits (*q.v.*) wear it in a casket round their necks. The figures are commonly of stone or glass. The Linga symbolizes the reproductive power of Nature. According to Monier-Williams, however, in the mind of a worshipper of Śiva it was never connected "with indecent ideas nor with sexual love, though impure practices have certainly been introduced in connection with the worship of Śiva's wife." One way of worshipping the Linga is to pour Ganges water over the stone image. There is a special Siva festival on the 27th of February when offerings are made to the Linga with prayer and fasting. "The Linga is bathed in milk, decorated, wrapped in *bilva* leaves, and prayed to; which ceremony is repeated at intervals with slight changes. All castes, even the lowest, join in the exercises" (E. W. Hopkins). See Monier-Williams; E. W. Hopkins; J. A. Dubois and H. K. Beauchamp.

LINGA SARIRA. An expression used in Theosophy (*q.v.*). It denotes the astral body, that is to say, the body formed of ethereal "astral" matter. It is the double of the physical body.

LINGAYITS. Lingavats, Lingāyits, or Lingāits is the name borne by a modern Hindu sect. They are a section of Śiva-worshippers, the followers of Basava, a priest of Śiva (*q.v.*). They are worshippers of the Linga (or phallus), which they wear "in a silver or metallic casket suspended round their necks with a cord like a necklace." The members of the sect are called also Jangamas, "vagrants." See Monier-Williams; E. W. Hopkins; J. A. Dubois and H. K. Beauchamp; R. V. Russell.

LITAVIS. One of the deities worshipped by the ancient Celts. Reverence was paid to Litavis in Britain as well as in Gaul. The goddess Litavis was paired with a god Cicolluis who corresponded to the Roman Mars.

LITHOMANCY. A species of divination. Lithomancy (Greek, *lithos*, a stone) was practised with stones. "The stone used for this purpose was washed in spring water by candle light, and the person engaged in divining, having purified himself, covered his face, repeated a form of prayer, and placed certain characters in a certain order. Then the stone was said to move of itself, and in a soft gentle murmur to give the answer" (James Gardner, *Faiths of the World*).

LITURGY OF THE ANCIENTS, THE. A Liturgy compiled by Edward Stephens (d. 1706), whose theological learning gained him the name "Abbat Stephens." The title of his Liturgy, printed in 1696, shows the nature of the "reformation" which he wished to introduce. It is: "The Liturgy of the Ancients, represented, as near as well may be, in English Forms. With a Preface concerning the Restitution of the most Solemn Part of the Christian Worship in the Holy Eucharist, to its Integrity, and just Frequency of Celebration." Stephens tells us in his Preface that he had received divine attestations that the reformation he was engaged upon, the restitution of a daily celebration of the Holy Eucharist in places proper for it and of a weekly celebration in all Churches, was the special work of God. He felt that he must obey God rather than man, and must prefer the authority of the Catholic Church before that of any society of men. Stephens was at first a barrister. While still a layman, he went to work to try to persuade people of the need of his reformation. He tried to influence the clergy, published pamphlets, and even petitioned Parliament. He exerted himself in this way for thirty years, but without success. When he saw no hope of having daily celebrations in public, he found an opportunity of having them in private. God, he says, brought together a little company of constant weekly Communicants, and amongst them one in Holy Orders according to the Church of England. These persons soon agreed upon three things. 1. To meet daily, at five in the morning, at a daily Communion. 2. To endeavour, as far as they could, in all things to follow the example of the ancient Christians. 3. To avoid giving offence to any, but especially to the Church of England. After nearly a year they were likely to lose the person who officiated. Stephens therefore took Holy Orders himself, and obtained permission from the Bishop of Gloucester to use his Church at Cripplegate. The celebration now became public, and the forms were suitably adapted. "While we had it in private, we used such enlargements of the Church Service as I thought most agreeable to the ancient Form: but when we came into the Church, we forbore most of that, and confined ourselves to the Church Forms, only supplying what I thought defective therein as well as I could out of other parts of our Liturgy." See Peter Hall.

LLEU. Lleu or Llew was one of the gods or divine heroes revered by the ancient Celts in Britain. He has been compared or identified with the Gaelic god Lugh or Lug (*q.v.*). His mother is said to have been Arianrod, a goddess who was associated with the god Gwydion (*q.v.*). Whether Gwydion was thought of as his father is uncertain. See Charles Squire, *Myth.*

LLUDD. Llûdd was one of the gods or divine heroes revered by the ancient Celts in Britain. The name also appears as Nûdd; and in Irish Mythology as Nuada. The god reappeared in British mythology as a king who gave the city which afterwards became London the name Caer Ludd. His name has been preserved in Lydney (Gloucestershire), where, as appears from inscriptions, he was regarded as a kind of god of war resembling the Roman Mars; and in Ludgate, where, according to legend, he was buried. In Welsh legend he has a wife, Gwyar. See Charles Squire, *Myth.*; cp. Reinach, *O.*

LLYR. The gods of the Celts in Ancient Britain are in Welsh documents sometimes referred to as the "Children of Llŷr." Llŷr is the British name. The Gaelic form of the name is Lêr. The wife of Llŷr appears as Iwerydd, that is to say, Ireland. The name of the god has survived in Leicester, which is for Llŷr-cestre. In the mythology the Gaelic Bron or the British Brân (*q.v.*) is represented as the son of Lir or Llŷr. See Charles Squire, *Myth.*

LOCI THEOLOGICI. As used by Aristotle and Cicero, the term *topoi* or *loci* is used to denote the sources or passages on which arguments are based. Similarly in theological language, the expression *loci theologici* has been used to denote the sources on which theological arguments are based. The Roman Catholic theologian, Melchior Canus (1523-1560), Professor of Theology at Salamanca, and afterwards Bishop of the Canaries, chose the expression for the title of his great work on the use of Scripture, the Councils, the Fathers, Philosophy, etc. The great Reformer Melanchthon (1497-1560) used the same expression to describe his own representation of evangelical dogmatics as distinguished from the *sententiae* of the Schoolmen. It was retained by the Lutheran theologians as a convenient expression to the middle of the seventeenth century. See Benham, Schaff-Herzog; the *Cath. Dict.*

LODHURR. Another name for the Scandinavian god Loki (*q.v.*).

LOFN. One of the deities of the Ancient Teutons. The goddess Lofn belonged to the retinue of Frija (*q.v.*) and Freyja (*q.v.*), and seems to have been a goddess of marriage.

LOGIA, THE. The name Logia has been given by scholars to a record of the sayings of Jesus which was used in the compilation of the First and Third Gospels. Papias of Hierapolis definitely states that Matthew made a collection of Sayings in Hebrew. He also says that "everyone interpreted them as he was able," which would seem to mean that they were translated into Greek by a number of persons. German scholars call this primitive source Q (from *Quelle* "source"). In the main the First and Third Gospels were based on two sources—this, and another corresponding to the Gospel of Mark. See Paul Wernle, *The Sources of Our Knowledge of the Life of Jesus*, 1907; C. F. Nolloth, *The Person of Our Lord and Recent Thought*, 1908; Arthur S. Peake, *Intr.*

LOHĀ-SUR. An Indian deity, the patron-god of the Agarias, a caste of iron-smelters and an offshoot of the Gond tribe. He is the Iron demon, to whom the Agarias offer a black hen. On special occasions they worship their smelting implements; and to these also they offer fowls.

LOKI. One of the gods of the old Scandinavians. Loki, "the closer," is represented as one of the Æsir (*q.v.*) and as the companion or rival of Wodan (*q.v.*) and Thor (*q.v.*). He is called also Loptr and Lodhurr, names which mean "the air" or "the hot air." His offspring include the Midhgardh-serpent (*q.v.*), the Fenris-wolf (*q.v.*), and Hel (*q.v.*). He is able to transform himself into various shapes (*e.g.*, that of a falcon) in order to carry out his plans. It is curious that he should appear in the twofold character of friend and enemy of the great gods. If, as has been suggested, he was a fire-god, equivalent to Agni (*q.v.*), the explanation may be that fire is at one time a friend (supplying warmth, etc.) and at another time a foe (bringing destruction). In Scandinavian mythology Loki is the personification of adroitness and cunning. In some myths Loki, Wodan, and Hœnir (*q.v.*) form a triad. According to one, when the first men were formed, Wodan gave them breath, Hœnir souls, and Lodhurr (Loki) colour and warmth. Logi, the fire-demon, has been explained as a doublet of Loki. See P. D. Chantepie de la Saussaye, *Rel. of the Teutons*, 1902; Reinach, *O.*

LONDON-AMSTERDAM TRUE CONFESSION. A Congregational Confession of Faith published in 1596 A.D. on behalf of the London fugitives who were living in and near Amsterdam. "In doctrine, its articles agree with Continental and Anglican Calvinism. As regards Church government, they carry further the Congregational principles of the Confession of 1589" (W. A. Curtis). Cp. LONDON CONFESSION OF 1589.

LONDON CONFESSION OF 1589. A Congregational Confession of Faith prepared by Henry Barrowe and John Greenwood. It was printed at Dort. It had been preceded in 1582 A.D. by Robert Browne's "Statement of Congregational Principles," published at Middelburg in Holland. "Less democratic than Browne's work in its view of the authority of the elders, it makes the same claim to New Testament warrant for the free election of pastors and teachers, elders, deacons, and widows, by the congregation" (W. A. Curtis).

LONO. A god worshipped by the Hawaiians. Sacred to him was the great New Year's festival. "On the twenty-third of the month Welchu, which nearly corresponded to November, Lono's image was decorated and, when night came on, all the people went to bathe in the sea. This rite of purification having been accomplished, men and women donned new clothing in preparation for the festival which began at sunrise on the morrow. During the four days of its continuance no fishing, no bathing, no pounding of *kapa*, and no beating of drums or blowing of conchs was permitted. Land and sky and sea were tabu to Lono, and only feasting and games were allowed" (Hutton Webster, *R.D.*).

LOPTR. Another name for the Scandinavian god Loki (*q.v.*).

LORD'S SUPPER. A name given to the Christian institution which commemorates the Last Supper of Jesus with his disciples. The name seems to have been borrowed from I. Corinthians xi. 20, "where, however, it probably refers to the Agape or Love-feast, which was held immediately before or after Communion" (W. R. W. Stephens, *Book of Common Prayer*). Other names are the Holy Communion, and the Eucharist (Thanksgiving).

LORETTO NUNS. An order founded by Mrs. Mary Teresa Ball in imitation of the Institute of the Blessed Virgin Mary (*q.v.*). In 1822 Mrs. Ball opened a large mansion at Rathfarnham, near Dublin, as a convent of "Our Lady of Loretto." Other convents were established not only in Ireland, but also in India and the Colonies. See *Cath. Dict.*

LOTUS, THE. In Hindu mythology the lotus flower is symbolical of the earth, and the creator of the world rests upon a lotus. Benares, which, with its two thousand temples, is a favourite place of pilgrimages, is called "the lotus of the world." The Egyptian sun-god Horus is represented as resting upon a lotus. This suggests to Prof. Elliot Smith (*Dr.*) that the flower represents his mother. "The familiar representation of Horus (and his homologues in India and elsewhere) being born from the lotus suggests that the flower represents his mother." But, since, according to his theory, the original form of Hathor was a shell-amulet (that is to say, a cowry-amulet), "it seems not unlikely that her identification with the lotus may have arisen from the confusion between the latter and the cowry, which no doubt was also in part due to the belief that both the shell and the plant were expressions of the vital powers of the water in which they developed" (p. 180 f.).

LUCIFERIANS. The party of Lucifer, bishop of Calaris (Cagliari) in Sardinia. Lucifer was a vigorous opponent of the Arians and a strong supporter of Athanasius. Constantius sent him into exile from 355 to 361 A.D. When in 361 the exiled bishops received permission to return to their sees, Lucifer went to Antioch, but he refused to hold communion with bishops and clergy who had through pressure consented to Arianism, that is to say, he would not accept the decision of the Council of Alexandria. According to Ambrose he separated himself from the Church, and according to Theodoret (*H.E.* iii. 5) he even framed new dogmas. But Jerome describes him as *beatus* and *bonus pastor*. He may have been a leader of a party; he would hardly seem to have been a schismatic. "The substance of Lucifer's controversial pamphlets consists of appeals to Holy Scripture, and they contain a very large number of quotations from both Testaments" (*Dict. of Christ. Biog.*). See J. H. Blunt; Wace and Piercy.

LUCOPETRIANS. Euthymius Zigabenus gives this name to the Euchites (*q.v.*) or a branch of them because one of their leaders, whose original name seems to have been Peter, came to be known as Lycopetrus (*lukopetros*, Wolf-Peter). He had proclaimed himself the Messiah and had promised to reappear after his death. It is said that on the third day after his death a wolf appeared to his disciples. After this they called Peter, their former leader, Lycopetrus. See J. H. Blunt.

LUG. Lug was a god or divine hero revered by the ancient Celts. The god, it is thought, reappears in Lugoves, a name for the Celtic genii, and in the town-name Lugdunum. The Gaelic Lug or Lugh has been compared or identified with the British Lleu or Llew; but more is known about the former. The Gaels seem to have regarded him first as a sun-god, and then as a fire-god or as both together. In Irish mythology his face is represented as shining like the sun. "He was the acknowledged master of all arts, both of war and of peace" (Squire). The Milky Way was described as Lug's Chain. See Charles Squire, *Myth.*; Reinach, *O.*

LUGAL-BANDA. A god in Babylonian mythology. "When the hearts of the other gods failed them, he alone recovered the Tablets of Fate, stolen by the bird-god Zû from Enlil's palace" (L. W. King, *Legends of Babylon and Egypt in relation to Hebrew Tradition*, 1918).

LUGAL-MARADA. A Babylonian deity. The name means "king of Marad." Lugal-Marada was a solar deity who had a temple at Marad, the native place of Gilgamesh. When Gilgamesh and Eabani had slain the divine bull Alû, sent against them by the goddess Ishtar (*q.v.*), Gilgamesh offered its horns to Lugal-Marada. See GILGAMESH EPIC. Lugal-Marada seems to be equivalent to Shamash (*q.v.*).

LUKE, THE GOSPEL OF. Like the Gospel of Matthew, the Gospel of Luke seems to have been based in the main on two documents, a document corresponding very closely to the Gospel of Mark (*q.v.*) and a document containing a collection of discourses and sayings of the Lord (the Logia, or Q). But the compiler used also other sources, written or oral, or both, for the Gospel of Luke contains a large amount of matter peculiar to itself. This matter comprises eighteen out of its twenty-three parables, including those of the Good Samaritan, the Prodigal Son, and Dives and Lazarus; the stories of the draught of fish (v. 1-12), the raising of the widow's son (vii. 11-19), the cure of a woman with a spirit of infirmity (xiii. 11-18), the cure of a man with dropsy (xiv. 1-7), the cure of ten lepers (xvii. 11-20), the healing of Malchus' ear (xxii. 47-54). It includes a number of short sayings: Satan's fall from heaven (x. 18-21); fire on earth (xii. 49); reply to a brother (xii. 14); reply to the greeting of a woman (xi. 27); the message to Herod Antipas (xiii. 32): and others. It includes a number of short narratives: the names of the ministering women (viii. 2, 3): Samaritans refusing hospitality to Jesus (ix. 51-57); a would-be disciple (ix. 61, 62); the seventy disciples (x. 1 ff.); Mary and Martha (x. 38 ff.); the story of Zacchaeus (xix. 2-11). P. Wernle thinks that some of these may have been derived from a lost gospel. The matter peculiar to Luke includes also certain sayings and incidents in the story of the Passion and the Resurrection: details of the agony in Gethsemane (xxii. 43, 44); the sending of Jesus to Herod (xxiii. 6-13); the daughters of Jerusalem (xxiii. 27-32); the first word from the cross (xxiii. 34); the two thieves (xxiii. 39-44); St. Peter at the tomb (xxiv. 12); the walk to Emmaus (xxiv. 13-33): the appearance of Jesus to the eleven (xxiv. 36 ff.); the ascension (xxiv. 50 ff.). These additions also, it has been thought, may have been taken from an older source. But this is quite uncertain. As Wernle says, "if Luke really made use of traditions, they were not necessarily written ones." Plummer, Harnack, and others have called attention to the fact that a very considerable portion of the matter peculiar to Luke is feminine in interest. Women figure prominently. Harnack suggests that these special traditions came from Philip and his four prophesying daughters. As regards Philip's daughters, "it is known that St. Luke made their acquaintance in Cæsarea, and it is very probable that on a later occasion he encountered them yet again in Asia. Papias, who himself saw the daughters, expressly states that they transmitted stories of the old days." Harnack further points out that another collection of stories in Luke is distinguished by the interest shown in the Samaritans, and that, according to the Acts of the Apostles (viii. 14), the great achievement of Philip was the evangelisation of Samaria. In his view, "this coincidence of interest in the feminine element, in prophecy (the Holy Spirit), and in the Samaritans, taken together with the general standpoint—*that of Jerusalem*—of this source peculiar to St. Luke, makes it probable that we have here a body of tradition which rests upon the authority of St. Philip and his daughters." Harnack thinks that the first two chapters of the Gospel of Luke are based upon a special tradition which Luke treated very freely. Sanday (*The Life of Christ in Recent Research*) thinks that "these two chapters—whatever the date at which they were first committed to writing—are essentially the most archaic thing in the whole New Testament, older really in substance—whatever may be the date of their actual committal to writing—than I. and II. Thessalonians." The Apostle Luke was a physician. It seems probable that it was actually his medical profession that led him to Christianity, "for he embraced that religion in the conviction that by its means and by quite new methods he would be enabled to heal diseases and to drive out evil spirits, and above all to become an effectual physician of the soul" (Harnack). Following Hobart (*The Medical Language of St. Luke*), Harnack maintains that "very nearly all of the alterations and additions which the third evangelist has made in the Markan text are most simply and surely explained from the professional interest of a physician." In the Third Gospel the representation of Jesus "is dominated by the conception of Him as the wondrous Healer and Saviour of the sick, as, indeed, the Healer above all healers." Harnack finds the same interest in medicine and healing in the Acts of the Apostles, and argues powerfully in support of the view that the Third Gospel and the Acts were composed by one and the same author, Luke the Physician. This was also the belief of the ancient Church. See Adolf Harnack, *Luke the Physician*, 1907; W. Sanday, *The Life of Christ in Recent Research*, 1907; C. F. Nolloth, *The Person of Our Lord and Recent Thought*, 1908; G. Currie Martin, *The Books of the N.T.*, 1909; Arthur S. Peake, *Intr.;* F. C. Conybeare, *New Test. Crit.*

LUKMĀN HAKIM. A Hindu deity, worshipped by the Kaderas (or Kanderas), a small caste of makers of fireworks, and reputed to have been the inventors of gunpowder. The Kadera is known also as a Golandāz, "ball-thrower," Bāndar, "rocket-thrower," or Hawāidār, maker of fireworks. Lukmān Hakīm is worshipped not in the house but in the shop, and with Muhammadan rites.

LULLARDS. Lullards (equivalent to Lollards) was a name given to a religious fraternity instituted at Antwerp about the year 1300. In time of plague the Lullards devoted themselves to the work of tending the sick and of carrying dead bodies to the grave. The word is derived from a root meaning "to sing softly," and has reference to their solemn processions. The proper name of the fraternity was "Cellite Brothers and Sisters" or "Brothers and Sisters of St. Alexius." In course of time the Lullards came to be regarded as heretics; and then the term Lullard became equivalent to "heretic." See J. H. Blunt; Brockhaus.

LUMAWIG. The supreme god of the Bontoc Igorot, an Indonesian people of the Philippines, who dwell in the Northern Luzon. Legend relates that he came down from the sky, married one of the Bontoc women, and lived at Chao-wi in the centre of the Bontoc district. "Certain large flat stones, arranged in a circle, are looked upon as the foundations of his house" (W. J. Perry, *The Megalithic Culture of Indonesia*, 1918). He is supposed to have taught the Bontoc to build their council house and men's house, and to have instructed them in the art of agriculture.

LUMINOUS TEMPLES. When in A.D. 636 a Nestorian mission arrived in China, the members obtained an imperial decree which authorized them to erect a temple. From the year 756 the Nestorian Churches became known as "luminous temples." When the Buddhist patriarch Zendo (b. 614 A.D.) died, the Emperor granted the temple in which he resided the honorific title Kōmyōji. According to A. Lloyd, this is only another form of "luminous temple." It is said that from the works of Zendo which were preserved in the library at the White Horse Monastery rays of light issued. See Arthur Lloyd.

LUPERCALIA. The festival known as Lupercalia was held in Rome on February 15 from early times in honour of Faunus (*q.v.*), a deity afterwards identified with the Greek Pan (*q.v.*). Faunus was worshipped under the name Lupercus, and the festival was held in a grotto on the Palatine Hill which was called the Lupercal. The god was evidently an ancient pastoral deity, a god of fertility. It has been thought that the object of the Lupercalian rites was, at least symbolically, to purify the land and thus to induce the god to give fertility to fields, flocks, and people. O. Seyffert describes the procedure as follows. " After the *flamen Dialis* had sacrificed some he-goats and a dog, two youths were touched on the forehead with a knife, smeared with the blood of the goats. It was then immediately wiped off with wool dipped in milk, whereupon they were bound to laugh. After the sacrificial feast the *Luperci* [as the priests were called], crowned and anointed, and naked, except for an apron of goatskin, ran round the ancient city on the Palatine with thongs cut from the skin of the sacrificed goats in their hands. On their course women used to place themselves in their way to receive blows from the thongs, which was believed to be a charm against barrenness." Possibly in the most ancient and primitive form of the rites the symbolism represented not purification but fertilization. See *Chambers' Encycl.;* O. Seyffert, *Dict.;* S. Reinach, *O.*

LUX MUNDI. A theological work, a collection of essays, published in 1889. The work produced a considerable amount of excitement, and was much criticised. The contributors were H. S. Holland, Canon of St. Paul's, who wrote on "Faith"; Aubrey Moore, Honorary Canon of Christ Church, who wrote on the " Christian Doctrine of God"; J. R. Illingworth, Rector of Longworth, who wrote on " The Problem of Pain, its bearing on faith in God," and on " The Incarnation in relation to Development"; E. S. Talbot, Vicar of Leeds, who wrote on " The Preparation in History for Christ": R. C. Moberly, Vicar of Great Budworth, who wrote on "The Incarnation as the Basis of Dogma"; the Hon. Arthur Lyttelton, Master of Selwyn College, Cambridge, who wrote on " The Atonement"; Charles Gore, Principal of Pusey House, Oxford, who wrote on " The Holy Spirit and Inspiration"; W. Lock, Sub-Warden of Keble College, Oxford, who wrote on " The Church"; F. Paget, Canon of Christ Church, Oxford, who wrote on " Sacraments"; W. J. H. Campion, Tutor of Keble College, Oxford, who wrote on " Christianity and Politics"; and R. L. Ottley, Vice-Principal of Cuddesdon Theological College, who wrote on " Christian Ethics." The writers were engaged together in the common work of University education at Oxford between the years 1875 and 1885. And they felt compelled both for their own sake and for the sake of others " to attempt to put the Catholic faith into its right relation to modern intellectual and moral problems." They met together not infrequently. The collection of essays, " Lux Mundi," is a combined effort to explain the Christian Creed. " We are sure that Jesus Christ is still and will continue to be the Light of the world. We are sure that if men can rid themselves of prejudices and mistakes (for which, it must be said, the Church is often as responsible as they), and will look afresh at what the Christian faith really means, they will find that it is as adequate as ever to interpret life and knowledge in its several departments, and to impart not less intellectual than moral freedom. But we are conscious also that if the true meaning of the faith is to be made sufficiently conspicuous it needs disencumbering, reinterpreting, explaining." Theology must take a new development. But development is not innovation, nor heresy. " The real development of theology is rather the process in which the Church, standing firm in her old truths, enters into the apprehension of the new social and intellectual movements of each age: and because 'the truth makes her free' is able to assimilate all new material, to welcome and give its place to all new knowledge, to throw herself into the sanctification of each new social order, bringing forth out of her treasures things new and old, and shewing again and again her power of witnessing under changed conditions to the catholic capacity of her faith and life." See *Lux Mundi*, edited by Charles Gore, twelfth edition, 1891.

LYCH-GATE. *Lich* is an Anglo-Saxon word meaning " corpse." Lych-gate or Lich-gate therefore means literally Corpse-gate. It is a gate at the entrance of a churchyard covered with a roof or shed. Here the bearers used often to pause and rest when bringing a corpse for interment. Lych-gates are still found in various parts of England, but they are rare in Scotland. According to Parker, " the term is also used in some parts of the country for the path by which a corpse is usually conveyed to the church." See Benham; J. H. Parker, *Gloss.*

M

M. God M is a designation used by anthropologists for a deity depicted in the MSS. of the Mayan Indians of Central America. He is usually represented as entirely black. Since he seems to be a god of chapmen or travelling merchants, like Yacatecutli, it has been suggested (Marian Edwardes and Lewis Spence) that his blackness may be symbolical of the tanned or bronzed skin acquired by travelling merchants in Central America. In the Codex Tro-cortesianus he is provided with the scorpion's tail.

MA. A goddess said to have been worshipped in Asia Minor. She seems to have been equivalent to the nature-goddess Atargatis.

MA'ASEROTH. The Jewish Mishnah, a collection and compilation completed by Rabbi Judah the Holy, or the Patriarch, about 200 A.D. (see MISHNAH), comprises a number of treatises or tractates which reproduce the oral tradition or unwritten law as developed by the second century A.D. There are sixty-three tractates, divided into six groups or orders (*sedarim*). Ma'asēroth is the seventh tractate of the first group, which is called *Zerā'im* (" Seeds ").

MA'ASER SHENI. The name of one of the Jewish treatises or tractates which reproduce the oral tradition or unwritten law as developed by the second century A.D. and are included in the Mishnah (*q.v.*), a collection and compilation completed by Rabbi Judah the Holy, or the Patriarch, about 200 A.D. The sixty-three tractates of the Mishnah are divided into six groups or orders (*sedarim*). Ma'asēr Shēni is the eighth tractate of the first group, which is called *Zerā'īm* ("Seeds").

MAAT. An Egyptian deity. Maat was the goddess of truth and justice. She was regarded as the daughter of Ra (*q.v.*) and wife of Thoth (*q.v.*). She is represented as wearing on her head, as a symbol of truth, an ostrich feather. Sometimes, in order to express the impartiality of justice, she is represented with bandaged eyes. In the Old Kingdom she is included already among the goddesses. See A. Wiedemann; Adolf Erman, *Handbook*.

MACHA. An ancient Irish deity. Sister of Bav, and wife of Neit, the god of battle, she had charge of one of the departments of battle and carnage, being active amidst the bodies of the slain. Human crania, which have been found in heaps, seem to have been offerings to the goddess.

MACCHIAVELLISTS. Those who belong to the school of thought of N. Machiavelli (1469-1527). Machiavelli attached great importance to religion, but simply as a means of keeping the people in check. He regarded it not as a principle implanted in the soul by God, but as a man-made political device. The device loses its value as soon as men see through it.

MACEDONIANS. The followers or the party of Macedonius, Bishop of Constantinople (341-360 A.D.), the most prominent of those theologians who denied the Godhead of the Holy Spirit. "Confessing that the Son was like the Father in substance, he held that the Holy Ghost was a creature, like the angels, and a servant of the Father and the Son" (*Cath. Dict.*). Those who held this opinion were called later Marathonians, after Marathonius, Bishop of Nicomedia. Another general name for the Macedonians was Pneumatomachi, "adversaries of the Spirit." The Macedonians were condemned in 374 by a Roman Synod, in 375 by an Illyrian Synod, and in 381 by the Second Oecumenical Council (Constantinople). Nevertheless, in Phrygia they continued to exist down to the fifth century. The first canon of Constantinople anathematizes especially, among other heresies, the heresy of "the Semi-Arians, or Pneumatomachi." See K. R. Hagenbach; J. H. Blunt: *Cath. Dict.*

MACMILLANITES. The followers of John Macmillan (1670-1753). Macmillan was expelled from the Scottish Kirk in 1703. In 1712 he established the "Reformed Presbytery," and became the first pastor of the Reformed Presbyterians. See CAMERONIANS.

MADAN MOHAN. The enchanter of love, one of the names of the Hindu god Krishna.

MĀDHAVA. Honey-sweet, or belonging to the Spring, vernal, one of the names of the Hindu god Krishna.

MĀDHAVACHĀRYA SECT. A Vishnuite sect of Southern India, the followers of a saint Mādhavachārya, also called Mādhavas. The founder sought to combine the worship of Krishna with that of Siva and Pārvati, and thus to reconcile the Sivites and Vishnuites. The members of the sect are called dualists, because they maintain that the human soul is different from the divine. "They admit a distinction between the divine soul and the universe, and between the human soul and the material world. They deny also the possibility of Nirvāna or the absorption and extinction of the human soul in the divine essence" (R. V. Russell).

MĀDHVAS. The followers of the Hindu religious teacher, Ānanda-tīrtha or Madhva. Madhva is said to have been born about the year 1200 A.D. He opposed the Non-duality doctrine of Śaṅkara and taught a Duality. It has been supposed that the Mādhvas were influenced by Christian doctrines, but the influence was more likely Muhammadan. According to Madhva, there is only one eternal Supreme Being. His chief name is Vishṇu or Hari. This Being is essentially different from the individual spirit, and from matter. The Supreme Spirit is independent; the human spirit is dependent. The Madhvas honour the Supreme Being in three ways: (1) by naming; (2) by worship; and (3) by branding. A child is given one of the names of Vishṇu. Worship is performed with the voice, the body, and the heart. The Mādhvas brand themselves with the circular discus and conch-shell as emblems of Vishṇu. See Monier-Williams; E. W. Hopkins.

MADHOSŪDAN. Destroyer of the demon Madho (honey or wine), one of the names of the Hindu god Vishnu.

MADHYAMAYĀNA. When the widened form of Buddhism known as Mahāyāna, or the Great Vehicle, was developed, the older form was called Hīnayāna, or the Little Vehicle. There arose also a third form, of a mediating nature, which received the name Madhyamayāna, or the Middle Vehicle. See VEHICLES, THE THREE.

MADIVĀLAYYA. The tribal deity of the Tsākalas of the Telugu country in India, a caste whose occupation is partly to prepare torches for processional or other ceremonial occasions.

MADRAS SYSTEM OF EDUCATION. A system originated by Andrew Bell (1753-1832), who was Superintendent of the Madras Male Orphan Asylum. Joseph Lancaster (1778-1838) tried the same system. See LANCASTERIAN SYSTEM OF EDUCATION.

MAGI. A priestly caste from whom, on account of their practice of astrology and the interpretation of dreams, the word magic is derived. Iranian scholars find a marked difference between the Persians and the Magi. The Magi were one of six tribes in Media. "They made a temporarily successful bid for political power when Gaumāta the Magus seized the throne in the character of Bardiya (Smerdis), the murdered brother of Cambyses. The Aryan aristocracy regained its power under the leadership of the great Darius, and an annual festival, the *Magophonia*, celebrated the downfall of the priests who had tried to be kings. After a generation or two we find the Magi firmly established as a sacred caste. Their general resemblance to the Brahmans is very suggestive in the light of Dr. D. B. Spooner's investigations. They kept their distinctive practices for centuries, and Greek witnesses expressly show that the Persians did not share them. Conspicuous among these were the exposing of the dead to vultures, and the practice of next-of-kin marriage" (J. H. Moulton). There is no proof that the Persians made use of the vultures before the Sassanian age; and they rejected the Magian doctrine of marriage, as well as other characteristics of the caste. According to Plutarch, the Magi sacrificed a wolf to the god of evil in a sunless place. Moulton notes that while this is akin to the spirit of Mithraism, the propitiation of evil powers never gained any footing in Parsism. "We may reasonably conjecture that only the Magi resident in Persia identified themselves with Zoroastrianism, and that a great many Magi living in other countries kept up their own special beliefs and usages, which might easily be credited to Zoroastrian Magi by misunderstanding." Those, however, who threw in their lot with Zoroastrianism (probably in the fifth century B.C.) profoundly modified its whole spirit. They introduced, for instance, the great development of ritual. Cp. F. W. Bussell.

MAGIC. According to J. G. Frazer (*The Magic Art*, 1911), the principles of thought on which magic is based resolve themselves into two: (1) that like produces like, or that an effect resembles its cause (the Law of Similarity); (2) that things which have once been in contact continue to act on each other at a distance after the physical contact has been severed (the Law of Contact or Contagion). From the first of these principles, "the magician infers that he can produce any effect he desires merely by imitating it"; from the second "he infers that whatever he does to a material object will affect equally the person with whom the object was once in contact, whether it formed part of his body or not. Charms based on the Law of Similarity may be called Homoeopathic or Imitative Magic. Charms based on the Law of Contact or Contagion may be called Contagious Magic." The same principles are believed to regulate the operations of inanimate nature. Magic is therefore a false science as well as a fallacious guide of conduct. "Regarded as a system of natural law, that is, as a statement of the rules which determine the sequence of events throughout the world, it may be called Theoretical Magic: regarded as a set of precepts which human beings observe in order to compass their ends, it may be called Practical Magic." The primitive magician, however, knows magic only on its practical side. To him magic is always an art, never a science. As regards the relationship of magic to religion, it has been much debated whether the former originated before the latter, or whether it is a degenerate form of religion. They have much in common. Like religion, magic has its ceremonies, sacrifices, lustrations, prayers, chants and dances. Frazer thinks that, though magic is found to fuse and amalgamate in many ages and in many lands, there are reasons for thinking that this fusion is not primitive, and that there was a time when man trusted to magic alone for the satisfaction of his higher cravings. "In the first place a consideration of the fundamental notions of magic and religion may incline us to surmise that magic is older than religion in the history of humanity. We have seen that on the one hand magic is nothing but a mistaken application of the very simplest and most elementary processes of the mind, namely, the association of ideas by virtue of resemblance or contiguity; and that on the other hand religion assumes the operation of conscious or personal agents, superior to man, behind the visible screen of nature. Obviously the conception of personal agents is more complex than a simple recognition of the similarity or contiguity of ideas; and a theory which assumes that the course of nature is determined by conscious agents is more abstruse and recondite, and requires for its apprehension a far higher degree of intelligence and reflection than the view that things succeed each other simply by reason of their contiguity or resemblance." A. C. Haddon, and Émile Durkheim.

MAGICAL PRAYERS AND NAMES. Papyri discovered in recent years have revealed the fact that Christians early adopted the pagan practice of using prayers and names as charms and amulets. "The name of Jesus together with gospel texts and certain liturgical formula were early used as amulets, and by the sixth century the sign of the cross and other symbols for Christ had quite widely taken on a magical import. Several of the early fathers speak of the Christian women wearing diamond editions of the gospels round their necks after the manner of Jewish *tephillin*, and the papyri show us the Lord's prayer as one of the most common devices to ward off evil. Wilcken and others have published a goodly number of Christian amulets from the sixth century, in which prayers to God and the local saints are made against the demons of asthma, croup, hydrophobia, insanity, indigestion, witchcraft, and pain. These amulets often end with the Lord's prayer" (Camden M. Cobern). In some of these conjurations the names of Greek, Roman, or Egyptian deities appear. In one, for instance, which has been assigned to A.D. 300, we find the names Jesus—Anoubis.

MAHĀ-BHĀRATA. Mahā-Bhārata or Great Bhārata is a name sometimes given to the great Epic poem of the Hindus, the Bhārata. The term means the Great Bhāratā. See BHĀRATA.

MAHĀBIR. An Indian deity, another name for Hanumān, worshipped by the Gārpagāris, a caste of village menials in India, whose occupation is to avert hail-storms.

MAHĀDEO. An Indian deity, the special god of the Dhangars, the Marātha caste of shepherds and blanket-weavers. The word means the great god, and is used as one of the names of Siva.

MAHATMAS. A term used in Theosophy. The name has been given to members of a great Brotherhood, persons who have reached a higher state of evolution than that of average humanity, and who possess the Secret Wisdom of Theosophy (*q.v.*). They "work ever for the service of their race with a perfect and selfless devotion, holding their high powers in trust for the common good, content to be without recognition, having power beyond all desires of the personal self" (Annie Besant). See Annie Besant, "Theosophy" in *R.S.W.*

MAHĀVAGGA. A Buddhist sacred book, one of the Khandhakas, in the first division of the Canon. See CANON, BUDDHIST.

MAHĀVIRA. Or Mahābīr, the strong one, one of the names of the Hindu god Hanumān.

MAHĀYĀNA. Mahāyāna, or the Great Vehicle, is the name that was given to a developed (widened) form of Buddhism. See VEHICLES, THE THREE.

MAHDI, THE. A term used in Muhammadanism. The word means "the Directed One," and is then used in the sense of "One who is ordained to direct others, as Guide or Leader." The Mahdi is an ideal figure, a kind of Messiah (*q.v.*), to whose coming all Muslims have looked forward. When he appears he is to set all things right. According to al-Bukhārī and other traditionists, utterances of the prophet Muhammad concerning him have been preserved. They include the following. "The world will not come to an end until a man of my tribe and of my name shall be master of Arabia. . . . The Mahdi will be descended from me, he will be a man with an open countenance and with a high nose. He will fill the earth with equity and justice, even as it has been filled with tyranny and oppression, and he will reign over the earth seven years. . . . Quarrelling and disputation shall cease amongst men, and then shall a man of the people of al-Madīnah come forth, and shall go from al-Madīnah to Makkah, and the people of Makkah shall make him Imām. . . . The Mahdī shall rule according to the example of your Prophet, and shall give strength and stability to Islām. He shall reign for seven years, and then die. . . . There shall be much rain in the days of the Mahdī, and the inhabitants both of heaven and earth shall be pleased with him. Men's lives shall pass so pleasantly, that they will wish even the dead were alive again." The Shī'ahs (*q.v.*) believe that the Mahdi has already appeared in the person of Muhammad Ibn Hasan al-'Askari. Ibn Hasan disappeared mysteriously about the year 878 A.D., when he was still a child. One tradition says that he entered a cave to seek for his father and was never seen to come out. He will emerge from his hiding-place and manifest himself before the end of the world. As to his remanifestation F. J. Bliss quotes an account obtained by Dr. Wortabet from a great Metawali leader. "At the appointed time he (the twelfth imam) will manifest himself to men, and will then be known by the name of Guide (El-Muhdy), and with Jesus, the son of Mary, will fill the whole world with the knowledge of God. . . . This set time is fast approaching. All this is a part of the settled faith of the Metawileh. Some of their learned men believe also that after the appearance of the Muhdy he will in due time die, and be succeeded by his own father, or predecessor in the office, who will be raised from death for this purpose; and a retrograde resurrection and succession will go one, until the twelve imams shall have risen and completed the regeneration of the world. After this will come the end, the judgment, and eternity." The Sunnis believe that the Mahdi has not yet appeared. See T. P. Hughes; F. J. Bliss.

MAIMINS. The Maimins or Dönmes are a Jewish sect of about 4,000 persons in Salonica. Jews by race, but Muhammadan by religion, they arose under the influence of Sabbatai Zevi.

MAIR. A Hindu deity, a family god worshipped by the Mochis, the occupational caste of saddlers and cobblers in India. He is represented in the house by a lump of clay.

MAIUMA. A nautical festival celebrated at Ostia in Italy, probably of Philistine origin.

MAIYA ANDHIYĀRI. An Indian deity, the goddess of the dark fortnight of the month, worshipped by the Dhanwārs (also called Dhanuhārs), a small primitive tribe in India. "She is worshipped in the house conjointly by husband and wife on any Tuesday in the dark fortnight of Māgh (January-February), all the relatives of the family being invited" (R. V. Russell). Other names of the goddess are Rāt Devi or the goddess of the night and Rāt Mai or the night mother.

MAJJHIMANIKĀYA. One of the Buddhist sacred books in the second division of the Canon. See CANON, BUDDHIST.

MAKARA. A figure in Hindu mythology, a composite creature on which the great Vedic god Varuna is represented as sitting. Elliot Smith (*Dr.*) suggests that the vehicle of Varuna corresponds to the composite animal or "sea-goat" of the Babylonian Ea-Marduk, and points out that the *Makara* was intimately associated with Indra as well as with Varuna. "The monster assumed a great variety of forms, such as the crocodile, the dolphin, the sea-serpent or dragon, or combinations of the heads of different animals with a fish's body" (see the illustrations, p. 88). The forms even include, according to Elliot Smith, one with the head of an elephant, "which was adopted as far east as Indonesia and as far west as Scotland." In a creation-story found in one of the MSS. of the Mayan Indians, one of the figures is a "female whale with alligator-feet." This seems to be another form of *Makara*.

MAKHSHIRIN. The name of one of the Jewish treatises or tractates which reproduce the oral tradition or unwritten law as developed by the second century A.D. and are included in the Mishnah (*q.v.*), a collection and compilation completed by Rabbi Judah the Holy, or the Patriarch, about 200 A.D. The sixty-three tractates of the Mishnah are divided into six groups or orders (*sedarim*). Makhshīrīn is the eighth tractate of the sixth group, which is called *Ṭohorōth* ("Purifications").

MAKKOTH. The Jewish Mishnah, a collection and compilation completed by Rabbi Judah the Holy, or the Patriarch, about 200 A.D. (see MISHNAH), comprises a number of treatises or tractates which reproduce the oral tradition or unwritten law as developed by the second century A.D. There are sixty-three tractates, divided into six groups or orders (*sedarim*). Makkoth is the fifth tractate of the fourth group, which is called *Neziḳin* ("Damages").

MAKUTU. A personified witchcraft in Maori mythology.

MALA ARAYANS. A class of hill tribes in Southern India. The Mala Arayans worship the spirits of their ancestors. The Arayans make "little cells of pieces of stone, the whole forming a box a few inches square; and, on the death of a member of any family, the spirit is supposed to pass, as the body is being buried, into a brass or silver image, which is shut into this vault; if the parties are very poor, an oblong smooth stone suffices" (S. Mateer, *Native Life in Travancore*, 1883). In memory of their ancestors, lamps are kept burning in these miniature cromlechs. See E. Thurston and K. Rangachari.

MALACHI, BOOK OF. One of the smaller prophetic books of the Old Testament. The work belongs to a period in which Judah is ruled by a governor (i. 8), and the Temple has been rebuilt (i. 10; iii. 1, 10); in which also the people made defective offerings (i. 7, 8, 12), and the priests despised the name of Jehovah (i. 6). "The conditions thus reflected are very similar to those which Nehemiah found when he visited Jerusalem about 445 B.C. In many ways Nehemiah's reform work, especially in eliminating the social evils and in improving the temple worship, was the fulfilment of the prophet's hope that Jehovah would speedily send his messenger to prepare the way for a better and nobler era. The presence of the evils which Nehemiah endeavoured to correct and the absence of any references to that great restorer of Judaism favour the conclusion that the book of Malachi was written not long before 445 B.C." (C. F. Kent). Cornill points out that the book is noteworthy on account of the way in which it anticipates the methods of discussion practised by the later rabbis. We have, in the style of Talmudic dialogue, assertion, objection, refutation. Kent even says that the work "also formulates in words which might almost have been taken from the mouth of Job the problems which are treated in the great wisdom book which bears his name." It is not unlikely that the work was anonymous. "Malachi" (which means "my messenger") was probably not intended to be understood as a personal name. In any case, nothing is known about a person Malachi. See C. Cornill, *Intr.*; G. H. Box; O. C. Whitehouse; C. F. Kent, *The Sermons, Epistles and Apocalypses of Israel's Prophets*, 1910.

MĀLIK. The name in Muslim theology of the angel who presides over Hell. "And they shall cry: 'O Malik! would that thy Lord would make an end of us!' He saith: 'Here must ye remain.'" (xliii. 77).

MALAKHBEL. A solar deity, of Mesopotamian origin, adopted by the Palmyrenes.

MĀLIS. The Mālis are described as the functional caste of vegetable and flower gardeners in India. The name has been derived from *māla*, a garland, and it is "a plausible hypothesis that the calling of the first Mālis was to grow flowers for the adornment of the gods, and especially for making the garlands with which their images were and still are decorated" (R. V. Russell).

MAMA ALLPA. A deity in Peruvian mythology, goddess of the earth and harvest.

MAMA COCHA. A deity in Peruvian mythology, goddess of water and mother of mankind.

MAMA OULLO HUACA. A goddess in Peruvian mythology, teacher of the arts of domestic life.

MANA. A term used in the Melanesian islands of the S. Pacific to denote a mystic power or influence. It seems to have been derived from Polynesia, where the root-idea is an overwhelming, supernatural power or energy in individual, personal beings. But the power, at any rate in Melanesia, could be imparted to impersonal things. According to Codrington (*The Melanesians*, p. 118, N. 1), it is regarded as "a force altogether distinct from physical power, which acts in all ways for good and evil; and which it is of the greatest advantage to possess or control. . . . It is a power or influence, not physical and in a way supernatural; but it shows itself in physical force, or in any kind of power or excellence which a man possesses. This mana is not fixed in anything, and can be conveyed in almost anything. . . . All Melanesian religion consists, in fact, in getting this mana for one's self, or getting it used for one's benefit."

MANA. A man-god, the principal deity of the Kanjars, various small communities of a gipsy character in India, who wander about the country. Māna is regarded as the founder and ancestor, as well as the teacher and guide, of the tribe.

MANANNÁN. Manannán, son of Lir (LLŶR), was one of the gods or divine heroes of the ancient Celts. He was the Gaelic god corresponding to the British Manawyddan (*q.v.*). He figures most prominently in Irish mythology. He was the patron of sailors and merchants. As such he made his journeys in a wonderful boat known as the "Wave-sweeper." He is also represented as a knight who rode on a marvellously swift steed known as "Splendid Mane." See Charles Squire, *Myth.*

MANAS. A term used in Theosophy (*q.v.*). The term is applied to the Ego in man, the Spiritual Intelligence. Mrs. Besant describes it as "the immortal entity, the link between Atma-Buddhi and the temporary personality" ("Theosophy" in *R.S.W.*).

MANASA DEVI. A Hindu deity, the queen of snakes, worshipped by the snake-charmers in India, the Saperas.

MANAWYDDAN. Manawyddan was one of the gods or divine heroes revered by the ancient Britons. He corresponds to the Irish god Manannán (*q.v.*). His characteristics are rather contradictory. "On the one hand he appears as a kind of culture-hero—hunter, craftsman, and agriculturist; while on the other he is the enemy of those gods who seem most beneficient to man" (Squire). See Charles Squire, *Myth.*

MĀNBHAOS. A caste belonging to the Marātha Districts of the Central Provinces and to Berār in India. By origin the Mānbhaos are a religious sect or order. They recognise only two of the Hindu deities, Krishna and Dattātreya, the latter a celebrated devotee of Siva, deified as an incarnation of the deity. They accept as their sacred book the Bhāgavat-Gīta, rejecting the other Hindu scriptures. There are three divisions of the order: the Brahmachāri or ascetics, who devote themselves to meditation, prayer and spiritual instruction, and beg for their living; the Gharbāri, who lead a mendicant life, but are allowed to marry; and the Bhope or Bhoall, who are purely secular and are allowed to follow any occupation they choose. "One of the leading tenets of the Mānbhaos is a respect for all forms of animal and even vegetable life, much on a par with that of the Jains. They strain water through a cloth before drinking it, and then delicately wipe the cloth to preserve any insects that may be upon it. They should not drink water in, and hence cannot reside in, any village where animal sacrifices are offered to a deity. They will not cut down a tree nor break off a branch, or even a blade of grass, nor pluck a fruit or an ear of corn. Some, it is said, will not even bathe in tanks for fear of destroying insect-life. For this reason also they readily accept cooked food as alms, so that they may avoid the risk of the destruction of life involved in cooking. The Mānbhaos dislike the din and noise of towns, and live generally in secluded places, coming into the towns only to beg. Except in the rains they wander about from place to place" (R. V. Russell).

MANCO CCAPAC. A figure in Peruvian mythology, reputed to be the founder of the royal Peruvian Incas. He is said to have founded Cuzco, the site of the ancient Inca capital, and to have taught the inhabitants the arts of civilisation. Born of the sun and moon, when he had completed his work, he ascended to heaven with his sister-wife Mama Oullo.

MANDAEANS. The Mandaeans are an oriental sect of which representatives still exist to the South of Bagdad. Their religion has grown out of a mingling of Babylonian, Persian, Jewish, and Gnostic elements. The word *Mandâ*, from which their name is derived, does in fact mean "gnosis." The rite to which they attach the greatest importance is baptism or ablution. This has given them the names, Sabians (*Subbā*) which means Baptists, Christians of St. John (the Baptist), and Disciples of St. John. The chief of their sacred books are five in number. They are: (1) "The Great Book," which is called also the *Ginza* or "treasure"; (2) "The Book of John"; (3) "The Completion," a book of hymns; (4) "The Divan," a book of ritual; and (5) a book on astrology. According to the Mandaeans, John the Baptist was the only true prophet. Jesus was one of the false prophets. The Supreme Being, "The Great Glory," can be known only after death. The revealed deity is "The First Life," from whom proceeded "The Second Life" and "The Spirit of Life." From "The Second Life" proceeded the Angels, one of whom, Gabriel, formed the earth and man. "The Spirit of Life" (*Mandâ d'hayyê*) is the Saviour, who revealed himself to man in three sons, of whom the chief was Hibil. Reinach thinks "it is not impossible that John the Baptist may have belonged to a primitive sect of Mandæans; if at this early period they already called themselves Nazarenes, we should have an explanation of the tradition which made Nazareth the birthplace of the Messiah, who was himself called a Nazarene." See V. Brandt, *Die Mandäische Religion*, 1889; J. H. Blunt; Reinach, *O.*; Brockhaus; *Chambers' Encycl.*

MANIBOZHO. A deity ("The Great Hare") in the mythology of the Algonquian Indians of North America, a god of the dawn and a culture-hero. He is supposed to have been the inventor of the Algonquian hieroglyphs, and the originator of all the arts and crafts.

MANICHÆISM. A movement in the third century, so called from Mani (*b.* 215 A.D.) of Ecbatana. Of Persian stock, he was brought into contact with the Gnostic sects known as Elkesaites and Mandeans. Mani regarded himself as the last and greatest of a series of prophets (including Adam, Noah, Abraham, and the phantom Christ), and described himself as "leader," "ambassador," and "Paraclete." His religion was one of physical redemption, and admits the worship of no personal redeemer. "As might be expected from its headquarters being in Babylon, the doctrines of the sect were in the main akin to the old Babylonian nature religion, modified by Persian Dualism, with some admixture, especially in the West, of the Gnostic Christianity of Basilides and Marcion. Owing partly to their minute and strict asceticism and their rigid morality, partly also to the great number 'of the cultured who sought for a rational and yet to some extent Christian religion, and who had exalted free inquiry, especially as regards the Old Testament, into a battle-flag' [Harnack], Manichæism obtained considerable influence in Christian circles, especially in North Africa, and at one time succeeded even in capturing Augustine" (H. B. Workman). Mani wrote six works in Syriac, and a "Holy Gospel" in Persian. The Gospel was written in opposition to the New Testament. See F. W. Bussell.

MĀNIKYA DEVI. The tutelary deity of the Nāgvansi, kings of Bastar in India before the fourteenth century.

MANITOU. A term used among the Algonquin of N. America to denote a mystic potentiality ascribed to beings whether human or non-human, living or not living. *Manitou* seems to be a force, and not a personal being.

MANNIKINS. Lucian (§ 16) states that in the vestibule of the great temple of Hierapolis there stood a pair of phalli (or pillars) of great size bearing the inscription: "I, Dionysus, dedicated these phalli to Hera my stepmother." He adds: "The Greeks erect phalli in honour of Dionysus, and on these they carry, singular to say, mannikins made of wood, with enormous pudenda; they call these puppets. There is this further curiosity in the temple: as you enter, on the right hand, a small brazen statue meets your eye of a man in a sitting posture, with parts of monstrous size" (transl. by H. A. Strong). The phalli are stated to have been thirty fathoms high (§ 28). We are told that a man mounted one of these twice every year and remained on the summit for seven days. It was believed popularly that "the man who is aloft holds converse with the gods and prays for good fortune for the whole of Syria, and that the gods from their neighbourhood hear his prayers." Lucian suggests that the custom was rather in honour of Dionysus, and that the ascent was made in imitation of the wooden mannikins.

MANLA. Manla is the Buddha in his character of a god of healing, the "Healing Buddha." A cure may be effected by touching his image. He is venerated in China and Japan, Tibet and Manchuria. In China he is known as the Healing Teacher and Medical King.

MANOHAR. The heart-stealer, one of the names of the Hindu god Krishna.

MANTRA. J. C. Oman gives the following explanation of the term "Mantra" from the "Classical Dictionary of India" by Garrett. "Mantra—a hymn of invocation or form of prayer in the Sanskrit language. Mantras are used in the performance of every religious rite. They are of various sorts, invocatory, evocatory, deprecatory, conservatory. They are beneficent or hurtful, salutary or pernicious. By means of them, it is believed that great and various effects may be produced. Some are for casting out evil spirits, some inspiring love or hatred, for curing diseases or bringing them on, for causing death or averting it. Some are of a contrary nature to others, and counteract their effect: the stronger overcoming the influence of the weaker. Some are potent enough, it is said, to occasion the destruction of a whole army; while there are others which the gods themselves are constrained to obey." John Campbell Oman, *Cults*, 1908.

MANU, LAWBOOK OF. The Code or Lawbook of Manu is one of the most remarkable of the literary productions of Brāhmanism. The work seems to be due to a number of authors, some of whom perhaps lived in the fifth century B.C., others in the second century B.C. The Hindus ascribe it to Father Manu, their semi-divine ancestor. A number of modern scholars think it to be an elaboration of a code that was current among the Mānavas who seem to have lived in a district in the North-west of India. According to the Code of Manu, "the root of all law is the Veda and the traditions of those who know the Veda." But a knowledge of the sacred texts and a participation in the holy ceremonies are permitted only to certain castes. "The enormity of all crimes depends on who commits them, and against whom they are committed. The three upper castes alone have religious privileges" (Hopkins). The four chief classes of men or castes are Brāhmans (priests), Warriors, Agriculturists, and Slaves or Servants. The philosophical views of the Code are not always in agreement. The philosophies of the Vedānta School (see VEDĀNTISM) and of the Sānkhya School (see SĀNKHYA) are both represented. Some of the precepts of the Code of Manu, as given by Monier-Williams, are: "Even though wronged, treat not with disrespect thy father, mother, teacher, elder brother. . . . Say what is true, speak not agreeable falsehood. . . . Pride not thyself on thy religious works; give to the poor, but talk not of thy gifts. By pride religious merit melts away, the merit of thy alms by ostentation. . . . Thou canst not gather what thou dost not sow; as thou dost plant the tree so will it grow. . . . Contentment, patience under injury, self-subjugation, honesty, restraint of all the sensual organs, purity, devotion, knowledge of the Deity, veracity, and abstinence from anger, these form the tenfold summary of duty." See Monier-Williams; E. W. Hopkins.

MAPONUS. Maponus, "the great youth," was one of the names given by the ancient Celts to a god of healing who presided over thermal springs and corresponded to Apollo (*q.v.*). Another name for the god was Grannus (*q.v.*). The name Maponus survived in Mabon, one of the heroes in Welsh mythology. Mabon, the son of Modron (probably equivalent to Matrona), appears as a companion of King Arthur. See E. Anwyl; Squire, *Myth*.

MĀPPILLAS. A hybrid Muhammadan race of the western coast of Southern India. The Māppillas seem to have resulted from the alliances of early Arab settlers on the Malabar coast with the women of the country. They are either Sunnis or Shiahs. The chief seat of their religious organisation is a college at Ponnāni, the Jammat mosque, said to have been founded in the 12th or 13th century A.D. The mosques of the Māppillas are quite different from those of any other Muhammadans. According to Fawcett (*Ind. Ant.* xxx., 1901), they are "much in the style of the Hindu temple, even to the adoption of the turret-like edifice which, among Hindus, is here peculiar to the temples of Siva" (quoted by E. Thurston and K. Rangachari). The Māppillas practise magic and witchcraft. "One of their methods of witchcraft is to make a wooden figure to represent the enemy, drive nails into all the vital parts, and throw it into the sea, after curses in due form" (E. Thurston and K. Rangachari). One of these figures was washed ashore at Calicut in 1903.

MARAI MĀTA. A Hindu goddess, the goddess of cholera, worshipped by the Kohlis, a small caste of cultivators in India. Also by the Korkus, a Kolarian tribe.

MARANG BURU. A Hindu deity, a mountain god who is supposed to control the rainfall; worshipped by the Mundas (also called Kols or Hos), a large tribe in Chota Nāgpur, India.

MĀRĀNS. The Mārāns or Mārāyans are described in the Madras Census Report (1901) as "temple servants and drummers in Malabar." Their traditional occupation is "sounding or playing on the panchavadya or five musical instruments used in temples" (Thurston and Rangachari). One of these is the conch-shell. The sounding of the asu and pani is left to the highest dignitaries. "The beating of the pāni is the accompaniment of expiatory offerings to the Saptamata, or seven mothers of Hindu religious writings, viz., Brāhmi, Mahēsvari, Kaumari, Vaishnavi, Varahi, Indrāni, and Chāmunda." See E. Thurston.

MĀRBOD. A Hindu deity worshipped by the Telis,

the occupational caste of oil-pressers and sellers in India. He is represented by the branch of a thorny creeper. "In the middle of the rainy season the Teli women sweep the house with the branches of a thorny creeper, which they call Mārbod, addressing to it the words, "Oh Mārbod! sweep away all diseases, pains, coughs, bugs, flies and mosquitoes" (R. V. Russell).

MARCELLIANS. The followers or the school of Marcellus, Bishop of Ancyra in Galatia. In his zeal to defend the Nicene faith against the Arians, Marcellus developed a form of Sabellianism (*q.v.*). The Marcellians are condemned with the Sabellians in the first canon of the Council of Constantinople (381 A.D.). Marcellus held that in the Divine Nature there was only one person (*prosōpon*), Father and Son being simply names or titles of Almighty God and His eternal Word. The Word was from all eternity in the One God. In the Incarnation this One God consented to expand or extend Himself. It is Jesus, and not the Logos (as it were, an attribute of God like the reason in man), who is the Son, the Image of God, the Christ, the Firstbegotten, the King. "And when He has accomplished the object of His coming, they [these titles] will cease to apply to Him; for He will leave the flesh, return to God, and be merely the Word as before; and His kingdom, as being the kingdom of the flesh or manhood, will come to an end" (J. H. Blunt). At the Council of Constantinople the words "Whose kingdom shall have no end" were added to the creed to guard against the Marcellian heresy. Marcellus based this part of his doctrine on I. Corinthians xv. 24-28. See J. H. Blunt; *Cath. Dict.*

MARCELLINIANS. The followers of a woman named Marcellina. She was herself a follower of Carpocrates (see CARPOCRATIANS), and came to Rome in the time of Pope Anicetus (*c.* 155 A.D.). She gained many adherents, and it is stated by Epiphanius (*Haeres.* xxviii.) that images of her were worshipped by her followers. See J. H. Blunt; Louis Duchesne, *Hist.*

MARCIANISTS. One of the names given to the Euchites (*q.v.*). They were so called after one of their leaders, Marcian, who lived in the middle of the sixth century.

MARCOSIANS. A Gnostic sect, the followers of one Marcus, who flourished in the middle of the second century and belonged to the school of Valentinus. The principal authority for his teaching is Irenaeus. To a great extent Marcus was in agreement with Valentinus; but he added features of his own. He found great mysteries in numbers and names, and considered it of vital importance to know the right name of each celestial power. The Marcosians had special formulae and sacraments of redemption. "Some conferred this redemption by baptism with special invocations; others added or substituted various anointings; others held that these applications could not procure spiritual redemption—only by knowledge could such redemption be effected. This knowledge included the possession of formulae, by the use of which the initiated would after death become incomprehensible and invisible to principalities and powers, and leaving their bodies in this lower creation and their souls with the Demiurge, ascend in their spirits to the Pleroma" (Wace and Piercy). Marcus was skilful as a magician. "The eucharistic cup of mingled wine and water was seen under his invocation to change to a purple red." The explanation given was that Charis, one of the highest Æons in the system of Marcus, had dropped some of her own blood into the cup. Marcus encouraged his female disciples to prophesy, choosing them for the purpose by lot. He is said also to have been guilty of immoral practices. "Some of his followers certainly claimed to have been elevated, by their knowledge and the redemption they had experienced, above ordinary rules of morality"; but this may have been a misapplication of the teaching of Marcus. The Marcosians do not seem to have been a large body. See J. H. Blunt; Wace and Piercy.

MARDUK. A Babylonian deity. The god Marduk became the patron deity of the city of Babylon, and as such was greatly glorified. He was not really one of the older gods. He became prominent in the days of Hammurapi, and from this time grew more and more powerful. The result of this was that to him were transferred qualities and powers which previously had belonged to other gods. In the Epic of Marduk (see below), for instance, he is more important than the members of the first triad, Anu (*q.v.*), Bel (*q.v.*), and Ea (*q.v.*). He is the creator of the heavenly bodies. It is he who, by defeating Tiâmat (*q.v.*), brings order out of chaos. True, he is the child of Ea, but he is the first-born son who has inherited all the virtues of his father and more. His name is even used as a title of other gods. Nergal (*q.v.*) is described as "the Marduk of warfare"; Nebo as "the Marduk of earthly possessions"; Ninib (*q.v.*) as "the Marduk of strength." Marduk is the "lord of the Anunnaki and Igigi." To Nebuchadrezzar he is the all-wise creator and king. The Epic of Marduk represents Bel and Ea as voluntarily transferring their own names to Marduk. Originally Marduk was a solar deity. It is natural therefore that he should be associated with the sun-god, Shamash (*q.v.*). He is also associated with Ramman (*q.v.*), but during the Cassite dynasty, Ramman seems to have been more prominent. Marduk does not appear even in the second triad. This consists of Sin (*q.v.*), Shamash, and Ramman. The consort of Marduk was Sarpanitum. Her name has been explained as meaning "silvery bright one." Marduk's great festival was the New Year's Day. The Zagmuk (*q.v.*) was converted into a Marduk festival. The Zu myth (*q.v.*) describes how Marduk recaptured the tablets of fate from the bird Zu. See Morris Jastrow, *Rel.*

MARDUK, EPIC OF. The Babylonian creation-epic, in which Marduk (*q.v.*), the head of the pantheon, is the principal figure. Marduk is represented as battling with a great monster, Tiâmat. In the beginning there existed only Apsu, the ocean, and Tiâmat, primaeval chaos. Both really represent the same thing, the one being masculine, the other feminine. Then the gods were created: first Lakhmu and Lakhamu, then Anshar and Kishar, next Anu, Bel and Ea. Tiâmat had as her associates great serpents, furious vipers, scorpion-men, and other monsters, of whom the chief was Kingu. Kingu is made ruler over all the gods. Tiâmat seems to have resolved to destroy them. Anshar sends Anu his son to pacify her, but in vain. Then he sends Ea, but with the same result. Finally he sends his son Marduk. The news of his coming is conveyed to the army of Tiâmat, "all the Igigi," by a messenger Gaga. Before Marduk goes forth he is encouraged by the gods. They give him a sign, which consists in his performing a miracle. He makes a garment first disappear and then reappear. He arms himself with a net of seven destructive winds, in addition to ordinary arms, and mounts his chariot. When he approaches Tiâmat, Kingu and his monsters are afraid. Marduk challenges Tiâmat to fight. They fight. Marduk envelops her in his net, plunges his spear into her, and kills her. Afterwards he captures her monsters, and takes from Kingu the tablets of fate which Tiâmat had given him. He cuts Tiâmat in two. Of one half of her he made the heavens. Of the other half, we may suppose, he made the earth. He makes a dwelling for Ea in front of Apsu that he may control this subterranean sea. Over Apsu he places Esharra, the vault of earth. He assigns to Anu, Bel, and Ea their districts. He sets up the stars and constellations, and divides the year into twelve months. He makes Nannar, the moon-god, and gives him control of the night. When he has completed his work, he is praised and adored by the Igigi. Bel and Ea, the great gods, give him their own names. In an epilogue all men are bidden to remember and acknowledge Marduk's great achievements. See Morris Jastrow, *Rel.;* Reinach, *O.*

MARGHANITES. The followers of Sayed Aly el Marghani. The Marghanites are a Muhammadan sect, of whose religion one of the features is a respect for the life of the cat. Marghani crossed the Red Sea from the Hedjaz to the Upper Nile valley in the first half of last century to preach the doctrine of Mohamed el Idrissi among the Nubian tribes. The sect is for the most part Muhammadan; but it has a cabalistic sign of its own which possesses mystic powers, and reveres its chief as a saint.

MARIMĀTA. A Hindu deity, a goddess worshipped by the Kaikāris or Kaikādis (also called Bargandis), a wandering tribe of basket-makers in India.

MARISTS. The Society of Mary is a religious order which was founded in 1898 by Père Colin (1790-1875) with the object of preaching foreign Missions. It was approved by Pope Gregory XVI. in 1836, when members of the order volunteered to preach the gospel in Western Oceania. The work of the Society made great progress, and was extended to all parts of the world. The members are known as the Marist Fathers. In 1817 a congregation of Marist Sisters was founded. It was approved in 1884, and has a number of convents in England. There are also Marist Brothers, a teaching confraternity founded by one of the Marist Fathers. The Marist Brothers have a number of schools in England and Scotland. See the *Cath. Dict.*

MĀRIYATTĀL. A Hindu deity, worshipped as a goddess of small-pox by the Paraiyans, a tribe or caste in India.

MARK, THE GOSPEL OF. Papias makes the following statement about the work of Mark: "And this also the elder said: Mark, having become the interpreter of Peter, wrote down accurately all that he remembered of the things that were either said or done by Christ, but not in their order. For neither did he hear the Lord, nor did he follow Him; but subsequently he attended Peter, who adapted his teaching to the needs of his hearers, but had no idea of making a connected narrative of the words of the Lord. So Mark, in thus writing down things just as he remembered them, made no mistake, for he made it his one care to omit none of the things that he heard, and to make no false statement in his record of them." According to this statement, the Apostle Peter was Mark's chief authority; and Justin Martyr even seems to refer to the Gospel of Mark as the Memoirs of Peter. We may, as A. S. Peake says, trust the statement of Papias "to the extent of recognising that reminiscences of Peter do lie behind the Second Gospel. Peter's prominence in it is not to be accounted for simply by the fact that he was the most important member of the apostolic band, for some of the incidents are too trivial to have found their way into a story of Christ's ministry had it not been for the personal interest which they had for Peter." But Mark does not merely reproduce the preaching of Peter. He "has so arranged his material as to reproduce some of the main lines of the historical development." The Gospel of Mark, though it is placed second in order in the New Testament, is really the earliest of the Gospels. In approximately its present form and compass it lay before the compilers of the First and Third Gospels, and was freely used by them. For discourses and sayings of Jesus they used, in addition, another, more primitive, source, the Logia. "With the exception of three or four incidents the whole matter of St. Mark's Gospel is to be found either in both or in one at least of the other evangelists. And the order in which his incidents are arranged is always attested by one or by the other. It is clear that they were anxious to lose nothing of his work which they could find room to embody; but, on the other hand, they must have recognised in it a serious deficiency, which they on their part were in a position to supply" (J. Armitage Robinson). One of the omissions in the earliest gospel was an account of the birth of Jesus. The purpose of the Gospel of Mark would seem to be to record simply the main events in the public life of Jesus, his deeds rather than his words. "It omits the longer discourses, with the exception of certain parables and the great declaration on the End. It leaves even the Sermon on the Mount without report. It gives few parables—only four of the parables proper, together with three of the minor or germ parables. It deals with the acts of Jesus rather than his words. It has many more miracles than parables—no less than eighteen. Most of these are miracles of healing, and most belong to the period before the Transfiguration" (S. D. F. Salmond). All this is natural enough in the earliest gospel. More importance would be attached to traditions about the birth of Jesus later. What impressed people at first was the fact that Jesus demonstrated the truth of his teaching by curing people of their ailments, intellectual and physical. In the Gospel of Mark great emphasis is laid on the fact that he "cast out devils" (evil thoughts, etc.). In metaphorical language, it is said that "unclean spirits, when they saw him, fell down before him, and cried, saying, 'Thou art the Son of God.'" The author or the reputed author of the Gospel would seem to have been the person who is described at one time as Mark or Marcus (Acts xv. 39; Col. iv. 10; II. Tim. iv. 11; Philem. 24; I. Pet. v. 13), at another as John (Acts xiii. 5, 13), at another as "John whose surname was Mark" (Acts xii. 25), and again as "John, who was called Mark" (Acts xv. 37). It is thought that he may have been identical with the young man who on the night on which Jesus was betrayed followed him, "having a linen cloth cast about him, over his naked body" (Mark xiv. 51, 52). The writer of the Gospel may have used Aramaic Sources, but the language in which he wrote his own work would seem to have been Greek from the beginning. The style is not that of a translator. The author wrote for Western readers. This is clear from the fact that he carefully interprets Aramaic terms (iii. 17, v. 41, vii. 11, 34, x. 46, xiv. 36, xv. 34), and explains Jewish customs, localities, etc. (vii. 3, 4, 32, xii. 42, xiii. 3, xv. 42). The last few verses of the Gospel (xvi. 9-20) are not part of the original work. An Armenian manuscript, discovered in recent years, speaks of the section as being "of the presbyter Ariston." By Ariston seems to be meant Aristion, who, according to Papias, was one of the disciples of the Lord. The Sinaitic MS. and the Sinaitic Syriac VS. close the Gospel with vs. 8. So also does the Vatican MS., though in this case a blank space is left. It is true that the majority of MSS. have the verses, but the authorities for their omission are supported by the language of the passage which "is very different from that of the rest of the Gospel" (Currie Martin), and by the fact that the ninth verse does not connect well with the eighth. It is possible that the original conclusion of the Gospel of Mark is to be found in the last chapter of the Gospel according to John. It should be added that in some MSS. and VSS. the Gospel has in place of xvi. 9-20 a shorter conclusion. But it is clear from the style that this again is not original. See Allan Menzies, *The Earliest Gospel*, 1901; S. D. F. Salmond, *St. Mark* in the "Century Bible"; J. Armitage Robinson, *The Study of the Gospels*, 1903; Oscar Holtzmann, *The Life of Jesus*, 1904; G. Currie Martin; Arthur S. Peake, *Intr.;* C. F. Nolloth, *The Person of Our Lord and Recent Thought*, 1908; F. C. Conybeare, *N.T. Crit.*

MARNAS. A deity worshipped at Gaza in the Graeco-Roman age. His temple was called Marneion. He is identified by Mark the Deacon with the Cretan Zeus. G. F. Hill (*Some Palestinian Cults in the Graeco-Roman Age*, 1912) compares Marnas with the Cretan word *marna* = maiden. Marnas and his consort Britomartis he identifies with the Cretan Zeus and the Cretan Artemis. It has been held more commonly that Marnas is a Syrian name = "Our Lord."

MARONITES. The Syrian body known as Maronites seem originally to have been a heretical sect, a remnant of the Monothelites (*q.v.*) and Monophysites (*q.v.*). The name is used of a body of heretics by John of Damascus, who wrote in the eighth century, and afterwards by Christian authors in Egypt. The Maronites themselves derive their name from an old monastery on the Orontes between Hamath and Emesa, dedicated to St. Maron, who would seem to have lived about 400 A.D. It is more likely that the name was derived from Maronea, a village thirty miles east of Antioch, or from Johannes Maron, the first Patriarch of the "Maronites." In any case, the home of the community was the Lebanon region from Tripoli to Tyre and the Lake of Genesareth. In course of time the Maronites spread all over Syria, and became a small, but to some extent independent, nation. Their liturgy is in Syriac, but the Gospels are read in Arabic, their spoken language. In 676 Johannes Maron, a monk of St. Maron, was appointed Bishop of Botrus by the papal legate in Antioch. After converting all the Monothelites and Monophysites in the Lebanon region he was elected Patriach of Antioch. Since that time the head of the Church of the Maronites has been called the "Patriarch of Antioch and all the East." The Maronites remained spiritually independent until 1182, when, through the influence of the Crusaders, they attached themselves to the Church of Rome. In 1445 they entered formally into union with the Roman Church. This union was made more complete in 1596, when a large measure of agreement, though not entire agreement, was reached with respect to doctrines. "The Maronites retained the celebration of the Lord's Supper under both kinds, the Syriac liturgy, the marriage of the priests, their own fast-days, their own saints, etc." (Schaff-Herzog). In 1736, through the efforts of J. S. Assemani, the Maronites accepted the Roman Catechism, the Gregorian Calendar, and the Tridentine explanation of the doctrine of transubstantiation; they agreed to confine the marriage of the clergy to the lower degrees, and to introduce the name of the Pope into the prayers, the Mass, etc. Long before this Pope Gregory XIII. had founded a College of Maronites (*Collegium Maronitarum*) in Rome (1584). Since 1860 the Maronites have been very much weakened through conflicts with the Druses. They are said to number now about 128,000. See Schaff-Herzog; the *Prot. Dict.;* the *Cath. Dict.;* Brockhaus.

MĀROTI. Son of Mārut, the Hindu god of the wind, one of the names of the Hindu god Hanumān.

MARRANOS. A name or rather nickname given to those Jews of Spain who in the fifteenth century were constrained to be baptised and to profess themselves Christians. The name means "The Damned." The Marranos became a separate class or sect, outwardly Christians, but, as Graetz says, at heart Jews. "As far as they could they observed the Jewish rites and customs, whether out of piety or habit. Even those who, upon philosophical grounds, were indifferent to Judaism, were none the less irreconcilably hostile to that Christianity which they were compelled to confess with their lips. Although they did not have their children circumcised, they yet washed the heads of the infants immediately after baptism. They were, therefore, rightly looked upon by the orthodox clergy either as Judaising Christians or as apostate heretics" (Graetz). They suffered sadly under the Inquisition. In the middle of the sixteenth century many of them took refuge in Bordeaux, and a flourishing congregation arose there (A.D. 1550-1750). Others followed their example and escaped to Holland. There still survives a remnant of them (about 6000) in the Balearic Islands, where they are known as Anusim ("forced converts") or Chuetas. See H. Graetz; and A. Ruppin.

MARRI. An Indian deity, worshipped in Saugor by the Chamārs (also known as Chambhārs), the caste of tanners and menial labourers in Northern India. He is a family god, represented by a lump of clay kept in the cooking-room of the house (Russell and Hīra Lāl).

MARROW MEN. In 1646 there appeared, in the form of a dialogue, a work on Justification and Sanctification with the title "The Marrow of Modern Divinity." The author was described simply as E.F., and it has been thought by some that he is to be identified with Edward Fisher (*fl.* 1627-1655), a writer of anti-puritan tracts. Later the book attracted the attention of Thomas Boston (1677-1732), who recommended it to others. In 1718 it was reprinted, a preface being added by Thomas Hog, minister of Carnock, Fifeshire. The book was condemned by the General Assembly in 1720. Thomas Boston, with eleven persons who shared his views, defended the book and opposed the action of the General Assembly. On this account they were called "the twelve apostles" and "Marrow Men." Another name given to them was the "Representers," because they complained of the Act of Assembly in a document called a "Representation." The Church of Scotland was at this time divided into Moderates and Evangelicals. Thomas Hog, who wrote the preface to the new edition of "The Marrow of Modern Divinity," was an Evangelical. The real question as regards the book, says John Hunt, was "the question of the extent of the use of reason in doctrines supposed to come by external revelation. The Moderates virtually said that whatever the Bible meant, or whatever their standards meant, they could not regard as coming from God any doctrine which they knew to be unworthy of God. The Evangelicals said that however incomprehensible or apparently in contradiction to our natural reason or conscience, any dogma may be, it is to be received on the authority of external revelation. Thomas Boston, speaking of the 'Marrow of Modern Divinity,' says that the Gospel method of sanctification and justification lies so far beyond natural reason, that all the rationalists, philosophers, and divines in the world could never have discovered it. But, on the contrary, if proposed for their acceptance on the ground of reason, they would have rejected it as foolishness." Another of the Marrow Men was Ralph Erskine (1685-1752). See John Hunt; J. H. Blunt; the *D.N.B.*

MARSYAS. A figure in Phrygian mythology. Marsyas was either a Phrygian satyr or Silenus (*q.v.*), or a shepherd or herdsman. In any case, he is represented as a skilful player on the flute, an instrument which was closely associated with the worship of Cybele (*q.v.*). Marsyas is said to have challenged Apollo (*q.v.*) to a musical contest. He played the flute, while Apollo performed on the lyre. Apollo, on being declared victor, tied Marsyas to a pine-tree and flayed him. The skin, it is said, was hung up in a cave at Celaenae, and used to thrill at the sound of melodies played on the flute. J. M. Robertson (*C.M.*, 1910, p. 321) thinks that originally Marsyas was apparently a Phrygian variant of Pan, figuring as Silenus, and that the story of his flaying may have grown out of the fact that his symbol was a wine-skin. J. G. Frazer writes as follows. "In this Phrygian satyr, shepherd, or herdsman who enjoyed the friendship of Cybele, practised the music so characteristic of her rites, and died a violent death on her sacred tree, the pine, may we not detect a close resemblance to Attis, the favourite shepherd or herdsman of the goddess, who is himself described as a piper, is said to have perished under a pine-tree, and was annually represented by an effigy hung, like Marsyas, upon a pine? We may conjecture that in old days the priest who bore the name and played the part of Attis at the spring festival of Cybele was regularly hanged or otherwise slain upon the sacred tree, and that this barbarous custom was afterwards mitigated into the form in which it is known to us in later times, when the priest merely drew blood from his body under the tree and attached an effigy instead of himself to its trunk." See O. Seyffert, *Dict.;* J. M. Robertson, *C.M.; P.C.;* J. G. Fraser, *Adonis, Attis, Osiris*, 2nd ed. 1907.

MARTYR. A term derived from Greek ("witness"), and used to denote a witness for Christ. It was used first of those who were witnesses for him by their faith alone, then of those who suffered for Him, and afterwards (from the middle of the third century) exclusively of those who suffered death for Him. Many accounts of martyrdom have come to light in recent years. One of these represents Diocletian "being inspired by the devil in the guise of a serpent." Another narrates with eagerness "the tortures of the martyrs crowned with red-hot helmets, or boiled, after strips were cut from their back, etc." (Camden M. Cobern). In the early Church works dealing with the lives of saints and martyrs were read regularly in the monasteries with the liturgies. In England a favourite book of private devotion used to be the work of John Foxe (1516-1587), popularly known as *The Book of Martyrs.*

MARUTS. The name in Hinduism for the storm-winds, the attendants upon Indra (*q.v.*) and Rudra (*q.v.*).

MASKS. There are many instances of the use of masks at funeral dances. It has been noted among the Bantu-speaking peoples of the interior of the Kamerun, among the inhabitants of the interior of Brazil, among the Chinese, and among the Bohemians. The masks represent various animals and demons, as well as human beings. It has been suggested that in some cases the idea seems to be to terrify the evil demons who were supposed to have been the cause of a death. In other cases the masked persons are presumed to represent the ghosts of the deceased: in the person of the masked dancer the ghost is still alive and able to visit his friends.

MASS, THE. The word Mass seems to be derived from a Latin word "missa," which is another form of "missio" and means "dismissal." Originally it was employed in law-courts and churches to denote dismissal from further attendance. Then in the churches it came to mean the services from which certain persons were dismissed. Thus the service for catechumens, who were dismissed after the Gospel and sermon, was called Missa Catechumenorum, and the rest of the service (including the Eucharist) for which the faithful remained Missa Fidelium. Later the term came to be used specifically of the Eucharist or Holy Communion. In the Anglican Prayer Book of 1549 the title of the Eucharist was "The Supper of the Lord and the Holy Communion, commonly called the Mass." In that of 1552 the term Mass, "which had been common for more than a thousand years in the Western Church," was dropped, "no doubt from its association with Roman ceremonial and teaching" (W. R. W. Stephens, *Book of Common Prayer*). According to Roman Catholic doctrine, "the Mass is a sacrifice of adoration, of praise and thanksgiving; it is also a sacrifice of propitiation for sin, and a means of obtaining all graces and blessings from God" (*Cath. Dict.*). According to Article xxxi. of the Thirty-nine Articles of the Church of England, "the sacrifices of Masses, in the which it was commonly said, that the priest did offer Christ for the quick and the dead, to have remission of pain or guilt, were blasphemous fables and dangerous deceits." The Roman Church recognises various kinds of Masses. High Mass is "Mass with incense, music, the assistance of deacon and sub-deacon, etc." Low Mass is "Mass said without music, the priest at least saying, and not singing, the Mass throughout." Missa cantata is "a Mass sung, but without deacon and sub-deacon and the ceremonies proper to High Mass." Votive Masses "are those which do not correspond with the office of the day, but are said by the choice (*votum*) of the priest. Requiem Mass is a Mass for the dead. It is so called from the opening words of the Introit: Requiem æternam dona eis, Domine. Missa Adventitia or Manualis is "a Mass for the intention of a person who gives an alms."

MASSACHUSETTS METAPHYSICAL COLLEGE. An institution founded and opened in Boston in 1881 by Mary Baker Eddy for giving instruction in the principles and practice of Christian Science (*q.v.*). Mrs. Eddy taught in this college for seven years, during which time over four thousand students studied there. She closed the college in 1889 in order to give the next two years of her life to the preparation of the revision of her book "Science and Health." It was re-opened in 1899 as auxiliary to her church. See Mary Baker Eddy, *Science and Health with Key to the Scriptures*, 1911: *Miscellaneous Writings*, 1910.

MASSILIENSES, HERESY OF THE. A designation sometimes used of Semipelagianism (*q.v.*).

MASSORAH, THE. The Massorah is the name of a branch of Hebrew learning. The term itself seems to mean "tradition." The tradition concerns the Hebrew text of the Old Testament, the Massorah being a collection of critical and explanatory notes. At first these notes were written on the margins of the manuscripts. Afterwards, the collection grew to such an extent that this by itself became impossible, and independent treatises were written. The authors of the Massorah "compiled lists of variations, noted and tabulated all singularities, counted the letters and words in each book," etc. (A. S. Geden). The earlier and simpler form of the Massorah is called "Massorah Parva." A later and expanded form is called "Massorah Magna." These two together are called "Massorah Marginalis." A third division has the name "Massorah Finalis." It is placed at the end of manuscripts. The scholars who compiled this body of learning are known as "Massoretes." The same name was given to those earlier scholars who invented a system of punctuation for the Hebrew text, which before their time had been unpointed. This system was based upon the traditional punctuation of the Schools and Synagogues. See C. H. H. Wright, *Intr. to the O.T.*, 1890: A. S. Geden, *Intr. to the Hebrew Bible*, 1909; Gesenius' *Hebrew Grammar*, 1910.

MASTERS. In Theosophy (*q.v.*) the term Masters, like that of Mahatmas (*q.v.*), is applied to members of a great Brotherhood, Brothers, who possess the Secret Wisdom of Theosophy.

MASWĀSI. An Indian deity, the mythical ancestress of the Dhanwārs (also called Dhanubārs), a small primitive tribe in India. She is held to be the wife of Karankot and the daughter of Maiya Andhiyāri. Since the Dhanwārs invoke her before they go hunting, she would seem to be the goddess of hunting.

MATAR DEO. One of the special deities of the Ahirs, a caste of cowherds, milkmen, and cattle-breeders in India. He is the protector of the pen or enclosure for cattle made in the jungle.

MATERA HUNDI. A Hindu deity, worshipped as the goddess of harvest by the Bonda division of the Porojas, a class of cultivators in India.

MATERIALIZING MEDIUMS. An expression used in spiritism (*q.v.*). The mediums are supposed to have the power of materializing the spirits of the dead. The spirits speak, play instruments, etc., and may be touched.

MĀTH. One of the gods or divine heroes revered by the ancient Celts in Britain. He was a great magician. C. Squire (*Myth.*) compares him with the Irish god Dagda (*q.v.*).

MĀTIDEO. An Indian deity, the god of hunting, worshipped by the Gadbas, a primitive tribe belonging to the Vizagapatam District of Madras, and by the Bhatras.

MATLALCUE. A Mexican deity, goddess of running water, wife of the great rain-god Tlaloc.

MATOWELIA. The chief god of the Mohave Indians of Colorado, who led his people across the prairies.

MATRES. Matres (mothers) or Matronae (matrons) is a term used of the mother-goddesses worshipped in ancient times by the Celts. The cult reached from Britain to Switzerland, and is supposed to have been spread by Celtic soldiers. "These mother goddesses frequently form groups of three; they bestow a blessing upon the fields and make them fruitful, and hence are frequently represented with fruits and flowers, with ears of corn or a horn of plenty" (Chantepie de la Saussaye). See *Rel. of the Teutons*, 1902.

MATTHEW, THE GOSPEL OF. It used to be thought that Papias in the first half of the second century A.D. was referring to the Gospel of Matthew when he said that "Matthew composed the Logia in the Hebrew language, and each one interpreted these as he was able." But it is now widely recognised that the work referred to by Papias was not our Gospel of Matthew, but an earlier document. The Gospel of Matthew, like the Gospel of Luke, would seem to have been based in the main upon two sources, a collection of discourses (*Logia*), and a narrative resembling our Gospel of Mark (*Urmarkus*). It was not the work of the Apostle Matthew, of whom comparatively little is known, but incorporates work of his. The Gospels of Matthew and Luke have a large amount of matter that is common to both. But there is also matter peculiar to Matthew, which shows that the compiler of this Gospel made use of other traditions, written or oral, or both. This matter peculiar to Mathew comprises the narrative of the birth and infancy of Jesus (chapters i. and ii.), the teaching about almsgiving and fasting in the Sermon on the Mount (vi.), certain parables (xiii., xviii., xxi., xxv.), certain sayings in xii. 5 ff., 11 ff., xviii. 10, xix. 10-12, xxv. 31-46, and the promise to Peter (xvi. 16 ff.). Some of the peculiarities may be further explained by the fact that "both Matthew and Luke had conceptions of the character and *rôle* of Jesus based partly on reflections of their own, partly on the growing prophetic gnosis of the age, in obedience to which they remodelled Mark's narrative" (F. C. Conybeare). The compiler of the Gospel of Matthew would seem to have been a Jewish Christian. This is suggested by the genealogy at the beginning of the book, by familiarity with Messianic prophecies, by the quotations from the Old Testament, which are not dependent upon the Septuagint, and by sympathy with the Jewish point of view (for which cp. v. 18, x. 6, 23, xv. 24, xix. 3, 28, xxi. 43, xxiv. 20). These characteristics might seem to imply that the work was composed in Palestine or Syria. But they do not preclude composition at Rome, which is favoured by the ecclesiastical character of the gospel and its interest in Peter. According to Currie Martin and others, the gospel has upon it the mark of the early Catholic Church. And "part at least of the Church in Rome was strongly Jewish in character." Th. Zahn thinks the work was composed about A.D. 85, Sanday about A.D. 80, Currie Martin about 90 A.D. See J. Armitage Robinson, *The Study of the Gospels*, 1903; C. F. Nolloth, *The Person of Our Lord and Recent Thought*, 1908; W. F. Slater, *St. Matthew* in the "Century Bible"; G. Currie Martin; Arthur S. Peake, *Intr.*; F. C. Conybeare, *N.T. Crit.*, 1910.

MATWĀLES. A special sect of the Koshtis (or Koshtas), the Marātha and Telugu caste of weavers of silk and fine cotton cloth in India. According to R. V. Russell and R. B. Hira Lāl, the Matwāles are so called because they drink liquor at their religious feasts. They worship, besides Siva and Sakti, Vishnu as Nārāyan.

MAULBRONN FORMULA. A formula drawn up by Luke Osiander and Balthasar Bidenbach as the basis on which the Lutherans might agree. It was a brief formula, designed as an improvement upon the lengthy formula suggested by James Andreæ, the Swabian and Saxon Formula of Concord (*q.v.*).

MAURICE HOSTELS. Settlement Houses established in connection with the Christian Social Union (*q.v.*) and named after Frederick Denison Maurice.

MAXIMIANISTS. The party of Maximianus. Maximianus was a Donatist deacon at Carthage, and is said to have been related to Donatus the Great. Primian, on being appointed bishop of the Donatists at Carthage (A.D. 391), found fault with Maximian and excommunicated him. He was himself condemned and deposed by a number of Donatist bishops, and Maximian was ordained bishop. Thus arose one of the divisions among the Donatists. "Notwithstanding the defection of the Maximianists, who appear to have rebaptized those who joined them, the validity of their baptism was not denied by the other Donatists, a point which Augustine frequently uses against them" (Wace and Piercy). See Wace and Piercy.

MĀYĀ. A term used in Hinduism. Māyā means "illusion." According to Vedantism (*q.v.*), all that really exists is the One Spirit. The individual soul or spirit, if it will only realize its true nature, is one with the eternal, infinite Being. Nothing else really exists. It is all Māyā or Illusion. Compare BERKELEYISM and CHRISTIAN SCIENCE.

MAYĀNDI. A Hindu deity, the god of the Paliyans, a caste in Madura and Tinnevelly, Southern India. He is usually represented by a stone, "preferably one to which nature has given some curious shape, the serpent form being especially valued" (E. Thurston and K. Rangachari).

MAZDEISM. Mazdeism is another name for Zoroastrianism (*q.v.*) or Parseeism. It is so called because one of the names of the principal gods of the system is Mazda. Mazda, otherwise known as Ahura-Mazda, Hormuzd, or Ormuzd, is the god of light, purity, and truth, the all-wise creator. Mazdeism is dualistic, the god of light being opposed by a god of darkness, Angra-mainyu, otherwise known as Ahriman.

MECHITARISTS. An order of Christian Armenian

monks founded by Peter Mechitar (1676-1749). A native of Siwas, the ancient Sebaste, Mechitar went to Constantinople and formed a congregation there in 1701. The hostility of some of the Armenians drove him from Constantinople, and he removed to Modon in the Morea. Here in 1712 his congregation was approved by Clement XI. In 1715, when war broke out and Modon was captured by the Turks, Mechitar took refuge in Venice. In 1717 he settled with his companions on the island of San Lazzaro. Here he continued his work and built an Armenian convent. Houses were afterwards established in Vienna (1810) and other places. The Mechitarists have devoted themselves to literary labours, and have done excellent and remarkable service in perfecting the Armenian language. They have made, printed, and published translations into Armenian of many European books. See *Cath. Dict.;* Brockhaus.

MEDIATING THEOLOGY. Pfleiderer gives the name Eclectic Mediating Theologians to a class of theologians who have sought, independently of definite philosophical systems, to reconcile the faith of the Church with the thought of their times. Typical of this class or school was Isaac August Dorner (1809-1884). One of his works was on the history of the development of the doctrine of the person of Christ ("Entwicklungsgeschichte der Lehre von der Person Christi": 2nd ed. 1845-56); another was a history of protestant theology ("Geschichte der protestantischen Theologie," 1867). Dorner maintains that "the method of Christian dogmatic theology must be not simply productive, but rather reproductive; still it must not be merely empirical and reflective, but also constructive and progressive. When the enlightened Christian mind is in harmony by its faith and experience with objective Christianity, which faith knows to be its own origin, and which is also attested by the Scriptures and the scriptural faith of the Church, then such a mind has to justify and develop its religious knowledge in a systematic form." Our knowledge of God is incomplete and relative, but it is real and growing. In revelation the divine power works, in part outwardly (in miracles), in part inwardly (in inspiration). Dorner taught that "the primary seat of inspiration must not be sought in books, but in men, and must not be separated from the general history of revelation. But though no specific difference can be proved between men endowed with the spirit and inspired men: still of the latter it is a distinctive and indeed unique characteristic, by virtue of their being vehicles of revelation, that without being personally absolutely incapable of error, they are yet preserved from it in their teaching and preaching, and proclaim only unerring truth, even in historical details, as the word of God" (Pfleiderer). In Denmark the school found an able representative in Hans Lassen Martensen (1808-1884), who wrote on "Christian Dogmatics" (4th German edition, 1897) and on "Christian Ethics" (6th German edition, 1893). In reference to the latter work, Martensen says: "The one-sided views against which we have to contend are those of one-sided ecclesiasticism, and one-sided individualism. Both negative the great problem of the modern age—the living union of Christianity and humanism. For a nomistic ecclesiasticism which suppresses all intellectual, and especially all scientific freedom, and an individualism which tries to isolate Christianity, and separate it from the varied spheres of human life, are alike un-Christian and inhuman. The problem will continue to be the presentation in life and doctrine of this union and combination of Christianity and genuine and free humanity." Johann Peter Lange (1802-1884), who wrote on "Dogmatics" (1849-51), tried to put new life into dogmatic theology with the help of theosophical speculation. Daniel Schenkel (1813-1885), who wrote a book on "Christian Dogmatics" (1858-59), and another on the character of Jesus ("Das Charakterbild Jesu," 4th ed. 1873), thought that theology ought thoroughly to revise its idea of religion. The Jesus of Schenkel is described by Pfannmüller as "an idealized and modernized Christ." Albrecht Ritschl (1822-1889), who wrote on "The Christian Doctrine of Justification and Atonement" (4th ed. 1895), felt the need of an altogether new theology, and sought to supply it. He founded a new school of theology, the Ritschlian School. Another representative of the Mediating Theology, though he differed very much from Ritschl, was Richard Adelbert Lipsius (1830-1892), author of a "Manual of Evangelical Protestant Theology" (3rd ed. 1893). According to Lipsius, "the Christian faith regards the existence and course of the world from the teleological point of view as the means of securing the divine purpose of the world—without prejudice to the scientific causal theory of the world. The same course of the world must be placed entirely under the point of view of natural causation, and also entirely under that of a divine purpose, since the divine teleology manifests itself as the power immanent in the course of nature" (Pfleiderer). See Otto Pfleiderer, *Development of Theol.;* G. Pfannmüller, *Jesus im Urteil der Yahrhunderte,* 1908; H. S. Nash, *Higher Criticism of the N.T.,* 1901.

MEDITATION. Meditation, as a form of Christian prayer (see PRAYER), has been defined as "the application of the three powers of the soul to prayer—the memory proposing a religious or moral truth, the understanding considering this truth in its application to the individual who meditates, while the will forms practical resolutions and desires grace to keep them" (*Cath. Dict.*). Meditation is of course a form of Mental or Silent Prayer.

MEDIUMS. A name given by spiritists to those persons who possess, or seem to possess, in a special degree the power of establishing communication between living beings and departed spirits. See SPIRITISM.

MEGALITHIC MONUMENTS. There are still to be found in various parts of the world sepulchral monuments of stone which were erected in ancient times. Many are to be seen even in Europe. Megalithic monuments include *dolmens*, or table-like structures formed of several slabs of stone, *cromlechs,* or stone circles, and *menhirs* or solitary upright stones. Examples of these three types of monument have been found in Palestine east and west of the Jordan, and would seem to have been the work of a pre-Semitic race. It used to be thought that the dolmens were tables or altars of stone, but there is a growing mass of evidence against this view. R. Munro points out (Hastings' *E.R.E.*) that, as used by some English archæologists, *cromlech* is almost synonymous with dolmen; but, as defined by Continental authorities, cromlech is exclusively applied to enclosures "constructed of rude standing stones placed at intervals of a few feet or yards, and arranged roughly on a circular plan—circle, oval, horse-shoe, or rectangle." Cromlechs sometimes surround dolmens, tumuli, and cairns. It is clear, from the discovery of bones, skeletons, etc., that use was made of most of the smaller cromlechs as sepulchres. But he finds it difficult to believe "that burial was the sole purpose of the large cromlechs such as Avebury, Stonehenge, the Giant's Ring near Belfast, Mayborough near Penrith, etc. This last consists of a circular mound composed of an immense aggregation of small stones in the form of a gigantic ring, enclosing a flat space 300 feet in diameter, to which there is access by a wide break in the ring. Near the centre of the area there is a fine monolith, one of several known to have formerly stood there." He thinks that such large enclosures must have been used not only as cemeteries, but also "for the performance of religious ceremonies in connexion with the cult of the dead." Menhirs, besides being sepulchral monuments, may sometimes have been erected for other purposes (as oracular stones, etc.). They are often isolated, but they are also found in groups, forming a circle (cromlech) or an avenue. The question of the origin of the megalithic monuments is interesting and important. It has been discussed recently (1912) at the meetings of the British Association for the Advancement of Science. Mr. T. Eric Peet, author of *The Stone and Bronze Ages in Italy* (1909), pointed out that the main point at issue is whether the megalithic monuments were built by a single race or by a number of entirely different races or peoples, and, in the latter event, whether they arose independently among various peoples or spread from a single centre. Prof. G. Elliot Smith suggested that the idea of megalith-building originated in Egypt soon after the invention of metal tools, and spread from tribe to tribe until the whole world was encircled by it. "No adequate explanation of the significance of dolmens, cromlechs, alignments and all the other works in stone associated with them, can be found unless due recognition is given to (*a*) the identity of the ideas which prompted their construction, and the essential resemblances in their plan; (*b*) their geographical distribution—their absence from large central continental areas, and their wide extent alone continuous coastal and insular territories; (*c*) the chronological sequence of their construction, the site of their earliest appearance being somewhere in the neighbourhood of the Eastern Mediterranean, and progressively later in date as we go either west or east—towards Ireland and Scandinavia, or Japan and the Pacific Islands, respectively; (*d*) the coincidence of their first appearance in most lands with the last phase of the Stone Age or the commencement of the Age of Metals; and (*e*) the improbability of theories of independent evolution, among widely separated races of mankind, of identical ideas which find expression in the same way in building of similar design and materials." Prof. Elliot Smith pertinently asked why, if the impulse to build megalithic funerary monuments was a phase of culture through which all mankind passed, the people of Central Europe were exempt from this instinct, when their littoral relatives in the Mediterranean area and on the north-west of Europe were stirred by it to cut rock-tombs and build dolmens. "Why also, if this hypothesis has any basis of fact, did the ancient inhabitants of Ireland not get their 'impulse' until more than a millennium later, and the people of Japan until two millennia later, than the people of Egypt?" See the "Discussion on Megalithic Monuments and their Builders" in the Report of the Meetings of the British Association (1912); W. J. Perry, *The Megalithic Culture of Indonesia*, 1918; Reinach, *O.*; Peter Thomsen, *Palästina und seine Kultur in fünf Jahrtausenden*, 1909; Brockhaus; Hastings' *E.R.E.*, *s.v.* "Death and Disposal of the Dead," vol. iv. 1911.

MEGARICS, THE. The Megaric School of Greek philosophers was so named because the founder was Euclides of Megara (455-380 B.C.?). It was also called the Eristic School on account of its misuse of dialectics. Euclides taught a one, only, universal existence, which is true in itself and is always the same. This one existence is the Good. It is known also by other names, such as God, Truth. The philosopher Stilpo developed the teaching in an ethical and moral direction, and by the union of Megaric and Cynic ideas paved the way for the Stoic School of Philosophy (see STOICISM). See C. J. Deter.

MEGILLĀ. The name of one of the Jewish treatises or tractates which reproduce the oral tradition or unwritten law as developed by the second century A.D., and are included in the Mishnah (*q.v.*), a collection and compilation completed by Rabbi Judah the Holy, or the Patriarch, about 200 A.D. The sixty-three tractates of the Mishnah are divided into six groups or orders (*sedarim*). Megillā is the tenth tractate of the second group, which is called *Mō'ēd* ("Festival").

MEGILLOTH. Literally "rolls," the Jewish designation of the five books of the Old Testament, Song of Songs, Ruth, Lamentations, Ecclesiastes, and Esther. These books are used in the service of the Synagogue, and are called Megilloth because they are written upon separate rolls. They are read on special occasions: Canticles on the eighth day of the Passover, Ruth on the second day of Pentecost, Lamentations on the 9th day of Ab, Ecclesiastes on the third day of the Feast of Tabernacles, and Esther at Purim.

ME'ILĀ. The Jewish Mishnah, a collection and compilation completed by Rabbi Judah the Holy, or the Patriarch, about 200 A.D. (see MISHNAH), comprises a number of treatises or tractates which reproduce the oral tradition or unwritten law as developed by the second century A.D. There are sixty-three tractates, divided into six groups or orders (*sedarim*). Me'ilā is the eighth tractate of the fifth group, which is called *Ḳodāshīm* ("Holy Things").

MELCHIORISTS. The followers of Melchior Hofmann (*d.* 1533) of Strassburg. Little is known about them; but they held millenarian views, and believed that Hofmann would return to earth with the prophet Elijah. J. E. Erdmann thinks that Melchior Hofmann gave Sebastian Frank (*c.* 1495-1543) the first impulse to devote himself to mysticism.

MEMRA. Memra is a Hebrew word meaning "word." It first came to be used to designate God, because the real name of the Divine Being was considered too sacred to be pronounced. It was then employed to denote some power which issued from God, and was, apparently, thought of as a kind of personality. In the Aramaic Targums both usages are found. In Exodus xix. 17 the Hebrew text has: "And Moses brought forth the people out of the camp to meet God." In the Targum of Onkelos (*q.v.*) this is translated: "Moses led the people forth to meet the *Word* of God." In Deuteronomy i. 30 the Hebrew text has: "The Lord your God goeth before you." In the Targum of Onkelos this is translated: "Jehovah, your God, whose *Word* leads you." Oesterley and Box quote a number of passages from the Targums to show that by the time they were written the "Word" had become a definite *personality*. The passages, however, do not necessarily prove this. All they need prove is that at this time devout Jews did not like to ascribe human actions or passions to God. In II. Samuel vi. 7 the Hebrew text has: "And the anger of the Lord was kindled against Uzzah; and God smote him there for his error; and there he died by the ark of God." Here the Targum of Jonathan explains that: "The Memra of God slew Uzzah." God Himself cannot be angry, and does not slay people. Compare II. Kings xix. 28 where the Targum of Jonathan has: "Thou hast angered my *Word*." But there can be no doubt that "the Word" came more and more to be thought of as a person commissioned by God to act for Him. In the philosophy of Philo the *Memra* has become the *Logos*, which is even "after the likeness of man." See W. O. E. Oesterley and G. H. Box.

MEN. The chief god of Antioch in early Christian times, a god of prophecy and healing. He is represented on the coins standing with one foot on a bull's head and wearing a Phrygian cap. He was paired with Demeter, and was closely associated with Artemis (Diana). In 1910-13 the sanctuary of Men-Askænos in Antioch was excavated by Sir William Ramsay. "It is suggestive that no temple of Men was found, but only this holy High Place on the top of the mountain, open to the sky, in the centre of which was the ancient hall of initiation, and the high trough or baptismal font where purifications were made by the worshippers. There is no doubt whatever that we may see in this newly-discovered sanctuary the famous hall of Phrygian mysteries. The hall proper was, doubtless, the central closed chamber. The soil above the stone floor of this chamber was full of animal bones and teeth, and beneath the floor the teeth of pigs and wild boars were found. Emblems of Men, a horned bull's head, and many engraved tablets were excavated" (Camden M. Cobern). H. R. Hall (*Ancient History,* 1913) thinks that Men was a moon-god; and that he was not of Anatolian origin, but was an Aryan or Proto-Iranian god introduced from the East.

MENĀCHŌTH. The name of one of the Jewish treatises or tractates which reproduce the oral tradition or unwritten law as developed by the second century A.D., and are included in the Mishnah (*q.v.*), a collection and compilation completed by Rabbi Judah the Holy, or the Patriarch, about 200 A.D The sixty-three tractates of the Mishnah are divided into six groups or orders (*sedarim*). Menāchōth is the second tractate of the fifth group, which is called *Kodāshīm* ("Holy Things").

MENANDRIANS. The followers of Menander, who, according to Irenaeus and Eusebius, was the successor of Simon Magus (*d.* 108 A.D.). Menander was a Samaritan belonging to Capparatea. He taught at Antioch, and his teaching seems to have been an early form of Gnosticism (*q.v.*). Menander seems to have taught that the Primary Power was unknown or unknowable, and that the world was made by angels, who proceeded from Ennoia (Supreme Thought). He claimed to be divine, and to have the power to overcome the angels and to give his disciples undying youth and eternal life. The Menandrians seem to have been absorbed in course of time by the Gnostics. See K. R. Hagenbach; J. H. Blunt; Louis Duchesne, *Hist.*

MENT. An Egyptian deity. The name is written also Mont (*q.v.*).

MERINTHIANS. Merinthians occurs as another name for the Cerinthians (*q.v.*).

MERSEBURG CHARMS. In 1841 G. Waitz, the German historian, discovered in the Cathedral at Merseburg in Saxony a tenth century manuscript, written in Old German and containing magic formulas or charms. Two of these charms are purely pagan and may be of the eighth century. They mention a number of old Teutonic deities: the Idisi; the gods Phol, Wodan, and Balder; the goddesses Sinthgunt and Frija. The Idisi are female beings who were active in battle. They seem to be identical with the Walkyries (*q.v.*). Wodan and Balder, unless the latter means simply "lord" here, are the well-known Teutonic gods. Phol has been supposed to be a corruption of Apollo. It has also been suggested that he is a figure borrowed from Christianity, and is none other than Paul the Apostle. Frija (*q.v.*) is the well-known Teutonic goddess. The goddess Sinthgunt is not otherwise known. See P. D. Chantepie de la Saussaye, *Rel. of the Teutons,* 1902.

MESSALIANS. Messalians was the original Syriac name of the religious sect which was afterwards known as the Euchites (*q.v.*). Both words, the one of Syriac, the other of Greek, derivation, mean "the praying people." The sect was found in Syria towards the end of the fourth century A.D.

MESSIAH, THE. The term Messiah is the Hebrew equivalent of the Greek *Christos,* and means "the one anointed." The Jews in course of time, particularly in the days when great calamities began to threaten the existence of the nation, developed the belief which has come to be known as the Messianic hope—the belief that God would send a hero chosen or anointed to be the Saviour of his people. The first prophet of the Messianic hope was Isaiah. In the Syro-Ephraimitish war of 735 B.C., when he was a young man, he looked for a king to come who should throw the great Assyrian king Tiglath-pileser IV. into the shade (Isa. ix. 2-6). Later, in the days of Sennacherib's second invasion of Judah (691 or after), when the prophet was an old man, he prophesied the coming of a ruler who should inaugurate a rule of ideal happiness and peace (Isa. xi. 1-9). "The prophecy is doubly significant, for it presents the noblest ideal of a ruler found in Hebrew literature, and also combines closely with it those popular hopes of the golden era, which were probably drawn from the traditions of Paradise, inherited from the primitive Semitic past. In its portrayal of the fruits that follow, as a result of a just and righteous rule, it possesses a perennial value" (C. F. Kent, *The Sermons, Epistles and Apocalypses of Israel's Prophets,* 1910, p. 475). During the Exile a new type of Messianic hope emerged. "Jehovah would care for his people as the shepherd cared for his sheep, and the land to which they would return would be renewed (Ezek. xxxiv. 11-31), while the nations would support Israel and fear Jehovah (Isa. xlix. 22, 23). Jehovah would make an everlasting covenant with his people (Isa. lv. 1-5), but the new nation would not be composed of all those who had been swept into exile and their descendants. It would rather be a righteous community, purified by suffering" (Hastings' *D.B.*). In the late canonical books the Messiah is not well defined, but the Book of Daniel, in its apocalyptic sections, contains the expectation of a political State founded by Jehovah in Palestine, if not of a distinct personal Messiah. For the Messianic expectations in the second century B.C. (Apocalyptic Literature) Dr. Charles gives as the chief authorities outside the Canon, the older sections of I. Enoch, the Book of Jubilees, the Testaments of the xii. Patriarchs, and I. and II. Maccabees. Here, no doubt on account of the part played by the family of Levi in the history of the times, the Davidic Messiah gives place to a Messianic King descended from Levi. In the first century, however, no doubt on account of the degeneracy of the great Maccabean family (descended from Levi), we find the hope of a Messiah sprung from Levi abandoned. In Enoch xxxvii.-lxxi. the Messiah appears as the supernatural "Son of Man" (xlvi. 3, xlviii. 2, lxix. 27). He is "the Christ" (xlviii. 10), "the Righteous One" (xxxviii. 2), "the Elect One" (xl. 5). In the Psalms of Solomon (or Psalms of the Pharisees), on the other hand, "the Messiah is conceived as embracing in his own person all the patriotic aspirations of the nation. The Messiah is, it is true, the righteous ruler of Israel, but he is no less assuredly the avenger of their wrongs on all the heathen nations. He is to be a militant Messiah of the house and lineage of David" (Charles; cp. W. Fairweather, *The Background of the Gospels*). Turning to the New Testament—in what sense, if in any, did Jesus regard himself as the Messiah? There can be little doubt that gradually he did come to regard himself as such, but only gradually. The conviction can hardly have been inborn. "To affirm this would be to quit the domain of what is humanly conceivable. Also his quiet growth and his baptism are insufficient to account for the origin of such an idea. It can only have sprung up in the light of great publicity. On the other hand, also, it must be said, the disciples can hardly have been the first to suggest the idea. For, since at Cæsarea Philippi he invites their opinion, he must himself already have been considering what his true character was. At all points he made them sharers in his world of thoughts. Indeed, until now, he had not given them the slightest occasion for spontaneously associating their Jewish ideal of the Messiah with his own person. On all the suggested assumptions, therefore, the psychological motives, on which everything depends, would be missing. Unless we would abandon all attempts to explain the matter, as most recent critics do, we must look for the rise of this sublime self-consciousness at a period between the baptism and Peter's confession. The prominence previously given to the purely religious and moral preaching in the life of Jesus then receives an excellent explanation. We can then, and then alone, realise how it was that Jesus could believe in the practical coming of the 'kingdom of God' as the result of obedience to religious and moral commands' (Arno Neumann, *Jesus*). In any case, when Jesus took up the Messianic ideal of his people, there can be no doubt that he transformed it in his own way. To him the Messiah would seem to have been beyond and above the king of the Davidic ideal. Moreover, he seems to have discarded the warlike features of the Messiahship. And "naturally, when the sword and spear were laid aside, prominence was given inevitably to the idea of a religious and moral revival of the people." At the same time Jesus was forced by circumstances to cling to the hope of a second coming from heaven. The Jews of course did not recognise Jesus as the Messiah, and continued to look for a saviour or salvation. During the Talmudic age, "the Messianic hope in its national character includes always the reunion of all Israel under a victorious ruler of the house of David, who shall destroy all hostile powers and bring an era of supreme prosperity and happiness as well as of peace and good-will among men. The Haggadists indulged also in dreams of the marvellous fertility of the soil of Palestine in the Messianic time, and of the resurrection of the dead in the holy land" (K. Kohler). In the Middle Ages, Maimonides in his commentary on the Mishnah and in his Code formulated a new kind of Messianic belief. His twelfth article of faith declares that "the Jew, unless he wishes to forfeit his claim to eternal life, must, in acceptance of the teachings of Moses and the prophets down to Malachi, believe that the Messiah will issue forth from the house of David in the person of a descendant of Solomon, the only legitimate king; and he shall far excel all rulers in history by his reign, glorious in justice and peace. Neither impatience nor deceptive calculation of the time of the advent of the Messiah should shatter this belief. Still, notwithstanding the majesty and wisdom of the Messiah, he must be regarded as a mortal being like any other and only as the restorer of the Davidic dynasty. He will die and leave a son as his successor, who will in his turn die and leave the throne to his heir. Nor will there be any material change in the order of things in the whole system of nature and human life; accordingly Isaiah's picture of the living together of lamb and wolf cannot be taken literally, nor any of the Haggadic sayings with reference to the Messianic time. We are only to believe in the coming of Elijah as a messenger of peace and the forerunner of the Messiah, and also in the great decisive battle with the hosts of heathendom embodied in Gog and Magog, through whose defeat the dominion of the Messiah will be permanently established" (quoted by Kohler). As far as Reform Judaism is concerned, the nineteenth century has seen another change of attitude. "Thus the leaders of Reform Judaism in the middle of the nineteenth century declared themselves unanimously opposed to retaining the belief in a personal Messiah and the political restoration of Israel, either in doctrine or in their liturgy. They accentuated all the more strongly Israel's hope for a Messianic age, a time of universal knowledge of God and love of man, so intimately interwoven with the religious mission of the Jewish people. Harking back to the suffering Servant of the Lord in Deutero-Isaiah, they transferred the title of Messiah to the Jewish nation. Reform Judaism has thus accepted the belief that Israel, the suffering Messiah of the centuries, shall at the end of days become the triumphant Messiah of the nations" (Kohler). It should be added that the idea of a Messiah is not confined to Judaism. Cheyne cites a Babylonian parallel (*Encycl. Bibl.*). The Egyptian "Admonitions of an Egyptian Sage" seems to refer to an ideal king, a kind of Messiah. In Buddhism we find the ideal king as the personification of Power and Justice, and also the ideal perfectly Wise Man (T. W. Rhys Davids, *Hibbert Lectures*, 1881). Zoroastrianism, again, "looked forward to the ultimate triumph of Ahura Mazdah, just as the Jews looked forward to the ultimate triumph of Yahweh and his Messiah" (G. A. Barton, *R.W.*). Cp. I. Husik.

METAPHYSICS. The term "metaphysic" was used by commentators on Aristotle to denote the books which came *after* the writings of the philosopher on Physics. Metaphysics then came to mean the inquiry into the ultimate nature of Being, an inquiry which comprehends morality, religion, and politics. Aristotle himself described this part of philosophy as First (that is to say, Fundamental) Philosophy, and the other part (Physics) as Second Philosophy. Some systems of thought (Positivism, Naturalism, Agnosticism, Materialism) are unmetaphysical, since they deny the possibility of metaphysical knowledge. The metaphysical inquiry is a search for truth, which is unending, because, as William James says, the only indefectible certain truth is the truth that the present phenomenon of consciousness exists. "No concrete test of what is really true has ever been agreed upon. Some make the criterion external to the moment of perception, putting it either in revelation, the *consensus gentium*, the instincts of the heart, or the systematized experience of the race. Others make the perceptive moment its own test—Descartes, for instance, with his clear and distinct ideas guaranteed by the veracity of God; Reid with his 'common-sense'; and Kant with his forms of synthetic judgment *a priori*. The inconceivability of the opposite; the capacity to be verified by sense; the possession of complete organic unity or self-relation, realized when a thing is its own other—are standards which, in turn, have been used. The much-lauded objective evidence is never triumphantly there; it is a mere aspiration or *Grenzbegriff*, marking the infinitely remote ideal of our thinking life. To claim that certain truths now possess it, is simply to say that when you think them true and they *are* true, then their evidence is objective, otherwise it is not. But practically one's conviction that the evidence one goes by is of the real objective brand, is only one more subjective opinion added to the lot. For what a contradictory array of opinions have objective evidence and absolute certitude been claimed! The world is rational through and through—its existence is an ultimate brute fact; there is a personal God—a personal God is inconceivable; there is an extra-mental physical world immediately known—the mind can only know its own ideas; a moral imperative exists—obligation is only the resultant of desires; a permanent spiritual principle is in every one—there are only shifting states of mind; there is an endless chain of causes—there is an absolute first cause; an eternal necessity—a freedom; a purpose—no purpose; a primal One—a primal Many; a universal continuity—an essential discontinuity in things; an infinity—no infinity. There is this—there is that; there is indeed nothing which some one has not thought absolutely true, while his neighbour deemed it absolutely false; and not an absolutist among them seems ever to have considered that the trouble may all the time be essential, and that the intellect, even with truth directly in its grasp, may have no infallible signal for knowing whether it be truth or no" (*The Will to Believe*, 1908, p. 15).

METATRON. In post-Biblical Judaism Metatron appears as the name of one of the beings intermediate between God and man. The derivation of the word is uncertain. It has been connected with the Latin *metator* in the sense of "guide," and even with the Zoroastrian Mithra (see MITHRAISM). It is more likely of Greek origin. Weber thinks it is a Hebrew form of the Greek *Metathronos* or *Metatyrannos*, which denotes one who ranks next to the ruler. The first mention of Metatron is found in the Babylonian Talmud. The office and work of Metatron are similar to those of the Memra (*q.v.*) and Logos. He represents God. And he does this especially when God has to come into contact with mundane affairs; hence his designation "Prince of the World." He is also called "Prince of the Presence," on account of his constant attendance on God. As in the case of Memra, it seems clear that Metatron takes the place of God whenever human actions and feelings are ascribed to the Divine Being. But, besides representing God, he can intercede with Him. He is called the "Mediator." Another name for Metatron was the "Great Scribe." He was so called because, like Enoch, with whom the Jerusalem Targum identifies him, he was supposed to write down the merits of Israel. In the Jerusalem Targum and in the Ascension of Isaiah (ix. 21) he is identified with Michael the Archangel. See W. O. E. Oesterley and G. H. Box.

METAWILEH. Metawileh is the plural form of Metawali, which is a synonym for Shi'ah (*q.v.*).

METEMPSYCHOSIS. The transmigration of the soul at the death of the body into some other body, either human, animal, or even material. See TRANSMIGRATION OF SOULS.

METHODISTS, NEW CONNEXION. The New Connexion Methodists are an offshoot of the original Methodists, the Wesleyan Methodists (*q.v.*). The body was founded in 1797 by Alexander Kilham, after whom the members were called Kilhamites (*q.v.*). At first they were called also "The New Itinerancy."

METHODISTS, PRIMITIVE. A Christian body which represents a secession from the Methodism of John Wesley (see WESLEYAN METHODISTS). They were so called because they reverted, as they claimed, to the original or primitive methods of Wesley and his followers. They did this by "preaching in the open air, holding camp meetings to promote revivals, singing through the street, praying and preaching anywhere and everywhere they could, so as to save souls." The ministers of the older community, the members of which are now called Wesleyan Methodists to distinguish them from the Methodist New Connexion, disapproved of these irregular proceedings. "These elders induced the Conference to denounce the holding of a great camp meeting, May 31, 1807, on Mow Cop hill on the borders of Cheshire and Staffordshire. It was promoted by Hugh and James Bourne, and was attended by thousands of people. The two enthusiastic brethren were refused their tickets of membership, and virtually driven from the society. Next a class leader, named William Clowes, was suspended for his sympathy and co-operation in the movement; and in the same year (1810) ten persons, who had been converted at a village service in Stanley, were refused admission to the society. These with Clowes and the Bournes formed the nucleus of the new community, which from that time continued to grow and flourish. Its members were mostly poor and uneducated; yet they were thoroughly devoted to its interests, and were, moreover, always ready to make great sacrifices to promote them. In their Conference the Primitive Methodists have two laymen to one minister; and they were amongst the first to encourage the public preaching of women" (J. A. Houlder).

METHURGEMAN. When Aramaic took the place of Hebrew as the spoken language of the Jewish people, it was necessary for someone in the Synagogue to interpret the original language of the Hebrew Scriptures. This person was called the Methurgeman or Targoman. See TARGUM.

MEVLEVITES. An order of Dervishes, founded in the thirteenth century by Jelālu-'d-Dīn, surnamed Er Rumi. They are known to Europeans as the Dancing Dervishes from their peculiar dance (*devr*), in which they imitate the planets circling round the sun. Rumi's great work, the *Mesnevi*, was dictated to Hasan, his friend and scribe, after the year 1258. The Mevlevites "pass through the severest trials in the noviciate: before the candidate can be received at all he must work as a 'jackal' at menial tasks for 1001 days; if he fail on one day, he must begin his servitude afresh." They profess "pantheist views and are regarded with disfavour and suspicion by the regular clergy; but they are tolerant and broadminded" (F. W. Bussell).

MEXTLI. The original name of the war-god of the ancient Mexicans. A more popular name was Huitzilopochtli (*q.v.*).

MICAH, BOOK OF. The prophet Micah, whose book is one of the twelve Minor Prophets, is described as the Morashtite, *i.e.*, as a native of Moresheth. The prophet Jeremiah quotes Micah iii. 12 and refers to him as prophesying "in the days of Hezekiah, king of Judah" (Jeremiah xxvi. 18). Whitehouse thinks that "the closely analogous passage, Micah i. 5-9, clearly proves that he prophesied in the reign of Ahaz, shortly before the overthrow of Samaria (722-1 B.C.)." The superscription to the book (i. 1) is no doubt due to an editor. The book may be divided into three sections. The first, chapters i.-iii., is a prophecy of denunciation and judgment. Samaria is to be punished for idolatry. So also Judah, which has been guilty not only of idolatry, but also of social and moral corruption. The second section, chapters iv.-v., opens with a Messianic passage (iv. 1-5) which in large part recurs in the book of Isaiah (ii. 2-4). There is another Messianic passage in v. 2-6 (Heb. 1-5) which makes definite reference to the overthrow of Assyria. The third section, chapters vi.-vii., is of the nature of a controversial dialogue between Jehovah and his people. In Chap. vii. 8-20, however, the standpoint changes. These verses are assigned by Cornill to an editor who revised the whole book. It seems hardly possible to ascribe the whole book to Micah. Robertson Smith thought that chapters i.-v. formed a single well-connected Book of Micah. Whitehouse thinks that "it is not possible to assign to Micah and the latter part of the eighth century more than chaps. i.-iii." In any case, chap. vi. 1-vii. 6 is different in character and style from the rest of the book, and H. Ewald, who thought that the section was composed by an anonymous writer in the reign of Manasseh, has found many followers. See *Encycl. Bibl.*; T. K. Cheyne, *Micah* in the "Cambridge Bible," 1882; J. Wellhausen, *Kleine Propheten*, 3rd ed.,

1898; W. Nowack, *Kleine Propheten*, 2nd ed., 1904; C. F. Kent, *Sermons, Epistles, and Apocalypses*, 1910; C. Cornill, *Intr.;* G. H. Box; O. C. Whitehouse.

MICHELIANITES. The name "Michelianer" was given to a German Pietistic sect founded in Württemberg by Johann Michael Hahn (1758-1819). Hahn was influenced by Jacob Boehme (1575-1624), the theosophist and mystic. The system of theology which he developed was of a theosophical nature. He professed to have received a special inward light. The Michelianites lived in expectation of a "restoration of all things." See J. H. Blunt; Brockhaus.

MICTLAN. Mictlan was one of the deities worshipped by the ancient Mexicans. He corresponded to Pluto. In the drear and dismal region over which he ruled, he was attended on by terrible demons. See Lewis Spence, *Myth.*

MIDDŌTH. The title of one of the Jewish treatises or tractates which reproduce the oral tradition or unwritten law as developed by the second century A.D., and are included in the Mishnah (*q.v.*), a collection and compilation completed by Rabbi Judah the Holy, or the Patriarch, about 200 A.D. The sixty-three tractates of the Mishnah are divided into six groups or orders (*sedarim*). Middoth is the tenth tractate of the fifth group, which is called *Ḳodāshim* ("Holy Things").

MIDER. Mider, a god of the Underworld worshipped by the ancient Gaels (Goidels), seems to have resembled the British god Pwyll (*q.v.*).

MIDHGARDH. A term used in the cosmology of the Ancient Teutons. By Midhgardh is meant "either the inhabited earth as the centre of the universe, situated between heaven and the lower world, or the centre of the earth conceived as a disk, surrounded by the sea (Midhgardh-serpent)." It is a fair place for men to inhabit. See P. D. Chantepie de la Saussaye, *Rel. of the Teutons*, 1902.

MIDHGARDH-SERPENT. The name of a sea-monster, a giant, in the mythology of the Ancient Teutons. He is said to be one of the offspring of the god Loki (*q.v.*). Sometimes he represents the sea. Legend tells of a struggle between the god Thor (*q.v.*) and the Midhgardh-serpent. See P. D. Chantepie de la Saussaye, *Rel. of the Teutons*, 1902.

MID-LENT SUNDAY. Another name for Lætare Sunday (*q.v.*), the fourth Sunday in Lent.

MIDRASH. The name of a branch of Rabbinical literature. The word occurs in the Hebrew text of the Old Testament, and means "exposition" or exegesis. This exegesis is sometimes legalistic or halakic (see HALAKAH), sometimes illustrative or haggadic (see HAGGADAH). The Midrashim (plural of Midrash) range from the second to the thirteenth century A.D. C. J. Ball (quoted by Oesterley and Box) points out that Jewish teachers had an inveterate tendency "to convey their doctrine, not in the form of abstract discourse, but in a mode appealing directly to the imagination, and seeking to arouse the interest and sympathy of the man rather than the philosopher. The Rabbi embodies his lesson in a story, whether parable or allegory or seeming historical narrative; and the last thing he or his disciples would think of is to ask whether the selected persons, events, and circumstances which so vividly suggest the doctrine are in themselves real or fictitious. The doctrine is everything; the mode of presentation has no independent value. To make the story the first consideration, and the doctrine it was intended to convey an afterthought as we, with out dry Western literalness are predisposed to do, is to reverse the Jewish order of thinking, and to do unconscious injustice to the authors of many edifying narratives of antiquity." For a list of Midrashim and further particulars about these expository commentaries, see C. A. Briggs, *Intr.;* W. O. E. Oesterley and G. H. Box.

MIḲWĀ'OTH. The name of one of the Jewish treatises or tractates which reproduce the oral tradition or unwritten law as developed by the second century A.D., and are included in the Mishnah (*q.v.*), a collection and compilation completed by Rabbi Judah the Holy, or the Patriach, about 200 A.D. The sixty-three tractates of the Mishnah are divided into six groups or orders (*sedarim*). Miḳwā'oth is the sixth tractate of the sixth group, which is called *Ṭohŏrōth* ("Purifications").

MILK AND HONEY. It was an ancient baptismal custom to give the newly-baptised milk and honey to drink. Sidney Heath explains the custom by a quotation from Clement of Alexandria. "As soon as we are born we are nourished with milk, which is the nutriment of the Lord: and as soon as we are born again, we become entitled to the hope of rest, the promise of Jerusalem which is above, where it is said to rain milk and honey, for by these material things we are assured of that heavenly food."

MILLENIAL CHURCH, THE. Another name for the Shakers (*q.v.*).

"MILL YARD" SABBATARIAN CHURCH. This church claims to be the mother Church of the Seventh-day Denomination. It is so called because from 1691 to 1885 the "Meeting House" of the denomination was in Mill Yard, Leman Street, Goodman's Fields, London. The exact date of the foundation of the Church is not known. John Trask, however, would seem to have been a member in 1618. Peter Chamberlen (1601-1683), afterwards physician to Charles II., was a leader of the Church. In 1691 the "Meeting House" in Mill Yard was purchased by the Church. The services are now held in Mornington Hall, Canonbury Lane, Islington, London. The distinctive features of the denomination consist in the beliefs "that Christians are required to keep the Sabbath according to the Commandment (commonly called Saturday) as was the practice of Christ and His disciples; also that it is their duty to follow Him through the watery grave of 'immersion' on confession of their faith, which is the only true baptism. Hence the title 'Sabbatarian' or Seventh-day Baptist." The seventh day is reckoned from Friday sunset to Saturday sunset.

MIMAMEIDHR. Literally "the tree of Mimir," a name for the sacred tree of the gods of the Edda. It is also called Yggdrasil's ash. See YGGDRASIL.

MIN. An Egyptian deity. The god Min "was worshipped in that part of Upper Egypt where the Nile and the Red Sea approach each other most closely, and which was therefore at all periods the starting point of the caravan route to the Eastern world" (Erman). Travellers sought his protection. He was the "lord of foreign lands." The figure of Min is ithyphallic. On his head are two feathers; on his upraised right arm he bears a scourge. Erman thinks it probable that Min is another name for the sun god. He also identifies Min with Amon (*q.v.*) of Thebes. The temple of Min was at Koptos. In the New Kingdom his name was regarded as another form of Horus (*q.v.*). According to Wiedemann, Min had as his sacred animal the ram; and he was the god of the generative power of nature, to whom harvest festivals were dedicated. See A. Wiedemann; Adolf Erman, *Handbook.*

MINIMS, THE ORDER OF. The Order of Minims, or rather of Minim-Hermits (Ordo Minimorum Eremitarum Sancti Francisci de Paula) was founded by St. Francis of Paula (?1416-1507). They were called Minims, "the least," to indicate that they regarded themselves as lower than the Franciscans (*q.v.*) who called themselves Minor (Friars Minor) "the less." In Paris before the Revolution they were called Bons Hommes. In Spain they were known as "Brothers of Victory." Francis of Paula (Paola) began by establishing communities in various places in Italy without any written rule. In 1473 his communities were approved by Pope Sixtus IV. under the title of the "Hermits of St. Francis of Assisi." In 1493, when the first Rule was composed by Francis and approved by Pope Alexander VI., the title of the order was changed to "Minim-Hermits of Francis of Paola." The friars of St. Francis had always observed a perpetual Lent. In 1501 this was established as a vow. In the same year Francis added a Rule for Tertiaries, affiliated persons of either sex who preferred to live in the world; and in 1502 the two Rules were approved by the Pope. In 1506 the two Rules, together with a third Rule for nuns, were approved and confirmed. The Minim-Hermit undertook to live under the vows of poverty, chastity, obedience, and of the life of Lent. He used to go barefoot or in sandals, but is now shod. Francis introduced the order into France, Spain, and Germany. See Schaff-Herzog; the *Cath. Dict.*

MINOAN WORSHIP. Discoveries in Crete and other centres of the Minoan-Mycenaean culture have furnished certain facts about the Minoan worship. According to L. R. Farnell, "the most striking figure in the Minoan worship was a great goddess, conceived mainly as a mother but here and there also as virginal, imagined as a mountain goddess, whose familiar animals were the lion and the snake, and ethnically related to the Phrygian Cybele and the ancestress of the Cretan Rhea and probably of some Hellenic goddesses. By her side is sometimes represented a youthful deity imagined probably as her lover or son. We discern also the figure of a sky-god, armed and descending through the air." But the predominant and immemorial cult seems to have been that of the goddess. "The Minoan imagination of the divinity was clearly anthropomorphic, but probably admitted the idea that it might occasionally be embodied in animal form; that is to say, the anthropomorphism was not yet stable." The divine ancestor would seem to have been worshipped. "As regards the ritual of this period, the famous sarcophagus found at Hagia Triada reveals a ceremony of blood-offering, in which the blood of the sacred ox is first caught in a receptacle, and then poured on an altar; we may take this as evidence of the idea of a mystic potency inherent in the blood of the victim." Four of the worshippers are represented as wearing the skin of the sacrificed ox. Another feature of Minoan worship is "a communion-service in which the mortal was absorbed into the divine nature by the simulated fiction of a holy marriage." See L. R. Farnell, *Greek Religion*, 1912; D. A. Mackenzie, *Myths of Crete*.

MINORESSES. Nuns of the second order of Francis of Assisi. For his male followers he chose the name Friars Minor. The Minoresses or Poor Clares were established in London in 1293 in a house which became known as "the Minories," and the name still survives in the neighbourhood.

MINORITES. Another name for the Franciscans (*q.v.*), or male followers of Francis of Assisi.

MINOR PROPHETS, THE. In the Jewish Canon (see CANON, OLD TESTAMENT) the second group of Old Testament books, The Prophets, is sub-divided into (1) The Former Prophets and (2) The Latter Prophets. The Former Prophets comprise Joshua, Judges, I. and II. Samuel, and I. and II. Kings. The Latter Prophets comprise Isaiah, Jeremiah, Ezekiel, and the Twelve Prophets. The Twelve Prophets were commonly called simply "The Twelve" and were counted as one book. Christian scholars further sub-divide the Latter Prophets into (a) The Major Prophets: Isaiah, Jeremiah, Ezekiel; and (b) The Minor Prophets: Hosea, Joel, Amos, Obadiah, Jonah, Micah, Nahum, Habakkuk, Zephaniah, Haggai, Zechariah, Malachi.

MINOTAUR. A figure (Bull of Minos) in Cretan mythology, a monster with the head of a bull and the body of a man. A special building, a labyrinth, was built for it, according to Cretan legend, at Knossos. Donald A. Mackenzie (*Crete*) remarks that the Minotaur overshadows all the other Cretan monsters, and thinks the fact highly suggestive. "Possibly the explanation is that the bull clan of Minos, which was established at Knossos, attained political supremacy over the whole island, with the result that its Minotaur became the chief deity. This would account also for the myths regarding the sea-bull forms of Poseidon and Zeus, and the notorious ceremonies associated with the bull-ring at Knossos. The Minos clan may have invaded and conquered the island." L. R. Farnell (*Greece and Babylon*, 1911) notes that "a few of the Zakro sealings show the sealed figure of a human body with bovine head, ears, and tail; and a clay seal-impression found at Knossos presents a bovine human figure with possibly a bovine head sealed in a hieratic attitude before a warrior in armour."

MIQUETANTEOT. One of the gods of the Nicarao (of Nicaragua). He was the lord of the underworld, and was equivalent to the Mexican Mictlantecutli.

MIRACLES. According to one definition, a miracle is "anything beyond human power, and deviating from the common action of the laws of nature" (*Chambers's Etymol. Dict.*). Miracles in this sense have, it is claimed, often been performed by prophets and other great religious leaders. Indeed, in ancient times a prophet was expected to prove his divine authority by the performance of marvellous works, and he did often prove it in this way. The marvellous works were believed at the time to be above Nature, supernatural, or contrary to Nature. Modern Science, on the other hand, will not concede that events have ever taken place in defiance of the laws of Nature. If marvellous things have taken place there must be laws of Nature which can explain them, though these laws may be new in the sense of being hitherto unknown. The matter may be illustrated by reference to what used to be called miracles of healing. Prophets by inspiring people with a faith, in them or in a divine power, of such strength as to remove instantly all fear have cured them of sickness and disease. Such healing is wonderful, but it is no longer described as miraculous, for it has been found to be in accordance with certain laws the working of which may still be tested and proved by experience. The remarkable fact in the case of the prophets is that they should have had intuitive knowledge of these laws. Are there other laws, still not generally known, of which they had intuitive knowledge? This is quite possible, and a cautious student would hesitate now to say that other wonderful works ascribed to them could not have been performed. It has to be borne in mind, however, at the same time that in ancient times objective and subjective phenomena were not clearly distinguished. We know that in modern times phantasms of the living, for instance, are seen not infrequently, and we know that they are only mental pictures telepathically transmitted. They will have been seen quite as frequently in ancient times, and were then no doubt taken to be real appearances. Telepathy (*q.v.*) explains many such phenomena. Miracles in the sense of wonderful events have happened, are happening, and will happen. Our highest conception of the nature of God excludes the possibility of their being confined to any one age or clime. God is no respecter of persons. If one person has been healed by the divine power, all can be healed. It is not a divine license, but a divine law.

MIRU. A wicked goddess in Maori mythology.

MISHNAH. The Jewish Mishnah (Hebrew *shānāh*, Aramaic *tenā*, "to repeat") comprises for the most part the discussions of the Rabbis who lived between A.D. 70 and about A.D. 200. These legal discussions were gradually codified and committed to writing by a succession of scholars known as Tannāim ("repeaters"), and the final codifier who gave the work its present form (*c.* A.D. 200) was Rabbi Jehudah the Holy (see TANNĀIM). After this the Mishnah itself became the subject of discussion by a succession of scholars who were called Amorāim (*q.v.*). These discussions received the name Gemārā ("supplement" or "completion": see GEMARA). The Gemārā is entirely of the nature of Haggadah (*q.v.*); the Mishnah is mostly, though not entirely, in the style of Halakhah (see the articles HAGGADAH and TALMUD. The Mishnah contains sixty-three treatises or tractates, which are arranged in six groups or sedārim. The names of the tractates (with the number of the groups to which they belong are as follows: 'Abōdā zārā (iv. 8); Ābōth (iv. 9); 'Ārākhīn (v. 5); Bābā Bathrā (iv. 3); Bābā Ḳammā (iv. 1); Bābā Mĕṣi'ā (iv. 2); Bĕkhōrōth (v. 4); Bĕrākhōth (i. 1); Bēṣā (ii. 7); Bikkūrim (i. 11); Chăgīgā (ii. 12); Challā (i. 9); Chullīn (v. 3); Dĕmái (i. 3); 'Ēdūyōth (iv. 7); 'Erūbīn (ii. 12); Giṭṭīn (iii. 6); Hōrāyōth (iv. 10); Kēlīm (vi. 1); Kĕrīthōth (v. 7); Kethūboth (iii. 2); Ḳiddūshīn (iii. 7); Kil'áyim (i. 4); Ḳinnīm (v. 11); Ma'ăsēr Shēnī (i. 8); Ma'ăsērōth (l. 7); Makhshīrīn (vi. 8); Makkōth (iv. 5); Mĕgillā (ii. 10); Mĕ'īlā (v. 8); Mĕnāchōth (v. 2); Middōth (v. 10); Miḳwā'ōth (vi. 6); Mō'ēd Kāṭān (ii. 11); Nāzīr (iii. 4); Nĕdārīm (iii. 3); Nĕgā'īm (vi. 3); Niddā (vi. 7); Ōhālōth (vi. 2); 'Orlā (i. 10); Pārā (vi. 4); Pē'ā (i. 2); Pĕsāchīm (ii. 3); Rōsh ha-Shānā (ii. 8); Sanhedrīn (iv. 4); Shabbāth (ii. 1); Shĕbū'ōth (iv. 6); Shĕbī'īth (i. 5); Shĕḳālīm (ii. 4); Sōṭā (iii. 5; Sukkā (ii. 6); Ta'ănīth (ii. 9); Tāmīd (v. 9); Ṭĕbūl Yōm (vi. 10); Tĕmūrā (v. 6); Tĕrūmōth (i. 6); Ṭohŏrōth (vi. 6); 'Ūḳṣīn (vi. 12); Yādáyim (vi. 11); Yĕbāmōth (iii. 1); Yōmā (ii. 5); Zābīm (vi. 9); Zĕbāchīm (v. 1). See *Encycl. Bibl.*, *s.v.* "Bibliographical Notes" (prefatory matter) and "Law Literature"; W. O. E. Oesterley and G. H. Box; A. S. Geden, *Intr. to the Hebrew Bible*, 1909.

MISSAL, THE. The Missal was one of the Service Books used in the Church of England before the Reformation of the 16th century. It was in four parts. (1) The Antiphoner, Gradual, or Grail contained those parts of the Service which were sung by the choir at High Mass. (2) The Lectionary contained the lessons from the Epistles of the New Testament. (3) The Evangelistarium contained the Gospels. (4) The Sacramentary which contained the prayers of the Mass. This last was called distinctively the Missal or Mass-book in the eighth century. Missals which contained more than the Sacramentary were afterwards called Completa Missalia. "The Roman Missal was carefully revised and printed under Pius V., who carried out a decree of the Council of Trent on the matter, and strictly enjoined the use of this Missal, or faithful reprints of it, in all churches which could not claim prescription of two hundred years for their own use. It was revised again under Clement VIII. and Urban VIII." (*Cath. Dict.*). From time to time new Masses have been added.

MITHRAISM. The doctrines and rites of the old Persian deity Mithras or Mithra. S. Reinach points out (*O.*) that the Iranians and Hindus, who about the year 1400 B.C. were still united, have several gods with similar names. One of these is Mithra (see MITRA). After the reign of Alexander the Great Mithra came to be worshipped in all the Oriental kingdoms. The introduction of the worship into the Roman provinces in the West is supposed to have taken place during the first half of the first century B.C. By the beginning of the second century A.D. it had spread throughout the Roman empire. "The immense popularity of his worship is attested by the monuments illustrative of it which have been found scattered in profusion all over the Roman empire. In respect both of doctrines and of rites the cult of Mithra appears to have presented many points of resemblance not only to the religion of the Mother of the Gods but also to Christianity. The similarity struck the Christian doctors themselves and was explained by them as a work of the devil, who sought to seduce the souls of men from the true faith by a false and insidious imitation of it. . . . However that may be, there can be no doubt that the Mithraic religion proved a formidable rival to Christianity, combining as it did a solemn ritual with aspirations after moral purity and a hope of immortality. Indeed the issue of the conflict between the two faiths appears for a time to have hung in the balance. An instructive relic of the long struggle is preserved in our festival of Christmas, which the Church seems to have borrowed directly from its heathen rival" (J. G. Frazer). S. Reinach (*Cults*) gives the following account of the god Mithra. "Mithra was a young god, beautiful as the day, who, clothed in Phrygian garb, sojourned of old among men and won their love by doing good. He was born of no mortal mother. One day, in a grotto or stable, he issued from a stone, to the astonishment of the shepherds who alone were present at his birth. Waxing in strength and courage, he overcame the pestilent creatures that infested the world. Most redoubtable of these was a bull, himself divine, whose blood, if shed upon the ground, would render it fruitful and cause miraculous crops to spring. Mithra gave him battle, gained the victory, plunged a knife into his breast, and by this sacrifice assured riches and peace to men. Then he ascended into Heaven, where he still keeps watch over the children of earth. He grants the petitions of them that pray to him. Those who are initiated into his mysteries, in caverns like that where he first saw the day, receive after death his powerful protection against those enemies beyond the tomb who threaten the tranquillity of the dead. Furthermore, he will one day give to them a better life, and has promised a resurrection. When the fate-appointed time comes round, he will cut the throat of another celestial bull, the source of life and felicity, whose blood shall revive the flagging energies of earth and restore a life of happiness to all who have believed on Mithra." The rites by which persons were initiated into the mysteries of the god were called sacraments (*sacramenta*). "One of them was baptism by blood—the blood of a bull; and there was also a baptism by pure water, as well as anointings of the forehead with honey. Further, it was the custom to consecrate bread and wine by certain formulae, and then to distribute the elements among the faithful." The head over the initiated was called Father, while the initiated were called Brethren. See J. G. Frazer, *G.B.*, Pt. iv. 2nd ed., 1907; O. Seyffert, *Dict.;* Reinach, *O.;* J. M. Robertson, *P.C.;* Reinach, *Cults*.

MITRA. Mitra is referred to in the Rig Veda in close connection with Varuna (*q.v.*) as one of the deities of the Hindus. It is said for example: "On their wonted path go Varuna and Mitra when in the sky they cause to rise Sūrya, whom they made to avert darkness." Hopkins thinks that, excluding those names which describe purely physical characteristics, Mitra is perhaps the oldest name for the sun, though in the Rig Veda he is always subordinate to Varuna. He points out that "Mithra in Persian keeps the proof that this title was given to the Indo-Iranic god before the separation of the two peoples." The name Mitra means "friend." See E. W. Hopkins.

MIXCOA. One of the gods of the Nicarao (of Nicaragua). He was the god of trade, and is equivalent to the Mexican Mixcoatl. Worshippers offered to him some of their own blood.

MIXCOATL. The Aztec god of hunting. The name means "Cloud Serpent," and the god is often represented as carrying a bundle of arrows. Mixcoatl was thus, like other gods of the chase, a thunder god as well.

MOABITE STONE, THE. Also called the Mesha Stone or the Mesha Inscription. A block of basalt inscribed by Mesha, king of Moab, and dedicated by him to the Moabite god Chemosh. The inscription is written in the Phoenician character, and the language differs very slightly from the Hebrew of the Old Testament. The Moabite Stone records Mesha's victory over the Israelites after the death of Ahab (ii. Kings i. 1), and dates from the ninth century B.C. It was discovered in 1868 at Dibân (Dibon) on the east of the Jordan, and is now preserved in the Museum of the Louvre at Paris.

MOCCUS. The name Moccus is found on inscriptions as that of one of the gods worshipped by the ancient Celts. Anwyl identifies the name with the Welsh *moch* "swine," and points out that old coins in Britain often bear the image of a boar. It would seem that in Italy the pig was offered to deities of the earth. This, together with its diet of acorns, suggests to Mr. Anwyl a connection between the pig and the earth-spirit or the oak-spirit. But in any case we know that in ancient times the boar was worshipped. See Anwyl.

MODALISTS. The Modalists were one of the schools of theologians produced by the doctrine of the Logos. They would not recognize any intermediary between God and the world. Jesus Christ, according to them, was an incarnation of the one God. "According to them the names of Father and Son corresponded only to different aspects of the same Person, playing transitory parts, and not to divine realities" (Duchesne). Modalism spread from Asia to Rome. Here early in the third century Praxeas became a leading exponent of it. In course of time, however, he was brought to admit that the doctrine was erroneous. Noëtus taught similar doctrines in Smyrna, for which he was excommunicated. He said: "I know but one God: it is no other than He who was born, who suffered, and who died." For this kind of teaching the Modalists were called also Patripassians. Epigonus, a disciple of Noëtus, opened a school in Rome. He was succeeded, first by Cleomenes, and then by Sabellius (see SABELLIANISM). See J. H. Blunt; Louis Duchesne, *Hist.*

MŌ'ĒD KAṬĀN. The title of one of the Jewish treatises or tractates which reproduce the oral tradition or unwritten law as developed by the second century A.D., and are incorporated in the Mishnah (*q.v.*), a collection and compilation completed by Rabbi Judah the Holy, or the Patriarch, about 200 A.D. The sixty-three tractates of the Mishnah are divided into six groups or orders (*sedarim*). Mō'ēd Kāṭān is the eleventh tractate of the second group, which is called *Mō'ēd* ("Festival").

MOGOUNUS. Mogounus or Mogons was one of the names given by the ancient Celts to a god who corresponded to the Roman Apollo (*q.v.*). Another name for the god was Grannus (*q.v.*).

MOLINISTS. The school of theologians founded by L. Molina (1535-1601), a Spanish Jesuit, in the sixteenth century. His work "On the Agreement of Free-Will with Grace and Predestination," published in 1588, marks the beginning of the struggle between the Jesuits and the Augustinian school of theologians known as Jansenists. See JANSENISTS.

MOLOKANEH, THE. The Molokaneh or "Milk-eaters" are a sub-sect of the Russian dissenters known as Bezpopovtzi. They were so called because on fast-days they lived on milk. The name which they chose for themselves was "the truly spiritual Christians" or the "Gospellers." They reject baptism by water: true baptism is a spiritual cleansing of the soul from sin. They reject all externals, such as temples, prayers, crossing. Their bishop and high-priest is Christ alone. Accepting the principle that "where the Spirit of the Lord is, there is liberty" (II. Cor. iii. 17), they refuse to be bound by State laws. See Schaff-Herzog; J. H. Blunt.

MOLOKI. A malignant spirit of whom the Bayaka of the Kasai district in the Congo State stood in awe.

MONARCHY MEN, FIFTH. See FIFTH MONARCHY MEN.

MONISM. As distinguished from Pluralism, Monism is that philosophy which traces back all phenomena to a single physical or spiritual principle. Physical (materialistic) Monism is represented by such a writer as Ernst Haeckel. "A broad historical and critical comparison of religious and philosophical systems, as a whole, leads as a main result to the conclusion that every great advance in the direction of profounder knowledge has meant a breaking away from the traditional dualism (or pluralism) and an approach to monism. Ever more clearly are we compelled by reflection to recognise that God is not to be placed over against the material world as an external being, but must be placed as a 'divine power' or 'moving spirit' within the cosmos itself. Ever clearer does it become that all the wonderful phenomena of nature around us, organic as well as inorganic, are only various products of one and the same primitive matter. Ever more irresistibly is it borne in upon us that even the human soul is but an insignificant part of the all-embracing 'world-soul'; just as the human body is only a small individual fraction of the great organised physical world." Again, "the monistic idea of God, which alone is compatible with our present knowledge of nature, recognises the divine spirit in all things. It can never recognise in God a 'personal being,' or, in other words, an individual of limited extension in space, or even of human form. God is everywhere. As Giordano Bruno has it: 'There is one spirit in all things, and no body is so small that it does not contain a part of the divine substance whereby it is animated.' Every atom is thus animated, and so is the ether; we might, therefore, represent God as the infinite sum of all natural forces, the sum of all atomic forces and all ether-vibrations." Spiritual Monism may be described in the terms of *The New Theology*. "The philosophy underlying the New Theology, as I understand it, is monistic idealism, and monistic idealism recognizes no fundamental distinction between matter and spirit. The fundamental reality is consciousness. The so-called material world is the product of consciousness exercising itself along a certain limited plane; the next stage of consciousness above this is not an absolute break with it, although it is an expansion of experience or readjustment of focus." See Ernst Haeckel, *Monism as connecting Religion and Science*, 1895; R. J. Campbell, *The New Theology*, New Popular Edition; and cp. Max B. Weinstein, *Welt-und Leben-Anschauungen*, 1910.

MONOLATRY. The term designates the worship of one God only in distinction from monotheism, which denotes the belief in the existence of one God only. C. F. Burney thinks that monolatry "embodies the true description of the early stage of Israel's national religion, because at this earlier stage Yahwe was thought of, not as the only Divine Being in existence, but as the only Divine Being with whom Israel as a nation had any concern, or to whom they were bound by any obligation. Yahwe, in short, was the national God, and, as national God, He made an exclusive claim upon Israel's allegiance, and would not tolerate the worship of any other god beside Himself. Such a view, however, of Israel's relationship towards Yahwe obviously did not hinder the belief that other nations might also have *their* national gods, and that these gods, though concerned only with their own nations, and in no position to exact worship or any other form of notice from Israel, were not merely false gods or idols, but had a real existence of their own." See C. F. Burney, *Outlines of Old Testament Theology*, 1903.

MONOPHYSITES. Monophysitism, the teaching of the Monophysites, represented a reaction against the too zealous protest against the teaching of Nestorius (see NESTORIANS). The first to protest was Eutyches (see EUTYCHIANISM), and the protest was carried farther. The distinctive tenet of the Monophysites, J. H. Blunt explains, "was developed out of the heresy of Eutyches, but was not identical with it: Eutyches maintaining that the Union of Christ's Divine and Human Natures in the Incarnation resulted in the ultimate extinction of the latter, so that the glorified Saviour is wholly and only Divine, while the Monophysites held that the two Natures were so united, that although the 'One Christ' was partly Human and partly Divine, His two Natures became by their union only one Nature (μονη φυσις). See William Benham; J. H. Blunt; Wace and Piercy.

MONOTHELITES. The Monothelites agreed with the Monophysites in holding that Christ had only *one* nature, and added the claim that since he had only one nature, he must have had only *one* will. "Monothelism was the simple and natural consequence of Monophysitism, and originated from the endeavours which the State Church made, in the seventh century, of conciliating the Monophysites" (Schaff-Herzog). Several attempts were made to establish the Monothelite doctrine, but in A.D. 680 the Council of Constantinople, with the co-operation of the Bishop of Rome, "adopted the doctrine of *two* wills and *two* energies as the orthodox doctrine, but decided that the human will must always be conceived as subordinate to the divine" (Hagenbach). See Schaff-Herzog; K. R. Hagenbach.

MONT. An Egyptian deity. The god had temples near Karnak and in Hermonthis. He was a god of war, and is represented with the head of a hawk. In the New Kingdom Amon-Re assumed the rôle of a number of other gods, including Mont of Thebes. In later times also Mont himself was often combined with Re the sun-god as Mont Re, "and as such he stands in the prow of the solar bark armed with a lance and ready to pierce the enemies who oppose the progress of the Sun" (Wiedemann). See Alfred Wiedemann; Adolf Erman, *Handbook*.

MONTANISM. Montanism may be regarded as an effort to retain or revive the liberty of prophesying. In itself the movement was not necessarily one to be condemned, but it arose at a difficult period in the history of the Church, and tended to encourage movements which were or might be dangerous. We read of prophets and of a kind of prophetic ministry in the New Testament, and it is not easy to understand why the prophets or their activity should suddenly have come to an end. Montanus was one of those who claimed that it had not done so as late as, or later than, the middle of the second century. It seems to have been about the middle of the second century that Montanus became active at Ardaban, a village in Phrygian Mysia. The worship of Cybele (identified with the Cretan goddess Rhea [*q.v.*]) had long prevailed in Phrygia, and it is thought that before his conversion to Christianity, Montanus was a priest of Cybele. In any case, he attracted attention by becoming at times ecstatic and in his transports uttering strange words. The kind of phenomena which were associated with his ecstasies have been observed even in modern times. He seemed to become as it were a passive instrument through which some other agent spoke. In other words he seemed, and in fact claimed to be, inspired. He himself represents the inspirer as describing his condition thus: "Behold the man is as a lyre, and I sweep over him as a plectrum." The inspiration of a prophet has often been described in this way. Dr. Lindsay points out that Athenagoras describes the Spirit of God as inspiring the prophets as "a flute-player breathes into his flute," and that the author of the "Cohortatio ad Gentes" says that "the divine plectrum descends from heaven and uses righteous men as an instrument like a harp or lyre." The description is a good one; but in ancient times the powers and operations of the Subjective Mind (*q.v.*) were not scientifically understood, with the result that a distinction could not easily be made between an utterance derived from a treasure-house of human thought and experience and an utterance transmitted, as it were telepathically (see TELEPATHY), from a Divine Mind. In any case, Montanus became a prophet, and soon two prophetesses attached themselves to him, Prisca or Priscilla and Maximilla, women who manifested the same spiritual phenomena. Montanus claimed that the person who spoken through him was the Paraclete (*q.v.*). As Dr. Salmon says, he does not seem to have claimed that he himself was the Paraclete. Through him the Paraclete was speaking and proclaiming a new dispensation. "The Paraclete confidently announced the speedy return of Christ, and the Vision of the Heavenly Jerusalem descending from above, which was to appear first in the clouds, and then rest on the earth, at a spot indicated. This was a plain on the further side of Phrygia, between the two little towns of Pepuza and Tymion. The three prophets transported themselves thither, when or wherefore is not precisely known: they were followed by an immense multitude. In some places the people were so entirely won over to the movement that all the Christians left. In the feverish expectation of the last day, country, family, and all earthly ties were disregarded. Marriages were dissolved; and community of goods and the most severe asceticism prevailed. This state of mental exaltation was fostered by the words of the possessed prophets; the voice of the Paraclete was heard, and his exhortations animated them afresh" (Louis Duchesne). The Montanists were orthodox in so far as they did not reject the sacred writings or the doctrines of the Church. Their heresy consisted in the belief that they received new revelations which supplemented and explained these. In such writings as the Gospel and Apocalypse of St. John they believed that they could find particular support for their views. A curious result of this was that, as a protest, a body arose, the Alogi (*q.v.*), which rejected the writings of St. John altogether. But if the Montanists were not unorthodox, the Church was not prepared at this critical time to tolerate long the doctrine of a progressive revelation. The promised Heavenly Jerusalem did not appear; but a terrestrial Jerusalem was established, the name of Pepuza being changed to that of New Jerusalem. The movement spread from the East to the West and caused divisions in the Church. The result was that in course of time Montanism was discouraged or condemned both in the East and in the West, in spite of its great moral austerity. This did not prevent the great Tertullian from becoming a Montanist. He was chosen head of the Montanists in Africa, and they were even called Tertullianists there. But the opposition to Montanism became more and more pronounced. Under the Emperor Constantine, according to Sozomen, they were exterminated everywhere but in Phrygia. Sterner measures were taken against them by later Emperors. The Emperor Justinian even sent soldiers against them. They were so harried that they set fire to their churches in which they had taken refuge. See Schaff-Herzog; T. M. Lindsay in the *Prot. Dict.;* the *Cath. Dict.;* Louis Duchesne, *Hist.;* G. Salmon in Wace and Piercy.

MONTO SECT. A Japanese Buddhist sect. Monto Sect is another name for the Shin Sect (*q.v.*).

MOORHOUSE LECTURESHIP. A lectureship founded in memory of the Australian episcopate of the Right Rev. James Moorhouse, D.D., St. John's College, Cambridge, Bishop of Melbourne 1876-1886. The electors, the Bishops of the metropolitan sees of Australia and Tasmania, and the Primate of New Zealand, may elect anyone in Holy Orders in the Church of England at home or abroad, or in a Church in communion with her. The subjects of the lectures must be: (1) the defence and confirmation of the Christian faith as declared in the Apostles' and Nicene Creeds; (2) questions bearing upon the history and authority of the Holy Scriptures of the Old and New Testaments; and (3) the social aspects of the Christian faith in their widest application. The lectures are delivered annually in St. Paul's Cathedral, Melbourne, and must be published afterwards.

MORALITIES. The "Moralities" of the Middle Ages, which were introduced into England from France, were a class of religious drama. But instead of Biblical characters and subjects being represented, the characters were allegorical representations of the virtues and vices. Moralities were more secular than Miracle-plays and Mysteries, and prepared the way for the regular drama. "Even in the oldest religious dramas, allegorical characters such as Mercy, Justice, the synagogue, etc., occur; and when the drama fell into the hands of the laity, it was quite natural that they, more especially under the influence of the Renaissance, should develop a taste for a drama of a more secular character—a drama which to a certain extent mirrored their own life, and expressed their own ideas" (Schaff-Herzog). See Schaff-Herzog; W. Benham; *Chambers's Encycl.*

MORAVIANS. The community of Christians known as Moravians had its origin in Bohemia, and the connection of Bohemian Christianity with England goes back to the 14th century. At various periods Bohemian refugees sought freedom of conscience in England. About the beginning of the 16th century there was a colony of Moravian Waldenses at Lerwick, and in 1583 we find a member of the Brethren's Church, John Bernardus, graduating B.D. at Oxford. In 1641 J. A. Comenius, Bishop of the Brethren's Church, visited England, and in 1716 Christian Sitkovsky. In 1734 A. G. Spangenberg came to London to make arrangements for sending out a colony of Moravian emigrants to do mission work among the Indians. In 1735 Bishop David Nitschmann brought to London a second party of emigrants for Georgia. Before the end of the year they sailed for America in company with John and Charles Wesley, Benjamin Ingham, and Charles Delamotte. In 1737 Count Zinzendorf came to London and rented a house in Chelsea. Here his daily meetings for household worship were attended by other Germans resident in London, and a small society was formed. When Peter Böhler came to London in 1738 he worked amongst the members of a small society which met in Little Wild Street. This Society was more fully organised on the lines of the Herrnhut "Band" system, and rules were drawn up for it by Böhler and John Wesley. Later in the same year its place of meeting was moved to a room in Fetter Lane. The Wesleys withdrew from the Society later (1740). During the years 1739-1741 a number of new Societies sprang up in various parts of the country. In 1741 Spangenberg opened a "Pilgrim House" or Central Office in Little Wild Street, London, and in 1742 a "Pilgrim Congregation" was settled for Yorkshire. On September 7th of the same year the Fetter Lane Society was registered as a Dissenting Congregation, under the name of "Moravian Brethren, formerly of the Anglican Communion"; and on November 10th it was "settled" as a Congregation of the Moravian Church. The General Synod of Hirschberg, held in 1743, decided that London was the "Pilgrim Congregation" or headquarters for England. In course of time Societies or Congregations were formed in Wales, Ireland, and Scotland. In 1860 a Theological College was opened at Fulneck. In 1878 this was moved to Fairfield, in order that use might be made of Owen's College, Manchester, and since 1904 it has been affiliated with the Theological Faculty of Manchester University. The Moravian Church is described as "that branch of the visible body of Christ which took a separate form at Litiz in Bohemia in 1457; which was crushed in its first home by Roman influence, as the result of the Thirty Years' War, and was renewed in 1722 at Herrnhut in Saxony." The Moravians have an episcopacy of their own, and the Church as a whole is represented by a constitutional body known as the General Synod. The Holy Scriptures are the only rule of faith and life. On individual points of doctrine no detailed standard is allowed to bind the conscience and quench the Spirit. All worship is scriptural and congregational, and is to be in Spirit and in Truth, and not in dead cold form. The Moravians "have always been distinguished for the simplicity of their evangelical faith and worship, the purity and beneficence of their lives, and the ardour of their missionary zeal" (J. A. Houlder). They exercised considerable influence upon the Wesleys. It was indeed at a meeting of the Moravian Brethren in London (1738) that John Wesley experienced his "conversion." See the *Moravian Church Almanack.*

MORISONIANS. The followers of James Morison (1816-1893), minister of Kilmarnock. In 1840 Morison published a tract on the Atonement, which resulted in his being suspended by the Presbytery. He taught that Christ died for all men alike; "that repentance is not sorrow for sin, but simply the change of mind from disbelief in salvation to belief; that those who ultimately will be condemned, will be condemned only for disbelieving the truth of Christ's dying for them, and consequently failing to secure forgiveness through Him; that all men are able of themselves to believe, and that Adam's fall has not so corrupted mankind as to render them liable to eternal punishment on account of his sin" (J. H. Blunt). In 1843, Morison, in conjunction with a number of other suspended ministers, formed "The Evangelical Union and affiliated Churches." In the same year they founded also a theological college with Morison as Principal. "The sect is of the Congregational kind, each separate congregation maintaining individual freedom; and consequently, although generally agreeing in maintaining Morisonian views, there is not in it any necessary unanimity in opinion" (J. H. Blunt). Morison retired from the ministry nearly ten years before his death. See J. H. Blunt; the *D.N.B.*

MORMON, THE BOOK OF. The sacred book of the Mormons, in addition to the Bible. It is regarded as divinely inspired, and as in perfect harmony with the Bible. It is claimed that the second inspired work is alluded to in the Bible itself in the Book of Ezekiel (xxxvii. 15-19). The "stick of Judah" there referred to is the Bible; the "stick of Ephraim" is the other record, the Book of Mormon. It is said that an angel named Moroni appeared to Joseph Smith, the Prophet of the Mormons, and told him that in A.D. 420 he had buried a sacred record in the hill Cumorah in the northern part of the State of New York. The plates of the work, with a Urim and Thummim, were committed to the care of Joseph Smith for translation. "Each plate was six inches wide and eight inches long, and not quite as thick as common tin. They were filled with engravings in Egyptian characters, and bound together in a volume, as the leaves of a book, with three rings running through the whole. The volume was something near six inches in thickness, a part of it being sealed. The characters on the unsealed part were small and beautifully engraved. The whole book exhibited many marks of antiquity in its construction, and much skill in the art of engraving. The Urim and Thummim consisted of two transparent stones set in the rim of a bow fastened to a breastplate. The unsealed portion of the plates was translated, and the whole were again taken charge of by the angel" (James H. Anderson). The part translated was published in 1830. This Book of Mormon purports to be an abridgment of the records of his forefathers made by the Prophet Mormon, father of Moroni. See J. H. Blunt; James H. Anderson, "The Church of Jesus Christ of Latter-Day Saints," in *R.S.W.*

MORMONS. The Mormons are the followers of Joseph Smith (1805-1844). Smith was born at Sharon, Windsor County, Vermont, in the United States of America. He became greatly interested in religion when he was little more than fourteen years old. This interest was in time rewarded, it is said. He received revelations from heaven which were noted down in the Book of Mormon (see MORMON, BOOK OF). In 1829 he was ordained first to the Aaronic Priesthood by John the Baptist, and then to the Apostleship by the Apostles Peter, James, and John. He then re-established the Church of Jesus Christ in preparation for the millennial reign of Christ on earth. He erected a temple in Kirtland, Ohio, and the State of Missouri became the chief gathering-place of the believers. But Smith's followers were not popular. Their neighbours persecuted them and drove them from their dwellings. Those who escaped, to the number of about twelve thousand, settled in Illinois and founded the city of Nauvoo. They were again persecuted, and on June 27, 1844, their Prophet, Joseph Smith, was assassinated. He was succeeded by a body of men called the Twelve Apostles. The President of these was one Brigham Young. Another temple was soon completed at Nauvoo. The Mormons again suffered cruel persecution. They were again driven into exile. This time they made their way into the valley of the Great Salt Lake, where in 1850 the Territory of Utah was created. Seventy-five per cent. of the inhabitants of Utah are Mormons. The Church of Jesus Christ of Latter-Day Saints, to give the Mormons their correct title, has thirteen Articles of Faith. 1. We believe in God, the Eternal Father, and in His Son, Jesus Christ, and in the Holy Ghost. 2. We believe that men will be punished for their own sins, and not for Adam's transgression. 3. We believe that through the atonement of Christ, all mankind may be saved, by obedience to the laws and ordinances of the Gospel. 4. We believe that these ordinances are: First, Faith in the Lord Jesus Christ; second, Repentance; third, Baptism by immersion for the remission of sins; fourth, Laying on of hands for the gift of the Holy Ghost. 5. We believe that a man must be called of God, by "prophecy, and by the laying on of hands," by those who are in authority, to preach the Gospel and administer in the ordinances thereof. 6. We believe in the same organization that existed in the primitive Church, viz., apostles, prophets, pastors, teachers, evangelists, etc. 7. We believe in the gift of tongues, prophecy, revelation, visions, healing, interpretation of tongues, etc. 8. We believe the Bible to be the word of God, as far as it is translated correctly; we also believe the Book of Mormon to be the word of God. 9. We believe all that God has revealed, all that He does now reveal, and we believe that He will yet reveal many great and important things pertaining to the Kingdom of God. 10. We believe in the literal gathering of Israel and in the restoration of the Ten Tribes. That Zion will be built upon this continent. That Christ will reign personally upon the earth, and that the earth will be renewed and receive its paradisic glory. 11. We claim the privilege of worshipping Almighty God according to the dictates of our conscience, and allow all men the same privilege, let them worship how, where or what they may. 12. We believe in being subject to kings, presidents, rulers and magistrates, in obeying, honouring and sustaining the law. 13. We believe in being honest, true, chaste, benevolent, virtuous, and in doing good to *all men;* indeed, we may say that we follow the admonition of Paul: "We believe all things, we hope all things"; we have endured many things, and hope to be able to endure all things. If there is anything virtuous, lovely, or of good report, or praiseworthy, we seek after these things. One of the features of Mormonism that have attracted special attention is the adoption of the patriarchal order of marriage. The Mormons point out that the prophets of God in ancient times had a plurality of wives, and regard this as a good example in agreement with the laws of God and of nature. "Many people revile against it, frequently because they are ignorant of its harmony with natural laws, but it ill becomes those who profess a belief in Christianity to say that God ever gave to His children a law that was sinful in its nature or pernicious in its effects; to thus reproach the justice and righteousness of the Almighty is blasphemy" (James H. Anderson). Plurality of wives does not, however, seem to have been ordained by Joseph Smith, but to have been proclaimed by Brigham Young, his successor. The faithful followers of Joseph Smith, the "Smithite" or "Josephite" Mormons, refused to accept the new ordinance or to follow Brigham Young to Utah. They adhered to the original principles of the first Prophet. "These 'Smithite' or 'Josephite' Mormons have spread and flourished exceedingly, and have missionaries in every English-speaking country, also in Norway, Sweden, and Switzerland" (L. Dougall in the *Manchester Guardian*). It appears from the United States census that between 1900 and 1906 their numbers increased from 21,773 to 40,851. See J. H. Blunt; James H. Anderson, "The Church of Jesus Christ of Latter-Day Saints," in *R.S.W.*

MORRIGAN. An ancient Irish deity. Sister of Bav, and wife of Neit, the god of battle, she had charge of one of the departments of battle and carnage, inciting men to deeds of strife and valour.

MÓRRIGU. A goddess of war worshipped in ancient Britain and associated with the god of war Llûdd (*q.v.*). See NEMETONA.

MOSQUES. Muhammadan places of worship. The primitive name was *masjid* "place of prayer." Towards the fourth century a distinction was made between great and small mosques. The Great Mosque was called first *masjid al-jamā'a*, and then simply *al-jāmi'*. After this the word *masjid* was reserved for the most part for mosques of the second rank. The original plan of the mosque, which is oriented in the direction of Mecca, is simple. It forms a large square court, surrounded with porticoes. Over these is a flat roof, supported by arches with stone columns or brick pillars. "The elements of this plan seem to be borrowed, on the one hand, from the Persian palaces of the Achæmenian type, perhaps, but indirectly, from the Egyptian palaces, and, on the other hand, from the Christian churches of Egypt and Syria" (Hastings' *Encycl., s.v.* Architecture). In some cases Christian churches were transformed into mosques. Examples of this are the Great Mosque at Damascus and the al-Aqṣā Mosque at Jerusalem. The mosques in Cairo include the great Mosque of Aḥmad ibn Ṭūlūn (879) and the great Mosque of the Nilometre (1092). In Isfahan in Persia a handsome mosque called *Masjid-i Shāh*, "Mosque of the King," was founded by Shah Abbas in 1612. In Tabriz there is a well-known specimen, the Masjid-i Kabud or Blue Mosque, which dates from the middle of the fifteenth century (A. V. Williams Jackson, *Persia*). J. C. Ewald Falls notes that in the Libyan desert an open circle of stones serves as a mosque (*Three Years in the Libyan Desert*, 1913).

MOUNT CARMEL, FRIARS OF OUR LADY OF. The title under which the order of Carmelites (*q.v.*) was confirmed by Pope Innocent IV.

MOUNT OF A HUNDRED FLOWERS, THE. The Mount of a Hundred Flowers is associated with Taoism (*q.v.*), one of the religions or ethical systems of China. The founder of Taoism, Lao-tsze (sixth century), recommended a life of simplicity, quiescence, purity, content, and inaction (or non-interference). Such a life, when faithfully practised, no doubt resulted in longevity. When Taoism degenerated, the later Taoists sought to attain longevity by more artificial practices. One of these was a practice known as Self-training. The ascetic sat cross-legged in an upright position, not, as in the case of the Buddhist, that he might attain to Nirvana (*q.v.*), but that he might lengthen out his days to an extent surpassing that of the old Taoists. "This attitude was believed to promote longevity, since it tended to keep the breath in the lungs, and thus to ward off death, which is the final result of the unceasing expirations. The fact also of remaining still, and excluded from the world, helped to suppress that other enemy of life, the passions" (R.K.D.). This ideal of longevity or even of eternal life is illustrated by the legend of the Mount of a Hundred Flowers cherished by the mountaineers of China. The Mount of a Hundred Flowers is a very sacred peak in the mountain range which runs from Peking across the provinces of Chih-li and Shan-tung. The mount is covered with wild flowers. "There, according to the legend, live, partly embedded in the soil, certain ancient Taoist hermits. By a long course of absolute conformity with Nature [*Tao*] they have attained immortality, and are now in the enjoyment of unearthly bliss. To use a Taoist phrase, their faces are washed by the rains of heaven, and their hair combed by the wind. Their arms are crossed upon their breasts, and their nails have grown so long that they curl round their necks. Flowers and grass have taken root in their bodies and flourish luxuriantly; when a man approaches them, they turn their eyes upon him, but do not speak" (Balfour). Some of these old sages are more than three hundred years old. See Robert K. Douglas, *Confucianism and Taouism;* Frederic H. Balfour, "Taoism," in *R.S.W.*

MOUNTAINS, SACRED. In ancient Egypt the sun was supposed to come forth from one mountain in the morning and to enter another in the evening. In the Babylonian Gilgamesh epic reference is made to "the mountain of the Sunset." The Hittite deities was associated with mountains. So also was the Israelite god Yahweh. In Palestine Lebanon, Hermon, Peor, Sinai or Horeb, and Carmel were all sacred mountains. Iamblichus (Vit. Pyth. iii. (15)) speaks of Mount Carmel as "sacred above all mountains and forbidden of access to the vulgar." Robertson Smith (*R.S.*) notes that in the oldest poetry of the Hebrews, when Yahweh rides over his land in the thunder-storm, he issues forth, not from heaven, but from Mount Sinai. Sinai or Horeb, which was obviously sacred before the theophany described in Exodus iii., is called "the Mount of God." It became specially sacred to Yahweh, who was perhaps originally a moon-god. C. F. Burney (*Book of Judges*, 1918) thinks that the mountain at which God revealed Himself to Moses under the name of Yahweh, "which is called Sinai in the narratives of J and P, must have been so called on account of an ancient connexion with the moon-god Sin, who gives his name to the whole district in which the mountain is situated ('the wilderness of Sin')." The Greeks, the Romans, the Gauls, and the Celts had their sacred mountains. So also have the Slavs, the Chinese, and the Hindus. In fact, the association of gods with mountains is world-wide.

MOUSE, THE. According to a story in I. Samuel vi., when the Philistines sent back to the Israelites the Ark of Yahweh, which they had captured, they sent back also "golden mice" as a votive offering. And Isaiah lxvi. 17 condemns the mystic sacrifice of mice as a heathen abomination. According to Maimonides, field-mice were sacrificed by the Harranians. The *Encycl. Bibl.* states: "Small votive offerings in the shape of mice have even been found (see Frazer, *Paus*, 5, 290), and it is possible that the worship of mice (especially white mice) may have originated not so much from the survival of a mouse-totem as to propitiate mice in general and to induce them not to ravage the cornfields (cp. Frazer, *Paus*, 5, 289f.)." Donald A. Mackenzie thinks that "the mouse feasts referred to by ancient writers may have been held to ensure long life among those who, like the Egyptians, connected the mouse with the moon, the source of fertility and growth and the measurer of the days of man." In Egypt the mouse was associated with the lunar god Thoth, and in Greece with Apollo. Homer refers to a Smintheus Apollo, that is to say, "Mouse Apollo." In several counties of England and in Scotland mice were at one time used as a cure for various child-ailments. They seem to have been used for the same purpose in ancient Egypt. Professor G. Elliot Smith writes (*A.E.*, p. 43): "The occasional presence of the remains of mice in the alimentary canals of children, under circumstances which prove that the small rodent had been eaten after being skinned, is a discovery of very great interest, for Dr. Netolitzky informs me that the body of a mouse was the last resort of medical practitioners in the East several millennia later as the remedy for children *in extremis*."

MOWLAWĪYEH. An order of Dervishes, founded by Jelal' ed-Din Mowla'wa (*d.* 1273 A.D.). These have been called the whirling dervishes. "The cap of the order, always a conspicuous object in a crowd, is of a yellowish white felt in the form of a truncated cone" (F. J. Bliss). See DERVISHES, WHIRLING.

MUDRĀS. A term found in Hinduism. Mudrās are mystical figures made by intertwining or twisting the fingers and hands. The figures are supposed to resemble various animals and objects, and to possess great power as occult forces. See Monier-Williams.

MUGGLETONIANS. A religious sect named after Lodowicke Muggleton (1609-1698). Muggleton in 1631 began to act as journeyman tailor to his cousin, John Reeve (1608-1658), who was a Puritan. In 1651-2 Muggleton professed to have received revelations, and in 1652 the two men gave out that they were the "two witnesses" of Revelation xi. In the same year they published the "Transcendent Spirituall Treatise." Reeve was supposed to represent Moses, and Muggleton, as the "mouth" of Reeve, Aaron. They claimed the power to curse and destroy their enemies. They asserted "that earth and water were not created, but self-originated; that the Evil One became incarnate in Eve; that the Father was the sufferer upon the Cross, having left Elijah to govern heaven, while He came to earth to die" (J. H. Blunt). Muggleton was imprisoned for blasphemy in 1653, and in 1677 was arrested again on the same charge and made to pay a heavy fine. He entered into controversy with the Quakers, and was replied to by William Penn (1644-1718) and George Fox (1624-1691). When Reeve died, Muggleton professed to have received a double portion of the Spirit. The Muggletonians survived into the nineteenth century. See J. H. Blunt; the *D.N.B.;* and *Chambers' Encycl.*

MUGTASILA. The Mugtasila or the Washers were a religious body which flourished about 215 A.D. on the Lower Tigris near the Arabian frontier. They seem to have been the ancestors of the Mandæans. Fâtâk, the father of Manes or Mani (see MANICHÆISM), may have founded the sect. In any case, he joined it, and Mani lived among the Mugtasila for some years. The descendants of the Mugtasila, the modern Mandæans, have a sacred book, "The Treasure" or "Great Book" or "Book of Adam," which "shows that in the doctrine of these baptizers there was a certain blending of old Babylonian legends with the teachings of the Bible" (Duchesne). Duchesne thinks that "a strange form of Christianity, recalling that of the serpent-worshipping sects, and Elkasaism especially, must have arisen in the second century, upon the ruins of the old Chaldean civilization." See Duchesne, *Hist.*; Wace and Piercy, *s.v.*, "Manes."

MUHAMMADANISM. The religion founded by Muhammad, son of Abdullah, of the Arab tribe of the Quraish, who was born at Mecca in 570 A.D. Left an orphan when he was five or six years old, Muhammad became the ward, first of his grandfather, and then of his uncle Abū Tālib. When twelve years old his uncle took him as a companion through parts of Syria, and on this journey he is said to have met a Christian monk who prophesied his future greatness. At the age of twenty-five he married a rich widow Khadijah, who became one of his earliest converts. Soon after he was forty years old he began to receive revelations. "From these revelations, treasured up, written down, and finally compared together and brought into harmony, the Qur'ān was formed, as it is known and read by the millions of adherents of Islām at the present day. No attempt, however, seems ever to have been made to preserve the chronological sequence of the revelations. It is tradition alone that associates the various utterances with particular epochs or circumstances of the Prophet's experience, and in tracing in outline the history of his outward life, and the development of his doctrine and character, it is upon tradition, more or less reliable and consistent, that dependence has to be placed" (A. S. Geden, *Studies*). It has been thought that he could neither read nor write (cp. Qur'ān, vii. 156), but this is not likely. And since, especially in later life, his inspired utterances fell from him while he was in a trance, it has been held that he suffered from some nervous disorder. Weil, in 1862, tried to prove that his symptoms pointed to epilepsy as opposed to catalepsy. "More recently Professor Margoliouth, in his *Life of Muḥammad* (p. 46), has urged the same based on such symptoms as this unconsciousness, the sound of a bell, the belief that someone is present, a resultant headache, violent perspiration, and others, such as turning of the head to one side, foaming at the mouth, reddening or whitening of the face, all which are characteristics of epilepsy. But as Sprenger (Vol. III., p. 65) rightly points out, the traditions are too contradictory to afford a sure basis. What is certain is the existence of some pathological condition in Muḥammad, resulting in trances, and it is not at all impossible that Sprenger's judgment (Vol. I. pp. 207f.) that it was some form of hysteria under which he suffered, may be correct" (D. B. Macdonald, *R.A.L.I.*). The Quraish showed such hostility to Muhammad's followers that in 615 A.D. some of them with his permission sought refuge in Abyssinia (the First Hijrah). Others (about 100) followed them less than a year later. In 622 A.D. the prophet himself was obliged to leave Mecca—this is the *Hijrah* or Flight which forms the starting-point of Muhammadan chronology throughout the world. His wife and uncle had died, and he had married a second wife 'Ayishah, daughter of Abū Bakr. He went from Mecca to Medina, a cosmopolitan city, in which he came into touch with and felt the influence of Jews, Christians, and Zoroastrians. Here the number of his adherents (*Muhārijūn*, or "emigrants" from Mecca; and *Ansār*, "helpers," or converts won in Medina) grew, in spite of the continued opposition of the Quraish, who now resorted to armed warfare. In 630 A.D. Muhammad marched against Mecca with an army and took possession of it. From this time his power and authority extended until they were established over practically the whole of Arabia. Before the prophet died (632 A.D.) he designated Abū Bakr as his successor. "The cardinal doctrine of Mohammed was the oneness and aloneness of God, whom he called Allah, 'The God.' The one God was conceived by him as a great human being or a transcendent man. He had hands, eyes, and human attributes. He was thought to be all-wise and all-powerful, and to be the absolute despot of the world. It was useless for man to hope to understand him, but God would be merciful if man submitted to him. Next in importance to the doctrine of God was the doctrine of the prophetic function of Mohammed. Through Mohammed, God made his final revelation; Mohammed was the seal of the prophets; no prophet was to come after him. . . . To these doctrines Mohammed added, from the time of his earliest ministry, a doctrine of material rewards and punishments. Believers were to be rewarded with a material paradise, and unbelievers were to be tortured in a very material hell. . . . The outward duties of believers were to pray five times a day, as well as to be just and kind to the poor. The doctrines of angels and of Satan were taken over from Judaism, though the figure of Satan was blurred by conceptions of the jinn inherited from Arabian heathenism" (G. A. Barton, *R.W.*). Abū Bakr's succession was accepted by the Sunnīs, the traditionalists, who follow the orthodox traditions of Islam, but was contested by the Shī'ahs, who contend that the right of succession belonged to Ali, the son-in-law of the Prophet. Of the first four Khalifs (successors), Abu Bakr, Omar, Othmān, and Ali, therefore, all but the last are held by the Shī'ahs to have been usurpers. When Othmān died, Mu'awiya, the governor of Syria and Damascus, refused to recognise Ali as his successor. The result was civil war, and Ali moved his capital from Medina to Kūfa, not far from ancient Babylon. Hasan, Ali's elder son, succeeded his father, but soon abdicated in favour of Mu'āwiya. Husain, his younger son, who had settled at Mecca, relying on help from Kūfa, contested the rule of Mu'āwiya's son and successor Yazid unsuccessfully, and was killed by the Khalīf's horsemen on the tenth of Muharram, the first month of the Muhammadan year, A.H. 61 (Oct. 10, 680 A.D.). "Husain is regarded as a martyr by the Shī'ah sect of the Muslims, who reverence him and his father with a passionate devotion. The memory of his name and fate is kept alive on the anniversary of his death by the yearly festival of the Muharram, with services and processions and lamentation" (Geden). The Khalīfs of the Quraish dynasty were succeeded by the Umayyads (661-750 A.D.), who took their name from Umayya, the great-grandfather of Mu'āwiya, and reigned at Damascus. At the close of this dynasty Muhammadanism had spread throughout North Africa and the south-western half of Spain, and in parts of Southern France. "The armies of this caliphate also carried the conquésts eastwards to the borders of India and into Turkestan and Samarcand beyond the Oxus and Jaxartes rivers" (Barton). In 750 A.D. the Ummayad dynasty was overthrown by Abul-Abbas, a descendant of Abbas, an uncle of Muhammad, and the 'Abbāsids were established in its place. The first of the Abbasid Khalīfs, Saffah, held his court at Anbār on the east bank of the Euphrates; but his successor, Mansūr, founded the city of Baghdād, which became the centre of Abbāsid power for five centuries—until the end of the dynasty, in fact. The Muslims of North Africa and Spain, however, refused to recognise the 'Abbasids. Abd-er-Rahman, a scion of the Umayyad house, was made ruler in Spain, and his descendants established a Spanish Khalīfate, which lasted until 1027 A.D. At Baghdād and Cordova literature and philosophy flourished, and a brilliant period of intellectual life began. The study of philosophy produced many sceptics, who were often called Mu'tazilites or Seceders. The power of the 'Abbasids gradually waned, and practically came to an end when Baghdād was captured by Mongol hordes in 1258 A.D. Another Khalīfate had risen at Kairwan in North Africa in 909 A.D., and had conquered Egypt in 968. This was known as the Fātimid Khalīfate. These Khalīfs who exercised a more or less independent rule at Cairo from 1258-1517 A.D., claimed to be directly descended from Fātimah, the daughter of the Prophet. In 1517, when Egypt was conquered by the Ottoman Turks, the office of Khalīf was sold to the Sultan of Turkey, who thus came to be regarded as the successor of the Prophet. Muhammadanism has made, and is still making, great missionary efforts. "In the course of the centuries it has penetrated India, China, Africa, and the isles of the Pacific, and has made many converts. . . . It is estimated that at present there are about 240,000,000 Mohammedans in the world. If this is true, they constitute nearly one-sixth of the population of the globe" (Barton). The sacred book of the Muhammadans is of course the Qur'ān (*q.v.*). "The *Qur'ān* is written in rhymed prose throughout. The portions rhymed, verses as we may call them, vary greatly in length. In the earlier chapters these verses are short, just as the style is lively and fiery; in the later chapters they are of lumbering length, prosaic and slow, and the rhyme comes in with often a most absurd effect. It is very plain that Muhammad's first utterances were in genuine *kāhin* form and *kāhin* spirit [*i.e.*, in the form and spirit of the Arab soothsayer]; that they boiled forth from him as though under uncontrollable external pressure" (D. B. Macdonald). His utterances seem therefore to have taken that form of language which is peculiar to the ecstatic life. There are other sources of authority for Muhammadan faith and practice besides the Qur'ān. These are the *Sunnat*, which means "usage" or "rule," and embraces the rule of faith or observance founded on the traditions; the *Ijmā'*, which means "unanimity," and denotes the unanimous consent of the early doctors and teachers regarding new rules and precedents; and the Qiyās, which means "measure" or "comparison," and is applied to analogical reasoning or inference based upon, and supplementary to, the Qur'ān, Sunnat, or Ijmā'. Muhammadan law above and beyond the revealed law of the Qur'ān was developed by four great orthodox schools, the leaders (*Imāms*) of which were Abū Hanīfah (*d.* about 768 A.D.), Ibn Mālik ibn Anas (*b.* 716 A.D.), Ash-Shāfi'ī (*d.* about 820 A.D.), and Ahmad ibn Hanbal (*b.* 780 A.D.). There are five so-called "pillars of religion." The first of these is the recital of the *Kalimah* or creed: "There is no god but God, and Muhammad is the Prophet of God" (cp. Qur'ān xlvii. 21, xlviii. 29). The second is *Salāt* or prayer (the five daily prayers). The third is Fasting, particularly the thirty days' fast of the month Ramadhān. The fourth is *Zakāt* or alms-giving. The fifth is the *Hajj* or pilgrimage to Mecca in the twelfth month of the Muhammadan year. This statement looks simple enough, but Muhammadan theologians and philosophers have found plenty of material for exposition and speculation in the doctrine of the unity of God. One of the most famons of these theologians and philosophers is al-Ghazzālī (1059-1109), who began by being a sceptic or Mu'tazilite, was converted, and ended by being a Sufi or mystic and a defender of the faith (see Macdonald for an interesting account of his religious experiences). The prayers may be offered individually and privately, or in a mosque (with a leader, *Imām*). "The form observed consists in the recital of passages from the Qur'ān, with other formulae or expressions of faith such as 'God is great,' accompanied by bowings and prostrations of the body. The summons to prayer is given by the *mu'azzin* from the minaret, or if there is no minaret from the side of the mosque" (Geden). Muhammadanism has produced many sects. The Shī'ahs, who quarrelled with the orthodox Sunnīs over the succession to the Khalīfate, have been mentioned already. The Shī'ahs were mostly Persians, and the Persians are still Shī'ahs. The Ismā'īlians took their name from Ismā'īl, the adopted son of ibn Maimun, the sixth Imām. They are a sub-sect of the Shī'āhs, and are sometimes called the "Seveners," because they claim that Ismā'īl (and not Mūsā) was rightfully the seventh and last Imām. The Druses or Druzes owe their name to ad-Duruzī, who was the Persian minister of al-Hākim (996-1020 A.D.), the sixth Fātimid Khalīf. They revere al-Hākim as the last and greatest incarnation of God. Their tenets, however, are those of a teacher named Hamzah rather than those of ad-Daruzī, who came to be regarded as a heretic. The Druses are still a numerous sect in the Hauran and mountains of Lebanon. The Assassins is a name given by Europeans to the Hashshāshīn, devotees of the drug *hashshīsh*. They were the followers of Hasan, the "Old Man of the Mountain," who claimed to be an incarnation of God. In the time of the Crusaders they were a terror throughout Syria, and well earned the name Assassins. The Sūfīs, who were influenced by Gnosticism and Greek mysticism, are mystics who attained to union with God through an "inner light." They rely upon knowledge gained by *ilhām* (a kind of inspiration) rather than upon that acquired by study. "Books and proofs they shun. Their path (*tarīq*), rather, is to cleave to spiritual striving, to remove blameworthy qualities, to sever all ties, to advance with the utmost zeal toward God. Whenever these things take place, God takes charge of the heart of his creature, and illumines it with knowledge, and opens the breast of the seeker so that he accepts guidance and trusts God; there is revealed to him the secret of the heavenly kingdom (*al-malakūt*), and there is cleared away from the surface of his heart the veil of error, and so the essences of divine things shine in it. All that he has to do is to prepare himself by simple purifying, by showing zeal joined to pure will, by thirsting and watching and expecting. If any turn thus to God, God will turn to him" (Macdonald). From among the Sūfīs the various orders of Darwīshes (Dervishes) have arisen, such as the Qādiriyah; the Maulāwiyah, or "dancing Darwīshes"; the Rufā'iyah, or "howling Darwīshes"; the Bakhtāshīyah, who are mostly soldiers; the Sanūsīyah, who show great hostility to European civilization. The Wahhābīs, who belong to the close of the eighteenth and beginning of the nineteenth centuries, represent a military and fanatical reform movement in Arabia. In recent years the Bābīs and Bahāīs of Persia have attracted great attention. The founder of the Bābīs, Mīrza 'Alī Muhammad (*b.* 1820), claimed to be the Bab or the "Door" through which it was possible to communicate with the "Concealed Imām (the twelfth Imām, who disappeared at the beginning of the fourth century after the Hijrah, 940-1 A.D.). Afterwards he proclaimed himself an incarnation of God. The Bahāīs were the result of a schism after the death of the Bab. They were founded by Bahā'ullah (*d.* 1892), who proclaimed himself "He whom God manifests," and claimed that his coming had been foretold by the Bab. Bahāism claims to be a universal religion. While Bābism has declined in numbers and influence, Bahāism has grown in importance, and has had considerable success in America. See, in addition to the works mentioned above, D. B. Macdonald, *Muslim Theology*, 1903; D. S. Margolionth, *Mohammedanism* in the "Home University Library"; I. Goldziher, *Mohammed and Islam*, 1917; F. W. Bussell.

MUJASSIMA. An Arabic word meaning "corporealists." It is another name for the Karrâmiyya (*q.v.*).

MUJTAHIDÎN. Mujtahid is an Arabic word meaning "one who exerts himself or takes pains." The term came to be used of learned doctors of Islâm who applied their minds diligently to problems of Muslim theology. It was thought by some that only the Companions of the Prophet could be true Mujtahidîn. "The majority of Muslim theologians, however, are of opinion that there may be true Mujtahidîn in any age and in any place, and that their unanimous agreement is to be accepted as conclusive in any legal or theological question." There are Mujtahids of different kinds. Some of them are authorities on the whole Law, others on the doctrines of a particular school of theology, and others on questions of special difficulty. See F. A. Klein.

MULAHIDA. An Islamic sect, referred to by Moiz Mohammed Haidar (*d.* 1551-2) in his History of the Moguls. "Most of the people of Badakshan are adherents of this sect; they hold the world to be without beginning or end: they do not believe in resurrection or a future state. They say that while the Prophet was alive all the faithful were bound to abide by the statutes of the Holy Law; but at the present day the whole duty of man is to speak fitting words and be faithful to their meaning. All other ordinances are futile: sexual intercourse with kindred is lawful and its enjoyment need not depend on marriage-rites; if one has a passion for someone—be it daughter or son or mother—it is lawful to gratify it if it be practicable. It is also lawful for them to take one another's lives or property." As *Ismaili* the sect still survives in Shignan and Roshan.

MULCTRA, THE. In Christian art, Christ, when represented as the Good Shepherd, sometimes has hanging on His arm a *mulctra* or milk-pail. This is interpreted as a symbol of the spiritual nourishment derived from Him as the Lamb. See Sidney Heath.

MULLO. A god worshipped by the continental Celts as the patron of mule-drivers. He was regarded by the Romans as equivalent to Mars.

MULUNGU. A term used among the Yao to denote a mystic potency in things. *Mulungu* seems to be a force, and not a personal being, and corresponds to the Melanesian *mana*.

MUMMERS. Les Mômiers or "the hypocrites" was a name given to the strict Calvinists in the French cantons of Switzerland, who were followers of Robert Haldane (1764-1842) and César Malan (1787-1864). Haldane lectured in his own house to theological students of the University of Geneva. Malan, forbidden by the Venerable Association of Pastors at Geneva to preach on such subjects as hereditary sin and predestination, also gathered his adherents round him in his own house, though without separating from the Established Church. Afterwards he built a small chapel for them, "Chapelle du Témoignage." See Schaff-Herzog.

MUMMIFICATION. It is thought by Professor Elliot Smith that the art of mummification, as practised in ancient Egypt, was mainly responsible for prompting the earliest great maritime expeditions of which the history has been preserved, and even supplied the foundation on which the knowledge of anatomy and the science of medicine has been built up. The practice of course had great religious significance, the object being to preserve the body of the deceased for a continued existence, not merely the corpse, but the body with its tissues. The Egyptian embalmer at the outset was eager (1) to preserve the actual tissues of the body with as little disturbance of its superficial appearance as possible, and (2) to preserve a likeness of the deceased as he existed in life. The first attempts to reproduce the features of the deceased were made upon the wrapped mummy itself. "In the earliest known (Second Dynasty) examples of Egyptian attempts at mummification the corpse was swathed in a large series of bandages, which were moulded into shape to represent the form of the body. In a later (probably Fifth Dynasty) mummy, found in 1892 by Professor Flinders Petrie at Medûm, the superficial bandages had been impregnated with a resinous paste, which while still plastic was moulded into the form of the body, special care being bestowed upon the modelling of the face and the organs of reproduction, so as to leave no room for doubt as to the identity and the sex" (G. Elliot Smith, *Dr.*, p. 16). In two cases the head, and not the whole body was covered with a layer of stucco. In the Pyramid Age a new procedure seems to have been devised—the making of a death-mask. The custom also arose of making a life-size portrait statue of the dead man's head ("reserve heads") and placing it in the burial chamber with the actual body. Then, in the Old Kingdom, a life-like stone statue of the deceased was made to represent him. The original idea of restoring the form of the mummy itself, however, was never abandoned, for even in the New Empire and in Roman times the wrapped mummy was sometimes modelled into the form of a statue. To convey to the statue the breath of life, as well as the vitalising fluids, the odour, and the sweat of the living body, certain ceremonies were performed. The physiological functions of the heart (the seat of knowledge and feeling) were stimulated by offerings of blood. Water being regarded as a fertilizing and vitalizing power, libations of water were made to restore to the body its vital fluids. Thus it happened that when in course of time gods came to be represented by statues, libations were regarded as an act of worship, and water became an essential part of any act of ritual rebirth. To give to the body the warmth, the sweat, and the odour of life, incense was burned before the corpse or statue. Later this custom of burning incense, like the custom of pouring out libations, came to be regarded purely and simply as a religious act of homage to a god. But the most important incident in the ritual of reanimating the mummy or the statue was the ceremony of imparting to it the breath of life by the "opening of the mouth." If the heart was the seat of knowledge and feeling, the breath of life was still regarded as necessary to set the heart working. Thus, "the ceremony of 'opening the mouth,' which aimed at achieving the restoration of the breath of life, was the principal part of the ritual procedure before the statue or mummy" (Elliot Smith, *op. cit.*, p. 43). Great importance was attached also to the painting of eyes on the wrapped mummy or on the statue. The eyes were regarded as one of the chief sources of vitality (cp. the article EYES). At first the Egyptians buried their bodies in the sand. Later on, they constructed coffins of wood and stone, and placed them in subterranean chambers. These chambers in which the body was housed developed into dwellings with many rooms. "But when the statue took over the function of representing the deceased, a dwelling was provided for it above ground. This developed into the temple where the relatives and friends of the dead came and made the offerings of food which were regarded as essential for the maintenance of existence" (*op. cit.*, p. 22). Recent archæological research has shown that "the early Egyptian Christians were mummified clear up to the Arab conquest, and used the old Egyptian forms connected with the burial rites to enforce their new doctrine" (Camden M. Cobern). It should be noted, in conclusion, that the practice of mummification has not been confined to Egypt. As Hartland says (Hastings' *Encycl.*, iv., p. 418), it is widely practised. It has been found more or less throughout the west of Africa and elsewhere. For instance, the Macleay Museum in the University of Sydney contains a mummy from Torres Straits, and the Anatomical Museum in the University of Manchester four Peruvian mummies. The Incas practised embalming not only for their kings, chiefs and priests, but also for the population in general. See G. Elliot Smith, *op. cit.*; also *A.E.*, 1911: *Migrations*, 1915; A. M. Blackman, "The Significance of Incense and Libations in Funerary and Temple Ritual," in the *Zeitschrift für Ägyptische Sprache und Altertumskunde*, Bd. 50, 1912.

MUNGILAMMĀ. A Hindu deity, bamboo goddess, worshipped by the Paraiyans, a tribe or caste in India.

MURATORIAN FRAGMENT. The Muratorian Fragment is so called because it was first published (in 1740) by Muratori. It is a list of the books of the New Testament, and was found in the Ambrosian Library at Milan in a manuscript of the seventh or eighth century. "The MS. had come from the Irish monastery of Bobbio, and the fragment seems to have been a copy of a loose leaf or two of a lost volume" (*Dict. of Christ. Biogr.*). C. R. Gregory thinks the volume may have been an apologetical book. "It is defective in the beginning, and breaks off in the middle of a sentence, and the mutilation must have taken place in the archetype of our present copy. This copy was made by an illiterate and careless scribe, and is full of blunders: but it is of the greatest value as the earliest-known list of N.T. books recognized by the Church" (*Dict.*). C. R. Gregory would date it about 170 A.D. See C. R. Gregory, *Canon*; J. Moffatt, *Intr.*; Wace and Piercy.

MURJIA, THE. A Mohammedan sect. The name is derived from a word meaning either (1) to postpone or (2) to cause to hope. The Murjia were so called either because they subordinate (postpone) works to intention (profession), or because they think that the judgment of the sinner will be postponed until the resurrection, or because they say that "disobedience joined with faith hurteth not," and in this way allow hope (cause to hope). See F. A. Klein.

MUSHABBIHA, THE. A Mohammedan sect the members of which held that God bore a resemblance to his creatures, having a body and members capable of motion. See F. A. Klein.

MUSHAF. Al-Mushaf is another name for the Qur'ân (KORAN). The word means the collection of leaves or sheets, and so the Volume. Other names for the Qur'ân are Al-Kitâb (*q.v.*) and Al-Furqân (see FURQÂN).

MUSLIM. A disciple of Muhammad, one who professes Islâm (*q.v.*). In the Qur'ân it is said (iii. 60): "Abraham was neither Jew nor Christian, but he was sound in the faith, a Muslim, and not of those who add gods to God."

MUSPELLSHEIM. Muspellsheim was one of the nine worlds in the cosmogony of the Ancient Teutons. It was located in the South.

MUSPILLI. The "Muspilli" is a Bavarian poem of over one hundred lines dating from the ninth century. It depicts the end of the world. There will be first a struggle between Elijah and the Antichrist, and then a universal conflagration. Chantepie de la Saussaye thinks that the mythology here is Christian and not pagan, but it has been adapted by the Teutons. See P. D. Chantepie de la Saussaye, *Rel. of the Teutons*, 1902.

MU'TAZILA. An Arabian sect, regarded by the Sunnis as heretics. As a body, they "entirely reject the eternal attributes of God, in order, as they say, to avoid the distinction of persons made by the Christians, and they hold that eternity is the proper attribute of God's essence, that God is omniscient, not by reason of His knowledge, is omnipotent, not by reason of His omnipotence, as the Sunnis say, but by reason of His essence." The Mu'tazila hold also that "all those verses of the Qur'ân which contain a comparison of God to creatures must be explained allegorically." They differ from the Sunnis on the important question of predestination, since they regard man as a free agent. They are also called Qadariyya, "either because they deny the *qadar* or predestination, or as others say, more correctly, because they assert man's power (*qadrat*) to act freely. They consequently believe that he deserves either reward or punishment in the next world in accordance with his actions." See F. A. Klein.

MUTUA DEO. A Hindu deity, worshipped by the Korkus, a Kolarian tribe in India. A village deity, Mutua Deo is represented within the village by a heap of stones.

MYLITTA. A Babylonian goddess, referred to by Herodotus. She is perhaps to be identified with the old Sumerian goddess Ninkharsagga, who came to be regarded as the goddess of birth, "the Lady of Child-bearing." According to Herodotus (i. 199), every Babylonian woman was obliged once in her life-time to present herself in the temple-precincts of the goddess Mylitta and to sacrifice her virginity to any stranger who might claim her. The stranger threw money into her lap and said, "I invoke the goddess Mylitta for you." The idea seems to have been to consecrate to the goddess "the firstfruits of the woman's virginity before marriage" (L. R. Farnell, *Greece and Babylon*, 1911).

MYRDDIN. The Myrddin who figures prominently in the Arthurian legend would seem to have been worshipped originally in ancient Britain as a god. In mythology he is described "as the master of all knowledge, owner of all wealth, and lord of Fairyland" (Squire, *Myth.*).

MYSTERIES. The Greeks, and afterwards the Romans, used the term Mysteries of certain secret and mysterious forms of worship which could only be participated in after solemn initiation. Some of these Mysteries were restricted to particular classes of persons (cp. THESMOPHORIA); others were open to anyone who was willing to be duly initiated. In course of time many foreign elements were introduced into the worship. The ceremonies "consisted usually in the recital of certain legends about the fortunes of the deity celebrated, which differed from the ordinary myths in many respects (*e.g.*, the names and genealogies), and were often accompanied by a dramatic representation, with which was connected the exhibition of certain holy things, including symbols and relics. In many cases the symbols were not hidden from the public eye, but their meaning was revealed to the initiated alone" (Seyffert). Compare, in particular, ELEUSINIAN MYSTERIES, ORPHICS, and MITHRAISM.

MYSTICISM, CHRISTIAN. Mysticism is the effort to enter into close touch or union with the Divine Being, with Eternal Life. The mystic seeks to penetrate into and to absorb himself in that Life which is infinite. "By getting rid of everything that makes for separation and distinction, by casting off the chains of what men call happiness, and by freeing himself from all the narrowness and insufficiency of the mere unit, the mystic believes that in extinction itself he gains an incomparably higher life and genuine blessedness" (Rudolf Eucken). Mysticism "strives to free human life more and more from every element of time, to make man younger every day, and to transport him entirely into a 'permanent present.' The man for whom time becomes as eternity and eternity as time, seems to escape all pain and to be brought into a state of pure bliss." Such a state of mind does not necessarily preclude joyous activity in the world. It may even bring quite the opposite of this. "The close connection between God and the world which mysticism stands for, may reduce both the visible world and time to an illusion and a dream, a morning-glow which disappears at the rising of the sun. But this may easily lead to the thought that the world and time, as expressions of eternal being, gain a closer connection and a greater significance." Rudolf Eucken thinks it a remarkable feature that in the present day Mysticism is regaining its old power of attraction. The Americans, it may be added, have discovered that mysticism of a kind, whether Christian or not, is of great practical value (see HIGHER THOUGHT). The Christian mystics are associated particularly with the Middle Ages. According to Inge, the mediæval mystics were "steeped in" Dionysius the Areopagite. The supposed works (sixth century) of Dionysius were translated into Latin by John Scotus Erigena (ninth century). At the same time Erigena worked up the theories of Dionysius "into a consistent philosophical system" (Inge). In the twelfth century Mysticism had in France, in particular, very eminent representatives. One of these was Bernard of Clairvaux (1091-1153). Another was Hugo of St. Victor near Paris (1097-1141). To a later period belongs, in France, Bonaventura (John of Fidanza), the "Doctor seraphicus" (1221-1274). In the fourteenth century Germany produced mystics of great fame and influence. One of these was Master Eckhart (c. 1260-1329), the "Doctor Ecstaticus," who has been described as the greatest of all speculative Mystics. According to Eckhart, God is Being. To God time is Now, which embraces together past, present, and future. The ground of the soul is an "uncreated and uncreatable light," a "soul-spark" which is divine. This spark enables man to penetrate intuitively into the kingdom of light. If we are to see and know God we must turn away our gaze from everything that belongs to time and space. Another of these Mystics was John Tauler (1300-1361), the "Doctor Illuminatus." His mysticism was less speculative. He has been classed as one of the Devotional Mystics. But he attached great importance to practical Christianity. If necessary, a man should interrupt his devotions in order to do a service for a sick person, "believing not only that God would be with him, but that He would vouchsafe him, it may be, even greater grace and blessing in that external work, undertaken out of true love, in the service of his neighbour, than he should perhaps receive in the loftiest contemplation." Jan van Ruysbroek (1293-1381), another "Doctor ecstaticus," was a famous Flemish mystic. Ruysbroek speaks of "being swallowed up in the unfathomable abyss of eternal happiness." Max B. Weinstein describes him as the most thoroughgoing theosophist of the Middle Ages. Another famous mystic was Henry Suso (von Berg; 1295-1366), who wrote a "Book of Eternal Wisdom." He was a pupil of Eckhart and friend of Tauler. Suso was an ascetic, a visionary, and a poet. The name of Thomas à Kempis (Thomas Hamerken of Kempen; 1380-1471) may be said to be a household word. Mysticism continued to be a force in Germany. In 1518 Martin Luther (1483-1546) published a remarkable work by an unknown writer, "German Theology," which is thought to have prepared the way for the Reformation and given it a mystical tone. The book seems to have been written about 1350. The author contends that "the more the Self, the I, the Me, the Mine, that is, self-seeking and selfishness, abate in a man, the more doth God's I, that is God Himself, increase in him." Sir Frederick Pollock finds much in common between this book and parts of the Ethics of Baruch Spinoza (1632-1677; see SPINOZISM). J. H. Blunt thinks that it exhibits the germ of the "Reine Vernunft" of Immanuel Kant (1724-1804). A different kind of mysticism was introduced by Paracelsus (Philippus Aureolus Paracelsus Theophrastus von Hohenheim; 1493-1541), who was a physician and chemist. His mysticism was affected by his acquaintance with astrology and astronomy, alchemy and medicine. It has been described as Nature Mysticism, or as Theosophy. According to Mrs. Besant ("Theosophy" in *R.S.W.*), Paracelsus was one of the disciples of the Secret Wisdom. "Now and then one of its disciples appeared in Christendom, and gave to the world some 'discovery' which started thought on some new and fruitful line; thus Paracelsus, with his 'discovery' of hydrogen, his magnetic treatment for the cure of disease, and his many hints at secrets of nature not even yet worked out." The followers of Paracelsus have been called Paracelsists. Another Reformation mystic and theosophist was Valentine Weigel (1533-1588). He founded a new system, and gave birth to a new school, Weigelians. He held that God is conscious in man of His own being, and that in pitying man He has pity on Himself. There were Weigelians even in the eighteenth century. Another famous Nature mystic was Jacob Boehme or Behmen (1575-1624), the shoemaker of Goerlitz. In 1612 he published a work, "Aurora oder Morgenröte im Aufgang," which was condemned by the Church authorities. Before this he had had wonderful visions and reveries. Boehme held that no knowledge is possible without opposition and division. All things consist of Yes and No. They are either divine or devilish or earthly. The Yes is the Divine itself, simply power and love. The No is the retort to the Divine. Through it the Divine is made manifest. It is a necessary contrary in which divine love becomes operative. God represents a polarity, a conflict with Himself. He is both Good and Evil. "For the holy world God and the dark world God are not two gods: they are a single God. He is in Himself all Being. He is Evil and Good, Heaven and Hell, Light and Darkness, Eternity and Time, Beginning and End. Wherever in a being His love is hidden, there His anger is manifest." Boehme's mystical work, "The Supersensual Life," was translated into English by William Law (1686-1761), the author of the "Serious Call." Law was a disciple of Jacob Boehme. The founder of Quietism (*q.v.*), Michael Molinos (1640-1696) is an example of Spanish mysticism. His teaching influenced the French mystic, Mme. Guyon (1648-1717). A "modern" Catholic mystic of great repute is St. John of the Cross (San Juan de la Cruz; 1542-1591). He is spoken of as a Doctor in Mystical Theology, "whose works are the most complete and luminous, the most sublime, and at the same time the most philosophically exact and precise, and whose authority is the highest which any private theologian can have" *(Cath. Dict.)*. See B. Puenjer; J. H. Blunt; Chr. Joh. Deter, *Abriss der Geschichte der Philosophie*, 1906; E. C. Gregory, *Introduction to Christian Mysticism*, 1908; Rudolf Eucken, *The Life of the Spirit*, 1909; Max B. Weinstein, *Welt-und Leben-Anschauungen*. 1910; William James, *Varieties of Religious Experience*; E. Underhill.

MYSTICISM, NON-CHRISTIAN. In Christian mysticism the aim is to enter into communion with a personal God. Where a personal God is recognised, the same aim is pursued in other religions. But before we come to the higher types of religion, it should be noticed that even in lower or primitive religions a sort of mysticism is common in which communion is sought with divine or supernatural powers. Primitive folk have their mysteries of initiation, in which a state of ecstasy is attained. To them various animals and things are holy and able to communicate holiness as being instinct with divine power or life. The heathen Semites had their mystic sacrifices. Robertson Smith notes, for instance (*R.S.*), that the Harranians offered sacrificial gifts to the dog, "and in certain mysteries dogs were solemnly declared to be the brothers of the mystae." We find traces of primitive mystical cults even in the Old Testament. It appears from Isa. lxv. 3 ff., lxvi. 3, 17, Ezek. viii. 10, that during the Exile there was a tendency to revive certain cults of a primitive type. "This tendency was not confined to the Hebrews, nor did it reach its chief development among them. The causes which produced a resuscitation of obsolete mysteries among the Jews were at work at the same period among all the Northern Semites; for everywhere the old national deities had shown themselves powerless to resist the gods of Assyria and Babylon. And among these nations the tendency to fall back for help on primitive superstitions was not held in check, as it was among the Hebrews, by the counter-influence of the Prophets and the Law. From this period, therefore, we may date with great probability the first rise of the mystical cults which played so large a part in the later developments of ancient paganism, and spread their influence over the whole Graeco-Roman world. Most of these cults appear to have begun among the Northern Semites, or in the parts of Asia Minor that fell under the empire of the Assyrians and Babylonians. The leading feature that distinguishes them from the old public cults, with which they entered into competition, is that they were not based on the principle of nationality, but sought recruits from men of every race who were willing to accept initiation through the mystic sacraments; and in pursuance of this object they carried on a missionary propaganda in all parts of the Roman Empire, in a way quite alien to the spirit of national religion." The naturalization of Oriental cults in Greece and Rome, however, led to the introduction there of a more personal element into religion. Thus the cult of the Thracian god Dionysos, a deity of Oriental origin (see Gladys M. N. Davis, *The Asiatic Dionysos*, 1914), as introduced into Greece, promised the realization of a personal salvation. In Rome the Oriental mystery-religions which exerted a wide influence were the cult of Cybele of Phrygia, of Isis of Egypt, and of Mithra of Persia. "These religions appealed to the imagination on account of their great antiquity, their elaborate myths, their mystic rites, their promises of regeneration and of salvation" (G. A. Barton, *R.W.*). We have noted references in the Old Testament to a lower type of mysticism which was condemned by the great prophets. We may presume that this was condemned all the more sternly, because the prophets themselves knew by experience the difference between the lower and higher types. The great prophet was a true mystic (cp. the article "The Language of the Prophets" in *The Quest*, July, 1919). He "is carried away by the divine power and speaks as the mouthpiece of God, using lofty poetic diction while in a state of ecstacy" (K. Kohler). In later Judaism, as Kohler notes, there has always been a current of mysticism. We find the beginnings of a developed form in the religion of the Essenes, in the allegorizing methods of Philo, in the speculations about the "Chariot" *(merkabah)* of the book of Ezekiel, and in the mystical interpretation of the O.T. book, the "Song of Songs." In the Merkabah Mysticism the Chariot, as J. Abelson says (*Jewish Mysticism*, 1913), became a kind of "mystic way" leading up to the final goal of the soul. "Or, more precisely, it was the mystic 'instrument,' the vehicle by which one was carried direct into the 'halls' of the unseen. It was the aim of the mystic to be a 'Merkabah-rider,' so that he might be enabled, while still in the trammels of the flesh, to mount up to his spiritual Eldorado." As regards the "Song of Songs" (or Canticles), the Rabbis saw in its imagery of human love and marriage a true symbol of the union of Israel with the Divine Father. "The intimate and secret experiences of the soul of the Jew, the raptures of its intercourse with God in senses which no outsider could understand, were best reflected in the language of that august and indefinable passion which men call love." But the Jews were not content simply to interpret O.T. writings mystically. They produced a large mystic literature which, though starting with the Old Testament, contains many new speculations. Famous examples of this literature are the book "Yetsirah" and the "Zohar." The *Sefer Yetsirah* (Book of Creation) is of uncertain authorship and date. Judah Halevi (end of 11th century) attributed it to Abraham. Reitzenstein (*Poimandres*), connecting it with Gnostic activities, assigns it to the second century. It has also been assigned to Rabbi 'Akiba (50-130 A.D.), on account of his skill in the mystic lore of numbers. But the most likely date is about the sixth century A.D., since, as Abelson points out, this century marks the beginning of the Gaonic epoch, in which several important Rabbinic-mystical works were composed. In any case, the work has been held in high esteem from the tenth century, and has exercised a great influence on the general development of Jewish Mysticism. "It is a mystical philosophy drawn from the sounds, shapes, relative positions, and numerical values of the letters of the Hebrew alphabet." Abelson notes that although the nucleus of much of the teaching is to be found in the Talmud, the Rabbis were not the originators, but borrowed from older sources, Egyptian, Babylonian, and Mandæan. He points out also that if Alexandrian Neoplatonism is the pith and core of the emanation doctrines of Plotinus, it is also the root of the emanation doctrines of the Book *Yetsirah*, the *Zohar*, and indeed of all branches of the mediaeval Kabbalah. The *Zohar* ("Shining" or "Brightness"; cp. Dan. xii. 3) is in particular the text-book of Jewish mediæval mysticism. Its authorship is uncertain, though it purports to be the record of a divine revelation to Rabbi Simeon ben Yoḥai (*b.* second century A.D.). It made its first appearance in Spain in the thirteenth century, obviously had a number of authors, and quite as clearly drew from various faiths and philosophies. Neoplatonism, Gnosticism, the Talmud and Midrashim, and Persian Sūfism all seem to have helped to form and fashion it. While the *Zohar* claims to be a commentary on the Pentateuch, it is really an independent compendium of Kabbalistic theosophy. The work emphasises the fact that in the phenomena of the world there is an esoteric as well as an exoteric really. The universe is the outward expression of the inner Divine thought. Man, "having the privilege to behold everywhere the Divine image—the world being an embodiment of God—can, if he will, make his way to the Invisible Author of all; can have union with the Unseen." In addition to such lofty teaching, the work is rich in angelology and in mediaeval astrology. The treatment of the problem of evil is noteworthy. "Evil, sin, and their personifications, the demons, are termed *kĕlīfoth*, i.e., the coverings, wrappings, externals of all existing things. Just as the covering (or husk) of anything is not the real thing and far inferior to it, so sin and evil are, as it were, the gross, inferior, imperfect aspects of creation. And as the world is an emanation of the Divine, it follows that whatsoever in the world is evil, and not of the Divine, cannot be real. Hence evil is that which has no being; it is a sort of illusion; it is a state of absence, negation; it is a thing which merely appears to be but is not" (Abelson). The general name in Jewish literature for every kind of mystical interpretation is Kabbalah ("esoteric tradition"). Its secret lore is described by Kohler as ill-adapted to the teaching of Judaism and as simply the reaction to the excessive rationalism of the Spanish-Arabic period. "The legalism and casuistry of the Talmud and the Codes appealed too much to the intellect, disregarding the deeper emotional sources of religion and morality; on the other hand, the mysticism of the Cabbalists over-emphasized the emotional element, and eliminated much of the rational basis of Judaism." In Arabic, Persian, and Turkish the word 'mystic' is represented by *Sūfī*, though this word is restricted to mystics who are Moslems, and at first (*c.* 800 A.D.) bore a humbler meaning. The Sūfīs are so called from *sūf* "wool," because they were ascetics who wore rough woollen garments. "The earliest Sūfīs were, in fact, ascetics and quietists rather than mystics" (R. A. Nicholson, *The Mystics of Islam*, 1914). In course of time, however, they came to regard asceticism as only the first stage of a long spiritual pilgrimage, and Dr. Nicholson thinks the essence of Sūfism is best displayed in its extreme type, which is pantheistic and speculative rather than ascetic or devotional. The Sūfī is a "traveller" by slow "stages" along a "path" the goal of which is union with Reality. When he attains illumination, he is endowed with a supernatural power of discernment. When he attains ecstasy he is united with God. "The whole of Sūfism rests on the belief that when the individual self is lost, the Universal Self is found, or, in religious language, that ecstasy affords the only means by which the soul can directly communicate and become united with God. Asceticism, purification, love, gnosis, saintship—all the leading ideas of Sūfism—are developed from this cardinal principle." The Sūfī obtains, as divine gifts, gnosis (mystic knowledge) and love; and "gnosis and love are spiritually identical: they teach the same truths in different language" (cp. further SUFIISM). Mysticism in India is characterised by Dr. E. Lehmann (*Mysticism in Heathendom and Christendom*, 1910) as a mysticism of *meditation* and of *renunciation*. "The mysticism of the Hindus did not originate in philosophy, any more than their religion from the first was a philosophical religion. The beginning was adoration, worship, and therein the earliest elements of mysticism are to be found." The Hindu mystic for the most part seeks a life of seclusion and meditation. Union with the divine principle, Brahma and Atman, is only to be attained by way of meditation. "Insight is what is needed, and Brahma, thus thought out, is meditation." But in practice ordinary meditation is found to be insufficient. It is therefore improved by art, "the art above all arts to which the Hindu applies himself assiduously, the art of raising himself above the life of this world by rapture, forgetting himself in ecstasy, and producing this ecstasy by penances—the art which in India is known as *Yoga*" (see YOGA). In China, according to Lehmann, the temperament of the people is absolutely opposed to anything of a mystical nature. Nevertheless, Laotze (*b.* 604 B.C.), the founder of Taoism (*q.v.*) and the second in importance of China's great sages, produced here a work in which are found all the properties of true mysticism. "It would seem as if here, in the Far East, the groundwork had been laid for that which in the subsequent peregrinations of mysticism should receive more solid form. The three chords which mysticism always strikes, namely, alienation from the world, the doing away with personality and with self, reverberate here also, and they sound—and this is the remarkable part of it—perfectly Chinese, although constantly clashing with the normal system of Confucian doctrines, with all its practical and personal activity." In addition to the works mentioned above, see J. C. Oman, *Mystics;* L. M. J. Garnett; Isaac Husik.

N

N. God N is a designation used by anthropologists for a deity depicted in the MSS. of the Mayan Indians of Central America. He has the head of an old man, and wears a head-ornament which contains the sign for the year of 360 days. He is described by Schellhas as "The God of the end of the Year."

NAASSENI. A name derived from the Hebrew word *nachash*, "serpent." It is equivalent to the name Ophites (*q.v.*).

NABU. A Babylonian deity. The god Nabu or Nebo is represented as embodying divine wisdom. Jastrow thinks that as the Babylonians associated wisdom with the watery deep, the origin of Nabu was aqueous. He thinks that Nabu and Ea (*q.v.*) were originally related. In any case, Nabu is referred to as the irrigator and fertilizer of fields, and became a patron of agriculture. He was especially the god of Borsippa, but in the days of Hammurapi he had to give place to Marduk (*q.v.*). He reappeared, however, as the son of Marduk, and in some cases received greater prominence than his father. The Assyrian kings paid him great homage, and several of them were named after him (Nabupolassar, Nebuchadrezzar, Nabonnedos). Marduk-baladan II describes himself as "worshipper of Nabu and Marduk." As the herald of the gods he was called Papsukal, the supreme messenger. His symbols were the stylus of the writer and the sceptre of the ruler. His consort would seem to have been originally Erua; afterwards it was Tashmitum (*q.v.*). In the Deluge-story (see DELUGE-STORY, BABYLONIAN) Nabu figures prominently among the gods who are active in storm. Nabu was sometimes identified with Nusku (*q.v.*). He came to be identified also with Mercury. In the procession on New Year's Day Nabu was carried in a magnificent ship. See Morris Jastrow, *Rel.*

NĀG DEO. A deity, really the cobra, worshipped by the Baigas and others. Nāg is an object of special veneration among the Barais (also known as Tambolis or Pansāris), who observe a festival in his honour called Nāg-Panchmi (Cobra's fifth).

NAGUALISTS. Members of a cult formed in Mexico after the conquest. "The Nagualists were supposed to have animal familiars, whose shape they could assume, and to hold regular 'witches' sabbaths.'" (T. A. Joyce, *M.A.*). It was the avowed object of the cult to eliminate Christianity.

NAHUM, BOOK OF. The original sections of the book of Nahum (chaps. i. 1, 11, 14; ii. 1, 3-13; iii. 1-19) are concerned with the approaching fall of Nineveh. This gives us the *terminus ad quem* for the date of the book. Nineveh was not overthrown until 606 B.C. On the other hand, its end had seemed near on several earlier occasions. If Herodotus is to be trusted, Cyaxares, the Mede, besieged it in 625 B.C. In any case, as C. F. Kent points out, in 626 B.C., when the great Assyrian king Ashurbanipal died, the people of Judah no doubt felt convinced that now at length the days of Nineveh were numbered. The *terminus a quo* for the date of the book is supplied by a reference to the capture and sack of Thebes. This took place about 660 B.C., and it seems to have been still vividly remembered at the time Nahum wrote. Nahum's prophecy therefore can hardly be dated later than 626 B.C. An introduction has been prefixed to the book by a later editor (chaps. i. 2-15; ii. 2). It takes the form of an acrostic psalm, which describes the just rule of Jehovah. As far as the original prophecy is concerned, "Nahum voices, in language of surpassing literary beauty and vigour, the universal cry of exultation which burst from the lips of a great family of nations, when at last the news came that Nineveh was falling" (C. F. Kent). See C. Cornill; G. H. Box; O. C. Whitehouse; C. F. Kent, *The Sermons, Epistles and Apocalypses of Israel's Prophets*, 1910.

NAKHIS. Literally "Nail" men. An order of Hindu ascetics, worshippers of Śiva (*q.v.*). They are so called because they allow their nails to grow long and to pierce through their clenched hands. See E. W. Hopkins.

NAKSHIBENDI. A Dervish order. Their service consists of one prayer called the *Iklah*, which is repeated a thousand and one times. "This number of pebbles is distributed among the brethren who are seated in a circle on the floor; and, as each one completes the mental recitation of an *Iklah*, he lays down before him a pebble until the whole number are deposited within the circle" (L. M. J. Garnett).

NAKTI DEVI. An Indian deity, the "Noseless Goddess." In Bilāspur she is the principal deity of the Bhainas. When a man dies, a cock is offered to her; when a woman dies, a hen.

NAMBŪTIRIS. The Nambūtiris or Nambūtiri Brāhmans are described by Thurston and Rangachari as the socio-spiritual aristocracy of Malabar in India. "The characteristic features of the Nambūtiri are his faith in God and resignation to his will, hospitality to strangers, scrupulous veracity, punctiliousness as regards the ordinances prescribed, and extreme gentility in manners. The sustaining power of his belief in divine providence is so great that calamities of whatsoever kind do not exasperate him unduly" (E. Thurston and K. Rangachari). The Nambūtiris devote much of their time to the study of the Vēdas, and are said to be probably more familiar with Sanskrit than any other Brāhmans. They are forbidden to use liquor and flesh. They may keep cows and buffaloes, but not the horse, which is a sacred animal. They are not allowed to swear or take an oath, but may make a solemn asseveration. Bathing is one of their most important religious duties. "All objects, animate or inanimate, organic or inorganic, are believed to be permeated by the divine spirit. Animals, trees, plants, and flowers are animate, and therefore venerated." Horses, snakes, and cows are worshipped, the last being held the most sacred of all animals. See E. Thurston.

NĀMDEO SECT. An Indian sect, founded by Nāmdeo

Sādhu, a Chhīpa or dyer, who is said to have been a contemporary of Kabīr, founder of the sect of Kabīr Panthīs (*q.v.*), and to have flourished in the twelfth or thirteenth century. "He was a great worshipper of the god Vithoba of Pandharpur, and is considered by the Marāthas to be their oldest writer, being the author of many Abhangs, or sacred hymns. He preached the unity of God, recognising apparently Vithoba or Vishnu as the one deity, and the uselessness of ceremonial" (R. V. Russell). To this sect belong many of the Darzis, the occupational caste of tailors.

NAME, CHANGE OF. In the Old and New Testaments we read of persons' names being changed. In Genesis xxxii. 28 it is represented that the name of Jacob was changed to Israel. Jesus gave his disciple Simon the name Peter (Luke vi. 14). The Apostle Paul was originally called Saul (Acts vii. 28). Prof. O. C. Whitehouse suggests (*Isaiah* in the "Century Bible") that the name Isaiah was perhaps not his original name. He may have assumed it in reference to his prophetic mission. It would almost seem that in certain circumstances it was a fairly common practice among the Hebrews to take or receive new names. The practice is found among the Arabs. Burton notes (*Al Madinah and Meccah,* new edition of Bohn, i. p. 14, N. 3) that "when a man appears as a Fakir or Darwaysh, he casts off, in process of regeneration, together with other worldly sloughs, his laical name for some brilliant coat of nomenclature rich in religious promise." In the West Indies, again, when two prominent men were very friendly, they would bind themselves together more closely by exchanging their names. The ceremony served to make the parties friends for all time. The Mehtars, the caste of sweepers and scavengers in India, worship a saint named Vālmīki. He was originally a hunter named Ratnakār. When he was purified and became a saint, Brahma changed his name from Ratnakār to Vālmīki. There are several definite examples of change of name in the Bible. It is possible that the change was made also in other cases—cases in which the Biblical writers have forgotten to mention the fact. In the Old and New Testaments the practice seems to be specially associated with what may be described as cases of a "call" or of conversion. But not exclusively. Naomi, if we may interpret the passage literally, became Marah. One of the kings of Judah is sometimes referred to as Azariah, sometimes as Uzziah. Prof. K. Marti suggests in his Commentary on Isaiah that Uzziah was perhaps the real name borne by Azariah before he ascended the throne. It is possible that David—which is probably an abbreviation of Dodiel, "darling of God"—was not the famous king's original name. David's original name may have been Elhanan, "God is gracious." In I. Samuel xvii. David, the son of Jesse, is said to have slain the Philistine giant Goliath. In II. Samuel xxi. 19 we read: "and Elhanan the son of Jaare-oregim the Bethlehemite slew Goliath the Gittite, the staff of whose spear was like a weaver's beam." In the parallel passage of the Book of Chronicles (I., xx. 5) we read: "and Elhanan the son of Jair slew Lahmi the brother of Goliath the Gittite, etc." In both these passages there are corruptions, and it is likely that the original and correct text was in both cases the same. In the first passage "oregim" ("weavers") has evidently crept in after Jaare from the following line. In the second passage "Lahmi the brother of" is evidently a corruption of "the Bethlehemite." In both passages "Jaare" and "Jair" are probably corruptions of "Jesse." Originally therefore the two texts may have read: "And Elhanan the son of Jesse the Bethlehemite slew Goliath the Gittite." Most modern critics assume that the story of David's killing Goliath is a later tradition, and that the exploit of Elhanan, one of David's warriors, was transferred to his royal master. It is hardly likely, however, that this could have happened. Possibly Elhanan and David were one and the same person. In II. Kings xxiii. 34 we are told that "Pharaoh-necoh made Eliakim the son of Josiah king in the room of Josiah his father, and changed his name to Jehoiakim" (similarly, II. Chronicles xxxvi. 4). In II. Kings xxiv. 17 we are told that the king of Babylon made Mattaniah brother of the father of Jehoiachin king in place of Jehoiachin, and changed his name to Zedekiah. Why should the king of Egypt have changed the name Eliakim "God establishes" to Jehoiakim "Yahweh establishes"? Why should the king of Babylon have changed the name Mattaniah, "gift of Yahweh" to Zedekiah "righteousness of Yahweh"? It is more likely that the two kings had already borne these two names. The Hebrew word for name is often used, in reference to Yahweh, in the sense of character. It may have been a common practice for persons when they changed their character to change their name. There is much to recommend the practice. The Tolstoy of later years, to take a modern example, felt himself to be an entirely different person from the Tolstoy of an earlier period.

NAMTAR. A Babylonian deity. Namtar was a god of pestilence. He appears in the service of Allatu (*q.v.*), the goddess of the nether world. In the story of the descent of Ishtar (*q.v.*) to the nether world, Allatu commands Namtar to smite Ishtar with disease. In the story of the conflict between Nergal and Allatu, Namtar is told by Nergal to announce to Allatu his approach. See Morris Jastrow, *Rel.*

NANÂ. A Babylonian deity. The name Nanâ means "the lady." Nanâ was the principal goddess of the city of Uruk. She was the planet Venus (*q.v.*), the daughter of Sin (*q.v.*), the moon-god. As the descendant of Anu (*q.v.*), she was called also Anunit. Shalmaneser II. calls her the consort of Nabu (*q.v.*). See Morris Jastrow, *Rel.*

NANAI. A nature-goddess of pre-semitic Babylonia, equivalent to the Babylonian Ishtar.

NĀNAKPANTHI SECT. An Indian sect founded by Bāba Nānak of the Lahore District (lived between A.D. 1469 and 1538-39), whose teaching paved the way for the development of Sikhism (*q.v.*). Nānak was a religious reformer who wished to abolish idolatry and superstition and to inculcate the worship of one invisible deity. "The burden of his teaching was that there is no Hindu and no Muhammadan. He believed in transmigration, but held that the successive stages were but purifications, and that at last the soul, cleansed from sin, went to dwell with its maker. He prescribed no caste rules or ceremonial observances, and indeed condemned them as unnecessary and even harmful; but he made no violent attack on them, he insisted on no alteration in existing civil and social institutions, and was content to leave the doctrine of the equality of all men in the sight of God to work in the minds of his followers. He respected the Hindu veneration of the cow and the Muhammadan abhorrence of the hog, but recommended as a higher rule than either total abstinence from flesh. Nothing could have been gentler or less aggressive than his doctrine, nothing more unlike the teaching of his great successor Govind" (R. V. Russell and R. B. Hīra Lāl). In 1901 the persons in the Central Provinces of India who returned themselves as Nānakpanthis numbered 13,000. See R. V. Russell and R. B. Hīra Lāl, *The Tribes and Castes of the Central Provinces of India,* 1916.

NANAKSHAHI. A mendicant order in India, a branch of the Nānakpanthis (*q.v.*). They are known also as Suthra Shāhis (*q.v.*).

NANDKISHORE. Nandkishore and Nandkumār, child of Nand (Krishna's foster-father), are names of the Hindu god Krishna.

NANGA. *Nanga* or *Mbaki* was a secret society among the western tribes of Viti Levu, the largest of the Fiji Islands. By initiation into the *nanga*, the youth of the tribe, it was supposed, were brought into relations with the ancestral spirits. "The sanctuary and lodge of the association formed the earthly dwelling-place of the spirits; it was a tabernacle as holy to these Fijians as was the structure in the Wilderness to the Israelites; there the first-fruits of the yam harvest were solemnly presented to the ancestors; and there the young men of Viti Levu were introduced to the mysteries of the tribe. When the *manga* enclosure was being raised for the initiatory performances, the people suspended all other work" (Hutton Webster, *R.D.*).

NANNAR. A Babylonian deity. Nannar was a name for the moon-god, who was worshipped at Ur. Nannar was called the "heifer of Anu," that is to say, the offspring of Anu (*q.v.*). He was also called the "lord of the crown." In the Epic of Marduk (see MARDUK, EPIC OF) it is said that Marduk made Nannar and gave him control of the night. Another name for the moon-god was Sin (*q.v.*).

NANTOSVELTA. A goddess in the mythology of the British Celts. She is connected in some way with the sun-god Sulis.

NĀRĀYANA. Nārāyana or Nārāyan is one of the names or forms under which the great Hindu god Vishnu (*q.v.*) was worshipped. In the Law-book of Manu (i. 10) Nārāyana is a name for the Universal Spirit, which was so called because it was thought of as moving on the waters. Monier-Williams points out that in harmony with this idea "Vishnu is often represented in sculptures, images, and pictures as Nārāyana in human form, reposing on the thousand-headed serpent and floating on the ocean." See Monier-Williams; E. W. Hopkins.

NARSINGHA. The man-lion, one of the incarnations of the great Hindu god Vishnu.

NASTRAND. In the religion of the Ancient Teutons, Nastrand (and not Hel [*q.v.*]) appears as a place of punishment in which sin is expiated. The doors of the Hall which stood on Nastrand faced northward; the Hall was "entwined with the backs of serpents." No sunlight penetrated its darkness; through the roof dripped venom. See P. D. Chantepie de la Saussage, *Rel. of the Teutons*, 1902.

NAT BĀBA. A Hindu deity, a village god worshipped by the Nats. He is a deified Nat. The term Nat (literally a dancer), according to R. V. Russell and R. B. Hira Lāl, seems to be applied indefinitely to a number of groups of vagrant acrobats and showmen in India.

NATIONAL PROTESTANT LEAGUE. A league in connection with the Church Association (*q.v.*). Its objects are: to maintain unimpaired "the Protestant Reformed Religion, established by law," and to defend it against all encroachments of Popery: to spread sound Protestant truth in the Church of England; to unite in prayer for the increase of spiritual religion; to co-operate with the Church Association in upholding Reformation principles; to educate the young in evangelical truth; to disseminate sound and wholesome literature; to secure the return of Protestant candidates at Parliamentary elections.

NATIONAL SOCIETY FOR THE EDUCATION OF THE POOR IN THE PRINCIPLES OF THE ESTABLISHED CHURCH. A Society founded in 1811. The Superintendent was Andrew Bell (1753-1832), founder of the Madras System of Education, which was similar to the Lancasterian System of Education (*q.v.*).

NATIONALSOZIALER VEREIN. A political association in Germany founded by Friedrich Naumann (*b.* 1860). It seeks, by working along national and Christian-socialist lines, to improve the condition of the working classes.

NATURAL THEOLOGY. As distinguished from Revealed Theology or Positive Theology, Natural Theology denotes the evidence of God's existence and character derived from a study of Nature. From the standpoint of the sceptic, the subject is discussed in the "Dialogues on Natural Religion" (1779) by David Hume (1711-1776); from the standpoint of an orthodox theologian of the old school in the "Natural Theology" (1802) of William Paley (1743-1805), Archdeacon of Carlisle. Natural Theology, as distinguished from Revelation (*q.v.*), seeks to find evidence of the existence and goodness of God in Nature. It has been claimed that Natural Theology is the only true theology, and that its revelation of God is complete and sufficient; but it has been objected that it leaves important questions unanswered. To say the least, it requires to be supplemented by Revelation. We may go further and say that the highest revelation of God is not physical in any sense but metaphysical. It is intuitional knowledge that comes by inspiration. A lifelong study of Nature may fail to reveal the goodness of God, whereas a sudden intuition may make it known in such a way that it will never again be doubted. Natural Theology works too much on the assumption that things are as they appear to be. See Schaff-Herzog.

NAUALA. A term used among the Kwakiutl of N. America to denote a mystic potentiality ascribed to beings whether human or non-human, living or not living. *Nauala* seems to be a force, and not a personal being, and corresponds to the Melanesian *mana*.

NAZARAEANS. Nazaræans (also written Nasaræans and Nassaræans) is the name of a Jewish sect referred to by Epiphanius (*Hær.* xviii.). J. H. Blunt suggests that they are to be identified with the Genistæ. The Genistæ (*q.v.*) are said to have claimed that they were the stock of Abraham; and the Hebrew word *netsir*, from which Nazaraeans may be supposed to be derived, means "branch." The Nazaraeans would have a patriarchal religion. Consequently they did special reverence to the patriarchs (including Moses and Joshua). They practised circumcision, were vegetarians, and refused to sacrifice animals. See J. H. Blunt.

NAZARENES. In the Gospels Jesus is represented as a Nazarene, that is to say, as one who belonged to Nazara or Nazareth in Galilee. In the Acts of the Apostles (xxiv. 5) the name appears as one used by opponents of the followers of Jesus. In the fourth century Epiphanius and Jerome give the name Nazarenes to a body of Jewish Christians. The Nazarenes were Christians who continued to observe the law of Moses. To what extent, if any, they were identical with a section of the Ebionites (*q.v.*) is a disputed point. Augustine says they were called Symmachians sometimes. This name may have been derived from that of Symmachus, one of the translators of the Old Testament into Greek, an Ebionite who flourished towards the end of the second century. See K. R. Hagenbach; J. H. Blunt; Louis Duchesne, *Hist.*

NAZARENES. A name by which the Mandæans (*q.v.*) refer to themselves. In this case the word would seem to be derived from *nazir*, "separated, or pure."

NĀZIR. The name of one of the Jewish treatises or tractates which reproduce the oral tradition or unwritten law as developed by the second century A.D., and are incorporated in the Mishnah (*q.v.*), a collection and compilation completed by Rabbi Judah the Holy, or the Patriarch, about 200 A.D. The sixty-three tractates of the Mishnah are divided into six groups or orders (*sedarim*). Nāzīr is the fourth tractate of the third group, which is called *Nāshīm* (" Women ").

NEBIIN. The Hebrew name (" Prophets ") of the second of the three groups into which the books of the Old Testament are divided. See PROPHETS, THE.

NECESSARIANISM or NECESSITARIANISM. Another name for Determinism (*q.v.*).

NEDĀRIM. The title of one of the Jewish treatises or tractates which reproduce the oral tradition or unwritten law as developed by the second century A.D. and are incorporated in the Mishnah (*q.v.*), a collection and compilation completed by Rabbi Judah the Holy, or the Patriarch, about 200 A.D. The sixty-three tractates of the Mishnah are divided into six groups or orders (*sedarim*). Nedārīm is the third tractate of the third group, which is called *Nāshīm* (" Women ").

NEGĀ'IM. The name of one of the Jewish treatises or tractates which reproduced the oral tradition or unwritten law as developed by the second century A.D. and are incorporated in the Mishnah (*q.v.*), a collection and compilation completed by Rabbi Judah the Holy, or the Patriarch, about 200 A.D. The sixty-three tractates of the Mishnah are divided into six groups or orders (*sedarim*). Negā'im is the third tractate of the sixth group, which is called *Ṭohorōth* (" Purifications ").

NEHALENNIA. One of the deities of the Ancient Teutons. Nehalennia seems to have been a goddess of fertility and navigation. She is known from inscriptions found on the island of Walcheren. " Her attributes are a dog, a basket with fruit, and the prow of a ship; at times she is represented as accompanied by Hercules and Neptune " (Chantepie de la Saussaye). The goddess herself is depicted on some of her monuments. See P. D. Chantepie de la Saussaye, *Rel. of the Teutons*, 1902; Reinach, *O*.

NEHEMIAH, BOOK OF. The Book of Nehemiah, though it now appears in Hebrew Bibles as a separate work, originally in the Jewish Canon formed one work with the Book of Ezra. In the Septuagint the two books still appear as one (Second Esdras). See EZRA-NEHEMIAH.

NEIT. An ancient Irish deity. Neit, Ned, or Nudd was the god of war. He is supposed to have had three wives, Neman, Morrigan, and Macha. These took charge of various departments of battle and carnage. Neit seems to have been equivalent to the god who was worshipped as Mars by the natives of Gaul.

NEMAN. An ancient Irish deity. Sister of Bav, and wife of Neit, the god of battle, she had charge of one of the departments of battle and carnage, afflicting her victims with madness.

NEMETONA. Nemetona is the name of one of the goddesses worshipped by the ancient Celts. She is paired with Mars, but it is not known what relationship was intended. From an inscription found at Bath it appears that she was worshipped in Britain. She has been compared or identified with another British goddess Nemon, " venomous." C. Squire suggests again that Nemon is probably the same as Mórrigu, who, as a goddess of war is associated with the British god of war Llûdd (*q.v.*). See Anwyl; Squire, *Myth.*; cp. Reinach, *O.*, 1909.

NEMOLIAKI. A sub-sect of the Russian dissenters known as Bezpopovtzi. It was founded by Cossak Zimin. The fundamentals of religion were to him and his followers spiritual prayer and a pure life based upon the study of the New Testament. Cossak Zimin believed that a new age started in 1666 A.D., the age of the Holy Ghost. In this age no external rites are needed. See Schaff-Herzog.

NEMON. A goddess of war worshipped in ancient Britain. She has been compared or identified with Nemetona (*q.v.*).

NEONOMIANS. A name given by the followers of Tobias Crisp, the Crispians (*q.v.*), to their opponents. Blunt quotes the following definition by one of their writers. " One that asserts the Old Law is abolished, and therein is a superlative Antinomian, but pleads for a New Law, and justification by the works of it, and therefore is a Neonomian."

NEO-PLATONISM. In Neo-Platonism ancient Greek philosophy took a religious and mystical turn. It was eclectic in the sense that with the ideas of Plato and Pythagoras were combined Oriental ideas and doctrines. Founded by Ammonius Sakkas of Alexandria (175-200 A.D.), the philosophy was developed and systematized by Plotinus of Lycopolis in Egypt. " All existence is referred, not to two principles, but only to one. God, or the primal Essence, is the simple unity that lies above all multiplicity. As such, God is without thought, because thinking requires plurality; and without will, because willing pre-supposes duality. God is the absolutely transcendent One, exalted above everything, above consciousness and unconsciousness, above rest and motion, above life and being. Hence God is entirely unattainable in our knowledge. Thinking must here abandon itself and become Not-thinking, if it is to apprehend God in blessed vision, and unite itself with Him. But at the same time God is the original source and ground of all things; finite things arise out of Him by emanation of what is absolutely simple unfolding itself into an ever-advancing series of finite things, that are always the more imperfect the farther they are removed from God. In all things, therefore, there is only one divine power and essence, but in different degrees of perfection, so that every higher existence embraces the lower with itself. Finite things long for a return to their origin, and this is especially true of the human soul, which, banished into this earthly life as a punishment for former sin, strives to soar aloft to its higher home. . . The highest goal is immediate intuition of the primal divine Being. This is the true philosophy, the perfection of the spirit, and likewise the highest happiness. By such intuition the soul becomes completely one with the primal Being, and sinks in ecstacy into deity " (Puenjer). Porphyry of Phoenicia (233-304), the disciple and biographer of Plotinus, further developed Neo-Platonism on its religious side. He even accused the Christians of stealing and adulterating the teaching of his master. Iamblichus of Coele-syria († 333), a disciple of Porphyry, is largely responsible for the degeneration of Neo-Platonism. He distinguished between gods, angels, and demons, and taught a system of theurgy and magic. The downward tendency was even more marked in the theosophical teaching of Proclus (412-485), who erected what has been described as " a veritable pantheon of pagan dogmas and philosophies." Synesius of Cyrene († *c.* 430), a disciple of the Neoplatonist Hypatia of Alexandria, afterwards became a Christian and was made Bishop of Ptolemais, but he did not entirely abandon his Neo-Platonism. It is possible that Boethius also, one of the last of the Neoplatonists, was a Christian. See Schaff-Herzog; J. H. Blunt; B. Puenjer; C. J. Deter.

NEO-PYTHAGOREANISM. Neo-Pythagoreanism bears much the same relation to Pythagoreanism that Neo-Platonism does to Platonism. Apollonius of Tyana in Cappadocia, who lived in the first century A.D., is regarded as its chief representative. He is said to have travelled to India, and to have learned there the secrets of the Brahmans. A strict ascetic and a worker of marvels, he made so great an impression on the people that he was worshipped as a god. The Emperor Alexander Severus gave him a place of honour in his private chapel by the side of Orpheus and Jesus. See Hastings' *E.R.E.*, s.v. "Apollonius of Tyana": Max B. Weinstein, *Welt- und Leben-anschauungen*, 1910.

NEPHTHYS. An Egyptian deity. Nephthys is the sister of Isis (*q.v.*). The name in Egyptian is Neb-hat, and means "Lady of the House." Nephthys is little more than one of the actors in the Osiris myth. When Set (*q.v.*) succeeded in killing Osiris, Isis his wife sought for the body without rest until she found it. Then she and her sister Nephthys sat down by it and made lamentation. Erman speaks of the lament as one "which has become the model of all funerary lamentations." The gods of Heliopolis formed an Ennead or company of nine. In the oldest list in the Pyramid Texts, and in the ritual of Abydos Nephthys appears as one of the Nine. See Alfred Wiedemann: Adolf Erman, *Handbook;* Edouard Naville, *The Old Egyptian Faith*, 1909.

NERGAL. A Babylonian deity. The god Nergal is one of the gods mentioned prior to the days of Hammurapi. He was the god of Cuthah, and his association with this city is referred to in the Old Testament (II. Kings xvii. 30). Nergal was the god of war and pestilence, and of the former more particularly in its violent, destructive, aspect. He was "king of the nether world." Sometimes he is described as the "god of fire," a description which seems to connect him with the sun in its destructive, burning, character. As ruler of the nether world, Nergal is chief of its monstrous, half-human demons. In the Gilgamesh Epic (*q.v.*) it is he who opens the earth and brings up the spirit of Eabani. With Nergal was identified another, originally distinct, god of plague and war Gir-ra. The name Gir-ra was at first read as Dibbarra (see DIBBARRA EPIC). A legend has survived among the Amarna tablets which makes Nergal the hero of a battle rather similar to that between Marduk and Tiâmat (see MARDUK, EPIC OF). A goddess Allatu of the lower world enters into conflict with the gods on high. Nergal is chosen to represent the gods. He has fourteen companions of the nature of demons. He sends the plague-demon Namtar to announce his arrival to Allatu. She is obliged to admit him. He drags her from her throne with the idea of killing her, but when she bursts into tears and offers to become his wife and to place "the tablets of wisdom" in his hands, he spares her. Nergal is sometimes associated with Ninib (*q.v.*) as a god of the chase. His symbol was a lion. Naturally he was identified with Mars. See Morris Jastrow, *Rel.*

NERTHUS. One of the deities of the Ancient Teutons. The goddess Nerthus was worshipped by the Ingævonic tribes, and mention is made by Tacitus of her temple and grove. He identifies her with Mother Earth. In her grove, we are told (*Germania*, xl.), is a consecrated chariot, which the priest alone is allowed to touch. On festivals this chariot, accompanied by the priest, is drawn about by cows. After such a procession, "the chariot, with its cover, and, if it appear credible, the deity herself, thereupon undergo ablution in a secluded lake. This service is performed by slaves, whom this very lake instantly swallows up." The festival of Nerthus was celebrated on an island; this seems to have been Seeland. A similar festival was held in Sweden in honour of the god Freyr (*q.v.*). The chariot of the god, however, was accompanied by a priestess. How exactly the goddess Nerthus was represented, whether by an image or by a symbol, is not certain. It is possible that there was nothing but an empty seat in the chariot or car. It should be added that the car had a cover. See P. D. Chantepie de la Saussaye, *Rel. of the Teutons*, 1902; Reinach, *O.*

NESTORIANS. The followers of Nestorius (*fl.* 431 A.D.), patriarch of Constantinople, who in turn was an adherent of Theodore of Mopsuestia. The tendency of Nestorianism was to fix attention on the human element in Jesus Christ. Objecting to the designation of the Virgin Mary as *theotokos*, "who gives birth to God," Nestorius followed Theodore of Mopsuestia in contending that "she only gave birth to a man in whom the union with the Logos had its beginning, but was incomplete until His baptism." Jesus Christ was not God but "God-bearer" (*theophoros*). Nestorius was condemned in his absence by the synod of Ephesus (431 A.D.), but Nestorianism was not checked in its career. "An energetic Nestorian Church, in its missionary zeal, carried the condemned tenets first to Edessa, and then, on the suppression of that school in 489, to the ends of the earth. Persia, India, China—as the tablets of Si-ngan-fu (636-781) bear evidence—alike witnessed their activity. From the eleventh century until almost blotted out by Tamerlane, the Nestorian Church was the largest Christian body in the world, whose patriarch at Bagdad was acknowledged by twenty-five metropolitans. On the conquest of Persia and the East by the Muslim, Nestorianism was thrown into an alliance, by no means unfriendly, with the new faith. To this we trace the rise in Mohammedan Spain in medieval times of a new form of this Nestorian doctrine to which the title of Adoptionism is more strictly applied" (H. B. Workman). Nestorian missions had great success in China. In fact, the activity of the missionaries covered a whole continent, and, according to Marco Polo (*c.* 1274 A.D.), the Nestorians had an unbroken series of see-towns along the trade-routes from Bagdad to Pekin. "The present patriarch of this dwindled sect lives in the Kurd Mountains near Lake Urumiyah, with a flock of 70,000 souls, the *Assyrian Christians*, sole remnants of a once mighty organization" (F. W. Bussell).

NETHINIM, THE. The Nethinim are a religious order referred to in the Old Testament. They are mentioned in Ezra-Nehemiah (*q.v.*) in the lists of those who returned from exile with Ezra. Another name for them, or for a section of them, was the "children of Solomon's servants" (Ezra ii. 55 = Nehemiah vii. 57). Five classes of Temple ministers are distinguished—priests, Levites, singers, porters, and Nethinim. As compared with the Levites, the Nethinim were clearly a subordinate class of Temple-servants. But with the priests and Levites they shared immunity from taxation (Ezra vii. 24); and, though they do not appear among the signatories to the covenant, it is clear that they "were really regarded as forming part of the privileged *personnel* attached to the temple-worship" (I. Benzinger). In Joshua ix. 27 (JE) it is said that Joshua made the Gibeonites "hewers of wood and drawers of water for the congregation, and for the altar of the Lord." This has suggested the identification of the Nethinim, who were regarded as foreigners, with the Gibeonites. E. L. Curtis and A. A. Madsen (*Chronicles*, 1910) think that probably the Nethinim "were of Canaanitish origin—most likely to be connected with the Gibeonites (Joshua ix. 23) and the foreigners mentioned in Ezekiel xliv. 7." Benzinger, on the other hand, regards this view as quite unhistorical. The post-exilic Nethinim were regarded as descendants of slaves who had been give "by David and his princes" to the Levites as their servants (Ezra viii. 20). This is on the whole an acceptable view of their origin. They would seem to have been foreign captives taken in war who were made temple-slaves. In course of time they became free men, and eventually perhaps even Levites. In any case, as time went on, "the distinction of rank between the Levites and the inferior grades of temple servants diminished more and more" (I. Benzinger). See I. Benzinger in the *Encycl. Bibl.*

NEW AND LATTER HOUSE OF ISRAEL, THE. A sect founded in 1875 by James White (1840-1885) and others. In 1876 White assumed the name James Jershom Jezreel. He professed to be the messenger of God and to have received divine revelations. In course of time he established the headquarters of his sect at Gillingham, near Chatham, in Kent, England. The members gave all their property to a common fund. They "allowed their hair to grow long, tucked it up at the back, and wore purple velvet caps" (*D.N.B.*). The death of Jezreel caused a division in the sect, and in course of time the members began to fall away. See the *D.N.B.*

NEW-BORN, THE. A religious sect in America in the eighteenth century. It was founded by Matthias Bowman (*d.* 1727), a German, who settled in Pennsylvania in 1719. The New Born believed in regeneration by inspiration and visions. They also held that by communion with God men could be deified and made incapable of sinning. See J. H. Blunt.

NEW HAMPSHIRE CONFESSION, THE. A Calvinistic Baptist Confession of Faith drawn up in 1833 A.D. by J. Newton Brown of New Hampshire. A confession in eighteen articles, it was adopted by the New Hampshire Convention, and has been accepted generally by American Baptists. "The language is often felicitous in its attempt to express the essence of Calvinism in terms which shall not repel" (W. A. Curtis).

NEW HOUSE OF ISRAEL, THE. Another name for the Southcottians (*q.v.*), the followers of Joanna Southcott (1750-1814).

NEW IDEALISM, THE. The religious philosophy known as "The New Idealism" is associated with the name of Rudolf Eucken, Professor of Philosophy in Jena. His philosophy has also been described as a "Religious" or "Spiritual" Idealism. Its central theme "is 'The Struggle for Spiritual Existence', and its central persuasion is this, that nothing short of an Independent Spiritual Life in intimate communion with our own can give to the struggle a meaning and a value. The conceptions of 'immanence' and 'independence' are not easy to define, but it should be noted that, from Eucken's standpoint, the immanence of the Spiritual Life within us implies at once its transcendence over us and its independence of us. By the very intimacy of its indwelling, the Spiritual Life awakens our reverence for its own distinctive standards, values, and obligations; and at the same time convinces us that its authority, which is spiritual only in relation to our freedom, is yet not of our own making, and exists in its own right." The New Idealism "is *mystical* in the stress is lays on the reality and immediacy of the Spiritual Life, and on the intimacy of personal union between the human and the divine: it is *activistic* in its insistence that all spiritual communion is a challenge to our moral nature, and can be mantained as an inspiration only through the earnestness with which we adopt its values as authoritative over our action; it is profoundly *humanistic* in the breadth and depth of its historical insight, and in its close identification of the welfare of our race with the dominance of these spiritual values" (L. J. Gibson and W. R. Boyce Gibson in "Preface" to *The Meaning and Value of Life*, 1909). See W. R. Boyce Gibson, *Rudolf Eucken's Philosophy of Life* (2), 1907; Rudolf Eucken, *The Meaning and Value of Life*, 1909; *Christianity and the New Idealism*, 1909; *The Life of the Spirit* (2), 1909.

NEW ISLAM. A Muhammadan sect founded in North India in recent years by Sir Sayed Ahmed Khan of Aligarh. According to E. M. Wherry, it represents really a restoration of the rationalism of the old Mutazillas. "Its followers are progressive, and number among them many of the most learned and intelligent Moslems of North India. The interesting feature of the movement is the readiness to give reason a place in the discussion of religious questions." By orthodox Muhammedans it is regarded as heretical. See E. M. Wherry.

NEW ITINERANCY, THE. An early name for the New Connexion Methodists or the Kilhamites (*q.v.*).

NEW JERUSALEM CHURCH. The disciples of Emanuel Swedenborg (1688-1772) first formed a society, "The Theosophical Society," for the purpose of "promoting the heavenly doctrines of the New Jerusalem, by translating, printing, and publishing the theological writings of the Honourable Emanuel Swedenborg." In 1788 the name "The New Church" was substituted, and an "Order of worship for the New Church signified by the New Jerusalem in the Revelation" was agreed upon. See SWEDENBORGIANS.

NEW MORAL WORLD. See OWENITES.

NEW PELAGIANS. A religious sect which appeared after the Reformation. They were found mostly in Holland. As the name New Pelagians or Pelagiani Novi implies, some of their views were those of Pelagianism (*q.v.*).

NEW THEOLOGY, THE. In January 1907 the preaching of the Rev. R. J. Campbell, who was then Minister of the City Temple, London, attracted considerable attention. His sermons were quoted in the religious and secular Press, and a controversy was soon raging under the newspaper heading "The New Theology." Mr. Campbell, feeling, with a number of his friends, that "recent criticisms of what has come to be called the New Theology ought to be dealt with in some comprehensive and systematic way," wrote a book to explain his teaching. This book was published in 1907 with the title *The New Theology*. The title could hardly be avoided. "My only reason for calling this book by that title," said Mr. Campbell, "is that a considerable section of the public at present persists in regarding me as in a special way the exponent of it [the New Theology]; indeed, from the correspondence which has been proceeding in the Press, it is evident that many people credit me with having invented both the name and the thing." The name was not really new. "The New Theology is only new in the sense that it seeks to substitute simplicity for complexity, and to get down to moral values in its use of religious terms. Our objection is not so much to the venerable creeds of Christendom as to the ordinary interpretations of those creeds." It is further explained as follows. "The New Theology is an untrammelled return to the Christian sources in the light of modern thought. Its starting-point is a re-emphasis of the Christian belief in the Divine immanence in the universe and in mankind. This doctrine requires to be placed effectively in the foreground of Christian preaching. In the immediate past, the doctrine of the Divine transcendence—that is, the obvious truth that the infinite being of God must transcend the finite universe—has been presented in such a way as to amount to a practical dualism, and to lead men to think of God as above and apart from His world instead of expressing Himself through His world. I repeat that this dualism is practical, not theoretical; but that it exists is plain enough from such statements as that of the present-day theologian who speaks of God's 'eternal eminence, and His descent on a created world.' This kind of theologizing leads straight to the conclusion that God is, to all intents and purposes, quite distinct from His creation, although He possesses a full and accurate knowledge of all that goes on in it and reserves to Himself the right to interfere. In what sense language like this leaves room for the Divine immanence it is difficult to see. The New Theology holds that we know nothing, and can know nothing, of the Infinite Cause whence all things proceed, except as we read Him in His universe and in our own souls. It is the immanent God with whom we have to do, and if this obvious fact is once firmly grasped, it will simplify all our religious conceptions and give us a working faith." The movement, it was claimed, was also related to Socialism. "The great social movement which is now taking place in every country of the civilized world towards universal peace and brotherhood, and a better and fairer distribution of wealth, is really the same movement as that which, in the more distinctively religious sphere, is coming to be called the New Theology. This fact needs to be realized and brought out. The New Theology is the gospel of the kingdom of God. Neither Socialism nor any other economic system will permanently save and lift mankind without definitely recognized spiritual sanctions—that is, it must be a religion. The New Theology is but the religious articulation of the social movement. The word 'theology' is almost a misnomer; it is essentially a moral and spiritual movement, the recognition that we are at the beginning of a great religious and ethical awakening, the ultimate results of which no man can completely foresee." Finally, the New Theology claimed to be the religion of science. "Science is supplying the facts which the New Theology is weaving into the texture of religious experience." The New Theology made considerable progress, and gave birth to a large organization which was called at first (June 1908) the "League of Progressive Thought and Social Service," or, more popularly, the "Progressive League," and afterwards the "League of Liberal Christian Thought and Social Service" (*q.v.*). The organ of the movement was "The Christian Commonwealth" (*q.v.*). It should be added that Mr. Campbell modified his views in course of time, and became a clergyman in the Church of England. See R. J. Campbell, *The New Theology*, New Popular Edition.

NEW THOUGHT, THE. The kind of idealistic and mystical philosophy which is sometimes called the "New Thought" is perhaps more fittingly designated the "Higher Thought" (*q.v.*).

NEWTON HALL. Newton Hall was so named after Sir Isaac Newton, who purchased the site for the Royal Society in 1710. For more than twenty years it has been used by the Positivists (see POSITIVISM) as a kind of Academy, a free School and Institute for the people. Free lectures have been given there on Positivist philosophy, science, morality, and religion. "The greater names in the Positivist Calendar of 558 Worthies of all ages and nations have been commemorated on special centenaries, those of musicians by appropriate musical pieces" (Frederic Harrison). In connection with Newton Hall pilgrimages, social parties, guilds, and libraries have been organized. "There is, on Positive principles, no road to stable religious convictions except by the way of knowledge of real things; and there is no royal road to real knowledge other than the teaching of competent instructors and the systematic study of science in the widest sense" (first Report, 1881). See Frederic Harrison in *Great Religions of the World*, 1902.

NGAI. A name given by the Masai to a power which is supernatural, supernormal, or awe-inspiring. By some writers it is pronounced *en-gai*. Hollis thinks that in *en-gai* "we have primitive and undeveloped religious sentiment where the personality of the deity is hardly separated from striking natural phenomena" (*The Masai*, p. xix.).

NICENE CREED. One of the three creeds in common use in the Christian Church. The Nicene Creed (which in its present form is more correctly described as the Nicæno-Constantinopolitan Creed) is so called because the greater part was framed at the Council of Nicaea held in A.D. 325. It ended originally with the clause "and I believe in the Holy Ghost." The final clauses appear in a work written by Epiphanius, Bishop of Salamis, in 374 A.D., and the creed in its present form, with the exception of the last three words of the clause, "Who proceedeth from the Father and the Son," was recognized by the Councils of Constantinople (A.D. 381) and Chalcedon (A.D. 451). The last three words of the clause quoted were inserted at a Council held at Toledo in A.D. 589, and the creed in its present form does not seem to have come into general use before the middle of the sixth century.

NICHIREN SECT. A Japanese Buddhist sect founded by Nichiren A.D. 1253. It was formed in opposition to the Shingon and Jôdo sects, and is of an aggressive and fanatical character. The founder wished to give the historic Buddha Gautama his rightful place, as compared with Amida, faith in whom is regarded as a heresy. But Hackmann points out that the historic Buddha is everywhere regarded in a mystical light. "The true Buddha is a greatness permeating all being, the great illumination which we must find in ourselves. Prayer, recitation of the sacred writings (or even of the sacred formula, "Namu myô hô renge kyô," which means "Praised be the book of the lotos of the good law!"), and a number of pious deeds, lead to the right communion with the Buddha of the true illumination." See H. Hackmann.

NIDDĀ. The title of one of the Jewish treatises or tractates which reproduce the oral tradition or unwritten law as developed by the second century A.D., and are incorporated in the Mishnah (*q.v.*), a collection and compilation completed by Rabbi Judah the Holy, or the Patriarch, about 200 A.D. The sixty-three tractates of the Mishnah are divided into six groups or orders (*sedarim*). Nidda is the seventh tractate of the sixth group, which is called *Ṭohorōth* ("Purifications").

NIFLHEIM. In the cosmogony of the Ancient Teutons, Niflheim was one of the nine worlds. It was located in the North.

NIHANGS. A fanatical order of Sikh ascetics. Another name for the Akālis (*q.v.*).

NIKUR. A Scandinavian water-spirit. In the Middle Ages he was identified with St. Nicholas, who became the patron of sailors.

NILKANTH. The blue-jay sacred to Siva, one of the names of the Hindu god Siva.

NIMĀNANDIS. The followers of the Hindu religious teacher, Nimbārka or Nimbāditya, who seems to have flourished about the twelfth century. They worship the goddess Rādhā in conjunction with Krishṇa. The religious philosophy of Nimbārka was called dualistic non-dualism. "He held that every man's spirit was capable of being absorbed into God's Spirit, and that such an end was to be aimed at" (Monier-Williams). Nimbārka is held to be an incarnation of the Sun-god. See Monier-Williams; E. W. Hopkins.

NIMĀVATS. A name by which the followers of Nimbārka or Nimbāditya, the Hindu religious teacher, are known. They are called also Nimānandis (*q.v.*).

NIMBADITYA SECT. Another name for the Indian sect, the Nimānandis (*q.v.*).

NIMBUS, THE. The nimbus or halo of light was at first an emblem of power. Thus it was used by the Byzantines to adorn the figure of Satan. It was used also to glorify the figures of men such as King Herod,

Trajan, Justinian, and Charlemagne. Its use to adorn the heads of gods and saints is found in Greek, Roman, Buddhist, Hindu, and Chinese mythology, as well as in the Christian religion. It does not appear in Christian art before the sixth century. Its use in pagan mythology suggests to Sidney Heath that it was a Christianised form of the solar disc. Its early forms were circular. Until about the fifteenth century it was placed, like a flat plate, on the back of the head. In the sixteenth and seventeenth centuries it takes the form of a circlet or ring hovering over the head. In the eleventh century the triangular form, and, in the case of living persons, the square form came into use. In the figure of Christ, the cruciform nimbus is common. See Sidney Heath and Francis Bond.

NINE HEADS OF AGREEMENT. A Confession of Faith defining points of agreement between Congregationalists and Presbyterians in London and district. They were published in 1691 A.D. "They are more Congregationalist than Presbyterian, anything like a Presbyterian system of courts being an impossibility at the time" (W. A. Curtis). And they exerted more influence in America than in England. See William A. Curtis.

NIN-GIRSU. A Babylonian deity. Nin-gir-su is one of the gods mentioned prior to the days of Hammurapi. He is sometimes identified with Ninib (*q.v.*). Nin-gir-su was "Lord of Girsu," a district of Lagash, and is described as the warrior of Bel (*q.v.*). He appears also as a god of agriculture. The ship in which he was carried in procession is called the "beloved ship." The consort of Nin-gir-su was Bau (*q.v.*). See Morris Jastrow, *Rel.*

NINGMAPA SECT. A sect in Lamaism, which has preserved many of the features of the ancient Bon religion of Tibet. The adherents pay special reverence to Padma Sambhava, the founder of Lamaism. The headgear and upper garments of these monks are red. See H. Hackmann.

NINIB. A Babylonian deity. The god Nin-ib was a god of war, invincible in battle. His temple was in Calah. He is also, like Nergal (*q.v.*), a god of the chase. Originally he seems to have been a solar deity, a personification of the sun. He was early identified with the solar deity Nin-girsu (*q.v.*). He is described as the offspring of Ekur, the earth, and as "the one who pursues his path over the wide world." Sargon celebrates him as "Nin-ib, who lays the foundations of the city." In the Deluge-story (see DELUGE-STORY, BABYLONIAN) he plays an active part in producing the storm. And it is he who tells Bel (*q.v.*) that Ea (*q.v.*) has allowed some of mankind to escape. His consort was Gula (*q.v.*). He was identified with Saturn (*q.v.*). It has been pointed out that the morning sun came to be represented by Ninib, the sun of the early spring by Marduk (*q.v.*), and the mid-day sun by Nergal. See Morris Jastrow.

NINIGI-NO-MIKOTO. A figure in Japanese mythology, grandson of Ama-Terasu, the Japanese sun-goddess.

NINKHARSAGGA. A goddess in the Sumerian pantheon, who assisted the gods Anu, Enlil, and Enki in the work of creation. Her principal seat was probably the city of Adab (Mod. *Bismâya*). The "Lady of the Mountains," she is described also as The Builder of that which has Breath, The Carpenter of Mankind, The Carpenter of the Heart, The Coppersmith of the Gods, The Coppersmith of the Land, and The Lady Potter. See L. W. King, *Legends of Babylon and Egypt in relation to Hebrew Tradition*, 1918.

NIRANKARIS. An Indian order of ascetics in the Punjab, related to the Udāsis. They worship Nirankal, the deity without shape or form, the supreme god of Nānak (founder of the Nānak-panthī Sect).

NIRGRANTHAS. Nirgranthas is another name for the Jains (*q.v.*). Possibly it is an earlier name.

NIRVĀNA. The term Nirvāna denotes literally "the state of a blown-out flame." Hopkins, however, points out that it has acquired three distinct meanings. To the Jains (see JAINISM) and to some of the Buddhists it means eternal blissful repose. To other Buddhists it has meant extinction and complete annihilation. To Buddha himself it meant the extinction of lust, anger, and ignorance. Gautama did not invent the term or the doctrine. The term occurs in the Mahā-bhārata. The idea, or one of the ideas associated with Nirvāna, is well expressed in a passage in the Bhagavad-gītā, to which Monier-Williams calls attention. "That Yogī who is internally happy, internally satisfied and internally illumined, attains extinction in the Supreme Being, and becomes that Being." A distinction is drawn between Nirvāṇa and Pari-nirvāṇa. Monier-Williams describes Pari-nirvāṇa as being "simply the absolute termination of a series of conscious bodily organization." As a rule Nirvāna does not mean extinction, for the state can be attained even in the present life. It is a state of absolute painlessness. This idea of Nirvāṇa is "the idea of, so to speak, floating in perfect repose and peace and cessation from all pain, and all work, and even all thought, on a kind of ocean of half conscious, half unconscious beatitude. It is not consciousness, neither is it unconsciousness. It is symbolized by a full-blown, perfectly formed lotus—a frequent emblem of perfection—reposing on a calm mirror-like lake" (Monier-Williams). See Monier-Williams, *Buddhism*, 1890; E. W. Hopkins; J. C. Oman, *Cults;* H. Hackmann.

NIRVANA SECT. An early sect of Chinese Buddhists. It flourished from 386 to 589 A.D., and "was one of the first sects to construct a 'Harmony' of the numerous miscellaneous Sūtras" (A. Lloyd). The Nirvana sect was in course of time absorbed by the Tendai (*q.v.*).

NISKAI. The Niskai, or the water-sprites, were a group of goddesses worshipped by the ancient Celts. There were several such groups, another of which was called Proximae (*q.v.*).

NJORDHR. One of the deities of the Ancient Teutons. In Norway the name of Njordhr is borne by a number of places. He is usually represented as god of the sea. The Finnish goddess Skadhi (*q.v.*) chose him in marriage, mistaking him for Balder (*q.v.*). Chantepie de la Saussaye points out that there is a close connection between Njordhr and Nerthus on the one hand, and between Njordhr-Nerthus and Freyr-Freyja on the other. He suggests that perhaps Njordhr has been deduced from Nerthus, and Freyja from Freyr. See P. D. Chantepie de la Saussaye, *Rel. of the Teutons*, 1902.

NOLLARDS. A name given to the Alexians (*q.v.*).

NOMINALISM. The Nominalist school of philosophy was founded by Roscellinus, who was born about 1050, and was Canon in Compiègne about 1090. According to Nominalism, Universals (*universalia*) are simply subjective products of abstraction; they are not real things, but only names. Real existence belongs only to individuals (existentia est singulorum). The watchword of the Nominalist school was "Universalia post rem." When Roscellinus came to apply this doctrine to the dogma of the Trinity, he incurred the charge of tritheism. "The 'person' is in his view the *substantia rationalis*, and in application to God this notion can signify nothing else. The three persons are eternal, and therefore there are three eternal persons. There are accordingly three separate persons, although they are one in will and power" (Puenjer). To satisfy the ecclesiastical authorities, Roscellinus recanted at the Council of Soissons in 1092, but privately he continued to hold the same views.

Nominalism was revived by William of Occam (*c.* 1280-1349), who was a pupil of Duns Scotus (1274-1308). "Only individuals, as individual things, have meaning. Universals as common conceptions are only abstractions made by our own understanding from these individual things (*conceptus mentis significantes univoce plura singularia*)." Puenjer points out that this teaching paved the way for "the empirical method of thought through observation of individual things and the derivation of universal principles from inductive experience." It at the same time excluded the approach to a Rational Theology. To faith is to be assigned all knowledge that transcends experience. "To faith also belong the precepts of morality; for, in virtue of his unlimited freedom, God could also sanction other precepts as good and just." The Nominalists included: Peter D'Ailly (1350-1425) and John Gerson (1363-1429), whose Nominalism developed into Mysticism; Gabriel Biel (*d.* 1495), Robert Holkot (*d.* 1349), and Raymond of Sabundi (*c.* 1430). See B. Puenjer; J. H. Blunt; C. J. Deter; Max B. Weinstein, *Welt- und Leben-Anschauungen*, 1910.

NONCOMALA. A deity in the mythology of the Indians of Costa Rica, the creator. After the creation of men, the god became angry with them and flooded the earth; but another deity, Nubu, succeeded in saving their seed.

NONCONFORMISTS. John Hooper (*d.* 1555), who was made Bishop of Worcester in 1552, but was afterwards deprived by Queen Mary and sentenced for heresy, has been called the "Father of Nonconformity," because he was unwilling to conform to the rites and ceremonies of the Church of England. Nonconformists was really a later name for the Puritans, the reformers who sought to purify the Church from error and corruption, though it was not generally used until the passing of the Act of Uniformity in 1662, when a body of clergymen seceded from the Church rather than conform. The name Dissenters was preferred afterwards. When many of the Nonconformists of the Church of England became Separatists or Sectaries, the name Puritan was generally limited to those reformers who remained in the Establishment.

NONJURORS. A name given to a body of clergymen and laymen in England who refused to take the oath of allegiance to William and Mary and seceded from the national Church (1691). They included five bishops. "Obedience to conscience, when it involves great sacrifice, deserves supreme respect, and the Church of England could ill afford to lose men of such spiritual lives and such single-minded integrity. But the theory of Divine right on which they acted is now completely discredited, and therefore their action cannot be approved" (M. W. Patterson). The succession of the nonjuring bishops was continued after the death of Sancroft (1693). "Many of their clergy served as chaplains in Jacobite families, and the schism was only finally closed at the beginning of the nineteenth century." A famous Nonjuror was William Law (1686-1761), author of *A Serious Call to a Devout and Holy Life*.

NORBERTINES. An order of regular canons founded by St. Norbert (*d.* 1134). In England they received the name White Canons. Another name for them is Premonstratensians.

NORMALISM. A term invented by Prof. T. W. Rhys-Davids. He explains it in his *Cosmic Law in Ancient Thought* (1917). "If one glances over the tables of contents to the best and latest treatises on the early religious beliefs of the four or five countries where early records have been found—such as de Groot on China, Hopkins on India, Jastrow on Mesopotamia, or Breasted on Egypt—one sees that they are mainly, if not quite exclusively, concerned with Animistic ideas or with the applications of such ideas. In the course of my ten years' lectures on Comparative Religion I came across quite a number of early religious beliefs and practices which by no stretch of ingenuity could be brought under Animism. They were not explained in the books, and could not be explained, by the theory of a detachable soul. I found myself forced to the conclusion that we must seek for at least one additional hypothesis, as far-reaching as Animism, and altogether different from it, before we could explain all the facts. I say 'at least one,' for it seemed at first that more than one would be required. But though the number of non-Animistic beliefs was very great, it was found possible to arrange them in more or less overlapping groups; and behind all the groups can be discerned, I venture to think, one single underlying principle. That principle is the belief in a certain rule, order, law. We must invent a name for it—a name that does not imply or suggest a law-giver, and that does not suffer from the disadvantage of being still in common use, and liable therefore to have vague and modern connotations wrapt up in it. Such a word is Normalism, with its convenient adjective Normalistic." Professor Rhys-Davids thinks that to this term we can attach a specific, scientifically exact, meaning.

NORNS. An order of supranatural beings in the religion of the Teutons. They were goddesses of war and fate. They are sometimes referred to as being three in number. Snorri Sturluson, as quoted by Chantepie de la Saussaye, writes as follows: "These maidens appoint the fate of men and we call them Norns. There are, however, still other Norns (*i.e.*, aside from the three already mentioned, Urdhr, Verdhandi, and Skuld), who come to every new-born child and dispense its fate. . . When the Norns determine the destinies of men, they divide the fortunes very unequally: to some they grant a life full of joy and honour, to others little happiness and glory; to some a long life, to others a short one. . . . The good Norns, who are of noble descent, dispense a happy fate." It often happened that two Norns bestowed a blessing on a child, whereas a third contributed something that impaired this blessing. They were active at marriages as well as at births. In some respects they resembled Walkyries (*q.v.*) and Swan-maidens; but Norns were sometimes worshipped, whereas these other divine beings were not. See P. D. Chantepie de la Saussaye, *Rel. of the Teutons*, 1902.

NOTIRZI. One of the deities of the Todas, a goddess.

NÛDD. The name of an ancient Celtic god or divine hero. Also pronounced Neit (*q.v.*) or Ned. The god was the same as Llûdd (*q.v.*).

NUDITY PARADES. Some of the Doukhobórs (*q.v.*) settled in Canada were persuaded that they ought strictly to follow the example of Jesus who gave up manual labour and went about preaching. Accordingly, they went on pilgrimages. On one occasion (1903) they decided to follow the example of Adam and Eve in Paradise. Before entering a town or settlement, both men and women stripped off their garments and presented themselves naked. The enthusiasts were stopped by the police and sent to prison.

NUMBERS, SYMBOLISM OF. In the Old and New Testaments there is frequent use of symbolical numbers. Seven, for instance, is a significant number. We read of a seven-branched candlestick, of a sevenfold sprinkling, of seven sacrificial lambs, of seven angels, seven stars, seven churches of Asia. As W. H. Bennett says (Hastings' *D.B.*), "a similar use of 'seven' is found in the Egyptian, Assyrian, and Persian religions, and is often derived from astral worship of the seven heavenly bodies, the sun, moon, and the five planets known to the ancients." In Egyptology there is frequent reference to the seven Hathors. The seven-headed dragon is found in the Scottish dragon-myth, as well as in the legends of Cambodia, India, Persia, Western Asia, East Africa, and the Mediterranean area. According to Elliot Smith, (*Dr.*), "the seven-headed dragon probably originated from the seven Hathors." The moon determined the earliest sub-division of time into months; and the moon-goddess (the Great Mother) "lent the sanctity of her divine attributes to the number twenty-eight." The number four derives its sanctity from the four cardinal points, and was associated especially with the sun. "Having invested the numbers four and twenty-eight with special sanctity and brought them into association with the measurement of time, it was a not unnatural proceeding to subdivide the month into four parts and so bring the number seven into the sacred scheme. Once this was done the moon's phases were used to justify and rationalize this procedure, and the length of the week was incidentally brought into association with the moon-goddess, who had seven *avatars,* perhaps originally one for each day of the week. At a later period the number seven was arbitrarily brought into relationship with the Pleiades."

NUMBERS, BOOK OF. The fourth book in the Hebrew Canon of the Old Testament (*q.v.*) is called *Arithmoi,* because it begins by giving an account of a numbering or census of the Israelites, made in the second year of the Exodus. This title was adopted for the Vulgate (*Numeri*), and then for the English Version. In the Hebrew Bible the book bears the name *Be-midbar,* this being the fifth word in the opening verse. The contents of the Book of Numbers are as follows: Chapters i.-x. 10 deal with the first census (i.) and the disposition of the camp and the tribes (ii.), with the number and duties of the Levites (iii.-iv.), with various laws, including those relating to the ordeal of jealousy and the Nazarite (v.-vi.), with the offerings of the princes of the tribes when the Tent of Meeting was consecrated (vii.), with the consecration of the Levites (viii.) and with the Passover (ix. 1-x. 10). Chapters x. 11-xx. 13 deal with the journey from Sinai to Kadesh (x. 11-xii. 16), with the sending of the spies (xiii.-xiv.), with laws relating to offerings, etc. (xv.), with the rebellion of Korah, Dathan, and Abiram, and the privileges of priests and Levites (xvi.-xviii.), with the rite of purification associated with the Red Heifer (xix.), with the death of Miriam and the episode of the "waters of strife" (xx. 1-13). Chapters xx. 14-xxxvi. 13 deal with the journey of the Israelites from Kadesh to the plains of Moab (xx. 14-xxi. 35), with the story of Balak and the prophet Balaam (xxii.-xxiv.), with various episodes, including the taking of a second census, and the appointment of Joshua as Moses' successor (xxv.-xxvii.), with a calendar for regulating the sacrifices for the stated festivals (xxviii.-xxix.), with the law of women's vows (xxx.), with a war of vengeance against Midian (xxxi.), with the assignment of territory east of the Jordan to Reuben, Gad, and part of Manasseh (xxxii.), with an itinerary of the marches to the Jordan (xxxiii. 1-49), with laws relating to the borders of Canaan, cities of refuge, etc. (xxxiii. 50-xxxvi. 13). The Sources which were used in the compilation of the Book of Numbers were the same as those used for the books of Exodus and Leviticus (see EXODUS, and LEVITICUS). Chapters i.-x. 28 are from P (the Priestly Writer). Chapters x. 29-xxv. 18 are largely narrative, and for the most part the narrative portions of Numbers belong to J and E. Sections here and there, however, are to be assigned to P (*e.g.,* xiii. 1-17a; xiv. 26-38; xv. 1-41; xvi. 1-35; xvi. 36 [Heb. xvii. 1]-xx. 13; xx. 23-29; xxv. 6-19). Chapters xxvi.-xxxvi. may be assigned almost entirely to P. The fragments of poetry in chapter xxi. are due to E who took them from the collection of poems known as the "Book of the Wars of the Lord" (*q.v.*). R. Kittel (*The Scientific Study of the O.T.*, 1910) thinks that probably in the story of the prophet Balaam (chaps. xxii.-xxiv.) we have a true description of an ancient seer. In chapter xxiv. 3-4 the ecstatic state is clearly described. "The outward eye closed, physically unconscious, the seer lies there and utters his oracle. But his inner eye is opened that he may see the face of the Almighty, his ear uncovered that he may hear His words and counsel." Kittel thinks that the oracles of Balaam are the oldest extant literary witness to an early form of a kind of Messianic hope. "They are probably the product of the early monarchic period, perhaps of the reign of Saul or the early part of the reign of David, since Saul's victory over Agag seems to be still fresh in the memory of the writer, and not yet eclipsed by the greater conquests of David. The climax of the oracles of Balaam is reached where he predicts that a star shall come out of Jacob and a sceptre from Judah, which will arise and defeat the enemies of Israel. Apparently the reference is to the expected Saviour. It may be possible that the successful David is meant, but even in that case the figure has been borrowed from the general conception of a future saviour." See *Encycl. Bibl.;* Carpenter and Harford-Battersby; B. Baentsch, *Numeri,* 1903; H. Holzinger, *Numeri,* 1903; G. B. Gray, *Numbers,* 1903; C. F. Kent, *Israel's Laws and Legal Precedents,* 1907; A. R. S. Kennedy, *Leviticus and Numbers* in the "Century Bible"; G. H. Box, *Intr.;* O. C. Whitehouse.

NUN. An Egyptian deity. The god Nun represents the primeval waters. He was the father of the gods, existing at first alone. From him came Ra (*q.v.*). Ra created out of himself the god Shu (*q.v.*) and the goddess Tefnet (*q.v.*). The offspring of Shu and Tefnet were Keb (*q.v.*), the god of earth, and Nut (*q.v.*), the goddess of sky. Keb and Nut gave birth to Osiris (*q.v.*), Set (*q.v.*), Isis (*q.v.*), and Nephthys (*q.v.*). See A. Wiedemann; Adolf Erman, *Handbook.*

NURTUNJA. A ritual instrument found among the northern Arunta and their immediate neighbours in Central Australia. It is "made up principally of a vertical support which is either a single lance, or several lances united into a bundle, or of a simple pole. Bunches of grass are fastened all around it by means of belts or little cords made of hair. Above this, down is placed, arranged either in circles or in parallel lines which run from the top to the bottom of the support. The top is decorated with the plumes of an eagle-hawk. This is only the most general and typical form; in particular cases, it has all sorts of variations" (Émile Durkheim). The nurtunja is fixed in the earth or carried by an officiant, and marks the central point of a religious ceremony.

NUSEIRIYEH. A branch of the Muhammadan Shi'ah sect. Unlike the Isma'iliyeh (*q.v.*), they agree with the Shi'ahs in finding the true Imām in Mūsā al-Qasim, the second son of Ja'afar as-Sādiq. Otherwise they have much in common with the Isma'iliyeh and the Druses. All three are secret cults in which an important part is played by initiation. According to F. J. Bliss, who gives an account of the Nuseiriyeh in Syria, they pray only in secret, or at any rate not before members of other sects. "At the ceremony of initiation wine is used, as it is also at the annual feast of the quddâs, which is the ordinary word for the Christian mass. Whether the Nuseiriyeh borrowed this use of wine from Christian sources or whether it is the survival of older heathen practices is not clear. Some influence of Christianity is indicated by the observance of Christmas. At the feast of the quddâs a bowl of wine, the symbol of light, is placed before the imam, who, after a service of reading, presents a cupful to each initiate present." The Nuseirîyeh believe in the transmigration of souls. They believe in seven incarnations of the Deity, that of 'Ali, the son-in-law of Muhammad, transcending all the rest in importance. They even hold that 'Ali created Muhammad, his father-in-law. As F. J. Bliss says, it is difficult to believe that such doctrines could have developed from the pure monotheism of Islam. But he points out that the followers of 'Ali "have always been characterized by minds hospitable to new ideas, or rather to the old ideas of other cults, including Persian Dualism and Christian Gnosticism." See F. J. Bliss.

NUSKU. A Babylonian deity. Nusku was a fire-god. He came to be identified with Nabu (*q.v.*) and amalgamated with Gibil (*q.v.*). He is the wise god, the messenger of the gods, and the bearer of the brilliant sceptre. He is spoken of as sprung from Ea (*q.v.*), and as the first-born of Bel (*q.v.*). See Morris Jastrow, *Rel.*

NUT. An Egyptian deity. Nut was a goddess, the female personification of the sky, wife of Keb (*q.v.*), god of the sky. Nut and Keb, who were themselves the offspring of Shu (*q.v.*) and Tefnet (*q.v.*), gave birth to Osiris (*q.v.*) and Set (*q.v.*), Isis (*q.v.*) and Nephthys (*q.v.*). Nut, the sky, at first lay upon Keb, the earth. The two had to be separated before the present world could be set in order. See Alfred Wiedemann; Adolf Erman, *Handbook;* Naville, *The Old Egyptian Faith*, 1909.

NZAMBI. A great goddess worshipped by the Bantu of South-West Africa.

O

O. Goddess O is a designation used by anthropologists for one of the deities depicted in the MSS. of the Mayan Indians of Central America. She appears only in the Madrid MS., where she is represented as an old woman.

OANNES. A figure in Babylonian mythology, a fish-like monster, who, according to Berossus, came up from the Erythraean Sea, where it borders upon Babylonia, to instruct the people. Oannes "taught them the use of letters, sciences and arts of all kinds, the rules for the founding of cities, and the construction of temples, the principles of law and surveying; he showed them how to sow and reap; he gave them all that contributes to the comforts of life. Since that time nothing excellent has been invented" (Maspero, *Dawn of Civilisation*, p. 546).

OATH. An oath is defined in the *Encycl. Brit.* (9th ed.) as "an asseveration or promise made under non-human penalty or sanction." It is sanctified by reference or appeal to a sacred person (God, for instance) or object (such as the Bible), and involves a curse in penalty of violation. If it is taken falsely, the sacred person or object will exact vengeance. Sometimes it is accompanied by some action, such as the lifting up of the right hand, or by some special ceremonial, which adds solemnity to the occasion. There are many examples of oaths in the Old Testament. The occasions are very varied. Among the old Arabs the sacred obligation to treat a guest as inviolable was often confirmed by oath at a sanctuary. The oath is a kind of covenant. When Hannibal made a covenant with Philip of Macedon, he swore before all the deities of Carthage and of Hellas, including "the sun, the moon, and the earth, rivers, meadows (?) and waters" (Robertson Smith, *R.S.*). In Babylonia the oath was the most solemn feature in connection with legal documents. In the earliest days it is taken in the name of the king, who, as representing the deity, has the quality of sanctity attached to him. "In the days of Hammurapi, the gods either take the place of the king or the name of the king is added to that of the gods, and frequently also the name of the city or temple in which the document is drawn up. The change points to the growing secularization of the royal office, leading to the substitution of the gods as a more solemn affirmation. The oath was taken by the 'raising' of the hand, and the place where it was taken was naturally in the temple. Before the civil courts, sitting outside of the temple, no oath could be taken, and when it became necessary in a suit brought before such a tribunal to introduce the oath, the case was transferred to the 'temple' judges" (Morris Jastrow, *Civ.*). Some Christian sects (such as the Friends and the Moravians) consider that they are forbidden by passages in the New Testament (Matthew v. 34, James v. 12) to take any oath, even in a Court of Justice.

OBADIAH, BOOK OF. The smallest prophetic book in the Old Testament. The book of the prophet Obadiah contains a denunciation against Edom for its hostility to Israel. It is stated that when aliens entered into the gates of Jerusalem and cast lots over it, Edom was as one of them. The Edomites not only exulted over the land of Judah in the day of its disaster, but even cut off its fugitives in the day of distress (vss. 11-14). The verses in which these statements are made evidently describe the capture of Jerusalem by Nebuchadnezzar. The prophecy, therefore, at least in its present form, must be later than the year 586. There are other verses in Obadiah (vss. 1-9) which exhibit many points of contact with an oracle against Edom found in the Book of Jeremiah (xlix. 7-22). On comparison, it would appear that the passages in Obadiah are more original. Ewald thinks that the prophecy of Jeremiah emanates from the fourth year of Jehoiachim. This obliges him, as Cornill says, to assume a third source common to both Jeremiah and Obadiah, "an original Obadiah, which Jeremiah freely, and our Obadiah, on the other hand, faithfully, reproduced." C. F. Kent thinks that the prophecy in Jeremiah xlix. is late and that the author quotes from

Obadiah. As a further indication of the date of Obadiah, in addition to the references to the destruction of Jerusalem, he points out that it is clear from vs. 7 that a great calamity has overtaken Edom itself. The allusion seems to be to "the expulsion of the Edomites from their territory by the Nabataeans, which took place sometime between 600 and 400 B.C." Kent would therefore assign the prophecy to some date between 500 and 450 B.C. He thinks that the second half of the prophecy comes from the same period as the first half. See C. Cornill, *Intr.;* G. H. Box; O. C. Whitehouse; C. F. Kent, *The Sermons, Epistles and Apocalypses of Israel's Prophets*, 1910.

ŌBAKU SECT. A Japanese Buddhist sect of the Zen (*q.v.*), founded in 1654 A.D. by Ingen, a famous priest from China. It was decided to read the Buddhist Scriptures and Services in modern Chinese. This was an important reform. "The great mass of the Buddhist worship is in a dead language, the Chinese of fifteen centuries ago; in the Ōbaku worship, the ordinary Sinico-Japanese of the modern literary style, has been, as it were, consecrated to the purposes of religion" (Lloyd). See Arthur Lloyd.

OBERLINVEREINE. The Oberlin Associations in Germany have worked on the lines of the philanthropist J. F. Oberlin (1740-1826), who, as pastor at Waldersbach in the Steinthal, did so much to improve the spiritual and material conditions of his people. Oberlin was not only the first to start Infant Schools, etc., but he made a desolate district fruitful by improving agriculture, constructing roads and bridges, etc. See the *Encycl. Brit.*, *s.v.* "Oberlin"; Brockhaus.

OBI. Obi was a name by which medicine-men or magicians were known in the West Indies. Longfellow uses the term in one of his dramas (*Giles Corey of the Salem Farms*): "He was an Obi man, and taught me magic; taught me the use of herbs and images." De Quincey has suggested a connection with the Hebrew term *Obh*. The Septuagint usually translates the Hebrew word by a Greek term meaning "ventriloquists." In Isaiah xxix. 4 it is said: "and thy voice shall be as an *obh* out of the ground, and thy words (speech) shall chirp out of the dust." In I. Samuel xxviii. 7 the witch of Endor is said to be the "possessor" of an *obh*. Leviticus xx. 27 is translated by Driver (*Deuteronomy*): "a man or a woman when there is in them an *ōb* or a *yiddeʿōni*." But "in them" might be translated "with them" or "among them." Kennedy thinks that the necromancer is "supposed to have a *daimon* or spirit in attendance upon him or even residing within him" (*Leviticus* in the "Century Bible"). See B. Edwards, *West Indies*, 1819; De Quincey, *Collected Works* (A. and C. Black), vol. viii., pp. 287 f., 412.

OBO. It is noted by Burton (*Al Medinah and Meccah*, new edition of Bohn, i., p. 155, N. 1) that "in Huc's travels we are told that the Tartars worship mountain spirits by raising an 'Obo'—dry branches hung with bones and strips of cloth, and planted in enormous heaps of stones."

OBJECTIVE MIND, THE. The study of psychic phenomena is supposed to have demonstrated that there exists in man a duality of mind. One of these minds is the ordinary mind which is active in the daytime. This is called the Objective Mind. The other mind, to which the name Subjective Mind has been given, as a rule is active only during sleep. This is what F. W. H. Myers (1843-1901) called the Subliminal Self (*q.v.*). See DUALITY OF MIND.

OBSCHIE, THE. The Obschie or "Communists" are a branch of the Russian Molokaneh (*q.v.*), who again are a sub-sect of the Russian dissenters known as Bezpopovtzi. They hold their property in common.

OBSERVANTINES. The Franciscans (*q.v.*), in course of time, became divided into two great branches, the Conventuals and the Observantines. The Conventuals have remained separate, but the Observantines in 1897 were reunited to the general body.

OCCASIONALISM. A system of philosophy founded by Arnold Geulinx (1625-1669), professor of philosophy at Leiden. Geulinx points out that there are many thoughts or modes of thinking in us which do not arise from ourselves. They come without our willing them, and they must be due to some other conscious power. Since these ideas are manifold, and are excited by means of the body, "they arise not from the body as at rest and continuing always the same, but from its movements. The body, however, and its movements are entirely without the capacity to excite thoughts, and hence the body is neither the efficient nor the occasioning, but merely the *occasional* cause of our thoughts. The body, on whose occasion, '*occasione cujus*,' those ideas that are independent of me arise in me, is my body. My union with this body is not my work; for birth and death take place without my knowing and willing. It is the work of One who works by means of the body and its motion upon me; and on the occasion of my willing, works in like manner upon body" (Puenjer). Further, God must be a Mind, and He is the only true Mind. Other minds are particular and limited. Geulinx declared that "ideas and eternal truths, such as that two and three are five, are in the divine mind, and in ours only when we see them in God, and consequently contemplate God Himself." See B. Puenjer; C. J. Deter; Max B. Weinstein, *Welt- und Leben-Anschauungen*, 1910.

OCTAPLA, THE. A name sometimes given in early times to Origen's Hexapla. See HEXAPLA.

OCTATEUCH. A word of Greek derivation which has sometimes been used as a collective title for the first eight (Greek *octo*) books of the Old Testament. The books are: Genesis, Exodus, Leviticus, Numbers, Deuteronomy, Joshua, Judges, Ruth.

OCTLI. A Mexican term denoting an intoxicating drink made from the maguey or American aloe. There were a number of gods of fertility who presided over *octli*. Among these were Tezcatzoncatl, Tepoztecatl, Izquitecatl, and Patecatl.

OCTOPUS, THE. It has been pointed out by Professor G. Elliot Smith that the goddess Aphrodite seems to have been associated not only with the cowry, the pearl, and the mandrake, but also with the octopus. This connection with the octopus and its kindred "played a very obtrusive part in Minoan and Mycenæan art; and its influence was spread abroad as far as Western Europe and towards the East as far as America. In many ways it was a factor in the development of such artistic designs as the spiral and the volute, and not improbably also of the swastika" (*Dr.*). In a sculptured representation of the Great Mother on a number of stone slabs from Manabi in Central America, the head of the goddess is a conventionalized octopus. This seems to demonstrate that the American Aphrodite was identified with the octopus. Again, wherever the swastika is found, it is supposed to be an amulet which has power to confer good luck and long life. "Both this reputation and the association with the female organs of reproduction link up the symbol with the cowry, the *Pterocera*, and the octopus. It is clear then that the swastika has the same reputation for magic and the same attributes and associations as the octopus: and it may be a conventionalized representation of it, as Houssay has suggested."

ODES OF SOLOMON. In 1909 Dr. J. Rendel Harris published under the title *Odes and Psalms of Solomon* a large Syriac manuscript of 64 leaves which he had discovered or recovered. In 1911 Professor F. C. Burkitt found another manuscript of the tenth century in the British Museum which also contains a large part of the Odes. The Psalms were known already. They were composed by various authors, and were collected by the Pharisees about half a century before Christ. The Odes, which are a distinct collection, are a new discovery. According to Harnack, we have here a Psalm-book of the time of Jesus, which was edited by the Christian community in Palestine about the year A.D. 100. It contains "all-important pieces of the Johannine theology together with their religious tone colour," which are epoch-making for the higher critic of John's gospel. "Dr. Harris and many other specialists regard the 'Odes' as the work of a Jewish Christian of the first century, though some think them to be wholly Jewish, adopted with certain Christian interpolations to form the earliest Christian hymnal" (Cobern).

ODHIN. Another form of Wodan (*q.v.*), one of the chief deities of the Ancient Teutons.

ODHR. Odhr is one of the deities referred to in Ancient Teutonic mythology. One legend relates that the goddess Freyja was the wife of Odhr. When Odhr went to distant lands, Freyja roamed about in search of him. She had already shed tears of gold. Probably, however, Odhr is identical with Odhin (see WODAN). See P. D. Chantepie de la Saussaye, *Rel. of the Teutons,* 1902.

ODHRERIR. The name in Norse mythology of the cauldron containing the magic mead made of honey mixed with the blood of Kvasir, the wisest of men. The potion was supposed to have power to confer wisdom and poetic inspiration. Odhin, for instance, received from the giant Mimir, the keeper of the cauldron, a draught which increased his wisdom.

OENOMANCY. A species of divination. Oenomancy (Greek *oinos,* wine) was practised by the ancients with wine. They found omens in "the colour, motion, and other circumstances connected with the wine used in libations to the gods" (James Gardner).

OGMIOS. The name Ogmios, though not found on inscriptions, is mentioned by Lucian (*c.* A.D. 170) as that of a god worshipped by the ancient Celts and corresponding to Heracles (*q.v.*). He is depicted as a white-haired old man who carries a lion-skin, a club, and a bow. Reinach thinks Ogmios was a culture-hero. The name resembles the Gaelic Ogma which was the name of the god of literature and writing, who is supposed to have invented the ogam alphabet. See Anwyl, *Celtic Religion*, 1906; Squire, *Myth.;* Reinach, *O.*

OGUN. A deity worshipped by the Yoruba tribes of the Slave Coast of Africa. In some parts of Yorubaland he seems to have taken the place of the deity Odudua.

ŌHĀLŌTH. The name of one of the Jewish treatises or tractates which reproduce the oral tradition or unwritten law as developed by the second century A.D., and are incorporated in the Mishnah (*q.v.*), a collection and compilation completed by Rabbi Judah the Holy, or the Patriarch, about 200 A.D. The sixty-three tractates of the Mishnah are divided into six groups or orders (*sedarim*). Ōhālōth is the second tractate of the sixth group, which is called *Ṭohorōth* ("Purifications").

O'HARAI. A ceremony of general purification in Shintoism, held twice a year. Expiatory offerings were brought by the people, and they were given absolution either by the emperor or by his representative.

OHONAMOCHI. A deity in the mythology of the Japanese, the earth god. His great shrine at Kitzuki, in Idzumo, is resorted to yearly by thousands of pilgrims. In Tokyo also a great festival is held in his honour.

OJHAS. A community in India the members of which were originally the soothsayers and minstrels of the Gonds. The name is derived from the word *ojh* meaning "entrail." According to R. V. Russell and R. B. Hīra Lāl, the name is Sanskrit and not Gond, and "is applied by the Hindus to the seers or magicians of several of the primitive tribes, while there is also a class of Ojha Brāhmans who practise magic and divination."

OKI. A term used among the Iroquois of N. America to denote a mystic potentiality ascribed to beings whether human or non-human, living or not living. *Oki* seems to be a force, and not a personal being, and corresponds to the Melanesian *mana*.

OLD CATHOLICS. The body known as the Old Catholics (Alt-Katholiken) arose in Germany in protest against the definition of Papal infallibility made by the Vatican Council in 1870. The Council was held under the presidency of Pope Pius IX. The proclamation was as follows: "If, therefore, anyone says that the Roman Pontiff possesses only the office of Inspection or Direction, but not the full and highest power of Jurisdiction over the Universal Church, not only in things pertaining to faith and morals, but also in those pertaining to the discipline and government of the Church spread over the whole world; or that he has only the more important share, but not the fulness of this highest power; or that such his power is not an ordinary and immediate one, as well over all and several Churches as over all and several pastors and faithful, let him be anathema." It was further taught and defined as a dogma divinely revealed that "when the Roman Pontiff speaks *ex cathedra, i.e.,* when in the exercise of his office as the Pastor and Doctor of all Christians, through his supreme apostolic authority, he defines the teaching which is to be received by the Universal Church regarding faith or morals, then, by virtue of the Divine assistance promised to him in St. Peter, he is invested with the infallibility with which it was the will of the Divine Redeemer that His Church should be endowed, in the definition of doctrine touching faith and morals; and that therefore such definitions of the Roman Pontiff are unalterable in themselves, and not by consent of the Church." This new doctrine met at once with considerable opposition, and was repudiated in particular by forty-two Professors of the University of Munich, the chief of whom was Döllinger (1799-1890). In 1870 an assembly was held at Nuremberg at which the Vatican declaration was rejected publicly by a still larger number of professors. Early in the next year Döllinger made his famous declaration in which he explained that "as a Christian, as a theologian, as an historian, as a citizen," he could not accept the new Vatican doctrine. This declaration came to be regarded in Germany, Austria, Switzerland, and France as the authoritative reply of the Old Catholics to the Vatican claim. On the 18th of April in the same year Döllinger was excommunicated by the Archbishop of Munich. This of course widened the breach. In September 1871 a conference of Old Catholics was held in Munich, and was attended by eight hundred delegates. The programme adopted was as follows: "The retention of the old Catholic faith; assertion of rights as Catholics; rejection of the new dogmas; retention of the constitution of the ancient Church, with omission of such declarations of the faith as were not in harmony with the actual belief of the Church; reform of the Church, with such co-operation of the laity as was consistent with its constitution; efforts towards the reunion of Christian confessions; reform of the training and position of the clergy; allegiance to the State, in opposition to the attacks of Ultramontanism; rejection of the Jesuits; solemn protest in favour of claims as Catholics upon the endowments of the Church." It was decided also to form Unions and Congregations. When this had been done, it became necessary to elect a bishop. The choice fell upon Joseph Hubert Reinkens (1821-1896), Professor of Theology at Breslau. He was consecrated at Rotterdam by the Jansenist Bishop of Deventer according to the Roman rite. The Old-Roman or Jansenist Church of Holland had been for nearly two hundred years a Catholic Church independent of Rome, but it had preserved the apostolic succession. Addis and Arnold state that the Dutch Jansenists (see JANSENISTS), unlike most other sects, remain just where they were on their separation from Rome. "They have retained valid orders, the celibacy of the clergy, the Mass and other services in Latin." The Old Catholics allow the laity to communicate in both kinds. They have abolished compulsory celibacy of the clergy, indulgences, the worship of the Blessed Virgin Mary, etc. They have made private confession voluntary. In 1876 the Old Catholics in Switzerland felt the need of a bishop. They elected Professor Eduard Herzog (*b.* 1841), and he was consecrated at Rheinfelden by Bishop Reinkens. R. S. Oldham points out that there has been an active sympathy between the Old Catholic Churches and the Churches of the Anglican Communion, and that Bishop Reinkens and Bishop Herzog have been welcomed as equals by English prelates at Lambeth, Farnham, and Cambridge. According to the same writer, the Old Catholics in 1889 numbered about 120,000 or 130,000. See J. H. Blunt; *Prot. Dict.*; *Cath. Dict.*, 1905; R. S. Oldham, "Old Catholicism," in *R.S.W.*

OLD INDEPENDENTS. A name assumed by David Dale and his followers. See DALEITES.

OLD TESTAMENT. The expression Old Testament is a Christian (cp. II. Corinthians iii. 14), not a Jewish, designation of the Hebrew canonical writings. It is Paul who speaks of the Jewish writing as ἡ παλαιὰ διαθήκη, and this the Authorised Version wrongly translates "Old Testament." The correct meaning of the Greek expression is the "Old Covenant." The canonical writings of the Jews were so named by the Christians because they describe the making of a covenant between Yahweh (Jehovah) and his people. Similarly the "New Covenant" (commonly called "New Testament" [*q.v.*]) was so called because this collection of writings describes the making of a new covenant, which was intended to take the place of the old one. It is convenient to retain the familiar expressions "Old Testament" and "New Testament." The Old Testament is a collection of books of different dates and of varied character. It includes Historical Books such as the Pentateuch and Joshua, Judges, I. and II. Samuel, I. and II. Kings, I. and II. Chronicles, etc.; Prophetical Books, such as Isaiah, Jeremiah, Ezekiel, and the Minor Prophets; Poetical Books, such as Psalms, Lamentations, Canticles; Wisdom Literature, such as Proverbs, Ecclesiastes; and Apocalyptic Literature, such as the Book of Daniel. Cp. CANON OF THE OLD TESTAMENT, and see the articles on the separate books.

OMECIHUATL. The name given to the moon by the Aztecs of Mexico. They called the sun Ometicutli (*q.v.*).

OMETECUTLI. Ometecutli, "twice Lord," was the name given to the sun by the Aztecs of Mexico. Lewis Spence thinks that when the Aztecs emerged from totemism the sun and the moon were probably the first deities worshipped by them. They called the moon Omecihuatl, "twice lady." See Lewis Spence, *Myth.*

ÖN. One of the gods of the Todas, the son of Pithi. He was the creator of buffaloes and of the Toda. The first Toda woman he created from a rib which he took from the right side of the first man. Eventually he departed to the world of the dead, and became ruler there.

ONKELOS, TARGUM OF. The Aramaic translation of the Pentateuch. The name Onkelos is the same as Aquila. The Targum on the Pentateuch is more literal than the Targum (of Jonathan) on the Prophets. See TARGUM.

ONNIONT. A figure in the mythology of the Huron Indians, a gigantic serpent with a great horn which it used for piercing mountains and rocks. A beverage made by the medicine-men, as they claimed, from pounded pieces of its horn was supposed to impart vigour to warriors.

ONTOLOGISM The philosophy known as Ontologism had its roots in the teaching of the Platonist Marsilius Ficinus (1433-1499), the author of a work called "Platonica Theologia" (1482). But the principles of Ficinus were developed first by Nicole Malebranche (1638-1715), and then by Vincenzo Gioberti (1801-1852). Ontologism means the "doctrine of Being." Malebranche taught that knowledge is not in ourselves; it is possible only *in* God. "There is in fact only One Reason: as only an infinite reason can grasp the idea of the infinite, and as it is only under this supposition that universal validity can belong to the cognitions of the innumerable individual men. The Universal Reason and the Intelligible Extension correspond to each other. God is the Universal Reason, and along with it He is the Intelligible Extension; and therefore He is the ground of all individual things. Our clear and distinct knowledge, in contrast to the unclear and indistinct knowledge of sense, is the knowledge which arises from universally valid thinking of reason or from ideas. These ideas are in God, and therefore we are also in God, in so far as we have ideas, and know by them; or conversely, we can know things really only in God" (Puenjer). The teaching of Gioberti are summarized in the seven propositions which were censured by the Roman Catholic authorities in a decree of the Inquisition, dated September 18, 1861. (1) An immediate cognition of God, at least habitual, is essential to the human intellect, so that without this it can have cognition of nothing, inasmuch as it is the intellectual light itself. (2) The being which we perceive by the intellect in all things, and without which we intellectually perceive nothing, is the divine being. (3) Universals, considered *a parte rei*, are not really distinguished from God. (4) The congenital knowledge of God as being in the simple sense of the term, involves in an eminent mode every other cognition, so that by it we possess an implicit cognition of every being under every respect in which it is cognoscible. (5) All other ideas are nothing but modifications of the idea in which God is intellectually perceived as being, in the simple sense of the term. (6) Created things are in God as a part is in a whole, not indeed in a formal whole, but in one which is infinite and most simple, which places its *quasi* parts outside of itself, without any division or diminution of itself. (7) Creation can be thus explained: God, in the special act in which He intellectually cognises and wills Himself as distinct from any determinate creature—*e.g.*, man—produces that creature. See B. Puenjer; J. E. Erdmann, vol. ii., 1890; *Cath. Dict.*

OONAWLEH UNGGI. A deity, "The Oldest Wind," in the mythology of the Cherokee Indians, a wind-god.

ONYCHOMANCY. A species of divination. Onychomancy was practised by examining the nails of a boy. "For this purpose they were covered with oil and soot, and turned to the sun. The images represented by the reflection of the light upon the nails gave the answer required" (James Gardner, *Faiths of the World*).

OPHIOLATRY. The worship of snakes. See ANIMAL WORSHIP.

OPHITES. A name (from Gk. *ophis*, "serpent")

given to a number of sects of a Gnostic character, because the serpent played a rôle in their symbolism. They were (1) Cainites, (2) Perates, (3) Sethians, (4) 'Gnostics' of Irenaeus, (5) Naassenes, (6) Barbelo-Gnostics, (7) Severians, (8) Nicolaitans, (9) Archontics, (10) Justinians. The serpent appears for the most part as the enlightener, and the benefactor of men. The original sect seems to have been the *Ophianoi* referred to by Origen. The members made the serpent an object of reverence. They made use of a seal, bearing the formula, "'I have been anointed with white ointment from the tree of life,' and mystical observances of various kinds played a great part in their worship" (Hastings' *Encycl.*). Irenæus connects all such sects with Simon Magus. E. F. Scott thinks that Ophitism represents in the main a primitive phase of the Gnostic movement. "It had its true antecedents in those theosophical sects which had grown up in Egypt and the East during the age of syncretism, and it marks the beginning of the alliance of those alien sects with Christianity. In this consists the historical importance of Ophitism. It reflects the Gnostic movement in its earlier stages, and helps us to determine the sources and intrinsic character of its beliefs" (*op. cit.*).

OPOCHTLI. A Mexican deity, a god of fishing and hunting. He was one of the Tlaloque, subsidiary deities associated with Tlaloc. To him was ascribed the invention of the fishing-rod and the harpoon. At the feast held in his honour the beverage called octli was imbibed; and the offerings made to him included maize, flowers, and tobacco.

OPUS OPERATUM. An expression which means literally "the work wrought." It was used by mediaeval theologians to denote the effect of the sacramental rites. Bellarmine ("De Sacramentis," ii. 1) explains that "that which actively, proximately, and instrumentally effects the grace of justification, is only that external act, called sacrament, and this is the sense of 'Opus Operatum,' the word *operatum* being taken passively, so that when we say the sacrament confers grace ex opere operato, our meaning is that grace is conferred by virtue of the sacramental act itself instituted by God for this end, not by the merit of the minister or the recipient" (quoted by Addis and Arnold). See *Cath. Dict.*

ORATORIANS. See ORATORY, THE FRENCH, and ORATORY OF ST. PHILIP NERI.

ORATORY, THE. A Church and Service carried on by John Henley (1692-1756). Henley began to deliver "orations" at an Oratory in Newport Market. In 1726 we find him established at an Oratory in Clare Market, London. In the same year The Oratory was planned, and on Sunday, July the 3rd, 1726, it was opened. The Oratory, he claimed, was an Ecclesiastical Institution. It was a Church. But it was more than this, for it was an Academy of the Sciences and Languages as well. As a Church, we are told, its principles are three. 1. In belief, a liberty of conscience from all secular restraints. 2. In morality, the religion of nature, of which revelation, in this respect, is only declarative. 3. In historical, or revealed religion, that of the primitive Church, in the first ages. Its view is impartially to examine the pleas of all religions, proposing that as the truest standard and centre of union. The Service of the Oratory is (1) in the model, primitive, (2) in the language, entirely scriptural. But sometimes the Primitive Liturgies shall be performed. Persons who have been eminent in, or great patrons of, arts and literature, if they have been virtuous, or penitents, shall be commemorated. As to the religious instruction. (1) In the sermons, it shall be performed with the most exact composition, speaking, and action. (2) Both in the sermons and lectures, it shall take in the whole circle of divinity, regularly, faithfully, clearly, and elegantly represented. In the morning, a sermon will be delivered; in the evening, a lecture will be read: the former on some part of practical theology; the latter, on the critical, historical, speculative, or literary parts of it. A special "Primitive Liturgy" was prepared for the use of the Oratory. It had eighteen Rubrics. 1. Let the Reading of the Liturgy be always performed according to the laws of speaking and action established in the Oratory, founded on a just impression in the mind and heart of the Reader, and a ready command and memory of the whole Service; the voice and gesture varying, as the thing requires. 2. Let all the Sermons and Orations be delivered according to the same rules of speaking and action. 3. Let the Lectures and Readings be read with distinctness and propriety in the speaking and address. 4. Let the Prayer before Sermon be (very short, and) entirely left to the discretion of the Preacher. 5. Let the Members of the Oratory form an Amicable Society, for mutual defence and convenience. 6. Let the Rules of the Primitive Church be observed in all things, as far as the prejudices of the world and the circumstances of things will allow. 7. Let nothing contrary to the Laws of the Realm be said or done in the Oratory. 8. Let the Sermons and Lectures be a complete and regular course of Practical and Primitive Theology, in all its branches. 9. On the Lord's-day, between Easter and Pentecost, let all pray standing: let all stand, when any part of the Gospel is read. 10. Feasts are all Lord's-days, all Sabbath-days or Saturdays; Easter-day, its Octave; the fifty days from Easter to Pentecost; Ascension, and Pentecost: besides the Feast of the Nativity, and Days of the Apostles, etc., of later institution. 11. The Men and Women are to sit separate in the Public Assemblies. 12. The Fasts are Passion-Week, especially Friday and Saturday, till day-break; all Wednesdays and Fridays (except between Easter and Pentecost) and the five middle Days before Passion-Week, till the ninth hour, or till evening. Alms, Devotion, Abstinence from Flesh and Wine, etc., are essential to Fasting. 13. The Litany should be said at noon, on Wednesdays and Fridays. 14. Let the Psalmody be before Prayers, and before and after Sermon, and before the Third Service at the Altar: one, two, three, or four verses, or more, as the Institutor directs. Let the Psalmodist say, To the Praise of God, let us sing a part of the — Psalm, verse the —, etc. 15. Let any eminent Preacher, properly recommended, be admitted to preach in the Oratory, and to use his own method of Prayer before Sermon, the Common Prayers not being always in themselves essential. 16. Let the Ostiaries [door-keepers] perform their duty; taking care that the avenue to the seat-door be properly guarded, and no disturbance arise in the time of Service. 17. Let all things be done decently, and in order: and the Laws of the Land, which favour Religious Assemblies publicly authorized, be strictly put in execution. 18. Let Primitive Antiquity be the constant search of the Oratory; and its prevailing maxims be gradually opened, settled, and put in practice. See Peter Hall; and the *D.N.B.*

ORATORY, THE FRENCH. The French Oratory was founded at Paris in 1611 by Cardinal de Bérulle (*d.* 1629), and was declared a royal foundation in 1612. A society of priests, it was approved by Paul V. in 1614, and received the title "Congregation of the Oratory of our Lord Jesus Christ in France." In 1616 it was established in the Rue St. Honoré. "To deepen devotion, promote professional studies, and spread an ecclesiastical spirit among the secular clergy, that through them the whole population might be reached and influenced, were the principal objects of the institute" (*Cath. Dict.*) Cardinal de Bérulle instituted a number of seminaries and colleges. At the time of the Revolution the French Oratorians resisted the Civil Constitution of the Clergy. In 1792 the Congregation of the Oratory was dissolved. In 1852, however, it was succeeded by "The Oratory of the Immaculate Conception," which adopted the same rule. See *Cath. Dict.;* Brockhaus' *Konversationslexikon.*

ORATORY OF ST. PHILIP NERI. The "Oratory" was the name given to a chapel which Philip Neri obtained permission to build over one of the aisles of the Church of St. Jerome in Rome (1558). It had long been a practice of his to gather round him a number of men and to instruct them in spiritual things. He began this practice as a layman, and continued it after his ordination (1551). At first he used a room of his own, then a larger room, and finally an oratory. These gatherings developed into evening services with hymns, popular devotions, and sermons. In 1564 a number of Philip's followers were ordained. In 1575 they obtained possession of the old church of the Vallicella. On its site Philip built the "Chiesa Nuova" (completed 1577). The Congregation was approved and confirmed by Gregory XIII. in 1575; its constitutions were approved by Paul V. in 1612. The members consist of simple priests who agree to a rule of life, but take no vows. Each house is independent. In 1847 the Congregation was introduced into England. In 1849 a house was opened in Birmingham, and soon after another in the Strand, London. The London house was eventually transferred to Brompton, and is now the Brompton Oratory. See *Cath. Dict.;* Brockhaus.

ORDEALS. Among the Pārdhis, a low caste of wandering fowlers and hunters in India, the primitive method of trial by ordeal is still practised. "If a woman is suspected of misconduct she is made to pick a pice coin out of boiling oil; or a pīpal leaf is placed on her hand and a red-hot axe laid over it, and if her hand is burnt or she refuses to stand the test she is pronounced guilty. Or, in the case of a man, the accused is made to dive into water: and as he dives an arrow is shot from a bow. A swift runner fetches and brings back the arrow, and if the diver can remain under water until the runner has returned, he is held to be innocent" (R. V. Russell).

ORENDA. A term used among the Iroquoian tribes of N. America to denote the potentiality that belongs to beings whether human or non-human, living or not-living. A hunter, a prophet, a bird, and even a storm possess *orenda.* Where this is superior in quality, it enables the possessor to overcome every kind of antagonistic orenda. Hewitt (as quoted by Émile Durkheim, p. 193) says: "The savage man conceived the diverse bodies collectively constituting his environment to possess inherently mystic potence . . . (whether they be) the rocks, the waters, the tides, the plants and the trees, the animals and man, the wind and the storms, the clouds and the thunders and the lightnings."

ORIEL SCHOOL. A party or school of theologians who were members of Oriel College, Oxford. The leader was Richard Whately (1787-1863), afterwards Archbishop of Dublin, who was fellow of Oriel College from 1811 to 1822. Other members of the party were John Davison (1777-1834), who become a Fellow in 1800; Edward Copleston (1776-1849), afterwards Bishop of Llandaff, who was Fellow of Oriel from 1795 to 1814 and Provost from 1814 to 1828; Thomas Arnold (1795-1842), afterwards Headmaster of Rugby, who became Fellow in 1815; and R. D. Hampden (1793-1868), afterwards Bishop of Hereford, who became Fellow in 1814. They were Broad Churchmen (see BROAD CHURCH), and were opposed by the Tractarians (*q.v.*).

'ORLĀ. The title of one of the Jewish treatises or tractates which reproduce the oral tradition or unwritten law as developed by the second century A.D. and are incorporated in the Mishnah (*q.v.*), a collection and compilation completed by Rabbi Judah the Holy, or the Patriarch, about 200 A.D. The sixty-three tractates of the Mishnah are divided into six groups or orders (*sedarim*). 'Orlā is the tenth tractate of the first group, which is called *Zerā'im* ("Seeds").

ORMUZD. The personification of Good in the dualistic religion of Zarathustra, Zoroastrianism (*q.v.*).

ORNITHOMANCY. A species of divination. Ornithomancy was practised by the ancient Greeks by means of birds.

OROTAL. A deity worshipped by the ancient Arabs of Egypt. In his honour worshippers shaved the fore part of their heads. Robertson Smith thinks that this was done as a formal initiation into the worship of the god. See W. Robertson Smith, *R.S.*

ORPHANS. A division or sub-division of the Hussites (*q.v.*). When John Ziska (1360-1424), the leader of the Taborites (*q.v.*) died, he was succeeded by the brothers Procopius. Some of the Taborites, however, contended that no one could properly succeed Ziska. They therefore formed a new division and called themselves Orphans.

ORPHEUS. The Greek hero Orpheus was revered by the Greeks as an earlier poet than Homer. They ascribed to him a wonderful power of song by which he was able to charm the wildest beasts and to move even trees and stones. When his beloved wife Eurydice died he descended to the underworld and by his power of song persuaded Persephone to allow him to carry back the beloved one to the upper world. Consent was given on condition of his not looking round, a condition which was not kept, with the result that Eurydice had to return. According to legend he met his end by being torn in pieces by the Thracian Mænads (women in a state of Bacchic ecstasy). He came to be regarded by the Greeks as a hero of civilisation who taught the Thracians the useful arts and induced them to give up cannibalism, besides being a wonderful poet and the founder of a religion. According to Reinach, "he was in reality an old totemic god of Northern Greece, whose violent death and resurrection were the articles of faith of a mystic form of worship." In consequence of his reputation as a poet, a number of poems were attributed to him (Orphic Poems). Some of these are hymns to gods and demons. "Concerning the dates and the manner of growth of these poems volumes of erudition have been compiled. As Homer is silent about Orpheus (in spite of the position which the Mythical Thracian bard acquired as the inventor of letters and magic and the father of the mysteries), it has been usual to regard the Orphic ideas as of late introduction. We may agree with Grote and Lobeck that these ideas and the ascetic 'Orphic mode of life' first acquired importance in Greece about the time of Epimenides, or, roughly speaking, between 620 and 500 B.C. That age certainly witnessed a curious growth of superstitious fears and of mystic ceremonies intended to mitigate spiritual terrors . . . We may suppose that the Orphic poems were collected, edited and probably interpolated, in this dark hour of Greece. 'To me,' says Lobeck, 'it appears that the verses may be referred to the age of Onomacritus, an age curious in the writings of ancient poets, and attracted by the allurements of mystic religions.' The style of the surviving fragments is sufficiently pure and epic: the strange unheard of myths are unlike those which the Alexandrian poets drew from fountains long lost. But how much in the Orphic myths is imported from Asia or Egypt, how much is the invention of literary forgers like Onomacritus, how much should be regarded as the first guesses of the physical poet-philosophers, and how much is truly ancient popular legend recast in literary form, it is impossible with certainty to determine" (Andrew Lang). Cp. ORPHICS. See Andrew Lang, *Myth, Ritual and Religion*, 1899; O. Seyffert, *Dict.;* Reinach, *O.*

ORPHIC POEMS. See ORPHEUS.

ORPHICS. The founder of the Orphic Mysteries and of the sect known as the Orphics is supposed to have been Orpheus (*q.v.*) The Orphics believed in re-incarnation, but they believed also that souls could escape the "cycle of reincarnation" by initiation into the mysterious Orphic mysteries. "To avoid new birth, certain magic formulae were learnt by heart: the dead man was allowed to drink the water of a living spring, whereupon he cast off his carnal nature in which sin inhered, and thus purified 'reigned among the heroes'" (Reinach). They believed also in original sin. "The soul was enclosed in the body as in a tomb or prison, to punish a very early crime committed by the Titans, the ancestors of man, who had treacherously slain the young god Zagreus." It needed to be purified by religious consecration and by the means of expiation taught by Orpheus. The cosmogony of the Orphics, as found in the poems attributed to Orpheus, is curious and interesting. At the beginning was Time (*Chronos*). "Time was when as yet this world was not." Time, personified, produced (gave birth to) Chaos, "the monstrous gulph," and Æther. In course of time Chaos produced a silver-white and shining egg. "We have now three primitive generations, time, chaos, the egg, and in the fourth generation the egg gave birth to Phanes, the great hero of the Orphic cosmogony" (Lang). J. M. Robertson finds here the origin of the Easter Egg; the Gnostics took it from the lore of the Orphics. Phanes, who is both male and female, has in him "the seed of all the gods." He is represented as being, in the form Phanes-Ericapæus-Metis, a kind of trinity. Phanes produces, as the last of a series of gods, Zeus, who swallows the rest, including Phanes, and then produces the real world. Orphism had great success, and spread throughout the Greek world and into Southern Italy. See Andrew Lang, *M.R.R.;* O. Seyffert, *Dict.;* Reinach, *O.;* Max B. Weinstein, *Welt- und Leben-anschauungen*, 1910.

ORTHIA. The name (recorded in the seventh century B.C.) of a goddess whose temple at Sparta has been excavated in recent years. Many archæologists are inclined to identify her with the great Nature-goddess mostly called Artemis. Prof. R. S. Conway suggests that she is equivalent to a goddess worshipped by the people known to the Romans as Veneti, the goddess Rehtia (*q.v.*).

ORTLIBERIANS. The Ortliberians (also Ortlibenses) are said to have been organised as a sect in the thirteenth century by one Ortlieb of Strassburg. In any case, they had much in common with the Amalricians (*q.v.*). "They held that the external orders of the Church are of no value, and that the rejection of them when conjoined with rigid asceticism leads to the highest perfection, and even to the reception of immediate divine revelation. Thereby man is raised to God; nay more, by a process of deification he attains, as his highest goal, complete oneness with God" (B. Puenjer). See J. H. Blunt; B. Puenjer.

OSIANDRIANS. The party of the Lutheran theologian, Andreas Osiander (really Hosemann; 1498-1552), who taught that Justification meant not merely a "declaring righteous," but a "making righteous." This teaching gave rise to the "Osiandrian Controversy." In 1549 Osiander went as Professor to Königsberg. The party disappeared after 1566, when Osiander's son-in-law Funch was executed for high treason. See J. H. Blunt; Brockhaus.

OSIRIS. An Egyptian deity. Osiris, Set (*q.v.*), Isis (*q.v.*), and Nephthys (*q.v.*) were supposed to be the offspring of Keb (*q.v.*) the god of earth and Nut (*q.v.*) the goddess of sky. Osiris became lord of the underworld, and we are told how he attained to this position in the Osiris myth or legend. Osiris became the husband of his sister Isis (*q.v.*), Set (*q.v.*) the husband of his sister Nephthys (*q.v.*). Keb made Osiris ruler of the world, giving him "the government over the two Egypts." He was a just ruler and a great warrior. But for some reason or other Set became his enemy and tried to kill him. Isis, the devoted wife of Osiris, guarded her husband and for a time succeeded in protecting him against Set. At length, however, by means of cunning Set contrived to achieve his purpose. Osiris was killed, and his body disappeared. Isis sought for it without wearying. When she found it she sat down by it with Nephthys, and the two made lamentation. Re took pity on her and sent Anubis (*q.v.*) from heaven to bury Osiris. Anubis set the dismembered body in order. Thereupon Isis breathed into the body new life. But Osiris was to live a new existence. He became king of the dead. In course of time Isis gave birth to a son, whom she brought up secretly in the Delta for fear of Set. This was Horus (*q.v.*). Attempts were made upon his life, but he escaped them. When Horus grew up, he fought with Set and was victorious. He lost an eye, however. And when Thoth (*q.v.*) healed him and restored it, Horus presented it as an offering to his father Osiris, who ate it. Herodotus identifies Osiris with Dionysos. According to Plutarch, Osiris is Good, "the reasoning power of the soul and law and order in the world" (Erman). Typhon, that is to say Set, is Evil, "the lack of sense, the indiscretion of the soul, and disease and disorder in the world." Osiris is commonly represented as a human being with a crown on his head and a sceptre and whip in his hand. In Busiris, one of the chief seats of his worship, however, he was represented as a pillar, the upper part of which was repeated several times. The precise meaning of this pillar is doubtful. Perhaps the most likely explanation is that the pillar stands for the backbone of Osiris. When his dismembered body was set in order, one of the most important parts of the undertaking was the restoration of the backbone. It was commemorated and celebrated annually at Busiris. The resurrection of Osiris became a guarantee for the resurrection of every man. "As surely as Osiris lives, so shall he live also: as surely as Osiris did not die, so shall he not die: as Osiris is not annihilated, so shall he too not be annihilated" (Egyptian text). Figures of Osiris which were buried with deceased persons have been found in Egyptian cemeteries. In some cases they were made of cloth and stuffed with corn. J. G. Frazer gives reasons for thinking that originally Osiris was in the main a corn-god, "a personification of the corn, which may be said to die and come to life again every year." He suggests that in prehistoric times the Egyptian kings actually personated Osiris, "the god of fertility in general and of the corn in particular." Osiris was also a tree-spirit, and probably he was this before he became a corn-spirit. Frazer thinks that "the backbone of Osiris" (the column with several cross-bars at the top; see above) represents the bare trunk and branches of a tree. The worship of Adonis at Amathus resembled so closely the Egyptian worship of Osiris that by some people the two were identified. See A. Wiedemann; J. G. Frazer, *Adonis, Attis, Osiris,* 1906; Adolf Erman, *Handbook;* Naville, *The Old Egyptian Faith,* 1909; Reinach, *O.*

OWENITES. The followers of Robert Owen (1771-1858), who was a contemporary of St. Simon (1760-1825; see SIMONIANISM, ST.). After being assistant in a draper's shop at Stamford in Northamptonshire, Owen went to Manchester, where in course of time he became manager of a large cotton mill. In 1799 he purchased for a Company the cotton-mills of David Dale (see DALEITES) at New Lanark, and married his daughter. He devoted himself zealously to philanthropic work, and opened schools for infants and others. In 1813 he produced a publication "A New View of Society, or Essays on the Principle of the Formation of the Human Character," which embodied a new social and religious creed. In 1817 he explained a scheme of "villages of unity and co-operation." From co-operation he advanced to Socialism and Communism, and wished to found a "New Moral World." The religion of the new system comprised eight articles or principles. 1. That all facts yet known to man indicate that there is an external or internal cause of all existences by the fact of their existence; that this all-pervading cause of motion and change in the universe is the power which the nations of the world have called God, Jehovah, Lord, etc.; but the facts are yet unknown to man which define what that power is. 2. That all ceremonial worship by man of this cause, whose qualities are yet so little known, proceeds from ignorance of his own nature, and can be of no real utility in practice; and that it is impossible to train men to become rational in their feelings, thoughts, and actions, until all such forms shall cease. 3. That it is man's highest duty to himself and his fellowmen to acquire an accurate knowledge of those circumstances which produce evil to the human race, and of those which produce good; to exert all his powers to remove the former from society, and to create around it the latter only. 4. That this invaluable practical knowledge can be acquired solely through an extensive search after truth, by an accurate, patient, and unprejudiced inquiry into facts, as developed by Nature. 5. That man can never attain to a state of superior and permanent happiness, until he shall be surrounded by those external circumstances which will train him, from birth, to feel pure charity and sincere affection towards the whole of his species; to speak the truth only on all occasions, and to regard with a merciful disposition all that has life. 6. That such superior principles and feelings can never be given to man under those institutions of society which have been formed on the mistaken supposition that man forms his feelings and convictions by his will, and therefore is responsible for them. 7. That under institutions formed in accordance with the Rational System of Society, these superior principles and dispositions may be given to the whole of the human race, without chance of failure except in the case of organic disease, and influenced only by the natural consequences of our actions. 8. The religion of the New Moral World will therefore consist in the unceasing practice of promoting the happiness of every man, woman, and child, to the greatest extent in our power, without regard to their class, sect, party, or colour. In the new constitution of Society all are to have absolute religious freedom, and no one is to be held responsible for his physical, intellectual, or moral organization. All are to be provided by public arrangements with the best of everything, including the best possible education. All children are to be educated together, and to be under the special care of the community. "Both sexes shall have equal education, rights, privileges, and personal liberty; their associations will arise from the general sympathy of their nature, uninfluenced by artificial distinctions." There is to be no useless private property and no individual punishment or reward. "Society shall not be composed, as at present, of single families, but of communities or associations of men, women, and children in the usual proportions, from three hundred to two thousand, as local circumstances determine." All the communities are to possess as far as possible the same advantages. Each community is to be governed by two Councils, one for the Home, the other for the Foreign department. The latter is for the purpose of keeping in touch with other associations or communities. If persons become diseased physically, intellectually, or morally, "the council shall remove them into the hospital for bodily, mental, or moral invalids, where they shall remain until they shall be recovered by the mildest treatment which can effect their cure." Towards the end of his life Robert Owen became a Spiritualist. See Owen's *Autobiography*, 1857-8; Edward Vansittart Neale, *The Characteristic Features of some of the Principal Systems of Socialism*, 1851; G. J. Holyoake, *History of Co-operation in England*, 1875; Mark Hovell, *Chartist Movement*, 1918; and the *D.N.B.*

OWL, THE. The owl, which is often associated with night and gloom, appears in the MSS. of the Mayan Indians of Central America as the symbolical bird of the god designated God A by anthropologists. Among the ancient Germans, according to Tacitus, every tree in the sacred forests had its genius, and this genius sometimes took the form of an owl.

OXFORD DECLARATION. A manifesto on "Eternal Punishment" drawn up and signed in 1864 by Edward Bouverie Pusey (1800-1882), Regius Professor of Hebrew at Oxford and Canon of Christ Church, and George Anthony Denison (1805-1896), Archdeacon of Taunton and Editor of the "Church and State Review" (1862-65). More than three thousand other clergymen signed the declaration.

OXFORD MOVEMENT, THE. Another name for the Tractarian Movement (*q.v.*).

P

P. God P is a designation used by anthropologists for a deity depicted in the MSS. of the Mayan Indians of Central America. In the Codex Tro-cortesianus he is provided with a blue background representing water, and himself has the fins of a frog. Schellhas therefore describes him as "The Frog God." He seems to be a god of agriculture.

PACARI TAMPU. The name (House of the Dawn)

in Peruvian mythology for the cave from which came the brothers who founded various Peruvian systems of worship. "The first brother would appear to represent the oldest religion of Peru, that of Pachacamac, the second that of a fetishtic stone-worship, the third that of Viracocha, and the last sun-worship pure and simple" (Edwardes and Spence).

PACHACAMAC. The two chief deities of the ancient Peruvians were Pachacamac and Viracocha (*q.v.*). Like Viracocha, Pachacamac was adopted by the Peruvians from an older civilisation. The name means "earth-generator," which in itself suggests a similarity to Viracocha. Both were civilising powers, and legend relates that there was in fact rivalry and conflict between them. According to the legend, Viracocha was defeated by Pachacamac and put to flight. Pachacamac thereupon "created a new world more to his liking by the simple expedient of transferring the race of men then upon earth into wild animals, and creating a new and higher humanity." Pachacamac would seem to have forced his way into the pantheon of the Incas after Viracocha. Lewis Spence points out that the god of volcanoes, earthquakes, and subterranean fire, Pachacamac, would naturally be hostile to the god of water, Viracocha. A legend of the Collas (S.W. of Cuzco) seems to imply that the order in which the Peruvian deities was introduced was: Pachacamac, Viracocha, the Sun. The myth, however, which was authorised, so to say, by the Incas themselves, implies the order: Viracocha, Pachacamac. See Lewis Spence, *Myth.;* J. M. Robertson, *P.C.*

PACT OF FRATERNITY, THE. A declaration of principles for the progress of humanity drawn up in 1836 by Giuseppe (Joseph) Mazzini (1805-1872) for a secret Association composed of German, French, Italian, and Polish exiles, and called "Young Europe." As a young man Mazzini had joined the secret association in Italy called the "Carbonari" (literally "charcoal-burners" or "colliers"). In 1830 he was intrusted with a secret mission, and, having been betrayed, was imprisoned in the fortress of Savona on the western Riviera. In prison he conceived the idea of founding a new religious and republican association, to be called "Young Italy." In 1831 he was banished to France. Here, at Marseilles, in the same year, his association was founded. The members swore to devote their lives to the mission of uniting their dismembered country into "one free, independent, republican nation." But Mazzini was not a mere politician. Republicanism with him "was a *faith* —the logical and necessary consequence of his religious faith in the oneness of humanity" (E. A. Venturini). A few years later he was obliged to flee to Switzerland. While he was there he founded "Young England." Banished from Switzerland towards the end of 1836, he took refuge in London. About this time he was distressed by religious doubts, but he succeeded in arriving at a confirmation of his first faith. "I came to my better self alone; without aid from others, through the help of a religious conception, which I verified by history." In London for some years he had a struggle for existence. During the whole of 1837 and half of 1838 he suffered "absolute poverty." But he sought to help his neighbours. He opened a school for poor Italian boys, and kept it open from 1841-1848. "During those seven years we gave both moral and intellectual instruction to several hundred youths and children who were in a state of semi-barbarism; and who, half afraid at first, and urged only by curiosity, came to our humble rooms at 5 Hatton Garden, to be gradually tamed and civilized by the gentleness and kindness of the masters; until at length they learned to rejoice with a certain conscious pride in the idea of returning to their country possessed of education." They attended the school between nine and ten o'clock at night, bringing their organs with them; they also met on Sunday evenings for a lecture. In 1848 he left London to take part in the Italian revolutions. In March 1849 he was appointed to form a Triumvirate with Saffi and Armellini at Rome. Soon afterwards the Republic fell before the French, and he returned to London. Here he founded the "European Association," and planned other revolutions. In 1870 he returned to Italy, and on the 10th of March, 1872, died at Pisa. Mazzini was no ordinary political agitator. He was a prophet, and a religious force of considerable significance. He was radically opposed to Materialism. In his essays "On the Duties of Man" (1844) he says that Italy has suffered and is suffering from two great sores, Macchiavellism and Materialism. He says elsewhere ("A Letter to the Members of the Œcumenical Council," 1870) that morally Materialism is disinherited of all criterion of right, or principle of *collective* education; scientifically it is based upon a periodical confusion in men's minds of the instruments of life with life itself; historically, it is inexorably, invariably representative and characteristic of a period of transition between one religious faith and another. As a matter of fact "there is no antagonism between matter and spirit." But Revelation is progressive. "Revelation, which is, as Lessing says, the education of the human race, descends continually from God to man; prophesied by genius, evoked by virtue and sacrifice, and accepted and proclaimed from epoch to epoch by the great religious evolutions of collective humanity." Every epoch of humanity has had and will have its own social, artistic, and religious expression. From time to time man will adopt a different solution of the great problem of life, but assuredly it will never be a mere negation (cp. "The Religious Side of the Italian Question," 1867). Each of these religions contains a truth destined to live for ever. "Each religion sets before mankind a new educational idea as its aim; each is a fragment, enveloped in symbols, of eternal truth. . . . Having accomplished its mission, that religion disappears; leaving behind the portion of truth it contained, the unknown quantity disengaged by it from its symbol, a new, immortal star in humanity's heaven. As the discoveries of science have revealed, and will reveal, star upon star, until our knowledge of the celestial system of which the Milky Way is zone and the earth a part, be complete, so the religious faculties of humanity have added, and will add, faith to faith, until the entire truth we are capable of comprehending be complete" ("Letter to the Œcumen. Council," 1870). Mazzini felt that he himself was living in a transition period. But a new religious faith was already dawning. "The religious synthesis, which is slowly but infallibly taking the place of the synthesis of the past, comprehends a new *term*—the continuous *collective* life of humanity—and this alone is sufficient to change the *aim*, the *method*, and the moral *law* of our existence. . . . When once all belief in the past synthesis shall be extinct, and faith in the new synthesis established, the State itself will be elevated into a church; it will incarnate in itself a religious principle, and become the representative of the moral law in the various manifestations of life" ("The Religious Side of the Italian Question," 1867). Mazzini did not believe in the miraculous as commonly understood, but in the gradual working out of divine law. "We believe in the Unknown: in the Mysterious—to be one day solved—which now encompasses us on every side: in the secrets of an *intuition* inaccessible to analysis; in the truth of our strange presentiment of an Ideal, which is the primitive fatherland of the soul; in an unforeseen power of action granted to man in certain rare moments of faith, love, and supreme concentration of all the faculties towards a determinate and virtuous aim—deserved therefore—and analogous to the power of revelation which the increased concentration of rays in the telescope communicates to the human eye: but we believe all these things the pre-ordained consequences of laws hitherto withheld from our knowledge" (Letter of 1870, as cited above). He believed in "*one heaven*, in which we live, and move, and love; which embraces—as an ocean embraces the islands that stud its surface—the whole indefinite series of existences through which we pass." He believed in an indefinite series of re-incarnations of the soul, from life to life, from world to world. He believed in the slow, progressive divinisation of man, in the possibility of slowly elaborating in man the angel. True priests and counsellors are those who have proved worthy to be such by long years of tried virtue and of study of things eternal. "Prophets and guides upon the weary pilgrimage of humanity are the men upon whose brow God has set the seal of genius sanctified by virtue; but forget not that the Divine element exists also in yourselves; never yield up the liberty of your immortal souls into the hands of your brother man" (Letter of 1870). In answer to the question, What is Life? he tells us that Life is Love; Life is movement, aspiration, progress; Life is communion (a word, he says, taught us by Christianity)—"communion with nature and with man, wheresoever he loves, struggles, or hopes, and with God." The social Gospel of Mazzini is inseparably connected with his religious convictions. "The first real, earnest religious Faith that shall arise upon the ruins of the old worn-out creeds, will transform the whole of our actual social organization, because every strong and earnest faith tends to apply itself to every branch of human activity; because in every epoch of its existence the *earth* has ever tended to conform itself to the Heaven in which it then believed; and because the whole history of Humanity is but the repetition—in form and degree varying according to the diversity of the times—of the words of the Dominical Christian Prayer: *Thy Kingdom come on Earth as it is in Heaven*" ("On the Duties of Man," 1844). Labour should be the basis of civil society, and the distribution of its fruits should be according to works. If a man will not labour, he should possess naught. The religious Word of the epoch is Association. "Association of labour, and the division of the fruits of labour, or rather of the profits of the sale of its productions between the producers, in proportion to the amount and value of the work done by each—this is the social future" ("Duties," 1844). We must strive to make of Humanity one single family. But property, though it is ill-constituted is not an evil. The *principle* of property is in fact eternal. "We must not seek to abolish property because at present it is the possession of the few: we must open up the paths by which the many may acquire it" ("Duties."). We must make it, however, the result of labour alone—labour rightly remunerated. Nor is wealth in itself an evil. "Wealth is sacred when diffused like healing balm upon the wounds both of mind and body, by which your brothers are afflicted; accursed, when employed to minister to selfish passion, pleasure, or pride" ("Letter" as cited above). It has already been said that Mazzini opened a night-school for working lads in London. He attached supreme importance to education. In his essays "On the Duties of Man" he says that his whole doctrine is included and summed up in this grand word. "The vital question in agitation at the present day is a question of Education. We do not seek to establish a new order of things through violence. Any order of things established through violence, even though in itself superior to the old, is still a tyranny. What we have to do is to propose, for the approval of the nation, an order of things which we believe to be superior to that now existing, and to *educate* men by every possible means to develope it and act in accordance with it." In a chapter on duties towards the family he says that the conception of the family is divine, and no human power can extinguish it. The Angel of the family is Woman. To her belong by nature equal rights with man. "Cancel from your minds every idea of superiority over Woman. You have none whatsoever. Long prejudice, an inferior education, and a perennial legal inequality and injustice, have created that *apparent* intellectual inferiority which has been converted into an argument of continued oppression. . . . In the sight of God the Father there is neither *man* nor *woman*. There is only the *human* being, that being in whom, whether the form be of male or female, those characteristics which distinguish humanity from the brute creation are united—namely, the social tendency, and the capacity of education and progress." In 1847 Mazzini published some very interesting "Thoughts upon Democracy in Europe." See P. A. Taylor, *Joseph Mazzini: A Memoir by E. A. V., With Two Essays by Mazzini*, 2nd ed. 1877; *Foreshadowings of the Coming Faith by Joseph Mazzini*, 1888.

PADAITHALAIDAIVAM. The name in Tanjore of one of the sea gods worshipped by the Pattanavans, a caste of fishermen in India. He is represented by a large conical heap of wet sand and mud.

PAGANALIA. An Italian festival of the old village communities. It was moveable, but was held after the winter-sowing in January. A pregnant sow was sacrificed to Tellus or Ceres. At this festival also "we are told that small images of the human figure, or masks, or simply round balls (*pilae*), were hung up on trees or doorways, and left to swing in the wind" (Warde Fowler). These figures were commonly called *oscilla*, whence the verb *oscillare*. J. G. Frazer has shown that swinging has been, and is, practised in various parts of the world as a religious or magical rite (see SWINGING). This suggests that the oscilla were imitations of men and women. As Frazer explains, in some cases the object of the swinging is to promote fertility, perhaps by clearing the air of dangerous influences. In the festival described by Virgil in the second *Georgic* (380 fol.), which seems to be some form of Paganalia, "the object would seem to be prosperity of the vine-crop" (Fowler). See O. Seyffert, *Dict.*; W. Warde Fowler.

PAGODAS. The Pagoda has developed out of the Dāgaba. The Dāgaba was at first simply the casket in which the Buddhists preserved the relics of their great saints. Then in course of time it came to denote not only the casket containing the relics but also the monument containing the casket. Next the monument grew to an enormous size, and Dāgabas became Pagodas. Monier-Williams gives a description (after Scott) of the great Rangoon pagoda, which contains relics of Gautama and his three predecessors. "The stately pile stands upon a mound—partly natural, partly artificial—cut into two rectangular terraces one above the other, the upper being 166 feet above the ground, and each side facing one of the cardinal points of the compass. The ascent is by very dilapidated steps, some of stone, some of 'sun-dried bricks, worn almost into a slope by the bare feet of myriads of worshippers.' From the centre of this springs, from an octagonal plinth, the 'profusely gilt *solid brick* pagoda', which has a circumference of 1355 feet, and rises to a height of about 328, 'or nearly as high as St. Paul's Cathedral.' On the summit is 'the Tee,' a gilt umbrella-shaped ornament with many tiers of rings, on each of which 'hang multitudes of gold and silver jewelled bells.' It was 'placed there at a cost of not much less than £50,000.' At the foot of the pagoda are four chapels, having colossal figures of Buddha at the sides, and their gilded interiors darkened by the vapour of thousands of burning tapers. 'Hundreds of Gautamas', large and small, white and black, gilded and plain, sitting, standing, and reclining, surround the larger images." Compare STŪPAS. See Monier-Williams, *Buddhism*, 1890; and H. Hackmann.

PAN. The worship of the Greek god Pan originated in Arcadia, where he was the divinity of hills, woods, and pastures, and the patron of hunters, herdsmen, and flocks. He is represented as having shaggy hair, a beard, a puck-nose, two horns, a tail, and goat's feet. He was supposed to wander by day "through hill and dale with the Nymphs, guarding the flocks, especially the goats, and chasing wild animals." At noonday, when he slept, hunters or shepherds could not blow their horns without incurring his wrath. He is supposed to have been fond of music and dancing, and to have invented the syrinx or Pan's pipe. In the forest he was wont to come upon the traveller unexpectedly and to inspire him with sudden terror ("panic"). As a god of hills, he had special mountains in Attica and Arcadia, which were named after him. Some of the rocks were called Pan's goats. As a god of woods, he was an oracular deity, a god of prophecy. The offerings which his worshippers brought to him consisted of the simple products of the country, milk, honey, must, cows, goats, or lambs. He was identified with Faunus by the Romans. And with him were associated young Pans (*Pānisci*), just as with Faunus were associated Fauns, and with Silvanus (*q.v.*) Silvanuses. See, further, FAUNUS. See O. Seyffert, *Dict.; Chambers' Encycl.;* J. M. Robertson, *C.M.*, 1910; J. G. Frazer, *G.B.*, Part V. vol. ii.

PANDĀRAMS. A kind of caste in India. According to H. A. Stuart (quoted by E. Thurston), Pandāram is "the name rather of an occupation than a caste, and used to denote any non-Brāhmanical priest."

PĀNDURANG. Yellow-coloured, one of the names of the Hindu god Vishnu.

PANENTHEISM. A term used by Dr. Inge to denote the belief in the immanence of a God who is also transcendent. "In its true form it is an integral part of Christian philosophy, and indeed of all rational theology." But, according to Inge, it is apt to degenerate into the worst form of pantheism.

P'AN-KU. The name of the first man in Chinese cosmogony. He is depicted as a giant with mallet and chisel, the implements used by him in his task of breaking the primeval rocks and shaping the world.

PANTHEISM. Pantheism has been defined in various ways. The word is said to have been used first in the title to one of Toland's books (1705). Weissenborn defines Pantheism as the system which identifies God and the *all of things*, or the *unity of things* (K. R. Hagenbach, *History of Christian Doctrines*, iii., p. 323). Six forms have been distinguished. (1) Mechanical, or materialistic pantheism: God being the mechanical unity of existence. (2) Ontological (abstract unity) pantheism: God being the one substance in all (Spinoza). (3) Dynamic pantheism. (4) Psychical pantheism: God being the soul of the world. (5) Ethical pantheism: God being the universal moral order (Fichte). (6) Logical pantheism (Hegel). The Christian mystics are loosely charged with being pantheists. But, as H. B. Workman says, however much they might play with pantheistic phrases, there are few of them who do not seek to conserve personality. "For the mystics were conscious that the originality of Christianity consists in its revelation through the person of Christ of the depth and inexhaustibleness of human personality. Accordingly, in the Christian mystics, dangerous as their language with reference to absorption may be at times, there is always an emphasis of purpose; in the later mystics, for instance, much is made of the will—and this in itself is fatal to pantheism."

PANTISM. Pantism, the theory of the All, differs, as Paul Carus points out, from Pantheism (*q.v.*), the theory which identifies the All with God. Pantism is "a theory according to which the All alone (or rather the conception of the absolute as the All) is possessed of reality, while all concrete existences are considered as a mere sham, an illusion, a dream" (Paul Carus, *History of the Devil and the Idea of Evil*, 1900.).

PĀRĀ. The name of one of the Jewish treatises or tractates which reproduce the oral tradition or unwritten law as developed by the second century A.D., and are incorporated in the Mishnah (*q.v.*), a collection and compilation completed by Rabbi Judah the Holy, or the Patriarch, about 200 A.D. The sixty-three tractates of the Mishnah are divided into six groups or orders (*sedarim*). Pārā is the fourth tractate of the sixth group, which is called *Ṭohorōth* ("Purifications").

PARABLES OF THE NEW TESTAMENT. The Gospels contain a large number of parables, and these may be regarded as only a selection of those spoken by Jesus. Jesus seems to have employed this figurative style of speech as a means of enforcing and elucidating his lessons. The parables were not always understood by His disciples. An explanation had to be sought privately. As an excuse for their own dullness they seem to have cherished the thought that the Master spoke in parables for the very purpose of disguising some of his message from the people. "In Mark iv. 10-12 = Matthew xiii. 10-15 = Luke viii. 9f. the idea of the Evangelists is that the Master specially favours the disciples by explaining to them figurative language which has been contrived in such a way as to disguise the truth from the people. As a matter of fact, the explanation was necessitated simply by their defective insight" (Arno Neumann). It is not likely that Jesus taught esoteric and exoteric doctrines. Some of the parables are certainly difficult for us to understand, but this is no doubt because they have not been preserved in quite their original forms. It is possible in some cases that two parables which were originally distinct have been made into one. There is another possibility with regard to some of the narratives in the New Testament. It is that parables have been converted into history. The story of the miraculous feeding of five thousand or four thousand people has been explained in this way. The story is to the effect that a multitude was fed with a few loaves and fishes, and that after it had been satisfied, a large quantity of food remained. It is suggested that originally this was a parable with a deep spiritual meaning. "The following figure will make the meaning quite clear:—When a mother divides a loaf of bread between twelve children, each one, of course, receives less than if there were only two children. But if she is able to share her love or her knowledge with twelve instead of with two, love and truth do not decrease, but increase. An explanation like this has not been invented by perplexed scholars: it has been rediscovered" (Arno Neumann). The Fourth Gospel does not contain a single real parable. See O. Holtzmann, *Life of Jesus*, 1904; Arno Neumann, *Jesus*, 1906; Paul W. Schmiedel, *The Johannine Writings*, 1908.

PARACELSISTS. The followers of Paracelsus (Philippus Aureolus Paracelsus Theophrastus von Hohenheim;

1493-1541), the theosophist or mystic. See MYSTICISM, CHRISTIAN.

PARACLETE. The term Paraclete (Gk. *paraklētos*) occurs four times in the Gospel of John (xiv. 16, 26; xv. 26, xvi. 7) and once in the First Epistle of John (ii. 1). In Job xvi. 2 it is used by Aquila and Theodotion in the plural to render the Hebrew word *mĕnaohămîm,* which means "comforters" ("wearisome comforters are ye all"). In Isaiah xl. 1, where the Hebrew has, "Comfort ye, comfort ye my people," the Septuagint renders by *paracaleite, paracaleite.* The Greek word *paraclēsis* frequently means "consolation." It also means "encouragement." Philo sometimes uses the word "*paraclētos* in the sense of "helper" or "adviser." The word, it is true, is passive in form and most naturally means "one called in," or "called to the side of another," and so "an advocate." This is perhaps the meaning in I. John ii. 1: "We have an Advocate with the Father, Jesus Christ the righteous." But it seems also, perhaps on the analogy of Hebrew usage, to have been used in an active sense and as the equivalent of the Hebrew *mĕnachēm,* "comforter." Origen and Chrysostom understand the word in this sense. The Hebrew word often means to "console" those who are mourning, but it also means to "encourage" (Gen. l. 21). In Psalm lxxxvi. the verb is made parallel to the verb *'āzar* "to help," and in Jeremiah xxxi. 13 to the verb "to cause to rejoice." The Paraclete, then, may be regarded as some agency which consoles, comforts, encourages, and helps. Used as an equivalent of the Hebrew term, there is in the word no idea of acting as an advocate or pleader. And in the Gospel of John the word is no doubt to be understood as the equivalent of *mĕnachēm.* Thus, John xiv. 16 says: "And I will pray the Father, and he shall give you another *Comforter* (not necessarily a person), that he may be with you for ever, the spirit of truth." Vs. 26 reads: "But the *Comforter,* the holy spirit, whom the Father will send in my name, he shall teach you all things, and bring to your remembrance all that I said unto you." In xv. 26 it is said: "But when the *Comforter* is come, whom I will send unto you from the Father, the spirit of truth, which proceedeth from the Father, he shall bear witness of me." Lastly, in xvi. 7, Jesus is represented as saying: "If I go not away, the *Comforter* will not come unto you; but if I go, I will send him unto you." And he explains that it is necessary for the Comforter to come to convince (not "convict" in the sense of condemn) the world of the true nature of sin, righteousness, and judgment. The Comforter, therefore, is the spirit of truth, which will comfort, help, encourage and enlighten men. Or as A. Juelicher expresses it: "in place of the Son about to return to the Father, the seemingly forsaken disciples are to receive the *patronus,* the "helper" κατ' ἐξοχην, the spirit of truth, who will take them up and lead them up, in the struggle for light and life, step by step, from victory to victory." See A. Juelicher in the *Encycl. Bibl.;* also the *Prot. Dict.;* and the *Cath. Dict.*

PARAKUTTI. One of the chief gods of the Nāyādis, a Hindu caste in Malabar. "Parakutti is he who aids them in their hunting expeditions, bringing the game to them, and protecting them from wild beasts" (E. Thurston and K. Rangachari). The other chief gods are Mallan and Malavazhi.

PARASHRĀM. One of the incarnations of the Hindu god Vishnu.

PARDHĀNS. The Pardhāns (also known as Pathāris, or Panāls) are described by R. V. Russell and R. B. Hira Lāl as an inferior branch of the Gond tribe whose occupation is to act as the priests and minstrels of the Gonds.

PARERMENEUTAE. An early religious body, the members of which declined to follow other men's judgments with regard to the Scriptures, and insisted on interpreting them themselves.

PARI-NIRVĀṆA. One of the forms of Nirvāṇa (*q.v.*).

PARIVĀRA. One of the Buddhist sacred books. A kind of appendix to the books in the first division of the Canon. See CANON, BUDDHIST.

PARJANYA. Parjanya is one of the rain-gods in Hinduism. Hopkins points out that he is identical with the Slavic Perkuna. He is a personification of the rain-cloud, and is therefore associated with Indra (*q.v.*). "Occasionally he is paired with Wind; and in the curious tendency of the poets to dualize their divinities, the two become a compound, *Parjanyavātā* ("Parjanya and Vāta")." Sometimes no distinction seems to be made between Parjanya and Indra. See E. W. Hopkins.

PARMĀRTHI SECT. A Vishnuite sect in India, which in 1901, according to the census, numbered 26,000 persons. Originally the adherents devoted themselves to the pure worship of Krishna, but later their worship, at any rate in the case of a considerable part of the sect, "has been degraded by sexual indulgence and immorality, and this appears to be the main basis of its ritual at present" (R. V. Russell).

PARMESHWAR. A god worshipped as the supreme deity by the Kurmis, the representative cultivating caste of Hindustān. He seems to be equivalent to Siva or Mahādeo.

PARNAPISHTIM. Parnapishtim or Utnapishtim is the hero of the Babylonian Deluge-story. To some extent he resembles the Noah of the Old Testament. See DELUGE-STORY, BABYLONIAN, and GILGAMESH EPIC.

PARRAPOTAMMĀ. A Hindu deity, a goddess supposed to cure cattle diseases, worshipped by the Paraiyans, a tribe or caste in India.

PARSON LOT. "Parson Lot" was the *nom-de-plume* assumed by Charles Kingsley (1819-1875) as the writer of some of the tracts known as "Politics for the People." On one occasion when the leading contributors to this series were assembled at the house of Frederick Denison Maurice (1805-1872), in some discussion Kingsley found himself in a minority of one. This prompted him to say jokingly "that he felt much as Lot must have felt in the Cities of the Plain, when he seemed as one that mocked to his sons-in-law." It was thereupon suggested that he should call himself "Parson Lot." See C. W. Stubbs, *Charles Kingsley and the Christian Social Movement,* 1899.

PARTHENOGENESIS. The myth that certain divine beings or culture-heroes have owed their birth to a mother without the co-operation of a father has been found to be widespread. For example, Isis, Cybele, Leto, Demeter, and Venus are all represented as "virgin" mothers. The Chinese culture-hero Hou Chi was born of a mother who conceived by treading in a footprint of God. The principal deity of the Uapes Indians of Brazil, Jurupari, was born of a virgin who conceived after drinking a draught of native beer. The idea may be a survival from a time when the fact of physical paternity was unknown. To this day many Australian tribes seem to have remained ignorant of this fact (see J. G. Frazer, *Adonis, Attis, Osiris,* 3rd ed., i., p. 99 ff.). It is said, for instance, that the Arunta is ignorant of the exact relation between generation and the sexual act, supposing every act of conception to be due to a sort of mystic fecundation. "According to him, it is due to the entrance of the soul of an ancestor into the body of a woman and its becoming the principle of a new life there. So at the moment when a woman feels the first tremblings of the child, she imagines that one of the souls whose principal residence is at the place where she happens to be, has just entered into her" (Émile Durkheim).

PARTHIANS, LETTER TO THE. Augustine quotes a verse from the First Epistle of John and says that it occurs in John's letter "to the Parthians." Since, however, the Greek word for "virgins" resembles the word "Parthians," it has been suggested that the one was mistaken for the other. It has been inferred from a passage in the Book of Revelation (xiv. 4) that perhaps the First Epistle of John was known by the title "To the Virgins." See G. Currie Martin, *Books of the N.T.*

PĀRVATĪ. Pārvatī is one of the deities worshipped by the Hindus. The name is one of those given to the wife of the god Śiva (*q.v.*). Another name is Durgā (*q.v.*).

PASSALORYNCHITES. A body of early mystics. They are perhaps to be identified with the Tascodrugites (*q.v.*).

PASSIONISTS. A Roman Catholic order founded in 1720 by Paul Francis Danei (1694-1775) or Paul of the Cross. The founder could not at first obtain papal sanction for his order; but in 1746 the rules of the congregation were approved by Benedict XIV. In 1867 Paul of the Cross was canonised by Pius IX. The real description of the order is: "Congregation of the Discalced Clerks of the most holy Cross and Passion of our Lord Jesus Christ." Its motto is "Jesu Christi passio sit semper in cordibus nostris." Paul of the Cross was very anxious to extend his work to England, and there are now a number of Passionist houses in this country. Soon after the Passionists obtained a footing in England (1842), they established themselves in the United States, where they now have a province. "The life of a Passionist is very austere. They fast three days in every week, besides Advent and Lent; they wear nothing on their feet but sandals; they rise at night to say Matins, and, indeed, recite the office in choir at all the canonical hours. They divide their time between contemplation and action; being indefatigable in giving missions and retreats, especially to persons living in community. Besides the three usual vows, they make a fourth—that they will do their utmost to keep alive in the hearts of the faithful the memory of our Lord's passion. On the day of their profession they make a vow of perseverance in the congregation. Nevertheless, they only take simple vows" (Addis and Arnold). See *Prot. Dict.;* and the *Cath. Dict.*

PASTORAL EPISTLES, THE. Three Epistles in the New Testament are commonly called the Pastoral Epistles because they deal with the ministry and are addressed to two pastors in the early Church. Timothy and Titus. The Epistles are First Epistle to Timothy, Second Epistle to Timothy, and the Epistle to Titus (*qq.v.*). The Epistles are attributed to Paul, but their genuineness is open to grave doubt. A. S. Peake summarises the arguments against the genuineness as follows: "It is strange that Paul should have written letters of this kind to such companions and disciples as Timothy and Titus, and that he should have felt it necessary to assert to them his apostleship and warn them to keep clear of heretical teaching. If the letters fall outside the period covered by the Acts they are probably not genuine, since Paul's imprisonment, there recorded, seems to have ended, not in release, but in death. As to organisation, we find much stress on ecclesiastical appointment, little on the spiritual gifts, and it is not quite like Paul to be occupied so much with details of this kind. The general emphasis on the importance of sound doctrine and the use of faith as almost equivalent to orthodoxy are strange in Paul. So too the tone of the letters is moralistic rather than evangelical, though the latter element is not absent. And finally the style is quite unique and unlike that of the other Epistles, and the ring of the letters does not remind us of Paul." Peake thinks that the Epistles contain not a little Pauline material, but that in their present form they cannot have come from Paul's hand. Currie Martin points out that in ancient writings it is not always a question only of authenticity or forgery. The question also of pseudonymity comes in. It was a practice among Jewish writers to produce a book under the name of some famous person (*e.g.*, Moses, Isaiah, Enoch) of an earlier day. "It is quite possible, therefore, that with no evil intention or purpose of leading readers astray, the name of the great Apostle may have been used by some of his friends and followers who were anxious to further his work, promulgate his ideas, and, in all probability, find a hearing for teaching that they knew was derived from himself in letters that, in their present form at least, do not emanate from him at all." See J. A. M'Clymont; G. Currie Martin; Arthur S. Peake, *Intr.*

PASTORAL STAFF. The official emblem of a bishop. See CROSIER.

PATERINES. The Paterines or Patarenes were Manichaean heretics who appeared in Italy in the eleventh century. A number of them were burned by the Archbishop of Milan. They were opposed to marriage, and regarded matter as evil. The name seems to have been suggested by Pataria, a designation of an evil quarter of Milan. It came to be used as a term of reproach. Those who reproached the Lombard married clergy were taunted with being Paterines (1057). In the twelfth century the Cathari are referred to as Paterines. See J. H. Blunt; *Cath. Dict.;* Brockhaus.

PATERNIANI. A Manichæan sect referred to by Augustine (*Hœres.* lxxxv.) and Prædestinatus (*Hœres.* lxxxv.). The Paterniani, who were also known as Venustiani, held that God created the upper part of the body, but the Devil the lower or sensual part. They were condemned by Pope Damasus I. (366-384). See J. H. Blunt.

PATRIPASSIANS. The Patripassians were a school of theologians produced by the doctrine of the Logos. They were so called because they held that He who became incarnate in Jesus Christ was none other than God the Father. Thus Noëtus said: "I know but one God; it is no other than He who was born, who suffered, and who died." The Patripassians were called also Modalists (*q.v.*). See J. H. Blunt; Louis Duchesne, *Hist.*

PATTHĀNA. A Buddhist sacred book in the third division of the Canon. See CANON, BUDDHIST.

PĀVADAIRĀYAN. The name in Tanjore of one of the sea gods worshipped by the Pattanavans, a caste of fishermen in India. He is represented by a large conical heap of wet sand and mud.

PE'Ā. The title of one of the Jewish treatises or tractates which reproduce the oral tradition or unwritten law as developed by the second century A.D. and are incorporated in the Mishnah (*q.v.*), a collection and compilation completed by Rabbi Judah the Holy, or the Patriarch, about 200 A.D. The sixty-three tractates of the Mishnah are divided into six groups or orders (*sedarim*). Pe'ā is the second tractate of the first group, which is called *Zerā'im* ("Seeds").

PEACH, THE. The oldest sacred books of China teach that the Universe has two souls or breaths, Yang (*q.v.*) and Yin (*q.v.*). Yang represents the heavens, and with them light, warmth, productivity and life. Yin represents the earth, and with it darkness, cold, and death.

The peach tree, like the cock, is associated with Yang. "The triumphal progress of the *Yang* in early spring is characterized by the flowering of the peach. Therefore this tree and the red, brilliant colour of its blossoms represent the destruction of the *Yin* or winter, and the spectral world which is identified with it. Therefore, from the oldest times to this day, branches, boards, and human images of peach wood have been fixed on New Year's day to doors and gates. At present those things are replaced by sheets of red paper, which nobody who has set foot on Chinese soil can have failed to notice. Red, in consequence, is under all circumstances a colour expressing felicity, seeing that felicity consists in destruction of spectres, the enemies of human welfare" (Degroot). See J. J. M. Degroot, *Rel. of the Chinese*, 1910.

PEARL AMONG WOMEN. One of the seven royal treasures which the king of kings, the ideal king, of the Buddhists, or rather of the pre-Buddhists, is supposed to possess. She is described as "graceful in figure, lovely in appearance, charming in manner, and beautiful in complexion, surpassing human beauty"; and it is said that "she had attained unto the beauty of the gods." See T. W. Rhys Davids.

PECTORAL CROSS. As a special privilege granted by the Pope, bishops, abbots, and sometimes canons and others are allowed to wear on the breast a small cross of precious metal as a mark of their office. This is called a pectoral cross.

PECULIAR PEOPLE. A religious sect founded at Plumstead near London in 1838, and called also "Plumstead Peculiars." They are Faith-healers, and have much in common with the American Tunkers (*q.v.*). Their principles are based on a passage in the Epistle of James (v. 13-15). "Is any among you suffering? let him pray. Is any cheerful? let him sing praise. Is any among you sick? let him call for the elders of the church; and let them pray over him, anointing him (or, having anointed him) with oil in the name of the Lord: and the prayer of faith shall save him that is sick, and the Lord shall raise him up; and if he have committed sins, it shall be forgiven him." The peculiar people put faith in prayer and in anointing with oil by the elders rather than in medicine and medical treatment (apart from surgery). Cp. CHRISTIAN SCIENCE.

PELAGIANISM. The doctrine and principles of the British monk Pelagius (*fl.* 400-418). He was often called Pelagius Brito to distinguish him from another Pelagius. He went from the British Isles, probably from Ireland, to Rome, where he made the acquaintance of Paulinus (353-431), Rufinus of Aquileia, and Cœlestius. In 410 he went with Cœlestius to Africa, where he met Augustine. From Africa he went alone after a few years to Palestine. Jerome was living at this time in Bethlehem. In 415 Pelagius was accused of heresy by Paulus Orosius, acting on behalf of the African Church. The matter came before a Synod at Jerusalem, with the result that it was decided to refer it to Pope Innocent I. Innocent I. died soon afterwards (A.D. 417), and was succeeded by Zosimus. Zosimus declared in favour of the orthodoxy of Pelagius, and in a circular letter to the African episcopate commanded that the charge of heresy should be abandoned. The Emperor Theodosius, however, having been induced to exert himself against Pelagius, he was condemned by African Councils in 417 and 418. In 418 Zosimus also, having reconsidered the matter, anathematized Pelagius and Cœlestius. In 431 Pelagianism was condemned by the third General Council, the Council of Ephesus. In the first canon any one who is of Cœlestius' opinion is "entirely cast off by the Synod from all Church communion, and suspended." The fourth canon declares: "The holy Synod gives it in charge, that all clergy who fall away, and either publicly or privately adhere to the opinions of Nestorius and Cœlestius, be deposed." Pelagius had been vigorously opposed by Augustine and Jerome. A favourite principle with Pelagius was the declaration, "I ought, therefore I can." "In his view, Augustine's doctrine of total depravity, and of the consequent bondage of the will, cut the nerve of all human effort. He insisted, accordingly, that man is able to do all that God commands. In keeping with this, he denied original sin, holding that since obligation implies ability, the power of choosing the good exists after the Fall precisely as before it. It is apparent that these positions rest upon a theory of freedom quite different from Augustine's. Augustine believed in freedom in the ordinary actions of life, but taught that in its highest form, as the power to keep God's law, freedom is a lost gift, which only grace can restore. By freedom Pelagius meant an equipoise of the will, which enables us at any time, whatever our previous history may have been, to choose between the evil and the good" (*Prot. Dict.*). Cp. further SEMI-PELAGIANISM. See J. H. Blunt; *Prot. Dict.*; *Cath. Dict.*

PELICAN. In mediæval art the pelican appears frequently as an emblem of Christ. The symbolism is explained by St. Augustine in a comment on Psalm cii. 6. "The pelican fervently loveth her young birds. Yet when they be haughty and begin to wax hot, they smite her in the face and wound her, and she smiteth them and slayeth them. And after three days she mourneth for them; and then striking herself in the side till the blood runs out, she sprinkleth it upon their bodies, and by virtue thereof they quicken again. In like manner Christ was beaten and buffeted by the children of men, and yet shed His blood to give them eternal life" (quoted by Francis Bond). The emblem is called the "Pelican in Piety" or the "Pelican in her Piety." The representation survives in a number of Churches (*e.g.*, in S. Nicholas Church, Yarmouth). See also Sidney Heath; and cp. W. Carew Hazlitt, 1905.

PENANCE. The Hindu view of penance is aptly described by S. G. Roberts, *Calcutta Review*, 1902, quoted by E. Thurston and K. Rangachari. "Briefly stated, it is that anyone who performs any penance for a sufficiently long time acquires such a store of power and virtue that the very gods themselves cannot stand against it. Hindu mythology affords many examples of this belief. Siva himself, in one of his incarnations, saved the whole Indian Olympus and the universe at large from a demigod, who, by years of penance, had become charged, as it were, with power, like a religious electric 'accumulator.' The early sages and heroes of Indian story had greater facilities for the acquisition of this reserve of power, in that their lives lasted for centuries or even æons."

PENITENTIAL PSALMS. A name given to seven of the psalms of the Old Testament, because they express repentance for sin. They are: Psalms vi., xxxii., xxxviii, li., cii., cxxx., cxliii. (in the Latin numeration, vi., xxxi., xxxvii., l., ci., cxxix., cxlii.). In the Roman Breviary they are placed together, and Pope Innocent III. ordered that they should be recited in Lent. It is not, however, obligatory to recite them in the private recitation of the Breviary. In the Breviary an antiphon "Ne reminiscaris" from Tobit iii. 3 is now attached to them. It was added, it is thought, in the sixteenth century. See the *Cath. Dict.*

PENTATEUCH. A term of Greek derivation which is commonly used as a collective title for the first five books of the Old Testament. The Jewish title is "The

Law" (Torah). The books are: Genesis, Exodus, Leviticus, Numbers, Deuteronomy. Modern criticism, however, has shown that the compiler of the sixth book of the Old Testament (Joshua) has made use of the same sources, and that in fact "the book of Joshua originally was an essential member of the group" (C. A. Briggs, *Hex.*). It is therefore more convenient and correct to speak of the Hexateuch.

PEOPLE OF GOD, THE. A sect founded by Mary Anne Girling (1827-1886) in Battersea, London. In 1864 she declared that in her the Deity had again become incarnate. Her followers settled in Hampshire. See the *D.N.B.*

PEPUZANS. Another name for the Montanists. They were so called because Pepuza in Phrygia became their headquarters. See MONTANISM.

PERATICI. Another name for the Essenes (*q.v.*). They were so called from their settlement at Peraea.

PERCHTA. Perchta is a figure in Teutonic mythology. She belongs more especially to Southern Germany. Sometimes she is represented as a goddess of fertility. In Switzerland and the Tyrol at the beginning of January a procession has long been held in her honour called the Perchtenlaufen or Berchtenlaufen. In Upper Germany Perchta or Berchta is represented as surrounded by the children who have died. See P. D. Chantepie de la Saussaye, *Rel. of the Teutons*, 1902.

PERES DU BEAU CHANT, LES. A name given to the fathers of the French Oratory on account of their interest in music. See ORATORY, THE FRENCH.

PERFECTIONISTS. A sect founded about the year 1831 by John Humphrey Noyes (1811-1886) in North America. Noyes established his community at Oneida Creek in New York State. The principles of the sect are that its members, being reconciled with God, are perfect; that the two sexes are equal; and that there should be a perfect community of families and goods. Since the members of the sect are perfect, all that they do must be good and pure. Their community of families means a community of women. Hence the Perfectionists are known also as "Free Lovers." Another name for them is Bible Communists. There are now four settlements in America. See J. H. Blunt; Brockhaus.

PERICOPE ADULTERAE. The section in the Gospel of John containing the story of the adulteress (John vii. 53-viii. 12) is thus designated. It is clearly an interpolation. It does not appear in a large number of manuscripts, and "in many a copy it has been merely added, often in a small hand, on the margin" (C. R. Gregory). The verses did not originally form part of the Gospel of John. The story seems to have been widely circulated (at first orally) and read. Eusebius says that it found a place in the Gospel according to the Hebrews. But there are many various readings. Dr. Gregory thinks that "there are in the whole New Testament no other dozen verses that exhibit such a manifold variation of reading." One of the variations, chiefly found in manuscripts on Mount Athos, makes the story, as described by Dr. Gregory, very dramatic. "At the close of the eighth verse, when Jesus again turns away from the Pharisees and again writes on the ground, we are told what He wrote. For the sentence is made to say: He wrote upon the ground the sins of each single one of them. Of course, that is aimed at these accusing Pharisees. We see the people crowding around Jesus. In the midst of the group are half a dozen or more scribes and Pharisees, who have brought the woman to Jesus and have stated her sin. They think to lay a snare for Him. They have no fear for themselves. The ninth verse completes the change that turns the tables upon the Pharisees. It does not read: And they when they heard it. It reads: And they when they read it. The Pharisees accused the woman. Jesus wrote on the ground, affecting not to hear them, as also an old reading suggests. They badger Him until He looks up at them and curtly says: He that is without sin among you let him first cast a stone at her. And then He stoops down and again writes upon the ground. What is He writing there? The foremost Pharisee is of course the oldest. It was his right to be in front. He looks down at the sand at the word that Jesus has just written, and sees there the name of a great sin that he has done, but which he thinks is known to no one. Like a flash his conscience wakens. Verse ninth says: And they, when they read it, being convicted by their conscience, went out one by one, beginning from the eldest unto the last. This oldest Pharisee has turned and edged his way out of the crowd as fast as he could. Jesus has swept His hand across the sand to smoothe it over, and has again written something. This word the next Pharisee reads, and recognising a hidden sin of his own, he too flees. And thus it goes on till the accusers are all away. And Jesus is left alone with the woman in the centre of the group of people. Jesus looks up at her and asks her—we can hear the scathing irony of the words—Where are they? Doth no man condemn thee? Yes, indeed, He may well ask where they are. They have gone off, thinking of their own sins. Their own thoughts are now accusing and perhaps weakly excusing them, but chiefly condemning them. And the woman answers: No man, Lord. And Jesus said: Neither do I condemn thee. Go thy way, and from henceforth sin no more." See C. R. Gregory.

PERIODEUTÆ. The Periodeutæ are mentioned by Cosmas Indicopleustes as an order of Nestorian itinerant preachers who were active in N.W. India (535 A.D.). Cosmas Indicopleustes was a Greek merchant who visited India.

PERUMAL. A synonym of Vishnu, the great Hindu deity. The name is taken by some of the Pallis, a caste in India.

PERUNU. Perunu was the supreme god of the ancient Slavs. There was a wooden idol of the god at Kief in 980 A.D., "with a silver head and a golden beard, holding in his hand a thunderbolt" (Reinach). This seems to be the god of the Slavs referred to by Procopius as forging thunderbolts and as being the sole master of the universe. He would correspond to some extent to Jupiter and Thor (*q.v.*). The name for Thursday among the Baltic Slavs is Perendan. Reinach thinks this implies that the god of thunder and of heaven had a name akin to Perunu. See Reinach, *O.*

PERVIGILIUM. This was the name given by the ancients to a vigil in honour of a deity. The "Pervigilium Venĕris" is also the name of a Latin hymn dating from the third century A.D.

PESACHIM. The name of one of the Jewish treatises or tractates which reproduce the oral tradition or unwritten law as developed by the second century A.D. and are incorporated in the Mishnah (*q.v.*), a collection and compilation completed by Rabbi Judah the Holy, or the Patriarch, about 200 A.D. The sixty-three tractates of the Mishnah are divided into six groups or orders (*sedarim*). Pesāchīm is the third tractate of the second group, which is called *Mō'ēd* ("Festival").

PETER, THE FIRST EPISTLE OF. The First Epistle General of Peter claims to be by the well-known apostle of that name, and the claim is strongly attested by the external evidence. The Epistle was known to the author of the Second Epistle of Peter, to Polycarp, to the author of the Teaching of the Twelve Apostles, and (according to Eusebius) to Papias. It is quoted as the work of Peter by Irenaeus, Clement of Alexandria, Tertullian and Origen. It is reckoned by Eusebius and Origen as one of the quite authentic books of the New Testament. It is not, it is true, included in the Muratorian Canon; but it is found in the earliest versions. The internal evidence is not so strong. No visit of Peter to the "sojourners of the Dispersion in Pontus, Galatia, Cappadocia, Asia, and Bithynia," to whom the letter is addressed is known. Paul was closely associated with them, and yet he is not mentioned. If the Babylon in v. 13 is a name for Rome, Mark and the author of the epistle were in Rome when it was written. Does this mean that Paul, who is not mentioned, was dead? The author seems to have made use of some of the Epistles of Paul (Romans xii. and xiii.; Galatians iii. and v.; Ephesians ii. and iv.), and his whole epistle is influenced by Pauline teaching. Prof. Peake thinks it is no use minimising the extent of the Pauline influence. "We may rather state the problem in this form. Granting that the dominant influence is that of Paul, is this incompatible with Petrine authorship? It should be observed that the influence of Christ's teaching is not wholly absent, and there are reminiscences which gain much of their point if they are seen to rest on the personal recollections of an eye-witness." Peake thinks it not unnatural that Peter should have come to assign a chief place to the death and resurrection of Christ, and points out that in this particular epistle the writer wishes, at a time when a State persecution has begun, "to encourage the readers to patient endurance, and even joy in their distress." But what was this State persecution? That is another difficulty. If Peter wrote the epistle, it must have been the persecution in the time of Nero. Ramsay thinks, however, that the relations of Church and State, as they are indicated in the Epistle, imply a date not earlier than 80 A.D. Others (*e.g.*, P. W. Schmiedel) think the date implied is not earlier than the edict of Trajan in his letter to Pliny. Others again (*e.g.*, Von Soden) assign the epistle to about 92-96 A.D. (reign of Domitian). On the other hand, Mommsen thinks that the circumstances do not preclude the time of Nero. If Peter was not the author of the Epistle, it has been suggested that it may have been written by Paul, Barnabas, or Silvanus. Barnabas is supposed to have written two other epistles, the Epistle to the Hebrews, and the Epistle of Barnabas. A number of writings were fathered on Peter (*e.g.*, the "Gospel of Peter," the "Preaching of Peter," the "Apocalypse of Peter). See the *Encycl. Bibl.;* J. A. M'Clymont; G. Currie Martin; Arthur S. Peake, *Intr.;* J. Moffatt, *Intr.*

PETER, THE SECOND EPISTLE OF. What is known as the Second General Epistle of Peter is one of the most puzzling books in the New Testament. In part it so closely resembles the Epistle of Jude that one writer must have copied the other (cp. II. Peter ii. 1-iii. 3 with Jude vss. 4-18). There are good grounds for thinking that it was the author of II. Peter who came second (see JUDE). In that case the author can hardly have been Peter. It is true that the author speaks in the name of Peter (cp. iii. 1; i. 16-18), but the style of the Epistle is different from that of the First Epistle of Peter. Again, there are references to the Epistles of Paul which can hardly be reconciled with Petrine authorship. "They are spoken of as if a collection of them had been formed; they had already been the object of considerable misinterpretation. What is most remarkable of all is that they are spoken of as Scripture" (A. S. Peake). Further, as Currie Martin says, the whole content of the Second Epistle of Peter "points to a much later period in the history of the Church than anything that could be covered by the life of the Apostle." The external evidence for the Epistle is very weak. Origen (third century) is the first to mention it, and he is doubtful about its authorship. Eusebius speaks of it as a work the genuineness of which was disputed. It is not included in the Muratorian Canon, nor in the old Latin or Syriac Versions. Other writings besides this were fathered on Peter, and Prof. Peake points out that the authenticity of the "Apocalypse of Peter" is better attested by the Early Church than that of the First Epistle of Peter. Currie Martin thinks the date of the Second Epistle must be later than 140 A.D. Peake also thinks it can hardly be much earlier than the middle of the second century. This seems to be suggested by the nature of the false teaching to which reference is made. "This date is also confirmed by the close relationship with the Apocalypse of Peter. No certain conclusion can be reached as to the place of composition, but the affinities with Philo and Clement of Alexandria point to Egypt, in which also the Apocalypse of Peter was probably written" (A. S. Peake). See J. A. M'Clymont; G. Currie Martin; Arthur S. Peake, *Intr.;* J. Moffatt, *Intr.*

PETER'S CHAINS, FEAST OF. A festival in honour of St. Peter observed in the Roman Church on the 1st of August. See LAMMAS DAY.

PHAISTOS DISK. A monument containing strange hieroglyphs which have not been deciphered yet. It originated perhaps in Lycia or Caria. According to Sir Arthur Evans, it may be a religious chant composed in honour of the Anatolian Great Mother.

PHANEBALOS. A deity worshipped at Ascalon in the Graeco-Roman age. It is doubtful whether the deity was a war-god or a solar god.

PHENOMENALISM. The term Phenomenalism is used sometimes to describe the philosophy of George Berkeley (1685-1753). Berkeley contends that so-called material things are in reality only phenomenal. They are appearances, and are not copies of real things. Matter is not an absolute substance. The only absolute substance is Mind or Spirit. See BERKELEYISM.

PHILADELPHIAN CHURCH. A name assumed by the followers of Joanna Southcott (1750-1814). See SOUTHCOTTIANS.

PHILADELPHIANS. A name assumed by the followers of Jane Lead or Leade (1623-1704). Jane Leade was an enthusiastic student of the mystical writings of Jacob Boehme (1575-1624). She herself claimed to have had prophetic visions. She gave an account of them in a work published in 1683, "The Revelation of Revelations." In 1695 she founded, with the help of her friends, a society described as "The Philadelphian Society for the Advancement of Piety and Divine Philosophy." The idea was to form a union of all persons of every church and sect who were really regenerate. The "Theosophical Transactions" of the Society were edited by Francis Lee (1661-1719). See J. H. Blunt; the *D.N.B.*

PHILEMON, EPISTLE OF PAUL TO. The Epistle of Paul the Apostle to Philemon is one of the briefest compositions in the Bible. It consists of only twenty-five verses. It is in fact a short private letter—so short and insignificant that in the fourth century A.D. certain writers thought it could not have been written by the Apostle Paul. In more recent times it has been held (*e.g.*, by F. C. Baur) to have been invented in order to depict the ideal relations that should subsist between master and slave. This view, however, has not found much acceptance. It is true that there is not much external evidence for the epistle. It is not referred to by many early Christian writers. But it is found in the Canon of Marcion and the Muratorian Canon; and it has been reasonably urged that the silence of early Christian writers is no doubt due to the fact that the Epistle is not of a doctrinal character. To many scholars the epistle seems thoroughly Pauline. "The internal evidence," says Prof. Peake, "is decisive. No one could have imitated Paul in so inimitable a way, nor could any plausible reason be assigned for its composition in Paul's name." Moreover, it is closely connected with the Epistle to the Colossians (cp. Colossians iv. 7-18; Philemon, vss. 2, 10-12, 23, 24). Philemon had a slave Onesimus who robbed his master and ran away to Rome, where he came under the influence of Paul and became a convert. The Apostle became much attached to him, but since the slave was the lawful possession of Philemon, he felt he could not retain him. When Tychicus returned to Asia the Apostle sent back the slave to his master. At the same time he sent a letter to Philemon pleading for a merciful reception and restoration. "Paul does not write an abolitionist pamphlet, but presents the necessary solvent of slavery in the doctrine of universal brotherhood in Christ Jesus" (G. Currie Martin). The Epistle may perhaps have been written at Rome in 62-63 A.D. See the *Encycl. Bibl.;* J. A. M'Clymont; G. Currie Martin; A. S. Peake, *Intr.;* J. Moffatt, *Intr.*

PHILIPPINES. A sub-sect of the Russian dissenters known as Bezpopovtzi. They refused to do military service or to swear allegiance to the Czar, and they observe only two Sacraments, Baptism and the Lord's Supper.

PHILOSOPHICAL SOCIETY OF GREAT BRITAIN. Another name for the Victoria Institute (*q.v.*).

PHISIOLATRY. The worship of the forces and phenomena of nature.

PHŒNIX. The phœnix was adopted in Christian art as a symbol of the resurrection. It is represented in the Catacombs of Rome by the side of St. Paul, and over the doorway of the ancient basilica of St. Paul at Rome is a sculptured figure of it. Sidney Heath quotes a passage by St. Clement of Rome which dwells upon the suitability of the emblem. "Let us consider that wonderful sign which occurs in the Eastern countries; that is to say, Arabia. There is a certain bird called a Phœnix. It is the only one of its kind, and it lives 500 years. When the time of its dissolution draws near that it must die, it makes itself a nest of frankincense, myrrh, and other spices, into which, when its time is fulfilled, it enters and dies. But as its flesh decays, a certain kind of worm is generated, which being nourished with the juice of the dead bird, puts forth feathers; and when it is grown to a perfect state, it takes up the nest in which the bones of its dead parent lie, and carries it from Arabia, in Egypt, to the city called Heliopolis." See further W. Carew Hazlitt.

PHOL. Phol seems to have been one of the deities of the Ancient Teutons. The name occurs in one of the Merseburg Charms (*q.v.*) in close conjunction with that of Wodan (*q.v.*). But Phol does not appear elsewhere, except in German place-names. It has been suggested that Phol is identical with Balder (*q.v.*), or is a corrupt form of the name Apollo. Another suggestion is that Phol is none other than the Apostle Paul. See P. D. Chantepie de la Saussaye, *Rel. of the Teutons,* 1902.

PHOTINIANS. The followers or school of Photinus. Photinus was bishop of Sirmium in Pannonia and a disciple of Marcellus of Ancyra (see MARCELLIANS). He was condemned by a synod held at Antioch A.D. 344, and afterwards by several other synods. In the first canon of the Council of Constantinople (381 A.D.) the heresy of the Photinians is anathematized together with that of the Sabellians, Marcellians, and others. These schools had much in common. Tyrannius Rufinus, presbyter of Aquileia, writing about 400 A.D., refers to Photinus as the successor of Paul of Samosata, from which it would appear that to a large extent he identified the teaching of the two men. Photinus agreed with other Monarchians in holding "that Jesus Christ was born of the Holy Ghost and the Virgin Mary; that a certain portion of the Divine Substance, which he called the Word, descended upon and acted through the man Jesus Christ; that on account of this association of the Word with the human nature Jesus was called the Son of God, and even God Himself: that the Holy Ghost was not a distinct Person, but a celestial virtue proceeding from the Deity" (J. H. Blunt). Photinus differed from Paul of Samosata in regarding the Divine element in Jesus' Person as "substantivum" or "ousiōdēs" (substantial), whereas Paul regarded it as "prosphorikon." Photinus held, with the later Sabellians "that there acted in and through the man Jesus an element from the nature of the Deity, impersonal, yet substantive, which is to be again resumed into the Deity." See J. H. Blunt; *Cath. Dict.*

PHOTISMS. A term applied to certain psychic phenomena associated with profound religious experiences. A knowledge of such experiences probably lies behind the Old Testament story of the Burning Bush (*q.v.*), the New Testament story of St. Paul's conversion, and the story in Church History of the Emperor Constantine's conversion (see CONVERSION). The appearance of luminous phenomena or photisms has been reported frequently. One of the examples given by William James is as follows. President Finney writes: "All at once the glory of God shone upon and around about me in a manner almost marvellous. . . . A light perfectly ineffable shone in my soul, that almost prostrated me on the ground. . . . This light seemed like the brightness of the sun in every direction. It was too intense for the eyes. . . . I think I knew something then, by actual experience, of that light that prostrated Paul on the way to Damascus. It was surely a light such as I could not have endured long." In some cases, however, the language is merely metaphorical. See William James, *The Varieties of Religious Experience,* 1906.

PHYLACTERIES. In the Gospel of Matthew (*q.v.*) Jesus is represented as saying (xxiii. 5), with reference to the Scribes and Pharisees: "But all their works they do for to be seen of men: they make broad their phylacteries, and enlarge the borders of their garments." The word phylacteries is Greek. It was used as the equivalent of the Hebrew word Tōtāfoth (FRONTLETS). In the Old Testament it is said (Deuteronomy vi. 8), with reference to the words of God: "And thou shalt bind them for a sign upon thine hand, and they shall be for frontlets between thine eyes." The practice of writing sacred words or formulas on pieces of parchment and using them as amulets and charms has been common among primitive folk. The passage in Deuteronomy may be understood in this way. It is possible, however, that originally the words were not intended to be taken literally. In any case, in course of time they came to be interpreted literally, and it became the custom to wear phylacteries. The phylactery was a small black square box made of skin. The box contained passages from the Old Testament (the Torah) written on parchment. It was attached to the arm or head of a person by long leather straps. The box, the parchment, and the straps had to be made of the skin of a "clean" animal. In the Targums the Aramaic equivalent of phylacteries is Tefillin (the Hebrew word in the Singular, *tefillah,* means "prayer"). This is the term which has come into common use among the Jews. They speak of the "Arm-Tefillah" (or Hand-Tefillah) and the "Head-Tefillah." The Tefillin are now worn during the daily morning service; but it is not considered necessary to wear them on Sabbaths or Holy Days. They are not worn by women; nor by boys until they are thirteen years old. See W. O. E. Oesterley and G. H. Box.

PIETISM. A religious movement in Germany in the seventeenth century. Its founder was P. J. Spener (1635-1705); its centre in course of time was Halle. The Pietists attached importance rather to a religion of the heart than to a religion of dead formalism and orthodoxy. In 1670 Spener held in his own house at Frankfort gatherings at which the Bible was read and explained. In course of time (about 1675) this institution came to be known as Collegia Pietatis, and the school of Spener as Pietists. In 1675 Spener published a work which attracted widespread attention: "Pia Desideria, or Earnest Wishes for the Good Improvement of the True Evangelical Church, with some Christian Proposals for that end." In 1686 Spener went to Dresden as Chief Court Preacher. Here amongst his pupils were A. H. Francke (1663-1727) of the University of Leipzig, P. Anton, and C. Schade. Francke established Pietism in Leipzig by instituting the Collegium Philobiblicum. At Francke's gatherings amongst other matters Luther's translation of the Bible was criticised. At this and at the simple life and dress of the Pietists the Theological Faculty of Leipzig, which was conservative, took offence. The Pietists had to leave the University of Leipzig. In 1691 Spener removed from Dresden to Berlin, as Provost of the Church of St. Nicholas. In 1692 Francke was appointed Professor at Halle, which now became the centre and home of Pietism. The famous Francke Institutions (*Franckesche Stiftungen;* Schools, Home for Orphans, Dispensary, Printing-house, etc.), which are so extensive as to form a town within a town, are a living witness to the practical Christianity of Pietism. Pietism as a theological movement, however, was opposed in various parts of Germany. The orthodox Lutheran party probably regarded it, as K. F. A. Kahnis (1814-1888) regarded it, as ministering indirectly to Rationalism. Two reforms in particular were demanded by the Pietists. "First, that the theological schools should be reformed by the aboliton of all systematic theology, philosophy, and metaphysics, and that morals and not doctrine should form the staple of all preaching; secondly, that only those persons should be admitted into the Lutheran ministry whose lives were examples of living piety" (J. H. Blunt). After the death of Francke in 1727 Pietism degenerated into a kind of fanaticism. See A. S. Farrar, *Crit. Hist. of Free Thought,* 1862; B. Puenjer; J. H. Blunt; Brockhaus; Chambers' *Encycl.*

PIGEONS. According to Lucian, pigeons were sacred in Hierapolis, and were not used for food. He tells us also that the lower half of Semiramis took the form of a pigeon. A special sanctity seems to have been ascribed to the pigeon by the Hebrews (cp. Lev. xix. 4, 49; Num. vi. 10).

PILLAN. The name (Supreme Essence) in the mythology of the Araucanian Indians of Chili for the supreme deity. Pillan seems to be a thunder-god resembling the Mexican Tlaloc.

PILLAR OF CLOUD AND FIRE. The Old Testament relates that after the Exodus of the children of Israel from Egypt, Jehovah went before the people in a pillar of cloud by day, and in a pillar of fire by night (Exodus xiii. 21 f.). On one occasion the pillar of cloud moved to the rear of the people to prevent the Egyptians from overtaking them (Exodus xiv. 19*b*, 20*b*.). This is the representation of the Jehovist (J). The Pillar of Cloud, as the Elohist (E) knows it, is a cloud which descends from time to time in front of the "Tent of Meeting" (*q.v.*) to indicate the divine presence (Exodus xxxiii. 7-11; Numbers xii. 5; Deuteronomy xxxi. 15). The Priestly Writer (P) thinks of the cloud as being present over the Tabernacle from its completion until the end of the wanderings of the children of Israel (Exodus xl. 38; Numbers ix. 16). By night there was fire in the cloud. A rationalistic explanation of the cloud would be that in front of the caravan was carried a fire which indicated the line of march by its smoke in the daytime and by its flames at night. It was the practice of the ancient Babylonians, Persians, and others to carry such a fire in a brazier. It is not impossible, however, that the conception of the pillar of cloud and fire originated in a spiritual experience (cp. BURNING BUSH). Moses, having once in an inspired and ecstatic state seen a burning light, would always associate the divine presence with fire and smoke. So when the children of Israel journeyed from Egypt Moses felt that Jehovah was leading them, and in front of them he saw, or believed he saw, some physical manifestation of the divine presence. G. B. Gray points out that the word used for cloud in this connection, *'ānān*, may mean a cloud of smoke as well as an atmospheric cloud. See *Encycl. Bibl.*

PILLAR-SAINTS. To stand on a pillar was an early form of asceticism. The practice was adopted by Christian ascetics and mystics, such as Simeon Stylites (A.D. 388-460) and Joshua Stylites (fl. A.D. 507), when apparently it had come to be regarded as pious because it was painful. This, however, was hardly the original idea. Lucian states that at the entrance to the temple of Hierapolis there were two phalli (or pillars) erected in honour of Dionysus, and that twice every year a man mounted to the top of one of them and remained there seven days. He describes his ascent by means of a chain (§ 29). Then he continues: "When he has climbed to the top, he lets down a different chain, a long one, and drags up anything that he wants, such as wood. clothing, and vases; he binds these together and sits upon them, as it were on a nest, and he remains there for the space of time that I have mentioned. Many visitors bring him gold and silver, and some bring brass; then those who have brought these offerings leave them and depart, and each visitor gives his name. A bystander shouts the name up; and he on hearing the name utters a prayer for each donor; between the prayers he raises a sound on a brazen instrument which, on being shaken, gives forth a loud and grating noise" (transl. by H. A. Strong). The man never sleeps. This is said to be from fear of a scorpion; but Lucian suggests that his wakefulness was due rather to his fear of falling off the pillar. It was believed popularly that the man mounted the pillar to be nearer to the god (cp. E. S. Bouchier).

PILZINTECUTLI. A Mexican deity, a sun-god.

PIONEER PREACHERS. A band of preachers who disseminated the gospel of the "League of Liberal Christian Thought and Social Service" (*q.v.*).

PIRQE ABOTH. The work which bears this title (literally "Chapters of the Fathers"; but often translated "Sayings of the Fathers") may be described as a Hebrew classic. It has been honoured with a place in the Hebrew Prayer Book. The work is included in the Mishnah as the ninth tractate of the fourth series. Its purpose, as H. L. Strack says, is in the first place to prove the continuity and consequently the authority of tradition, and in the second place to give practical advice. The opening portion of the book professes to give in chronological order the names of the oldest scribes who were members of what is known as The Great Synagogue (*q.v.*). The line is traced up to Hillel and Shammai. There follow sayings by men of the House of Hillel up to Gamaliel ben Jehudah (*c.* 230 A.D.), by Hillel himself, by Hillel's disciple, Johanan ben Zakkai, and by Johanan's five disciples. The rest of the book contains a number of sayings by Tannāim (*q.v.*), some anonymous sayings, and sayings by Jehudah ben Temâ, by Ben Bag Bag, and by Ben He He. The collection is probably to a considerable extent the work of Rabbi 'Aqibâ, but the original collection was supplemented. The following is an example of one of the sayings in the latter portion of the book. "Rabbi José ben Qosma said, 'Once I was walking along the road, when a man met me and greeted me and I returned his greeting. He said to me, Rabbi, what place do you come from? I said, I come from a great city, a city of sages and scribes. He said to me, Rabbi, if thou wilt consent to dwell with us in our place, I will give thee a million denars of gold and precious stones and pearls. I said to him, My son, if you were to give me all the silver and gold and precious stones and pearls in the world I could only dwell in a place where the Law is, for at the hour of a man's decease it is not silver or gold or precious stones or pearls that can accompanying him, but only the law and good deeds'" (vi. 9 *b*). In 1877 Charles Taylor published an edition of *The Sayings of the Jewish Fathers* with critical and illustrative Notes. H. L. Strack's edition, *Die Sprüche der Väter* (1888), gives the Hebrew text with notes.

PIRZĀDA SECT. A religious sect in India. It has "a kind of reformed creed, based on a mixture of Hinduism and Islām" (R. V. Russell and R. B. Hira Lāl).

PISCINA. Piscina, literally a pool for fish, is one of the names used by ancient writers for the Christian baptismal font. According to Optatus (*c.* A.D. 371), "the name piscina, given to the baptismal font of which the water, the element of fishes, purifies us from all stain and becomes the means of salvation, is derived from fish, symbolising Him from whom we are nourished, healed, and redeemed" (quoted by Sidney Heath).

PISHĀRATIS. A sub-caste of the Ambalavāsi caste in India. The name appears also as Pishārodis. "Their primary occupation is to prepare garlands of flowers for Vaishnava temples, but they frequently undertake the talikazhakam or sweeping service in temples. . . . They are strict Vaishnavites, and the ashtākshara, or eight letters relating to Vishnu, as opposed to the panchākshara or five letters relating to Siva, forms their daily hymn of prayer" (E. Thurston).

PITHI. Pithi or Pūthi or Pithioteu is one of the gods of the Todas. He is said to have been born in a cave.

PIX, THE. The pix or pyx was a box in which the consecrated wafer, or the host, was placed. For the use of the term Sidney Heath quotes the second of the ordinances for the government of the army made in the reign of Richard II. (1386). "Also that no man be so hardy to touche the sacrament of the aulter nor the pyxe wherein it is enclosed upon payne to be draune, hanged, and his hedde to be smeten of."

PIZLIMTEC. A tribal deity, god of singing, in the religion of the Mayan Indians.

PLACENTA, THE. The ancient Egyptians made a statue of a deceased person for the "soul" to dwell in after death. They made the statue because they were not able to make an adequately life-like reproduction of the dead man's features upon the mummy itself or its wrappings. Then gradually the idea took shape that the life-substance could exist apart from the body as a "double" or "twin" (*ka*) which animated the statue. What was there to substantiate this curious idea of a double? An answer to this question has been suggested by Elliot Smith and others. "When an infant is born it is accompanied by the after-birth or placenta to which it is linked by the umbilical cord. The full comprehension of the significance of these structures is an achievement of modern science. To primitive man they were an incomprehensible marvel. But once he began to play with the idea that he had a double, a vital essence in his own shape which could leave the sleeping body and lead a separate existence, the placenta obviously provided tangible evidence of its reality. The considerations set forth by Blackman, supplementing those of Moret, Murray and Seligman, and others, have been claimed as linking the placanta with the *ka*" (G. Elliot Smith, *Dr.*, 1919). The *ka* is conceived as a double who is born along with the individual, and then as a kind of guardian angel who inhabits the statue of a deceased person. "This material conception of the *ka* as a double who is born with and closely linked to the individual is, as Blackman has emphasized, very suggestive of Baganda beliefs and rites connected with the placenta. At death the circumstances of the act of birth are reconstituted, and for this rebirth the placenta which played an essential part in the original process is restored to the deceased. May not the original meaning of the expression "he goes to his *ka*" be a literal description of this reunion with his placenta? The identification of the *ka* with the moon, the guardian of the dead man's welfare, may have enriched the symbolism." A Chinese work recommends the storing away of the placenta in a felicitous spot under the salutary influences of the sky or the moon in order that the child may be ensured a long life.

PLATONISM. The philosophy of Plato (427-347 B.C.), whose real name was Aristocles, is a form of Idealism. He denied the real existence of the objects of sense which are changing continually. Real Being belongs only to Ideas, which are unchangeable and eternal. The objects of sense are but imperfect copies of Ideas, the perfect types. And the highest Idea of all is the Idea of the Good. This is the foundation or first cause of knowledge and of all Being. This, "the Good in itself," is God. It is explained in the *Republic* (bk. vi.) that as the sun is the cause which makes things to be and to grow and to become visible, so the Good is of such power and beauty that it bestows Truth and Being upon everything that is an object of knowledge, and as the sun is high above the visible, so the Good in itself is high above Knowledge and Truth. From the point of view of religion, the important question with regard to Platonism is: Does it comfort and console men? Or the question may be put in another way: What then is Plato's conception of happiness? The answer may be given in the words of Rudolf Eucken. "His conception of happiness involves an energetic negation and rejection of the usual human existence: all the happiness which is there offered and commended seems to him fleeting, external, and illusory. But science reveals to the thinker the possibility of contemplating an external order of things which, in accordance with his characteristic tendency towards grandeur and vividness of conception, becomes coordinated into a whole, the world of ideas. This ideal world, with all its superiority, is not intrinsically alien to us, but he who strives with all his might to attain it can gain complete possession of it and make it his own life and being. In this appropriation of a real and perfect world the thinker finds a happiness which is beyond comparison with anything else that life offers. But even the individual life of man takes another course when a higher world is thus revealed to him: it is in particular the combination of scientific thought with the formative activity of art which everywhere reveals great tasks and leads to genuine happiness. . . . In the possession of such happiness, which is grounded in his own nature, man may feel himself superior to all fate, for this inner harmony cannot be destroyed or even diminished by anything that comes from outside. Thus Plato sketches that magnificent picture of the suffering just man, who is misjudged and persecuted even unto death, but through all the attacks upon him actually gains in inward happiness. . . . The chief distinction of this doctrine of happiness lies in the fact that it brings the internal disposition and its manifestation, the good and the beautiful, into the closest connection, but represents the whole as finding its joy and motive force immediately in itself. Here all petty calculation of private advantage, all thoughts of reward and punishment, have sunk out of sight." See O. Seyffert, *Dict.;* C. J. Deter: Rudolf Eucken, *The Life of the Spirit*, 1909; Max B. Weinstein, *Welt- und Leben-anschauungen*, 1910.

PLEROMA. Pleroma means literally "that which is filled" or "that with which a thing is filled" or the "full number." The term is used in Gnosticism (*q.v.*) of the complete number of æons or ineffable beings. See VALENTINIANS.

PLUMSTEAD PECULIARS. A designation of the Faith-healers who are better known as Peculiar People (*q.v.*).

PLYMOUTH BRETHREN. The followers of J. N. Darby. The body known as Plymouth Brethren in the British Empire and in America are on the Continent commonly called Darbyites (*q.v.*).

PLYNTERIA. An Athenian festival, the washing festival of the goddess Athene, held on the twenty-fifth or twenty-ninth of Thargelion. Athene's image was carried in procession to the sea and bathed in the waters. Plutarch says that on that day "the Praxiergidæ solemnize their secret rites: they remove all the ornaments from her image and cover it up"; and according to Xenophon, "none of the Athenians would venture to transact any serious business on this day" (both quoted by Hutton Webster). Hutton Webster thinks it probable that at one time the Plynteria was "a rite of purification preliminary to the bringing-in of the first-fruits, and hence a rite which must have existed long before its ascription to the protecting deity of Athens." See Jane E. Harrison, *Prol.;* and Hutton Webster, *R.D.*

POKUNT. A term used among the Shoshune of N. America to denote a mystic potentiality ascribed to beings whether human or non-human, living or not living. *Pokunt* seems to be a force, and not a personal being.

POLYGLOT. A term applied to editions of the Bible containing the text in several languages. The most important Polyglots are: (1) the Complutensian Polyglot which Cardinal Ximenes had published at Alcala (Complūtum) in six volumes (1514-1517); (2) the Antwerp Polyglot, which was published in eight volumes (1569-72); (3) the Paris Polyglot, which was produced in ten volumes (1629-45); and (4) the London Polyglot in ten languages, edited by Bryan Walton (1600?-1661) in six volumes (1654-57). In 1669 a Lexicon in two volumes by Edmund Castell (1606-1685) was added to Walton's Polyglot. Bagster's Polyglot, published in 1831, gives the Old Testament in Hebrew, Greek, Latin, English, German, Italian, French, and Spanish; and the New Testament in nine languages. The Polyglot published by Stier and Theile in Germany (five editions, 1875-94) is in Hebrew, Greek, Latin, and German.

PO-NAGAR. The goddess of agriculture among the Chams of Binh-Thuan in Indo-China. J. G. Frazer explains that the tilling of the earth seems to be regarded as "a crime which must be perpetuated secretly and afterwards atoned for." The owner of the land pretends to be unaware who has ploughed it, and then brings offerings to Po-Nagar and the other deities. When the rice has grown high enough to hide pigeons, offerings are again made, and finally first-fruits are presented. See J. G. Frazer, *Spirits of the Corn*, 1912.

POOR CLARES. An order of nuns (called in French Clarisses) founded by Clara Sciffi of Assisi (1194-1253), who had come under the influence and inspiration of Francis of Assisi. Clara Sciffi practised a very severe form of asceticism. Under the constitutions drawn up by Cardinal Ugolino, the Nuns of St. Clare, "observed a perpetual fast, and on three days of the week in Lent fasted on bread and water; they lay on boards; their habit was rough and of coarse material; and they could not speak to one another at any time without the superior's leave" (*Catholic Dictionary*). In the rule written by St. Francis in 1224, and approved by Pope Innocent IV. in 1246, the severity of these practices was mitigated somewhat. In a rule drawn up in 1264, and approved by Pope Urban IV., the practices were further mitigated. This led to a division of the order into two branches, the Urbanists, who adopted the mildest form of the rule, and the Clarisses, who adhered to the stricter rule. In 1436 Colette of Corbie founded the Congregation of St. Colette for the observance of the stricter rule. In 1631 Francisca of Jesus Maria founded the Congregation of the Strictest Observance. Another apostle of strict asceticism, Peter of Alcantara, in 1676 founded the Congregation of the Hermitesses of Alcantara. See Schaff-Herzog; the *Cath. Dict.*

POOR OF LYONS, THE. The name "Pauperes de Lugdūno" was given to the followers of Peter Waldus, the Waldenses (*q.v.*), on account of the poverty which they assumed in imitation of the apostles.

POOR PRIESTS. An order of itinerant preachers instituted by John Wycliffe (*d.* 1384). They were sent about the country, the Midlands and the South of England, to propagate his gospel and principles. They received the name Lollards.

POPOL VUH. A book of the annals of the Quiché Indians of Guatemala. It contains the Quiché legends and myths.

POPOVTZI. One of the two classes into which the Russian dissenters or Raskolniks (*q.v.*) are divided. The Popovtzi have priests and bishops, whereas the other class of dissenters, the Bezpopovtzi have no regular priests.

PORENUTIUS. It appears from Saxo Grammaticus that Porenutius was one of the gods worshipped by the ancient Slavs. He had five faces, one of them being on his breast.

PORT-ROYALISTS. The Jansenists (*q.v.*) have been called Port-Royalists. The Abbé de St. Cyran, Jansen's friend, founded a Jansenist Society which in 1638 removed from Paris to the monastery of Port Royal des Champs near Versailles.

POSEIDON. The Greek god of the Sea, son of Cronus and Rhea. According to Homer, he was a younger brother of Zeus, according to Hesiod, an elder brother. He was identified by the Romans with Neptune. "Rejected as patron of Athens, in favour of his accomplished niece, he was understood to have a special regard for the Isthmus of Corinth, that focus of navigation from east and west. His sceptre was the trident fishing spear of the Mediterranean; and he rode forth in a chariot drawn by dolphins, sea-horses, or other marine monsters. Horses came into his province as well as waves, an idea not far to seek in the comparison of leaping and rearing billows that has occurred to many a poet" (A. R. Hope Moncrieff).

POSEIDONIASTAE. A name given to some of the merchants of Delos in the second century B.C. They were so called after their divine patron Poseidon.

POSITIVISM. A system of religion founded by Auguste Comte (1797-1858), a French mathematician and philosopher, author of *Cours de Philosophie Positive* (1839) and *Traité de Sociologie* (1851-54). Comte contended that only phenomena can be known, and these only relatively. The sciences fall into two classes, abstract and concrete, the latter being first in time. A theory of concrete phenomena, which is really scientific, can be established only when the general laws which rule phenomena have been understood. A science is made "positive" when its truths are linked with those of the other sciences, and worked out to their logical consequences. "Positivism raises each science in succession from its empirical condition, and incorporates it with every other positive science as a co-ordinated and coherent body of doctrine" (J. H. Blunt). As regards an Absolute Supreme Power, since our powers of mind are finite and relative, we cannot prove its existence. The power of which we have positive proof is Humanity. This is a Power whose operations go backward into the dim past and forward into the distant future. It is a power that is present in us and with us. Positivism is the Religion of Humanity. "The revelation, the inspiration, the incarnation so long and passionately dreamed of by the religious souls of men through such a long vista of ages, are realized at last. The true revelation of the will of the great Being is science itself. Human genius and love is that Inspiration. The sum of demonstrated Law is the Gospel. The Bible of the Hebrews, the Gospel of Christ and of Paul, becomes a real, but a simple, part of the true Gospel. There is no one Book of the Law. All great books alike reveal the Law. All great thinkers and teachers, all true workers and rulers have been inspired. There is no single incarnation of the son of a carpenter and a maiden of Judah. Humanity is incarnate in all great men in a supreme degree; it is incarnate in every worthy man and woman alike; every son of Humanity, who does not repudiate his birthright, is the son of Man, is a Christ, is or may be, the Messiah, of some honest family or home; every daughter of Humanity is, at least in nature, the mother or the sister of some Christ to be—is herself a transfigured type of Humanity itself" (Frederic Harrison). It is claimed that the Positive creed is scientific, founded on real scientific bases. There are organized bodies of Positivists throughout the world. In England different bodies emphasize different aspects of the Positivist synthesis, but they all agree in essential principles. The school or educational centre of Positivism in London is Newton Hall (*q.v.*). Comte attached great importance to Love as the principle of Sociology. This great principle he termed *Amour d'autrui* or Altruism. His motto was "Vivre pour altrui." See J. H. Blunt; Frederic Harrison, "Positivism" in *Great Religions of the World*, 1902; "Humanity" in *Religious Systems of the World*, 1908; C. J. Deter.

POT, THE MOTHER. It is pointed out by G. Elliot Smith (*Dr.*) that the Proto-Egyptian biologist, groping after some explanation of the natural phenomenon that the earth and seed were made fruitful by water, formulated the idea that water was the repository of life-giving powers. The realization that animals could be fertilized by the seminal fluid would seem to have been brought within the scope of the same theory. Just as water fertilized the earth, so the semen fertilized the female. Then, as both the earth and women could be fertilized by water, they were homologized one with the other. "The earth came to be regarded as a woman, the Great Mother. When the fertilizing water came to be personified in the person of Osiris, his consort Isis was identified with the earth which was fertilized by water" (p. 29). A new view then developed. Woman was regarded no longer as the real parent of mankind, but as the matrix in which the seed was planted and nurtured during the course of its growth and development. "Hence in the earliest hieroglyphic writing the picture of a pot of water was taken as the symbol of womanhood, the 'vessel' which received the seed" (p. 178). This idea of the Mother Pot is found in India as well as in Babylonia, Egypt, and the Eastern Mediterranean. Among the Dravidian people at the present day the seven goddesses are often represented by seven pots. According to E. Thurston and K. Rangachari, the Padma Sālēs in the Madras Presidency of India celebrate annually a festival in which their god and goddess are represented by two decorated pots placed on a model of a tiger. The idea is widespread also among the Celtic-speaking peoples. "In Wales the pot's life-giving powers are enhanced by making its rim of pearls. But as the idea spread, its meaning also became extended. At first it was merely a jug of water or a basket of figs, but elsewhere it became also a witch's cauldron, the magic cup, the Holy Grail." etc. (G. Elliot Smith, p. 181).

PRAGMATISM. A system of philosophy with which are closely associated the names of the American philosophers William James and John Dewey and the English philosopher F. C. S. Schiller. The term, which is derived from the Greek *pragma* "practice," was first employed (1878) by Charles Peirce of America. William James explains that the pragmatic method in itself implies not particular results, but simply an attitude of orientation. "The attitude of looking away from first things, principles, 'categories,' supposed necessities; and of looking towards last things, fruits, consequences, facts." To the pragmatist Truth in our ideas and beliefs means their power to work. It means that "ideas (which themselves are but parts of our experience) become true just in so far as they help us to get into satisfactory relation with other parts of our experience." As regards its attitude towards theology, it is pointed out that pragmatism has no *a priori* prejudices against this. "If theological ideas prove to have a value for concrete life, they will be true, for pragmatism, in the sense of being good for so much. For how much more they are true will depend entirely on their relations to the other truths that also have to be acknowledged." If a theological idea is pragmatically successful, its truth ought not to be denied. In Pragmatism the "only test of probable truth is what works best in the way of leading us, what fits every part of life best and combines with the collectivity of experience's demands, nothing being omitted. If theological ideas should do this, if the notion of God, in particular, should prove to do it, how could pragmatism possibly deny God's existence?" If it be asked whether pragmatism is optimistic or pessimistic, the answer is that it is best described by a term that denotes a position midway between optimism and pessimism: pragmatism is melioristic. It should be added, finally, that pragmatism favours pluralism. "Pragmatism, pending the final empirical ascertainment of just what the balance of union and disunion among things may be, must obviously range herself upon the pluralistic side. Some day, she admits, even total union, with one knower, one origin, and a universe consolidated in every conceivable way, may turn out to be the most acceptable of all hypotheses. Meanwhile the opposite hypothesis, of a world imperfectly unified still, and perhaps always to remain so, must be sincerely entertained. This latter hypothesis is pluralism's doctrine. Since absolute monism forbids its being even considered seriously, branding it as irrational from the start, it is clear that pragmatism must turn its back on absolute monism, and follow pluralism's more empirical path." See William James, *Pragmatism*, 1907.

PRAJĀPATI. Prajāpati, "lord of creatures," is a designation of the Father-god in the religion of the Hindus. Originally no doubt it was a title of the Sun. Then it came to be used as a title of the chief god. The name occurs in a passage that anticipates the later development of a trinity. With reference to Vishnu (*q.v.*) it is said: "Having the form of Brahmā he creates; having a human body (as Krishna) he protects, in the nature of Siva he would destroy—these are the three appearances or conditions (*avasthas*) of the Father-god (Prajāpati)." See Monier-Williams; E. W. Hopkins.

PRANA. A term used in Theosophy (*q.v.*). Mrs. Besant explains that it denotes "the animating life-principle of the personality" (*R.S.W.*).

PRANNĀTHI SECT. A Hindu sect, named after its founder, Prannāth. Its adherents are called also Dhāmis (*q.v.*).

PRAYER. Man has been described as a praying animal, and it has been claimed that prayer is a human instinct. This is hardly true of prayer in a high sense of the word. "Nobody dreams of propitiating gods or spirits by prayer while magic is universally practised," says Andrew Lang (*Magic and Religion*). Prayer is intuitional rather than instinctive. The truth about its value has come to men by Revelation (*q.v.*). Prayerlessness is characteristic either of a savage state or of a degenerate civilisation. In either case it is due to a lack of real knowledge. In the latter case the knowledge was at one time present, but it has run to seed. Prayer, where it has not become mechanical, is characteristic of a high stage of culture. The Egyptians, Babylonians, Arabians, Jews, Romans, Greeks, and early Christians have given us examples. The Hebrew Psalms and the Babylonian Psalms (*q.v.*) contain beautiful prayers. J. A. Farrer (*Paganism and Christianity*) quotes a beautiful prayer to Zeus, composed by Simplicius (sixth century A.D.). It is as follows: "I beseech Thee, O Lord, the Father and Guide of our reason, to make us mindful of the noble origin Thou hast thought worthy to confer upon us; and to assist us to act as becomes free agents; that we may be cleansed from the irrational passions of the body and may subdue and govern the same, using them as instruments in a fitting manner; and to assist us to the right direction of the reason that is in us, and to its participation in what is real by the light of truth. And, thirdly, I beseech Thee, my Saviour, entirely to remove the darkness from the eyes of our souls, in order that we know aright, as Homer says, both God and Man." In the best sense of the word, prayer of course assumes that the Supreme Power is good and is knowable. The truth of this assumption is vouched for by a knowledge which is intuitional. And goodness involves righteousness, justice, impartiality. God is no respecter of persons. This of itself means that prayers cannot always be answered, because they are such as a good and impartial ruler cannot grant. A benefit granted to one individual or to one nation could often be granted only at the expense of another individual or another nation. This has been well expressed by Matthew Arnold in the poem "Consolation." Prayer must ever be made with humility and with resignation to the will of a good and impartial God. What can be objected to the practice is that it has so often been misused and abused. But so long as the petition is a good one, it is better to have prayed in vain than never to have prayed at all. W. M. Salter complains (*Ethical Religion*) that "men have heretofore conceived of the Supreme Power of the world as a personal being like themselves; and they have had so slight a notion of the order of nature and the fixity of nature's laws that they have thought they might pray to him and ask him to do for them what they could not do for themselves." This is true, but the moral should be not that men should give up praying, but that they should learn to pray rightly. Salter thinks that prayer to what he chooses to call the Unknown God "involves a double vice—first, distrust of the beneficence of that order through which he is already manifested, and which holds fast whether we pray or not; second, a despair of our ability to act as proximate causes and to bring about the results we wish ourselves." But no intelligent person prays for the suspension of a law which he knows to be beneficent. Discrimination has to be exercised. One cannot abolish divine laws, but one can pray to understand them. And one can, by prayer, abolish violations of divine laws. Who shall say that Slavery was not abolished by prayer? And as to the second point, man does not despair of his own ability, but, believing in a God of Goodness, Power, and Love, he naturally seeks His help. And this leads us to the highest kind of prayer. Prayer is not merely a petitioning for some material benefit, but is also an act of praise and adoration. It is also, and pre-eminently an act of communion with God. As such it has power to bring such substantial benefits as health and happiness. This kind of prayer was better understood and more widely practised in days when faith was more fervent and thought was less materialistic. Its power was well known in the early days of Christianity, and though in many quarters effectual prayer has become a lost art, the power has never ceased to operate. Prayer of course need not always be vocal. Mental or Silent Prayer is of the highest value. Here a distinction has been drawn between Meditation (*q.v.*), Affective Prayer, and Contemplation. In Affective Prayer "the soul goes straight to God by affection of the will without need of formal discourse or reasoning" (*Cath. Dict.*). Contemplation "is either natural or infused in an extraordinary manner by God, and in the latter the soul is said to be passive—*i.e.*, to be in some special sense moved by God." See Schaff-Herzog; Benham; Vernon Staley, *The Catholic Religion*, 1893; the *Cath. Dict.*; P. Vivian, *The Churches and Modern Thought*, 1908; Reinach, *O.*

PRAYER-CYLINDER. A contrivance which figures prominently in Lamaism. The prayer-cylinder, which has commonly been called a prayer-wheel or prayer-mill, may be regarded as an improved or developed form of the ordinary charm-papers or mantras (*q.v.*). "The sacred formula (or a number of them) is printed on a long strip of paper rolled round the cylinder, which is enclosed in a box, and by means of a stick, which is the axle on which it revolves, it is fastened to a handle or in a case. Every turn of the cylinder sets the word in motion, and makes its wholesome influence operative." The prayer-cylinder can be held in the hand and swung. Or it can be set in motion in a still more mechanical way —by the power of wind or water. See H. Hackmann.

PRAYING-FLAGS. Flags inscribed with prayer-formulas are used in that form of Buddhism known as Lamaism. Monier-Williams found a whole village near Dārjiling decorated with flagstaffs from which long flags were flying. "Every time the wind, which happened to be blowing fresh, extended the long flags, a vast number of prayers were credited to the inhabitants who were themselves all absent, and probably hard at work either in the fields or at Dārjiling." See Monier-Williams, *Buddhism*, 1890.

PRAYER-OIL. The name in the Eastern Church for the sacrament of Unction. See EXTREME UNCTION.

PRAYING PEBBLE. Muhammadans of the Shi'ah sect, according to F. J. Bliss, should always carry with them a *sejdi*, "or praying pebble, a cake of baked clay, made of earth from Mecca or Medinah or Kerbela, or some other notable place of visitation. This is to be placed on the ground before him so that his forehead may touch it in the due course of prostration. In case it is lost or unavailable, he may substitute as a reminder a round stone or a bit of green paper, or leaves from any plant that does not bear fruit." F. J. Bliss speaks of having handled a sejdi octagonal in shape and measuring one inch and three-quarters across. See F. J. Bliss.

PRAYING-SHAWL. This is a kind of shawl worn by Jews in the Synagogue. It has taken the place of the ancient "garment with fringes" (see FRINGES). The Hebrew term is Talith (*q.v.*).

PRAYING-WALLS. Praying-walls are a feature in that type of Buddhism known as Lamaism. They are stone-structures set up at the side of high-roads. In the walls are inserted slabs inscribed with prayer-formulas. "Passing travellers acquire merit by keeping them on their left side, so that they may follow the letters of the inscription without necessarily repeating the words" (Monier-Williams). See Monier-Williams, *Buddhism*, 1890.

PREACHING BROTHERS. Preaching Brothers, Fratres Praedicantes, was the original name of the Dominicans (*q.v.*).

PREADAMITES. The French Calvinist Isaac de la Peyreyre in a book published in 1655 maintained that there must have been Preadamites, men before Adam, on the earth. "He held that Adam was the progenitor of the Jews only, and that the Flood, which was local merely, did not destroy the nations who had inhabited the earth long before Adam's creation" (*Cath. Dict.*).

PRE-ANIMISM. The term *pre-animistic* was invented by R. R. Marett to denote a stage in the evolution of religion anterior to that known as Animism, in which the rites are addressed to impersonal forces like the Melanesian *mana* and the North American *orenda*. According to Edward Clodd ("Pre-Animism" in *The R.P.A. Annual*, 1917), "the root idea in this Naturism, or *Pre-Animism*, as it may be called, is that of power everywhere—power vaguely apprehended but immanent, and as yet unclothed with supernatural or personal attributes."

PRECISIANS. Another name for the Puritans (*q.v.*).

PRESBYTERIANS. The first Presbyterian church in England was formed at Wandsworth in 1572 under the pastorate of John Field. It was part of the programme of the Puritan reformers to remodel the Church on Presbyterian lines. They insisted on the "parity of ministers," and held that the Episcopacy ought to be abolished. "Each single congregation was to be ruled by a minister and elders, forming a *consistory;* the minister was to be admitted to his ministry by a *conference*, a wider assembly, which representatives of the different churches in the district were to attend" (M. W. Patterson). The minister was to be called and elected by a congregation, and the elders were to be associated with him in the government of his church. "In each congregation *deacons*, who were not an order of ministry, were to be chosen to look after the poor. A whole series of councils was arranged: representatives from each congregation were to form the *conference* of a district; above the conferences were to be *synods provincial, synods national*, and ultimately *synods international*. Each of these was to be attended by representatives of the councils immediately subordinate. This presbyteral scheme of government was supposed to be enjoined by Scripture. The divine right of Presbyterianism was matched against the Anglican's divine right of Episcopacy." Through the zeal and energy of John Knox (1505-1572), and after the triumph of Protestantism in 1560, Presbyterianism was established in Scotland; and in 1567 Knox obtained confirmation of the Presbyterian reformation in the Scottish Parliament. When the Westminster Assembly met in 1643, a "Solemn League and Covenant" was taken, and in St. Margaret's Church was subscribed by the members of the House of Commons. "This bound the part of the nation under the control of Parliament to a new ecclesiastical system, which should exclude Popery, Prelacy, Superstition, Heresy and Schism; and which was to be similar to that of Presbyterian Scotland, and was to be imposed, as far as possible, on Roman Catholic Ireland. The Assembly then proceeded to arrange the form of the new system. The draft was finished and sent up to the Parliament in July, 1645, and duly confirmed: but owing to disputes on the question of the independence of the Church, the carrying out of the scheme was delayed, and as a matter of fact it never came into full operation" (J. A. Houlder). By 1646, however, there were twelve presbyteries in London, and in 1647 the First Provincial Synod met there. In 1649, when a Provincial Synod met at Preston, there were nine presbyteries in Lancashire. From the year 1694 the Presbyterians in England began to decrease in numbers, and to decline as a separate organisation. During the eighteenth century several secessions from the Church of Scotland took place. Thus some "United Societies" of Covenanters formed themselves into a "Reformed Presbyterian Church," independent of the State. In 1733 Ebenezer Erskine led a secession which formed the "Associate Presbytery" or the "Secession Kirk." A further secession in 1752 led to the establishment of the "Relief Church." These two bodies combined in the "United Presbyterian Church," in 1847. In 1843 a body called the "Evangelical Union" arose, which in 1896 was amalgamated with the "Congregational Union of Scotland." In 1843 David Welsh and Thomas Chalmers led another secession which resulted in the "Free Church of Scotland." Subsequently the Free Church united with the "Reformed Presbyterian Church." Attempts to unite the various sections of the Free Presbyterian Church were in course of time successful to this extent that at a meeting of the Synods of the Presbyterian and the United Presbyterian Churches at Liverpool in 1876 these two bodies agreed to constitute themselves the Presbyterian Church of England." This union resulted in constant and steady progress.

PRESENTATION OF THE BLESSED VIRGIN MARY, ORDER OF THE. In some of the Apocryphal Gospels it is said that Mary was presented in the temple when she was three years old and stayed there until her marriage. The Order of the Presentation was founded in 1777 by Nano or Honora Nagle (1728-1784), of County Cork, Ireland, with the object of instructing the poor. The nuns took simple vows, renewable from year to year; and were not enclosed, but visited the houses of the poor. In this form the institution was confirmed in 1791 by Pope Pius V. When, however, in 1805 Pius VII. made it a religious order, he introduced solemn vows and strict enclosure. The order has many houses in Ireland. See the *Cath. Dict.;* the *D.N.B.*

PRIESTHOOD. In Babylonia priesthoods had developed in the prehistoric period. Elaborate liturgies were developed later. "As time advanced, the duties of the priests were differentiated; some gave themselves to the ordinary duties of a priest, while others were set apart for the observance of omens, and still others for the recitation of the incantations which were supposed to drive out the demons of sickness" (G. A. Barton, *R.W.*, p. 29 f.). The priesthood in Babylonia was the learned class. "In addition to the purely religious duties in connection with the temple service, the priests were also the scribes, the judges and the teachers of the people—all three functions following naturally from the religious point of view involved in writing, in legal decisions and in knowledge in general. The tradition once established, the priests continued to act as the official scribes in the case of the thousands upon thousands of legal and commercial documents that have come down to us from all periods, though, to be sure, in later days we occasionally come across a scribe who does not appear to have been a temple official" (Jastrow, *Civ.*, p. 273). In ancient Egypt the priesthoods as finally organized consisted of various classes of priests, prophets, and others with different duties. "Greek writers tell of festivals at which priests acted out the myths of the gods. At some of the temples (probably at all) schools existed for the instruction of candidates for the priesthood in the mysteries of their work and the culture of their time" (Barton, p. 51). Among the Hebrews, the priests, apart from their ordinary duties, acted as scribes and codifiers of the laws. The priests of Zoroastrianism under the Achaemenians were the Magi (originally a Median tribe) who had gradually attained power through royal patronage. The completion of the Avesta by the addition of the Yashts and the Vendidad was probably due to their influence. The priests of the Avesta "formed a hereditary caste, the members of which were alone competent to offer sacrifices or perform the rites of purification; the priest was born, not made. They lived on the proceeds of their ritual, which were strictly defined by law, and also on the numerous fines they exacted in return for indulgences. They were, in short, a regular clergy" (Reinach, *O.*, p. 63). In India the priests are known as Brahmans (*q.v.*). In the Greek states of the classic period, the priests were never associated in communities, nor set apart as instructors, like the Druids of Gaul. They learned the ritual of a god, not in seminaries for priests, but by serving him. "Thus the Greek priests never constituted a clergy like those of India, Persia or Gaul; the only attempt at such a constitution was the one Grote has compared to the foundation of the Society of Jesus, the confraternity formed in Southern Italy by Pythagoras, which was a failure" (*ibid.*, p. 91). In Germany in primitive times the king was also the priest.

PRIESTS OF CALVARY. Another name for the Calvarians (*q.v.*).

PRIMIANISTS. The party of Primianus, who in A.D. 392 succeeded Parmenian as Donatist bishop of Carthage. The arbitrary action of Primian in finding fault with some of his deacons and in excommunicating Maximian resulted in a Donatist schism. There arose two hostile parties, Primianists and Maximianists (*q.v.*).

PRIMITIVE CHRISTIANITY, SOCIETIES FOR PROMOTING. See SOCIETIES FOR PROMOTING PRIMITIVE CHRISTIANITY.

PRIMITIVE IRISH METHODISTS. The Primitive Irish Methodists are "primitive" in the sense that they hold fast to John Wesley's original intention, that of forming Societies which were to remain a part of the Church of England. See WESLEYAN METHODISTS.

PRIMITIVE METHODISTS. An offshoot of the original Methodists, the Wesleyan Methodists (*q.v.*). Primitive Methodism represents an effort to revive the field-preaching methods of Wesley, Whitfield, and others. Soon after the formation of the body known as the Kilhamites or the New Connexion Methodists, members of the parent body began to hold "revival services" in Cornwall, Lancashire, Staffordshire, and elsewhere. When in 1807 the American Methodist Lawrence Dow introduced "camp-meetings" into Staffordshire, his methods were approved and adopted by two local Methodist preachers, William Clowes and Hugh James Bourne. The members of the old Methodist body in general, however, did not approve of this kind of revival, and decided in the Conference of 1807 that "even supposing such meetings to be allowable in America, they are highly improper in England, and likely to be productive of considerable mischief. And we disclaim all connection with them." The expulsion of Bourne (1808) and Clowes (1810) led to the formation of a new sect and to the secession from Wesleyan Methodism of a number of congregations and preachers in Lancashire and Cheshire. The new body increased rapidly, and has become flourishing and important, especially in the northern counties. It has a large theological college in Manchester, Hartley College (named after a great benefactor, Sir W. P. Hartley, of Liverpool), which is affiliated to the Manchester University. See J. H. Blunt.

PRISCILLIANISTS. One of the names by which the Montanists were known in the time of Epiphanius. Prisca or Priscilla was one of the women who, as prophetesses, were associated with Montanus of Phrygia. See MONTANISM.

PROCESSIONAL ROAD. In recent excavations carried out in Babylon under the superintendence of Dr. Robert Koldewey an interesting discovery was made in the space between the palace and the chief temple. "A sacred procession street was laid bare, a *via sacra* built high above the low houses of the city and along which the images of the numerous gods and goddesses, who formed a court around Marduk, were carried in procession on festive occasions, and more particularly on the New Year's Day, which was the most solemn occasion of the year. The walls along this street were lined with glazed tiles representing a series of lions surmounted by rows of rosettes and other ornamental designs. The street was paved with large blocks of a composite material and contained at frequent intervals a dedicatory inscription indicating the name of the street as "Aiburshabu," "may the enemy not wax strong," and the name of the builder as the great Nebuchadnezzar. A magnificent gateway, known as the Ishtar gate and consisting of an outer and inner gate, formed the approach to the street. The six square towers of the gateway contained on all sides a series of glazed tiles with alternate representations of horned dragons and unicorns, so arranged that a group of dragons running as a pattern around the four sides of the tower was succeeded by a group of unicorns similarly arranged. It was found that there were eighteen such alternate groups, one above another (Morris Jastrow, *Civ.*).

PROFANITY. Professor G. T. W. Patrick distinguishes two kinds of swearing, asseverative or legal, and ejaculatory or profane. The latter he defines as "the ejaculatory or exclamatory use of a word or phrase, usually the name of the deity or connected in some way with religion or other sacred things, having no logical connection with the subject in hand, and indicative of strong feeling, such as anger or disapproval." This definition would include the severer forms of profanity, such as cursing, and blasphemy, as well as the milder and more common forms. As far as religion is affected, such profanity makes use of: names of deities, angels, and devils; names associated with the sacred matters of religion (*e.g.*, Cross); names of saints and sacred persons (*e.g.*, Holy Moses); names of sacred places (*e.g.*, Jerusalem); and terms relating to the future life (*e.g.*, Heavens, Hell). There is of course also a vulgar kind of profanity which scoffs at religion and holds it up to ridicule. This is described usually as blasphemy Profanity may be said to be common to all religions. The vice was common among the Hebrews and the Arabs. It is common still in countries which are not irreligious (*e.g.*, England and America). How is the habit, which is considered sinful by strictly religious people, to be accounted for? Professor Patrick, examining the matter psychologically, offers a noteworthy explanation. Profanity is a reaction in the civilized man against the suppression of the combative instinct in his primitive nature. Profane outbursts are like the "*noises* which an animal may make in order to 'strike terror to the heart' of the opponent, such as the growl, the snarl, the roar, the bellow, and the hiss, all of which are, like the curse or oath of anger in human beings, harmless in themselves, but useful as indirect means of defense, since they induce in the opponent the reactions of flight instead of combat." Profane oaths do this because "they possess that which all weapons possess, the power of producing a shock in the one against whom they are directed."

PROPHECY OF AHIJAH. A record referred to in II. Chronicles (ix. 29). We read as follows: "Now the rest of the acts of Solomon, first and last, are they not written in the history (or "acts" or "words") of Nathan the prophet, and in the prophecy of Ahijah the Shilonite, and in the visions of Iddo the seer concerning Jeroboam the son of Nebat?" It is probable that "these sources were not independent works, but were either sections of the canonical books" or of the Book of the Kings of Israel and Judah. "Nathan the prophet appears at the beginning of Solomon's reign (I. Kings i.), Ahijah near its close (I. Kings xi. 29 ff.), hence in *the acts* or *history of Nathan* and in *the prophecy of Ahijah* we probably have references to I. Kings. Whether this is so in the visions of Iddo the seer is more doubtful. This may refer to the Chronicler's other source (*cf.* xii. 15; xiii. 22); yet the unknown prophet of I. Kings xiii. is called by Josephus *Jadon*, a name equivalent to Iddo (Ant. viii. 8, 5), and he may thus have been known at the time of the Chronicler" (E. L. Curtis and A. A. Madsen). See E. L. Curtis and A. A. Madsen, *Chronicles*, 1910.

PROPHESYINGS. The Prophesyings inaugurated in England in 1571 were religious exercises suggested by the passage in the New Testament: "Ye shall all prophesy one by one that all may learn and all be comforted" (I. Corinthians xiv. 31). "Every fortnight the clergy of a district met on a week-day in the chief town under a moderator or president; each minister would then for a quarter of an hour or so handle the same passage of Scripture. The whole prophesying took some two hours, and at its close the moderator would sum up the discussion and prescribe a text for the next meeting" (M. W. Patterson). By means of these Prophesyings preaching was improved and knowledge increased. But Queen Elisabeth was told that they promoted Puritanism, and sought to suppress them. Edmund Grindal (1519?-1583), Archbishop of Canterbury, was suspended for refusing to carry out the Queen's order. In the reign of James I. the Puritans wished to revive the Prophesyings, but they were opposed by the King. See J. H. Blunt; M. W. Patterson, *Hist.*

PROPHETS, THE. The title of the second of the three groups into which the books of the Old Testament are divided. They are sub-divided into two smaller groups. (1) The Former Prophets (Nebiim rishônim): Joshua, Judges, I. and II. Samuel, I. and II. Kings. These are what we should call historical writings. (2) The Latter Prophets (Nebiim akharônim): Isaiah, Jeremiah, Ezekiel, the twelve Minor Prophets. These are strictly prophetical writings. Certain historical books are regarded as prophetical writings (The Former Prophets), because the prophets were regarded as the writers of the age. "The idea was that the history of each successive generation was written by a contemporary prophet; and as the prophetic literature in the narrower sense does not begin until the reign of Jeroboam II. in Israel and Uzziah in Judah, the narratives of whose reigns fall in the second half of the Second Book of Kings, it was natural that the great bulk of the historical writings (Joshua-II. Kings xiv.) should be roughly described as the work of the older prophets" (W. Sanday, *Inspiration*, 1903). The order of the books as given by the Talmud and Jerome is somewhat different. The Talmud has: Joshua, Judges, Samuel, Kings, Jeremiah, Ezekiel, Isaiah, Minor Prophets. Here the position of Isaiah (last instead of first of the great prophets) is remarkable. The Talmud accounts for this order "by saying that the Books of Kings end with desolation, that Jeremiah is all desolation, that Ezekiel begins with desolation and ends with consolation, and that Isaiah is all consolation, so that desolation is fitly joined to desolation and consolation to consolation; an idea which is not without its pathos and beauty, but which belongs rather to the time when the harps were hung up and the Rabbis were occupied with the wistful retrospect of their past history, than to the simpler motives at work when the books were first collected. That the place assigned to Isaiah has been affected by the incorporation of the last twenty-seven chapters, which are really later than Jeremiah and Ezekiel, would be a welcome supposition if it were probable, but it appears more likely that Jeremiah was placed next to the later chapters of II. Kings, with which his book is so closely connected, and Isaiah immediately before his contemporary Hosea" (W. Sanday). The order given by Jerome is: Joshua, Judges and Ruth, Samuel, Kings, Isaiah, Jeremiah and Lamentations, Ezekiel, Minor Prophets. See G. Wildeboer; H. E. Ryle, *Canon*.

PROPHETS, MOHAMMEDAN. The Mohammedans believe that the prophets have been sent by God, and as an act of free grace. They make a distinction, however, between ordinary prophets and apostles. The apostles, such as Moses, Jesus, and Mohammed, were prophets entrusted with a special message and book. Prophets cannot sin. They may have sinned before they became prophets, but not afterwards. It is not possible to ascribe to prophets want of intelligence, dulness, concealment of the message, unfaithfulness, or falseness. "God has given the prophets and apostles the power to perform miracles, *i.e.*, the doing of things contrary to custom in proof of their prophetic mission, and the truthfulness in what they deliver to men as a divine message. One single miracle is considered sufficient to prove the prophetic character of him who performs it." See F. A. Klein.

PROSTITUTION, RELIGIOUS. There are several references in the Old Testament to the heathen practice of religious prostitution. In Hosea iv. 14, for instance, reference is made to "holy" or "consecrated" women, that is to say, women who sacrificed their virtue in honour of Astarte. The practice was common in ancient sanctuaries, and "the temples of the Semitic deities were thronged with sacred prostitutes" (Robertson Smith, *R.S.*): but anything of the kind was forbidden by the Deuteronomic Code of the Hebrews (Deut. xxiii. 17 f.). It is found in the religion of Babylonia and Assyria. Women took a large part as priestesses in the temple service—as singers, "howlers" (in lamentation), musicians, exorcisers, etc. "We find also several classes of holy women leading a secluded life in special homes which would correspond to our cloisters and nunneries, and who were regarded as constituting in a measure the harem of the god to whose service they were dedicated. Some of these were "sacred prostitutes," and it is in connection with this class of priestesses that rites were practised in the temples which, while probably regarded as purely symbolical to promote fertility among mankind and in the animal world, were unmistakably obscene, or at least degenerated into obscene rites" (Morris Jastrow, *Civ.*).

PROTESTANT ALLIANCE, THE. The Protestant Alliance was instituted in 1845. With it are associated a number of other similar Societies, including the Scottish Protestant Alliance. The object of the alliance is to maintain and defend, against all that it considers encroachments of Popery, the Scriptural doctrines of the Reformation and the principles of civil and religious liberty, as the best security under God for the temporal and spiritual welfare of the British Empire. For this purpose it makes in the main two great efforts. (1) "To unite the Protestants of the Empire in a firm and persevering demand, both in Parliament and out of it, that the national support and encouragement given to Popery should be discontinued. In this demand would be included all endowments of Popery in every form and of every kind, drawn from the public revenues, the concession of rank aud precedence to Romish Ecclesiastics, and the allowance of conventual establishments not subject to the inspection and control of the Law." (2) "To extend, as far as may be practicable, the sympathy and support of British Christians to those in foreign countries who may be suffering oppression for the cause of the Gospel; and to seek to call forth the influence of the British Government to obtain for Protestants, when residing in Roman Catholic countries, religious liberty equal to that which is granted to Roman Catholics in Great Britain and its dependencies, especially the liberty of public worship, and of burying their dead according to their own rites; and above all, freedom in the use and circulation of the Word of God." The Alliance professes to be non-political.

PROTESTANT FRIENDS. Another, and later, name for the Friends of Light (*q.v.*). The Free Congregations (*q.v.*) formed in Prussia in 1841 adopted the name Friends of Light. In course of time this was changed to Protestant Friends.

PROTEVANGELIUM, THE. A name given to a verse in the Book of Genesis (iii. 5). The verse belongs to the Jahwistic narrative. It reads: "I will put enmity between thee and the woman, and between thy seed and her seed; it shall bruise thy head, and thou shalt bruise his heel." This has been called the first announcement of the gospel of redemption. Christ, it is interpreted, will destroy the power of sin and Satan (bruise the Serpent's head), though at the cost of suffering (since Satan bruises his heel). But, as A. R. Gordon says, the words can hardly "be regarded as a prophecy of the final victory of Good. At the most, they imply only unceasing conflict between good and evil." Prof. Skinner thinks it "possible that in its primary intention the oracle reflects the protest of ethical religion against the unnatural fascination of snake-worship. It is psychologically true that the instinctive feelings which lie at the root of the worship of serpents are closely akin to the hatred and loathing which the repulsive reptile excites in the healthy human mind; and the transformation of a once sacred animal into an object of aversion is a not infrequent phenomenon in the history of religion (see Gres. *l.c.* 360). The essence of the temptation is that the serpent-demon has tampered with the religious instinct in man by posing as his good genius, and insinuating distrust of the goodness of God; and his punishment is to find himself at eternal war with the race whom he has seduced from their allegiance to their Creator. And that is very much the light in which serpent-worship must have appeared to a believer in the holy and righteous God of the Old Testament." R. Kittel interprets the passage to mean that at some time in the history of the human race certain individuals or one individual will arise who will bring the moral war to victory in the name and on behalf of the whole race. "Closely connected with this idea is that of the saviour of the future, which is thus transferred from the naturalistic to the moral sphere." He thinks it quite possible that we ought to ascribe the passage to a much earlier date than the Jahwistic document itself, and that it is really the "first Gospel." See W. H. Bennett, *Genesis* in the "Century Bible"; A. R. Gordon, *The Early Traditions of Genesis*, 1907; J. Skinner, *Genesis*, 1910; R. Kittel, *The Scientific Study of the O.T.*, 1910.

PROVERBS, BOOK OF. The Book of Proverbs belongs to that class of Hebrew literature known as Wisdom-literature, of which there are several examples in the Old Testament (Proverbs, Job, Ecclesiastes). It is a collection of sententious maxims (*mĕshālīm*) which enforce a practical rather than a speculative wisdom. C. H. Toy points out (*Encycl. Bibl.*) that this wisdom has much in common with the thought of the preceding and contemporary literature. It accepts monotheism; takes monogamy for granted; and retains the traditional division of mankind into good and bad. As in the Prophets and the Psalms, miracles play little or no part, except as reminiscences. On the other hand, its character is relatively non-national, little stress being laid on national institutions, laws, and hopes. Characteristic of the Wisdom-literature is its conception of virtue. As regards this, "in Job and Proverbs and the succeeding books we meet a conception of the moral life which, while not without a point of connection with the prophetic thought, still goes far beyond anything in the earlier literature; virtue is practically identified with knowledge. Knowledge, it is true, is a necessary condition of obedience, and is so spoken of in the Prophets (Is. i. 3, vi. 9, Jer. iv. 22, v. 4); but the sages treat it as if it were the same thing as obedience. The central fact in the books just named is wisdom, which is made to include all the duties of life from the lowest to the highest. The ideal person, he who stands for the right against and above the wrong, is the wise man. . . Instead of the simple demands of earlier times, the sole worship of Yahwè and obedience to his ritual and moral laws, there has now arisen a science of living, in which intellectual insight is the central faculty, it being assumed that he, and only he, who sees will do" (C. H. Toy in *Encycl. Bibl., s.v.* "Wisdom Literature"). The Book of Proverbs is called in the Hebrew Bible *Mishlē*, this being the first word in the description "Proverbs of Solomon" (*Mishlē Shĕlōmōh*). In the Vulgate the title is "Parabolæ Solomonis." Certain portions of the book have special superscriptions. Thus chapters x. 1-xxii. 16, in which has been found the real kernel of the Book of Proverbs, has the superscription "Proverbs of Solomon." The verses, many of which are antithetical in structure, are independent wholes. Chapters xxii. 17-xxiv. have the superscription "Words of the Wise." Chapter xxx. professes to be the "Words of Agur the son of Jakeh." Chapters xxv.-xxix. are ascribed to the literary activity of Hezekiah. They have the heading: "These also are Proverbs of Solomon, which the men of Hezekiah, king of Judah, copied out." Prof. Driver thinks that the statement may be correct. The opening section, chapters i.-ix., "forms a treatise of moral instruction specially intended for young men, presented in the form of exhortations by a father to his son to take Wisdom as his guide"

(O. C. Whitehouse). It is doubtful whether King Solomon can be regarded as the author even of the oldest section of the book (chaps. x. 1-xxii. 16), though no doubt contemporary and even older proverbs have been incorporated. A number of scholars assign chapters i.-ix. to a period a little before the Exile. Others regard practically the whole of the Book of Proverbs as post-exilic. The use of Solomon's name would be suggested by his reputation for wisdom. C. H. Toy thinks that, as regards rhythm, "the line in Proverbs has usually three beats (a form which may be called ternary), sometimes two (binary), sometimes four (quaternary). . . . In a few cases it is difficult to detect rhythm at all; but in such cases there is ground for supposing the trouble to be in the text." See C. H. Toy, "Proverbs" and "Wisdom Literature" in the *Encycl. Bibl.;* and *Proverbs* in the *I.C.C.*, 1899; C. Cornill, *Intr.;* G. H. Box; O. C. Whitehouse.

PROXIMAE. Proximae, the kinswomen, was the name given by the ancient Celts to a group of goddesses. There are other such groups. Edward Anwyl (*Celtic Religion*, 1906) thinks that "these grouped goddesses take us back to one of the most interesting stages in the early Celtic religion, when the earth-spirits or the corn-spirits had not yet been completely individualised." Cp. MATRES.

PSALMS, BOOK OF. In the Canon of the Old Testament (*q.v.*) the Book of Psalms (Hebrew *Sepher tĕhillīm;* Greek *Psalmoi*) is one of the books of the Third Division or Hagiographa (*q.v.*). It is a collection of religious poems of various date, and also, though a large proportion of the poems were popularly ascribed to David, of various authorship. The ascription of so many psalms to David was due no doubt to his fame as a minstrel and to the tradition that he organised the worship and music of the temple. The Psalms are divided in the Hebrew Bible into five books, the five-fold division having perhaps been suggested by that of the Pentateuch. The five books are: (1) Psalms i.-xli.; (2) xlii.-lxxii.; (3) lxxiii.-lxxxix.; (4) xc.-cvi.; (5) cvii.-cl. In the first three books (for the most part) many of the Psalms have titles or superscriptions. Often these are of the nature of musical directions. Sometimes they are notes as to authorship. Thus eleven psalms are said to be by or to belong to "the Sons of Korah" (xlii., xliv.-xlix., lxxxiv., lxxxv., lxxxvii., and lxxxviii.). One psalm is ascribed to "Ethan the Ezrahite" (lxxxix.), and another group to "Asaph" (l., lxxiii.-lxxxiii.). Such superscriptions indicate that there are psalters within the Psalter. This is clearly the case. There are a number of psalms each of which is called "a song of degrees (or ascents)." These are Psalms cxx.-cxxxiv. There are Jewish traditions which explain that they were so called because at the Feast of Tabernacles they were sung by the Levites on the fifteen steps or degrees leading from the temple-court of the women to that of the men. Robertson Smith, however, thinks (*Encycl. Bibl.*) that they must originally have been a hymn-book intended not for the Levites, but for laymen who went up to Jerusalem at the great pilgrimage feasts. He thinks that the title of this hymn-book was simply "Pilgrimage Songs." Other groups of psalms have been distinguished and described as the *Hodu*-psalms (cv.-cvii.), the *Hallelujah*-psalms (cxi.-cxiii., and cxlvi.-cl.) and the *Hallel*-psalms (cxiii.-cxviii.). These groups, apart from other considerations, indicate that the Psalter is a compilation. A large number of the Psalms were not composed by David. Prof. Cheyne writes (*E. Bi.*): "That the song of triumph in II. Sam. xxii. (= Ps. xviii.) and the 'last words of David' in xxiii. 1-7 (both highly religious compositions) are Davidic, is not, on grounds of criticism, tenable. Nor can any of the psalms in the Psalter be ascribed with any probability to David." But this is an extreme position. As O. C. Whitehouse and R. Kittel say, there is no reason why David should not have composed songs for religious worship (cp. II. Sam. i. 17 ff., iii. 33 ff.). However great David's shortcomings were, it may be claimed as a historical fact, as Kittel says, that he was deeply religious. His biographers do not fail to tell us his faults. They also depict him in his greatness. "And when they do this, they describe him as a man of extraordinary genius, head and shoulders above his contemporaries, both as a man and as a religious personality. As a man full of genuine magnanimity, he laments the death of his bitterest enemy in accents of unalloyed sorrow, is chivalrously faithful to a friend even unto death, and he frankly admits his guilt to the prophet. And as a religious personality he is in keeping with the spirit of his day, which he truly reflects, and is not free from superstitions and eccentric religious tendencies. He reveals this side of his character in his lifelong child-like simplicity, which was more pronounced perhaps in David than in any of his contemporaries—in this respect again proclaiming himself to be a man in the truest sense of the term. But this characteristic of his nature is due to the influence of true religion. It is the expression of strong, genuine, deep piety" (Kittel). H. Ewald has ascribed sixteen psalms to David (iii., iv., vii., viii., xi., xv., xviii., xix. 1-6, xxiv. 1-6, xxiv. 7-10, xxix., xxxii., lx. 6-9 [Heb. 8-11], lxviii. 13-18 [Heb. 14-19], cxliv. 12-14, cl.). The religious lyric in Israel no doubt goes back to an ancient date. "We find very early traces of religious poetry in Egypt, which has many affinities with the poetry of the psalms, and in the Babylonian penitential psalms we are taken back to a period prior to 3000 B.C." (R. Kittel). See S. R. Driver, *The Parallel Psalter*, 1898; F. Baethgen, *Die Psalmen*, 1904; T. K. Cheyne, *Book of Psalms* (translation), 1905; C. Cornill, *Intr.;* G. H. Box; O. C. Whitehouse; R. Kittel, *The Scientific Study of the Old Testament*, 1910.

PSATHYRIANS. The followers of Theoctistus Psathyropola (the "cake-seller") of Constantinople about 390 A.D. They were Arians. They held "that the First Person of the Trinity was in a proper sense Father, and so to be styled before the Son existed; while their opponents, the followers of the Antiochene Dorotheus, maintained that He was only a Father after the existence of the Son" (G. T. Stokes). See J. H. Blunt; Wace and Piercy.

PSEUDEPIGRAPHA. The Pseudepigrapha of the Old Testament are apocryphal and apocalyptic writings which were "falsely" ascribed to certain authors with well-known names. See APOCALYPTIC LITERATURE and APOCRYPHA OF THE OLD TESTAMENT.

PSEUDO-DIONYSIAN WRITINGS. The writings which purport to have been composed by Dionysius the Areopagite seem to have been written in Syria by a Christian bishop between about 490 and 500 A.D. The writer assimilated much of the teaching of the great Hellenistic philosopher Proclus (410-485 A.D.); and, in fact, according to F. von Hügel, his writings "constitute the most wholesale adoption of non-Christian philosophy ever, so far, endorsed by the official Christian Church."

PSYCHICAL RESEARCH, THE SOCIETY FOR. The Society for Psychical Research was founded at the beginning of 1882, and incorporated in August, 1895, "for the purpose of making an organised and systematic attempt to investigate various sorts of debatable phenomena which are *primâ facie* inexplicable on any generally recognised hypothesis. From the recorded testimony of many competent witnesses, past and present, including observations recently made by scientific men of eminence in various countries, there appeared to be, amidst much illusion and deception, an important body of facts to which this description would apply, and which, therefore, if incontestably established, would be of the very highest interest. The task of examining such residual phenomena had often been undertaken by individual effort, but never hitherto by a scientific society organised on a sufficiently broad basis." The principal departments of work at present undertaken by the Society are five in number. 1. An examination of the nature and extent of any influence which may be exerted by one mind upon another, otherwise than through the recognised sensory channels. 2. The study of hypnotism and mesmerism; and an inquiry into the alleged phenomena of clairvoyance. 3. A careful investigation of any reports, resting on testimony sufficiently strong and not too remote, of apparitions coinciding with some external event (as, for instance, a death) or giving information previously unknown to the percipient, or being seen by two or more persons independently of each other. 4. An inquiry into various alleged phenomena apparently inexplicable by known laws of nature, and commonly referred by Spiritualists to the agency of extra-human intelligences. 5. The collection and collation of existing materials bearing on the history of these subjects. "The aim of the Society is to approach these various problems without prejudice or prepossession of any kind, and in the same spirit of exact and unimpassioned inquiry which has enabled Science to solve so many problems, once not less obscure nor less hotly debated. The founders of the Society have always fully realised the exceptional difficulties which surround this branch of research; but they nevertheless believed that by patient and systematic effort some results of permanent value might be attained." The Society publishes "Proceedings," and a Monthly Journal is issued to members and associates. The Society for Psychical Research, it may be said, is having a considerable influence upon the thought of the age.

PSYCHIC PHENOMENA OF RELIGIOUS EXPERIENCE. It is still a common belief in some quarters that the religious experiences of the Hebrew prophets, of the early Christians, and even of the Christians of the Middle Age differed widely from those of the adherents of other religions, and from those of modern Christians. By a curious process of reasoning it is claimed that in distant ages the power of the Spirit manifested itself in marvellous ways, and then changed its method of operation. Whenever in modern times it has been reported that marvellous things have happened the disposition has been to smile or even to scoff. It is true that the Society for Psychical Research has brought about a change, but the prejudice against such investigations and against the trend of thought which such investigations represent is amazingly strong. Yet, if marvels happen at all, why they should happen in one age and not in another, no one has been able satisfactorily to explain. To many people the simplest explanation seems to be that they never have happened. And of course the simplest explanation is often the wrong one. The truth is that what were understood as marvels in distant ages do happen still. It is impossible to suppose that the Divine Power, which is the same yesterday, to-day, and for ever can ever have left itself without unmistakeable evidence in any age. Marvels do happen quite similar to some of those which happened in the days of the Hebrew Prophets and the Early Christians. There can no longer be any doubt that people in these days are being healed bodily and reformed morally in a way that seems miraculous. One need only refer to such works as W. Soltau's *Hat Jesus Wunder getan?* H. Dresser's *Health and the Inner Life* (1907), the book published in 1908 with the title *Religion and Medicine*, and Hugo Muensterberg's *Psychotherapy* (1909). Marvels still happen. But there is a fundamental difference between our age and the early ages to this extent that at least in some cases the progress of the Science of Mind, which is still new, has taught us to interpret the marvellous phenomena of religious experience in another way. We are better able to distinguish between subjective and objective phenomena. This is a matter of far-reaching significance. The failure in ancient times to make this distinction not only fostered an extravagant belief in palpable marvels, but influenced the whole style and language in which even ordinary historical events were described. The profound and remarkable subjective experiences of men like Moses, for instance, dictated the style in which the history of his people was written. One example may be taken, though it may not be the best for our purpose. We are told that when the people of Israel journeyed from Egypt, Jehovah went before them in a pillar of cloud by day and in a pillar of fire by night. This is none other than the fire and smoke which Moses saw subjectively in his vision of the Burning Bush, and which he ever afterwards associated with the Divine Presence (see further BURNING BUSH, and PILLAR OF CLOUD AND FIRE). The Bible is probably full of instances of the kind, and in this respect no sharp line of distinction can be drawn between the Old Testament and the New. Profane history in any age is but a poor reflexion of historical truth. Sacred history, history written from a religious standpoint, bears a still slighter resemblance to history as the term is commonly understood. But let this fact be emphasized at once, the style in which sacred history is composed bears witness to religious experiences which stirred men to their inmost depths. And the history does reflect and enshrine in great measure that knowledge which is of priceless worth, the knowledge of divine truth. This is the treasure hid in a field which one would do well to search out and buy at any price. To interpret sacred history too literally then is to misunderstand it. This was pointed out long ago by De Quincey, a rather conservative writer when he came to deal with theology. The language of sacred books is coloured by religious experience. And yet, where the writer is not a mere second-hand reporter or editor, but one who has himself had exceptionally profound religious experiences, divine inspiration may be said to cling to every word. In a sense the idea expressed by Verbal Inspiration is still true. Be that as it may, the claim that certain books as a whole are inspired is well supported. It is supported powerfully in one way by the effect which they produce when they are rightly understood. The philosophy known as Pragmatism seems to be based upon the principle that the truth of a philosophy will be demonstrated by its practical results. The principle is a right one. Experience shows that there is nothing wrong with Inspiration and Revelation, but only with the way in which they have been understood. Certain books are inspired. The point that requires to be emphasized is that by the time inspiration has reached a book it has passed through several processes or stages. According to Mr. Laurie Magnus ('*Religio Laici' Judaica*, 1907), even traditional Judaism "recognizes at least three elements in the inspired text, as we receive it. First, the message; next, the interpreter; lastly, the audience. Human agents were chosen to communicate the divine will, and something doubtless was lost in the first process of transmission. Further, the transmitting agent had to make his communication to a heterogeneous audience, and that second process of removal from the original Voice involved a fresh adaptation of the message. The Pentateuchal formula is commonly: 'And the Lord spake unto Moses, saying, Speak unto the children of Israel, and say unto them.' Now taking the thing quite literally, it is obvious that in any attempt to repeat to a large mixed class the words of a supreme authority, a certain admixture must take place. There is not only the mind of the transmitter, but the mind of the receivers to be considered. Each will colour the message on its way; and there will be in the resultant text the element of Moses and the element of the children of Israel, as well as the original code." This, according to Mr. Laurie Magnus, is the view of traditional Judaism. But we can go even deeper to the root of the matter. God is spirit. This of itself suggests that he would not use a human language. The general experience of mankind supports the suggestion that he does not do so. When God inspires, Spirit communes directly with spirit. The language of God is the language of the soul. Light is thrown on this matter by the experience known as Conversion (*q.v.*). A sudden conversion is the result of inspiration. It is not as a rule the inspiration of a religious genius; but it is real inspiration, though of a lesser degree. What happens? A person suddenly receives a subjective message, a divine intuition. He feels, or rather he knows, that an important change has taken place in him. He knows that somehow or other his outlook has been radically altered. He experiences a sense of relief, of happiness, unknown before. Ask him what exactly has happened. That is to say, ask him to translate his subjective, his divine message into the language of human speech. In most cases he cannot do it. Probably the most he can do is to repeat mechanically old formulas, perhaps the old formulas of his childhood religion, which seem to have some connection with his present state of mind and may express his new feeling but not his new knowledge. The divine intuition never ceases to influence his life. It does not fail to colour his language, but it may never receive adequate expression in human speech. The man's faith cannot be explained in such a way as to satisfy merely intellectual inquiries. He has, however, the kind of knowledge that made Job proof against all the attacks of those who sought to destroy his faith in God, the kind of knowledge which all persons whose religion is not a mere form do somehow or other obtain. Such is an ordinary case of sudden conversion. Now the inspiration of a prophet or a religious genius, we may suppose, differs from the inspiration of ordinary conversion, not in kind but only in degree. The difference seems to be that it comes with greater power and does in course of time receive more or less adequate expression. Yet even in this case, as far as ordinary language is concerned, only more or less adequate, by no means perfect, expression. Inspired persons are always more inspired than their spoken or written utterances. The priests of some of the Zen sects in China and Japan seem to have realized this, though they may be mistaken in thinking themselves inspired. Mr. Arthur Lloyd writes of them (*The Religion of Half Japan*, 1911): "It is difficult to talk with them on purely spiritual issues, because they hold that Truth is not communicated orally from mouth to ear, but without the intermediary of words, by a kind of wireless telegraphy from heart to heart." Bodhidharma, an Indian priest, who arrived in China in the year 526 A.D. and played a prominent part in the development of the Zen sects, is quoted as having said: "You cannot get Buddhism from books. If you want Enlightenment, you must get it as S'akyamuni did, as the great Kaśyapa did, as Nāgārjuna and Vasubandhu did—by meditation. Books will only tell you about it—meditation and contemplation will *procure* it for you." The divine message to a prophet, like the divine message to an ordinary converted person, is received subjectively or telepathically. It comes as a kind of intuition. We know that in the case of ordinary telepathic messages, the message only in rare cases rises from the sub-conscious mind to the waking mind. It requires some peculiarly endowed person to bring even a simple message to the surface. The prophets were peculiarly endowed. But even in their case, we may suppose, the difficulty of translating profound subjective religious experiences or intuitions into the language of the ordinary speech of a particular period and place is almost insuperable. And when at length, perhaps after a long interval, the inspired words are written down, they may be supposed to give but a poor reproduction of the original inspiration. The inspiration is there. It is there in and behind the mere words, and in some subtle way it does not fail to make itself felt. It is never really lost. This explains the power of the Bible. Read as a whole, it does succeed in giving very forcible expression to divine intuitions. In days when it was read with a simple childlike faith it did often work marvels. Another of the phenomena of religious experience seems to point in the same direction as Conversion, the phenomenon known as Speaking with tongues (see TONGUES, GIFT OF). In many cases it is the result of a real religious experience, a divine inspiration. Here again what seems to happen is that people try to express in human language a message which has been received in a different way, that is to say, subjectively or telepathically, with the result that they only succeed in uttering strange unintelligible sounds. We have reference to this kind of experience in the New Testament (I. Corinthians xii. 10, xiv. 2, 14, 23). J. Massie (I. and II. Corinthians in the "Century Bible") explains that "there appears to have been in those days of infant Christianity an inarticulate yearning to praise, an inexpressible joy, which because it had no vocabulary commensurate with its requirements, broke forth in unintelligible utterance." He adds: "Surely such incoherence when joy is overwhelming is not beyond conception; perhaps it is not altogether contrary to experience." The messages of God pass directly and subjectively to the minds or souls of men. It is true that reference is often made to a voice. Those who have had remarkable religious experiences often testify to having distinctly heard a voice. We are often told in the Bible that men heard the voice of God. There is no reason to doubt that a voice was heard, but as heard it was hardly the voice of God. Such a voice is heard subjectively. If two persons are together it will be heard as a rule by one, but not by both. If, however, the two persons are in very close sympathy, it may be heard by both, just as the same remark is sometimes made by two persons at the same moment. In any case, the voice is really secondary. It is the voice, subjectively heard, not of God but of man. It is said that on the occasion of Paul's conversion he was not the only person who heard the voice. We read: "And the men that journeyed with him stood speechless, hearing the voice, but beholding no man." This is possible, for Paul was just in that condition in which he might have acted as a medium. But it may be that the statement does not necessarily mean more than that the men who were with Paul heard him carrying on a conversation with, as they thought, some unseen person. The knowledge, then, which comes through inspiration differs, it would seem, from the knowledge acquired through the ordinary efforts of the intellect. It is intuitional, and is conveyed by a different language, a language, if we can call it such, of its own. But it need not come by an immediate or direct inspiration as in the case of a sudden conversion. In many cases no doubt it is inherited. A religious genius transmits it subjectively to his disciples, and these transmit it to others. For there is truth in the idea of an Apostolic Succession, and an Elisha does inherit the mantle of an Elijah. It may be transmitted by an inspired book, if the ordinary intellect is not allowed to assert itself too uncompromisingly. In some way or other, one must suppose, it is a knowledge within the reach of all. For experience seems to teach that if the pursuit of religious truth is persevered in, sooner or later, however black for a time the prospect may be, the light will burst forth. The trouble is that so many people too soon abandon the pursuit in despair, adopt some party label, Agnostic, Rationalist, and so forth, accepting all its shibboleths without more ado, and henceforth think no more. Books have been referred to in the course of the article.

PSYCHO-ANALYSIS. That there was some inkling of the Freudian psycho-analytic method of treating nervous disorders many centuries ago is shown by a narrative in Lucian's tract *The Syrian Goddess*. According to this story (§§ 17 and 18), the stepson of Stratonice, wife of the king of the Assyrians (*i.e.*, Syrians, the king thought of being probably Seleucus Nicator of Antioch), was enamoured of his stepmother. He lost his colour, and became daily more frail. Seen by a doctor, the doctor could find no definite disease, and perceived that the malady was erotic. He noted that when the stepmother was near, the patient became worse: he paled, sweated, trembled, and suffered from violent beating of the heart. The doctor summoned the patient's father, and explained to him that the malady was due to a wrongful action. Slightly dissembling the truth, he said: "he has no painful symptoms; he is possessed by love and madness. He longs to possess what he will never obtain; he loves my wife, whom I will never give up" (transl. by H. A. Strong). The father pleaded for his son, explaining his guilt as involuntary. Thereupon the doctor professed to be scandalized, and asked: "What would you do, if it were your wife?" The father replied that even if his son were enamoured of his own stepmother, he would not begrudge him his life. The doctor then announced that the object of the young man's love was actually his father's wife. On hearing this the father decided to give up his wife and kingdom; and the young man was cured. In the words of Professor R. C. Cabot (*What Men Live By*, 1915), the essence of the Freudian doctrine is this: "People suppress and try to bury a disappointed hope or an evil desire; but accidentally they bury it alive, so that it struggles and shrieks beneath the weight of daily life piled on top of it." Jane E. Harrison (*Rationalism and Religious Reaction*, 1919) observes with truth that, if Dr. Freud's books are in some ways unpleasant reading, no one now doubts the substantial soundness of his conclusions or the reality of his cures. "He *can*

> Pluck from the memory a rooted sorrow,
> Raze out the written tablets of the brain.

He *does*

> Cleanse the stuffed bosom of that perilous stuff
> Which weighs upon the heart.

A host of obscure diseases—on the borderland of insanity—diseases gnawing at and corrupting the very sources of life, are caused, he finds, by repressed emotions, and most of all by repressed desires. Such diseases are hysterias, claustro- and other *phobias*, multiple personalities, and the like." To find a remedy, "the suppressed desire is to be fished up, brought into relation with the conscious, harnessed to reality, sublimated." For a popular exposition of Freudian and other Psycho-analytic methods, see Wilfrid Lay, *Man's Unconscious Conflict*, 1918.

PSYCHOLOGICAL HEDONISM. See HEDONISM.

PSYCHO-THERAPEUTIC SOCIETY. This Society, which was established in 1901, rightly claimed to be scientific, charitable, and useful. It deserves notice here because it had also a religious significance. The Rev. Clinton A. Billig, for instance, came to England to study the Society's methods, and "returned to his church in America to put their ideas into practice." As in the case of the "Church and Medical Union," the institution was clearly another of the results of the modern sympathetic study of faith-healing. "The Society exists for the Study, Investigation, and Practice of Health Reform, Medical Hypnotism, Suggestive Therapeutics, Curative Human Radiations, and Drugless Healing, with due regard to Diet, Hygiene, and the observance of Natural Laws of Health, and Monthly Lectures and Instruction Classes are held in connection with these interesting and important subjects." At the time of its institution it could be said that "the only Philanthropic Institution in the United Kingdom at which Free Treatment may be obtained along the above Psychological and Mental Lines." The Society published a journal, which was called "The Health Record." See the *Ninth Annual Report* of the Society, 1910.

PTAH. One of the deities of the ancient Egyptians. The root from which Ptah seems to be derived is common in the Semitic languages in the sense "to open." The meaning of Ptah, as the name of a god, however, is uncertain. In the Book of the Dead (*q.v.*) it is Ptah who performs the ceremony of "opening the mouth" for the dead; but, as Wiedemann says, this function was probably suggested by his name. From the earliest times Ptah has been associated with Memphis. The god is depicted as a bandaged mummy. Two hands, however, are represented in front of the body, in which is held a sceptre symbolizing truth and just measurement. Ptah is the divine sculptor, and became the patron deity of artists and artizans. He is called "Father of the mighty fathers, father of the beginnings, he who created the sun egg and the moon egg." Under the name Ptah Tatûnen he is depicted at Philae sitting in front of a potter's wheel and turning the egg of the sun or moon. See Alfred Wiedemann, *Rel.*; Adolf Erman, *Handbook*; Edouard Naville, *The Old Egyptian Faith*, 1909.

PUERIS SIMILES. A name given to a sect of Anabaptists, who sought to carry out the precept of Jesus reported in the New Testament, and to become like little children. They seem to have mistaken childishness for childlikeness.

PUGGALAPAÑÑATTI. A Buddhist sacred book in the third division of the Canon. See CANON, BUDDHIST.

PUISLAM. Puislam or Putiya Islam (new Islam) is a name given to converts to Islam among the Mukkuvans, the caste of sea fishermen on the Malabar coast of India. The Puislams also follow the pursuit of fishing.

PULLUVANS. The Pulluvans of Malabar are described as astrologers, medicine-men, priests and singers in snake groves. They are sometimes known as Vaidyans, physicians. Their special deities include Velayuthan, Ayyappa, Rāhu, Mūni, Chāthan, Mukkan, Karinkutti, and Parakutti.

PURĀNAS. Purāna is a term used in Hinduism. It means "ancient lore." In the late Vedic period Purāna means "ancient history" (details about ancient history) as distinguished from Ithāsa, "story." The term is used also of parts of the Epic. But it came to be applied particularly to writings held sacred by sectarian worshippers of Siva (*q.v.*) and Vishnu (*q.v.*) of a much later date. They were written after the sixth century A.D., and, according to Hopkins, perhaps as late as 1500 A.D. He thinks that "what is ancient in them is a more or less fugitive resemblance to the epic style and matter; what is new is the more pronounced sectarianism with its adventitious growth of subordinate spiritualities and exaggerated miracles." See E. W. Hopkins.

PURGATORY. The idea of Purgatory (from Latin *purgo* "to cleanse") as a developed doctrine may be said to be the work of the Roman Catholic Church. The position, if certain principles are accepted, is a logical one. The purest of earthly souls can hardly be fit to pass immediately into the spiritual presence of God. Purgatory is thought of therefore, not indeed as a place of probation, for those who reach it have already shown their fitness to enter heaven, but as a place of purification. It is "a place in which souls who depart this life in the grace of God suffer for a time because they still need to be cleansed from venial, or have still to pay the temporal punishment due to mortal sins, the guilt and the eternal punishment of which have been remitted" (*Cath. Dict.*). Not only is there such a place, but the sufferings of those who are there may be relieved by the prayers of the faithful. The eighth article of the Profession of the Tridentine Faith or the Creed of Pius IV. states: "I firmly hold that there is a purgatory, and that the souls therein detained are helped by the suffrages of the faithful. Likewise, that the saints reigning with Christ are to be honoured and invoked, and that they offer up prayers to God for us, and that their relics are to be had in veneration" (quoted in Schaff-Herzog). It has been widely believed that the purification in purgatory is by fire, and that not merely spiritual but material. This was the belief of Thomas Aquinas, Bonaventura, Gerson, and other doctors of the Middle Ages. On this point, however, the Greek differed from the Latin Church, and at the Council of Florence (1439) they agreed to differ. The doctrine of a purgatorial fire was opposed by the Cathari, the Waldenses (*q.v.*), and other sects. The Reformers protested against the whole theory. See Schaff-Herzog; *Chambers's Encycl.*; the *Prot. Dict.*; the *Cath. Dict.*; K. R. Hagenbach.

PURIM, THE SARAGOSSAN. A yearly anniversary celebrated by a few of the Jews resident at Jerusalem on the 17th of Shebat (February) to commemorate the deliverance of the Jews of Saragossa from a plot framed against them about the year 1420. The plot was due to a Christian Jew named Marcus of Damascus, who sought to rouse the anger of Alphonso V., the king of Arragon, against his Jewish brethren, and, like Haman of old, was foiled and punished. See J. E. Hanauer, *Folk-lore of the Holy Land*, 1910.

PURIST CONTROVERSY, THE. A controversy which arose at the beginning of the seventeenth century concerning the text of the New Testament. "The Purists maintained that to deny that God gave the New Testament in anything but pure classical Greek was to imperil the doctrine of inspiration. The Wittemberg Faculty, in 1638, decreed that to speak of barbarisms or solecisms in the New Testament was blasphemy against the Holy Ghost" (M. R. Vincent, *Text. Crit. of the N.T.*, 1903).

PURITANS. A name given to reformers in the Church of England, because they sought to purify the Church from what they regarded as error and corruption. The Puritan controversy began to become acute during the reign of Elizabeth. Originally it was confined for the most part to forms, ceremonies and vestments used in divine worship, but in course of time it was extended to the nature and government of the Church and its relation to the State. "In the first of the Admonitions to Parliament (1572), which was written by Field and Wilcox, and constituted one of the most important Puritan manifestoes of the day, although there was a discussion of forms of worship and clerical vestments, it was said, 'Neither is the controversy between them and us as for a cap, a tippet, or a surplice, but for great matters concerning a true ministry and regiment of the Church according to the Word. Which things once established, the others melt away of themselves'" (A. C. M'Giffert). In the second Admonition of the same year, the policy of the Church appears as the principal subject of discussion. "In this document prelacy was attacked, and presbyterianism declared to be the only lawful government because taught in the Scriptures, the independence of the Church was asserted, and its subjection to the State rejected in good Calvinistic fashion. Strict ecclesiastical discipline was also insisted upon in the spirit of Calvin." M'Giffert notes that the same general position is maintained by Walter Travers in his work *A Full and Plain Declaration of Ecclesiastical Discipline out of the Word of God, and of the Declining of the Church of England from the same* (1574), which became the recognised text-book of puritanism. The controversy came indeed to centre more and more round questions of polity and discipline, though doctrine also became involved owing to the fact that the Puritans emphasised a high and rigid Calvinism. "When they gained control of the government under the Commonwealth, they immediately undertook to put their principles into practice and to reform the Church in accordance with their long-cherished ideas. The Westminster standards (1645 ff.) were for a short time the official standards of the English Church. They represented an extreme Calvinism in theology, Presbyterianism in polity (though without the assertion of its exclusive divine right), and Puritanism in worship. With the Restoration in 1660 the old Anglican order was re-established, and Puritanism was again proscribed, and since the Revolution of 1688 it has existed only in the form of legalised dissent." In Scotland, through the zeal of John Knox, "Calvinism in doctrine, Presbyterianism in polity, and Puritanism in worship were permanently stamped upon the Protestantism of the country, and in 1690, after the English revolution, the Westminster standards were made binding by law upon the Scottish Church." The Puritans started with the idea of reforming the Church from within. When in course of time many of them, finding it impossible to remain in the Church, were obliged to form independent churches of their own, or in other words, when they became Separatists or Sectaries, the name Puritan came in general to be limited to "those Episcopalians who, whilst remaining in the Establishment, still sought to bring about its further reformation" (J. A. Houlder).

PUSEYITES. Persons belonging to the theological school of Edward Bouverie Pusey (1800-1822), Regius Professor of Hebrew at Oxford. The tractarian movement (*q.v.*) came to be called Puseyite on account of the prominent part taken in it by Professor Pusey. Pusey himself, however, writing in 1870, says: "I never was a party leader. I never acted on any system. My name was used first to designate those of us who gave themselves to revive the teaching of forgotten truth and piety, because I first had occasion to write on Baptismal Regeneration. But it was used by opponents, not by confederates" (*Eirenicon*). See the *D.N.B.*

PUSHAN. One of the names of the Sun, as a deity, in the religion of Hinduism. The meaning of the name is nearly equivalent to that of Savitar (*q.v.*). He is the guardian of cattle and the god "with braided hair." He is depicted also as warlike, but his characteristics are in the main bucolic. He is represented as using the goad and as directing the furrow. He is the finder of lost cattle. In the last part of the Rig Veda he escorts the souls of the departed to heaven. See E. W. Hopkins.

PUSHPAKANS. The name of a class of Ambalavāsis in Malabar and Travancore, Southern India. They are so called from *pushpam*, a flower, because their employment is to bring flowers and garlands to the temples.

PUZI. Puzi or Purzi is one of the deities worshipped by the Todas. Perhaps she is identical with Teikirzi.

PWYLL. A god of the Underworld worshipped by the ancient Celts in Wales. His wife was Rhiannon, who seems to be identical with the earlier Rigantona, "the great Queen." Pwyll resembles in some respects the Gaelic Mider.

PYRE, FESTIVAL OF THE. According to Lucian (§ 49), this was the greatest of the spring festivals of the Syrians. He gives the following description of the sacrifice. "They cut down tall trees and set them up in the court; then they bring goats and sheep and cattle and hang them living to the trees; they add to these birds and garments and gold and silver work. After all is finished, they carry the gods around the trees and set fire under; in a moment all is in a blaze" (transl. by H. A. Strong).

PYRRHONISTS. An ancient school of sceptic philosophers. The Pyrrhonists were so called because they followed in the footsteps of Pyrrho of Elis (*c.* 360-270 B.C.). According to Pyrrho, part of the problem of philosophy is to know how things are constituted and what our attitude towards them should be. He decided that the correct attitude is to say nothing about things, to suspend one's judgment. We must not say "things are so," but "so it appears to me." We must say "Perhaps" or "I assert nothing definitely." Pyrrhonism was revived by Ænesidemus of Cnossus, a younger contemporary of Cicero (106-43 B.C.). According to Ænesimus, the true sceptic avoids carefully every kind of dogmatism. He will not assert that there can be only probability. "He neither affirms, nor denies, nor doubts, but merely investigates" (Erdmann). See J. E. Erdmann.

PYTHAGOREANS. The followers of Pythagoras of Samos (584-500 B.C.), who was the first person to describe himself as a philosopher. Little is known of Pythagoras himself. Our knowledge of Pythagoreanism is chiefly derived from Aristotle, who in turn seems to have been dependent upon the oral communications of Pythagoras's disciple Philolaus. Pythagoras is said to haye travelled through Asia Minor, Phoenicia, and Egypt. Then he settled in Crotona (520-509 B.C.), where he founded a society whose members by a secret covenant pledged themselves "to a pure and devout life, to the closest friendship with each other, to united action in upholding morals and chastity as well as order and harmony in the common weal" (Seyffert). They were known as Esoterics or Exoterics. They seem in particular to have developed the theory of numbers. Number is the principle of things. Measure and harmony constitute the highest law of the All. But the doctrine that may be ascribed to Pythagoras with most confidence is that of the transmigration of souls, though even this he seems to have borrowed from the Orient. The body is regarded as a prison of the soul, which latter belongs to the higher world. At death the soul leaves the body. At first it hovers in the air; then it passes into another organism, a higher one, if it has been good, a lower one, if it has been evil. Pythagoras himself is said to have identified certain armour in the temple of Hera as that which he bore before Troy in an earlier existence, and to have recognized in a certain dog the soul of a deceased friend. Gautama the Buddha professed to have an equally good memory. It is thought that the asceticism of the Pythagoreans influenced the Essenes of Palestine and the Therapeutae. They abstained from wearing woollen garments and from eating flesh and beans. Pythagoras, it is said, drank only water, and preferred to eat honey and bread. Cp. NEO-PYTHAGOREANISM. See *Chambers's Encyclopædia;* O. Seyffert, *Dict.;* C. J. Deter; Reinach, *O.*, 1909; Max B. Weinstein, *Welt- und Leben-anschauungen*, 1910.

Q

Q. The letter Q, as an abbreviation of the German word *Quelle* "Source," is used by New Testament scholars as a designation of the sections of the Gospel story which are common only to Matthew and Luke (the Double Tradition). The matter is for the most part of the nature of discourse, and the original document would seem to have been identical with the "Logia" referred to by Papias as composed by Matthew. The work of Matthew is said to have been composed in Hebrew, and it is hardly possible to conclude that it was the same as our Gospel of Matthew. See Arthur S. Peake, *Intr.;* F. C. Conybeare, *Hist. of N.T. Crit.*, 1910.

QADARIYYA. Another name for the Arabian sect called MU'TAZILA (*q.v.*).

QADIRĪYEH. The mother order of the most influential group of Dervish orders. It was founded by 'Abd-el-Qādir ej-Jilani (*d.* 1165), a descendant of the prophet Muhammad. The founder was buried at Baghdad, and his shrine there "has ever continued to attract crowds of pilgrims whose voluntary gifts add greatly to its revenues" (F. J. Bliss). The order has now a number of more or less independent offshoots. F. J. Bliss mentions for example that in Algeria and Tunisia there are three important monasteries which are independent not only of the mother *zawiyeh* or monastery but even of each other. See T. P. Hughes; F. J. Bliss.

QAT. An object of prayer and worship in Melanesia. "Qat appears to hover between the estate of a lowly creative being, born of a rock, and that of a culture-hero, and rather resembles the Zulu Unkulunkulu" (Andrew Lang, *Social Origins*, 1903).

QĪAS. An Arabic word meaning "measuring or

measure." The Qîas is the fourth foundation of Islâm. It denotes "the reasoning by analogy of the learned doctors of Islám, the Mujtahidín, with regard to certain difficult and doubtful questions of doctrine and practice, by comparing them with similar cases already settled by the authority of the Qur'án, Sunna or Ijmá' and thus arriving at the solution of undecided questions." The doctors were not all agreed as to the value of Qîas. There were two parties, one of which was called the People of Qîas or the people of private opinion, while the other was described as the People of Tradition. See F. A. Klein.

QOSH. The name of an Edomite god. The name has been preserved in compound proper names. Qôsh would seem to have been a storm-god, like Adad (*q.v.*), and to have been the national god of the Edomites. He may also have been a moon-god. See E. Schrader; A. Jeremias.

QUADRIVIÆ. The ancient Celts worshipped certain goddesses in groups. One of these groups was called Quadriviæ, or the goddesses of cross roads. Another was known as Proximae (*q.v.*).

QUAHOOTZE. One of the chief deities, apparently a war-god, in the mythology of the Indians of the Nootka Sound country in North America.

QUAILS. According to Athenæus (ix. 49, p. 392 *d.*), the Phoenicians sacrificed quails to the Tyrian Baal, to commemorate the resurrection of Heracles. This may be a misunderstanding. Robertson Smith points out that, as a matter of fact, the ancients regarded quail's flesh as dangerous food, but seem to have made an ointment from the brain to cure epilepsy. With this we may compare the use of the mouse (*q.v.*).

QUAKER BAPTISTS. Another name for the Keithians (*q.v.*), the followers of George Keith.

QUAKERS. The name Quakers was originally a nickname given to a religious body which arose about 1650 A.D. The founder of the body was George Fox (1624-1691). Another of the original leaders of the movement was James Naylor (1612-1660). James Naylor, writing in 1653, "quotes many texts of Scripture to shew that the earth trembled and quaked, that Isaac trembled exceedingly, that Moses feared and quaked, that the Lord bade His disciples quake for fear, and that therefore saints ought to be Quakers" (*Dict. of Sects*). Originally the followers of George Fox called themselves "The people of the Lord" or "The people of God," or "Children of Light," or "Friends." Then, in reference to their nickname, they described themselves as "the people called Quakers" or "the poor Quakers" or "the despised Quakers," or "The people of God, in scorn called Quakers." Later they described themselves as the Society of Friends, and this is now regarded as their correct name. See FRIENDS, SOCIETY OF.

QUAKERS, SHAKING. Another name for the American sect known as Shakers (*q.v.*).

QUASIMODOGENITI. A Latin expression meaning "as newly-born." In France and Germany it is a designation of Low Sunday. The name was suggested by the first words of the introit in the Mass (I. Peter ii. 2).

QUATUOR CORONATI. Quatuor Coronati was the name given to four Christian soldiers, Carpophorus, Severus, Severianus, and Victorinus, who were martyred for refusing to obey the command of the Emperor Diocletian, when he required his troops to offer sacrifice to Aesculapius (*q.v.*). They were flogged to death. See Wace and Piercy, *s.v.* "Sirmium, Stonemasons of."

QUEEN OF HEAVEN. In the Book of Jeremiah (vii. 17-20, xliv. 15-30) reference is made to *meleketh hashshāmayim*, and the words have been rendered "the queen of heaven" (on the supposition that *meleketh* is equivalent to *malkath*). In the Revised Version of Jeremiah vii. 17 f. we read: "Seest thou not what they do in the cities of Judah and in the streets of Jerusalem? The children gather wood, and the fathers kindle the fire, and the women knead the dough, to make cakes to the queen of heaven, and to pour out drink offerings unto other gods, that they may provoke me to anger." The word *meleketh*, however, has also been taken to be equivalent to *mel'eketh*, which means "work." It has then been supposed (*e.g.*, by Jewish scholars) that the worship of "the work (cultus) of heaven" was the same as the worship of "the host of heaven" (Jer. viii. 2, xix. 13, Deut. iv. 19, xvii. 3, etc.). But the interpretation "queen of heaven" is more likely. The worship would seem to have been that of one of the heavenly bodies. In Babylonian mythology the goddess Ishtar (*q.v.*), who was regarded as the planet Venus (*q.v.*), is called *bēlit shamē* and *sharrat shamē*; and, as G. F. Moore says, the latter exactly corresponds in meaning to malkath *hashshāmayim*. Thus the cult would seem to have been of Babylonian origin. It was probably introduced into Judah in the reign of Manasseh. "The description points to its prevalence among the poorer classes, who have to collect firewood and do all the work themselves. From xliv. 19 we learn that the cakes 'pourtrayed' (RVmg.) the goddess. By this is meant, either that they were modelled to represent her, or that her image or symbol was impressed on them" (A. S. Peake). See G. F. Moore in the *Encycl. Bibl.*; A. S. Peake, *Jeremiah*, vol. i., in the "Century Bible," 1910.

QUEST SOCIETY, THE. The objects of the Quest Society are: (1) To promote investigation and comparative study of religion, philosophy and science, on the basis of experience; and (2) to encourage the expression of the ideal in beautiful forms. The Society is essentially a body of seekers and learners. Its objects briefly indicate the general tendency of its programme, which is designed to help those who are seeking for a better understanding of the purpose of life and the means of self-realization. The Society desires especially to promote inquiry into the nature of religious and other supranormal experiences and the means of testing their value, to strengthen that love of wisdom which stimulates all efforts to formulate a practical philosophy of life, and to emphasise the need of a vital science to crown and complete the discoveries of physical research. It also interests itself in whatever throws light on the nature and purpose of art, in the expression of the ideal in forms of beauty, and generally in works of inspiration and of the creative imagination. The endeavour of the Council is to provide the members and guests of the Society with the most competent lecturers procurable on the many subjects which fall within the wide field of its interests. The Honorary Secretary is Mrs. L. M. Mead (47, Campden Hill Road, Kensington, London, W.8).

QUETZALCOATL. Quetzalcoatl, which means "Feathered Serpent," was one of the deities of the ancient Mexicans. He was not originally a god of the Aztecs, but was adopted by them from the Toltecs, whom they drove out. His worship was more humane than that of the Aztec gods, Huitzilopochtli (*q.v.*) and Tezcatlipoca (*q.v.*). And legend relates that it was resented and resisted by Tezcatlipoca. The myth represents that Quetzalcoatl suffered a kind of persecution. "It tells that he was once high-priest at Tula, in Anahuac, where, ever clothed in white, he founded a cultus, and gave beneficent laws to men, teaching them also the arts of agriculture, metal-work, stone-cutting, and civil government; the while a king named Huemac held with him the secular rule, and framed the law book of the nation. But the God Tezcatlipoca came to earth in the guise of a young merchant, who deceived the king's daughter, and again in the guise of an old man, who persuaded Quetzalcoatl to drink a mystic drink, whereupon he was seized with an irresistible impulse to wander away" (J. M. Robertson). Quetzalcoatl wandered about for a time, and at length disappeared. His worshippers expected him to return, and when Cortes came, the appearance of the white man was regarded by the Aztecs as a fulfilment of their expectation. According to Robertson, Quetzalcoatl was god of the air. D. Brinton and A. Réville see in him the east-wind which brings the beneficent rain, but is driven away for a time and then again returns. Lewis Spence, on the other hand, points out that Quetzalcoatl was "Lord of the Dawn." He holds him to have been a culture-god. It is probable, he thinks, that "Quetzalcoatl was one of those early introducers of culture who sooner or later find a place among the deities of the nation they have assisted in its early struggles towards civilisation. By the strife between Tezcatlipoca and Quetzalcoatl is typified the struggle between culture and barbarism." The worshippers of Quetzalcoatl did not approve of human sacrifice. E. B. Tylor thinks too that Quetzalcoatl was a real, and not a mythical, personage. Lewis Spence points out that he is represented sometimes as quite European in appearance, with fair beard, blue eyes, and white complexion. To J. M. Robertson, who is fond of finding parallels to a Christian Christ who, according to him, never existed, Quetzalcoatl is not a man who was converted into a god, but a god who was converted into a man: he is the "Mexican White Christ." See Lewis Spence; J. M. Robertson, "The Religions of Ancient Mexico" in *R.S.W.;* Reinach, *O.;* J. M. Robertson, *P.C.*

QUIATEOT. One of the gods of the Nicarao (of Nicaragua). He was the lord of rain, thunder, and lightning. Sacrifices of boys and girls were made to him.

QUIETISM. As the name suggests, Quietism implies an effort to reach a state of quietude. The mystic system of religion known as Quietism originated, as a modern movement, with Michael Molinos (1640-1696), a Spanish priest. In 1675 Molinos published "Guida Spirituale," a work which sets forth the principles of his method. The title of the English translation of the work, published in 1688, explains its nature as follows: "The Spiritual Guide which disentangles the soul and brings it by the inward way to the getting of perfect contemplation and the rich treasure of eternal peace." Molinos maintained "that our perfection consists in an uninterrupted act of contemplation and love; that in this state the soul does not consciously reflect either on God or itself; that true prayer is this state of quietude, and that in prayer the first act of faith, the first intention of resignation prevails to constitute the whole act of worship" (C. H. H. Wright and C. Neil). The spirit of this teaching seemed to be quite opposed to the ordinances and institutions of the Church. Molinos was condemned by the Inquisition in 1685, and was imprisoned. In 1687 he was prevailed upon to recant sixty-eight of his erroneous propositions. Molinos was evidently tempted to carry his doctrine, in theory at least, to extremes. This is clear, it has been thought, when we read such statements as this: "It is never good to love thy neighbour to the detriment of thine own spiritual good. To please God in purity ought to be the only scope of thy works." Madame Guyon (Jeanne Bouvier de la Motte; 1648-1717) adopted a modified form of Quietism. In 1684 she published her well-known work, "Moyen Court et très facile pour faire l'Oraison," which appeared in English as "A Short and Easy Method of Prayer." This and other writings were examined by a Commission in 1694 and declared to contain erroneous doctrines. One of the Commission was Jacques Bénigne Bossuet (1627-1704), who regarded Madame Guyon's ideas as "a mass of extravagances, illusions, and puerilities." Madame Guyon found a sympathizer in her friend Fénelon (1651-1715), Archbishop of Cambray, who adopted rather similar views. In his "Explication des Maximes des Saints sur la Vie intérieure" (1697) he defended the principle of holy indifference and of disinterested love. He was opposed by Bossuet, and in 1699 was condemned by Pope Innocent XII., whereupon he submitted. E. C. Gregory describes the teachings of Madame Guyon and Fénelon as "practical, lofty, inspiring, and second to none for the lift and insight which they afford." See E. C. Gregory, *Intr. to Christian Mysticism;* J. H. Blunt; *Prot. Dict.; Cath. Dict.*

QUIMBYISM. The principles and teaching of Phineas Parkhurst Quimby (1802-1866). Quimby was born in Lebanon, New Hampshire, but two years afterwards his parents moved to Belfast. His father was a blacksmith, and the son did not receive a good education. Phineas Quimby, however, according to his son, "had a very inventive turn of mind, and was always interested in mechanics, philosophy, and scientific subjects." When the French mesmeriser Charles Poyan visited America about the year 1836, Quimby became interested in the new science. He began to experiment himself, believing the new power to be animal magnetism. In course of time, however, he came to realize that the real factor was the influence of one mind upon another. This led him to develop a science of mental healing. "To reduce his discovery to a science, which could be taught for the benefit of suffering humanity, was the all-absorbing idea of his life. To develop his 'theory' or 'the truth,' as he always termed it, so that others than himself could understand and practise it, was what he laboured for. Had he been of a sordid and grasping nature, he might have acquired unlimited wealth; but for that he seemed to have no desire" (Dresser). Quimby lost faith in the efficacy of Mesmerism. "Instead of putting the patient into a mesmeric sleep, Mr. Quimby would sit by him; and, after giving him a detailed account of what his troubles were, he would simply converse with him, and explain the causes of the troubles, and thus change the mind of the patient, and disabuse it of its errors and establish the truth in its place; which, if done, was the cure." Quimby claimed that "mind was spiritual matter and could be changed"; that "disease was an error, or belief, and that the truth was the cure." In 1859 he went to Portland, where he practised until 1865. Annetta G. Dresser went to Quimby as a patient in 1862, and she has given an account of her experience. She says that her first interview with him marked a turning-point in her life. He had a large practice. "People were coming to Mr. Quimby from all parts of New England, usually those who had been given up by the best practitioners, and who had been persuaded to try this new mode of treatment as a last resort. Many of these came on crutches or were assisted into the office by some friend; and it was most interesting to note their progress day by day, or the remarkable change produced by a single sitting with the doctor. I remember one woman who had used crutches for twenty years, who walked without them after a few weeks." Mary Baker Eddy was one of those who visited Quimby. Annetta G. Dresser says she well remembers "the day when she was helped up the steps to his office on the occasion of her first visit for mental treatment." She adds: "She was cured by him, and afterwards became very much interested in his theory. But she put her own construction on much of his teaching, and developed a doctrine which is for the most part a one-sided interpretation of the Quimby philosophy." The two statements in the last sentence are a little difficult to understand. The first admits the original and independent bent of Mrs. Eddy's mind; the second looks like an attempt to weaken this admission (see CHRISTIAN SCIENTISTS). See Horatio W. Dresser, *Health and the Inner Life*, 1907.

QUINTILLIANISTS. Another name for the Priscillianists (*q.v.*), followers of Montanus (second century). Quintilla seems to have been the name of a prophetess (see Augustine, *Hær.* xxvi., xxvii.).

QUR'ĀN. A more correct spelling of the word commonly known as KORAN (*q.v.*).

QUR'ĀN-READERS. A name given by Muhammad to persons who were well-versed in the Qur'ān (see KORAN).

R

RĀ. One of the deities of the ancient Egyptians. Rā was one of the names of the Sun god, or rather of the Sun. The deity is depicted with the body of a man and the head of a hawk. He holds in one hand the sign of life, and in the other a royal sceptre. Above his head is represented the solar disk surrounded by the symbol of power over life and death, the coil of the uraeus. The serpent was supposed to protect the sun against its enemies who tried to oppose its progress. The hawk's head indicates either that the passage of the sun across the heavens is like the flight of the hawk, or perhaps that the sun is supposed to have the form of a sparrow hawk. The latter is the view of Wiedemann. "Probably this bird of prey—which now hovering high in air seems to disappear into the blue heaven and to merge itself in the sun, and anon shoots down suddenly to earth like a ray of light—was regarded as the messenger and even as part of the Sun god, and hence it was concluded that he himself bore the form of a sparrow hawk." In course of time other gods were combined with Rā. Amon-Rā, for instance, became for a thousand years the most prominent of all the gods of Egypt. See Alfred Wiedemann; Adolf Erman, *Handbook;* Edouard Naville, *The Old Egyptian Faith*, 1909.

RAB. A Hebrew word meaning "master" or "teacher." It was employed as a title for the doctors of the Talmudic Schools (the Amorāim; see TALMUD). Abba Arikha (A.D. 175-247) of the Babylonian School was called simply Rab as being the teacher *par excellence.* He founded (A.D. 219) the College at Sura on the Euphrates. "The Palestinian Amoraim who had been ordained by the Patriarch (*Nasi*) bore the title of Rabbi; those of Babylonia who had received ordination bore the title of Rab" (W. O. E. Oesterley and G. H. Box). The title "Rabban" was reserved for Patriarchs and heads of the Sanhedrin. Instead of Rab, "Rabba" or "Rabbah" was also used. Rabbana, "our teacher," was another title. It was given in particular to Rab Ashi of Babylonia. See J. W. Etheridge, *Intr. to Heb. Lit.*, 1856; W. O. E. Oesterley and G. H. Box.

RABBA. Also written "Rabbah," a Hebrew word used as a title. See RAB.

RABBAN. Literally "master" or "teacher," a Hebrew word used as a title. See RAB.

RABBANA. Literally "our Teacher" or "our Master," a Hebrew word used as a title. See RAB.

RABBI. A Hebrew word meaning "my master" or "my teacher" and used as a title. See RAB.

RACOVIAN CATECHISM, THE. The Racovian Catechism of 1605-9 A.D. is a Socinian statement of doctrine. W. A. Curtis speaks of it as one of the longest of Catechisms, controversial and argumentative, theological rather than religious, rationalistic yet also supernaturalistic. "The positions maintained are in many cases far removed from those of present-day Unitarianism, and they are maintained on Scriptural grounds. . . . The work abounds in flashes of true insight, and in the evidences of minute scholarship. Not a few of its criticisms of prevailing theories have a permanent value, some, indeed, have passed into commonplaces of modern thought" (W. A. Curtis). See William A. Curtis.

RĀDHA. A Hindu goddess, the beloved of Krishna.

RAKELIMALAZA. The name of a Malagasy god. It means "renowned, although diminutive." It is curious that horses were not allowed to enter his sacred place. But other animals and objects were also excluded, such as guns, gunpowder, pigs, onions, sifotra (explained as a shell-fish resembling a snail), sitry (explained as a small animal resembling the young crocodile), striped or spotted robes, anything of a black colour, goats, meat distributed at funerals, cats, and owls. See J. G. Frazer, *Spirits of the Corn*, 1912.

RĀKSHASAS. An order of demons in Hinduism. They are mentioned in the Rāmāyaṇa (*q.v.*) as opponents of gods and men. They devour men, and disturb religious rites. They have the power of transforming themselves. One of the most hideous of these monsters is called Virādha. The chief of them, however, is Rāvaṇa. He has a brother, Vibhishaṇa, who is represented as a virtuous demon. See Monier-Williams; E. W. Hopkins.

RĀMA. One of the divine beings worshipped by the Hindus. Rāma was originally a man. He became one of the human incarnations of the god Vishṇu (*q.v.*), the other being Krishṇa (*q.v.*). He was the son of a king, it is said, but his father banished him to the southern forests. Here the tyrant-demon Rāvaṇa, king of Ceylon, carried off his wife Sītā. The hero Rāma, assisted by

Hanumān (*q.v.*), who was probably chief of an ape-like tribe but is represented as a monkey-like semi-divine being, recovered her. After his death Rāma was deified. His exploits are described and enlarged upon in the Epic called Rāmāyaṇa (*q.v.*), "The Wandering of Rāma," of which he is the hero. "From Kaśmīr to Cape Comorin the name of Rāma is on every one's lips. All sects revere it, and show their reverence by employing it on all occasions" (Monier-Williams). Rāma was commonly called Rāma-candra, that is to say, "the moon-like Rāma." See Monier-Williams; E. W. Hopkins; J. A. Dubois and H. K. Beauchamp.

RĀMACANDRA. Rāma-candra, that is to say, "the moon-like Rāma," is a common designation of Rāma (*q.v.*).

RAMADÂN, FAST OF. Ramadân is the ninth month of the Muslim calendar. It is sacred because in this month God is supposed to have sent down the Kur'ân. In it every Muslim, male and female, if of mature years, is required to fast thirty days (not nights). "O believers! a Fast is prescribed to you as it was prescribed to those before you, that ye may fear God, for certain days" (Qur'ân ii. 179-180). The fast begins as soon as two reliable witnesses have seen the new moon of the month of Ramadân. "As to the month Ramadân in which the Koran was sent down to be man's guidance, and an explanation of that guidance, and of that illumination, as soon as any one of you observeth the moon, let him set about the fast" (ii. 181). If the new moon of Ramadân cannot be seen distinctly, one witness suffices; "but when the beginning of the fast rests on the testimony of one witness only, the fast must be continued and cannot be broken till the appearance of the new moon of the following month (Shawwal) is affirmed by two trustworthy witnesses" (Klein). Various forms of abstinence have to be observed. The traditional practice of the Prophet has to be followed. For instance, the Suhûr, the meal taken a little before daybreak, has to be delayed as long as possible. A date or a little water should be taken before prayer. Alms should be bestowed, and the Qur'ân should be read. See F. A. Klein.

RAMAITES. Worshippers of the Hindu man-god Rāma. Some of the Hindus maintain that Vishnu (*q.v.*) was incarnated in Krishna (*q.v.*), others in Rāma. Rāma "is celebrated throughout India as the model son, brother, and husband, who was banished by his father to the southern forests." When Sītā, his wife, was carried off by Rāvaṇa, Rāma by a heroic effort succeeded in recovering her with the help of a chieftain Hanumān. Rāma thus became the hero of the great Indian Epic, the Rāmāyaṇa (*q.v.*). When after his death Rāmā was made into a god, Hanumān also was regarded as divine. The Ramaites have split up into parties on the question of free-will. The Southern, Calvinistic, Ramaites are called Ten-galais. The Northern Ramaites, who hold that free-will must be exercised, are called Vada-galais. The Ramaites agree, however, in accepting Rāma as the human *avatar* of Vishnu, and in acknowledging Vishnu as the deity. In conjunction with Vishnu, they worship his wife Lakshmī. See Monier-Williams; E. W. Hopkins.

RĀMĀNANDIS. The followers of the Hindu religious teacher Rāmānanda, who is said to have been born in the thirteenth century. "They worship Vishṇu under the form of Rāma (the hero of the Rāmāyaṇa) either singly or conjointly with his wife Sītā, and they are not, like the Rāmānujas, hyper-scrupulous about the privacy of their meals" (Monier-Williams). They worship also the divine ape, Hanuman. A number of Rāmānanda's disciples founded new sects. See Monier-Williams; E. W. Hopkins.

RĀMĀNUJAS. The followers of the Hindu religious teacher, Rāmānuja, who was born about A.D. 1017. Rāmānuja settled at Śrī-raṅgam near Trichinopoly, and it is said that he did not die until 1137. In opposition to the doctrine of Śaṅkara (see SMĀRTAS), he acknowledged a triad of principles: (1) the Supreme Spirit; (2) the separate spirits of men; and (3) non-spirit. The spirits of men he regards as essentially different from the Supreme Spirit. He holds that "God is himself both the creator (Kartā) of the world and the substantial cause or material out of which it is formed" (Monier-Williams). He believes that periodically human spirits are re-absorbed into God. He distinguishes five ways or stages in which the Supreme Being can be worshipped, each of them higher than the other. The lowest is in forms and images; the highest is the worship of the internal Spirit. Rāmānuja himself appointed seventy-four special teachers. In the thirteenth century one of his followers undertook to purify the faith of the Master and remove incrustations. He caused divisions by regarding the doctrines of the Northern Brāhmans as purer than those of the Southern. Two parties or schools arose: the Vada-galai or northern school, and the Ten-galai or southern school. The two schools developed some differences of doctrine. For instance, they differ on the question of free-will. Both parties agree in branding themselves with the discus, the conch-shell, the club, and the lotus as emblems of Vishṇu, and in preparing and eating their food in great secrecy. See Monier-Williams; E. W. Hopkins.

RĀMAVATS. A name sometimes given to the followers of the Hindu religious teacher Rāmānanda. They are called also RĀMĀNANDIS (*q.v.*).

RĀMĀYANA. Two sacred writings among the Hindus are called Rāmāyana, "the wandering of Rāma." (1) A great legendary heroic poem, composed by Vālmīki, and based upon the ancient legends of Eastern India. (2) A later poem composed in the sixteenth century by the great Hindu poet, Tulasī-dās. "What the Divine Song and the Bhāgavata Purāna are to the Krishnaite, the older (epic) Rāmāyana of Vālmīki and Tulasīdāsa's new poem (of the same name) are to the Ramaite" (E. W. Hopkins). See Sir Monier Monier-Williams; E. W. Hopkins.

RĀMBAKSH. The gift of Rāma (King of Ayodhia, a great incarnation of Vishnu), one of the names of the Hindu god Rāma.

RĀMCHANDI. A Hindu deity, a goddess, perhaps the personification of Mother Earth, worshipped by the Koltas (also known as Kolitas or Kultas), an agricultural caste of the Sambalpur District and the adjoining Uriya States in India.

RĀMCHANDRA. The moon of Rāma (King of Ayodhia, a great incarnation of Vishnu), one of the names of the Hindu god Rāma.

RĀMCHARAN. The footprint of Rāma (King of Ayodhia, a great incarnation of Vishnu), one of the names of the Hindu god Rāma.

RĀMJI DEO. A god worshipped in Hoshangābād by the Jāts, the representative cultivating caste of the Punjab in India. Another god worshipped in the same place is Bairam Deo. The chief deity of the Jāts, however, is Siva or Mahā-deo. They worship also their swords and horses.

RAMMAN. A Babylonian deity. The older name of the god was perhaps Adad (Syrian Hadad), Ramman being only an epithet. Ramman, "the thunderer," was the god of storms. During the Cassite dynasty Sin (*q.v.*), Shamash (*q.v.*), and Ramman (*q.v.*) formed a second triad of gods. Afterwards he was held in high honour by Nebuchadrezzar I. as the god of battle. He was not only the thunderer, but also the bringer of lightning. He even appears also as a solar deity associated with the sun-god, Shamash (*q.v.*). As the bringer of rain he had a two-fold character: at one time he was the producer of destruction, at another of blessings. But it was more natural to contrast Ramman as the destructive power with Shamash as the beneficent power. In the description of the storm in the Deluge-story (see DELUGE-STORY, BABYLONIAN) Ramman is of course made to take a chief part. In the Zu myth (*q.v.*) he is called upon by the other gods to attack Zu, who has stolen the tablets of fate (*q.v.*). He declines the contest, with the excuse that Zu by gaining possession of the tablets has become invincible. The consort of Ramman was the goddess Shala (*q.v.*). See Morris Jastrow, *Rel.*

RAN. One of the deities of the Ancient Teutons. Ran is represented as goddess of the sea. She drags men down into her depths. She is the wife of the sea giant Ægir (*q.v.*). Her nine daughters represent "the surf and the turbulent waves of the sea." See P. D. Chantepie de la Saussaye, *Rel. of the Teutons*, 1902.

RANDALLITES. The followers of Benjamin Randall (1749-1808), better known as Free-will Baptists. Randall was at first an ordinary Baptist, but he became convinced that every man's will is free to the extent that he can choose or refuse salvation. This conviction led to a division among the Baptists.

RANTERS. (1) A name sometimes given to the Primitive Methodists (*q.v.*). (2) A sect which was prominent in England during the Commonwealth. They are said to have declared that sin is imagination; or that they were unable to sin, being in the state of Adam before the Fall. Richard Baxter (1615-1691) says that they used blasphemous oaths and curses; "and this all uttered as the effect of knowledge and a part of their religion, in a fanatic strain, and fathered on the Spirit of God." They are said also to have practised community of women. See J. H. Blunt.

RAPPISTS. The followers of George Rapp (1757-1847). They are also known as the Harmony Society, or the Harmonists, or the Harmonites (*q.v.*).

RASHNU. A deity worshipped by the Persians as a god of justice. With Mithra he decides the fate of the soul after death. "After death," writes Prof. Geldner (*Encycl. Bibl.*, *s.v.* Zoroastrianism), "at the end of the third night, the soul arrives at the head of the Cinvatō-Peretu, or Accountant's Bridge, over which lies the way to heaven. Here takes place the revealing and disclosure of all its past life, the *judicium particulare*. The angel Mithra and the angel Rashnu make up the account and reckoning (*SBE* 24^{258}), or Rashnu the Just weighs the good and the evil deeds over against each other in the impartial balance that does not vary a hair's breadth in favour of any man, not even a monarch (*SBE* 17^{48})."

RASKOLNIKS. A general designation of Russian schismatics or dissenters. The term is derived from a word meaning "cleft." The great schism was the result of a much-needed revision of the books used by the Established Church of Russia, the Greek-Eastern Church. When the Patriarch Nikon (1652-1658 A.D.) effected this reform, the Church was divided into Staroveri or the "Old Believers" (the dissenters) and Nikonians or the "New Believers." The original Raskolniks "held sacred certain points modified by the revision; namely, they used only the unrevised service-books; they crossed themselves with two fingers and not with three; they repeated hallelujah only twice; they used seven and not five altar-breads in the Eucharistic service; they used only an eight-pointed cross; during divine services they turned from left to right, 'according to the sun,' and not from right to left; they attended only their own churches, and regarded the outsiders as impure; they said Isoos (Jesus) instead of Iisoos; they never shaved their beard, being afraid of spoiling God's image; they never used tobacco, or practised vaccination" (Schaff-Herzog). See Schaff-Herzog; J. H. Blunt.

RATIONALIST PRESS ASSOCIATION. The objects of this Association are "to stimulate the habits of reflection and inquiry and the free exercise of individual intellect; to promote a rational system of secular education; to assist in publishing the works of capable thinkers, and in popularising the great discoveries of modern science and scholarship; to re-issue, in cheap form, notable books of a critical, philosophical, or ethical character; and generally to assert the supremacy of reason, as the natural and necessary means to all such knowledge and wisdom as man can achieve." Rationalism is defined as "the mental attitude which unreservedly accepts the supremacy of reason and aims at establishing a system of philosophy and ethics verifiable by experience and independent of all arbitrary assumptions."

RATU-MAI-MBULU. A deity worshipped in the Fiji Islands. The name means Lord from Hades. "Through him the earth gives her increase. In December he comes forth from Mbulu, and pours sap into the fruit-trees, and pushes the young yam shoots through the soil. Throughout that month it is *tabu* to beat the drum, to sound the conch-shell, to dance, to plant, to fight, or to sing at sea, lest Ratu-mai-Mbulu be disturbed, and quit the earth before his work is completed" (Basil Thomson, *The Fijians*, 1908).

RĀVULOS. A class of temple servants in Southern India associated with the Mālis and the Mūnis. "The Rāvulos blow conches (shells of *Turbinella rapa*) in the Saivite temples and at Brahmans' weddings, sell flowers, and regard themselves as superior to the other two. The Mālis do service in Saivite or Vaishnavite temples and sell flowers, but the Mūnis are employed only in the temples of the village goddesses" (Madras Census Report, 1901, quoted by E. Thurston).

RECEPTIONISTS. A term used of those who hold a certain doctrine as to the presence of Christ in the Eucharist. "Christ is present, according to this doctrine, not in the Sacrament, but in the worthy receiver: not by virtue of the act of Consecration, but by virtue of each act of Communion" (B. J. Kidd, *The Thirty-nine Articles*, 1908).

RECORDING ANGELS. A class of angels referred to in the Qur'ān. "Think they that we hear not their secrets and their private talk? Yes, and our angels who are at their sides write them down" (xliii. 80). They observe men's actions and write them down. "Yet truly there are guardians over you—illustrious recorders—cognizant of your actions" (lxxxii. 10). "Of such angels every man is said to have two, one standing on the right to write down his good actions, the other on his left to write down his bad actions; they are constantly watching and always present except on certain occasions. These angels never change, but remain with man till his death, and then stand at his grave, praising and writing down his reward, if he was a believer: cursing him to the day of the resurrection if he was an infidel" (Klein). See F. A. Klein.

RECTOR. The clergyman who is in perpetual charge of an Anglican church is commonly called a vicar. If the tithes are not impropriate, he is called a Rector. But the tithes often are impropriate. In former times it became a not uncommon practice to transfer the revenues of a benefice to a layman on the understanding that he would make suitable provision for the carrying out of the cure of souls. Where this has happened the Rector is a layman. The clergyman who performs the spiritual duties is called the Vicar. He may, in addition to other emoluments, receive the "small tithes" of the parish, but the "great tithes" belong to the Rector. The same title Rector is given to the head of some of the Colleges at Oxford; and to the head of some of the Universities in Scotland (equivalent to Chancellor elsewhere). In Scotland and in the Episcopal Churches of the United States all incumbents are now called Rectors.

RECUSANTS. A name given to those theologians who rejected the papal Bull "Unigenitus" (1713), which condemned the views of the Jansenist leader Pasquier Quesnel (1634-1719). See JANSENISTS.

RED. Red is said to be pre-eminently the lucky colour of the Hindus. According to R. V. Russell and R. B. Hira Lāl, this is due to the important part played in former times by the blood-covenant and blood-offerings. Among the lower castes the blood of animals is still offered to the deities. "But the higher castes of Hindus have abandoned animal sacrifices, and hence cannot make the blood-offering. In place of it they smear the stone with vermilion, which seems obviously a substitute for blood, since it is used to colour the stones representing the deities in exactly the same manner. Even vermilion, however, is not offered to the highest deities of Neo-Hinduism, Siva or Mahādeo and Vishnu, to whom animal sacrifices would be abhorrent." It is offered to Hanumān.

REP-CAP BUDDHISTS. In course of time the Tibetan Buddhists split up into two chief bodies or parties, a strict party and a lax or less strict party. They came to be distinguished by the colour of their clothing, the strict party wearing yellow, the lax party red. The Yellow-cap Buddhists (*q.v.*) maintained celibacy. One of the changes made by the Red-cap Buddhists consisted in allowing the monks under certain conditions to marry. The real founder of the Red-cap Buddhists was Padma-sambhava, who was the first to make a Tibetan version of the whole Buddhist Canon. The Tibetans gave him the title Guru Rimpo Che, "the glorious teacher." He is said to have founded the monastery of Samye in 749 A.D. See Monier-Williams, *Buddhism*, 1890; H. Hackmann.

RED POTTAGE. According to the writer of the Epistle to the Hebrews, Esau sold his birthright to Jacob for "one mess of meat" (xii. 16). The Old Testament narrative (Gen. xxv. 29-34) is interpreted by commentators on the Bible in the same way. It is supposed that Esau was simply ravenous with hunger. "He fancies himself dying! Anything for a good meal!" (Peake's *Commentary on the Bible*, 1919). But that he should have valued his birthright so lightly has long been a puzzle to readers of the Bible. Is it likely that he did so? It is not. The narrative has been misunderstood. Esau came in from the field, not merely faint from hunger, but faint from exhaustion. "Behold," he says, "I am going to die. What good is the birthright to me?" Jacob had boiled some pottage. What the ingredients were is not certain. That it was a "lentil stew" (vs. 34) is probably a later assumption. All that we know is that it was red. Esau sees the red stuff and exclaims (vs. 30), "Let me swallow the red, this red!" It is not food he wants, but medicine. The red stuff which he caught sight of in his extremity was, or seemed to him to be an elixir of life. For this, that is to say, for a draught which would give him rebirth and new life, he was willing to barter his birthright. A kind of beer coloured red, red wine, and other red potations have served among various peoples as substitutes for blood, which was an elixir of life. If blood was life ("the blood that is the life thereof"), it would obviously seem a rational procedure to offer blood to persons whose vitality was defective. "It became an elixir to restore youth, to ward off danger to life (by adding to the vital substance), and to increase the supply of vitality to the dead, in whom life was not regarded as ended but simply reduced in volume" (Elliot Smith, "The Giver of Life," in *Journ. of the Manch. Eg. & Or. Soc.*, 1918, p. 55). Cp. ELIXIR OF LIFE.

REEVITES. The followers of John Reeve (1608-1653), who was associated with Lodowicke Muggleton as one of the founders of the Muggletonian theology. See MUGGLETONIANS.

REFA'IYEH. An order of Dervishes, founded by Sheikh Ahmed er-Refa'i (*d.* 1182 A.D.). They have been called the howling dervishes, because during the *zikr* ("remembrance"), a performance which consists of a chanting recitation of the divine name, accompanied by a swaying of the body or even by a whirling dance, they shriek. The frenzy induced by the *zikr* leads the Refa'iyeh "into horrible demonstrations of their boasted immunity from the burning of fire, such as licking red-hot irons, biting them and cooling them in the mouth" (F. J. Bliss). They relate that their founder "once put his legs in a basin of burning coals, but was cured by the holy breath and saliva of 'Abd-el-Qādir." See T. P. Hughes; F. J. Bliss.

REFORMED EPISCOPAL CHURCH. A dissentient episcopal community. It "retains the historical succession through an American seceded bishop; not as in itself necessary or important, but that the validity of its ministerial acts may be unimpeachable by those who think otherwise" (J. A. Houlder).

REFORMED PRESBYTERIAN CHURCH. A secession from the Church of Scotland. See PRESBYTERIANS.

REFRESHMENT SUNDAY. Another name for Lætare Sunday (*q.v.*), the fourth Sunday in Lent.

REHTIA. A goddess worshipped by the people known to the Romans as Veneti. She had a temple near the modern town of Este, the ancient Ateste, about 15 m. S. of Padua, and her cult seems to have flourished in the third century B.C. The objects presented to the goddess as votive offerings included bronze statuettes of race-horses, rectangular bronze nails, and bronze alphabetic tablets. Professor R. S. Conway infers upon the latter that the goddess "was regarded as a being of superior intelligence, who took a particular interest in written symbols, and might be expected to be influenced by their proper use." The name Rehtia means "straightness." So also does Orthia, the name of a goddess whose temple at Sparta has been excavated in recent years. This, with other resemblances, suggests a possible identification of the two deities. See R. S. Conway, "Some Votive Offerings to the Venetic goddess Rehtia," *Journal of the Royal Anthropological Institute*, vol. xlvi., Jan.-June, 1916.

REINCARNATION. The doctrine is held by a number of the Hindu castes or sects. For instance, by the Taonlas, a small non-Aryan caste of the Uriya States in India, the members of which are generally farm-servants and labourers. "They believe in re-birth, and when a child is born they proceed to ascertain what ancestor has become reincarnate by dropping rice grains coloured with turmeric into a pot of water. As each one is dropped they repeat the name of an ancestor, and when the first grain floats conclude that the one named has been born again" (R. V. Russell). The Turis, a non-Aryan caste of cultivators, workers in bamboo, and basket-makers use grains of rice for the same purpose.

RELIC SUNDAY. What was called Relic Sunday was observed on the third Sunday after Midsummer-day.

It was so called because "holy relics in the churches and other ecclesiastical institutions were exhibited for worship or public curiosity" (W. Carew Hazlitt).

RELIGION. The etymology of the word religion is doubtful; and the thing itself is difficult to define in such a way as to include all varieties. E. B. Tylor defines it simply and briefly as being "a belief in spiritual beings." To S. Reinach it means "a sum of scruples which impede the free exercise of our faculties"; to Feuerbach "it is a desire which manifests itself in prayer, sacrifice, and faith." According to Max Müller, "religion is a faculty of the mind which enables a man to grasp the infinite independently of sense and reason." According to A. Réville, "Religion is the definition of man's life by the connection of the human with that mysterious spirit, the power of which over the universe and himself he recognises and with which he feels himself united." According to Goblet d'Alviella, "religion is a certain method by which man realises his relation to the superhuman and mysterious powers upon whom he regards himself as dependent." Marie-Jean Guyau defines religion as follows: "Religion is a universal sociomorphism. The religious sense is the sense of dependence in relation to wills which primitive man places in the universe." A more comprehensive definition is that given by Jean Réville. "Religion is essentially a principle of life, the feeling of a living relation between the human individual and the powers or power of which the universe is the manifestation. What characterises each religion is its way of looking upon this relation and its method of applying it." W. Warde Fowler approves the definition of an American writer: "Religion is the effective desire to be in right relation to the Power manifesting itself in the universe." He thinks that this definition at any rate suits very well the early Roman religious ideas. "The 'Power manifesting itself in the universe' may be taken as including all the workings of nature, which even now we most imperfectly understand, and which primitive man so little understood that he misinterpreted them in a hundred different ways. The effective desire to be in right relations with these mysterious powers, so that they might not interfere with his material well-being—with his flocks and herds, with his crops, too, if he were in the agricultural stage, with his dwelling and his land, or with his city if he had got so far in social development—this is what we may call the religious instinct, the origin of what the Romans called *religio*." Perhaps one of the best definitions of religion is that of J. G. Frazer. "By religion I understand a propitiation or conciliation of powers superior to man which are believed to direct and control the course of nature and of human life." What Tolstoy understands to be *true religion* he defines as follows. "True religion is the establishment by man of such a relation to the Infinite life around him, as, while connecting his life with this Infinitude and directing his conduct, is also in agreement with his reason and with human knowledge" (*What is Religion?* 1902). W. Trotter (*Instincts of the Herd in Peace and War*, 1916) rightly emphasises the fact that religious feeling is "a character inherent in the very structure of the human mind, and is the expression of a need which must be recognised by the biologist as neither superficial not transitory."

RELLYANISTS. The followers of James Relly (1722?-1778). Relly was at first one of the preachers attached to George Whitefield (1714-1770). About the year 1761, however, he became a Universalist and a leader of the movement in London. See UNIVERSALISM.

REPHAIM. The term *rephā'im* is found in the Old Testament, and is used in two different senses. In some passages (*e.g.*, Genesis xv. 20, Joshua xvii. 15) it is a proper name for an old race of giants. In other passages the word denotes "shades" or "ghosts." The literal meaning, it has been suggested, may have been "sunken, powerless, ones" from the root *rāphā* "to sink." Another suggestion, however, is that the word comes from rāphā in the sense "to hurl down." It was first applied to a race of giants. When they were hurled down to Shĕōl they became its chief inhabitants and gave their name to the rest of the inhabitants. Cheyne (*Encycl. Bibl.*) thinks "the word ought to mean 'the terrible,' or 'the wise,' or the like." He adds that "in the later Old Testament books the condition of those in Shĕōl is portrayed in very gloomy colours; but these books do not express the primitive popular belief. No doubt *Rephā'īm* is a mutilated or modified form of some primitive religious term." In Job xxvi. 5 it is said: "the shades (rephā'īm) tremble beneath the waters and the inhabitants thereof." Other references are found in Isaiah xiv. 9, xxvi. 14 (parallel to "dead"), Psalm lxxxviii. 11 [10] (parallel to "dead"), Proverbs ii. 18, ix. 18, xxi. 6. See *Encycl. Bibl.*

REPRESENTERS. Another name for the Marrow Men (*q.v.*). They were so called on account of a Representation which they drew up protesting against the condemnation by the General Assembly of the teaching contained in the work "The Marrow of Modern Divinity" (reprinted, 1718).

REQUALIVAHANUS. This name has been found on an inscription, and seems to be that of a god worshipped by the Ancient Teutons. The name suggests the darkness either of a forest or of the lower world. See P. D. Chantepie de la Saussaye, *Rel. of the Teutons*, 1902.

RESTORATIONISTS. A religious sect which was an offshoot from the American Universalists. It was formed in the year 1831. The Restorationists were persons who had accepted the teaching of Hosea Ballow of Boston. Ballow taught that sin is inseparably connected with the living body, and that when the body dies and the soul is set free, no sin remains to be punished.

REVELATION. It is a firmly-rooted religious conviction that, apart from the knowledge which man obtains in an ordinary way, there is a divine knowledge which is revealed to him by inspiration. Psychology is lending more and more support to this belief or conviction. See INSPIRATION, and PSYCHIC PHENOMENA OF RELIGIOUS EXPERIENCE.

REVELATION, THE BOOK OF. The Latin title of the book of the New Testament which in Greek is called the Apocalypse. As the Greek indicates, it belongs to the literature now described as Apocalyptic. It is therefore probably pseudonymous, written not by but in the name of one of the Johns. It can hardly have been written by the John of the fourth Gospel, from which it differs greatly in style and character. Irenaeus assigns the Revelation to the end of the reign of Domitian. See A. S. Peake, *The Revelation of John*, 1919.

RHABDOMANCY. In ancient times it was a widespread practice to take omens from the flourishing or withering of cuttings or slips. Robertson Smith thinks we have an example of this in the Old Testament story of the budding of Aaron's rod (Numbers xvii.). He writes: "We have such an omen in Aaron's rod (Numb. xvii.); and Adonis rods, set as slips to grow or wither, seem to be referred to in Isa. xvii. 10 *sqq.*, a passage which would certainly gain force if the withering of the slips was an ill omen." B. Baentsch also thinks that the story of the rod indicates that the ancient Israelites were familiar with rhabdomancy and practised it in the worship of Jehovah. G. B. Gray finds different parallels to the story of Aaron's rod. One of these is the story of Hercules' club. Concerning this Pausanias (as translated by J. G. Frazer) says: "They say that Hercules leaned his club against this image [a Hermes], and the club, which was of wild olive wood, struck root in the ground, if you please, and sprouted afresh; and the tree is still growing." See W. Robertson Smith, *R.S.;* B. Baentsch, *Numeri* (Commentary on the Book of Numbers), 1903; G. B. Gray, *Numbers* in the *I.C.C.*, 1903.

RHÆTIAN CONFESSION, THE. The "Confessio Rhætica" was composed by Saluz Gallicius. It was "intended to establish a uniform system of doctrine in place of the existing theological chaos, in which Anabaptist, Lutheran, Zwinglian, Romanist, Socinian, and pantheistic teachings mingled" (W. A. Curtis). The Confession was approved in 1552 A.D. at a Synod of the Reformed Churches in the Rhætian Alps. See William A. Curtis.

RHEA. The Rhea of Greek mythology was originally a Cretan nature-goddess. She is fabled to have been the daughter of Uranus and Gæa, and the wife of the Titan Cronus, her brother. She was called the Mother of the Gods, because she was supposed to have given birth to the Olympian deities, Zeus, Hades, Poseidon, Hera, Hestia, and Demeter. The Cretan Rhea was identified in early times with the Asiatic nature-goddess Cybele. See, further, CYBELE. According to Lucian, a goddess with the same name was worshipped in Syria.

RHEINBERGERS. Another name for the Collegiants (*q.v.*) or followers of John James, Hadrian, and Gisbert van der Kodde in Holland. They were called Rheinbergers because after a time they removed to Rheinberg near Leyden.

RHETORIANS. The followers of the Alexandrian Rhetorius. The Rhetorians seem to have been anti-dogmatists. According to Philaster, they found no harm in any heresy. According to Prædestinatus, they thought Christian fellowship should be maintained with all who believed in the Incarnation. See J. H. Blunt.

RIDWÂN. The name in Muslim theology of the angel who has charge of heaven, the keeper or guardian of Paradise.

RIFAJE, ORDER OF THE. An order of dervishes in the Nile valley. The members throw stones at their chests, eat burning coals, and stick iron nails in their eyes.

RIGANTONA. Rigantona, "the great Queen," was the name of a goddess worshipped by the ancient Celts. It is thought that the goddess survived in Rhiannon, a figure in Welsh mythology, the wife of the divine hero Pwyll (*q.v.*). See Anwyl; Charles Squire, *Myth.*

RIG VEDA. The Rig Veda is one of the chief collections of hymns held sacred by the Hindus. It is the earliest of the Vedas (see VEDISM). It may go back to about 2000 B.C. or even to 3000 B.C. Hopkins, however, thinks that the bulk of it is to be assigned to about 1000 B.C. He divides the hymns of the Rig Veda into three classes: first, those in which the older divinities are specially adored; second, those in which the sacrificial gods are specially prominent; third, those in which polytheism is giving place to a more systematic pantheism. "In each category there are hymns of different age and quality, for neither did the more ancient with the growth of new divinities cease to be revered, nor did pantheism inhibit the formal acknowledgment of the primitive pantheon." See E. W. Hopkins; Reinach, *O.*

ROGATIANI. The followers of the Donatist Rogatus (flourished about A.D. 372-3). See DONATISM.

ROGERIANS. The followers (*c.* 1677) of one John Rogers in New England. They were a branch of the Puritan Ranters (*q.v.*), and opposed worship on the Lord's Day as being idolatrous.

ROMAN PSALTER, THE. The Roman Psalter was the first (383) of the three revisions of the Book of Psalms made by Jerome. It was so called because it was introduced by Pope Damasus, at whose request it was made, into ecclesiastical use in the Roman Church. It remained in general use until the time of Pope Pius V., when the Gallican Psalter (*q.v.*) was substituted. The third version, made direct from the Hebrew, was never admitted to public use. Cp. VULGATE.

ROMANS, EPISTLE TO THE. The Epistle to the Romans is one of the four "practically non-disputed" Epistles of the Apostle Paul. Even so uncompromising a critic as P. W. Schmiedel holds that the genuineness of at least the four principal Epistle of Paul (the *Hauptbriefe*) is unassailable. They have of course been attacked, but only by scholars who are notorious for the extremeness and extravagance of their criticism. The Epistle to the Romans was declared by Luther to be the chief book of the New Testament, and by Coleridge to be the most profound work ever written. It is just the kind of work that Paul, with his intellectual training and spiritual experience was qualified to write. As Currie Martin says, "no epistle is more clearly his than is this one." The external evidence for the epistle is equally strong. It seems to have been used by the author of the First Epistle of Peter (compare I. Peter ii. 5 with Romans xii. 1; and I. Peter iii. 8-9 with Romans xii. 16-18), and to have been known to the authors of the Epistle of James and the Epistle to the Hebrews. It is quoted by Clement of Rome. There are reminiscences of it in the Letters of Ignatius and in the Epistle of Polycarp. It is included in the Canon of Marcion and in the Muratorian Canon. It is one of the Epistles ascribed to Paul by Irenaeus. What has already been said does not mean that there are no difficulties in the Epistle. There are a number. What, for instance, was the composition of the Church to which it was addressed? Baur thought that it was in the main Jewish Christian. This would account for the many quotations from the Old Testament and allusions to "the Law." But these, it is thought by many scholars, are explained by the supposition that there was a Jewish Christian element in the Church. Currie Martin admits that there are parts of the Epistle which seem to bear very distinctly upon Jewish life and thought, but he thinks "they are so written as to be quite applicable to Jews who formed part of a church the majority of whose members were Gentiles." Prof. Peake points out that for some of those passages which have been supposed to postulate Jewish readers, parallels may be quoted "from Epistles which were certainly not written to Jews." Another difficulty is presented by the facts (1) that chapters xv. and xvi. seem to have been lacking in Marcion's copy of the Epistle, and (2) that the Doxology in chapter xvi. vss. 25-27 is in some manuscripts placed at the end of chapter xiv., in others is found in both places, and in others is omitted altogether. These facts have suggested the theory that different sections of the Epistle were addressed to different Churches. "Renan made the ingenious suggestion that the main part of the Epistle was sent to several Churches, but with different endings in each case, i.-xi. with xv. to the Romans, i.-xiv. with xvi. 1-20 to the Ephesians, i.-xiv. with xvi. 21-24 to the Thessalonians, and i.-xiv. with xvi. 25-27 to an unknown Church. The Epistle came to its present form through a combination of these separate endings" (A. S. Peake). The theory is intended also to remove the difficulty that as the Epistle stands the Apostle sends greetings to many persons in a Church which he had not visited. On the other hand he had laboured among the Ephesians; the warning in xvi. 17-20 would suit Ephesus better than

Rome; and some of the persons greeted were, we know, closely connected with Asia Minor. Those who defend the integrity of the Epistle emphasize the fact that Rome was a place to which all roads led, and many of Paul's friends may easily have found their way there. And, as Prof. Peake says, "in spite of the very large acceptance which the hypothesis that the greetings were sent to Ephesus has received, it is still rejected by several of the most eminent scholars, including Harnack, Zahn, Sanday and Headlam, Denney, Ramsay and Lietzmann." A comparison of Romans xv. 22-26 with Acts xx. 1-3, xxiv. 17-19, I. Corinthians xvi. 1-4, II. Corinthians viii. 1-4, ix. 1. 2 suggests that the Epistle was written about the year 58 A.D. It would seem to have been written soon after the Second Epistle to the Corinthians. See R. J. Knowling, *The Witness of the Epistles*, 1892; the *Encycl. Bibl.*; J. A. M'Clymont; G. Currie Martin; Arthur S. Peake, *Intr.*; J. Moffatt, *Intr.*

ROMANTICISM, MODERN FRENCH. The romantic view of the world, which may be described as Romanticism, has been well described by William James. "Look at the last runnings of the romantic school, as we see them in that strange contemporary Parisian literature, with which we of the less clever countries are so often driven to rinse out our minds after they have become clogged with the dulness and heaviness of our native pursuits. The romantic school began with the worship of subjective sensibility and the revolt against legality of which Rousseau was the first great prophet: and through various fluxes and refluxes, right wings and left wings, it stands to-day with two men of genius, M. Renan and M. Zola, as its principal exponents—one speaking with its masculine, and the other with what might be called its feminine, voice. I prefer not to think now of less noble members of the school, and the Renan I have in mind is, of course, the Renan of latest dates. As I have used the term gnostic, both he and Zola are gnostics of the most pronounced sort. Both are athirst for the facts of life, and both think the facts of human sensibility to be of all facts the most worthy of attention. Both agree, moreover, that sensibility seems to be there for no higher purpose—certainly not, as the Philistines say, for the sake of bringing mere outward rights to pass and frustrating outward wrongs. One dwells on the sensibilities for their energy, the other for their sweetness; one speaks with a voice of bronze, the other with that of an Æolian harp; one ruggedly ignores the distinction of good and evil, the other plays the coquette between the craven unmanliness of his Philosophic Dialogues and the butterfly optimism of his Souvenirs de Jeunesse. But under the pages of both there sounds incessantly the hoarse bass of *vanitas vanitatum, omnia vanitas,* which the reader may hear, whenever he will, between the lines. No writer of this French romantic school has a word of rescue from the hour of satiety with the things of life—the hour in which we say, 'I take no pleasure in them'—or from the hour of terror at the world's vast meaningless grinding, if perchance such hours should come. For terror and satiety are facts of sensibility like any others: and at their own hour they reign in their own right. The heart of the romantic utterances, whether poetical, critical, or historical, is this inward remedilessness, what Carlyle calls this far-off whimpering of wail and woe. And from this romantic state of mind there is absolutely no possible theoretic escape. Whether, like Renan, we look upon life in a more refined way, as a romance of the spirit; or whether, like the friends of M. Zola, we pique ourselves on our 'scientific' and 'analytic' character, and prefer to be cynical, and call the world a 'roman expérimental' on an infinite scale—in either case the world appears to us potentially as what the same Carlyle once called it, a vast, gloomy, solitary Golgotha and mill of death." See William James, *The Will to Believe*, 1908.

RONSDORF SECT. A sect of religious enthusiasts in Germany, founded by Elias Eller (*b.* 1690). They were also called Zionites (*q.v.*).

ROSARY, IN HINDUISM. The rosary is used in Hindūism by the worshippers of Śiva (*q.v.*) and Vishnu (*q.v.*). That of the Śaivas generally consists of thirty-two or sixty-four berries of the Rudrāksha tree (Elæocarpus Ganitrus) on a string. Sometimes, however, the rosary is made of the teeth of dead bodies. The rosary of the Vaishṇavas consists of one hundred and eight beads made of wood of the Tulasī shrub (see TULASI). The rosaries are usually carried and used in the recitation of prayers or of the names of the deity; but sometimes they are worn as necklaces. Monier-Williams, in describing the devotions of a naked ascetic, describes the use as follows: "Hanging over his left shoulder and under his right arm was the sacred cord of three coils of cotton—the mark of his second birth—and his right hand was inserted in a Gomukhi or rosary bag. I asked what he was doing. 'He is counting the beads of his rosary,' said a bystander, 'and each time he tells his beads he repeats one of the 1008 names of the god Śiva over and over again, but this operation must on no account be seen, and so the hand and rosary are concealed in the bag.'" See Monier-Williams; E. W. Hopkins.

ROSENFELDERS. The followers of a German fanatic Hans Rosenfeld, who professed (*c.* 1763) to be the Messiah, and proposed to rule the world with the assistance of twenty-four elders. In 1782 proceedings were taken against him, with the result that he was imprisoned.

RŌSH HASH-SHĀNĀ. The title of one of the Jewish treatises or tractates which reproduce the oral tradition or unwritten law as developed by the second century A.D. and are incorporated in the Mishnah (*q.v.*), a collection and compilation completed by Rabbi Judah the Holy, or the Patriarch, about 200 A.D. The sixty-three tractates of the Mishnah are divided into six groups or orders (*sedarim*). Rōsh hash-shānā is the eighth tractate of the second group, which is called *Mō'ēd* ("Festival").

ROSICRUCIANS. In the seventeenth and eighteenth century the name Rosicrucians was assumed by members of certain secret societies. The derivation of the name is matter of dispute. The most likely explanation perhaps is that given in a Rosicrucian pamphlet, "Fama Fraternitatis" published in Germany in A.D. 1614. According to this pamphlet the Rosicrucian fraternity was founded by a German, Christopher Rosenkreutz (*b.* A.D. 1388), who had travelled in the East and learned from wise men there valuable secrets. On his return to Europe he founded the fraternity with the object of reforming human knowledge. The Rosicrucians professed to have a special knowledge of alchemy, medicine, and the healing art. Another explanation of the name is that it is derived from the two Latin words *rosa* "rose" and *crux* "cross." In that case the reference would be to certain symbols. The Rosicrucians were not all of one mind. According to J. H. Blunt, however, they agreed upon the following points: "first, that the only true knowledge was to be derived by analysis of all bodies by the agency of fire; secondly, that God operates by the same laws in the kingdom of Grace as in the kingdom of Nature, and that there is therefore a complete analogy and coincidence between science and religion; thirdly, that a divine soul or energy is diffused through the fabric of the universe—this incorporeal existence being by some called 'Achæus,' by others the Universal Spirit." The Rosicrucian doctrines were of the nature of theosophy (*q.v.*). See B. Puenjer; J. H. Blunt; *Chambers' Encycl.;* Brockhaus.

ROSIN BIBLE. A popular designation of an edition of the Bishops' Bible (*q.v.*) published in 1609. It was so called on account of a passage in Jeremiah viii. 22 ("Is there no balm in Gilead?"), which was rendered, "Is there no rosin in Gilead?"

ROSKOLNIKS. The designation of Nonconformists or Schismatics in Russia, that is to say, of those who have seceded from the Greek Church. They arose chiefly in the seventeenth century in opposition to the revision of Holy Scripture and the liturgical books, and in the eighteenth century in opposition to the reforms of Peter the Great (1689-1725).

ROSMERTA. A goddess worshipped by the ancient Celts. She is paired, perhaps either as mother, sister, or wife with Mercurius, Mercury.

ROSMINIANS. The founder of the Fathers of the Institute of Charity or the Rosminians (1828) was the Italian philosopher Antonio Rosmini (1797-1855). He desired the members of his society to devote themselves wholeheartedly to every branch of charity. This desire was fulfilled, and during the first ten years of the society's existence its operations "consisted in giving retreats, preaching, sick-visiting, taking care of prisons and hospitals, teaching, missions abroad, literary work, and almsgiving" (*Catholic Dictionary*). The rule of the Institute of Charity was approved by Gregory XVI. in 1838, and in 1839 Rosmini was nominated its Superior-General. See *Cath. Dict.;* Brockhaus.

ROWITES. Another name for the English Campbellites (*q.v.*), the followers of John McLeod Campbell (1800-1872), who was Minister of Row, Dumbartonshire.

RUDRA. A deity in Hindu religion. Rudra, "the ruddy one," appears as an important deity in the Veda. He is the Vedic prototype of Śiva (*q.v.*). He is closely associated with the Rain-god, Indra (*q.v.*) and the Fire-god, Agni (*q.v.*). Rudra is the god of gales and tempests. But he is present in health-giving winds as well as in storm-winds. In course of time he became more and more comprehensive. His terrific and ungodlike character was "kept well in the background, and his epithet 'the blessed or auspicious one (Śiva)', who brought life out of death, who re-created after dissolution, passed into his principal name" (Monier-Williams). The storm-winds are called Rudras or Maruts. They accompany Rudra and Indra. In a Marut hymn, as translated by Müller, it is said: "Truly they are terrible and powerful; even to the desert the Rudriyas bring rain that is never dried up. The lightning lows like a cow, it follows as a mother follows after her young, when the shower has been let loose. Even by day the Maruts create darkness with the water-bearing cloud, when they drench the earth." Originally there were seven Maruts. Afterwards the number was greatly increased. See Monier-Williams; E. W. Hopkins.

RUGIEVIT. Rugievit was the name of one of the gods worshipped by the ancient Slavs. He appears to have been a god of war. He had seven faces.

RŪFĀ'I. A Dervish order founded by Achmet Rūfa in the twelfth century, and known to Europeans as the "Howling Dervishes." The devotees cut themselves with knives and lancets, eat pieces of glass, snakes, and live coals; but the founder of the order is said to have conferred upon them the power of miraculously healing their wounds. "The knives, red-hot irons and coals, and other instruments used by the Rūfa'i Order in their extraordinary religious exercises, are called by the symbolic name of 'Roses'" (L. M. J. Garnett).

RUKHMINI. A Hindu goddess, the bright or shining one, a consort of Vishnu.

RUMBALD. It was formerly a custom among the fishermen of Folkestone, on returning from a fishing expedition, to set apart eight of the largest and best whiting, to be sold separately. With the money thus obtained they made a feast on Christmas Eve, which they called a rumbald. It has been suggested that originally the feast was held in honour of St. Rumbald. According to Francis Bond, there are eight dedications to St. Rumbald in England. See W. Carew Hazlitt.

RUNCARI. A Waldensian sect, the members of which held that since sin is of the heart, no part of the body that is below the waist can commit sin.

RUTH, BOOK OF. One of the books of the Old Testament. The events with which it deals are said to have belonged to the period of the Judges. The book might therefore be expected to follow the Book of Judges (*q.v.*). This is the place assigned to it by the Septuagint, Josephus, and the English Bible. In the Hebrew Canon, however, it appears among the Hagiographa as one of the five "Rolls" or Megilloth (*q.v.*). Conservative scholars explain that it was classed with the Megilloth because, like them, it was set apart for special use in the Synagogue. Higher critics find in its separation from the historical books support for the view that the origin of the book belongs "to a period when the collection of the historical books had already been closed" (C. Cornill). Cornill describes the story as "a charming idyll." The story is this. In the days of the judges, Elimelech, a man of Bethlehem, goes with Naomi, his wife, and their two sons, to sojourn in the land of Moab. Here the two sons marry Moabite women, Orpah and Ruth. Naomi soon loses her husband and both her sons. She decides to return to Bethlehem, and her daughter-in-law clings lovingly to her and refuses to leave her. When they have settled in Bethlehem, Ruth goes to glean in the field of Boaz, a kinsman of Elimelech. She finds favour in his eyes, and is treated with exceptional kindness. Naomi, having noted this, thinks of a means of suggesting to Boaz that he should marry Ruth. Boaz is willing to do so, but he knows of a nearer kinsman who has a better claim. When the other kinsman refuses to press his claim, Boaz marries Ruth. She becomes the ancestress of David. Conservative scholars maintain that the events of the book occurred about a hundred years before the time of David. The marriage of an Israelite with a Moabite, it is argued, would have seemed offensive to a pious Israelite of post-exilic times. The higher critic, on the other hand, thinks that the time-indication (ch. i. 1) "presupposes the rigidly fixed chronological system of the Deuteronomic Exilic History of Israel" (Cornill). The conservative scholar explains peculiarities of language as "instances of the spoken patois"; the higher critic finds in them post-exilic Aramaisms. The conservative scholar finds no reference to the levirate law of Deuteronomy (xxv. 7-9) in Ruth iv. 7; the higher critic finds that in Ruth "a custom which was current in the times of Deuteronomy is expressly explained as if it were an antiquarian curiosity" (Cornill). If the book is post-exilic, it may be regarded as a protest against the strict view regarding intermarriage with foreign wives, the view enforced by Ezra and Nehemiah (see Ezra ix., x.; Neh. xiii. 23-29). Perhaps Prof. Whitehouse is right in thinking that "the present book may have arisen from a pre-exilian documentary basis, and have owed its present form to a writer who, like the author of the Book of Jonah, was opposed to the narrower traditions of the time of Ezra and Nehemiah." See C. H. H. Wright, *Intr. to the O.T.*, 1890; C. Cornill, *Intr.;* G. H. Box; O. C. Whitehouse.

RYŌBU-BUKKYŌ. Another name for the Japanese religion known as Ryōbu-Shinto (*q.v.*).

RYŌBU-SHINTŌ. In the sixth century A.D. Buddhism was introduced into Japan from Korea and China. It did not, however, displace the old religion, which now came to be known as Shintō, that is to say, "The way of the Genii, or Spirits." The two religions borrowed from each other, and the mixed form of faith that resulted came to be known as Ryōbu-Shintō. In 1868 Shintoism was made the State religion. To distinguish it from Ryōbu-Shintō, the ancient faith is called "pure Shintō." See SHINTOISM.

S

SA'ADĪYEH. An order of Dervishes, founded by Sa'ad-ed-Din ed-Je'bawi (*d.* 1335 A.D.); also called Jebawīyeh.

SABATATI. A name given to the followers of Peter Waldus, the Waldenses (*q.v.*), because they wore wooden shoes.

SABAZIUS. A Phrygian deity. Sabazius is the Phrygian Jupiter or Dionysus. According to Cumont, Sabazius was frequently confounded with Attis, a confusion due to the great similarity of their mysteries. "By means of an audacious etymology that dates back to the Hellenistic period, this old Thraco-Phrygian divinity has been identified with 'Yahveh Zebaoth,' the Biblical 'Lord of Hosts.' The corresponding expression in the Septuagint has been regarded as the equivalent of the *kurios Sabazios* of the barbarians. The latter was worshipped as the supreme, almighty and holy Lord. In the light of a new interpretation the purifications practised in the mysteries were believed to wipe out the hereditary impurity of a guilty ancestor who had aroused the wrath of heaven against his posterity, much as the original sin with which Adam's disobedience had stained the human race was to be wiped out. The custom observed by the votaries of Sabazius of dedicating votive hands which made the liturgic sign of benediction with the first three fingers extended (the *benedictio latina* of the church) was probably taken from the ritual of the Semitic temples through the agency of the Jews. The initiates believed, again like the Jews, that after death their good angel (*angelus bonus*) would lead them to the banquet of the eternally happy, and the everlasting joys of these banquets were anticipated on earth by the liturgic repasts. This celestial feast can be seen in a fresco painting on the grave of a priest of Sabazius called Vincentius, who was buried in the Christian catacomb of Praetextatus, a strange fact for which no satisfactory explanation has as yet been furnished. Undoubtedly he belonged to a Jewish-pagan sect that admitted neophytes of every race to its mystic ceremonies." The worship of Sabazius was introduced into Greece and Italy. It invaded every Latin province, and extended as far as the most remote limits of Germany. See Franz Cumont, *Oriental Religions in R.P.*, 1911.

SABBATIANS. 1. The followers of a Jew Sabbatius. Sabbatius had been converted and had been made a presbyter by Marcian. His sect was an offshoot of the Novatians. Sabbatius contrived to have himself made a bishop. The Sabbatians were condemned by the Council of Constantinople (A.D. 381; seventh canon). See the *Ecclesiastical History of Socrates* (Bohn); *The Canons of the First Four General Councils*, Oxford, 1880. 2. The followers of a Jewish fanatic, Sabbatai Z'vi (1626-1676), of Smyrna, who declared himself to be the Messiah. Afterwards he became a Muhammadan. See H. Graetz, *History of the Jews*.

SABBOTNIKI. A Jewish sect in Russia. They live according to the Jewish law. In the Jewish colonies of Palestine, where some of them have settled, they are known as "Gerim."

SABELLIANISM. The doctrine of Sabellius and his school. Sabellius was a presbyter at Rome towards the end of the second century. Modalism (*q.v.*) had been introduced into Rome by Praxeas, who, according to Tertullian, "had put to flight the Paraclete, and crucified the Father." The Modalists received the name Patripassians (*q.v.*). About 230 A.D. this kind of teaching led to the excommunication of Noëtus of Smyrna. Noëtus declared: "I know but one God; it is no other than He who was born, who suffered, and who died." Epigonus, a disciple of Noëtus, opened a school in Rome and acted as head of it. He was succeeded first by Cleomenes, and then by Sabellius. According to Dionysius, Bishop of Rome, Sabellius blasphemed by "saying that the Son himself is the Father, and *vice versâ*." Novatian refers to Sabellius as being one "who calls Christ the Father." The Modalists made great use of the term "Monarchy" to describe their strict monotheism, and their movement is known as Modalist Monarchianism. A form of the Apostles' Creed known (*c.* 400 A.D.) to Tyrannius Rufinus, Presbyter of Aquileia, begins: "I believe in God the Father Almighty, invisible and impassible." Commenting on the last three words, Rufinus says: "They were added in our Church, as is well known, on account of the Sabellian heresy, called by us 'the Patripassian,' that is, which says that the Father Himself was born of the Virgin and became visible, or affirms that He suffered in the flesh" (*Commentary on the Apostles' Creed*). Sabellius was excommunicated by Callistus, Bishop of Rome (219-222). His doctrine was afterwards developed or, it might be said, modified. The three *prosōpa* or *personae* of God came to be regarded as three characters of God. It was held that "the same Person is the Holy Ghost, so far as He manifests Himself in the Christian Church, and by parity of reasoning the Son, so far as He appeared in Christ" (*Cath. Dict.*). He who gave the law as Father, He who became flesh in Christ as Son, and He who descended on the Apostles as Holy Ghost, was one and the same Person or Hypostasis. See C. A. Heurtley, *On Faith and the Creed*, 1889; J. H. Blunt; *Prot. Dict.*; *Cath. Dict.*; Louis Duchesne, *Hist.*

SABHORAIM. Literally "thinkers" or "explainers," a name applied to the Jewish scholars of the sixth century who supplemented the work of the

Amoraim (see TALMUD) by giving "the finishing touches to the compilation of the Babylonian Talmud" (Oesterley and Box). See J. W. Etheridge, *Intr. to Heb. Lit.*, 1856; W. O. E. Oesterley and G. H. Box; A. S. Geden, *Intr. to the Heb. Bible*, 1909.

SABIANS. Another name for the Mandæans (*q.v.*). The word means "Baptists," and they were so called because they paid special reverence to John the Baptist and made baptism their most important rite.

SABITUM. A Babylonian deity. Sabitum appears as a sea-goddess in the Epic of Gilgamesh (see GILGAMESH EPIC). When Gilgamesh wishes to cross the ocean, "the waters of death," he has to ask Sabitum to help him.

SACRAMENTS. Robertson Smith (*R.S.*) contends that the sacramental meal stands out as the very essence of the ritual of Semitic sacrifice. In course of time the primitive crudity of the ceremonial was modified, but originally in the shedding of the blood of a victim upon the altar and the eating of the flesh by worshippers there were two significant features: "the conveyance of the living blood to the godhead, and the absorption of the living flesh and blood into the flesh and blood of the worshippers." The fundamental idea of sacrifice throughout the Semitic field "is not that of a sacred tribute, but of communion between the god and his worshippers." In the field of Egyptian religion, Dr. A. M. Blackman has shown how great a part is played by rites of a sacramental character. In the religion of the Greeks, Dr. L. R. Farnell (*Greek Religion*) points out that "in the earlier period at least, and frequently also in the later, the offering of the animal at the altar was felt to be something more than a bribe to the deity. The holy spirit of the altar passed into the animal that was consecrated and brought into contact with it; and those who afterwards partook of it might be conscious of eating holy flesh and thus enjoying temporary communion with the spirit of the divinity." He thinks that in other details of the Homeric sacrifice and in ritual records of the later period we can discover clear traces of sacramental communion. In the Eleusinian Mysteries, again, the means of grace seem to have included "a form of sacrament, the drinking of the sacred cup into which the personality of the goddess might be infused by transubstantiation." In the mysteries of the Orphic brotherhoods the means of grace "were a ritual of purification more elaborate than the Eleusinia and fixed as a perpetual rule of life, and at times a mystic sacrament, in which the initiated drank the blood or devoured the body of his god. The form was savage, but the act was pregnant of religious consequences." The term *sacraments* is applied by Tertullian (*c.* 200 A.D.) to the Mithraic ceremonies of initiation, "which comprised baptism, purification by honey, the use of consecrated water, bread and wine: they were regulated by the priests called 'fathers' of whom the 'father of fathers' was the chief" (S. Reinach, *O.*). In the Christian Church there was for centuries great vagueness as to the number of sacraments owing to the fact that the word *sacramentum* was used in the Old Latin and Vulgate versions as the equivalent of the Greek *mustērion*. Protestants now recognize only two sacraments, Baptism and the Lord's Supper. The Roman Catholics recognize seven: Baptism, Confirmation, the Eucharist, Penance, Extreme Unction, Holy Orders, and Matrimony. "The Protestant view is grounded on the fact that baptism and the Supper are the only two ritual observances which spring directly out of the historical revelation of Jesus Christ as given in the New Testament, which rest clearly upon His personal appointment, and are bound up with His own word" (*Prot. Dict.*). It should be added that in the light of more recent researches, Robertson Smith's theory of sacrifice requires to be modified. The sacrificial meal came in course of time to be interpreted in the way in which he has interpreted it, but its original significance does not seem to have been such as he imagined (see Émile Durkheim).

SACRIFICE. It is pointed out by Robertson Smith (*R.S.*, p. 213 f.) that in ancient times the oblation at an altar had so central a place among certain prescribed rites and ceremonies of worship that "among the Greeks and Romans the words ἱερουργια and *sacrificium*, which in their primary application denote any action within the sphere of things sacred to the gods, and so cover the whole field of ritual, were habitually used, like our English word sacrifice, of those oblations at the altar round which all other parts of ritual turned. In English idiom there is a further tendency to narrow the word sacrifice to such oblations as involve the slaughter of a victim." It is convenient to include both kinds of oblation under the term sacrifice. What the sacrificial act really means, and why in the antique religions it should be the typical form of all complete acts of worship, is, as Robertson Smith says, a difficult problem, and one which does not belong to any one religion. In the Semitic field the only system of sacrifice of which we have a full account is that of the second temple at Jerusalem. This, of course, is not primitive, but it contains primitive elements. The Levitical law of the Hebrews recognises three main types of sacrifice: the whole burnt-offering; the sacrifice followed by a meal consisting for the most part of the flesh of the victim; and the sin-offering. The whole burnt-offering and the sacrifice followed by a meal are often mentioned in the older literature. So also is the use of sacrifice as an atonement for sin (especially the burnt-offering); but before the time of Ezekiel there is little trace of a special kind of sacrifice devoted to this purpose. The pre-exilic literature makes certain distinctions. It distinguishes between animal and vegetable oblations; between offerings which were consumed by fire and such as were simply set forth on the sacred table; between sacrifices in which the gift was wholly made over to the god and such as were partaken of by the god together with his worshippers. "To the latter class belong the *zebaḥim*, or ordinary animal sacrifices, in which a victim is slain, its blood poured out at the altar, and the fat of the intestines with certain other pieces burned, while the greater part of the flesh is left to the offerer to form the material of a sacrificial banquet" (*R.S.*, p. 217). Among the offerings from the vegetable kingdom made by the Hebrews, the chief were meal, wine, and oil. Wine was used also even in Arabia, where it was scarce. Milk was offered by the Arabs and the Carthaginians, but not apparently by the Hebrews. Fruit in its natural state was used by the Carthaginians, and probably by the ancient Hebrews. The Babylonians offered dates, figs, cucumbers, butter, and oil (Jastrow, *Civ.*, p. 277). The Egyptians filled the trunks of animal victims with honey, raisins, figs, incense, myrrh, etc. The most important oblations among the Semites and other peoples, however, are animal sacrifices. According to Robertson Smith, the leading idea in the animal sacrifices of the Semites "was not that of a gift made over to the god, but of an act of communion, in which the god and his worshippers unite by partaking together of the flesh and blood of a sacred victim" (p. 227). He therefore draws a sharp line of distinction between the cereal oblation, "in which the dominant idea is that of a tribute paid to the god," and animal sacrifices, "which are essentially acts of communion between the god and his worshippers." In animal sacrifices the victim is a sacred animal. The Harranians sacrificed swine and, according to Maimonides, field-mice (cp. Isa. lxvi. 17). At Rhodes, "where religion is throughout of a Semitic type, four horses were cast into the sea as a sacrifice at the annual feast of the sun" (*R.S.*, p. 293). The Babylonians, according to lists embodied in Gudea's inscriptions, offered oxen, sheep and goats, doves and various other domesticated birds, chickens, ducks and geese (?), and various kinds of fish (Jastrow, *Civ.*, p. 277). The ancient Egyptians sacrificed gazelles, antelopes, and wild goats; but, according to Herodotus, the sacrifice to one of the principal goddesses consisted of bullocks. The importance of the bullock in Hebrew sacrifice is well known. Among the Hindus the victims included horses; among the Chinese sheep and pigs. But if the practice of sacrificing animals is wide-spread, hardly less prevalent is that of offering a human victim. Indeed, "in the later ages of antiquity there was a very general belief," says Robertson Smith (p. 361), "that in strictness the oldest rituals demanded a human victim, and that animal sacrifices were substitutes for the life of a man." D. G. Brinton (*R.P.P.*, p. 189) states that "traces of human sacrifice are discovered in the early history of even the noblest religions, and the rite extended so widely that scarce a cult can be named in which it did not exist." Porphyry gives examples of human sacrifices, of which many subsisted within the Roman Empire down to the time of Hadrian (*R.S.*, p. 366). Among the Saracens the favourite victims were young and beautiful captives. Among the Carthaginians, too, choice captives were sacrificed. In an Old Testament narrative (I. Sam. xv. 33), the captive king Agag seems to be treated as a human victim. Prisoners of war were sacrificed to the Norse god Odhin. Virgins and young children were sacrificed to the Mexican god Tlaloc. Human victims were offered to the Aztec god Xipe; to god F (*q.v.*) of the Mayan Indians; to the Frisian god Forseti; to the Teutonic god Tiwaz. They seem also to have been offered to Danu, the Mother of the gods among the Irish Celts. "The ancient Germans laid it down that in time of famine beasts should first be slain and offered to the gods. Did these bring no relief, then men must be slaughtered; and if still there was no aid from on high, then the chieftain himself must mount the altar; for the nobler and dearer the victim, the more pleased were the gods!" (Brinton, *R.P.P.*, p. 188). One is tempted to think that human sacrifice must have been more primitive than animal sacrifice. It would be a natural development for animals to be substituted in course of time for human beings. Cp. the article BLOOD.

SADĀSHEO. Siva the everlasting, one of the names of the Hindu god Siva.

SADDUCEES. The Sadducees were so called after Zadok, who was high-priest in the reign of Solomon (I. Kings ii. 35; Ezekiel xl. 46). The name has been wrongly connected with a Hebrew word meaning "just." The Sadducees were the Jewish aristocracy. "They were partly the courtiers, the soldiers, the diplomatists, and other superior officials who had risen into prominence in the Maccabaean war, and partly the old high-priestly families who had fallen into the background in the early stages of the revolt, but who came once more to the front under Simon Maccabaeus" (W. D. Morrison). They were the successors of the Hellenists. They were more a political party than a religious sect; but in so far as they were the latter, some of their views were remarkable. We are told in the New Testament (Acts xxiii. 8): "the Sadducees say that there is no resurrection, neither angel nor spirit; but the Pharisees confess both." Josephus says (*Antiquities* i. 4) their doctrine was that souls perish with the body. They differed widely from the Pharisees. And not only in these matters, but also in their estimation and interpretation of Holy Scripture. The Pharisees attached great importance to oral tradition. The Sadducees would acknowledge only the letter of the written law, which they interpreted with great literalness. In the time of Jesus the party of the Sadducees was no longer the great patriotic party that it had been under the Hasmonaeans. For the most part they cherished and discussed their ideas of enlightening the people privately. They proclaimed them in public only on very rare occasions, especially when they seemed to have an opportunity of refuting the views of their opponents, the Pharisees. It is natural that they should have crossed swords with Jesus. As Neumann says, "the Pharisees and Sadducees were at one in their hatred of this Messiah who smote them with the sword of the Spirit and the scourge of His words." The idea that the Messiah would suddenly appear in the heavens, surrounded by angels, and would awaken the dead to judgment, must have been particularly obnoxious to the Sadducees. The party disappeared soon after the destruction of Jerusalem. See W. D. Morrison, *The Jews under Roman Rule*, 1890; Oscar Holtznann, *The Life of Jesus*, 1904; J. H. Blunt; Arno Neumann, *Jesus*, 1906.

SĀDHUS. The word means literally "holy men," and corresponds to "clergy." The disciples of the Hindu religious reformer, Svāmi Nārāyana, who was born near Lucknow about 1780, are divided into two classes—Sādhus, "holy men," and Grihasthas, "householders." The latter term corresponds to "laity." Svāmi Nārāyana was an assumed name. His real name was Sahajānanda. A Vaishṇava, Sahajānanda became disgusted with the debased practices of the Vallabhas (*q.v.*). About 1800 he left his home to study under a chief Guru, Rāmānanda-Svāmi. In 1804 the Guru went to Ahmedābād, and Sahajānanda followed him. The latter in course of time collected about him a large band of disciples of his own. His popularity provoked such jealousy that he was obliged to escape from Ahmedābād to a place called Jetalpur. Here he was arrested and imprisoned, but was soon released. The place became the focus of a great religious gathering, and thousands of persons enrolled themselves as his followers. His influence has been attributed to a mesmeric power. Monier-Williams, however, thinks it probable that he "owed his success to a remarkable fascination of manner combined with consistency of moral character, and other qualities which singled him out for a leader." His doctrines are a protest against the Vallabhas. His crusade against them was principally carried on from Wartāl as a centre, a village to which he retired for seclusion and in which he erected a temple to the Supreme Being, Nārāyaṇa (Krishṇa, Vishṇu). His sect is said to number now not less than a quarter of a million persons. The clergy devote themselves completely to the Supreme Being, suppressing their passions and seeking to purify the life of all. Some of the precepts of Svāmi-Nārāyaṇa, as given by Monier-Williams, are as follows: "Abstaining from injury is the highest of all duties. Holy men should patiently bear abusive language, or even beating, from evil-minded persons, and wish good to them. Every day all my followers should go to the Temple of God, and there repeat the names of Krishṇa. The story of his life should be listened to with the greatest reverence, and hymns in his praise should be sung on festive days. All males and females who go to Krishṇa's temple should keep separate and not touch each other. On no account let it be supposed that difference in forms (or names) makes any difference in the identity of the deity. Those males and females of my followers who will act according to these directions shall certainly obtain the four great objects of all human desires—religious merit, wealth, pleasure, and beatitude." See Monier-Williams; E. W. Hopkins.

SADITES. An order of Dervishes. "All claim powers of healing, and there are divisions with different rights; one may eat glass but not serpents, another serpents but no glass. Some sects or brotherhoods are antinomian, that is, consider all acts (even the vilest) as indifferent when done in a state of coma or ecstasy; the soul is then supposed to be in heaven and both unconscious of bodily deeds and not responsible for them" (F. W. Bussell).

SAGA. One of the deities of the Ancient Teutons. The goddess Saga, who is associated with water, belongs to the retinue of Frija (*q.v.*) and Freyja (*q.v.*).

SAKHĀRĀM. The friend of Rāma (King of Ayodhia, a great incarnation of Vishnu), one of the names of the Hindu god Rāma.

ŚĀKTISM. Śāktism is a form or kind of worship among the Hindus. It is connected closely with Śaivism or the worship of Śiva (*q.v.*). In fact it is the worship of the female side of Śiva, the female energy. Monier-Williams points out that the duality of the divine nature (male and female) is first enunciated clearly in the Brāhmaṇas and Upanishads. According to Manu, the Self-existent divided his own substance and became half male half female. Śiva came to be depicted sometimes as a male on his right side and a female on his left side. But it is the latest of the sacred writings, the Tantras, that make the female energy, personified as a goddess, a special object of worship. In course of time a large section of the Hindus devoted themselves exclusively to the worship of the female side of Śiva and Vishṇu, to the worship of Durga or Kali, wife of Śiva, of Rādhā, wife of Krishṇa, of Sītā, wife of Rāma, of Ambā or Devī, the Mother-goddess, and of Śakti, the great Power of Nature. Śakti, however, came to be regarded by the worshippers of the female energy as the embodiment of all the powers and virtues of all the other deities, male and female. As might be expected, Śaktism developed into gross sensuality. "In Śāktism we are confronted with the worst results of the worst superstitious ideas that have ever disgraced and degraded the human race. It is by offering to women the so-called homage of sensual love and carnal passion, and by yielding free course to all the grosser appetites, wholly regardless of social rules and restrictions, that the worshippers of the female power (Śakti) in Nature seek to gratify the goddess representing that power, and through her aid to acquire supernatural faculties, and even ultimately to obtain union with the Supreme Being. Incredible as it may appear, these so-called worshippers actually affect to pride themselves on their debasing doctrines, while they maintain that their creed is the grandest of all religions, because to indulge the grosser appetites and passions, with the mind fixed on union with the Supreme Being, is believed to be the highest of all pious achievements" (Monier-Williams). See Monier-Williams; E. W. Hopkins; J. A. Dubois and H. K. Beauchamp.

SĀLAGRĀMA. Sālagrāma is one of the objects worshipped by the Hindus. It is a black pebble; and "what the Linga is to Sivaite the Sālagrāma is to the Vishnuite" (Hopkins). Sacrifices are offered to it daily, for it is regarded as a metamorphosis of Vishnu (*q.v.*) or Krishna (*q.v.*). Thus the Sālagrāma stone is a god. On the other hand the sacred Tulasi-plant (see TULASI) is a goddess, and in some parts of India the Tulasī is married annually to the Sālagrāma. To indicate this union a Tulasī leaf is always kept on the Sālagrāma stone. Sālagrāma stones are handed down from father to son as precious heirlooms. Even the water in which they have been washed is precious. "There is nothing more efficacious for the remission of sins, no matter how grievous they may be, than to possess some water in which the *salagrama* has been washed. Forgiveness of sins may even be obtained by simply touching the water which has been thus sanctified" (Dubois and Beauchamp). See Monier-Williams; E. W. Hopkins; J. A. Dubois and H. K. Beauchamp.

SALAMANDER, THE. The salamander seems to be used in Christian art to symbolise fire. It was an old superstition that the creature lived in fire or at any rate that it could endure the flames of fire. According to Gregory of Nazienzen it could extinguish fire also. It is depicted, as a lizard or serpent, on Church-fonts (*e.g.*, at Norton and Youlgrave, Derbyshire), and is supposed to symbolise baptism with the "Holy Ghost and Fire." See Sidney Heath and W. Carew Hazlitt.

ṢALM. A god mentioned in an Aramaic inscription (*c.* the fourth century B.C.).

SALVATION ARMY, THE. William Booth (*b.* 1829), the founder of the Christian body known as the Salvation Army, was originally a minister of the Methodist New Connexion. He left that Church in 1861 in order to take up independent evangelistic work. The result was his "East London Mission," which, with the extension of its activities, became the "Christian Mission." The Mission then began to acquire halls, etc., for its meetings, and steps were taken to give it a legal title to its property. "In January, 1877, finding that the semi-democratic conference committee system which he had inaugurated did not run smoothly, and was not likely satisfactorily to accomplish the end in view, Mr. Booth established a system of government more closely allied to the autocracy of Wesley; and, with the consent of his fellow workers, constituted himself its head" (J. A. Houlder). The new organisation was called The Salvation Army. "With the name *army* came military phraseology. Prayer was termed *knee-drill*, the leader a *general;* evangelists, *officers;* and candidates, *cadets.* A semi-military attire was assumed, barracks were built instead of separate residences, and when the army went out to take a place by storm, it was with banners displayed and bands of music" (William Benham, *Dict.*). The Salvationists wage war against the devil, and seek to convert and to "save" those who are in danger of being lost souls. By means of their brass bands, etc., they aim at reaching a class of the community which is unmoved by other religious appeals. In 1880 the Army began to extend its operations beyond the British Isles, and to enter upon a world-wide crusade.

SAMARITANS, THE. An account of the origin of the Samaritans is found in the Old Testament in II. Kings xv. When the Israelites were deported from the province of Samaria, Sargon, king of Assyria, brought colonists from Babylonia and elsewhere to take their place. These colonists seem to have come from Babylon, Kutu, and Sippar; as well as from Hamath in northern Syria. The Hebrew population which remained in Samaria mingled with the foreign colonists with the result that a new Semitic group was evolved. In B.C. 538 the Davidic prince Zerubbabel and the priest Joshua, with the permission of Cyrus, proceeded to Judah in order to rebuild Jerusalem and the Temple. They found the Samaritans firmly established and possessing some measure of power in the North. After the Jews had begun to rebuild the Temple, the Samaritans desired to help them; and when their aid was declined, they became hostile and thwarted the Jews for some years (Ezra iv. 4, 5). Finally, the Samaritans, claiming to be the true successors of ancient Israel, built a temple of their own on Mount Gerizim and adopted the Law as their sacred book (see SAMARITAN PENTATEUCH). The Samaritans have survived down to the present time. "A little group of them, less than a hundred, still live together at Nablus, the ancient Shechem, under the shadow of their sacred mountain Gerizim, and worship Jehovah as did their ancestors at the same holy site. Of all the many petty peoples which lived in Palestine in ancient times, they alone remain" (C. F. Kent). Not long ago little was known about them. But since the visits of Edward Robinson (1838 and 1852) to Shechem our information has accumulated year by year. A number of Samaritan manuscripts have been brought to Europe. "Beside many texts of the Hebrew Pentateuch and its Targum, we have extensive theological treatises and Midrashim, commentaries which show some exegetical skill, chronicles whose defect is their chronology, grammatical and scientific works, and, most important of all for studying the spirit of the Samaritan religion, tomes of their liturgy" (J. A. Montgomery). An anthropological study of the Samaritans has revealed the fact that they have become Hebrews of the Hebrews. Dr. Montgomery thinks that the study of their religion and manners shows further that they are really nothing less than a Jewish sect. Their religion "is a monotheism identical with that of Judaism, whose very terms they use throughout, while it bitterly opposes any attempt to associate with God other deities, as in polytheism, or to find in him any distinctions, as in Christianity. It is a spiritual religion, which not only rejects any representation of Deity, but even eschews, after the letter of the Second Commandment, all pictorial designs. It is moreover an ethical religion which has flowered in just such virtues and which is circumscribed by just such limitations as mark what is known as orthodox Judaism." The head of the Samaritan church is the high-priest. The priests, who are also the doctors of the Law, observe the Nazarite rule, allowing no razor to touch their head. The laymen wear white robes in the services. They do not use the Tephillin, because the law is to be observed spiritually. When the priest reads the Law he wears a talith without fringes. The only sacrifice celebrated by the Samaritans is the Passover. Montgomery describes the solemnity as "a veritable *Haj*, or pilgrim-feast." As regards the treatment of the dead, he points out that "it is not forbidden to the Samaritans, as has been frequently stated, to handle their dead, except in the case of the high-priest." It is the custom to burn candles before burial at the head and foot of the corpse. The dead are placed in coffins, which is an exceptional practice in modern Palestine. "The mourning ceremonies last until the following Sabbath, the community going each day to the tomb, where they read and pray. On the Sabbath the community again visit the tomb, where they partake of a meal, while further approprite services are held in the synagogue. The Samaritans appear to-day to make a point of forgetting their dead, and have no subsequent commemorations, except their visits to the tombs of the Patriarchs. However, the liturgy contains requiem hymns." See *Encycl. Bibl.*; C. F. Kent, *The Kings and Prophets of Israel and Judah*, 1909; J. A. Montgomery, *The Samaritans*, 1907.

SAMARITAN PENTATEUCH, THE The Samaritan Pentateuch is to be carefully distinguished from the Samaritan Targum. The Samaritan Targum is a version; the Samaritan Pentateuch is simply the Hebrew text of the "five books of Moses" written and preserved in the Samaritan character. When the Jews after their return from exile proceeded to rebuild the temple, the Samaritans offered to help them. This help was declined. The Samaritans thereupon left or were driven away and formed a separate community in Samaria. About the year 333 B.C. Darius Codomannus gave a certain Manasseh, grandson of the high-priest Eliashib (Nehemiah xiii. 23-31; Josephus, *Antiquities* xi. 7, viii.), permission to erect a temple on Mount Gerizim. He seems to have taken with him a copy of the Book of the Law in Hebrew. This became the only Sacred Scripture of the Samaritans. A few changes were made in order to magnify the importance of Mount Gerizim and to adapt the book to the new worship. "The value and authority of the Samaritan text of the Pentateuch has been variously estimated. By De Rossi it was regarded as an independent witness to the original, and therefore of equal weight with the Hebrew; others have estimated it even higher. These views are now generally abandoned, and it is conceded that for critical purposes no great value can be attached to the Samaritan form of the text" (A. S. Geden). See *Encycl. Bibl.*, *s.v.* "Text and Versions"; A. S. Geden, *Intr. to the Heb. Bible*, 1909.

SAMARITAN TARGUM, THE. A Targum (see TARGUM) or version of the Pentateuch based on the Samaritan Pentateuch (*q.v.*). It is in the Samaritan dialect. There seems to have been a Greek translation of this version, since the Fathers of the third and fourth centuries speak of a *Samareitikon*.

SĀMA VEDA. The Sāma Veda is one of the three principal Vedas (see VEDISM) or collections of hymns held sacred by the Hindus. The Sāma Veda is a liturgical collection of hymns for special (Soma) sacrificial ceremonies.

SAMPSAEANS. An early Christian sect, worshippers of the sun. They are called by Epiphanius (*Haer.* liii. 2) *hēliakoi*.

SAMUEL, BOOKS OF. The two books of Samuel originally formed one book. The original work was divided by the authors of the Septuagint into the First and Second Book of Kingdoms. Afterwards Jerome gave the books the title, The First and Second Book of Kings. Samuel gave his name to the work in the Hebrew Canon, not because he was its author, but because he plays a large and prominent part in the narrative. The history covered extends from the birth of the prophet Samuel to the close of the life of King David. The contents of the books have been divided as follows: (1) Eli and Samuel (I. Sam. i.-vii.); (2) Samuel and Saul (I. Sam. viii.-xiv.); (3) Saul and David (I. Sam. xv.-xxxi.); (4) David (II. Sam. i.-xx.); (5) Appendix of miscellaneous matter (II. Sam. xxi.-xxiv.). These narratives are composite, having clearly been compiled from a number of sources. There are different and divergent accounts of the same events: for instance, in the origin of the monarchy and the appointment of Saul as king; and of the introduction of David to Saul (cp. I. Sam. ix. 1-x. 16 with x. 17-27, and I. Sam. xvi. 14-23 with I. Sam. xvii. 1-xviii. 5). There are marked differences in the style of different sections. The compilers of the Books of Samuel would in fact seem to have drawn upon several different cycles of stories. C. F. Kent distinguishes early Judean Saul narratives, early Judean David narratives, later Ephraimite Samuel narratives, very late Popular Prophetic Traditions, and Popular Judean David stories. The early Judean Saul narratives, which present sympathetically and appreciatively the character and work of Israel's first king, include chaps. ix. 1-x. 16, xi. 1-11, 15 *b*, xiii. 1-xiv. 46. The early Judean David narratives comprise: I. Sam. xvi. 14-xvii. 11, 32-40, 42-49, 51-54, xviii. 6-8, 12-16, 20-29*a*, xix. 1-17, xx. 1-39, xxi. 1-9, xxii. 1-xxiii. 14*a*, xxv. 2-xxviii. 2, xxix.-xxxi.; II. Sam. i. 1-4, 11, 12, 17-iii. 1, 7-v. 13, 17-24, vi., viii. 7-10, ix. 1-xxi. 14, xxiii. 8-39, xxiv. Kent thinks that "viewed either as literature or as historical sources, the early Judean David narratives are unsurpassed by any others in the Old Testament. The pictures which they give of the actors and events in this epoch-making period in Israel's history are not only interesting and full of life and local colour, but they may be accepted as substantially true, even in detail, to the historical facts. They and the related Saul stories probably represent the first extensive Hebrew writings." Kent assigns the early Judean Saul and David stories to the reign of Jehoshaphat (876-851 B.C.). No use is made in the Books of Samuel of the Early Ephraimite prophetic narratives. But later Ephraimite Samuel narratives, in which the interest is religious and the purpose didactic, are found in I. Sam. i. 1-v. 1, vii. 2*b*-viii. 22, x. 17-25, xii. and xv. These, according to Kent, were committed to writing some time after the days of the prophet Hosea and before the reformation of King Josiah (621 B.C.). Examples of very late Prophetic Traditions, which are rather of the nature of Jewish *midrashim* (see MIDRASH), are found in I. Sam. xv. 35 *b*-xvi. 13, xix. 18-xx. 1*a*. Finally, Popular Judean David Stories are found in I. Sam. xvii. 12-31, 41, 50, 55-58, xviii. 1-5, 10, 11, 17-19, 29*b*, 30, xxi. 10-15, xxiii. 16-xxiv. 22, II. Sam. i. 5-10. According to Kent, most of these were committed to writing "before the late prophetic editor compiled his history of the period—that is before the first capture of Jerusalem in 597 B.C." H. P. Smith and W. R. Harper distinguish in like manner between an early and a later history of the times of Saul and David. To these additions were made by a first and a second Deuteronomist redactor. To the first are due I. Sam. x. 25 *b*-27, xi. 12-14; to the second I. Sam. ii. 1-11, xiii. 1, xx. 1-xxi. 1; II. Sam. xxi 15-21, xxii. 1-23, xxix. According to Harper, the contemporary literary sources may include: the Song of Hannah (I. Sam. ii. 1-10; according to Whitehouse and others, on the other hand, a post-exilic production); David's Elegy on Saul and Jonathan (II. Sam. i. 19-27); David's Lament over Abner (II. Sam. iii. 33, 34); Nathan's parable of the ewe lamb (II. Sam. xii. 1-15); the "last words of David" in a more original form; Psalm xviii. (II. Sam. xxii.). The prophet Samuel, who has given his name to these books, was probably the founder of certain prophetic schools. "In his days, it appears that the prophets had united together to make a common cause against the Canaanitish influences. Bands of ecstatic men—looking like madmen—went through the land preaching a holy war, and sweeping away everything that hindered their progress. . . . Samuel gathered them together and took them into his service, and so began to refine their innate passionate and unruly natures and to guide their energies to new paths" (R. Kittel, *The Scientific Study of the O.T.*, 1910). See *Encycl. Bibl.*; H. P. Smith, *The Books of Samuel* in the *I.C.C.*, 1899; A. R. S. Kennedy, *I. and II. Samuel* in the "Century Bible"; W. R. Harper, *The Prophetic Element in the Old Testament*, 1905; C. F. Kent, *Israel's Historical and Biographical Narratives*, 1905; G. H. Box, *Intr.*; O. C. Whitehouse.

SAMYUTTANIKAYA. One of the Buddhist sacred books in the second division of the Canon. See CANON, BUDDHIST.

SANCTUARY. Persons accused of a crime formerly enjoyed the right of seeking "sanctuary" in certain churches. At first only the altar and inner buildings could be used for the purpose, but since refugees were not allowed to eat or sleep in a church, the boundaries of asylum were enlarged. Sometimes they extended to a mile on every side of the building. The boundary-lines were marked by four crosses known as Sanctuary Crosses. Durham Cathedral has preserved a famous Sanctuary Knocker (of the 14th century). It has the form of a dragon's head with a ring in the mouth. See Sidney Heath.

SANDAN. Sandan or Sandes was a Hittite deity. On the Hittite sculpture of Ivriz he is associated with corn and grapes. He has a beard, and wears the Hittite dress and hat. According to Garstang, he is the original of the bearded and robed Apollo of Lucian (§ 35).

SANDEMANIANS. The followers of Robert Sandeman (1718-1771), who adopted and developed the views of John Glas (see GLASSITES). In 1760 Sandeman formed a congregation in London; but in 1764 he went to America and in the following year founded a congregation at Portsmouth in New Hampshire. In 1851 there were six churches in England and six in Scotland. Michael Faraday was one of the elders of the congregation in London. Sandeman taught that faith is "a bare belief of the bare truth"; it does not differ from belief in ordinary human evidence. The Sandemanians had a number of peculiar observances. "They observe various primitive practices with great strictness: *e.g.*, weekly administration of the Lord's Supper, with a weekly offertory; love-feasts, *i.e.*, the dining together between morning and afternoon services; the kiss of charity at the admission of a new member, and at other times; washing each other's feet as an occasional work of mercy; abstinence from things strangled and from blood; community of goods, in so far as that they consider the whole of their property liable for calls on behalf of the Church and the poor, and condemn the storing up of money for future and uncertain use" (Blunt). Believing that the lot is sacred, they disapprove of all games of chance. They refuse to hold communion with other denominations. See J. H. Blunt; and the *D.N.B.*

SANDRAUDIGA. The name of a goddess worshipped by some of the Ancient Teutons. A stone discovered at Breda in the Netherlands was consecrated to her by the "priests of the temple" (cultores templi).

SANHEDRIN. The name of one of the Jewish treatises or tractates which reproduce the oral tradition or unwritten law as developed by the second century A.D. and are incorporated in the Mishnah (*q.v.*), a collection and compilation completed by Rabbi Judah the Holy, or the Patriarch, about 200 A.D. The sixty-three tractates of the Mishnah are divided into six groups or orders (*sedārīm*). Sanhedrin is the fourth tractate of the fourth group, which is called *Nezīkīn* ("Damages").

SANJŌGIS. The Sanjōgis of Southern India are described as an Oriya class of religious mendicants, who wear the sacred thread, and acts as priests for Pānos and other lowly people. "The name indicates connection, and that they are the connecting link between ordinary people and those who have given up earthly pleasures (Sanyāsis). The Sanjōgis follow the ordinary as well as the ascetic life" (E. Thurston).

SĀNKHYAS. The Sānkhyas are adherents of the Hindu dualistic philosophy known as the Sānkhya system. Colebrooke describes the system as "partly heterodox, and partly conformable to the established Hindu creed." Two schools, having much in common, are distinguished as the Sānkhya and the Yoga. The Sānkhya system was founded by Kapila. It teaches "that the soul is simply a part of God, and that the wisdom acquired by *yoga*, or contemplation, ends in either actual or spiritual unity with God" (Dubois and Beauchamp). See E. W. Hopkins; J. A. Dubois and H. K. Beauchamp.

SANNYASI. Literally "one who renounces," a Brahman ascetic. The state of a Sannyāsi is the fourth stage in the life of a good Brahman. At this stage all worldly ties are renounced. The ancient lawgiver Manu "ordained that the discharge of household duties is incompatible with the attainment of greater nearness to the Supreme Being, and that therefore every twice-born man as he advances in life is bound to give up all family ties" (Monier-Williams). The Sannyāsi does not really die. He passes from this world in a kind of trance. Consequently his body must not be burned but buried. See Monier-Williams; E. W. Hopkins; J. A. Dubois and H. K. Beauchamp.

SANRON SECT. A Chinese and Japanese Buddhist sect. It flourished in China during the Sui dynasty (589-618 A.D.), and was introduced into Japan in 624 A.D. Its teaching was metaphysical. The sect was called also the *Ichi-dai-kyōshu*, or "Sect of the Teachings of Buddha's whole life," for "it made it a feature of its teachings that it professed to accept every one of the many thousand volumes of the Mahāyāna Canon as of equal authority, without assigning to any single one a pre-eminent place among its compeers" (A. Lloyd). It aimed at the greatest comprehensiveness. But it was not a success in Japan, and no longer exists as a separate organization. See Arthur Lloyd.

SAOSHYANT. A term in Zoroastrianism meaning "deliverer" or strictly "he that shall deliver." According to the *Gathas*, certain persons will arise as the "future deliverers of the provinces." The deliverance will take place at the Great Consummation, which Zarathustra expected to come soon.

SARASVATI. A deity in Hinduism. Sarasvatī is a goddess, the wife of Brahmā (*q.v.*). In the Rig Veda, however, she is a river-goddess, and is not connected with Brahmā. She became the goddess of language and literature. In Bengal a festival is held in her honour in the Spring, when pens, inkstands, paper, etc., are worshipped as representing the goddess (cp. LAKSHMI). "Sarasvatī is almost the only fair goddess. She is represented not as a horror, but as a beautiful woman sitting on a lotus, graceful in shape, a crescent on her brow" (Hopkins). See Monier-Williams; E. W. Hopkins.

SARPANITUM. A Babylonian deity. The goddess Sarpanitum appears after the time of Hammurapi as the consort of Marduk (*q.v.*). She was popularly regarded as the "offspring-producing" goddess, and seems to have been worshipped as one who possessed secret knowledge and protected the foetus. Sarpanitum was amalgamated with a water goddess Eurua, who also appears as the consort of Marduk. Her place of worship in E-Sagila was called "the gate of widespread splendour." Her festival was on the 25th day of the third month, Siwan. See Morris Jastrow, *Rel.*

SARUM, USE OF. The term *Use* was applied to different modes of celebrating the Mass or Holy Communion. One of the most important of these was the Use of Salisbury or Sarum. Osmund, Bishop of Salisbury (1078-1107 A.D.), seems to have begun in his Cathedral a revision of the Service Books, which was completed by Bishop Poore (1215-1242 A.D.). The Use of Sarum then became a model in many parts of England, especially in the South. "The Sarum Liturgy, like the other ancient Liturgies, had two main divisions commonly called the 'Ordinary' and the 'Canon' of the Mass. The 'Ordinary' contained the variable parts of the Service; the 'Canon' or Rule, corresponding to what in Eastern Liturgies is called the *Anaphora* or offering, contained the fixed portion, which never varied" (W. R. W. Stephens, *Book of Common Prayer*).

SARVĀSTIVĀDINS. One of the early Buddhist sects of the School of the Hīnayāna (*q.v.*). The Sarvāstivādins believed in the real existence of the universe and the soul, and in the reality of life after death.

SASKYAPA SECT. A sect in Lamaism, which attaches special importance to magic. It treasures a number of forms of incantation which have been handed down to it from its special patron the Bodhisattva Manjuśrī. The hoods and upper garments of these monks are red. See H. Hackmann.

SĀSTHAN. The chief deity of the Kānikars, a jungle tribe inhabiting the mountains of South Travancore in Southern India.

SĀTĀNIS. A class of temple servants in Southern India. They are described by H. A. Stuart as "a mixed religious sect, recruited from time to time from other castes, excepting Paraiyans, leather-workers, and Muhammadans. All the Sātānis are Vaishnavites, but principally revere Bāshyakar (another name for Rāmānuja), whom they assert to have been an incarnation of Vishnu. The Sātānis are almost entirely confined to the large towns. Their legitimate occupations are performing menial services in Vishnu temples, begging, tending flower gardens, selling flower garlands, making fans, grinding sandalwood into powder, and selling perfumes. They are the priests of some Sūdra castes, and in this character correspond to the Saivite Pandārams" (quoted by E. Thurston).

SATNĀMIS. The Satnāmis, "worshippers of the true name," are a modern Hindu sect. It seems to have been founded by Jag-jīvan-dās, who flourished about A.D. 1750. The doctrines are based on the theology of the great reformer Kabīr (see KABIR PANTHIS). The Satnāmis are Vaishnava Theists. Their name is taken from the name which they give to God, Satnām. The following are some of their principles and precepts, as given by Monier-Williams: "God pervades the universe. He is present in every single thing. The title Lord (Sāhib) should be added to every object in which God is present. God is the spring and source of everything good and evil. Idols must not be worshipped. The ordained religious teacher (Guru) is holy. Even the water in which his feet are washed is holy, and should be drunk by his disciples. Distinctions of caste are not to be observed. Fasts need not be kept." See Monier-Williams; E. W. Hopkins.

SATURN. An ancient Roman deity, a god of seed-time and harvest. The name Saturninus is derived from a root meaning "to sow." In an inscription it occurs as Saeturnus. The special festival of the god was called Saturnalia (*q.v.*). In course of time Saturn came to be identified with the Greek god Kronos. Kronos, defeated in a war which Zeus waged against him, fled to Italy, was received by Janus, and settled at the foot of the Capitoline Hill. Thus, "Saturn, the old homely deity of the Latin husbandmen, was transformed into a divine king, who ruled the happy aborigines of the Italian peninsula with paternal mildness and beneficence, taught them agriculture and the usages of a simple and innocent civilisation" (*Chambers' Encycl.*). See O. Seyffert, *Dict.*; J. G. Frazer, *G.B.*, Pt. I., vol. ii., 1911.

SATURNALIA. A festival held on December 17 in honour of the Roman god Saturn (*q.v.*). Sacrifices were offered and a banquet was held in the open air. "The festival was also celebrated in private society; schools had holidays, law-courts were closed, all work was stopped, war was deferred, and no punishment of criminals took place for seven days from December 17 to 23" (O. Seyffert). It was a kind of Christmas. People presented gifts to one another, especially wax tapers and dolls, and gave themselves up to every kind of amusement and entertainment. An ancient account of the Saturnalia was discovered and published some years ago by Franz Cumont of Ghent. "From that account we learn that down to the beginning of the fourth century of our era, that is, down nearly to the establishment of Christianity by Constantine, the Roman soldiers stationed on the Danube were wont to celebrate the Saturnalia in a barbarous fashion which must certainly have dated from a very remote antiquity. Thirty days before the festival they chose by lot from among themselves a young and handsome man, who was dressed in royal robes to resemble the god Saturn. In that character he was allowed to indulge all his passions to the fullest extent; but when his brief reign of thirty days was over, and the festival of Saturn was come, he had to cut his own throat on the altar of the god he personated" (J. G. Frazer). In 303 A.D. a Christian soldier, St. Dasius, was put to death for refusing to play the part of Saturn at the Saturnalia. Saturn was the god of seed, and the Saturnalia was the festival of sowing celebrated in December, "when the autumn sowing was over and the husbandman gave himself up to a season of jollity after the long labours of summer and autumn" (Frazer). J. G. Frazer thinks that formerly the part of the god Saturn was played by the Roman king himself, and that in the licence accorded to the human representatives of Saturn may perhaps be detected a trace of the Sacred Marriage. In some ways the festivals of the new yams, celebrated by the Ashantees early in September, resembles the Saturnalia. So also does the festival of the new fruits celebrated by the Caffres of Natal and Zululand at the end of December or the beginning of January (*G.B.*, Pt. v. vol. ii., 1912). See O. Seyffert, *Dict.*, 10th ed. 1908; J. G. Frazer, *G.B.*, Pt. i., vol. ii., 1911.

SATURNINIANS. The followers or school of the Gnostic Saturninus or Saturnilus, who flourished about the time of Trajan (98-117 A.D.). The Saturninians, or most of them, abstained from animal food of every kind; and they held marriage and the procreation of children to be the work of Satan. According to Saturninus, there is one Supreme, unknowable God, the Father, who created the angels, archangels, powers, etc. Seven of these angels created the visible world. "They created man after the likeness of a brilliant vision, which had appeared to them for a fleeting moment from the Supreme God; but at first their work was imperfect. Primitive man crawled on the ground, unable to stand erect. God took compassion on him, because He recognised his likeness to Himself: He sent, therefore, a spark of life which completed his creation. After man's death, this spark of life is set free, and returns to its primary cause" (Duchesne). One of the angels is the God of the Jews, a Demiurge. The Saviour came to destroy the power of this Demiurge, and to save those men who were capable of salvation. This Saviour emanated from the Supreme God. He was not born, and had no human body. He was a man only in appearance, not in reality. See J. H. Blunt; *Cath. Dict.;* Louis Duchesne, *Hist.*

SATYRS. The Satyrs of Greek mythology were spirits or demons who lived in mountains and woods. They are represented as having ears like those of a goat, bristling hair, and short tails. Following in the train of Dionysus, they made merry with pipe and flute. "They were considered as foes to mankind, because they played people all kinds of roguish pranks, and frightened them by impish tricks" (Seyffert). Dr. A. B. Gough points out that at the earliest period to which we can trace them, Satyrs, Seileni, Cyclopes, and Centaurs were very similar to one another, but in course of time they were differentiated. In the Old Testament demons of a similar kind seem to be referred to as Se'īrīm, a term which means literally "hairy ones." Since a word Se'īrīm also means "he-goats," it has been assumed that these Hebrew demons were goat-shaped, but the assumption is not necessary. The Se'īrīm were wild and semi-human in appearance. In Isaiah xiii. 21 they are spoken of as dancing amid the desolate ruins of Babylon. The Se'īrīm have been connected by some scholars with an Egyptian god corresponding to Pan (*q.v.*). It is possible, however, that they may preserve a hint of early traditions concerning some tribe or tribes of real men, "hairy beings" who were supposed to dwell (and play pranks) in the desert, were regarded as formidable, and looked upon as devils. Jane Harrison (*Prolegomena*, 2nd ed., 1908) thinks that the Satyrs of the Greeks were to Homer and Pindar "the representatives of an actual primitive population." They were in fact identical with the Satrae, a wild Thracian tribe. See *Encycl. Bibl.;* O. Seyffert, *Dict.;* Alfred B. Gough, *The Primitive Savage in Early Art and Tradition*, 1910.

SĀUGATAS. The Sāugatas are a division of the Buddhists who believe that the essence of religion consists in kindness. Compare SITTARS.

SAVADAMMAN. The goddess of the weaver caste in Coimbatore, India, an avatar of Parvati, the wife of the great Hindu god Siva.

SAVIOUR. The title Saviour was given in ancient times to deities, and to eminent men, such as kings, princes, and heroes. In the Old Testament it is used of ordinary men (Neh. ix. 27) and of God. In the New Testament the term is applied to God (Luke i. 47, etc.) and to Jesus Christ or the Messiah (Luke ii. 11; Acts v. 31; II. Peter i. 11). J. M. Robertson points out (*Pagan Christs*, 1911) that the title was given by the Greeks to Zeus, Helios, Artemis, Dionysos, Herakles, the Dioscuri, Cybele, and Æsculapius. But there is nothing remarkable in this. The word is an ordinary one. The important question is: Was it used of Jesus in an ordinary sense? The fact is that it was not. It was always used in a moral sense. It was popularly understood to mean that Jesus, by converting men from sin, would save them from the future punishment which would otherwise befall them. In Jesus' own understanding of the term, it evidently had a more spiritual meaning. This is clear from the famous utterance: "For whosoever would save his life shall lose it; and whosoever shall lose his life for my sake and the gospel's shall save it" (Mark viii. 35; Luke ix. 24; Matthew xvi. 25). To save a man is to bring him to realize fully in this present life that to live in a material way and sense is not really to live at all. The material sense of life must be lost that the spiritual and real sense of life may be gained; and when this is gained eternal life is already present. This is the sense in which Jesus was the Saviour: he saved men from a false sense of life, and so from death. Cp. Thayer-Grimm, *Greek-English Lexicon to the N.T.*, 1896.

SAVITAR. A Vedic deity, the "vivifier," who in the morning awakens the universe and men from sleep. Savitar is a form under which Surya, the Sun, is invoked. The daily formula of supplication addressed to Savitar (the *Sāvitri*) runs: "On the surpassing splendour of that divine Vivifier let us meditate; and may he enlighten our minds."

SAVOY DECLARATION, THE. The "Savoy Declaration" was the result of the Conference held at the Savoy Palace in London. Though arranged by Cromwell, the Conference did not meet until some weeks after his death. Its task was to draw up a new Confession of Faith which should satisfy the Independents, and there were representatives of one hundred and twenty Congregational Churches. The new Confession (1658 A.D.) consists of a "Preface" which urges "toleration in matters non-essential among Churches that held the necessary foundations of faith and holiness" (W. A. Curtis); a "Declaration of Faith" which comprises "the doctrinal matter of the Westminster Confession slightly modified"; and what is called the "Institution of Churches," a System of Polity providing for the organization and constitution of Congregationalism. See William A. Curtis.

SAVUS. One of the gods worshipped by the ancient Celts. He was paired with the goddess Adsalluta.

SAXNOT. Another form of Seaxneat (*q.v.*), the name of an Anglo-Saxon deity.

SAYBROOK PLATFORM, THE. In the declaration known as the "Saybrook Platform" (1708 A.D.), the Connecticut Churches of America adopted the Boston Declaration of 1680 A.D. (which accepted the Savoy Confession and the Cambridge Platform) together with the Nine Heads of Agreement (*q.v.*) which the Congregationalists and Presbyterians of London agreed upon in 1691 A.D. In 1801 A.D. the Connecticut Churches further adopted a "Plan of Union." See William A. Curtis.

SAYINGS OF THE FATHERS. The English title of a collection of sayings and maxims of some of the Jewish Doctors. The Hebrew title of the work is *Pirqê Ăbôth* (*q.v.*).

SCHWENKFELDIANS. The followers of Caspar von Schwenkfeld (1490-1561), who was a nobleman of Silesia and a Councillor to the Duke of Liegnitz at the time of the Reformation. He was at first in sympathy with the ideas of the Reformation, but afterwards sought to develop a Protestant theology of his own along the lines of mysticism and religious enthusiasm (cp. his work "Bekanndtnus uud Rechenschaft von den Hauptpunkten des christl. Glaubens," 1547). As early as 1527 he explained a new doctrine of the Holy Eucharist which he professed to have received by special revelation. "This was that our Lord's words of Institution are to be understood as if He had said 'My Body is this'—a spiritual food, which nourishes the soul as bread does the body, 'My Blood is this'—a spiritual drink, which nourishes the soul as wine does the body. His theory went on to maintain that the Sacraments are not means, but only signs of grace, and that the benefit which they signify comes, not in, through, or with them, but directly from God" (J. H. Blunt). Schwenkfeld was banished from Silesia in 1527, and settled at Strassburg. Luther opposed him bitterly and gave him the nickname "Stenckfeld." In 1725 many of the Schwenkfeldians removed to Saxony. A few years later they emigrated to Pennsylvania and formed congregations there. See J. H. Blunt; Brockhaus.

SCIENCE. As employed by the author of "Science and Health," the term Science is used interchangeably with the expressions Divine Science, Spiritual Science, Christ Science, and Christian Science (*q.v.*).

SCIENCE AND HEALTH. The title of the work by Mary Baker Eddy, which has become the textbook of Christian Scientists (*q.v.*). Mrs. Eddy claims that the book was entirely the result of a study of the Bible. The real meaning of the Bible, however, dawned upon her as a revelation. "The Scriptures were illumined; reason and revelation were reconciled, and afterwards the truth of Christian Science was demonstrated. No human pen nor tongue taught me the Science contained in this book, SCIENCE AND HEALTH; and neither tongue nor pen can overthrow it. This book may be distorted by shallow criticism or by careless or malicious students, and its ideas may be temporarily abused and misrepresented; but the Science and truth therein will forever remain to be discerned and demonstrated" (*Science and Health*, p. 110). The first edition of "Science and Health" was published in 1875. A revised edition was published in 1891. Many persons testify to having been cured of various diseases simply by reading the book. The work may be borrowed from any Christian Science Reading Room. See Mary Baker Eddy, *Science and Health with Key to the Scriptures*, 1911.

SCIENTIFIC STATEMENT OF BEING, THE. The Scientific Statement of Being may be described as the "Creed" of Christian Scientists (*q.v.*). It is as follows: "There is no life, truth, intelligence. nor substance in matter. All is infinite Mind and its infinite manifestation, for God is All-in-all. Spirit is immortal Truth; matter is mortal error. Spirit is the real and eternal; matter is the unreal and temporal. Spirit is God, and man is His image and likeness. Therefore man is not material; he is spiritual." See Mary Baker Eddy, *Science and Health*, 1911, p. 468.

SCILLITAN MARTYRS. The Scillitan Martyrs are so described because they came from the town of Scillita in Africa. They were twelve persons who were martyred at Carthage about 180 A.D., when Praesens II. and Condianus were consuls. The *Acts* of these martyrs have been preserved in two forms. G. T. Stokes thinks that "to the Biblical critic these Acts in both shapes are interesting, as indicating the position held by St. Paul's Epistles in 180 in the N. African Church. The proconsul asked the martyr Speratus what books they kept laid up in their bookcases. He replied, Our books, or as the Latin version puts it, the four Gospels of our Lord Jesus Christ, and in addition the Epistles of Paul the holy man." See Wace and Piercy.

SCOTTISH UNITARIAN ASSOCIATION. This was founded in 1813 by James Yates (1789-1871) in conjunction with Thomas Southwood Smith (1788-1861), the sanitary reformer. See UNITARIANS.

SEAL OF PROPHECY. This name was given to a large mole which the prophet Muhammad had on his back. It was supposed to be the divine seal predicted by the Scriptures. T. P. Hughes quotes Shaikh 'Abdu'l-Ḥaqq as saying: "it was a piece of flesh, very brilliant in appearance, and according to some traditions it had secretly inscribed *within* it, 'God is one and has no Associate.'" See T. P. Hughes.

SEAXNEAT. Seaxneat appears as one of the deities worshipped by the Anglo-Saxons. The god seems to be identical with the Ancient Teutonic Tiu (*q.v.*).

SE-BAPTIST. The origin of this name is explained in Daniel Neal's "History of the Puritans" (ii. 49, 1732). "Mr. Smith was a learned man and of good abilities, but of an unsettled head, as appears by the preface to one of his books, in which he desires that his last writings may always be taken for his present judgment. He was for refining upon the Brownists' scheme, and at last declared for the principles of the Baptists; upon this he left Amsterdam, and settled with his disciples at Ley, where, being at a loss for a proper administrator of the ordinance of baptism, he plunged himself, and then performed the ceremony upon others, which gained him the name of a Se-Baptist. He afterwards embraced the tenets of Arminius, and published certain conclusions upon those points in the year 1611, which Mr. Robinson answered; but Smith died soon after, and his congregation dissolved."

SEBEK. An Egyptian deity, the crocodile-god, worshipped at Ombos and in other towns of the Fayyūm. Sebek, who is represented as a crocodile or as a man with a crocodile head, developed into a deity that was essentially evil.

SECESSION KIRK. A secession from the Church of Scotland, which took place in 1733. See PRESBYTERIANS.

SEEKERS. Richard Baxter (1615-1691), writing in

1650, refers to a sect of Puritans with this name. He mentions them in connection with the Familists (*q.v.*), to whom they seem to have been related. They were seekers for the true Church, Ministry, Scripture, and Ordinances, believing them to have been lost. The Scriptures as commonly accepted they regarded as uncertain. Another of their tenets was that present miracles are necessary to faith. See John Hunt; J. H. Blunt.

SEIDHR. A Norse form of witchcraft or magic. It was employed usually to bring harm, but sometimes also to protect against harm or to divine the future. The man who practised it was called *Seidhmadhr*, the woman *Seidhkona*. The magician sat on a raised seat and sang suitable songs. See P. D. Chautepie de la Saussaye, *Rel. of the Teutons*, 1902.

SEKHMET. An Egyptian deity. The goddess Sekhmet, "the mighty one," is represented with the head of a lioness. The head is crowned with the solar disk and uraeus serpent. In her hand she carries a knife. Since the head of Sekhmet resembles that of Bast (a cat's head), the two goddesses have been connected. Erman thinks the two developed originally from a single sky goddess, Hathor (*q.v.*). Hathor was the goddess of love and joy. Bast delights in dancing and music. A Philae text says with reference to Isis Hathor: "Kindly is she as Bast, terrible is she as Sekhmet." In the New Kingdom deities are combined in a curious way. "In the temple at Koptos the goddess Mut of Thebes was called at one time Bast, and at another time Sekhmet of Memphis, although she was neither cat- nor lion-headed, but figured as a vulture" (Erman). See A. Wiedemann; Adolf Erman, *Handbook*.

SELF-DETERMINATION. Self-determination is a philosophical position that stands midway between Determinism (*q.v.*) and Indeterminism (*q.v.*). "All voluntary action is motived—so far Determinism is true; but Determinism is wrong when it assumes that the relation between motive and action is the same as the relation between cause and effect in the physical world. For motives are the motives of a self, and are not to be taken as isolated phenomena. And it is this self which ultimately chooses or rejects. What is free, then, is not some pure faculty of willing, but rather the self. Deliberation and uncertainty arise because this self is of such a nature that certain elements, *e.g.* impulses, in it may conflict with certain other elements" (A. Butler).

SEMINARISTS. A term applied to the English Romanists who were trained in the Seminary at Douay founded by William Allen (1532-1594), Fellow of Oriel College, Oxford, in 1568. Allen was anxious that there should be an unfailing supply in England of Romanist priests thoroughly instructed in the Tridentine theology and in the general learning of their age. One of his students was Edmund Campion (1540-1581). See M. W. Patterson, *Hist.*; the *D.N.B.*

SEMIPELAGIANISM. Semipelagianism, a modified form of Pelagianism (*q.v.*) was a reaction against the Augustinian views of predestination and grace. It has been called the heresy of the Massilienses, because it was defended by the monks of Marseilles in opposition to the teaching of Augustine. "The monks objected to the Augustinian doctrine that the number of the elect was absolutely fixed by the decree of God. They made predestination the mere foreknowledge of God that some would, others would not, persevere. They also held that God allowed some infants to die without baptism, some adults without hearing the Gospel, only because He knew they would have made no use of these graces had they been offered" (*Cath. Dict.*). They maintained also that the desire to be healed by Christ was due to the use of the natural human faculties. The doctrines of Semipelagianism were further developed by the monk Cassian who had come to Marseilles from the East and founded the monastery of St. Victor there (*c.* 415 A.D.). Cassian wrote a work called "XXIV. Conferences" (423-428). In this he declared, among other things, that Job's victory over Satan and the Centurion's faith in the power of Jesus to heal were due to their own natural efforts. The next prominent Semipelagian was Faustus, Abbot of Lerins and afterwards Bishop of Riez (*d.* 491). His book "De Gratia Dei et Humanæ Mentis Libero Arbitrio" was condemned by a number of African bishops who had been exiled to Sardinia. Finally in 529 Semipelagianism was condemned by the Synod of Orange, in South Gaul, and the sentence was confirmed by Pope Boniface II. The Synod, presided over by Cæsarius of Arles (*d.* 542), passed four canons. (1) That by the sin of Adam free-will has been so perverted and weakened that none have since then been able to love God, or believe in Him, or to do good actions for His sake, unless Divine grace has prevented them. (2) After grace has been received by baptism, all baptized persons are able by the divine assistance and co-operation, to do all things that belong to the soul's salvation, if they are willing to work with faith. (3) We not only do not believe that some persons have been predestined to evil by the divine power, but we pronounce anathema against all who incline to hold such an opinion. (4) We also profess and believe that in every good work it is not we who begin, and who are afterwards assisted by the mercy of God; but God Himself first inspires faith and love, without any previous good works on our part, so that we faithfully demand the sacrament of baptism, and after baptism are able, with His assistance, to accomplish what is pleasing to Him. Whence it is most clearly to be believed that the marvellous faith of the thief whom the Lord summoned to Paradise, of the centurion Cornelius to whom an angel was sent, and of Zacchæus who was found worthy to entertain our Lord, was not natural but the gift of God. See J. H. Blunt; *Prot. Dict.*; *Cath. Dict.*

SEMIRAMIS. A goddess who figures in mythology as founder with Ninus of Nineveh. She is represented as the daughter of Derceto, the fish-goddess. Originally she would seem to have been a historical character, Sammuramat, wife of Samsi-Adad (*c.* B.C. 820), of Assyria.

SENGEN. A Japanese deity, goddess of the sacred mountain of Fuji, to which pilgrimages are made.

SENSUALISM. The term Sensualism is used sometimes to describe the philosophy of George Berkeley (1685-1753). He contends that we have knowledge only of our feelings. Material things are nothing else but so many physical qualities or combinations of physical qualities. Appearances cannot be regarded as copies of real things. They are only objects of experience. See BERKELEYISM.

SENTENTIARIES. A name given to the pupils of Peter Lombard (*d.* 1164), called Magister Sententiarum, or to those who studied his great compendium "Sententiarum Libri Quattuor." See SUMMISTS.

SENUSSI. A Muhammadan brotherhood, founded by an Algerian, Sidi Mohammed ben Ali es-Senûsi (*d.* 1859). His son, Sidi Mohammed el-Bedr (1844-1902) played an active part as the Mahdi for some years in the east of North Africa. His followers believe that he still lives. "On a white horse, surrounded by white gazelles and antelopes, he wanders unseen through the desert, makes long journeys, and then suddenly appears among his adherents at fixed places, sometimes in two places at once" (J. C. Falls, *Three Years in the Libyan Desert*, 1913). The rule of the Senussi order is strict. It requires abstemiousness, and prohibits the use of tobacco, coffee, dancing, and music. See T. W. Arnold; Oskar Mann, "Mohammedanism," in *G.R.W.*

SEPHARIM GENUZIM. The expression means "books hidden away." We find in the Talmud echoes of controversies about some of the Jewish sacred books which finally secured a place in the Canon. The question raised was whether certain books (*e.g.*, Proverbs and Ezekiel) were really suitable for use in the Synagogue, or whether it would not be better to withdraw (gānaz) them. *Sepharim genuzim* never include books which are uncanonical in the sense of heretical. The Jews call these *Chītsōnim*, that is to say, libri extranei. To withdraw a book was not the same as to pronounce it uncanonical. In the Talmudic treatise *Shabbāth* (30 *b*) we read: "Some desired also to withdraw (*ganaz*) the book of Proverbs from use, because it contained internal contradictions, but the attempt was abandoned, because the wise men declared, 'We have examined more deeply into the Book of Ecclesiastes and have discovered the solution of the difficulty; here also we wish to enquire more deeply.'" The Book of Ezekiel also was in danger of being hidden away because in several points it seemed to be in conflict with the law of Moses (*Menachoth*). As to this we read in the Talmud (*Shabbāth* 13 *b*, *Chagīgā* 13 *a*, *b*): "But as for Hananiah, the son of Hezekiah, blessed be his memory—if it had not been for him, the Book of Ezekiel would have been hidden, because its words contradict the words of the Torah. What did he do? They brought him 300 measures of oil; and he sat down and explained it." See G. Hölscher, *Kanonisch und Apokryph*, 1905.

SEPTUAGINT, THE. This Greek translation of the Old Testament, which was the Bible of Greek-speaking Jews, was called the Septuagint because it was supposed to have been made by seventy or seventy-two Jewish elders. The full title in Latin is "Interpretatio septuaginta virorum (or seniorum)," and in Greek it is referred to as the version *κατα τους ἑβδομηκοντα*. The tradition as to how the translation was planned and prepared is given in the Epistle of Aristeas, a Jewish-Alexandrine production which must have been written earlier than 198 B.C. The work purports to be a letter written by Aristeas, an officer of King Ptolemy II. Philadelphus (284-247 B.C.), to his brother Philocrates. It tells how the king's librarian, Demetrius Phalereus, advised the king to add a Greek translation of the Law of the Jews to the royal library of Alexandria. The king sends to the High Priest Eleazar at Jerusalem and begs him to send scholars to undertake the work. "The high priest is filled with joy at the request of the king, and seventy-two men, six from every tribe, are sent to Alexandria with a copy of the Law written in golden letters. During seven days they have daily audiences of the king, and excite the admiration of all by the wisdom with which they answer the seventy-two questions proposed to them in philosophy, politics, and ethics. Thereafter they are transported to the island of Pharos, where, in a beautiful residence, they engage diligently in the work of translation. Every day they all translate, each one by himself, a portion of the Law, and then, after comparison of the various renderings, they produce a common text. In seventy-two days the work is completed" (F. Buhl, *Canon and Text of the Old Testament*, 1892). Philo (*c.* 20 B.C.-45 A.D.) adds that all the translators were inspired to choose the same expressions (cp. INSPIRATION). The Church Fathers further embellish the story by stating that each of the translators was shut up in a separate cell. There is no reason to doubt that Ptolemy Philadelphus encouraged the Greek translation in its earliest form, which included only the five books of the Law. This was the first Greek Bible. The other books followed in due course. In the Preface to Ecclesiasticus, Ben Sira, who arrived in Egypt in 132 B.C., implies the existence of a Greek version of the Former and Latter Prophets and of some at least of the Hagiographa, as well as of the Law. He says: "For things originally spoken in Hebrew have not the same force in them, when they are translated into another tongue: and not only these, but the law itself, and the prophecies, and the rest of the books, have no small difference, when they are spoken in their original language." This may be taken to mean that the books had been translated before 132 B.C. There is a footnote to the Greek version of Esther which says that it was brought to Egypt in the fourth year of Ptolemy and Cleopatra. If, as seems probable, Ptolemy VI. Philometor is referred to, the date would be 178 B.C. It is probable, however, that some of the books of the Hagiographa (*q.v.*) were not translated much before the beginning of the Christian era. The different styles in which books are translated is a further indication that the translations were the work of a number of authors. Some of the translations are extremely literal; others are very paraphrastic. The Septuagint, as we have it, includes our Apocrypha. The apocryphal books are not printed as an appendix, but are placed among the canonical works; and, in general, the books of the Greek Bible are placed together according to similarity of character or subject. Some other peculiarities call for remark. The apocryphal additions to Esther are distributed through the Book of Esther. Some of the apocryphal additions to Daniel, including the writings known to us as "The Song of the Three Holy Children" and "The Prayer of Azarias," are distributed through the Book of Daniel. The Epistle of Jeremy is appended to Baruch. Further, I. and II. Samuel and I. and II. Kings are regarded as four books of "Kingdoms" (*basileiōn*); our Ezra-Nehemiah is called Second Esdras; while First Esdras ("Greek Esdras") "consists of an independent and somewhat free version of portions of II. Chronicles and Ezra-Nehemiah, broken by a long context which has no parallel in the Hebrew Bible" (H. B. Swete, *Intr. to the O.T. in Greek*, 1900). The order of books in Swete's standard edition of the Septuagint is as follows: The Pentateuch in the usual order, Joshua, Judges, Ruth, four books of Kingdoms, I. and II. Chronicles, I. and II. Esdras, Psalms, Proverbs, Ecclesiastes, Song of Solomon, Job, Wisdom of Solomon, Wisdom of Sirach, Esther, Judith, Tobit, Hosea, Amos, Micah, Joel, Obadiah, Jonah, Nahum, Habakkuk, Zephaniah, Haggai, Zechariah, Malachi, Isaiah, Jeremiah, Baruch, Lamentations, Letter of Jeremiah, Ezekiel, Daniel, Susanna, Bel and the Dragon, and the four books of Maccabees. The common or accepted text of the Septuagint is found in the Hexapla of Origen. Lucian (died A.D. 311) of Antioch issued a revised text, and Hesychius (died in Egypt A.D. 310-11) another. Paul de Lagarde published a restoration of part of the Lucianic recension in 1883. Cp. further GREEK VERSIONS. See H. B. Swete, *Intr.*; A. S. Geden, *Intro. to the Heb. Bible*, 1909.

SERAPHIC BRETHREN. A name by which the Franciscans (*q.v.*) are sometimes known.

SERAPHIM. Heavenly beings referred to in the Old Testament in connection with the vision of the prophet Isaiah. Isaiah saw the Lord sitting on a high throne. "Above Him were standing the seraphim. Each one had six wings. With twain he was covering his face, and with twain he was covering his feet, and with twain he was flying." As this (Isa. vi. 2) is the only mention of the Seraphim in the Old Testament, their precise nature is doubtful. An identical word, found in the Singular, means "a (fiery) serpent." In Isaiah xiv

29, xxx. 6 it occurs in the expression "flying serpent" (or, dragon). This would suggest that the Seraphs were serpentine in form. It would appear also from Isaiah vi. that these attendants on Jehovah had human hands and voices and six wings. The Serāphīm have been compared with the Egyptian *Seref*, a winged griffin, which is represented as the guardian of graves, etc., and, according to Pietschmann, was a feature in the religion of Syria as well as in that of Egypt. Assyriologists compare the name *sharrāpu*, "the burner," which is used of the Babylonian solar fire-god Nergal (*q.v.*). Cheyne (*Encyclopaedia Biblica*) inclines to the view that the Serāphīm were originally serpents (cp. Isa. xiv. 29; Nu. xxi. 8). "Arabian and Hebrew folklore placed flying serpents, with burning venemous bite, in the desert, and Hebrew mythographers may have represented winged serpents as the guardians of the dwelling of the Deity." But why should we seek to ascribe any particular form to the Seraphim? They were probably thought of simply as "dazzling (burning; Hebrew *sāraph* "to burn") ones." Their brightness was so dazzling that probably as a rule no form could be distinguished. In so far as the picture seen by Isaiah assumed a form, it took the shape of six wings, two at the top, two at the bottom, and one on either side. It is useless to seek a parallel figure in mythology and folklore. The Seraphim, as seen by Isaiah, belong, like Moses' vision of the burning bush (see BURNING BUSH), purely to the realm of psychic phenomena. True, we are told that one of the Seraphim flew to Isaiah with a live coal in his hand and touched his mouth with it. But the words were hardly intended to be taken literally. It is not possible to describe in human speech the kind of experience that Isaiah had. When the attempt is made to do so, words have to be used which are in reality quite inadequate and very liable to be misunderstood. See *Encycl. Bibl.*; Hastings' *D.B.*; O. C. Whitehouse, *Isaiah* in the "Century Bible."

SERAPIS. An Egyptian deity, or rather a deity half Egyptian and half Greek. Serapis belongs to the Hellenistic Period in Egypt. He is identical with Wser-hap, the deceased Apis bull (see APIS). "The soul of the Apis was supposed to have been received into heaven as the Osiris Apis, and was regarded henceforth almost as a Double of Osiris. It was indeed in this form that Osiris was generally recognized by the Greeks, who, having endowed him with attributes derived from Pluto and Asklepios, named this half Greek, half Egyptian deity Sarapis or Serapis" (A. Wiedemann). Serapis was worshipped throughout the Roman Empire. See Adolf Erman; Alfred Wiedemann.

SERMON ON THE MOUNT, CHRISTIAN. A discourse of Jesus, so called because in the Gospel according to Matthew (chap. v.) it was delivered on a mountain. It might equally well be called the Sermon in the plain, since in the Gospel according to Luke (vi. 17, 20-49), it is said to have been delivered in a plain. Our most valuable source for the Christianity of Christ, the Sermon on the Mount is in its present form an artificial combination of sayings of the Lord (Arno Neumann, *Jesus*, 1906). "The discourse, which in both Evangelists begins with the beatitudes and ends with the parable of the prudent and the foolish builder, is in Mt. interspersed with a great number of sayings of the Lord, which Lk. gives in other parts of his gospel; and even what is peculiar to Mt. in the discourse may have been taken from another setting" (Oscar Holtzman, *Life of Jesus*, 1904).

SERMON ON THE MOUNT, MUHAMMADAN. A sermon delivered by Muhammad on the occasion of his last pilgrimage to the Kaaba. It was delivered on the Mount of 'Arafah, the "Mount of Recognition," situated twelve miles from Mecca. Here the pilgrims stay on the ninth day of their pilgrimage. To account for the name of the Mount there is a legend recounted by Burton (and quoted by T. P. Hughes). "When our first parents forfeited heaven for eating wheat, which deprived them of their primeval purity, they were cast down upon earth. The serpent descended upon Ispahān, the peacock at Cābul; Satan at Bilbays (others say Semnān or Seistān), Eve upon 'Arafāt, and Adam at Ceylon (Sarandib). The latter, determining to seek his wife, began a journey, to which the earth owes its present mottled appearance. Wherever our first father placed his foot, which was large, a town afterwards arose; and between the strides will always be country. Wandering for many years, he came to the Mountain of Mercy, where our common mother was continually calling upon his name, and their *recognition* of each other gave the place the name of *'Arafah*." The sermon of Muhammad, which has been only partly preserved, is given by Syed Ameer Ali. "Ye people! listen to my words, for I know not whether another year will be vouchsafed to me after this year to find myself amongst you. Your lives and property are sacred and inviolable amongst one another until ye appear before the Lord, as this day and this month is sacred for all; and remember ye shall have to appear before your Lord, who shall demand from you an account of all your actions. Ye people, ye have rights over your wives, and your wives have rights over you . . . treat your wives with kindness . . . verily ye have taken them on the security of God, and made them lawful unto you by the words of God. And your bondsmen and bondswomen. See that ye feed them with such food as ye eat yourselves, and clothe them with the stuff ye wear; and if they commit a fault which ye are not inclined to forgive, then part from them, for they are the servants of the Lord, and are not to be harshly treated. Ye people! listen to my words, and understand the same. Know that all Moslems are brothers unto one another. Ye are one brotherhood. Nothing which belongs to another is lawful unto his brother, unless freely given out of good will. Guard yourselves from committing injustice. Let him that is present tell it unto him that is absent. Haply he that shall be told may remember better than he who hath heard it." See T. P. Hughes; Syed Ameer Ali, *Islām*, 1906.

SERPENT, BRAZEN. It is of interest to note that a bronze figure of a cobra has been found in the "High Place" at Gezer (cp. II. Kings xviii. 4).

SERPENTINIANS. Another name for the Ophites (*q.v.*).

SERVITES. The Servites or the "Religious Servants of the Holy Virgin" were founded in 1233 by seven merchants of Florence. These merchants met together on the Festival of the Assumption, and agreed to renounce the world. They sold their goods, took up their abode in a house outside the city, practised great austerity, and begged their bread in the streets. They next built a convent on the top of Monte Senario. In 1306 Juliana Falconieri, niece of one of the seven merchants, Alexis Falconieri, founded the Servite Third Order, a branch for women. In 1487 Innocent VIII. "bestowed on the Servites equal privileges and prerogatives with those enjoyed by the other four mendicant orders—viz., the Franciscans, the Dominicans, the Augustinian Hermits, and the Carmelites" (Cath. Dict.). The Servites are well represented in Italy, Austria, and Germany. See *Prot. Dict.*; *Cath. Dict.*, 1905; Brockhaus.

SET. An Egyptian deity. Set was the personification of Evil, of such things as drought, darkness, disease, etc. As such he was greatly feared by gods and men alike. The kings of the Old Kingdom, in order to be on good terms with the powers of Good and Evil, represented themselves as being Set as well as Horus (*q.v.*). In late times fear was converted into hatred, and his adherents were persecuted. In the New Kingdom he became known as Sûtekh, a name which is simply a lengthened form of Set. His figure was human, but he is represented with the head of an animal, perhaps that of a camel. He holds a sceptre. In the Osiris myth, Set is the wicked brother of Osiris and is defeated by Horus. Herodotus in his identification of Greek with Egyptian gods, identifies the gigantic Typhon with Set. See Alfred Wiedemann; Adolf Erman *Handbook;* Naville, *The Old Egyptian Faith*, 1909.

SEVEN BISHOPS, THE. In 1687 James the Second of England issued a Declaration of Indulgence which provided that Roman Catholics, as well as Protestant Nonconformists, should have full right of public worship. In 1688 he ordered the clergy of the Church of England to read it publicly in their churches. Thereupon seven bishops drew up, and presented to the King, a petition protesting against the Declaration. They said, moreover, that they could neither read it themselves nor order it to be read. In consequence of this action it was read only in a few churches. The King had the bishops arrested and prosecuted. When, however, the trial took place, the bishops were acquitted. The seven rebels were: (1) William Sancroft (1617-1693), Archbishop of Canterbury; (2) Thomas Ken (1637-1711), Bishop of Bath and Wells; (3) William Lloyd (1627-1717), Bishop of St. Asaph; (4) Francis Turner (1638?-1700), Bishop of Ely; (5) John Lake (1624-1689), Bishop of Chichester; (6) Thomas White (1628-1698), Bishop of Peterborough; and (7) Sir Jonathan Trelawny (1650-1721), Bishop of Bristol. See M. W. Patterson, *Hist;* and the *D.N.B.*

SEVENTH DAY MEN. A name given afterwards to those who were called originally Traskites (*q.v.*).

SEVERIANS. The Severians were an Encratite body or sect. According to Eusebius (*H.E.* iv. 29) they were so named from one Severus who flourished soon after Tatian. According to Epiphanius he preceded Tatian. The statement of Eusebius, who is supported by Theodoret and Jerome, is more likely to be correct. Eusebius tells us also that the Severians used the Law, the Prophets, and the Gospels, but interpreted them in their own way; but they rejected the Pauline Epistles and the Acts of the Apostles, and abused the Apostle Paul. G. Salmon suggests that this shews Ebionite features, and that " these Severians may have been of Ebionite origin, for great diversity probably existed between the teaching of persons classed together as Encratites. The Severians are described by Epiphanius (*Hær.* 45) with all the features of an Ophite sect; but evidently from hearsay only, as he speaks of the sect as having almost died out" (*Dict. of Christian Biogr.*, *s.v.* "Encratites"). According to Augustine (*Haer.* xxiv.), the Severians' belief that matter is essentially evil led them to deny the resurrection of the body. See J. H. Blunt; Wace and Piercy.

SEWĀRĀM. Servant of Rāma (King of Ayodhia, a great incarnation of Vishnu), one of the names of the Hindu god Rāma.

SGĀNA. A term used among the Haida of N. America to denote a mystic potentiality ascribed to beings whether human or non-human, living or not living. *Sgāna* seems to be a force, and not a personal being, and corresponds to the Melanesian *mana*.

SHABBĀTH. The title of one of the Jewish treatises or tractates which reproduce the oral tradition or unwritten law as developed by the second century A.D. and are incorporated in the Mishnah (*q.v.*), a collection and compilation completed by Rabbi Judah the Holy, or the Patriarch, about 200 A.D. The sixty-three tractates of the Mishnah are divided into six groups or orders (*sedarim*). Shabbāth is the first tractate of the second group, which is called *Mō'ēd* (" Festival ").

SHADDAI. One of the names given to God in the Old Testament. The precise meaning of the word is uncertain. Rabbinic scholars understood it to mean " he who is sufficient " (*she-day*). The Vulgate has " omnipotens." Some modern scholars have explained it to mean " almighty " (from *shādad* " to deal violently "); others " the high one " (from Assyrian *šadû*, " high "). Others would pronounce the word *shēdi*. This would mean " my sovereign lord " (literally, " my protecting spirit "). By others the word has been connected with a root *shadah* " to pour forth." The reference would then be to God as the rain-giver. See the *Oxford Heb. Lex*.

SHAITĀN. A name of the devil in Muslim theology. Another name is IBLĪS (*q.v.*).

SHAKERS. The Shakers, as founded in 1776 in North America by Ann Lee (1736-1784), were an offshoot of the Society of Friends or the Quakers (*q.v.*). In 1758 Ann Lee had joined in England some seceders from the Society of Friends, who had already received the nickname " Shaking Quakers " or " Shakers." She became head of these in 1770, being elected " spiritual Mother in Christ." In 1774 she went to America and founded a Shaker Society there. Ann Lee professed to be a prophetess and worker of miracles. The Shakers believe that sacraments are unnecessary, that celibacy is a holier state than matrimony, and that goods should be held in common. The name Shakers was suggested by a peculiar kind of jerk or movement which they used at their religious services. They called themselves also " The United Society of Believers " and " The Millennial Church." See J. H. Blunt; the *D.N.B.*; Brockhaus.

SHALA. A Babylonian deity. The goddess Shala appears as the consort of Ramman (*q.v.*). The name Shala means simply " lady." Jastrow suggests that it may have been applied also to other goddesses. See Morris Jastrow, *Rel.*

SHAMAN. A term used by anthropologists to denote those who exercise the functions of priest, sorcerer, and medicine man. Its adoption was suggested by its use among the Tunguz, a tribe of South-Eastern Siberia.

SHAMANISM. Shamanism is a term used to describe the religion of the Turanian races of Siberia. The term was suggested by Shaman, the name for the Siberian priest-magician. The Shaman undertakes to cure disease, or avert death, or safely conduct souls to the other world. In the performance of their magical rites, they work themselves up into a state of ecstasy or delirium to the sound of music. According to Reinach, the priests are actually chosen from among epileptics or persons who know how to work themselves up into a state of ecstasy. They deal in talismans, and sacrifice horses to good and evil spirits. In order to knit one another closely together, to form a Blood Brotherhood, they drink or mingle blood. F. J. Gould, following A. Réville, gives a lively description of the priest-magician. A strange figure suddenly appears. " Amid his rags little bells tinkle, and rude images of beasts and fishes, shaped out of old iron and connected by iron rings, clash together as he advances. These figures are endowed with magical virtue. The sorcerer's head-dress is decorated with two iron horns. In one hand he holds a magic rod enveloped in rat or sable skin; with the other he continually beats a sort of tambourine; both hands being gloved with bearskin. He leaps and capers, crosses his legs in a wild dance, howling and tambouring all the time. When his ecstasy has reached its pitch his look becomes fixed. He falls as if in a swoon, oblivious of all around. At length the prophetic spasm passes off. The Shaman quietly rises, and is ready to declare to his questioners the decision of the gods." The Shaman invests all the mysterious phenomena of nature with spirits, good and evil. These spirits he believes he can control. The chief spirit is Ukko, the Heaven-god. The term Shaman is a corrupt form of Sramana, a name which was given to Buddha and then to all Buddhist priests. See F. J. Gould, *Concise Hist. of Rel.*, 1907; Reinach, O., 1909; E. H. Parker, *Studies;* Max B. Weinstein, *Welt- und Leben-anschauungen*, 1910.

SHAMASH. A Babylonian deity. Shamash was the sun-god. Important as he was, he was regarded as subordinate to the moon-god, Sin (*q.v.*), and his name means "servitor." In the early days he was worshipped particularly at Sippar. He was called the king or the shepherd. He is the light which gives life, and banishes darkness, that is to say, misfortune and disease. He is the judge who decides the fates of men. Righteousness represents his light; wickedness the absence of his light, darkness. This righteousness in connection with Shamash comes to be more emphasized under the Assyrian kings. Shalmaneser II. calls himself "the sun" of the world. He describes Shamash as the messenger of the gods, the lord of law. But Shamash is still the warrior who gives help in battle. Sargon II. called one of the eastern gates of his palace "Shamash, who grants victory." In the Gilgamesh Epic (*q.v.*) Shamash is represented as the patron of Gilgamesh, who has given into his hand "sceptre and decision." He is the patron also of Etana (See ETANA). Etana beseeches Shamash to give him "the plant of birth." The eagle who helps Etana in his search for the plant would seem to have been sent by Shamash. But afterwards it loses the favour of Shamash and is destroyed by a serpent with the help of the sun-god. In the same legend there is a reference to a conflict between Shamash and Zu, which implies that Shamash had caught Zu in his net. In the Zu-myth (*q.v.*), however, in the form in which it has been preserved to us, Marduk (*q.v.*) appears as the conqueror of Zu. Shamash is sometimes called Malik. His consort appears as Malkatu. See Morris Jastrow, *Rel.*

SHANKAR. He who gives happiness, one of the names of the Hindu god Siva.

SHAPE-SHIFTING. The belief that persons may be re-born in a new shape is almost universal. In the new birth the form may not be human, and the sex may be changed. The Warramunga and Urabunna, two of the tribes of Central Australia, according to Spencer and Gillen, believe that with each successive birth the sex changes.

SHEBI'ITH. The Jewish Mishnah, a collection and compilation completed by Rabbi Judah the Holy, or the Patriarch, about 200 A.D. (see MISHNAH), comprises a number of treatises or tractates which reproduce the oral tradition or unwritten law as developed by the second century A.D. There are sixty-three tractates, divided into six groups or orders (*sedarim*). Shebī'ith is the fifth tractate of the first group, which is called *Zerā'im* ("Seeds").

SHEBŪ'ŌTH. The name of one of the Jewish treatises or tractates which reproduce the oral tradition or unwritten law as developed by the second century A.D. and are incorporated in the Mishnah (*q.v.*), a collection and compilation completed by Rabbi Judah the Holy, or the Patriarch, about 200 A.D. The sixty-three tractates of the Mishnah are divided into six groups or orders (*sedarim*). Shebū'ōth is the sixth tractate of the fourth group, which is called *Neziḳīn* ("Damages").

SHEḲALIM. The name of one of the Jewish treatises or tractates which reproduce the oral tradition or unwritten law as developed by the second century A.D. and are incorporated in the Mishnah (*q.v.*), a collection and compilation completed by Rabbi Judah the Holy, or the Patriarch, about 200 A.D. The sixty-three tractates of the Mishnah are divided into six groups or orders (*sedarim*). Sheḳālim is the fourth tractate of the second group, which is called *Mō'ēd* ("Festival").

SHEKHINAH. The word Shekhinah is derived from a Hebrew root meaning "to dwell" (*shākēn*). It is used in the Talmud (*q.v.*) of some divine influence which dwells with men. This influence seems at times to be regarded as a person. In the "Sayings of the Fathers" it is said that "two that sit together and are occupied in words of Torah have the *Shekhinah* among them." Oesterley and Box compare the passage in the Gospel of Matthew (xviii. 20): "Where two or three are gathered together in My name, there am I in the midst of them." The Shekhinah seems in fact to correspond sometimes to what Christians understand by the Holy Ghost. It also corresponds to the Logos. "*Shekhinah* is sometimes equivalent to *Memra* (Logos), but we may distinguish between them by regarding the one as the medium of a *passive*, the other of an *active* manifestation; the one a creative, the other as over-shadowing or indwelling. The two are brought together by St. John, in whose theology the conceptions assume a new definiteness, and the medium becomes a Mediator: *The Word (Logos) became flesh and tabernacled among us* (i. 14)" (Taylor in *Sayings of the Jewish Fathers*). See W. O. E. Oesterley and G. H. Box.

SHEN. A Chinese term. The *shen* are good souls or spirits, a sub-division of Yang (*q.v.*), the light-soul of the universe. A man's *shen*, also called *hwun*, "immaterial, ethereal, like heaven itself from which it emanates, constitutes his intellect and the finer parts of his character, his virtues" (J. J. M. de Groot). The evil spirit or *kwei* is responsible for the passions and vices in a man. But the universe is full of shen and kwei. "The gods are such *shen* as animate heaven, sun, moon, the stars, wind, rain, clouds, thunder, fire, the earth, seas, mountains, rivers, rocks, stones, animals, plants, things—in particular also the souls of deceased men. Innumerable kwei swarm everywhere." De Groot points out that "in effect, each member of the human race, since he has a *shen*, is a god, and each god may become a man by descending into a human body." See J. J. M. de Groot, *Rel. of the Chinese*, 1910.

SHEN NUNG. A legendary emperor of China, who is supposed to have reigned from 2838 to 2698 B.C. He is reputed to have been miraculously conceived, and to have taught his people agriculture and the uses of certain plants in medicine.

SHEO PRASAD. Gift of Siva, one of the names of the Hindu god Siva.

SHESH NĀG. A figure in Hindu mythology. One of the superstitions held by the Kurmis, the representative cultivating caste of Hindustān, is concerned with Shesh Nāg. "When an astrologer is about to found a house he calculates the direction in which Shesh Nāg, the snake on whom the world reposes, is holding his head at that time, and plants the first brick or stone to the left of that direction, because snakes and elephants do not turn to the left but always to the right. Consequently, the house will be more secure and less likely to be shaken down by Shesh Nāg's movements, which cause the phenomenon known to us as an earthquake" (R. V. Russell).

SHEWBREAD. The Hebrew expression translated Shewbread (from Luther's *Schaubrot*) means literally "bread of the face" or "presence-bread" (*lechem hap-*

pānim). It is also described as "the continual bread" or "bread of ordering" or "hallowed bread." In I. Samuel xxi. 4-6 we are told that David, when ordinary bread could not be found, commandeered shewbread. "So the priest gave him holy bread, for there was no bread there but the shewbread, that was taken from before Jehovah in order to put hot bread there the day it was taken away" (after C. F. Kent). Shewbread was bread which was set before Jehovah in the sanctury, the original idea being that he would accept it as his food. A. Jeremias thinks that the name "bread of the countenance" has reference to beholding God in the mysteries of the cult. He compares the Babylonian texts of ritual, according to which twelve loaves were laid before the deity. They had to be made of fine flour, and to be sweet. The custom of offering food to the gods was widespread in ancient times. Among the Romans, banquets (*lectisternia*) were sometimes offered to the twelve great gods (cp. Isaiah lxv. 11; Baruch vi. 30). See *Encycl. Bibl.*; A. Jeremias, *The O.T. in the Light of the Ancient East*, 1911; S. R. Driver, *The Book of Exodus*, 1911.

SHI'AH, THE. A Muslim sect which differs from the Sunnis on the question of the Imâmate (see IMÂM). The name means "followers or companions." The Shî'ahs maintain that 'Ali was really the first legitimate Imâm, and that he, and not Abu Bakr, was the immediate successor of the Prophet. They would only recognise 'Ali and his descendents. "Many of the Shî'ahs carried their veneration for 'Ali and his descendants so far that they transgressed all bounds of reason and decency, though some of them were less extravagant than others. The branch of the 'Ghália' (extravagant, fanatic) raised their Imâms (descendants of 'Ali) above the degrees of created beings and attributed to them divine properties. Some affirmed that 'Ali was not dead, but would return again in the clouds and fill the earth with justice. They held the doctrine of metempsychosis, and what they call the immanency, the indwelling of God in man." See F. A. Klein.

SHIĀMSUNDAR. The dark and beautiful one, one of the names of the Hindu god Krishna.

SHIBBOLETH. A Hebrew word meaning "a flowing stream." According to a story in the Old Testament (Judges xii. 6), it was made a test of dialect during a battle between Gileadites and Ephraimites. "And the Gileadites seized the fords of the Jordan to intercept the Ephraimites; and when one of the survivors of the Ephraimites would say: Let me cross, the men of Gilead would ask him: Art thou an Ephraimite? And if he answered: No, they would bid him say Shibboleth; and if he said Sibboleth, and could not pronounce it as they did, they took him, and slaughtered him at the fords of the Jordan" (G. F. Moore's translation, "The Sacred Books of the Old and New Testaments," 1898).

SHI-KING. One of the Chinese Classics. The *Shï* is the "Book of Odes" (*q.v.*). *King* simply means "Classic."

SHINGON SECT. A Japanese Buddhist sect founded by Kôbô Daishi (A.D. 806). Hackmann describes it as "the *mantra* school of Japan," because it attaches special importance to the magic word or spell (see MANTRA). The teaching of the school is of a mystical and esoteric character. See H. Hackmann.

SHIN SECT. A Japanese Buddhist sect founded by Shinran Shonin A.D. 1224. It was originally called the Jôdoshin sect. It attaches the greatest important to faith. "This faith is an inward firm conviction of the good-will and help of the deity, more especially of Amida, who almost entirely holds the position of a highest god in the Western sense. Faith is the foundation of the whole religious life. Compared with the power of faith, all other religious devices—prayer, good works, asceticism, a monastic life—are of secondary value." In this sect no special importance is attached to monasticism or celibacy. The priests are allowed to marry and to live an ordinary human life. They are said to be disposed to adopt Western methods; but their faith in Buddhism remains unimpaired. See H. Hackmann.

SHINTŌISM. When Buddhism was introduced into Japan from Korea and China, some term was needed to designate the ancient faith of the Japanese as distinct from the new religion. The term chosen was in Japanese Kami-no-michi, and in Chinese Shinto. Both expressions mean the "Way of the Genii, or Spirits." In course of time Shinto borrowed features from Buddhism. It then became necessary to distinguish between this mixed religion and Pure Shintōism. The former received the name Ryobu-Shinto or "double religion." Although Buddhism was favoured by the ancient nobility, in 1868 Shintoism was decreed to be the State or Established Religion. The Government undertook to pay a large sum of money annually for its maintenance. And whereas for several centuries Buddhist and Shinto priests had officiated in turns at the same altars in the same temples, the temples had to be declared either Shinto or Buddhist. G. A. Cobbold points out that, as far as the practice of the people is concerned, this has made little difference. "The people still practise the observances of both religions alike; the only difference being that, to effect this, they have now to visit two temples instead of one. A new-born child, for instance, is taken by its parents to both Shinto and Buddhist temples, for the purpose of solemn dedication." D. Goh thinks that Shintoism cannot be classified as one of the religions of the world. It is simply the State religion of Japan, in its main and original features a simple religion of filial piety (reverence for ancestors) and patriotism (reverence for the Imperial dynasty). He holds that Shintō is distinguished by five peculiarities. One of these is that it has no sacred books or moral code. The absence of sacred books is not, however, a peculiarity. The Druids, for example, had no sacred (that is to say, written) books. And it hardly seems true to say that Shintoism has no moral code. Another peculiarity is said to be that Shintoism makes no distinction between the mythology and the history of the nation. This is not, however, a peculiar feature, but is common to other religions (*e.g.*, the religions of the ancient Americans, Celts, and Teutons). A third peculiarity is said to be that, as regards a future state, Shintōism, though it believes in the eternal existence of spirits, recognises no Paradise or Hell. But the fact seems to be that some of the real principles or doctrines of pure Shintōism are uncertain. D. Goh himself declares that Shintōism has been corrupted by contact with Buddhism. There does not really seem to be much that is peculiar to Shintōism. Its development appears to have been very similar to that of other religions. Reverence has been paid not only to heroes, sovereigns, and other men, but also to animals, such as foxes and serpents, and to natural objects, such as trees, rocks, rivers, mountains, etc. These and other features suggest on the whole a common and well-known line of development. There are some special points which have remarkable parallels in other religions. Shintoists believe that the human breath may cause ritual defilement. The priests, therefore, when they offer sacrifice, wear masks. Similarly we learn from Saxo Grammaticus that the priests of the Slav deity Svantovit (*q.v.*) were not allowed to breathe in the temple. Whenever they wanted to breathe they had to go outside. Again, the symbol of the ancient Mexican god Tezcatlipoca (*q.v.*) was a mirror of metal or stone; and a mirror is one of the chief symbols in Shintoism. As regards Shinto worship, the first historical emperor, Jimmu Tenno, who is said to have ascended the throne on the seventh of April 660 B.C., was deified, and is worshipped in a thousand temples. From him every Mikado has claimed direct descent. Jimmu Tenno himself, it is said, was fifth in descent from the sun-goddess Ama-terasu, who in turn was born from the left eye of the creator of Japan, Izanagi. The heroes of Japanese mythology and history, who are the chief objects of worship in Shintōism, are all the children of Izanagi. Properly speaking, there is no public worship. The priests perform a service of their own every morning and evening. The ordinary person when he wishes to worship in a temple, goes to one and attracts the attention of the deity by ringing a bell or sounding a gong. Then, after throwing down a coin, he prostrates himself, says a silent prayer, and finally claps his hands. Forms of prayer, though they exist, are not necessary. It is enough "to frame a wish without uttering it, and most Shintôists content themselves with turning to the sun in the early morning, rubbing the hands slowly together, and bowing" (I. Bishop). But if there is no public worship, worship in the home is not neglected. Every house has its Kamidana, or god-shelf, on which stands a miniature temple of wood. Here are placed paper-covered tablets inscribed with the names of the patron deities of the household, as well as the monumental or ancestral tablets of the family. And here also are offered sprigs of the sacred evergreen *cleyera japonica*, rice beer, and a portion of the rice cooked daily for the household. One of the gods whose names are written on the paper-covered tablets is always Ten-shôkô-daijin, the chief deity of Isé, the centre of Shintô. The Ten-shôkô-daijin tablet contains inside "some shavings of the wands used by the priests of Isé at the two annual festivals, and is able to protect its possessor from misfortune for half a year" (I. Bishop). One of the emblems of Shintōism is a slender wand to which are attached strips of white paper. Another is a structure, commonly made of wood, which is called "birds' rest," because the birds offered to the gods used to rest on it. The rope of rice straw, another emblem, hangs across temple entrances or house doors or round sacred trees. But the chief symbol, which has been mentioned already (see also IZANAGI), is the mirror. Above the altar in many Shintō temples a large circular steel mirror is to be seen. In a box below a sword and a stone are commonly kept. As votive offerings stone lanterns are erected in the grounds of the temples. Isé is a kind of Mecca to the Shintoists, and throughout the year pilgrimages are made to its temples. Relics of Isé are taken home as precious treasures and potent charms. The number of Shinto gods is endless. In addition to those already mentioned, two of the most popular gods are Binzuru (*q.v.*), the medicine god, and Daikoku (*q.v.*), the household god and guide, whose image is to be found in every home. Reinach notes that there is evidence of fire-worship in Shintōism. The custom of "passage through fire" is a ceremony or ordeal of purification. In earlier times, it is said, human sacrifice was in vogue, but afterwards clay statuettes were substituted. See G. A. Cobbold, *Rel. in Japan*, 1894; K. Florenz, "Die Religionen der Japaner" in *Orientalische Religionen*, 1906; D. Goh and I. Bishop, "Shintōism," in *R.S.W.*, 1908; Reinach, *O.*, 1909; Max B. Weinstein, *Welt- und Leben-Anschauungen*, 1910.

SHORTER CATECHISM, THE. The Shorter Catechism was one of the results of the consultations of the Westminster Assembly of Divines (*q.v.*). It was prepared in 1647 by a small committee, which made use of the Westminster Confession (*q.v.*), the Larger Catechism, and a number of other catechisms In 1648 it was approved by the Church of Scotland, in which "it became at once, and has remained, a household book, a Bible in miniature, and the working Creed of the nation" (W. A. Curtis). Curtis speaks of the Catechism as "an acknowledged masterpiece, a triumph of happy arrangement, of condensed and comprehensive instruction, of lucid and forceful expression." See William A. Curtis.

SHU. An Egyptian deity. The god Shu was the "supporter of the heavens." Shu and the goddess Tefnet (*q.v.*) were the offspring of Re (or Râ), the Sun-god. Shu appears as a man with a feather on his head. When represented with Tefnet, however, he appears as a lion. The offspring of Shu and Tefnet, Nut, the sky, and Keb, the earth, had to be separated by Shu. Shu came to be regarded as the protector against evil spirits and other foes. In the later magic his figure, "represented as a young prince in his chariot slaying lions," possesses great efficacy. See A. Wiedemann; Adolf Erman, *Handbook*.

SHU-KING. One of the Chinese Classics. *Shu* is the "Book of History" (*q.v.*). *King* simply means "Classic."

SHUNAMITE'S HOUSE, THE. According to a narrative in the Old Testament (II. Kings iv.), the prophet Elisha was entertained by a Shunammite woman. It appears that there existed formerly in London an establishment called "The Shunamite's House," in which were lodged clergymen who came to London to preach at Paul's Cross. Walton in his *Life of Hooker* (1581) speaks of it as "a house, so called, for that, besides the stipend paid the preacher, there is provision made also for his lodging and diet, for two days before, and one after his sermon." See Robert Nares, *Glossary*, 1822.

SIBI. A Babylonian deity. The god Sibi is mentioned in the Dibbarra Epic (*q.v.*). He is described as "a warrior without rival." Since Sibi means "seven," it has been suggested that the god is a personification of the seven evil spirits. See Morris Jastrow, *Rel.*

SIDEROMANCY. A species of divination. Sideromancy was practised in ancient times "by placing straws on red-hot iron, and drawing inferences as to the will of the gods from the manner of their burning" (James Gardner, *Faiths of the World*).

SIKHISM. The Sikhs, literally the "disciples," are a body which was founded in India by the great religious teacher Nānak (1469-1538 A.D.), who was himself a follower of Kabīr (see KABIR PANTHIS). Nānak's disciples idolized him after his death, and, amongst other things, declared that his birth had been proclaimed by all the Hindū gods. He was announced as a saviour of the world. In any case, after studying diligently the religion of Vishnu (*q.v.*) in the sacred books, he became an earnest teacher and a zealous reformer. Living in a part of India in which there were many Muhammadans, his ideal seems to have been to unite the Hindūs and Muhammadans in a common form of theistic religion. He acknowledged One Supreme Lord, whom he preferred to call Hari (Vishnu), but to whom he gave also other names such as Brahmā, Govinda. The Universe is evolved out of the Supreme Being. It is a kind of extension of himself (cp. SPINOZISM). Separation between God and the human soul or between God and the world is caused simply by Māyā (*q.v.*) or Illusion. Reduced to a single formula, it has been pointed out that the principles of Nānak amounted to the Unity of God and the Brotherhood of Man. The practical application of these principles "led to the formation of a new nationality, the disciples of the great teacher becoming a republican fraternity, which gradually consolidated into a separate nation by the necessity for struggling for the liberty they claimed " (F. Pincott). Instead of Hindūs and Muhammadans being drawn together, Sikhs and Muhammadans became bitterly opposed to one another as political bodies with conflicting aims and ambitions. Nānak was succeeded by nine other chief Gurus. The fourth Guru, Rām-dās, built the lake-temple at Amṛitsar. The fifth Guru, Arjun, united the Sikhs more closely by compiling for them their first bible, the Granth or Book, by making Amritsar the centre and metropolis of Sikhism, and by ruling the Sikhs as a kind of pontiff. Arjun was imprisoned as a rebel, and perhaps was killed by the Muhammadans. From this time the Sikhs began to develop their warlike propensities. When the ninth Guru was cruelly tortured by the Muhammadan Emperor Aurangzib, the Sikhs became, as Monier-Williams says, a nation of fighting men. It was under the tenth Guru, Govind, that the Sikhs became a nation. They now assumed the name Singhs or "Lions of the Punjāb." Govind completed their organization. He compiled a second bible and wrote a book for it called the Book of the tenth Guru. "In his own supplement Govind adhered to the religious teaching of the Ādi-Granth, but he introduced precepts the direct object of which was to rouse the martial ardour of his followers" (Monier-Williams). The original Granth came to be called Ādigranth, the First Book, to distinguish it from this later and larger compilation. The new Granth was to take the place of the last of the Gurus, to be a Granth-Sāhib. The Sikhs have a special objection to the worship of images, but they have made their sacred book into a kind of idol. Monier-Williams found that at Amṛitsar "the Granth is, in fact, the real divinity of the shrine, and is treated as if it had a veritable personal existence." It is said that many of the Sikhs have now returned to the ordinary practices of the Hindus. See Monier-Williams; E. W. Hopkins; Sir Lepel Griffin in *Great Religions of the World*, 1902; F. Pincott in *R.S.W.*; J. C. Oman, *Cults*.

SILENUS. A god of Asia Minor. A divinity of woods and fountains, people tried to catch him and to make him prophesy and sing to them. It is said that King Midas of Phrygia thus learned all kinds of wisdom. Silenus came to be regarded as the teacher and constant companion of Dionysus. To him Dionysus owed his highest aspirations and much of his success and fame. To his inspiration was due the cultivation of the vine and the keeping of bees. In the famous group in the Vatican at Rome he is represented as nursing the infant Dionysus. With him were associated *Silenuses (Sileni)*, woodland deities corresponding to the young Pans and the Fauns (see FAUNUS). Silenus and the Silenuses are supposed to have taught men the use of the flute. In later art the god presents a degraded figure. He appears "as a little old man, pot-bellied, with bald head and snub nose, his whole body very hairy; never without his skin of wine, always drunk, and hence usually riding on an ass, and led and supported by the other Satyrs" (O. Seyffert). See O. Seyffert, *Dict.*; J. M. Robertson, *C.M.*; J. G. Frazer, *G.B.*, Pt. v., vol. ii.

SILVANUS. An ancient Italian deity, worshipped originally as a god of woods and trees. He resembled Faunus (*q.v.*). In course of time Silvanus came to be regarded as the protector of the house, of shepherds and flocks, and of boundaries. He came also, like Faunus, to be identified with the Greek god Pan (*q.v.*). And Silvanus was supposed to have his Silvanuses (*Silvani*), just as Pan had his young Pans, and Faunus his Fauns. On this see further FAUNUS. See O. Seyffert, *Dict.*

SIMIA. A Syrian deity. A daughter of Hadad, she was worshipped at Hierapolis. In Latin inscriptions she appears as Juno Regina. Simia is associated with Aphrodite and Hadad, and is represented with a dove on her head.

SIMONIANISM, ST. The School of thought founded by Count St. Simon (1760-1825), who seems to have been influenced by the philosophy of Jean Jacques Rousseau (1712-1778). The origin and aims of St. Simonianism are described admirably by Edward Vansittart Neale (1810-1892), who became one of the first members of the Christian Social Union. "St. Simon was nurtured among the stirring scenes of the last half of the Eighteenth Century. Sprung from an ancient family of French noblesse, he grew up to manhood while the power of the *Grand Monarque* was still unbroken. He took an active part in that war of American Independence, the prelude to the great European movement, becoming a colonel under Washington at the age of twenty-three. He saw society shaken to its basis by the hurricane of the French Revolution, terminating in the dazzling but brief effort of Napoleon to create a new European unity by military power." After producing several preliminary works which aimed at explaining methods of reorganizing society upon a new basis, he published his "Treatise du Nouveau Christianisme," which soon after his death became the foundation of the system known as St. Simonianism. The philosophy of the Simonians had an essentially religious character. "The destination of mankind, they taught, bound up in God with that of the globe they inhabit, was accomplished progressively. The end of man was happiness, which he could obtain only by a religious union with those of his own race and with the world which surrounds him. The grandest desire which mankind could form for social and individual happiness was that of the religious and political association of all nations among themselves, of all the families of the same nation, and of all the individuals of the same family, and of the harmony between the two halves of the human race, the man and the woman, whose union by the institution of marriage forms the type and germ of all other associations. Association was defined to be the union of men to work together and enjoy peaceably the fruits of their labour: the worth of man in association would be measured by the special portion which he could personally accomplish of the common task; this constituted his capacity, otherwise called his personality or liberty. But men were born with unequal and different capacities; this was the law of God, a holy law, which man should love as the condition of his progress. In consequence association implied a hierarchy, that is a division of different tasks according to men's different vocations or aptitudes, and a combination of efforts by the subordination of the inferior to the superior capacities, terminating in the result of the union of all in one social work which had as its basis the desires and the wants of all, and as its object the moral, intellectual, and physical amelioration of all; and was so arranged that every one would take part in it according to his capacity, and share in the results according to his work. In its complete form association would consist of artists, or priests; men of science, or theologians; and men of industry, otherwise called theurgists; and its outward object would be the embellishing and making useful to man the terrestial globe. The progress of mankind consisted in the degree of perfection attained in acting upon this law of association. In the most imperfect stage of human progress, from man's appearance upon the earth to the Christian era, the nature of the work assigned to each man and the reward allotted to him had depended upon his birth. Castes, slavery, serfdom, inheritance, the servitude of the most numerous class, *l'exploitation de l'homme par l'homme*, with their consequences, war, ignorance, misery, and disease, were the characteristics of this period; as, in the opposite stage, the emancipation of the most numerous class by the abolition of all the privileges of birth, with its results peace and love, the moral amelioration of mankind by the continual progress of religion expressed by the fine arts, their intellectual amelioration by the continual progress of science, and their physical amelioration by the continued progress of industry, would characterise the future, after the adoption of the perfect law announced by St. Simon." Unfortunately these doctrines lent themselves to abuses. To community of property was added afterwards community of women, and in 1832 St. Simonianism had to be suppressed by the French Governmen. Auguste Comte (1798-1857), however, was a disciple of St. Simon, and in his own philosophy, Positivism (*q.v.*), revived much of the teaching of his master. See Edward Vansittart Neale, *The Characteristic Features of some of the Principal Systems of Socialism*, 1851; J. H. Blunt; cp. Giuseppe Mazzini, *Thoughts upon Democracy in Europe*, 1847.

SIN. A Babylonian deity. Sin was the moon-god, who, as Nannar, in the early times was worshipped particularly at Ur, and was regarded as more important than the sun-god, Shamash (*q.v.*). The worship of Sin is particularly associated with Harran. But after the time of Hammurapi, Nannar and Sin became identical. Nannar was the "illuminator," and this character was transferred to Sin. Sin was represented as being the father of the goddess Ishtar (*q.v.*). As in the case of Marduk (*q.v.*), the child seems in course of time to a large extent to have taken the place of the parent. When, moreover, the lunar cycle was accommodated to the movements of the sun, Shamash naturally became more prominent than Sin. The Assyrian kings refer to sin as a war-god who inspires terror. The consort of Sin was Nin-gal. The ship in which Sin was carried in procession was called "ship of light." See Morris Jastrow, *Rel.*

SIN-EATER. A name which has been applied to a person who figured in funeral observances in Great Britain. He ate some food placed on the chest of the deceased, and by so doing was supposed to relieve the latter of his sins and take them upon himself. The practice may have come to be interpreted in this way, but its original significance was probably identical with that of the so-called corpse-cakes (*q.v.*) in the Highlands of Bavaria.

SINGBONGA. A Hindu deity, the sun, worshipped by the Turis, a non-Aryan caste of cultivators, workers in bamboo, and basket-makers in India. Singbonga is also the chief deity of the Mundas (also called Kols or Hos), a large tribe in Chota Nāgpur.

SINGHBĀHANI. A Hindu deity, a goddess worshipped by the Tameras, the professional caste of coppersmiths in India. She is represented riding on a tiger.

SINTHGUNT. An old Teutonic goddess mentioned in one of the Merseburg Charms (*q.v.*).

SIRMIUM, STONEMASONS OF. The famous Stonemasons of Sirmium were five Christians belonging to Pannonia who were martyred in the reign of Diocletian. They were employed in the imperial quarries, and worked with such skill that they excited the jealousy of the pagans. Ordered by the emperor to make, among other statues, a statue of Aesculapius (*q.v.*) they refused to do so. Thereupon their enemies were able to obtain an order for their execution. The five Christian stonemasons—one of them originally a pagan—were put in lead coffins and thrown into the Save. See Wace and Piercy.

SIRONA. Sirona appears as the name of one of the goddesses worshipped by the ancient Celts. She is paired with Grannus (*q.v.*), the Celtic Apollo. E. Anwyl thinks that probably the name meant "the long-lived one," and was used of the earth-mother.

SISTERHOOD OF ST. MARGARET'S, EAST GRINSTEAD. A Church of England Sisterhood founded in 1854. The Sisters are engaged in the conduct of Orphanages and Homes of Rest, in working ecclesiastical embroidery, and in education. Their books include "services in honour of the Saints, Invocation of Saints, Offices for the Dead, and for Corpus Christi Day" (Walsh). See Walter Walsh, "Sisterhoods, Ritualistic," in the *Prot. Dict.*

SISTERS OF THE CHURCH. A Church of England Sisterhood mainly devoted to educational work. The Sisters also conduct Convalescent Homes and Orphanages. They publish tracts and books of devotion, "several of them teaching Auricular Confession, Prayers for the Dead, and the Eucharistic Sacrifice" (Walsh). See Walter Walsh, "Sisterhoods, Ritualistic," in the *Prot. Dict.*

SISTRUM. A kind of rattle borrowed by the Romans from the Egyptians. The instrument, as shaken before Hathor or Isis or some other deity, was rounded at the top and had four transverse bars. Andrew Lang compares it with the "bull-roarer" (Australian *turndun*) used as a call to the ceremonial observance of tribal ritual. In ancient Egypt it was used also as a musical instrument. Cp. BULL-ROARER and CHURINGA.

SITA. A Hindu goddess, the wife of Rāma.

SITALA DEVI. An Indian deity, the Hindu goddess of small-pox, worshipped by the Parwārs, a sub-caste of the Jains.

SITARĀM. Rāma (King of Ayodhia, a great incarnation of Vishnu) and Sita, his wife, one of the names of the Hindu god Rāma.

SITTARS. The name Sittars taken by a modern sect in Southern India is equivalent to the old term Siddhas, "saints" or "perfect ones," which is used in reference to attendants upon Indra (*q.v.*), and to those who are initiated into the mysteries of Śaktism (*q.v.*). The Sittars may have been influenced either by Islam or by Christianity. The essence of religion they understand to be "kindness to all." Hopkins thinks that they seem to be the modern representatives of the Buddhistic division called Sāugatas (*q.v.*). "In these sects there is found quietism, a kind of quakerism, pure morality, high teaching, sternest (almost bigoted) monotheism, and the doctrine of positive altruism, strange to the Hindu idolator as to the Brahman." See E. W. Hopkins.

SIVA. Siva is one of the principal Hindu deities. He has developed out of the Vedic deity Rudra (*q.v.*). He is one of the triad, Brahmā, Vishnu (*q.v.*), and Siva; for at one time Brahmā was regarded as the Creator, Vishnu as the Preserver, and Siva as the Dissolver and Reproducer. Orthodox Brāhmans are generally worshippers of Śiva, or Vaishṇavas, worshippers of Vishnu. The ference for the worship of one or the other. The Hindus of modern times are usually either Śaivas, worshippers of Śiva, or Vaishṇavas, worshippers of Vishnu. The Śaivas worship one personal god Śiva as the Supreme Being. Monier-Williams points out that Śiva is represented as less human and more mystical than the incarnated Vishṇu. "The character in which he is most frequently worshipped is that of an omnipotent God, taking the place of Brahmā the Creator, and granting new life to all created things, but only through death and disintegration. Hence he is not represented by the image of a man, but by a mystic symbol—perhaps the best symbol of delegated creative power—which is not dressed or fed or put to sleep like Vishṇu's idols, but is supposed to be in a condition of perpetual heat and excitement, and requires to be cooled and appeased by constant sprinklings (abhisheka) of cold Ganges water and cooling Bilva leaves applied throughout the day by those who worship him." This symbol is the Linga (*q.v.*), which is often made of white stone, just as Vishnu is represented by a black stone, the Sālagrama (*q.v.*). Although Śiva never became incarnate in the sense that Vishnu did, he assumed a distinct personality and a variety of characters. His worshippers gave him more than a thousand names or epithets (1008). These include: The Mother (Mātā); The Father (Pitā); Extinction (Nirvāṇam); The Great Illusionist (Mahāmāyah); The White One (Śuklaḥ); The Mule (Haya-gardabhiḥ). Of his many characters, Monier-Williams thinks that five stand out prominently. 1. Śiva personifies the dissolving and disintegrating powers of nature. 2. He personifies the reproductive power of nature. 3. He is the type of asceticism and self-mortification. 4. He is the learned sage and contemplative philosopher. 5. He is the jovial mountaineer, who is fond of hunting, dancing, and drinking. The wife of Śiva appears with several names, which include Durgā or Kālī. The female energy corresponding to Śiva is called Śakti (see ŚAKTISM). See Monier-Williams; E. W. Hopkins; J. A. Dubois and H. K. Beauchamp.

SIVACHARS. According to the Mysore Census Report, 1901, the Lingāyats call themselves Vīra Śaivas, Sivabhaktas, or Sivachars. " The Vīrasaiva religion consists of numerous castes. It is a religion consisting of representatives from almost every caste in Hindu society."

SIX PRINCIPLE BAPTISTS. A body of Baptists in America, descendants of the Baptists of the first Baptist Church founded at Providence in Rhode Island (1639) by Roger Williams (1604?-1683). They called themselves " The Ancient Order of the Six Principles of the Doctrine of Christ and His Apostles." The principles were: repentance from dead works, faith in God, the doctrine of baptisms, laying on of hands (Confirmation), resurrection of the dead, and eternal judgment. See J. H. Blunt; cp. the *D.N.B.*

SJOFN. One of the deities of the Ancient Teutons. The goddess Sjofn belonged to the retinue of Frija (*q.v.*) and Freyja (*q.v.*), and seems to have been a goddess of love.

SKADHI. One of the deities of the Ancient Teutons. The goddess Skadhi, daughter of the giant Thjazi, and wife of the god Njordhr (*q.v.*), was Finnish. She is represented as hunting game with bow and arrow. Temples and groves are said to have been consecrated to her. See P. D. Chantepie de la Saussaye, *Rel. of the Teutons*, 1902.

SKANDA. Skanda, often called Kārttikeya and more often still Su-brahmaṇya, is one of the gods of the Hindus. He is one of the sons of Śiva (*q.v.*). To the extent that Skanda is the leader of the hosts of good demons against the evil demons he is the god of war. His name Su-brahmaṇya, however, means " very pious or sacred." His brother, Ganesa (*q.v.*), is represented as being unmarried, but Skanda has two wives. " These, like their husband, are believed to grant children, to prevent the attacks and thwart the malice of devils, and when evil spirits have actually taken possession of any one, to be capable of casting them out " (Monier-Williams). The difference between Skanda and Ganesa seems to be that Skanda leads the demon-host as a warrior, whereas Ganesa controls it as a king. The demons of Skanda who possess people are represented as being both male and female. It should be added that the animals of Skanda are the cock and the peacock. See Monier-Williams; E. W. Hopkins.

SKOPTZI. The Skoptzi or " Self-mutilators " are a branch of the Russian Khlisti (*q.v.*), who again are a sub-sect of the Russian dissenters known as Bezpopovtzi. They adhere closely to the principle contained in Matthew v. 30: " And if thy right hand causeth thee to stumble, cut it off, and cast it from thee, for it is profitable for thee that one of thy members should perish, and not thy whole body go into hell." They are ascetics, and practise flagellation and self-mutilation. Their own name for themselves is Karablik, a term meaning " a small ship." The Skoptzi do not observe Sunday, and they reject the doctrine of the resurrection of the body. See Schaff-Herzog; J. H. Blunt.

SMĀRTAS. One of the three principle classes into which the Hindus are divided for religious classification. The Smārtas believe in the Tri-mūrti, the three personal gods, Brahmā, Śiva, and Vishṇu; but they regard them " only as co-equal manifestations of the one eternal impersonal Spirit, and as destined ultimately to be re-absorbed into that Spirit and so disappear " (Monier-Williams). The spirit of man is identical with that one Spirit which is the essence of the Universe. The Smārta Brahmans are followers of the great eighth century teacher Śaṅkara. Śaṅkara, who was a strict Brāhman and " a typical representative of Brāhmanical doctrines," founded a number of monasteries in India. He would seem to have regarded Śiva and Vishṇu as equal manifestations of the Universal Spirit, though most modern Smārta Brāhmans have a preference for the worship of Śiva. According to Śaṅkara, " the separate existence of the spirit of man, as distinct from the one Universal Spirit, was only illusory. Illusion (Māyā), too—existing from all eternity—was the only material or substantial cause (upādāna-kāraṇa) of the external world, though this eternally creative Illusion was powerless to create the world except in union with the one Spirit " (Monier-Williams). See Monier-Williams; E. W. Hopkins.

SMECTYMNIANS. The name of a theological school or party. The leaders of the party were Stephen Marshal, Edmund Calamy (1600-1666), Thomas Young (1587-1655), Matthew Newcomen (1610?-1669), and William Spurstowe (1605?-1666). When Joseph Hall (1574-1656), Bishop of Exeter, published the " Divine Right of Episcopacy " (1640), these five men entered into a controversy with him and sought (1641) to refute his claim in a work " Smectymnuus." The title of the work was suggested by the initial letters of the names of the authors, and the party has been called the " Smectymnians." See John Hunt.

SNAKE-GODDESS. Snake-goddesses figured in Minoan worship. At Knossos a representation of a group of these was discovered. Some of them are well described by H. R. Hall (*A.A.*). "The two weird women stand there, figures of polychrome-faience a little over a foot high, attired in the latest Minoan female fashion of their day, and holding at arm's-length with strong and imperious gesture writhing and twisting serpents. A ' spotted snake with double tongue ' curls itself round the high head-dress of the chief figure, while on the head of the other, above what looks like a wreath, sits a spotted cat, with face looking straight at the worshipper." Mr. Hall points out that the association of the cat with the snake seems to have been a definite item of Minoan superstition, since it is paralleled elsewhere.

SNAKE WORSHIP. Among the Kunbis, the great agricultural caste of the Marātha country in India, " if a man dies of snake-bite they make a little silver image of a snake, and then kill a real snake, and make a platform outside the village and place the image on it, which is afterwards regularly worshipped as Nāgoba Deo " (R. V. Russell).

SNOTRA. One of the deities of the Ancient Teutons. The goddess Snotra, who belonged to the retinue of Frija (*q.v.*) and Freyja (*q.v.*), is represented as a goddess of wisdom.

SOCIALISM. See, in addition to the articles below, FOURIERISM, SIMONIANISM ST., and OWENITES.

SOCIALISM, CHRISTIAN. The need of the movement known as Christian Socialism was suggested by the great social distress of the working classes which culminated in the great Chartist demonstration of April the 10th, 1848. In May, 1848, Frederick Denison Maurice (1805-1872) and his friends commenced the publication of a series of "Tracts for the Times" in which they proposed to "consider the questions of the relation of the capitalist to the labourer, of what a government can or cannot do, to find work or pay for the poor." The friends with whom Maurice had taken counsel were Charles Kingsley (1819-1875), Julius Charles Hare (1795-1855), Alexander John Scott (1805-1866), J. M. Ludlow, Charles Blackford Mansfield (1819-1855), J. W. Parker (1792-1870), and Thomas Hughes (1822-1896). The tracts were also described as "Politics for the People." The contributors, in addition to Maurice, Kingsley, Ludlow, Mansfield, and Scott, included Richard Whately (1783-1863), Archbishop of Dublin, R. C. Trench (1807-1886), Archbishop of Dublin, Connop Thirlwall (1797-1875), Bishop of St. David's, Arthur Penrhyn Stanley (1815-1881), Dean of Westminster, Professor Connington, Dr. Guy, James Spedding (1808-1881), Daniel Macmillan (1813-1857), founder of Macmillan's publishing company, Lord Sidney Godolphin Osborne (1808-1889), Sir Edward Strachey, and Sir Arthur Helps (1813-1875). All these Dr. Stubbs describes as pioneers of the Christian Social movement in England. Charles Kingsley adopted as a *nom de plume* the name "Parson Lot." It was under this name that he wrote his famous pamphlet "Cheap Clothes and Nasty." In the summer of 1849 a series of meetings were held at the house of Maurice, with the result that a Co-operative Association of Tailors was formed. The next step was the establishment in 1850 of the Society for the Promotion of Working-men's Associations, "the practical application of Christianity to the purposes of trade and industry." With this was associated the plan of publishing Tracts on Christian Socialism. The new Society enlisted the sympathies of a number of new workers. These included Dr. Walsh, Augustus Vansittart, E. Vansittart Neale (1810-1892), founder of the Central Co-operative Agency and one of the first members of the Christian Social Union (*q.v.*), Cuthbert Ellison, a friend of Thackeray, Charles Sully, and Lloyd Jones (1811-1886), a disciple of Robert Owen (1771-1858). E. Vansittart Neale found the capital for starting two Working Builders' Associations, and he established the first London Co-operative Stores. Mr. Neale in a lecture on the characteristic features of Socialism, after passing in review the principal systems, seeks to justify the designation Christian Socialism. "The remarks which I have made upon the systems of the Social Reformers with whom we have been occupied to-night, must serve as my justification for claiming the epithet Christian as the proper distinctive adjunct to Socialism, and calling upon all Socialism to announce itself as Christian, if it would be at once truly social and historically just. We have in these systems the theories of four independent, fearless, original minds, earnest in their own views, propounding them as exclusively the truth on the questions to which Socialism relates. Now if we are not to commit ourselves to any of these teachers alone, if we assume that each one saw some side or portion of social truth; if, therefore, we are to seek for a principle which shall harmonize them among themselves, I know not where we shall find one unless we accept as true that profound saying of the gospel, which I select as pre-eminently expressive of the tone of many others of the Christian precepts: 'Except ye become as little children ye cannot enter into the kingdom of God.' For consider what, according to these several authors, Socialism demands: A fearless trustfulness towards God, a readiness to be guided by our natural superiors, a disposition for enjoyment, a general feeling of interest in the objects around us, an absence of the pride of outward distinction, a readiness to be satisfied with the exercise of our powers as such without troubling ourselves as to the reward; all these are qualities which according to one or another of our socialist philosophers, are to make up true Socialism. And do not these constitute the very essence of childhood in its healthy manifestations, that is the essence of that character which Christianity eighteen centuries since declared to be an indispensable condition of man's true well-being? I say then, if as socialists we would be just, we must acknowledge Socialism to be the offspring of Christianity." It has been stated recently by a number of clergymen that, as far as the ultimate aims are concerned, there is no difference between Christian Socialism and Socialism as commonly understood. In that case the real difference of opinion now is as to the means. Socialism is itself of the nature of a religion. While, however, one section of Socialists, Christian Socialists, identify Socialism with Christianity and the best work of the Christian Church, the other section, composed of Secular Socialists, repudiates Christianity, and asserts that it has been a hindrance rather than a help to the cause. To the one section belong such men as Canon S. Holland, Father Adderley, and Mr. R. J. Campbell; to the other such men as Robert Blatchford. To describe Socialism, therefore, either as Christian or Secular is convenient and appropriate. To regard the term "Christian" in this application as being a natural and inevitable description of Socialism is uuwise. The Gospel of Jesus is indeed democratic. God is, in his view, no respecter of persons. But his message seems to have been essentially religious. He seems to have taught that, whatever a person's outward circumstances may be, he may develop within himself a peace of God which passeth all understanding. The words of Jesus, as W. Herrmann says, seem to have been intended to "reveal to us that spirit which enables us to gain independence in the inward man—that is to say, true life." It may well be asserted that Jesus was as much an individualist as a socialist. See the *Tracts on Christian Socialism;* J. M. Ludlow, *Christian Socialism and its Opponents*, 1851; Professor Maurice, *The Reformation of Society*, 1851; Edward Vansittart Neale, *The Characteristic Features of some of the Principal Systems of Socialism*, 1851; Thomas Ramsay, *Is Christian Socialism a Church Matter?* 1851; C. W. Stubbs, Charles Kingsley and the *Christian Social Movement*, 1899; A. Harnack and W. Herrmann, *Essays on the Social Gospel*, 1907.

SOCIALISTS, SACRED. Sacred Socialists was the name of a small band of men who formed a kind of branch of Robert Owen's followers under the leadership of James Pierrepont Greaves (1777-1842). Greaves was of a mystic turn of mind, and was influenced by the writings of Jacob Bœhme (1575-1624). Greave's Socialism, in contrast to the rather materialistic system of Robert Owen, was of a spiritual character. He had in view "the soul's spiritual ends and the interior world." He would seek to discover scientific arrangements to make human beings everywhere and at all times dwell without the wants or wishes of wealth, without desire for individual accumulation, or any inequality of condition."

The great need is for the soul to be "possessed and exercised by the Love Spirit." This should make the "science of the influence of circumstances and the individual man both correspond with the universal man, and by this universal man hold through all ages the individual man and his sciences under control, and secure him from misery and inferiority, which could only be done by enlarging the antecedent parental relationship so as to secure to the new beings a superior organ." Greaves' system is somewhat ascetic in character, as E. Vansittart Neale points out. "The use of cold water abundantly, abstinence from all but vegetable diet, and all drinks but water; and, for the attainment of the highest state, the union of what he calls the life, light, and love natures, the use only of undyed and flowing robes of linen, above all, marriages between 'unions of Spirit, selected pairs in sympathetic harmony with Love'; these are some of the conditions which he proposes." Greaves was Secretary of the London Infant School Society. See Edward Vansittart Neale, *The Characteristic Features of some of the Principal Systems of Socialism*, 1851; and the *D.N.B.*

SOCIETIES FOR PROMOTING PRIMITIVE CHRISTIANITY. The theologian who conceived the idea of forming these Societies, William Whiston (1667-1752), in spite of his eccentricity, deserves, as Leslie Stephen has pointed out, more attention than has usually been given to him. He may be said to some extent to have anticipated movements which have attained important dimensions in recent years. William Whiston was born in 1667, his father, Josiah Whiston, at the time of his birth being Rector of Norton in Leicester. He was educated at home by his father until 1684, when he went to Tamworth School. Two years later he was entered at Clare Hall, Cambridge, where we are told his motto was "plain living and high thinking." He worked eight hours a day, chiefly at mathematics; and the plainness of his living is shown by the fact that his expenses amounted to less than £100 for three years and a half. His industry was rewarded in 1693, when he became a Fellow and Tutor of his College. His next step was ordination, which led to his appointment as Chaplain to John Moore (1646-1714), Bishop of Norwich, a position which he held from 1694 to 1698. Meantime he had devoted himself to the study of the "Philosophiae Naturalis Principia Mathematica" (1687) of Isaac Newton (1642-1727). The next important event in his life was the publication of his first book, "A New Theory of the Earth" (1696), the object of which was to confirm the story of Genesis on Newtonian grounds. In 1698 Bishop Moore presented him with the living of Lowestoft, Suffolk. After the publication of his first book, others followed in rapid succession. We learn that in 1710 his writings made "a great noise in Germany." He had already in 1703 succeeded Sir Isaac Newton as Lucasian Professor of Mathematics at Cambridge. But his theological investigations leading him to regard a form of Arianism as the most primitive type of Christianity, he was banished from Cambridge at the end of 1710, and in 1711 we find him settled in London. Proceedings were taken against him on account of his teaching; but they did not lead to any definite action, and apparently they did not disturb Whiston's equanimity. "Continuing to act boldly, according to my duty and conscience, [I] enjoyed a great calm within, how roughly soever the waves and billows abroad seemed ready to overwhelm me. Nor do I remember that during all the legal proceedings against me, which lasted in all four or five years at Cambridge and London, I lost my sleep more than two or three hours one night to that account." In January 1711 Whiston's address is: Lower end of Cross-street, Hatton Garden. The nearest church in those days was St. Andrew's, Holborn, of which in 1713 the famous Dr. Henry Sacheverell (1674?-1724) became Rector. In 1711 Whiston published his book "Primitive Christianity Revived." On Easter Day, 1715, he says, "we began to have a solemn assembly for worship, and the Eucharist, at my house in Cross-street, Hatton Garden, according to the form in my Liturgy (about fifteen communicants present)." This assembly was held three times a year for several years. The title of the book containing the liturgy is as follows: "The Liturgy of the Church of England, Reduced nearer to the Primitive Standard, Humbly proposed to Public Consideration by William Whiston, M.A. (A.D. 1713)." On July the 3rd, 1715, in pursuance of Whiston's proposals "for erecting Societies for promoting Primitive Christianity," such a Society was erected" and "met weekly at the Primitive Library, which was at my house in Cross-street, Hatton Garden." It lasted until June 28, 1717. On the institution of the Society, Joshua (Josiah?) Martin (1683-1747), "the most learned of all the people called Quakers that I ever knew, offered himself to be a member, and was readily received as such. I then proposed that we should use some short collects, taken out of our Common-Prayer Book, before we began and after we ended every meeting, to implore the blessing of God upon our enquiries. To which proposal all readily agreed but Mr. Martin, who entirely scrupled joining with us in such prayers, unless when the Spirit moved him. Which occasioned a good deal of difficulty to the Society. Yet at last we agreed to leave him to himself, to stay either with his hat on or off, as he pleased, and he gave us leave to say our prayers ourselves; nor did he disturb us, nor was he afterward an unuseful member, when he came to the Society." Whiston fasted regularly on Wednesdays and Fridays; thus he "kept the old rule of Christians." But it was not always easy to induce others to follow his example. "Now although Mr. Rundle [Thomas Rundle (1688?-1743), Bishop of Derry, 1735-43] was at first so zealous for religion, as a member of our Society, yet did not he keep himself in so temperate and abstemious a way of living as one that seemed disposed to be a confessor ought to use himself to; which made that real confessor Mr. Emlyn [Thomas Emlyn (1663-1741)] then say, 'that Mr. Rundle did not seem cut out for such sufferings as confessors are to expect.' Accordingly Mr. Rundle once invited me to eat a cheese-cake, as he termed it, with Mr. Talbot [? William Talbot (1659?-1730)] and himself; to which invitation I agreed, without suspicion of any particular design. But when I came, I found such a collation of wine and sweet-meats prepared, as little corresponded to the terms of the invitation. After some time the grand secret was disclosed, and I was informed that they were both determined to sign the Thirty-nine Articles, and take Holy Orders and preferment." In 1719 Whiston published "A Letter of Thanks to the Bishop of London [John Robinson (1650-1723)] for his late Letter to his Clergy against the Use of New Forms of Doxology," and rebuked the bishop "in a way of banter or ridicule." On the Queen's remonstrating with him, he said: "When the Bishop will beg St. Paul's and St. Peter's, etc., pardon (for calling their doxologies new and heretical doxologies), I will beg his pardon." It was the publication of this letter that gave rise to a scene in St. Andrew's Church in which Dr. Sacheverell and Whiston were the actors. The Rector ordered Whiston to leave his church. This was his parish church. After the altercation with Dr. Sacheverell, he seems to have attended either St. George's, Queen's Square, or St. Dunstan's in the East. He was not exactly a *persona grata* in any church. The Athanasian Heresy, as he called the established doctrine, whenever he was specially reminded of it, as at the reading of the Athanasian Creed, excited his anger to an almost intolerable degree. (In 1746 he made a solemn resolution regarding it. He decided "to go out always from the public worship of the Church of England, whenever the reader of Common Prayer read the Athanasian Creed," which he esteemed "a public cursing of Christians." He put this resolution into practice for the first time at Lincoln's Inn Chapel on October the 28th, 1746. When Mr. Rawlins began to read the Creed he went out, coming in again when it was over. He acted in the same way on November the 30th when Mr. Harrison began to read it at St. George's Church, Queen's Square. Later on he contented himself with sitting down while it was read). In 1720 certain friends wished to propose Whiston as a member of the Royal Society, but the proposal was dropped on account of the opposition of Sir Isaac Newton, the President. In 1721 Whiston published "The Longitude and Latitude found by the Inclinatory or Dipping Needle"; and towards the end of the same year a large subscription was made by his friends for the support of his family and for the carrying on of his experiments. William Whiston held strong views on the question of second marriage. Leslie Stephen has pointed out that "in many respects he strongly resembles the Vicar of Wakefield, who adopted his principles of monogamy." He thinks "it is not improbable that Whiston was more or less in Goldsmith's mind when he wrote his masterpiece." He addressed Dr. Hoadley (Benjamin Hoadly, 1676-1761) in the following terms: "In direct contradiction of the laws of Christ, you left your first church, and though now advanced to a more lucrative bishopric, during a good part of the year you abandon the duties of your ecclesiastic office, to become a political member of our civil constitution. Though a very old man, and in express contradiction to the letter of the Holy Scriptures, you have married a second time a young woman. These notorious practices, together with your injudicious and unlearned treatise on the Lord's Supper, will hand you down in no very favourable light to posterity." In 1724 Whiston removed from Cross Street to Great Russell Street, over against Montague House. In 1730 he published his "Memoirs of the Life of Dr. Samuel Clarke." It was in 1737 that he published the work by which he is known most widely, "The genuine Works of Josephus, the Jewish Historian, in English." This was followed by various works on his pet subjects. In addition to the Athanasian Creed, another stumbling block to Whiston was the inclusion of Canticles (*q.v.*) among the Canonical Books. Thus he once inquired of Bishop Sherlock (1678-1761) "how the Church of England could pretend to be so pure and primitive, as she has long boasted herself to be, while she still retains the Book of Canticles in her Bible, and the Athanasian Creed in her Common Prayer Book." The Bishop made no answer. In 1745 was published the "Primitive New Testament in English." Whiston's "darling motto" was "Consider well and act steadily." His "immoveable Guide and Standard" he found in the Apostolical Constitutions and Canons. The Athanasian Creed he calls "that shame and reproach of the public worship of the Church of England." He notes that he "continued in the Communion of the Church of England till Trinity Sunday, 1747." His conscientious scruples in politics and religion brought him to the verge almost of abject beggary. See especially his *Memoirs of my own Life*; also the *D.N.B.*

SOCIETY OF THE HOLY TRINITY. A Church of England Sisterhood founded in 1845. The Sisters devote themselves to education, nursing, and visiting. There is an inner circle called "Sisters of the Sacred Heart." See Walter Walsh, "Sisterhoods, Ritualistic," in the *Prot. Dict.*

SOCIETY OF THE SACRED MISSION, THE. An Anglican Brotherhood which trains working-men for the foreign mission field. Those who seek admission to its training institution promise to serve for their whole life without pay, receiving only the necessaries of life. They also undertake to remain unmarried. See BROTHERHOODS, MODERN ANGLICAN.

SOCIETY PEOPLE. Another name for the Cameronians (*q.v.*).

SOCINIANS. The Socinians took their name from two Italian theologians, Lælius Socinus (1525-1562) and his nephew, Faustus Socinus (1539-1604). Lælius Socinus was a lawyer, who seems to have felt that jurisprudence ought to rest upon a positive divine basis. He searched the Scriptures to find this basis, and in his search found himself confronted by a number of problems. His nephew Faustus Socinus corresponded with him. He also studied the manuscripts of his uncle. After spending some years in Switzerland, he settled in Poland, which at this time was a haven of refuge for liberal theologians. Unitarianism was already strongly entrenched in Poland, but it was infected with Anabaptist notions. Socinus set to work to form a compact community, and to formulate a consistent system of theology. In 1605, immediately after his death, appeared the Rakow or Socinian Catechism (*Catechismus Racovensis*), which is a good compendium of the theology. It is not, however, a confession of faith, for the Socinians recognised no authoritative Confessions. It was called the Rakow Catechism from the city of Rakow where the general synod of the Socinians met yearly. But interesting as the Catechism is, the doctrinal system of the Socinians is best drawn from the *Bibliotheca Fratrum Polonorum* (eight volumes, 1656), in which a number of the writings of the leading Socinians are included. The editor was Andreas Wissowatius (*d.* 1678). One of the most prolific writers and daring thinkers was J. Crell. A study of the Socinian writings makes it clear that their doctrines are very different from those of modern Unitarianism (*q.v.*). In some ways the Socinians held firmly to a positive supranaturalism. "The genuine Socinianism decidedly desiderates a divine revelation. This revelation is not regarded as some sort of internal working of the divine spirit upon man, but as a purely external communication of truths of a practical and theoretical nature" (Puenjer). The revelation is to be found in the Bible, particularly in the New Testament. The writers wrote under the impulse and at the dictation of the Divine Spirit. At the same time it was held that only the essential parts were divinely inspired in the sense of being free from error. Man has to exercise his Reason, which is his spiritual eye. Only through Reason can he receive, know, comprehend, and judge the divine revelation. But Reason is not allowed an unlimited right of criticism. "On the contrary, it is always emphatically maintained by the Socinians that religion is above reason, because it is revealed by God." Miracles are not contrary to reason, but above reason. "A distinction between what is above reason and what is contrary to reason is attempted, by holding that it is entirely different to say that a thing cannot be conceived, and to conceive that a thing cannot be." Puenjer points out that "in the application of this principle, reason is regarded as the supreme, indisputable judge of religious doctrines; and an unlimited rationalism is thus introduced." From this position Socinianism proceeded to criticise the profoundest Christian dogmas, and "almost all that has been presented with reference to Christianity in this connection, even to the present day, may be found already contained in the writings of Faustus Socinus." The Socinians found the doctrines of the Trinity and the

Deity of Christ to be contrary to Reason. Christ was not a deity. At the same time they held that he was more than a man, having been conceived of a Virgin and being perfectly holy. They found that the doctrine of Satisfaction also was open to severe criticism. "Satisfaction is impossible in the abstract, as well as in the concrete. It is impossible *in abstracto,* because a satisfaction by *obedientia activa* and a satisfaction by *obedientia passiva* mutually exclude each other. . . . In like manner, satisfaction is impossible *in concreto,* and chiefly because we have brought upon us eternal death, while Christ only underwent bodily death." The Socinians flourished in Poland. They were more successful in Holland than in Germany. Compare, further, UNITARIANS. See Schaff-Herzog: B. Puenjer; J. H. Blunt.

SODALITY. In the Roman Catholic Church the term sodality is used of a religious association of lay persons, male or female, or both male and female. "meeting together at stated times under ecclesiastical direction, for the performance of pious exercises, and recommending to each of its members conformity in life and conversation to a body of rules, framed in order to promote the honour of God, devotion to the Blessed Virgin, the spread of good works, and the spiritual advancement of those who faithfully observe them" (the *Cath. Dict.*).

SOLIFIDIANISM. The name given to the teaching of Martin Luther (1483-1546), according to which man is saved by faith alone and not by works.

SOLOMON'S SERVANTS, CHILDREN OF. The "children of Solomon's servants" (Ezra ii. 55, 58; Nehemiah vii. 57, 60, xi. 3) would seem to have been another name for the Nethinim (*q.v.*). They were perhaps slaves of Solomon who were made temple-servants (see I. Kings ix. 20 *f.*).

SOMA. An alcoholic drink made in India. In Vedic times it was esteemed so highly by the Aryans that they made it one of their principal gods, but its use is now prohibited by the higher castes of Hindus. "It is said in the Rig-Veda that Soma grows upon the mountain Mūjawat, that its or his father is Parjanya, the rain-god, and that the waters are his sisters. From this mountain, or from the sky, accounts differ, Soma was brought by a hawk. He is himself represented in other places as a bird; and as a divinity he shares in the praise given to Indra. It was he who helped Indra to slay Vritra, the demon that keeps back the rain. Indra, intoxicated by Soma, does his great deeds, and indeed all the gods depend on Soma for immortality Divine, a weapon-bearing god, he often simply takes the place of Indra and other gods in Vedic eulogy. It is the god Soma himself who slays Vritra, Soma who overthrows cities, Soma who begets the gods, creates the sun, upholds the sky, prolongs life, sees all things, and is the one best friend of god and man, the divine drop (*indu*), the friend of Indra. As a god he is associated not only with Indra but also with Agni, Rudra, and Pushān" (Hopkins, quoted by R. V. Russell).

SOMLAI. A Hindu deity. Somlai (or Devi) is one of the principal deities of the Lohārs, the occupational caste of blacksmiths in India.

SOMMONOCODON. A Siamese deity. He seems to have been a form of Buddha.

SONG OF SOLOMON. Another name for the book of Canticles (*q.v.*).

SONG OF SONGS. Another name for the book of Canticles (*q.v.*).

SŌṬĀ. The name of one of the Jewish tractates or treatises which reproduce the oral tradition or unwritten law as developed by the second century A.D. and are incorporated in the Mishnah (*q.v.*), a collection and compilation completed by Rabbi Judah the Holy, or the Patriarch, about 200 A.D. The sixty-three tractates of the Mishnah are divided into six groups or orders (*sedarim*). Sōṭā is the fifth tractate of the third group, which is called *Nāshīm* ("Women").

SOUTHCOTTIANS. The followers of Joanna Southcott (1750-1814). Joanna Southcott was at first a Methodist. In 1792, she says, she began to receive divine revelations. These were written down and sealed, to be opened some years later. In 1801 she began to publish "prophecies" which had been revealed to her ten years before. When she was sixty years old she announced that, through supernatural conception, she would bear a son who was to be Shiloh or the Prince of Peace and was to introduce the Millennium. "Since this powerful visitation of the Lord came to me," she says in her *Second Book of Wonders,* "like that in ninety-two [1792], I have fresh things revealed to me every day. I am awaked every morning between three and four o'clock: I sit up in my bed till the day breaks; and have communications given to me as soon as I am awake. When the day breaks I rise and go down into the dining-room by myself; the moment I enter the room I feel as though I was surrounded with angels; feeling a heavenly joy which I cannot describe, and which has taken from me my natural appetite." A London physician, Dr. Reece, who visited Joanna Southcott four months before her death, believed her to be pregnant in spite of her age and virginity. Only a *post mortem* examination convinced him of his mistake. She died on December the 27th, 1814. Her followers believed that she would revive. In 1825 one Charles William Twort announced that he was the Shiloh whose advent had been prophesied. He published epistles, which were sealed with a special seal and signed "Zion, the Lord is here." The epistles were called "Epistles of Shiloh." Another writer of similar epistles was a George Turner of Leeds (1821). John Wroe (1782-1863) came under his influence, and in 1822 claimed to succeed him. His followers afterwards called themselves Christian Israelites (*q.v.*). Joanna Southcott's publications include "The Book of Wonders" (1813-14) and "Prophecies concerning the Birth of the Prince of Peace" (1814). See J. H. Blunt; the *D.N.B.;* and *Chambers' Encycl.*

SOUTH INDIA UNITED CHURCH. A union of Congregationalists, Methodists, and Presbyterians. At the first General Assembly, held in 1908, a basis of union was adopted. This included a Confession in five articles. The Church reserved the right to revise its general Confession of Faith whenever the consensus of opinion of the United Body demands it. See W. A. Curtis.

SPIDER. The spider was sometimes used by the early Christians in exorcisms. This "is shown by a very curious Latin text, recently published, in which the exorcist denounces his enemy in the name of the Lord Jesus Christ, declaring that he shall not be able to 'cross the river' because of the 'fiery spider'" (Cobern).

SPINOZISM. The principles of Benedict or Baruch de Spinoza (1632-1677). He was the son of a Jewish merchant of Amsterdam. At a comparatively early age Spinoza showed a great interest in learning. He was encouraged and helped in his studies by the Chief Rabbi of Amsterdam, Saul Levi Morteira. But he lost the sympathy of his Jewish friends, and even of his own family, when he developed religious views which were considered heterodox. He was excommunicated in 1656, and had to leave his father's house and earn his living as best he could before he was twenty-four years old. The study of Descartes (Cartesius, 1596-1650) had given him a deep and abiding interest in philosophy. After the publication of Spinoza's *Principia Philosophiae Cartesianae*, he was offered the chair of Philosophy in the University of Heidelberg. He declined it, being unable to comply with one of the conditions of acceptance, namely, that he would not teach anything contrary to the established religion. The persons with whom he corresponded included Henry Oldenburg (1615?-1677), first Secretary of the Royal Society, and G. W. Leibnitz (1646-1716). Spinoza died of consumption in 1677, when he was only forty-five years old. His work, *Tractatus Theologico-Politicus* (1670) caused a great sensation, and its sale was prohibited nearly everywhere. In it he contends that the Word of God had been greatly misunderstood, and that the Bible required to be re-examined and re-interpreted. Prophecy he explains in a natural way, denying that it was a gift peculiar to the Jewish people. Miracles, he argues, in the sense of interferences with Nature, do not happen. Nothing contrary to Nature can possibly happen. Miracles have been understood in the Old Testament where they were not intended. Metaphorical language has been misinterpreted, understood literally. The authorship of books of the Old Testament was not such as commonly it has been supposed to be. The Pentateuch and other books were written long after the events which they describe. The Pentateuch was written, not by Moses, but by Ezra. The books of Chronicles were perhaps written by Judas Maccabaeus. The Psalms were collected in the days of the Second Temple. The Word of God is a living revelation from the Divine Mind, and is not confined to any one book, or indeed to any book. Holy Scripture supplies, not a body of speculative theology, but a collection of simple rules or principles. The spheres of theology and philosophy are distinct. The main principles of a universal faith are as follows: "That there is a God, a Supreme Being, who is most just and merciful, by whose example every man ought to regulate his life; secondly, that this God is One, which opinion is absolutely necessary to make a man adore, admire, and love God—for devotion, admiration, and love, are caused by that excellency which is in one above all others; thirdly, that He is everywhere present, or that all things are known to Him, for if anything were hidden from Him, or if men did not think that He seeth all things, we might doubt of His equity and justice, whereby He governeth all things; fourthly, that He hath supreme power and dominion over all things, that He doth nothing by compulsion, but of His own goodwill and pleasure; fifthly, that the worship of God, and obedience to Him, consists only in justice and charity towards our neighbours; sixthly, that only they who obey God by such a course of life will be saved; and others, who are slaves to their lusts and pleasures, will be condemned; lastly, that God pardoneth the sins of those that repent, because there is no man living without sin; therefore, if this were not an article of faith, all would despair of salvation" (after Sir Frederick Pollock). Spinoza contends that everyone should be free to think what he likes and to say what he thinks. In his *Ethics* (1677), published after his death, Spinoza seeks to construct from human reason a mathematically demonstrated system of ethics. The work, in part, treats of God, who is regarded as the foundation of all existence. Substance is that which stands under (Lat. *substans*) all appearance, making it seem real. The one absolute eternal substance is God. God is the cause of all things, but He is immanent and not transient. Whatever exists, exists in God, and without God nothing can exist or be conceived. The one eternal Substance has eternal Attributes. Of these Attributes there are only two which can be apprehended by man, Extension (*Extensio*) and Thought (*Cogitatio*). Everything material is a Mode of God's Extension; everything intellectual is a Mode of His Thought. The material runs quite parallel to the intellectual. The order and connexion of ideas is the same as the order and connexion of things. From the infinite power or infinite nature of God has followed necessarily the immanent, invisible Cause, *Natura naturans*, and the visible Material, *Natura naturata*. Nothing happens by chance. The *Ethics* treats also of the mind. The body of man is a Mode of God's Extension: the mind of man is a Mode of God's Thought. Particular things are only Modes of expressing God's Attributes in a definite way. "In so far as our mind perceives things truly, it is part of the infinite intelligence of God; and it is as much matter of necessity that all clear and distinct ideas of the mind should be true as that the idea of God in our mind is a truth." As to the Human Will, it is not absolutely free. As to Good and Evil, they are only relative ideas. True existence is knowledge; the highest knowledge is the knowledge of good. The greatest good is intellectually to know and to love God. That part of the human mind which experiences the intellectual love of God is eternal. Happiness is not merely the reward of virtue; it is virtue itself. According to Sir Frederick Pollock, the central idea of Spinoza's philosophy is that of the union of man with the order of the world, or, in other words, with God. Spinoza's private life was blameless. He lived very simply. Heinrich Heine (1797-1856) has said that the only life with which that of Spinoza can be compared is the life of Jesus Christ. See *Spinoza: Four Essays by Land, Kuno Fischer, J. Van Vloten, and Ernest Renan*, 1882; B. Puenjer; Kuno Fischer, *Geschichte der neuern Philosophie*, vol. i., pt. 2, 4th edition, 1897; J. H. Blunt; C. J. Deter; *R.S.W.*; Rudolf Eucken, *The Life of the Spirit*, 1909; Max B. Weinstein, *Welt- und Leben-Anschauungen*, 1910.

SPIRITISM. A belief in the continued activity of departed spirits and of their interference in mundane affairs may be said to be characteristic of primitive religion. It is not necessarily on that account a wrong belief. The child, the savage, the primitive man may in some ways be in closer touch with the reality of things than are mature, educated, and cultured persons. Education, as commonly understood, is not necessarily identical with real advancement. An uneducated person who has been endowed with an intuitional understanding of reality has received a gift of priceless value compared with the accumulation of a stock of educated beliefs. But truth is unfolded gradually. The spiritism of the savage is in most cases probably nothing more than an inkling of the truth. In any case, the term Spiritism is now used to denote not certain beliefs prevalent among primitive folk, but certain views and practices which have been adopted by a number of educated persons in modern times. The modern belief in spiritism may be said to date from 1847. In this year extraordinary phenomena are said to have been observed in an American family of German origin named Fox. John Fox, with his wife and three daughters, had settled in the county of Wayne, New York. His eldest daughter married soon afterwards. It is said that not many days after the wedding strange noises began to be heard in the house. They were repeated so often that the Fox family grew quite accustomed to them. One evening Catherine Fox, the youngest daughter, rapped with her fingers and is said to have heard raps in response. The girl called her mother's attention to this remarkable experience. The author of the phenomena, it is said, was then invited to count ten by means of raps, and did so. "To similar demands were then given quite comprehensible answers by means of raps. When the unknown being was asked whether it were a man, there was no reply. But when asked if it were a spirit, clear and rapid blows took the place of an evident affirmative" (Joseph Lapponi). It is said that neighbours were called in to witness these occurrences. "Thus was modern Spiritism born in America, and from the first it was undertaken to enter into communication with the supposed author of the singular phenomenon by means of a conventional language, based on the number of the raps given. Afterwards other means of communication were found." The next stage was reached when it was realized that communication with a so-called spirit depended on the presence of some persons rather than of others. In the case of the Fox family, the spirit was more communicative when Catherine Fox was present. This suggested that certain persons possess in a special degree the power of establishing communication with the spirit-world. To such persons the name "medium" was applied. With the help of mediums people were anxious to communicate with their departed friends. This led to the establishment of spiritistic unions and circles. In 1852 spiritism was introduced into Scotland. It soon spread into England, Germany, France, and Russia. In 1858 it was introduced into Italy. It was natural that the table round which those who were interested in spiritism sat should be used for rapping. This gave rise to table-rapping and table-turning. This early kind of spiritism, in which questions and replies were made by means of raps, was called "typtological spiritism." The mediums were called "typtological mediums." In course of time writing was introduced. This kind of spiritism was called "graphological spiritism." The mediums were called "graphological mediums." It was next held that the medium was possessed for a time by a spirit, and during this possession acted like an automaton. The mediums were called "possessed mediums" and the spiritism "spiritism by invasion." A further development of spiritism was called "visible spiritism," because it was claimed that the spirits were visible not only to the mediums, but also to those who assisted at the *séances*. The final development has been "spiritism of materialization." Here the mediums are called "materializing mediums," because they are supposed to be able to materialize the spirits of the dead. The spirits can touch or be touched, speak, play instruments, etc. All this kind of thing lends itself to imposture, and frauds have been practised. Nevertheless, it can hardly be doubted that mediumship does produce remarkable phenomena which require examination and explanation. When carefully examined, they can be explained without resorting to a belief in the return of spirits from the dead. T. J. Hudson claims that they can be explained by three well-supported propositions. 1. The mind of man is dual—objective and subjective. 2. The subjective mind is constantly controlled by suggestion. 3. "The subjective mind, or entity, possesses physical power; that is, the power to make itself heard and felt, and to move ponderable objects." The most difficult of these propositions is the third. Hudson, however, claims to have seen enough to *know* the reality of the leading physical phenomena. But he explains all the phenomena telepathically (see TELEPATHY). They are produced not by spirits, but by persons possessed of peculiar powers, in other words, by mediums. Lapponi, on the other hand, believes that they are produced by immaterial beings. "In view of the imprint of intelligence, of will, of tendencies, of affections, and of passions that undeniably characterize many of the singular manifestations which we are considering, it seems quite logical to admit that the phenomena point to the existence of immaterial beings who prove their existence by means of these singular manifestations." See T. J. Hudson; Joseph Lapponi, *Hypnotism and Spiritism*, 1907; *Der Spiritismus und seine Geschichte* in the "Miniatur-Bibliothek"; Archdeacon Colley, *Sermons on Spiritualism*, 1907.

SPIRITUAL HEALING. Spiritual healing is not identical with mental healing. They have much in common, it is true, but spiritual healing is definitely religious. The difference is illustrated by the operations of the Psycho-therapeutic Society (*q.v.*) and Christian Science (*q.v.*). The former system was purely mental; the latter is strictly spiritual. In both cases the aid of Mind is invoked. But on the one hand, it is Human Mind; on the other hand, Divine Mind. The healing power in Christian Science is the full realization of the goodness of God and of the unreality of evil, the acceptance of a new view of mind and matter. Mental healing requires a great effort of the human mind. Spiritual healing requires no effort, because the mind that heals is the omnipotent Divine Mind. There have been mental healers in all ages. Jesus Christ, it has been claimed, was the first to reveal the science of Spiritual Healing. T. J. Hudson maintains (1) "that Jesus Christ was the first who correctly formulated the exact conditions necessary and indispensable to the exercise of the power to heal the sick by psychic methods"; and (2) "that the conditions which he declared to be necessary to enable him to exercise that power are the same conditions which are indispensable to-day." An essential condition in both healer and patient is *faith*. This was "the key to health and to heaven." This faith, as explained by Christian Science, springs from a discernment of spiritual truth. Week after week persons testify, orally and by writing, that they have been healed of diseases by Christian Science. The testimonies are given with such obvious truthfulness and sincerity that it is impossible to doubt the genuineness of the cures. This suggests that Jesus possessed a secret, which was afterwards lost; and that this secret has been rediscovered in modern times. "If the nineteenth century was materialistic and critical, the first half of the twentieth century promises to be mystical and spiritual" (*Religion and Medicine*). See Horatio W. Dresser, *Health and the Inner Life*, 1907; T. J. Hudson, *Psychic Phenomena*, 1907 (tenth impression); E. Worcester, S. McComb, and I. H. Coriat, *Religion and Medicine*, 1908.

SPIRITUAL SCIENCE. Another designation of Christian Science (*q.v.*). The author of "Science and Health" (*q.v.*) uses the expressions Divine Science, Spiritual Science, Christ Science, Christian Science, or Science alone interchangeably.

SPIRITUALISM. The term Spiritualism is commonly used to denote a belief that certain phenomena are due to the influence of departed spirits, this influence being put into operation through a living person called a "medium." A belief in such phenomena, however, is more correctly described as Spiritism (*q.v.*). Spiritualism means strictly a belief either that soul or spirit is the only reality, or that spirit, if not the only reality, possesses a real existence apart from matter. It denotes the opposite to materialism (*q.v.*), a belief in matter as the real and all-important existence. All Christians are spiritualists. They are not all spiritists.

SPRING AND AUTUMN ANNALS. The book called "Spring and Autumn Annals" was composed by Confucius (551-479 B.C.). It was accepted by the Chinese as one of their five Classics. The Annals are those of the State of Lu, and extend from 722 to 484 B.C. Prof. Giles speaks of the annals as "bald entries set against each year." No allusion is made to any interposition in human affairs on the part of God. In the Commentaries on the book, which are more interesting, the Supreme

Being is alluded to sometimes. See H. A. Giles, *Religions of Ancient China*, 1905.

SRAOSHA. The name (meaning "Obedience") of an angel in Zoroastrianism, an Angel of Judgment. Among the Parsis, when a person dies the relatives for the first three days after death address prayers to Sraosha on his or her behalf. When each day the hour approaches (midnight) for the soul's destiny to be formally determined, a special ceremony is performed in honour of Sraosha. Another ceremony takes place on the dawn of the fourth day when the soul takes it flight to its permanent abode.

SRI VAISHNAVA. A Vishnuite sect in India, another name for the Rāmānujis and Rāmānandis. The name characterises them as the principal or original Vaishnava sect.

STAR IN THE EAST, THE ORDER OF THE. An order founded at Benares, India, on January 11th, 1911. According to the founders, there is in many parts of the world to-day a rapidly growing expectation of the near coming of a great spiritual Teacher. In all the great faiths at the present time, and in practically every race, there are people who are looking for such a Teacher; and the hope is being expressed quite naturally in each case, in the terms appropriate to the religion and the locality in which it has sprung up. It is the object of the Order of the Star in the East, so far as is possible, to gather up and unify this common expectation, wherever and in whatever form it may exist, and to link it into a single great movement of preparation for the Great One whom the age awaits. The objects of the Order are embodied in a declaration of six principles, the acceptance of which is all that is necessary for membership. (1) We believe that a Great Teacher will soon appear in the world, and we wish so to live now that we may be worthy to know Him when He comes. (2) We shall try, therefore, to keep Him in our mind always, and to do in His name and, therefore, to the best of our ability, all the work which comes to us in our daily occupation. (3) As far as our ordinary duties allow, we shall endeavour to devote a portion of our time each day to some definite work which may help to prepare for His coming. (4) We shall seek to make Devotion, Steadfastness, and Gentleness prominent characteristics of our daily life. (5) We shall try to begin and end each day with a short period devoted to the asking of His blessing upon all that we try to do for Him and in His name. (6) We regard it as our special duty to try to recognise and reverence greatness in whomsoever shown, and to strive to co-operate, as far as we can, with those whom we feel to be spiritually our superiors. The official organ of the order is *The Herald of the Star*.

STATES, THE FOUR FORMLESS. According to Buddhism four kinds of trances and four kinds of formless states are produced by deep meditation. See TRANCES, THE FOUR.

STATIONS OF THE CROSS. The Stations of the Cross (*via Crucis, via Calvarii*) are pictures depicting incidents in the Passion of Jesus. "Usually, they are ranged round the church, the first station being placed on one side of the high altar, the last on the other" (*Catholic Dictionary*). The pictures are used in a form of devotion originated by the Franciscans (*q.v.*), the guardians of the holy places in Jerusalem. The devout, by contemplating the pictures, are able in spirit to follow Jesus' footsteps on the path of His Passion. In 1694 Innocent XII. "declared that the indulgences granted for devoutly visiting certain holy places in Palestine could be gained by all Franciscans and by all affiliated to the order if they made the way of the cross devoutly—*i.e.*, passed or turned from station to station meditating devoutly on the stages of the history" (*Cath. Dict.*). In course of time the indulgences have come to be extended, by authority, to all churches. The authorized Stations of the Cross are fourteen. (1) Christ before Pilate; (2) the receiving of the cross; (3) Christ's first fall; (4) His meeting with His mother; (5) Simon of Cyrene bearing the cross; (6) the wiping of Christ's face with a handkerchief by Veronica (a legend of the Middle Ages); (7) His second fall; (8) His words to the women of Jerusalem; (9) His third fall; (10) His being stripped of His garments; (11) His crucifixion; (12) His death; (13) the taking down of His body from the cross; (14) His burial. See *Prot. Dict.; Cath. Dict.;* cp. F. W. Farrer, *The Life of Christ as represented in Art*, 1894.

STEEPLE. The tower of a church, etc., together with any superstructure standing upon it, such as a spire or lantern. Morris Jastrow thinks there is a direct and continuous line of tradition leading from the Babylonian *zikkurat* or stage tower to the towers of the Mohammedan mosques (note the Mohammedan tower at Samarra on the Tigris, of the ninth century A.D., which was clearly modelled on the pattern of a Babylonian *zikkurat*) on the one hand, and to the belfries, campaniles and steeples of Christian churches on the other. "In Babylonian and Assyrian architecture the tower is always separate from the temple proper—as though to symbolize the independent origin of the two structures, the mountain-*motif* and the house-*motif*. Generally the tower is back of the temple, at times to one side, but, even when it is accorded a position immediately adjacent to the temple, as in the case of the two zikkurats attached to the temple of Anu and Adad at Ashur, one standing to the right, the other to the left of the double temple, the tower is yet a distinct structure, the ascent being independent of the temple. In the case of many mosques the Babylonian-Assyrian tradition is followed through the virtual independence of the minarets as adjuncts to the mosque, though in others the minaret is directly attached and eventually becomes a steeple placed on or at the side of the mosque. Similarly in the church architecture of Italy we find a tower built quite independently of the church as in the case of St. Mark's in Venice and of the cathedrals in Florence and Pisa, while in Norman architecture the belfry becomes attached to the church, and in Gothic architecture the tower becomes a steeple placed on the church, and with a complete departure from its Babylonian-Assyrian counterpart is looked upon as a symbol of the spirit of Christianity, calling upon its followers to direct their thoughts heavenward" (*Civ.*).

STHULA SARIRA. An expression used in Theosophy (*q.v.*). It denotes the physical body in man.

STIGMATA. The word Stigmata means marks or brands. St. Paul speaks (Galatians vi. 17) of bearing in his body the marks (*stigmata*) of the Lord Jesus. He is speaking metaphorically. It is claimed, however, that there have been a number of cases in which marks have appeared on the bodies of very devout persons resembling the wounds of Jesus. It is claimed further that these marks were miraculous. St. Francis of Assisi (1182-1226) in 1224 saw in a vision a man fastened to a cross. After this there appeared on the body of St. Francis the mark of the stigmata of Jesus—the wounds on the hands and feet and in the side. These marks were concealed from most people during the life of St. Francis, but on his death they were seen by a number of persons, by fifty of the Brethren and very many seculars. Pope Benedict XII. instituted a Feast of the Stigmata of St. Francis. St. Catherine of Siena (1347-1380) told her confessor, Raymond of Capua, that the Lord had impressed upon her the stigmata. Painters were forbidden by Sixtus IV. to represent her stigmatisation, but "a special feast in commemoration of it was granted to the Dominicans by Benedict XIII." (*Cath. Dict.*) In 1694 the marks of the crown of thorns and of the crucifixion are said to have appeared on Veronica Giuliani. In 1831 she was canonized. The stigmata of Anna Katharina Emmerich (1774-1824), who became a nun, are said to have bled every Friday from the year 1812. Louise Lateau (1850-1883) was another noted example of stigmatization. The phenomenon was not confined to Catholics. Mary Anne Girling (1827-1886), for instance, who founded the sect known as "The People of God," is said to have had a similar experience. Formerly, when stigmatization was not regarded as miraculous, it was treated as imaginary or fraudulent. We now know that it need not be either the one or the other. Stigmata may arise, not through miracle, but through concentration of the human mind. This has been proved by experiments in "hypnotism." For instance, in the Hospital Marie at St. Petersburg, a man was told that after warming himself at a stove, which had not been lighted, a redness would appear on his arm and blisters would break out. He touched the door of the cold stove and uttered a cry of pain. This was followed first by a redness and swelling on the arm and then by a number of blisters (Olston, p. 174 f.). The writers of "Religion and Medicine" have in fact good reason for saying that much in the experience of the mystics and monks of the Middle Ages "which has been rejected by the scientific mind as incredible, and accepted by the religious mind as miraculous, is now seen to be neither one nor other, but a reality to be explained in terms of psychical processes." They make special reference to stigmatization. "Perhaps the most striking of these phenomena is that of stigmatization which has, however, been paralleled in our own time in the case of some hysterical patients. From St. Francis of Assisi and Catherine of Siena to the famous case of Louise Lateau there has been a succession of susceptible souls who by intense mental concentration on the sufferings of the Saviour, on the wounds in His hands and feet and side, have in some way, inexplicable to physiology, so affected the bodily organism as to reproduce in it the sorrows of the Crucified. And thus in a very real sense they may be said to have borne branded on their bodies the marks of the Lord Jesus'." See *Prot. Dict.; Cath. Dict.;* A. B. Olston, *Mind Power*, 1906; E. Worcester, S. McComb, and I. H. Coriat, *Religion and Medicine*, 1908.

STOICISM. The Stoic School of Greek philosophy was founded by Zeno of Citium in Cyprus (362-264 B.C.), who is said to have had Phoenician blood in his veins. He was influenced greatly by early schools of philosophy, for he had been in turn the disciple of the Cynic Crates, the Megaric Stilpo, and the Academic Polemon. He was even accused of being a plagiarist or an eclectic without any originality. Stoicism was so called because Zeno opened a school of his own in the *Stoa Poikilē*, a colonnade in Athens adorned with pictures. Zeno was succeeded by his disciple Cleanthes from Assos in the Troad (331-232 B.C.), and Cleanthes by Chrysippus of Soli in Cilicia (282-209 B.C.). These three constitute what has been called the Older Stoa. They were followed by a number of other Greek philosophers known as the Middle Stoa, and these by a number of Roman philosophers usually known as the Later Stoa. The Roman philosophers were L. Annaeus Seneca (3-65 A.D.), Epictetus, who left Rome in 94 A.D. and went to live and teach in Nicopolis in Epirus, and Marcus Aurelius Antoninus, who was Emperor from 161 to 180 A.D. The Stoicism with which we are most familiar is that of the Roman period. Only fragments of the writings of Zeno, Cleanthes, and Chrysippus have been preserved. The philosophy of the Stoics embraced three great branches of knowledge, Logic, Physics, and Ethics. Logic in their use of the term was of wide scope. To quote W. L. Davidson, "not only did it cover to them what has been regarded by many as alone Logic, namely, 'the science and art of reasoning' or of 'thought,' but it included also Rhetoric (or the art of style) and Epistemology (or Theory of Knowledge)." Physics meant to the Stoics not merely what it means to the modern physicist, but also, and even more, "the metaphysical interpretation of the universe." "Their great achievement was their Cosmogony or Theory of the world, and their Theology or philosophical conception of God. Their physics, therefore, was pre-eminently Ontology: it was Science of Being—occupied with the three great entities, God, the World, and the Human Soul." Again, Ethics to the Stoics meant Practical Philosophy. "As philosophy was to them a substitute for religion, it was, above all things, their aim to make it a rule of life, 'a way of living'—not merely, as now, a necessary part of a University curriculum, but a power operative for good in daily action. If, then, men were to be guided in their conduct, it was not enough to teach them to reason, or to harangue, or to speculate. You may feed the imagination on cosmogony, you may sharpen the intellect by logic, you may train literary faculty through rhetoric, but you cannot nourish the soul, or produce a robust, manly character, unless you bring your cosmogony into a definite immediate relation with living, and utilize your logic and your eloquence for the defence and establishment of life-directing truth" (Davidson). It is an interesting fact that the leading Stoics were of non-Hellenic nationality. "Zeno was from Citium, a Phoenician colony in Cyprus, and himself belonged to the Semitic race. . . . Of his disciples, Persæus came also from Citium; Herillus was from Carthage; Athenodorus from Tarsus; Cleanthes from Assus in the Troad. The chief disciples of Cleanthes were Sphærus of the Bosporus, and Chrysippus from Soli in Cilicia. Chrysippus was succeeded by Zeno of Sidon, and Diogenes of Babylon; the latter taught Antipater of Tarsus, who taught Panætius of Rhodes, who taught Posidonius of Apamea in Syria. There was another Athenodorus, from Cana in Cilicia; and the early Stoic Archedemus is mentioned by Cicero as belonging to Tarsus. The names of Nestor, Athenodorus, Cordylion, and Heraclides may be added to the list of Stoical teachers furnished by Tarsus. Seleucia sent forth Diogenes; Epiphania, Euphrates; Scythopolis, Basilides; Ascalon, Antibius; Tyre, Antipater; Sidon, Boëthus; Ptolemais, Diogenes" (Sir A. Grant, *The Ethics of Aristotle*, quoted by W. L. Davidson). See W. L. Davidson, *The Stoic Creed*, 1907; C. J. Deter, *Gesch. der Philosophie*, 1906; Max B. Weinstein, *Welt- und Leben-anschauungen*, 1910.

STONE OF DESTINY, THE. The "Stone of Destiny" is a name by which an ancient piece of rock now enclosed in the British Coronation Chair is known. The stone and chair are kept in Edward the Confessor's Chapel in Westminster Abbey. The stone is that upon which in early times the Scottish monarchs were crowned at Scone, in Perthshire. It was brought from Scotland by Edward I. There was an old prophecy in rhyme concerning it:

> "If fates go right, where'er this stone be found,
> The Scots shall monarchs of that realm be crowned."

The prophecy was fulfilled, it has been said, in 1603 when James the Sixth of Scotland and the First of England was crowned, at Westminster, seated on the Coronation Chair with the Stone of Destiny beneath it. As regards the origin of the stone it has even been claimed that this is the identical piece of rock that served the Old Testament patriarch Jacob for a pillow, or the piece of rock from which water flowed when Moses struck it.

The truth, however, is that for one reason or another the worship of stones or pieces of rock has been common in primitive religions. It appears from Irish mythology that Ireland too had its "Stone of Destiny," a mysterious stone "which would cry out with a human voice to acclaim a rightful king" (C. Squire). It is true indeed that some people would identify this stone with the "Coronation Stone" in Westminster Abbey; but there is every reason to believe that there were a number of such stones, and, as Charles Squire says, "it is more probable that it [the Irish 'Stone of Destiny'] still stands upon the hill of Tara, where it was preserved as a kind of fetish by the early kings of Ireland." See H. O. Arnold-Forster, *Our Great City*, 1907; Squire, *Myth.*

STONES, SACRED. An early example of a stone being held sacred is found in the O.T. story of Jacob. Jacob called the place where he rested on a stone and saw the vision of a ladder reaching to heaven Bethel (Gen. xxviii. 10-22). The term bætyls or bætuli, applied to sacred stones, is probably a Graecized form of Bethel. The Phoenicians of Paphos represented Astarte by a cone-shaped stone. The Arabiau deity Dusares was worshipped in the form of a large stone, and on coins of Seleucia Zeus Casius appears as a stone.

STRANGERS. The ascribing of a semi-supernatural character to strangers is very general. As a being possessed of unknown powers for good or ill, "he must be either repulsed at once as a foe or received and treated with extraordinary respect" (E. S. Hartland, *Ritual*). The former course would be adopted only when hostility was suspected. "The latter course has given birth to laws of hospitality recognized all over the world, however the exact procedure may differ among different peoples. But even in this case the stranger is looked upon with suspicion until he has undergone what M. van Gennep calls rites of aggregation to the group or society to which he has come. These rites may be of the most simple character, such as spitting upon his host or drinking a cup of water or coffee from his host's hand; or they may involve a trial of strength, an exchange of gifts, the offering of sacrifices or entry into a blood-covenant" (p. 285 f.).

STRANNIKI. A sub-sect of the Russian dissenters known as Bezpopovtzi. The Stranniki or "the Travelers" are so called because they do not remain anywhere more than a few days. They believe that Christians are already living in the future age and the new heaven, and that men rise from the dead whenever in the present life they repent and lead a good life. See Schaff-Herzog.

STUNDISTS. A pietistic and evangelical sect in Russia. They are descended, it is thought, from Russian soldiers who seceded from the Greek Church through the influence of German missionaries. Down to the year 1905 they were persecuted by the Government. They are said to number half a million.

STŪPAS. Stūpa is one of the names for the receptacle in which the Buddhists preserve the relics of their great saints. At first the ashes or remains were placed under heaps or tumuli. These heaps were called Ćaityas and afterwards Stūpas. Then Ćaitya came to denote a relic-structure in an assembly-hall, and Stūpa a relic-structure outside in the open air. The ashes, teeth, nails, etc., were deposited in a casket, and the casket was deposited inside the Ćaitya or Stūpa. The casket was called in Pāli Dāgaba. In course of time this term Dāgaba or Pagoda came to denote not only the casket but also the monument, and Pagodas have developed into immense buildings (see PAGODAS). It should be added that Ćaityas and Stūpas were not always used to hold relics. Sometimes they were simply monuments in the form of pyramids. Hackmann points out that the Sanskrit word Stūpa meant originally "a tuft of hair" and then acquired the meaning "a dome-shaped monument." See Monier-Williams, *Buddhism*, 1890; H. Hackmann.

SUA. A culture-god, and apparently a solar deity, in the mythology of the Muysca Indians of Central America. He is known also as Nemquetaha or Bochica.

SUBJECTIVE MIND, THE. It is believed by students of psychic phenomena that there are in man two minds. One, the objective mind, is active in the daytime; the other, the subjective mind, is active during sleep. The latter was called by F. W. H. Myers (1843-1901) the Subliminal Self (*q.v.*). See DUALITY OF MIND.

SUBJECTIVISM. The term Subjectivism is used sometimes to describe the philosophy of George Berkeley (1685-1753). Berkeley contended that the material world exists subjectively, and not objectively. It is a mistake to think that an objective world of matter exists outside of us. Matter is not an absolute substance. The only absolute substance is spirit. See BERKELEYISM.

SUBLAPSARIANISM. A doctrine held by the less extreme Calvinists. When God created man, he did not decree his fall, but he foresaw it. See INFRALAPSARIANISM.

SUBLIMINAL SELF. Students of psychic phenomena believe that they have discovered in man a duality of mind. The one mind is the conscious mind, and is active in daily life; the other mind is subconscious, and as a rule is active only during sleep. Another name for the conscious mind is the objective mind. The subconscious mind is then called the subjective mind. F. W. H. Myers (1843-1901) designated this the Subliminal Self. See DUALITY OF MIND.

SUBRAHMANYA. Another name for Skanda (*q.v.*), one of the gods of the Hindus.

SUBSTANCE. In philosophical and theological usage Substance does not denote anything material or solid, but the essence which makes a thing what it is. As used by Aristotle, the substance "is regarded as an independent existence, a permanent subject of which the accidents are predicated, and to which they belong as its qualities or states" (Chambers's *Encyclopaedia*). In the philosophy of Spinoza, Substance is the all-comprehending Reality. "It is infinite, and manifests itself in an infinite number of finite forms or 'modes.' It has two main attributes, Thought and Extension, the *res cogitans* and the *res extensa*" (A. Butler). The founder of "Christian Science" defines Substance as follows: "Substance is that which is eternal and incapable of discord and decay. Truth, Life, and Love are substance, as the Scriptures use this word in Hebrews: 'The substance of things hoped for, the evidence of things not seen.' Spirit, the synonym of Mind, Soul, or God, is the only real substance. The spiritual universe, including individual man, is a compound idea, reflecting the divine substance of Spirit" (Mary Baker Eddy, *Science and Health*, 1911). Compare TRANSUBSTANTIATION.

SUCCUBI. Female demons who were supposed to visit men and have sexual intercourse with them.

SUCELLUS. Sucellus, "the good striker," appears as the name of one of the deities worshipped by the ancient Gauls. He is represented as wearing a wolf-skin and as holding a long mallet. The god would seem originally to have been worshipped as a wolf. Afterwards he was represented as a man. We are reminded of Silvia the she-wolf, who was reputed to have been the mother of Romulus and Remus; and of the ancient Roman god Silvanus, the forester, who would seem also originally to have been a wolf. A Celtic god is often paired with a Celtic goddess, though it is uncertain what the relationship is supposed to be. The goddess who is paired with

Sucellus is Nantosvelta. See Anwyl, *Celtic Religion*, 1906; Reinach, *O.*

SÚFIISM. Súfiism is the name given to a kind of mysticism practised by Mohammedans. The word is derived either (1) from an Arabic word meaning "wool," or (2) from an Arabic word meaning "purity," or (3) from the Greek word *sophia* "wisdom." In the first case the Súfis would be so called because they wore woollen clothes. In any case, the early Súfis devoted themselves to a life of devotion and seclusion. They renounced pleasures and amusements, and despised riches and honours. Later Súfiism seems to have borrowed from Indian philosophy. "Its chief doctrines are that the souls of men differ in degree, but not in kind from the Divine Spirit, of which they are emanations, and to which they will ultimately return; that the Spirit of God is in all He has made, and it in Him; that He alone is perfect love, and beauty, and that hence love to Him is the only real thing and all besides is mere illusion; that this present life is one of separation from the Beloved; that the beauties of nature, music and art revive in man the divine idea and recall his affections from wandering from God to other objects." The highest state of bliss is oneness with God, absorption in the Eternal. The Súfis are required blindly to obey their leader, the Murshid. See F. A. Klein.

SUITENGU. A deity worshipped by the Japanese as a god of the sea. He has a temple at Tokyo.

SUKKĀ. The title of one of the Jewish treatises or tractates which reproduce the oral tradition or unwritten law as developed by the second century A.D. and are incorporated in the Mishnah (*q.v.*), a collection and compilation completed by Rabbi Judah the Holy, or the Patriarch, about 200 A.D. The sixty-three tractates of the Mishnah are divided into six groups or orders (*sedarim*). Sukkā is the sixth tractate of the second group, which is called *Mō'ēd* ("Festival").

SULIS. A deity worshipped by the British Celts as a sun-god.

SULPICIANS. In 1650 (or a few years earlier) M. Olier founded the theological seminary of St. Sulpice in Paris. The Sulpicians, "a society of priests who devote themselves to the care of theological seminaries" (*Cath. Dict.*), derive their name from this institution.

SUMMISTS, THE. The Summists is a designation of certain mediaeval theologians who compiled theological *Summae*. The name is said to have been suggested by the work of Hugo of St. Victor (1097-1141) entitled "Summa Sententiarum." The first of the Summists was Robert Pullen (or Robertus Pullus; *d.* 1147?), who was born in England. Pullen published a work "Sententiarum Libri Octo." A more famous Summist was Peter Lombard (Petrus Lombardus; *d.* 1164), a pupil of Abelard. His work "Sententiarum Libri Quattuor," which became the standard compendium of dogmatic theology for some centuries, gained him the title "Magister Sententiarum." His students were called Sententiaries. The most remarkable of the Summists was Alanus ab Insulis (really Alain; 1114-1202), who became known as "Doctor Universalis." He wrote an important work, "De Arte, seu de Articulis Catholicae Fidei, Libri Quinque." His poem "Anticlaudianus" made him even more famous. See J. E. Erdmann, *Hist. of Philosophy*, vol. i., 1890.

SUN WORSHIP. The Kurmis, the representative cultivating caste of Hindustān, observe Raviwār as the day sacred to Vishnu or the Sun, Sunday. "A man salutes the sun after he gets up by joining his hands and looking towards it, again when he has washed his face, and a third time when he has bathed, by throwing a little water in the sun's direction. He must not spit in front of the sun nor perform the lower functions of the body in its sight. Others say that the sun and moon are the eyes of God, and the light of the sun is the effulgence of God, because by its light and heat all moving and immobile creatures sustain their life and all corn and other products of the earth grow" (R. V. Russell).

SUNDAY SCHOOLS. The *Catholic Dictionary* claims that before Sunday Schools were thought of in England, one was established at St. Sulpice (1699) by St. J. B. de la Salle, and that even before this similar schools, open on festivals, had been established at Milan (c. 1580) by St. Charles Borromeo. The St. Sulpice Sunday School was open from noon to three o'clock. In both cases the purpose was to give secular instruction. These were not Sunday Schools in the modern sense; and it could no doubt be shown that such schools as they were were found here and there at a much earlier date. The founder of modern Sunday Schools as an organised system was Robert Raikes of Gloucester (1735-1811). Raikes started by collecting a few children from the streets on Sundays and instructing them or having them instructed in religious knowledge. In 1785 a society was formed to establish and maintain Sunday Schools in all parts of the kingdom. In 1803 the "Sunday School Union" was founded, to promote Sunday School work and raise its standard. The Union is unsectarian, but mainly nonconformist. A series of simultaneous "International Lessons" are drawn up for three months in advance, in order that the same lessons may be studied by all schools belonging to the Union. For these lessons careful expository notes by duly qualified writers are published a week or two in advance. "Other helps are published and supplied at the lowest possible prices, and public training, lessons, lectures, and examinations are also carried on" (William Benham). The American Sunday School Union, a development of earlier Unions (since 1791), was established in 1824. See William Benham; the *Cath. Dict.*; *Chambers' Encycl.*; the *D.N.B.*

SUNNA. Sunna would seem to have been one of the deities of the Ancient Teutons. The name seems to occur as that of a goddess in one of the Merseburg Charms (*q.v.*). It is possible, however, that the reading, "Then charmed it Sinthgunt, Sun(na) her sister; then charmed it Frija, Vol(la) her sister," should rather be, "Then charmed it Sinthgunt, Sun's sister; then charmed it Frija, Vol's sister." See P. D. Chantepie de la Saussaye, *The Rel. of the Teutons*, 1902.

SUNNA, THE. Sunna is an Arabic word meaning "way, rule, mode of acting or conduct." The term is used to describe the traditional sayings, actions, etc., of Muhammad. These are rules and patterns for all devout Muslims. This kind of information is also called Hadith. It ranks next in importance to the Qur'ān. "The science of Tradition is considered the noblest and most excellent after that of the Qur'án, and its study the next in importance to that of the Holy Book. Muhammad himself is said to have encouraged his followers to keep and transmit his sayings" (Klein). There is the Sunna of Saying, which consists of oral laws and utterance derived from the Prophet; the Sunna of Action, which consists of his deeds and practice; the Sunna of Approbation or Confirmation, which consists of his silent sanction of acts done by others. In course of time it was thought necessary to have the oral traditions sifted and written down. Khalif 'Umar II. (99-101 A.H.) ordered this to be done about one hundred years after Muhammad's death. There are six collections of exceptional authority, called "The Six Books." (1) The traditions of Bukhâri *b.* A.H. 194), which professes to include only genuine traditions. Klein quotes a learned doctor of Islâm as saying: "The collection of Bukhári is the most excellent book of Islam after the Book of God." (2) The traditions of Muslim (*d.* 261 A.H.), a disciple of Bukhâri. This again was supposed to include only genuine tradition. (3) The traditions of Abu Dâud (*d.* 275 A.H.). (4) The traditions of Tirmidhi (*d.* 279 A.H.). (5) The traditions of An Nisâ'i (*d.* 303 A.H.). (6) The traditions of Ibn Mâjâ (*d.* 273 A.H.). See F. A. Klein.

SUPAY. Supay was one of the deities worshipped by the ancient Peruvians. He was the god of the dead, and corresponded to Pluto.

SUPERMAN, THE. The German term *Uebermensch* "superman," used by Goethe in "Faust," is employed by Friedrich Nietzsche (1844-1900) to describe the ideal man of his philosophy. In 1888 Nietzsche became insane, and his last literary production, *Der Antichrist,* in its extravagance already bears the stamp of insanity. Influenced at first by Schopenhauer (1788-1860), the disciple went far beyond his master. Nietzsche is usually regarded as a gloomy pessimist and a brutal materialist. He is of course in some respects pessimistic and materialistic. But probably he is very much misunderstood. He is thought to have done young people in Germany much harm. But young people will have read his works, without understanding them, with the idea of finding in them something (outrageous) which is not necessarily there. Forbidden books are always attractive to certain people, and a reputation for outrageousness acts as a powerful suggestion. Certain people want to be outraged. Writers like Ibsen and Nietzsche are the tools which they sharpen for themselves. It has been rightly observed that the strength of Nietzsche's Superman "could hardly be won and maintained without the austerest self-discipline" (A. Butler). One can do Nietzsche justice without accepting or admiring his philosophy. "Nietzsche represents a passionate individualism in opposition to the social and democratic tendencies of the present time. His ideal is the powerful individual who has risen above the 'slave-morality' of Christian civilisation, with its sympathy and compassion, its indulgence towards weakness, and its weak love of neighbours and enemies. The mass, he thinks, has by mere force of numbers overcome the strong individuals whose power he conceives to be the only intrinsic good. The mass has made morality, determined the scale of life's values; and it has done this, thinks Nietzsche, in its own interest and in the strength of mere majority" (Butler). According to Nietzsche, we need a transvaluation of all values ("Umwertung aller Werte"). See C. J. Deter, *Geschichte der Philosophie,* 1906; Arthur Butler, *Dict. of Philosophical Terms.*

SUPERNATURAL RELIGION. The title "Supernatural Religion" was given to a work by Walter R. Cassels, which appeared in 1874, and created a considerable stir. The author contended that the Gospels of Matthew and Mark as they have been preserved to us are not those referred to by Eusebius. He also discussed from a rationalistic standpoint the questions of Miracles, the Incarnation, the Resurrection, and the Ascension. The book was replied to by Bishop J. B. Lightfoot (1828-1889) in his *Essays on the Work called "Supernatural Religion."* F. C. Conybeare, himself a keen critic and advanced theologian, thinks that Lightfoot succeeded in refuting Cassels' thesis that our Gospel of Luke is merely a later edition of Marcion's Gospel, as well as his contention with regard to Eusebius. He thinks that Cassels' book has other grave shortcomings. "In general it underestimates the external evidence in favour of the age of the Synoptic gospels; and its author has no clear idea either of the relations in which they stand to each other, or of the supreme importance of ascertaining those relations correctly. He moved exclusively in the circle of Baur's ideas, and had neglected other German books of equal weight, like those of C. H. Weisse and C. G. Wilke, published in 1838." Cassels' great opponent, Lightfoot, however, held no superiority in critical outlook, "though he was a better scholar and, within the narrow circle of his premises, a more careful and accurate worker." See F. C. Conybeare, *Hist. of N.T. Crit.;* cp. P. Vivian, *The Churches and Modern Thought,* 1908.

SUPPLEMENTARY HYPOTHESIS, THE. This name has been given to one of the theories put forth by the Higher Critics (see CRITICISM, HIGHER) to explain the composition of the Hexateuch. It was preceded by the Documentary Hypothesis (*q.v.*) and the Fragmentary Hypothesis (*q.v.*). All that was best in these it adopted. Their mistakes it corrected. The Supplementary Hypothesis is largely associated with the name of the German scholar W. M. L. De Wette (*b.* 1780), because he prepared the way for it. After some hesitation, De Wette rose above the two earlier hypotheses and pressed "for the *unity* of the Pentateuch in its present form as the *plan* of one mind. He first stated that Deuteronomy is an independent part of the Pentateuch, composed in the age of Josiah. He subsequently adopted into his system the improvements suggested by other Biblical scholars who followed in his footsteps" (C. A. Briggs). A later scholar, F. Bleek (1793-1859), put the Supplementary Hypothesis into shape. According to him, the original narrative of the Elohist (the writer who uses the divine name *Elohim*) was supplemented by the Jahvist (less correctly Jehovist; the writer who uses the divine name *Jehovah*). H. Ewald (1803-1875) afterwards showed that throughout the Pentateuch it was possible to distinguish the Elohistic and Jahvistic (Jehovistic) documents. It was then discovered that this was true of Joshua as well, so that it became convenient to speak of the Hexateuch. In 1853 H. Hupfeld of Halle independently revived the discovery of C. D. Ilgen (see DOCUMENTARY HYPOTHESIS), who had claimed that a number of documents were used in the composition of Genesis. He analysed the book of Genesis very carefully, and was able to discriminate an Elohist, a Second Elohist, a Jahvist (Jehovist), and a Redactor. He found that the Redactor differs from the other three, "in that he is distinguished for the conscientiousness with which he reproduces the ancient documents, word for word, and the skill with which he combines them in the unity and order which characterize his work" (C. A. Briggs). Heinrich Ewald (1803-1875), a many-sided and brilliant scholar, found in the Elohistic document a Book of Origins, which had drawn upon older writings: a biography of Moses, the Book of the Wars of Jehovah (*q.v.*), and the Book of the Covenants. This framework (German "Grundschrift) was supplemented at later dates by the Second Elohist, the Jahvist, the Redactor, and the Deuteronomist. According to E. Schrader (writing in 1868), "there are two chief documents: the Annalistic (Elohist) and Theocratic (2d Elohist), composed, the former in the earlier part of the reign of David, the author a priest who used earlier written sources; the latter soon after the division of the kingdom in the northern realm, 975-950 B.C., also using ancient documents. The third prophetic narrator (Jehovist) combined the two, freely appropriating, and rejecting, and enlarging by numerous additions, making a complete and harmonious work, in the reign of Jeroboam II., 825-800 B.C., in the northern kingdom. The Deuteronomist in the prophetic spirit composed the law of Moses contained in Deuteronomy, and became the final *redactor* of the Pentateuch in its present form, immediately before the reform of Josiah, 622 B.C., being a man closely associated with the prophet Jeremiah." In

England the Supplementary Hypothesis was advocated by Samuel Davidson (1806-1899). Cp HEXATEUCH. See C. A. Briggs, *Hex.;* A. Duff, *Hist. of O.T. Crit.*, 1910.

SUPRALAPSARIANISM. A doctrine held by the extreme Calvinists. When God created man, he decreed his fall, both foreseeing and permitting it. He overruled it for man's redemption. "It is logically the most consistent type of Calvinism, but borders on fatalism and pantheism, and hence was excluded from the Reformed Confessions, all of which deny emphatically that God is the author of sin" (Schaff-Herzog).

SURA. The Qur'ân is divided into Suras. The word Sura means a row or series. As used of the Qur'ân, it corresponds roughly to our chapter. Each Sura has a special title which is supposed to relate to its contents. Thus, the first is called "Mecca," the second "The Cow," the third "The Family of Imran," etc. The verses are designated 'Āyât, which means literally "signs" or "miracles." They are so called because each verse was supposed to be a miracle. In Sura xvii. vs. 90 Muhammad is reported to have said: "Verily, were men and genii assembled to produce the like of this Koran, they could not produce its like, though the one should help the other." There are one hundred and fourteen Suras of different lengths. Every Sura, except the ninth, is prefaced by the words: "In the name of God, the Merciful, the Compassionate."

SURĀDEVI. A Hindu deity, goddess of wine, worshipped by the Sundis, the liquor-distilling caste of the Uriya country in India. The Sundis regard her as their mother.

SŪRYA. The chief of the Vedic solar deities, the son of Dyaus or the sky. He is closely associated with Agni, and sometimes seems to be identified with him. The car in which he makes his daily journey is drawn by seven mares.

SUSA-NO-O. A figure in the mythology of the Japanese. He was born from the nose of Izanagi, and, whatever he was at first seems to have developed into a god of the underworld. From one of his children the Mikado is supposed to be descended.

SŪTEKH. An Egyptian deity. Sûtekh is a later and lengthened form of the name Set (*q.v.*).

SUTHRA SHĀHIS. A mendicant order in India, an offshoot of the Nānakpanthis (*q.v.*). They are said to have been founded by a disciple of Nānak. Their distinctive badges are the Seli, a rope of black wool bound round the head like a turban, and the Syāhi, the ink which they use to draw a black line on their foreheads. See R. V. Russell.

SUTTAPIṬAKA. The second division of the Buddhist Canon. See CANON, BUDDHIST.

SUTTAVIBHANGA. One of the Buddhist sacred books in the first division of the Canon. See CANON, BUDDHIST.

SUTTEE. Suttee or Satī is the designation of the Hindu practice of burning the widows of deceased persons. A good wife showed her devotion by burning herself on the funeral pile of her husband. The practice seems to have originated in the noble caste of Rajahs. It was an honour claimed first by the pet wife, then by the first wife, and finally by any devoted wife. Dubois gives vivid descriptions of the Suttee ceremony. One relates to the case of a widow, aged about thirty years, who had decided to accompany her dead husband to the funeral pyre. "The news having rapidly spread abroad, a large concourse of people flocked together from all quarters to witness the spectacle. When everything was ready for the festival, and the widow had been richly clothed and adorned, the bearers stepped forward to remove the body of the deceased, which was placed in a sort of shrine, ornamented with costly stuffs, garlands of flowers, green foliage, etc., the corpse being seated in it with crossed legs, covered with jewels and clothed in the richest attire, and the mouth filled with betel. Immediately after the funeral car followed the widow, borne in a richly decorated palanquin. On the way to the burning-ground she was escorted by an immense crowd of eager sight-seers, lifting their hands towards her in token of admiration, and rending the air with cries of joy. She was looked upon as already translated to the paradise of Indra, and they seemed to envy her happy lot." On her way she distributed leaves of betel, which were treasured as relics. On leaving the palanquin, she dragged herself or was dragged to a pond not far from the pyre. Into this she plunged before being led to the pyre, which "was surrounded by Brahmins, each with a lighted torch in one hand and a bowl of ghee in the other." At length the fatal signal was given. "The poor widow was instantly divested of all her jewels, and dragged, more dead than alive, to the pyre. There she was obliged, according to custom, to walk three times round the pile, two of her nearest relatives supporting her by the arms. She accomplished the first round with tottering steps; during the second her strength wholly forsook her, and she fainted away in the arms of her conductors, who were obliged to complete the ceremony by dragging her through the third round. Then, at last, senseless and unconscious, she was cast upon the corpse of her husband. At that moment the air resounded with noisy acclamations. The Brahmins, emptying the contents of their vessels on the dry wood, applied their torches, and in the twinkling of an eye the whole pile was ablaze. Three times was the unfortunate woman called by her name. But, alas! she made no answer." There is no authority for the Suttee custom in the Hindu religious books. The Hindu theistic reformer, Rāmmohun Roy (b. 1774) denounced the practice, and in 1829 it was abolished by statute throughout British India. But it is said still to prevail on the borders of British territory in the Independent Hill States. E. W. Hopkins is inclined to think that the present existence of widows is more horrible than death on the funeral pyre. See Monier-Williams; E. W. Hopkins; J. A. Dubois and H. K. Beauchamp; J. Campbell Oman, *Cults*.

SUWĀ'H. An Arabian deity mentioned in the Qur'ân (lxxi., 22). The idol Suwâ'h is supposed to have been antediluvian. Legend says that after lying under water for some time after the Deluge, it was discovered by the pagan Arabs. Suwâ'h was worshipped in the shape of a woman. See E. H. Palmer, *The Qur'ân*, 1880, in the "Sacred Books of the East"; E. M. Wherry, *Comprehensive Commentary on the Qurân*, 1896.

SVANTOVIT. Svantovit is said to have been the chief god of the ancient Slavs. Saxo speaks of his worship on the island of Ruegen. He was represented, it seems, as having four heads and necks, and as holding in one hand a bow and in the other a drinking-horn. "Near the idol were a saddle and bridle destined for the white horse of the god, which only the priest might mount" (Reinach). Thus the god was, amongst other things, a god of war. The horse was used also in some form of divination. See Reinach, *O.*, 1909.

SVARGA. Svarga is one of the paradises or heavens in Brāhmanism. It is the heaven presided over by Indra (*q.v.*), and the paradise to which orthodox Brāhmans hope to be transported. In the centre is the palace of Indra, adorned with gold and precious stones, and there is another palace for his wife Sati. In the paradise thrive the Kalpa-tree with its golden fruit of exquisite flavour and the cow Kamadhenu with its delicious milk. These supply food for the gods. The Kalpa-tree has in fact "the power of satisfying all the desires of men who put their trust in it," and the cow Kamadhenu "can, among other things, grant milk and butter in abundance to anybody who invokes her with sincere faith and devotion" (Dubois and Beauchamp). See Monier-Williams; J. A. Dubois and H. K. Beauchamp.

SVARTALFAHEIM. Svartalfaheim would seem to have been one of the nine worlds in the cosmogony of the Ancient Teutons.

ŚVETĀMBARAS. The Śvetāmbaras or "white-attire men" are one of the two main bodies into which the Jains (*q.v.*) have split up. They were so called because they insisted on the need of wearing some attire (in their case, white), whereas the other body, the Digambaras or "sky-attire men," on principle wore no covering.

SWABIAN AND SAXON FORMULA OF CONCORD. A German Confession drawn up by James Andreæ of Tübingen in 1575 A.D. In 1573 Andreæ suggested as the basis on which the Lutherans might agree the substance of six irenic lectures. Martin Chemnitz, the famous pupil of Melanchthon, criticised this document, with the result that Andreæ then drew up the Swabian and Saxon Formula of Concord. This was rather lengthy, and as an improvement Luke Osiander and Balthasar Bidenbach at once drew up a brief formula, the Maulbronn Formula. These two formulas were superseded by the Book of Torgau (*q.v.*). See William A. Curtis.

SWADDLERS. A nickname bestowed upon the early Methodists by Roman Catholics in Ireland. It is supposed to have been suggested by some reference made by John Cennick (1718-1755) in a sermon to the "babe wrapped in swaddling-clothes."

SWALLOWS. In the mythology of the Dragon, the monster is represented as being fond of roasted swallows. This partiality of dragons for swallows was due, according to Elliot Smith (*Dr.*), to the transmission of a very ancient story of the Great Mother, who in the form of Isis was identified with the swallow. "In China, so ravenous is the monster for this delicacy, that anyone who has eaten of swallows should avoid crossing the water, lest the dragon whose home is in the deep should devour the traveller to secure the dainty morsel of swallow. But those who pray for rain use swallows to attract the beneficent deity. Even in England swallows flying low are believed to be omens of coming rain—a tale which is about as reliable as the Chinese variant of the same ancient legend."

SWĀMI-NARAYAN SECT. A Vaishnava sect in India, founded by Sahajānand Swāmi (b. A.D. 1780). He was made a Sādhu of the Rāmānandi order (see RAMANANDIS), and was nominated Rāmānandi's successor. Then he became head of a new sect, named after him, although his tenets did not differ much from those of Rāmānandi. He preached with such success in Gujarāt that in 1901 there were about 300,000 members of his sect there. He taught the worship of one sole deity, Krishna or Nārāyana, identified with the sun. By his followers he seems to have been regarded as a new incarnation of Vishnu. "It is said that he displayed miraculous powers before his disciples, entrancing whomsoever he cast his eyes upon, and causing them in this mesmeric state (Samadhi) to imagine they saw Sahajānand as Krishna with yellow robes, weapons of war, and other characteristics of the god, and to behold him seated as chief in an assembly of divine beings" (Russell and Hīra Lāl). He prohibited the use of animal food, intoxicating liquors, and drugs. His followers were required to abstain from promiscuous intercourse with women, theft, robbery, false accusations, and suicide. They were taught also to bear injury without retaliation. See R. V. Russell.

SWEDENBORG SOCIETY. In 1810 a few private persons formed a Society in London for the purpose of publishing the writings and disseminating the views of Emanuel Swedenborg. Chiefly through the efforts of John Clowes (see article below), the translator of many of Swedenborg's works, a similar institution, had been established in Manchester in 1782. The London Society may be regarded as a continuation of the Manchester Society. "Thus the voluminous writings of an author unknown to the public in general were, shortly after their publication, taken under the especial guardianship of a few earnest Christian men, deeply impressed, from a careful study of their contents, with a sense of their unspeakable value to the Church at large." It is pointed out that three things require to be distinguished carefully by the reader of Swedenborg's works. (1) The claims of Swedenborg to supernatural illumination. (2) The records of events heard and seen by him in the spiritual world. (3) The doctrines he has delivered, as derived from, and confirmed by, the express and undoubted statements of the Divine Word, and illustrated by rational considerations.

SWEDENBORGIANS. The disciples and followers of Emanuel von Swedenborg (1688-1772). His real name was Swedberg. His father Jesper Swedberg (1653-1735) was Bishop of Skara in West Gothland. After studying at Upsala University, Emanuel sought to extend his knowledge and experience by travel. He acquired an extensive knowledge of physical science, and on his return to his own country he started a scientific journal called "Dædalus Hyperboreus" (1716-1718). He was brought to the notice of Charles XII., and in 1716 was appointed Assessor Extraordinary in the Royal College of Mines at Stockholm. When Charles XII. was besieging Frederickshall, a fortress in Norway, Emanuel Swedberg's mechanical skill was of great service to him. In 1719 Swedberg was ennobled by Queen Ulrica Eleanora, successor of Charles XII., and his name was changed to Swedenborg. After this he began a literary career of great fruitfulness, publishing papers on the longitude, algebra, physics, mechanics, etc. In 1724 he was invited to become Professor of Mathematics in the University of Upsala, but declined. In 1734 he published at Leipsic, at the expense of the Duke of Brunswick, a work in three volumes on the various methods of mining and smelting and on the origin of creation, *Opera Philosophica et Mineralia*. The first volume was called "Principia, or the First Principles of Natural Things, being New Attempts towards a Philosophical Explanation of the Elementary World." In the same year he published a more metaphysical and theological work entitled "Philosophical Argument on the Infinite, and the Final Cause of Creation; and on the Mechanism of the Operation of Soul and Body." After more travels, he published in 1740 his "Economy of the Animal Kingdom." The year 1743 marks the turning-point in his life. In this year he claims to have received supernatural revelations. In one of his most important works, published some years later, "True Christian Religion," he says: "I foresee that many who read the Memorable Relations annexed to each chapter of this work, will believe them to be the fictions of imagination; but I protest in truth they are not fictions, but were really seen and heard; not seen and heard in any state of the mind in sleep, but in a state of complete wakefulness; for it has pleased the Lord to manifest himself to me, and to send me to teach those things which will belong to his New Church, which is meant by the New Jerusalem in the Revelation. For this purpose he has opened the interiors of my mind or spirit, by which privilege it has been permitted me to be with angels in the spiritual world, and with men in the natural world at the same time, and that now for twenty-seven years." In 1745 he published a philosophical work called "The Worship and Love of God," but he had not yet reached the complete change in the direction of his life. His characteristic philosophy is to be gleaned from the works that followed. In 1747 he resigned his assessorship in order to devote all his time and energies to his spiritual work. His philosophy was developed in "Arcana Cœlestia," an exposition of the Books of Genesis and Exodus (1749-56); "Heaven and Hell" (1758); "The Last Judgment and the Destruction of Babylon" (1758-1763), described as "being a relation of things heard and seen"; "The White Horse, mentioned in the Revelation, chap. xix." (1758); "Angelic Wisdom concerning the Divine Love and the Divine Wisdom" (1763); "Angelic Wisdom concerning the Divine Providence" (1764); "The Apocalypse Revealed" (1766); "Conjugal Love and its Chaste Delights" (1768); "The True Christian Religion" (1771). The "Arcana Cœlestia" was written in London while Swendenborg was living at 26 Great Bath Street, Coldbath Fields, Clerkenwell. He died in London on the 29th of March, 1772. His disciples before his death were not many. One of them was Thomas Hartley (1709?-1784), who translated one of Swedenborg's works. After Swedenborg's death, his writings gradually became better known. John Clowes (1743-1831), Vicar of S. John's, Manchester, in 1780 founded a Swedenborgian printing society, which in 1781 began to issue translations of Swedenborg's works made by Clowes himself. In 1783 Robert Hindmarsh (1759-1835), a Clerkenwell printer, formed a small Swedenborgian Society, which met at S. Paul's Coffee-House, St. Paul's Churchyard. Out of this grew "The Theosophical Society" which was "instituted for the purpose of promoting the heavenly doctrines of the New Jerusalem, by translating, printing, and publishing the theological writings of the Honourable Emanuel Swedenborg." It held its meetings in New Court, Middle Temple. In 1788 Robert Hindmarsh opened a chapel in East Cheap: the name of the Society was changed to "The New Church"; and an "Order of worship for the New Church signified by the New Jerusalem in the Revelation" was agreed upon. Hindmarsh acted as priest, and was charged afterwards to ordain others. In 1793 he built a chapel in Cross Street, Hatton Garden. In the same year a chapel was opened in Peter Street, Manchester. In 1815 three orders of ministers were established. The doctrines of Swedenborg have been summarized by J. Clowes. As regards the Sacred Writings, he thinks no one else has explained so clearly their divine original, and the nature of their divine inspiration. "He not only venerates their Divine authority on all occasions, therein grounding, and thereby confirming every doctrine which he delivers; he was not only well read in the sacred oracles, almost above the example of any other person, in the present or former times; but he likewise asserts, and proves indisputably, that there is contained in the Holy Books an *internal spiritual sense* heretofore little known, to which the outward literal sense serves as a basis, or receptacle, answering or corresponding thereto in a *figurative, allegorical,* or *symbolical* way, as a type answers to its archetype, or as a representative to the thing represented. He shews that in this internal sense consists the spirituality and Divinity of the Sacred Writings, whereby they *essentially* differ from all other books whatsoever; and that by virtue of this sense they are adapted, not only to the use of men on earth, but of angels in heaven: containing the great eternal laws of that Order, whereby the heavens are formed, preserved, and governed, and whereby man is reformed, regenerated, and restored to heavenly order: being thus accommodated to the instruction and perfecting of all intelligences from the highest to the lowest" (p. 50 f.). As regards the Christian life, Swedenborg declares that a man cannot be saved by charity, or faith, or good works alone; by a moral life without a spiritual life, or by a spiritual life without a moral life: by divine grace without his own free exertions, or by his own free exertions without divine grace. "A truly Christian life is a life which leads to heaven; and to be led to heaven is the same thing as to be formed in the image, likeness, and spirit of heaven, according to our Lord's declaration, '*The kingdom of heaven is within you.*' A truly Christian life, therefore, is that which tends most perfectly to open and form in man the image, likeness, and spirit of heaven. But whereas man consists of different parts or principles, each of them capable, in its degree, of receiving this heavenly image, likeness, and spirit, therefore this heavenly image, likeness, and spirit cannot be fully opened and formed, unless it be opened and formed in each part or principle. These parts or principles are, in general, the *will,* the *understanding,* and the *act* or *operation* thence proceeding. A truly Christian life therefore hath respect to these three several parts or principles of man, to open and form each of them according to the image, likeness, and spirit of heaven. The *will* is thus opened and formed by *charity,* with all its heavenly attendant graces and virtues. The *understanding* is thus opened and formed by *faith,* with all the bright knowledges and perceptions of holy truth thereto appertaining. And, lastly, the *act* or *operation* is so formed by *good works,* or an obedient practice of the things which charity and faith dictate. A truly Christian life, therefore, or a life which leads to heaven, is a life of charity, of faith, and of good works *conjointly*" (p. 57 f.). As regards qualifications for admission into the kingdom of heaven, poverty is not necessarily one of them. "It is the *love* of wealth, and not the mere *possession* thereof, which is a hindrance to man's salvation. These writings clearly prove that it is self-love and the love of the world that oppose and obstruct man's entrance into heaven; because these two kinds of love are *principally* opposite to the pure love of God and of our neighbour; in which the life of heaven consists, and by which it is opened and formed in man. In living therefore a life which leads to heaven, the chief difficulty is, according to the testimony of Baron Swedenborg, to remove self-love and the love of the world, with their various attendant concupiscences, so that the love of God and neighbourly love may have free admission into the heart, and formation in the life. It is therefore of no consequence, in this respect, whether a man be rich or poor as to his *outward circumstances,* because in either case he may *remain* in self-love and the love of the world, or he may *purify himself* from those unclean affections" (p. 63 f.). The New Church demands a new state of mind, not a radical change in the external state of civil society. "There will, therefore, still continue to be a difference of station, of office, and of character amongst men, but the pride and vanity arising from that difference will be removed and lost; for every member of the New Jerusalem, from the highest to the lowest, will consider himself as a *servant of the public,* in the station appointed for him by an all-wise Providence, to promote the common good under the influence of the same common spirit of good-will and charity. And thus, though there be a difference of office, employment, and character, yet all being influenced by one and the same spirit, 'the first will be last, and the last first.' *Kings* therefore, and those who are in authority, will execute judgment and justice in the earth. *Priests,* and those who have spiritual administration, will *wait on their ministry,* publishing the pure laws of spiritual order and truth from the pure love thereof. *Soldiers* will be courageous from principle, and will be valiant in defence of the just laws of nations, but without violence, injustice, or cruelty. *Merchants* will pursue commerce, not in the spirit of covetousness, but of universal good-will, to open the doors of communication between distant people, in the way of mutual comfort, convenience, and benevolence. *Mechanics* will be skilful and industrious, each in his several occupation, but without vice and artifice. *Scholars* will study the sciences, not in the pride thereof, but in the pure affection of truth." Swedenborg says little about forms of external worship, though he evidently attached importance to the outward rites of Baptism and the Lord's Supper. In other respects he seems to have felt that people should be free to use such forms as best suited their spiritual requirements. They are even warned to be slow to reject those forms of worship which are publicly sanctioned and in which they have been educated. Like certain other religious leaders, apparently he himself had no idea of founding a sect. Swedenborg's philosophy is essentially spiritual. "According to the testimony of the Sacred Writings, as opened by Baron Swedenborg, every man hath communication and association with the invisible world of spirits—whether he knows it or not—according to the nature, quality, and extent of his wisdom, as grounded in, and derived from, that love. If, therefore, the ruling principles of man's will be formed according to heavenly love, which is love to the Lord, and love towards his neighbour, and the ruling persuasions of his understanding be formed according to the wisdom of such love —which is the genuine truth of the holy commandment or Word of God—he then lives, wills, thinks, speaks, and acts proportionably from heaven, and in conjunction therewith, and is in invisible association continually with the blessed inhabitants thereof, being internally, as to his spirit, united to, and one with them." See the biographies by Schaarschmidt (1862), W. White (1867, new ed. 1871), and J. J. Garth Wilkinson (2nd ed. 1886); R. L. Tafel, *Documents concerning the Life and Character of Swedenborg*, 3 vols., 1875-77; J. Clowes, *Outlines of Swedenborg's Doctrines*, 1873; the publications of the "Swedenborg Society"; J. H. Blunt; and *Chambers' Encycl.*

SWEET SINGERS. 1. A band of religious enthusiasts in Scotland (1681) who followed a person called John Gib of Borrowstounness. They abandoned their ordinary occupations, turned their backs on what is commonly accepted as civilised life, and fasted and prayed in the open fields. They received the name Sweet Singers from their habit of chanting some of the Psalms. See J. H. Blunt. 2. Another name for the English Ranters (*q.v.*) of the seventeenth century.

SWINE. Among the Hebrews, Syrians, and Saracens swine's flesh was taboo, as indeed it was among all the Semites. The reason seems to be that the pig was at one time a sacred animal, especially as we are told that it possessed magical powers (Cazwīnī, i. 393, cited by Robertson Smith). "According to Al-Nadim, the heathen Harranians sacrificed the swine and ate swine's flesh once a year. This ceremony is ancient, for it appears in Cyprus in connection with the worship of the Semitic Aphrodite and Adonis. In the ordinary worship of Aphrodite swine were not admitted, but in Cyprus wild boars were sacrificed once a year on April 2" (Robertson Smith, *R.S.*). In Egypt, Osiris, Isis, and especially Set, were identified with the pig; and throughout the Eastern Mediterranean the pig was identified also with the Great Mother and associated with lunar and sky phenomena. "In fact at Troy the pig was represented with the star-shaped decorations with which Hathor's divine cow (in her rôle as a sky-goddess) was embellished in Egypt. To complete the identification with the cow-mother, Cretan fable represents a sow suckling the infant Minos or the youthful Zeus-Dionysus as his Egyptian prototype was suckled by the divine cow" (G. Elliot Smith, *Dr.*). The Mesopotamian god Rimmon when worshipped as a tempest-god was known as "the pig." According to Elliot Smith, the use of the words χοιρος by the Greeks, and *porcus* and *porculus* by the Romans, reveals the fact that the terms had the double significance of pig and cowry-shell. "As it is manifestly impossible to derive the word 'cowry' from the Greek word for 'pig,' the only explanation that will stand examination is that the two meanings must have been acquired from the identification of both the cowry and the pig with the Great Mother and the female reproductive organs. In other words, the pig-associations of Aphrodite afford clear evidence that the goddess was originally a personification of the cowry." In New Guinea the place of the sacrificial pig may actually be taken by the cowry-shell.

SWINGING. A number of examples of the practice of swinging in various parts of the world as a religious or magical rite have been collected by J. G. Frazer. At a feast held by the Dyaks of Sarawak at the end of harvest, "when the soul of the rice is secured to prevent the crops from rotting away," a number of old women are accustomed to rock to and fro on a rude swing. In the East Indian island of Bengkali swinging is one of the ceremonies performed to secure a good catch of fish. The ancient Athenians kept an annual festival of swinging. "Boards were hung from trees by ropes, and people sitting on them swung to and fro, while they sang songs of a loose or voluptuous character. The swinging went on both in public and private." The festival was explained as an expiation for a suicide or suicides by hanging. Swinging was also a feature of the great Latin festival, *Feriae Latinae*. J. G. Frazer suggests that "perhaps we can reconcile the two apparently discrepant effects attributed to swinging as a means of expiation on the one side and of fertilisation on the other, by supposing that in both cases the intention is to clear the air of dangerous influences, whether these are ghosts of the unburied dead or spiritual powers inimical to the growth of plants." Swinging is still practised as a festal rite in Greece and Italy. See J. G. Frazer, *G.B.*, Pt. iii., 1912.

SYMBOLICS. The Christian creed known as the Apostles' Creed was called the Symbolum Apostolicum. Used as the baptismal confession, it was called a "symbol" as being a kind of watchword by which Christians were recognized. Luther and Melanchthon adopted the word and used it of other creeds. P. C. Marheineke (1780-1846) adopted the word Symbolics in 1810 to describe the study of the origin, contents, and history of the various Christian creeds. See Schaff-Herzog.

SYMBOLISM. Camden M. Cobern has pointed out that in the early Christian centuries it was the practice of Christians in all lands to use the native symbolism wherever possible to express their religious ideas. At Deir-el-Bahari Dr. Naville found the embalmed body of a Christian. The deceased held in his right hand a cup containing a red liquid and in his left what appeared to be a handful of wheat. These, according to Naville, were emblems of the Eucharist. "On the left shoulder is the swastika (卐) which was used as a Christian emblem from the earliest times not only in the Roman catacombs but also in Egypt. Yet the lower part of the robe covering the deceased contains a painting of two jackal-headed gods, probably Anubis and Apuat, adoring the sacred bark of Socharis" (Cobern).

SYMMACHIANS. A name by which the Ebionites (*q.v.*) are sometimes referred to. They were so called after Symmachus, the author of one of the Greek versions of the Old Testament.

SYN. One of the deities of the Ancient Teutons. The goddess Syn, who belonged to the retinue of Frija (*q.v.*) and Freyja (*q.v.*), is represented as protecting people who have to take an oath.

SYNAGOGUES. Jewish places of worship. The word Synagogue is Greek and means "assembly" or "congregation." The Hebrew (post-Biblical) expression for the Synagogue is *Beth ha-keneseth*, "House of Assembly." The institution seems to have arisen in the Greek period. "It probably did not become a regular institution in Palestine till after the beginning of the Maccabean period, and seems to have grown up first in the Dispersion. By the time of the New Testament, as everybody knows, Synagogues had become a widespread institution, and it was owing to their existence that Judaism was able to perpetuate itself after the destruction of the Temple" (W. O. E. Oesterley and G. H. Box). The remains of ancient Synagogues have been discovered in Palestine in recent years. "In April and May, 1905, the German Oriental Society excavated a Hebrew synagogue of the Roman period at Tell-Hum. It was 78 feet long by 59 feet wide, was built of beautiful white limestone almost equal to marble, and was in every way more magnificent than any ever before found in Palestine, that in Chorazin being the next finest. Its roof was gable-shaped, and it was surprizingly ornamented with fine carvings representing animals, birds, fruit, etc.; though in some cases these ornamentations had been intentionally mutilated. In January, 1907, Macalister and Masterman reported that they had made sufficient excavations at Khan Minyeh to prove that it was not the ancient Capernaum, as it contained no pottery older than the Arab time. This report being accepted, Tell-Hum is left without a rival in its claim to be Capernaum, and makes it probable that the synagogue excavated there is the very one referred to in Luke 12, 5" (Cobern). The Synagogue of course has its peculiar institutions and ceremonies, but it differs from the Christian Churches in having, according to K. Kohler, no sacraments. "Its institutions, such as the festivals, aim to preserve the historic memory of the people; its ceremonies, called 'signs' or 'testimonies' in the Scripture, are to sanctify the life of the nation, the family, or the individual." The Jew becomes a member of the Jewish community by right of birth. The most important institution of the Synagogue is the Sabbath. "The highest point of religious devotion in the synagogue is reached on the New Year's day and the Day of Atonement preceding the Feast of Sukkoth." Kohler thinks that the weakness of the Synagogue was its Orientalism, which was marked particularly by its former attitude to women. Full rights of membership have only been accorded them in our own time, owing to the reform movement in Germany and Austria.

SYNOPSIS. The name Synopsis has been given to works in which, for convenience, the texts of the Synoptic Gospels (Matthew, Mark, and Luke) are printed in parallel columns. It is a more scientific term than "Harmony" (see HARMONIES OF THE GOSPELS).

SYNOPTIC PROBLEM. The three Gospels which present on the whole a common view of the Gospel story, the Gospels of Matthew, Mark, and Luke, present also a problem of great difficulty. For many as are the sections in which they are in agreement, there are many others in which they differ from one another considerably. "It is this combination of agreement and difference that has given rise to what is known as the Synoptic Problem. The problem is to frame a theory which shall account for the relations between the first three Gospels, setting them in their chronological order, tracing the sources from which they have been compiled, and explaining both the coincidences and differences which they present" (A. S. Peake). See Allan Menzies, *The Earliest Gospel*, 1901; J. Armitage Robinson, *The Study of the Gospels*, 1903; C. E. Scott-Moncrieff, *St. Mark and the Triple Tradition*, 1907; Paul Wernle, *The Sources of Our Knowledge of the Life of Jesus*, 1907; A. S. Peake, *Intr.*

SYNOPTICS. In Scientific Theology the name Synoptics has been given to the Gospels of Matthew, Mark, and Luke. *Synopsis* means "common view." These gospels have so much in common that they may be "viewed together." There are indeed many differences, but, as compared with the Gospel of John (*q.v.*), the other three gospels may be regarded together. See SYNOPTIC PROBLEM.

SYRIAN CHRISTIANS. A community in India. According to a tradition cherished by the Syrian Christians in Southern India, the Apostle St. Thomas founded seven churches in Cochin and Travancore, and then extended his labours to the Coromandel coast, where he was martyred. The apostle is supposed to have landed about 52 A.D. In the second century Demetrius of Alexandria is said to have been requested by natives of India to send a Christian teacher to them. Pantaenus of Alexandria, who undertook to go, and sailed between 180 and 190 A.D., found some "to whom Bartholomew, one of the apostles, had preached," already in possession of the Gospel of Matthew in Hebrew. The traditions in fact (whatever their value) waver between St. Thomas and St. Bartholomew. According to Dorotheus of Tyre (254-313 A.D.) and Jerome (390 A.D.), St. Thomas was martyred at Calamina in India. According to Rufinus, his remains were taken from India to Ephesus. It has been urged by some that the Thomas who introduced the Gospel into India was rather Thomas the Manichæan. He is supposed to have gone to India in 277 A.D. But still a third Thomas is associated with the evangelization of India. About the middle of the fourth century one Thomas Cana, a Syrian merchant, is said to have conducted a mission to the Malabar coast to improve the conditions of the Christians there. In any case, from this time until the arrival of the Portuguese in India the natives of Malabar seem to have welcomed the visitations and teachings of Nestorian and Jacobite Bishops without troubling to distinguish between them. In the sixteenth century they seem to have come under the authority of the Nestorian Patriarch of Mesopotamia. When the Portuguese came, they lost little time in converting the Malabar Church into a branch of the Roman Church (A.D. 1599). But the conduct of the Jesuits led before long to a split in the Malabar Church and the rise of two parties, the Romo-Syrians and the Jacobite Syrians, who acknowledged the spiritual supremacy of the Patriarch of Antioch. The Romo-Syrians are now known as Catholics of the Syrian rite. The converts made among the various castes of the Hindus by the Portuguese formed a third party, known as Catholics of the Latin rite. A long dispute between the claims of Rome, Babylon, and Antioch sharpened the divisions of the Malabar Church. In 1893 Titus Mar Thoma was chosen to preside over a Reformed Party of Jacobite Syrians, who prefer to be known as St. Thomas' Syrians. The original Jacobite Syrians are under Mar Dionysius, and owe allegiance to the Patriarch of Antioch. There are besides the Chaldæan Syrians who are so called because in 1856 a large section of the Syrians asked the Catholic Chaldæan Patriarch of Babylon to send them a Chaldæan Bishop, which he did in 1861. It seems that "while the Jacobite Syrians have accepted and acknowledged the ecclesiastical supremacy of the Patriarch of Antioch, the St. Thomas' Syrians, maintaining that the Jacobite creed was introduced into Malabar only in the seventeenth century after a section of the church had shaken off the Roman supremacy, uphold the ecclesiastical autonomy of the church, whereby the supreme control of the spiritual and temporal affairs of the church is declared to be in the hands of the Metropolitan of Malabar. The St. Thomas' Syrians hold that the consecration of a Bishop by, or with the sanction of the Patriarch of Babylon, Alexandria, or Antioch, gives no more validity or sanctity to that office than consecration by the Metropolitan of Malabar, the supreme head of the church in Malabar, inasmuch as this church is as ancient and apostolic as any other, being founded by the Apostle St. Thomas; while the Jacobites hold that the consecration of a Bishop is not valid, unless it be done with the sanction of their Patriarch. The St. Thomas' Syrians have, however, no objection to receiving consecration from the head of any other episcopal apostolic church, but they consider that such consecrations do not in any way subject their church to the supremacy of that prelate or church" (E. Thurston and K. Rangachari). The Catholics of the Syrian rite use the liturgy of the Church of Rome in Syriac; the Catholics of the Latin rite use the same in Latin. The Chaldæan Syrians use the Roman liturgy, but they have introduced differences in practice. According to Thurston and Rangachari most of the Syrians of the present day trace their descent from the higher orders of Hindu society, and, in spite of being Christians, many of them observe certain customs more or less prevalent among high-caste Hindus. See E. Thurston.

T

TA'ANITH. The name of one of the Jewish treatises or tractates which reproduce the oral tradition or unwritten law as developed by the second century A.D. and are incorporated in the Mishnah (*q.v.*), a collection and compilation completed by Rabbi Judah the Holy, or the Patriarch, about 200 A.D. The sixty-three tractates of the Mishnah are divided into six groups or orders (*sedarim*). Ta'anith is the ninth tractate of the second group, which is called *Mō'ēd* ("Festival").

TABLETS OF FATE. In Babylonian mythology the possession of the tablets of fate gives power and authority over gods and men. In the Epic of Marduk Tiâmat gives them to Kingu, from whom Marduk takes them after he has conquered Tiâmat. In the Zu myth we find Bel or En-lil in possession of them. The storm-god Zu snatches them from him and escapes to the mountains. Marduk is the only god who ventures to attack Zu. He is successful, and captures the tablets of fate. Thus he gains the power formerly possessed by Bel. See MARDUK, EPIC OF; ZU MYTH.

TABOO. The word *taboo* is Polynesian, and means withdrawn from current use. "The field covered by taboos among savage and half-savage races in very wide, for there is no part of life in which the savage does not feel himself to be surrounded by mysterious agencies and recognise the need of walking warily. Moreover, all taboos do not belong to religion proper, that is, they are not always rules of conduct for the regulation of man's contact with deities that, when taken in the right way, may be counted on as friendly, but rather appear in many cases to be precautions against the approach of malignant enemies—against contact with evil spirits and the like. Thus alongside of taboos that exactly correspond to rules of holiness, protecting the inviolability of idols and sanctuaries, priests and chiefs, and generally of all persons and things pertaining to the gods and their worship, we find another kind of taboo which in the Semitic field has its parallel in rules of uncleanness. Women after childbirth, men who have touched a dead body and so forth, are temporarily taboo and separated from human society, just as the same persons are unclean in Semitic religion. In these cases the person under taboo is not regarded as holy, for he is separated from approach to the sanctuary as well as from contact with men; but his act or condition is somehow associated with supernatural dangers, arising, according to the common savage explanation, from the presence of formidable spirits which are shunned like an infectious disease. In most savage societies no sharp line seems to be drawn between the two kinds of taboo just indicated, and even in more advanced nations the notions of holiness and uncleanness often touch" (W. Robertson Smith, *R.S.*). Among the Syrians, and indeed among all the Semites, swine's flesh was taboo; it might not be eaten. Among the Syrians again the dove was taboo; it might not be touched. Among the Israelites it was not permitted to touch the sacred ark; and among the natives of Central Australia no ordinary person dares to approach a *churinga*.

TABORITES. The Taborites were one of the sections into which the followers of John Hus (1369-1415; see HUSSITES) were divided. Tabor means "tent," and the Taborites or "men of the tent" were so called because in 1419 they met and encamped on a mountain near Prague in Bohemia in order to received the Communion in both kinds. Unlike the Calixtines (*q.v.*), the more peaceful section of the Hussites, the Taborites sought to promote and defend their principles by the power of the sword. They were led by John Ziska (1360-1424). In 1419 he marched into Prague and committed acts of pillage and violence. This was the beginning of that vandalism and iconoclasm that deprived Bohemia of most of its beautiful churches. The Taborites regarded the Word of God as the sole authority in religious matters. They lived in expectation of the personal descent of Christ. From their fourteen articles, published in 1420, it appears that they rejected all polite literature, the decrees of the Fathers, the use of holy oil, the use of consecrated water in Baptism, the practice of having sponsors, auricular confession, office books, vestments, etc., fasts, and in fact the whole ritual of the Church. In 1422 Ziska defeated the Emperor Sigismund in a battle near Deutschbrod. In 1424 he died. He was succeeded by the brothers Procopius. Some of the followers of Ziska, however, refused to acknowledge that anyone could properly succeed their old leader. They therefore called themselves Orphans and formed a new body, though they were willing to fight with the Taborites against the common foe. Warfare continued, and the Taborites won a number of victories. At length in 1434 they were severely defeated at Boehmischbrod. In 1453 they were again defeated and dispersed. Those who remained formed the nucleus of the Bohemian Brethren (*q.v.*). See J. H. Blunt: *Prot. Dict.; Cath. Dict.;* Brockhaus.

TALITH. The Talith is a kind of shawl made of silk and ornamented with fringes. It is worn by orthodox Jews in the Synagogue. In the Old Testament one of the commands given to the Jews is this (Deuteronomy xxii. 12): "Thou shalt make thee fringes upon the four corners of thy vesture wherewith thou coverest thyself." This original garment was a piece of linen or wool large enough to cover the whole body. In course of time it became necessary to avoid attracting attention by wearing fringes or tassels on the outer garment. A smaller garment with fringes was therefore worn underneath the ordinary clothing. The modern praying-shawl is called Talith (a corruption of the Greek *stolē*), and a distinction is made between the "Little Talith" and the "Large Talith." The Large Talith corresponds to the ancient "garment with fringes." The fringes have again been attached to it, so that now both the Large Talith and the Little Talith have them. See W. O. E. Oesterley and G. H. Box.

TALMUD, THE. The Talmud, the great literary production of the Jewish Schools, consists of the Mishnah and the Gemara. The Mishnah for the most part reproduces the traditional discussions of the Rabbis who lived between 70 A.D. and about 200 A.D. These discussions seem to have been written down about 200 A.D. After this the Mishnah (*q.v.*) was discussed in the Schools of Palestine and Babylonia, and the new discussions received the name Gemara. The Rabbis who were active in the Schools from 220 to 500 A.D. are designated Amoraim, "Speakers" or "Interpreters." The Palestinian or Jerusalem Talmud was completed towards the end of the fourth century or during the fifth century A.D. The Babylonian Talmud was completed about 500 A.D. The Mishnah is the text, to which the Gemara is a kind of commentary. In both recensions of the Talmud the Mishnah is the same. The Gemara is not identical, that of Babylon being very much amplified. In neither case is the Gemara complete. Certain tractates are omitted in each, and these are not the same in the two Gemaras. The Mishnah consists of sixty-three tractates or treatises which are arranged in six groups or Sedārim. For the names of these see MISHNAH. The discussions in the Mishnah are mostly of the kind called Halachah: those in the Gemara are entirely of the kind known as Haggadah. Halachah means literally the act of walking or going. Then it comes to mean (1) a walk (life) in accordance with the Law, (2) the Law in accordance with which the walk of life must be guided. Haggadah means literally "telling" or "recitation." Halachah aims at establishing legal rules. Haggadah is homiletical. See further HAGGADAH and HALACHAH. Throughout the Talmuds are also found what are known as *Baraitha* sections. Baraitha means in Aramaic "the outside" or "the external." It denotes a Tannaite tradition (see TANNĀIM) which has not been incorporated in the Mishnah. The Baraitha sections are in Hebrew, whereas the Gemara is in Aramaic. Moreover, the Baraithas are in the style of both halachah and haggadah. C. A. Briggs (*Intr.*) gives an example of Baraitha and Gemara from the tractate Bābā Bathrā. Part of it is as follows: (Baraitha) "The rabbins have taught that the order of the Prophets is, Joshua and Judges, Samuel and Kings, Jeremiah and Ezekiel, Isaiah and the Twelve (minor prophets)"; (Gemara) "How is it? Hosea is first because it is written, 'In the beginning the Lord spake to Hosea.' But how did he speak in the beginning with Hosea? Have there not been so many prophets from Moses unto Hosea? Rabbi Jochanan said that he was the first of the four prophets who prophesied in the same period, and these are: Hosea, Isaiah, Amos, and Micah. Should then Hosea be placed before at the head? (*Reply*): No, since his prophecies had been written alongside of Haggai, Zechariah, and Malachi, and Haggai, Zechariah, and Malachi were the last of the prophets, it was counted with them. (*Question*): Ought it to have been written apart and ought it to have been placed before? (*Reply*): No; since it was little and might be easily lost. (*Question*): How is it? Isaiah was before Jeremiah and Ezekiel. Ought Isaiah to be placed before at the head? (*Reply*): Since the book of Kings ends in ruin and Jeremiah is, all of it, ruin, and Ezekiel has its beginning ruin and its end comfort, and Isaiah is all of it comfort; we join ruin to ruin and comfort to comfort." See J. W. Etheridge, *Intr. to Heb. Lit.*, 1856; *Encycl. Bibl.*, *s.v.* "Law Literature"; W. O. E. Oesterley and G. H. Box; A. S. Geden, *Intr. to the Heb. Bible,* 1909.

TAMAGOSTAD. The chief god of the Nicarao (of Nicaragua). He seems to have been equivalent to the Mexican Oxomoco. With the help of the goddess Cipaltonal, he created the earth and mankind.

TAMBALAS. A class of Hindu priests in Southern India. They are described as Telugu-speaking temple priests.

TAMFANA. Tacitus (*Annals*, i., 51) mentions a temple of a goddess Tamfana, which was levelled to the ground by Germanicus. Tamfana was worshipped by the Marsi, and seems to have been a goddess of fertility. Her festival was in the autumn. See P. D. Chantepie de la Saussaye, *Rel. of the Teutons*, 1902.

TĀMĪD. The title of one of the Jewish treatises or tractates which reproduce the oral tradition or unwritten law as developed by the second century A.D. and are incorporated in the Mishnah (*q.v.*), a collection and compilation completed by Rabbi Judah the Holy, or the Patriarch, about 200 A.D. The sixty-three tractates of the Mishnah are divided into six groups or orders (*sedarim*). Tāmīd is the ninth tractate of the fifth group, which is called *Ḳodāshīm* ("Holy Things").

TAMMUZ. The name of a god worshipped in Babylonia. It appears from a Sumerian Dynastic List that the Sumerians believed him to have been a man who reigned in Erech for a hundred years. He seems also to be described as a hunter: "Dumuzi, the hunter (?), whose city was . . ., ruled for a hundred years" (L. W. King, *Legends of Babylon and Egypt in relation to Hebrew Tradition*, 1918). This description, as Professor King points out, recalls the death of Adonis in Greek mythology. Tammuz became a god of vegetation, and reference is made to the annual festival of mourning for the death of the god in Ezekiel viii. 14. This annual mourning for Tammuz (or Adonis) is "the scenic commemoration of a divine tragedy in which the worshippers take part with appropriate wailing and lamentation" (W. Robertson Smith, *R.S.*); and it is thought that in point of form it supplies the closest parallel to the fasting and humiliation on the Hebrew Day of Atonement. The mother of Tammuz was Ishtar, but in course of time she came to be regarded as his wife, just as the Egyptian Isis became the wife of Osiris. Both the Babylonians and the Hebrews named the fourth month of the year after the god.

TAMU. A deity worshipped by the Caribs of Brazil as a culture-god. He is said to have taught the people the art of agriculture.

TANIT. A goddess referred to in Carthaginian inscriptions. In one passage she is described as "The Great Mother." Elsewhere she is addressed as the "Lady Tanit, the Face of Baal."

TANNAIM. The word means "Teachers" (literally "repeaters" or "reciters"; Aram. *tenā*, Heb. *shānāh* "to repeat"). It is a name given to the Jewish Rabbis who flourished from A.D. 10 to A.D. 220 and were the predecessors of the Amoraim (*q.v.*). Hillel and Shammai, the famous leaders of rival schools of learning, belonged to the first generation of them (A.D. 10-80). To the second generation (A.D. 90-130) belonged Rabban Gamaliel II. and Rabbi Akiba ben Joseph. To the third generation (A.D. 130-160) belonged Rabbi Meir, Rabbi Simon ben Jochai, and Rabbi Simon b. Gamaliel, disciples of Rabbi Akiba. To the fourth generation (A.D. 160-220) belonged Rabbi Jehudah ha-Nāsi or "the Prince" (A.D. 160-210). He was also called Rabbi Jehudah the Holy, "Our master the saint," or simply Rabbi, *i.e.*, the Rabbi *par excellence*. It was he who finally compiled and codified the Mishnah (*q.v.*) in its present form. And it was during his presidency that the centre of Jewish learning was transferred from Jamnia to Tiberias. See J. W. Etheridge, *Intr. to Heb. Lit.;* W. O. E. Oesterley and G. H. Box; A. S. Geden, *Intr. to the Heb. Bible*, 1909.

TANTRA. Tantra is a term found in Hindūism. It denotes a kind of sectarian tract or rite-book. In Śāktism (*q.v.*) they are held in such high honour that they are said to constitute its bible. They are generally believed to have been revealed by Śiva (*q.v.*). "As a general rule they are written in the form of a dialogue between the god Śiva and his wife; and every Tantra ought, like a Purāṇa, to treat of five subjects—the creation, the destruction of the world, the worship of the gods, the attainment of superhuman power, and the four modes of union with the Supreme Spirit" (Monier-Williams). Many of the Tantras deal with the use of charms and spells, Yantras (*q.v.*), Bijas (*q.v.*), and Mudrās (*q.v.*), alchemy, etc. See Monier-Williams; E. W. Hopkins.

TAOISM. Taoism is one of the religions of China, or it might be better to say, Taoism has become one of the superstitions of China. For Taoism, as expounded by its reputed founder, was a philosophy rather than a religion, and when it came to be regarded as a religion, it had degenerated into a superstition. According to R. K. Douglas, Taoism was originally a purely politico-ethical system. It passed, in fact, through three stages. There was first the pure Taoism which was systematized about 600 B.C. by Lao-tsze, but had been in existence since about 1100 B.C. This flourished until about 200 B.C. There was secondly the Taoism as developed by the followers of Lao-tsze, Lieh-tsze and Chwang-tsze. There has been, thirdly, the Taoism of modern times, which is so degenerate that it hardly deserves the name. The Yellow Emperor Hwang Ti (2700 B.C.) is supposed to have bequeathed to his people a number of valued and venerable precepts. And, according to E. H. Parker, "there can be little doubt that Lao-tsze in the sixth century B.C. simply gave a name (*Tao*) to a floating group of ethical principles already for many centuries spread far and wide over China, and already known as the Maxims of Hwang Ti." The difficulty is to know what exactly Lao-tsze meant by the term Tao. It appears in the title of the book in which he expounded his philosophy, the Tao-teh-King (*q.v.*). The word *King* means "classic" or "orthodox work" and was added subsequently when the work came to be regarded as classical. The subject of the book is therefore Tao-têh, an expression which was already in use in the "Book of Changes" and the "Book of Rites." E. H. Parker explains Têh as follows: "Têh is an emanation from *Tao*, and signifies that rule of action which naturally follows from faith in *Tao;* not charity or forgiveness, as many have thought: its modern signification as a noun is "virtue," "efficacy," "power for good"; and, again, in verbal senses, "to be grateful for," "to like one for," "to take credit to one's self for"" (*Chinese Religion*, p. 71). From this one would suppose that the word corresponds to our -ism (or value). But Prof. Parker decides in favour of the word "Grace," which, in view of its theological associations, seems unfortunate. For *Tao*, he tells us, Lao-tsze himself could not find a suitable definition or circumlocution. Literally "the road," it is here simply a makeshift like the letter X as used in our expression X Rays. He decides in favour of "Providence," which again seems unfortunate. The primary meaning of the word *Tao* is "The Way." In this sense it was used frequently by Confucius (equivalent to Greek *methodos*). J. Legge thinks that of the three English terms that suggest themselves, the Way, or the Reason, or the Word, the most suitable is the Way in the sense of Method. He goes so far as to say: "If Methodism and Methodist had not been so well appropriated in English, I should have recommended their employment for Tâoism and Tâoist." But, as R. K. Douglas says, to Lao-tsze it seems to have meant more than the way. It is something impalpable. "You look at it, and cannot see it. You listen to it, and you cannot hear it. You try to touch it, and you cannot reach it. You use it, and cannot exhaust it. It is not to be expressed in words. It is still and void; it stands alone and changes not; it circulates everywhere and is not endangered. It is ever inactive, and yet leaves nothing undone. From it phenomena appear, through it they change, in it they disappear. Formless, it is the cause of form. Nameless, it is the origin of heaven and earth; with a name, it is the mother of all things. It is the ethical nature of the good man and the principles of his action." F. H. Balfour would translate the word by Nature or Principle—Nature, that is to say in the sense of Spinoza's *natura naturans* (see SPINOZISM), "the abstract Cause, the initial Principle of life and order, the hypostatic quiddity which underlies all phenomena, and of which they are a manifestation only." Other meanings that have been suggested are: The Absolute in the sense of Schelling, and Substance in the sense of Spinoza. The Tao-teh-King, as rendered in English by Prof. E. H. Parker, the latest translator, does not create such a favourable impression as one would expect from quotations in other books; but his renderings no doubt follow the original more closely. Prof. Parker, in addition to his translation, gives a summary of the teaching of the Tao-teh-King. The following are quotations from the summary: "Providence [*Tao*], without origin itself, is the origin of everything; being without body and without palpable existence; invisible, imperceptible, spontaneous, and impalpable. Heaven and Earth have their beginnings in it; that is, in this eternal principle of pure being which determines the Universe. . . . It knows no distinction between spirit, mind, and matter, between what men call existence and non-existence; it contains all potentialities. . . . Providence [*Tao*] is incorruptible, perfect, eternal. . . . Providence is always restful, yet never idle; knows no time, limits, or wants; has no inclinations or preferences; and absorbs or takes unto itself those who regulate their conduct by faith in it. . . . A man who regulates his conduct by and has faith in Providence avoids display and self-assertion; is humble, modest, calm, ready for all emergencies, and fearless of death. . . . He is always rich, because contented: his body is always safe, for the mind has no apprehensions: he has no ill-will, and devotes his efforts to the amelioration of others. . . . He prefers reality to appearances, and strives for pure truth. . . . The natural powers should be economized, and all agitation, mental or physical, studiously avoided. . . . Do not trouble to have any fixed aim in life. The man who has attained to a mental oneness with Providence [*Tao*] is superior to the highest rulers. . . The King should avoid luxury, over-legislation, and over-taxation, which tend to the poverty, evasiveness, and misery of the people. . . . Too much cooking spoils the fish, as too much handling irritates the people. . . . The people should not be raised from their ignorance to the intellectual level of their rulers. . . . Restrictions tend to hamper industry; consequently these should be as few and as simple as possible. At the same time, mechanical skill should not be too much encouraged, as it leads to excessive effort, emulation, and luxury." To bring oneself into complete harmony with Tao (Substance, Truth, Principle)—this is the great ideal. As R. K. Douglas points out, Taoism is a kind of mysticism. Such was the Taoism of Lao-tsze. Lieh-tsze and Chwang-tsze thought to improve upon it, with the result that it began to degenerate. Lieh-tsze (fifth century B.C.) was fond of depicting ideal states of society in the form of dreams. He makes one of the Emperors dream, for instance, of a country "where the people were without rulers, for they were masters of themselves—were without passion, for they controlled their desires. They regarded life without pleasure and death without dread, and therefore were overtaken by no untimely fates. They knew neither relations nor connections, and so were free from love and hate. . . . They walked in water without being drowned, they threw themselves into the fire without being burnt, and they might be cut and struck without receiving hurt. They mounted into the air and walked as on the ground. They slept in space as though they were on their beds, and the clouds and the mists interfered with them not" (R. K. Douglas). This allegory, as Douglas says, foreshadows the way in which Taoism was to degenerate. Chang-tsze (four century B.C.) followed his master more closely. According to Douglas, his main theme was the vanity of human effort. "If the world were but left to itself, people would wear that which they spun and eat that which grew. The mountains would be without paths, and the waters without ships. All created things would rejoice in life. Wild animals would wander in troops, and trees and shrubs would flourish, among which birds and beasts might roam. Then would men enjoy a golden age. No knowledge would separate them from virtue, and no desires would taint their purity." Chwang-tsze came in time to believe that life was largely a matter of mere phantasmata or deceptive appearances. The later Taoists devoted themselves to alchemy and magic, putting their faith in charms and in the elixir of life. The old Taoism was further corrupted by the introduction of Buddhism into China in A.D. 65. Nevertheless, there are still to be found Taoists who cherish the old ideal—"men who are almost entirely uncontaminated by the follies and impostures of modern popular Taoism, and who may be said to represent the true Apostolic Succession in the Taoist Church" (F. H. Balfour). See Joseph Edkins, *Religion in China*, 1878; James Legge, *The Religions of China*, 1880; R. K. Douglas, *Confucianism and Taoism;* H. A. Giles, *Religions of Ancient China*, 1905; Frederic H. Balfour, "Taoism," in *R.S.W.;* E. H. Parker, *Studies;* J. J. M. De Groot; *Rel. of the Chinese*, 1910; Max B. Weinstein, *Welt- und Leben- Anschauungen*, 1910.

TAO-TEH-KING. One of the sacred books of the Chinese. Composed or compiled by Lao-tsze, it gives the principles and precepts of pure or original Taoism (*q.v.*).

TAPU. A Polynesian term. According to R. R. Marett, it "serves as perhaps the chief nucleus of embryonic reflection with regard to mystic matters of all kinds; in some of the islands the name stands for the whole system of religion."

TARANIS. One of the deities worshipped by the ancient Celts, the god of thunder. See TEUTATES, and compare ESUS.

TARANUCUS. Taranucus, "the thunderer," was one of the names given by the ancient Celts to a god who corresponded to the Roman Jupiter.

TARGOMAN. Literally "interpreter," corresponding to the modern "Dragoman." An official of the Jewish synagogue who interpreted the Hebrew Scriptures in the language of the people. Cp. METHURGEMAN and TARGUM.

TARGUM. The designation of a Jewish version of certain books of the Old Testament. After the Exile, Aramaic took the place of Hebrew as the spoken language of the people. Consequently, the text of the Hebrew Scriptures became unintelligible to the general public. It became necessary therefore in the Synagogue service, an important part of which consisted in readings from the Law and the Prophets, to have someone to interpret the original language. As the reader in the Synagogue read a passage of Scripture, an interpreter, *Methurgeman*, rendered the sense in Aramaic, the language of the people. Naturally this translation was apt to become paraphrastic. In the case of the Law, an effort seems to have been made to give the translation as literally as possible, though even here the interpreter was tempted to explain and to expound. In the case of the Prophets, a free paraphrase was almost unavoidable. In any case, it was not necessary to guard against it so carefully, as the reading from the Prophets (introduced at a later date) was of minor importance. The frequent repetition of these interpretations will have resulted in their assuming in course of time a more or less fixed or stereotyped form. These interpretations or translations were called Targums. Transmitted at first orally, they were afterwards committed to writing, though it was forbidden to use these written translations in the Synagogue service. The Targums originated in Palestine, but were not held in high esteem there. Amongst the Babylonian Jews, by whom they were adopted, they received greater honour. The Torah (Law) Targum of the Babylonians is called the *Targum Onkelos*. It seems clear that Onkelos is a variation of Aquilas, which again is the same as Aquila, the name of the author of a very literal translation (Gk.) of the Old Testament. The Targum was so called either through confusion, or because it was made in the literal style of Aquila. The Babylonian Targum on the Prophets is called the *Targum of Jonathan*, *i.e.*, of Jonathan ben Uzziel. It has been suggested that Jonathan is equivalent to Theodotion, the name of the author of another (fragmentary) translation (Gk.) of the Old Testament. The two names, the one Hebrew, the other Greek, have the same meaning. In that case this Targum may have been so called because it was made in the style of Theodotion, *i.e.*, in a freer and more paraphrastic style. The Palestinian Torah (Law) Targum has been preserved in two forms, the one complete, the other fragmentary.

The complete form has been called *Targum Jonathan* (Pseudo-Jonathan). This has been owing to a mistake. The real name was *Targum Yerushalmi* (Jerusalem Targum). The abbreviation T.Y. was wrongly interpreted Targum Yonathan (Jonathan). The Palestinian Targum on the Prophets has only been preserved in fragments. The Targums on the Hagiographa were confined to Palestine, and were never recognised officially. There were no Targums on the books of Daniel and Ezra, which belong to this group. There is also a Samaritan Torah (Law) Targum. See F. Buhl, *Canon;* C. A. Briggs, *Intr.;* W. O. E. Oesterley and G. H. Box.

TARTARUS. The Greek Tartarus in earlier times was a dark abyss below the surface of the earth. In later times it came to correspond to Hades; it denoted the lower regions, the place of torment in which the wicked were punished. See O. Seyffert, *Dict.*

TASCODRUGITES. A name given to a religious sect which arose in Galatia in the fourth century. The name is formed from the Greek words *taskos* " a wooden nail " and *drouggos* " a nose." According to Epiphanius (*Hær.* xlviii.), the Tascodrugites were so called because while praying they placed the finger on the nose. They are said to have rejected the Creeds and Sacraments (so Theodoret). They are perhaps to be identified with the Passalorynchites, a body of early mystics. This name is formed from the Greek words *passalos* " a gag " and *rugchos* " a muzzle." The Passalorynchites seem to have been so called because they placed a finger across the mouth and nose to prevent the possibility of speaking. See Schaff-Herzog, *Religious Encyclopaedia;* J. H. Blunt.

TASHMITUM. A Babylonian deity. Tashmitum appears as a goddess in the time of Hammurapi. She is the consort of Nabu (*q.v.*). Originally the consort of Nabu was Erua. When Erua was amalgamated with Sarpanitum (*q.v.*) and assigned to Marduk (*q.v.*), a new consort had to be found for Nabu. The new consort was Tashmitum (" revelation "). She is always coupled with Nabu (" Nabu and Tashmitum "), and never appears alone. Jastrow thinks that originally the name was a title given to Nabu. It was afterwards converted into a goddess. See Morris Jastrow, *Rel.*

TATTOOING. In a passage in the Old Testament (Leviticus xix. 28) tattooing is referred to as one of the heathen practices which the Israelites must avoid. They are forbidden to " tattoo any marks " upon them. The reference is perhaps to marks which indicated consecration to a special deity and served as signs by which members of the same cult recognized one another. Reinach mentions that among the negroes tattoo-marks attest dependence on a particular fetish, and among the Polynesians alliance with the god of the tribe. Bertholet notes that the people of Mecca make three incisions in each cheek of their children to protect them against the evil eye. Robertson Smith points out that in Lev. xix. 28 tattooing " is immediately associated with incisions in the flesh made in mourning or in honour of the dead." This, he thinks, " suggests that in their ultimate origin the *stigmata* are nothing more than the permanent scars of punctures made to draw blood for a ceremony of self-dedication to the deity." According to Lucian (§ 59), the Syrians all tattooed themselves, some on the hands and some on the neck. Tattooed bodies of Nubians of the time of the Middle Empire (*c.* 2000 B.C.) have been found. The practice has been noted also among some of the tribes in the Sudan. See W. Robertson Smith, *R.S.;* A. Bertholet, *Leviticus*, 1901; Reinach, *O.*

TAUROBOLIUM. A Roman sacrifice connected with the worship of the Asiatic goddess Cybele (*q.v.*). A priest having sacrificed a bull, " its blood was made to drip between the boards of the floor upon the head of the person who made the offering, and was supposed to render him divine " (Reinach, *O.*).

TA-URT. An Egyptian goddess, the female hippopotamus, a goddess of maternity. She was reputed to be the mother of Osiris, and was in fact fused with Isis.

TAWAF. The Arabic name for the ceremony of going round the Ka'ba. See HAJJ, THE, and compare CIRCUMAMBULATION.

TAYAMMUM. An Arabic name for the practice of using sand, instead of water, in ablutions. Where water is scarce or not to be found, the Muslim is allowed to use fine clean sand or earth as a substitute. In the Qur'ân (v. 9) it is said : " And if ye have become unclean, then purify yourselves. But if ye are sick, or on a journey, or if one of you come from the place of retirement, or if ye have touched women, and ye find no water, then take clean sand and rub your faces and your hands with it." Klein describes the practice more fully. " In order to perform the Tayammum, the Muslim places both his hands, the fingers being joined together, on the ground covered with clean sand or dust and then carefully wipes with it his face once, proposing to himself the lawfulness of prayer after this kind of ablution; then, if he has any ring on his finger, he takes it off, places the palms of his hands on the dust again, this time with his fingers spread out, and then rubs his arms up to his elbows." See F. A. Klein.

TEACHING OF THE TWELVE APOSTLES. See DIDACHE.

ṬEBŪL YŌM. The name of one of the Jewish treatises or tractates which reproduce the oral tradition or unwritten law as developed by the second century A.D. and are incorporated in the Mishnah (*q.v.*), a collection and compilation completed by Rabbi Judah the Holy, or the Patriarch, about 200 A.D. The sixty-three tractates of the Mishnah are divided into six groups or orders (*sedarim*). Ṭebūl Yōm is the tenth tractate of the sixth group, which is called *Ṭohorōth* (" Purifications ").

TEFILLIN. The word Tefillin is Hebrew (or rather Aramaic), and means literally " prayers." In the Jewish Targums it is used as the equivalent of the Greek term Phylacteries (*q.v.*). Phylacteries were so called because they consisted of small boxes containing prayers written on parchment. The Hebrew name for them in the Old Testament is Totâfoth (*q.v.*).

TEFNET. An Egyptian deity. Egyptian legend represents the Sun-god Ra (*q.v.*) as creating out of himself two supporters of the heavens, the god Shu (*q.v.*) and the goddess Tefnet. These in turn gave birth to Keb (*q.v.*), god of the earth, and Nut (*q.v.*), goddess of the sky. In the Book of the Dead (*q.v.*) Shu and Tefnet, together with Atûm appear as rulers of Heliopolis. Tefnet is represented as a lioness, or as a human being with the head of a lioness. In Nubia she was regarded as the mother of Thoth (*q.v.*). In Abydos the goddess created by Re was not Tefnet, but the frog Hekt (*q.v.*). See A. Wiedemann; Adolf Erman, *Handbook.*

TEIKIRZI. Teikirzi, sister of Ön (*q.v.*), is one of the chief deities of the Todas. She seems to have become their ruler when Ön left them to rule the world of the dead. According to one legend, when the people of Mysore came to fight against her, she turned them into stones.

TEIKUTEIDI. One of the gods of the Todas.

TEIPAKH. Teipakh or Tirshti, brother of Teikirzi, is one of the chief gods of the Todas, a river god.

TEKMORIAN GUEST-FRIENDS. An anti-Christian secret society established on the imperial estates of Pisidian Antioch. They are referred to in an inscription

(A.D. 300) found by Sir William Ramsay in 1882. "These 'brothers of the sign' spoke of the pagan devotees as saints' (ἅγιοι), and doubtless sought to rebuild the decayed temples and to win new votaries to the old faith in their homeland, which had become wholly Christian by an imitation of the languages and virtues of the new Way" (Cobern).

TELEPATHY. The word telepathy has been coined to express the power of one mind to communicate with another directly, that is to say, without the aid of the ordinary organs of sense. Telepathy is not necessarily a religion, but it is of vast religious significance. It re-establishes the importance of prayer (*q.v.*), re-enforces the value of worship, and gives new meanings to old creeds. It establishes communication between sympathetic minds among mortals; it renders possible real communion between a divinely disposed human mind and the divine mind itself. The efficacy of mental and spiritual healing is largely due to telepathy. A healthy mind can impart healing to a mind that is sick. Thomson Jay Hudson maintains that "the power of telepathic communication is as thoroughly established as any fact in nature." This is due to the work of the London Society for Psychical Research. Telepathy is the normal means of communication between subjective minds. "The reason of the apparent rarity of its manifestation is that it requires exceptional conditions to bring its results above the threshold of consciousness. There is every reason to believe that the souls, or subjective minds, of men can and do habitually hold communion with one another when not the remotest perception of the fact is communicated to the objective intelligence. It may be that such communion is not general among men; but it is certain that it is held between those who, from any cause, are *en rapport*. The facts recorded by the Society for Psychical Research demonstrate that proposition. Thus, near relatives are oftenest found to be in communion, as is shown by the comparative frequency of telepathic communications between relatives, giving warning of sickness or of death. Next in frequency are communications between intimate friends" (T. J. Hudson). It would seem that "the subjective minds of those who are deeply interested in one another are in habitual communion, especially when the personal interest or welfare of either agent or percipient is at stake." In any case, "it is certain that telepathic communication can be established at will by the conscious effort of one or both of the parties, even between strangers." Albert B. Olston thinks "telesthesia" would be a better term than "telepathy." See Albert B. Olston, *Mind Power*, 1906; T. J. Hudson, *Psychic Phenomena;* and cp. Prentice Mulford, *The Gift of the Spirit*, 1908 (second edition).

TELLUS. Tellus or Tellus Mater was an Italian goddess worshipped as mother-earth. She was the goddess of marriage and of fruitfulness. As the latter, a festival of sowing was held in her honour in January. In April cows in calf were sacrificed to her. A male deity, Tellumo, was also worshipped. See O. Seyffert, *Dict.*

TEMPLARS. Following the example of two knights, one from Burgundy, the other from Northern France, who in 1119 undertook to defend pilgrims in the Holy Land, a small body of men took an oath to the Patriarch of Jerusalem and constituted themselves a religious community and a military order. "The members lived in chastity, poverty, obedience; and found their chief active duty in guarding the public roads in Palestine. Baldwin the king gave them the (so-called) Temple of Solomon in the Holy City, and they derived their name from it. They devoted themselves to reclaiming and converting to penitence and sacred uses the rabble of excommunicate and stranded knights who had come to the Holy Land rather for plunder than holy ends. Later, the Templars were for this reason immune from sentences of excommunication pronounced by bishops and parochial ministers" (F. W. Bussell). The rules of the Order were drawn up in 1128, and in the course of two centuries the Templars became the richest corporation in Christendom, and a force to be reckoned with by Emperors and Popes. They enjoyed all sorts of papal privileges (control of their own churches and churchyards, freedom from tithe, etc.). But their career was not uncheckered. They had to meet charges of treachery and corrupt practice. For instance, when the Emperor Conrad III. failed to take Damascus in 1149, this was said to be due to a secret understanding between the Templars and the garrison. The fact that the Templars carried on their rites of initiation in secret excited curiosity and unfavourable comment. "Chapters were held in guarded rooms with strictest privacy and at break of day; no participant might reveal what took place at each lodge-meeting *even* to a brother-member. Suspicious or prurient minds invented the usual tales about esoteric societies: at his reception, the postulant spat on the crucifix, denied Christ, and was required to bear sexual outrage without complaint. At the Mass the words *Hoc est Corpus Meum* were omitted, and on Good Friday the Cross was trampled underfoot. A form of devil-worship was used —either of a black cat or a black idol called Baphomet." In France it was even believed that the Templars roasted children. Modern apologists have sought to prove the innocence of the Templars, and in large measure seem to have succeeded in their efforts, though "it is beyond question that the Templars had long and profitable dealings with the Assassins" (Bussell). It may be recalled that charges similar to some of those brought against them have frequently, and even in our own days, been brought against the Jews. In 1312 by papal Bull most of the estates of the Templars were transferred to the Knights of St. John.

TEMPLE SOCIETY. A religious community founded in 1848 by Christian Hoffmann. Other names for them are the Temple Union and the Jerusalem Friends (*q.v.*).

TEMŪRĀ. The title of one of the Jewish treatises or tractates which reproduce the oral tradition or unwritten law as developed by the second century A.D. and are incorporated in the Mishnah (*q.v.*), a collection and compilation completed by Rabbi Judah the Holy, or the Patriarch, about 200 A.D. The sixty-three tractates of the Mishnah are divided into six groups or orders (*sedarim*). Temūrā is the sixth tractate of the fifth group, which is called *Ḳodāshīm* ("Holy Things").

TENDAI SECT. A sect or school of Japanese Buddhists. They are so called because the headquarters of the sect are on a mountain in China which bears the same name. The teaching is of the nature of mysticism.

TENDENCY THEORY, THE. A theory concerning the composition of the New Testament writings, associated chiefly with the name of the German critic, F. C. Baur (1792-1860). The use of the word "tendency" in this connection (Tendenz) is German rather than English. A Tendenz-schrift is "a piece of writing written with a (polemical) purpose"; a Tendenz-roman is what we call "a novel with a purpose." F. C. Baur claimed to show that the New Testament writings are not purely historical, but were written with a purpose (Tendenz). The first Christians were soon divided into two parties, Jewish Christians and Pauline Christians. Each was rather bitterly opposed to the other; and there was a fundamental opposition between Paul and the original apostles. The New Testament writers are supposed to share in this conflict, and often to write with the purpose of supporting the claims of the one party or the other. In Baur's criticism, "each book was assigned its position in time and space by reason of the conscious relation of its author to the supposed mortal conflict between the two wings of Apostolic Christianity" (H. S. Nash). There was, of course, an element of truth in Baur's contention. Unless we adhere to the old idea of verbal inspiration, it is hardly possible not to admit that to some extent the New Testament writers, like all writers of this class of works, are likely to have written with a special purpose or tendency (Tendenz). But in the sense in which Baur pressed the theory, the matter was greatly exaggerated. He did a service, however, in calling attention to the tendency and in putting people on their guard. Herbert Spencer has done a similar service in pointing out (*Study of Sociology*) that in every field of study—in Science as well as in Theology—this tendency or bias has to be guarded against. See R. W. Mackay, *The Tübingen School and its Antecedants*, 1863; H. S. Nash, *Higher Criticsm of the N.T.*, 1901.

TENEBRAE. In the Roman Catholic Church the name Tenebrae is given to the Matins and Lauds of the three last days of Holy Week. They are said or sung on the previous afternoon or evening. As a sign of sorrow, the lessons of the first nocturn are taken from the Book of the Lamentations of Jeremiah. The name Tenebrae ("darkness") seems to be due to the practice of extinguishing lights. "At the beginning of the office fifteen lighted candles are placed on a triangular candelabrum, and at the end of each psalm one is put out, till only a single candle is left lighted at the top of the triangle. During the singing of the Benedictus the candles on the high altar are extinguished, while at the antiphon after the Benedictus the single candle left alight is hidden at the Epistle corner of the altar, to be brought out again at the end of the office" (the *Catholic Dictionary*). The darkness is supposed to represent the gloom of the time when Jesus, the light of the World, was taken away. See the *Cath. Dict.*

TENJIN. Also called Temmangū, a Japanese deity, god of learning and caligraphy. His vehicle is a cow, and with his worship is associated the plum-tree.

TEN-SHOKO-DAIJIN. Ten-shôkô-daijin figures in the Japanese religiou known as Shintōism (*q.v.*) as the chief god of Isé, the centre of Shintō. Isé is in the province of Yamato in Central Japan. The name of the god Ten-shôkô-daijin is always one of those inscribed on the paper-covered tablets or tickets which are placed on the household "shelf for gods" (*Kamidana*).

TENT OF MEETING. The Tent of Meeting, *Ohel Mō'ēd*, was a tent pitched outside the camp of the Israelites by their leader Moses (Exodus, xxxiii. 7 ff.). It was so called because here Jehovah met Moses and spoke to him, revealing himself in a pillar of cloud which descended in front of the door of the tent. Tent of Meeting, as Driver says (Deuteronomy), is practically equivalent to Tent of Revelation. Exodus xxxiii. 7-11 represents E's conception. J's conception seems to be the same (see Numbers, xi. 24-26). In D there is no reference to such a tent. In P the Ohel Mō'ēd is referred to 131 times. The Tent of Meeting was a simple, portable tent-sanctuary. The use of portable shrines and of tents as sanctuaries seems to have been familiar to the ancient Semites. And, as I. Benzinger says (*Encyclopaedia Biblica, s.v.* "Tabernacle") "it is noteworthy that the portable chapels of the heathen Semites were mainly used for divination (cp. *Journ. of Phil.* 13, 283 f.), just as the Mosaic tabernacle is described by the Elohist, not as a place of sacrifice (such as the tabernacle of the Priestly Code is), but as a place of oracle." We hear of an *Ohel Mō'ēd* again at Shilo (I. Samuel ii. 22) and at Gibeon (II. Chron. i. 3, 6, 13). See *Encycl. Bibl.;* the Oxford *Hebrew and English Lexicon.*

TEPEYOLLOTL. A Mexican deity, a cave-god. He was represented as bear-headed.

TERAPHIM. A term used in the Old Testament with reference to idolatry. The word seems to denote a particular kind of idol, for in Genesis xxxi. 30, 32 the *Terāphim* are designated *elohim* ("gods"). We have no very definite information about their form or character. It is thought that it cannot certainly be inferred from Genesis xxxi. 34 that the images were small, or from I. Samuel xix. 13, 16 that they were large and in the form of a man. In Hosea iii. 4 they are mentioned with the ephod (*q.v.*), sacrifices, and maṣṣēbahs (sacred pillars) as a natural part of the apparatus of religion. Laban had terāphīm in his house; the Ephraimite Micah had an ephod and terāphīm in his sanctuary (Judges xvii. f.). In I. Samuel xix. 13, 16, the reference to the terāphīm in David's house implies that it or they might be found in every household. They seem in fact to have been household gods (*penates*). It has been suggested that they were images of the ancestors. This, it is thought, explains their use as oracle-givers (in connection with the oracular ephod in Judges xii. f., Hosea iii. 4: cp. I. Samuel xv. 23, Zechariah x. 2, Ezekiel xxi. 26, 27). In II. Kings xxiii. 24 they are associated with mediums and wizards. The Plural form probably denotes a singular idea, being what is known in Hebrew syntax as a "Plural of Majesty." On the assumption that the word denotes images of ancestors, it has been connected with *rephā'īm* (*q.v.*) which is used of "shades" or "ghosts." See *Encycl. Bibl.;* W. H. Bennett's *Genesis*, and J. Skinner's *Kings* in the "Century Bible."

TERATISM. A term derived from the Greek word *teras* "power." The use of the term is suggested by R. R. Marett to denote supernaturalism in pre-animistic religion.

TERMINISM. The teaching of pietistic theologians (see PIETISM) in the seventeenth century, according to which God has fixed a limit (*terminus gratiæ*) to the period within which persons can be converted, repent, and be forgiven. The teaching gave rise to a Terministic Controversy.

TERMINUS. Terminus was the Roman god who protected the stones that marked boundaries. Such a stone was set with great ceremony. An animal was slaughtered, and its blood was sprinkled over the hole in which the stone was to be set. The stone itself was anointed and decorated. In Rome there was an annual ceremony in February in honour of the landmarks. This was called the Terminalia. See O. Seyffert, *Dict.*

TERTIARIES. Francis of Assisi was perhaps the first to introduce an order of persons called Tertiaries (Tertiarii). In any case he was the first to organize the institution properly. In the Franciscan foundation they constituted a third order, and were called by St. Francis Brothers and Sisters of Penance. They were intended to be representatives of a life intermediate between that of the world and the cloister, an order, "the members of which, men and women, should be bound by rule to dress more soberly, fast more strictly, pray more regularly, hear Mass more frequently, and practise works of mercy more systematically than ordinary persons living in the world" (*C.D.*). The desire of many tertiaries to live in community and take solemn vows, while continuing to conform to the rule of the Third Order, led to the institution of a number of congregations of tertiary monks and nuns. The example of the Franciscans was followed by the Dominicans (*q.v.*) and other monastic orders. See Schaff-Herzog; the *Cath. Dict.*

TERTULLIANISTS. Tertullian was born at Carthage about the middle of the second century A.D. He was converted to Christianity about 185, and afterwards defended it with great skill and zeal against pagans and heretics. Later, however, he became attracted by the austerity of the Montanists (see MONTANISM). About 202 he openly joined them, and became head of the Montanists of Africa, who often called themselves after him Tertullianists. He wrote Montanist works, including a treatise in seven books on ecstasy, "De Extasi," which has not survived. In itself Montanism was not unorthodox, so that Tertullian was still a great champion of the fundamental truths of Christianity. What repelled him in the Church was the lax discipline of so many of its members. As J. M. Fuller says, he remained "staunch to the faith of that church whose discipline and ritual he abjured or carried with him to a schismatic body. . . . His theology, if developed by Montanism, is in substance that which the Church accepted, and accepts." Cyprian (200-258 A.D.), Bishop of Carthage, greatly admired his writings. See Louis Duchesne, *Hist.;* Wace and Piercy.

TERŪMŌTH. The name of one of the Jewish treatises or tractates which reproduce the oral tradition or unwritten law as developed by the second century A.D. and are incorporated in the Mishnah (*q.v.*), a collection and compilation completed by Rabbi Judah the Holy, or the Patriarch, about 200 A.D. The sixty-three tractates of the Mishnah are divided into six groups or orders (*sedarim*). Terūmōth is the sixth tractate of the first group, which is called Zerā'īm ("Seeds")

TESHUP. A Hittite deity. Teshup is the god of thunder, and corresponds to the Babylonian Ramman (*q.v.*) or Adad. A. Jeremias thinks that Jupiter Dolichenus, whose emblems are the same, "is Ramman-Teshup imported into Rome and Germania by Syrian traders." It has been suggested that the idea of the double hammer, which is the symbol of the Babylonian Ramman-Adad and of the European Thor (*q.v.*) "passed into Europe from pre-Mycenæan Crete, where Zeus appears with the double hammer." See A. Jeremias, *The O.T. in the Light of the Ancient East*, 1911.

TETEOINNAN. A Mexican deity, the patroness of doctors and midwives. She was also the goddess of ripe maize.

TETRAGRAMMATON, THE. A technical expression for the Hebrew divine name, consisting of four letters, which was considered too sacred to be pronounced. The letters are Y-h-v-h. They are volcalized Yehovah, but the vowels are those of another word, Adonay, meaning "My Lord." When Adonay itself precedes, the word Y-h-v-h is given the vowels of Elōhīm, the Hebrew word for "God," and the word is pronounced "Elōhīm." The true pronunciation of the word Y-h-v-h was lost at an early date. There is a word *hayah* or *havah* in Hebrew, which means "to be" or "to become." Many modern scholars, therefore, think that the original pronunciation of the word was Yahveh, which would mean "he who is" (third pers. m. Imperf. of the verb *havah*). It is possible, however, that the word never had a meaning. The letters may have had some mystical and mysterious significance. If they were pronounced, certain vowels of course had to be added. But vowels were not added in order to form a known word. There are examples of such mystical words in other religions. See, further, YAHWEH.

TETRAPLA, THE. An edition of the Septuagint compiled by Origen. See HEXAPLA.

TETRATHEISM. In the controversies with regard to the Christian doctrine of the Trinity (*q.v.*), some of the contraversialists were accused of being Tetratheists, that is to say, persons who recognized four Gods. The charge was brought for instance against Damianus of Alexandria (see DAMIANITES), who, by distinguishing between God Himself, as the autotheos, and the Father, seemed to introduce a fourth Person. Gilbert of Poitiers (Bishop of Poitiers, 1142 A.D.), called "Peripateticus," also seemed to teach a kind of tetratheism. He acknowledged the unity of the Father, the Son, and the Spirit. But he maintained that they are one only in reference to the *quo est* (the substantial form), not in reference to the *quod est* (the divine essence as such). Jerome of Prague is charged with having taught that in God or in the Divine Essence there is not only a Trinity of persons, but also a quaternity of things, and a quinternity, etc. See K. R. Hagenbach; J. E. Erdmann, *Hist. of Philosophy*, 1890.

TEUTATES. Teutates, the "god of the people," was one of the names given by the ancient Celts to a god who corresponded to the Roman Mercury. He is mentioned by Lucan (*c.* A.D. 60) with Taranis, the god of thunder, and Esus (*q.v.*), as a deity who demanded human sacrifices. Reinach and Anwyl point out that these were local deities. They did not constitute, as has been supposed, a Celtic Trinity. See Anwyl; Reinach, *O.*

TEUTONIC KNIGHTS. The Teutonic Knights were a German military-religious order that arose during the Crusades. In 1190, during the siege of Acre, some German merchants provided a hospital for wounded Christians called the Hospital St. Mary of the Germans in Jerusalem. The persons connected with the hospital then formed themselves into a religious order like the Brothers of the Hospital of St. John the Baptist (see HOSPITALLERS). This order became in a few years a military order, the Order of the Teutonic Knights, and was approved by the Pope in 1199. "The Knights, in addition to the usual monastic vows, bound themselves to tend the sick and wounded and wage incessant war upon the heathen" (Chambers). In 1240 they were invited by the Duke of Masovia in Poland to help him defend his frontiers against the heathen Prussians. In 1252 they were strengthened by amalgamation with the Order of Christ or Brethren of the Sword, which had already taken possession of Livonia. Acting together, they "became possessed of all the territory between the Vistula and the Memel, the coast-line reaching from Narva, on the Gulf of Finland, to the south-western point of Pomerania" (Schaff-Herzog). They acted with great harshness, but gradually civilized the country. In the fifteenth century they lost much of their territory, and in 1525 they were driven from the country. In 1809 Napoleon I. formally abolished the order. See William Benham; Schaff-Herzog; the *Cath. Dict.; Chambers's Encycl.*

TEZCATLIPOCA. Tezcatlipoca, which means "Shining Mirror," was the name of one of the deities worshipped by the ancient Americans. As a Sun-god, he was held to be the brother of Huitzilopochtli (*q.v.*): but he was the god of the cold season, whereas Huitzilopochtli was the god of the warm season. Spence thinks that Tezcatlipoca may have been originally a wind demon of the prairies, and then in another clime, an ice-god. The latter character is suggested by his season and by the shining mirror. In any case he became to the Aztecs, nominally at least, the greatest god. According to D. Brinton (*American Hero Myths*, 1882), Tezcatlipoca was "the most sublime figure in the Aztec Pantheon." He was the Creator and the "Soul of the World." He was the God of Justice and Retribution, "in whose mirror the thoughts and actions of men were reflected" (Spence). He is called also the "Night Wind." He was supposed to wander from one part of the city of Mexico to another, and the inhabitants erected for him in the streets stone resting-places or seats. At one of the annual festivals of Tezcatlipoca, as the Winter Sun, a young male captive of great beauty was sacrificed. He was chosen a year before, and during this year he lived in regal splendour, and was worshipped. A victim for Huitzilopochtli was sacrificed at the same time. During the year he acted as a kind of companion to Huitzilopochtli, but was not worshipped. This victim was called the "Wise Lord of Heaven." See Lewis Spence, *Myth;* J. M. Robertson, "The Religions of Ancient Mexico" in *R.S.W.;* Reinach, *O.;* J. M. Robertson, *P.C.*

THĀKUR DEO. An Indian deity, the god of the village land and boundaries among the Baigas who inhabit the eastern Satpūra hills in the Mandla, Bālāghāt and Bilaspur Districts. The Baigas offer him a white goat. He is worshipped by the Bhainas as the deity of cultivation.

THĀKURĀNI MĀTA. An Indian deity, also called Burhi Māta, the goddess of smallpox and rinderpest, worshipped by the Gadbas, a primitive tribe belonging to the Vizagapatam District of Madras.

THARGELIA. The Thargelia was a feast held in Athens in honour of Apollo (*q.v.*). Firstfruits were offered to him; and to induce him to refrain from sending parching heat and pestilence, two persons, a man and a woman, were sacrificed. They were sacrificed on the seashore, and when their bodies had been burned, the ashes were thrown into the sea. In course of time, however, for the latter custom a more humane practice was substituted. The victims were thrown into the sea from a height, but they were caught as they fell. Instead of being condemned to die, they were banished from the country. The victims seem to have been of the nature of scapegoats who bore away the sins of the people (cp. AZAZEL). See O. Seyffert, *Dict.;* J. M. Robertson, *P.C.*

THEATINES. An Order of "Regular Clerks" (*Clerici regulares Theatini*) founded in 1524 by Cajetan of Thiene, Boniface of Colle, and Bishop Caraffa of Chieti or Theate (whence their name) who afterwards became Pope Paul IV. Cajetan was the real originator of the foundation. "The reform of the lives of Christians, and especially of the irregularities too common at that time among the clergy, presented itself to him as the object to which God willed him to devote his life" (*Cath. Dict.*). The Order was confirmed by Paul III. in 1540 and by Pius V. in 1568. The members renounced all property or rents and refused to ask for alms, relying simply on Providence and on the freewill offerings of the faithful. From Italy the movement spread to Spain, Poland, Bavaria, and France. In 1583 Ursula Benincasa founded an order of Theatine nuns. The Theatines are sometimes called Cajetani or Chietini. See Schaff-Herzog; the *Cath. Dict.*

THEISM. Theism was defined by Charles Voysey (*Religious Systems of the World*, 1908) as "a belief in a God whom we can thoroughly trust and love, and whom to obey is a delight; a belief based on indisputable facts and capable of expansion and elevation with every addition to our knowledge and with every rise in our moral nature." The earliest use of the term he finds in the works of Lord Bolingbroke, though in his day he and other writers of the same school were called Deists and not Theists. The first writers in England to give the term a definite and formal signification were Francis William Newman (1805-1897), Frances P. Cobbe (who wrote in 1863), and Theodore Parker (who wrote in 1834). The Herzog-Schaff *Encyclopaedia* explains the term thus: "Theism in its etymological and widest acceptation is a generic term for all systems of belief in the existence of the Divine. Thus understood, it includes pantheism, polytheism, and monotheism, and excludes only atheism; but this acceptance of the term is rare. Common usage has determined that theism must be identified with monotheism, and consequently opposed to polytheism and pantheism, as well as to atheism." Cp. DEISM.

THEISTIC CHURCH, THE. A Church and Congregation established by Charles Voysey (*b.* 1828). Voysey was at first a clergyman of the Church of England. He was curate of St. Mark's, Whitechapel, London, but had to give up his curacy after a few years on account of a sermon which he preached against endless punishment. In 1864 he became Vicar of Healaugh in Yorkshire, but he did not become more orthodox. The extreme orthodox party at length moved the Archbishop of York to take legal proceedings against him. The case was finally taken to the Judicial Committee of the Privy Council. Voysey was deprived of his living and ordered to pay costs. Since 1885 his Services were held in Swallow Street, Piccadilly, London. He has explained his religion in a number of books and in a great many sermons. In three sermons on "Objections to Theism" will be found a summarized statement. "The Theistic view," he says, "begins with a refusal to discuss the mystery of the mode of God's existence and of the mode of His relation to the cosmos. Theism also repudiates the idea of God's omnipotence when the term is used to cover impossibilities or absurdities. All that Theism affirms of God's power is that He is perfectly able to carry out His purposes and can never suffer final obstruction or defeat. And because this cannot be proved it is wholly a matter of belief, but a belief which is entirely rational, based upon overwhelming probability and upon induction so large and comprehensive as almost to amount to certainty." Only One Being is the Author of all the order, beauty, and progress of the cosmos. "Theism does not concern itself with the problem of the origin of matter or whether it be self-existent. Theism is satisfied with the abundant proofs of the superiority of mind over matter and with the obvious fact that matter is controlled and regulated by mind." From the higher faculties of human nature, Theism infers the nature of the faculties of the Author of those faculties. "Man knows that before all things the order of the world ought to be right, and that conviction he gained solely from God who gave him a conscience and made him a moral being. This enables Theism to affirm as a matter of certainty that the purposes of God are good and only good, in the best sense of producing true and lasting welfare." This of course is nothing more than an inference. It is wholly a matter of faith, but it is a most reasonable faith. Again, the conviction that God is able and willing "to accomplish His good purposes down to the very last and smallest detail" is an inference from tokens around and within us. Man is not constructed to be a blind worshipper of sheer Power and even sheer Intellect. "There must be something more to excite his reverence and to win his homage. So Theism seeks some moral ground as a basis for belief in the adequate power of God to carry out His good purposes. And here it lies all ready in the human heart. It would be against reason, against conscience and against love for any Being to dare to create a single sentient being only for fruitless suffering and annihilation, still worse to create for endless degradation and torment." But all these considerations involve the existence of the two worlds—the material and the spiritual. "If either be denied it disqualifies the denier from accepting the proofs. If there be nothing more than the body, the whole of religion and morality too tumbles down like a house of cards. Granting now the goodness of God's purposes and His certain ability to carry them out; in this life we cannot see the final issue.

We can only believe in it and hope for it. But our faith and hope are enormously increased by analysing the processes which are already going on before our very eyes wherein the good purposes of God are being wrought. Even here and now we can see what steps are being taken by the Great Ruler of our lives and destiny to promote our highest welfare." If the process is slow, it is sure and is "gradually mending the life that now is and giving promise of the life that is to come." See Charles Voysey, *Objections to Theism*, 1905; *Religion for all Mankind*, 1903.

THEODICY. The term Theodicy denotes the attempt to vindicate the wisdom and goodness of God in the creation and government of the world, and to rebut the charge that these are brought into question by the existence of evil and sin. An early example of a theodicy is provided by the Book of Job in the Old Testament. But in its true philosophical form the most famous theodicy is the *Essais de Théodicée* (1710) of G. W. Leibnitz (1646-1716). This was written to refute P. Bayle's claim that the doctrines of faith were irreconcilable with reason. According to Leibnitz "metaphysical evil—the defect and inadaptation that is to be seen in the world—is due to the Finiteness of created things. Physical evil or pain exists as a punishment or as a hindrance to greater evil. Moral evil or sin is not willed by God, yet it is an indispensable means of achieving the good. Good is positive, while Evil is only negative" (A. Butler). See Schaff-Herzog; C. J. Deter.

THEODOTIANS. The first Theodotus to whom the Theodotians owed their name was a tanner of Byzantium, who went to Rome in the time of Pope Victor I. (193-202 A.D.). He taught that Jesus, though born of a virgin, was only a man. He exhibited, however, a very high degree of piety and holiness; and at his baptism in Jordan the Christ descended upon Him. From this time he was able to work miracles. He did not, however, become God until after His resurrection. For this teaching Theodotus was excommunicated. The second Theodotus, a disciple of the first, was a banker. Another disciple was named Asclepiades. A fourth disciple was the Artemon or Artemas, against whom, according to Eusebius, a book "The Little Labyrinth," from which he gives extracts, was written. "The Little Labyrinth" was probably composed by Hippolytus (*fl.* 190-235), the author of the *Philosophumena*. The Theodotians seem to have recognized, besides God, a divine power called Christ, or the Holy Ghost. Theodotus the banker seems also to have worshipped Melchisedech, and to have identified him with the Son of God, the Holy Spirit. Melchisedech he ranked higher than the Christ, who was God only by adoption. The Theodotians seem to have accepted the Church Canon of Scripture, but they had versions of their own. They were familiar with positive philosophy, and did honour to such sages as Aristotle, Theophrastus, and Euclid. See J. H. Blunt; Louis Duchesne, *Hist.*

THEOLOGIA GERMANICA. The mystical work, "Theologia Germanica," whose author is unknown, had a considerable influence on the thought of Germany, and is even supposed to have paved the way for the Reformation. Written about 1350, it was published by Martin Luther (1483-1546) in 1518. See MYSTICISM, CHRISTIAN.

THEOLOGICAL VIRTUES. The virtues Faith, Hope, and Charity are called theological virtues, because they have God for their immediate object. According to the *Catholic Dictionary*, "these virtues are supernatural, because they are beyond the reach of man's natural powers, and because they enable him to attain a supernatural end."

THEOLOGY. Theology is the science which teaches about God. The term was used by Plato and Aristotle to denote teaching about the Greek Gods. Among Christians the word came into use in the third and fourth centuries. In Scholasticism it came to be used more definitely of the whole body of Christian doctrine, and this use of the term prevails at the present day. The field embraced is so wide that it has been very much sub-divided. Natural Theology is the knowledge of God gained by the study of Nature. Positive or Revealed Theology is the knowledge of God revealed through Inspiration. Dogmatic Theology deals with the history, development, and exposition of Christian doctrines. Moral Theology deals with the regulation of conduct as dictated by the principles of Revelation. Mystical Theology treats of the communion of the soul with God in prayer and other spiritual exercises. Pastoral Theology explains the duties of the parish priest. Theology is further sub-divided into Anthropology, the teaching about man; Christology, the teaching about the person and work of Christ; Pneumatology, the teaching about the Holy Spirit; Soteriology, the teaching about Salvation; Ecclesiology, the teaching about the Church, its Sacraments, etc.; and Eschatology, the teaching about the last things, about the state of the soul after death, etc. See Schaff-Herzog.

THEOPATHY. A term invented by William James to describe one of the varieties of religious experience. "In gentle characters, where devoutness is intense and the intellect feeble, we have an imaginative absorption in the love of God to the exclusion of all practical human interests, which, though innocent enough, is too one-sided to be admirable. A mind too narrow has room but for one kind of affection. When the love of God takes possession of such a mind, it expels all human loves and human uses. There is no English name for such a sweet excess of devotion, so I will refer to it as a *theopathic* condition." Mr. James' description of this kind of experience will be felt by many persons to be wanting in sympathy and understanding. See William James, *The Varieties of Religious Experience*, 1906.

THEOPHILANTHROPISTS. In 1776 David Williams (1738-1816), afterwards founder of the Royal Literary Fund, opened a chapel in Margaret Street, Cavendish Square, London. He described himself as a Priest of Nature, and used a special form of theistic service called a "Liturgy on the universal principles of Religion and Morality." This undertaking became known in France through Voltaire (1694-1778). In France some of the deists thought this kind of religion—the ruling principles being simply a love of God and a love of man—a good substitute for Christianity. One D'Aubermenil established a new kind of worship in which a perpetual fire represented the Deity. His disciples were called Theoandrophiles. Out of this sect grew the Theophilanthropists. In 1796 the French Directory authorised Theophilanthropism, and placed at its service twenty churches in Paris. The new creed acknowledged God, virtue, and the immortality of the soul. The Theophilanthropists held festivals in honour of Socrates (*b.* 470 B.C.), St. Vincent de Paul (*b.* 1576 A.D.), Jean Jacques Rousseau (1712-1778), and George Washington (1732-1799). In course of time the new religion fell into disfavour, and was deprived of its churches. In 1802 there was no church left, and the Theophilanthropists disappeared. See J. H. Blunt; Reinach, *O.*

THEORIÆ. Theoriæ was a name given by the Greeks to sacred embassies sent by individual States, partly at their expense, to the great national festivals and to the festivals of friendly States. The ambassadors were treated as honoured guests. See O. Seyffert, *Dict.*

THEOSOPHICAL SOCIETY, THE. 1. A Society instituted in 1784 "for the purpose of promoting the heavenly doctrines of the New Jerusalem, by translating, printing, and publishing the theological writings of the Honourable Emanuel Swedenborg." In 1788 the name of "The New Church" was substituted. See SWEDENBORGIANS. 2. A modern Society, the objects of which are stated to be: (1) to form a nucleus of the Universal Brotherhood of Humanity, without distinction of race, creed, sex, caste or colour; (2) to encourage the study of comparative religion, philosophy and science; (3) to investigate the unexplained laws of nature and the powers latent in man. According to a statement in *The Times* (May 30, 1913), the Theosophical Society is composed of students, belonging to any religion of the world, or to none, who are united by their approval of the above subjects, by their wish to remove religious antagonisms, and to draw together men of goodwill, whatsoever their religious opinions, and by their desire to study religious truths, and to share the results of their studies with others. Their bond of union is not the profession of a common belief, but a common search and aspiration for Truth. They hold that Truth should be sought by study, by reflection, by purity of life, by devotion to high ideals, and they regard Truth as a prize to be striven for, not as a dogma to be imposed by authority. They see every religion as an expression of the Divine Wisdom, and prefer its study to its condemnation, and its practice to proselytism. Peace is their watchword, as truth is their aim.

THEOSOPHY, MODERN. Theosophy as interpreted by the Theosophical Society has been explained in a statement in *The Times* (May 30, 1913). It is the body of truths which forms the basis of all religions, and which cannot be claimed as the exclusive possession of any. It offers a philosophy which renders life intelligible, and which demonstrates the justice and love which guide its evolution. It puts death in its rightful place, as a recurring incident in an endless life, opening the gateway of a fuller and more radiant existence. It restores to the world the Science of the Spirit, teaching man to know the Spirit as himself, and the mind and body as his servants. It illuminates the Scriptures and doctrines of religions by unveiling their hidden meanings, and thus justifying them at the bar of intelligence, as they are ever justified in the eyes of intuition. Members of the Theosophical Society study these truths, and Theosophists endeavour to live them. Theosophy, as understood by Mrs. Annie Besant, is explained in an article in the *Religious Systems of the World*. It claims to be a great body of Secret Wisdom which is in the hands of a Brotherhood. The Brothers are also described as Adepts, Masters, or Mahatmas. They are "living men, evolved further than average humanity, who work ever for the service of their race with a perfect and selfless devotion, holding their high powers in trust for the common good, content to be without recognition, having power beyond all desires of the personal self." Theosophy postulates, to start with, the existence of an Eternal Principle. The Universe, visible and invisible, is built up of "spirit-matter." There are seven Kosmic planes of manifestation. The substance in all is the same, but each plane is denser than its predecessor. Each plane has its own characteristics. The first plane is that of pure Spirit. The second is that of Mind or loftiest spiritual intelligence. The fourth is that of animal passions and desires. The fifth is "that of the vivid animating life-principle, as absorbed in forms." The sixth is the astral plane, "in which matter is but slightly rarer than with ourselves." The seventh is the plane with which we are familiar, the plane of the objective universe. Mrs. Besant explains that "a plane may be defined as a state, marked off by clear characteristics; it must not be thought of as a place, as though the universe were made up of shells one within the other like the coats of an onion." A man may pass from one plane to another. And it is a mistake to think that the intangible is necessarily unreal. "All the mightiest forces are those which are invisible on this plane, visible though they be to senses subtler than our own." It is possible to pass from plane to plane because man himself is the universe in miniature. He is built up of seven "principles," or in other words "is himself a differentiation of consciousness on seven planes." Each of these states of consciousness has a distinctive name. The Spirit in man is called Atma. Its vehicle is Buddhi, the Spiritual Soul. The Spiritual Intelligence is called Manas. This is the Ego, the immortal entity, in man. The Emotional and Passional Nature is called Kama. The Animating Life-principle in man is called Prana. The Astral Body, formed of ethereal "astral" matter, is called Sthula Sarira. The *individual* and true man, imperishable and immortal, is made up of a trinity, Atma-Buddhi-Manas. The other states characterize the transitory and perishable *person*. "The consciousness of the normal man resides chiefly on the physical, astral, and kamic planes, with the lower portion of the Manasic. In flashes of genius, in loftiest aspirations, he is touched for a moment by the light from the higher Manasic regions, but this comes—only comes—to the few, and to these but in rare moments of sublime abstraction. Happy they who even thus catch a glimpse of the Divine Angoeides, the immortal Ego within them. To none born of women, save the Masters, is it at the present time given by the law of evolution to rise to the Atmic-Buddhic planes in man; thither the race will climb millenniums hence, but at present it boots not to speak thereof" (Annie Besant). Theosophists attach supreme importance to the doctrine of Re-incarnation. In Theosophy this does not mean that the Ego in man may become incarnate in lower animals, but that it may dwell successively in a number of personalities. The vast differences, mental and moral, between men is explained by this reincarnation of the Ego. By reincarnation men rise or fall as the result of good or bad action. There is an immutable law of cause and effect. This law is called Karma or "action." There must be "Re-incarnation under Karmic law, until the fruit of every experience has been gathered, every blunder rectified, every fault eradicated; until compassion has been made perfect, strength unbreakable, tenderness complete, self-abnegation the law of life, renunciation for others the natural and joyous impulse of the whole nature." Mrs. Besant explains in a beautiful passage that the doctrines of Re-incarnation and Karma, that is to say, of One Universal Spirit common to all humanity, inevitably result in the Universal Brotherhood of Man.

THERAPEUTÆ. An order of hermits among the Hellenistic Jews of Egypt. They are described in the "De Vita Contemplativa," a work which is commonly supposed to have been written by Philo of Alexandria. It is a mistake to regard them as an Alexandrian variety of the Palestinian Essenes, though, like these, they were ascetics and vegetarians. The members of the order included both men and women: but they all lived apart, devoting themselves to the study of the sacred writings and to spiritual exercises. Once a week they assembled together for common worship, men and women apart: and every fifty days they observed a great festival in which a sacred meal and choral songs were prominent features. They cultivated a *bios theōrētikos*, a life of study and contemplation. W. Staerk compares them with the Egyptian philosopher-priests and -prophets, of whom we hear in the time of Nero. He suggests that the Therapeutae were in fact imitators of the Egyptian hermits, and, like these, exercised a kind of mysticism, partly oriental and partly hellenistic. See W. Staerk, *Neutestamentliche Zeitgeschichte*, 1907.

THESMOPHORIA. A Greek festival in honour of Demeter, the goddess of agriculture and fertility and the foundress of marriage. It was celebrated at Athens in particular, and only by virtuous married women. On the last day of the festival the goddess was invoked as Kalligeneia, the goddess of fair children. See O. Seyffert, *Dict.*

THESSALONIANS, FIRST EPISTLE TO THE. The Apostle Paul visited the important city of Thessalonica and made converts there, especially among the Gentiles. He left Thessalonica and went to Athens (I. Thess. iii. 1). Thence he sent Timothy back to Thessalonica (iii. 2), and Timothy rejoined him at Corinth (iii. 6; Acts xvii. 5). From Corinth, it would seem, was sent the First Epistle to the Thessalonians. It was written soon after his visit, but probably not until about six months had elapsed. It was written at a time when Paul believed that he himself might live to see the sudden realization of the Second Coming of Christ. He assures those to whom he writes that if this should happen in his and their lifetime, their friends who had already died would not be at a disadvantage. "The difficulty created with reference to the destiny of those members of the Church who had died before the Second Coming points to a very early stage in the history of the Thessalonian Church. The question must have been obsolete long before Paul's death. . . . The organisation is in a rudimentary stage; we meet with no technical titles for the officials" (A. S. Peake). Prof. Peake thinks that "the Epistle must have been written in Paul's lifetime, and it may therefore be taken for granted that it was written by Paul himself." The external evidence for the Epistle is sufficiently adequate. It was included in the Canon of Marcion, and is found in the Muratorian Canon. Irenaeus definitely quotes it as one of the letters of Paul. It is included in the Syriac and Old Latin Versions. Naturally such an early letter differs in some respects from those that followed. But it contains, as Currie Martin says, "the germ of many ideas which were afterwards more fully developed in later communications of the Apostle." See R. J. Knowling, *Witness;* J. A. M'Clymont; G. Currie Martin; Arthur S. Peake, *Intr.;* J .Moffatt, *Intr.*

THESSALONIANS, SECOND EPISTLE TO THE. Certain close resemblances between the Second Epistle to the Thessalonians and the First have led some scholars to believe that the Second was modelled on the First by a writer who assumed the name of Paul with the idea of correcting some of the ideas of the earlier letter. In the First Epistle the Second Advent is imagined to be imminent; in the Second it is not imminent, but is to be preceded by another event which itself still lies in the future. The really difficult section in the Epistle is chapter ii. vss. 1-12, which is in the style of Apocalypse. A solution of the difficulty would be to remove this particular section as an interpolation. But strong objections may be urged against this. Prof. Peake thinks "it would be out of the question to rescue the authenticity of the Epistle by sacrificing this section as a later interpolation. The Epistle was written for the sake of that paragraph; remove it and we cannot understand what object could be served by the composition of the rest. If ii. 1-12 is not the work of Paul the authenticity of the whole must be surrendered." The section speaks of the Son of Perdition who opposes and exalts himself against all that is called God or that is worshipped, and sits in the temple of God, setting himself forth as God. It says that the Mystery of Lawlessness is already at work, but there is one that restrains until he shall be taken out of the way. The Lord will come, and will slay the Lawless One with the breath of his mouth. Attempts have been made to identify the Son of Perdition and the One that Restrains with various historical persons and empires. The former, for example, with Nero or even with Luther; the latter with the Roman Empire, and even with the German Empire. Currie Martin thinks that the Son of Perdition represents the Judaizing teachers who figure so prominently in the Epistle to the Galatians (*q.v.*), and that the One that Restrains represents the Roman power. Prof. Peake thinks the Son of Perdition represents a form of heathenism. "There is nothing that so closely corresponds to Paul's description as the deification of the Roman Emperors, which had gone to insane lengths with Caligula. Paul's language especially reminds us of Caligula's orders to have his statue placed in the temple at Jerusalem. The mystery of lawlessness was already at work in Paul's time, held in check for a time by Claudius the reigning Emperor, but destined on his removal to receive its final consummation in a monster of impiety who would be slain by Christ at the Second Coming. It was not unnatural that concurrently with this there should be a great apostasy within the Christian Church itself, such as is also predicted in the Gospels." The external evidence for the Second Epistle to the Thessalonians is fairly strong. The Epistle seems to be quoted by Polycarp in his letter to the Philippians. Justin Martyr seems to be acquainted with the second chapter. The Epistle is mentioned by Irenaeus. It is included in the Canon of Marcion and in the Muratorian Canon. See R. J. Knowling, *Witness;* J. A. M'Clymont; G. Currie Martin; Arthur S. Peake, *Intr.;* J. Moffatt, *Intr.*

THIASUS. The Greek term Thiasus was used (1) of "a society which had selected some god for its patron, and held sacrifices, festal processions, and banquets at stated times in his honour" (Seyffert); (2) of the festivals held in honour of Dionysus; and (3) of the mythical retinue of Dionysus. See O. Seyffert, *Dict.*

THNETOPSYCHITAE. Certain Arabian heretics (see ARABES) were given this name by John of Damascus and Nicetas.

THOMASITES. The followers of John Thomas of Brooklyn, United States of America (1805-1871). They are better known as Christadelphians (*q.v.*).

THOR. One of the chief deities of the Ancient Teutons. He was worshipped by the Frisians and Saxons as Thuner, by the Anglo-Saxons as Thunor, and by the High Germans as Donar. But originally Thor was the chief god of Norway. Sweden too came to pay him very great honour. He was the god of thunder and lightning, wind and rain. As such he was naturally also the patron god of agriculture. The Norwegians took the cult to Iceland. When Odhin (see WODAN) was introduced into Norway he became a formidable rival to Thor, but the Thunder-god continued to exercise great power, and at times thought it necessary to frustrate the plans of Odhin. Thor is called "the roarer." He is also called "god of the chariot" and "riding Thor," and is represented as driving a chariot drawn by two he-goats. He has red hair and beard. His strength is symbolised by a hammer, iron gauntlets, and a girdle of strength. In Norse mythology he is made the son of Wodan. In the Snorra Edda (see EDDA) and the Eddic songs he is represented as having great contests and adventures with the giants, in which his hammer plays a great part. His name has been preserved in the English Thursday and the German Donnerstag. See P. D. Chantepie de la Saussaye, *Rel. of the Teutons,* 1902.

THORGERDH HOLGABRUDH. One of the deities of the Ancient Teutons. The goddess Thorgerdh Holgabrudh was Finnish. Jarl Hakon, when he was fighting with the Jomsvikings, in order to gain her help, sacrificed to her his young son. Mention is made of her image. In one place, we are told, it stood on a car or wagon together with those of Irpa and Thor (*q.v.*). See P. D. Chantepie de la Saussaye, *Rel. of the Teutons,* 1902.

THOUGHT-TRANSFERENCE. See TELEPATHY.

THOTH. An Egyptian deity. Thoth is the moon god, and is represented as ibis-headed. In the judgment scene described in the Book of the Dead (*q.v.*) Thoth acts as the "scribe of the gods." When the heart of the dead is weighed in the balance, he writes down the result on his tablets. He was the god of writing, the god of letters, the tutelary deity of scribes. His skill in magic made him the god of medicine, since magic and medicine were closely connected. Again, since the moon determined the measurement of time, Thoth became the god of time. At the beginning of the New Kingdom the Pharaohs were named after him (*e.g.*, Thothmosis, "Son of Thoth"). He is identified by the Greeks with Hermes. See Alfred Wiedemann; Adolf Erman, *Handbook;* Naville, *The Old Egyptian Faith,* 1909.

THREE DENOMINATIONS. A designation used of the Presbyterians, Independents (Congregationalists), and Baptists in 1727 as representing the majority of Dissenters in England. The three denominations obtained the privilege of appealing directly to the king by means of the presentation of joint addresses.

THREE-REFUGE FORMULA. The formula known as the three-refuge formula was the only prayer used by the early Buddhists. It is the prayer which the novice is required to repeat three times at the ceremony at which he is admitted into the order of monks. It runs: "I go for refuge to the Buddha; I go for refuge to the Law; I go for refuge to the Order." Monier Williams points out that it resembles the Gayatri Prayer (*q.v.*) of the Veda in being composed of three times eight syllables (in the original). It is still regarded by many of the Buddhists as the only legitimate prayer. See Monier-Williams, *Buddhism,* 1890; H. Hackmann.

THRESHOLD, THE. The threshold of a house or temple figures in the religion of certain peoples as a sacred spot or a dangerous point. According to Herodotus (ii. 48) every Egyptian sacrificed before the door of his house a hog to Osiris (*q.v.*). According to H. Clay Trumbull, in modern Egypt the incoming master of a house may be welcomed by a threshold sacrifice. In modern Syria it is unlucky to tread on a threshold; and in Upper Syria the friends of a bridegroom sometimes carry the bride across the threshold of the bridegroom's house. The Hebrew word for Passover, *pesah*, is derived from a root meaning "to leap, dance." This has suggested that perhaps the Passover was so called because, after the performance of a special rite, the Israelites, in recognition of the sanctity of the threshold, leaped over it or performed a ritual dance near it. In Zephaniah (i. 9) it is said: "And I will punish all who leap over the threshold, who fill the house of their lord with violence and deceit." T. K. Cheyne paraphrases this (*Encycl. Bibl.*): "And on that day I will punish those who, though they leap with scrupulous awe over the sacred threshold, yet bring with them into Yahwè's house hands stained with cruelty and injustice." But the reference here may be to some superstitious practice of foreign origin. The threshold of the house has been regarded by many peoples as the favourite abode of demons or the ghosts of the dead. W. Warde Fowler mentions that among the Romans a man who returned home after his supposed death in a foreign country was made to enter the house by the roof instead of by the door. He might be a ghost or have evil spirits about him, and against such the door had to be kept barred. There was a curious Roman ceremony immediately after the birth of a child, the object of which was "to prevent Silvanus, who may stand for the dangerous spirits of the forest, from entering in and vexing the baby" (Warde Fowler). St. Augustine mentions a protecting spirit of the entrance to a house named Limentinus. See H. Clay Trumbull, *The Threshold Covenant,* 1896; the *Encycl. Bibl.;* W. Warde Fowler, *Religious Experience of the Roman People.* 1911.

THRITA. The second of the two chief gods of healing in the Iranian pantheon. He is equivalent to the Indian Trita. He is, like Trita, an old, wise, very beneficent deity, and a bestower of long life. "Though he is not explicitly represented as a curer of diseases, his connection with the plant of life, the soma, makes him a powerful healer. While Thrita offered the haoma-sacrifice in primeval times, Trita is the great preparer of soma" (A. Carnoy, "The Iranian Gods of Healing," *Journal of the American Oriental Society,* vol. 38).

THRONE BEARERS. A class of angels referred to in the Qur'ân. "And the angels shall be on its sides, and over them on that day eight shall bear up the throne of thy Lord" (lxix. 17). "They who bear the throne and they who encircle it, celebrate the praise of their Lord and believe in Him, and implore forgiveness for the believers" (xl. 7). The usual number is four, which is to be augmented to eight on the day of resurrection. See F. A. Klein, *The Religion of Islâm.*

THUGS, THE. A Hindu sect, worshippers of Kālī (*q.v.*) as goddess of destruction. The Thugs or Thags murdered people as a religious act. But they always strangled their victims, because they objected on principle to the spilling of blood. E. W. Hopkins even thinks that "the sect originated among the Kāli-worshippers as a protest against blood-letting." The Thugs are described by Lieutenant Reynolds as "mostly men of mild and unobtrusive manners, possessing a cheerful disposition." After strangling their victims, they robbed them. The bodies they buried. They did not kill women. The Thugs were suppressed by the year 1840. See Monier-Williams; E. W. Hopkins; and R. V. Russell.

THUNDERING LEGION, THE. Eusebius (v. 5), on the authority of Apollinarius and Tertullian, says that this name was given to a legion of Christian soldiers in the army of the Roman Emperor Marcus Aurelius. He gives the following story to account for the name: "But it is said that Marcus Aurelius Caesar, the brother of the former, when about to engage in battle with the Germans and Sarmatians, and his army was suffering with thirst, was greatly at a loss on this account. Then, however, those soldiers that belonged to the Melitine legion, as it was called, by a faith which has continued from that time to this, bending their knees upon the earth whilst drawn up in battle array against the enemy, according to our peculiar custom of praying, entered into prayer before God. And as this was a singular spectacle to the enemy, a still more singular circumstance is reported to have happened immediately: that the lightning drove the enemy into flight and destruction, but that a shower came down and refreshed the army of those that then called upon God, the whole of which was on the point of perishing with thirst" (*Eccles. Hist.*, Bagster's English edition). Neander has sought to show that the story is a mixture of truth and fiction. Duchesne writes: "The precarious position of the army is undoubted. And we also know that the Romans in their extremity invoked all the different divine powers whose rites the soldiers affected. But when the column commemorative of the victories of Marcus Aurelius in Germania was erected in the Campus Martius, the miracle was ascribed to the gods of the State. In those celebrated bas-reliefs, Jupiter Pluvius is still to be seen with the saving torrential rain—which enabled the legions to escape thirst and defeat—streaming from his hair, his arms, and his whole person." See William Benham; Louis Duchesne, *Hist.*

THUNER. The name by which the Teutonic deity Thor (*q.v.*), the god of thunder, was known to the Frisians and Saxons.

THUNOR. The name by which Thor (*q.v.*) was known to the Anglo-Saxons.

TIÂMAT. A Babylonian deity. The goddess Tiâmat with the god Apsu (*q.v.*) is represented in the Epic of Marduk (see MARDUK, EPIC OF) as existing from the first. The two deities are virtually identical, one being the male, the other the female principle. Both personify primaeval chaos. Tiâmat both in sound and meaning resembles the Hebrew word *Tĕhôm.* Tiâmat appears as a great monster with a train of other monsters, chief of which is Kingu. The other gods are created after Tiâmat, and there ensues a battle between them and Tiâmat with her monsters. In this battle Marduk is the champion and representative of the other gods. The result is that Marduk (Order) conquers Tiâmat (Chaos).

TIHAX. A tribal deity, god of the stone knife, in the religion of the Mayan Indians.

TIJANIYAH. A Muhammadan religious order in Africa. The order, which has Wahhabite tendencies (see WAHHÂBIS), sought at first to spread its faith by the power of the sword. "But," says Oskar Mann, "the real inward conversion only took place when, laying aside their swords, the victors began to be teachers of the subjugated heathen in the truest sense of the word; and, according to travellers' reports, this peaceful work is being carried on without interruption at the present day" (Oskar Mann). See T. W. Arnold, *Preaching of Islam*, 1896; Oskar Mann, "Mohammedanism," in *G.R.W.*

TIMOTHY, THE FIRST EPISTLE TO. The First Epistle to Timothy, one of the Pastoral Epistles (*q.v.*), is ascribed to the Apostle Paul by Irenaeus and in the Muratorian Canon, but was rejected by Tatian, Marcion, and Basilides. It is possible that it is quoted by Polycarp. There are passages in the Epistle (*e.g.*, iii. 16) which look very like fixed liturgical formulae, and its descriptions of Christian life suggest a somewhat developed organisation. The references to false teaching point, it is thought, to a form of Gnosticism such as flourished in the second century. But it is not necessary to suppose this. As A. S. Peake says, "it must be remembered that similar allegations have been made with reference to the Colossian heresy, but probably erroneously." The false teaching was evidently Jewish in origin (cp. i. 7), though there may have been associated with it foreign elements. According to Hort, there is no reference in the "antitheses of knowledge falsely so called" (vi. 20) to the work of Marcion called *Antitheses.* The word "antitheses" describes "the endless contrasts of decisions founded on endless distinctions which played so large a part in the casuistry of the scribes as interpreters of the Law." Others have thought that the false teachers were Essenes. Harnack places the Epistle as late as 140 A.D. But, as Currie Martin says, so late a date is hardly possible. See M'Clymont; G. Currie Martin; Arthur S. Peake, *Intr.;* J. Moffatt, *Intr.*

TIMOTHY, THE SECOND EPISTLE TO. It is not unlikely that what is now called the Second Epistle to Timothy really preceded what is now known as the First Epistle. "The picture given of Timothy is very hard to accept as historically accurate if this is really later than the first epistle, for he is dealt with as a younger and less strong personality than in the first epistle" (Currie Martin). But in any case, there are the same difficulties of language, teaching, and relationship to the Acts of the Apostles, as in the First Epistle. Attempts have been made to get over some of the difficulties by regarding the Epistle as composite. Two or three letters have been found in it. One theory is that these comprise (*a*) i. 1-iv. 8 (with the addition perhaps of iv. 19-21) and (*b*) iv. 9-18. Another theory is that they comprise (*a*) ii. 14-iii. 9 and (*b*) iv. 9-15 and 19-21 and (*c*) the remainder of the Epistle. The passage ii. 11-13 seems to be part of a Christian hymn. There are not so many references to false teaching as in the First Epistle, and these are indefinite. A special feature of the Epistle is the large number of proper names. There are twenty-three, of which ten are mentioned elsewhere. "The letter contains a very beautiful portraiture of the Christian minister in the twofold aspects of the writer as a man with his course completed, and of the ideal set before the younger preacher with his work largely before him. These remain of permanent value to all time, whatever decision we may come to with regard to the authorship" (G. Currie Martin). See J. A. M'Clymont, G. Currie Martin; Arthur S. Peake *Intr.;* J. Moffatt, *Intr.*

TIQQUNE SÔPHERIM. Literally "corrections of the Scribes." The expression is used of emendations proposed by the Jewish Scribes for certain passages in the Old Testament which they thought had been altered because they offended against a sense of propriety. There are eighteen of these passages. To take an example, the present text of Genesis xviii. 22 says that "Abraham was still standing before Jehovah." The Scribes think that the original text said, "Jehovah was still standing before Abraham," but that it was not considered fitting that Jehovah should be represented as waiting upon a man. See A. S. Geden, *Intr. to the Heb. Bible*, 1909.

TITI USI. A Samoan village deity. The god, whose name means Glittering Leaf Girdle, was worshipped at the new moon, when all work was suspended for a day or two.

TITUS, THE EPISTLE TO. One of the Epistles of the New Testament known as the Pastoral Epistles (*q.v.*). It appears from this letter that Titus, to whom it is addressed, was in charge of the work of the Church in Crete. Titus was a Gentile who was converted by the Apostle Paul. With Paul and Barnabas he visited Jerusalem (Galatians ii. 1-4). The Epistle to Titus has the same linguistic and stylistic characteristics as the Epistles to Timothy. Like the other Pastoral Epistles, it refers to false teaching of a semi-Jewish character (i. 10, 14; iii. 9). In the case of Crete, a corruption of Christian doctrine can easily be understood, for the character of the Cretans was proverbially bad. The Epistle itself in i. 12 refers to a description of them by Epimenides (600 B.C.). "One of themselves, a prophet of their own said, Cretans are always liars, evil beasts, idle gluttons." It has been thought that the letter is not a unity. "Attempts have been made, not very satisfactorily, to split this letter into Pauline and non-Pauline sections, the only part about which there is absolute unanimity among such critics being that the last few verses are certainly to be attributed to the Apostle" (Currie Martin). See J. A. M'Clymont; G. Currie Martin; Arthur S. Peake, *Intr.;* J. Moffatt, *Intr.*

TIU. One of the gods of the Ancient Teutons. It has been suggested that Tiu is identical with Irmin, the eponymous hero of the Irminsleute or Hermiones. He was one of the chief gods of the Frisians; and was worshipped by the Anglo-Saxons as Tiw, and by the Norsemen as Tyr. But his worship was common to all the Teutons. Tiu appears often as a god of war, but originally he seems to have been a sky god. The sword would seem to have been one of his symbols, and sword-dances to have been performed in his honour. The sword-dances were accompanied by sacrifice. The name of the god survives in the English Tuesday. See P. D. Chantepie de la Saussaye, *Rel. of the Teutons*, 1902.

TIWAZ. An ancient deity worshipped by many of the Teutonic tribes. According to Tacitus, the Semnones offered human sacrifices to him. Originally a sky-god and storm-god, he developed into a god of war and justice, and is associated by Latin writers with Mars. Our name Tuesday represents Tiwes-daeg. The Norse name of the god is Tyr.

TIYANS, RELIGION OF THE. The Tiyans are described as the Malayālam toddy-drawing caste of Malabar, Cochin, and Travancore in India. Their religion is connected largely with Sakti worship, that is to say, the worship of the life principle in nature. The Hinduism of Malabar "is very largely imbued with the lower cult, which, with a tinge of Hinduism, varied in extent here and there, is really the religion of the people at large all over Southern India. The Tiyans have a large share of it. To the actions of evil and other spirits are attributable most, if not all, of the ills and joys of life. The higher Hinduism is far above them. Nevertheless, we find among them the worship of the obscure and mysterious Sakti, which, unfortunately, is practised in secret." Every individual is believed to be a spark of the divinity and to be capable of attaining godhood. The Tiyans regard the Sakti goddess, Bhagavati, as their own guardian spirit. And it may be said that "Sakti worship is perhaps more peculiarly theirs than others', owing to their being able to use arrack, a product of the palm, and therefore of their own particular métier. The highest merit in Sakti can be reached only through arrack" (E. Thurston).

TIYARS. A small caste of boatmen and fishermen in India. On the special festival of the goddess Durga, they make to her offerings of fish and lotus flowers. "In honour of Durga they observe a fast on the four Tuesdays of the months of Chait and Kunwār (March and September). In Chait they also worship their hooks and nets" (R. V. Russell.

TLALOC. Tlaloc was the name of one of the earliest deities of the ancient Mexicans. The name means "the nourisher," for Tlaloc was the god of rain. His seat in the mountains was also called Tlaloc, and that in heaven Tlalocan. Naturally, as god of rain, he was also god of fertility. When rain was wanted he had to be propitiated by the sacrifice of sucking infants. If they wept on the way to the sacrifice, this was a sign that there would be plenty of rain. Tlaloc would be kind. "One-eyed and open-mouthed, he delighted in the sacrifice of children, and in seasons of drought hundreds of innocents were borne to his temple in open litters, wreathed with blossoms and dressed in festal robes" (Lewis Spence). His children, the Tlalocs, would seem to have been the rain-clouds. His wife, Chalchihuitlicue, "the lady Chalchihuit," or Cioacoatl, was the goddess of Water. Prayer was made to her when children were baptised. See Lewis Spence, *Myth.;* J. M. Robertson, "The Religions of Ancient America," in *R.S.W.; P.C.*

TLAZOLTEOTL. Tlazolteotl was one of the deities worshipped by the ancient Mexicans. She was the goddess of love, and lived in a beautiful garden. Here she was attended on by musicians, jesters, dwarfs, and others. She first espoused the Rain-god Tlaloc, but afterwards forsook him in favour of Tezcatlipoca (*q.v.*). With her worship were associated a number of grossly sensual practices. See Lewis Spence, *Myth.;* J. M. Robertson, *P.C.*

T.N.K. A formula used in the later (Massoretic) Hebrew literature to designate collectively the three divisions of the Jewish Bible:—the Law (T), the Prophets (N) and the Writings (K). The formula is thus an abbreviation of the three Hebrew words, *Torah, Nebi'im*, and *Kethubim*.

TOBACCO. In the West Indies tobacco is found to have played a part in religion. Its importance in religious ceremonial "is shown by the fact that it was known by the same word, *cogioba*, as prayer, and to pray and to offer tobacco were alike called 'making cogioba'" (T. A. Joyce, *C.A.W.I.A.*). The tobacco was inhaled through a Y-shaped tube, the two branches being placed in the nostrils. The priests inhaled tobacco in order to produce a state of ecstasy, in which they communicated with the unseen powers. In healing the sick, both doctor (priest) and patient were rendered ecstatic by the use of tobacco. This enabled the doctor to discover the cause of the sickness. Among the Bribri of Costa Rica the incantations of the medicine-men, when they seek to control the rain, to cure ill-luck, or to banish snakes, "consist in blowing clouds of tobacco-smoke in certain directions." Tobacco was offered to the Mexican god Opochtli. Even in Ireland, according to W. G. Wood-Martin, the tobacco-pipe has become a religious symbol. "In many parts of the country new clay pipes and packets of tobacco are distributed among the funeral guests, who sit around and smoke while the grave is being dug. It is believed that it is the duty of the ghost of the last arrival in a churchyard to watch the other graves, and attend upon their occupants; but the recently made spirit hankers after tobacco, and dearly loves a last smoke, so unused tobacco and unused pipes are not removed from the graveyard; the guests are, however, at liberty to take away the pipes they themselves have smoked."

TOHIL. A deity in the religion of the Mayan Indians. He was worshipped as a thunder-god by the Quiché of Guatemala, and resembles the Mexican god Quetzalcoatl.

ṬOHORŌTH. The title of one of the Jewish treatises or tractates which reproduce the oral tradition or unwritten law as developed by the second century A.D. and are incorporated in the Mishnah (*q.v.*), a collection and compilation completed by Rabbi Judah the Holy, or the Patriarch, about 200 A.D. The sixty-three tractates of the Mishnah are divided into six groups or orders (*sedarim*). Tohorōth is the fifth tractate of the sixth group, which is called *Tohorōth* ("Purifications").

TONATIUH. A Mexican deity, the sun. He is represented as carrying a sun-disc.

TOLSTOYANS. Followers of Count Leo Tolstoy (1828-1910), the Russian social reformer. Tolstoy was educated in the faith of the Orthodox Greek Church. But he gradually lost the faith of his childhood. From the age of sixteen he ceased to attend the services of the Church. "I no longer accepted the faith of my childhood, but I had a vague belief in *something*, though I do not think I could exactly explain what" (*How I came to Believe*). In early manhood, he tells us, he gave free rein to his passions. After serving in the Crimean War, he became an author. At St. Petersburg he associated with the authors of the day, and "met with a hearty reception and much flattery." But as time went on he became more and more disgusted with his own life and with the life of the people around him. He went abroad and made the acquaintance of many eminent and learned men. On his return he organised schools for the peasantry. He went abroad again to study methods of teaching. Returning to Russia, he accepted the office of a country magistrate or arbitrator, and began to teach the uneducated people in the schools, and the educated classes in journals which he published. But the work was a constant worry to him, "trying to teach, without knowing how or what," and he became ill. On his recovery, he married (1862); and family life for a time diverted his thoughts. In 1874 his mental difficulties became again a source of worry and depression. "Till I know the reasons for my own acts, I can do nothing—I cannot live." Life no longer seemed to have any meaning for him. He sought for its meaning in Art, Poetry, Science, and Philosophy, but in vain. He next sought for its meaning in life itself, in the men who surrounded him. The life of those who occupied the same position as himself offered no satisfactory solution of his difficulties. Having failed here, he decided to study the life of the labouring classes. This seemed to suggest that throughout mankind there was given to the meaning of life a sense which he had neglected and despised. He was forced to the conclusion that besides the reasoning knowledge which he once thought the only true knowledge, "there was in every living man another kind of knowledge, an unreasoning one, but which gives a possibility of living—faith." This led him to turn his attention to religion again, especially to Christianity. But he could not discover among the so-called believers of his own class the faith he sought. Once more he studied the lives of the people, and became "convinced that a true faith was among them, that their faith was for them a necessary thing, and alone gave them a meaning in life and a possibility of living." After living among them for two years, the life of his own circle of rich and learned men became repulsive and lost all its meaning. "The life of the working classes, of the whole of mankind, of those that create life, appeared to me in its true significance. I understood that this was life itself, and that the meaning given to this life was a true one, and I accepted it." The tormenting feeling which Tolstoy had had was really, he felt afterwards, a searching after God. "This search after a God was not an act of my reason, but a feeling, and I say this advisedly, because it was opposed to my way of thinking; it came from the heart." Gradually he returned to "a belief in God, in moral perfectibility, and in the tradition which gives a meaning to life." He decided to renounce the life of his own class, and to adopt the simple life of the working classes. He also returned to the Orthodox Faith. But he found after a time that he could not continue to be an orthodox member of it. He wished to be a brother to men of every creed, and he was horrified because in time of war Russians slew their brethren in the name of Christian love. He withdrew from the Orthodox Church. His criticisms of orthodox Christianity have since been very searching; and in 1901 he was excommunicated by the Russian Synod. In 1895 Tolstoy had renounced his property in copyright, land, and money. When Tolstoy came back to Christianity and re-read the Gospels again and again, he discovered a new meaning in sayings of Jesus. He found, for instance, that when Jesus said, "Resist not evil," he gave utterance to a principle of supreme importance. "He says with perfect clearness and simplicity: 'The law of resistance to evil by violence, which you have made the principle of your lives, is false and unnatural.' He gives another basis—the non-resistance of evil, which, according to his teaching, can alone deliver mankind from evil. He says: 'You think that your laws of violence correct evil; they only increase it. For thousands of years you have tried to destroy evil by evil, and you have not destroyed but increased it. Do what I say, and you will know the truth of this'" (*What I believe*, 1884). Again, when Jesus condemned the use of oaths, he fully meant what he said. "Jesus said, 'But I say unto you, Swear not at all.' This expression is as simple, clear, and unhesitating as the words 'Judge not' and 'Condemn not,' and requires as little explanation; particularly as it is further explained that whatever is required of us more than the answer Yea, or Nay, is from the source of evil." War is the most frightful wickedness; and to take a military oath is to rebel against the precepts of the Gospels. Our evil social conditions are due to violence. "The cause of the miserable condition of the workers is slavery. The cause of slavery is legislation. Legislation rests on organised violence. It follows that an improvement in the condition of the people is possible only through the abolition of organised violence" (*The Slavery of Our Times*, 1900). Governments ought to be abolished—but not by violence. People must be persuaded that disciplined armies are not necessary, except for keeping the masses of the people in slavery. "People must feel that their participation in the criminal activity of Governments, whether by giving part of their work, in the form of money, or by direct participation in military service, is not, as is generally supposed, an indifferent action, but besides being harmful to oneself and to one's brothers, is a participation in the crimes unceasingly committed by all Governments, and a preparation for new crimes which Governments, by maintaining disciplined armies, are always preparing." They must feel this and communicate the feeling to others. They must not think of meeting violence with violence. "The inconsistency of violence as a means of communion between men, its incompatibility with the demands of contemporary conscience, is too obvious for the existing order to be able to continue. But external conditions cannot change without a change in the inner spiritual condition of men" (*The One Thing Needful*). The means of deliverance lies only in one thing, "the inner work of each man upon himself." Tolstoy was the prophet of the simple life. It is natural that he should have become a vegetarian. But he did not maintain that in order to be moral, people must cease to eat meat. "I only wish to say that for a good life a certain order of good actions is indispensable; that if a man's aspiration toward right living be serious, it will inevitably follow one definite sequence; and that in this sequence the first virtue a man will strive after will be abstinence, self-renunciation. And in seeking to be abstinent a man will inevitably follow one definite sequence, and in this sequence the first thing will be abstinence in food, fasting. And in fasting, if he be really and seriously seeking to live a good life, the first thing from which he will abstain will always be the use of animal food, because, to say nothing of the excitation of the passions caused by such food, its use is simply immoral, as it involves the performance of an act which is contrary to the moral feeling—killing; and is called forth only by greediness, and the desire for tasty food" (*The First Step*, 1900). As an ideal, Tolstoy seems to have recommended also abstinence from marriage. "The Christian's ideal is love to God and to one's neighbour; it is the renunciation of self for the service of God and one's neighbour. Whereas sexual love, marriage, is service of self, and therefore in any case an obstacle to the service of God and man; consequently, from a Christian point of view, a fall, a sin." He repeats this teaching in a number of letters to correspondents. One more example. "If man be already living a human, spiritual life, then being in love and marriage will be for him a fall: he will have to give part of his powers to his wife or family or the object of his love. But if he be on the animal plane, the eating, working, writing plane, then being in love will be for him an ascent, as with animals and insects" (*The Relations of the Sexes,* 1901). Tolstoy disapproved of the current conceptions of Art, and offered a new definition. "To evoke in oneself a feeling one has once experienced, and having evoked it in oneself, then, by means of movements, lines, colours, sounds, or forms expressed in words, so to transmit that feeling that others may experience the same feeling—this is the activity of art. Art is a human activity, consisting in this, that one man consciously, by means of certain external signs, hands on to others feelings he has lived through, and that other people are infected by these feelings, and also experience them" (*What is Art?* 1898). The result of false conceptions of Art has been that "the ecclesiastical and patriotic intoxication and embitterment of the people" has been perpetuated (cp. *Guy de Maupassant,* 1898). See, in addition, to the works quoted above: *The Kingdom of God is Within You,* 1894; *What to do; On Life,* 1902; *What is Religion?* 1902; *Popular Stories and Legends.*

TONGUES, GIFT OF. A religious phenomenon to which special reference is made in the New Testament. In the Acts of the Apostles (ii.) we are told that soon after the death of Jesus, when the disciples were assembled together on the day of Pentecost, they were suddenly filled with the Holy Spirit and began to speak with other tongues. The passage ought to be quoted. "And when the day of Pentecost was fully come, they were all with one accord in one place. And suddenly there came a sound from heaven, as of a rushing mighty wind, and it filled all the house where they were sitting. And there appeared unto them cloven tongues, like as of fire, and it sat upon each of them. And they were all filled with the Holy Ghost, and began to speak with other tongues, as the Spirit gave them utterance. And there were dwelling at Jerusalem Jews, devout men, out of every nation under heaven. Now when this was noised abroad, the multitude came together, and were confounded, because that every man heard them speak in his own language. And they were all amazed, and marvelled, saying one to another, Behold, are not all these which speak Galileans? And how hear we every man in our own tongue, wherein we were born?" (*vss.* 1-8). It is clear from this report that the disciples were stirred and agitated in a way that seemed very strange. They uttered strange sounds. These sounds were understood to be words spoken in foreign languages. And this view is shared by many Christians. With God all things are possible, it is argued. It is true that, in the Christian view, God is omnipotent; but it is widely felt now that God does not arbitrarily break through the natural order of things, and that where two explanations of an event are possible the simpler and more natural one is to be preferred. In the present case there is a more natural explanation. The study of this class of phenomena has revealed the fact that often when people's religious feelings are deeply stirred and agitated they fall into a kind of trance and mutter sounds which are unintelligible. Unsympathetic persons will describe their condition by saying that they have become afflicted with hysteria. And it is true that excessive religious emotion is often a disease. But it is bad logic and worse taste to say that because two persons are similarly agitated the causes are always the same. This is to suggest that there is no difference, to take an instance, between heartfelt grief and the hysterical sobbing of a criminal. In the Acts of the Apostles we have the report of a true spiritual experience. The language of the Holy Spirit is different from the language of men. It cannot, especially at first, easily be translated into human speech. If the attempt is made, it only results in language which is incoherent and unintelligible. No one knew this better than St. Paul, who had made the experience at his conversion (see CONVERSION). Consequently we find him giving the true explanation of the Gift of Tongues (I. Corinthians xiv.). A few quotations are necessary. "For he that speaketh in an unknown tongue, speaketh not unto men, but unto God; for no man understandeth him, howbeit in the spirit he speaketh mysteries." . . . "He that speaketh in an unknown tongue edifieth himself; but he that prophesieth edifieth the church." . . . "Now, brethren, if I come unto you speaking with tongues, what shall I profit you, except I shall speak to you either by revelation, or by knowledge, or by prophesying, or by doctrine? And even things without life giving sound, whether pipe or harp, except they give a distinction in the sounds, how shall it be known what is piped or harped? For if the trumpet give an uncertain sound, who shall prepare himself to the battle? So likewise ye, except ye utter by the tongue words easy to be understood, how shall it be known what is spoken? for ye shall speak into the air." The whole chapter should be read. People have been known to show a knowledge of a foreign language which has not been acquired in the ordinary way. But this also has admitted of an ordinary psychological explanation. It has been due to the abnormal working of the subjective mind (see SUBJECTIVE MIND). Compare, generally, CONVERSION, ECSTASY, INSPIRATION.

TOPE. Tope is one of the names for a Buddhist Stūpa (*q.v.*). Tope is a corrupt form of the Pāli Thūpa, which again is equivalent to the Sanskrit Stūpa.

TORTOISE. A Hindu legend relates that the world was fished up out of the waters by the god Brahma (*q.v.*), with the help of a boar, a fish, and a tortoise. The tortoise figures prominently in the religion of the Chinese. One of the precepts of the "Book of Rewards and Punishments" (*q.v.*) is, "Don't needlessly kill tortoises and serpents." In ancient times the shell of the tortoise and the stalks of a particular kind of grass were supposed to possess spiritual powers and to be very efficacious in divination. The tortoise would become an object of reverence on account of its longevity. "To explore what is complex, to search out what is hidden, to hook up what lies deep, and to reach to what is distant, thereby determining the issues for good or ill of all events under the sky, and making all men full of strenuous endeavour, there are no agencies greater than those of the stalks and the tortoise shell" (after Giles). Russell and Hīra Lāl note that among the Bhunjias of India great reverence is paid to the tortoise. "They call the tortoise the footstool (*pīdha*) of God, and have adopted the Hindu theory that the earth is supported by a tortoise swimming in the midst of the ocean." In the mythology of the Hurons, the earth is supported by a great tortoise. See Robert K. Douglas, *Confucianism and Taouism;* Herbert A. Giles, *Religions of Ancient China,* 1905; Reinach, *O.*

TOTĀFOTH. Totāfoth is the Hebrew word which is translated "Frontlets" (*q.v.;* Deuteronomy vi. 8). The Greek equivalent is Phylacteries (*q.v.*).

TOTEMISM. Totemism, as Salomon Reinach says, is difficult to define. The word *totem* or rather *otam* (mark or sign) was adopted at the beginning of the eighteenth century from the Indians of North America. It was found to be the term employed by the Ojibway, an Algonquin tribe, to designate usually the animal or plant the name of which the clan bears, and which is recognised as an ancestor, a protector, and a rallying sign. "Totemism seems to have been as widespread as the animism from which it is derived; we find it to some extent everywhere, if not in the pure form and unmixed with more recent religious conceptions, at least as a survival more or less clearly defined. The religions of Egypt, of Syria, of Greece, of Italy and of Gaul are all impregnated with totemism" (Reinach, *O.*, 1909). That the Semites passed through the totem stage seems clear from the facts adduced by Robertson Smith (*R.S.*). Professor Zapletal (*Der Totemismus und die Religion Israels*, 1901) has opposed this view, and denied that the Israelites were totemists, but without success, as Stanley A. Cook has shown ("Israel and Totemism" in the *Jewish Quarterly Review*, April, 1902). But in the light of new discoveries, the data collected by Spencer and Gillen among the tribes of Central Australia, it is felt that Robertson Smith's general conception of totemism and especially his theory of a "totem sacrament" will not stand. Dr. Frazer (as quoted by Cook) says that Robertson Smith's theory inferred "a totem community united in reverence, awe and love of the totem animal, solemnly and sorrowfully killing it once a year, and partaking of its flesh, not as common food to fill their stomachs, but as a means of entering into a mystic communion with the divine animal." What are the facts? "We find a community of which the greater part regularly kills and eats the animal in question whenever they can lay hands on it, whilst the remaining section (which has the animal for its totem) does its best to multiply the creature in order that all the rest of the people may devour it. And since, in order to breed the animal for eating, they think it necessary to have part of its substance in their bodies, they do ceremonially partake of its flesh, not in order to acquire certain mysterious divine qualities, but ultimately in order that the majority of their fellows may feed on roast kangaroo, roast emu, or whatever it may be. Instead of a mystic religious rite like the Christian sacrament of the Eucharist (which was clearly in Robertson Smith's mind), we see a magical ceremony of the most practical and business-like intention." Dr. Frazer thinks that the relation of the group to the totem cannot properly be described as worship. The most primitive form of totemism he finds now among the Arunta of Central Australia. The Arunta have a peculiar theory of conception. "The child has neither the totem of his father nor that of his mother, but the one whose centre is at the spot where the mother believes that she felt the first symptoms of approaching maternity. For it is said that the Arunta is ignorant of the exact relation existing between generation and the sexual act; he thinks that every conception is due to a sort of mystic fecundation. According to him, it is due to the entrance of the soul of an ancestor into the body of a woman and its becoming the principle of a new life there. So at the moment when a woman feels the first tremblings of the child, she imagines that one of the souls whose principal residence is at the place where she happens to be, has just entered into her. As the child who is presently born is merely the reincarnation of this ancestor, he necessarily has the same totem; thus his totem is determined by the locality where he is believed to have been mysteriously conceived" (Émile Durkheim). Durkheim gives a brief summary of Frazer's theory. "At the exact moment when the woman realizes that she is pregnant, she must think that the spirit by which she feels herself possessed has come to her from the objects about her, and especially from one of those which attract her attention at the moment. So if she is engaged in plucking a plant, or watching an animal, she believes that the soul of this plant or animal has passed into her. Among the things to which she will be particularly inclined to attribute her condition are, in the first place, the things she has just eaten. If she has recently eaten emu or yam, she will not doubt that an emu or yam has been born in her and is developing. Under these conditions, it is evident how the child, in his turn, will be considered a sort of yam or emu, how he regards himself as a relative of the plant or animal of the same species, how he has sympathy and regard for them, how he refuses to eat them, etc. From this moment, totemism exists in its essential traits: it is the native's theory of conception that gave rise to it, so Frazer calls this primitive totemism *conceptional*." The weakness of this theory is that it assumes too much, for the probability is that this so-called primitive totemism was preceded by the better known type, hereditary totemism, either in the paternal or the maternal line. Salomon Reinach in his *Cults* has formulated a code of (animal) totemism. 1. Certain animals are neither killed nor eaten, but man rears specimens and tends them. 2. Mourning is worn for the accidental death of a member of a particular animal species; and it is buried with the same honours as a member of the clan. 3. Occasionally the alimentary interdiction applies only to a part of the animal's body. 4 When animals, ordinarily spared, are killed under the stress of urgent necessity, the slayers address excuses to them, or strive by various artifices to extenuate the violation of the taboo: in other words, the murder. 5. The tabooed animal is mourned for after it has been ritually sacrificed. 6. Men put on the skins of certain animals, especially in religious ceremonies. Where totemism exists, these animals are totems. 7. Clans and individuals take the names of animals. Where totemism exists, these animals are totems. 8. In many instances, the clan carries the image of an animal on its ensigns and arms. The individual may paint this image on his body, or tattoo himself with it. 9. The totemic animal, if dangerous, is supposed to spare the members of the totemic clan, but only when they belong to it by birth. 10. Animal totems help and protect the members of the totemic clan. 11. Animal totems foretell the future to the faithful, and serve them as guides. 12. The members of a totemic clan frequently believe themselves related to their animal totem by the bond of a common descent.

TOUTIŎRIX. Toutiŏrix, "lord of the people," was one of the names given by the ancient Celts to a god who corresponded to the Roman god Apollo (*q.v.*). He was a healing god. He would seem to have been confounded with Theodoric the Goth. The worship of the Celtic Apollo under the name Grannus (*q.v.*) was adopted by the Roman soldiers. See Anwyl; Squire, *Myth.*; Reinach, *O.*

TRACTARIAN MOVEMENT, THE. The Tractarian Movement, like other new and important movements in the history of the Church, was produced by a crisis. The Church of England was, or seemed to be, in a perilous condition. At a time when reforms were being demanded on all hands, a time when Reform was in the air, the time of the Reform Bill (1831), it is reputed to have been weak, spiritless, and impotent—so much so indeed that it appeared to be open to easy and successful attack and to be in danger of losing some of its privileges. Dean Church in his book "The Oxford Movement" gives a forcible description of the state of affairs. "The idea of clerical life had certainly sunk, both in fact and in the popular estimate of it. The disproportion between the purposes for which the Church with its ministry was founded and the actual tone of feeling among those responsible for its service had become too great. Men were afraid of principles; the one thing they most shrank from was the suspicion of enthusiasm. . . . The typical clergyman in English pictures of the manners of the day, in the *Vicar of Wakefield*, in Miss Austen's novels, in Crabbe's *Parish Register*, is represented, often quite unsuspiciously, as a kindly and respectable person, but certainly not alive to the greatness of his calling. He was often much, very much to the society round him . . . but there was much—much even of what was good and useful—to obscure it. The beauty of the English Church in this time was its family life of purity and simplicity; its blot was quiet worldliness." Dean Church points out that "the fortunes of the Church are not safe in the hands of a clergy, of which a great part take their obligations easily. It was slumbering and sleeping when the visitation of days of change and trouble came upon it." It is clear that great efforts were needed to strengthen and revive the Church at this critical period. In July 1833 Hugh James Rose (1795-1838), Rector of Hadleigh in Suffolk, Richard Hurrell Froude (1803-1836), William Palmer (1803-1885), and the Hon. A. P. Perceval met together at Hadleigh to discuss plans for putting new life into the Church. At this consultation, which lasted about a week, it was decided that a great effort should be made to maintain doctrine and discipline. Froude was Fellow of Oriel College, Oxford. Conferences were also held here, in which John Henry Newman (1801-1891), Fellow and Tutor of Oriel, and John Keble (1792-1866), Fellow and Tutor of Oriel and author of "The Christian Year" (1827), also took part. The result was an attempt to form an "Association of Friends of the Church." The objects of this Association were: "(1) To maintain pure and inviolate the doctrines, the services, and the discipline of the Church; that is, to withstand all change which involves the denial and suppression of doctrine, a departure from primitive practice in religious offices, or innovation upon the apostolic prerogatives, order, and commission of bishops, priests, and deacons. (2) To afford Churchmen an opportunity of exchanging their sentiments, and co-operating together on a large scale." This, however, did not prove to be the best plan, and was not attended by great success. In the same year, 1833, John Keble preached a sermon on National Apostasy which is supposed to mark the initiation of the Oxford Movement. In any case, it was decided by the "Friends of the Church" to follow up this line of teaching, and to do so by issuing "Tracts for the Times," the aim of which was to prove that the doctrines of the Church of England are identical with those of the primitive Catholic Church. On account of these tracts the movement became known as Tractarian. Keble, who wrote seven of the tracts, insisted upon "deep submission to authority, implicit reverence for Catholic tradition, firm belief in the divine prerogatives of the priesthood, the real nature of the sacraments, and the danger of independent speculation" (Church). The first tract, published in 1833, was written by J. H. Newman. Others followed down to 1841, when Tract xc. put an end to the series. The chief writers, besides J. H. Newman and J. Keble, were R. H. Froude, E. B. Pusey, and Isaac Williams (1802-1865). The latter wrote a remarkable tract, No. 80, on "Reserve in communicating Religious Knowledge." But Tract xc. is the most famous, or, according to bitter opponents of Tractarianism, the most infamous of all. It was an essay by Newman on the Thirty-nine Articles. "His aim was to determine how far as a matter of fact the Articles were capable of a 'Catholic' interpretation, and to what extent they were directed against Roman doctrine. He drew a distinction between Romanism as a popular working system and Roman authoritative dogma. While he did not go the full length of stating that the Articles were not directed at all against Rome's authoritative dogma, he pointed out that the Tridentine decrees had not been ratified when the Articles were first drawn up, and that therefore the Articles were not directed against *them*. The general drift of the tract was to show that the articles were directed against the dominant errors of popular Romanism, and not for the most part against Roman dogma. The general conclusion was that, after the gloss placed upon the Articles by Calvinists and other Protestants had been removed, they were capable of a perfectly 'Catholic' interpretation, and did not condemn prayers for the dead, the doctrine of the eucharistic sacrifice, the belief in some form of purgatory, etc." (M. W. Patterson). The tract was at once repudiated (March 8, 1841) by four Oxford tutors: T. T. Churton, Henry Bristow Wilson (1803-1888), who afterwards contributed to "Essays and Reviews," John Griffiths (1806-1885), who afterwards become Warden of Wadham College, and A. C. Tait (1811-1882), who afterwards became Archbishop of Canterbury. Soon afterwards (March 18, 1841) it was condemned by the Hebdomadal Board. The Bishop of Oxford also, and later other bishops, expressed disapproval of the tract. In 1842 Newman retired to Littlemore, not far from Oxford, where he had established a kind of monastery. Fuel was added to the flames in 1844 when W. G. Ward (1812-1882), an extreme Tractarian, who claimed the right, as a member of the Church of England to hold "the full cycle of Roman doctrine," published his book "The Ideal of a Christian Church." Newman had resigned the living of St. Mary's, Oxford, in 1843. In 1845 he was received into the Roman Church. But the Tractarian Movement could not be arrested. The Tractarians were reinforced by such notable men as W. F. Hook (1798-1875), who became Dean of Chichester, J. B. Mozley (1813-1878), who later became Regius Professor of Divinity at Oxford, R. W. Church (1815-1890), Dean of S. Paul's, W. E. Gladstone (1809-1898), Sir John Taylor Coleridge (1790-1876), and Sir Roundell Palmer (1812-1819). The centre of the movement was no longer in Oxford. The Oxford Movement was ably opposed and denounced by such Broad-churchmen as R. D. Hampden (1793-1868), Bishop of Hereford, A. P. Stanley (1815-1881), F. D. Maurice (1805-1872), and Charles Kingsley (1819-1875). Whatever the merits of the movement, unless it is wisely guided, it is exposed by its insistence on authority to grave dangers. What D. Hampden said about the Tractarians has, at the least, an element of truth in it (*Some Memorials of Renn Dickson Hampden*, 1871, p. 90). See R. W. Church, *Hist. of the Oxford Movement*, 1891; W. Walsh, *Secret Hist. of the Oxford Movement;* M. W. Patterson, *Hist.;* J. H. Blunt; *Prot. Dict.*

TRADITIONALISM. L. G. A. de Bonald (1754-1840) is regarded as the author of Traditionalism (cp., however, FIDEISM). This system of philosophy has been described as the "philosophy of antiphilosophy" (Madame de Staël) or the "extreme of anti-rationalism" (*Cath. Dict.*). In its stricter form, as expounded by de Bonald, "this system reduces the intellect to a merely receptive faculty, capable of acquiring knowledge by instruction, which comes originally from God by a primitive revelation given to the first progenitors of the human race" (*Cath. Dict.*). In its modified form, as expounded by Bonnetty, "it restricts the absolute necessity of a traditional instruction derived from revelation to metaphysical, religious, and moral truth, admitting the capacity of the human mind to discover other intellectual truths by its innate power." Traditionalism was condemned by the Congregation of the Index in 1855, and again by the Vatican Council in 1870. See Addis and Arnold; Reinach, *O.*

TRADUCIANS. Traducianism, the opposite of Creationism, is one of the theories as to the origin of the soul. The Traducians hold that "both soul and body are derived from the human parents, and that, therefore, the Fall of Adam was naturally the direct cause of the sinfulness which attaches to human beings from the very beginning of their existence" (*Prot. Dict.*).

TRANCES, THE FOUR. The deep meditations of Buddhists are supposed to produce four kinds of trances and four kinds of formless states. This is the teaching of the Buddha himself. "Of one who has entered the first trance the voice has ceased; of one who has entered the second trance reasoning and reflection have ceased; of one who has entered the third trance joy has ceased; of one who has entered the fourth trance the inspirations and expirations have ceased; of one who has entered the realm of infinity of space the perception of form has ceased; of one who has entered the realm of the infinity of consciousness the perception of the realm of the infinity of space has ceased; of one who has entered the realm of nothingness the perception of the infinity of consciousness has ceased; of one who has entered the realm of neither perception nor yet non-perception, the perception of the realm of nothingness has ceased; of one who has entered the cessation of perception and sensation, perception and sensation have ceased. Of the priest who has lost all depravity, passion has ceased, hatred has ceased, infatuation has ceased." See H. Hackmann, *Buddhism*.

TRANSMIGRATION OF SOULS. The belief that at death the soul passes into another body has been widely held. According to Herodotus (II., 123) the Egyptians believed that the soul at death entered immediately upon another existence. "After three thousand years, during which it had experienced all the various forms of life that exist on land, in the water and in the air, it would once more re-enter a human being" (Adolf Erman, *Handbook*). But though Herodotus describes the belief correctly, he is perhaps wrong, as Erman thinks, in ascribing it to the Egyptians. In any case, it is held by Brahmans, Buddhists, and Greeks, is found to prevail among certain primitive people, and is even cherished by many individuals in modern civilised countries. The Hindu "feels himself at one with all about him; he thinks that his soul, before animating his body, may have existed in beings of every kind, organic and even inorganic, and believes that, after his death, it will pass into a great variety of bodies" (Reinach). The doctrine was one of the distinguishing marks of the Greek Pythagoreans (*q.v.*). And the Orphics (*q.v.*) believed that by initiation into the Orphic Mysteries their souls were spared the "cycle of reincarnation." The Romans to some extent borrowed the belief from the Greeks. There are traces of it also among the ancient Celts. The Algonquins believed that the soul of a dead child might enter another mother and be born again. Natives of Africa and Australia sometimes think that white men are the reincarnations of the souls of black men. Redskins, Esquimaux, and Zulus believe that the souls of dead men enter animals. The doctrine of the transmigration of souls as taught in Europe and America (United States) has naturally changed its character to some extent. "Animals, birds, fish, and reptiles are re-embodied. To deny a spirit to one form of intelligence is to deny it to all forms, man included. The animal re-appears in a series of births, each birth giving to its spirit a new form. Each of these is a slight improvement on the last, if the animal is in its wild or natural state. Progression, improvement, and continual change from a coarser to a finer organisation, are not confined to man. . . The spirit of an animal can actually be re-embodied in a man or woman, and its prominent character will appear in that man or woman" (Prentice Mulford, *The Gift of the Spirit*, 1908). See F. J. Gould, *Concise Hist. of Rel.*, vol. i., 1907; Reinach, *O*.

TRANSUBSTANTIATION. In instituting the Lord's Supper, Jesus said of the bread, "Take, eat, this is my Body which is given for you," and of the wine, "Drink ye all of this, for this is my Blood of the New Testament." The Council of Trent decreed that in the Lord's Supper or Eucharist there is a "change of the whole substance of the bread into the body, of the whole substance of the wine into the blood [of Christ], only the appearances of bread and wine remaining; which change the Catholic Church most fitly calls transubstantiation." The term "trans-substantiatio" was first used by Hildebert, Archbishop of Tours (*d.* 1134). But some such doctrine was at least as early as Paschasius Radbertus (*fl.* 844-865). In the eleventh century, Berengarius (c. 1000-1088), after attacking those who maintained a carnal presence of the Body and Blood, was forced by Pope Hildebrand to recant (1079), and the terms of his recantation reveal the kind of doctrine that had become current. "The bread and wine placed upon the altar are, by the mystery of holy prayer and the words of the Redeemer, converted into the true, actual, and life-giving flesh and blood of our Lord Jesus Christ, and are, after consecration, the true body of Christ which was born of the Virgin, and which hung on the cross an offering for the salvation of the world, not only in the way of a sign and in virtue of a sacrament, but also in propriety of nature and truth of substance." After this the schoolmen, members of the Realist school, set to work to improve the doctrine. Emphasis was laid on the Aristotelian distinction between substance and accident. Essence or substance is that which makes a thing what it is, its inner reality. An accident or quality is that which inheres in substance as its substratum. A substance may remain the same, while its accidents or qualities change. Applying this teaching, it is maintained that in the Lord's Supper the change in the elements is substantial. The bread and wine are changed substantially into the body and blood of Christ. "In one respect, however, this substantial change differs from all other substantial changes. In other cases, when one substance changes into another, the accidents also change. Here the accidents of bread and wine remain unaltered; and so long as they remain, the body and blood of Christ also remain concealed beneath them" (*Catholic Dictionary*). The doctrine, as thus improved, was in 1215 proclaimed by the Fourth Lateran Council, and in 1551 re-affirmed by the Council of Trent. See *Prot. Dict.; Cath. Dict.*, 1905; B. J. Kidd, *The Thirty-nine Articles*, 1906; cp. K. R. Hagenbach.

TRAPPISTS. A Roman Catholic order, a branch of the Cistercian order. They were so called after the Cistercian monastery of La Trappe in La Perche near Séez, which was founded in 1140 by Count Rotrou. The order was founded in 1663 by Armand Jean de Rancé (1626-1700), titular Abbot of La Trappe, with the idea of reforming the lives of the monks there. The Abbot began by reviving the Strict Observance of the Cistercian order, and proceeded to introduce a still stricter discipline of La Trappe. The most remarkable feature of this discipline was the imposition of silence. The monks were not allowed to speak to one another on any occasion. Each monk had manual work assigned to him; the food was vegetarian. The Trappists were expelled from France in 1790. In 1817, however, some of them were again in possession of La Trappe. In 1892 they were reorganized. They now have about sixty monasteries. See *Prot. Dict.; Cath. Dict.*; Brockhaus.

TRASKITES. The followers of John Trask. Born in Somersetshire, about the year 1617, he became a preacher in London. With some difficulty he seems to have taken Holy Orders. He had a loud voice "which indeed had more strength than anything else he delivered" (Fuller). His followers were enjoined to fast; to sell all their possessions and give to the poor; and "to eat their bread with quaking, and to drink their water with trembling." Everything was to be done according to the law of Scripture. A disciple, Hamlet Jackson, led Trask to carry this principle farther than he thought originally of doing. Thus he regulated the dress and domestic life of his followers, and required them to observe the Sabbath, Saturday, instead of Sunday. Trask and his wife were in course of time brought before the Star Chamber and reproved by Bishop Andrewes. He was also put in the pillory, while his wife was imprisoned. The Traskites came in time to be called also Seventh-day Men. See J. H. Blunt.

TRAVEL DOCUMENT, THE. Scholars have given the name "The Travel Document" to certain sections of the Acts of the Apostles (xvi. 10-17; xx. 5; xxi. 18; xxvii. 1: xxviii. 16), which are distinguished from the rest of the book by the fact that the writer speaks of himself as an eye-witness of the things which he records, using the pronoun "We." The section has been called also "The 'We' Section" or "The Journey Record." See, further, ACTS OF THE APOSTLES.

TREACLE BIBLE. A popular designation of the Bishops' Bible, published in 1568. It was so called on account of a passage in Jeremiah viii. 22 ("Is there no balm in Gilead?"), which was rendered, "Is there no treacle in Gilead?"

TREASURE OF MERITS. The Treasure of Merits (Thesaurus Meritorum) is an expression used by Roman Catholics to denote the fund of good works accumulated by Christ and the saints. The trustee of this fund is the Pope. See the article INDULGENCES.

TREASURES, THE SEVEN ROYAL. The Buddhist ideal king, or king of kings, is represented as being "possessor of the seven royal treasures. One of these is the Wheel (*q.v.*), the second is the White Elephant (see ELEPHANT, WHITE), the third is the Horse (see HORSE, TREASURE OF THE), the fourth is the Gem (*q.v.*), the fifth is the Pearl among Women (*q.v.*). The sixth and seventh are two faithful servants, a Treasurer and an Adviser.

TREES, SACRED. There is abundant evidence, says Robertson Smith (*R.S.*, p. 185), that trees were adored as divine in all parts of the Semitic area. The sacred date-palm was worshipped by the Arabs. "It was adored at an annual feast, when it was all hung with fine clothes and women's ornaments." At Mecca there was a tree which is described as a "tree to hang things on." The goddess Al-'Ozzā was believed to reside in a sacred acacia. The Syrians, the Phoenicians, and the Canaanites all seem to have worshipped trees. Without its sacred tree no Canaanite high place was complete. Tree worship was common in Phrygia and Greece. The ancient cypresses of Heracles at Daphne were believed to have been planted by the god himself. In Babylonian-Assyrian art a "favorite scene was the representation of the semi-divine beings in front of the sacred tree, appearing again in many variations" (Jastrow, *Civ.*, p. 421). In the Old Testament we are told that Abraham planted a sacred tree in Beersheba. "It was under an oak at Shechem that Jacob hid his treasures; it was under an oak that Gideon met the angel of the Lord and there built an altar, and, long before, the nurse of Rebecca was buried at Bethel under an oak" (S. G. Smith, *Rel. in the Making*, p. 118). The ancient Germans seem to have believed that they were the offspring of their sacred trees. "In the sacred forests, every tree had its genius, which took the form of an owl, a vulture or a wild cat. The guardian spirit of a family inhabited a tree near the dwelling; the gods of the Edda had their own sacred tutelary tree, Yggdrasil. He who cuts down a tree destroys a genius" (Reinach, *O.*, p. 133). The oak seems to have been the sacred tree of the chief god of the Baltic Slavs. The walnut was also sacred among them. Like the ancient Germans, they had their sacred woods. Sacred trees are found also in Japan. "In most American stories where we hear of the first of men emerging from the underworld, it is by climbing a tree. This tree also supports the sky, and is so represented in the native books of the Mayas and Nahuas. The Yurucares of Bolivia relate that their god Tiri, when he would people the earth with men, cleft a tree, and from the opening came forth the various tribes of the world" (Brinton, p. 151).

TRIAD SOCIETY. A secret sect in China, known also as Heaven and Earth Society or the Hung League, and said to have been founded in the year 1674. One of the founders was an ardent student of Taoist occultism. This accounts for the mingling of Buddhist and Taoist elements in the ritual. The original object of the Society was the extinction of the dynasty, and its members were frequently engaged in rebellions. The ceremonial for initiation, called "Entering the Hung doors," is very complicated. As many as thirty-six oaths are taken by the initiate. See S. Couling.

TRIANGLE. The triangle was used in Christian art to symbolise the Trinity. In the Catacombs, for instance, the equilateral triangle appears. Sidney Heath suggests that this was perhaps the earliest symbol of the Trinity.

TRIMBAK. The three-eyed one, one of the names of the Hindu god Siva.

TRINE BAPTISM. Trine Baptism is the designation of the usual form of Christian baptism. The person baptized is immersed three times in the water, or is sprinkled with water three times, in the name of the Father, the Son, and the Holy Ghost. Eunomius, the Arian, introduced baptism by single immersion and rejected the use of the trinitarian formula.

TRINITARIAN BIBLE SOCIETY. The Trinitarian Bible Society exists "for the circulation of Protestant or uncorrupted versions of the Word of God." The British and Foreign Bible Society was formed in 1804. In the early years of its existence three things gave offence to a number of its members. 1. The aid of Unitarians was invited. 2. The meetings were not opened with prayer. 3. It printed and circulated "For Catholics" what the objectors describe as "erroneous Romish Versions, made by Roman Catholics." The third point in particular led to disruption. Separate Societies were formed in Edinburgh, Glasgow, and Aberdeen. In 1861 these were amalgamated into the "National Bible Society of Scotland." In England the objectors agitated for some time for alterations in the policy of the British and Foreign Bible Society. Their efforts were not successful, however, and in 1831 they founded "The Trinitarian Bible Society." The British and Foreign Bible Society removed the second of the three causes of offence on June the 8th, 1857, by resolving that their meetings should be opened with prayer. As regards the third cause of offence, some of the versions objected to have been withdrawn; but versions to which the Trinitarian Bible Society objects are still printed and circulated. See the pamphlets and leaflets of the Trinitarian Bible Society.

TRINITIES. The belief that a special sanctity attaches to the number three is widespread. It is natural therefore to find in many primitive faiths myths, idols, rites, etc., so devised as to reflect and inculcate a belief in the triplicate nature of divinity. "Such is the case, and it is easy to quote examples, whether we turn to the Indians of America or the Indians of Hindostan, whether we touch on the triads of ancient Egypt or those of the Druids, whether we recall the three Norns of Teutonic myth or the three Fates of the Hellenes" (D. G. Brinton, *R.P.P.*, p. 121). Dr. Brinton quotes Westcott as saying (*Symbolism of Numbers*, p. 7): "It is impossible to study any single system of worship throughout the world without being struck with the peculiar persistence of the triple number in regard to Divinity."

TRINITY, HOLY. The doctrine of the Holy Trinity—the Trinity in Unity, and Unity in Trinity—is one of the profound mysteries of Christian doctrine. It is a doctrine which was formulated by the Church when it became necessary to construct Symbols, Creeds, or Confessions. It was one of the fruits of doctrinal development. Dr. F. C. Conybeare thinks that both the name and the idea of a divine Trinity were derived from an Alexandrine source, "for Philo taught that the divine being or nature is a three-in-one and one-in-three, and two of the persons with which he fills up his formula—namely, the king and father, and the son or Logos—are identical with those which Christian orthodoxy put forward in this scheme." In any case, the doctrine was first elaborated in the Creeds. In the Nicene Creed (325 A.D.) Jesus Christ is said to be "of the substance (*ek tēs ousias*) of the Father, God of God, Light of Light, Very God of Very God, begotten, not made, consubstantial (*homoousion*) with the Father." In the Constantinopolitan Creed (381 A.D.) He is said to be "Begotten of His Father before all worlds, God of God, Light of Light, very God of very God, Begotten, not made, being of one substance (*homoousion*) with the Father." The Holy Ghost is said to be "The Lord: and the Giver of Life, Who proceedeth from the Father, Who with the Father and the Son together is worshipped and glorified, Who spake by the Prophets." The Council of Chalcedon (451 A.D.) confirmed the Creeds of the Councils of Nicaea and Constantinople. The Creed which defined the doctrine of the Holy Trinity most fully was that commonly called the Creed of St. Athanasius. He was not the author. It seems to have been called after him because it embodied, or was supposed to embody, his teaching. It really belongs to the sixth, seventh, or eighth century. Here the Catholic Faith is said to be this: "That we worship one God in Trinity, and Trinity in Unity, neither confounding the Persons, nor dividing the substance." We are forbidden by the Catholic Religion to say that there are three Gods or three Lords. There are not three Lords, but one Lord. "And in this Trinity none is afore or after other, none is greater or less than another: but all the three Persons are co-eternal together and co-equal." See *The Definitions of the Catholic Faith, and Canons of Discipline*, Oxford, 1874; C. A. Heurtley, *On Faith and the Creed*, 1889; *Cath. Dict.*; F. C. Conybeare, *M.M.M.*

TRIPITAKA. "The Three Baskets," the designation of the threefold division of the Buddhist Canon. See CANON, BUDDHIST.

TRISACRAMENTARIANS. A name given to those Reformers who held that only three sacraments are necessary to salvation—Baptism, Penance, and the Eucharist.

TRITO-ISAIAH. Chapters lvi.-lxvi. of the Book of Isaiah (*q.v.*) have been called Trito-Isaiah because they clearly form a group of prophecies different from those of Isaiah (chapters i.-xxxix.) and Deutero-Isaiah (chapters xl.-lv.). Language, style, and historic background are different, and imply a different date and authorship. See ISAIAH, BOOK.

TROJANU. A god Trojanu appears among the deities worshipped by the ancient Slavs. He seems to have been a demon who was popularly identified with the Roman Emperor Trajan.

TRUCE OF GOD. In the Middle Ages the institution called a Truce of God was intended to limit the right of private warfare and to mitigate its violence. Hostilities were to cease during certain solemn or sacred hours. These were from Thursday to Sunday evening every week, the whole seasons of Advent and Lent, and the octaves of certain festivals. "Respect was shown to Thursday as the day of Christ's ascension; to Friday as that of His Passion; to Saturday because on that day He lay in the grave; and to Sunday because it was the day of His resurrection" (*Cath. Dict.*). The institution was first proposed in 989 A.D. It was first practised in Aquitaine (after 1027), but afterwards spread throughout France. In 1042 it was introduced in England and Italy. It was discussed at a number of Councils, and was confirmed by the Second and Third Lateran Councils (1139 and 1179). See William Benham; the *Cath. Dict.*

TRUE BRITISH CATHOLIC CHURCH, THE. A Church founded at Manchester by Thomas Deacon (1697-1753), one of the Nonjurors (*q.v.*). In 1733, with the aid of Scotch bishops, Deacon was consecrated a nonjuring bishop. In 1734 he published a "Complete Collection of Devotions, both Public and Private," in two parts. The first part was devoted to the "Public Offices of the Church," the second part to a "Method of Daily Private Prayer." The Collection of Devotions is founded upon two principles. 1. That the best method for all Churches and Christians to follow is to lay aside all modern hypotheses, customs, and private opinions, and to submit to all the doctrines, practices, worship, and discipline, not of any Particular, but of the Ancient and Universal Church of Christ, from the beginning to the end of the fourth century. 2. That the Liturgy in the Apostolical Constitutions is the most ancient Christian Liturgy extant; that it is perfectly pure and free from interpolation; and that the book itself, called the Apostolical Constitutions, contains at large the doctrines, laws, and settlements, which the three first and purest ages of the Gospel did with one consent believe, obey, and submit to, and that as derived to them from Apostolical men: that therefore the said book, where it does not disagree with the tradition of the Primitive Catholic Church (as upon examination it will hardly ever be found to do, but on the contrary may be corroborated thereby, and by the consentient testimony of the holy Fathers of the three first centuries), ought to be received, submitted to, and allowed its due authority. If these two principles were once put in practice, Deacon believed, a truly Catholic union would be restored among all Christian Churches. "That I may contribute my mite towards so desirable an end, I have here ventured to present the world with what in my humble opinion will be the only means to attain it; which is what some will call a *new*, but which I presume to recommend to every pious Christian as the *oldest*, and therefore the *best*, Collection of Devotions extant in the whole Christian world. This I dare venture to say, because I have omitted no practice or ceremony that appears to be supported by antiquity, universality, and consent; and because I have taken in all the Devotional part of the Apostolical Constitutions (except a few particulars foreign to the present purpose), at the same time that I have herein included such parts of the Common Prayer Book of the Church of England, as were necessary to complete the design." See Peter Hall, *Fragmenta Liturgica*, 1848, and the *D.N.B.*

TRUMPETS, SACRED. The trumpet figures in Minoan religious worship; large imitation trumpets of clay, with serpents round them, have been discovered in a household shrine. The conch-shell served the same purpose.

TSUL 'KALU. A deity in the mythology of the Cherokee Indians, a hunter-god.

TUATHA DE DANANN. A name for the gods of the Irish Celts, meaning "Tribe of the goddess Danu." They were worshipped by the race which drove out the older inhabitants of Ireland.

TUEBINGEN SCHOOL. A School of theology in Germany of which the real founder was Ferdinand Christian Baur (1792-1860). In 1835 appeared the famous "Life of Jesus" by David Friedrich Strauss (1808-1874), in which the mythical theory was applied rigorously to the gospel history. "The author's method is to apply the principle of myth to the whole extent of the story of the life of Jesus, to find mythical narratives, or at least embellishments, scattered throughout all its parts" (Strauss). The book caused a sensation, and the author was fiercely attacked. But Strauss's work was appreciated and defended by his Tuebingen teacher, F. C. Baur, and the critical method was continued and developed by Baur's School. Baur had already published (1831) his essay on the Epistles to the Corinthians, "Die Christuspartei in der korinthischen Gemeinde, der Gegensatz des paulinischen und petrinischen Christenthums in der ältesten Kirche, der Apostel Petrus in Rom," in which he sought to show that in the early Church there was opposition between a Pauline and a Petrine party. This was followed by works on the other books of the New Testament, works which were characterised by what came to be known as "Tendenzkritik" (cp. TENDENCY THEORY). Baur found the New Testament writings to be "products of a definite party movement," and he thought it possible to determine "their place in the history of primitive Christianity by means of their supposed dogmatic or ecclesiastical '*Tendenz*'" (Pfleiderer). Baur and Strauss were reinforced by Eduard Zeller (1814-1908), Albert Schwegler (1819-1857), Karl Planck (1819-1880), and Karl Köstlin (1819-1894); and the Tuebingen School had an organ in the "Theologische Jahrbücher." Planck and Köstlin, however, tried to correct the extravagances of A. Schwegler. They were followed by Albrecht Ritschl (1822-1889), who carried his corrections so far that, from being a sympathiser, he became an opponent of the School (so in the second edition of his book, "Die Entstehung der altkatholischen Kirche," 1857). Other opponents were G. V. Lechler (1811-1888), B. Weiss (*b.* 1827), Eduard Reuss (1804-1891), H. Ewald (1803-1875), and Karl Hase (1800-1890). But the Tuebingen School found again able defenders in such scholars as A. Hilgenfeld (1823-1907), who was editor of "Die Zeitschrift für wissenschaftliche Theologie"; Volkmar, author of "Jesus Nazarenus und die erste christliche Zeit" (1882); and Holsten. Hilgenfeld preferred to speak of his method as "Literarkritik," not as "Tendenzkritik." Other important representatives of the School were Adolf Hausrath (*b.* 1837), who was also a novelist (George Taylor), and Otto Pfleiderer (*b.* 1839). An important work by Hausrath was his "Neutestamentliche Zeitgeschichte." "As this work is further distinguished by a beauty of style rare in German theologians, it has attracted attention even among the laity, and contributed much to the diffusion of the results of modern research" (Pfleiderer). Pfleiderer, referring to his own book, "Das Urchristenthum," writes as follows. "In it I have tried to show that the development of primitive Christianity into the Catholic Church must not be conceived as a continued struggle and gradual reconciliation between Paulinism and Jewish Christianity, as Baur had thought; nor (with Ritschl) as a falling away from the apostolical religion and a degeneration of Paulinism; but as the natural evolution of the Christian Hellenism introduced by Paul, which soon cast off the Pharisaic elements in Paul's doctrines, and developed, on the one hand, in a speculative direction, into the Johannine theology of Asia Minor; on the other, in a practical direction, into the Church life of Rome (Epistle of James). But notwithstanding my difference from Baur, both in my general view and in my estimate of individual books (especially the Apocalypse, the Gospels of Matthew and Mark, the Acts and others), I shall never forget how much I, with all our generation, owe to the epoch-making achievements of the great Tübingen Master." See R. W. Mackay, *The Tübingen School and its Antecedents,* 1863; Otto Pfleiderer, *The Development of Theol.;* and Henry S. Nash, *Higher Crit. of the N.T.*

TUISCO. A god whose praise was sung, according to Tacitus, by the ancient Germans. He is said to have been "born of the earth."

TUI TOKELAU. A Polynesian deity. At Fakaofo, or Bowditch Island, in the Union group, he was worshipped during the month of May, when all work was laid aside. The people assembled from the three islands, and prayed for life, health, and an abundant supply of fish and cocoanuts.

TULASI. The Tulasī (*Ocymum sanctum*) is a plant or shrub worshipped by the Hindus. In the first instance it would seem to have owed its worship to its many medicinal properties. Its leaves, which have a sweet aromatic scent, were used to prevent colds, chills, and other complaints. In course of time it became sacred to Vishnu (*q.v.*), and even came to be identified with the wife of Vishnu or Krishna (*q.v.*). On the other hand, the Sālagrāma stone is regarded as a metamorphosis of Vishnu or Krishna themselves; and every year in some parts of India the Tulasī plant is married to the Sālagrāma stone. The plant is to be found in nearly every Hindu household in India; and persons who are well-to-do have one planted in the courtyard of the house in such a position that it is possible to practise circumambulation (see CIRCUMAMBULATION). The Tulasī is particularly a woman's deity. Daily the women walk round it, pray to it, or make offerings of flowers and rice to it. "In one village, especially," says Monier-Williams, "I watched a woman who was in the act of walking 108 times round the sacred plant with her right shoulder always turned towards it. Her simple object, no doubt, was to propitiate the goddess with a view to securing long life for her husband and gaining a large family of sons for herself." When a man is dying a Tulasī plant is placed near him, or some of its leaves are put on his face and chest. To its medicinal properties was added the power of removing sin and purifying from defilement. See Monier-Williams; E. W. Hopkins; J. A. Dubois and H. K. Beauchamp.

TUMBLERS. A nickname given to the American Tunkers (*q.v.*) on account of the attitude which they assume when they are being baptised.

TUNKERS. A religious sect in America. The name is derived from a German word *tunken* "to dip." As the word suggests, the sect originated in Germany. It appeared at the beginning of the eighteenth century in Rhineland and Westphalia. In 1719 the members for the most part removed to America. The Tunkers at first lived a kind of monastic life. They recognize only adult baptism, and this is effected by trine immersion. They practise the "Lavipedium," that is to say, on special occasions they wash one another's feet. They celebrate "Love-feasts" and give one another (members of their own sex) the kiss of charity. They decline to take oaths, and to engage in litigation, politics, or war. They anoint the sick with oil, and do not much favour the use of medicine. At first their services resembled those of the Quakers (*q.v.*). Now they have deacons, ministers, and bishops, all of whom are usually unpaid. See J. H. Blunt; *Chambers' Encycl.;* and Brockhaus.

TUPAN. A deity worshipped by many Brazilian tribes. "The Tupan of the Indians of the period immediately subsequent to the discovery of Brazil was by no means a beneficent deity, but typified the thunder, or any agency terrible or majestic" (Hastings, *Encycl.*, *s.v.* Brazil). By the first missionaries in the southern part of Brazil, however, he was identified with God the Father. He hovers over the people in the form of a great bird.

TURLUPINS. The name by which the Brethren of the Free Spirit (*q.v.*) were known in France.

TURNERITES. The followers of George Turner (*d.* 1821). Turner himself was a follower of Joanna Southcott. See SOUTHCOTTIANS.

TVASTRI. A figure in Hindu mythology, corresponding to Vulcan. He is represented in the Vedas as the architect of the universe, and in the Purānas is regarded as divine. He carries a club, and has three eyes.

TWELVE NIGHTS, THE. It is an old Teutonic belief that the souls of the departed dwell in the air, and that sometimes at night they rush through the air in a kind of procession. This happens especially during the Twelve Nights, which fall usually between Christmas and Epiphany. Company WILD HUNT. See P. D. Chantepie de la Saussaye, *Rel. of the Teutons,* 1902.

TWENTY-FIVE ARTICLES, THE. A recension of the Thirty-nine Articles, made by Wesley and adapted to the special circumstances of his Methodist Episcopal Church in America. "The Twenty-five Articles, as they are called, were adopted by Conference in Baltimore in 1784, with the exception of xxiii., recognizing the independence of the United States, which was not approved till 1804. They reveal Wesley's precise attitude to the Thirty-nine" (W. A. Curtis).

TWENTY-FOUR, THE. A name given to the Old Testament in the Talmudic period. The twelve Minor Prophets are counted as one book. So also are I. and II. Samuel, I. and II. Kings, I. and II. Chronicles, Ezra and Nehemiah, respectively. Jerome (*Prologus Galeatus*) gives an enumeration of twenty-two books. This number is obtained by combining Ruth with Judges, and Lamentations with Jeremiah. In our English versions the books are counted as thirty-nine. It should be noted that the number twenty-four corresponds to the number of letters in the Greek alphabet, and twenty-two to the number of letters in the Hebrew alphabet.

TYPTOLOGICAL SPIRITISM. The early kind of spiritism in which questions and replies were made by means of raps. It is also described as spirit-rapping. See SPIRITISM.

TYR. The name given to Tiu (*q.v.*) in Norse mythology.

TZAPOTLATENAN. A Mexican deity, a goddess of medicine. She was a deified woman.

U

UATCHET. An Egyptian deity, symbolised by a winged serpent, tutelary goddess of the north of Egypt. The Greeks called her Buto, and identified her with Leto. When the god Set sought to kill the child Horus, his mother Isis fled with him to Uatchet, who, to escape Set, took the form of a shrew mouse.

UBBONITES. Ubbonites or better Ubbenites were a body of Anabaptists (*q.v.*) formed by Ubbo Philipps of Leuwarden in 1533. The Ubbonites rejected divorce, and "differed from the rest of the Anabaptists by denying that the kingdom of Christ was an earthly kingdom in which the pious were to exterminate the wicked" (Schaff-Herzog). See Schaff-Herzog.

UBIQUITARIANS. A name given to those Lutheran theologians in Germany who maintained that the body of Christ was everywhere (*ubique*). Others asserted that the body was present in many places (*multipresence*), that is to say, in those places in which he had promised to be. According to this school, it might be in several places at the same time.

UDĀSIS. An Indian order of ascetics belonging to the Nānakpanthi or Sikh faith. The order was founded by Sri Chand, younger son of Nānak (founder of the Nānakpanthi sect). They venerate the Granth of Govind Singh, as well as the Adi-Granth of Nānak. According to R. V. Russell, "in the Central Provinces members of several orders which have branched off from the main Nānakpanthi community are known as Udāsi."

UITZILOPOCHTLI. A Mexican deity, the warrior-god.

UIXTOCIUATL. A Mexican deity, goddess of salt.

UKEMOCHI. A deity in Japanese mythology, goddess of food or cereals.

UKEWALLISTS. A division of the Mennonite Baptists. They derived their name from Uke Walles, a native of Friesland. Uke Walles became associated with one John Lens, and the two together developed a doctrine which gave offence to the orthodox Mennonites. Their teaching was influenced by the belief that there was hope of salvation even for a Judas Iscariot. They were thus in line with a number of modern thinkers who hold the view that Judas, terrible as his crime was, was not an ordinary criminal (see De Quincey's theological essays).

UKHAT. A figure in the Babylonian Epic of Gilgamesh (see GILGAMESH EPIC). In Babylonian mythology the goddess Ishtar (*q.v.*) is represented as having in her train the Kizrêti, Ukhâti, and Kharimâti. These are three classes of sacred prostitutes. In the Epic of Gilgamesh, Ishtar sends Ukhat to entice Eabani (*q.v.*), the divine hero created by the goddess Araru, away from the animals with which he is living. This she succeeds in doing. He follows her to Uruk to be a companion to Gilgamesh.

UKKO. Ukko is the chief deity, or rather the chief of the spirits, worshipped by the Shamans. He is the Heaven-god. See SHAMANISM.

'UKṢIN. The name of one of the Jewish treatises or tractates which reproduce the oral tradition or unwritten law as developed by the second century A.D. and are incorporated in the Mishnah (*q.v.*), a collection or compilation completed by Rabbi Judah the Holy, or the Patriarch, about 200 A.D. The sixty-three tractates of the Mishnah are divided into six groups or orders (*sedarim*). 'Ukṣin is the twelfth tractate of the sixth group, which is called *Ṭohorōth* (" Purifications ").

ULEMA. Ulema, an Arabic word meaning " learned ones," is used in Muhammadan countries to denote the body of learned men consisting of theologians, doctors of divinity, and lawyers. These are all in one way or another interpreters of the Koran (*q.v.*). They include the *imâms*, who are readers of the public prayers in the mosques; the *muftis*, who are barristers and assessors; and the *mollas* or *kâdis*, who are magistrates.

ULLR. One of the deities of the ancient Teutons, whose name has been preserved in a number of place-names. The god Ullr was worshipped in Sweden. He was regarded as a stepson of Thor (*q.v.*) and as one of the Æsir (*q.v.*). He is the god of the bow, shield, hunt, etc. People used to swear by the ring of Ullr. Chantepie de la Saussaye points out that the identification with Holler, the " inferni dominus," is uncertain. See P. D. Chantepie de la Saussaye, *Rel. of the Teutons*, 1902.

ULTRAMONTANE. The word Ultramontane is used to designate that party in the Roman Catholic Church which recognizes the Pope's claim to absolute authority over the whole Church of Christ, as well as his personal Infallibility. The word means literally " Beyond the Mountains " (*i.e.*, the Alps). Originally it was used by the Italians of the French, the Germans, and others. Then it came to be used of the Italians themselves by the northern nations.

UMĀ. Umā is one of the names given to Śiva (*q.v.*), the great god of the Hindus. Monier-Williams points out that in Bengal when Umā, the wife of Śiva, is worshipped as a type of beauty and motherly excellence, she is always regarded as a virgin. Another name for the wife of Śiva is Durgā (*q.v.*). Durgā in a hymn is described as " Umā, the slayer of demons." See Monier-Williams; E. W. Hopkins.

UMBILICAL CORD. It is noted by D. G. Brinton (*R.P.P.*, p. 194) that various rites and opinions connected with the umbilical cord are widely prevalent among primitive peoples. " As it united the unborn infant to the life of the mother, it was generally held to retain that power in a mystical sense. Among the American Indians it was a frequent custom to carry it to a distance and bury it, and it became the duty of the individual, in his later life, to visit alone from time to time that spot, and perform certain ceremonies." Cp. PLACENTA.

UMBILICANIMI. Another name for the Hesychasts. They were so called because they believed that if they remained perfectly still in a bent position with their gaze intently fixed in the direction of the navel (Latin *umbilicus*), they could attain spiritual illumination or the " inner light."

UMBRELLA. The use of the umbrella as a symbol of sovereignty in Asia prevailed centuries before its adoption by Europeans as a protection against the weather. Among the ancient Egyptians it served to distinguish persons of quality, and among the Assyrians royal personages. The modern state umbrellas of China and Burma have a long history. R. V. Russell and R. B. Hīra Lāl note that " when one of the early Indian monarchs made extensive conquests, the annexed territories were described as being brought under his umbrella; of the king Harsha-Vardhana (606-648 A.D.) it is recorded that he prosecuted a methodical scheme of conquest with the deliberate object of bringing all India under one umbrella, that is, of constituting it into one state." Over the " Wheel of Light " which symbolises Buddha in Buddhist architecture is placed an umbrella. Nor is the importance attached to the umbrella peculiar to Orientals. Rajendra Lāl Mitra points out (*Indo-Aryans*) that " the Greeks used it as a mystic symbol in some of their sacred festivals, and the Romans introduced the custom of hanging an umbrella in the basilican churches as a part of the insignia of office of the judge sitting in the basilica." According to W. W. Skeat (*The Past at our Doors*), from about the year 1717 a " parish " umbrella was used in England by the priest at open-air funerals. Russell and Hīra Lāl suggest that this ecclesiastical use may have been derived from its employment as a symbol in Italian churches. According to Skeat, some kind of umbrella as a protection against the weather was used in England at least as far back as 1709, though usually Jonas Hanway is said to have been the first person to use an umbrella in the open street (1750.) The Muhammadans associate with the umbrella a sun-symbol (*aftāda*). The fact that both were carried over the head of a royal personage suggests to Russell and Hīra Lāl that " the umbrella represents the sky, while the king's head might be considered analogous to the sun." It was part of the principal business of the Dahāits (or Dahāyats), a caste of village watchmen in India, to carry the royal umbrella above the head of the king. See R. V. Russell.

UMM-ATTAR. A goddess referred to in the Sabaean inscriptions of South Arabia. The name means Mother-Attar (or Mother-Astarte).

'UMRA, THE. A Muslim pilgrimage of less importance than the Hajj (*q.v.*). It must not be performed on the 8th, 9th, or 10th of Zu'l-Hijja, for these days are claimed for the Hajj. The Prophet himself is reported to have said: " Join the 'Umra with the Hajj, for truly the joining of both brings a blessing on your days and your possessions, and wipes out your sins and purifies you." The 'Umra " can be performed before or after the great pilgrimage, jointly with or separately from the same. It is not of the same importance or meritoriousness, nor a duty of the same obligation as the Hajj; but still it is a Sunna duty in imitation of the Prophet's example and in obedience to his exhortation." See F. A. Klein.

UNCTION. See EXTREME UNCTION and ANOINTING.

UNDINES. Paracelsus of Hohenheim (1493-1541), whose writings are full of astrological, cabbalistic, and theosophical ideas, as well as of apolocalyptic and mystic fancies, saw spirits everywhere. Amongst these were female water-spirits called Undines, who could intermarry with human beings and in bearing children could themselves receive human souls.

UNION OF PROTESTANT FRIENDS. A religious body founded in Germany in 1841 by Leberecht Uhlich (1799-1872). The members were also called Friends of Light (*q.v.*).

UNION STATEMENT, THE. A Confessional statement drawn up in the United States in 1906 A.D. with a view to uniting Congregationalists, Methodist Protestants, and United Brethren. It has met with wide acceptance. W. A. Curtis speaks of it as bearing the same character as the Commission Creed (*q.v.*).

UNITARIANS. It has been claimed with justice that

Unitarianism is older than the Christian Church. The Jews themselves, of course, were Unitarians, and it can hardly be doubted that the Jewish Christians remained such for a long time. No emphasis is laid on Trinitarianism (see TRINITY) in the writings of the New Testament. The doctrine is one that was developed gradually by the Church. And it was not accepted without protest. The stubborn resistence of Arius, which brought him into conflict with Athanasius, is famous (see ARIANISM). Unitarianism is the more modern form of protest, and it is not identical with that of Arius. In any case, the early movement failed, and a Trinitarian Creed was formulated, which became the authoritative religion of the Christian Church. For some centuries Trinitarianism was too strongly entrenched and too powerfully supported to be resisted with any hope of success. A change came at the time of the Reformation, not because the Reformers were anti-Trinitarian, but because criticism and questioning along one line led to criticism and questioning along others. The time was ripe for the birth of Modern Unitarianism. Among the students who were seized by the ardour of the Reformation was Servetus, the Spaniard. He is commonly regarded as a Unitarian. In some respects he was, but his system has been described by M. Reville as a crude mixture of rationalism, pantheism, materialism, and theosophy. His teaching was so little to the taste of the Reformers that in 1553 he was burned at the instance of John Calvin. More in the line of direct development of Unitarianism were Lælius Socinus and his nephew Faustus Socinus (1539-1604), though Unitarians are not described correctly as Socinians (*q.v.*). J. W. Chadwick thinks there is no name of which Unitarians have more reason to be proud than that of Socinus, so great a leap did the uncle and nephew of this name make "out of the darkness of the ancient and the mediæval, into the light and beauty of the modern world." But the first organised Unitarian Church arose in 1565 in Poland, a country remarkable at that time for its religious liberty, whither Socinus and Georgio Blandrata had fled. "The history of Polish Unitarianism is a history of efficient organization, and a success so positive that it drew upon itself the arm of persecution with its utmost strength, a decree of expulsion marking the first centennial of Blandrata's arrival in Poland" (Chadwick). From Poland Unitarianism spread to Transylvania, where it met with remarkable success. In 1660 the Unitarians were driven out of Poland. In Transylvania also great efforts were made to repress them, but though the number of their churches was greatly reduced, they succeeded in maintaining themselves. After 1857 they began to revive, and they are now growing stronger continually. Their Church government is partly Episcopalian, partly Congregational. In England a number of persons were burned in the sixteenth century for holding views similar to those of the Unitarians. In 1654 all the antitrinitarian books of John Biddle (1615-1662) were ordered to be burned by the common hangman. But in the seventeenth century such efforts at repression had little chance of success, for the objectionable views were largely shared by such men as John Milton, John Locke, and Sir Isaac Newton. Nevertheless, the first Unitarian Church in England was not established until 1774. Its founder was Theophilus Lindsey (1723-1808), a clergyman of the Church of England, "one of the holiest of men, one of the gentlest, purest, truest that the world has ever known" (Chadwick). He resigned his living, and started the first Unitarian Church in Essex Street, Strand. The chapel was afterwards removed to Kensington, and the Essex Street establishment was converted into Essex Hall, the headquarters of the British and Foreign Unitarian Association. In 1787, under James Freeman (1759-1835), who also had changed his views, King's Chapel, Boston, "the oldest Episcopal Church in New England, became the first Unitarian Church of America" (Schaff-Herzog). In England a great impetus was given to the movement by Joseph Priestley (1733-1804). Priestley, famous both as a man of science and as a theologian, was educated for the presbyterian ministry, and had charge of various churches. But his views on the inspiration of the Bible and on the doctrines of the Church became very liberal, and in 1791 for these, as well as for liberal views in politics, his house in Birmingham was destroyed by a mob. In 1794 he emigrated to New York. In Philadelphia he was instrumental in organising a Unitarian Church. In America nearly all the members of the new Church were drawn from the Congregationalists, just as in England they were from the Presbyterians. Here a great leader arose in the person of William Ellery Channing (1780-1842). Greater as a preacher and a practical reformer than as a theologian, his preaching was "so fervent that about half the churches in Massachusetts accepted Unitarianism, and it numbered among its adherents many statesmen, writers, and thinkers, eminent throughout the world" (Brooke Herford). These included Longfellow, Lowell, and Ralph Waldo Emerson (1803-1882). At Lexington, Massachusetts, was born Theodore Parker (1810-1860), a leader who had studied well all the philosophical and critical literature of the time. J. W. Chadwick thinks that, compared with the philosophy of Schelling or Fichte, that of Theodore Parker was as a mountain to a cloud. To him "God, Immortality, the Moral Law were intuitional certainties of irrefragable stability. It was as if he had set aside a public supernatural revelation only to substitute for it a private one in each several mind and heart." He was too outspoken to please even the Unitarians of his own time, but he is now regarded as one of the chief representatives of modern Unitarianism. In England the greatest modern representative of Unitarianism has been James Martineau (1805-1900), a philosopher as well as a theologian. The Unitarians do not impose a creed or dogmatic articles of faith on the members of their congregations or on their ministers. Their churches for the most part have free and open trusts. This accounts for considerable differences of belief among them. "Some Unitarians believe that Jesus Christ wrought miracles; others reject as legendary those parts of the Bible which record such 'wonderful works,' and yet claim to be 'Christians'; some pray to their God 'through Christ'; others humbly seek direct access to the spirit of their Heavenly Father, and in the most solemn moments of their lives would be 'alone with the Alone'; some call themselves 'Christian Theists,' or simply 'Theists'; others cherish a firm faith that a special and peculiar revelation of the will of God was made through an accredited and supernaturally endowed 'Messiah'" (H. W. Crosskey). It is a principle with all alike that the human intellect must be free to reject what is unreasonable. And reason requires them, they hold, to believe in one God, whose one supreme demand of them is a noble life, and in a Kingdom of Heaven the realization of which is possible in the present life. It requires them to believe in the rise rather than in the fall of man. It requires them above all to believe in the goodness of God. "Parker's great premise, from which flowed forth the sum of his religion, was '*God is absolutely good.*' And by that he meant good with the same goodness that man strives after and can admire. For did he not find in all men, and in himself most deeply, a wondrous spiritual sense by which, when the brave, the noble, the pure, the generous, the holy, was once set before them, they admired and revered, and by which, conversely, when baseness and cowardice, and avarice, and corruption, were truly painted for them, they dissented and abhorred? And how could such sense lie so deeply engrained in man, unless it came to him, an inalienable gift and inheritance, from Him who created man? Parker knew in this way that, whatever more that awful Power which men name God might be, by whatsoever immensity he might transcend the scope of the bounded understanding of mankind, *that*, at least God must be; he knew that any theology which made God act in such fashion as an enlightened conscience would condemn in the human father of children, capriciously, cruelly, revengefully, must be by that very fact a lie, and that they who thought to hold off such criticisms by rebuking the man that would dare judge God, quibbled with conscience, and aimed a death-blow at true religion" (R. A. Armstrong). Theodore Parker liked to speak of God not only as "Our Father," but also as "Father and Mother" (compare the "Father-mother God" of Christian Scientists). See R. A. Armstrong, *Latter Day Teachers*, 1881 (the quotation is from a reprint for the Theodore Parker Centenary, 1910); J. W. Chadwick, "The Unitarian Church in England and America," in *Common-Sense Theology*, 1893; Brooke Herford, *A Brief Account of Unitarianism*, 1903; Schaff-Herzog; J. H. Blunt; Henry W. Crosskey, "The Unitarians" in *R.S.W.*

UNITAS FRATRUM. Literally "The Unity of the Brethren." Unitas Fratrum is claimed by the Moravians as the correct and original name of their Church (see MORAVIAN CHURCH). In 1457 remnants of the Calixtines (*q.v.*) and Taborites (*q.v.*: see also HUSSITES) united to form a religious body of Bohemian (and Moravian) Brethren with the name "Unitas Fratrum." The unity was to consist of a brotherhood of Christians of every denomination. This was the beginning of the Moravian Church. See BOHEMIAN BRETHREN.

UNITED BRETHREN IN CHRIST. A sect formed in America in 1800 by a German Reformed Lutheran, P. W. Otterbein (1726-1813). Otterbein had gone to America in 1752 to take charge of a congregation at Lancaster in Pennsylvania. He soon conceived the idea of trying to unite members of different sects on a broad religious basis; and congregations, composed of Lutherans, Reformed Lutherans, Mennonites, and Methodists were formed in several States. Otterbein was then appointed Superintendent. In course of time the original freedom as regards doctrine and rites had to be restricted, and "the subsequent form into which the sect settled was very similar to that of the Moravians" (J. H. Blunt). See J. H. Blunt; Brockhaus.

UNITED GREEKS. A name used to include "all who follow the Greek rite and, at the same time, acknowledge the authority of the Pope—*i.e.*, the United Melchites in the East; the Ruthenian Catholics, who use the Greek liturgy in a Slavonic version; the Greek Catholics of Italy; and the Catholics of the Greco-Roumaic rite in Hungary and Sibenbürgen" (*Cath. Dict.*).

UNITED PRESBYTERIAN CHURCH. A body formed in 1847 by the union of two other bodies, the "Associate Presbytery" or "Secession Kirk" and the "Relief Church," which had seceded from the Church of Scotland. See PRESBYTERIANS.

UNITED SOCIETY OF BELIEVERS, THE. Another name for the Shakers (*q.v.*).

UNITY OF CHRISTENDOM, ASSOCIATION FOR THE PROMOTION OF THE. An Association founded in 1857. At first the members were drawn from the Church of Rome and the Greek Church as well as from the Church of England, but after a few years the Pope required the Roman Catholic members to withdraw. "The members are required to pray daily for the restoration of visible unity between the Church of England, the Church of Rome, and the Eastern Churches, while the clergy are required to offer the 'Holy Sacrifice' at least once in three months for the 'intention' of the Association" (Walsh). See Walter Walsh, "Ritualistic Secret Societies," *Prot. Dict.*

UNIVERSAL COMMUNITY OF CHRISTIAN BROTHERHOOD. A name assumed by the religious community which is commonly known as the Doukhobórs (*q.v.*).

UNIVERSALISM. Universalism claims "that all souls will finally be saved, that evil is temporary, that good is permanent, and will achieve a complete and perfect triumph in the divine economy" (Schaff-Herzog). It claims to be based on the two fundamental principles of Christianity: (1) the parental love of God; (2) the solidarity of mankind, a mankind which is to be conformed to the image of the Son of God. God is infinite, eternal, and unchangeable; and man, the child of God, was made in His image and likeness. The Universalist "sees the whole creation in one vast, resistless movement, sweeping towards the grand finality of universal holiness and universal love" (Schaff-Herzog). A disciple of what has been called the Larger Hope, he protests vehemently against the doctrine of Eternal Punishment. God is love. "The terms are equivalent. They can be interchanged. God is not anger though He can be angry, God is not vengeance though He does avenge. These are attributes, love is essence. Therefore, God is unchangeably love. Therefore, in judgment He is love, in vengeance He is love—'love first, and last, and midst, and without end.' But in fact the traditional creed knows nothing of what love really is. For love is simply the strongest thing in the universe, the most awful, the most inexorable, while the most tender. Further, when love is thus seen in its true colours, there is less than ever an excuse for the mistake still so common, which virtually places at the centre of our moral system sin and not grace. This it is which the traditional dualism has for centuries been doing, and is still doing. Doubtless retribution is a most vital truth. Universalists rejoice to admit it; nay, largely to *base* on it their system; but there is a greater truth—which controls, and dominates the whole, the truth of Love. We must not, in common phrase, put the theological cart before the horse. Retribution must not come first, while love brings up the rear; nor must we put the idea of probation before that of God's education of His human family. In a word, to arrive at truth is hopeless, so long as men virtually believe in a quasi-trinity—God and the Devil, and the Will of Man." So writes a modern Universalist (Thomas Allin). Universalism as a denominational creed was preached first by James Relly (1722?-1778). Originally one of Whitefield's preachers, about 1761 he became a Universalist. One of his disciples was John Murray (1741-1815), who in 1770 went to America and, after preaching in various places for some years, established a number of churches in the New England and Middle States. A famous American Universalist was Hosea Ballou (1771-1852), but his views differed considerably from those of John Murray. In course of time Universalism made great progress in the United States, and the Universalists became a powerful denomination. See Schaff-Herzog; *Chambers's Encycl.*; Thomas Allin, *Universalism Asserted as the Hope of the Gospel*, 9th ed., 1905.

UNIVERSALISTIC HEDONISM. See HEDONISM.

UNIVERSAL RESTORATIONISTS. Another name for the American Restorationists (*q.v.*).

UNKULUNKULU. A term (meaning "the old, old one") used among the Kaffirs to denote a mystic potency in things. The conception seems to be that of a force, like the Melanesian *mana*, and not of a personal being.

UNNIS. Unni in Travancore, Southern India, is a title common to four castes of the Ambalavāsi group: the Pushpakans, Brāhmanis, Tīyattunnis, and Nattu Pattars. The Pushpakans prepare flower garlands for use in the temples, and assist to prepare materials for the daily offering. The Brāhmanis (also called Pappinis) are so called because they perform for the Sūdra population of Travancore some of the priestly functions of the Brāhmans. The word Tīyattu seems to be a corruption of Daivamattu, which denotes dancing to please the deity. This would explain the name Tīyattunnis. The Nattu Pattars (also known as Pattar Unnis and Karappuram Unnis) are said to be mostly agriculturists. The Brāhmanis and Tīyattunnis show a partiality for the deity Bhadrakāli. See E. Thurston.

UPANISHADS. The Upanishads are a class of literature held in sacred esteem by the Hindus. They are tractates containing the oldest philosophical speculations of the Indians, and are based upon the Vedas, being intended to supplement them. E. W. Hopkins says "it is known that the Upanishads, as a whole, *i.e.*, the literary form and philosophical material which characterize Upanishads, were earlier than the latest Brahmanic period and subsequent to the early Brahmanic period; that they arose at the close of the latter and before the rise of the former." See Monier-Williams; E. W. Hopkins; J. A. Dubois and H. K. Beauchamp.

URBANENSES. A small sect of Donatists (*q.v.*) in Numidia mentioned by St. Augustine.

URBANISTS. A branch of the Franciscan order Poor Clares (*q.v.*).

URDHR. One of the three Norns or fates in Norse mythology. She had a fountain at the foot of the ash Yggdrasil, the waters of which had wonderful power to purify.

URDHVABAHUS. Literally "Up-arms." An order of Hindu ascetics, worshippers of Siva (*q.v.*). They are so called because they raise one or both arms over the head and keep them raised for years. Monier-Williams saw one of these ascetics whose arm "was quite withered, and his fist was so tightly clenched that the nails were growing through the back of his hand." See Monier-Williams; E. W. Hopkins.

URIEN. Urien is represented sometimes as a god of the ancient Britons corresponding to the god Brân.

URSULINES. An order founded by Angela Merici (1470-1540) in 1537 with the object of instructing young girls and nursing the sick. The members, the "Company of St. Ursula," met at first in the kitchen of Angela's house, and it was not her wish to impose strict conventual rules. In 1544 the Order was confirmed by Pope Paul III. Soon afterwards a uniform costume was introduced. "They wear a black dress bound by a leathern girdle, and a black cloak without sleeves, and a tight-fitting fabric about the head, with a white veil and a longer black veil" (Schaff-Herzog). In 1594, by the help of Françoise de Bermont, they were introduced into France; and in 1610 a monastery for Ursulines was established at Paris. This meant a change in their mode of life. Pope Paul V. made the order subject to the rule of St. Austin. These nuns, "religious" Ursulines, "were to be strictly enclosed; they were to take solemn vows; and were to add a fourth, that of instructing the young" (*Cath. Dict.*). But others, "congregated" Ursulines (*Ursulines congrégées*), were unwilling to abandon the mode of life intended by St. Angela. In 1639 the Order was introduced into Canada, where in 1682 it was affiliated to the congregation of Paris. The Ursulines have a number of houses in Ireland and England. See Schaff-Herzog; the *Cath. Dict.*

USHEBTI. A term used in Egyptian religion. The Ushebtis were small statuettes in the form of mummies. They were inscribed with magic formulæ, and placed in the tombs. It was believed that they would come to life in the other world and work in the fields of Aalu for him in whose tomb they had been placed. Originally, it would seem, a man's servants were sacrificed at his tomb that they might accompany him. The use of Ushebtis was an improvement on this practice. Erman mentions that "in some cases the deceased had 365 ushebtis, so that each of these little men served him for one day in each year." See A. Wiedemann; Adolf Erman, *Handbook*.

UTILITARIANISM. Modern Utilitarianism is associated with the names of Jeremy Bentham (1748-1832) and J. S. Mill (1806-1873). Bentham was the author of the phrase "the greatest happiness of the greatest number." He held that the true and proper aim of life is Pleasure or Happiness or Utility. But the Utilitarianism of Bentham and Mill differs from the utilitarianism of the ancient Epicureans (see EPICUREANISM) in being social and universalistic. The happiness that is to be sought is not merely that of self, but also of others.

UTNAPISHTIM. Utnapishtim or Parnapishtim is the hero of the Babylonian Deluge-story. See DELUGE-STORY, BABYLONIAN, and GILGAMESH EPIC.

UTO. An Egyptian deity. Uto, who has the form of a serpent, is more commonly called Buto (*q.v.*). Her city was Buto. See Adolf Erman, *Handbook*.

UTRAQUISTS. The term is derived from the Latin words *sub utrâque specie*, "in each kind," and has been used to describe those who claim that in the Holy Eucharist the laity should receive the cup as well as the bread, (*e.g.*, CALIXTINES [*q.v.*]).

UXELLIMUS. Uxellimus, "the highest," was one of the names given by the ancient Celts to a god who corresponded to the Roman Jupiter.

V

VĀC. In Hinduism Vāc appears as the name of a female divine being. It is in fact one of the names for the female side of the god Brahmā, in addition to Sāvritī or Sarasvati. It appears in one of the hymns of the Rig Veda. Since Vāc means "speech" or "word," the application of this name Vac has been compared with that of the Greek Logos. "In the Brahmanic period Vāc becomes more and more like the Greek Logos, and it may truthfully be said that in this period 'the Word was God'" (Hopkins). Hopkins points out, however, that Vāc—the word itself is feminine—is simply one of many female abstractions. See E. W. Hopkins.

VĀDA GODS AND SHRINES. The Vādas are a caste of sea fishermen on the coast of Ganjam and Vizagapatam, Southern India. They make clay figures of their gods and put them in shrines. "Separate families appear to have separate shrines, some consisting of large chatties (earthern pots), occasionally ornamented, and turned upside down, with an opening on one side. Others are made of brick and chunam (lime). All that I have seen had their opening towards the sea. Two classes of figures are placed in these shrines, viz., clay figures of gods, which are worshipped before fishing expeditions, and when there is danger from a particular disease which they prevent; and wooden figures of deceased relations, which are quite as imaginative as the clay figures. Figures of gods and relations are placed in the same family shrine" (H. D'A. C. Reilly, quoted by E. Thurston and K. Rangachari). The chief sea goddess of the Vādas is said to be Orusandlamma, who is represented with four arms. She has a brother, Ramasondi, who rides an elephant. Marulupōlamma, another sea-goddess, "is housed in a small shed made of date palm leaves" (Thurston). The goddess Būlokamma is worshipped at the burial-ground. The goddess Kalimukkamma "is represented by a paper or wooden mask painted black, with protruding tongue," and has for her shrine a low hut made of straw. She has a brother Bāithari. Other goddesses are Peddamma or Polamma, Maridiamma, Samalamma, who is associated with a god Bengali Bābu, represented as wearing a hat and riding on a black horse, Rājamma, a goddess, represented as carrying a sword and riding on a black elephant, Yerenamma, a goddess, represented as carrying a sword and riding on a white horse, Bhāgirathamma, represented as having eight or twelve hands and as riding on an elephant, and Koralu Sakthi. See E. Thurston.

VADIANI. The Audiani (*q.v.*) are referred to by Augustine as the Vadiani.

VAGANTES. "Clerici vagantes" was the name given to ordained clerks who roamed about in search of employment. It was forbidden by a canon of the Council of Chalcedon (451 A.D.) to confer an "ordinatio absoluta sive vaga" without any "titulus ordinationis." Nevertheless, the evil continued, and there were many "clerici acephali" or "clerks without head," that is to say, "missionary bishops and priests who recognized no jurisdiction or any settled authority, but hung loose on the Christian community" (Schaff-Herzog). It was finally enacted that a bishop who ordained a clerk without giving him an office must support him at his own table. See Schaff-Herzog.

VAIKUṆTHA. Vaikuṇṭha is one of the paradises or heavens of the Hindus. It is the heaven of Vishnu (*q.v.*). The heaven of Śiva (*q.v.*) is Kailasa; that of Krishna (*q.v.*) is Go-loka. To Vaikuntha the faithful followers of Vishnu are transported. "It is above *Kailasa*, and occupies a most charming site; hence the name *Vaikuntha*, signifying 'Pleasant.' Gold and precious objects of all sorts sparkle on every side. In the midst of this enchanting abode rises a superb palace inhabited by Vishnu and his wife Lakshmi; close to them are Pradyumna, their eldest son, and a host of other children. . . . In this abode, as in the rest, there are flowers, trees, quadrupeds, birds, and especially peacocks in great numbers" (Dubois and Beauchamp). See Monier-Williams; J. A. Dubois and H. K. Beauchamp.

VALDENSES. Another name for the Waldenses (*q.v.*).

VALENTINIANS. The followers of the Egyptian Gnostic Valentinus (d. *c.* 160). Valentinus went from Alexandria to Rome about 140 A.D. By 200 A.D. his followers seem to have become very numerous. His theology or philosophy is full of symbolism. The original, invisible, and ineffable Existence is a self-existent Abyss, *Buthos*, whose consort is Silence, *Sigé*. Buthos and Sigé give birth to Mind, *Nous*, who is a being like the Supreme Buthos, and to his consort Truth, *Alētheia*. These four form a tetrad of æons. Mind and Truth give birth to Word, *Logos*, and his consort, Life, *Zōē*. Word and Life give birth to Man, *Anthrōpos*, and his consort, the Church, *Ecclesia*. These together form an ogdoad of æons. Word and Life further give birth to five other pairs, and Man and Church to six other pairs. This completes a Plēroma of thirty æons, an Ogdoad, a Decad, and a Dodecad. The Ogdoad consists of higher æons. Wisdom, *Sophia*, one of the two last æons in the Dodecad (the other being Will, *Thelētos*), is seized by an irregular passion to know the Father, the Abyss. She is stopped by the æon *Horos*, the Boundary set round the Pleroma. But she has already conceived an illegitimate being through her contact with Chaos. This is called *Hachamoth*, the Desire of Wisdom (Hebrew *chokhmah*, "wisdom"). To introduce order and harmony into the Pleroma, Mind and Truth, the second pair of æons, now produce a sixteenth pair, Christ and the Holy Spirit. After this all the æons combine to produce a thirty-third æon, Jesus, the Saviour. Through the sending to Hachamoth of, first, the Christ, and secondly Jesus, three kinds of substance arose in the universe, material inanimate substance (*hulikē*), psychic animate substance (*psuchikē*), and pneumatic or spiritual substance (*pneumatikē*). This is the world of the Kenoma. Hachamoth, expelled from the Pleroma, forms the Demiurgos out of psychic animate substance. The Demiurgos, without knowing it, makes the universe an inferior copy of the Pleroma. He creates mankind, material and psychic. Some of these, through Hachamoth, catch a spark of the spiritual substance, and become superior or spiritual men. The spiritual men do not need to be saved; the material men cannot be saved. The psychic men can be saved if they are helped. "The scheme of Redemption is intended for them. The Redeemer is formed of four elements. The first, without being actually material, has the semblance of matter; the semblance is sufficient, as matter does not need salvation. The second element is psychic, the third pneumatic, the fourth divine: this is Jesus, the last æon. These three last elements then proceed respectively from the Demiurge, Hachamoth, and from the Pleroma. The æon Jesus did not, however, descend into the Redeemer until the moment of his baptism; at the moment of his being brought before Pilate, he returned to the Pleroma, taking with him the pneumatic or spiritual element, and leaving the psychic element, clothed with his material semblance, to suffer" (Duchesne). Finally Hachamoth and the spiritual men will pass into the Pleroma. The Demiurgos and the best of the psychic men will follow. See R. A. Lipsius, *Valentinus und seine Schule*, 1887; J. H. Blunt; Louis Duchesne, *Hist.;* Max B. Weinstein, *Welt- und Leben-Anschauungen*, 1910.

VALESIANS. A sect mentioned by Epiphanius (*Hæres.* lviii) and other early writers. They are said to have held Gnostic views. One of their practices was to mutilate themselves. See J. H. Blunt.

VALHALLA. Another form of the term Walhalla (*q.v.*).

VALI. One of the gods of the Ancient Teutons. Vali, who is called also Ali and Bous, is represented as the son of Wodan (*q.v.*). In the myth of Balder (*q.v.*) Vali avenges Balder, who is his brother. With Vidharr (*q.v.*) he is one of the survivors in the final world-catastrophe. See P. D. Chantepie de la Saussaye, *Rel. of the Teutons*, 1902.

VALKYRIE. A name in Teutonic mythology for warrior women who waited on the heroes of Valhalla. Their ruler was the goddess Freyja. They were symbolized by swans, which were in fact supposed to be transformed Valkyries.

VALLABHACHARYA SECT. A Vishnuite sect in India, founded by Vallabha (*b.* A.D. 1479), after whom the members are called also Vallabhas (*q.v.*). Another name for the order is Vishnu-Swāmi.

VALLABHAS. The followers of the Hindu religious teacher, Vallabha or Vallabhāćārya, "Teacher Vallabha." Vallabha is said to have been born about A.D. 1479. He is said to have shown great precocity at the age of seven, and at the age of twelve to have formulated a new form of the Vaishṇava creed. He travelled for some years, and then settled in Benares. Here he composed a number of works, including a commentary on the Bhāgavata-purāṇa. He disapproved of fasting and self-mortification. The body ought to be reverenced and fostered because the soul contained in it is a portion of the Supreme Soul. This doctrine exposed him to the charge of Epicureanism. His creed has been called Pushṭi-mārga, "the way of eating, drinking, and enjoying oneself." Vallabha taught, or professed to teach, a pure non-duality: individual human spirits are like sparks from the Supreme Spirit; in essence the two are identical. His teaching in general lent itself to abuse. His successors acquired such power and renown that they received the title Mahārājas, "great kings." They have indulged in great luxury and sensuality. Men and women do homage to them as representatives, or incarnations, of Krishṇa. They devour the leavings of their food and the dust on which they have trodden. They drink the water in which their feet have been washed. In a peculiar rite called Self-devotion, they make over to Krishṇa's vicars upon earth body, soul, and property, "and women are taught to believe that highest bliss will be secured to themselves and their families by the caresses of Krishṇa's representatives" (Monier-Williams). See Monier-Williams; E. W. Hopkins.

VĀLMIKI. A saint (also called Bālmik or Bālnek), the reputed author of the Rāmāyana, worshipped by the Mehtars, the caste of sweepers and scavengers in India. Vālmīki was originally a hunter called Ratnakār.

VALLUVANS. A Hindu caste, the members of which are described as the priests of the Paraiyans and Pallans.

VĀM-MĀRGI SECT. Also known as Bām-Mārgi, and Vāma-Chari. An Indian sect which worships the female principle in nature (the female energy being known as Sakti). The membership of the sect is kept secret as far as possible. "Among the Vām-Mārgis both men and women are said to assemble at a secret meeting-place, and their rite consists in the adoration of a naked woman who stands in the centre of the room with a drawn sword in her hand. The worshippers then eat fish, meat and grain, and drink liquor, and thereafter indulge in promiscuous debauchery" (R. V. Russell and R. B. Hīra Lāl). They are said to worship in their houses a figure of the double triangle drawn on the ground or on a metal plate. See R. V. Russell.

VANAHEIM. Vanaheim would seem to have been one of the nine worlds in the cosmogony of the Ancient Teutons.

VĀNAPRASTHA. In the religion of the Hindus the Vānaprastha is the anchorite. The life of an anchorite, according to Manu, is one of the four stages in the life of a good Brāhman. The Vānaprastha has been treated with the greatest respect. By repressing the animal passions, by mortifying the flesh, and by practising meditation, they strove to gain perfect wisdom and purity. They rejected the claims of caste and wealth, rank and honours, land and women, cold and heat, wind and rain, pain and sickness. By meditating for a long time every day they sought to attain complete and blessed union with the Divine Being. When the Vānaprasthas died their bodies were burned in order that the purification of their souls might be completed by fire. See Monier-Williams; J. A. Dubois and H. K. Beauchamp.

VANIR, THE. A group of ancient Teutonic deities. It consists of a masculine deity Njordhr corresponding to a feminine deity Nerthus, and a masculine deity Freyr corresponding to a feminine deity Freyja. They seem to have been the gods of the Ingævonic peoples, and to have passed from their home, the Isle of Seeland, to Sweden and then to Norway. Mythology tells of a great war between the Vanir and the Æsir (*q.v.*), in which the Vanir were victorious. In one account Gullveig, also called Heidhr, "the sorceress," appears as queen of the Vanir. This Gullveig seems to be identical with Freyja (*q.v.*). Chantepie de la Saussaye thinks the war between the Vanir and the Æsir cannot be explained as a nature-myth, but points to an ethnic difference between the two. See P. D. Chantepie de la Saussaye, *Rel. of the Teutons*, 1902.

VANISTS. A name given by Richard Baxter (1615-1691) to the Antinomians in New England, because he thought they were disciples of Sir Henry Vane (1613-1662), who was Governor of Massachusetts from 1636 to 1637. Vane was a religious enthusiast, and in Massachusetts came under the influence of Anne Hutchinson (1590?-1643), who preached against the Massachusetts clergy. Ann Hutchinson was tried for heresy in 1637, condemned, and banished from the colony.

VARUNA. One of the chief deities in Hinduism,

Varuṇa is one of the forms of the Sun. In a hymn to Varuṇa from the Atharva-veda, as given by Monier-Williams, it is said: "The mighty Varuṇa, who rules above, looks down upon these worlds, his kingdom, as if close at hand. . . Whate'er exists within this earth, and all within the sky, yea, all that is beyond, king Varuṇa perceives." Varuna appears in turn as a rain-god, a day-god, and a night-god. In the early Rig Veda "he is the covering sky united with the sun, or he whose covering is rain and dew" (Hopkins). Hopkins thinks that at the time when the Vedic Aryans became Hindus, Varuna may have been the great god that he appears in the great hymn of the first book of the Rig Veda composed in his honour, but beyond this period "lies one in which Varuna was by no means a monotheistic deity, nor even the greatest divinity among the gods." See Monier-Williams; E. W. Hopkins.

VARUNI. A deity in Hindu mythology, the goddess of wine. She was held to be the consort of Varūna. See above.

VĀSUDEVA. Vāsudeva is the name or form under which the Bhāktas (*q.v.*) worship the great Hindu deity Vishnu (*q.v.*). He is represented as being the father of Krishṇa (*q.v.*), who was one of the incarnations of Vishnu. Hopkins quotes a model prayer from the Vishnu Purāna, which runs: "Glory to Vāsudeva, him of perfected wisdom, whose unrevealed form is (known as) Brahmā, Vishnu, and Siva." See Monier-Williams; E. W. Hopkins.

VATICAN, THE. The Vatican comprises a group of buildings in Rome on the right bank of the Tiber and on the Vatican Hill. The Palace, built by Pope Symmachus (498-514), rebuilt by Innocent III. (1198-1216), and continually enlarged from the time of Nicholas III. (1277-1281), has for centuries been the chief residence of the Pope. The Sistine Chapel, built by Bacio Pintelli for Sixtus IV. (1471-1484) in 1473, is adorned by the work of Michael Angelo and Raphael. The Vatican Library contains priceless treasures, Biblical, Classical and Literary. See Schaff-Herzog.

VATICAN COUNCIL. The Vatican Council was a General Council which met on the 8th of December, 1869, and was prorogued on the 20th of October, 1870. It was not dissolved, and consequently, as a Roman Catholic writer says, it is not yet concluded (*Cath. Dict.*). The Council defined the dogma of Papal Infallibility, and the Pope (Pius IX.) confirmed the decree. Other important matters were discussed, such as Discipline, and the preparation of a Short Catechism. See *Cath. Dict.*

VAUD CANTON, FREE CHURCH OF THE. The Free Church of the Vaud Canton in Switzerland was founded in 1845, as a protest against the high-handed measures of the Established Church. See Schaff-Herzog.

VAUDOIS. Another name for the Waldenses (*q.v.*).

VAYANIS. A section of the Mādigas in Southern India. The Vayanis (also known as Vayinis, Vaguniyans, or Parvinis) "play on a single-stringed mandoline, and go about from village to village, singing the praises of the village goddesses" (Thurston and Rangachari).

VĀYU. One of the nature-gods of the Vedic Aryans. Vāyu, the wind, is associated closely with Indra (*q.v.*), the Rain-god. In the cosmogony of Manu, *vāyu*, air, was the second of the five elements created. See Monier-Williams.

VEDANTISM. The Vedānta school of Brāhmanism is a metaphysical school which was founded by the great teacher Saṅkara who lived at about the beginning of the eighth century A.D. According to Vedantism, all that really exists is the One Spirit, Atmā or Brahmā. The Ego is really one with the infinite eternal Being. All else is Maya or Illusion. "In other words, the separate existence of man's spirit and of all natural phenomena is only illusory" (Monier-Williams). This being so, one who is seeking union with the One Spirit or true happiness will strive to escape from Illusion. "True wisdom consists in obtaining deliverance from this illusion by diligent contemplation of Self, by persuading oneself that one is the unique, eternal, and infinite Being, and so forth, without allowing one's attention to be diverted from this truth by the effects of *Maya*" (Dubois and Beauchamp). The soul is hindered from enjoying union with the One Spirit by a belief in matter, which is really an illusion. See Monier-Williams; E. W. Hopkins; J. A. Dubois and H. K. Beauchamp; Max B. Weinstein, *Welt- und Leben-Anschauungen*, 1910.

VEDISM. Vedism is that form of Indian religion represented by the Veda, a compilation of songs, prayers, etc. The authors of these compositions are supposed to have been inspired men or Ṛishis. At this stage the powers worshipped were the forces of Nature (Sun, Fire, etc.). The hymns, which belong to different dates, the earliest going back perhaps to the fifteenth century B.C., are arranged in three principal collections or Vedas. (1) The Ṛig-veda is a collection of hymns for devotional recitation. (2) The Yajur-veda is a liturgical collection of hymns for sacrificial ceremonies. (3) The Sāma-veda is a liturgical collection of hymns for special sacrificial ceremonies (Soma). (4) The Atharva-veda is a collection of later hymns composed by the Atharvans, a special class of priests. This Veda came to be used in magic. "It is a sort of conjuring book, professing to teach the magic art of injuring by means of spells and enchantments" (Dubois and Beauchamp). See Monier-Williams; E. W. Hopkins; J. A. Dubois and H. K. Beauchamp; J. C. Oman, *Cults*; Reinach, *O.*

VEHICLES, THE THREE. Triyāna, or "the three vehicles," is a term used by the Tibetans in reference to three schools or kinds of Buddhism. Hackmann points out that "the picture of a vehicle was frequently used in Buddhism to symbolize the doctrine, which bore the disciples across the world to the goal of Nirvâṇa." When in Northern India the more original Buddhism underwent a change, being developed and widened, the new form received the name Mahāyāna or the Great Vehicle. The older form was then called Hinayāna or the Little Vehicle. There also arose a third form, of much less importance, called Madhyamayāna, or the Middle Vehicle. In general the inhabitants of Nepāl, Tibet, China, Manchuria, Mongolia, and Japan prefer the Great Vehicle; those of Ceylon, Burma, and Siam the Little Vehicle. The Mahāyāna teaches the existence of many Bodhisattvas. It develops a theism and polytheism which are far removed from the original creed of Buddhism. See Monier-Williams, *Buddhism*, 1890; E. W. Hopkins; H. Hackmann.

VELCHANOS. A Cretan god. He seems to have been the only male deity of the Cretans. Later, the Northern Greeks identified him with Zeus. "In Crete, however, the god preserved most of his old Minoan idiosyncracy, and all sorts of barbarous tales were told about him which the other Greeks would have nothing to do with. The Cretans, for instance, said that he had died, and pointed out the mountain, with the sacred cave, where his death had taken place" (H. R. Hall, *A.A.*). On rings from Mycenae and on a coffin (or *larnax*) from Milatos, Zeus-Velchanos is represented as a youth armed with spear and shield and descending from the sky.

VENDÎDÂD. The Vendîdâd (literally "laws given against demons") is one of the divisions of the Zendavesta (*q.v.*), the oldest collection of writings sacred to the old Persians. It consists of laws, rules for exorcising demons, myths, etc., and seems to be the latest section of the Zendavesta.

VENKATRĀMANA. One of the special deities of the Stānikas, a class of temple servants in Southern India. The other special deity is Ganapati.

VENUS. A Latin goddess who came in course of time to be identified with the Greek goddess of love, Aphrodite (*q.v.*). Originally Venus was worshipped in particular by gardeners and vinedressers as a goddess of Spring who presided over flower-gardens and vines. She came to be regarded as the mother of the Roman people, and in her honour as such (*Genetrix*) Caesar and Hadrian erected temples. The first day of April was a day sacred to her. Venus sometimes appears of double sex, just as in Sparta sometimes Aphrodite was represented as bearded. See O. Seyffert, *Dict.;* Reinach, *O.*

VENUSTIANI. Another name for the Manichæan sect, Paterniani (*q.v.*).

VERETHRAGHNA. One of the most prominent angels (Victory) in the religion of the Later Avesta, the angel of war.

VERMITTLUNGS-THEOLOGIE. A German expression for that type of theology which seeks to reconcile the religion of the Churches with the claims of modern science. See MEDIATING THEOLOGY.

VERONICA. The name Veronica was given by mediæval writers to face-cloths from the catacombs "on which Christian reverence and affection have painted the features of the Saviour" (Dict. of Christ. Biogr.). Such a face-cloth was described as *vera icon* "true image." Matthew of Paris (ad ann. 1216) speaks of "the representation of our Lord's face, which is called Veronica." A late legend (but earlier than the eleventh century) converted the face-cloth into a woman. It told how one Veronica accompanied Christ on his way to the Cross and offered him her veil as a *sudarium*. After he had wiped the perspiration from his face with it, his features were found impressed upon the linen. See the *Cath. Dict., s.v.* "Christ, Appearance of"; Wace and Piercy; Sidney Heath; Francis Bond.

VER SACRUM. Ver Sacrum or "Sacred Spring" was the name given to a kind of vow taken by the Italian tribes in critical times. They undertook to sacrifice all the produce of the coming spring. Children who were born then were dedicated to heaven, and banished from the country as soon as they were grown up. The last vow was made in the Second Punic War, though it was not fulfilled until 195-194 B.C., twenty-one years afterwards. See O. Seyffert, *Dict.*

VERSCHOORISTS. The followers of James Verschoor (*d.* 1700), of Flushing, in the seventeenth century. They are said to have attached importance to a knowledge of Hebrew, and even to have been called Hebrews. Verschoor was influenced by the views of J. Cocceins (1603-1669), founder of the Federal Theology (*q.v.*), and of Baruch Spinoza (1632-1677). See B. Puenjer; J. H. Blunt.

VERSIONS OF THE BIBLE. See the separate headings.

VERTUMNUS. Vertumnus, "the changer," was the name of an Italian god of fruits. He was supposed to preside over the changing year, and is depicted as a gardener holding a pruning knife in his hand and fruits in his lap. He was popularly believed to have the power of transforming himself into various shapes. Naturally the produce of gardens and orchards was offered to him. See O. Seyffert, *Dict.*

VESPERS. Vespers or "Evensang" is one of the seven "Hours" or Services of the Breviary (*q.v.*). The hour is 6 p.m.

VESTA. A Latin goddess corresponding to the Greek goddess Hestia. The goddess and guardian of fire, and so of the private and public hearth, she was so important as to be worshipped by the State, as well as by the family. The worship was introduced from Lavinium by Numa, who also built the Temple of Vesta. Vesta came to be worshipped as the goddess of every sacrificial fire. The fire in her temple which served as her symbol could not be allowed to go out without danger to the State. See O. Seyffert, *Dict.;* Reinach, *O.*

VESTALIA. A festival in honour of the Latin goddess Vesta (*q.v.*). It was observed on the ninth of July. "The matrons of the town walked barefooted in procession to her temple, to implore the blessing of the goddess for their households, and to offer sacrifice to her in rude dishes, in remembrance of the time when the hearth served generally for the baking of bread" (Seyffert). The bakers and millers also took part in the festival, and placed crowns on the mills. See O. Seyffert, *Dict.*

VESTALS. Vestals or Vestal Virgins were priestesses in the temple of the Latin goddess Vesta (*q.v.*). Their chief duty was to tend the sacred and eternal fire, the symbol of the goddess. They were under the control of the pontifex. When they entered upon their duties, they had to be not more than ten years of age. "The time of service was by law thirty years, ten of which were set apart for learning, ten for performing, and ten for teaching the duties. At the end of this time leave was granted to the Vestals to lay aside their priesthood, return into private life, and marry" (Seyffert). If any of them broke their vows, they were beaten with rods and buried alive. There is no need to see in this anything more than a severe form of punishment intended to act as a deterrent. J. M. Robertson (*Pagan Christs*, 1911) compares the custom of Suttee (*q.v.*), and the custom among the Peruvians with whom good widows, especially those of the Incas, were at one time expected to bury themselves alive when their husbands died. But it is difficult to see the connection between good widows and bad virgins! See O. Seyffert, *Dict.;* Reinach, *O.*

VESTRY. In the ancient church-building Vestiarium or Vestry was the name of the room in which the vestments of the clergy and the sacred vessels of the church were kept. It must often have been very spacious, for several of the Councils of Carthage as well as the Synod of Arles were held "in secretario ecclesiæ," and secretarium was equivalent to vestiarium. In modern times in the English Church a Vestry came also to denote a meeting of the ratepayers of a parish, held, not necessarily in a vestry, to discuss the affairs of the parish. See Schaff-Herzog; *Chambers's Encycl.*

VIATICUM. The Latin term viaticum means "provision for a journey" (cp. the Greek *ephodion*). As an ecclesiastical term it came to be applied to the Holy Communion when administered to persons who were thought to be dying. In this application the word would mean provision for the last journey. In the thirteenth canon of the Council of Nicæa the Holy Communion is described as the "last and most necessary *ephodion* (viaticum)." In the Middle Ages the Viaticum followed Extreme Unction (*q.v.*). In the Roman Catholic Church the Viaticum is now given first. See *Prot. Dict.; Cath. Dict.*

VIBHANGA. A Buddhist sacred book in the third division of the Canon. See CANON, BUDDHIST.

VICAR. The ordinary meaning of the word Vicar (Lat. *vicarius*) is a representative or substitute (qui alterius vices agit). In the Roman Catholic Church the Apostle Peter is described as the Vicar of Christ, because, it is held, he was appointed by Christ his substitute on earth as the head of the Church. The office passed from Peter to the Bishop of Roman, who became both Vicar of St. Peter and Vicar of Christ (Vicarius S. Petri,

Vicarius Christi). In the early Catholic Church, however, all bishops were Vicars of Christ. The Pope, the one Vicar of Christ, has his own vicars. There are Vicars-Apostolic. These were formerly bishops or archbishops or even ordinary but specially delegated ecclesiastics; but now they are nearly always titular bishops "stationed either in countries where episcopal sees have not yet been established, or in those where the succession has been interrupted" (*Catholic Dictionary*). There are Vicars-general both in the Church of Rome and in the Church of England. In the Roman Catholic Church he is also called "official" (officialis). "In Transalpine countries the name of 'official' is commonly given to the ecclesiastic administering the *contentious* jurisdiction of the bishop, and that of 'vicar-general' to him who exercises his *voluntary* jurisdiction" (*Cath. Dict.*). A bishop is not obliged to have a vicar-general, but he may have two or more. In the Church of England some of the bishops have a vicar-general. The Archbishop of Canterbury, for instance, has one. The *London Diocese Book* (1912) explains that for the Province of Canterbury "The Vicar-General's Office grants marriage licences throughout the province, transacts the legal business relating to the Consecration of Bishops, and legalises the appointment of clergy to churches within the Archbishop of Canterbury's jurisdiction." There are also in some of the cathedrals of the Church of England Vicars-Choral, clergy or laymen, who assist the Dean and Chapter in matters relating to the choir and music. Further, the clergyman who is in permanent charge of an Anglican church is commonly called the Vicar, though he is sometimes called the Rector (*q.v.*). The Roman Catholic Church has its Vicars-forane, who resemble the Anglican Rural Deans. "A vicar forane is either a dignitary or at least, if possible, a parish priest, who is appointed by the bishop to exercise a limited jurisdiction in a particular town or district of his diocese" (*Cath. Dict.*). See Schaff-Herzog; William Benham; the *Cath. Dict.*

VICTORIA INSTITUTE, THE. The Victoria Institute or Philosophical Society of Great Britain has three primary objects. 1. To investigate fully and impartially the most important questions of Philosophy and Science, but more especially those that bear upon the great truths revealed in Holy Scripture. 2. To associate men of science and authors who have already been engaged in such investigations, and all others who may be interested in them, in order to strengthen their efforts by association; and by bringing together the results of such labours, after full discussion, in the printed Transactions of an Institution, to give greater force and influence to proofs and arguments which might be little known, or even disregarded, if put forward merely by individuals. 3. To consider the mutual bearings of the various scientific conclusions arrived at in the several distinct branches into which Science is now divided, in order to get rid of contradictions and conflicting hypotheses, and thus promote the real advancement of true Science; and to examine and discuss all supposed scientific results with reference to final causes, and the more comprehensive and fundamental principles of Philosophy proper, based upon faith in the existence of one Eternal God, Who in His wisdom created all things very good.

VICTORINES. The Victorines were a mediaeval school of theologians whose chief centre was the Augustine monastery of St. Victor in Paris founded by William of Champeaux. The Victorines have been described as "the religious Anthropologists or teachers of piety, the pietists of the twelfth century." They approved of a solitary life, a life devoted to contemplation. They differed from the Summists (*q.v.*) in being inclined to neglect the doctrinal side of theology. Richard of St. Victor (*d.* 1173?), a native of Scotland, attached special importance to mystic contemplation. Walter of St. Victor, who succeeded Richard, inveighed against the writers of Summaries and the Dialecticians (such as Socrates, Aristotle, and Seneca). See J. E. Erdmann.

VIDHARR. One of the gods of the Ancient Teutons. Vidharr is represented as the son of Wodan (*q.v.*), and as the slayer of the monster known as the Fenris-wolf (*q.v.*). With Vali (*q.v.*) he is one of the survivors in the final world-catastrophe. According to F. Kauffmann, he is the great Teutonic god of the forest. He is represented as a god of great strength, only second to that of Thor (*q.v.*). See P. D. Chantepie de la Saussaye, *Rel. of the Teutons*, 1902.

VIDHYĀDHAR. The lord of learning, one of the names of the Hindu god Ganpati or Ganesh.

VIGILANCE SOCIETIES. In the United States of America the name Vigilance Societies has been given to "illegal associations which spring up from time to time in all parts of the country for the compulsory improvement of local morals, and the punishment of those who either refuse or fail sufficiently to reform their lives" (Chambers's *Encycl.*). One of these societies has been known as the White Caps, because the members, who have been in the habit of visiting the homes of supposed offenders for the purpose of whipping them or of destroying their property, have concealed their faces by wearing white hoods.

VIGILS. Originally a Vigil was the watch kept on the night before a feast. In the eleventh or twelfth century the term came to denote both the day and night preceding a feast. In the Roman Catholic Church the practice of keeping Vigils has been retained only in the Matins and Lauds and the midnight Mass before Christmas. The Vigil was spent in watching (Latin *vigilare*) and prayer. In course of time it became also a fast. The Prayer Book of the Church of England contains a Table of Vigils. See W. R. W. Stephens, *Book of Common Prayer*, 1901; *Cath. Dict.*

VIGNEŚA. Vigneśa, "Lord of Obstacles," is another name for Ganesa (*q.v.*), one of the gods of the Hindus.

VIHANSA. Vihansa, as appears from an inscription, was the name of a goddess worshipped by some of the Ancient Teutons.

VINĀYAK. The remover of difficulties, one of the names of the Hindu god Ganpati or Ganesh.

VINAYAPIṬAKA. The first division of the Buddhist Canon. See CANON, BUDDHIST.

VINTIUS. Vintius was one of the deities worshipped by the ancient Celts. He seems to have been a god of the wind. He was identified with the Roman god Mars.

VIRACOCHA. Among the ancient Peruvians Viracocha was a name for divine beings in general, as well as the name of one of the chief deities. Viracocha means "Foam of the Water." The god is supposed to have emerged from the sacred waters of Lake Titicaca. The creator, he first created the sun, the moon, and the stars. When he created men, he first made them stone figures. Viracocha was taken over by the Incas from an earlier civilisation. Lewis Spence points out that the story of Viracocha's creation clashes with the legend of the solar origin of the Incas. To the Incas he was the water-god, the fertiliser of the country round about Lake Titicaca. The lake was his sister and consort, Cocha. The worship of Viracocha would seem to have been rather more humane than that of the Mexican gods. Compare further PACHACAMAC. See Lewis Spence; J. M. Robertson, *P.C.*

VIRGIN BIRTH, THE. The orthodox Christian faith teaches that Jesus, the founder of Christianity, was "conceived of the Holy Ghost, born of the Virgin Mary" (Apostles' Creed). It is believed also by many Christians that with a view to her future destiny she was specially sanctified from the womb. "It was to the pure maiden of Nazareth, thus chosen and prepared by God, that the angel Gabriel came, bearing the offer from God of an honour so amazing, that compared with it, every earthly honour is as nothing. The angel's message was nothing less than that Almighty God would, with her consent, take human form in her womb. . . . Then arose in Mary's mind the wondering question, how could she, a virgin, bear a child? Had ever a maiden become mother without the agency of human father? . . . It was then that Gabriel announced to Mary that the agency of the human father would be superseded, and that, through the power of God, a virgin-birth would be accomplished. He assured her that in conceiving and bringing forth her Child, her virgin-chastity would remain, that she would still be a virgin. He taught her that she should fulfil the mother's part, God the Holy Ghost quickening the powers of nature. 'And the angel answered and said unto her, the Holy Ghost shall come upon thee, and the power of the Highest shall overshadow thee: therefore also that Holy Thing which shall be born of thee shall be called the Son of God.'" What did this announcement involve to Mary? "She must have seen, by a pure womanly instinct, that there lay before her a time of keenest trial, of suspicion and agonizing doubt. If she accepted her amazing destiny, would not the finger of reproach be pointed at her as the Holy Child grew in her womb? How could she explain her condition even to those nearest and dearest to her? How terrible must the facing of all this have been to one whose soul was as pure as the driven snow? What would Joseph, to whom she was about to be married, think of her? What he *did* think we know; for we are told at first 'he was minded to put her away privily,' to hide her from the shame which he began to think she had brought upon herself. Only a voice from heaven reassured him, and relieved him from the painful suspicion. Beyond all this, there was the thought of the strangely mysterious association with Almighty God and His deep purposes, and all it would cost her to maintain such a dignity, which must have tempted the Blessed Virgin to hesitate in accepting the Divine call. . . . The decision lay with Mary, and we may well thank God that it was the right decision. In the face of all that awaited her, by the grace of God, the Blessed Virgin accepted with complete self-surrender the wondrous call of God, and uttered the eventful words—'Behold the handmaid of the Lord: be it unto me according to Thy Word.' In that central moment, the everlasting Son of the Father, Who took upon him to deliver man, did not abhor the Virgin's womb. He began to take human form, and Mary became the Mother of God" (Vernon Staley, *The Catholic Religion*). Such is the orthodox belief, which is based upon a literal interpretation of narratives in the First and Third Gospels. It is the belief held by orthodox Christians. But it is a belief which, in this form, is no longer held by many persons who claim to be called Christians. Apart from the question whether the nativity-narratives are an original part of the primitive Gospel story, it is felt by many that they are only an effort to express in human language a spiritual truth. Jesus was the son of a Virgin in the sense that he was the first-born son of one Mary who conceived him in perfect innocence and purity. He was the son of a Virgin in the sense that he was spiritually conceived as a perfect man in the mind of Mary long before she was betrothed to Joseph. This is the real meaning of the nativity stories. Jesus was not born like an ordinary child. All material thought was excluded, and the spirit reigned supreme. God is Spirit, and Jesus or the Christ was the true and only-begotten Son of the Father. See Vernon Staley, *The Catholic Religion*, 1893; Oscar Holtzmann, *The Life of Jesus*, 1904; Arno Neumann, *Jesus*, 1906.

VISHNU. Vishnu is one of the principal deities in Hinduism. He is one of the triad, Brahmā, Vishnu, and Śiva. If Brahmā is the Creator, Vishnu is the Preserver and Śiva the Dissolver and Reproducer. Monier-Williams points out that Vishnu is the most human, and the most humane in his character and sympathies, and consequently is the most popular. His divine nature has been imparted to certain chosen men, and in a measure to all good men. "Whether, in fact, Vishṇu be connected with light, with heat, with air, or with water, it is evident that his function is that of a divine Pervader, infusing his essence for special purposes into created things, animate and inanimate; for example, into stones, such as the black Śālagrāma; into rivers, such as the Ganges; into trees and plants, such as the Tulasī; into animals, such as a fish, a tortoise, a boar; and lastly, into men" (Monier-Williams). Orthodox Brāhmans are worshippers of Vishnu and Siva (*q.v.*) alike. Other Brāhmans reveal a tendency to prefer the worship of one or the other. The Hindus of modern times are generally either Vaishṇavas, worshippers of Vishnu, or Saivas, worshippers of Śiva. The Vaishṇavas worship one personal god Vishnu as the Supreme Being, especially in the form of his two incarnations Rāma (*q.v.*) and Kṛishṇa (*q.v.*). They believe that Vishnu has power to deliver his worshippers in this life from disease and sin, and from evils inflicted by cruel beasts, wicked men, and invisible demons. They believe that when this life is over he has power to transport them to his blissful paradise, Vaikuṇṭha (*q.v.*). In the Purāṇas it is said that he has four arms and holds in his four hands a wheel, a conch-shell, a club and a lotus-flower. He is also represented as riding on the semi-human bird Garuḍa to the help of his worshippers. His worshippers have given him a thousand names and epithets. These include: the Holy Being, the Pure Spirit, the Way, the Truth, the Father, the Holy of the Holy. Vishnu has become incarnate in nine forms, and is to become incarnate in yet another. The first was The Fish (Matsya); the second The Tortoise (Kūrma): the third The Boar (Varāha): the fourth The Man-lion (Nara-sinha); the fifth The Dwarf (Vāmana); the sixth Rāma with the Axe (Paraśu-rāma); the seventh Rāma-candra, "the moon-like Rāma"; the eighth Kṛishṇa (*q.v.*); and the ninth Buddha. The tenth is to be in the form Kalki or Kalkin. He will appear in the sky on a white horse and with a flashing sword in his hand, ready to destroy the wicked, redeem the good, renew creation, and restore the age of purity. Vishnu is represented as having a wife Lakshmī or Śrī. She is the goddess of beauty and fortune. See Monier-Williams; E. W. Hopkins; J. A. Dubois and H. K. Beauchamp.

VISHNU-SWAMI. A Vishnuite sect in India, founded by Vallabha (*b.* A.D. 1479), after whom the members are called also Vallabhas (*q.v.*).

VISHWANATH. Lord of the universe, one of the names of the Hindu god Siva.

VISIBLE SPIRITISM. The designation of that kind of spiritism in which the spirits have been supposed to be visible not only to the mediums but also to those who assist at the *séances*.

VISION, BEATIFIC. What is known as the Beatific Vision is, in human language, the bliss of seeing God face to face (cp. in the New Testament, I. John iii. 2, I Cor. xiii. 12). The Council of Florence declares that the "souls of those who after receiving baptism have incurred no stain of sin whatsoever, or who after incurring such stain have been purified, in the body or out of the body . . . are at once received into heaven and clearly see God Himself as He is, in three Persons and one substance, some, however, more perfectly than others, according to the diversity of their merits." In consequence of some of the cruder, anthropomorphic conceptions of the ancient Hebrews, according to which a theophany was accompanied by flames of fire, etc., it was believed that no man could see God's face. In course of time, however, after the development of the Christian conception, it came to be realized that God, who is incorporeal, can be seen by the eyes of the soul. But, according to the schoolmen, for beatific vision the intellect requires to be illuminated by what is metaphorically spoken of as the "light of glory" (Council of Vienne). "Just as the natural eye, in order that it may see, requires first the presence of the object, and then light, in order that the image of the object may be received, so the intellect, in order to see God, requires not only the proximity of the divine essence, but also an interior disposition by which it is elevated to an act above its natural powers" (*Cath. Dict.*). See Schaff-Herzog; *Prot. Dict.; Cath. Dict.*

VISIONS. The seeing of visions is one of the common phenomena of religious experience. In ancient times and among primitive peoples visions are believed to be objectively real. Modern psychology and psychical research have demonstrated that they are subjective and unreal. They may be explained by the working of Telepathy (*q.v.*) and the Subconscious Mind (*q.v.*). Certain persons have the power of calling up images in the minds of other persons. "The percipient sees a vision representing the incident sought to be communicated by the agent. He sees the image of the object or person which the agent desires him to see. Thus, when a person consults a medium he generally expects and desires to learn something of his deceased friends. The medium goes into the subjective condition for that purpose. The visitor's mind is full of anticipation and hope that he will be put into direct communication with the loved and lost. Presently the medium sees a vision of some person. He believes that he sees a spirit. He describes it, and it is found to correspond with one of the visitor's deceased friends. The visitor recognizes the description, and says so. He asks for the name, and it is given. Then the medium sees a vision known only to the visitor and the deceased. He describes the incident, not, perhaps, as a vision which he sees, but as a statement of fact imparted to him by the spirit. The visitor very likely knows that the medium knew nothing of him or of the deceased before that hour. He is convinced that the medium has seen and conversed with the spirit of his dead friend, and he is a convert to spiritism from that moment. Now, has the medium actually seen a spirit, or has he merely read the sitter's subjective mind? Is there any more reason for supposing that he has seen a spirit of a dead man than there is for supposing that a mind-reader sees the spirit of the Jack of clubs when the image of that card is telepathed to him? Obviously not. The conditions are precisely the same in both cases. The percipient sees the image of that which is in the mind of the agent" (T. J. Hudson). The agent of course need not be a professional medium. The faculty is common to many persons who do not use it professionally. It has often happened that a person in great danger or at the point of death has been able to transmit an image of his condition to someone with whom he is *en rapport*. Cp. APPARITIONS. See T. J. Hudson.

VISIONS OF IDDO THE SEER, THE. A record referred to in II. Chronicles (ix. 29) as one of the compiler's sources. See PROPHECY OF AHIJAH.

VISPARAD. The Visparad is one of the divisions of the Zendavesta (*q.v.*), the oldest collection of writings sacred to the old Persians. It seems to have been intended to supplement the Yasna (*q.v.*), the liturgy of sacrifice. It consists of litanies and invocations.

VISWAKARMA. An Indian deity, the celestial architect, worshipped by the Barhais (also known as Sutārs, Kharādis, or Mistris), the caste of carpenters. On the Dasahra festival the Barhais worship also their trade implements. Viswakarma is worshipped also by the Urias (also known as Sānsias), a caste of masons and navvies of the Uriya country.

VITALIANS. The Antiochenes called the Apollinarians (q.v.) Vitalians, because Vitalis became an Apollinarian bishop.

VITTOBA. Vittoba is the name of one of the modern gods of the Hindus, an incarnation of the Supreme Triad. Sir Alfred C. Lyall states (*Asiatic Studies*) that he is one of the four most popular gods in the province of Berar in Central India. He thinks that not so very long ago he must have been a notable living man. By the Dhangars. the Marātha caste of shepherds and blanket-weavers, he is worshipped on Wednesdays.

VITUCADRUS. Vitucadrus, "the brilliant in energy," was one of the names given by the ancient Celts to the war-god, a deity who corresponded to the Roman god Mars.

VIVASVAT. The name of a deity in Hinduism. Vivasvat, or, as the name is also written Vivasvant, is the Sun. In the Rig Veda Yama (*q.v.*), the first man, and his sister and wife Yima are said to be children of Vivasvat. Vivasvat corresponds to the Iranian Vivangvant. In the Avesta, Yima (Yama) is said to be the son of Vivanghvant. See Monier-Williams; E. W. Hopkins.

VIZTEOT. A god worshipped by the Nicarao (of Nicaragua). He was the god of hunger.

VOLLA. Volla, it has been thought, was one of the deities of the ancient Teutons. The name Volla or Vol occurs as that of a goddess in one of the Merseburg Charms (*q.v.*). The words may be read either, "Then charmed it Sinthgunt, Sun(na) her sister; then charmed it Frija, Vol(la) her sister," or "Then charmed it Sinthgunt, Sun's sister; then charmed it Frija, Vol's sister." Volla, however, seems to be the same as Fulla, who is referred to elsewhere as the handmaid of Frija (*q.v.*). See P. D. Chantepie de la Saussaye, *Rel. of the Teutons*, 1902.

VOLOSU. Volosu is one of the gods worshipped by the ancient Slavs. He was the god of flocks. Volosu has been identified with St. Blasius.

VOLUNTARYISM. Voluntaries are those who contend that the Churches and their clergy ought to be supported solely by the contributions of their congregations. Voluntaryism would separate entirely the Church and the State by disestablishment and disendowment.

VOLUNTEERS OF AMERICA. A philanthropic and Christian movement in the United States organized on military lines. It was founded in 1896, and may be compared with the Salvation Army (*q.v.*) and Church Army (*q.v.*) in England. See F. M. Colby and A. L. Churchill, *The New International Year Book*, 1910.

VOMITING AS A RELIGIOUS RITE. In the celebration of the festival of first-fruits among the Creek Indians of North America, vomiting appears as a rite of purification. In order to purge their sinful bodies, the men drank a bitter decoction of button-snake root which caused vomiting. The same practice is still observed by the Yuchi Indians of Oklahoma. The rite is supposed to have been instituted by the Sun. " He taught the Indians to steep the button-snake root and the red root in water and to drink the decoction, in order that they might vomit and so purify their bodies against sickness during the ensuing year. They think that if they did not thus purge themselves before eating the new corn, they would fall sick. The chief of the town is charged with the solemn duty of preparing the nauseous concoction, and he is assisted by four boys who have been initiated into the mysteries. The pots containing the stuff are decorated on the rim with a pattern representing the sun, and they stand east of the fire near the middle of the public square. The order of drinking is regulated by the rank of the drinkers. . . . When they feel the inward workings of the draught, they step out of the square and discharge the contents of their stomachs in a place set apart for the purpose " (J. G. Frazer, *Spirits of the Corn*, 1912). At a public religious ceremony (agricultural) in Santo Domingo, West Indies, the participants, in order to attain a condition of ceremonial purity, made themselves vomit by thrusting sticks down their throats. Afterwards " bread was offered to the idol and then distributed by the priests among those present, who took it home and carefully preserved it until the next year as a powerful amulet against fire and hurricanes " (T. A. Joyce, *C.A.W.I.A.*). Originally at least, those present would seem to have eaten some of the bread. This would account for the purification of the body by vomiting.

VOR. One of the deities of the Ancient Teutons. The goddess Vor, who belonged to the retinue of Frija (*q.v.*) and Freyja (*q.v.*), is represented as a goddess of vows and oaths.

VOTAN. A tribal deity in the religion of the Mayan Indians. He was worshipped as a culture-hero, and was equivalent to Itzamna.

VOWS. Vows and votive offerings are well defined by G. F. Moore in the *Encycl. Bibl.* " A vow is a voluntary obligation solemnly assumed toward God to do something not otherwise required, but believed to be acceptable or influential with him. The promise may be either simple or conditional. In the former case it is usually a pledge to perform at a future date—for example, at the next recurrence of a feast— an act of worship which is less convenient or suitable at the time the vow is made; and the motive may be any which would prompt man to the act itself, such as gratitude to God, the desire to secure his favour, etc. A conditional vow is commonly made in circumstances in which the urgent need of God's protection or help is felt, as in illness, an attack by the enemy, or for the obtaining of a greatly desired end, such as the birth of a child, the increase of flocks and herds, victory in battle, and the like. In such a case a man solemnly binds himself, if God does for him what he wishes, to do such and such a specified thing for God." Thus a vow often has the force of an oath. In ancient religions conditional vows were the common accompaniment of prayer. " The thing vowed might be anything with which it was conceived that God would be pleased —a sacrifice, a service, a dotation of gold and silver, houses and lands, cattle, or persons to God, that is, to the temple. It might also be an interdict imposed by the maker upon himself for a time or for life in the use of things otherwise lawful; thus fasting, abstinence from particular kinds of food—as the grape and its products in the Nazirite's vow—from the wearing of ornaments, sexual intercourse, etc., were often vowed. Such arbitrary self-denial was thought, like the scrupulous observance of the similar restrictions imposed by religion itself, to be a proof of devotion." There are many examples of vows in the Old Testament. Examples in Greek and Roman religion are also familiar. In Egypt innumerable votive offerings have been found. In Arabia votive offerings frequently consisted of weapons. In Buddhism the monks had imposed upon them ten vows of abstinence called the ten precepts: " abstinence from destroying life, from theft, from impurity, from falsehood, from strong drink; abstinence from eating at forbidden times, from dancing, singing, music and spectacles, from garlands, scents and finery, from high or broad couches, and from receiving gold or silver " (A. S. Geden, *Studies*). In the Christian Church the practice of making vows was adopted at an early period, and two classes of vows in particular came to be recognised. " *Vota realia* were vows to present a material gift: and in Roman Catholic countries examples of such gifts may still be seen in the offerings of wax candles, or in the models of ships which are suspended in certain churches by sailors who have been delivered from the danger of shipwreck. *Vota personalia*, again, were vows bearing directly upon personal conduct. The vow to go on a pilgrimage is an example, but the most frequent and important of personal vows were those of abstinence or self-limitation, which, again, reached their crowning height in the great monastic vows of poverty, chastity, and obedience, whereby devotion to God was supposed to reach its consummation through a definite entrance upon what came to be known as the *status religiosus* " (*Prot. Dict.*).

VOZDYKHANTZI. The Vozdykhantzi or " the Sighers " are a sub-sect of the Russian dissenters known as Bezpopovtzi. They believe that after the seventh thousandth year from the creation of the world a third spiritual reign began, the reign of the Holy Ghost. The Holy Ghost is to be served by means of sighing and spiritual prayers. See Schaff-Herzog.

VULCAN. Vulcanus or Volcanus is the name of the Roman god corresponding to the Greek god Hephæstus. He was the god of fire and of the forge. As such, he was also a beneficent god of Nature, husband of Mai or Majesta, the goddess of Spring, and on the other the god of conflagrations. His chief festival was the Volcanalia, kept on the twenty-third of August. On this occasion it was customary to throw certain fish into the fire on the hearth. See O. Seyffert, *Dict.*; Reinach, *O.*

VULGATE. The term " Vulgate " or " Vulgata editio " was used by Jerome of the Septuagint Version as compared with the original Hebrew; of the common or corrupt text of the Septuagint as contrasted with the text in Origen's Hexapla; of the Old Latin version which was made from the Septuagint; and of the New Testament of the Old Latin Version. The Council of Trent (1545-1563) declared Jerome's own version to be the " vetus et vulgata editio " of the Scriptures as being the common and authentic version of the Church, and from that time the term has been used of this version alone. The work was undertaken by Sophronius Eusebius Hieronymus, commonly called Jerome (331-420), at the request of Pope Damasus. In the first instance (383) he was asked to revise the current Latin version of the New Testament. He therefore produced a revised version of the Gospels. Whether he revised the rest of the New Testament in the same way we do not know. His next task was to revise the Psalms. The revision which he made at this time (383) was made by comparison with the Septuagint and is known as the Roman Psalter, because Pope Damasus introduced it into ecclesiastical use in the Roman Church, in which use it remained until the time of Pope Pius V. At St. Peter's and in the Ambrosian rite it is still retained. In 387 Jerome made a more careful revision by comparison with the text of

Origen's Hexapla. This is known as the Gallican Psalter, because it is said to have been introduced into Gaul by Gregory of Tours. In 1566 Pope Pius V. assigned this the place of honour formerly held by the Roman Psalter. Jerome next revised the rest of the Old Testament by comparison of the Hexaplar text. But apart from the Psalms, only the Book of Job in this revision has been preserved. It now became his aim to make his revised version of the Old Testament direct from the Hebrew, and with this intent he learned Hebrew at forty-five years of age under the guidance of a converted Jew. In 392 he began a translation of the Books of Samuel and Kings, and he published them with the Preface *Prologus galeatus*, which gives an account of the Hebrew Canon. The rest of the books, including a large part of the Apocrypha, followed, and the work was completed in 405. No revision or translation at this time seems to have been made of Wisdom, Ecclesiasticus, or the Books of Maccabees; and other books, such as Esther, Judith, and Tobit were translated in haste. In the age in which Jerome lived a thorough knowledge of Hebrew was impossible. With this qualification, " it is admitted on all hands that Jerome's version from the Hebrew is a masterly work, and that there is nothing like it or near it in antiquity " (*Cath. Dict.*). The demand for Jerome's undertaking was due to the existence at the end of the fourth century of a great variety of Latin renderings. " Three groups of Old Latin manuscripts are recognised, each representing a distinct type of text: (1) African, agreeing generally with quotations in Tertullian and Cyprian; (2) European, either independent or based on the African; (3) Italian, formed on the European type, and revised with the aid of later Greek manuscripts. Many of the Old Latin manuscripts, however, present texts which cannot be assigned to either of these classes " (M. R. Vincent). Jerome's labours were devoted mostly to the Old Testament. " In all parts of the New Testament, except the Gospels, his revision was cursory. The texts which preceded his version remain to us only in fragments, and are to be gathered, largely, from citations by the Fathers. These patristic citations may be found, not only in writings composed before Jerome, but also in later compositions, since a long time elapsed before Jerome's work obtained general currency. Down to the end of the sixth century different texts were used at the writer's pleasure. Accordingly, we find in some exclusively an old text, in others only Jerome's version, while others again employ both." In course of time the text of Jerome's version became corrupt through scribal errors. Another revision was needed. At the request of Charlmagne, Alcuin (735-804) undertook to revise the Latin text in 802. He did so by comparing older Latin manuscripts. Other revisions were made, and in the thirteenth century valuable lists of variant readings were drawn up called " Correctoria biblica." When printing was invented, the Latin Bible was one of the first books printed. When later Cardinal Ximenes (1437-1517) issued his *Complutensian Polyglot* (1502-1517) he issued a revised Latin text. But Robert Stephanus (1503-1559) was the first to produce (in 1528) a really critical edition based on the collation of a number of manuscripts. After this the Roman Church felt the need of a pure and authentic text. This was undertaken by Pope Sixtus V. (1585-1590), and the Sixtine edition was published in 1590. This in 1592 was withdrawn by Pope Clement VIII., and in the same year the Clementine Vulgate was published. This was decreed to be the standard and authorised text of the Roman Church. See Schaff-Herzog; *Cath. Dict.*; the *Encycl. Bibl.*; J. Paterson Smyth, *The Old Documents and the New Bible*, 1890; Marvin R. Vincent, *Text. Criticism of the N.T.*; K. Lake, *Text. of the N.T.*, 1904; C. R. Gregory.

W

WADD. An Arabian deity, mentioned in the Qur'ân (lxxi., 22). The Arabic word means " love." The idol Wadd is supposed to have been worshipped originally by the antediluvians. The worship was adopted by the pagan Arabs, who gave Wadd the shape of a man. He is said to have represented the heaven. See E. H. Palmer, *The Qur'ân*, 1880, in the " Sacred Books of the East "; E. M. Wherry, *Commentary on the Qurán*, 1896.

WADDAHGUDJAELWON. A deity in the religion of the Euahlayi tribe of Australia. A goddess, she has charge of spirit-babies. These she sends " to hang promiscuously on trees, until some woman passes under where they are, then they will seize a mother and be incarnated " (K. Langloh Parker, *The Euahlayi Tribe*, 1905).

WĀGHYAS. An order of mendicants in India, belonging to the Marātha Districts and Bombay. They are devotees of the god Khandoba, an incarnation of Siva. " In Bombay the Wāghyas force iron bars through their calves and pierce the palms of their hands with needles. To the needle a strip of wood is attached, and on this five lighted torches are set out, and the Wāghya waves them about on his hand before the god " (R. V. Russell).

WAFERS. The small cakes used in the Latin Church in the celebration of the Holy Eucharist or Holy Communion are called wafers. These are a convenient substitute for broken pieces of bread. They are made without leaven, and it has been contended that this has been the practice from Apostolic times. As a matter of fact, the practice of the ancient Church is uncertain. In all probability either leavened or unleavened bread was considered suitable. In the Oriental Church, except in the case of the Maronites and Armenians, unleavened bread is used. See *Prot. Dict.*; *Cath. Dict.*

WAHHÁBIS. A Mohammedan sect founded by Muhammad Ibn 'Abdu'l-Wahháb (A.D. 1691-1765). Wahháb, on returning to his native village after visiting Mecca and other places, became a religious teacher. He had become convinced that the Mohammedans were not living in strict accordance with the real and primitive principles of their faith. "The use of omens and augurals, the veneration of sacred shrines and the tombs of saints, the use of intoxicating drugs, the wearing of silk and satin and all sorts of luxury which had found favour in the Muslim world were all opposed to the principles of true religion, and Islám must be purged of these idolatrous practices" (Klein). Wahháb naturally met with a good deal of opposition. His protector, however, Muhammad ibn Sa'úd, became the founder of the Wahhábi dynasty, by marrying Wahháb's daughter. Sa'úd's grandson, also named Sa'úd, was a great reformer, and established the Wahhábi rule at Mecca and Madina for nine years. He died A.D. 1814. The Wahhábis describe themselves as the Unitarians. See F. A. Klein; and R. V. Russell.

WAKAN. A name given by the North American Indians to a power that is supernatural, supernormal, or awe-inspiring. It is described as a force, and not as a personal being. All life is wakan. "It is not a definite and definable power, the power of doing this or that; it is Power in an absolute sense, with no epithet or determination of any sort. The various divine powers are only particular manifestations and personifications of it; each of them is this power seen under one of its numerous aspects" (Émile Durkheim).

WAKEMANITES. The followers in 1855 of Rhoda Wakeman in New Haven, Connecticut. She professed to be a divinely inspired prophetess and to have risen from the dead. She exercised so great an influence over her adherents that she persuaded them to kill a man, with his own consent, who was supposed to be possessed of an evil spirit. See J. H. Blunt.

WALDENSES. The Waldenses are a religious body who have inhabited for centuries the valleys of the south of France and north of Italy. Another form of the name is Vallenses. This has been derived from the Latin, French, and Italian word for "valley" (Latin *vallis*), and explained as equivalent to "valesmen." It has also been contended that the Waldenses or Vallenses date back to Apostolic times. The truth seems to be that the sect was organized about 1177 in Lyons by Petrus Waldus. Waldus had come forward in 1160 as a reformer of the abuses of the Church. The Waldenses (also Vaudois) are identical with the "Poor of Lyons" or Leonists, the Sabatati or Sabôtiers (from their wooden shoes), and the Humiliati. Petrus Waldus is also called Peter of Waldo, Pierre de Vaud, and Pierre de Vaux. He was a merchant of Lyons, who came to feel that the ideal life meant a return to the simplicity and poverty of Apostolic times. In 1170 he had portions of the Bible translated into the Provençal dialect. He then trained a number of his followers as preachers of the Gospel. They were excommunicated by the Archbishop of Lyons, and forbidden to preach by Pope Alexander III. (1179). In 1184 the Waldenses were condemned at the Council of Verona. Nevertheless, they spread rapidly. The Waldenses had no idea originally of separating from the Church. They were driven to this, however, by the opposition of the ecclesiastical authorities. They now denied the authority of the Church and the efficacy of her ordinances. The Church of Rome was the Babylon and the harlot of the Apocalypse; the Waldenses represented the true Church of Christ; laymen, and even women, were entitled to preach; consecration and absolution by a bad priest were invalid, whereas absolution by a good layman was valid: tithes and religious endowments were unlawful; much of the ceremonial of Baptism was unnecessary; in the Eucharist, transubstantiation was only subjective; Extreme Unction was useless. As a Roman Catholic writer puts it, "they made a clean sweep of all the beautiful and touching ceremonies—all the salutary institutes—with which the Church had surrounded the life of Christians here below" (*Cath. Dict.*). Great and violent efforts were made to suppress the Waldenses, and they suffered cruel and continual persecution. In 1530 they entered into communication with the Swiss and German Reformers. Georges Morel and Pierre Masson were sent to meet J. Œcolampadius (Heussgen; 1482-1531) in Basle, Berthold Haller in Bern, Wolfgang Capito (Koepfel; 1478-1541), and Martin Bucer (or Butzer; 1491-1551) in Strassburg. The result seems to have been that the Waldenses were willing to abandon some of their extravagant tenets, and to make some of their other tenets conform more closely to those of the Reformers. In 1532 they renounced communion with the Roman Catholic Church. In 1556 they expressed to the German Reformers their belief in the Old and New Testament, the Apostles' Creed, the Athanasian Creed, the Creeds of the first four Councils, the Holy Sacraments as instituted by Christ, the Ten Commandments, and submission to divinely appointed superiors. In 1630, when they suffered from a dearth of pastors, ministers went to their help from Geneva and Lausanne. This involved a still closer approximation to the theology of the Protestant Reformers. In 1655 they accepted the Confession of Augsburg. In the same year and in 1685 supreme efforts were made to crush them. The latter was so far successful that thousands of the Waldenses were killed, imprisoned, or exiled. Some of the exiles returned in 1689, and more between the years 1690 and 1696. But they were not safe until 1848, when the Turin Edict of Emancipation was signed. The Waldenses are said to number now more than 20,000. See Karl Mueller, *Die Waldenser*, 1886; J. A. Chabrand, *Vaudois et Protestants des Alpes*, 1886; J. H. Blunt; *Prot. Dict.; Cath. Dict.;* Brockhaus.

WALHALLA. In Scandinavian mythology Walhalla or Valhalla, "the Hall of the Slain," is a mansion of the gods into which are admitted warriors who have been slain in battle. It was the paradise of these heroes. Here in the Viking period they are represented as leading a life not only of joyous feasting, but also of continuous combat. See P. D. Chantepie de la Saussaye, *Rel. of the Teutons*, 1902.

WALI, A. A term used in Muslim theology. F. A. Klein explains that a Muslim saint or Wali is so called (from a root meaning "to possess" or "to be in charge of") "because God takes charge of his concerns and also because he himself only cares for the worship of God. He is able to do things contrary to custom, and such acts are called 'beneficence.' Such miracles do not appear in his lifetime, but after his death. Such a saint, if no miracles appear through him, is not a true Wali." See F. A. Klein.

WALKERITES. The followers of John Walker (1768-1833), a Fellow of Trinity College, Dublin. In 1804 Walker left the Church of England, and founded a Calvinistic sect, "The Church of God." The Walkerites have also been called Separatists. See the *D.N.B.*

WALKYRIES. Goddesses of the Edda. They are goddesses of war, who decide which of the warriors are to fall in the battle and which of them will win the crown of victory. It is they who admit the warriors to the banquet in the halls of Walhalla (*q.v.*). Chantepie de la Saussaye thinks that the Walkyries of the Viking period may be connected "on the one hand with the warlike Teutonic women of the ancient times, and on the other hand with the goddesses of battle and victory." In Norse mythology they are found in the train of Odhin (*q.v.*). They are the "battle-maidens" who give victory to Odhin's favourites or conduct them to Walhalla. Sometimes they assume the form of swan-maidens. The Walkyries seem to have much in common with the Norns (*q.v.*). See P. D. Chantepie de la Saussaye, *Rel. of the Teutons*, 1902; Reinach, *O.*

WALPURGIS NIGHT. The day sacred to St. Walpurga, sister of St. Wilibald or Willibald (700?-786), who became Bishop of Eichstädt, was the first of May. The eve of this, the night between 30th April and 1st May, was called "Walpurgis Night." Walpurga or Walburga (*d.* 779?) was born in England. When her brother Wilibald went to Germany, she went with him and became abbess of Heidenheim, near Eichstädt. The 1st of May was the date of one of the most important of pagan festivals, that on which was celebrated the beginning of summer. In consequence of this, a number of superstitions became associated with Walpurgis Night. Witches were supposed to indulge in revels at the ancient places of sacrifice, especially on the Brocken, the highest of the Harz Mountains, riding thither on broom-sticks and he-goats. See the *D.N.B.*; and Brockhaus.

WĀMAN. The dwarf, one of the incarnations of the Hindu god Vishnu.

WAND, MAGIC. Among the Hebrews a certain sacredness or magic power seems to have been ascribed to sceptres, rods, or wands. Moses carried in his hand a divine rod (*maṭṭeh hā-'elōhīm*, Exod. iv. 20, xvii. 9). With this rod he smote the waters (Exod. vii. 20, xiv. 16), and the rock (Num. xx. 11). In II. Kings iv. 29 the staff of a prophet seems intended to serve instead of the presence of the prophet himself. In Hosea iv. 12 a staff is even referred to as speaking. In early Egyptian religion the gods are represented as carrying a staff such as every Bedouin cuts for himself at the present day, and the goddesses are provided with a simple reed (Adolf Erman). The wand of the king or priest, which was known as "the great magician," had power to cause the dead to be born again; and Elliot Smith notes (*Dr.*) that such beliefs and stories of a magic wand are found to-day in scattered localities from the Scottish Highlands to Indonesia and America. He points out also (p 155) that the papyrus sceptre of Astarte is regarded at times as an animate form of the mother-goddess. With this may be compared J. G. Frazer's statement (*The Magic Art*, 1911, I. p. 365) that "the sceptre of king Agamemnon, or what passed for such, was worshipped as a god at Chaeronea; a man acted as priest of the sceptre for a year at a time, and sacrifices were offered to it daily." In ancient Mexico (as noted by Marian Edwardes and Lewis Spence, p. 189) the traveller's staff was worshipped as a symbol of Yacatecutli. It was sprinkled with sacrificial blood; incense was burned before it; offerings were presented to it; and prayers and genuflections were made to it. The Mexican Quetzalcoatl was represented as a traveller with a staff in his hand; and Jizō, the god of travellers among the Buddhists of Japan, carries a pilgrim's staff. In all such cases we may assume that the staff had a religious significance. The Iranian priests used in their magic practices bundles of magic wands called *baresmân*. These were gathered with certain rites. The so-called "staffs of office" depicted by the cave-dwellers of the Reindeer Age probably played some part in magic ceremonial (so S. Reinach, *Cults*). The staffs are often marked with regular notches. This suggested to Bernadin, who compares the genealogical staffs of the Maoris, that the notches were intended to recall the chief's genealogy.

WANINGA. A ritual instrument found among the southern Arunta, the Urabunna and the Loritja in Central Australia. It has no one unique model. "Reduced to its most essential elements," it "consists in a vertical support, formed by a long stick or by a lance several yards high, with sometimes one and sometimes two cross-pieces. In the former case, it has the appearance of a cross. Cords made either of human hair or opossum or bandicoot fur diagonally cross the space included between the arms of the cross and the extremities of the central axis; as they are quite close to each other, they form a network in the form of a lozenge. When there are two crossbars, these cords go from one to the other and from these to the top and bottom of the support. They are sometimes covered with a layer of down, thick enough to conceal the foundation. Thus the waninga has the appearance of a veritable flag" (Émile Durkheim). The waninga is fixed in the earth or carried by an officiant, and marks the central point of a religious ceremony.

WARBURTON LECTURESHIP. A Lectureship founded in 1769 by William Warburton (1698-1779), Bishop of Gloucester, author of "The Divine Legation of Moses" (part i., 1737, part ii., 1741). The object of the lectures is "to prove the truth of revealed Religion in general and of the Christian in particular from the completion of those prophecies in the Old and New Testaments which relate to the Christian Church, especially to the Apostacy of Papal Rome." The Lectures are delivered in the Chapel of the Society of Lincoln's Inn, London; and the lectureship may be held for four years.

WARRENITES. The followers of Samuel Warren (1781-1862). Warren was a Wesleyan preacher in Lancashire. In consequence of a dispute, however, with the Wesleyan body, he was expelled from his chapel in 1835. He found many sympathisers. These banded themselves together first as "Associated Methodists" and afterwards as the "United Methodist Free Churches." Warren himself in 1838 took holy orders in the Church of England, and in 1840 became Rector of All Souls, Ancoats, Manchester.

WAS SEASON. A sacred season among the Singhalese and Burmese Buddhists. The season lasts three months. The name *Was* is supposed to have meant originally the rainy season. During these three months the monks must give up the practice which they follow during the rest of the year, that of wandering as mendicants from place to place, and must remain in a temple where it is a duty of the laity to supply their needs. The Burmese monks must deny themselves their pantomimic dances. The month after *Was* is called the "clothing," because during this month the laity make special gifts of clothing to the monks. Hackmann mentions a curious custom in connection with the "clothing month." Sometimes a number of outfits, by a united effort on the part of the laity, are completed in a single day. See H. Hackmann.

WATER-DEMONS. Water-demons, having a form that resembles somewhat that of the Egyptian hippopotamus-goddess Taueret, figure frequently in Late Minoan and Mycenaean art.

WATER-WALKING. It is noted by Rendel Harris (*Boanerges*, 1913) that among the Argonauts, as described by Apollonius Rhodius, Euphemus, the swiftest of men, could run on the sea without merging his feet. Traces of the same idea are found in Indian literature.

WATERLANDERS. A name given before 1664 to the less strict division of the Mennonite Baptists. They were so called because most of them lived in a district in the North of Holland called Waterland. They are also known as Johannites.

WATTS'S NAZARENES. A name given to bells cast by Hugh Watts (1582?-1643), of Leicester. The name was due to a favourite inscription.

WAUKHEON. A deity in the mythology of the Dakota Indians, a personification of the thunder-cloud. He was opposed by Unktahe, the water-god.

WAY OF THE CROSS. See STATIONS OF THE CROSS.

WEIGELIANS. The followers or school of the mystic and theosophist, Valentine Weigel (1533-1588). See MYSTICISM, CHRISTIAN.

WEIGHING OF SOULS. The weighing of the heart or soul in the Hall of the Truths, where Osiris presided as judge and was assisted by Thoth, Anubis and Horus, is a familiar feature in the Old Egyptian religion. We meet with the same idea in Christian art. St. Michael is represented as weighing the souls of the departed. Sometimes we find represented also a little imp who is trying to pull down the scales. It seems clear, as Francis Bond says (*Dedications*), that St. Michael "has succeeded to the functions of the pagan Hermes or Mercury, who is himself derivative from Egyptian Art."

WELSH CALVINISTIC METHODIST CHURCH, THE. A Methodist body in Wales which arose under the influence of John Wesley and George Whitefield, but adopted the Calvinistic theology of the latter. Whitefield's friend, Howell Harris (1714-1773), had already formed various societies similar to those of Wesley. In 1743, at a meeting at which Whitefield was present, a union of these societies was regularly constituted, and rules were laid down for the government of the community. The community, however, "though organised in 1743, did not separate from the Established Church for nearly seventy years afterwards" (J. A. Houlder).

WEN TI. A Chinese deity, also called Wên Ch'ang Ti Chün, the god of literature. It is thought that originally he was a man named Chang, and that he experienced many reincarnations. He is identified with part of the constellation *Ursa Major*. See S. Couling.

WEPWAWET. An Egyptian deity. The deity has the head of a jackal. In the old religion the word denotes two gods (the word meaning the "guides") who direct the dead in the paths of the underworld. In the religion of the late period, when it had become the fashion to represent the gods as birds, Wepwawet has become a sparrow with the head of a jackal. In Herodotus (II., 122) the Wepwawet gods seem to appear as two wolves. See Adolf Erman, *Handbook*.

WERTHEIM BIBLE. A translation of the Bible, made by Johann Lorenz Schmidt (*d.* 1751). It seems to have been intended to popularize the results of English Deism, French Encyclopedism, and German Aufklaerung (*q.v.*). The Bible was to be explained on the principle that nothing can be true which contradicts reason. "Instead of transporting himself into the thoughts and the poetical spirit of the Bible, he treats it as a text-book of the Leibniz-Wolffian philosophy, renders it in the dullest prose of a cold intellectuality, and puts general intellectual conceptions into the place of its images and similes" (Puenjer).

WESLEYAN METHODISTS. Wesleyan Methodists or Wesleyans represent the parent body among a number of sects that arose as a result of the work of John Wesley. The term *Méthodistes* was used in France early in the seventeenth century to describe certain theologians who sought to reunite the Huguenots with the Church by stating precisely and fairly the case on both sides. The name was not chosen or favoured by John Wesley. When, after having taken his Master's degree, Wesley returned to Oxford (1729), he attached himself to a number of students who with his brother Charles Wesley were in the habit of taking the Sacrament weekly. In this way and in other ways these students became noted for a certain seriousness and regularity, and by other students they were nick-named Methodists. They cultivated holiness, studied diligently the Bible, and devoted themselves to Christian and philanthropic work. "They were tenacious of all the doctrines and discipline of the Church of England, and were scrupulously strict in observing the rubrics and canons" (*Prot. Dict.*). At this time John Wesley, among other practices, "seems to have been in favour of the strict observance of saints' days and holy days, confession, constant communion, the mixture of water with the sacramental wine." In 1735 Wesley went to Georgia in America as a missionary to the Indians. On the voyage he was brought into contact with some Moravians (*q.v.*), and seems to have been much impressed by them. In America he met the Moravian pastor A. G. Spangenberg. Wesley returned to England in 1738. In London he met the Moravian pastor Peter Boehler, who had been ordained by Zinzendorf in 1737 for work in South Carolina. He became interested in a "Religious Society" founded in London by his friend James Hutton. For this society he and Peter Boehler drew up rules, and on May the 12th, 1738, it was organised more fully on the lines of the Herrnhut "Band" system. At a meeting of this society on May the 24th, 1738, Wesley had that profound religious experience which marked the great turning-point in his life. In July, 1740, Wesley withdrew from the Society, whose pastor at the time was Philip Henry Molther, and formed a separate society. The new society met in a preaching-house in Windmill Hill (now Windmill Street) called the Foundery. The service was very simple. But Wesley was accustomed to preach in the open-air in various parts of the country. Before the opening of the Foundery, the foundation-stone had been laid in Bristol of another "preaching-house." This involved Wesley in debt, and a meeting was held in 1742 to consider how the money could be raised. The plan adopted led to the institution of "classes." The classes were originally companies into which the Society was divided to facilitate the collection of money by "leaders of the classes." The members of the classes were visited by their respective leaders. In course of time, instead of being visited, each class met together, and the Class Meeting became an instrument for regulating Christian life and conduct and deepening religious experience. In this sense Class Meetings have not suffered much change. "They are usually small gatherings of some dozen to twenty people for strictly devotional purposes, and for giving and getting sympathy and mutual advice in leading a godly life. . . They vary as infinitely as the characteristic of the leader, or person who is accountable to Methodism for those put under his or her spiritual charge; as infinitely as the characteristics of the members. In some cases it is a stiffer, in some a more homely meeting. But in every case the word of God is accepted as the rule of life, and the little groups try to help each other to conform to it; and membership in one of these classes constitutes membership in the Methodist Society" (Mrs. Sheldon Amos). In 1743 John Wesley issued a document entitled "The Nature, Design, and General Rules of the United Societies in London, Bristol, Kingswood, and Newcastle-upon-Tyne." Full members of the Society of "the People called Methodists" were required to conform to these rules, though in course of time they were altered somewhat. Persistent failure to observe them meant exclusion from the Society. The institution of Classes led in time to the institution of smaller groups called "Bands." These submitted to even stricter rules. There arose further "Select Bands" with whom Wesley took counsel. The "Bands" met together quarterly to observe "love-feasts," the food being only a little plain cake and water. The occasion was and has remained one for recounting spiritual experiences. Speaking of such "love-feasts," Mrs. Sheldon Amos says: "As I remember them, they were occasions on which pieces of currant-bread and water were passed from pew to pew in the chapel, and then, interspersed with singing and prayer, one short speech after another was made by whoever chose, about the life of Christ in the heart. One would be full of joy and praise for help in trouble, or added and sharpened delight in happy circumstances. Another would tell of heavy-heartedness and clinging faith and hope in God. There was always a feeling of special approach to the presence of God, and I think these meetings were good." An interesting feature of Wesleyan Methodism is the extent to which laymen were invited to help Wesley. They were at first lay-helpers. Then the lay-helper became also a lay-preacher. "The pastoral office is shared with the men and women leaders of classes, the ecclesiastical rule of the Church is shared with laymen (and in the lower branches theoretically with women), and even the office of preaching is shared very largely with lay preachers who live by their own labour and give their Sundays to preaching in their own neighbourhoods, and sometimes in distant parts of the country. The office of a local preacher is one that has always been held by men of the most various attainments and positions in the world, and much of the vigorous life of the Methodist Society is owing to the fact that the ministry is thus felt to be not a far-off office, but one of the functions of the Christian life exercisable by anyone whose capacity for teaching is recognised by a number of his fellows. Many a useful local preacher has wished to be a minister set apart and ordained, but his suitability for Orders has not been clear to the authorities" (Mrs. Sheldon Amos). In 1744 Wesley held a Conference of lay-preachers and sympathetic clergymen. This became a "Yearly Conference of the People called Methodists." In 1784 Wesley drew up a "Deed of Declaration," which nominated one hundred preachers as the Conference, and provided for the filling up of vacancies as they occurred. This made Wesleyan Methodism a distinct denomination. This was not John Wesley's original desire. The beginning of the cleavage was made when in 1741, in consequence of exclusion from the Communion Table of the Church, Charles Wesley began to administer the Lord's Supper in "unconsecrated" preaching-houses. The Wesleys had intended their Society to work in connection with the Church. "In John Wesley's idea Methodism was not to found a Church. He permitted no Methodist service to be held in church hours, and even to the present day in quiet villages the same filial respect is shown to the National Church. The change came when the numbers of persons excluded from the Communion, and treated as pariahs by the clergy, grew so great that it was a practical inconvenience for them to be unable to use the best hours of the Sunday for the services to which they were attached" (Mrs. Sheldon Amos). Mrs. Sheldon Amos thinks that "the spirit of dissent which now exists in Methodism is an unnatural excrescence, and will die down again as soon as fresh life in the Church of England causes the hand of brotherly love to be stretched out." John Wesley was himself an ordained clergyman of the Church of England. In 1763 Wesley ordained that the preachers should preach nothing contrary to the teaching of his four volumes of Sermons and his Notes on the New Testament. This is still the rule. Wesley believed that in the Primitive Church bishops and presbyters were the same order. Consequently he held that presbyters have the same right to ordain. To meet the needs of the Methodist missions in North America, in 1784 he ordained Dr. Coke, who was already a priest of the Church of England, "Superintendent" (virtually equivalent to Bishop), and Richard Whatcoat and Thomas Vasey "Elders." In 1789 he ordained Henry Moore and Thomas Rankin "Presbyters" that the sacraments might be administered to the Methodists of England, and that the power to administer them might be transmitted to others. The members of Wesley's Society were called also Precisians. Wesley himself explains that a true Methodist is none other than a true Churchman: in his observance of the rules of the Church for the practice of personal piety he is precise and methodical. See J. H. Blunt; *Prot. Dict.*; *R.S.W.*; J. A. Houlder.

WESSOBRUNN PRAYER, THE. The manuscript now known as the Wessobrunn Prayer was discovered in the cloister of Wessobrunn in Bavaria. The prayer is in prose, but prefixed to it are nine lines of alliterative verse. It is written in Old High German, and dates from the eighth or ninth century. It is concerned with "the almighty God, who, ere earth and sky, tree and mountain were, ere sun and moon shone, ere the sea was, when all about was void, was already then surrounded by many good spirits, he the most bounteous of men, the holy God" (de la Saussaye). Chantepie de la Saussaye considers the prayer to be wholly Christian. J. Grimm, K. Müllenhoff, and others believe it to be a fragment of genuine Teutonic paganism. See P. D. Chantepie de la Saussaye, *Rel. of the Teutons*, 1902; Brockhaus.

WESTMINSTER ASSEMBLY. The Assembly of Divines was constituted in 1643. Both Houses of Parliament had resolved to set up a government "most agreeable to God's word, most apt to procure and preserve the peace of the Church at home, and in nearer agreement with the Church of Scotland and other Reformed Churches abroad." The Assembly of Divines therefore was appointed by the Long Parliament, "to be consulted with by the Parliament for the settling of the government and liturgy of the Church of England, and for vindicating and clearing of the doctrine of the said Church from false aspersions and interpretations." It consisted of one hundred and fifty-one members, who met first in the Chapel of Henry VII. in Westminster, and afterwards in the Jerusalem Chamber in the Deanery. "Ten weeks were devoted to the revision of the Thirty-nine Articles to bring them into unequivocally Calvinistic form on the lines of the Lambeth Articles and of Ussher's Irish Articles, and the first fifteen were finished, and supplied with Scripture proofs" (W. A. Curtis). The Assembly next prepared a Confession of Faith (see WESTMINSTER CONFESSION), Catechisms (see LARGER CATECHISM, and SHORTER CATECHISM), and a Book of Discipline. See William A. Curtis.

WESTMINSTER CONFESSION, THE. The Westminster Confession was the result, or rather the chief of the results, of the consultations of the Westminster Assembly of Divines. It was submitted to Parliament in December 1646, and again in April 1647 with the addition of Scripture proofs. In Scotland it was approved by the Assembly of 1647 as "most agreeable to the Word of God, and in nothing contrary to the received doctrine, worship, discipline, and government of this Kirk." In 1648, by order of Parliament, it was issued in English and Latin, "and enjoyed, until the Restoration, the unique distinction of being the Confessional standard of the whole United Kingdom" (W. A. Curtis). In 1649, the Scottish Parliament having approved it, the Assembly ordained that "in every house where there is any who can read, there be at least one copy of the Shorter and Larger Catechism, Confession of Faith, and Directory for family worship." W. A. Curtis points out that "though not intended by its English authors to be imposed on the individual conscience as a document for subscription, it was promptly so used in Scotland." In 1690, under William and Mary, it obtained the royal sanction. According to Curtis, the Westminster Confession does for the whole system of Calvinistic doctrine what the Canons of Dort (1619) did for one doctrine. "It was the last great Creed-utterance of Calvinism, and intellectually and theologically it is a worthy child of the *Institutes*, a stately and noble standard for Bible-loving men. While influenced necessarily by Continental learning and controversy, it is essentially British, as well by heredity as by environment; for not only is it based upon the Thirty-nine Articles, modified and supplemented in a definitely Calvinistic sense at Lambeth and at Dublin, but it literally incorporates Ussher's Irish Articles, accepting their order and titles, and using, often without a word of change, whole sentences and paragraphs. . . . It still remains, in spite of changing times and altered formulae of adherence, the honoured symbol of a great group of powerful Churches throughout the British Empire and the great American Republic, embracing within their membership a large proportion of the foremost representatives of the world's highest material, social, educational, moral, and religious interests. The English-speaking Presbyterian Churches throughout the world without exception adhere either to it or to some comparatively slight modification of it; while its hold, direct or indirect, upon Congregationalists and Baptists and others is a further tribute to its power both of education and of revival." See William A. Curtis.

WHALE, THE. It is noted by Donald A. Mackenzie (*Crete*) that in Palæolithic times the spines of fish were laid as charms on the bodies of the dead; and also that the Ligurian and Cretan Neolithic people seem to have used the backbones of whales as charms. Among the Peruvians of the coast in Incan times the whale was worshipped, and was called Mamacocha or "Mother Sea."

WHEEL, THE. One of the seven royal treasures of the ideal king, or king of kings, of the Buddhists (or rather of the pre-Buddhists) is the treasure of the wheel. This wheel became one of the symbols of Gautama. It has six, eight, or even a thousand spokes. Hackmann thinks that by the rolling wheel, as applied to Gautama, the spiritual ruler of the world, is typified the spread of his teaching. The wheel is supposed to appear to the ideal king when, after purifying himself, he ascends to the upper story of his palace to keep the sacred day. Rhys Davids explains that the wheel was suggested by the Vedic poetry, which describes the sun as rolling across the space of heaven in his victorious course. "And like the sun, when the wondrous wheel appears to the great king, it rolls onwards to the very extremities of the world conquering and to conquer. But the wheel of the ancient sun-worship is now subordinated to the king who has purified himself." See T. W. Rhys Davids; H. Hackmann.

WHEEL OF LIFE. What is called a "wheel of life" figures prominently in Lamaism. The wheel is painted on the walls of the verandas of temples. It has six spokes, and the divisions between the spokes represent six regions in which a new existence may be found. These are: the region of the heavens; the region of the semi-celestial Titans; the region of the man world; the region of the animal world; the region of ghosts; and the region of the hells. Entwined about the wheel is the figure of a demon. See H. Hackmann.

WHITE BRETHREN. A body of religious enthusiasts who were prominent in Italy early in the fourteenth century. They were so called because they wore white robes and hoods. Their leader professed to be Elijah, the herald of the Second Advent, and he wished to lead his followers to a crusade against the Turks in the Holy Land. The White Brethren came into conflict with some of the papal troops of Boniface IX. They were dispersed, and their leader was captured, and burned as a heretic. See J. H. Blunt.

WHITE CANONS. A name given in England to the Premonstratensians. They are also known as Norbertines, because the order was founded by St. Norbert (*d.* 1134). They were called White Canons because their habit was white.

WHITE CAPS. A name given to members of one of the American Vigilance Societies (*q.v.*) from their practice of wearing white hoods in order to conceal their faces.

WHITE DOVES. A religious sect in South Russia which came into prominence in 1876 by coming into conflict with the authorities.

WHITE FATHERS. A Roman Catholic congregation founded in Algiers in 1868 by Cardinal Lavigerie (1825-1892).

WHITEFIELDITES. The followers of George Whitefield (1714-1770), who became domestic chaplain to Lady Huntingdon (1748). See HUNTINGDON'S CONNEXION.

WHITE FRIARS. A name by which the Carmelites (*q.v.*) were known in England.

WHITE HORSE, THE MONASTERY OF THE. The oldest monastery in China is called "the Monastery of the White Horse." A. Lloyd says that in Japan also the White Horse is held in reverence. In several temples a white horse is kept constantly. In certain Japanese provinces in which As'vaghosha is regarded as the patron saint of silk culture, "he is said to have appeared as a thousand white horses, to have made a thousand white birds sing, to have assumed the forms of countless silk-worms, to have spun thousands of cocoons, to have saved many thousands of living creatures" (Lloyd). In any case, the White Horse played an important rôle in the development of religion in China. In 64 A.D. the Chinese Emperor Ming-ti is said to have dreamed night after night that he saw standing before him a man clothed in golden raiment. He held in his hand a bow and arrows and pointed to the West. Ming-ti was so much impressed that he decided to send men to the West to search for "the true man" who had appeared to him. His messengers started for India. On their way they met two monks who were leading over the mountain passes a white horse laden with Scriptures and Buddhist images. Ming-ti's messengers felt that they had found what they wanted, and that it was unnecessary to continue their journey. The monks accompanied them to the Chinese capital and were lodged in a monastery which has since been known as "the Monastery of the White Horse." One of the books which the two monks are supposed to have brought with them is known as the "Sutra of the Forty-Two Sections," a collection of *logia* or short pithy sayings. The origin of the collection is not certain. It has even been suggested that the two monks were not Buddhist missionaries, but Christian disciples of St. Thomas. The suggestion is supported by A. Lloyd, who urges several considerations in support of it. Although we know of such logia among early Christians, there are no similar *logia*, Lloyd believes, "in the whole range of Buddhist Sūtra literature, except those which were compiled about this period for like purposes." *On the whole* the *main* contents of the collection will be found "to be not in disagreement with Christian doctrines, and far more suitable for Christian purposes than the Epistle of St. James (which has been claimed as a Buddhist writing) would be for the use of disciples of S'akyamuni." The component parts of the character which was introduced to represent Buddha are said to represent a man with a bow and arrows. Lloyd suggests that the character is capable of another signification besides the one usually given—" the three first letters of the *name* of the Perfect Man, our cherished monogram IHC, the man with the bows and arrows!" Curiously enough, in the Book of Revelation (vi. 2) we read: " And I saw, and behold, a white horse, and he that sat thereon had a bow; and there was given unto him a crown: and he came forth conquering and to conquer." The mission of the White Horse was not followed up by the Buddhists of India, a fact which seems to A. Lloyd to point to "its not having been a Buddhist mission at all, for the Buddhists would surely not have neglected to follow up so gracious an invitation from so powerful a monarch as Ming-ti." See Arthur Lloyd.

WHITE LOTUS SOCIETY, THE. The White Lotus Society was an association of Buddhist monks and laymen founded by Eon (died A.D. 416) of China, for the joint adoration of Amida Butsu (the Buddha Amida). It was the first body of the kind. The place of its origin was Rozan, south of the Yangtze, where Eon laboured and had the support of friends who were known as the " eighteen sages of Rozan." According to A. Lloyd, Eon devoted himself to a monastic life and the worship of Amida, without troubling very much about the Amida Scriptures. " It has been said that he was a Manichæan: the White Lotus Society still exists in China, I am told, and its members sing hymns which it is hard to distingnish from Christian ones." See Arthur Lloyd.

WHITE QUAKERS. The religious body which received the name of " White Quakers " was founded in Ireland by Joshua Jacob (1805?-1877), after he had been disowned by the Society of Friends (1838). The members of the sect were so called because they wore undyed garments. Their leader objected to the use of newspapers, bells, clocks, and watches. He was imprisoned for two years on a charge of misappropriating money belonging to some orphans. Afterwards (about 1849) he established a community at Newslands, Clondalkin. " The members of this establishment lived in common, abstaining from flesh-food, and making bruised corn the staple of their diet, flour being rejected " (*D.N.B.*). See the *Dictionary of National Biography.*

WHITE SUNDAY. A name given to the first Sunday after Easter, because in the Roman Catholic Church the newly-baptised wore their white robes for the last time. It is called in the Missal and Breviary " Dominica in Albis." Other names are Quasimodogeniti (*q.v.*) and Low Sunday.

WHITE WEEK. A name given to the week after Easter, because during this week the newly-baptised catechumens appeared in their white garments.

WHITSUN-FARTHINGS. Whitsun-farthings or smoke-farthings were offerings formerly made at Whitsuntide to the cathedral by persons in the diocese who lived in a house with a chimney.

WHITSUNTIDE. The Prayer Book of the Church of England speaks of the week following Whit Sunday as Whitsun Week and of the Monday as Whitsun Monday. Whit Sunday is, like Pentecost, the fiftieth day after Easter Day. It has been suggested that Whitsun is a corruption of *Pfingsten*, the German name for Pentecost. Another conjecture is that Whit Sunday was called originally White Sunday on account of the white garments worn by catechumens. The Feast commemorates the bestowal of the gift of the Spirit upon the apostles and the foundation of the Christian Church. A writer of about the fourteenth century seems to assume that Whit is equivalent to Wit or Wisdom (see W. Benham).

WILBURITES. One of the divisions of the Society of Friends (see QUAKERS), being the followers of John Wilbur. When Elias Hicks caused a schism in the Society in America by his rationalism, some of the orthodox party, led by Joseph John Gurney (1788-1847), of Norwich, England, thought that further secession would be avoided if the stringency of their doctrines were relaxed a little. John Wilbur opposed this tendency, and the Wilburites became the strictly orthodox party.

WILD HUNT. What is known as the " Wild Hunt " or the " Furious Host " is an old Teutonic legend. Sometimes at night a great noise was heard, or seemed to be heard, in the air. This was supposed to be a wild hunt in which huntsmen shouted, and dogs bayed, while a host of spirits rushed along with them. Originally, it would seem, the Wild Huntsman was Wodan (*q.v.*). The shouting and baying represent the howling and raging of the tempest sent by the Wind-god. Since Wodan was also god of the dead, the souls of the departed were thought of as accompanying him. There are various versions of the legend. " The Wild Hunt is at times in pursuit of an animal, a boar, cow, deer, or again of a woman, the *Windsbraut*. When a storm is raging, the host draws near. The beginning of the winter, the ill-famed Twelve Nights, is more especially its chosen time " (Chantepie de la Saussaye). See P. D. Chantepie de la Saussaye, *The Rel. of the Teutons*, 1902; *Chambers' Encycl.;* Brockhaus.

WILEMITAE. Another name for the Bohemian Brethren (*q.v.*).

WILHELMIANS. The followers of one Wilhelmina of Milan (*d.* 1281). She asserted that the angel Raphael announced her birth to her mother. Influenced by the teaching of the Abbot Joachim (1130-1200), she further declared herself to be an incarnation of the Holy Spirit. Sent to save Saracens, Jews, and false Christians, she would, she said, suffer as Christ did, and afterwards rise from the dead. See J. H. Blunt.

WILKINSONIANS. 1. A branch of the Brownists (*q.v.*). They took their name from their leader Wilkinson. The Wilkinsonians declared that they were Apostles like Peter and Paul. 2. The followers of Jemima Wilkinson (1753-1819) in America. She said that she had risen from the dead and was perfect. She claimed also to work miracles and to prophesy. The designation which she herself gave to her followers was that of " Universal Friends." See J. H. Blunt.

WILLIAMS'S LIBRARY, DR. A Library founded in 1716 by Daniel Williams (1643?-1716). From 1687 to 1716 Dr. Williams was Presbyterian minister at Hand Alley, Bishopsgate, London. He also became lecturer at Painters' Hall, but in 1694 he was dismissed from his lectureship in consequence of a book which he had published, " Gospel Truth " (1692). He left large sums of money for religious and scholastic work. Dr. Williams's Library is primarily a Theological Library intended for the use of ministers, students, and other persons engaged in the study of Theology, Ecclesiastical History, Comparative Religion, and kindred subjects. But it is also serviceable to students of History, Philosophy, Economics, the History of Language, and Literature, including Classical Literature both ancient and modern. There is no subscription, and the readers are not confined to any particular denomination.

WINEBRENNERIANS. The followers of John Winebrenner (1797-1860), who was originally a minister of the German Reformed Church in Harrisburg, Penn. He was in charge of four churches in which there was a " revival." The revival led in course of time to separation from the German Reformed Church. The new congregations became " spiritual, free, and independent churches." In 1830 a conference was held to decide upon the constitution of " The Church of God," as the new body was called. It was decided that churches should consist of " believers only "; that they should be " without sectarian or human name "; that they should have " no creed and discipline but the Bible "; that they should be under no foreign jurisdiction; and that " they should be governed by their own officers, chosen by a majority of the members of each individual church." Winebrenner presided over the Conference, which inaugurated an Annual Conference or Eldership. The ministers were called elders. Baptism, Feet-washing, and the Lord's Supper constitute " positive ordinances of perpetual standing in the church." The third of these should be " administered to Christians only, in a sitting posture, and always in the evening." See J. Winebrenner in Rupp's *Religious Denominations*, 1844; Schaff-Herzog.

WINGED DISC, THE. The winged disc or solar disc is a figure composed of a disc, representing the sun, and two wings, one on each side of it. There is perhaps reference to it in the Old Testament (Malachi iv. 2: " the sun of righteousness shall arise with healing in his wings "; see however, the *Journal of the Manchester Egyptian and Oriental Society*, 1917, p. 67.). In any case, it has been a common religious symbol in ancient Egypt, Babylonia, and elsewhere. According to Professor Elliot Smith, indeed, it originated in Egypt, and was carried thence all over the world. " The winged disc with a pair of serpents is the commonest and most distinctive symbol of the ancient Egyptian religion, and is constantly found carved upon the lintels of the great doors of the temples. It appeared in a great variety of forms in Egypt and was widely adopted and distributed abroad, especially by the Phoenicians (see Count d'Alviella, " The Migration of Symbols," 1894, p. 204 *et seq.*)." It is found in Asia Minor, Assyria, Babylonia, and Persia, as well as in Carthage, Cyprus, Sardinia, and elsewhere in the Mediterranean. " In modified forms it occurs in India and the Far East, and ultimately it re-appears in America in a practically complete form and in precisely homologous situations, upon the lintels of doors in sun-temples. But the curious feature of these American winged discs is that they are invariably reversed; and the body of the serpent, which even in the Egyptian models is often conventionalized into a lattice-like pattern, is now replaced by a geometrical design. This only becomes intelligible when it is compared with the (reversed) Egyptian original " (G. Elliot Smith, *Anc. Egypt. Civ.*, 1916, p. 31). In most cases the design is still further modified in a characteristically American manner. Often the place of the sun's disc is taken by the face of the god. The American development of the winged disc is essentially geometrical, and Dr. Rivers has pointed out that the transformation of a naturalistic into a geometrical design is usually due not to simplification, but to a blending of different cultural influences.

WISDOM-LITERATURE. A name given to those Hebrew writings which deal with problems of practical religion. Prof. Cornill points out that the Hebrew Wisdom-literature " is not philosophic, but theological, or—if the term be preferred—theosophical speculation." Prof. Toy (*Encycl. Bibl.*) classes it as a kind of philosophy. " Inasmuch as it seeks to discover what is permanent and universal in life (which is the aim of philosophy), it may be described as the pre-Philonic Hebrew philosophy." The writings which belong to this class are: Job, some of the Psalms, Proverbs, Ecclesiasticus, Ecclesiastes, Wisdom of Solomon. The most remarkable of these is the Book of Job. See *Encyl. Bibl.*; C. Cornill, *Intr.*

WISDOM OF JESUS THE SON OF SIRACH, THE. Another name for the apocryphal book of Ecclesiasticus. It is also known as The Book of Ben Sira. Jesus the son of (Ben) Sira or Sirach is claimed as the author.

WITCHCRAFT. According to Grimm the word Witch is derived from the Gothic word *veihan* (German *weihen*), which meant originally " to perform (rites)." The earlier meaning of the term was " a woman regarded as having supernatural or magical power and knowledge " (Findlater). The word then came to denote (in the Middle Ages, for instance) a woman who was supposed to have formed a compact with the devil, or with evil spirits, in virtue of which she was able to work supernaturally and to do harm to men and beasts. The *Catholic Dictionary* defines Witchcraft as " a power, real or supposed, of producing, in concert with an evil spirit, effects beyond the reach of natural means and operations." A belief in magic and sorcery is found everywhere in ancient times, and even in modern times among primitive folk. But a distinction has been made between authorised and unauthorised exponents of the art. While the medicine-man has inspired people with a kind of religious awe, the witch has filled them with a sense of terror. The evils of real witchcraft are manifest, and real witches deserved to be ruthlessly exterminated. The danger was, and proved to be a terrible reality, that harmless persons might in spite be accused of practising witchcraft. In Africa " countless millions of human beings have been slain as sorcerers and witches on the accusation of professional witch-doctors " (J. M. Robertson, *P.C.*). In Europe, in the thirteenth century, began a war of extermination against witches which developed into a horrible mania. In this war the innocent suffered with the guilty. It seems indeed to be a law of human progress that innocent persons must suffer or be sacrificed. If the innocent had not suffered, the superstition involved in the burning and drowning of witches would have persisted longer. It is customary to lay all the blame for the hunting down of witches upon the Church. " No saint, no pope, no Christian scholar rebuked the great crime of the Middle Ages. In the fifteenth and sixteenth centuries pope after pope solemnly sanctioned and encouraged it. Innocent III., in 1484, gave a fearful impetus to the slaughter throughout Europe, urging the Dominican monks on with awful effect. The Reformers joined in the error, and Protestant lands were just as much desecrated as Catholic. No estimate of the number of victims is possible, but details such as a French judge boasting that he has accounted for 900 witches in fifteen years, or a Swiss judge dealing with 1,000 cases in one year, give some idea. The horror that was added to life by the hunts of Inquisitors, and the monstrous nature of their courts, can hardly be realised." So writes Joseph McCabe (*The Bible in Europe*, 1907). The Church and the Bible were to blame. But if " not a saint or prelate, from Francis of Assisi to Wesley, was moved to protest," as he says, one wonders what must have been the mental condition of the mass of the people or what it would have been without the Church. The natural inference is that to a large extent the excesses were due on the one hand to an impatient religious zeal and on the other hand to the interference of a lawless lay element. The history of witchcraft shows that the persecution of witches is often due to popular superstition. J. C. Oman (*Cults*, 1908) thinks that since 1802 thousands of witches in India " must have perished in out-of-the-way places at the hands of their superstitious countrymen, with the knowledge and connivance of the equally superstitious village police." One of the methods of testing witches has been that of the trial by water. " In Ḥadramaut, according to Macrīzī, when a man was injured by enchantment, he brought all the witches suspect to the sea or to a deep pool, tied stones to their backs and threw them into the water. She who did not sink was the guilty person, the meaning evidently being that the sacred element rejects the criminal" (W. Robertson Smith, *R.S.*). The idea of the Witches' Sabbath which once prevailed throughout Europe had an ancient pagan foundation. It was believed "that certain women, having made a bargain with the devil, betook themselves to the 'Sabbath' on grotesque steeds, and there acquired redoubtable powers for evil" (Reinach). See *Chambers's Encycl.; Cath. Dict.;* W. E. H. Lecky, *History of Rationalism in Europe;* E. B. Tylor, *P.C.;* H. C. Lea, *Hist. of the Inquisition of the Middle Ages,* vol. iii., 1887; G. Steinhausen, *Quellen und Studien zur Geschichte der Hexenprocesse*, 1898; Reinach, *O.*

WODAN. Wodan or Odhin was one of the chief deities of the Ancient Teutons. Tacitus regarded him as the supreme deity, and speaks of him as Mercury. He was one of the chief gods of the Frisians and the Saxons. He figures prominently in one of the Merseberg Charms (*q.v.*), which were discovered at Merseburg in Saxony. The cult was widespread among the Anglo-Saxons. Wodan was worshipped also by the Norsemen. Norse literature suggests, however, that Thor (*q.v.*) was more generally worshipped in Norway as the national deity, and that Wodan was introduced from outside. Originally he would seem to have been a god of the Istvæones mentioned by Tacitus. The name Wodan is derived from a root meaning "to blow," and Wodan is the wind god. Since wind may be harmful or beneficial, it is natural that he should have been also a god of war and a god of agriculture and fertility. He is the commander of the "Furious Host" or the leader in the "Wild Hunt" (*q.v.*). He is represented as riding on a dapple-grey horse or on a steed known as Yggdrasil, and as being a great wanderer or traveller. In Norse literature and in German popular tradition he has become god of the dead, especially of fallen heroes, whom he welcomes to Walhalla (*q.v.*), the happy meeting-place. He developed further into a god of wisdom, of secret wisdom and the magic arts. A triad is sometimes formed by Loki (*q.v.*), Hoenir (*q.v.*), and Wodan. When the first men were formed, Loki is said to have given them warmth and colour, Hœnir souls, and Wodan breath. Wodan's name survives in the English Wednesday. See P. D. Chantepie de la Saussaye, *Rel. of the Teutons,* 1902; *R.S.W.;* Reinach, *O.*

WOLFENBUETTEL FRAGMENTS. In 1777 G. E. Lessing (1729-1781), who since the year 1770 had been Librarian at Wolfenbuettel, published a work, "Wolfenbuettelsche Fragmente eines Ungenannten." The fragments were very bold in their criticism of the origins of Christianity, and when the authorship became known a considerable stir was created. The author was Hermann Samuel Reimarus (1694-1768), who had been Professor of Hebrew at the Gymnasium of Hamburg. See Gustav Pfanmueller, *Jesus im Urteil der Jahrhunderte,* 1908.

WORD, THE MAGIC. Morris Jastrow remarks (*Civ.*, p. 428) that "to have a name" according to ideas widely prevalent in antiquity was to exist. Hence in an Assyrian Creation-tablet, to express the idea of non-existence of heaven and earth, it is said that they were not named. In the O.T. book of Genesis (i.), God has only to pronounce the word "Light" for light to come into existence. For this D. G. Brinton (*R.P.P.*, p. 91) compares a corresponding myth among the Quiché Indians of Central America. The maker of the world calls forth, *Uleu!* Earth, and at the word the solid land grew forth (*Popol Vuh, le Livre Sacré des Quiches,* p. 10). "It is to be noted that the magical influence of the word is *independent of its meaning.* It is distinctly *not* the idea, image, or truth which it conveys to which is ascribed its efficacy. On the contrary, the most potent of all words are those which have no meaning at all or of which the sense has been lost. . . . The same fact is abundantly shown in the cabalistic jargon of classical and mediæval diviners, and in the charms drawn from contemporary folklore. Indeed, the famous cabalist, Pico de Mirandola, asserts that a word without meaning has most influence over the demons" (Brinton, p. 92). Even long communications may be made in articulate sounds which convey no thought whatever.

WORTHIES, THE NINE. A select number of heroes in the world's history. The heroes are: Joshua, David, and Judas Maccabæus (161 B.C.) among the Jews; Hector of Troy, Alexander the Great (323 B.C.), and Julius Caesar (44 B.C.) among the pagans; and King Arthur of Britain (542 A.D.), Charlemagne of France (814 A.D.), and Godfrey of Bouillon (1100 A.D.) among Christians.

WROEITES. The followers of John Wroe (1782-1863). They called themselves Christian Israelites (*q.v.*). Wroe was himself a follower of Joanna Southcott, from whom the Southcottians (*q.v.*) received their name.

WURRAWILBEROO. Two demons in the religion of the Euahlayi tribe of Australia. They come to earth sometimes in whirlwinds; try to catch the spirits of the dead; and bring disgrace on women. "Wurrawilberoo is said to snatch up a baby spirit sometimes and whirl along towards some woman he wishes to discredit, and through the medium of this woman he incarnates perhaps twins, or at least one baby" (K. Langloh Parker, *The Euahlayi Tribe,* 1905).

WYCLIFFITES. The followers of John Wycliffe (1325-1384). See LULLARDS.

X

XARATANGA. A Mexican deity, an earth and maize goddess.

XAVERIAN BROTHERS. A Roman Catholic order established in North Brabant, Holland, in 1846, by Theodore James Ryken. The Brothers undertook to devote their lives to the Christian education of youth. Ryken called himself Brother Francis Xavier in honour of Francis Xavier or Xaver (1506-1552), the Apostle of the Indians. He opened a college at Bruges, and called it St. Francis Xavier's College. The Brothers have worked also in England since 1848, and in the United States since 1854. In the United States its sphere of work is very extensive. See *Cath. Dict.*

XCACAU. A tribal god of fertility in the religion of the Mayan Indians.

XEROPHAGY. The Greek word *xērophagia* means "dry food." The term Xerophagy occurs in Greek and Latin writers as the equivalent of fasting.

XILONEN. A Mexican goddess, protectress of the young maize-ear.

XIPE. A god worshipped by the Aztecs. Human sacrifice was a feature in the worship, victims being crucified.

XISUSTHROS. The name given by writers who depend upon Berosus as that of the hero of the Babylonian deluge. It is a distortion of the expression Adra-Khasis which is found in the Gilgamesh Epic (*q.v.*) as an epithet for Parnapishtim. Adra-Khasis was read Khasis-adra and then Xisusthros. See Morris Jastrow, *Rel.*

XIUHTECUTLI. Xiuhtecutli was one of the gods worshipped by the ancient Mexicans, the Fire-god. The name means "lord of fire." As the other name of the god, Huehueteotl, "the old god," suggests, he was one of the oldest deities. There are points of resemblance between him and both Tezcatlipoca (*q.v.*) and Huitzilopochtli (*q.v.*). As in the case of the former, his connection with the sun was represented by a mirror. As in the case of the latter, a dough image of the god played an important part in one of his festivals. The image was raised on a cross. Afterwards it was thrown down, and the fragments were eaten by those who took part in the festival. Xiuhtecutli, besides being the god of thunder and lightning, was the divinity of the domestic hearth. Lewis Spence mentions that a piece of bread and a libation were consecrated to Xiuhtecutli by the members of an Aztec family every morning on rising. Among his emblems are the fire-snake and the butterfly. At his chief feast living victims were cast into a large brazier. See Spence, *Myth.*; J. M. Robertson, "The Religions of Ancient America," in *R.S.W.*; *P.C.*

XMUKANE. A tribal deity, a disease-god, in the religion of the Mayan Indians.

XOCHBITUM. A tribal deity, god of singing, in the religion of the Mayan Indians.

XOCHIPILLI. A Mexican deity, god of flowers, dance, song and games.

XOCHIQUETZAL. A Mexican deity, goddess of flowers, love and pregnancy. She was also the patroness of weaving and embroidery.

XOLOTL. A Mexican deity, god of twins and monstrosities. He is represented as dog-headed.

XPIYAKOK. A tribal deity, a disease-god, in the religion of the Mayan Indians.

XTOH. A tribal god of fertility in the religion of the Mayan Indians.

Y

YACATECUTLI. A Mexican deity, god of the guild of travelling merchants. His symbol, the staff of the traveller, was treated as a god. Incense was burned to it; offerings of flowers, tobacco, etc., were presented to it; prayers and genuflections were made to it. To the god himself, slaves, fattened for the purpose, were often sacrificed.

YĀDAYIM. The title of one of the Jewish treatises or tractates which reproduce the oral tradition or unwritten law as developed by the second century A.D. and are incorporated in the Mishnah (*q.v.*), a collection or compilation completed by Rabbi Judah the Holy, or the Patriarch, about 200 A.D. The sixty-three tractates of the Mishnah are divided into six groups or orders (*sedarim*). Yādáyim is the eleventh tractate of the sixth group, which is called *Ṭohorōth* ("Purifications").

YAHWEH. The pronunciation of the Hebrew divine name Y-h-w-h (or Y-h-v-h) adopted by modern Christian scholars. The Jews refrained from pronouncing the sacred name Y-h-w-h. Wherever this name occurs in the Old Testament they pronounce it Adonay (My Lord), or sometimes Elohim (God). Christians have long been accustomed to pronounce the word Y-h-w-h, Yehovah or Jehovah (using the vowels of Adonay). Modern Christian scholars, however, believe that the true pronunciation, which the Jews had forgotten at an early period, is Yahweh or Jahveh. There is a verb *hayah* or *havah* in Hebrew which means "to be" or "to become" and makes its Imperfect or Future tense Yahweh. Yahweh might mean "he who exists (absolutely)" or "he who is self-existent" or "he will be (with us)." Or it might even mean "he who causes to be," or "he who calls into existence." The name is used in the Old Testament as the peculiar name of the God of Israel distinguishing him from the gods of other nations. For another suggestion regarding the pronunciation of the name, see the article TETRAGRAMMATON, THE.

YAJUR VEDA. The Yajur Veda is one of the sacred books of the Hindus. It belongs not to the strictly Vedic period, which is represented by the Rig Veda (*q.v.*) and Atharva Veda, but to a following period. With the Sāma Veda (*q.v.*), the Yajur Veda introduces a new period, the Brahmanic period. The Yajur Veda contains the sacrificial formulae used by the priests. To these formulae explanatory remarks have been added. See Monier-Williams; E. W. Hopkins.

YAMA. Yama is one of the deities in Hinduism. At first he was regarded as a man, the "first of mortals," corresponding, it would seem, to the Hebrew Adam. In course of time, however, he came to be regarded as the king of the dead, the god of departed spirits. In one of the hymns of the Rig Veda addressed to the "god of departed spirits" the following lines (as translated by Monier-Williams) occur:

> To Yama, mighty king, be gifts and homage paid.
> He was the first of men that died, the first to brave
> Death's rapid rushing stream, the first to point the road
> To heaven, and welcome others to that bright abode.

As the first man Yama had a twin sister Yamī, and both of them were children of Vivasvat the Sun. The older mythology made Yamī the wife also of Yama and the mother of mankind. When Yama became king of the dead his abode was the upper sky, and two four-eyed watch-dogs guarded the approach to it. Sometimes his abode seems to be thought of as being actually in the sun. It is said, for instance: " my home is there where are the sun's rays." Yama's friend and even messenger is Agni (*q.v.*). Finally Yama developed (*e.g.*, in the Epic Poems) into the stern Judge who condemns and punishes the dead. He is " the Punisher," or " the King of Justice," or " the Rod-bearer," or the " Noose-bearer." He is represented sometimes as holding in his hand a noose, " with which he binds the spirit and its subtle frame after drawing it from the sick man's body " (Monier-Williams). But if a man dies with the wonderful Tulasī plant near him, however many sins he may have committed, Yama cannot look upon him. See Monier-Williams; E. W. Hopkins.

YAMAKA. A Buddhist sacred book in the third division of the Canon. See CANON, BUDDHIST.

YAMI. In Hinduism Yamī is the sister of the first man Yama (*q.v.*), who when he died became king of the dead. In the older mythology she is represented as being also his wife and the mother of mankind. Both are children of Vivasvat, the Sun. See Monier-Williams; E. W. Hopkins.

YĀNĀDIS, RELIGION OF THE. The Yānādis are a tribe which inhabits the Telugu country in India. Their headquarters is the island of Srīharikota in the Nellore district. Their places of worship are called dēvara indlu, " houses of the gods." " They worship a household god, a village goddess of local importance, and a deity of wider repute and influence. Chenchu Dēvudu is invariably the household god. Poleramma or Ankamma is in charge of a local area for weal or woe. Subbarāyudu, Venkatēswaralu, Panchala, Narasimhulu, and others, are the gods who control destinies over a wider area. The Yānādis are their own priests. The objects of worship take various forms: a wooden idol at Srīharikota; bricks; stones; pots of water with margosa (*Melia Azadirachta*) leaves; images of gods drawn on the walls of their houses; or mere handfuls of clay squeezed into shape, and placed on a small platform erected under an aruka tree, which, like other Hindus, they hold sacred " (E. Thurston and K. Rangachari). The Yānādis worship their ancestors. " A belief lingers that the pious are *en rapport* with the deity, who converses with them and even inspires them. The goddess receives animal sacrifices, but Chenchu Dēvudu is a strict vegetarian, whose votaries are bound, at times of worship, to subsist on a single daily meal of roots and fruits. The Yānādis, like Hindus, wear sect marks, and are even divided into Vaishnavites and Saivites. They are supposed, during worship, to endow inanimate objects, and the spirits of geographical feature, with life and mind, and supernatural powers " (*ibid.*). See E. Thurston

YANG. The Chinese believe that there are two supreme powers in the Universe, one of which, Yang, is the source of light, warmth and life, while the other, Yin, is the source of darkness, cold and death. The Yang is associated closely with the heavens, the Yin with the earth. The soul of man is supposed to consist partly of Yang and partly of Yin matter, three parts of the former and seven parts of the latter. Naturally the sun contains the greatest quantity of the vital energy known as Yang. Amongst other things which contain a certain amount of it is the cock, which is regarded as an emblem of the sun. According to De Groot, an ancient Chinese book says that " the cock is the emblem of the accumulated Yang (*i.e.*, the sun) and of the South. Etherial things which partake of the character of fire and of the Yang element have the property of flaming up; hence, when the Yang rises above the horizon the cock crows, because things of the same nature influence each other." The blood from a cock's comb is supposed to have the power of reviving a person who is dying. The Yang vital energy counteracts the influence of the earthly matter Yin. See J. J. M. de Groot, *R.S.C.*, 1892-97.

YANTRA. A term found in Hinduism. The Yantras are supposed to possess a power and efficacy equal to those of the Mantras (*q.v.*). They are mystic diagrams drawn on tablets of metal, " generally combinations of triangular figures like the inverted triangles of the Freemasons " (Monier-Williams). A Yantra may be combined with a Mantra. A diagram with six or eight sides, and with a Mantra underneath, is supposed to have great potency. See Monier-Williams.

YARIBOL. A deity worshipped by the Palmyrenes.

YASHTS. The Yashts are one of the divisions of the Zendavesta (*q.v.*), the oldest collection of writings sacred to the old Persians. They are hymns and invocations addressed to various Iranian gods.

YASNA. The Yasna is one of the divisions of the Zendavesta (*q.v.*), the oldest collection of the writings sacred to the old Persians. It is a liturgy of sacrifice, and includes the Gāthas, sacrificial hymns which are the oldest part of the Zendavesta and constitute the original or old Avesta.

YAZATAS. The Yazatas or Yazads are a class of angels in Zoroastrianism, who seem to rank below the Amesha Spentas (Ameshaspands).

YEBĀMŌTH. The name of one of the Jewish treatises or tractates which reproduce the oral tradition or unwritten law as developed by the second century A.D. and are incorporated in the Mishnah (*q.v.*), a collection or compilation completed by Rabbi Judah the Holy, or the Patriarch, about 200 A.D. The sixty- three tractates of the Mishnah are divided into six groups or orders (*sedarim*). The work Yebāmōth is the first tractate of the third group, which is called *Nāshīm* (" Women ").

YEK. A term used among the Tlinkit of N. America to denote a mystic potentiality ascribed to beings whether human or non-human, living or not living. *Yek* seems to be a force, and not a personal being, and corresponds to the Melanesian *mana*.

YELLOW-CAP BUDDHISTS. When in course of time the Buddhists in Tibet split up into two chief bodies or parties, a strict party and a lax or less strict party, they came to be distinguished by the colour of their clothing, the strict party wearing yellow, the lax party red. The Yellow-cap Buddhists were founded in the fifteenth century by Tsong Khapa (*b.* 1355 or 1357), whose followers were also known as the Gelugpa Sect (*q.v.*). His idea was to institute a religious reform, and he has been compared with Martin Luther (1483-1546). He felt that the discipline of Buddhism had been corrupted by the laxity of the Red-cap school, especially by the marriage of monks. The monastery called Galdan, which he built not far from Lhāssa, became the first centre of his teaching and influence, but his movement spread rapidly. " Undeniably, Tsong Khapa's chief merit was that he caused his followers to revert to the purer monastic discipline, especially to the rule of celibacy. He also purified the forms of worship, and greatly restricted without altogether prohibiting the use of magical rites. Tsong Khapa, too, is said to have re-established the original practice of retirement for religious meditation at certain seasons, although as there was no rainy season in Tibet, another period had to be chosen " (Monier-Williams). When Tsong Khapa died in 1419 A.D., he is supposed to have ascended to heaven. His ascension is celebrated in a Festival of Lamps (see LAMPS). It should be added that Tsong Khapa's reformation had a precursor in the eleventh century. At that time Brom Ton, a disciple of Atīsha, founded a sect called Kadampa. He insisted on great strictness in the monastic life. See Monier-Williams; H. Hackmann.

YEN LO. The Chinese name for Yama (*q.v.*), the Hindu god of the dead.

YESHWANT. The glorious, one of the names of the Hindu god Krishna.

YETSIRAH, THE BOOK. The Book Yetsirah (*Sefer Yetsirah*) or Book of Creation, is a Jewish mystical work of uncertain authorship and date. It probably originated about the sixth century A.D. See MYSTICISM, NON-CHRISTIAN.

YEWE ORDER. A secret religious society of men and women in Togo, West Africa. The members are not amenable to the laws, and the doctrine and practice of the society are said to be lewd and licentious. "On being initiated everyone receives a new name, and thenceforth his or her old name may never be mentioned by anybody under penalty of a heavy fine. Should the old name be uttered in a quarrel by an uninitiated person, the aggrieved party, who seems to be oftener a woman than a man, pretends to fall into a frenzy, and in this state rushes into the house of the offender, smashes his pots, destroys the grass roof, and tears down the fence. Then she runs away into the forest, where the simple people believe that she is changed into a leopard. In truth she slinks by night into the conventual buildings of the order, and is there secretly kept in comfort till the business is settled. At last she is publicly brought back by the society with great pomp, her body smeared with red earth and adorned with an artificial tail in order to make the ignorant think that she has really been turned into a leopard" (J. G. Frazer). See J. G. Frazer, *The G.B.*, Pt. II., 1911.

YEZIDIS. The Yezidis or Devil-worshippers are a sect found chiefly in the Caucasus, Armenia, and Kurdistan, and having their headquarters in the province of Mosul, Mesopotamia. The origin of the name is obscure. It may be derived from Yazid or Yazd, a town in Iran. Among Christians in the villages near Mosul the name applied to the Yezidis is Daisanites or followers of Bardesanes. "According to the belief of the Yezidis, God, the creator of heaven and earth, first made from his own essence six other divinities, the sun, the moon, and the principal stars, and these joined with him in creating the angels. The devil, who was God's own creation, rebelled against his lord and was cast into hell. He afterward repented of his sin, did penance for seven thousand years, and shed tears of contrition which fill seven vessels that will be used at the Day of Judgment to quench the fires of the seven hells. God in his mercy pardoned the recreant, restored him to heavenly rank, made him one with himself, and forbade the angels to look with scorn upon their reinstated brother. Inasmuch as God's grace thus forgave and exalted even Satan himself, man should not look with hatred upon this so-called representative of evil. On this account the Yezidis never allow the name of Satan to pass their lips, avoiding even a syllable that suggests the word, and shrinking with horror from any mention of the devil by others" (A. V. Williams Jackson, *Persia Past and Present*, 1906). The Yezidis are afraid to pour boiling water upon the earth lest they should scald the face of the little devils. They worship the sun, the moon, and the stars. They also pay divine honours to a metal cock called Tâous. According to Williams Jackson, this is really a peacock conventionalized so as almost to resemble a cock. But Lidzbarski has suggested that Tâous is a corruption of Tamuz, the Babylonian deity. This lends support to Williams Jackson's statement that "the Yezidi religion shows distant survivals of the old Assyro-Babylonian worship of the sun, moon, and stars, for the faith appears to have retained the sun-god Shamash under the form of Sheikh Shems, and the moon-god Sin as Sheikh Sinn, an emanation of God himself." Alphonse Mingana contends that the Yezidi sacred books are spurious. See A. V. Williams Jackson, as cited above; Alphonse Mingana, "Devil-worshippers," in the *Journal of the Royal Asiatic Society*, July, 1916.

YGGDRASIL. The ash of Yggdrasil is the sacred tutelary tree of the gods of the Edda. It is a great cosmic tree, and its trunk forms the axis of the world. Another name for it is "the tree of Mimir," Mimameidhr. In the Icelandic prose Edda, *Gylfayinning* it is said: "Three roots stretch out in three directions under Yggdrasil's ash. Hel dwells under one, the frost giants under the other, the race of men under the third." Chantepie de la Saussaye thinks that the idea of Yggdrasil's ash does not belong to popular belief but is due to the imaginations of the scalds (minstrels). See P. D. Chantepie de la Saussaye, *Rel. of the Teutons*, 1902; Reinach, *O.*

YIH-KING. One of the Chinese Classics. *King* means "Classic." *Yih* is the "Book of Changes" (*q.v.*).

YIMA. An Iranian deity. Yima is the son of the sun. There is a close connection, it would seem, between the Iranian Yima and the Hindu Yama. In the Avesta (*q.v.*) the *soma* (*haoma*) is first prepared for man by the sun. In the Rig Veda "it is Yama the son of Vivasvant (x. 58.1; 60.10) who first 'extends the web' of (*soma*) sacrifice (vii. 33. 9, 12)." See E. W. Hopkins.

YIN. According to the Chinese, Yin, the source of darkness, cold and death, is one of the two supreme powers in the universe, the other being the source of light, warmth and life, Yang (*q.v.*).

YOGA. Yoga is the name of a doctrine or practice which has prevailed in India for many centuries. Mr. J. C. Oman quotes the following explanation by "the Apostle of the New Dispensation," Babu Keshub Chunder Sen. "What does yoga literally mean? Union. The English word which makes the nearest approach to it is Communion. The created soul, in its worldly and sinful condition, lives separate and estranged from the Supreme Soul. A reconciliation is needed; nay, more than mere reconciliation. A harmonious union is sought and realized. This union with Deity is the real secret of Hindu yoga. It is a spiritual unification, it is consciousness of two in one; duality in unity. To the philosophical and thoughtful Hindu this is the highest heaven. He pants for no other salvation; he seeks no other *mukti* or deliverance. Separation, disunion, estrangement, a sense of distinction, duality, the pride of the eye, this is to him the root of all sin and suffering; and the only heaven he aspires to is conscious union and oneness with Deity. He is ever struggling and striving to attain this blessed condition of divine humanity. Once in possession of it, he is above all sorrow and distraction, sin and impurity, and he feels all is serene and tranquil within. All his devotions and prayers, his rites and ceremonies, his meditations and his self-denials, are but means and methods which help him on to this heaven." This explanation may be supplemented by one given by William James from the work "Vivekananda" (*Raja Yoga*, London, 1896). The Yogi (disciple) finds "that the mind itself has a higher state of existence, beyond reason, a superconscious state, and that when the mind gets to that higher state, then this knowledge beyond reasoning comes. . . . All the different steps in yoga are intended to bring us scientifically to the superconscious state or samâdhi. . . . Just as unconscious work is beneath consciousness, so there is another work which is above consciousness, and which, also, is not accompanied with the feeling of egoism. . . . There is no feeling of *I*, and yet the mind works, desireless, free from restlessness, objectless, bodiless. Then the Truth shines in its full effulgence, and we know ourselves —for Samâdhi lies potential in us all—for what we truly are, free, immortal, omnipotent, loosed from the finite, and its contrasts of good and evil altogether, and identical with the Atman or Universal Soul." The Yogis are in great repute in India as healers of diseases, and as philosophers and saints of great knowledge and power. See *Yoga: Objective and Subjective*, Calcutta, The Brahmo Tract Society, 1884; *Yoga Vasishta Maha Ramayana*, 4 vols., Calcutta, 1891-99; Karl Kellner, *Yoga: Eine Skizze*, 1896; William James, *The Varieties of Religious Experience*, 1906; J. C. Oman, *Cults*.

YOGIS. The Yogis worship Siva. Their principal festival is the Shivrātri (Siva's night), " when they stay awake all night and sing songs in honour of Gorakhnāth, the founder of their order " (R. V. Russell and R. B. Hīra Lāl). They worship also the cobra on the Nāg-Panchmi day. Russell and Hīra Lāl say of their philosophy: " The Yoga philosophy has indeed so much substratum of truth that a man who has complete control of himself has the strongest will, and hence the most power to influence others, and an exaggerated idea of this power is no doubt fostered by the display of mesmeric control and similar phenomena. The fact that the influence which can be exerted over other human beings through their minds in no way extends to the physical phenomena of inanimate nature is obvious to us, but was by no means so to the uneducated Hindus, who have no clear conceptions of the terms mental and physical, animate and inanimate, nor of the ideas connoted by them. To them all nature was animate, and all its phenomena the results of the actions of sentient beings, and hence it was not difficult for them to suppose that men could influence the proceedings of such beings " (Russell).

YŌMĀ. The title of one of the Jewish treatises or tractates which reproduce the oral tradition or unwritten law as developed by the second century A.D., and are incorporated in the Mishnah (*q.v.*), a collection or compilation completed by Rabbi Judah the Holy, or the Patriarch, about 200 A.D. The sixty-three tractates of the Mishnah are divided into six groups or orders (*sedarim*). The work Yōmā is the fifth tractate of the second group, which is called *Mō'ēd* (" Festival ").

YOUNG EUROPE. The name given to an association founded in Switzerland by Guiseppe (Joseph) Mazzini (1805-1872). See PACT OF FRATERNITY.

YOUNG ITALY. An association founded at Marseilles in 1831 by Guiseppe (Joseph) Mazzini (1805-1872). See PACT OF FRATERNITY.

YOUNG MEN'S CHRISTIAN ASSOCIATION. The first of these Associations was founded in London in 1844. On June the 6th of this year twelve young men met in a room in St. Paul's Churchyard to establish " a society for improving the spiritual condition of young men engaged in the drapery and other trades." The idea was to arrange for religious meetings, such as Bible Classes and Prayer Meetings, in the business houses in the centre of London. Branch and Corresponding Associations soon sprang up in different parts of the Metropolis and throughout the country. They all adopted the same name, but each of them adapted its agencies to the varying circumstances and necessities of young men. The objects and methods of the Associations have always been dictated by the principles held in common by Evangelical Churches. In 1855 a general conference of delegates from the Associations of Europe and America was held in Paris, and a basis of Alliance of the Young Men's Christian Associations was agreed upon. This basis reads as follows: " Young Men's Christian Associations seek to unite those young men who, regarding the Lord Jesus Christ as their God and Saviour, according to the Holy Scriptures, desire to be His disciples in their doctrine and in their life, and to associate their efforts for the extension of His Kingdom among Young Men." The Associations in no way enter into competition with the existing Churches, and have no desire to enter upon functions proper to the Churches. In 1882 a " National Council of Young Men's Christian Associations " was formed. In June, 1899, at a joint meeting of British and Colonial representatives held at Dublin a constitution was adopted for the " British and Colonial Union of Young Men's Christian Associations." A good idea of the character and scope of the work of Young Men's Christian Associations may be gained from a description of the building which has been erected as a memorial to the founder of the original Association, George Williams. " In the basement there are a large gymnasium with gallery, a swimming bath with shower-baths, a rifle-range and bowling-alley, and a self-contained, fully-equipped Boys' Department, consisting of lounge, meeting-rooms, reading-room, games-room, and locker-rooms, etc. The entrance hall with its circular staircase, which is a feature of the ground floor, rises through two stories and has a saucer dome springing from the entablature over the columns. On the ground floor are also the large hall, the small hall, a club restaurant, and a public restaurant. The large hall rises through two stories, and has a flat curbed ceiling, with an organ. On the first floor are the principal social and club rooms. On the second floor is the Technical College, consisting of a library, a laboratory, lecture-rooms, examination-rooms, class-rooms, and a photographic section, with work- and printing-room, dark-rooms, and enlarging-rooms. The third floor contains the kitchen and larders, and the manager's flat; the remainder of this floor, together with the whole of the fourth floor, excepting the assistant manager's rooms, is occupied by bedrooms, of which there are upwards of two hundred, with baths and lavatory accommodation." See the *English Year Book of Y.M.C.A.'s*, 1910.

YOUNG WOMEN'S CHRISTIAN ASSOCIATIONS. These Associations are established on the same basis as the Young Men's Christian Associations (*q.v.*). The first Association was founded in 1857 by the Dowager-Lady Kinnaird.

YŪDZŪNEMBUTSU SECT. A Japanese Buddhist sect founded by Ryonen Shōnin (1072-1132 A.D.), a monk of Hieizan. In a vision Amida, so he thought, appeared to him and advised him to leave the Hieizan monastery, for it was a " den of thieves." At the same time he was told to change the Nembutsu (a term meaning " thinking of Buddha ") to an intercessory prayer, " One man for all men, all men summarized in *One*, one devotion for all, all devotions summed up in one " (A. Lloyd). The sect is still in existence, but is not very popular. See Arthur Lloyd.

YUISHIKIKYŌ, THE. The Yuishikikyō or the Oneness sect is another name for the Japanese Hossō sect (*q.v.*). The doctrine of Oneness is " one of the key-notes of the Hossō teaching " (Arthur Lloyd).

Z

ZABIANS. The name Zabians has been used in various ways. To Arabian, Persian, and Jewish writers of mediæval times all who were not Magians or Muhammadans, Jews or Christians, were Sabæans or Zabians. In the Koran the term is used of the ancestors of the Mandæans (*q.v.*), who were non-Christian Gnostics. In Syria the descendants of the ancient Hellenized heathens were called Zabians. They were so called because they claimed as their patriarch one Zābī, son of Seth (or of Adam, or Enoch, and so on). See *Chambers's Encycl.*

ZĀBIM. The name of one of the Jewish treatises or tractates which reproduce the oral tradition or unwritten law as developed by the second century A.D. and are incorporated in the Mishnah (*q.v.*), a collection and compilation completed by Rabbi Judah the Holy, or the Patriarch, about 200 A.D. The sixty-three tractates of the Mishnah are divided into six groups or orders (*sedarim*). Zābīm is the ninth tractate of the sixth group, which is called *Ṭohorōth* (" Purifications ").

ZABULUS. Zabulus occurs in Patristic writings as a corrupted form of Diabolus or the Devil.

ZACCHÆANS. A name used by Epiphanius (*Hæres.* xxvi. 3) in reference to Gnostics (*q.v.*).

ZADOKITES. A body of Jewish reformers who arose in the second century B.C. within the priesthood, and were known in the first century as " the Sons of Zadok." According to a document (*Fragments of a Zadokite Work*) discovered by Dr. Schechter, and supposed by C. H. Charles (*Religious Development*) to have been written between 18 and 8 B.C., they were called also " the penitents of Israel," acknowledged as leaders " the Star " and " Law-giver," and were members of a " New Covenant " and " Covenant of Repentance," which involved a great spiritual change. The author of this work " hated the orthodox Pharisees, declaring that they made void the written law by raising a body of oral tradition as a ' wall ' about it. But he was almost equally opposed to his brethren the Sadducees, declaring the Prophets as well as the Law to be a religious authority, teaching a blessed immortality, the existence of angels, the advent of the Messiah, a high moral code, and the wickedness of divorce " (Cobern).

ZAG-MUK. The Babylonian name for New Year's Day. It might be the first day of the month sacred to a deity. This was the case with the goddess Bau (*q.v.*). When Marduk (*q.v.*) became the central figure of the pantheon, New Year's Day came to be his special day, and the Zag-muku became a Marduk festival. On this occasion there was a solemn procession through a handsomely paved route. " The union of Nabu and Marduk was symbolized by a visit which the former paid to his father, the chief of the Babylonian pantheon. In his ship, magnificently fitted out, Nabu was carried along the street known as Ai-ibur-shabû, leading from Borsippa across the Euphrates to Babylon " (Jastrow). The New Year's Festival of Marduk was a specially propitious time for seeking oracles in the temple of the god, for during this festival he decided the fate of men for a whole year. See Morris Jastrow, *Rel.*

ZAHILA, ANNALS OF. A book of the annals of the Kakchiquel Indians of Guatemala.

ZĀHIR PIR. A Muhammadan saint worshipped in Saugor, India, by the caste of sweepers and scavengers.

ZAKAR. One of the minor Babylonian gods in the period of Hammurapi. He seems to have been worshipped in Nippur, and to have been closely related to Bel and Belit (*qq.v.*). See Morris Jastrow, *Rel.*

ZALMOXIS. The god of the Getai, a Thracian tribe. This seems to have been their only deity. During thunderstorms they tried to intimidate him by shooting arrows at the sky.

ZAMAMA. A Babylonian deity belonging to the second Babylonian period. He is called a " god of battle," and his temple the " house of the warrior's glory." He was worshipped in the city of Kish in northern Babylonia. His consort is called simply Ninni, " the lady." Zamama seems to have had the character of a sun-god. See Morris Jastrow, *Rel.*

ZANZALIANS. Another name for the Jacobites, who are supposed to have derived their name from Jacobus Baradæus, a Syrian monk. Baradæus had also the surname Zanzalus, whence the designation Zanzalians.

ZCERNOBOCH. Zcernoboch or Chernobog was one of the gods worshipped by the ancient Slavs. He is called " the black god," which would seem to mean the evil god. Salomon Reinach thinks there must have been also a god Bielbog, " the white god," that is to say, the good god, for the name has survived in certain place-names. See Reinach, *O.*

ZEALOTS. In the New Testament one of the apostles is described as " Simon called Zēlōtēs " (Luke vi. 15; Acts i. 13). He is also called Kananaios (Matthew x. 4; Mark iii. 18). The latter word, Kananaios, is simply a Greek form of the Hebrew term *kannā* " zealous." Zēlōtēs is the real Greek equivalent. The Zealots were an offshoot of the Pharisees. They believed in taking violent measures to introduce the Kingdom of the Messiah. Their principles were very much those of the Assassins (*q.v.*).

ZEBĀCHIM. The Jewish Mishnah, a collection and compilation completed by Rabbi Judah the Holy, or the Patriarch, about 200 A.D. (see MISHNAH), comprises a number of treatises or tractates which reproduce the oral tradition or unwritten law as developed by the second century A.D. There are sixty-three tractates, divided into six groups or orders (*sedarim*). Zebāchīm is the first tractate of the fifth group, which is called *Ḳodāshīm* (" Holy Things ").

ZEBEDEE-STONES. A name (also Sebedei) for thunderstones in use among peasants in Denmark. They were carried by persons who believed that they made them immune from thunder. The name seems to have been suggested by the reference to the Sons of Zebedee in the New Testament.

ZECHARIAH, BOOK OF. One of the longest of the books of the Old Testament known as the Minor Prophets. The book itself tells us (chap. i. 1) that Zechariah was the son of Berechiah, son of Iddo. In the book of Ezra (chaps. v. 1; vi. 14) he is said to have been the son of Iddo. It appears from the same book that the prophet Zechariah was contemporary with Haggai (see HAGGAI, BOOK OF). The book of Zechariah itself assigns dates to some of the prophecies contained in it. Chapter i. 1-6 is said to have been written in the eighth month of the second year of Darius (Hystaspis), that is to say, in November 520 B.C. Chapters i. 7-vi. 8 are said to have been written in the eleventh month of the same year, that is to say, in February 519. Chapters vii.-viii. are said to have been written in the ninth month of the fourth year of Darius, that is to say, in December 518. These chapters are concerned with the rebuilding of the Temple and the Messianic hopes associated with it. They may well have been composed by Zechariah and have constituted the original book of Zechariah. The remaining chapters bear a different character, and would seem to have been the work of two other authors. Some scholars have been led by references in chapters ix.-xi. to Ephraim (ix. 10-15; x. 7; xi. 14), diviners (x. 2), and Assyria (x. 10), to assign them to a period previous to the fall of Samaria. Chapters xii.-xiv., with their reference to false prophets (xiii. 2-6) and the absence of any reference to the Northern Kingdom, have been assigned to the closing years of the Judaean Kingdom (seventh century B.C.). A number of scholars, however, now regard both these sections as post-exilic. The reference to the Greeks in chapter ix. vs. 13 has suggested to some that the oracles in chapters ix.-xiv. were composed during or after the period of Alexander the Great (between 332 and 280 B.C. Whitehouse points out that there are many reminiscences of older oracles (cp. xiv. 8 with Ezekiel xlvii. 1-12). He thinks that "probably some old pre-exilian oracles belonging to the eighth and seventh centuries have been worked into the texture of these prophecies in chaps. ix. ff." Cornill favours the view that chapters ix.-xi. were composed by a contemporary of Hosea or Isaiah. He thinks that all the arguments brought forward in favour of the time of Hosea and Isaiah "receive an entirely satisfactory explanation if the authorship is attributed to a later secondary writer, who was steeped in the ideas of Ezekiel and dependent upon that prophet." In Cornill's opinion, the post-exilic composition of chapters xii.-xiv. also is indisputable. The idea which dominates this section, of a violent attack by all the heathen upon Jerusalem and God's people, was first coined by Ezekiel under the impression produced by the actual destruction of Jerusalem and the Temple. "Ch. xiv. 8 also is obviously an exaggerated imitation of Ezek. xlvii. 1-10, while the specially Deutero-Isaianic type of language is equally in evidence in xii. 1 and xiv. 16, and xiii. 1 goes back to Numb. xix." See C. Cornill, *Intr.;* G. H. Box; O. C. Whitehouse; C. F. Kent, *The Sermons, Epistles, and Apocalypses of Israel's Prophets*, 1910.

ZEMI. A religious term used in the West Indies. The term is explained by J. W. Fewkes. "The name was apparently applied to gods, symbols of the deities, idols, bones or skulls of the dead, or anything supposed to have magic power. The dead or the spirits of the dead were called by the same term. The designation applied both to the magic power of the sky, the earth, the sun and the moon, as well as to the tutelary ancestors of clans. *Zemis* were represented symbolically by several objects, among which may be mentioned (1) stone or wooden images, (2) images of cotton and other fabrics enclosing bones, (3) prepared skulls, (4) masks, (5) frontal amulets, (6) pictures and decorations on the body" (quoted by T. A. Joyce, *C.A.W.I.A.*).

ZEN SECT. A Japanese Buddhist sect, founded by Eisai (A.D. 1191). The founder attached great importance to contemplation and meditation as religious exercises. The Zen at first even opposed altogether the use of books. But they changed their attitude in this respect afterwards. We are told that "the Zen school always laid special stress on the training of the will, for the regulation of all passion and for the conquest of physical desires"; and "because such exercises proved useful for the development of knightly and warlike valour, many of the nobles (*samurai*) in early times, as well as military officers until quite recently, took part in these self-denying and hardening practices." See H. Hackmann.

ZENDAVESTA. The Zendavesta is the most ancient collection of books held sacred by the Zoroastrians and modern Parsees. The word Avesta denotes the original documents. Zend denotes the *glossae* or commentaries to these. The compound word has been explained as "commentary lore." The writings were ascribed to Zoroaster or Zarathustra, the founder of Zoroastrianism, who lived before the sixth century B.C., but they are really of various dates. The Zendavesta includes the Yasna, the Visparad, the Vendîdâd, and the Yashts. The Yasna is a liturgy of sacrifice and contains the Gâthas, or sacrificial hymns, which are the most ancient part of the Zendavesta, with documents relating to them. The Visparad consists of litanies and invocations, which, it would seem, were intended to supplement the Yasna. The Vendîdâd (literally, "laws against the demons"), which seems to be the latest section of the Zendavesta, comprises laws, rules for exorcising demons, myths, etc. The Yashts are hymns and invocations addressed to various Iranian gods. There is a wide divergence between the original or Old Avesta, the Gâthas, and the later or New Avesta. The later Avesta is more polytheistic and introduces such things as the worship of sun, moon, and stars, of Haoma, Mithra, etc. See J. Darmesteter in *Sacred Books of the East;* V. Henry, *Le Parsisme*, 1905; Reinach, *O.*, 1909; *Chambers' Encycl.;* Brockhaus.

ZEPHANIAH, BOOK OF. The superscription to the book of the prophet Zephaniah states that he was the great-grandson of Hezekiah, and that he prophesied "in the days of Josiah the Son of Amon King of Judah." The Hezekiah would seem to have been the well-known king of that name. Since the prophecy itself denounces idolatrous customs, Baal-worship, star-worship, apostasy from Jehovah, and other such things, the prophet's activity must be placed before Josiah's reform of the cultus in 621 B.C. Another indication of date is supplied by the description of the "Day of Jehovah" in chapter i. Robbery and plunder, the blast of the trumpet and the cries of war, bloodshed and devastation, suggest to the prophet some terrible world-catastrophe. Zephaniah's thoughts would seem in fact to have been influenced by the invasion of "the foe from the North," the Scythians, in 626 B.C. Though the Scythians did not actually invade Judah, the people of Judah watched their progress with alarm. C. F. Kent thinks that the great reformation under Josiah was one of the fruits of Zephaniah's preaching. "It is more than possible that Zephaniah was the companion of the young Josiah, and the one who influenced the king to abandon the policy of his father and grandfather and to follow the guidance of the disciples of Isaiah and Micah." Parts of chapter iii. have been regarded as later additions to the book (*e.g.*, vss. 1-8 and 11-13). Cornill, however, thinks that chapter iii. need only be regarded as to some extent mutilated. See C. Cornill, *Intr.;* G. H. Box; O. C. Whitehouse; C. F. Kent, *The Sermons, Epistles, and Apocalypses of Israel's Prophets*, 1910.

ZEUS. Zeus is represented as the greatest of the Greek gods. According to a Cretan legend, his mother

Rhea gave birth to him in a cave of the island, and the goat Amalthea suckled him. His sister and consort was Hera, the queen of the gods. As the god of the sky and its phenomena, thunder and lightning, wind and rain, he was worshipped on high mountains, especially on the Thessalian Mount Olympus. On Mount Lycæus in Arcadia he was worshipped with human sacrifice as the Lycæan Zeus. In the Troad the summit of Mount Ida was sacred to him. In the representation of Homer, he is the beneficent father of men, as well as the wise ruler of Nature, "the father of gods and men" (Homer). "He gives to all things a good beginning and a good end: he is the saviour in all distress: to Zeus the saviour (Gr. *sōtēr*) it was customary to drink the third cup at a meal, and in Athens to sacrifice on the last day of the year. From him comes everything good, noble, and strong, and also bodily vigour and valour, which were exhibited in his honour, particularly at the Olympian and Nemean games. . . . From him, as ruler of the world, proceed those universal laws which regulate the course of all things, and he knows and sees everything, the future as well as the past. Hence all revelation comes in the first instance from him" (Seyffert). Zeus was regarded also as the protector of house, home, and hearth. His favourite children were Athene and Apollo. In Roman mythology the corresponding god to Zeus is Jupiter. It should be noted that the transformation of Zeus into the omnipotent and omniscient ruler of the world and father of men was a gradual process. See O. Seyffert, *Dict.;* Brockhaus; and cp. J. M. Robertson, *P.C.*

ZHIKKO. One of the principal Shinto sects in Japan. According to G. A. Cobbold, the members of the sect, which was founded A.D. 1541, recognize one deity, who is eternal, absolute, and of infinite benevolence. There seem, however, to be "vague references to a Trinity engaged in the work of Creation." See G. A. Cobbold, *Religion in Japan*, 1894.

ZIKKURAT. The Babylonian name for what has been described as a staged tower. The Babylonians supposed the gods to dwell on mountains. Consequently when they proceeded to built a temple they first piled up a mountain-like mound of earth to serve as the foundation plane. The tower might consist of a number of stages or stories, but the average number seems to have been three. It was quadrangular in shape. The zikkurat at Nippur was called "house of oracle." See Morris Jastrow, *Rel.*

ZIKR. The Muhammadan zikr (a "remembrance," that is to say, a remembrance of God) is a religious ceremony or an act of devotion practised by the various orders of Dervishes. As T. P. Hughes says, the performance is very common in all Muhammadan countries, since nearly every devout Muhammadan belongs to some order of Dervishes; but the zikr is not always quite the same. It consists in repeating the divine name according to set formulas. There is a private zikr for individual use. "The private zikr is either 'secret' (zikr-el-kha'fi), that is, to be recited mentally or in a low voice, or 'vocal' (zikr-ej-ja'li), that is, to be said aloud" (F. J. Bliss). In the secret zikr, according to E. Sell, the dervish closes his eyes and with "the tongue of the heart" repeats the words "Allah the Hearer," "Allah the Seer," "Allah the Knower." Then, with alternate inhaling and exhaling of breath, he repeats phrase by phrase the creed of the unity. The repetition may be made hundreds of times. In the vocal zikr, the worshipper, who is seated, varies his position from time to time and shouts the phrases of the creed with a voice that grows louder and louder. The congregational zikr is said by a number of dervishes in concert after a leader. "It is usually conducted on Thursday evening (the eve of the sacred day) at the dervish house. According to the order to which they belong, the participants squat on their heels, stand on their feet, or begin sitting and later change to standing. The chanting is accompanied by the bending of the body in different directions. Sometimes the zikr takes the form of a rude dance, to execute which the worshippers form a circle or a row, holding each other's hands, advancing and retreating in unison, and stamping with the feet. Beginning slowly to repeat the divine name with clear enunciation and solemn dignity, they gradually work themselves up into such a state of excitement that the rapidly uttered words become mere sounds without meaning. The swaying body keeps pace with the tongue. Physical exhaustion naturally follows this furious exercise of lungs and limbs" (F. J. Bliss). There is another kind of zikr, practised by the uninitiated. This is called the imitation zikr. It is commonly held in mosques. "According to strict doctrine, through the imitation zikr laymen may obtain protection against their enemies, but not that mystical union with God produced by the zikr of initiation." See T. P. Hughes; F. J. Bliss.

ZIMMIS. The name given by Muhammadans to subjects who, instead of embracing Islâm, pay a poll-tax (*Jizza*, from a root meaning "to satisfy" or "to compensate"), and are allowed to continue to profess their own religion, so long as it is not a gross form of idolatry. The poll-tax is either paid voluntarily to prevent war, or is imposed after conquest. "The Zimmi must distinguish himself from the Muslim by wearing different clothes 'lest he receive the marks of honour and respect due to the Muslim only.' He is to be kept in a state of subjection and abject humiliation. He must not ride on saddles like Muslims. When the Muslim stands, he may not sit. No Muslim ought to show him respect and honour. If he meets him in the street he must make him go aside. They must not live in large numbers in the midst of Muslims, and, if they possess houses of their own, they must be forced to sell them to Muslims. Their houses must be lower than those of Muslims. A Zimmi loses his right of protection if his country becomes a land of warfare or if he does not pay the poll-tax. If he should insult the Prophet he is to be killed." See F. A. Klein.

ZINZENDORFIANS. The followers of Nikolaus Ludwig von Zinzendorf (1700-1760). Zinzendorf was originally a pietist of the school of P. J. Spener (1635-1705). He became the leader of the revival of the Unitas Fratrum or the Church of the Bohemian (and Moravian) Brethren (see BOHEMIAN BRETHREN). Believing in the union of Christendom, he allowed members of various denominations to make his estate in Saxony a place of refuge. In 1721 the refugees were joined by the greater part of the remnant of the Bohemian Brethren. Zinzendorf's settlement received the name Herrnhut, "The Lord's Watch"; the settlers became known as Herrnhuter. In course of time it occurred to the Count to unite his tenants into "a church within the church" (ecclesiola in ecclesia). In 1727 the Herrnhuter received the Holy Ghost and felt themselves to be a close spiritual brotherhood. "They also gradually adopted the *ecclesiastical* forms, discipline, and orders of the Ancient Church of the Brethren's Unity of Bohemia and Moravia, and then as the *Renewed "Unitas Fratrum"* took up their position as a distinct Protestant Church, in the midst of the other Reformed Churches" (*The Moravians: Who and What are They?*). See, further, MORAVIANS.

ZIONISM. The movement among the modern Jews known as Zionism aims at the return of the Jews as a political unity to Zion. But it is a religious movement in the sense that this return is a going back to the centre of the ancient faith, and is regarded as a fulfilment of the predictions of the ancient prophets. Associated with this is the revival in Palestine of the ancient and classical language as a spoken speech. The movement began by the establishment in Palestine of Jewish colonies. In 1880, through the generous help of Baron Edmond de Rothschild, of Paris, a great impetus was given to the work. Later, Baron de Hirsch left his fortune to the Jewish Colonization Association, which has devoted part of it to the colonization of Palestine by Jews. M. Gaster speaks of the movement as follows: "We are standing at the beginning of this movement, which alone will assist in solving one of the most perplexing problems in modern sociology; will free Europe of an element which, in spite of all phrases to the contrary, is still considered as alien, and will be treated as such according to circumstances. There are some, among the richer Jews, who have vested interests and narrow conceptions; they are held fast in the meshes of self-delusion and cannot differentiate between the rights and duties of a citizen and the historical obligations of a national and religious life; they are still holding aloof from this movement. The vast masses, however, the sufferers and toilers of the earth, have rallied enthusiastically round it. In one way or another, realized sooner or later, with the assistance of all, or carried out in spite of many, this is the sign under which Judaism enters the new century." See M. Gaster, "Jews and Judaism" in *Great Religions of the World*, 1902; N. Sokolow, *History of Zionism, 1600-1918*, vol. i., 1919.

ZIONITES. A sect of religious enthusiasts in Germany in the 18th century. It was founded by Elias Eller (*b.* 1690), and his followers were called Zionites because his wife prophesied that the New Zion was about to be established. The sect has also been called the Ellerian Sect; and the Ronsdorf Sect from the name of the place with which Eller was closely associated. See Brockhaus.

ZIPAKNA. A tribal deity in the religion of the Mayan Indians. He is described as the creator of mountains.

ZIPALTONAL. One of the deities worshipped by the ancient Americans before the time of the Aztecs. Zipaltonal was a goddess, the wife of Fomagazdad. See FOMAGATA.

ZIUSUDU. The hero of the Deluge story in the recently discovered Sumerian Version. "The name of the hero, Ziusudu, is the fuller Sumerian equivalent of Ut-napishtim (or Uta-napishtim), the abbreviated Semitic form which we find in the Gilgamesh Epic. For not only are the first two elements of the Sumerian name identical with those of the Semitic Ut-napishtim, but the names themselves are equated in a later Babylonian syllabary or explanatory list of words. We there find 'Ut-napishte' given as the equivalent of the Sumerian 'Zisuda,' evidently an abbreviated form of the name Ziusudu; and it is significant that the names occur in the syllabary between those of Gilgamesh and Enkidu, evidently in consequence of the association of the Deluge story by the Babylonians with their national epic of Gilgamesh. The name Ziusudu may be rendered 'He who lengthened the day of life' or 'He who made life long of days,' which in the Semitic form is abbreviated by the omission of the verb. The reference is probably to the immortality bestowed upon Ziusudu at the close of the story, and not to the prolongation of mankind's existence in which he was instrumental" (L. W. King, *Legends of Babylon and Egypt in relation to Hebrew Tradition*, 1918). Dr. King notes that the character of Ziusudu presents a close parallel to the piety of Noah.

ZOHAR, THE. A famous Jewish work, the chief text-book of Jewish mediæval mysticism. It purports to be the record of a divine revelation to Rabbi Simeon ben Yoḥai (*b.* second century A.D.), and is for the most part in the form of utterances made by the Master to his disciples. But the work made its first appearance in Spain in the thirteenth century, and is clearly due to a number of writers. See MYSTICISM, NON-CHRISTIAN.

ZOOLATRY. The worship of animals. See ANIMAL-WORSHIP.

ZOROASTRIANS. The ancient Persian religion has been called Zoroastrianism after Zoroaster (the Greek form of the name Zarathustra), who is commonly supposed to have been its originator. Zoroaster is thought to have been a Mede or Bactrian; but very little is known about his life, and his historical existence is doubtful. If he existed, he would seem to have flourished about 1100 B.C. It is claimed that, although in the later parts of the Avesta he appears in a mythical garb, in the Gâthâs, which are perhaps the earliest parts, he is represented in such a simple way as to suggest a real person. In any case, as L. H. Mills says, he "was probably only the last visible link in a far extended chain. His system, like those of his predecessors and successors, was a growth. His main conceptions had been surmised, although not spoken before." J. M. Robertson thinks that the name Zarathustra is simply an ancient title for a kind of priest-king. According to legend, Zoroaster was born by the side of a river, and was in danger of being slain as an infant; later "he was brought by angels before Ahura Mazda (the great Lord of Wisdom), who conversed with him at length and revealed his laws to him" (Reinach). The teaching of the Zoroastrian religion is found in the sacred book or collection called the Avesta (*q.v.*), or rather in parts of it. The system is dualistic, being based upon the doctrine of a conflict between the powers of light, represented by Ormuzd (*q.v.*) and his angels the Amshashpends (*q.v.*), and the powers of darkness, represented by Ahriman or Ahura-mazda (*q.v.*) and his demons or Devas. Fire, as being a means of purification, is symbolical of Ormuzd. Victory over the powers of darkness can only be achieved by means of veracity, purity, ritual exactitude, and the active pursuit of agriculture. See further the separate articles. Also J. Darmsteter, *Ormazd et Ahriman*, 1876; *Le Zendavesta*, 1892; Reinach, *O.*, 1909; J. M. Robertson, *P.C.*; J. H. Moulton, *The Treasure of the Magi*, 1917.

ZOTZIHA CHIMALCAN. A tribal deity in the religion of the Mayan Indians. He was worshipped in the form of a bat.

ZUCCHETTO. The name of a skull-cap worn over the tonsure by Roman Catholic clerics.

ZÛGOTH. Zûgôth, which means "pairs," is a hebraized form of a Greek word. The word was used as the designation of the chief teachers of the Law from 150 to 30 B.C. According to Hebrew tradition one of each successive pairs of teachers was the President (*Nasi*) of the Sanhedrin, while the other was the Vice-President (*Ab beth din*). The most famous pair were Hillel and Shammai. See W. O. E. Oesterley and G. H. Box.

ZUHUYKAK. A tribal deity, protectress of children, in the religion of the Mayan Indians.

ZUIMACO. An earth-goddess worshipped in the West Indies (Antilles).

ZUME. A deity in the mythology of the natives of South America. The name is Paraguayan; but the Tamu of the Caribs, the Kamu of the Arawaks, and the Kabol of the Carayas represent the same god. It was Zume who taught the people the arts and crafts. He is therefore a culture-hero.

ZU MYTH. Zu is a Babylonian deity, a storm-god in the form of a bird. He seeks to take from En-lil or Bel the tablets of fate which have come into his possession. He would secure these in order to be able to decree divine decisions and give commands to the Igigi (*q.v.*). He goes to the dwelling of En-lil to attack him. He snatches the tablets of fate from his hands and flies away with them to the mountains. By losing the tablets, En-lil loses his power. Anu (*q.v.*) calls upon one of the gods to attack Zu. Ramman (*q.v.*) is promised great honour and glory if he will do so, but he thinks Zu invincible. In the end it would seem that Marduk (*q.v.*) undertakes the task and recaptures the tablets. In this way he gains the power that formerly belonged to Bel. See Morris Jastrow, *Rel.*

ZWICKAU PROPHETS. The Zwickau prophets were enthusiast followers of Martin Luther (1483-1546), who believed themselves to be divinely inspired. They were led by Nicholas Stork, Mark Thomas, Thomas Muenzer (*c.* 1489-1525), all of Zwickau, and by Mark Stuebner. The prophets rejected infant baptism, and required people to be rebaptized in the spirit. They believed that a new government, the kingdom of heaven, was to be established on earth. The conditions of the apostolic age were to be re-introduced. Cp. ANABAPTISTS. See Brockhaus; J. H. Blunt.

ZWINGLIANS. The followers of Ulrich (Huldreich) Zwingli (1484-1531), the founder, with John Calvin (1509-1564), of the Reformed Church. The Zwinglians were the early Swiss Protestants. In 1506 Zwingli became parish priest at Glarus in Constance. From 1512 to 1515 he acted also as chaplain to the Swiss troops when they were in Italy. In 1516 he became preacher in the monastery at Einsiedeln, to which pilgrims resorted to worship the Black Virgin. It was here that his career as a reformer began, for he preached that Christ alone can forgive and save. In 1519 he was appointed chief pastor of Zürich and preacher in the Cathedral. From this time he began to show increasing zeal as a reformer, and to make his influence widely felt. He at once preached against the sale of Indulgences (*q.v.*). In 1522 he protested against the Catholic commands as to fasting. In the same year he was instrumental in obtaining the civil abolition of clerical celibacy. In January 1523 he debated at Zürich with the vicar-general of the Bishop of Constance, and set forth sixty-seven theses of reformed doctrine. After this disputation the Reformation was inaugurated officially by the adoption of Zwingli's theses by the city. As the result of a second debate in October 1523 the Mass was condemned and the worship of images abolished. In 1524 Zwingli married a widow, Anna Meyer. In the following year he administered the Sacrament of the Lord's Supper in both kinds to the people. In 1528 another disputation was held at Bern, and Zwingli set forth ten propositions. In these he contended that the Christian Church is born of the Word of God; that Christ alone is its head, He alone is our salvation; that Holy Scripture does not teach a real, corporeal presence in the Holy Communion; that the doctrine of the Mass is contrary to Scripture; that Christ is the only mediator and intercessor; that the doctrine of Purgatory (*q.v.*) and the adoration of pictures and images are contrary to Scripture; that marriage is lawful to all; and that immorality in the clergy is more dishonourable than in the laity. The result was that Bern also decided for the Reformation. In 1529 war broke out in Switzerland between the Protestant and Catholic Cantons. In the same year the Swiss and German Reformers conferred together. They met at Marburg. The Germans were represented by Martin Luther (1483-1546), Justus Jonas (1493-1555), Philipp Melanchthon (1497-1560), Andreas Osiander (1498-1552), and others. The Swiss were represented by Zwingli, John Œcolampadius (1482-1531), Martin Bucer (1491-1551), and others. Luther submitted to the Conference fifteen articles. As to fourteen of these both parties were quite agreed. As to the fifteenth, however, there was a fundamental and insuperable difference of opinion. Luther held fast to a real corporeal presence of the body and blood of Christ in the Holy Communion. Zwingli rejected the real presence in every form, and maintained that there was only a symbolical presence, the rite being only commemorative of Christ's death. In 1530 Zwingli published his German version of the Bible. In 1531 war broke out again between the Protestant and Catholic Cantons. At Cappel the men of Zürich were defeated on October 11, 1531, and Zwingli was one of the slain. He was succeeded by Henry Bullinger (1504-1575). See B. Puenjer; J. H. Blunt; *Prot. Dict.; Chambers' Encycl.; Brockhaus' Encyclopaedia;* cp. M. W. Patterson, *Hist.*